A COLLECTION OF READINGS ▣ THIRD REVISED EDITION

Personal Character
and
Cultural Milieu

compiled and edited by

DOUGLAS G. HARING
SYRACUSE UNIVERSITY

 SYRACUSE UNIVERSITY PRESS

THIRD REVISED EDITION © 1956, SYRACUSE UNIVERSITY PRESS

SECOND PRINTING 1962   SYRACUSE, NEW YORK

THIRD PRINTING 1964

LIBRARY OF CONGRESS CATALOG CARD 48-2993

Compiler's Preface

The original edition of this book aimed at a specific need. Under crowded postwar conditions, few college or university libraries could provide periodicals or technical symposia in sufficient quantity to permit assignment of articles for student reading. A dearth of textbooks also made it extremely difficult to offer courses that dealt with culturally fostered patterns of personal character. The outstanding textbook on the subject—Kluckhohn and Murray's *Personality in Nature, Society and Culture*, had not yet appeared. Its authors generously informed me of its proposed contents; this made it possible to economize by excluding from this book any paper that they planned to reprint. In the second edition I also avoided reprinting papers that had appeared in *A Study of Interpersonal Relations*, ed. by Patrick Mullahy, and in *Readings in Social Psychology*, ed. by Newcomb, Hartley, and associates. The present third revision omits—regretfully—some papers that appeared in the earlier editions in order to add important new material.

This compilation stresses anthropological data; consequently pertinent psychological and psychiatric papers are omitted. Ethnological sources vary widely in accessibility and many important items are almost certainly absent from the average college library. Hence this is not a "book of readings" as much as it is a collection of papers that the compiler and some of his professional friends have wanted to place in the hands of students.

Four articles are published here for the first time: Margaret Mead writes on photography in personality research; and reports of specific field investigations are presented by Edward and Margaret Norbeck, Ronald L. Olson, and Betty B. Lanham. These authors have placed their papers at my disposal generously and their ready cooperation has been pleasant and memorable.

Part One, essentially introductory, presents some concepts, goals, and field techniques of anthropology, plus a discussion of social research in relation to scientific method. There is a list of readings for students who have not studied anthropology previously.

Part Two is the book—a series of papers that present varied data and interpretations on the common theme of culturally fostered patterns of personal character. It purposely avoids organization of materials to fit an intellectual scheme. Papers are arranged alphabetically by authors, and chronologically under each author. Instructors can fit the materials into diverse schemes of organization, according to their own plans, or in conjunction with textbooks such as *Personality in Nature, Society and Culture* (Kluckhohn, Murray & Schneider; N. Y. 1953) or *Culture and Personality* (John J. Honigmann; N. Y. 1954), or Weston La Barre's *The Human Animal* (1954).

The conceptual neutrality inherent in the mechanical, card-index sequence of papers, is not quite accidental, nor does it completely exempt the compiler from possible charges of bias. Self-conscious avoidance of obvious bias probably leaves intact the idiosyncrasies of the compiler, although these may be estimated from my introductory chapter ("Anthropology: One Point of View"). The selection of papers, however, is not strictly personal; I have been guided by much correspondence and many conversations with users of the book, and have responded to pleas for inclusion of specific articles. The aim is to supplement the library facilities of small colleges and of many large universities, rather than to propagate the compiler's point of view. The attempt to bring together material useful to my colleagues in teaching turned out to be useful in another way; the earlier editions have sold unexpectedly in foreign countries where the cost of American journals hampers efforts of local scholars to keep abreast of trends of thinking in the United States. The present edition, in view of this situation, stresses the thinking and research of North American anthropologists. They are presented in their own words, unedited, and complete with footnotes.

The compiler cherishes no illusions about complete coverage of the field. Accounts of the use of psychological tests, such as the Rorshach, in exotic societies have been omitted deliberately. They are reported in psychological literature, and the General Bibliography indicates some of the sources. Even the strictly anthropological material is limited; important cultural areas, such as India, the Levant, Russia, North Africa, and South America, are not represented. Australia, Melanesia, and Polynesia; the Philippines, Java and Sumatra; southeast Asia with the rich cultures of Thailand and Burma; central Asia from Tibet to the myriad tribes of Asiatic Russia—these merely suggest parts of the world that afford rich data excluded by present limitations of space. Aside from Dr. Hu's enlightening article on "face" no data from China could be included.

The General Bibliography aims to be inclusive rather than selective. Nearly all items have been verified from the originals, but in some cases—especially when an item has been listed to facilitate references made in a reprinted article—time and available labor have not sufficed for verification. Bibliographies compiled by Margaret Mead and by Weston LaBarre have provided considerable help.

One basic debt must be acknowledged. It was my privilege to participate in Dr. Franz Boas' seminar at Columbia University in the spring of 1927, in which he chose "The Individual and Society" as the topic for a term of study and discussion. A roster of the participants in that seminar would indicate that Boas' influence in the reorientation of anthropology to take account of the types of personality fostered by each specific society is much greater than many writers on "culture and personality" have realized. My own interest in the subject dates from that experience. This explicit acknowledgment—nearly three decades later—seems necessary because some recent writers accuse Boas of purblind neglect of the individuals whose ideas and activities constitute "culture."

Each of the authors whose work is included has granted permission so graciously that printed words of thanks are inadequate. Editors of journals and other scientific publications also have acted generously. Since authors are not guaranteed remuneration for the use of their writings, the price of the book is being held as low as rising production costs permit. The compiler is keenly conscious of the courageous investment on the part of Syracuse University Press.

Several professional colleagues have given assistance and counsel unstintedly. Verbal acknowledgment does not discharge the compiler's debt to them, and at the very least they should not in any way share in blame for the shortcomings of the book. Dr. Margaret Mead has given time to the revised edition as generously as she contributed to the original edition, when she provided suggestions and criticisms, loaned reprints, and cheerfully endured a barrage of inquiries. The lucid paper that Dr. A. I. Hallowell made available for the first edition has lost none of its pertinence. Dr. Clyde Kluckhohn has answered inquiries and placed his own writings at my disposal. Dr. George B. Wilbur, editor of *American Imago*, offered sound comment on the original plan. The compiler, however, made final decisions and assumes sole responsibility for the outcome. To Mr. Donald Bean, Director of Syracuse University Press, I owe appreciation for quick insight and cordial support. Mrs. Arpena Mesrobian of the Press has mastered a thousand and one details, carried the bulk of the proofreading, and maintained unruffled good temper throughout. My wife, Ann T. Haring, has read sheafs of galley proofs with painstaking care. Mr. David Tillson has attended to many details and has read much of the proof when my absence from the University required a dependable substitute.

The introductory chapter, "Anthropology: One Point of View," was written under unanticipated pressure and I have been fortunate in friends who gave time to reading the manuscript: Dr. Earl Bell, chairman of the Department of Sociology and Anthropology, Dr. Marguerite Fisher of the Department of Political Science, and Dr. William Mangin, my colleague in anthropology—all of Syracuse University—have helped materially. So have some of my graduate students: Carol Fisher, Betty Lanham, Joy Neale, and David Tillson. To Dr. Mary H. Marshall, Peck Professor of English Literature at Syracuse University, I am grateful for criticisms of style and for a notable diminution in the literary infelicities at which I am naturally adept. The residual shortcomings derive from my own limitations.

DOUGLAS G. HARING

Syracuse University
June, 1956

Contents

PART ONE

ASPECTS OF AN ANTHROPOLOGICAL APPROACH TO PERSONAL CHARACTER

PART TWO

SELECTED PAPERS

ix

Part One

ASPECTS OF AN ANTHROPOLOGICAL
APPROACH TO PERSONAL CHARACTER

THE FIELD OF ANTHROPOLOGY

Students of anthropology presumably encounter this book only after they have acquired general knowledge of the many aspects of that subject. The general reader—and readers who have special knowledge of psychology, psychiatry, sociology and allied sciences—may wish to read something that will provide a sense of proportion before dealing with the specialized materials in the present compilation. One or more of the following books will contribute to that end.

Anthropology Today, an Encyclopedic Inventory. Chicago, 1953.

Boas, Franz, *The Mind of Primitive Man.* Rev. ed., N. Y., 1948.
———, Anthropology, *Encyclop. Soc. Sci.* N. Y., 1930. vol. 2:73-110.
———, The Aims of Anthropological Research, *Science* 76:605-613.

Chapple, E., & C. S. Coon, *Principles of Anthropology.* N. Y., 1942.

Coon, Carleton S., *Reader in General Anthropology.* N. Y., 1948.
———, *The Story of Man.* N. Y., 1954.

Gillin, John, *The Ways of Men.* N. Y., 1948.

Goldenweiser, A. A., *Early Civilization.* N. Y., 1922.
———, *Anthropology.* N. Y., 1937.

Herskovits, M. J., *Man and His Works.* N. Y., 1948.
———, *Cultural Anthropology.* N. Y., 1955.

Hoebel, E. A., *Man in the Primitive World.* N. Y., 1949.
———, J. D. Jennings, & E. R. Smith, *Readings in Anthropology.* N. Y., 1955.

Kluckhohn, Clyde, *Mirror for Man.* N. Y., 1949.

Kroeber, A. L., *Anthropology.* Rev. ed., N. Y., 1948.

Linton, Ralph, *The Study of Man.* N. Y., 1936.
———, *The Tree of Culture.* N. Y., 1955.

LaBarre, Weston, *The Human Animal.* Chicago, 1954.

Lowie, Robert H., *Primitive Society.* N. Y., 1920.
———, *Introduction to Cultural Anthropology.* Rev. ed., N. Y., 1940.

Murdock, G. P., *Social Structure.* N. Y., 1949.

Shapiro, H. L., ed., *Man, Culture, and Society.* N. Y., 1956.

Thomas, W. I., *Primitive Behavior.* N. Y., 1937.

Titiev, Mischa, *The Science of Man.* N. Y., 1954.

Yearbook of Anthropology. Wenner-Gren Foundation for Anthropological Research, Inc. New York, 1955—.

ANTHROPOLOGY: ONE POINT OF VIEW

Douglas G. Haring

Accounts of far-off peoples who follow strange customs always have afforded fascinating reading. The anthropologist, however, is not a seeker after the bizarre; his is the task of understanding the whole fabric of life, whether among remote tribes or great nations. The better he knows the people whom he studies, the less does he emphasize the sensational. In retrospect he strikes a balance in his memories. Perhaps he encountered squalor and discomfort, poisonous reptiles, mouse-sized cockroaches, problems of obtaining diet suited to his urbanized digestion, the loneliness of living among a people whose language he comprehended imperfectly, and endless drudgery to clarify customs that in native eyes were too simple to require explanation. He also remembers warm friendships, generous hospitality, eager cooperation of those who understood his purposes, and the deep satisfaction of transcending barriers of race, language, and custom. Sometimes fortune places him among a people whose gracious age-old tradition might contribute to enrichment of his own civilization, and among whom he enjoys his quota of creature comforts. His scientific goal, however, outweighs comfort and discomfort. If in his record, readers can sense the human realities beneath quaint details that catch their fancy, he has accomplished one of his objectives. After all, in his own land he too is a native, whose ways seem queer to an outlander, and his responsibility to his own people includes deeper understanding of mankind.

Anthropology is many sciences in one. "The science of man" hardly could be otherwise. Different anthropologists focus diverse interests upon special aspects of the human drama. In general there emerge four main foci of anthropological research: physical anthropology, ethnology, comparative linguistics, and prehistoric archaeology.

Physical anthropology, a biological science, is the study of *genus homo* as a mammalian species whose evolutionary history and affiliations with other species are to be discovered. To the extent that a physical anthropologist can be distinguished from a human biologist, his unflagging interest in all sorts of people in all parts of the world places him among the anthropologists. He visits Eskimos, Hindus, Hottentots and Americans, measures individuals and makes physiological and chemical tests that help to clarify "racial" characteristics. In the role of a human palaeontologist, he measures ancient bones exhumed by archaeologists and examines them microscopically and chemically. His major goal is exploration of the world-wide range of variations in human bodies; to that end he mobilizes every feasible technique of biological and medical research.

Ethnology, also called *social anthropology*, is a social science. Other social scientists—sociologists, economists, political scientists—usually operate within the orbit of Euro-American civilization. Ethnologists, however, travel afield though sometimes they study their own society. They seek out all possible variations in social living, compare them, and constantly amend and enlarge their perspective to comprehend the endless gamut of human possibilities. Often it is said that the subject matter of ethnology is "culture." This means that ethnological research focuses on whatever behavior human beings learn from their fellows in the diverse and manifold situations observable throughout the world. "Culture" is an abstraction comparable to such terms as "society," "civilization," and "institution." The observed phenomena back of these elusive abstractions are human ideas and actions.[1] Some human behavior is not cultural; man does not learn how to digest food or how to maintain the rhythm of his heartbeat. He does learn, however, the patterns of talk, of action, of environmental adjustment—all the behavior involved in living with other people. Much of this learning is accomplished subtly and without conscious effort; some of it requires concentrated hard work. He learns thousands of complex patterned activities such as wearing clothes, shaking hands, applying cosmetics, buying a ticket and boarding a train, solving mathematical problems, understanding the meanings of words and the framing of sentences. Much cultural behavior is covert, invisible to anyone, known only to the "thinker." But even the patterns of thinking are acquired and vary with the language learned.

Culture is not an entity, thing, or force that acts on people. No one is "moulded by culture." *Cultural behavior* denotes whatever human beings do or think according to patterns learned from other people. Almost never does a person act in a way that has not been learned; his "originality" consists in recombining known behavior in new patterns. Man is limited to the cultural resources current, or at least accessible, in his own society. His individual repertory of behavior, like that of each of his neighbors, has drawn upon the cultural patterns in vogue in their time and place—including "book learning"—and each has selected behavior congenial to his individual situation.

The ethnologist aims to record all forms and aspects of cultural behavior throughout the world. Ethnology is not confined to the "primitive" and exotic; its scope embraces the whole pattern of living of every people, whether "primitive" or "civilized." This includes political, economic, social, and religious behavior: folklore, arts, science, magic, law, morals, ideals, beliefs, philosophy, dress, etiquette, technology—in short, whatever human beings do or think. Ethnologists draw upon the research techniques of the special social sciences and gladly cooperate with other scientists—e.g., ecologists, psychiatrists, and geologists. On-the-spot observation and description of a specific people is called ethnography; comparison of societies, strictly speaking, is ethnology.

Comparative linguistics also is a cultural science which concentrates upon the most ubiquitous element of cultural behavior: namely, language. The linguistic anthropologist may or may not attain fluency as a speaker of many languages. His task is to compare languages, analyze their structure, phonetics, vocabularies and thought-patterns. Often he starts with philology and the history of languages, and thus he works largely in the area of learning called the humanities. In recent years linguistic research has attained high precision of technique. Its findings shed light upon the diverse workings of human minds as they operate in and through different linguistic matrices.

Prehistoric archaeology is understood by the general public somewhat more clearly than are other branches of anthropology. The division of labor between two areas of archaeological research, however, is less well-known. Arbitrarily a distinction of convenience is drawn between classical archaeology and prehistoric archaeology. In broad philosophical perspective this distinction is meaningless, but it is useful in practice. The *classical* archaeologist is affiliated with the historians of our own culture; it is he who unearths the ruins of ancient Greece or Troy, Carthage, Egypt, or Babylon. He verifies and amplifies written history as he excavates inscriptions, buildings, even documents on perishable material. The architecture of a ruined temple carries more interest for him than do the skeletons in ancient graves. The *prehistoric* archaeologist, however, works with less imposing, more enigmatic material. He excavates the buried remains of the simpler peoples—and some complex non-European civilizations—beyond the boundaries of the Western "classical" world. His techniques were developed under the aegis of general anthropology. Always he pays strict attention to human skeletal remains, to bits of wood that might help to date his finds, to potsherds and flint tools, and to whatever tokens of ideas and beliefs he can discover. One prehistoric archaeologist remarked pointedly that at least 98% of human history falls in the province of prehistoric archaeology; and as estimates of the duration of man's occupation of the planet stretch into millions of years, the comment gains force. Thus the prehistoric archaeologist studies the physical anthropology and the ethnology of extinct peoples by excavating their remains.

* * * *

A philosopher engaged in classifying the sciences logically might not place these four anthropological sciences in a single category. Certainly their practitioners differ in training and in research methods: biologist, social scientist, linguist, and archaeologist. Each has his problems and ways of working, and each talks his specialized scientific jargon. How then do these four kinds of scientists accept the common label, "anthropologist"? The answer lies not in philosophy but in practical necessity. Given the common goal of exploring the universe of man and his works—a common orientation toward discovery of other kinds of people and other ways of living—their actual labors of exploration bring them together. Indeed, any kind of anthropologist often finds himself in situations that demand knowledge of all four fields.[2] Should he be the first student of a hitherto unknown tribe—say in New Guinea or the Brazilian rain forest—he is beset by the certainty that imminent contacts with traders, missionaries or alien governments will shortly modify the tribal culture, perhaps even the very bodies of the tribesmen. He is observing a way of life that has evolved over centuries, possibly millennia; these phenomena may be evanescent and perhaps no one else will be in a position to record the facts. Whatever he can record—data of physical anthropology, of ethnology, of language—will be useful to future research and may even carry unsuspected theoretical importance. Lacking time for archaeological excavation, he can still be alert to promising sites and tokens of their significance. The charge that an anthropologist is a jack-of-all-trades inheres in the cost and circumstances of field research. A well-financed expedition conducted by specialists in each branch of anthropology, plus, say, a geographer and a psychiatrist, is a Utopian dream that rarely materializes. Even if such large specialized expeditions were possible, they might fail of their purposes by introducing too many foreigners and too much new material equipment to the tribe, and thereby disrupting an established way of living.

Present-day anthropologists are not called upon as frequently as were their predecessors to pioneer in study of completely unknown peoples. Yet no matter how often a tribe has been studied, there always is more to learn; and since even non-literate peoples change their customs, repeated studies are needed to chart the changes. The way thus opens for the specialist to pursue his interests, but he still needs the cooperation of other specialists. The physical anthropologist needs the ethnographer, since bodily characteristics of any people are related to modes of livelihood, family customs, foods and their preparation, ways of child rearing, and religious or magical practices. As for the ethnographer, he must learn the local language if he would study the culture, for local modes of thought are embodied in the implicit logic of the language. A professional linguist is called for; in the absence of a specialist, the ethnographer records the language as fully as he can. He may wish for an archaeologist; he notes sites that might yield materials that would indicate the history of the people. On the other hand, an archaeologist usually needs an ethnographer to interpret some of his findings. The proliferation of refined techniques of research in every field of anthropology makes it almost impossible for an individual to be expert in all of them. A few decades ago it was possible for such men as Boas and Thurnwald and Dixon and Kroeber to contribute mightily to all branches of anthropology. Even then, many an anthropologist working far from libraries and laboratories has longed for a few days' aid from a botanist, geologist, or physician. Always there is so much in the field to observe and record, so much necessary knowledge is inaccessible, and time is brief.

Scientific problems as yet unformulated may haunt the working ethnographer. He has read the works of ethnographers of the past and has wished that they had recorded details that became significant in the eyes of a later generation. If only Mariner or Lewis and Clark, or L. H. Morgan or Bastian had recorded more details of child-training or of native dreams—or if Codrington or W. H. R. Rivers or Boas had known how eagerly another generation would pore over scientifically collected native autobiographies! So the field ethnographer wonders what he is missing, what is before his eyes that a subsequent generation will need and miss because he could not foresee the course of scientific development. The late Ralph Linton, for example, studied archaeology in the Marquesas Islands in 1920-1922, while his team-mate, Edward Handy, recorded ethnographic data. The indigenous culture was dying along with its bearers; Handy recorded that he could not describe birth customs because no babies were born during their stay. Years later, in association with the psychoanalyst Kardiner, it fell to Linton to marshal ethnographic data on the Marquesas for purposes unforeseen in 1920. By that time the traditional Marquesan culture was practically extinct.

The *unity of anthropology* inheres in the circumstance that no specialized investigation of human beings and their affairs stands alone. At the moment it is fashionable for writers to call for "integrated research" by coordinated effort of specialists in different disciplines. It could be argued that anthropology never has operated otherwise. Even the narrowly defined specialties—such as study of decorative art, investigation of tribal diets, or ethnozoology (study of uses made of animals by a human society)—can be pursued fruitfully only if the investigator is conversant with the cultural resources, family patterns, bodily idiosyncrasies, history, and ideological goals of a people.[3] The numerous sub-specialties in anthropology are united by their common focus on the human species and its activities.

Another source of unity in anthropological diversity is the restless urge to discovery. Other sciences also are concerned with human biology, with sociocultural phenomena, with language, or with archaeology. Their practitioners, however, do not usually range so far afield. Once a scientist transcends the intangible cultural boundaries that delimit the Euro-American heritage to enter deeply into the life and lore of an Asiatic or African nation or a culturally peripheral tribe, his research becomes anthropological—not by some mystic alchemy of geography, but by the personal necessity of adjusting to people whose cultural universe is more or less incommensurable with his previous experience. Armed with perspective acquired by living in an alien culture, anthropologists sometimes study their own civilization. Their researches in the European tradition are anthropological by virtue of the investigator's point of view; they are not differentiated from sociology or psychiatry by specific tricks of method or research technique.

Whatever their specialized interests, anthropologists generally direct attention outward beyond the confines of their native milieu. The most fundamental qualification of an anthropologist is first-hand understanding of one or more peoples of contrasting culture. An anthropologist without field experience is comparable to a biologist who never has looked through a microscope; his insight falls short of what it might have been. Intimate protracted living among an alien people effects emotional reorientation in the observer; the exotic culture becomes familiar, comprehensible, no longer alien. Neither Orientals nor any other people are hidden in inscrutable mystery. All of their behavior has been learned, and what one person can learn another can learn. The ethnographer in a foreign land needs time, patience, and effort. He learns to meet the demands of etiquette, friendship, and obligation that any society imposes on all who enter it. Basic emotional adjustment to a culturally different society is not achieved quickly; it may require years, even though a trained observer can accumulate an impressive body of data in a few months. Through long residence one comes to know how the people around him *feel* in every situation. He does not feel that way himself, for he has been reared in a different society; but he comes to understand. The natives are the ultimate judges of the quality of his insight. These facts explain the excellent ethnographic records made by persons innocent of ethnological training who, through long residence, had come to know a foreign people intimately. Mere physical presence in an alien society means nothing; many a trader, official, or missionary spends half a lifetime abroad without transcending the caricatures of native life that enliven the nostalgic table-talk of expatriates.

It is also true that study of anthropological data and theories, *per se,*

cannot guarantee that the student will live graciously and with perceptive understanding among folk culturally different from himself.
Training and knowledge of theory help immensely, but the observer's
flexibility and sensitiveness determine what he will perceive and assimilate.

The distinctive contribution of anthropology and especially of ethnology in the world of contemporary science is not the theories advanced by anthropologists. It is *the constant provision of an ever-
widening variety of data descriptive of human behavior under all sorts
of cultural, geographic, and psychological conditions.* Scientists—and
historians, physicians, philosophers, and other artists—utilize these data
ever more widely to test theory and to extend the scope and catholicity of their outlook. Whatever else anthropologists do, they inject
into many a discussion the crucial comment, "But in Bali (or Timbuc-
too, or Samoa, or Okinawa) it doesn't happen that way!" If these in-
terpellations sometimes become monotonous, they do stimulate thinkers to transcend provincial culture-bound assumptions and to envision
mankind more accurately and sympathetically. Anthropology stands
or falls with the accuracy and completeness of data of original research in the field.

What new insights and cues for fresh research might come to a student who could become thoroughly acquainted with as many as fifty
different peoples in as many parts of the world cannot be discovered.
No one lives long enough to achieve such a goal. Most ethnologists devote their productive years to study of one tribe or group of related
peoples. With advancing age the ethnographer becomes acutely aware
of the shortcomings of his efforts. The ethnologist who attempts to
compare numerous diverse societies must depend largely upon study
of the published works of others who have studied different peoples;
he draws upon his personal experience in contrasting cultural situations
to interpret and appraise descriptions of peoples whom he cannot
know at first hand.

*   *   *   *

Hypotheses devised in other sciences—sociology, psychology, economics, political science, genetics—are often tested in anthropological
researches. For example, the revision of former concepts of instinct
was due in part to anthropological findings. As late as 1920, textbooks
of psychology still included lists of human "instincts" such as construction, gregariousness, maternal love, ownership, kindliness, incest-
avoidance, and aggression. That human behavior suggests such concepts
no one questions, but simplistic explanations in terms of ready-made
inborn "instincts" have disappeared, largely because they were not
observed in the postulated forms in study of exotic peoples. Or again,
Margaret Mead visited Samoa in 1925 to test Stanley Hall's theories

of adolescence in a culturally different situation. The result was abandonment of the doctrine that "storm and stress" inevitably characterize adolescence.

The social sciences are limited by inability to use precise laboratory methods. If this disadvantage were due merely to complexity of the phenomena, experiments still might be devised to settle many questions. Human social behavior, however, is cultural (i.e., learned from other people). New behavior may be learned by anyone at any time and substituted for former behavior. These facts invalidate laboratory studies of social phenomena. To suggest a crude example, it would be ludicrous to select two individuals of opposite sex, place them in a laboratory, and instruct them to fall in love so that the process might be analyzed. Even should the subjects thereupon "fall in love" there is slight reason to expect that two other subjects would duplicate the first experiment. Failure to develop crucial controlled experiments, however, does not mean that social and psychological hypotheses cannot be tested. A hypothesis that holds under varying and contrasted cultural conditions is validated to that extent. If in a contrasting cultural milieu, the hypothesis no longer fits the facts, it is not valid universally, whatever its local applicability. Some hypotheses can be tested against published anthropological data without recourse to field research.

Anthropologists formulate their own hypotheses about human behavior and social phenomena—hypotheses that almost invariably involve complex ramifications in other sciences. While an anthropological hypothesis can be tested for consistency in different societies and against findings in other branches of anthropology, and should hold good in linguistics and physical anthropology and ethnology, verification may extend into the biological laboratory, the psychiatric clinic, or urban sociology.

A moment's reflection upon the nature of a scientific theory in contrast to a purely speculative theory may yield perspective upon much of the history of anthropology. Science begins—and, having made its theories, ends—with observation. In previous paragraphs the basic role of accurate observation and recording has been stressed. But given accurate observation, recorded as facts, what then? The next operation, and usually the most crucial one in any science, is classification. Classification may be explained very simply; it consists in putting together the facts that are alike, and so forming "classes." This simplicity is altogether deceptive, for a major stumbling block in all research is the problem of finding the meaningful and pertinent basis of classification.

Moreover, there is no one "best" classification of facts. If an oversimplified example may be used, suppose that the contents of office waste-baskets are to be classified. All that is necessary—so it seems—is to put like objects together: paper in one pile, discarded chewing gum in another, pencil stubs by themselves, cigarette butts in a pile of their own, and so on. So far, no meaningful pattern emerges other than a worm's eye view of certain habits of the office staff. Since most of the items are papers, a sub-classification is called for. The various pieces of paper are sorted by size, and neat rows of piles appear. Then some original person says, "But size isn't important. We should know whether expensive paper is being wasted; let's sort out the different kinds of paper." Promptly the neat piles are torn to pieces and a different lot of "classes" emerges. If color of the paper happened to be important, the previous classes would be broken up again and new ones formed, in which each "pile" or category would contain paper of the same color.

Classification, then, may occur in protean ways, depending on the interest of the classifier—or speaking more exactly, upon the criteria of classification. Scientifically, the most useful and meaningful classification is one that brings the same objects together in a class when criteria are altered. Thus Linnaeus worked out the basis of a classification of animal species in which use of additional criteria tends to bring out sub-groups, but which does keep the same animals together and lends meaning to the term *species*. Such a self-consistent and inclusive classification sets people thinking; in the case of the Linnaean system, Charles Darwin was among those who thought deeply and fruitfully. For classification suggests interrelations between classes, and a scientific theory is usually an attempt to state some perceived relation between classes of data. The term hypothesis usually denotes a suspected relation of this sort, and a hypothesis automatically suggests lines of research that might verify or disprove the hypothesis.

The thorniest problems of anthropology center in the classification of cultural data.[4] Perhaps the vague concept of "national character" presents the most complex classificatory problem. First comes the question of whether the individual members of a given population can be classified scientifically on the basis of differences in personal character. That divers personalities occur is granted by every field observer. How to identify different types of person with precision, how to accomplish that identification so easily and surely that the several types may be enumerated—these problems are not solved. Assuming that some partial solution is feasible, another question emerges: if societies are characterized by predominance of specific types of person, the term "national character" would gain precision of meaning. But can entire societies be classified scientifically? That question has not been answered satisfactorily. The following paragraphs indicate some of the steps by which this issue has emerged.

* * * *

The belief that people of different nations and tribes differ in "personality" or "national character" is as old as history. Men are interested perennially in exotic peoples and enjoy travellers' tales—the more grotesque the better. Consciously or unconsciously, historians attribute certain personal characteristics to entire nations. Many a book of history embodies some theory of persisting national characteristics. Inevitably history presents selected facts. The historian delves in manuscripts, studies archaeological findings, and endeavors to omit the "nonessential" and to include the "significant."

Sometimes a historian recognizes his principle of selection and states it; more often he works intuitively without fully realizing that his tastes and predispositions play a major role in the selection and arrangement of facts. Among recent historians, David Potter has analyzed lucidly the age-old practice of assuming some "national character" as typical of people of a specific nation, and selecting facts in the light of such assumptions.[5] He argues that ethnology and psychiatry have developed to the point where "national character" can be described objectively and analyzed, and that historians can well afford to investigate the evidence before accepting stereotyped lore about "national character."

The ethnologist also is a historian, whether or not he admits it. By the time that he can publish a report of a field investigation, the situation that he studied has changed, perhaps radically. Ethnographic reports usually are written in the present tense; it is common to speak of this way of writing as the "ethnographic present." No trick of grammar, however, can obscure the fact that ethnographic reports are historical documents. Like other historians, an ethnographer uses some principle of selection. He cannot put in books all that he observes. He is a wise man if he knows the criteria that determine his inclusion and exclusion of materials.[6] In ethnographic studies that are confined to solution of specific problems, the selection of relevant material may become more objective than in broad general cultural surveys.

Ethnologists have not clarified their underlying interest in "national character" much more readily than have the historians. A careful review of the history of anthropology in the light of this issue might be very fruitful. Overwhelmingly, anthropological research has centered implicitly or explicitly in attempts to explain and clarify the elusive differences and resemblances between peoples. Whether or not such differences are subsumed under the category of national character, the persisting goal is explanation of the fact that people of one tribe or nation differ from people of another.

In the nineteenth and early twentieth centuries certain widespread assumptions enabled many writers to feel that differences in national character had been explained. They believed that such differences arose in different "racial instincts," reinforced by inheritance of acquired characteristics, and unified for each people by the "social mind." This latter idea was a consequence of thinking about a society as if it were an organism or "social body."[7] Such beliefs were inseparable from convictions of racial superiority and inferiority. The extreme position taken by Houston Stewart Chamberlain—i.e., the inherent superiority of the "Nordic race" and consequent necessity of avoiding contamination of this precious stock lest civilization perish—won acclaim in Germany with the political support of the Kaiser, who circulated Chamberlain's writings among German army officers. In the United States, Chamberlain's doctrine was proclaimed by Madison Grant, Lothrop Stoddard, William McDougall, and Charles W. Gould, who offered allegedly scientific findings in support of their dogma.[8] This procedure assumed that heredity—i.e., race—provided a basic principle of classification of societies. These ideas were accepted widely until the nineteen-thirties.

The anthropologists of Darwin's generation paid relatively little attention to these issues. Their field researches had convinced them that "common human" characteristics outweighed the differences between peoples. Unique local features they generally attributed to differential retardation of human social evolution in various parts of the world. Fascinated by the idea of evolution, they worked out speculative sequences of human accomplishment from "the beginning" up to the achievements of European and American civilization. They assumed that all peoples pass through the same evolutionary stages in the same order, and consequently explained differences between peoples as due to unequal rates of progress. "Primitive" peoples were not essentially unlike themselves, but were simply retarded by circumstances of environment. Thus, the Iroquois Indians of New York State were regarded as exemplifying a condition that had prevailed among the Romans not very long before the beginning of recorded history.[9] To these writers, stages of cultural evolution afforded an ultimate basis of classification, and differences in "national character" were merely different stages of evolution of the societies involved; they assumed a universal human mentality that would automatically move on to the next stage when conditions were ripe for the change.

The subsequent generation of American anthropologists, of whom Franz Boas, A. L. Kroeber, and Robert Lowie may be regarded as more or less typical, focused their energy upon substantiating or refuting these varied assumptions about tribal and national characteristics. Eagerly they followed every clue that physical anthropology, ethnology, and linguistics could provide to test these alternative explanations of history: whether in terms of evolutionary stages, or in terms of race and Lamarckian inheritance of national traits. It was essential to subject ideas of evolution, or of race, heredity, and cultural phenomena to precise description and analysis, to obtain and verify data of cultural behavior in many societies, and to consider the doctrine of evolutionary stages against this factual background. It was necessary also to make certain whether specific bodily—i.e., racial—features are or are not correlated with mentality. The relation of language to heredity required meticulous investigation. There must be verified knowledge of the extent to which human behavior is determined by heredity, geography, and other factors adduced to explain differences in "national character."

That generation carried out these tasks thoroughly. Anthropologists alone could not solve the problems; in biology, for example, hundreds of thousands of experiments failed to verify a single instance of inheritance of learned behavior or other "acquired characteristics." The new science of genetics, pioneered by Thomas Hunt Morgan, removed heredity from folklore and the superstitions of stock-breeders. Abetted by new knowledge of cell structure based in the staining of tissues, the geneticists moved closer toward understanding of the function of chromosomes and genes. Meanwhile the sociologists and social psychologists—notably Floyd H. Allport[10]—disposed of the organic analogy in discussions of societies, and with it the notion of a "social mind."

The anthropologists, fortified by abundant data of tribes and nations unknown to L. H. Morgan and his contemporaries, found no factual support for doctrines of unilinear evolution. Each society—or at least each group of adjacent and related societies—is a product of its own unique history. That evolution occurs hardly needs proof; but it is evident that it does not proceed in uniform sequences everywhere in the world.[11] Iroquois Indians, when Columbus discovered America, were not in any "stage" of Roman evolution; they were in the contemporary stage of their own history. Inventions made anywhere in the world may spread elsewhere, and this fact of diffusion alone upsets any fixed sequence of evolutionary stages. "National character" is not explained in terms of different degrees of advancement on a fixed evolutionary scale.

The anthropologists reached a more important conclusion which has been confirmed by data of subsequent research: namely, that race, language, and "general culture" do not explain each other. Given a start in childhood, normal human beings of any race learn any language or any culture. No measurable bodily feature predisposes its bearer toward specific linguistic or other cultural behavior. Language and culture are totally learned, and man cannot function culturally or linguistically unless he "learns how." No one has shown that one racial

stock learns with greater facility than another. A so-called race com-
prises the entire gamut of individual ability from idiot to genius; human
differences are individual, not uniform within a race. E. B. Tylor had
first defined culture as learned "capabilities and habits,"[12] but a generation was required to clarify the implications of this concept. Boas and
his contemporaries concluded that neither race nor climate and topography, nor evolutionary stage, nor any single cultural feature such as
economics, can explain the patterns of any society.

Boas himself insisted that historical events afford the most tenable
explanations of specific cultural phenomena although he recognized
that, as far as non-literate peoples are concerned, the relevant historical events never could be known adequately. He insisted that ethnographers exert all possible effort to record the customs and bodily
characteristics of every tribe and nation before the spread of European civilization swept the lesser peoples into extinction. His generation
of anthropologists succeeded in discrediting simplistic explanations of
"national character" in terms of racial heredity, evolutionary stage,
geographic influences or other single-factor mysticisms. This conclusion carried the implication that classifications of societies by criteria of
race, evolutionary stages, religious systems, economic systems, etc.,
could not yield categories meaningful for explanation of cultural and
social systems.

* * * *

Human behavior does not vary capriciously and at random. The
possible forms and patterns of behavior, if not infinitely numerous, exceed the imagination of anyone who knows no culture other than his
own—as every ethnographic report demonstrates. But always the observed behavior varies within a finite range of what is known at a
specific time and place, and newly introduced features are modified to
fit what already is current in the local society. This integration of
specific cultural items to achieve a seemingly consistent whole[13] is
not a "process of culture." "Culture" does not act, for it is nothing
more and nothing less than whatever people are doing and thinking.
Individuals act. Integration can occur in only one locus—in a human
individual.[14] Each person adjusts his habits to what he must do, what
he can do, and what he wants to do, in terms of his view of himself
and his own role and the demands of his associates. The fact that the
many individuals in a society attain similar adjustments makes it possible to speak of societal patterns. No matter how individuals in the
same society may differ in each other's eyes, the very fact that their
selection of behavior patterns is confined to a specific time in history
and a specific region of the world with its local culture insures similarities in their behavior that are perceived after careful research as
societal patterns. "Society" is a convenient abstraction in discussing

interdependent multi-individual activity, and societal patterns are discovered in summation of observations of many participating individuals.[15]

Since participants in the same society draw upon the same cultural
base, face similar situations, and generally acknowledge ideals of character that emerge from a common tradition, the individual patterns of
integration of behavior in that society are similar in some respects. No
one's behavior can be interpreted apart from the total cultural context,
and ethnologists have come to insist on this principle. A revolution in
anthropological thinking had preceded this conclusion. Early anthropologists had attempted to follow the example of taxonomists; they
classified artifacts and cultural features as if they were so many species
of plants and animals, and did so on the basis of a vaguely defined
postulate of "universal human mentality." Museums contained cases of
arrow points neatly arranged by shape and size and material, regardless
of the part of the world from which they had come. Other cases contained tools, costumes, or pottery, similarly classified. Sir James Frazer's
monumental work, "The Golden Bough," attempted to classify customs and beliefs on the basis of similarity of content, regardless of cultural context, and without critical scrutiny of sources. Largely through
the insights of Bastian and Boas, it came to be realized that classification solely by external form usually is meaningless in dealing with
human behavior and artifacts. At the American Museum of Natural
History, the famous Northwest Coast Indian display was organized by
Boas according to tribes. The several tribal exhibits were arranged in
geographical sequence. Each object—canoe paddle, wooden box, mask,
totem pole, or blanket—received meaning, not by comparison with a
superficially similar object from another part of the world, but by
study of its functions in relation to the activities of the people who had
made and used it. It was becoming clear that the cultural behavior and
artifacts of each tribe or people possessed a kind of unity and could
not be understood out of context.

Subsequently Malinowski insisted vigorously upon a "functionalist"
interpretation of all socio-cultural phenomena.[16] Regardless of Malinowski's zest for controversy, his basic insight was the same as that of
Boas, namely, that every act, every human relationship, every idea or
artifact has meaning only in relation to the cultural resources and social
behavior of the people among whom it is observed.

Anthropologists thus came face to face with a problem that many
historians and sociologists already had approached speculatively. Can
entire societies be classified, and how? If cultural traits can be classified
only as items in a total cultural integration typical of the society of
their provenance, then can these numerous societies be classified as
wholes? One such classification emerged as ethnologists attempted to

map culture areas. In such maps societies of a region are classified in terms of their resemblances to and differences from neighboring societies.

Every tribe, nation, or sub-group within a nation is unique in many respects. Nevertheless every group resembles in many ways the adjacent peoples—resemblances unpredictable in detail, but varying within the ascertainable range of knowledge available within the area. This situation underlies the abused but valuable concept of *cultural areas*.[17] No one expects to find a community of Tibetan lamas in the heart of an American city, nor does one encounter Plains Indians in full ceremonial regalia in Central China. Every continent and sub-continent includes peoples who differ culturally among themselves; within these large regions, however, cultural similarities often outweigh the differences. Thus, African peoples south of the Sahara usually organize politically on the monarchial pattern, while American Indians north of the Rio Grande knew nothing of kings and based tribal organization on relatively democratic councils. Tailored clothing (i.e., cut, fitted, and sewed) is as characteristic of northeastern Asia and much of aboriginal North America as flowing robes are characteristic of Western Asia and North Africa. The fact that Japanese dwellings resemble the houses of southeastern Asia and Indonesia rather than those of China becomes significant in another way when Japan's extensive cultural borrowings from China are considered; Japanese culture is shown by house-forms and other details to depend also on Oceanic sources. It is enlightening in study of cultural phenomena to construct maps of the distribution of languages, house forms, types of clothing, religious ideas, forms of land tenure, patterns of social organization—of any cultural features whatever.

Granting that speed and variety of intercommunication constantly break down cultural divisions and create new ones, cultural areas still may be mapped for specific historical epochs and they reveal patterns of cultural interdependence. Automatically such maps effect valid classifications of societies; they show which societies are most alike and which ones differ sharply. These geographically-revealed classifications are not artificial, but natural in that they have come about through interchange of ideas, artifacts, and other cultural features over considerable periods of time. Specific practices and folkways thus appear in their wider context; in cultural comparisons, the unit of comparison should be the entire cultural area, not the individual tribes within such an area, unless sharp divergencies appear in some respects between tribes otherwise similar. Study of culture-distribution maps solves some historical problems and raises others; consequently there exists a considerable body of discussion concerning "culture areas."[18] Regardless of fine points of theory, it often is feasible to forecast, before visiting a people or tribe, the rudiments of what to expect culturally. Maps aid enormously in analysis of problems posed by local absence of an expected feature, even as they aid in interpreting the presence of a cultural element.

Geographically-oriented classification of societies in cultural areas, however, does not exhaust the possibilities of classification. One contemporary scheme offers considerable promise as far as it goes. Eliot Chapple and Carleton Coon formulated operational definitions of "institution" and "specialist" and proposed that societies be classified in terms of complexity, on the basis of numbers of institutions and the proportions of the several populations who function as specialists. These strictly socio-economic categories cut across culture areas; the "centrally located" societies are more complex than the marginal societies. The categories may be used in culturally different societies. No psychological questions of "personality type" are involved. Messrs. Chapple and Coon caution against applying to a whole people such facile labels as "mystic," "fanatic," "theocratic," etc.[19]

An inductively derived approach to classification of societies in psychological terms was presented by the late Richard Thurnwald.[20] During the second World War he retired to the country and spent years in careful analysis of the voluminous field-records of a lifetime of research in Africa, New Guinea, the Solomon Islands, and Southeastern Europe in an effort to discover inductively any generalizations that his data might offer. His hypotheses were then tested against data of India and Western Asia, the Mediterranean world, and the Americas. One theory, advanced tentatively and with the strict caution that it must not be interpreted as a general theory of social evolution, centered in certain general psychological differences that appear again and again in various cultural areas. These are the differences in type of personality developed in sedentary agrarian societies and the types developed in migratory herders and sea-rovers.

Tillers of the soil, notoriously, have little or no opportunity to range afield and so to broaden their experience. Nor do peasants learn how to organize masses of men for action; their energies are concentrated on intensive exploitation of the possibilities of earth, sunshine, and rain. The emergencies that confront them—drought, flood, insect pests—are not overcome by human effort, apart from large-scale organization to provide irrigation, famine relief, or scientific control of pests and plant diseases. Normally incapable of such organization, they remain helpless in time of catastrophe—including invasion by hostile plunderers. But herders and sea-rovers live a different kind of life. The herder must learn to direct and control masses of animals; he must learn to fight off wild beasts, to protect himself against human marauders, and to act decisively in emergencies. The seafaring peoples learn analogous skills—to organize the crew of a ship, to deal with hostile natives of a strange port, to save themselves in a storm. Both herders and seafarers learn much about other peoples and tribes. They learn the art of war, and more important, they often have advance information of the coming of an attacking horde.

The conventional interpretation of these historically verifiable differences in outlook and experience is evident in numerous theories of conquest of the sedentary peoples by the rovers. Political theorists have asserted that political states arise in conquest, and cite as evidence of past conquests the existence of numerous tribes in which a mobile aristocracy rules over a sedentary agricultural population. Such conquests have occurred and are commonplaces of history. Thurnwald, however, discovered even more numerous occasions on which sedentary tribes, having come into contact with rovers, perceived the advantages of an alliance, and initially cemented the merger by intermarriage. In exchange for protection and organizational "know-how" the peasants offered cereal foods, products of handicrafts that require a fixed base of operations, and a stable place of residence for the wanderers. Such peaceful mergers eventuated in domination of the sedentary population by a hereditary aristocracy precisely as military conquest accomplished the same end; in either case two culturally different peoples, usually speaking different languages, achieved a new and often mutually beneficial integration.

For present purposes, the contribution of Thurnwald's analysis resides in his delineation of the psychological contrast between the typical individual in a sedentary agricultural tribe, and the typical member of a mobile tribe. Here is a classification of societies in terms of aspects of personality characteristic of each society—not universally applicable, but inductively derived.

*   *   *   *

Advances in the study of characteristic differences in personal character among different peoples stem from research in several sciences. To select one contribution arbitrarily, Boas' colleague at Columbia University, the sociologist F. H. Giddings, envisioned methods of scientifically studying societies—methods curiously eclipsed after his death. He asserted that the initial step in study of a society is observation of the kinds of people that it includes, and determination of their relative numbers.[21] Giddings harbored no illusions about the difficulty of defining "kinds" of people. He pointed out, however, that all human beings gossip; i.e., they constantly discuss kinds of people, instantly recognize "my kind of person" and seek out their own kind in preference to other—allegedly worse—kinds.[22] Granted the difficulty of rigorous classification of individuals, he pointed out that enumeration of certain crudely defined kinds of persons is feasible in any society: witness census data of single, married, widowed, and divorced; of persons of different ages; of those engaged in various occupations; or of members of associations with declared purposes. Such attributes serve as cues by which people habitually sort themselves in search of congenial company or in attempts to achieve various ends by co-operation. To the extent that different kinds of persons can be identi-fied and counted, Giddings argued that a society may be evaluated ob-jectively on the basis of the contrast between the kinds of people who are encouraged and rewarded and the kinds of people who suffer dis-advantages. This recognition by sociologists of the presence in any large society of numerous kinds of persons—the current locution is "per-sonality types"—has not received due weight in some studies of "na-tional character." Here was the essence of a meaningful classification of the individuals who compose a society. Moreover, such classification suggested the possibility of a scientifically-based classification of so-cieties according to the dominant (or most frequent) personality type discovered in census enumerations of "kinds" within each society.

Ethnologists of the 1920's rarely possessed the inclination or the technical training that could have analyzed psychological or personality types within the societies they studied. But individual anthropologists —of whom Edward Sapir was outstanding—were turning to psycho-analysis and psychiatry for light on individual mentality and character. Since heredity in racial units, geography, evolutionary stages, and other short-cut explanations no longer sufficed to explain cultural differences, and since it was becoming ever clearer that "culture" is a psychological phenomenon, this shift of interest was overdue.[23] Some anthropolo-gists investigated psychoanalysis because they objected to Freudian notions of a "racial unconscious" that postulated universal hereditary memories, deeply buried in unconscious functioning, of alleged prime-val events for which anthropology could discover no evidence. In due course the anthropologists developed extensive common interests with the psychoanalysts. Some of these interests involved observation of neurotic and psychotic behavior among non-literate peoples, with con-sequent discussion of the question, "What is normal?" Other common interests appeared as both groups discovered that they were concerned with the whole life of man rather than with artificially isolated seg-ments of human affairs.

More fundamentally, ethnologists realized that psychoanalysts and psychiatrists were concerned with cultural phenomena. All three groups of scientists were studying *what people know and what they think about*. Intent on therapy, the psychoanalysts had been forced to examine specific "mental content" and to reconstruct the circum-stances in which individual emotional habits had been learned. On the other hand, the orthodox psychologists were trying to circumvent the limitations of specific cultural behavior in order to arrive at general principles of mental functioning. The ethnologists' studies of "culture" approached a common focus with the psychoanalysts' interest in *what ideas* individuals had learned, and the circumstances under which learning had occurred. Necessity was pressing the ethnologists to investigate differences in personality and mental operations among alien peoples, and that necessity drove them to psychologists and psychiatrists to obtain research techniques. So ethnographers began to use mental tests, projective tests such as the Rorschach, and tried also to understand psychoanalytic concepts in hope of deeper insight into the emotional life of their subjects in the field. Ethnology was coming to grips with the question, "What kinds of persons are observed in a specific society?"

Data had been accumulating to indicate that in small tribes, at least, the number of models for personal character is limited. Sometimes there appears but one tribal ideal of male character, with another for females. Both small tribes and great nations often—perhaps usually—exhibit consciously formulated ideals of personal character. These are asserted in folklore and exhortation to the young, and effort is directed to developing children along desired lines. Field researches also disclose that occasional individuals in a society find the local ideal of character uncongenial, and the analogy with maladjustment in Euro-American societies carries weight.

Margaret Mead and Ruth Benedict, among others, experimented with the possibility of classifying societies on the basis of predominant personality characteristics—in statistical language, modal personality types. Benedict borrowed Nietzsche's terms, Apollonian and Dionysian, and applied them to the Pueblo Indians, and to the Crow and Kwakiutl, respectively. She did not regard these as hard and fast categories, and she insisted that "It would be absurd to cut every culture down to the Procrustean bed of some catchword characterization."[24] Subsequently various writers, including Benedict and Mead, called attention to guilt feelings as dominant motivations in some tribes, and to fear of shame or ridicule as outstanding motivation in others. This suggested characterization of some societies as "shame cultures," others as "guilt cultures." These should not be accepted as simple categories of classification,[25] and their exponents regarded them as hypotheses for investigation, not as rigid universal categories.[26]

No one scheme of classifying societies—save perhaps the culture area procedure—meets the demands of rigorously scientific procedure. Contemporary ethnologists, however, devote much time to investigation of the prevalence of specific personality types or patterns in specific societies. This problem is central in many of the papers that have been collected in the present book. It is possible that among the simpler peoples, at least, types of personality may be distributed geographically and could be represented on maps just as house-forms, religious rituals, and other cultural phenomena are shown on the distribution maps that delimit culture areas. If so, the probability that phenomena of "personality type" are cultural—i.e., learned from associates—is strengthened by the same sort of evidence that demonstrates the independence of language and family organization from racial and purely geographic determination.

The trend of psychiatric investigation indicates that personal character depends overwhelmingly upon individual learning and experience, without neglecting the subtle, but strictly individual, facts of heredity. Psychiatrists agree that "personality" must be interpreted against the background of each individual's cultural equipment and social situation. The psychoanalysts have acted from the beginning as if this were the case; otherwise they would not analyze each individual patient, his relations with other people, his past experiences and subtly repressed impulses. They agree that a given patient is like other people in general, but for therapy they depend on the effort to understand his *unique* individuality.

The conclusions proclaimed by Boas and his generation of anthropologists, namely, that race, language, and general culture vary independently and do not explain each other, probably will be amplified by adding another independent variable. For styles in personal character also appear to vary independently of race, language, and broad cultural patterns of social organization, religion, and technology.[27]

Most ethnographers gladly leave to specialists the detailed investigation of the psychology of individual natives. In the search for ways of accumulating reliable data of individual behavior in culturally different societies the ethnographer accepts all the help that psychologists and psychiatrists can offer. The ethnographer's fundamental interest centers in the broad similarities of personal character that appear within a specific cultural milieu, not in every idiosyncrasy of every individual native. For example, in some respects a Chicago gangster, a Boston nun, and a Los Angeles real estate dealer are alike; all of them, traveling abroad, would find it difficult to conceal their North American origin. Sooner or later Europeans or Asiatics probably would recognize each of these contrasting individuals as an "American." Thus ethnologists seek to define the aspects of personal character that are fostered by the specific cultural milieu of each society. To the extent that such societal aspects of personality are identifiable and verifiable, they offer criteria of classification of societies. Some writers think that "national character" is defined when these distinctive features that nearly everyone in the same society exhibits are described. Abram Kardiner's distinguished contribution, for example, centers in his concept of "basic personality structure" and this includes discovery of the aspects of personality that are exhibited by the majority of persons in a society.

The specific obligations of ethnology, accordingly, include description of the ideals of personal character acknowledged by each people studied; of the ways in which these ideals are imparted to the young and the circumstances in which children and young people come to incorporate the ideals into their own habit systems—i.e., super-ego formation; and of the different types of persons in the society and their problems of adjustment to prevailing standards. If description of these phenomena discloses a clear-cut predominant personality type, that society is to that extent amenable to classification in terms of "national character."

* * * *

With all this attention to differences between peoples, the allied problem of universal human similarities has received much attention. Certain general conclusions may be summarized. These depend on physical anthropology and other biological sciences, as well as upon ethnology.

1. Human beings are living organisms. All organisms resist environmental forces, grow in spite of them, utilize them in order to live. At any moment an organism is the complex resultant of the interaction of hereditary factors in a variable but specific dynamic milieu and incorporates past growth and behavior. Each plant or animal grows in the form characteristic of its species and attains a definite size. Within limits set by the genes it may modify its form or behavior to cope with environmental conditions. It can be explained only in terms of what it has done about environment, and but slightly in terms of what environment has done to it. When it no longer resists environmental energies, it loses its characteristic shape and behavior; it is dead, no longer a living organism. Carelessly one says, "The sun tanned my skin." All that the sun can do, however, is to burn, sometimes fatally. The organism tans itself in adaptation to the sun. Organic viability is measured by adequacy and versatility of resistance to and utilization of environmental energies. These biological facts contravene the notion that external forces mould human beings. The pupils in a two-million-dollar school building are not twice as well educated as those in a one-million-dollar structure. *What man does about his environment outweighs anything that environment does to him*, short of violent death. In final analysis, human beings make themselves. The accessible cultural resources determine and limit opportunity to learn, not what one ultimately becomes. The tremendous range of cultural variation makes it easy to underestimate these elemental organic facts.

Human organisms are everywhere similar; all belong to a single species of primates: *homo sapiens*. Glandular secretions, blood chemistry, and other biochemical tests indicate identity of species; evidences of subtle biochemical differences in races do not justify regarding them as separate species. All human types are inter-fertile, and are not fertile with other animal species. Organic functions are practically identical throughout mankind. Innumerable aspects of cultural behavior are related to organic similarities; thus, all men eat, sleep, reproduce, breathe, and carry on other organic functions. Culturally they differ in the manner, time, and occasions of performing these functions. Most alleged "cultural universals" turn out to be biologically based. Since all human organisms are born, mature, and decline in the same way, every society contains people of different ages, as well as of both sexes. This biological fact enters into all social organization, but the manner of such organization varies with the cultural milieu.

2. Human nervous systems represent a special aspect of the biological identity of the species. To a degree observed in no other species, the nervous systems of human beings provide for indefinite modifiability of individual behavior involved in environmental adjustment. Only the nervous mechanisms that control functioning of the vital visceral organs operate in the stereotyped manner so characteristic of lower animals. Stated otherwise, human beings may eat all sorts of foods at any time of day, prepared and served in an infinite variety of ways. This is the cultural aspect of eating; but once masticated, from the moment of swallowing, the food is identically digested and assimilated. The urban socialite nibbling at a canapé and the aboriginal Australian eating roasted grubs, swallow, digest, and assimilate their food identically. Since emotional behavior involves specific visceral tensions and chemical conditions within the body, all human beings are capable of the same basic responses of fear, anger, tenderness, or anticipation. But the circumstances that evoke these responses and the complexes of ideas associated therewith differ with the cultural repertory of the individual. The organic mechanism that responds is everywhere the same; characteristic of that mechanism is extreme versatility of learning and adaptation that permits individuals of different societies to learn quite different habits of response. Human beings who use different languages may reason quite differently, depending on the inherent logic of their respective languages. The neural mechanisms that do the reasoning, however, are substantially identical. Boas' two dicta are pertinent: "the one the fundamental sameness of mental processes in all races and in all cultural forms of the present day; the other, the consideration of every cultural phenomenon as the result of historical happenings."[28]

3. Another aspect of organic similarity requires special mention. This is the identical mechanical functioning of sensory organs, with allowance for differences in habit and practice, in mankind every-

where. For example, optical mechanisms are identical in all human beings. Thus, ancient Greek architects recognized the unpleasant optical illusion that leads us to see a straight cylindrical column as narrower in the middle than at the ends; they corrected for that illusion by making columns thicker in the middle. The Indians of Vancouver Island recognized the same illusion and corrected the shape of their totem poles in the same way. Universal aspects of music are related in analogous fashion to the mechanical functioning of the ear.

4. Human beings perceive their bodies alike, and generally hit upon similar analogies between the body and its environment. Thus, in many languages openings in other objects are called by words that denote the mouth. Objects whose form resembles the sexual organs are usually named accordingly, and symbolic use of such objects is similar in societies otherwise quite different. The bole of a tree and the human torso often are called by the same name—in English, the word "trunk." Such ready analogies between the body and non-human objects do not imply a "racial unconscious" or a mystical instinct of some kind; they are explicable in terms of obvious analogies. Similarly, the facts of birth and parent-child interdependence evoke the same general analogies among many different peoples. Again, much human conduct is related to the fact that the head, which includes valuable organs such as eyes, ears, and mouth, happens to be at the top of the human body. Ideas of the relative superiority of that which is "above" or "up" and the inferiority of what is "below" or "down" show widespread uniformity. It is interesting to speculate upon the changes in language and custom that would be necessary if bodies were suddenly transformed to place the head at ground level.

5. Certain physical facts about human organisms may carry the same or similar cultural consequences everywhere. For example, possibilities of action may be limited physically. The "rule of the road" derives from the fact that when two people travelling in opposite directions meet, they must pass on one side or the other. Only two possibilities—left or right—are available for cultural standardization, and if any rule is established, it must be one or the other. Actual physical uniformities and limitations differ from psychological—hence cultural—interpretations of physical facts. E.g., every human body occupies space; hence the number of people who can assemble in a place is limited physically. Such a fact of physics is subject to varied psychological and cultural interpretations but is not altered thereby.

6. Most clearly demonstrable of all cultural similarities are those consequent upon diffusion of an idea or invention from one people to another. The universal use of fire, of clubs as weapons, and of stone tools have been attributed to "instinct" despite lack of evidence. Diffusion of these practices is suggested by archaeological data, and by

analogy with world-wide diffusion of other cultural items—such as the smoking of cigarettes—that has occurred in contemporary times and can be verified amply. The more complex the invention or artifact, the greater the probability that it has been diffused and not invented independently. Historically, it is possible to trace the diffusion of numberless items of cultural behavior, from war and communism to use of motor cars and electric lights.

7. More controversial are certain psychological operations that psychoanalysts have postulated as universal. Ethnological data refute some of the Freudian claims to universality of phenomena that he observed in his nineteenth-century European clientele. His interpretations of totemism and allied phenomena have been attacked sharply;[29] probably much of his use of mythological and ethnographic data available in his day should be evaluated in the light of the near-impossibility of expressing what he had to say with the linguistic equipment of his generation. Psychoanalysts have been trying to describe phenomena for which no precise vocabulary existed, and it was necessary at the outset to resort to all sorts of devices in hope of communicating psychoanalytic discoveries. In time, however, cultural data underwent re-examination and various writers became convinced that ethnological data often support the Freudian discovery of unconscious and repressed behavior—phenomena that explained neurotic behavior and that appeared to characterize human mentality and emotion in every society. There is increasing acceptance of the idea that folklore, dreams, shamanism, and various emotionally-disturbed states observed among "primitive" peoples involve analytically-discovered processes such as repression, projection, fixation, and introjection.

Whether Freud's interpretations of specific symbols are applicable universally, or whether each society develops a unique cultural repertory of symbolic representation of repressed impulses, is a problem that calls for ethnographic research. Interpretation of symbolism in any society should be discovered inductively by study of that society, not postulated for all mankind on the basis of Euro-American clinical experience. Interpretation of symbols used by non-Euro-American peoples remains speculative until there are ethnologically-sophisticated psychoanalysts capable of working with such peoples.[30] Better yet, indigenous analysts educated in psychiatry and psychoanalytic technique, but working in their own language among their own people, are almost certainly prerequisite to dependable interpretation of symbolism observed beyond the limits of Euro-American culture. Such analysts will need to chart inductively the symbolisms of their own culture even as Freud and others discovered European and American symbolisms. Such problems cannot be solved in terms of the generalized "culture" of a people; they must be approached by intensive study of individuals, just as the original analytic discoveries were achieved by Freud and his associates.

* * * *

These comments on various anthropological topics have so far avoided careful definition of the terms "personality" and "national character." The selected papers that compose this volume differ in use of these and other terms, and readers will bring to the materials their own varying concepts. In lieu of a rigorous definition, the essentials of an operational definition of "person" may be considered. The abstraction, "personality," may be defined in so many ways that no attempt is made to add one more definition to the confusion.

The term "person" is meaningless save as it refers to a human being. Observation of a person is impossible except as a living human organism is observed. Not all human organisms, however, justify the term, person. Newly-born infants are not yet persons. Some organically defective individuals never become persons; they never learn to feed and care for themselves or to communicate with others, even though they live for decades. A normal human baby learns rapidly, and integrates the learned behavior in its own unique fashion. Gradually this acquired action system of cultural behavior assumes a uniquely individual configuration and the child becomes recognizable as an individualized human being. From this time on he is not merely a living human organism, he is becoming a person. No one else exhibits precisely the same combination of habits and knowledge, no one else can remember the same events in the same sequence and with the same emotional emphasis, no one else responds to the same patterns of stimulation in the same way (since stimulation always includes the previous experience of the individual). In this context, a definition set forth elsewhere with supporting evidence is repeated: "A person is a human organism who has grown and developed habitual patterns of behavior through participation in social life."[31]

Far from presenting a final and authoritative picture of human beings and their cultural worlds, anthropology teems with unsolved problems. Otherwise this book would be superfluous. The following essays present many aspects of the investigation of culturally fostered patterns of personal character. Some important contributions are omitted because of sheer lack of space, others by accident of the compiler's range of competence. It should be clear, however, that diverse problems of individual adjustment in socio-cultural situations are under active investigation and that no one point of view can defend claims to finality. Like all science, anthropology is a continuing adventure—the intimate and emotionally-weighted adventure of man's attempts to understand himself.

NOTES

1. Definitions of "culture" are collected and analyzed in *Culture: A Critical Review of Concepts and Definitions*, by A. L. Kroeber and Clyde Kluckhohn, *Papers of the Peabody Museum, Harvard University*, vol. 47 #1 (1952). The present writer, dissatisfied with the usual definitions, has stated his position in "Is Culture Definable?" *Amer. Sociological Rev., 14* (1949): 26-32, and in more elementary form in Mosher et al, *Introduction to Responsible Citizenship* (New York, 1941), Ch. 2-10.

2. Cf. editorial, "Applied Anthropology," in *Human Organization* 14 #2 (1955):pp. 2-3.

3. One modest but distinguished student of primitive music always studied expertly the social and religious organization of a tribe, although no one could persuade her to publish her sociological data. Her usual comment was, "But I'm no sociologist. I simply had to know those things in order to understand the music!"

4. Space forbids discussion of the most extensive project of classification of cultural data thus far attempted: the Cross-Cultural Survey at Yale University. For the categories developed in classification of data of cultural behavior from hundreds of peoples, see G. P. Murdock *et al.*, *Outline of Cultural Materials: 3rd revised edition* (New Haven, 1950). For data of child training and personality characteristics, *cf.* J. W. M. Whiting and I. L. Child, *Child-Training and Personality, a Cross-Cultural Study* (New Haven, 1953).

Perhaps the Yale Cross-Cultural Survey may claim spiritual descent from Herbert Spencer's ambitious project of classifying social phenomena the world over; *cf.* his *Descriptive Sociology* (London, 1874 *et seq.*)

5. David M. Potter, *People of Plenty* (Chicago, 1954). Chapter I.

6. What is a *significant fact?* Mary Elizabeth Johnson has written:

"Since societal data are descriptive of people and the observer himself is a human person, the more pertinent and accurate the facts, the more difficult is the attainment of freedom from the bias inherent in personal logic; therefore all classifications of societal data require the most critical scrutiny to make certain that categories are truly inductive. Emotionally convinced of the profound truth of his personal evaluations, the investigator all too easily groups facts in an order consistent with his personal logic; the patterns that emerge from such biased classification are more likely to be descriptive of the personal logic of the observer than of the phenomena investigated.

"The organization and analysis of data descriptive of social phenomena usually involve the problem of the significance of some facts as contrasted with other facts. In scientific classification, a fact may be deemed important when its inclusion or exclusion alters the interpretation of other facts and involves the interrelation of numbers of facts. This criterion contrasts with emphasis upon facts as significant merely because they are emotionally important in personal logic or because knowledge of them leads people to change their behavior—as for example, when knowledge of the facts of deaths in childbirth arouses a community to build a new hospital. In scientific description of social life it is essential to restrict the term *significant fact* to those facts whose inclusion or exclusion alters the meaning of other facts."

D. G. Haring and M. E. Johnson, *Order and Possibility in Social Life* (New York, 1940). Pp. 451-452.

7. Cf. Thomas Hobbes, *Leviathan* (London, 1651); published in Everyman's Library, with an introduction by A. D. Lindsay (London and New York, n.d.). Two centuries later, Herbert Spencer's *Principles of Sociology*, vol. I (New York, 1901) contains, under the topic, "The Inductions of Sociology," the following chapter headings: "A Society is an Organism," "Social Growth," "Social Structures," "Social Functions," "Systems of Organs," etc. Consult any good work on social theory.

8. Houston Stewart Chamberlain, *Foundations of the Nineteenth Century* (Berlin, 1899), English tr. by Lord Redesdale, 2 vol. (New York and London, 1910); Madison Grant, *The Passing of the Great Race* (New York, 1916); Lothrop Stoddard, *The Rising Tide of Colour* (New York, 1920); Wm. McDougall, *Is America Safe for Democracy?* (New York, 1921); Charles W. Gould, *America a Family Matter* (New York, 1920). For less biased, more scientific studies, cf. papers and references in Franz Boas, *Race, Language, and Culture* (New York, 1940); Friedrich Hertz, *Race and Civilization* (New York, 1928); F. H. Hankins, *The Racial Basis of Civilization* (New York, 1926); E. A. Hooton, *Up from the Ape*, rev. ed. (New York, 1946); H. L. Shapiro, *Migration and Environment* (London & New York, 1939); Wm. C. Boyd, *Genetics and the Races of Man* (Boston, 1950); C. S. Coon, S. M. Garn, and J. B. Birdsell, *Races . . . A Study of the Problems of Race Formation in Man* (Springfield, 1950); and the magnificent source translations assembled by Earl W. Count, *This is Race* (New York, 1950).

9. Such schemata of cultural evolution were devised by many writers, of whom Lewis Henry Morgan, *Ancient Society* (New York, 1877), and Herbert Spencer, *Principles of Sociology*, 3 vols. (New York, 1901), may be regarded as typical.

10. *Institutional Behavior.* (Chapel Hill, 1933).

11. Cf. Robert H. Lowie, *Primitive Society* (New York, 1920).

12. Edward B. Tylor, *Primitive Culture* (London, 1871), p. 1.

13. The seeming consistency usually involves rationalization, polite fictions, and the amazing capacity of human minds for reconciling contradictory acts and ideas in the interests of complacency.

14. D. G. Haring, "Note concerning 'integration'," *Bull. Amer. Assn. Univ. Profs., 29 #5* Dec. 1943).

15. D. G. Haring and M. E. Johnson, *Order and Possibility in Social Life* (New York, 1940), Chapter 24.

16. Cf. B. Malinowski, "Anthropology," *Encyclopaedia Britannica*, 13th ed. (1926), vol. *29* (Supp. vol. I). Malinowski's "functionalism" was based in the organic analogy; he thought in terms of "social physiology." So was that of Radcliffe-Brown, who, however, recognized the analogy for what it was and used it cautiously. Cf. A. R. Radcliffe-Brown, "The Methods of Ethnology," *So. African Jnl. of Science, 20* (1923):124-147.

17. For a beautiful statement of the general idea, cf. A. A. Goldenweiser, *Early Civilization* (New York, 1922), pp. 118-123.

18. E.g., the Wissler-Dixon controversy: Clark Wissler, *Man and Culture* (New York, 1923); Roland B. Dixon, *The Building of Cultures* (New York, 1928); and other works in that debate. Cf. also the differences in the 1923 and 1948 editions of A. L. Kroeber, *Anthropology* (New York); A. A. Goldenweiser, "Diffusionism and the American School of Historical Ethnology," *Amer. Jnl. Sociology, 31* (1925): 34-37; M. J. Herskovits, "A Preliminary Consideration of the Culture Areas of Africa," *Amer. Anthrop. 26* (1924): 50ff; R. S. Naroll, "Draft Map of the Culture Areas of Asia," *S. W. Jnl. Anthrop.,* 6 (1950): 183-187; A. L. Kroeber, *Cultural and Natural Areas of Native North America* (Berkeley, 1939). A clear summary of the so-called diffusionist controversy appears in B. Schrieke, "The evolution of culture in the Pacific in relation to theories of the 'Kulturhistorische' and the 'Manchester' schools of Social Anthropology," *Proc. 3rd Pacific Sci. Congress, Tokyo, 1926*, vol. II, pp. 2423-2441.

19. Eliot D. Chapple and Carleton S. Coon, *Principles of Anthropology* (New York, 1942), pp. 36-41, 138-141, 281-292, and Chapter 18; Carleton S. Coon, *A Reader in General Anthropology* (New York, 1948), Appendix.

20. R. Thurnwald, *Der Mensch Geringer Natur-Beherrschung, Sein Aufstieg Zwischen Vernunft und Wahn* (Berlin, 1950).

21. Franklin Henry Giddings, *Studies in the Theory of Human Society* (New York, 1922); *The Scientific Study of Human Society* (Chapel Hill, 1924). For summaries of some of his contributions, *cf.* D. G. Haring and M. E. Johnson, *op. cit.*

22. Giddings' apt phrase, "consciousness of kind," unfortunately provided a handy slogan to denote his ideas, and his sound contribution was neglected by those who dismissed his work by repeating that slogan. In his later years Giddings often expressed regret that he ever had coined that phrase.

23. Cf., elsewhere in this book, Clyde Kluckhohn's paper, "The influence of psychiatry on anthropology in America during the last 100 years." Will some psychiatrist or psychoanalyst return the compliment and write a scholarly history of "The influence of anthropology on psychiatry in America during the last 100 years"?

24. Ruth F. Benedict, *Patterns of Culture* (Boston, 1934), p. 228. Chapters 7 and 8 show that she recognized clearly that both small tribes and populous nations may acknowledge more than one ideal type of character.

25. Gerhard Piers and M. B. Singer, *Shame and Guilt, a Psychoanalytic and Cultural Study*. Springfield, Ill., 1953.

26. Along with many other sociologists, F. H. Giddings had attempted a psychological classification of societies, in *Readings in Descriptive and Historical Sociology* (New York, 1906). His categories were: sympathetic societies, congenial societies, approbational societies, despotic societies, authoritative societies, conspirital societies, contractual societies, and idealistic societies. Subsequently Giddings abandoned this entire scheme in disgust.

Among anthropologists, L. Lévy-Bruhl (*Primitive Mentality*, New York, 1923; *How Natives Think*, New York, 1920) followed out some of Durkheim's ideas and classified societies as "primitive" or "civilized" on the basis of psychological differences that he ascribed to a special "primitive mentality." More recent anthropological classifications include R. Redfield's psychological distinctions between folk-societies and urban societies (*The Primitive World and Its Transformations*, Ithaca, 1953; *The Folk Culture of Yucatan*, Chicago, 1941). Obviously the problem of classification has not been solved.

27. Unpublished data of the writer's researches in Japan and the Ryūkyū Islands indicate that identical family and kinship systems may coexist with decidedly contrasting patterns of temperament and personality. Cf. "Japanese National Character," reprinted in this volume.

28. Franz Boas, *Primitive Art* (Oslo, 1927) p. 1.

29. Sigmund Freud, *Totem and Taboo* (Vienna, 1913, tr. by A. A. Brill, New York, 1918). A. L. Kroeber, "Totem and Taboo: an Ethnologic Psychoanalysis," (1920) and "Totem and Taboo in Retrospect," (1939) both included in his *The Nature of Culture* (Chicago, 1952).

30. The need for such analysts has not been diminished by Jung's attempts to carry analytic technique into cultural materials divergent from Euro-American ideas—nor can his interpretations be verified in the present state of research.

31. D. Haring and M. Johnson, *op. cit.*, p. 379. See Books II and III for supporting evidence, with due allowance for advances in knowledge since 1940.

HOW AN ANTHROPOLOGIST WORKS IN THE FIELD:
AMONG A NON-LITERATE PEOPLE

Bronislaw Malinowski, 1922. *Argonauts of the Western Pacific*, pp. 4-25. London and New York, E. P. Dutton and Company, Inc. Reprinted by permission of E. P. Dutton and Company, Inc.

Malinowski's studies of the Boyowan people of the Trobriand Islands, off the eastern tip of New Guinea, mark an epoch in ethnographic research. A keen, tireless observer, Malinowski recorded numberless details of every phase of native behavior. His untimely death prevented completion of the series of books in which he described Boyowan society (cf. General Bibliography).

Perhaps no one else has presented so vividly the daily routine of a field anthropologist, the problems of rapport with the people, and ways of observing and recording data, as did Malinowski in the pages that follow.

Although Malinowski's field research was completed before the development of specialized techniques of studying individuals, his active interest in the persons around him earned him a place among those who pioneered in the study of the psychological aspects of primitive tribes. He was among the earliest anthropologists to utilize Freudian concepts (Malinowski, 1927).

HOW AN ANTHROPOLOGIST
WORKS IN THE FIELD

Bronislaw Malinowski

Imagine yourself suddenly set down surrounded by all your gear, alone on a tropical beach close to a native village, while the launch or dinghy which has brought you sails away out of sight. Since you take up your abode in the compound of some neighbouring white man, trader or missionary, you have nothing to do, but to start at once on your ethnographic work. Imagine further that you are a beginner, without previous experience, with nothing to guide you and no one to help you. For the white man is temporarily absent, or else unable or unwilling to waste any of his time on you. This exactly describes my first initiation into field work on the south coast of New Guinea. I well remember the long visits I paid to the villages during the first weeks; the feeling of hopelessness and despair after many obstinate but futile attempts had entirely failed to bring me into real touch with the natives, or supply me with any material. I had periods of despondency, when I buried myself in the reading of novels, as a man might take to drink in a fit of tropical depression and boredom.

Imagine yourself then, making your first entry into the village, alone or in company with your white cicerone. Some natives flock round you, especially if they smell tobacco. Others, the more dignified and elderly, remain seated where they are. Your white companion has his routine way of treating the natives, and he neither understands, nor is very much concerned with the manner in which you, as an ethnographer, will have to approach them. The first visit leaves you with a hopeful feeling that when you return alone, things will be easier. Such was my hope at least.

I came back duly, and soon gathered an audience around me. A few compliments in pidgin-English on both sides, some tobacco changing hands, induced an atmosphere of mutual amiability. I tried then to proceed to business. First, to begin with subjects which might arouse no suspicion, I started to "do" technology. A few natives were engaged in manufacturing some object or other. It was easy to look at it and obtain the names of the tools, and even some technical expressions about the proceedings, but there the matter ended. It must be borne in mind that pidgin-English is a very imperfect instrument for expressing one's ideas, and that before one gets a good training in framing questions and understanding answers one has the uncomfortable feeling that free communication in it with the natives will never be attained; and I was quite unable to enter into any more detailed or explicit conversation with them at first. I knew well that the best remedy for this was to collect concrete data, and accordingly I took a village census, wrote down genealogies, drew up plans and collected the terms of kinship. But all this remained dead material, which led no further into the understanding of real native mentality or behaviour, since I could neither procure a good native interpretation of any of these items, nor get what could be called the hang of tribal life. As to obtaining their ideas about religion, and magic, their beliefs in sorcery and spirits, nothing was forthcoming except a few superficial items of folk-lore, mangled by being forced into pidgin-English.

Information which I received from some white residents in the district, valuable as it was in itself, was more discouraging than anything else with regard to my own work. Here were men who had lived for years in the place with constant opportunities of observing the natives and communicating with them, and who yet hardly knew one thing about them really well. How could I therefore in a few months or a year, hope to overtake and go beyond them? Moreover, the manner in which my white informants spoke about the natives and put their views was, naturally, that of untrained minds, unaccustomed to formulate their thoughts with any degree of consistency and precision. And they were for the most part, naturally enough, full of the biassed and pre-judged opinions inevitable in the average practical man, whether administrator, missionary, or trader; yet so strongly repulsive to a mind striving after the objective, scientific view of things. The habit of treating with a self-satisfied frivolity what is really serious to the ethnographer; the cheap rating of what to him is a scientific treasure, that is to say, the native's cultural and mental peculiarities and independence—these features, so well known in the inferior amateur's writing, I found in the tone of the majority of white residents.[1]

Indeed, in my first piece of Ethnographic research on the South coast, it was not until I was alone in the district that I began to make some headway; and, at any rate, I found out where lay the secret of effective field-work. What is then this ethnographer's magic, by which he is able to evoke the real spirit of the natives, the true picture of tribal life? As usual, success can only be obtained by a patient and systematic application of a number of rules of common sense and well-known scientific principles, and not by the discovery of any marvellous short-cut leading to the desired results without effort or trouble. The principles of method can be grouped under three main headings; first of all, naturally, the student must possess real scientific aims, and know the values and criteria of modern ethnography. Secondly, he ought to put himself in good conditions of work, that is, in the main, to live without other white men, right among the natives. Finally, he has to apply a number of special methods of collecting, manipulating and fixing his evidence. A few words must be said about these three foundation stones of field work, beginning with the second as the most elementary.

Proper conditions for ethnographic work. These, as said, consist mainly in cutting oneself off from the company of other white men, and remaining in as close contact with the natives as possible, which really can only be achieved by camping right in their villages. It is very nice to have a base in a white man's compound for the stores, and to know there is a refuge there in times of sickness and surfeit of native. But it must be far enough away not to become a permanent milieu in which you live and from which you emerge at fixed hours only to "do the village." It should not even be near enough to fly to at any moment for recreation. For the native is not the natural companion for a white man, and after you have been working with him for several hours, seeing how he does his gardens, or letting him tell you items of folk-lore, or discussing his customs, you will naturally hanker after the company of your own kind. But if you are alone in a village beyond reach of this, you go for a solitary walk for an hour or so, return again and then quite naturally seek out the natives' society, this time as a relief from loneliness, just as you would any other companionship. And by means of this natural intercourse, you learn to know him, and you become familiar with his customs and beliefs far better than when he is a paid, and often bored, informant.

There is all the difference between a sporadic plunging into the company of natives, and being really in contact with them. What does this latter mean? On the Ethnographer's side, it means that his life in the village, which at first is a strange, sometimes unpleasant, sometimes intensely interesting adventure, soon adopts quite a natural course very much in harmony with his surroundings.

Soon after I had established myself in Omarakana (Trobriand Islands), I began to take part, in a way, in the village life, to look forward to the important or festive events, to take personal interest in the gossip and the developments of the small village occurrences; to wake up every morning to a day, presenting itself to me more or less as it does to the native. I would get out from under my mosquito net, to find around me the village life beginning to stir, or the people well advanced in their working day according to the hour and also to the season, for they get up and begin their labours early or late, as work presses. As I went on my morning walk through the village, I could see intimate details of family life, of toilet, cooking, taking of meals;

I could see the arrangements for the day's work, people starting on their errands, or groups of men and women busy at some manufacturing tasks. Quarrels, jokes, family scenes, events usually trivial, sometimes dramatic but always significant, formed the atmosphere of my daily life, as well as of theirs. It must be remembered that as the natives saw me constantly every day, they ceased to be interested or alarmed, or made self-conscious by my presence, and I ceased to be a disturbing element in the tribal life which I was to study, altering it by my very approach, as always happens with a new-comer to every savage community. In fact, as they knew that I would thrust my nose into everything, even where a well-mannered native would not dream of intruding, they finished by regarding me as part and parcel of their life, a necessary evil or nuisance, mitigated by donations of tobacco.

Later on in the day, whatever happened was within easy reach, and there was no possibility of its escaping my notice. Alarms about the sorcerer's approach in the evening, one or two big, really important quarrels and rifts within the community, cases of illness, attempted cures and deaths, magical rites which had to be performed, all these I had not to pursue, fearful of missing them, but they took place under my very eyes, at my own doorstep, so to speak. And it must be emphasised whenever anything dramatic or important occurs it is essential to investigate it at the very moment of happening, because the natives cannot but talk about it, are too excited to be reticent, and too interested to be mentally lazy in supplying details. Also, over and over again, I committed breaches of etiquette, which the natives, familiar enough with me, were not slow in pointing out. I had to learn how to behave, and to a certain extent, I acquired "the feeling" for native good and bad manners. With this, and with the capacity of enjoying their company and sharing some of their games and amusements, I began to feel that I was indeed in touch with the natives, and this is certainly the preliminary condition of being able to carry on successful field work.

But the Ethnographer has not only to spread his nets in the right place, and wait for what will fall into them. He must be an active huntsman, and drive his quarry into them and follow it up to its most inaccessible lairs. And that leads us to the more active methods of pursuing ethnographic evidence. . . . Good training in theory, and acquaintance with its latest results, is not identical with being burdened with "preconceived ideas." If a man sets out on an expedition, determined to prove certain hypotheses, if he is incapable of changing his views constantly and casting them off ungrudgingly under the pressure of evidence, needless to say his work will be worthless. But the more problems he brings with him into the field, the more he is in the habit of moulding his theories according to facts, and of seeing facts in their bearing upon theory, the better he is equipped for the work. Preconceived ideas are pernicious in any scientific work, but foreshadowed problems are the main endowment of a scientific thinker, and these problems are first revealed to the observer by his theoretical studies.

In Ethnology the early efforts of Bastian, Tylor, Morgan, the German Völkerpsychologen have remoulded the older crude information of travellers, missionaries, etc., and have shown us the importance of applying deeper conceptions and discarding crude and misleading ones.[2]

The concept of animism superseded that of "fetichism" or "devil-worship," both meaningless terms. The understanding of the classificatory systems of relationship paved the way for the brilliant, modern researches on native sociology in the field-work of the Cambridge school. The psychological analysis of the German thinkers has brought forth an abundant crop of most valuable information in the results obtained by the recent German expeditions to Africa, South America and the Pacific, while the theoretical works of Frazer, Durkheim and others have already, and will no doubt still for a long time inspire field workers and lead them to new results. The field worker relies entirely upon inspiration from theory. Of course he may be also a theoretical thinker and worker, and there he can draw on himself for stimulus. But the two functions are separate, and in actual research they have to be separated both in time and conditions of work.

As always happens when scientific interest turns towards and begins to labour on a field so far only prospected by the curiosity of amateurs, Ethnology has introduced law and order into what seemed chaotic and freakish. It has transformed for us the sensational, wild and unaccountable world of "savages" into a number of well ordered communities, governed by law, behaving and thinking according to consistent principles. The word "savage," whatever association it might have had originally, connotes ideas of boundless liberty, of irregularity, of something extremely and extraordinarily quaint. In popular thinking, we imagine that the natives live on the bosom of Nature, more or less as they can and like, the prey of irregular, phantasmagoric beliefs and apprehensions. Modern science, on the contrary, shows that their social institutions have a very definite organisation, that they are governed by authority, law and order in their public and personal relations, while the latter are, besides, under the control of extremely complex ties of kinship and clanship. Indeed, we see them entangled in a mesh of duties, functions and privileges which correspond to an elaborate tribal, communal and kinship organisation. Their beliefs and practices do not by any means lack consistency of a certain type, and their knowledge of the outer world is sufficient to guide them in many of their strenuous enterprises and activities. Their artistic productions again lack neither meaning nor beauty.

It is a very far cry from the famous answer given long ago by a representative authority who, asked, what are the manners and customs of the natives, answered, "Customs none, manners beastly," to the position of the modern Ethnographer! This latter, with his tables of kinship terms, genealogies, maps, plans and diagrams, proves an extensive and big organisation, shows the constitution of the tribe, of the clan, of the family; and he gives us a picture of the natives subjected to a strict code of behaviour and good manners, to which in comparison the life at the Court of Versailles or Escurial was free and easy.[3]

Thus the first and basic ideal of ethnographic field-work is to give a clear and firm outline of the social constitution, and disentangle the laws and regularities of all cultural phenomena from the irrelevances. The firm skeleton of the tribal life has to be first ascertained. This ideal imposes in the first place the fundamental obligation of giving a complete survey of the phenomena, and not of picking out the sensational, the singular, still less the funny and quaint. The time when we could tolerate accounts presenting us the native as a distorted, childish caricature of a human being are gone. This picture is false, and like many other falsehoods, it has been killed by Science. The field Ethnographer has seriously and soberly to cover the full extent of the phenomena in each aspect of tribal culture studied, making no difference between what is commonplace, or drab, or ordinary, and what strikes him as astonishing and out-of-the-way. At the same time, the whole area of tribal culture *in all its aspects* has to be gone over in research. The consistency, the law and order which obtain within each aspect make also for joining them into one coherent whole.

An Ethnographer who sets out to study only religion, or only technology, or only social organisation cuts out an artificial field for inquiry, and he will be seriously handicapped in his work.

Having settled this very general rule, let us descend to more detailed consideration of method. The Ethnographer has in the field, according to what has just been said, the duty before him of drawing up all the rules and regularities of tribal life; all that is permanent and fixed; of giving an anatomy of their culture, of depicting the constitution of their society. But these things, though crystallised and set, are nowhere *formulated*. There is no written or explicitly expressed code of laws, and their whole tribal tradition, the whole structure of their society, are embodied in the most elusive of all materials: the human being. But not even in human mind or memory are these laws to be found definitely formulated. The natives obey the forces and commands of the tribal code, but they do not comprehend them; exactly as they obey their instincts and their impulses, but could not lay down a single law of psychology. The regularities in native institutions are an automatic result of the interaction of the mental forces of tradition, and of the material conditions of environment. Exactly as a humble member of any modern institution, whether it be the state, or the church, or the army, is *of* it and *in* it, but has no vision of the resulting integral action of the whole, still less could furnish any account of its organisation, so it would be futile to attempt questioning a native in abstract, sociological terms. The difference is that, in our society, every institution has its intelligent members, its historians, and its archives and documents, whereas in a native society there are none of these. After this is realised an expedient has to be found to overcome this difficulty. This expedient for an Ethnographer consists in collecting concrete data of evidence, and drawing the general inferences for himself. This seems obvious on the face of it, but was not found out or at least practised in Ethnography till field work was taken up by men of science. Moreover, in giving it practical effect, it is neither easy to devise the concrete applications of this method, nor to carry them out systematically and consistently.

Though we cannot ask a native about abstract, general rules, we can always enquire how a given case would be treated. Thus for instance, in asking how they would treat crime, or punish it, it would be vain to put to a native a sweeping question such as, "How do you treat and punish a criminal?" for even words could not be found to express it in native, or in pidgin. But an imaginary case, or still better, a real occurrence, will stimulate a native to express his opinion and to supply plentiful information. A real case indeed will start the natives on a wave of discussion, evoke expressions of indignation, show them taking sides—all of which talk will probably contain a wealth of definite views, of moral censures, as well as reveal the social mechanism set in motion by the crime committed. From there, it will be easy to lead them on to speak of other similar cases, to remember other actual occurrences or to discuss them in all their implications and aspects. From this material, which ought to cover the widest possible range of facts, the inference is obtained by simple induction. The *scientific* treatment differs from that of good common sense, first in that a student will extend the completeness and minuteness of survey much further and in a pedantically systematic and methodical manner; and secondly, in that the scientifically trained mind, will push the inquiry along really relevant lines, and towards aims possessing real importance. Indeed, the object of scientific training is to provide the empirical investigator with a *mental chart*, in accordance with which he can take his bearings and lay his course.

To return to our example, a number of definite cases discussed will reveal to the Ethnographer the social machinery for punishment. This is one part, one aspect of tribal authority. Imagine further that by a

similar method of inference from definite data, he arrives at understanding leadership in war, in economic enterprise, in tribal festivities—
there he has at once all the data necessary to answer the questions
about tribal government and social authority. In actual field work,
the comparison of such data, the attempt to piece them together, will
often reveal rifts and gaps in the information which lead on to further
investigations.

From my own experience, I can say that, very often, a problem
seemed settled, everything fixed and clear, till I began to write down a
short preliminary sketch of my results. And only then did I see the
enormous deficiences which would show me where lay new problems,
and lead me on to new work. In fact, I spent a few months between
my first and second expeditions, and over a year between that and the
subsequent one, in going over all my material, and making parts of it
almost ready for publication each time, though each time I knew I
would have to re-write it. Such cross-fertilisation of constructive
work and observation I found most valuable, and I do not think I
could have made real headway without it. I give this bit of my own
history merely to show that what has been said so far is not only an
empty programme, but the result of personal experience. In this volume, the description is given of a big institution connected with ever
so many associated activities, and presenting many aspects. To anyone who reflects on the subject, it will be clear that the information
about a phenomenon of such high complexity and of so many ramifications, could not be obtained with any degree of exactitude and
completeness, without a constant interplay of constructive attempts
and empirical checking. In fact, I have written up an outline of the
Kula institution at least half a dozen times while in the field and in the
intervals between my expeditions. Each time, new problems and difficulties presented themselves.

The collecting of concrete data over a wide range of facts is thus
one of the main points of field method. The obligation is not to enum-
erate a few examples only, but to exhaust as far as possible all the cases
within reach; and, on this search for cases, the investigator will score
most whose mental chart is clearest. But, whenever the material of the
search allows it, this mental chart ought to be transformed into a real
one; it ought to materialise into a diagram, a plan, an exhaustive, synoptic table of cases. Long since, in all tolerably good modern books
on natives, we expect to find a full list or table of kinship terms, which
includes all the data relative to it, and does not just pick out a few
strange and anomalous relationships or expressions. In the investigation
of kinship, the following up of one relation after another in concrete
cases leads naturally to the construction of genealogical tables. Practised already by the best early writers, such as Munzinger, and, if I

remember rightly, Kubary, this method has been developed to its fullest extent in the works of Dr. Rivers. Again, studying the concrete
data of economic transactions, in order to trace the history of a valuable object, and to gauge the nature of its circulation, the principle
of completeness and thoroughness would lead to construct tables of
transactions, such as we find in the work of Professor Seligman.[4] It is
in following Professor Seligman's example in this matter that I was
able to settle certain of the more difficult and detailed rules of the Kula.
The method of reducing information, if possible, into charts or synoptic tables ought to be extended to the study of practically all aspects of
native life. All types of economic transactions may be studied by following up connected, actual cases, and putting them into a synoptic
chart; again, a table ought to be drawn up of all the gifts and presents
customary in a given society, a table including the sociological, ceremonial, and economic definition of every item. Also, systems of magic,
connected series of ceremonies, types of legal acts, all could be charted,
allowing each entry to be synoptically defined under a number of
headings. Besides this, of course, the genealogical census of every community, studied more in detail, extensive maps, plans and diagrams,
illustrating ownership in garden land, hunting and fishing privileges,
etc., serve as the more fundamental documents of ethnographic research.

A genealogy is nothing else but a synoptic chart of a number of
connected relations of kinship. Its value as an instrument of research
consists in that it allows the investigator to put questions which he
formulates to himself *in abstracto*, but can put concretely to the native
informant. As a document, its value consists in that it gives a number
of authenticated data, presented in their natural grouping. A synoptic
chart of magic fulfils the same function. As an instrument of research,
I have used it in order to ascertain, for instance, the ideas about the
nature of magical power. With a chart before me, I could easily and
conveniently go over one item after the other, and note down the
relevant practices and beliefs contained in each of them. The answer
to my abstract problem could then be obtained by drawing a general
inference from all the cases. I cannot enter further into the discussion
of this question, which would need further distinctions, such as between a chart of concrete, actual data, such as is a genealogy, and a
chart summarising the outlines of a custom or belief, as a chart of a
magical system would be.

Returning once more to the question of methodological candour, I
wish to point out here, that the procedure of concrete and tabularised
presentation of data ought to be applied first to the Ethnographer's
own credentials. That is, an Ethnographer, who wishes to be trusted,
must show clearly and concisely, in a tabularised form, which are his

own direct observations, and which the indirect information that form the bases of his account. The Table on the next page will serve as an example of this procedure and help the reader of this book to form an idea of the trustworthiness of any statement he is specially anxious to check. With the help of this Table and the many references scattered throughout the text, as to how, under what circumstances, and with what degree of accuracy I arrived at a given item of knowledge, there will, I hope, remain no obscurity whatever as to the sources of the book.

CHRONOLOGICAL LIST OF KULA EVENTS WITNESSED BY THE WRITER

FIRST EXPEDITION, AUGUST, 1914–MARCH, 1915.

March, 1915.   In the village of Dikoyas (Woodlark Island) a few ceremonial offerings seen. Preliminary information obtained.

SECOND EXPEDITION, MAY, 1915–MAY, 1916.

June, 1915. A Kabigidoya visit arrives from Vakuta to Kiriwina. Its anchoring at Kavataria witnessed and the men seen at Omarakana, where information collected.

July, 1915. Several parties from Kitava land on the beach of Kaulukuba. The men examined in Omarakana. Much information collected in that period.

September, 1915. Unsuccessful attempt to sail to Kitava with To'uluwa, the chief of Omarakana.

October-November, 1915. Departure noticed of three expeditions from Kiriwina to Kitava. Each time To'uluwa brings home a haul of *mwali* (armshells).

November, 1915–*March*, 1916. Preparations for a big overseas expedition from Kiriwina to the Marshall Bennett Islands. Construction of a canoe; renovating of another; sail making in Omarakana; launching; *tasasoria* on the beach of Kaulukuba. At the same time, information is being obtained about these and the associated subjects. Some magical texts of canoe building and Kula magic obtained.

THIRD EXPEDITION, OCTOBER, 1917–OCTOBER, 1918.

November, 1917–*December*, 1917. Inland Kula; some data obtained in Tukwaukwa.

December–February, 1918. Parties from Kitava arrive in Wawela. Collection of information about the *yoyova*. Magic and spells of Kaygau obtained.

March, 1918. Preparations in Sanaroa; preparations in the Amphletts; the Dobuan fleet arrives in the Amphletts. The *uvalaku* expedition from Dobu followed to Boyowa.

April, 1918. Their arrival; their reception in Sinaketa; the Kula transactions; the big intertribal gathering. Some magical formulae obtained.

May, 1918. Party from Kitava seen in Vakuta.

June, July, 1918. Information about Kula magic and customs checked and amplified in Omarakana, especially with regard to its Eastern branches.

August, September, 1918. Magical texts obtained in Sinaketa.

October, 1918. Information obtained from a number of natives in Dobu and Southern Massim district (examined in Samarai).

To summarise the first, cardinal point of method, I may say each phenomenon ought to be studied through the broadest range possible of its concrete manifestations; each studied by an exhaustive survey of detailed examples. If possible, the results ought to be embodied into some sort of synoptic chart, both to be used as an instrument of study, and to be presented as an ethnological document. With the help of such documents and such study of actualities the clear outline of the framework of the natives' culture in the widest sense of the word, and the constitution of their society, can be presented. This method could be called *the method of statistic documentation by concrete evidence.*

Needless to add, in this respect, the scientific field-work is far above even the best amateur productions. There is, however, one point in which the latter often excel. This is, in the presentation of intimate touches of native life, in bringing home to us these aspects of it with which one is made familiar only through being in close contact with the natives, one way or the other, for a long period of time. In certain results of scientific work—especially that which has been called "survey work"—we are given an excellent skeleton, so to speak, of the tribal constitution, but it lacks flesh and blood. We learn much about the framework of their society, but within it, we cannot perceive or imagine the realities of human life, the even flow of everyday events, the occasional ripples of excitement over a feast, or ceremony, or some singular occurrence. In working out the rules and regularities of native custom, and in obtaining a precise formula for them from the collection of data and native statements, we find that this very precision is foreign to real life, which never adheres rigidly to any rules. It must be supplemented by the observation of the manner in which a given custom is carried out, of the behaviour of the natives in obeying the rules so exactly formulated by the ethnographer, of the very exceptions which in sociological phenomena almost always occur.

If all the conclusions are solely based on the statements of informants, or deduced from objective documents, it is of course impossible to supplement them in actually observed data of real behaviour. And that is the reason why certain works of amateur residents of long standing, such as educated traders and planters, medical men and officials, and last, not least, of the few intelligent and unbiassed missionaries to whom Ethnography owes so much, this is the reason why these works surpass in plasticity and in vividness most of the purely scientific accounts. But if the specialised field-worker can adopt the conditions of living described above, he is in a far better position to be really in touch with the natives than any other white resident. For none of them lives right in a native village, except for very short periods, and everyone has his own business, which takes up a considerable part of his time. Moreover, if, like a trader or a missionary or an official he enters into active relations with the native, if he has to transform or influence or make use of him, this makes a real, unbiassed, impartial observation impossible, and precludes all-round sincerity, at least in the case of the missionaries and officials.

Living in the village with no other business but to follow native life, one sees the customs, ceremonies and transactions over and over again, one has examples of their beliefs as they are actually lived through, and the full body and blood of actual native life fills out soon the skeleton of abstract constructions. That is the reason why, working under such conditions as previously described, the Ethnographer is enabled to add something essential to the bare outline of tribal constitution, and to supplement it by all the details of behaviour, setting and small incident. He is able in each case to state whether an act is public or private; how a public assembly behaves, and what it looks like; he can judge whether an event is ordinary or an exciting and singular one; whether natives bring to it a great deal of sincere and earnest spirit, or perform it in fun; whether they do it in a perfunctory manner, or with zeal and deliberation.

In other words, there is a series of phenomena of great importance which cannot possibly be recorded by questioning or computing documents, but have to be observed in their full actuality. Let us call them *the imponderabilia of actual life*. Here belong such things as the routine of a man's working day, the details of his care of the body, of the manner of taking food and preparing it; the tone of conversational and social life around the village fires, the existence of strong friendships or hostilities, and of passing sympathies and dislikes between people; the subtle yet unmistakable manner in which personal vanities and ambitions are reflected in the behaviour of the individual and in the emotional reactions of those who surround him. All these facts can and ought to be scientifically formulated and recorded, but it is necessary that this be done, not by a superficial registration of details, as is usually done by untrained observers, but with an effort at penetrating the mental attitude expressed in them. And that is the reason why the work of scientifically trained observers, once seriously applied to the study of this aspect, will, I believe, yield results of surpassing value. So far, it has been done only by amateurs, and therefore done, on the whole, indifferently.

Indeed, if we remember that these imponderable yet all important facts of actual life are part of the real substance of the social fabric, that in them are spun the innumerable threads which keep together the family, the clan, the village community, the tribe—their significance becomes clear. The more crystallised bonds of social grouping, such as the definite ritual, the economic and legal duties, the obligations, the ceremonial gifts and formal marks of regard, though equally important for the student, are certainly felt less strongly by the individual who has to fulfil them. Applying this to ourselves, we all know that "family life" means for us, first and foremost, the atmosphere of home, all the innumerable small acts and attentions in which are expressed the affection, the mutual interest, the little preferences, and the little antipathies which constitute intimacy. That we may inherit from this person, that we shall have to walk after the hearse of the other, though sociologically these facts belong to the definition of "family" and "family life," in personal perspective of what family truly is to us, they normally stand very much in the background.

Exactly the same applies to a native community, and if the Ethnographer wants to bring their real life home to his readers, he must on no account neglect this. Neither aspect, the intimate, as little as the legal, ought to be glossed over. Yet as a rule in ethnographic accounts we have not both but either the one or the other—and, so far, the intimate one has hardly ever been properly treated. In all social relations besides the family ties, even those between mere tribesmen and, beyond that, between hostile or friendly members of different tribes, meeting on any sort of social business, there is this intimate side, expressed by the typical details of intercourse, the tone of their behaviour in the presence of one another. This side is different from the definite, crystallised legal frame of the relationship, and it has to be studied and stated in its own right.

In the same way, in studying the conspicuous acts of tribal life, such as ceremonies, rites, festivities, etc., the details and tone of behaviour ought to be given, besides the bare outline of events. The importance of this may be exemplified by one instance. Much has been said and written about survival. Yet the survival character of an act is expressed in nothing as well as in the concomitant behaviour, in the way in which it is carried out. Take any example from our own culture, whether it be the pomp and pageantry of a state ceremony, or a picturesque custom kept up by street urchins, its "outline" will not tell you whether the rite flourishes still with full vigour in the hearts of those who perform it or assist at the performance or whether they regard it as almost a dead thing, kept alive for tradition's sake. But observe and fix the data of their behaviour, and at once the degree of vitality of the act will become clear. There is no doubt, from all points of sociological, or psychological analysis, and in any question of theory, the manner and type of behaviour observed in the performance of an act is of the highest importance. Indeed behaviour is a fact, a relevant fact, and one that can be recorded. And foolish indeed and short-sighted would be the man of science who would pass by a whole class of phenomena, ready to be garnered, and leave them to waste, even though he did not see at the moment to what theoretical use they might be put!

As to the actual method of observing and recording in field-work these *imponderabilia of actual life and of typical behaviour*, there is no doubt that the personal equation of the observer comes in here more prominently, than in the collection of crystallised, ethnographic data. But here also the main endeavour must be to let facts speak for themselves. If in making a daily round of the village, certain small incidents, characteristic forms of taking food, of conversing, of doing work are found occurring over and over again, they should be noted down at once. It is also important that this work of collecting and fixing impressions should begin early in the course of working out a district. Because certain subtle peculiarities, which make an impression as long as they are novel, cease to be noticed as soon as they become familiar. Others again can only be perceived with a better knowledge of the local conditions. An ethnographic diary, carried on systematically throughout the course of one's work in a district would be the ideal instrument for this sort of study. And if, side by side with the normal and typical, the ethnographer carefully notes the slight, or the more pronounced deviations from it, he will be able to indicate the two extremes within which the normal moves.

In observing ceremonies or other tribal events it is necessary, not only to note down those occurrences and details which are prescribed by tradition and custom to be the essential course of the act, but also the Ethnographer ought to record carefully and precisely, one after the other, the actions of the actors and of the spectators. Forgetting for a moment that he knows and understands the structure of this ceremony, the main dogmatic ideas underlying it, he might try to find himself only in the midst of an assembly of human-beings, who behave seriously or jocularly, with earnest concentration or with bored frivolity, who are either in the same mood as he finds them every day, or else are screwed up to a high pitch of excitement, and so on and so on. With his attention constantly directed to this aspect of tribal life, with the constant endeavour to fix it, to express it in terms of actual fact, a good deal of reliable and expressive material finds its way into his notes. He will be able to "set" the act into its proper place in tribal life, that is to show whether it is exceptional or common-place, one in which the natives behave ordinarily, or one in which their whole behaviour is transformed. And he will also be able to bring all this home to his readers in a clear, convincing manner.

Again, in this type of work, it is good for the Ethnographer some-times to put aside camera, note book and pencil, and to join in himself in what is going on. He can take part in the natives' games, he can fol-low them on their visits and walks, sit down and listen and share in their conversations. I am not certain if this is equally easy for every-one—perhaps the Slavonic nature is more plastic and more naturally savage than that of Western Europeans—but though the degree of success varies, the attempt is possible for everyone. Out of such plunges into the life of the natives—and I made them frequently not only for study's sake but because everyone needs human company—I have car-ried away a distinct feeling that their behaviour, their manner of being, in all sorts of tribal transactions, became more transparent and easily understandable than it had been before.

Finally, let us pass to the third and last aim of scientific field-work, to the last type of phenomenon which ought to be recorded in order to give a full and adequate picture of native culture. Besides the firm outline of tribal constitution and crystallised cultural items which form the skeleton, besides the data of daily life and ordinary behaviour, which are, so to speak, its flesh and blood, there is still to be recorded the spirit—the natives' views and opinions and utterances. For, in every act of tribal life, there is, first, the routine prescribed by custom and tradition, then there is the manner in which it is carried out, and lastly there is the commentary to it, contained in the natives' mind. A man who submits to various customary obligations, who follows a traditional course of action, does it impelled by certain motives, to the accompaniment of certain feelings, guided by certain ideas. These ideas, feelings, and impulses are moulded and conditioned by the cul-ture in which we find them, and are therefore an ethnic peculiarity of the given society. An attempt must be made therefore, to study and record them.

But is this possible? Are these subjective states not too elusive and shapeless? And, even granted that people usually do feel or think or experience certain psychological states in association with the per-formance of customary acts, the majority of them surely are not able to formulate these states, to put them into words. This latter point must certainly be granted, and it is perhaps the real Gordian knot in the study of the facts of social psychology. Without trying to cut or untie this knot, that is to solve the problem theoretically, or to enter further into the field of general methodology, I shall make directly for the question of practical means to overcome some of the difficulties involved.

First of all, it has to be laid down that we have to study here stereo-typed manners of thinking and feeling. As sociologists, we are not in-terested in what A or B may feel *qua* individuals, in the accidental course of their own personal experiences—we are interested only in what they feel and think *qua* members of a given community. Now in this capacity, their mental states receive a certain stamp, become stereotyped by the institutions in which they live, by the influence of tradition and folk-lore, by the very vehicle of thought, that is by language. The social and cultural environment in which they move forces them to think and feel in a definite manner. Thus, a man who lives in a polyandrous community cannot experience the same feelings of jealousy, as a strict monogynist, though he might have the elements of them. A man who lives within the sphere of the Kula cannot be-come permanently and sentimentally attached to certain of his posses-sions, in spite of the fact that he values them most of all. These ex-amples are crude, but better ones will be found in the text of this book.

So, the third commandment of field-work runs: Find out the typical ways of thinking and feeling, corresponding to the institutions and culture of a given community, and formulate the results in the most convincing manner. What will be the method of procedure? The best ethnographical writers—here again the Cambridge school with Had-don, Rivers, and Seligman rank first among English Ethnographers— have always tried to quote *verbatim* statements of crucial importance. They also adduce terms of native classification; sociological, psycho-logical and industrial *termini technici,* and have rendered the verbal contour of native thought as precisely as possible. One step further in this line can be made by the Ethnographer, who acquires a knowledge of the native language and can use it as an instrument of inquiry. In working in the Kiriwinian language, I found still some difficulty in writing down the statement directly in translation which at first I used to do in the act of taking notes. The translation often robbed the text of all its significant characteristics—rubbed off all its points—so that gradually I was led to note down certain important phrases just as they were spoken, in the native tongue. As my knowledge of the language progressed, I put down more and more in Kiriwinian, till at last I found myself writing exclusively in that language, rapidly taking notes, word for word, of each statement. No sooner had I arrived at this point, than I recognised that I was thus acquiring at the same time an abundant linguistic material, and a series of ethnographic documents which ought to be reproduced as I had fixed them, besides being utilised in the writing up of my account.[5] This *corpus inscriptionum Kiriwiniensium* can be utilised, not only by myself, but by all those who, through their better penetration and ability of interpreting them, may find points which escape my attention, very much as the other *corpora* form the basis for the various interpretations of ancient and prehistoric cultures; only, these ethnographic inscriptions are all decipherable and clear, have been almost all translated fully and unambiguously, and have been provided with native cross-commentaries or *scholia* obtained from living sources.

Our considerations thus indicate that the goal of ethnographic fieldwork must be approached through three avenues:

1. *The organisation of the tribe, and the anatomy of its culture* must be recorded in firm, clear outline. The method of *concrete, statistical documentation* is the means through which such an outline has to be given.

2. Within this frame, the *imponderabilia of actual life*, and the *type of behaviour* have to be filled in. They have to be collected through minute, detailed observations, in the form of some sort of ethnographic diary, made possible by close contact with native life.

3. A collection of ethnographic statements, characteristic narratives, typical utterances, items of folk-lore and magical formulae has to be given as a *corpus inscriptionum*, as documents of native mentality.

These three lines of approach lead to the final goal, of which an Ethnographer should never lose sight. This goal is, briefly, to grasp the native's point of view, his relation to life, to realise *his* vision of *his* world. We have to study man, and we must study what concerns him most intimately, that is, the hold which life has on him. In each culture, the values are slightly different; people aspire after different aims, follow different impulses, yearn after a different form of happiness. In each culture, we find different institutions in which man pursues his life-interest, different customs by which he satisfies his aspirations, different codes of law and morality which reward his virtues or punish his defections. To study the institutions, customs, and codes or to study the behaviour and mentality without the subjective desire of feeling by what these people live, of realising the substance of their happiness—is, in my opinion, to miss the greatest reward which we can hope to obtain from the study of man.

These generalities the reader will find illustrated in the following chapters. We shall see there the savage striving to satisfy certain aspirations, to attain his type of value, to follow his line of social ambition. We shall see him led on to perilous and difficult enterprises by a tradition of magical and heroical exploits, shall see him following the lure of his own romance. Perhaps as we read the account of these remote customs there may emerge a feeling of solidarity with the endeavours and ambitions of these natives. Perhaps man's mentality will be revealed to us, and brought near, along some lines which we never have followed before. Perhaps through realising human nature in a shape very distant and foreign to us, we shall have some light shed on our own. In this, and in this case only, we shall be justified in feeling that it has been worth our while to understand these natives, their institutions and customs, and that we have gathered some profit from the Kula.

NOTES

1. I may note at once that there were a few delightful exceptions to that, to mention only my friends Billy Hancock in the Trobriands; M. Raffael Brudo, another pearl trader; and the missionary, Mr. M. K. Gilmour.

2. According to a useful habit of the terminology of science, I use the word Ethnography for the empirical and descriptive results of the science of Man, and the word Ethnology for speculative and comparative theories.

3. The legendary "early authority" who found the natives only beastly and without customs is left behind by a modern writer, who, speaking about the Southern Massim with whom he lived and worked "in close contact" for many years, says: " . . . We teach lawless men to become obedient, inhuman men to love, and savage men to change." And again: "Guided in his conduct by nothing but his instincts and propensities, and governed by his unchecked passions. . . ." "Lawless, inhuman and savage!" A grosser misstatement of the real state of things could not be invented by anyone wishing to parody the Missionary point of view. Quoted from the Rev. C. W. Abel, of the London Missionary Society, "Savage Life in New Guinea," no date.

4. For instance, the tables of circulation of the valuable axe blades, "The Melanesians of British New Guinea," 1910, pp. 531, 532.

5. It was soon after I had adopted this course that I received a letter from Dr. A. H. Gardiner, the well-known Egyptologist, urging me to do this very thing. From his point of view as archaeologist, he naturally saw the enormous possibilities for an Ethnographer of obtaining a similar body of written sources as have been preserved to us from ancient cultures, plus the possibility of illuminating them by personal knowledge of the full life of that culture.

Amamians participate in one of the great civilizations, since they have long been a part of Japan. They also have much in common with the smaller peripheral societies. This dual orientation I shall sketch briefly. Thanks to Japanese public schools, Amami people know standard Japanese and are literate. They are proud of more than eight hundred years of recorded history, and of the longer era of legend that awaits verification by competent archaeologists. For three and a half centuries they have been integrated in the Japanese political system, although their status was that of serfs until about 1875. Locally published newspapers and periodicals are supplemented by more expensive reading matter imported from Japan Proper. Some households have radio, and in the larger places news and advertising are dispensed over public address systems. Urban Amamians are at home in movies and dance halls, bingo games, cockfights, athletic meets, and well-stocked shops. The endless rains and steep mountains afford hydroelectricity for the city and most of the hamlets. Ocean-going ships call regularly at Naze, while motor sampans provide cheap inter-island transportation. Roman Catholic, Buddhist, and Shintō missionaries carry their doctrines to most of the hamlets. The intelligentsia include highly educated individuals who wield considerable influence. Often a peasant will interrupt his toil to tell with glowing eyes of his son in some university in Japan. Agricultural extension services have introduced scientific agriculture and stock-breeding. When some farmers regaled me with tales of antiquity, their notions of social evolution sounded strangely familiar; I wondered if such theories underwent parallel independent development until I traced the doctrines to local intellectuals armed with L. H. Morgan's "Ancient Society." All these things are *modan*—the Japanese version of "modern."

Amami's simpler past, however, still lingers. Sixteen local dialects, unintelligible to the average Japanese, survive in as many mountain-girt hamlets or isolated islands. Despite ready means of travel, extreme poverty isolates the peasants, whose world is circumscribed by the practical question, "Do we eat rice today, or do we merely wash down cycad mush with the water used to wash yesterday's rice?" Shamanism, magic, and witchcraft are ubiquitous. City people laugh at superstition, but fear to venture into a strange village, lest the very water be charged with a deadly spell by the hissed imprecations of a witch. An ancient cult of living female deities—the *Noro*—survives in the countryside. Beliefs in goblins, in tree-spirits, in fearsome half-human, half-animal offspring of the unholy revels of practitioners of black magic, in sinister powers acquired by ghastly manipulations of blood drawn from the snipped-off tongue of a starving dog, in the efficacy of moxa cautery and acupuncture, in the unwavering benign guardianship maintained over a man by the spirit of his elder sister, in the busy mischief of ghosts and sprites—such beliefs are no monopoly of villagers. Each tiny hamlet—often out of touch with the hamlet across the mountain—preserves its dialect, its special folklore, songs, dances, festivals, technology, poetry, and economic organization; no single village is typical. In eight hundred years Buddhist missionaries have made but limited headway: perhaps because Buddhist priests usually are male and Amami tradition accords primacy to women in religious matters, perhaps because Amamian love of pork—a trait related to South Sea influences—conflicts with Buddhist taboos on meat. Family patterns and the status of women avowedly conform to Confucian and feudal-Japanese models. The rationalizations indeed are Confucian, but the real freedom of women, the investment of romantic love with glamour, and the lavishing of affection upon both consanguine and affinal kindred suggest that the human warmth of early Japan and the South Seas has outlasted what Sir George Sansom once called "the Confucian malady."[1] Under a hand-to-mouth economy very little money passes through the hands of farmers and fisherfolk. Even urban industries, such as the weaving of *tsumugi*—an exquisite *ikat*-dyed silk textile—continue as handicrafts refined by scientific research. In the city and larger villages population has outrun physical accommodations; for example, water for washing and bathing is scarce despite abundant rainfall. Amamian personality manifests distinctive features that survive even after migration to Japan Proper; the expatriates foregather in Japanese cities and nostalgically review the good old days back home. Thousands of young Amamian laborers work at Army projects on Okinawa; what is happening to them is anyone's guess.

Against this background of modern and not-so-modern Amami the ethnographer seeks to describe and to understand. The following discussion of field procedure is frankly in personal terms, since a depersonalized ethnographic report closes an important avenue to appraisal of the findings. The ethnographer is a human being precariously adjusted to human beings culturally different from himself. Only as the pattern of that personal adjustment is revealed can the trustworthiness of his account be estimated.

Conditions were unusually favorable for research. Both the Pacific Science Board and the United States Army left me almost ideally free in the research and in writing of findings. I could not cover the entire island, much less the rest of the archipelago. Although I visited many villages and talked with many farmers, my contacts with the city outnumbered those with the rural districts—in part because I lived at an Army base, in part because my native helpers at first were reluctant to venture into villages where they had no kin, and in part from lack of time to establish adequate rapport with the country folk. Except for a few Communists, no one showed hostility toward the study; everywhere I met with kindness and eager hospitality. Two suspicions had to be allayed: first, that I was a new kind of American counter-intelligence agent; second, that I might be working for the supposedly defunct secret police of Japan. When after six weeks children shouted a new dialect epithet, my translator was delighted; he said, "They just called you 'missionary.' That means that people have decided that you are not an Army agent, even though you do live at the Base." By the time that the missionary role had become clearly inappropriate, children and adults had learned my name and created a special category for me.

The usual caution that restrains an ethnographer from involvement in native politics was reinforced by the strict rule of the United States Army forbidding Americans to enter in even the slightest way into Ryūkyū politics. Some political facts, however, were patent and inescapable. Amamians were upset profoundly over their political divorce from Japan Proper. The strange regime of military government that lumped Amami with Okinawa and interposed an incomprehensible boundary between Amami and Japan had disarranged the patterns of social expectation. Across that boundary, in Japan, were friends and relatives, fiancees and relatives by marriage, children in college, business connections, pensions, old-age insurance, veterans' benefits, and sentiments of past legend and future hope. Geographically a close neighbor, Okinawa long had been viewed with rural resentment toward the city slicker, and except for its northern tip was a place where no relatives lived and whence no conceivable aid could come.

Once Amamians accepted me as a free agent bent on faithful description of their customs and ideas, they manifested an ambivalent combination of fear lest they unwittingly violate my neutrality and drag me into politics, and deep urgency lest I fail to perceive their desperate longing to rejoin Japan. I began to wonder how the people of the State of Maine might respond if suddenly they were cut off from the United States and incorporated into French Canada. At least the Amamians were grateful for American aid and friendship; they worried lest their agitation for reversion to Japan be construed as hostility toward the United States. This tense situation could have biased the research; it was apparent, however, that any honest survey would list as an outstanding fact the universal desire to rejoin Japan. This insistent political hope motivated much of the ready cooperation with the ethnographer; certainly it did not obstruct any phase of the study.

Desire to win my backing for reversion to Japan, however, was not the sole factor in acceptance of the ethnographer. I am convinced that even now, with reversion an accomplished fact, an anthropologist would be equally welcome. For the people literally adopted the study;

they wanted to be studied; they were pathetically eager to have their customs recorded, to be noticed in the far-off world that reached them only through books and radio. Elsewhere in the Amami Archipelago similar feelings were manifest. Unable to visit the island of Okierabu, I did get a half-hour chat with longshoremen who were unloading cargo there from a ship on which I was a passenger. They inquired why I was living on Amami, and hearing the reason, shouted in chorus, "Don't waste time studying those people on that bleak barren island! Come down here and study us: we have no poisonous snakes; we have sunshine; we are friendly; and we'd give a foreign scientist a big welcome!" These people feel forgotten; self-pity is a congenial emotion, and it is epitomized in references to "The Forgotten Islands." The visiting ethnographer symbolized their longings for a breach in the isolation. Apart from objective findings, I should have been less than human had I failed to respond and accept this emotional load, knowing full well that no one man could cope with the hopes and dreams of a whole people.

The inherent assets of the situation transcended this emotional complication. The hearty welcome that met my arrival puzzled me until I learned that Japan's senior scientist, the ethnographer Dr. Kunio Yanagita, who is especially revered on Amami for his studies of Amamian culture, had generously written letters on my behalf. The two daily newspapers took pains to report my project carefully; they made it clear that this was the sort of research that anthropologists conduct in their own countries; that it involved no assumption of the inferiority of the people studied; and they continued to provide an open channel to the people. Another asset was the prestige of science among Amamians. They are proud of Amamian scientists who have attained eminence in Japan; Government schools, agricultural and marine experiment stations, and other local research have convinced even the peasants that the future belongs to science. When the press announced that a real live scientist had arrived in their midst, the people were eager to help, even to submit to psychological dissection. Their easy friendliness and sense of humor made the investigation doubly pleasant.

How the islanders enjoyed it when, hard-pressed to imbibe murderous potions of *shōchū*, and having failed to convince them of the imperative need for abstinence on the part of a diabetic, I protested, "But I came to observe your customs; how can I tell how you act when you are drunk if I also get drunk?" This was repeated all over the island, and scarcely a week would pass without some bibulous pedestrian embracing me and saying, "You wanted to study drunks, now come with me and watch me, 'cause I'm drunk!"

Amamians do what they can to encourage science. A pathetically ill-housed museum, stocked with books, a collection of shells, and archaeological specimens, was crowded with eager students. The Assistant Curator was a brilliant young self-taught anthropologist. The Trustees of the Museum generously placed him at my disposal for the duration—with the one reservation that, since he was their best accountant, they would need him at the end of each month. Not every ethnographer finds a native anthropologist awaiting him in a supposedly backward area! In addition, several capable local antiquarians stood ready to discuss lore and custom, to obtain singers for the tape recorder, or to introduce me to some village mayor. Even now they answer my letters of inquiry.

Knowing the workings of gossip and curiosity respecting a foreign visitor, I deliberately planted correct information about myself in the fountainhead of gossip channels—a *geisha* house. By dropping in for lunch, when the girls were not occupied professionally, I gave answers complete with snapshots to their questions about my personal history, family and grandchildren, job, income, prospects, and all normal topics for gossip. This worked so well that later on all this information—plus normal accretions—returned to me from the familiar spirit of a local shaman in trance as he disclosed my past sins and future fortunes. Obviously the spirit was not above un-spectral consorting with *geisha* girls.

I employed no informants in the conventional sense. They were scarcely needed, for information piled up faster than I could digest it. I did hire two young translators: one to render into English the newspapers and other local periodicals, the other to act as interpreter. His translations of interviews insured my hearing everything twice and gained time for note-taking. When unusually heavy downpours curtailed our activities we held informal sessions on the aims and results of anthropology. Invariably these sessions were followed by bursts of initiative that often disclosed new data.

Several associations coöperated voluntarily. The Federation of Women's Clubs sponsored questionnaires on marriage, kinship, and family life, criticized and amended my schedules, mailed them to their many local clubs, and coaxed back the late returns. In 1951, Naze witnessed the opening of its first photographic supply store, followed by organization of a camera club. Together with the Colonel in command of the United States Civil Administration unit, I offered prizes for a photographic contest that stressed handicrafts, customs, and scenery. The Physicians' Association volunteered active coöperation, and I regret deeply that limited time prevented taking advantage of that offer. Government offices, especially the Statistical Office, provided whatever information I requested; despite lapses during war years and defects in reporting, their records were invaluable. Since the United States Army had analyzed the political and economic data, I used only the population records. At the Boys' High School many of the boys kept diaries for two months for my use, in exchange for my giving a weekly class in English pronunciation. At the Girls' High some twenty girls persuaded aged persons to dictate their autobiographies; these documents fall short of Professor Dollard's standards, but they shed light on history, customs, and—dimly—on psychology. Teachers, both urban and rural, were willing, perceptive, informed aids in research.

Studies already made locally provided much help. Hard-pressed by rising expenses, the teachers had just published a detailed study of family budgets and costs of living. The dean of local historians, Mr. E. Kazari, had devoted a lifetime to the study of Amamian folk music and folklore, and I gleaned richly from his store of knowledge. The Amamian anthropologist, Mr. F. Yamashita, entrusted me with his definitive study of tattoo designs collected from the backs of hands of aged persons now deceased; this I hope to publish for him.

In order to analyze printed media of communication, all locally published newspapers, periodicals, and other materials were assembled on a set day of each month, filed, and translated. The leading bookstores regularly provided lists, with quantities, of books and periodicals imported from Japan Proper.

Daily research procedures and my own participant activities were recorded in a log that ultimately covered 346 closely-typed pages. Two significant items of personal participation can be mentioned here: one was attendance at a concert of folk music, from which by sheer accident I did not depart at the intermission as American guests had usually done; thereby I unwittingly passed a test important in native eyes. The other was delivery of a short speech at an educational conference staged by visiting faculty from Michigan State University, attended by most of the teachers on the island. Proceedings were conducted through translators. Out of courtesy I had been asked to speak briefly. The evening before the conference, three of the Army's Japanese interpreters descended in force on my quarters and announced that they would work all night if need be to help me prepare and deliver a speech in Japanese, and that they would give me no choice— I *must* speak in Japanese. They rendered my ideas into fluent phrases quite beyond my normal capacity. This necessitated reading the speech, and in the very middle, the electricity began to fail. Had the lights gone out completely I should have lost face irretrievably; through sheer luck the current rallied and so did I. This speech in Japanese settled the question of popular acceptance of the ethnographer. Thereafter, wherever I went, someone who had been present would greet me as an old friend, show me off to the villagers, and explain the study. Immediately the people would answer questions gladly, pose for pictures, and surfeit me with coöperation. Even the secrets of the *Noro* cult eventually began to drift into my ears.[2]

The Wenner-Gren Foundation generously supplemented my equipment with a 16mm movie camera, a tape recorder, and moderate funds for film. Unaccustomed to either a movie camera or tape recorder, I learned the hard way; these mechanical aids, however, are invaluable. Even if film and tape records had proved worthless, the interest generated among the people by their use would have been worth-while. Professional artists volunteered to record folk songs. Friends sought out old persons who were expert in use of obsolescent local dialects. Several villages begged to provide folk dances (which were out of season) for the movies. Young men once lugged a heavy motor-generator set on narrow paths over a mountain pass to insure current for the tape recorder. Although I was chronically starved for film and for sound tape, I managed to record many folk songs, specimens of eight dialects, movies of crafts and dances, *et cetera*. Rain, lack of film, and urgent obligations incurred as host to intestinal parasites cancelled out numerous precious opportunities.

Movies are invaluable to record technology, dances, rituals (if cameras are permitted), and any other activity that conforms to a set pattern. The intricate handicraft dyeing and weaving of Ōshima *tsumugi*—perhaps the most precise and exacting handicraft ever observed—yielded to cinema recording in spite of my ignorance of textiles and weaving. Without the movie camera I should have been helpless to describe this process. Margaret Mead has shown the value of cinema records of the behavior development of infants; I fared badly, however, in photographing babies, for most of my visit fell in winter when Amami infants are bundled in shapeless masses of cloth. Furthermore, I hesitated to expend precious film on babies reared in strict accordance with a Japanese version of Dr. Spock's "Pocket Book of Baby and Child Care."

Ethnographic movies are records, not spectacles. If the subjects habitually frequent cinema shows, they invariably emulate Tyrone Power or Rita Hayworth when a lens points their way. This tendency is minimized in photographing a folk dance, a ritual, or a handicraft in process. To the extent that conditions are rearranged to suit the camera and rehearsals are held, bias is introduced—perhaps so subtly that the ethnographer does not detect the change in emphasis. Photographing without prior rehearsal consumes extra film and may yield indifferent entertainment, but it can obtain a reliable ethnographic record; and an accurate record with minimum disturbance of customary routine is a defensible goal when the ethnographer has but one movie camera and no technical assistant, and deals with a native situation unamenable to control.

For still photography a telephoto lens is invaluable—as in recording children's play. Unfortunately I did not acquire such a lens until my final month on Amami. Working in Amami's unrelenting rain, high-speed lenses are essential; I feel quite sure that I could defend the title of the world's most experienced rainy-day Kodachrome photographer! Two cameras were always ready for instant use, one for color, the other for black and white. Anything worth recording on either may merit a duplicate shot with the other film; this avoids copying color positives to obtain half-tone reproductions. All cinema shots should be paralleled by still pictures—not only as insurance against accidents, but as a source of illustrations. Unfortunately this procedure requires two photographers. It hardly needs saying that a humid hot climate requires extreme precautions in preserving film and in protection of lenses against mould.

Fundamental in studying a literate people is the question of imparting the results of the research to the people studied. This crucial problem of ethnographic research is unknown in the physical and biological sciences. The subjects of social research are self-naming, self-explaining, and self-categorizing. Still more important, they want to know the results, and unlike laboratory rats, they regard one's findings with emotion. This problem may be dramatized by the incident of an Amamian psychopath who regarded himself as a movie producer. Maladjusted individuals often seek the company of foreigners, and he attached himself to me—partly in hope of borrowing the movie camera and getting free film. Unsuccessful in this scheme, he asked the Assembly for a government appropriation to finance a grandiose scheme of publicizing Amami. There he delivered a speech to the effect that I plotted to slander Amami, that my pictures were limited to pornographic movies of nudes; and he talked the Assembly into appropriating 100,000 *yen*. Hotly the legislators resolved to purge the island of my nefarious activities. Some lucky fate, however—perhaps the familiar spirit of my friend the shaman—worked for me. That very morning the infrequent mails had returned from Hawaii several hundred feet of processed film. Unaware of the goings-on in the Assembly, I sought out the projection facilities at the United States Information Center and looked at the film. At the adjoining Government offices, clerks and secretaries were seeking diversion while their bosses deliberated. The grapevine spread word that I was showing movies, and in a twinkling I had a packed house. Delighted with the pictures, the clerks scurried for their desks just as the legislature adjourned. The moment he entered his office, each Assemblyman heard a glowing account of my pictures before he had a chance to mention the events of the legislative day. Not one of the gentlemen of the legislature repeated the slander against my pictures; instead, I received invitations to photograph athletic meets, parties, customs, festivals, black rabbits—anything.

This was only one of the occasions when a situation was saved, not by my ingenuity or ethnographic technique, but by sheer luck. I urge ethnographers to keep their good luck charms in working order—as Sumner would have phrased it, to give due attention to "the aleatory interest."

In addition to keeping the public constantly informed concerning my activities, I invited leading citizens to view the pictures and listen to records just before I left. They knew exactly what I carried away from Amami. At the showings, their comments opened new insights, verified information, and corrected blunders. Unfortunately I cannot afford to show appreciation by providing the Amami Museum with duplicate cinema films and many of the still pictures; my resources, however, were taxed by the necessity of giving hundreds of prints to those who had posed for pictures.

As far as they can be written before leaving the field, reports of the research should be read in the native language to native critics. This was done with my preliminary reports to the Pacific Science Board and the United States Army—except for recommendations made to the Army. Reading such a document in Japanese sorely tried my linguistic skill, but Amamian friends were patient. These critics were picked to include some of the best-educated and most thoughtful islanders. They corrected numerous mistakes and verified points where I was unsure. Such procedure gives the people confidence in anthropological research, and should prepare the ground for subsequent investigations. Later, I showed pictures to a group of Amamians in Tōkyō; they were enraptured with glimpses of home and volunteered independent confirmation of many facts. For example, reticence in discussing the *Noro* cult had left me dubious of some findings: a Tōkyō lady who had been born and reared in a hereditary *Noro* household on Amami—and who as the wife of a Japanese scientist understood the real aims of research —eagerly verified details and added more information.

Another valuable experience in Tōkyō I owed to the unfailing thoughtfulness of Dr. Yanagita. He assembled a group of Japanese ethnologists to whom I presented a summary of my findings. Their questions and comments forced me to rethink a number of points, verified others, and gave me the benefit of their experience.

Every philosopher knows, as Suzanne Langer has observed brilliantly, that the choice and formulation of a question define the range of the answers. I think that introduction of technically refined questionnaires or public opinion schedules into a non-Euro-American milieu may involve serious bias that the investigator fails to note because he is steeped in the logic of his own culture. When the Amami Federation of Women's Clubs revised my schedules, I took the hint: Why not let the people themselves make out the questions? Even if such procedure should miss some pet interest of the ethnographer, it would be enlightening to see what kind of questions they would frame. Unfortunately I cannot demonstrate this technique; the box that contained all the relevant schedules, replies, and translations of studies made in this way, as well as translations of the native press and all data of kinship and associations, was lost en route to the United States. I can only indicate what I attempted to do.

The first use of native ingenuity was in a survey of associations in Naze. I employed an intelligent and influential man to locate all possible associations and secure descriptive data. A member of the Assembly, he already knew many groups, and political aspirations whetted his appetite for further contacts. Data of this sort lay beyond my reach as an American, since rumor had it that the Army was about to revive the former Japanese police rules governing registration of associations. So I instructed the investigator to keep all names of individuals in a notebook that would be confidential in his hands without my ever seeing it. His integrity vouched for my good faith, and he obtained a considerable body of data. As his study progressed, many officers of associations said, "It's all right; give him our names—he won't get us into trouble!" The questions and categories that he formulated were appropriate to the Amami situation and to the local concept of an association—a concept foreign to American thinking.

Another study dealt with mate selection and family customs. The investigator was a respected teacher of Home Economics in the Girls' High School. In the homes of hundreds of former students, now wives and mothers, she was a very welcome guest. I offered a list of questions and suggested that she revise it. She came up with an interview schedule different from anything I would have devised; in some respects I questioned its value; in others it was highly satisfactory. After that study she came with an idea of her own: she had been teaching about birth and infant care; she wanted the facts as they had been discovered by midwives. Would I help her plan an interview schedule for the midwives? Promptly I offered to pay the costs of her study if she would share the results. The data thus obtained on the experience and opinions of Naze midwives are no model of interview technique, but some questions and answers are significant. She handed me the results just as I left Amami and there was no time to discuss them with her; they were translated in Tōkyō. Happily, they were not included in the box that went astray.

My general conclusions may be stated briefly. Unusual opportunities combine with special problems in study of a literate people whose numbers are small enough to render conspicuous an ethnographer in their midst. Ethical questions implicit in all ethnographic research come to focus when the people studied are sure to read whatever appears in print about themselves. On occasion, such a people may tend to center hopes and dreams in the ethnographer as a link with the outside world, and thus to complicate his scientific and ethical problems. This is a facet of the durable question of whether the rich cultural repertory of a literate people can be surveyed in the way that has yielded so many valuable studies of peripheral tribes. Certainly the picture of the ethnographer at work that was set forth so brilliantly by Malinowski[3] scarcely pertains at all to a relatively populous, completely literate society—and increasingly, ethnographers will be dealing with this type of situation as literacy is more widely diffused.

A people who read and discuss what they read should be taken into the ethnographer's confidence. Of course he must respect confidential information, but otherwise he has everything to gain and nothing to lose by the sort of publicity that invites verification. If individuals suspect that the ethnographer is misinformed or purblind on any topic, someone undertakes to set him right. Carrying this principle a step further, the ethnographer should enlist native minds in various aspects of planning the investigation in hope of escape from his own cultural limitations. Native critics can contribute richly to verification of findings. On the other hand, the ethnographer can bring insights to the culture that offer to the natives new understanding of their own ways of living, and their support of the research is enhanced whenever some aspect of their culture of which they are but dimly aware is clarified to their surprised satisfaction.[4]

Beyond correction of factual blunders, what criticisms have Amamiams voiced? First, that too little time was allotted for the study; I did not even experience the full round of the calendar of annual events. This implies that the pace of Amamian life is leisurely and that American haste annoys Orientals. "Take more time; you'll understand better!" "At least come back and study us some more!" Secondly, the ethnographer was criticized for not living in native style. This shortcoming was related to my dietary needs as a diabetic; it was mitigated in the eyes of Amamian friends by the circumstance that in Japan Proper I had lived in native style.

The major criticisms from other quarters run parallel, although they are oriented quite differently. Some United States Army personnel and some Japanese assert that the report was pro-Amamian in bias. I have not heard this criticism from Army men who have been stationed on Amami. Japanese objections on this ground seem to refer to quite different aspects of the report: in Japanese eyes, Amami is backwoods, not worth the time of a foreign scientist; and to some Japanese my picture of Amami seemed more favorable than the portrait of Japan in some of my other writings. I hope that time, and more complete publication of findings, will impart a mellower perspective.

Certainly no amount of sympathy with native culture would justify the slightest distortion of fact. In the work of any honest scientist this may be taken for granted, but one cannot guard too carefully against unrecognized bias. One can only endeavor to hold to a mature and inclusive objectivity that recognizes the emotional responses involved. If I have stressed the emotional aspects of living in Amami during the reversion agitation, it is because the situation forced upon me a deeper understanding of what I once wrote about the late Professor Thurnwald: ". . . if they [ethnographers] study exotic peoples, they remain under an ethical obligation to consider ways in which their findings may aid those peoples to survive and attain the goals they seek. Professor Richard Thurnwald . . . never subscribed to the doctrine that the fate of those whom he studied did not concern him. . . . The ethnographer cannot forget that he is dealing with people whose very existence may be threatened by the civilization that he represents."[5]

NOTES

1. George B. Sansom, *Japan, a Short Cultural History* (New York: Century Co., 1931), p. 110.

2. D. G. Haring, *The Noro Cult of Amami Ōshima: Divine Priestesses of the Ryūkyū Islands* (Sociologus, vol. 3, pp. 108-121, Berlin, 1953).

3. Bronislaw Malinowski, *Argonauts of the Western Pacific* (London: George Routledge and Sons, Ltd., 1922), pp. 2-25.

4. In this connection, some of Reik's ideas are interesting (Theodor Reik, *Surprise and the Psycho-analyst*, London: Kegan Paul, Trench, Trubner and Co., Ltd., 1936).

5. D. G. Haring, "The Social Sciences and Biology" (in *Beiträge zur Gesellungs- und Völkerwissenschaft, Professor Dr. Richard Thurnwald zu seinem achtzigsten Geburtstag gewidmet,* Berlin: Verlag Gebr. Mann, 1950), p. 135.

HOW AN ANTHROPOLOGIST WORKS IN THE FIELD: SOLUTION OF A SPECIFIC PROBLEM

Clyde Kluckhohn, 1938, "Participation in Ceremonials in a Navaho Community," *American Anthropologist*, Vol. *40*: 359-369. Reproduced by courtesy of the author and of the Editor of the *American Anthropologist*.

Prior to this study by Dr. Kluckhohn, students of the Navaho Indians often made statements such as "The Navaho are very religious." Scientifically-minded readers ask what such a phrase as "very religious" really means. Kluckhohn set out to find an answer. This paper shows how well-planned observation, supplemented by statistical summaries, can remove such questions from the vague realm of personal impressions and provide factual answers.

Descriptions of behavior in any society rarely justify statements such as "The Crow enforce the mother-in-law taboo," or "New Yorkers spend the hours of darkness in night clubs." These generalizations ignore differences in individuals. Precise description replaces broad generalizations with statistical frequency distributions and tables that show percentages of a population who can be classified in different categories. The clear cut "laws" of the exact sciences give way to descriptions of the behavior of numerous individuals. Statistical tables of contingency or correlation show how many persons who act in one way also act in some other way. Time is the only aspect of social phenomena that has been measured adequately, and the following study shows that measurement of time spent in a specific activity increases the accuracy of observations.

PARTICIPATION IN CEREMONIALS IN A NAVAHO COMMUNITY

Clyde Kluckhohn

In general, descriptions of the ceremonial behaviors of non-literate societies have tended to be restricted to accounts of observed ceremonies and descriptions of the formal ceremonial patterns with little attention to either the extent of participation or the affects of participants. I propose to treat the first of these somewhat neglected questions from data gathered among the four hundred odd Navaho in the region between Ramah and Atarque, New Mexico.[1] To what extent the trend of these data would be paralleled if material was gathered on similar questions among other Navaho groups is an interesting question and would, in my opinion, merit investigation. There is also the query: Would figures gathered in this society a generation or more ago have shown a comparable intensity of ceremonial activity? I doubt it. This inference cannot be proved, of course, but it is perhaps worth recording my feeling that the present almost hysterical frequency of ceremonials is related to the fact that only recently has this Navaho group felt the full impact of our culture.

The treatment will center on the following questions: What ceremonials are known? How many ceremonial practitioners are there? What ceremonials have been held during a specific period of time? What ceremonials have sample individuals held during their lifetimes? What proportion of family income is devoted to ceremonial activity? In addition, various supplementary information will be incorporated with a view to filling out a highly concrete picture of the extension and diversity of "religious" behavior and knowledge.

While the central aim will be to describe as concretely as possible ceremonial participation in this society, the discussion relates very readily to two connected problems of some general interest. In anthropological literature one continually reads such statements as the following: "The Navaho are a very religious people," or, more specifically, "The Navaho spend a great deal of their time in ceremonials." It would seem to me interesting and perhaps useful to examine such statements as these on the basis of fairly full information about this particular group of Navaho during a particular period of time. The results of the examination may perhaps also throw some light on an even more general problem in which anthropologists are much interested at present. The author of a general text on anthropology published recently states: "Every culture tends to have certain preferred modes of feeling and reacting." Now our problem may be phrased as follows: To what extent does an inductive analysis of the behaviors of the individuals making up a particular Navaho group support the generalization that a preferred Navaho mode of reacting is ceremonial? Comparably complete data for time and energy devoted to other activities are lacking, but I think that the data which follow give at least some crude measure of the amount of time and energy which goes—directly or indirectly— into ceremonial activities.

A very large number of ceremonials are (or in the recent past have been) carried out by the Navaho. The members of this group have participated in a much smaller number. Three varieties of ceremonial participation are open to them. First, they may attend or take active part in ceremonials given in other Navaho communities. This opportunity is relatively little exercised at present, although in years past individuals went rather frequently as far as the Navaho Reservation proper to attend such nine-day ceremonials as Mountain Top Way and Night Way. But during the past summer forty-one individuals (mostly young men) are known to have spent a total of ninety-three days attending four different performances of Enemy Way. During the preceding winter a party of nine individuals were present for the final day and night of a Night Way carried out north of Gallup. The ceremonial practitioners of this peripheral community are not in great demand outside, but two of the singers and three of the diagnosticians officiate from time to time in the three nearest Navaho societies. Data over a two year period indicate that each singer carries out about one five-night ceremonial a year among the Danoff and Two Wells Navaho and about one every second year among the Alamo-Puerticito Navaho. Each of the three diagnosticians apparently do motion-in-the-hand from two to five times yearly for Navaho from these outside groups.

Second, these Navaho may attend or assist in ceremonials given for members of their own community by singers from outside. (The ceremonial is almost invariably given at the home of the patient.) During the six months from March fifteenth to September fifteenth of this past year nine singers (mainly from the nearest Navaho groups) spent sixty-two days in conducting twenty ceremonials.[2] Outside singers are seldom imported to conduct a ceremonial fully known to any member of the community.[3] In stubborn cases, outside diagnosticians are sometimes consulted. This occurred five times in the six months period referred to: once by star-gazing, once by listening, three times by motion-in-the-hand.[4]

Coming to the third form of participation, twenty song ceremonials are known by one or more living members of the society. Only seven of these last for more than part of a night or day. It is worthy of remark that only one individual knows one hunting ceremonial and that no living individual knows a war ceremonial. Moreover, it is to be noted that only one singer in the group knows the nine-day version of any ceremonial, or any ceremonial involving the presence of masked personators of the gods. Only one nine-day ceremonial has been given during the past five years. This is the more remarkable in that, according to the traditional ideology, children can be given their ceremonial initiation only at this kind of ceremonial. The connections of the fact are, however, probably primarily economic, for there are few families in this group who are even well-to-do by Navaho standards. But even after one has made all of these qualifications one is, I think, impressed by the elaboration of ceremonial knowledge in a culture which from other points of view—e.g., the technological—is relatively undifferentiated.

This impression is fortified by consideration of the number of individuals having direct ceremonial knowledge. Twenty out of the sixty-nine adult men of the community conduct ceremonials. In addition, nine women and seven men are diagnosticians. In short, thirty-six individuals are to some degree involved in this aspect of behavior. But there is wide variation among these in amount of ceremonial knowledge. The Navaho distinguish between true singers and what Morgan has called "curers."[5] The term "singer" tends—by this group at all events—to be reserved for those practitioners who know at least two ceremonials of three or more nights' duration.[6] Such ceremonials I shall hereafter, simply for convenience, refer to as major ceremonials. There are three singers in this society. One knows five major ceremonials[7] (and the legend for three of these) and two one-night ceremonials.[8] A second knows four ceremonials in the first category (with the four legends) and two in the second. The third knows two and one respectively (and one of the concomitant origin legends). Of the seventeen curers one knows one five-night ceremonial (without the legend) and one one-night, another knows one three-night ceremonial (but not the legend) and is learning a five. A third knows one two-night and two one-night rites. A fourth knows the brief form of three ceremonials. Three know only the two-night Blessing Way. The others know one one-day or one-night ceremonial only (mainly various "blackenings"). All of the diagnosticians know only the one means of divination, that of motion-in-the-hand.

There is a somewhat corresponding variation in the proportion of time devoted to ceremonial activities. The most popular singer stated that he sang about five days out of every two weeks. Actually my figures show that in the six months from March fifteenth to September fifteenth last year he sang eighty-one days in twenty-nine ceremonials.[9] Another singer sang eighty-two days in twenty-three ceremonials during this period. The third sang only twelve in seven, but he is in extreme old age. The data indicate that an estimate of five days out of every fourteen for the two singers is not far from correct. As for the curers, one spent nineteen days, another eighteen in the period which my data cover, while two others spent only a day each. The mean is about nine days in six months. According to my data, three of the diagnosticians were called upon about once a week, others once or twice in the whole period. My records include sixty-four instances of divination during the sample period. (Of these one was carried out to locate a lost animal.)[10]

Let us now approach the problem from another angle. I have a record which I believe to be substantially correct—except for some probable omissions—of the 148 ceremonials[11] held during this period.[12] (This includes, of course, ceremonials conducted by local and by imported singers, but an asterisk indicates that the ceremonial is not known by any member of this group.) There were 27 Chiricahua Apache Wind Way; 26 Shooting Way, Female Branch; 25 blackenings[13]; 23 Blessing Way; 8 Hand Trembling Evil Way; 2 Hand Trembling Way; 8 Life Way, Female Shooting Branch; 2 Enemy Way*; 2 Navaho Wind Way*; 2 (brief form) Eagle Way*; 1 (brief form) Mountain Top Way*; 1 Beauty Way*; 1 Big Star Way*. Three hundred eighty-nine nights (and portions of days) during this period were devoted to ceremonials. Now remember that at every ceremonial not only the singer and patient, but usually at least one assistant and some members of the patient's immediate family are present. Further, at the last night of any longer ceremonial more distant relatives and neighbors gather.[14] The average number present for the last night of the ceremonials I witnessed was thirty-one. Most of these people were present during the greater part of the final day also. On the basis of these and other data I have calculated that during this six months sample period, the average adult man of the community spent 0.32 of his waking hours in ceremonial activity, the average adult woman 0.18.[15] Obviously, these figures convey an impression of spurious accuracy. But I think I am safe in saying that adult men in the community tend, on the average (at least during this portion of the year),[16] to devote one-fourth to one-third of their productive time to ceremonials[17]; adult women one-fifth to one-sixth. The figure for men would probably have been higher in the not very distant past, for a larger number of younger men would almost certainly have been engaged in systematically learning the ceremonials. At present only four men under late middle age are studying—and two of these very half-heartedly.

It will be noted that the facts presented thus far deal entirely with

the knowledge and behaviors relating to song ceremonials and diagnoses. To the best of my knowledge no member of the group knows
any of the prayer ceremonials. During the sample period, however, at
least one prayer ceremonial (lasting two nights) was carried on by a
man from the Two Wells region.

Naturally there are other features of "religious" behavior in this
Navaho society, but it has thus far proved impossible to secure comparably complete data. It is not that there are no purely individual
religious activities nor that the religious behavior of these Navaho is
never mainly spontaneous. But the facts are peculiarly difficult to secure, and, when secured, do not lend themselves to objective treatment,
particularly since they can almost never be observed directly. What
information I have on non-ceremonial religious activities may be summarized as follows.

I have no evidence of overt manifestations of sentiments relating to
the supernatural which can be described as strictly spontaneous.[18] But
certain practices have a considerable element of spontaneity. Most
notable among these are perhaps certain forms of "witchcraft." But
while members of this society gave various generalized ideological data
on this subject I got almost nothing on behaviors. A number of investigators have commented upon the unwillingness of the Navaho to
attribute this type of anti-social behavior to any individual of their
own acquaintance. They appear to dread the vengeance of the witch
as a consequence of any such revelations. Almost without exception
they are keenly conscious of several forms of witchcraft, but their
anecdotes of specific instances deal without exception, in my experience, with individuals who lived at least a hundred miles away, and who
are most often declared now to be dead. Most informants from this
group stoutly denied that anyone in their own community was even
suspected of witchcraft. Three informants did refer to the possibility
that one man, generally regarded as worthless, might be a witch. One
informant brought forward as a bit of evidence in favor of this hypothesis the report that the man had been seen to pick up human faeces.
This was the closest approach to any account of actual behaviors.

And so we shall proceed to socially approved non-ceremonial "religious" activities. A large number of informants reported that they had
secret "good luck" songs designed to protect or increase flocks and
herds and other forms of property; indeed it would seem the normal
pattern that an adult man should know one or more such songs. No
rigidly set context appears to give rise to an individual's singing these
songs. He may sing one when some minor disaster has actually occurred,
when he feels a premonition of one, or simply when he is out alone attending to sheep or cattle or riding alone on a journey. But the behavior
cannot be regarded as completely spontaneous since the song he sings

is never improvised to suit mood or occasion.[19] The other known forms of individual religious activity are strictly formalized. A brief prayer is commonly recited as a rock is added to the wayside altars.[20] Nine of the older men of the community chant a certain prayer and sing a song when they build a sweat house and when they take a sweat bath. The same song is always sung and sung only under these circumstances. Likewise, several older men sing a song and say a prayer when they plant their maize in the spring. Most of the men of middle age and older possess bags of pollen and on certain occasions[21] they scatter pollen and utter brief prayers.

As to brief ceremonies:[22] two of the singers know a number of optional ceremonies which may be incorporated in their ceremonials at the request of the patient or his family. But since they are never performed independently[23] they do not seem relevant to our present purpose. Formerly (and to some extent at the present time) each extended family group sent a party annually to collect salt at the Salt Lake some thirty miles to the south of the southern extremity of this community's territory. The party camped half a mile from the lake, and before visiting the lake (and preferably at sunrise) a short prayer was repeated by the members of the party who were familiar with it. One informant was of the opinion that only six adult men of the community know the prayer now. On reaching the lake, bits of turquoise were placed in crevices in the encrusted salt at the edge and the prayer was repeated. This ceremony has apparently not been carried out for several years. On the Navaho Reservation new hogans are frequently consecrated by the singing of the hogan songs from Blessing Way. This has not been done by any Ramah-Atarque Navaho for at least five years. One informant remembered a ceremony to bring rain which had been carried on in the Navaho country proper in his father's time. But no member of this society has ever witnessed or participated in such a ceremony.

Various life crises are also marked by ceremonies. During the sample period three girl's adolescence ceremonies were carried out by Blessing Way singers. In the Navaho country proper, marriage is often solemnized by songs and prayers preceding and following an eating together of man and girl and members of their families. But for some years the marriage ceremony (when any was held at all) in this area has been limited to the eating of mush from a basket. At death there is a minimum of ceremony. But those who have disposed of a body must undergo a four-day ritual purification. Immediately on returning, they wash in cold water and keep silence for at least fifteen minutes. They then remain together for four days in some one place to which no one else comes. Finally, they purify themselves with sweat baths.

Returning now to the ceremonials some little additional light may be thrown on our problem in another way. In how many ceremonials have typical individuals been patients during their lifetimes? Rather typical examples are a man and a woman who were putatively past sixty, who were neither rich nor poor by the standards of this community, who had in other ways shown themselves reliable informants with good memories. The woman had spent 83 days as the patient in ceremonials (women are rather more frequently patients than men), the man 71. These roughly represent the mode of about 50 case histories, making allowance for age differences. But the variation is enormous, of course. An old woman, who was perpetually ailing, had spent nearly 500 days in her lifetime—keeping both her immediate and extended families almost continually bankrupt! One of the singers, on the other hand, had had ceremonials held over him for only thirty-seven days of his life. And one man—presumably about fifty—had had but a single three-night ceremonial during his lifetime. Extensive interviewing failed to reveal a single individual over thirty who had not been the patient in at least one ceremonial. On the other hand, fully half of those under thirty had never had a ceremonial over them.

Besides approaching this problem from the point of view of time spent in ceremonial activities, it may also be approached from the point of view of proportion of family income (measured mainly, of course, on the basis of goods consumed) expended upon ceremonials. Fees paid to local individuals vary with degree of relationship[24] and various other factors, but seem to average about the equivalent of two dollars for diagnosis by motion-in-the-hand, the equivalent of five dollars for a one-night ceremonial, twelve dollars for Blessing Way, roughly three dollars and a half per night for Life Way ceremonials, thirteen dollars for a three-night ceremonial, twenty to twenty-five dollars for a five-night ceremonial.[25] They are considerably higher for outside singers[26] and diagnosticians. The fee for the same ceremonial repeated by the same singer is very small. Indeed the patient is considered to have a right to have the ceremonial repeated three times for a conventionalized gift of calico and a basket. But in every case the fee represents but a part of the total cost, for the singer, his assistants, and all visitors must be fed throughout the duration of the ceremony. My figures here are necessarily but approximations,[27] of course, but they suggest—for the six month period—a crude average of close to twenty percent of the annual income. Here also the figures would doubtless have been higher not many years ago because of the fees and "royalties" which learners pay to their teachers. The proportion varies from as high as about sixty percent of annual income for one family to zero for another—not counting time spent in attendance at ceremonials which might otherwise have been devoted to economically productive activities. There is a rough correlation with economic status, except in cases of really

serious illness when a poor family will dispose of everything and borrow from relatives and neighbors to make possible a whole succession
of different ceremonials for the sick individual. Last summer one of the
poorest families in this group hired singers for almost forty days out of
sixty. At all events one gets a decided impression that these families devote a higher proportion of their "budgets" to ceremonials than does
the average family in our society to church, physician, and theatrical
entertainment combined

In short, the evidence which has been presented seems to create a
strong presumption in favor of the hypothesis that ceremonials are a
focal point of the actions of this Navaho society. It goes without saying
that ceremonial behaviors are intimately bound up with other types,
and that, while ceremonial action clearly seems to be a favored mode
of conduct, it does not by any means always transcend other considerations.[28] It is true, of course, as Hill has shown,[29] that all ceremonies and
ceremonials are, among other things, means of food production by
controlling supernatural forces, and so, all "ceremonial" factors are, to
some extent, also "economic" factors. Indeed, as Hill says, "So thorough have been the adjustments of the ritual and material sides of the
culture that to the Navaho mind they appear indistinguishable." Nevertheless, to the observer, the fact that so much of the attack on problems
which we may abstract as "economic" is in this Navaho culture cere-
monialized remains interesting and important.

Navaho hogan; mother with sick child. Sand painting is part of curing ritual.
Photo courtesy of American Museum of Natural History.

NOTES

1. The two seasons' field work which supplied the data for this paper were supported by grants from the Division of Anthropology of Harvard University. The paper has had the benefit of helpful criticism from Dr. Leland C. Wyman and Mr. Harry Tschopik, Jr.

2. Within the last fifteen years singers have been brought from rather distant points on the Navaho Reservation to give such ceremonials as Red Ant Way and Plume Way so that most adults in the group have witnessed a considerably greater range of ceremonials than would be suggested by the data of the last two years. Inquiry revealed, however, sixteen individuals between about twenty and about thirty-five who had never attended any portion of a nine-night ceremonial.

3. It is clear that at least four singers in the Danoff and Two Wells regions have a fairly regular practice among the Ramah-Atarque Navaho. They have been seen (e.g., at "chicken pulls" and "squaw dances") under circumstances which strongly suggested that they were "looking for business."

4. For a description of these varieties of diagnosis see Leland C. Wyman, *Navaho Diagnosticians* (American Anthropologist, Vol. 38, pp. 236-46, 1936).

5. William Morgan, *Human Wolves Among the Navaho* (Yale University Publications in Anthropology, No. 11; 1936). See also Leland C. Wyman and Clyde Kluckhohn, *Navaho Classification of Their Song Ceremonials* (Memoirs, American Anthropological Association, No. 50, 1938) for terminology generally and for phonemic recordings of Navaho terms.

6. Dr. Wyman tells me that, in his experience, one who knows thoroughly a single five-night ceremonial is called "singer."

7. This does not imply, of course, all possible details, variations, and concomitant ceremonies connected with these ceremonials. Indeed my impression is that the knowledge of these singers is somewhat meagre as compared with that of certain singers of the Reservation. For example, this first singer knows a total of only seven sandpaintings for his four ceremonials. The second knows but five, the third but two. No curer can make more than a single sandpainting.

8. Although he does not sing Blessing Way, this singer knows enough songs from it to conduct the girl's adolescence rite.

9. These and subsequent statistics are based upon: (1) direct observation by the writer and by two graduate students (Harry Tschopik, Jr. of Harvard University and John Adair of the University of Wisconsin) who were carrying on other investigations in the area but kindly kept careful notes on these particulars; (2) systematic and repeated interviewing of all singers, curers, and diagnosticians; (3) statements made by other members of the community in interview material on other subjects. So many cross checks were available that no datum was included which was not documented by at least three independent sources.

10. I have a number of records for past years of motion-in-the-hand being used to find lost animals, children, jewelry, etc. No one in this group remembered its being used within the past generation for hunting. Some of the older men recalled its use in war.

11. Of these, thirty-three are known to have been "repeats" of the cycle of four by the same singer. This must be borne in mind in comparing the number of ceremonials (148) with the number of diagnoses (63). If one adds to this last figure the number of repeats and the number of Blessing Ways (to which—at all events among these Navaho—diagnosis is only very exceptionally a preliminary), one gets 119. From this two must be subtracted, for in two cases two diagnosticians were called in before a ceremonial was decided upon. There were 31 cases (148-117), excluding Blessing Ways, in which diagnosis did not precede the first carrying out of a ceremonial by a given singer. Actually there are only three instances where a major ceremonial was not based upon the advice of a diagnostician. The other twenty-eight cases mainly are "blackenings" to which diagnosis, apparently, is

not felt as a necessary prerequisite, although it was carried out in two recorded cases.

12. As a matter of fact, I have records for the same six months' period in 1936. The figures for these and other facts treated in this paper differ but little for the two years, but since I have reason to believe that the 1937 data are somewhat more accurate in detail I present these only.

13. Of these 8 were Moving Up Way, 4 Big Star Way, 3 Enemy Way, 2 Enemy Monster Way, 1 Evil Way, Male Shooting Branch. (All of these are known by members of this group.)

14. Some of these, while not precisely "assistants," are in demand because they "know the songs."

15. The wide individual range which went into these averages must not be forgotten. Some men do not average one day in two weeks.

16. It is difficult to say whether the frequency of ceremonials is greater or less during the period from September 15th to March 15th. Statements of informants on the general question were conflicting, and attempts to secure a comparably complete record of actual ceremonials showed plainly that even singers could not be relied upon to give in June a trustworthy record of ceremonials they themselves had conducted during, say, the preceding November. On the other hand, numerous cross-checks indicated that the lists given for the three months immediately before the arrival of the observer in the field could be regarded as substantially complete and accurate. It should be remarked that, within the sample period, August shows a slightly greater concentration of ceremonials than can be explained on the principle of random sampling, and August is also, with little doubt, both the freest of the six months from pressing economic activities and also one of the most prosperous months of the year for the Navaho.

17. This includes of course time spent (1) as singer, curer, diagnostician, or assistant, and travel directly arising out of these activities, including, e.g., trips to the mountains to gather plants; (2) as patient; (3) attendance at ceremonials, including travel to and from secular activities.

18. Except possibly for brief verbal references to the "actions" of natural phenomena.

19. Songs are, of course, improvised on various secular occasions and also in connection with the girl's dance of Enemy Way.

20. Cf. Father Berard Haile, *Origin Legend of the Navaho Enemy Way* (Yale University Publications in Anthropology, No. 17, 1938), p. 72.

21. For example, at least two old men say a prayer and sprinkle pollen in front of their hogans at sunrise each morning.

22. I use "ceremony" as opposed to "ceremonial" in the way recently proposed by Father Berard (*op. cit.*).

23. An exception is the brief ceremony against bad dreams centered around a Blessing Way song. I know of this ceremony being carried out twice in the six month period.

24. From a son to a father, for example, only a token payment may be given, but some sort of fee is essential to the efficacy of the treatment.

25. These fees are in addition to the basket and calico which must be given to any singer who sings all night.

26. I was unable to obtain trustworthy information (i.e. with at least one independent verification) in more than about one-third of the cases. Here are some of the actual data: diagnosis—two dollars cash, one goat, "one cheap ring," two old ewes; one-night ceremonial—an old Pendleton blanket and a bracelet, five dollars cash, one big sheep, an unwounded buckskin, four strings of coral beads, a kid (from an older brother), a ewe with her lamb, a young, broken horse (to an outside singer); Blessing Way—big buckskin and string of beads, three sheep, six dollars cash and two lambs, six sheep and two dollars, saddle horse, eleven dollars

cash; four-night Life Way—one old ram; six-night Life Way—ten dollars and two wether lambs; eleven-night Life Way—six dollars and four ewes (from a sister's daughter); five-night ceremonial—sixteen dollars cash, ten sheep, good saddle horse, shawl and five dollars cash, a yearling calf and five dollars cash, ten dollars and two sheep, a buckskin and seven dollars, five sheep, two sheep and a string of turquoise beads, a buckskin (from a sister's son), fifty dollars cash (to an outside singer), a heifer and a colt and twelve young ewes (to an outside singer). It is interesting to note that those who do Blessing Way appear to be best paid in proportion to the time involved and those who do Life Way least well paid. But the data are insufficient for generalization even as respects this group. It is perhaps worth observing explicitly that singers appear to be paid more per day than almost any Navaho can earn within our economic system. Several informants stated that fees were normally higher in winter—"because horses are poor."

27. A careful study of the books of all trading stores in the region by Mr. John Adair makes possible estimates of family income and expenditure which are considerably better than guesses. Actually, from a close study of the accounts one can actually tell when a family held a major ceremonial. I should like to express my gratitude to Mr. Adair for his material and also to the traders in the region (notably Messrs. Shephard, Hall, Williamson, Bond, Lambson, Ashcroft) for magnificent cooperation.

28. To give concrete illustrations: (1) Unless there is some peculiar urgency, a family with many sheep will not arrange a ceremonial at the height of lambing or shearing seasons! (2) In the year following a big pinyon crop a marked increase in intensity of ceremonial activity has been observed.

29. Willard W. Hill, *The Agricultural and Hunting Methods of the Navaho Indians* (Yale University Publications in Anthropology, No. 19, 1938). I am very much indebted to Dr. Hill for allowing me to see this important work prior to publication. I did not read it until after this paper was already completed.

HOW AN ANTHROPOLOGIST WORKS IN THE FIELD:
PHOTOGRAPHY IN FIELD RESEARCH

Margaret Mead, 1956. Some Uses of Still Photography in Culture and Personality Studies. Not published previously. Photographs and quotations reproduced from the following sources:

> *Growth and Culture. A Photographic Study of Balinese Childhood,* by Margaret Mead and Frances Cooke MacGregor (New York, 1951). G. P. Putnam's Sons. By courtesy of the authors and G. P. Putnam's Sons.
>
> *Balinese Character* by Gregory Bateson and Margaret Mead (New York, 1942). New York Academy of Sciences. By courtesy of The New York Academy of Sciences.
>
> Projective Testing in Manus, by courtesy of Lenora Schwartz.
>
> Projective Testing, Pondram's Return from the Dead, and Marriage Old, Middle, and New, by courtesy of Theodore Schwartz.
>
> *Manus Religion* by Reo F. Fortune, Plate IX. By courtesy of The American Philosophical Society.
>
> Broadway Bench Sitters, New York, by courtesy of Kenneth Heyman.
>
> Rickey at 2½, by courtesy of Paul Byers.

Dr. Mead concentrates in the following paper upon one aspect of photography in ethnography: the analysis of personality. With her associates, she has opened up a new field to students of personality on the one hand, and to sensitive users of the camera on the other. The manifold applications of photography in anthropology are increasing steadily (cf. for example, *Photography for Archaeologists,* by M. B. Cookson. London, 1954). Students are invited to study Dr. Mead's procedures, and to estimate possible implications of other photographs elsewhere in this book.

SOME USES OF STILL PHOTOGRAPHY IN CULTURE AND PERSONALITY STUDIES

Margaret Mead

Since the beginning of the study of human behavior there has been a standing controversy between those who believed that the way to deal with complexity was to ignore it, reduce complex materials to a few manageable variables, and those who have insisted on maintaining the integrity of the material in spite of our inability to analyze it in ways which could be "measured." This latter group of us have insisted that, until methods of handling organizational complexity were developed, we preferred to use that incalculable but superior computer, the human observer, and his or her "intuition," or wealth of experience which could be condensed into rapid perception.

At the same time we have been continually on the lookout for better methods of recording, rather than methods of reducing poor and incomparable types of recording to apparent meaningfulness by such devices as rating scales. This has meant that just in proportion to interest in complexity there has been an interest in the new recording methods made possible by the development of technology during the last thirty years, as expressed by miniature cameras, rapid winders, faster films, new methods of lighting, cine film, slow motion, sound recording, and equipment like the Chapple interaction chronograph. As fast as these new methods become available, they are being pressed into service to supplement, in visual and auditory terms, the observations of the trained human observer without sacrificing the richness of the material. Undoubtedly, in time, kinesthetic, tactual, olfactory, and gustatory recording devices will be developed also. Students of methodology may be interested in the extent to which it has been those who emphasized the complexity of the materials, who have been the most ready to use technical aids.

Still photography was the first technical aid to be given full utilization, partly because of costs and problems of power and light in the field necessary for cine and sound, and partly because our methods of analysis were still so rudimentary that such complex sequences as those provided by tape recording and cine film were still relatively intractable to analysis. Furthermore, still photography can be reproduced in a familiar form—the book—and cross comparisons in spatial terms, in the single composite plate or slide, or by spreading hundreds of prints out on accessible flat surfaces, are easy and practicable. All records which involve time as a major dimension and so must be presented sequentially—as must a tape recording or a cine film—present far tougher problems to a student working in a comparative science. One can set up two projectors to run simultaneously, but not ten, and even two present serious problems. For comparative purposes film has to be reduced to sets of stills, and tapes to visual patterns, or one has to rely on the memories of specially gifted individual investigators.

Thus, in the use of mechanical aids, we have at present several developments: 1: the use of still photography, which preserves the complexity of the original material and can be analyzed with an approach to simultaneity in which the memory of the investigator is at a minimum during the analysis; 2: cine film and tape recordings, in which the record is much more complete but in which the investigator's skill is more of a factor *during* the analysis; 3: records of the Chapple (6) interaction type, or the work of Goldman-Eisler (11), in which the observer is involved initially and his skill is as important as in any of the original types of investigation without technical aids, but the machine types of recording and analyzing increase the accuracy of data which is initially dependent upon coding at the time of the observation; and 4: records which are *entirely* dependent upon the human observer at the time they are made, but whose complexity can be handled by computers so that much more complex patterns can be analyzed.

The use of still photography in field research, and in the examination of expressions of emotion, has progressed steadily since Darwin's day (8), but, until the development of miniature cameras and mechanical devices for sequence shots and hand loading of bulk film, it remained a matter of single shots or very short sequences. Difficulties involved in photographing a live field situation in which real emotions were expressed led to the use of actors, or laboratory-produced emotions, which in turn distorted the material. Difficulties in using photography as a major tool in the tropics, before the development of modern methods of preserving and processing film, prevented the use of partially clothed people and retarded the use of the whole body. Studies of whole unclothed bodies tended to be limited to infants in clinical and laboratory situations, as in the studies made by Gesell (10) and McGraw (15). Restriction of studies to faces and to clothed bodies thus retarded the development of models of expressive and communicative behavior (5). The static quality of the single shot and the posed photograph was such a handicap, that for early studies of gesture, like that made by Boas and Efron (9), the sketches of an artist were preferred. Such vivid sketches as those of Covarrubias (7) were able to convey much more of a movement pattern than any sequence of slow single shots. Finally, photography was very expensive, both initially and for reproduction: line drawings were much cheaper.

Still photography as a major research tool, rather than a helpful little supplement which showed the main characters, and the way the landscape, houses and material objects "looked," had to wait on the inventions which overcame these difficulties: a camera which would take a long sequence without reloading, a method of hand loading bulk film (this dealt summarily with the matter of cost, and has improved from the appalling type of labor necessary in 1936 to usable daylight loaders), speed of film, and methods of lighting so that real people could be taken in real situations, wherever located. The problem of processing the thousands of shots for later work has not yet been satisfactorily solved. We have gone from diapositive film strips, which meant slow search for any special frame by passing the film strips through a projector (the method used in preparing *Balinese Character*), to mass printing of eight strips at a time, which obscures fine details because of differences in exposure, to electronically controlled enlargement processes which, while solving the problems of visibility and exposure, are still too expensive. With the present state of budgets on the one hand, and the general amateur-oriented standards of professional film processers, all work with photography demands the individual technical and *manual* attention of the scientist-photographers themselves.

Technology is changing so rapidly that many of the methods which we used in the 1953 Admiralty Island expedition—taking along generators, using flood lights and clumsy, complicated flash equipment that needed recharging, are no longer necessary. Greatly improved flash equipment, which in turn will probably be out of date before this article is printed, and much faster film, are together already making enormous changes. So it is not feasible to make any specific recommendations, beyond emphasizing the types of technical help needed (for speed, lens and film and flash equipment; distance shots, telephoto lenses; scope, wide angle lenses; cheapness, as with loaders for bulk film; preservation of film in the field, dry boxes and special preservatives), and methods of processing and storing the results.

It should also be emphasized that none of these advances replace complete, accurate accompanying notes and detailed written catalogues which make it possible to place each photograph in its original context, and to cross reference photography by time, subject, personalities, etc., for future use. Here again, if one member of the team has a good time-place memory, this will save thousands of dollars which would otherwise go to make an elaborate system of cross reference, as one searches for a picture which shows the foot used like a hand "by a man," or "a scene in which a child is trailing a toy on a long string," or "an instance which shows an anthropomorphic and a non-anthropomorphic offering together." In time electronic methods of search which can be built directly from photographs may solve part of this problem.

The plates which are used to illustrate this article have been taken from the initiating work of Gregory Bateson (1), Tax and Eisley (19), and subsequent work done by my collaborators and students which

---

PLATE I: BALANCE IN BALI

This plate illustrates the motif of the perfectly integrated body image.

1. A small boy learns to stand and walk. His father has set up for him in the houseyard a horizontal bamboo supported on two posts (*penegtegan*). The boy learns to walk by using this as a support.

The topology of this arrangement is the precise opposite of that of the play-pen of Western culture. The Western child is confined within restricting limits and would like to escape from them; the Balinese child is supported within a central area and is frightened of departure from this support.

When unsure of his balance, he holds onto his penis. This method of reassurance is common in Balinese baby boys.

I Karba, aged 414 days; I Kenjoen, his cousin, aged 317 days, behind him.

Bajoeng Gede, March 26, 1937. 6 F 20, 21

2. A baby girl unsure of her balance. She clasps her hands in front of her abdomen.

I Kangoen.

Bajoeng Gede. April 21, 1937. 7A 15.

3. A small boy scratches his leg. He was waiting in the road, uncertain whether his playmate was following. His natural movement is to raise his leg, rather than to stoop.

Bajoeng Gede. April 19, 1937. 6 W 19.

4. Painting of a woman transforming herself into a witch (*anak mereh*). She goes out alone at night, sets up a little shrine and makes offerings on the ground to the demons. She dances before the shrine with her left foot on a fowl, and becomes transformed into supernatural size and shape. The fantasy that the body is as integrated as a single organ is here danced out in grotesque balance, and leads to a nightmare transformation or ecstatic dissociation of the personality. The drawing illustrates the close association between grotesque posture and the ecstasy of witchcraft (cf. fig. 6).

Painting by I. B. Nj. Tjeta of Batoean.

Purchased Feb. 2, 1938. Reduced x 1/3 linear.

Cat. No. 548.

5. A girl stoops to pick up part of an offering. The flexibility of the body and the emphasis on the buttocks continue into later life, and occur even in those who are unusually heavily built.

I Teboes; I Tjerita behind her.

Bajoeng Gede. April 26, 1937. 7 H 18.

6. Decorative panel on a temple wall. This figure stands as one of a series of representations of transformed witches (*lejak*) and graveyard spirits (*tangan-tangan, njapoepoe,* etc.).

Poera Dalem, Bangli. Nov. 23, 1936. 3 J 5.

Figs. 2, 3, 5, 6, 7 and 8 and amended captions from Plate 17 (pp. 88 and 89) of "Balinese Character: A Photographic Analysis" by Gregory Bateson and Margaret Mead, New York Academy of Sciences, 1943.

PLATE I

1 2

3 4

5 6

has derived from that work. This paper is not meant to draw on all the variety of excellent photographic studies of primitive peoples or contemporary peoples which now exist, but simply to present a discussion of method in cases where the intent, the procedures, the culture, and the conditions under which the work was done are all known to me. The student who wishes to compare the work of many different photographers and artists on the same culture can do no better than compare the existing materials on Bali, which provide a full gamut of methods and approaches.[1]

We may now turn to some of the specific contributions to culture and personality research made by rapid sequence photography.

The use of large numbers of photographs, that is of the order of 20,000 per year's field observations, makes it possible to give some quantitative weighting to one's material. So it is possible to express quantitatively the use of crowd scenes[300], in which a given hand posture occurred[100], and another[200], or to state that photographic observations of Child A[400] are being compared with photographic observations of Child B[300]. As it is never possible to record one millionth of what one takes in through one's senses about a scene in the time available for a written note, such photographic records with the placement of each individual in a complex scene are invaluable checks on the bases of one's generalizations. Large numbers of photographs, especially photographs taken in depth, make it possible to check new hypotheses, not developed in the field, as for example the correlation between the body touching others and the mouth falling open in Bali. Individuals and events in the background of a photograph provide checks on the amount of bias which obtains in the choice of action in the foreground. Thus the greater anxiety of children in the presence of the witch form of trance than in the presence of child trance dancers representing "angels," which was a generalization not made in the field, could be tested against the faces of children in the background of many trance scenes photographed in Bali.

From a great series of photographs of all varieties of scene and behavior it is possible to cross reference, in simultaneous presentation, some theme or emphasis which would otherwise have to be presented in verbal sequence which could only touch on the single regularity being noted. Thus in Plate I, on balance in Bali, we see types of balance, children learning to walk, a girl working with offerings, a child standing watching in the street, a painting and a carving, in which the full scene is preserved while the single cross reference is made. Franz Boas once said that the trouble with a monograph was that one always needed all the other chapters for the point one was making. The reproduced photograph of a scene provides "the other aspects" of that scene, and reduces the chances of the verbal description doing violence to the material. Such composite presentations as Plate I bring to the user (note that we have no word which corresponds exactly to the word "listener" or "auditor" for the person who actively experiences visually; *viewer*, although now coming into use in connection with TV, is a name for a machine; *spectator* implies non-participation; *audience*, although used of moving picture attenders, refers primarily to hearing) corrective visual details in connection with any abstraction from the material, enriching the experience of the non-visualizer, and correcting the fluid imagery of the visualizer. The same pictures may be arranged in many different cross sequences, thus illustrating the patterns or styles in a culture which are so much more subject to pictorial than verbal description.

Rapid sequence shots can substitute for cine film as a device for recording a large number of points in a sequence, and the more rapid the shooting the lower the degree of intervention of the photographer. (While cine film provides more detail and longer smooth sequences, unless a motor is used on the movie camera, the circumstance of rewinding introduces an arbitrary cut-off, and the photographer introduces a personal choice point when he takes his finger off the button. Both reduce the natural superiority of the cine film over the still sequential record.) A rapid sequence of stills is presented in Plate II, Sibling Rivalry in Bali, with the accompanying protocol which places the material in context. It is during scenes of this sort that the field worker often develops new insights about the culture, and, if these are recorded on the spot, then later one can go back to the exact visual situation which gave rise to the insight. Furthermore, if a large number of such sequences of interpersonal relations are shot immediately on entering the field, it is possible to check the effect of a developed hypothesis in the distortion of the field worker's perception, by going back to the photographs which were taken *before* the insights were articulated. (We have no way of knowing, of course, at what stage they were inarticulately present in the mind of the observer.)[2]

An intermediate use of photography, between being chiefly a recording device and chiefly a communication device, is to facilitate communication among members of a team, between co-workers in the preparation of a joint report, or between workers in different fields where analysis of photographs which can be used as shared experience permits a form of rapid and accurate communication which words can not supply. Thus photographs can be not only a partial substitute for shared field work, but also serve to facilitate the very difficult task of collaborative writing. Joint selection of words or phrases is far more complicated and less satisfactory than joint agreement on a series of photographs which are to be presented together and make several

continued on page 90

PLATE II: SIBLING RIVALRY IN BALI

The mother's behavior is a conventional game which is often played—especially when there is an audience of visitors in the house. It consists of putting the new baby in the knee baby's lap and urging the latter to treat the rival as "younger sibling."

Margaret Mead's verbal record of the sequence of behavior reads as follows:

"Njawa (the knee baby, a girl) runs over and hangs on mother.

"Njawa tries to suck.

"Njawa given the baby to hold by her mother.

"Refuses, elbows sticking out.

"Men Njawi (the mother) says '*Gisiang! gisiang!*' ('Hold it! hold it!')

"Njawa puts her face down by the baby's.

"Njawa's arms tentatively around baby; she plays with her own mouth.

"Men Njawi says '*Gisiang!* ('Hold it!') Njawa giggles self-consciously."

"Njawa puts her face down to baby.

"Njawa pokes baby's chest with her finger, and then puts her finger behind her and rubs it off vigorously on the back of her sarong.

"Men Njawi says 'Sit better; put your legs out,' and she straightens Njawa's legs and lays baby on them. Says '*Gisiang!*' Mother stern (fig. 1).

"Njawa says '*Ngelawang.*' ('It's resisting.')

"Men Njawi repeats this, laughing, 'She says it's resisting.' The baby is really absolutely passive and good.

"Njawa ignoring baby leans against breast (figs. 3 and 4).

" '*Poeles.*' ('It's asleep'—probably said by the mother.)

"Njawa looks at baby, finger in mouth" (fig. 6).

Putting the verbal record and the photographs together, the events fall into eight groups:

1. Njawa attempts to suck (recorded verbally), and the mother replies by placing the baby in Njawa's lap.

2. Njawa withdraws.

3. Njawa puts her face down in contact with that of the baby (recorded verbally), then smiles at the photographer.

4. Njawa withdraws from the baby to play with her own mouth (recorded verbally) and the mother renews her insistence on attention to the baby.

5. Njawa again "kisses" the baby (recorded verbally).

6. Njawa repudiates the baby—poking it and then wiping her finger (recorded verbally). To this the mother responds with a vigorous effort to make her attend to the baby. The mother straightens Njawa's legs, etc.

7. The mother's attention shifts away from the children (fig. 3) and Njawa sucks at the breast (fig. 4), which is what she wanted to do at the beginning of the sequence.

8. Njawa looks at the baby with a triumphant expression, showing her teeth (recorded verbally without comment on the facial expression, fig. 6).

The two sets of data complement each other on a number of points, and neither gives the whole story without the other. The camera did not record Njawa's initial attempt to suck nor any of the mother's behavior when she was most energetically trying to make Njawa attend to the baby. While this was happening the photographer had to move and refocus the camera, but the camera did record Njawa's exhibitionistic attention to the photographer, her final successful effort to suck and her facial expression when she looked at the baby at the end of the incident.

The sequence illustrates the knee baby's ambivalence, and her attempt to make loving the baby more palatable by exhibitionism. It also illustrates the characteristic inconsistency of the mother's behavior—in first making a considerable effort to prevent the knee baby from sucking by making her pay attention to the new baby, and later permitting her to suck. It is true that

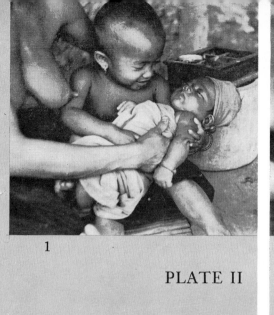

1

PLATE II

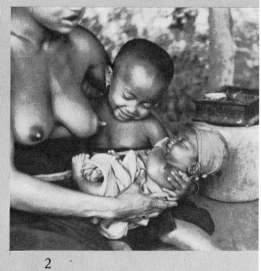

4

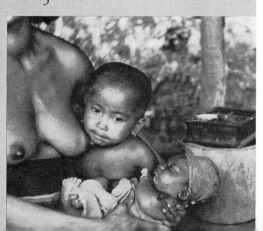

2

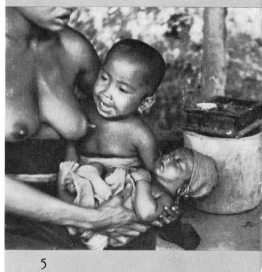

5

3

6

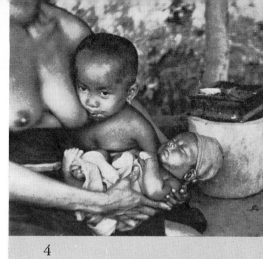

the mother's attention reverts to the knee baby after the sucking, but no rebuke followed, and the photographs show no sharp movement of the mother's body or left hand.
Men Njawi with I Njawa and I Koewat. Bajoeng Gede. April 30, 1937. 7V 34, 35, 36, 37, 38, 39.

This is a condensation of the notes which accompany Plates 71 and 72 and figs. 1 to 6 of Plate 72 (pp. 196 through 199) from "Balinese Character: A Photographic Analysis" by Gregory Bateson and Margaret Mead, New York Academy of Sciences, 1942. The references to the figures on Plate 71 and the figures themselves which show the first part of the sequence are omitted here, but the details from the notes of Margaret Mead are given to provide context.

PLATE III: INATTENTIVE HANDS. Bali

The way in which Balinese children are carried, either in a cloth sling or in an arm which uses the sling as a model, sets a style in which the child can be treated safely attached to the body of the adult, like one of the adult's own limbs, and needing no continuous attention. The child is habitually relaxed in the sling, the spread position of the thighs provides a fit rather than a hold on the body of the carrier, so that ordinarily there is no holding on, or grasping or tensing behavior in the child to which the attention of the carrier needs to respond. Under these circumstances, the adult gives minimal attention, a light contact with the wrist (figs. 3 and 5), treating the carried baby as a convenient arm rest (figs. 2 and 7), or the hands may hang completely flaccid, permitting the sling to do all the work (fig. 9), or the child to lean against the seated body (figs. 6 and 8).

1. I Baroek, 11½ months, in arms of her mother (Men Kesir). Own yard. Baroek rests in sling and on mother's knee, mother looks away, and the right hand, although lying along Baroek's side, makes no contact with the child. *2/11/39. 35 W 38.*

2. I Doemoen (age unknown) in the arms of her mother (Men Kesir). Our yard. This is the same mother (fig. 1)—more than two years earlier—carrying the child who died sometime after I Baroek was born, late 1938. Here, although Men Kesir is smiling at Doemoen, her left hand is inattentive. *10/10/36. 2 W 6.*

3. I Tongos, 8 weeks, being suckled by his mother (Men Tongos) in his own yard. Again her hand is unrelated to the child. *1/21/37. 4 Ga 29.*

4. I Marta, 14½ months, her head resting against her father (Nang Marti). Own yard. Her head rests against his shoulder, but his hands are unrelated to her. *2/11/39. 35 T 14.*

5. I Karba, 24½ months, being suckled by his mother (Men Oera). Our veranda. Karba is held at such a precarious angle that his mother's firm hold on his left knee is necessary; nevertheless, her left hand hangs loose, although his head rests against the forearm. *3/1/38 21 R 30.*

6. I Raoeh, 25½ months, being suckled by his mother (Men Goenoeng). Own yard. Her hands are lightly cupped and unrelated to him. She has just been stroking the chicken that is now being held by I Poendoeh (the child nurse). *3/3/38. 22 F 15.*

7. I Tabeng (age unknown) in arms of child nurse (I Ngembon), beside father (Nang Lintar) and older sister (I Meres). Own yard. Ngembon's hand

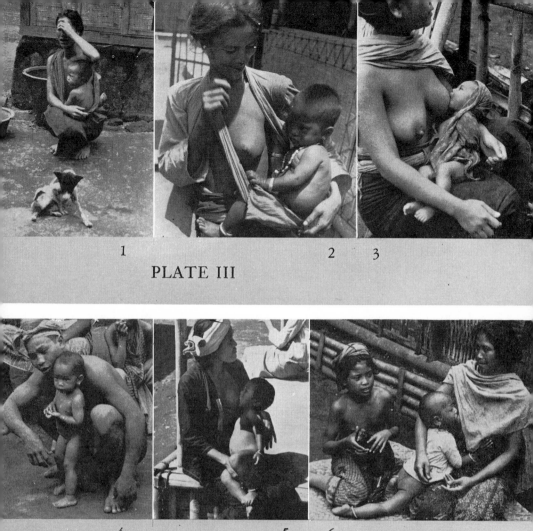

1   2   3

PLATE III

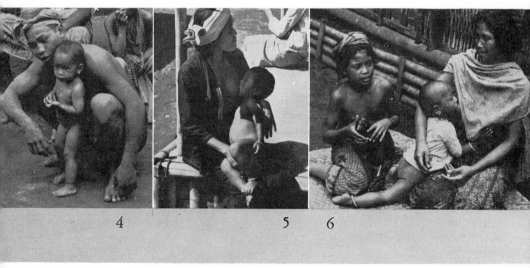

4   5   6

7   8   9

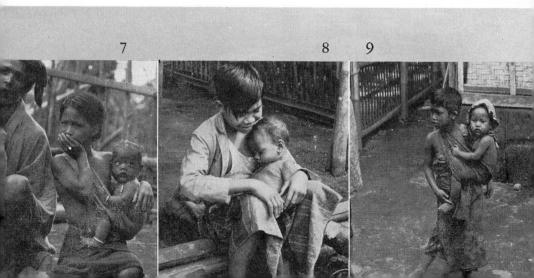

points of differential priority, simultaneously. *Balinese Character* is an example of such collaboration between Gregory Bateson, Claire Holt, and myself.

Plate III illustrates the research use of photographic records to communicate with workers in another field. After I returned from Bali, I became interested in the Gesell categories as interpreted by Frances Ilg, and when I met Frances Macgregor, who was a professional photographer now interested in combining research and photography, it occurred to me that it might be possible for someone with her training to use the photographs which we already had, for a preliminary test of the cross cultural usefulness of the Gesell categories. As a first step in developing the project, and without discussing any hypotheses with her, I left her alone with a large series of enlargements. With no directive categories to guide or restrain her, she selected the mothers' hands as of key interest, and wrote:

> The hands of Balinese mothers, fathers, and even of child nurses, while not actively engaged in administering to the babies' needs or teaching them, commonly assume a limp, passive, and detached expression even though the child may be suckling or troubled. Not only do the hands offer little physical support (more often it is the wrist or arm), but expressions of tenderness, security, anxiety, or tenseness, as conveyed by the hands, are lacking.

Plate III is a presentation of this insight after the analysis of the 4000 photographs used in *Growth and Culture*, which includes two further presentations of hands: Attentive Hands (Plate XLI) and Firm Hands (Plate XXXIX).

Plate IV, also from *Growth and Culture*, presents a further step in this use of already gathered photographs for research purposes, the results of a series of sessions in which our Balinese photographs of young children of known ages were roughly grouped in Gesell categories, and worked over with us by members of the Gesell group, with differ-

---

hangs limp from wrist while Tabeng, firmly held in sling, rests foot against her lap.

2/12/39. 36 M 27.

8. I Sami, 7 months, after a period of very active play, falling into a momentary sleep in arms of I Sambeh (younger brother of Nang Ngendon). Own

yard. Sambeh's hands lie completely lax and inattentive.

4/30/37. 7 P 10.

9. I Baroek, 11½ months, in arms of her sister child nurse (I Kesir). Own yard. Kesir's hands are inattentive, her left finger just touches Baroek's ankle.

2/12/39. 36 C 12.

Figures 1-9 and captions for Plate XL (pp. 142-143) of "Growth and Culture: A Photographic Study of Balinese Childhood" by Margaret Mead and Frances Cooke Macgregor, based on photographs by Gregory Bateson, analyzed in Gesell Categories, New York, G. P. Putnam's Sons, 1951.

ences and contrasts noted for further exploration. Out of this procedure, which would have been impossible without a large amount of simultaneously available visual material, the contrast in Balinese and New Haven American children's squatting sequence was developed.[3]

With Plate V, "Ricky at 2½," I turn to the work of Paul Byers, a professional photographer also interested in using insights from the behavioral sciences as a communicative device. Paul Byers is concerned with combining insight into the behavior of a child, or of a family group, using his own presence as a stranger and the photographic process as initial exploratory tools. From a large number of shots, ranging from about 100 to 200, he then constructs a *new* statement about the relationships observed, which will stand on its own without verbalizations of any sort. This procedure, conducted within the framework of professional children's photography, the end product of which is a compact, bound book of photographs, but also has to produce single pictures, pictures for wallets, for Christmas presents, for Grandmothers, sets formal limits to the exploration, and dictates an ethical sensitivity which will become increasingly important to field workers as their subjects become more conscious of the implications of visual images. His work underlines the extent of the photographer's responsibility for saying something with his pictures, about his subjects, to his subjects, which he not only feels to be true, but which must be arranged in a form which they can accept, deal with, and, when possible, learn from.

Plate VI, "Broadway Bench Sitters," by Ken Heyman, also a professional photographer interested in developing photography as a combined research and communication tool, has been prepared for this discussion to show how, by the use of different lenses, the photographer can give levels of context and place sequences of behavior meaningfully within them, and to demonstrate the use of a telephoto lens in reducing the awareness of the subjects.

Photographs may also be used to "bring home" to the reader and student the extent and intensity of some comparison or contrast. Here again, the larger the number of photographs, the greater the possibility of demonstrating points which arise in the course of analysis. (After completing our combined Bali and Iatmul field trip, we found many instances where we had, without being aware of it at the time, photographed sequences of behavior which provided some close and valuable parallel to material from the other culture, in such matters as response to a younger sibling's pain, or the handling of sibling rivalry in children of the same age.) Furthermore, extreme contrasts, as between the Manus of 1928-29 and the Manus of 1953-54, can be given with greater credibility through photographs than by verbal descriptions. Plate VII, "Marriage, Old, Middle and New, Manus 1928, 1946, 1953-54," illustrates this point. The 1946 photograph taken by an unknown American soldier illustrates a further way in which photographs taken from some different point of view can be combined with purposeful research materials.

I have selected Plates VIII and IX by Theodore and Lenora Schwartz, my collaborators in our recent field trip in the Admiralty Islands, to

---

PLATE IV: SQUATTING. Bali

In their squatting behavior there is found one of the most marked differences between Balinese and American children. The Balinese squat is much lower, the buttocks often resting on the ground (figs. 1, 4, 7), and the squatting position occupies a different position in the maturational sequence. American children tend to go from frogging to creeping to all fours or to standing, with the squat following later; the Balinese children, with hardly any creeping, go from sitting to squatting to standing, rising from the squat rather than sinking down into it. Here again a number of factors can be mentioned as explanatory; the presence of squatting as a usual form among Balinese adults, the wide spread of the hips that is associated with being carried on the hip for such a long period, the narrow circle within which a Balinese child is usually permitted movement so that movement up may be substituted for movement away from a given position, the extreme fluidity of Balinese movement, and the emphasis that has been placed on balance during the time the child was learning to stand alone.

1. I Karba, 18½ months, and I Marti, 16 months, with a *kapeng* (a copper coin) in our yard. Notice the very low squat, buttocks touching the ground.
   8/20/37. 14 L 15.
2. I Karba, 20 months, and I Ngen-

don, 11 months, playing with ball and spoon. Our yard.
   10/11/37. 17 I 27.
3. I Kenjoen, 17 months, and I Marti, 16 months, in our yard. Same scene as in fig. 1. Playing marbles.
   8/20/37. 14 M 24.
4. I Marti, 11 months, in wide low squat, playing with I Karba, 13½ months. Our yard.
   3/21/37. 6 C 9.
5. I Tongos, 10½ months, pausing in a near squat, after going on all fours, one leg dragging. I Karba, 20 months, standing with ball. In Nang Goenoeng's yard, afternoon of play.
   10/9/37. 16 Y 38.
6. I Sepek, 10½ months, squatting and maintaining his balance without his hands touching. In own yard, at his delayed *otonin* ceremony. His father (Nang Degeng) watches, holding the next older child (I Leket) sprawled in front of him.
   4/30/37. 7 S 39.
7. I Marta, 14½ months, squatting and looking over her shoulder. Own yard.
   2/11/39. 35 T 29.
8. I Raoeh, 25½ months, squatting, arms in balancing position, in front of his older brother (I Goenoeng) while his child nurse (I Poendoeh) does the hair of his mother (Men Goenoeng). Our yard.
   3/3/38. 22 E 29.

Figs. 1-8 and captions from Plate XXV (pp. 112-13) of "Growth and Culture: A Photographic Study of Balinese Childhood" by Margaret Mead and Frances Cooke Macgregor, based upon photographs by Gregory Bateson, analyzed in Gesell Categories, New York, G. P. Putnam's Sons, 1951.

illustrate two other aspects of photography. Lenora Schwartz made extensive use of the Lowenfeld Mosaic Test (14), a test which has a great advantage over many projective tests in that it results in a visible product rather than a verbal one, thus making cross cultural administration and comparison a great deal easier. Dr. Lowenfeld and her collaborators were accustomed to making notes of the behavior of the individual during the test, but they had no way of recording this behavior in detailed simultaneity and the record therefore consisted primarily of one or more completed mosaics. Mrs. Schwartz discovered that the movements of the Manus while making mosaics were as important as the finished design, and Plate VIII gives a demonstration of the difference between saying: "The subject overflowed the borders of the tray . . . ", and a visual presentation of what happened.[4]

The final Plate IX is designed to demonstrate the very significant role played by steadily improving technology. Since the beginning of pho-

continued on page 98

PLATE V: RICKY AT 2½ YEARS, U.S.A.

This plate is designed to express the multiple aspects of a child's relationships to himself, to other people, and to things. The placement of each picture in relation to each other picture is important, emphasizing as it does different degrees of intimacy, and echoing moods. The plate itself is a condensation of methods through which the photographer, in a selected series of photographic shots, arranged in new sequences or patterns, communicates to the family of a child new insights about the child and the place of the child in his total environment. Such a presentation is designed to be completely self-explanatory, as a communication to those who are already familiar with the details. No captions are needed or desirable. It has been found that persons who want one picture want an image, while those who want multiple pictures are *looking at the child*.

The explanatory notes on this page are prepared, not as captions to the pictures, but as a communication to stu-

dents using photography as a tool.

1. Child to stranger: Ricky turns from watching TV to gaze comfortably at the photographer.

2. Ricky watching and listening to a children's story on TV. There is an over-all suggestion of relaxation but he is involved with his mouth and hands as in fig. 7.

3. Ricky, facing his mother who does not appear in the picture, playing a TV rhythm game with sand blocks. Ricky is playing with his mother.

4. Child and mother: Ricky on his mother's lap in the intimacy and warmth of the bath ritual.

5. Child and father: Ricky plays with toys in his father's presence.

6. Child and maternal grandmother: Ricky, on his grandmother's lap, relates himself to the book.

7. Child and toy: Ricky is gently exploring a toy, too complicated for full understanding but which he does not force or manhandle.

Selections from a photographic family album, made for Ricky's parents, by Paul Byers.

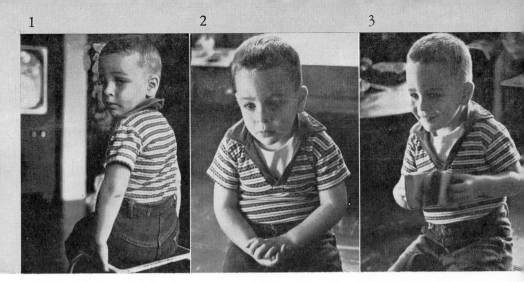

PLATE V   RICKY AT 2½ YEARS

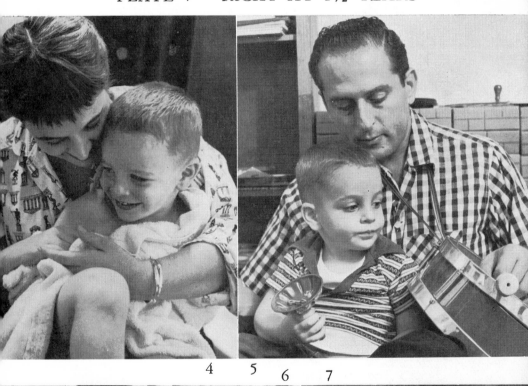

1

2

PLATE VI: BROADWAY BENCH SITTER.
New York, Summer 1955

This plate has been designed to emphasize the importance of using the camera to convey contexts in which the wider situation is essential to understanding the detail. All photographs were taken with a Leica M 3.

1. The Over-All *shot* is a photograph taken at a distance to show if possible the entire area. Such photographs can later be used as the basis for maps, diagrams, etc.

2. The Intermediate Shot is important for showing group interaction, especially when several individuals or groups are involved. In this picture a telephoto lens was used at about 40 feet from the subjects. This decreases the subjects' awareness of the photographic process.

3. A Wide-Angle Lens makes possible this kind of shot at close quarters and in interiors.

4-7. Sequence Shots With Telephoto Lens. Sequence shots of this sort are made possible by the use of rapid film advance mechanisms now available on some of the new 35 mm cameras. In this type of shot it is necessary to support the camera and Telephoto Lens by a stationary tripod. None of the individuals here were aware that they were being photographed.

In preparation for a study of this sort the photographer observes the scene for some time, using the period of observing and moving about both to provide him with background for his selections and to become an inconspicuous part of such a crowded and impersonal environment.

Plate prepared especially from original photographs by Ken Heyman.

3

tography, when the early travelers had to use wet plates, through Geoffrey Gorer's vividly described adventures with a changing bag, through the flash light bulbs which I had carried into the interior of New Guinea in 1931, all of which were damaged in transit, and Gregory Bateson's laborious hours inside a black mosquito net, cutting and rolling film by hand, in 1936-38, we have been limited in what we could photograph by problems of equipment, light and power. The developments during and since World War II make it possible to photograph as we never

continued on page 104

PLATE VII: MARRIAGE, OLD, MIDDLE AND NEW. Manus, 1928, 1946, 1953-54

Photographs may be used to convey changes in total adjustment, scene and posture, which it would be hard to convey in any other way. These pictures bridge a quarter of a century of intensive cultural change from the pre-Christian state of 1928-29, through the period of missionization, to the present cult position in which the people of Manus have their own version of Christianity. Marriage practices have changed from arranged marriage, child betrothal, and the use of protective mats or shawls in strict avoidance practices between affinal relatives (fig. 5), and a marriage ceremony in which the bride is an economic counter, dressed from head to foot in native currency and objects for affinal exchange (fig. 6), through a period when economic practices and their accompanying bridal costumes were relatively unaltered (fig. 6), to present day marriage in modern dress, a simple church ceremony, with bride and groom each supported by one attendant (fig. 1). Husbands and wives, once constrained and unable to use each other's names, are now encouraged to show demonstrative public affection, and this new style has been adopted not only by the young (fig. 2), but also by the old men who lived within the former style for many years.

1. Marriage in Church, of Martin Paliau of Bunai and Ludwika Molong of Peri, June 13, 1954. Peri.

2. Karol Matawai, son of Talikai and his wife, Aloisa Ngakakes, Dec. 14, 1953.

3. Pokanau, and his fourth wife, Benedikta Nyaulu, Sept. 10, 1953.

4. Nyalen, bride of Malean (Alois Manoi as of 1953), showing bridal canoe, bride dressed in currency, Jan. 26, 1929. Photographed by R. F. Fortune (substituted for Fig. 4 by Margaret Mead used in Plate XI of New Lives for Old).

5. Betrothed Peri girl, Taliye, wearing calico head covering so she could hide from her in-laws. 1919. Photographed by Margaret Mead.

6. Wedding of Johanus Lokus and Pipiana Lomot in Peri in 1926. Catholic ceremony illustrating how the old forms of marriage, represented by the bride's finery, remained.

Figures 1, 2 and 3, are from the American Museum Admiralty Island Expedition, 1 and 2 photographed by Theodore Schwartz, 3 by Lenora Schwartz, 5 by Margaret Mead, 6 by an unknown American soldier, and 4 by R. F. Fortune, reproduced from "Manus Religion" by R. F. Fortune, Philadelphia, The American Philosophical Society, Vol. III, 1935, Plate IX. (Replaces Fig. 4 on original plate.) The whole plate is reproduced from "New Lives For Old, Cultural Transformation, Manus, 1928-53," New York, William Morrow and Co., 1956.

PLATE VII

MARRIAGE: OLD, MIDDLE
AND NEW: Manus

1928, 1946, 1953-54

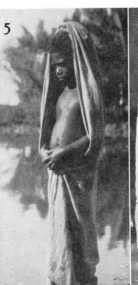

PLATE VIII: PROJECTIVE TESTING. Manus, 1954

Lenora Schwartz administering the Lowenfeld Mosaic test.

1. Small child responding to test situation but not taking test.

Lenora Schwartz' notes read: "Child of Ferdinand Pomat. The child wandered around the house perhaps feeling the excitement that the other children spread—that something was going on inside the house. When it came around to his turn he walked in shyly, looking more at the observer than at the mosaic pieces. Although he picked up the pieces, he never let his eyes move away from the observer. The pieces are piled in a corner of the board; he then seems to relax for a moment, places his head on his hand and seems to wonder—what next (fig. 3). He sits for five minutes in this position, then quietly gets up and leaves."

2-6. Kanawi taking the Mosaic test.

Lenora Schwartz' notes read: "Kanawi has been waiting all morning for his turn to come in and try or play with whatever the other children were doing (although he was not quite sure what was going on in M. M.'s house). He walked immediately over to the table and with the utmost pleasure he sighed, and then with a wonderful smile he let out with an *ay-ja ja!* There was no hesitation about picking up the colorful pieces of the mosaic. He picks up a handful of green equilaterals and spreads them out over the lower part on the board. This is quickly followed by picking up the blue equilaterals and placing them between the green pieces. We note that this is done with complete regularity in that the pieces are placed in a straight line so that you get green, blue, green, blue. We get the feeling that he has a definite direction. This direction being a desire to get the pieces going somewhere.

"One of the qualities that we note in Kanawi, himself, is his beautiful motor behavior in which he continually moves in and out of groups and captures the interest of the other children to the point where he inevitably becomes the leader in all motor activity. It is here with the mosaic pieces that again we feel he leads the pieces around, not so much to get anywhere but just to get them moving. There is complete involvement as he uses both hands and still maintains a calm and deliberate placing of the objects. His right hand places and readjusts the pieces, while his left hand holds the pieces which are waiting to be placed. Black is now lined up, still using the equilaterals. He picks up one black and brings it down to the bottom row which has now turned white. The white were placed above the green, blue row, but between the pieces as well. Red is now brought in (equilaterals). This is started at the right side and brought up to the top. Yellow (equilaterals) move up and across the top of the board. We see that each piece (so far) has been placed separately, becoming part of the lines mainly due to direction, shape and color rather than physical attachment. The board (or the space on the board) is now filled. He turns around and just continues to line the colorful pieces on the bench beside him.

"Up to this point Kanawi has shown a great deal of restraint and worked by sitting in one position. He reaches over as far as he can and, when he can no longer spread the pieces without moving, he stands up and with a handful of mixed colors he quickly moves across the floor following the long bench and placing the pieces down, each one following the other in complete regularity. Every time his hand empties he walks back to the box. His head keeps facing the bench so that his head seems to be facing his back as his body moves forward. He tries not to leave the performance visually, although his body moves away from it, in order to get

PLATE VIII

more pieces to continue what he has started. His facial expression changes each time he returns to continue. A smile appears as he returns to his creation of order in line and color.

"One line across the long bench has now been completed. He starts a second row. Now he uses the scalenes. Before he finished what was still in his hand he anticipated a lack of materials to finish this row and went back to the original creation on the board. Picking up the pieces carefully he goes back and continues his second row. We feel that pleasure is continually mounting and now, when he returns to complete his third row, he touches every single piece with his forefinger. He sighs, both with pleasure and a quality of exhaustion, as if he has done a whole day's work and still has so much to do.

Now he walks back and forth looking over the pieces with his hand spread out in space moving over the pieces. We feel now that in this spatial relationship he is actually touching the pieces, although he does not touch them closely enough to disturb them. He gets down on his knees at the end of the bench, looks over the long rows. Completely unclothed, free in all his movements, he stretches his arms up in the air, pulling his body with him, and then contracts with his hands placed on the bench. He reminds one of a ball of energy expanding and contracting for the mere pleasure of enjoying itself. He finally stands up, looks over the row again, and bringing his head down to the table he makes a sound of *ay—ay*, closing his eyes as if the pleasure is almost unbearable."

Peri village, Manus, May 20, 1954. From photographs of the American Museum of Natural History Admiralty Island Expedition, 1953-54. Photographed by Theodore Schwartz.

PLATE IX: PONDRAM'S RETURN FROM THE DEAD. Manus, 1954

Theodore Schwartz has prepared the following account to accompany this plate:

"On the morning of February 26, 1954, I was called to attend a man who was dying. I took medical supplies and the Leica camera which was always carried and went to a dimly lit house in the Usiai end of the village. (The Usiai were a tribe who had moved from the interior to the new amalgamated villages on the beach, which grew out of cult triggered movements of cultural transformation after the war.) I was told the man had died, but was again showing signs of life. Though it might have been cerebral malaria, sudden and drastic in its effects, his temperature and pulse were normal. After an hour his stiffened body relaxed and he began chewing weakly on

the betel nut that had been placed in his mouth. He began to speak with his hands, explaining to his anxious sons that he had been dead, had gone to heaven, had seen and spoken to Jesus and his ancestors, and had brought back a vital message. Others in the village had had similar experiences. I have collected several accounts of such resurrections. The belief was founded primarily on native interpretation of the Christian story of the Resurrection. Pondram, the subject of these photographs, was a quarrelsome old man with ten quarrelsome sons, who was occasionally a trouble maker, but of little importance or moral preeminence in the village. Now, as the news went around, the house was filled with Usiai, eagerly and respectfully watching as his hands unfolded the message

1

2

3

could before. Plate IX presents three shots from a long sequence of a scene which has been reported from many cultures and many periods of history, but never, as far as I know, photographed before—a man who had "returned from the dead," demonstrating to his awed fellow villagers the exact structure of Heaven!

In conclusion I should like to stress that success in the fields of anthropology and psychology, in fact in all fields dealing with human behavior, is not only dependent upon an ability to communicate with an audience of fellow scientists and a supporting public, but upon an ability to do this communicating without doing violence to the "humanity" of the subjects. This has meant in practice that those whose literary skill would have placed them within the historical humanities have both had a tremendous advantage and have also been distrusted as too literary or too artistic. In this situation photography can serve a double purpose: it can reassure those whose conception of science makes them distrustful of the use of the arts, by presenting more "objective" evidence, and it can enable those to whom words come less easily than images to use a different method of exposition. Linking a disciplined theoretical approach with high photographic skill adds a new dimension to the field of culture and personality.

---

from heaven. Thirty-six pictures were taken catching the dim light from a doorway by using the widest aperture of a fast lens, at a shutter speed of 1/15 of a second. It was possible to make a photographic record which demonstrates visibly the emotional impact of a cult experience bringing the support of Heaven to a new and rapidly changing culture."

1. "Pondram is guiding another man in the construction of a gate like that he had seen at the entrance to the broad, clean road in Heaven where all of the houses, lined in straight rows, were made of galvanized iron. The type of gate Pondram saw had figured in the earlier cult outbreak in 1947. Pondram is seated on an army cot mattress left over from the American occupation."

2. "The gate, almost completed, with a firewood turnstile patterned on the heavenly one, being supported by one of the village officials. Pondram's gate, a revival of the earlier cult, was later built at the entrance of one of the elaborate cemeteries which figured in the cult of 1954. Pondram's report was validated several days later by a younger man's dream."

3. "Pondram is showing that the food of the native is unfit for human consumption. He has taken a bite of an uncooked taro and spit it out in disgust. The enameled plate and spoon on his mattress were used as props while he ate an invisible meal from them as he expressed approval of the use of the clean and durable acquisitions from European material culture. His son, who had supported his body in death, watches."

Bunai village, Manus, Feb. 26, 1954. From photographs of the American Museum of Natural History Admiralty Island Expedition, 1953-54. Photographed by Theodore Schwartz.

NOTES

1. Cf. Gregory Bateson, Hugo Bernatzik, Miguel Covarrubias, Geoffrey Gorer, Philip H. Hiss, Colin McPhee, and Beryl de Zoete and Walter Spies.

2. The development of this method of checking one's developing and changing perceptions was one of the bases for a grant made to me by the Social Science Research Council, for the Balinese field trip in 1936.

3. For a detailed description of this entire research procedure see Mead, M., and Macgregor, F. C., *Growth and Culture*, pp. 189-208.

4. For a full Manus protocol recorded by Lenora Schwartz, see Lowenfeld, M., *The Lowenfeld Mosaic Test*, pp. 317-325.

REFERENCES

1. BATESON, GREGORY, and MEAD, MARGARET. 1942. *Balinese Character: A Photographic Analysis.* ("Special Publications of the New York Academy of Sciences," Vol. II.) New York: The Academy.

2. BELO, JANE. 1949. *Bali: Rangda and Barong.* ("American Ethnological Society Monographs," No. 16.) New York: J. J. Augustin.

3. BERNATZIK, HUGO A. 1937. "Bali, the Wonder Island" in *Südsee (Travels in the South Seas).* London: Constable & Co., Ltd. Pp. 145-158.

4. BIRDWHISTELL, RAY. (In Press.) *An Introduction to Kinesics.* Louisville, Ky.: University of Louisville Press. Originally published by the Foreign Service Institute, Department of State, Washington, D. C. (1952).

5. BRUNER, J. S. and TAGIURI, RENATO. 1954. "The Perception of the People," in *Handbook of Social Psychology*, ed. G. Lindzey, Vol. II, Chap. 17. Cambridge, Mass.: Addison-Wesley.

6. CHAPPLE, E. D. 1949. "The Interaction Chronograph: Its Evolution and Present Application," *Personnel*, Vol. 25, No. 4, pp. 295-307.

7. COVARRUBIAS, MIGUEL. 1937. *Island of Bali.* New York: Knopf.

8. DARWIN, CHARLES. 1955. *Expression of Emotion in Men and Animals* (first edition, 1872). New York: Philosophical Library.

9. EFRON, D. 1941. *Gesture and Environment.* New York: King's Crown Press.

10. GESELL, ARNOLD, *et al.* 1934. *An Atlas of Infant Behavior.* New Haven: Yale University Press. See Mead, M., and Macgregor, F. C., *Growth and Culture*, for a full bibliography of the relevant Gesell group publications.

11. GOLDMAN-EISLER, F. 1955. "Speech-breathing Activity.—A Measure of Tension and Affect during interviews," in *The British Journal of Psychology*, Vol. XLVI, Part I, Feb. 1955, pp. 53-63.

12. GORER, GEOFFREY. 1936. *Bali and Angkor or Looking at Life and Death.* London: Michael Joseph.

13. HISS, PHILIP HANSON. 1941. *Bali.* New York: Duell, Sloan and Pierce.

14. LOWENFELD, M. 1954. *The Lowenfeld Mosaic Test.* London: Newman Neame.

15. McGRAW, MYRTLE. 1935. *Growth.* New York: Appleton-Century.

16. MEAD, MARGARET, AND MACGREGOR, F. C. 1951. *Growth and Culture: A Photographic Study of Balinese Childhood.* New York: G. P. Putnam's Sons.

17. MEAD, MARGARET. 1954. "Manus Restudied," in *Transactions of the New York Academy of Sciences*, Ser. II, Vol. 16, pp. 426-432.

18. MEAD, MARGARET. 1956. "Applied Anthropology, 1955," in *Some Uses of Anthropology*, J. Casagrande and T. Gladwin, eds. Washington, D. C. 1956. Washington Society of Anthropology.

19. TAX, SOL, *et al*, (eds.). 1953. *An Appraisal of Anthropology Today.* Chicago: University of Chicago Press.

20. ZOETE, BERYL DE, and SPIES, WALTER. 1939. *Dance and Drama in Bali.* Preface by Arthur Waley. New York and London: Harper & Bros.
    Cf. also McPHEE, C., 1947, and MEAD, M., 1956.

THE SCIENTIFIC STUDY OF SOCIAL PHENOMENA

Douglas G. Haring, 1947. "Science and Social Phenomena," *American Scientist*, vol. *35:* 351-363. Reprinted by courtesy of the Editor of *American Scientist*.

Primarily designed to emphasize differences in approach in the social sciences and natural sciences, and to assert the validity of scientific method in study of human societies, this paper called forth two types of criticism.

First, some anthropologists do not accept the assertion that the loose abstraction, "culture," should give way to the more specific term, "cultural behavior." Nevertheless the writer insists that effective rapproachement between workers in the biological, psychological, and cultural sciences requires an operational concept such as "cultural behavior" in place of the almost indefinable pseudo-entity, "culture." (Cf. A. L. Kroeber and Clyde Kluckhohn, "Culture: A Critical Review of Concepts and Definitions," *Papers of the Peabody Museum*, Harvard University, vol. *47.*)

Second, the paragraph ending with general statement (7) has been criticized justly. The word "choice" has been used loosely and could be interpreted in terms of the crude rationalism evident in Adam Smith's discussion of "the economic man." Men are rational only now and then; most human choices are determined emotionally and unconsciously. The observed phenomenon is that a person demonstrably capable of two or more different responses in a specific situation actually behaves in but one way at a time. Only individuals whose cultural repertory is so meager that they know only one response in a situation can escape the necessity of choice—whether effected consciously and rationally or naively and emotionally.

The paper that follows is based upon an unpublished essay, "Cultural Phenomena—Toward Redefinition," delivered in 1936 before the American Anthropological Association. The main ideas appear with supporting data in *Order and Possibility in Social Life* (Haring and Johnson, 1940). Dr. Gregory Bateson arrived independently at all of the important ideas and embodied them in a paper presented at the American Anthropological Association in 1946. Another paper, "Sex and Culture," in the present volume, carries his approach somewhat further. Another paper, "Bali: The Value System of a Steady State" (see Bibliography) is relevant and important both for its data and method.

SCIENCE AND SOCIAL PHENOMENA

Douglas G. Haring

Insistent voices demand that ethical standards and knowledge of human affairs catch up with the physical sciences. Some people assume that, like the shaman, the scientist works magic, albeit of a new and cataclysmic variety. If only scientists would study Society, they might achieve miracles of the order of atomic disintegration!

Certain basic differences between the exact sciences and the sciences of human behavior, however, require emphasis. Despite unsettled problems of electronics the exact sciences continue to rely upon the principle of dynamic equivalence in all study of macroscopic phenomena.[1] The concept of dynamic transformations that do not deviate from strict equivalence is implicit in every scientific equation. A practical test of the completeness and accuracy of research in the exact sciences is ability to substitute measured quantities for every term of such an equation and thereby to satisfy both the equation and intellectual curiosity. Until that is done either the completeness of the research or the descriptive adequacy of the equation remains in question.

Social scientists are accustomed to the taunt that since no equations sum up the "laws" of social phenomena their work remains unscientific. If science be envisioned narrowly in terms of discovery of law and consequent predictability the charge is deserved. If, however, science be viewed as "description, in complete and very simple terms, of the motions occurring in nature" (Kirchhoff), then legitimate scientific aims include also the description of motions unamenable to summary as laws. The ultimate aim is to bring within range of comprehension every aspect of the universe that can be subjected to rigorous observation, and social phenomena are a tangible aspect of that universe. The attempt to study social phenomena cannot be evaded, however tenuous and inadequate the current results. Some sociologists ape the exact sciences and write equations that curiously interweave observed facts and speculatively derived concepts. To say the least, such equations fall short of representing precise measurements of observed phenomena.

The crucial fact is that social phenomena never admit of statement in terms of dynamic equivalence. All social occurrences are reducible to the behavior of human individuals—organic responses to stimulation.

The structure and function of living organisms insure that no response is equivalent dynamically to the related stimulus. Stimulation involves a dynamic disturbance, often extremely complex in its mechanism, of the vital processes of an organism. Response, also dynamic, is readjustment of the organism in position, form, internal chemistry, or other physiological or homeostatic conditions. Such readjustment continues in changing patterns until the disturbance ceases or is evaded—or failing adequate adaptation, until the organism dies.[2]

The energy of response without exception derives from food and oxygen obtained by the organism from the environing energy complex,[3] transformed and stored through the internal economy of the organism. Within the organic biochemical mechanism dynamic equivalence is observable. Very few of the energy transformations involved in behavior are amenable to adequate measurement, but none of the available evidence contravenes the assumption that the laws of dynamics are descriptive of metabolic processes. Stimulation, however, is effected by energy sequences differing from those that accomplish responses. Whether stimulation be internal or external the stimulating energy is imparted to and transformed within the sense receptors. Even when the stimulating events appear to be neural changes within the cerebral cortex the same principle holds; each neuron responds by discharge of its own stored energy and the energy of the stimulation does not travel through the organism. The energy of response, whether manifest externally or confined to internal changes, never derives from the energy of stimulation. The structural and functional patterns of organic mechanisms confirm this statement.[4]

In human behavior the indefinite range of individual modifiability in pattern of response emphasizes the dynamic hiatus between stimulation and the form of the response. Behavior evoked by a specific stimulus can be predicted in simple organisms because of the sharp limitation of the range of possible responses. In the higher vertebrates, however, indefinite possibilities of modification in pattern of response forbid machinistic prediction.[5] The best that can be done is a forecast of probabilities based on observation of well-established habits in the individual subject. Even then forecasts are precarious; at any moment the subject may "get a new idea" or "change his mind." Attempted mathematical formulations of the relation between a stimulating situation and a pattern of response provide little more than symbolic statements of an analogy[6] or of a capricious probability—something basically different from equations descriptive of physical and chemical events. In summary: (1) *All significantly related events of social phenomena are dynamically inequivalent.*

Another characteristic of social phenomena is sequential occurrence. Herbert Spencer differentiated coexistence and sequence by pointing out that coexistent phenomena are observed repeatedly and in any order. Patterns of structure are not altered by changes in the order in which their elements are observed; thus they occur as coexistences. Sequential phenomena, however, are observed in only one order and that order is irreversible.[7] The elements of organic structure coexist; anatomy, a science of structure, aims to describe such elements and the patterns of their spatial arrangement. Organic behavior, however, occurs only as sequence. Observation of behavior is observation of patterns of motion and time affords a universal coordinate in study of social phenomena. Consequently "social statics," "cross-section studies of Society," and a soundly physical use of the term *structure*[8] in description of social phenomena are inept if not impossible. Hence, (2) *all social phenomena are sequential.*

Social phenomena consist in varied, kaleidoscopically changing sequences of *interstimulation and response*[9] on the part of two or more sentient human organisms—*i.e.*, persons. Stimulation frequently eludes observation since practically all human somatic responses incorporate modifications based in previous behavior. "Memory" enters into all stimulation and modifies every response. Patterns of interstimulation and response are learned and cannot be explained in terms of the morphology or inherited structure of the persons involved.

Human individuals differ by heredity and growth, by the infinitely diverse combinations of habit that constitute individual behavior repertories, by experiences and memories. As social units no two persons are precisely alike. Moreover the personnel of any social situation or community changes constantly. Individuals depart and newcomers enter a situation; specific persons die unpredictably; infants are born and grow into adults uniquely different from their forebears. No program of political or economic revolution contemplates changes in a society as radical as those effected unobtrusively by deaths and births in less than fifty years. A one hundred percent replacement of the personnel of a society by different individuals constitutes a radical change, to say the least. During an individual's lifetime he changes profoundly: the child becomes a man, the pattern of friendships alters, occupations are shifted, a radical turns conservative, and the same individual participates in different families. From day to day the fleeting constellations of persons within a community shift and regroup. Inventions provoke irreversible alterations in societal constitution and economic behavior. At any moment no community or group exactly resembles any other community or group. If likeness exists that fact must be *discovered* by painstaking observation; it may not be postulated, despite superficial resemblances in persons and in material environments. The discovered resemblances in many communities tempt observers to gloss over the basic uniqueness, which nevertheless persists as an underlying fact:

(3) *Every human community, grouping, or social situation is unique.*[9a]

The sequential occurrence of social phenomena and the facts of incessant change emphasize the evanescent character of so-called societal stability. Given indefinite individual modifiability in behavior, diversity and change are normal aspects of existence and stability appears as a very special kind of achievement. A subtle fallacy pervades studies of "social change"—an assumption that a static condition is normal and that change is surprising if not anomalous. Historically of course there have been interminable ages when the limited knowledge at men's disposal allowed meager scope for certain kinds of social change. But as the range of learnable behavior increases, the wonder is not that societies change but rather that there ever should occur a semblance of stability: (4) *A central problem in social science is description of the circumstances that attend relative societal stability.* The foregoing discussion indicates a possibility that no uniformity in such circumstances will be discovered. Many investigators, however, ignore the problem.

Social behavior, in contrast to the relatively invariable patterns of visceral and homeostatic behavior, is learned in pattern. The hoary debate over nature vs. nurture is pointless; the real question is whether, in any specific problem, the biological approach or the cultural approach is more fruitful of significant results. The term *cultural behavior* denotes all human functioning that conforms to patterns learned from other persons. A popular dichotomy of "culture" into non-material (or "spiritual") culture and material culture arises in fallacious classification. Behavior cannot be classified scientifically in the same category with material objects despite the enormous involvement of material objects in almost every act of human behavior. Stimulating situations generally include physical products of cultural behavior—artifacts—which, however, acquire significance in relation to cultural activities rather than as physico-chemical entities *per se.* Description and analysis of cultural phenomena are confused by forcing into one category phenomena as distinct as human behavior and the material products and implements of such behavior.

Cultural behavior is observed in the sequential responses of individuals and may be distinguished from the relatively invariable patterns of physiological functioning by observation of the learning process.[10] The fallacy of "culture" or a "cultural whole" arises in reification of generalized observations of cultural behavior. Numerous individuals learn similar patterns of such behavior, and uncritical thinkers abstract these forms as "culture traits." Culture and culture traits never act and never provide a valid subject of an active verb. These words denote possibly useful but loose and probably misleading abstractions. The patterns of cultural behavior, however, may be discovered in observation of persons in action. (5) *Cultural behavior is observable and scientifically definable; "culture" is not.*

Fundamental qualitative differences characterize the patterns of cultural behavior. Viewed as patterns of activity, there can be no scientific comparison of banking with music, mathematics with farming, or philosophy with dancing. No measurements based on explicitly denotable,[11] quantitatively fixed units reduce cultural activities that differ in pattern to common terms. The only common element is the fact that human organisms do all the behaving. Organically similar, human bodily mechanisms provide for a degree of individual modifiability in behavior patterns that enables almost anyone to learn almost anything. So long as life processes are maintained, the patterns of behavior by which organic needs are met may vary endlessly and assume non-comparable forms. Approximate uniformity is observed only when numerous persons learn the same form and action patterns of cultural behavior. Hence, (6) *differing patterns of cultural behavior are incommensurable.*

Human individuals typically learn more than one way of responding in a specific type of situation. Associative memory involves the recall and mental rehearsal of past performances. Two or more patterns of action are compared in retrospect and in prospect in estimation of their relative effectiveness. Cultural behavior usually is purposeful; both goals and means of attainment are envisioned in advance of action. Because behavior is sequential and only one major pattern of activity may be performed at a time choice is inevitable. One decides whether to act in terms of pattern A, pattern B, or pattern C. He verbalizes the criteria of his judgment by saying, "A is better than B," or "C is harder than A." Judgments of better, worse, pleasant, unpleasant, beautiful, ugly, right, or wrong enter into all choices among behavior alternatives and provide a major theme of conversation. Persons may not explicitly state goals and means; they often remain unconscious of motivating mechanisms, but in any case cultural behavior is marked by evaluation and purpose. Given ability to learn varied patterns of response to any stimulation plus ability to remember, both purpose and evaluation are inescapable. Rarely if ever does social behavior occur according to mathematical probability or so-called statistical chance: (7) *Cultural behavior involves purposeful selection of patterns of response in terms of subjective criteria.*

Relatively few individuals devise completely new ways of thinking or acting. The behavior of parents and associates provides models that children copy consciously or unconsciously. Even the rare innovator speaks the language of his companions, eats, dresses, and plays as they do. Upon analysis innovations turn out to be rearrangements and new combinations of cultural behavior already current. For example, the atomic bomb did not spring full-blown from an inventor's brain. It was possible only after mathematics, physics, chemistry, industrial technology, and other complex cultural behavior (*i.e.*, knowledge) had been achieved bit by bit and had become accessible to inventors. Even a flint arrow point presupposes knowledge of tools, a bow, arrows, and the properties of stone. Human social activities invariably follow patterns already current and learned individually by each participant.[12] Save as he personally learns the details of a pattern of action an individual remains unable to participate: a Mormon elder suddenly placed in a Buddhist temple hardly could perform the ritual with facility. This indicates another basic generalization and a corollary: (8) *Human beings never behave socially in ways whose patterns they have not learned.* (9) *In any locality individuals manifest patterns of cultural behavior that are current among their associates.* The spatial—usually geographical—distribution of persons who exhibit specific patterns of cultural behavior may be shown on maps.

The question of the "unit of social research" has been discussed *ad nauseam*. Proposed units are denoted by terms such as "a social relation," " a group," "a culture trait," "a unit of social distance," "a community," or "a social process." These alleged units can be reduced to judgments passed upon something human individuals do or have done together. Not one of them is amenable directly to observation. The one tangible, explicitly denotable phenomenon involved is a living human organism. Two or more such organisms engaged in interstimulation and response constitute a social phenomenon. Human beings can be counted; and the forms of their overt behavior are observable. The descriptive adequacy of techniques of observation is ascertainable within definable limits of error. (10) *The objective unit of observation is a human being behaving.*

The foregoing ten summary statements constitute almost the opposite of a system of social science. Neither axioms nor postulates, they state observed aspects of social phenomena that are basic in all scientific study of human affairs. They also carry devastating implications for many existing formulations. Workers in the exact sciences have been fortunate in their choice of phenomena that so generally occur in patterns conformable to the laws of thermodynamics. Social scientists confront less tractable phenomena. While social phenomena do not contravene the laws of thermodynamics, they are unamenable to description in equations representative of measured dynamic equivalences. A rough dynamic analogy cites the audion valve and similar devices in which infinitesimal energy discharges release larger quantities of stored energy, but even the miracles of electronic engineering are simple compared to the intricate dynamics of many human beings behaving in a community. In the community thermodynamic analysis is meaningless.

The important facts are specific persons, ideas, beliefs, and goals of action. Social science requires techniques of observation fitted to the phenomena and the results do not fall into the clear-cut formulae of scientific laws. Scientific laws appear only when measurable dynamic equivalence is the subject of description.

From this point of view the fundamental task of science is descriptive. Even the most abstract scientific law is valid only insofar as it affords accurate description of observed events. Ability to predict is a happy accident for which workers in the exact sciences may thank their choice of phenomena. Prediction in this exact sense underlies all engineering and differs from forecasting that deals in approximations. If such prediction be the sole criterion of science, the study of human societies must be left to speculative philosophy—or worse, to the lunatic fringe. Fortunately hope of scientific description of social phenomena need not be abandoned. Once the special character of the phenomena and the consequent limitations upon method are clarified, such description affords practically useful data.

Impressed by the intangible, unobservable aspects of human behavior, some writers deny the practical effectiveness of any science of societies. In all fields of research, however, the seemingly intangible and unobservable have discouraged investigators. Experience shows that meticulous observation, classification, and analysis of the grosser, directly observable phenomena gradually narrow the limits of the unknown. Every advance in instruments and techniques of observation extends knowledge; simultaneously it becomes clear afresh that science is not about to run out of subject matter. Granting the abiding persistence of unknown, unobservable phenomena, it still is true that each extension of verified knowledge permits wider and surer control of the known.

So also in study of social phenomena, careful observation reveals the limits within which the intangible continues to defy formulation. It is possible to circumscribe the intangible aspects of social behavior by study of the tangible and thereby to delimit possibilities and impossibilities with respect to practical policy. To offer a crude illustration, a population count indicates the feasibility of specific plans. If a village contains no more than one hundred people, establishment of a symphony orchestra is out of the question. If the hundred persons are Irish Catholics, this cultural fact indicates the futility of Zionist propaganda in that community. If more than half of the hundred have passed the age of sixty, no great expenditure for schools is probable. The Ancient Order of Hibernians, however, might be able to stage a successful if slightly subdued picnic. In such a community all sorts of intangible human feelings and aspirations remain unobservable scientifically. For practical purposes, however, the limits of possibility in the major concerns of the community are ascertainable.

In any social situation from a sewing bee to a nation the individual participants can be counted. Persons so counted may be classified roughly by kinds; every individual is a specific *organic kind* and also one or more *behavior kinds*. Those organically alike can be classified inductively by age, sex, physical fitness, and bodily characteristics. These categories of organic kind are limited in intrinsic social significance but gain importance wherever custom emphasizes a specific bodily feature. Thus in parts of the United States the numbers of persons differing in skin color are major social facts. Persons differing in sex are treated differently and are expected to behave differently. In all societies differences in age indicate differing social roles. A count of individuals of specific bodily dimensions is important to a clothing manufacturer though meaningless in relation to religion. Understanding and wise practical action are facilitated by knowledge of the numbers of persons of each organic kind who are present in any social situation.

Individuals differ also in habitual behavior. Those who behave repeatedly in specific ways can be counted and classified. Some behavior kinds are defined by law and may be counted readily—as for example, marital status, citizenship, eligibility to vote, property ownership, and in some countries caste or social class. Other gross classifications by behavior kind include membership in associations or parties, income, occupation, place of nativity, mother tongue, duration of schooling, place of residence, religious affiliation, genealogical affiliation, parenthood, buying habits, *et cetera*. Any community is understood more adequately when its members are counted and classified by major behavior kinds. Observation of *social composition* by organic kinds and behavior kinds is the foundation of any research into specific human situations. It provides answers to the first great question of social research, namely, *Who are present?*

The second question in social research is, *What are they doing?* The initial step in the answer is clear description of specific patterns of cultural behavior and the recording of their occurrences. Techniques of observation include the time-honored pencil and notebook, the clumsy and expensive but superbly adequate cinema and sound recorder, and description of artifacts both as products of technological behavior and as implements of other behavior. Description of cultural behavior is facilitated by analysis of records of past activities, such as newspapers, historical documents, minutes of meetings, audited financial accounts, records of time consumed in work or play, recorded interviews, legal records and court transcriptions, "case records," diaries, biographies, *et cetera*. Records of verbal statements afford data of what people say; the content of such utterances may or may not be verifiable, but the fact of utterance is a fact of cultural behavior. Use of language is cultural behavior and description of a people alien to the observer or to his readers necessarily includes adequate data of their language and its distinctive patterns of thought and concepts.

Whatever the cultural behavior under observation—from church services to street walking—the individuals who manifest that behavior may be counted and the frequency of performance recorded for each person. The observer does not count "behavior patterns" nor does he count "kinds of behavior." He counts persons whom he classifies in inductive categories of *behavior kind;* i.e., an individual is classified as "the kind of person who manifests behavior pattern X" (10). Persons so classified may be observed further to determine the frequency of performance of "behavior pattern X" for each individual; such procedure yields subcategories of a form analogous to a statistical frequency distribution. If the time spent by each person in the activity be measured, a genuine frequency distribution is obtained.[13]

Overt indications of emotional behavior are included in description of the pattern observed. Although the emotional aspects of behavior elude direct observation, it may be noted that unexpressed emotion does not constitute a *social* phenomenon.[14] Similar reasoning applies to thoughts and ideas. Granted that much cultural behavior is implicit and unobservable, the fact of practical import is that unexpressed ideas and thoughts do not enter into interstimulation and response. When through speech or other expression they acquire social significance, ideas or strong emotions automatically come within range of observation. The intangible aspects of cultural behavior raise fewer problems for scientific observation than does the physical fact that one observer cannot be in two or more places at once. The practical difficulty is reaching enough people at any moment to observe the pertinent cultural behavior that might have been accessible to observation.

Many patterns of cultural behavior are not observable completely in the performance of any individual. Only as numerous persons coordinate their activities are these more complex patterns effected. Such patterns of organization of multi-individual responses appear everywhere, from the conduct of a shamanistic ritual to the administration of a railway or an army. The term institution, commonly employed to denote this class of phenomena, often involves fallacies of reification and personification. A more strictly descriptive emphasis leads to the term *institutional behavior.*

Still more comprehensive patterning of sequences of interstimulation and response among large numbers of individuals appears when data accumulated by many observers over large areas and long time intervals are assembled, classified, summarized, and analyzed. Discovery of these *societal patterns* is possible as the physical limitations of any single observer are transcended. For example, patterns of population change are not amenable to direct observation by an individual. Systematic recording of births, deaths, marriages, migrations, and other demographic phenomena in many places over long periods of time affords data that may be summarized and analyzed statistically to yield broad patterns of population change not otherwise observable. Similarly, the comprehensive societal patterns of cultural behavior in a large population are discovered through analysis of data from many sources and covering a considerable time interval. These societal patterns are perceived dimly if at all by the participants; they emerge in intellectual synthesis on the part of a student thoroughly and deeply conversant with the entire range of descriptive data. The sociological or ethnological analyst who previously has studied the diverse cultural behavior of many peoples in their different societies may thereby acquire intellectual and emotional habits that facilitate discovery of these broader societal patterns.

Persons habituated to research in the exact sciences almost uniformly comment at this point, "So what? All this is mere description. Where are your general laws and theoretical formulations?" The answer is implicit in the ten general statements that preface this discussion—especially statements (1), (2), and (3). The fact of dynamic inequivalence of stimulus and response interposes a significant distinction between social phenomena and physico-chemical phenomena. Scientific laws state *constant* relations between varying phenomena—relations whose constancy depends upon the first law of thermodynamics.[15] The intricate organic phenomena of response to stimulation and individual modifiability in behavior enable human beings to behave in ways determined by individual habit and choice. Stimulus and response are not related as physical "cause and effect" and consequently the attempt to describe the stimulus-response nexus in thermodynamic terms is totally meaningless in social situations. The concept of scientific law is not pertinent. Even the bald statement that no scientific laws of social phenomena are discoverable is misleading though "true," since it implies the pertinence of the concept of law in the physical sense.

After all, what is the value of scientific laws? Such value assumes two major aspects: first, insight into the universe is deepened and broadened by knowledge of the laws of the exact sciences; second, practical activities are furthered by increased control of environment.

What, then, is the value of scientific description of unique local social situations, involving detailed study of cultural behavior and, in synthesis, discovery of general societal patterns? The answer is twofold: first, insight into the universe is deepened and broadened by knowledge of man and his cultural activities; second, practical activities are furthered by increased control of situations and wiser planning based on ascertained possibilities and impossibilities.

The quest for cause and effect relations in human affairs has be-devilled all of the social sciences. Endless statistical series—often based in pseudo-measurement—have been tabulated and analyzed to discover correlations and multiple correlations. Sociologists, economists, political scientists, and ethnologists have emerged from their lairs proudly waving coefficients of correlation and hopefully predicting events that rarely occur on schedule. Insofar as statistical analyses and contingency or correlation procedures summarize and present facts of description their utility is very great. If Fact M always, or frequently, is accompanied by Fact P, the demonstration of co-occurrence contributes mightily to discovery of soundly derived societal patterns. Here, however, enters the temptation to conclude, as in the physical sciences, that the presence of Fact M somehow compels—or at least strongly invites—the presence of Fact P in all circumstances. Such indeed is a defensible inference when the relation between M and P can be shown by physico-chemical analysis to involve a more or less uniform pattern of dynamic interchange. But if either M or P symbolizes facts of cultural behavior, future co-occurrence of these two items depends upon the accidents of human learning and choice. Should the people whose behavior is under observation alter the patterns of their cultural behavior—i.e., "change their minds" or "get a new idea"—either M or P or both may disappear in the future in wholly capricious fashion. The former association of M and P becomes an item of history and affords no basis of prediction. All social data become historical data almost as soon as they can be recorded.

A practical basis of forecasts of social behavior, however, is discovered in two aspects. First, discovery of the limits of physical or biological or geographical possibility indicates the range within which future human behavior probably will occur. Second, the fact that persons do not behave in ways they have not learned (8) sets practical limits to the range of behavior that may be expected. These limits change as new cultural behavior is introduced and learned, but fortunately such innovation usually can be observed and the limits redefined. This latter basis of social forecasting may be stated alternatively as a function (in the mathematical sense) of the persistence of habits. Perhaps it is impossible for an individual simultaneously to change all of his habitual behavior to new patterns. That some of his habits will change is probable; rarely is it predictable that he will change any specific habit in a given time interval. The majority of his present habits, however, will recur in subsequent behavior. If this holds for individuals, it is equally pertinent to the behavior of many individuals. Human lack of originality is the mainstay of the forecaster in the social sciences.

Here is a clue to the problem of societal stability (4). The smaller the range of knowledge (called the "cultural base" among sociologists) available in a society, the greater the probability that present behavior will be repeated with minimum change in pattern. The more highly diversified the available cultural repertory, on the other hand, the more readily can individuals abandon former behavior in favor of new patterns.[16] The problem of societal stability emerges as a function of individual modifiability of patterns of human behavior. Animal aggregations, including the so-called insect societies, exhibit age-long stability of patterns of interstimulation and response. The predominance of invariable or instinctive behavior in the action systems of the articulate phylum and the lower vertebrates assures immunity against social innovation. By virtue of his unique nervous system with its potentialities of individual modifiability,[17] man depends for his patterns of action upon the accumulated knowledge current among his fellows. As such knowledge increases in diversity and number of patterns, populations become more heterogeneous with respect to behavior kinds and their diversified social behavior manifests more rapid changes in pattern. Thus for man alone, societal stability as a goal becomes increasingly difficult of attainment. For societies in which innovation occurs as frequently as in those of America and Europe, social order may become impossible of maintenance unless research discloses feasible methods of reconciling stability and innovation. The pertinence of the democratic ideal, which favors discovery of ways by which different behavior kinds may live together without seeking to annihilate each other, is notable.

Societal stability[18] founds in the learning of similar patterns of emotional response by large numbers of persons. The fundamental emotional habits that determine individual social choices are learned in infancy, even before language is learned. This intangible behavior loosely called emotional ultimately determines individual acceptance or rejection of such new behavior patterns as one may encounter. Study of the ways in which infants learn, and of what they learn, contributes more fundamentally to cultural forecasting than many investigators suspect.[19]

Political adventurers have discovered that relative societal stability may result from limitation of the range of ideas and patterns of action accessible for learning by the individuals who compose a population—hence the wave of censorship of news, radio, research, schoolbooks, *et cetera*. Such attempts by the fearful to circumscribe the possibilities of societal change may be expected to increase unless research discloses ways of achieving psychological and societal security despite rapid extension of knowledge. The issue is far more crucial than the frightened wails of those who want morals to catch up with knowledge would indicate. Even as the attainment of cultural behavior opened new vistas of achievement to the human species, the very accumulation of achievement creates fresh problems that cannot be solved by precedent. Evolution is irreversible; social living is sequence and the past cannot be recreated. If new social inventions are to solve the problem, they will occur if and when research provides the requisite knowledge and insight. The general acceptance of such innovations, however, is another matter and cannot be predicted. The human species may prefer blind adherence to traditional societal patterns despite impending extermination.

NOTES

For critical reading and helpful comment appreciation is due to Drs. GREGORY BATESON, DAVID B. STOUT, MISCHA TITIEV, and GEORGE B. WILBUR. The author, however, accepts sole responsibility for the content of the paper.

Supporting data for the main statements appear in *Order and Possibility in Social Life* by D. G. HARING and M. E. JOHNSON (*New York*, 1940). Reference to that work will reveal the nature of present dependence upon a variety of sources, many of which are quoted there at length. Especially important are ideas derived from the late F. H. GIDDINGS, who first insisted that social phenomena be envisioned as interstimulation and response although he never abandoned the quest for scientific laws of society. His contribution is summarized with quotations in the above-cited source. See also his *Studies in the Theory of Human Society* (*New York*, 1922).

REFERENCES

1. Throughout this paper the word "dynamic" is used in the physical sense. Those sub-microscopic phenomena that raise questions respecting dynamic equivalence are not directly pertinent in study of social phenomena; observable social phenomena are confined to decidedly macroscopic events. See P. W. BRIDGEMAN, The Nature of Thermodynamics (*Cambridge*, 1941).

2. JENNINGS, H. S. The Method of Regulation in Behavior and in Other Fields. *Jour. Exp. Zool.*, II, 473 ff (1906). Quoted *in extenso* in *Order and Possibility in Social Life*, cited above.

3. The phrase "environing energy complex," borrowed from the neurologist C. J. HERRICK, is preferable to the omnibus term "environment" because it emphasizes the physico-chemical character of all stimulation. Only as the organism stimulated interprets physical stimulation in psychological terms does this environing energy complex acquire personal and cultural aspects. For example, a spoken word impinges upon the ear as a pattern of sound waves; only in the mental operations of the hearer does it become a word rather than a noise.

4. DODGE, RAYMOND. Conditions and Consequences of Human Variability. *New Haven*, 1931.

5. "Mechanism" as used in this paper denotes any structural-functional pattern of physico-chemical events; "machine" denotes a mechanism limited by structural pattern to a fixed sequence of energy transformation. Anything from a cloud to a horse may be described physically as a mechanism. A machine is a special case of stable structural pattern such as a bicycle or a human elbow joint.

6. Mathematical formulae become vague analogies when their terms represent, not measured quantities, but hypothetical items or unobservable pseudo-quantities that might be used if they could be observed and measured.

7. SPENCER, HERBERT. First Principles (*London*, 1862. 4th ed., *London*, 1880). Part II. Chapter 3, Section 47.

8. *I.e.,* to denote an observable pattern of coexisting physically constituted parts.

9. The phrase "interstimulation and response" is chosen deliberately instead of the popular sociological term "interaction" because the word "interaction" in physics implies dynamic equivalence.

9a. Uniqueness is a distinctive, though not exclusive, aspect of social phenomena. Every macroscopic object, if described in sufficient detail, is unique. Communities and social situations, however, owe their uniqueness to complexities of a higher order that involve incommensurable aspects unamenable to measurement. The physico-chemical sciences afford no valid analogy to the phenomena of cultural behavior, although the dynamics of electronic computing machines provide an illuminating analogy to the individual nervous system.

10. In *The Range of Human Capacities* (*Baltimore*, 1935), DAVID WECHSLER implies that measurement of any morphological or physiological feature in numerous subjects yields distribution curves that increase in skewness with the complexity of the function measured. FLOYD ALLPORT, as in his "The J-Curve Hypothesis of Conforming Behavior" (*Jour. Soc. Psych.*, V, 141-181. May, 1934), shows that when cultural behavior is measured the distribution curves are so highly skewed that he refers to them as "J-curves." Insofar as behavior can be measured, does extent of skewness in distribution curves afford a technique for differentiation between behavior that is invariable in pattern in the species, and behavior that is individually modifiable, hence cultural?

11. ALLPORT, FLOYD H. "Group" and "Institution" as Concepts in a Natural Science of Social Phenomena. *Publ. Amer. Socio. Soc.*, XXII, 83-99.

12. Superficial discussions of learning sometimes ignore the subtler aspects of individual modifiability in human behavior. Psychoanalysts have shown how behavior that appears spontaneous and "original" can be followed through devious "transferences," "displacements," and other mental legerdemain back to the learned behavior (*i.e.,* remembered experience) from which it derives. In this paper, the word *learn* carries all the implications of this inclusive process.

13. The general technique of such observation of cultural behavior is illustrated in CLYDE KLUCKHOHN, Participation in Ceremonials in a Navaho Community, *American Anthropologist 40*, 359-369 (1938). See also E. D. CHAPPLE, and C. S. COON. Principles of Anthropology (*New York*, 1942, esp. pp. 36-41, 281-296.

14. Individual psychology may not ignore unexpressed emotion. Social stimulation, however, is accomplished by overt behavior past and present; ideas or "emotions" that never attain overt expression scarcely afford adequate stimulation to other persons. Overt expression may be very subtle but if the behavior affords stimulation to another person it must be overt in some way. Perhaps this begs the disputed question of whether unexpressed emotion occurs; that issue is left to the physiologist, psychologist, and psychoanalyst, whose answers probably will not alter the point under analysis here. This emphasis by no means diminishes the social importance of behavior that ultimately issues from repressed and unexpressed aspects of the individual psyche.

15. Or, from another angle, relations whose constancy leads to the first law of thermodynamics.

16. This general statement of the relation of social variability to the range of available knowledge cannot be dignified with the label, "scientific law." It is verified by observation of peripheral societies in contrast to civilized societies, and also is deducible from the nature of the learning process in human beings. The range of available knowledge, while not amenable to measurement, is disclosed in observation of social behavior.

17. The discussion of invariable and individually modifiable aspects of animal response is based on C. J. HERRICK, Introduction to Neurology, 5th ed. (*Philadelphia and London*, 1931).

18. The term stability is preferred to the popular term, societal equilibrium, because of the obvious physical analogy involved in the word equilibrium—an analogy misleading when applied to human behavior, as indicated in (1), (3), and (6) above.

Study of the meanings of the verb "to found" will justify the somewhat unusual use in the present sentence. This use is recommended in similar context as a valuable addition to precision of statement.

19. The several uses of the term "pattern" call for more precise analysis. It is hoped that the phenomena denoted are sufficiently clear to avoid serious confusion. See the book cited under "Notes," above, pp. 436-440.

Part Two

SELECTED PAPERS

PEDAGOGICAL SUGGESTIONS

The selected reports and essays that follow are reproduced unabridged from the scattered journals and symposia in which they originally appeared, except for three that were written 'especially for this book. The order of presentation is arbitrary, since authors appear in alphabetical sequence and when more than one paper from the same author is included, these are placed together in chronological order. Merely to read these papers in sequence is confusing; some organized plan of study is indispensable.

This compilation deliberately avoids the provision of a plan. No two teachers use the same materials in the same way or in like context. The present arrangement leaves a teacher free to select and arrange materials without the handicap of a scheme imposed by the compiler. Probably no one will use all of these materials, and each teacher will send his students elsewhere for important items not included here. Most of the writers represented herein have published other, sometimes much more important, works. The General Bibliography at the end of the book will suggest abundant additional materials. Students should be cautioned to read any of these contributions with careful attention to the date of its writing.

At the moment, there are two generally-used textbooks in this field of study: Kluckhohn, Murray, and Schneider, *Personality in Nature, Society and Culture* (Rev. ed., N. Y., 1953), and J. J. Honigmann, *Culture and Personality* (N. Y., 1954). Kluckhohn and associates present their own scheme of study, and reprint some of the best contributions to the field from forty-seven different authors. The present compilation purposely omits all of the papers that they have included; if students are not required to purchase their book, it should be available for constant reading. Honigmann has provided a more conventional and very useful textbook, but has not quoted other authors. Teachers who wish to follow a basic textbook will do well to use either of these two books.

Students should have ready access to certain other books that assemble important articles in this field. Notable titles are the following:

Mullahy, Patrick, ed., *A Study of Interpersonal Relations.* N. Y., 1949.
   (A compendium of relevant papers from the journal, *Psychiatry.*)
Newcomb, Hartley, *et al., Readings in Social Psychology.* N. Y., 1947.
Sargent, S. S., and M. W. Smith, eds., *Culture and Personality.* N. Y., 1949.

Reviews of earlier editions of the present compilation also provide critical comment in addition to suggestions of important papers that had to be omitted because of limited space. *Cf.* review by Weston LaBarre, *Social Forces*, May, 1950; also review by Benjamin Paul, *Journal of Abnormal and Social Psychology*, January, 1949. Critical discussions of the "culture and personality" school of research and analysis include Leites, 1948; Lindesmith and Strauss, 1950; papers by Hallowell and by Mead in *Anthropology Today: An Encyclopedic Inventory* (Chicago, 1953) and the discussions of those papers in *An Appraisal of Anthropology Today* (ed. by Tax, Eiseley, Rouse, and Voegelin; Chicago, 1953). Other critiques may be found by consulting the General Bibliography.

Of great importance in the study of personal character in relation to cultural setting are the studies of "brain-washing" by the Chinese Communists. Unfortunately the excellent analyses that are beginning to appear in print were not available when this book went to press; it is suggested, however, that courses in this field make use of such papers as Lifton, 1956; Schein, 1956; Moloney, 1955-a, together with the journalistic accounts that provide background in Hunter, 1951. Lifton's article refers to most of the relevant literature in its footnotes.

THE USE OF ETHNOGRAPHIC REPORTS ON CULTURAL BEHAVIOR IN DIFFERENT SOCIETIES

Each student should select from one to three non-Euro-American peoples with whose ways of living he is unfamiliar. Each of these tribes or nations should be studied as thoroughly as available sources permit.

The first reading of an ethnographic report often evokes the complaint that the mass of trivial detail is overwhelming. If one seeks insight, however, he needs to remember that human existence is for most people a round of trivial events. Few persons encounter so-called "great issues"; those who do still spend most of their time in a round of everyday routine. Only as the trivial is apprehended emotionally does one begin to grasp the pattern of living of any people. Everyone has read accounts of the survivors of some major disaster—as a flood or a bombing—which express amazement at the "courageous" way in which these sufferers take up the round of minor everyday affairs after the disaster. Without becoming unsympathetic, it may be asked, "What else can they do?" If they are alive, they continue as nearly as possible with the daily routine. Insight must be insight into routine and into petty concerns, or the "great issues" never come into focus.

Many ethnographic reports, especially the older ones, devote slight attention to psychological issues, child rearing, or variations in individual behavior. Nevertheless, such reports can facilitate insight into the patterns of living to which every person born into a society must adjust. It usually is possible to discover the modal composition of households—who may be expected to dwell together, who wields authority, which children expect to remain in the household, which children will leave it as they mature, to whom the members of this household can turn when their difficulties exceed their resources, who can demand or expect help from them, and so on. The seemingly dry catalogues of information concerning kinship, exogamy, descent, or property rights can be used to attain a vivid mental picture of actual people living together.

Students may be encouraged to analyze ethnographic reports by extracting and organizing data indicative of ideals of character and tribal or national goals; then to bring together whatever data may be provided on means of fostering these ideals in the young.

The general bibliography at the end of this book refers to numerous well-known ethnographic reports. Such works, to distinguish them from psychological and theoretical analyses, are marked with an asterisk (*).

The following books, available in most University libraries, contain brief summaries of cultural patterns in various non-Euroamerican societies:

Benedict, Ruth F., *Patterns of Culture.* Boston, 1934. Penguin Books.

Coon, C. S., *A Reader in General Anthropology.* N. Y., 1948. (Invaluable: reproduces important reports with minimum abridgment.)

Eggan, Fred, ed., *Social Anthropology of North American Indians.* Chicago, 1937. (Papers on special topics, but useful for brief presentations.)

Goldenweiser, A. A., *Early Civilization,* N. Y., 1922.

Haring, D. G., and M. E. Johnson, *Order and Possibility in Social Life.* N. Y., 1940. Book I.

Hoebel, Jennings, and Smith, *Readings in Anthropology.* N. Y., 1955.

Kroeber, A. L., and T. T. Waterman, *Source Book in Anthropology.* Berkeley, 1920; N. Y. 1931.

Linton, Ralph, ed., *Most of the World.* N. Y., 1949.

Lowie, R. H., *Introduction to Cultural Anthropology.* rev. ed. N. Y., 1940.

Mead, Margaret, ed., *Cooperation and Competition Among Primitive Peoples.* N. Y. 1937.

Mead, M., and N. Calas, eds., *Primitive Heritage.* N. Y., 1953.

Murdock, G. P., *Our Primitive Contemporaries.* N. Y., 1934.

To locate tribes, use: Leyburn, J. G., *Handbook of Ethnography,* New Haven, 1931.

THE SIGNIFICANCE OF RACIAL
DIFFERENCES

Those unfamiliar with anthropological findings on the subject of racial differences will raise the question of possible determination of personal character by racial inheritance. Since no specific discussion of these findings is included in this book, reference is made to the following titles:

Benedict, Ruth F., *Race: Science and Politics*. N. Y., 1943.

Boas, Franz, *Anthropology and Modern Life*. rev. ed., N. Y., 1932.

Boyd, Wm. C., *Genetics and the Races of Man*. Boston, 1950.

Coon, C. S., S. M. Garn, and J. P. Birdsell, *Races . . . A Study of the Problems of Race Formation in Man*. Springfield, Ill., 1950.

Count, Earl W., *This is Race: An Anthology Selected from the International Literature on the Races of Man*. N. Y., 1950.

Dunn, L. C., and Th. Dobzhansky, *Heredity, Race and Society*. Penguin Books, N. Y., 1946.

Gates, R. R., *Human Genetics*. 2 vol. N. Y., 1946.

Gillin, John, *The Ways of Men*. New York, 1948.

Haring, D. G., *Racial Differences and Human Resemblances*. Syracuse, 1947. (Pamphlet.)

Haring, D. G., and M. E. Johnson, *Order and Possibility in Social Life*. New York, 1940. Chapter 15.

Hooton, Earnest A., *Up from the Ape*. rev. ed., N. Y., 1946.

Klineberg, Otto, *Race Differences*. N. Y., 1935.

Montagu, M. F. Ashley, *Man's Most Dangerous Myth: The Fallacy of Race*. N. Y., 1942.

Weidenreich, Franz, *Apes, Giants, and Man*. Chicago, 1946.

GREGORY BATESON

1942. "Some Systematic Approaches to the Study of Culture and Personality," *Character and Personality*, vol. *11*: 76-82. Reprinted by courtesy of the author and of the Editor of the *Journal of Personality*.

1943. "Cultural and Thematic Analysis of Fictional Films," *Transactions of the New York Academy of Sciences*, Series II, vol. *5*: 72-78. Reprinted by courtesy of the author and of the New York Academy of Sciences.

1947. "Sex and Culture," from a symposium entitled "Physiological and Psychological Factors in Sex Behavior," *Annals of the New York Academy of Sciences*, vol. *47*, Article 5, pp. 647-660. Reprinted by courtesy of the author and of the New York Academy of Sciences.

Essential to the understanding of Dr. Bateson's method and point of view is his book *Naven*, an ethnographic study of a tribe in New Guinea, as well as his joint work with Margaret Mead, *Balinese Character, a Photographic Analysis*. Another paper, "Bali: The Value System of a Steady State," will repay careful study. Two other pertinent essays are reprinted in *Readings in Social Psychology* by Newcomb, Hartley, and associates. Another constitutes a chapter in *Personality and the Behavior Disorders*, edited by J. McV. Hunt. Jointly with Jurgen Ruesch, he has more recently published *Communication, the Social Matrix of Psychiatry*—a tangible indication of the close interrelation of the work of anthropologists with that of psychiatrists.

SOME SYSTEMATIC APPROACHES TO THE STUDY OF CULTURE AND PERSONALITY

Gregory Bateson

If physics were able to offer us only the very elaborate description of gases based upon molecular structure and the principle of indeterminacy, it would still be the duty of that science to give us the simpler, but less true, formulae which assume that gas is a fluid. In the social sciences we are still very far from giving anything like complete descriptions of the phenomena of human life, and now, when the urgency of international affairs and the internal instability of our own communities press upon us, it is more than ever urgent for us, social scientists, to provide whatever simple shortcuts we can to aid in the solution of practical problems. We do not know all the answers, but we must make our hunches available wherever they may be of practical use.

The purpose of the present paper is to make available certain recipes for thinking about people and cultures. Examples have been derived from the greater civilizations, and these examples are also in some measure based upon guesswork. No adequate field work has been done in England or in Germany, but the examples can be backed up by field work done among primitive peoples, where it can be shown that phenomena of the same order do actually occur. The possible applications of these principles to international affairs are discussed at the end of the paper.

The type of analysis which has come to be called "culture and personality" is based upon the notion that some degree of uniformity of character structure occurs among the individuals who participate in any given set of cultural behaviors, and gradually we are building up a vocabulary which shall be sufficiently abstract to describe these uniformities. Clearly, on a simple episodic level, we cannot expect uniformity. Chance differences in life history, differentiations of class within the community, and discrepancies of hereditary make-up will all tend to scatter the individuals away from any phenomenal norm, and the first step in the problem of applying characterological terminology to individuals *qua* participants in a particular culture is, therefore, to arrive at a vocabulary which shall transcend these differences.

1. *Vocabulary Based upon Contexts of Learning.*[1] It is possible to step from a crude episodic level of statement to a somewhat more abstract level by considering in any context of learning not what is learned in the ordinary sense, but the structure of the context in which learning occurs. If we assume that the learning subject not only acquires the specific learned behavior, but also acquires an expectation that the universe will be, to some extent, structured in the same terms as the context in which the learning occurred, then it follows that, by considering these contexts carefully, we may get a clue to the individual's *Weltanschauung*. Thus we arrive at a vocabulary for describing the individual's character structure in terms of how he may be expected to read coherence into his experiences and his own behavior. With this hypothesis a very considerable number of terms which have long been in loose general use become susceptible of precise definition. "Determinism," "instrumentalism," "anxiety," are obvious examples of words which can be either defined or refined by stating more critically the structure of the contexts in which these habitual characteristics are acquired. We could define "determinism" by finding out how the context of learning might be rigged to give the experimental subject a *sense* of determinism, and we could refine the notion of "anxiety" by discriminating those types which result from repeated experience of sequences in which punishment follows gratification from those types which result from sequences in which punishment follows upon some misstep in instrumental-behavior.[2]

The practice of looking at the context in which learning occurs rather than at what is learned is still rewarding when we come to deal with interpersonal sequences. For example, it enables us to discriminate very sharply between different sorts of dominance-submission behavior. In the upper classes of England, the behavior of the child towards its parent (and to a lesser degree, that of the parents towards the child) is inculcated indirectly by a nurse. This means that the patterns of dominance and submission are, in some measure, seen, not as interpersonal, but rather as being in accord with an impersonal or external structure of the universe. It means that, in applying such a term as "superego" to the English, we are using the word in a rather special sense, not to describe an image of a disciplinary parent introjected through sharp face-to-face encounters with that parent, but rather a second-hand picture, likely to have somewhat different dynamic properties.

A further application of this approach can be seen if we study such a book as Madariaga's *Englishmen, Frenchmen, and Spaniards.*[3] The book as it stands has probably not had the recognition it deserves, because in substance it says that the French are cognitive, the English connative, and the Spaniards affective. And even though Madariaga does not use this terminology, the ideas in which he is dealing are so close to these unfashionable psychological terms as to be unacceptable. If, however, we regard his descriptions as referring to types of learning experience, it seems likely that Madariaga has hit on an important descriptive clue, and our next task would be to show that, in the early contexts of childhood learning, the French emphasize discrimination, the English perhaps the continuity of goal orientation, and the Spaniards perhaps the apparent impossibility of altering the timing of emotional climaxes.

2. *Vocabulary Based upon the Elements of Interpersonal Behavior.*[4] When we observe the progressive changes which occur in interpersonal relationships, going towards mutual love and hate, we find, of course, that these processes consist in interaction in which, for example, A's behavior is both a response to B's previous behavior and a stimulus to B's future behavior. Such interaction sequences have been studied with great exactness by Chapple,[5] who, by ignoring the content and meaning, has been able to arrive at very revealing mathematical descriptions of the timing of such behavior, and has been able to show the presence of an invariable constant, differing from one individual to another. No doubt this method will be very revealing when applied to other cultural settings.

When we come to consider the content of such sequences, as distinct from the time relations, we can discriminate two contrasting patterns:

(a) Symmetrical sequences, in which A's behavior is fundamentally similar to B's and where the exhibition of *more* of this behavior by B leads to the exhibition of more by A. In this category, we could put boasting matches, various forms of competitive rivalry, armaments races, etc.,[6] all of them sequences in which the stimulus for more aggressive behavior is the greater aggression of the other side. This stimulus we may tentatively express in the form $(y - x)$, where x is own strength, y is the strength of the other side, and the resulting behavior has positive value when y is greater than x.

(b) Complementary sequences, in which A's behavior is fundamentally different but complementary to that of B. In this category we would place dominance-submission, succoring-dependence, etc., and significantly, in the case of dominance-submission, the stimulus for more positive or assertive behavior is roughly to be expressed in the form $(x - y)$, which will indicate that, when the opponent is stronger than the self, the behavior will become negative, and submission will replace dominance.

We know that, to some extent, standardization as between these two great categories of motivation is possible. One of the basic contributions of Christian ethics has been the notion that pity (some sudden reversal of the personality) should occur when x is very much greater than y in a complementary relationship. And one of the great contributions of Anglo-Saxon culture has been the more or less successful attempt to outlaw complementary or bully-coward relationships in favor of "fair play," which we may translate as an injunction to foster symmetrical motivations.

3. *Vocabulary Based upon Combinations of Elements of Inter-Personal Behavior.*[7] If we regard dominance-submission, succoring-dependence, etc., as elementary themes in human behavior, it is possible to go one step further by asking how, in any given culture, these themes are combined together. To an Englishman looking at America, a conspicuous peculiarity of the American parent-child relationship is the way in which the child is encouraged to certain sorts of boastful and exhibitionistic behavior while still in a position somewhat subordinate to and dependent upon the parents. It seems that in the American North, exhibitionism is linked with dependence and submission, rather than with dominance and succoring as in England. This reversed linkage seems to constitute the mechanism by which the American child is encouraged to independence, by being admired whenever he shows off self-sufficiency. In fact, the American parent-child relationship contains within itself factors for psychologically weaning the child, while in England among the upper classes, the analogous breaking of the succoring-dependence link has to be performed by a subsidiary institution, the boarding school. It is interesting to consider the effects of patterns of this order in such contexts as those of colonial administration. Colonies cannot be sent to a boarding school, and we may observe that England has had very great difficulty in weaning her non-Anglo-Saxon colonies, while these colonies have had corresponding difficulty in attaining maturity—in sharp contrast with the history of the Philippines.

The possible applications of this type of study can only be treated very briefly in this paper, but it is necessary at least to indicate some areas in which insights of this kind might be applied:

1. If our hypothesis that the context in which learning occurs is vitally significant for character structure is correct, then it is clear that some standardization of character will occur in all forms of mass learning, whether in the class room listening to a single teacher, or in the radio audience listening to a forum. Brubacher[8] has pointed out that the use of discussion in teaching does not avoid standardization of the pupil but rather runs a risk of standardizing in the pupils either a habit of disagreement or a frame of mind in which decision is no longer sought after. Similarly, we ought to ask ourselves about the slick perfection of our movies and radio programs. As the matter is at present

organized, the context of production in these industries is such that the attention of the performer is majorly focused upon split-second timing and loaded juxtapositions. His ardor is necessarily concentrated upon this aspect rather than on the emotional or intellectual content of the performance. This probably makes of the performance a context in which the audience is standardized towards a passive acceptance of these tricks and techniques, rather than towards active emotional or intellectual participation.

2. We must examine the mechanics of interpersonal behavior between people of different character structure—so that we may enjoy these differences instead of stubbing our toes against them. When such differences have been laid down in mutually irrelevant cultural settings, we cannot expect any simple complementary or symmetrical fitting to occur; and therefore we must look to possible catalysts or media of communication by which the discrepancies shall be automatically adjusted. Differences of language we are all aware of and have to negotiate somehow, and it is possible that some *lingua franca* or some special techniques in the teaching of languages might help to correct the international stereotypes and so improve international relations. A *lingua franca* should not be a Procrustean bed of objective expression, but a tool so flexible that a Frenchman or an Englishman should be able to express himself in it in forms appropriate to his own national character, so that his listener would be constantly aware of these peculiarities. Or, if we are to learn each others' languages, we might do well to concentrate on learning to *understand* rather than to speak. In New Guinea, neighboring peoples often do this. Conversation between them is then rapid, since each uses his own language, and real differences are less blurred by superficial objective understanding.

The mechanics of interpersonal relations carried on by means of a third language (e.g., diplomatic French), which is itself replete with cultural emphases foreign to both of the speakers, are too complex to consider here.

3. In the field of organization, approaches of this kind have many appplications. For the maintenance of psychological efficiency or "morale," functions must be distributed in ways that are congenial to the character structure of the participants. In organizing an hierarchical system in the American North, it is essential that the subordinate members should have opportunities for conspicuous achievement and that the superior members, if they are to be dominant in policy, should also be appreciative spectators of the carrying out of this policy. There is a continual danger of organizational structures being copied blindly from one nation to another, and still more danger that propagandists in one nation may try to borrow themes which have been successful in another—and only understanding of the peculiarities im-

plicit in their own cultural environment can show where such borrowing is appropriate.

It takes years of experience and training to produce a man who will have good "intuition" in matters of this kind, but it would be possible to train men quickly so that they would supplement their undeveloped "intuition" by asking, in any context, some at least of the questions which science can underline as significant.

NOTES

1. The analysis of contexts of learning and the theories based upon them, contained in Hilgard, E. R., and Marquis, D. G., *Conditioning and learning* (N. Y.: Appleton-Century, 1940), provided the stimulus for developing this approach.

2. For a schematic outline of the permutations of contextual structure in simple learning experiments, cf. Bateson, G., Comments on "The Comparative Study of Culture and the Purposive Cultivation of Democratic Values," by Margaret Mead. (In *Science, philosophy, and religion*, Second Symposium, published by the Conference on Science, Philosophy, and Religion, New York, 1942, pp. 81-97).

3. Madariaga, S. de, *Englishmen, Frenchmen and Spaniards, An Essay in Comparative Psychology* (Pref. Note by Alfred Zimmern). London: Oxford Univ. Press, 1931.

4. This approach is an elaboration from the theory of schismogenesis (Bateson, G., *Naven*, Cambridge Univ. Press, 1936), supplemented by a modification of F. L. Richardson's equations ("Generalized foreign politics," Monograph Supplement No. XXIII, *Brit. J. Psychol.*, 1939).

5. Chapple, E. D., "Personality" differences as described by invariant properties of individuals in interaction, *Proc. Nat. Acad. Sci.*, 1940, *26*, 10-16; and Chapple, E. D. & Lindeman, E., Clinical implications of measurements of interaction rates in psychiatric interviews. *Appl. Anthrop.*, 1942, *1*, 1-11.

6. Cf. Dollard, John, The dozens: dialectic of insult, *Amer. Imago*, 1939, *1*, 3-25.

7. Cf. Bateson, G., National Character and Morale. *In* Civilian Morale, Second Yearbook of the Society for the Psychological Study of Social Issues, Goodwin Watson, editor, Boston and New York: Houghton-Mifflin, 1942.

8. Brubacher, John S., Education towards a democratic world order, a paper read at the 3d Conference on Science, Philosophy and Religion, New York City, August 28, 1942.

CULTURAL AND THEMATIC ANALYSIS
OF FICTIONAL FILMS

Gregory Bateson

This paper is a preliminary report on a piece of research now in progress at the Museum of Modern Art Film Library. The purpose of this research is to derive some notion of the psychological implications of Nazism from the study of Nazi propaganda films. This involves the application of anthropological methods of analysis to a variety of German cultural materials—the analysis of film material provided by the Film Library and of verbatim interviews of Germans and social scientists familiar with German conditions conducted under the auspices of the Council on Inter-cultural Relations.

Anthropological analysis consists always of two parts. First, the recognition of significant themes and second, the verification that these themes are in fact characteristic of the culture that we are studying. In this research the themes are exemplified in the films and the verification has been done by interview techniques.[1] As usual in such research, the peculiarities of daily life and daydream are referred back to the family setting and especially to the position of the child in that setting. This procedure can be justified by the fact that the most formative years of an individual's life are spent in that setting, but the practice of referring the remainder of a culture to the family background is also necessary on practical grounds. It enables us to compare one culture with another. All societies have the institution of the family, but not all societies have Hinduism or age grades. Thus, by referring the peculiarities of Hinduism to the family structure, instead of *vice versa*, we arrive at systematic statements which are comparable from one culture to the next.

This method of referring cultural peculiarities to the family is specially suitable for the analysis of Nazi propaganda. In America we tend to think of propaganda as consisting of a large number of separate utterances, pious sentiments or jokes, inserted into the more or less propagandically neutral matrix of communication. Publicity methods were developed on the basis of rather simple psychological theories of association and Watsonian conditioning and have been comparatively little influenced by *Gestalt* Psychology or psychoanalysis. The significant propaganda in the German films is, however, not of this sort. It consists not of isolated utterances but of themes built into the structure of the plot in such a way that the audience, while enjoying the plot, will necessarily accept the underlying themes as basic premises which need never be articulately stated. The underlying themes, which are expertly woven into a background for the promotion of Nazism, are the themes of pre-Nazi German family life—are, in fact, the themes which cultural analysis is best equipped to recognise.

This use of the family is characteristic of the Nazi film, "*Hitler-junge Quex,*" made by Ufa and released in September, 1933.

The hero of this film is Heini, a preadolescent boy, the son of a violent father and a drudge mother. His parents are of lower middle class and have fallen in the world as a result of the inflation and the father's war wounds. The father hurts himself in a minor food riot which results from the stealing of apples by two hungry Communist boys. He is helped home by Stoppel, an organizer of Communist youth. He lives in a poor Communist district of Berlin. Stoppel helps the mother to dress the father's wound. The father asks the mother for money to get some beer. She says that she has no money, and a violent scene follows, the father ransacking all the containers in the house in search of the mother's hiding place. At this moment Heini returns from his work in a printing shop, arriving so that we see the climax of the scene between the parents through the eyes of the son. At the printing shop Heini had received a tip of one mark. He secretly gives the mark to his mother. She gives it to the father, who then goes off to get his beer. Stoppel is impressed by Heini's character and contacts him with a view to enlisting him in the Communist Youth.

After Stoppel has left, the mother opens the window and lets in the music of the merry-go-round at the fair. Heini is thus reminded of a wonderful knife which he has seen in a lottery in one of the side shows. He asks his mother for money to enter this lottery, which he is sure that he will win. She gets money from her hiding place in the coffee grinder and gives it to him. Heini goes to the lottery and loses.

Stoppel appears at Heini's elbow, comforts him and invites him to join a hike of the Communist Youth on the following day. Heini accepts.

On the hike Heini sees the Hitler Youth, a company of whom are on the same train, going hiking to the same woods. He is disgusted by the gross behavior of the Communists and especially by a kiss which Gerda, one of the Communist girls, forces upon him. Finally he wanders in the dark, away from the Communist camp, till he hears the Song of the Hitler Youth coming from the Nazi camp. He gazes through the bushes at the Nazis who are celebrating the Summer Solstice. The Nazis find him, accuse him of spying and send him away. He sleeps by himself on the ground and next morning after watching the Nazis with longing eyes he goes home to his mother.

He tells her he was with the Nazis and how wonderful they were. His mother is worried but not angry with him. She even lets him sing the Nazi Youth song (without warning him that the father is in the next room). The father hears the song and comes in furious. He compels Heini to sing the "Internazionale," boxing his ears while he sings.

Next day at school Heini again meets Gerda and resists her advances. He approaches Fritz, a boy leader of the Nazis, and is invited to supper with Fritz and Fritz's sister, Ulla. Gerda meanwhile has been told by Stoppel to vamp Grundler, a weak Nazi boy, and while Fritz and Heini go off to supper, Gerda and Grundler go off to seek "Turkish Delight" at the fair.

Fritz and Ulla ask Heini to come to the opening of their new Nazi club room (*"Heim"*). Heini hesitates because he has no key with which to return home after the meeting. Finally he accepts when put on his mettle by Fritz.

The father meanwhile has been persuaded by Stoppel to sign Heini into the Communist Youth. When Heini comes home the father at once informs him that he is to go that night to the Communist Local. Heini says, "Do I get a house key?" The father says, "Of course—you are now a grown man, and a grown man has a house key." The father then makes a long friendly speech to Heini about the difficulties of life and how "you young ones must help us older people." Heini is almost in tears and says later to his mother, "Father is not so bad—I cannot lie to him—he gave me a house key." He is determined, however, not to go to the Communist meeting.

He goes out that evening but meets Stoppel, who draws him aside into a doorway and tells him that the Communists are going to raid the Nazi home and that he is to help in the raid. Heini manages to slip away without taking an active part, but when the police come he is picked up.

The police tell him to "go home to Mother." The Nazis think he has set the Communists onto them and accuse him of treachery.

(We are given no further information about the events of that night, nor do we see Heini use the house key to return to the bosom of his family.)

Next day Stoppel tells Heini that he was a hero because he did not tell anything to the police and that tonight they will get dynamite from the cache in the Marschstrasse and blow up that nest of Nazis. Heini protests and finally says he will warn them. Stoppel is very much shocked and tells Heini that that is something which one does "only once in life" but in the end Stoppel shrugs his shoulders and dismisses the matter.

When Stoppel leaves, Heini rushes to the telephone to warn Fritz and Ulla. Ulla answers the telephone but Fritz tells her not to listen to that traitor. Ulla is worried by Heini's mention of dynamite but she obediently hangs up, and Heini is left talking into a dead phone. In despair he tries to persuade the police to interfere but they treat him as a child. He then tries to find Stoppel but cannot.

Suddenly while Heini is in the fair looking for Stoppel there is a violent explosion—the Nazis have blown up the dynamite—and Heini returns home whistling the Youth Song.

His mother is in a state of despair because Heini has betrayed the Communists and she tries to persuade him to make up with Stoppel. She fails, and Heini goes to bed while the mother sits weeping. Finally she turns on the gas to kill both herself and Heini, and the screen is filled with the fumes (which billow like a flag).

Heini awakes in the hospital. A nurse says, "There is somebody to see you." Heini says, "My mother?" But it is the Nazi boys and Ulla. They give him a uniform and a mirror in which to admire himself. After they have gone the nurse comes; and while she is removing the Nazi cap from his head she tells him that his mother will never come.

While Heini is convalescing, his father and the District Leader of the Nazis happen to visit him simultaneously, and the question is discussed—"Where does the boy belong?" The Nazi wins this discussion by a verbal trick, and Heini goes to live in a Nazi clubhouse outside the Communist district.

The Communists are waiting for vengeance, but in spite of the District Leader's opposition Heini wants to return to the Communist district to distribute leaflets for the 1933 election. Grundler has been falling lower and lower under Gerda's influence and now he and Gerda destroy all the available Nazi leaflets. Fritz has been wounded in an election riot so that Heini and Ulla are brought together by substituting Heini for Ulla's brother. They work together in the printing shop to prepare new leaflets and when the work is completed Ulla gives Heini a sisterly kiss. Heini then goes to distribute the leaflets in the Communist district. He is hunted and encircled by the Communists in the darkened streets and takes refuge in one of the tents in the deserted fair.

Accidentally he touches a mechanical figure of a drummer and the figure starts to beat its drum, thus betraying him. Heini is stabbed (presumably by Wilde, the sinister leader of the Communists, who has the original knife which Heini coveted). The Nazis come and find Heini dying. His last words are, "Our flag billows before . . . ." The sound track takes up the Youth Song and the flag appears on the screen, giving place to marching columns of Hitler Youth.

In this plot Heini's conversion to Nazism depends essentially upon the contrast which he is shown between the Nazis' picture of themselves and the Nazis' picture of "Communism." But this is not the only message which the propagandist conveys. At the beginning of the film the propagandist seems deliberately to build up an association between the mother and Communism. It is the mother who goes and opens the window and lets in the degenerate music of the fair, and the fair is the setting in which the Communists are most at home. And it is the mother who gives Heini the money to enter the lottery to try to win a knife from this depraved environment. Stoppel, the Communist organizer, is also associated with the mother, joining her in aiding and placating the father. In this way the audience is encouraged to accept unwittingly, the basic premise that ideology is related to the family structure.

Also at the beginning of the film we are shown Heini as a hero rescuing his mother from the father's violence by self-sacrifice. As the film progresses, we see these self-sacrificing attitudes shifted from the mother to the nation and the position of Communism shifted from its association with the mother to a very much more dramatic association with the father. The basic premise, that ideology is connected with the family structure, is allowed to persist, but the straw-man association between Communism and the mother is smashed when the father compels Heini to sing the "Internazionale," boxing his ears in time with the song. In this way the propagandist confers on Nazism not merely the virtue of Heini's preference for it, but also the whole fanatical gamut of emotions which are evoked in the Oedipus situation.

The contrast presented between Nazism and Communism on the hike is interesting in that it shows another aspect of Nazi psychology. One of the basic premises of the film which is nowhere articulately expressed is that Communism and Nazism are psychologically related. We see, for example, the behavior of the Nazi boys at the railroad station when one of the Communists throws chewed food into the face of one of the Nazis. Their instinct is to break their ranks and to lapse into disorderly aggression. Similarly, in Grundler, the weak Nazi, we see how normal heterosexual temptation may undermine the Nazi character until he becomes depraved like "Communists." The assumption is that without discipline pure Nazis degenerate into the picture which they themselves have drawn of "Communism." In other words, this particular picture of "Communism" has no factual relationship to the real thing but is a self-portrait of Nazism—a portrait of what the Nazis think that they themselves are like under the veneer of discipline.

From this point of view it is interesting to observe the large number of oral and anal characteristics which the film maker showers upon "Communism." The apple which fills the first frame and which is there sympathetically treated—it is a desirable apple, stolen by the

Communist boy under stress of hunger—is a symbol, whose oral and sexual implications are fully worked out. Continually we see the "Communists" indulging their mouths, eating coarsely, Gerda kissing Heini, and Stoppel pushing a banana into Gerda's mouth.

This curious double formation in Nazi character is likely to be of considerable importance after the war and it might almost be said that the closing of this split in the Nazi personality—between the over-pure and the over-dirty—will be essential for the stabilization of Europe. The split is not, however, merely of Nazi origin. It is older than that and is perfectly recognizable in German films of the early twenties (e.g. "The Street," "Variety," "M") and we are probably justified in regarding as an expression of the same split, the curious behavior of German troops at the end of the last war who found time during their retreat to soil their billets. In fact the problem of Germany is in part a problem of preventing a pendulum from swinging too far into aggressive purity in good times and into degenerate self-contempt in bad. And the extreme high point reached by this pendulum during the heyday of Nazism probably denotes an increased capacity for a later fall.

As we have seen, the lines for such a fall are clearly laid down in this film of 1933.

We cannot here examine in detail the methods of treating this split but, one incident in the film is suggestive. The film as a whole implies that Nazism is the total destruction of the family. In order to create a violent emotional adherence to Nazism the family itself is unscrupulously sacrificed. The woman's place may be in the home but she need not expect that home to contain a husband or children over six. These others, the men and the boys and the unmarried girls, will be absorbed into "Youth" organizations which free them from accepting the responsibilities of adult human status. The one feature of the film which appears discrepant with this treatment is the propagandist's implicit and probably unconscious confession that there is another way. The symbol of adult human status, which Heini is not allowed to use, is the house key—a symbol which while conferring freedom also confers the promise of return to the family.

NOTE

1. The writer was intimately connected with work done by E. H. Erikson and since published. ("Hitler's Imagery and German Youth," by Erik Homburger Erikson. Psychiatry, 1942, Vol. 5, pp. 475-493). The present research supports a number of Erikson's conclusions based on other types of German material. Acknowledgment must also be made to The American Museum of Natural History for the use of facilities.

SEX AND CULTURE

Gregory Bateson

It is certainly too early to try to introduce rigor into those anthropological hypotheses which mention sex as a causal factor, or which seek to explain the diversities of sexual behavior by referring to the cultural milieu. Even the word, *sex*, is used by us in a series of different senses, varying from observable and definable copulatory behaviors to a hypothetical drive, or drives, which are believed to influence a very wide and undefinable category of behaviors. It is even doubtful whether we should, at this time, attempt to sharpen our definitions, and not rather wait until some clarity begins to appear, as we amass more data. Definitions and abstractions are, after all, only "right" or "wrong" in so far as they form part of hypotheses which experience can test. Such hypotheses as we have today, relating sex to culture, are still so vague that very much more exploratory work will be needed before the abstractions involved can be sharply defined.

There is, however, a serious drawback to such a *laissez faire* attitude towards theory. It is, unfortunately, easy to construct hypotheses with vague concepts, and such hypotheses are usually impossible to prove or to disprove. The current theories of personality and character formation already contain an excessive number of parentheses (compensation, bisexuality, etc.), any one of which can be invoked to explain why behavior in a given case does not conform to hypothetical expectation. This building-up of parenthetical variables has reached such a point that today it is almost unkind to demand of any theorist: "What conceivable fact could disprove your hypothesis?"

There are, however, two possible approaches which may be of use: not to introduce rigorous hypotheses before the science is ready for them, but rather to suggest the sorts of question which we ought to be asking; and to delimit the orders of hypothesis to which we should look forward.

The first of these approaches will only be mentioned at this stage. It consists in asking metascientific questions about that order of hypothesis which would relate a concept or set of phenomena derived from one scientific field (physiology) to concepts and phenomena derived from another field (cultural anthropology). We are attempting to argue from a narrower sphere of relevance, the individual's internal environment, to a wider sphere which includes almost the whole of human behavior and the external environment. All such transitions from a narrower to a wider sphere of relevance are known to be fraught with difficulty, and we may expect *a priori* that very simple alterations in the narrower sphere will be represented by excessively complex changes in the wider. A small change in atomic structure may denote a total change at the molecular level. Similarly, even so simple a matter as a difference in physical stature might determine very complex differences of culture or society. Physiological sex is known to have causally powerful and complex ramifications within the individual, and, *a priori*, we may expect the social and cultural ramifications of this set of phenomena to be so complex that "sex" will almost cease to be a useful category for the ordering of phenomena at this wider level. Indeed, we know already that those social extensions of "sex" which anthropologists call the "family" and the "kinship system" are crucial to the whole of culture, in the sense that all behavior can be related back to these concepts, just as the same whole can be related back to hunger and the economics of food.[1-2-3] This fact, that the effects of any phenomenon within the narrow sphere ramify throughout the *whole* of the wider sphere, indicates that we may not make much headway in attempting to trace the manifold cultural expressions of physiological sex. It is possible, however, that we might make advances by an inverse approach: that, from cultural data, we might be able to derive hypotheses about the narrower physiological sphere. This inverse procedure has an advantage, in that our hypotheses are the more likely to be subject to experimental testing.

The second approach to hypotheses which will relate sex and culture, consists in asking what sorts of data anthropologists do, in fact, collect. This can be followed up with the question: "What types of verifiable hypothesis can be suggested or tested by data of this kind?"

Actually, there appears to be considerable confusion among other scientists, and among anthropologists themselves, about the nature of the data with which the cultural anthropologist works. Therefore, this matter must be made categorically clear. We too often think that the abstractions which we draw are a part of the data from which they are drawn and regard ourselves as studying "culture," or "social organization," or "diffusion," or "religion," or "sex." The creatures which we study are talking mammals and, whether they be natives of New York or of New Guinea, their talk is filled with abstract terms. Thus, we easily fall into the fallacy of assigning a false concreteness to these same abstractions. It is, therefore, salutary, at times, to leave all these abstractions aside for the moment and look at the actual objective data from which all the abstractions are drawn.

There are, I believe, only three types of data in cultural anthropology:

(1) *An identified individual in such-and-such a recorded context said such-and-such, and was heard by the anthropologist.* More than half of all our data take this form, and our main effort in fieldwork goes into the astonishingly difficult task of collecting such items. We do not always succeed, for various reasons. Sometimes, the individual is imperfectly identified. We may have insufficient information about his past experience and position in the kinship system and social organization. Still more often, we may have only an incomplete understanding of the context in which he spoke. But this remains our ideal type of datum.

(2) *An identified individual in such-and-such a recorded context was seen by the anthropologist to do so-and-so.* Here again, the ideal record is not always complete. The identification of the individual and the recording of the context present the same difficulties as in (1), above. In addition, we face very serious technical difficulties when we attempt to record bodily movements. Even with photographic or cinematic techniques, this is almost impossible, and the record, when obtained, can only with very great difficulty be translated into a verbal form for analysis and publication.

(3) *Artifacts (tools, works of art, books, clothes, boats, weapons, etc.), made and/or used by such-and-such individuals in such-and-such contexts.* These are, in general, the easiest data to collect, and the most difficult to interpret.

There are, at present, no other types of objective data in cultural anthropology.[4]

From inspection of this list of types of data, certain traps in anthropological deduction appear. The most serious of these is baited with the temptation to confuse verbal with behavioral data. Objectively, we may know that an individual said such-and-such about himself, or about some other individual; but we do not know, objectively, whether what he said is true. The objective fact—the only basis upon which we can build—is that he *said* such-and-such. Whether his statement is true or false, must be immaterial to any hypotheses which we may construct, unless (as sometimes, though rarely, happens) we have other objective data bearing upon the truth or falsity of the original statement. The importance of this point can scarcely be overemphasized when we are considering the validity of hypotheses relating to sex—a matter about which human beings are not only reticent and dishonest, but even totally unable to achieve an objective view of their own behavior or that of others.

An example may help to make clear how the anthropologist must proceed in such a case, and how he may construct hypotheses without assuming the objective truth of the verbal datum. Let us suppose that the anthropologist hears and records, *verbatim*, the statement of a man who claims: "I copulate with my wife n times every night." This may be an important objective datum, because within it are implicit numerous indications about the psychology of boasting and the psychological role of sex in that man's life. The next question which the anthropologist asks himself will not be: "Is the man's statement objectively true?" He will rather seek for those data which will enable him to place the man's statement in the cultural setting. He will want to know whether boasting and the use of sex activity for the enhancement of self-esteem are culturally acceptable. He will want to know whether such behavior is felt to be aggressive, and against whom the aggression is probably directed, and so on. He will therefore note, first and foremost, who is present on the occasion, and how these other people react to the boasting. He will look to see whether any of those present are markedly superior or inferior in status to the speaker, and whether any women are present; and he may later try to draw comments from the bystanders, after the original speaker has left the group. But in all this, he will not be trying to verify the truth of the original statement, and he will not, in general, care whether that statement is true. At most, he may carry a little suspended query in the back of his mind, a note that this is something about which he does not know, just to remind himself that every hypothesis suggested by the recorded statement must be so constructed that the truth or untruth of the statement will be irrelevant to the hypothesis.

The cultural anthropologist, in fact, is in the peculiar position of studying mammals which talk, and it is necessary to underline this fact to the minds of those who study less articulate and, therefore, less deceptive creatures. The circumstance that our subjects can talk to us, and to each other, is the great advantage which we have over the animal experimenter. However, it is very important not to abuse this advantage. To avoid such errors, stringent precautions must be observed, and these precautions necessarily limit the nature of the hypotheses which we can construct and verify.

Another peculiarity of the data collected by cultural anthropologists is the extreme complexity of each individual datum. The requirement that each datum include full identification of the individual and description of the context, is perhaps never fully met in practice. The fact remains, however, that a very large number of circumstances are always relevant, in the sense that a small change in any one of them might reverse, or drastically change, the form of the behavior which we are recording. There is, therefore, almost no possibility of handling the data statistically. The contexts, the individuals, and the behaviors are too various for their combinations and permutations to be handled in this way. The unit data of which any sample is composed are too heterogeneous to be legitimately thrown together into a statistical hopper. Moreover, the data are not selected at random, but according to circumstances which are forced upon the anthropologist rather than contrived by him. Anthropological informants, of which we do not use very many, are not a random sample of any population. Rather, they are carefully selected and carefully trained individuals, and the characteristics (accuracy, intelligence, articulacy, special interests, special social status, etc.) which make a man a good informant are not statistically normal in any population. Moreover, the selection is performed by the informants at least as much as by the anthropologist. The man who is in some way deviant, psychologically, sexually, physically, or by social experience, is more likely to want to talk to the anthropologist, and is likely to withstand such interviews with a minimum of boredom. The normal, non-deviant individual rarely, if ever, becomes a regular informant.[5]

The fact that our data are not suitable for statistical analysis means that they must be handled in other ways. This can be done, just because the unit datum is so complex. It is not necessary to discover hundreds of specimens of *Archaeopteryx lithographica*, in order to satisfy the scientific world that this creature existed and had a number of phylogenetically significant features. The existing samples, consisting of one nearly perfect skeleton, one imperfect skeleton, and one single feather, are more than sufficient, simply because an *Archaeopteryx* skeleton is a complex object. In the same way, the data of the cultural anthropologist, if they are a valid base for theory, are so because they are complex. "This given complex pattern of events occurred"; and this unique occurrence is one of the bricks which must form the material for our theoretical constructions.

This peculiarity of our data, like the unreliability of verbal statements, is a factor which must limit our hypotheses. Neither the single *Archaeopteryx*, nor any number of single specimens of different species, would suffice to demonstrate whether evolution is a continuous or discontinuous process, nor to answer the many sorts of questions which can only be answered by statistical analysis of random or representative samples. Similarly, anthropological data will not suffice to test hypotheses which would require statistical validation, and we must, therefore, avoid hypotheses of this kind. Ideally, we should concentrate upon those hypotheses of which it may be expected that the single exception will disprove the rule.

Within the limitations outlined above, cultural anthropologists have a vast mass of objective data, directly relevant to sex. We cannot report, of course, anything about frequency or characteristics of "normal" sexual intercourse, because such behavior is only accessible to observation under circumstances so exceptional as to preclude use of the term, normal, *e.g.*, copulation on orgiastic occasions, or specially staged for the observer and distorted by his presence, or included in traditional dramatic performances.

On the other hand, we have a large mass of information about native notions and psychological attitudes towards sex behavior, and we have information about how these various native attitudes and notions compare, and fit in, with other ideas which the same natives have on other subjects, such as achievement, sadism, humor, prestige, caste, etc. We know a great deal about the stylization of the differences between the sexes, and the roles of the two sexes in daily life and parenthood. We have collected hundreds of fantasies about copulation, love, homo-sexuality, incest, and so on. Then again, we have a mass of information on the economic aspects of sex behavior: dowries, bride prices, affinal exchanges, prostitution, etc. And masses of gossip about so-and-so's reputed sexual or courtship behavior, data which reflect on the cul-turally conventional attitudes towards various types of sexual normality and abnormality, and data on the sanctions which the people carry out (or say that they would carry out) in certain types of deviant cir-cumstances.

The problem is to introduce theoretical order into this confused jumble of data, arbitrarily separated from the remainder of our data by their evident relevance to the concept of "sex" which is derived from the physiological sphere of relevance.

Two generalizations can be drawn from all this material: first, that cultures differ markedly among themselves and, second, that a high degree of consistency obtains among the data on any one culture.[6]

These two generalizations suggest that the regularities which occur within one society[7] are of a different order from those which occur within an individual organism, and the matter can, perhaps, best be made clear by discussing this difference. If a biologist were allowed to make an exhaustive study of several different tissues derived from a single species of animal, and then were presented with another tissue differing from all those which he had so far studied, it would be almost impossible for him to determine whether this last specimen was or was not taken from the same animal species. The cultural anthropologist, on the other hand, if presented first with data upon several sorts of individuals in a given society, will probably be able to recognize that the data referring to other sorts of individuals in that same society do, in fact, have that provenience. Moreover, in their attempts to solve this problem, the biologist and the anthropologist will look for clues of quite different sorts. The biologist will look for characteristics of the cells so basic that they persist even through tissue differentiation. For example, he may attempt to count the chromosomes. The anthropologist, on the other hand, will look first for details of language and other very superficial learned characteristics, and if details of this sort are not available, he will look for more basic patterns and regularities which will be diagnostic of the *acquired* character structure of the individuals. It is significant that the biologists talk about "differentiation" of cells and tissues, while the anthropologists talk about the "acculturation" of individuals. The problem stressed by the biologist is: "How do genetically similar cells become different one from another, and how do they maintain these differences in spite of a homogeneous environment internal to the individual organism?" The problem for the cultural anthropologist, on the other hand, is: "How do individuals, who presumably differ among themselves in innate characteristics, become similar and remain sufficiently similar to understand each other, in spite of very evident differences in individual experience?"

In fact, to the cultural anthropologist, man appears not mainly as a physiological mechanism, nor yet as a creature endowed with instinctive urges and innate patterns of response. He appears to us, above all, as a creature which *learns*. The fact of human flexibility under environmental experience determines the major focus of our scientific attention.

Let us now return to the problems of "sex." If learning is the basic concept for the cultural anthropologist, then we can take a first step in relating "sex" to "culture," by examining the relations between sex and learning, bearing in mind that the phenomena connected with learning are to give us the definition of those sorts of regularity and homogeneity which we observe to be characteristic of each single culture. This definition still remains to be drawn.

To the anthropologist, it appears that all human sexual behavior is, in some degree, learned. The human infant apparently develops, at a very early age, a considerable reflex equipment. Its genitalia are erectile in response to various physical stimuli, and this tumescence is early associated with specifically interpersonal stimuli. This reflex equipment is precocious in the sense that the neural connections are present before the infant has the muscular development necessary to put the whole mechanism to work.

In this, there is nothing peculiar about sexuality, and the same sort of precocity is recognizable in other forms of behavior. The infant also shows what appear to be inherited reflex arcs for walking, swimming, arboreal suspension, and balance in an upright posture. For all of these activities, it appears that neural connections are established before the muscular development is adequate, and the rudimentary responses, which indicate the existence of these neural connections, fade out. A period of "latency" occurs not only in regard to sexual, but also locomotor behavior.[8]

Now, the crucial question about sexual latency is: *"Is it learned?"* Is the change from genital responsiveness to unresponsiveness to be ascribed to topological changes in the neural network, induced in that network by impulses which pass through it? The obvious alternative to such a hypothesis would be to ascribe the change in responsiveness to changes in the endocrine system and to hope that a fuller knowledge of maturation will enable us to account for these changes in endocrine balance without again being pushed back upon a theory of changes in the neural network induced by experience.[9]

From what little we know, it appears to me that we must assume that latency is learned, rather than due to a hypothetical endocrine change. The necessary shift in endocrine balance has not been observed,[10] and it appears, rather, that concentrations of androgens and estrogens in children's urine show a progressive rise through childhood to a peak at puberty. Moreover, the hypothesis that latency is learned will have the additional recommendation that it can be applied not only to sexual but also to locomotor latency, for which an endocrine theory can less readily be imagined.

Granting that learning probably plays a part in causing latency, the next question must be: "What are the stimuli or contexts which determine this learning?" Here we know, from anthropological data, that marked differences exist between cultures. In American and English cultures, we know that, among adults, even the notion of infantile sexuality is strongly resisted; masturbation of the child by parents or nurses is strongly deprecated (and, therefore, probably accompanied by guilt reactions on the part of the adult, when it occurs); and masturbatory behavior on the part of the child is sharply discouraged. Therefore, for these cultures, we must expect that latency will be induced not only by experience of own muscular insufficiency, but also by positive extinction or inhibition of tumescence. In sharp contrast to this, we know of cultures in which masturbation of the child by the parent is common and not deprecated. Even among these cultures, we may expect sharp differences which will be significant for the character formation of the child. The reason given by Italian peasants for this masturbation of the child is "to put it to sleep," and we may presume that, in Italy, the child is given some sort of sexual climax or other satisfactory experience. In Bali, on the other hand, our observations show that the child is not given satisfaction and, instead of going to sleep, becomes more restive. Indeed, from the mother's evident enjoyment both of the baby's responsiveness and of the temper tantrum which often follows, it would appear that the purpose of the masturbation is rather to wake it up. It is easy to see that the Anglo-Saxon and Balinese systems of handling may induce latency, though very different types of latency in the two areas. What sort of latency, if any, is induced by the Italian system, is not so clear.

These contrasts indicate very clearly that the social contexts which accompany the onset of latency are important for sexual learning. They may determine the individual's attitude towards sexual behavior and the part which these behaviors will play in his character. The matter becomes still more complex when we go on to consider the culturally stylized sexual play, masturbation, and courtship behaviors of the latency period, and the rewards and punishments which determine the role of these behaviors in the individual's character. These experiences will label the sexual patterns as safe or dangerous, approved or disapproved, as important sources of self-esteem and prestige, or as important sources of sensual pleasure.

Still later, the onset of puberty can be seen as a further set of learning and character-forming contexts, and the problems are analogous to those which we discussed in connection with latency. Here, the case for ascribing the change in responsiveness to endocrine factors is perhaps a little stronger, but it is possible that the importance of these factors has been exaggerated. There are, in addition, a host of interpersonal and social factors which push the individual into puberty. The sexual initiative of other persons; the value which the individual himself has been trained to place upon sexual adequacy and sexual conformity; his desire to acquire the respect of his fellows of the same sex and of possible sexual partners; all of these, in addition to his endocrines, may push him towards puberty. Further, the psychology of that puberty, when attained, will be determined by the specific qualities of the latency which has been broken down, and by the dynamics of the beginning of puberty. The individual who is pushed into active sexual life, by his physiological needs, at a period when he still feels that social pressures are on the side of latency, will learn something very different from what is learned by the individual who enters upon sexuality in an attempt to conform to social pressures before he is driven to this by physiological need.

The role played by sexual behavior and experience in determining character structure, and the inverse role of experience in determining sexual behavior, could be elaborated almost *ad infinitum*. To relate human sexual behavior to learning is easy, though at every turn we come upon new problems and new hypotheses requiring data for their verification. However, there is still another order of hypothesis which must be considered before we can be said to have related sexual behavior to culture.

It was suggested, above, that the data on a given culture show an internal regularity, or consistency, not simply deducible from the operation which we performed in defining the limits of the single culture in terms of causal interdependence of all events within this margin. We noted, also, that there is a contrast between physiology and cultural anthropology in that, though both sciences deal with spheres of relevance definable in terms of causal interdependence of events within the sphere, the physiologist is preoccupied with differentiation, while the anthropologist is preoccupied with acculturation. Our next step will be to define more sharply these regularities within the single culture, and to relate them to the theory of learning.

What has so far been said about learning could be deduced from any learning theory, such as that of *association*, which will describe learning as the setting-up of a classification of perceived objects and events, linked to a classification of responses and to a rudimentary linear value system which will discriminate the pleasant from the unpleasant. Such a system will, for example, account for the simple forms of sexual symbolism. Balinese carvings, for instance, illustrate a large number of types of symbolic distortion of the human body. The breasts may be equated with buttocks; the head may be equated with male genitalia; the mouth may be equated with the vulva; and so on.[11] All of these distortions can be seen as due to simple associational learning.

We find, however, in our cultural data, something more than this. If we take the data from a given culture and sort them by subject matter, putting all the data which refer to sex in one heap, the data referring to initiation in another, the data referring to death in another, and so on, we get a very remarkable result.[12] We find that similar types of order are recognizable in every heap. We find that, whether we are looking at the sex data, or the initiation data, or the death data, the system of classification of perceived objects and events (the *eidos* of the culture) is still the same. Similarly, if we analyze the heaps of data to obtain the system of linked responses and values (the *ethos*) of the culture, we find that the ethos is the same in each heap. Briefly, it is as if the same sort of person had devised the data in all the heaps.

Two obvious hypotheses which might account for this finding can, I believe, be ruled out. We cannot assume that these ethological and eidological regularities are simply due to innate human characteristics, because very different kinds of ethos and eidos have been analyzed out of different cultures. And we cannot say that the ethological and eidological uniformities are due to the uniform working of peculiarities of the mind of the analyst, because in different cultures the same analyst obtains different results.

It would, I believe, be impossible to deduce these results, the uniformity within one culture and the contrast between cultures, from the simple associational learning theory from which we started.[13]

However, these ethological and eidological uniformities within the single culture, and the corresponding contrasts between cultures, are precisely what we would expect if, in addition to the processes postulated in simple learning, there is a carry-over from learning in one context which will influence later behavior in quite different contexts. Various theories of this type have been put forward[14-15-16] and, in general, the experimental findings indicate that some such postulate may be necessary even at the animal level. At the human level, the carry-over from one context to others can be demonstrated in the phenomena of "transfer" of learning, and especially in the experimental increase in learning proficiency from one context to another of similar formal structure.[17]

Such a postulated carry-over from one context of learning to another will give us a theoretical system which will permit us to speak of changes in *character*, instead of limiting us to the mere addition or subtraction of associational links. We can very easily see how such a theory would give precision to qualities of the order of "optimism," "pessimism," "fatalism," "initiative," "level of aspiration," and the like, and lead us to expect that qualities of this sort, learned by experience in one sort of context, will be carried over into other contexts of very various types. This, I suggest, is the explanation of the ethological and eidological uniformities characteristic of each human culture.

We are driven, I believe, to conclude that what is learned in contexts associated with sex will be carried over into contexts associated with quite different spheres of life—initiation, death, trade, etc.— and that, *vice versa*, what is learned in these other contexts will be carried over into specifically sexual life.

Such a conclusion will reduce the title of the present paper to nonsense, by indicating that *sex* is scarcely a useful concept for the analysis of human cultures; a conclusion which was foreshadowed in our *a priori* metascientific examination of any attempt to relate phenomena in the physiological sphere of relevance to phenomena in the cultural sphere.

Our excursion into theory has not, however, been fruitless, because it has lent anthropological support to a type of hypothesis connected with learning, and this type of hypothesis is such that it can be tested and made more precise by further anthropological work, and by laboratory experiments. In addition, we have demonstrated that, in the psychological analysis of anthropological data, it is not useful to classify these data according to the sorts of physiological need to which they appear relevant. It is, however, very rewarding to classify these data according to the formal characteristics of the contexts of behavior. It is important to note that the Balinese baby is subjected to the same formal sequence, both when the mother refuses to respond to its temper tantrum and when she cheats it of sexual climax, and that the mother's behavior in both these contexts is an effect of her own past character-formation, as determined by experiences similar to those to which she is now subjecting the child. From such a beginning, we can go on to look at other types of Balinese data, and recognize that the same formal sequence recurs in certain ceremonials in which young men attack a masked figure representing the Witch. They are power-less against her, and fall into a state of disassociation in which they symbolically turn their aggression against themselves, thus achieving an introverted climax.[18]

From such a systematic analysis of the contexts of learning and the native interpretations of context which are implicit in cultural data, we may hope to build a formal science of culture.

NOTES

1. Malinowski, B. The Sexual Life of Savages. George Routledge & Sons, Ltd. London. 1929.

2. Malinowski, B. Coral Gardens and Their Magic. 2 vols. George Allen and Unwin, Ltd. London. 1935.

3. Richards, Audrey. Hunger and Work in a Savage Tribe. George Routledge & Sons, Ltd. London. 1932.

4. In defining the contexts of human behavior, many types of non-anthropo-logical information may be necessary. For this purpose, the field anthropologist may have to borrow from almost any of the other sciences. In practice, the "context" of behavior is usually limited to a narration of those factors which the anthropologist deems important and is able to describe. Merely permissive cir-cumstances are usually omitted. For example, meteorological and geophysical cir-cumstances always play a part in permitting an interview to take place, but these factors will usually not be mentioned in the record, unless the anthropologist believes that the shape and content of the conversation was thereby affected. More serious is the common omission of physiological circumstances: the ap-petitive state of both subject and interviewer, and so on. It is usually impractical to record these in anthropological fieldwork. However, the related sciences of psychoanalysis and experimental psychology are already benefiting from their closer association with the physiological laboratory, and we should certainly look forward to a time when physiologists will collaborate in anthropological field-work and amplify the scope of the available data.

5. There is some variation among cultures in this respect. Among the Iatmul, where verbal articulacy is highly developed, my informants were certainly more culturally normal than among the Balinese, where verbal skill is rare.

6. Operationally, it is probably necessary to define a "culture" as an aggregate of collected objective data of the kinds mentioned above. This definition may later be amplified, if necessary, by inclusion of some references to the type of order imposed on the data by the scientist. If, however, we limit ourselves to the minimum operational definition, the demarcation between one "culture" and another will have to be defined in terms of causal integration. If we fall into the error of defining this demarcation in terms of homogeneity, saying that culture A shall be separated from culture B if the data included under A differ markedly from the data included under B, then we shall have great difficulty in dealing

with the differentiation of occupational, age, and sex groupings within the single culture. Still more serious, the generalization in the text above will be a mere endowing of our data with a characteristic of our own operations. If, on the other hand, we delimit our cultures by saying, "Data shall be assigned to a single culture so long as causal interdependence among the data can be recognized," ignoring for the moment the problem of the delimitation of cultures in the time dimension and the related problems of culture contact, we shall, at least, postpone these troubles.

7. Operationally, the "society" may be defined as an aggregate of those individuals actually mentioned in the data which constitute a single culture, *plus* those others about whom data can be presumed to belong to the same aggregate.

8. We have, unfortunately, no comparative data about the occurrence of these various types of latency in different cultures, where different methods of handling, carrying, and exercising the baby occur. Even for sexual latency, the data are very poor, and it is perfectly possible that, in some cultures, the potentiality for genital tumescence does not disappear in childhood. It is, however, to be expected that, in all cultures, there is a period during which the child ceases to show specifically sexual desires directed towards adults.

9. A third possibility (that all types of latency are due to topological changes in the neural network, but that these changes are a function of maturation and not brought about by the passage of neural impulses) would also be tenable. This hypothesis will, however, differ somewhat from conventional notions about maturation, in that it must account for the breaking or inhibition of previously existing arcs.

10. Neustadt, R., & A. Myerson. Quantitative sex hormone studies in homosexuality, childhood, and various neuropsychiatric disturbances. Am. J. Psychiat. 97: 542-551. 1940.

11. Specimens of these carvings, collected by the writer, were exhibited at the conference. The collection of about 1200 carvings has been deposited at the American Museum of Natural History, New York, N. Y.

12. Bateson, G. Naven. Cambridge University Press. 1936. (This book is an experiment in analyzing a New Guinea culture, on these lines.)

13. The logical proof of this assertion is, however, beyond my powers, and probably not feasible until the concepts of *eidos* and *ethos* and, indeed, the whole of *gestalt* psychology have been much more critically defined than is possible today.

14. Frank, L. K. The problems of learning. Psych. Rev. 33: 329-351. 1926.

15. Maier, N. R. F. The behavior mechanism concerned with problem solving. Psych. Rev. 47: 43-58. 1940.

16. Bateson, G. Comment on M. Mead's The Comparative Study of Culture and the Purposive Cultivation of Democratic Values. In: Science, Philosophy, and Religion, 2nd Symposium. New York, N. Y. 1942.

17. Hull, C. Mathematical-Deductive Theory of Rote Learning. Yale University Press. 1940. (This book gives experimental curves for increase in proficiency in rote learning, but does not deduce this increase from a postulate system.)

18. For photographs of the ceremonial, *see* Bateson, G., & M. Mead. Balinese Character, a Photographic Analysis. Special Pub., No. 3, N. Y. Acad. Sci. 1942.

JANE BELO

1935. "The Balinese Temper," *Character and Personality*, vol. 4: 120-146. Reprinted by courtesy of the author and of the Editor of the *Journal of Personality*.

Miss Belo's portrayal of the people of Bali—an island adjoining Java to the eastward—provides background for other studies by Margaret Mead and Gregory Bateson. See also Miss Belo's other articles, listed in the Bibliography of this book. Like the other Indonesian peoples, the Balinese have derived their culture in large part from India. Students of the region assert that many aspects of ancient Hindu culture have been preserved more fully in Bali than elsewhere.

THE BALINESE TEMPER*

JANE BELO

In examining the psychological character of a people such as the Balinese, who number more than a million, we have no choice but to take up one by one the simple habits of the individual which are common to the people as a whole, noting the patterns occurring in the adult, and how the child by his early conditioning is molded into a personality essentially Balinese. If, in an effort to cast light upon problems of personality, one wished to set forth special traits, special individual developments to be found among the Balinese, one would find it difficult to make one's self understood unless some picture had previously been drawn of the people's psychological nature, as evidenced in the general character of their ways of behaving. For what are among them universal traits might be mistaken for individual deviations. Therefore it seems advisable to describe the general trend of personality development against a background suggesting the tenor of the life, the modes of feeling and of activity, which may range from a subdued stillness to states of exalted animation without being excluded from the habitual and universal trends.

By the Balinese temper I mean the nature and ways of the people as a whole. In my presentation individual examples will serve as illustrations of the general trends, and in certain cases indicate deviations from them. I believe that the Balinese exemplify by their behavior how closely the individual may be required to conform to patterns laid down by the social group, with what rhythmic and unstrained ease he may, under such laws, accomplish the tasks exacted of him, and in what apparent contentment he may exist, when no problem is without an answer in his scheme of things. A description of the making of such adjustments, and the formation of the personality through them, may be of interest because of the foreignness of the setting, of the society in which they are made. My method will consist in an enumeration of a series of patterns of behavior, beginning with the simplest, which give to the outsider his initial impression. The simplest passages of behavior differ from our own no less than do the highly complex thought

*This study is based on four years' acquaintance with the people, during which I resided with my husband, Colin McPhee, in a wholly Balinese village, making studies of the arts, music, legends, and rituals in their intimate correlation with Balinese life.

157

mechanisms, so closely interlocked with them. Ordinary behavior, the way of walking, of sitting, of greeting acquaintances, of taking nourishment, speech-habits, gesture, and facial expression, all these differ from our own, and all are founded not only on the way of life, but on the people's conception of it, and of the place of the individual in relation to it. And conversely, the higher concepts are built up out of component units, the simpler habits of ordinary behavior. In a discussion of the Balinese temper we shall have to consider both phases, and we shall find them often interdependent and inseparable.

BEARING AND PACE

To a Westerner, the most striking characteristic in the ordinary behavior of a Balinese is the absolute poise and balance of his bearing, noticeable in his posture, his walk, his slightest gesture. All mature men and women have this poise, and even the small children develop it with remarkable rapidity. Almost never does one see a stooped or curving back even among the old people, and clumsiness and lack of coördination are rare. The impression is that of a nation favored with an unusually fine physique, with natural dignity and ease in every motion. But together with the impression of ease, one remarks a sort of *carefulness* in the bearing, as if each foot were placed in its appointed place, each turn of the head or flick of the wrist calculated not to disturb an equilibrium delicately set up, and hanging somewhere unseen within the individual. One learns that the Balinese is never unconscious of his position in space, in relation to *kadja*,[1] North, which is the direction of the mountains, and *kelod*, South, the direction of the sea; and in relation to his position above the ground, which should not be higher than that of his social superior. It would seem that a great deal of the "carefulness" in the manner of the Balinese springs from his habit of adjusting his position according to the laws of his cosmology and his social group. The other great factor is the habitual avoidance of any impulsive movement which could shock or otherwise momentarily disturb the feeling of well-being in the body.

The individual Balinese moves slowly, with deliberation. Westerners, seeing for the first time films representing the Balinese at their daily tasks, are immediately struck by the slow tempo of their actions. If a man seated in one pavilion of his house-court suddenly wishes to show something which is in another pavilion, he will rise to his feet and saunter across the intervening space, quite as if he were going for a casual stroll. He will never hurry, as we would, eager to grasp the object which has come to mind. There is plenty of time, and to hurry would be unusual, unnecessary, and stupid—a waste of energy. Walking along the roads, each individual progresses with an even, measured step. The custom is to walk in single file, probably because the trails are narrow, and even today when the gravel covered motor roads are used for long distance walking, there is only a narrow track at the side which is comfortable to bare feet. Rarely does one individual walking in single file pass another, for all go at the same rhythmic pace. This pace seems to be kept over long distances as well as short, and is hardly influenced when the walker carries a medium load (about forty pounds). Women carry such a load with facility, balanced on their heads. Men usually carry much heavier weights, divided in two parcels, one of which is slung at either end of a bamboo pole balanced on the shoulder. Invariably when the load is heavy (a hundred pounds or so) the man with the shoulder bar proceeds at a short run, almost a trot, and he keeps up this pace without ever slowing down to a walk. The idea is not to get there more quickly; but the motion of the trot vibrates the pliant shoulder-bar, so that the weights at either end swing up and down, thus relieving the pressure on the shoulder. This pace however has become customary to people heavily laden, and a woman bearing on her head one of the large offerings of rice, fruit, and cakes (often a cone four or five feet high) will proceed with the same accelerated steps that the men use under their heavy shoulder-bars.

A test of the evenness of the habitual pace, kept up over long distances, came on the occasion of an annual ceremony at a temple on the southernmost shore. A Balinese whose house stood next to mine visited the temple on that day, accompanied by his two wives and two children, approximately eight and ten years old. All carried offerings and supplies of food and betel for the journey, but no member of the little group could be said to be heavily laden. They started "in the hour before dawn," which would be about five o'clock in the morning. When I arrived at the temple by motor they were seated outside taking their meal, having already made their prayers and presented their offerings. Shortly afterward they must have started homeward, for I passed them on my return, proceeding at an even steady pace along the road. At half-past three in the afternoon they reached home, apparently not the least exhausted by their walk of over fifty miles, as registered on the speedometer of my car. Even if one assumes that they spent only half-an-hour at the temple, they covered the fifty miles in ten hours, averaging certainly no less than five miles an hour. The road led up and down over several steep hills, and at least half of the way through arid fields, with no tree to give shade. This family, whose expedition I was able to time, was only one of hundreds visiting the temple on that day, and their excursion was in no sense unusual.

PHYSICAL EXERTION AND WELL-BEING

A great part of the land lying between the high mountain district and the shore is formed in longitudinal ridges which run parallel to each other, and no great distance apart. Between these ridges are the steep-walled ravines, where the rivers flow, and where are found most of the drinking and bathing springs. Villages are apt to be placed on the high ground, so that in inter-village traffic, walkers going North and South follow an easy up or down grade along the top of the ridge. But a person travelling East and West finds many a steep climb and precipitous descent along his path. Every member of the family is accustomed to go down at least once a day to the river or the bathing-place for his bath, and many must climb up and down several times in a day—the women and girls carrying water for household needs, the men going to and fro in their work in the steeply terraced rice-fields, the small boys escorting their special charges, the ducks and the water buffalo, down from the dry ground for their daily immersion. Mothers carry babies on their hips, at the same time balancing a forty-pound jar of water on their heads, yet never do they waver in their erect posture nor vary their slow even pace on the steep and often slippery incline. Little girls of five or six already carry a coconut-shell full of water on their heads. Gradually the weight of water is increased, until, on reaching maturity, the slender girl can manage as heavy a load as her mother and aunts. Neither do the aged women shirk the task. Kintil, whom I judged to be no less than sixty, and who lacked only a few months of being a great-grandmother, made the daily descent of more than two hundred feet along an almost vertical trail, and, in wet weather or dry, never failed to carry up her jar of water. She would, I believe, hate to give up carrying water, for that would constitute an admission of her failing strength.

There is an undercurrent of superstition in the Balinese mind that to "give up" will *cause* weakness, and increased vulnerability to the dangers of illness. For illness is conceived as imposed from the outside by malevolent forces, which lurk everywhere, ready to rush into the body of anyone whose strength and purity (both physical and spiritual) are for the time below the normal, outbalanced by the share of weakness and impurity which form a part of every human being. That is why people who have undergone a trying ordeal are not spared and pampered, but urged to get up and go on as if nothing had happened to them. Women who have just given birth to a child go down to the river for their bath as soon as the three days of sequestration within the house are passed; and this sequestration (during the period of "uncleanness" following the birth) is as much to protect the village from contamination by the mother and child as to protect the latter from the attacks of evil spirits, to which they are especially vulnerable at this time. Rantoen went down to her bath as soon as she could walk following an exhausting bout of fever, and she attempted to carry up her jar of water, although the household was well supplied.

Probably this unnecessary exertion brought on the relapse—she fell down on the trail, then clambered up with her empty jar and went to bed for several more days. But the desire for the daily bath is so strong in the Balinese who dwell in the hot regions that they will take any risks rather than forego it. The bath at the end of a long day in the heat is considered essential to the feeling of well-being within the body. "If I have my bath, I shall feel well," argues the Balinese, even in illness. And Rantoen undoubtedly believed she would regain her strength more quickly if she carried up the jar of water.

The same refusal to admit weakness and to spare the sick person was shown in two cases which I witnessed. A boy fainted, and remained unconscious for an hour and twenty minutes. His relatives showed great concern, and exerted themselves tirelessly to bring him to, blowing in his ears and eyes, rubbing his feet and hands, going to fetch arak and hot peppers which they put down his nostrils. But when at last he had regained consciousness they insisted that he should walk home, a distance of half a mile or more, and refused either to allow him to be carried or to remain in a strange house. The best thing was for him to walk home as if nothing had happened. On another occasion a woman was found unconscious in a field, knocked in the head with an axe. When she had been brought to and her wound attended, she was forced to attempt to walk the hundred yards to her house, although she was a tiny thing and her husband or any one of the men present could have carried her with ease. They did support her under the arms, and on arrival at the house, lift her onto her bamboo couch. But no matter how weak, she was not to be carried home like a corpse.

ORIENTATION IN SPACE

The question of position is so significant to the Balinese because of their acute consciousness of their position in relation to the surrounding space of their world. There are three ways for a man to be: erect (standing or "going"); seated (sitting or squatting); and recumbent (the words for sleeping and lying down are the same). Even children never stand on their heads nor turn somersaults. There is felt to be something wrong about the inverted position, with the head where the feet ought to be; and one of the best-known demons, who is pictured on the astrological calendar standing on his hands, is called Kala Soengsang, to be translated Demon Upsidedown. Babies are never seen to crawl—they are held or carried until old enough to stand on their two feet. Only animals walk on all fours. I have spoken elsewhere of an incest punishment in which the offending pair are forced to crawl on all fours to a pigs' drinking trough.[2] To fall down is considered an unlucky sign, a presage that worse things may happen, occasioned by the evil forces which are only "trying their strength" in causing the harmless fall. When one of the members of my household fell and broke her arm, the entire group seemed more concerned over the fact that she had fallen than over the actual injury. They said that several of them had fallen, that now things were getting worse, and that the place should by all means be purified by a great *metjaroe* ceremony, to drive away the demons and bad spirits who were growing bolder. Falling is a shock which upsets the nice balance of well-being, just as the feeling of a rush of blood to the head in an inverted position is uncomfortable, and must therefore be wrong.[2a] Fathers and grandfathers who hold their young children in their laps for hours at a time never swing them about nor cast them in the air as ours are apt to do. Men and women will always endeavor to keep their erect posture, their even pace, their absolute balance, regardless of obstacles in the way, and to cultivate this tendency in the child. White men who scamper down a hillside, in excess of good spirits and momentum, or who leap over a stream, will always evoke laughter in the Balinese who walks sedately on, stepping into the water as if it did not exist, so long as the even measure of his gait is not interrupted. Because his feet are bare and the water warm, there would seem to be no reason to exert himself to jump over the stream. If it were not that the Balinese never jump, one would say that their habits are only better adjusted than ours to a climate uniformly hot, where it is better to conserve one's energy for those exertions required in the daily work. But the systematic avoidance of all shocks and pains and disturbances of the circulation of the blood characteristic of all adult Balinese would indicate that a more specialized consciousness of the body is involved. And this theory is supported by the fact that the average Balinese, although he has plentiful supplies of distilled arak and palm-wine, does not like to get drunk. The feeling of confusion, the lack of his usual surefootedness and sense of equilibrium, are so unpleasant to him that he does not often risk the experience. And the whirling of the universe which precedes nausea is positively terrifying. Then he is indeed *lost*.

Malay people have a term for the sensation of being lost, *keliru*. In the Balinese language the word is *paling*. To be *paling*, they say, is "not to know where North is"; in other words, he is *paling* who has lost his sense of direction, or who has lost the sense of his own position in relation to the geography of his world. One man whom I knew was taken for a trip in a motor car. He fell asleep during the ride. When the car stopped, he awoke, and leaping out, looked about him desperately, crying, "Where's North, where's North? I'm *paling*."

So accustomed are the Balinese to know where they are in relation to the points of the compass that all instructions of direction are given in these terms, rather than in "right and left," or such designations as "towards me," "away from the wall," etc. The Balinese says "when you come to the cross-roads, take the turn to the West"; "pull the table southward"; "he passed me going North"—not "going towards the market"; even among musicians, "hit the key to the East of the one you are hitting." When for any reason this sense of direction is temporarily lost, when, as we phrase it, a man feels "turned around," he is not only uncomfortable but he is quite unable to function. We once sent a small boy of eight to a distant village where he was to learn to dance, living in the house of his teacher. Riding in the car, the child lost his sense of direction. When we visited him three days later, he had not begun his lessons, for he was still *paling*. "How can I tell him to turn to the East, to advance towards the North, when he is *paling?*" said the teacher. The boy was returned to his village, where, once on familiar ground, he found himself. After several days he went back to the house of the teacher, intently watching every curve of the winding road. But it was no good—he was again *paling*. He grew anxious, and was unable to eat and sleep. Then someone thought of taking him out into the fields, where he could see the high cone of the Goenoeng Agoeng, the highest mountain, rising to North. He was cured of his trouble on the spot, and had no recurrence of it during the six weeks of his stay in the village. He seemed happy there and made great progress with his dancing.[3]

As a rule the small children are not bothered with the responsibility of direction, for they play within the circumscribed limits of the particular *bandjar* (division of the village) which is theirs, or in the outlying rice fields. On this ground they are at home. When they visit other villages they go in the company of their parents or near relatives, an older brother or cousin, who knows the way. But their consciousness of position in space develops naturally together with the use of language, and the words "kadja," "kelod," "koaeh," and "kangin" are frequently heard in the chatter of the four and five year olds. When such a group was making drawings at my house, they arranged between them which was to have the South wall, which the East, and so on.

Every Balinese sleeps with his head either to the North (in North Bali, South; see footnote 1) or to the East. He may not even lie down for a moment in the opposite direction, for the feet are dirty and may not be put in the place of the head. To lie in the reversed position is said to be "lying like a dead man," although the Balinese in South Bali are not buried with their heads to the South. The implication is that only a dead man, who could not help himself, would lie in this dangerously wrong way.

SENSE OF SOCIAL ORIENTATION

By imitation of their elders the children soon learn also on which "level" they should sit at formal gatherings. Within the courtyard

of the Balinese house are a number of pavilions, each on a foundation
of sandstone varying in height from two to four feet. On the platforms
so formed are couches of bamboo, constructed between the pillars
which support the roof. It is customary to sit either upon the clay
floor of the foundation-platform or on the couches, which also may
vary in height. Thus are provided a hierarchy of sitting-places, whose
relative height may be easily ascertained, as the pavilions are without
walls.

In family groups no particular attention is paid to the arrangement
of levels, and a little girl does not have to stop to think whether or
not she is sitting higher than grandfather. But on the advent of a visitor,
especially if he be of higher caste than the family of the host, politeness requires that he be given the highest place. At a wedding which I
attended of a young man of noble birth, a nephew of the Radja, or
Regent of the district, the most formal rules were observed in the seating of the guests. On the floor of the highest pavilion sat the High
Priests. On a near-by lower pavilion sat the men of rank, and across
the court on a still lower pavilion, the women of the family, also of
noble birth. Some chairs were provided for the male guests of the
"advanced" type, but these were avoided by the more humble members
of the group. Even those seated on chairs were on a level inferior to
that where the High Priests sat, crosslegged on the floor. Servants and
retainers, people of low caste, came and went through the court.
Other pavilions for their use were provided in a rear court, where
they would eventually receive a share of the feast; but if any man
wished to be seated in the court of honor, he might, after making a
reverence with joined hands, squat down on the ground anywhere
without fear of offending his social superiors. When all were assembled, the Radja appeared. He marched across the courtyard, mounted
the steps of the pavilion where the High Priests sat, and seated himself crosslegged on the bamboo couch which formed the highest level
within the court.

THE PLACE OF THE CHILDREN

On occasions such as this when the strictest etiquette must be observed the children are not much in evidence, so quiet are they. Small
babies may be present, but they are not heard to cry, for at the first
whimper they are given the breast of the mother. This applies to
children up to two and three years old, provided no younger brother
or sister has taken their place. Aunts, cousins, and elder sisters (from
the age of eight or nine) habitually carry or hold children of this age.
But it is not customary for a woman other than the mother to suckle
the child. A youngster may scuttle across the intervening space which
divides the women from the men, scramble into its father's lap, and sit

there quiet and solemn-eyed. This is not in the least embarrassing to
the fathers, who are extremely affectionate and proud to show off their
young. It is not unusual to see a player in the gamelan orchestra holding on his knees for two or three hours his small child, while he reaches
around it, beating the keys of his resounding instrument.

As the children grow older, the boys tend to clan together in groups
of their own age, whereas the girls stay more closely beside their
mothers. One often sees a gang of small boys playing in the village
street, flying kites made of a leaf, or a captive dragon-fly, or playing
"jacks" or gambling games with pebbles. In contrast to their elders,
they do run, skip, and tumble, but rarely does the play take a rough
turn. Quarrels consist of brusque words and threatening gestures on the
part of the stronger child, while the weaker immediately assumes an
attitude of submission, or, if he is struck, utters a plaintive "ado!"
equivalent to our "ouch!" The utterance of this pain-word seems to
satisfy the oppressor, who desists. I never witnessed nor heard of a
case where one small boy "beat up" another. Certainly the hierarchy of
ages recognized in any family group tends to discourage fighting, for
every child knows that he is allowed to "speak down to," scold, and
order about his younger brothers and cousins, just as he himself is
spoken down to and ordered about by brothers and all relatives older
than he. The system works smoothly, for if one is humiliated by an
elder, one may take out one's venom on a younger member of the
familiar group. The accumulation of ill-humor does not fall too heavily
upon the youngest child, for he can always take refuge behind the
protective skirts of the mother, who is older, and therefore in authority, over his oppressor. So are the scales balanced.

Very small girls are sometimes seen in the company of the boys who
play in the streets. But by the time the girls reach the age of responsibility—seven or eight—they are more apt to remain in the housecourt
with the mother, taking a part in her work. Or if they are seen
along the road, they carry on their hip a younger child entrusted to
their care.[4] These diminutive nursemaids saunter up and down, or
stand watching the play of the boys, prevented from joining in the activity by the responsibility, and the actual weight of their charges.
Girls do not play games, for gambling is a man's occupation. Neither
can they share in one of the boys' favorite diversions, that of drumming away for hours on the instruments of the village orchestra, which
are generally left in an open pavilion accessible to the children. This is
another occupation which belongs to the men. The girls stand by
watching, and do not think of trying their hand at it, although they
are not actually forbidden to do so. I have known one or two girls,
dancers, who had developed quite a proficiency as musicians, but their
cases were exceptional. In the same way girls are not expected to paint

and draw. When I sent out a call to a number of villages for the drawings of children from four to ten years, and distributed materials sufficient for all, not a single girl sent in a drawing, nor would the little girls of my own village attempt any drawings even under repeated encouragement. Yet these same girls are learning from their mothers the complicated arts of making offerings, cutting designs from palmleaf, and weaving.

BEHAVIOR AT THE PLAYS

Whenever there is a performance of dancing, drama, or the shadow-show, the entire village attends. The audience is packed closely around the four sides of the "stage"—an oblong of level ground marked off with bamboos. The first arrivals squat as near as possible, folded up into the least possible space and pressed against each other, the late comers stand in rows eight or ten deep at the back, the rear-most able to catch only an occasional glimpse of a performer's headdress. In this tight formation the audience remains from the beginning, which for a play may be anywhere between the hours of nine and midnight, to the end which comes about dawn. The whole temper of the audience is, from the actor's standpoint, ideal—watching, concentrated as one man, happy and pleasantly disposed in the warm contact of a large group of their kind, in festive mood, ready to enjoy themselves to the utmost. On the appearance of a hero, particularly graceful and gorgeous in his attire, a whispered "Bèh!" of admiration issues from a hundred mouths; and when the clowns cavort, or a rough joke is made, the entire audience rocks with mirth, the high shrieks of the women's laughter rising above the guffaws of the men. The smallest children, from two or three years upward, constitute the first rows of the audience surrounding the stage. They arrive long before the performers have any thought of beginning, and sit, in quiet expectancy, sometimes for several hours before the play begins. If for any reason a child arrives late, he will with confidence squeeze his way through the crowd, pushing past people of higher rank and superior in age, to a good place in the very front. During the performance, the children watch every detail of the action with intentness.[5] Generally even the tiniest ones stay through the night, although they fall asleep for hours at a time, and only manage to wake up for the most exciting parts, battles, or the enacting of bewitchment.

Older boys and girls, especially those who have passed adolescence, come to the performance in groups of two or three friends; the girls with their arms entwined about each other, the boys often holding hands. Such a group of boys will arrange to sit down in a place immediately behind a group of girls, so that, as the press in the audience increases, they will be huddled more and more together. It would be unseemly to stroke or to caress a member of the opposite sex in public. But if a girl is so placed that she must lean against one's knee, or her shoulder touch one's shoulder and her sleepy head droop, who can find fault? In the dim light—for the stage is illumined by only one or two flickering oil lamps, and the audience is in almost complete obscurity—flirtation is favored. Occasionally a girl rises and leaves the audience, to be followed after a short interval by the youth who has been seated near her. One supposes that a rendezvous has been arranged for a few moments of stolen love in the surrounding darkness.

DEVELOPMENT OF DECORUM

By the time boys and girls have fully matured, they must behave with the decorous composure proper for adults. A boy of fifteen who belonged to my household was sometimes guilty of acts of clumsiness or thoughtless irresponsibility. He broke a plate in the washing of it, or he quietly made away with half a jar of the master's jam. These misdemeanors I was apt to excuse on the grounds of his youth. But the mature men were more stern with him. "Among us," they said, "a boy of that age is considered already big. He may not behave like a small child." Very marked was the change which came in Tjamploen, a talented little dancing girl, as she passed adolescence. When I first knew her she was a wiry child of eleven or twelve, the points of her breasts barely beginning to show. At that age she was a little devil, nervous and full of life, wriggling about, always up to some prank or mischief. A gifted mimic, she would make fun of anyone or anything, and go off into hilarious laughter at her own jests, bending her slim body back and forth, slapping her thighs, or the shoulder of any person who happened to be near her. Two years later she had grown tall, and her breasts had rounded out. She was no longer eligible to dance in the group of three little *lègong* dancers of her village, although it was to a large extent her own talent which had made these dancers famous, so that they were in demand to play at festivals in the surrounding district. Tjamploen trained a new set of six-year-old dancers for her village. Then she was engaged by various other villages within a radius of ten or fifteen miles to train their dancers. The fact of her growing up was forcibly impressed upon her by the change in her social function. She began to behave with dignity: to carry herself decorously, to sit down carefully with both legs to one side, not sprawling anywhere, to speak when she was spoken to, to keep upon her face an habitual expression of composure. As she learned manners, she lost a great deal of the vivid spontaneous charm of her personality. But in restraining her wild ways, she acquired a new charm, that of a demure and gracious feminine creature. When still another year had passed (which would make her about fourteen or fifteen), I saw her dance again, demonstrating before a new pupil. By this time the restraint in her bearing had become natural to her, and the change was strangely reflected in her dancing. She went through the dance in which she had so excelled as a child, without the slightest deviation from the traditional motions, postures, and step-figures which she had always used— and yet the whole flavor of the dance was different. Instead of the wiry, electric little body whose stick-like arms bent in sharp angles, accenting the beat of the music, whose fingers quivered in the classical hand positions, whose little head sat stiffly on a rigid neck, whose feet stamped out with tense exactitude the vibrant music—instead of this stylized, puppet-like figure was a woman, with rounded arms, and hands of classical perfection, on her face a blank composure almost beautiful, who moved forward sedately, or glided sideways with easy grace, her curves softening the intended angles of the postures. This smooth performance of an accomplished dancer, now grown to maturity, had a beauty of its own. But it was not *lègong* dancing as it should be. Seeing it, one could not help agreeing with the Balinese, who say that only children can dance *lègong*. For the very grace and womanliness of a bigger girl infuse a disturbing element into the dance, which is in its essence sexless, impersonal, acute, and pure in its stylization.

Tjamploen still laughs, and makes jokes, and her eyes snap with merriment. But her role has changed from that of a talented child to that of an unwed maiden, whose behavior shows modesty and restraint, for those are the qualities which will attract a desirable husband.

ETIQUETTE IN SPEECH, POSTURE, AND MANNERS

I have tried to give a suggestion of the strict order in the behavior of the Balinese people, and how this order is dictated by their way of life, their social and religious concepts, which hold them to a rigid pattern of what is fitting. In the use of language, as in other matters, definite and complex rules must be followed. The Balinese language, rich in terms with minutely differentiated meanings, is also stratified into words of all levels, which may be roughly subdivided into High and Low Balinese. Low Balinese is the familiar and current language, used between members of a family and to all friends and intimates, except when there is a disparity of caste between the speakers. A man of low caste must address his social superior in High Balinese, and he will be answered in Low. The matter is further complicated when a man of intermediate caste is being discussed, for the commoner must choose a word in referring to him neither so low as to be insulting to the ears of the noble he is addressing, nor so high as to be discourteous, for the very highest words should be reserved for reference to the noble himself.[6] Special words are to be used only in reference to animals, and to apply one of these lowest words to a man constitutes an un-

forgiveable insult. Strangers who meet address each other in High
Balinese, asking "Whence do you come? Where are you going?,"
and follow this immediately with a leading question designed to discover the rank of the interlocutor, so that the language appropriate to
him may be at once adopted. There is no "farewell" in the language.
Visitors must ask their host's permission to depart, and the answer to
this request may be either the common "yes," a dismissal, or a choice
of a polite word for "go," carrying a courteous inflection because of
the relative highness of the word used.

Less complex, but equally rigid, rules prescribe the actual way of
sitting. Both men and women habitually squat on their heels, and this
is the position most readily assumed when anyone stops for a moment
what he is doing, either for conversation or for a short rest from hard
labor (and it may be noted in passing that the Balinese seem to take,
automatically, a rest of five or ten minutes out of every hour of hard
work; look at any ten men at work in the sun, and two will be sitting
under a tree; half an hour later, two others will be resting). The
squatting position may also be held over long periods, in the fulfillment
of any task conveniently done on or near the ground, such as the
playing of certain musical instruments, or the chopping and hashing of
foodstuffs on a wooden block, in preparation for a feast. In taking the
position the Balinese, be he a man of eighty or a child of eight, lowers
himself with the back held straight, at the same time pulling the loin-
cloth with his two hands tight over the thighs, so that the folds will
not hang and expose him indecently. Women are of course, equally
modest, and the little girls learn this trick earlier than the boys, for
they are generally given a strip of cloth to wrap around them at the
age of four or five, whereas the boys run naked several years longer.

Women sit with their legs bent back from the knees, both legs to
one side. They may not take the crosslegged position which is proper
for the men. A high priest, who has a right to the place of honor, will
on entering a European house choose not the most softly cushioned,
but the highest chair, and he will cross his legs upon the seat of it.
Certain ascetics of noble caste, who have bound themselves to strict
rules of behavior, may not sit down to eat facing in any direction except North or East. In the palaces of the nobility men of humble rank
may sit or squat, but they are not allowed to stand or walk while a
prince is seated. When they have to move about, fulfilling orders, they
advance in a half-crouching position. So strongly felt is the matter of
relative height that a man may ask one's permission before venturing
to climb up a coconut tree to bring one refreshment.

The Balinese prefer to eat alone, and it is forbidden to speak to anyone who is eating. To speak to him would anger the god that is in
him.[7] In some villages there used to be a fine imposed on any man who

entered another's house and disturbed him while he was eating. Of this fine part was paid directly to the affronted person, part to the community, in compensation for disturbing the peace. Within the household there is no sitting down to a family meal. Each member takes his leaf-plate of rice at his own pleasure, carrying it off into a corner, often turning his back on his friends and relatives.[8] It is only proper to take food in the right hand while eating, although of course both hands are used in the preparation of it. Along the roads, at the markets, and at all performances are little stalls where refreshments are sold. But I have known several Balinese who said it was improper to eat in the street, and that they were "too ashamed" to do it.

The feeling of modesty—no other word seems to apply—attached to eating does not apply to drinking, and anyone will drink anywhere, without making a fuss about it. Similarly no shame is felt for urinating, which is done by both men and women along the public roads, in the open fields, anywhere except within the housecourt or on holy ground. But for defecating the people retire to relative privacy, "where the pigs are," out of sight. The many pigs and dogs act as scavengers, and may be relied upon to do away with all the filth.

Where there are gushing springs, bathing places are constructed, with walls dividing off the place of the women from that of the men. When the rivers are used for bathing, the sexes divide into groups, the men taking the upstream position, the women the downstream. But within each group modesty is shown, and the genitals may not be exposed even to a member of the same sex. The men cover themselves with one hand, the women lift their skirts gradually, and suddenly plunge waist deep in the water. Dressing and undressing may be done in public by both men and women, for their clothes are of such a nature that they can be changed without immodesty.[9]

MANIFESTATIONS OF THE EMOTIONAL LIFE

The Balinese are universally afraid in the dark, and the fear of *léjaks*, living male and female sorcerers in supernatural form, is intensified between the hours of midnight and dawn, when these creatures are supposed to roam. Even grown boys and men will not visit at night unholy places such as the graveyard, the crossroads, certain trees and bridges where supernatural manifestations are frequent. They are afraid to walk along the dark village streets at night, unless accompanied, but if a man must go alone he sings in a loud voice to frighten away the *léjaks*, or to keep his spirits up. His housecourt is his haven. The encircling clay walls, the high ceremonial entrance gate, and the magic strip of wall immediately within this gate (to block the path of evil spirits) give him a feeling of security, sleeping upon the open pavilions. But he prefers not to sleep alone. If he has passed the age when he wishes to sleep next his wife, he will take one or two of his little sons to bed with him. Small children sleep with their parents, grandparents, or huddle in a group together. When a group of men who are strangers are passing through a village, they may take shelter for the night in the men's communal pavilion which stands by the roadside—an unprotected place. They curl up as close as possible to each other, like young puppies, the body of one curving around that of his neighbor, with often an arm or a leg thrown over him. A group may be so compact that if one turns over the whole group must turn. The language contains terms for light and heavy sleepers, but as a rule they sleep soundly and are hard to rouse. They are afraid to awaken each other, lest the soul of the sleeper be wandering. But the taboo seems to imply more danger to the one doing the awakening than the one awakened, for a boy who says "I do not dare to wake him" will show no objection if a foreigner takes upon himself the responsibility of awakening one of his fellows.

As has been mentioned, a man may not touch a woman, even his wife, before others. He may not touch a woman's clothes, nor should his clothes touch hers, as, for instance, in a trunk. If it is necessary to pack them together, the man's clothes must be on top. But in the privacy supplied by darkness the taboos are lifted. Lovers and married people may caress each other freely. Favorite caresses are the *tjioem*, the affectionate or passionate "sniff" which replaces our kiss, and the *saling ngaras*, "exchange of strokings," a term applied to the rubbing of cheek on cheek, both slowly turning their heads from side to side, so that the lips do come into play as they brush past each other. Love-scenes depicted in the paintings, and described in the literature, suggest that many of the refinements of the art of love which belong to Hindu tradition have been taken over by the Balinese. But for reasons of their own, which have already been made sufficiently clear, the Balinese do not use the reversed posture, nor may the woman be above. In sexual play only the left hand may be used, since the right is used for eating.

A woman is popularly supposed to have within her a *manik*. The term *manik* is applied to jewels, and to a sprite which sits in coconut trees, and is pursued by Kilap Krèbèk Geroedoeg, Thunder-and-Lightning, who, when he catches the *manik*, causes the coconut tree to be burnt up. But the *manik* in a woman is of a different sort. In sexual intercourse her *manik* is repeatedly "hit," and this contact causes it to become larger and larger until it becomes a child. After the birth of the child, she gets a new *manik*. It is possible, though by no means sure, that the Balinese conceive orgasm of both man and woman to be caused when the male organ finally achieves contact with the *manik*.[10]

Although a free display of the affection between the sexes, except in private, is forbidden, the Balinese have a strong tendency to hold on to and caress each other in all relations where no sexual connotation is implied. Fathers and mothers, grandfathers and grandmothers, love to fondle the young children, to press their faces into them and "sniff" them, just as in the relation between a man and a woman. Two girls, two boys, or two bearded ancients will stroll along a road holding hands, or with their arms about each other. Such gestures should not be misconstrued as evidences of homosexuality, for they are no more than the habitual expressions of a demonstratively affectionate people.

Manifestations of anger are remarked much less frequently than those of love, fear, and affection in the everyday life. An equable temper is certainly the characteristic one among the Balinese. If a man is easily angered, he is said to have *kapala angin*, a Malay expression meaning "a windy head." Although one often hears voices raised in explosive and admonitory speech, they can hardly be said to be expressing anger, for among the adults, as among the children, superiors have always the right to call down their inferiors, an elder brother to speak harshly to a younger, a man to "order" (never simply to ask) his wife to do something for him. Each Balinese is habituated to thinking of himself as relatively more or less powerful than all the other members of his familiar group. And if he is less powerful, he obeys naturally and usually without remonstrance. By contrast, in larger groups, such as communal organizations, whose members are on a less intimate footing with each other, great care is taken to preserve the equality between the members. Each man is reluctant to appear to be giving an order or dictating in any way to his social equal. For this reason, in any group of workers the man whom we would call the "foreman" seems always inefficient and lacking in administrative powers; and the resulting accomplishment has a lively, if haphazard, character, brought about by the enthusiasm of the various individuals working together virtually without a leader. One has the impression that it is fear of angering his fellows which prevents the Balinese from assuming a dominant attitude towards persons outside of his familiar group.

When anger does appear, it usually follows the pattern of the Malay "running amok," also recognized in Bali. The literature is filled with episodes in which a man, even a prince or Radja, who is overcome with grief or thwarted in his desires, "becomes confused in his mind, and retires to his sleeping-apartment, where he lies for many days and many nights, refusing both food and drink." This brooding state is the first stage in the pattern, when the man remains alone, nursing his grievances, until he has worked himself into a trance-like state, and he will have the strength to rush out and commit deeds of violence. Tales of warriors describe the stirring up of anger before going into combat; and all war dances have brooding passages interspersed between the gestures and expressions of fierce and terrifying advance. Bravery in itself is not highly valued. It is considered more natural for a man to be under the sway of fear than of anger. A man shows no embarrassment over his fear—he says quite simply "I do not dare," whether the project in question is a midnight visit to the graveyard, or climbing a coconut tree on a day of the astrological calendar when it is forbidden. The things which a man will not dare to do are those which the experience of his forebears has shown to be unwise, and to behave with intrepidity without good reason would be to court disaster, not only for himself but perhaps for the whole community.

DEVIANTS

We have seen that in such a social scheme each individual has his place, and he has only to do what is expected of him to fit with nicety into the life of the group. But there are occasions when an individual finds it impossible to conform, and at these times disturbance and maladjustment appear. Certain temperaments, for instance, are not amenable to the national habit of submissive obedience. Women with fiery dispositions may run away from their husbands, taking shelter with their own families, and refusing to return, or departing with a lover.[11] A small boy of eight told the following story of his rebellion against his father's authority, the events described having occurred when he was no more than six or seven:

"My father beat my mother too hard, and I became too angry. Then my father beat me very hard. I followed him when he went out to work in the ricefields. I took money from the pocket of his jacket which he had laid down on the edge of the fields. I ran away. For a month I did not go home.

"With the money I bought rice in the market, and I stayed out all day in the rice fields, and I never saw my father and my mother. At night I would go into the house of one of my other fathers (uncles) and sleep with the children. My father and mother did not know where I was. Then one day my mother saw me. She wept, and begged me to come home. I went home.

"My father was only silent."

In this encounter, since the father did not beat him on his return, the child seems to have triumphed over the man.

Another deviant is Madé, who rebelled not so much against paternal authority as against the prescribed rules of tradition. He is a young man of impulsive temperament, with ways unusually quick and nervous in a Balinese, quick to laugh and quick to be angered, extremely efficient when engaged in tasks which interest him, lazy and unreliable at all other tasks. Born in a small hamlet far from the town, and at several miles' distance from the motor road, he decided when still a boy to become a chauffeur. He left his farmer parents, and went to live with relatives in the town. There he attended school, learned to speak Malay, and began to pick up from older boys the knowledge of his chosen trade. He served his apprenticeship with them, receiving their teaching in return for the performance of menial duties. When he had sufficient knowledge, he in turn got a job as chauffeur, and was able to marry, buying with the money he earned the rice which he had not been able to raise on his family land. (So strong is the farming background in Balinese life that any man who has had employment and loses it automatically goes back to tilling the land until he can find new work.) Although Madé is skillful as a driver and mechanic, he is not very successful. The very qualities which made him turn from the environment and occupation to which he was born, and to which his forebears had for generations conformed, impede his progress as a chauffeur. He refuses to carry out orders unless it pleases him. He is impatient with any part of his work which is not mechanical. He will drive tirelessly for several hundred miles, and cheerfully apply himself to any necessary repairs in a breakdown. But if after a short journey he is asked to lift out a parcel from the car, he calls another to do it for him—a very unusual thing in Balinese who are not of high caste, as they are universally reluctant to ask their equals to serve them. Another unusual quality is his lack of the sense of relaxation common to most Balinese. Generally they will sit for hours without impatience, waiting for something to happen, and they seem to find pleasant the state of doing nothing. Often they drop off to sleep. But Madé could not be left alone for ten minutes in a car; he would be off on some errand of his own, to bargain for coconuts or to flirt with some pretty girl at a market stall. He took rebukes from his masters with ill grace, flaring up in insolence, or sulking and glowering to himself. To cover up his impetuosity and his shirking of explicit orders, he developed habits of dishonesty. All these things caused him to make an unsatisfactory chauffeur, and he repeatedly lost his position, whether he worked for Europeans, or for Chinese or Arab car owners. He is an impulsive spender, vain about his costume and the prestige afforded him by his possessions. The money that he earns is soon gone, and he will probably never save enough, as many of the young men do, to buy a secondhand car of his own. This is the case of an unusually ill-adapted Balinese. It is curious to note that such a type cannot adjust itself to the new order any more than to the old. He makes many friends and many enemies among the Balinese. Men and women respond to his spontaneous charm, his vivacity and gayety as a companion. But in his friendly relations he is always getting into trouble, for he will not stick to the rules of the game.

THE FORCE OF TRADITION

It is in contemplating the character of such a man that one realizes, in contrast, how closely the majority of the Balinese do conform to the scheme laid down by tradition, and how well-mannered, balanced, and relaxed they appear. The babies do not cry, the small boys do not fight, the young girls bear themselves with decorum, the old men dictate with dignity. Every one carries out his appointed task, with respect for his equals and superiors, and gentleness and consideration for his dependents. The people adhere, apparently with ease, to the laws governing the actions, big and small, of their lives. Since the material conditions of their existence have remained for many hundreds of years static, it has been possible for these laws to grow up, to be sifted and tested over a long period, until they have reached a code eminently suitable to the people whom they govern. For this reason it becomes easy for the child to take over the ways of his elders—the more forcibly impressed upon him because of the weight of tradition behind them, and the fear of transgressing the laws which have been shown by experience to be acceptable to the ever-present gods and demons. Actually the child is afforded no choice at all under the sanction of the community. He has only to obey the prescriptions of tradition to become an adult happily adjusted to the life which is his. And if the child is a girl, she begins very early to feel how her rôle is differentiated from that of a boy. The women accept without rancor the rôle of an inferior. It is simply that they have their being on a different plane from the men. In a society with so many stratifications, that of age within the family, of rank and of relative wealth as between families, the place of woman as an inferior is not seen as a hardship. The system of stratification works smoothly, as a rule, and all those individuals who conform to it seem happy. It is a part of the very order which gives to the life of the Balinese its stability.

WHEN THE RULES MAY BE BROKEN

The Balinese way of life even provides an organized release from the rigid code, times when individuals who feel the need of it may break almost all the rules of decorum. These are the occasions of intense and fevered group activity. There is no space here to describe these manifestations in detail, and a few examples of what I mean must suffice. In the prolonged and enthusiastic rehearsals of musicians, actors, and dancers, when all work together in a group, no attention is paid to relative rank, and a performer of noble birth takes his place in equality with the group—he sits on a level with his social inferiors, and bows to their will in matters of artistic production, if their talent be superior to his. At communal feasts men who are accustomed to eating in private gather in groups to partake of the unusual viands and delicacies which they have prepared. Here the taboos do not quite break down, for although they regale themselves with relish, no conversation is allowed between the members feasting together. At the celebration of cremations, several hundred men together cast off their habitual carefully poised bearing, and taking up the body of their friend, or the tower which is to convey him to the cremation place, they shout, they leap, they lift their arms in threatening gestures, they whirl around and around in a mass of vigorously stamping, kicking, and entangled limbs, falling down, trampling upon their fellows, hurling themselves into a pool of mud and besplattering each other with howls of glee. Again, a group of villagers wishing to divine the will of the gods goes into trance—tears stream down the face of a young girl, a woman sobs hysterically, an old man trembles as in an ague, a youth with rolling eyes and thrashing limbs tries to force burning coals into his mouth. Or in a ceremony for the propitiation of the King of Demons, in the form of a grotesque figure of a lion, a group of men and boys clusters about, shouting, prancing, pressing with all the strength of both arms the point of a kris into their own naked chests. One holds the handle of the weapon on the ground, with the point upward, and hurls his body upon it, throwing both feet in the air so that he will strike with all his weight. The term *riboet*, a Malay word meaning "storm," is applied to a group in such an excited state. Acting under the powerful stimulus of mass-emotion, each man forgets to be cautious, to be dignified, to be afraid. The minor fears of pain and bodily disturbance are for the time forgotten. When the frenzy is carried to the pitch of trance, the

Dance in Bali. Active trance. *Photo by Margaret Mead and Gregory Bateson, courtesy of American Museum of Natural History.*

In repose. *Photo by Jane Belo, courtesy of American Museum of Natural History.*

Balinese is to a great extent in a state of anaesthesia, able to dance upon hot coals or to wound himself with a dagger (although they themselves say that if the trance is sufficiently deep the flesh will resist the dagger and no wound will be sustained).But even without trance, every individual who participates in the excitement is free to break the rules without experiencing fear or shame for his unusual behavior. He is secure in the consciousness that he is one of many, that the crowd moves as he does.

It has seemed necessary to mention, however briefly, these forms of activity which are in sharp contrast to the slow deliberate tempo, the quiet dignity and balanced equilibrium of the habitual movements. For the Balinese at their daily tasks lead a life of reserved, steady—almost plodding—application to hard labor, made easier by the absolute lack of tension or of any pressure from the sense of time, and by the rhythmic flow of their motions interspersed with suitable periods of rest. But this existence, they say, is dull and lonely without festivals and celebrations. Luckily their religion provides many occasions for celebration, and at these times the people burst forth in a riot of true *fun*, when all together they adorn themselves, they take part with enthusiasm in the elaborate preparation of offerings and the decoration of the temples, they enjoy to the utmost presentations of dancing, music, and drama, which the religion prescribes. It is significant that the audience for these presentations takes as much delight in them as the performers. Their own arts are to them completely satisfying, a fulfillment in the life of the people for whom they have been evolved. At such festivals one is impressed by the joyousness, the gayety with which the Balinese seem carried away. And just as these joyous occasions punctuate the dreary round of everyday life, so do the occasions of wild frenzy break into it, affording the individual a necessary release. If it were not for these organized departures from the habitual tempo, it would not be possible for the individual to conform, at all other times, to the rigid order of behavior which is exacted from him. And therefore we must recognize the two aspects, the quiet, relaxed, and peaceful tenor of the private life, and the intense and spontaneous exaltation of group activity, both of which are essential to the Balinese temper.

INTERPRETATION

In conclusion, perhaps, it will be well to stress once more the ease and relaxation in the ordinary behavior of the Balinese, so that an impression will not be left that any strain is caused by need to maintain a balanced equilibrium and a perfect orientation in social and geographical respects. On the contrary, the rules by which they abide seem to supply a simplification of behavior. For the Balinese life is divided into two phases quite opposed to those of the modern city dweller in our world; the Balinese works in relaxation, and in his pleasure finds intense stimulation, whereas our city dweller works under a strain of intense stimulation, and for his pleasure seeks relaxation. If there should be any doubt of the difference in tension between the two psychological types, let us imagine how the city dweller would react to certain conditions in Balinese life, as, for instance, living in a courtyard shared by ten or fifteen members of his immediate family, divided only by pavilions without walls; or sleeping in such close proximity as has been described, with a number of others; or enjoying a dramatic performance lasting for eight or nine hours, crouched in a press of bodies comparable only to one of our subway jams. These things do not offend nor put any strain upon the Balinese, because of the relaxation of his mood. Likewise he is able to wait for long periods without showing impatience, and to accept with composure frustration of his plans, saying simply, "It did not happen." It may be said that the agricultural way of life, requiring suitable physical exertion, and producing in a direct way the food supply, so that there may be no anxiety about it for anyone, contributes to the mental poise of the people; also that the children are surrounded with affection, and given very early a part in the work of the family group, so that they grow up feeling beloved and useful, which gives to them as individuals a sense of security. And because the rules for orientation, posture, facial expression, speech, and so forth are so universally accepted, they soon become habitual, and are carried out automatically by the people without any conscious application, without any of the strain which they would cause to us. The immutability of all the laws of conduct relieves the individual of any responsibility except that of obeying them. He does not doubt their rightness, since they have always been so. And since they are his habits, he does not have even to think of them. Beyond this, his only cares are specific misfortunes, which may always occur, but which he considers outside his power to control. Illness, flood, and famine, these are signs of the anger of the gods, and of the dominance, for the time, of the forces of evil. The religious concepts make the cause clear, and they supply, too, the remedy. Offerings must be prepared, purifications and celebrations carried out, for the propitiation of the demons and the glorification of the gods. Although it may seem to us that the Balinese lives in ever present fear of demons and of evil spirits, the strain is actually not great because the remedy is known and prescribed. Even in some cases charged with much superstitious fear, such as the birth of unlucky twins or the occurrence of certain forms of incest, when the entire village is rendered unclean, tradition takes care of the wrong by requiring temporary banishment of the offenders and elaborate purification rituals. In this way the burden of responsibility is lifted from the offenders and their fellow-villagers who are affected. Tradition tells them what to do in compensation for the wrong. When it is done, no weight of sin or guilt rests on the individual. He has in such matters, as in all other aspects of his life, no choice, no decisions to be made, only the responsibility to maintain the order which he and his society consider established and proved. To judge how suitable and how desirable is such an order, we can only take the evidence of Balinese behavior as it appears to us. If we see in the equilibrated, delicately adjusted, and essentially unstrained behavior of the people the clue to their happy temper, we must conclude that a static traditional culture such as theirs, solving all problems, prescribing every act, does form a desirable background against which well-balanced personalities may be reared.

NOTES

1. The mountains which form the central part of the island are conceived as the abode of the gods, and the highest and most holy place. The sea is by contrast the lowest place, and although there is also a god of the sea, the sea and the seashore are conceived as unholy, and all that is filthy must be cast there, or into the rivers which carry their own filth down to the sea. As the present observations were made in South Bali, for the sake of convenience *kadja* is translated North and *kelod* South. On the other side of the mountains, in North Bali, *kadja* means South, and *kelod* North, since the relative position of the inhabitants to the mountains is reversed. *Kangin*, East, and *kaoeh*, West, remain the same in both localities.

2. See the author's paper, "On Rites and Customs Connected with the Birth of Twins in Bali," in the *Tijdschrift voor Indische Taal, Land & Volkenkunde*, Batavia, 1935.

2a. The Balinese do not express in words the idea that to upset balance is wrong, but they do express it in their affective response. A look of pain, of fear, or of anxiety appears on the face of an adult who tumbles, or of a child who is held upside down, which far surpasses in feeling the response we should expect, and is comparable only to the responses called out by other "wrongs" against the social and religious laws.

3. It is probable that an important factor in what we know as homesickness is the dislocation of the sense of direction in unfamiliar surroundings. In the life of the civilized being, who continually moves about and changes the habitual interior from which he orients himself, this sense must be seriously disturbed. Wild animals seem to be perfectly oriented. And domesticated animals manifest uneasiness and make definite attempts to orient themselves, or to return to familiar surroundings, when they are removed from one place to another.

4. Boys also carry babies, without shame, in imitation of their fathers who habitually dandle the small children.

5. In connection with the close integration of the Balinese children with the life of their elders, one sees a parallel with the gentle and maternal Arapesh people, as described by Margaret Mead. She says of their children, ". . . games are played very seldom. More often the times when children are together in large enough groups to make a game worth while are the occasions of a feast, there is dancing and adult ceremonial, and they find the rôle of spectatorship far more engrossing." And again, ". . . early experience accustoms them to be part of the, whole picture, to prefer to any active child-life of their own a passive part that is in-

tegrated with the life of the community" (*Sex and Temperament*, New York, William Morrow and Company, 1935, pp. 57-58).

6. It is as if we were to choose between the expressions "he has eaten," "he has dined," and "he has partaken of his repast."

7. Here again, indigestion as a disturbance of bodily well-being is to be feared and avoided.

8. In my own house I often surprised a boy or girl crouching alone in a dark cupboard absorbing the allotted plateful of rice, while a merry group who were not at the moment eating sat chatting without.

9. For the breasts, of course, the women show no modesty at all. It is only the region from the knees to the waist which must never be exposed. The Balinese feel about exposure of the thighs of women as Westerners feel about their breasts, and a woman in a Western bathing suit is extremely shocking to them for that reason.

10. The reproductive function of semen is not unknown to them, as is illustrated in the popular legend of the creation of Kala, to whom Civa gave birth alone, by producing a single drop of semen. The parallel with the *manik* idea is, however, interestingly carried out in the legend, for it is only on being repeatedly struck by the arrows of the gods that the drop of semen becomes alive, gets arms and legs, a head, genitals, etc., and finally stands up and shouts, a fully formed Kala. It is difficult to tell whether the theme of the repeated striking refers to the rhythmic motion of copulation, or to an idea that a single sexual act is not sufficient to cause the development of the embryo, and that the man must continue to "strike" during gestation, so that the child will grow.

11. For cases of runaway wives see the author's "Study of a Balinese Family," *American Anthropologist*, 1936, XXXVIII, No. 1.

RUTH FULTON BENEDICT

1934. "Anthropology and the Abnormal," *The Journal of General Psychology*, vol. *10*: 59-80. Reproduced by permission of the author and of the Editor of *The Journal of General Psychology*.

This article presents in condensed form the thesis of *Patterns of Culture*, published in the same year. Because *Patterns of Culture* is widely known and available in inexpensive form, students in courses using the present compilation will probably be required to read it. Among the many reviews and critical comments, attention is directed to a review by A. L. Kroeber (*American Anthropologist 37*: 689-690) in 1935, and one by Elgin Williams ("Anthropology for the Common Man," *American Anthropologist 49*: 84-90) in 1947. See also "The Amiable Side of Kwakiutl Life" (Codere, 1956).

Equally important is Dr. Benedict's book on the Japanese, *The Chrysanthemum and the Sword* (1946). Written in wartime without benefit of field research in Japan, it was based on literary sources, Japanese theatrical films, and study of Japanese individuals in the United States. Nevertheless it offers a clear statement of personal characteristics that Japanese exhibited at the time—or at least, that were admired in Japan. (See J. W. Bennett and M. Nagai, "The Japanese Critique of the Methodology of Benedict's 'The Chrysanthemum and the Sword,'" *American Anthropologist 55*: 404-411.) Discussions of Japanese character elsewhere in this book may well be read against the background of *The Chrysanthemum and the Sword*.

Easily accessible and important papers by Mrs. Benedict occur in most college libraries; one is in *Readings in Social Psychology* by Newcomb, Hartley and associates; another is in Kluckhohn, Murray and Schneider, *Personality in Nature, Society, and Culture*.

Dr. Benedict's pioneer researches and analytical insights have contributed richly to the present cooperation of anthropologists with psychologists and psychiatrists. Her influence is apparent at almost every point in the field of "culture and personality" studies.

ANTHROPOLOGY AND THE ABNORMAL
Ruth Fulton Benedict

Modern social anthropology has become more and more a study of the varieties and common elements of cultural environment and the consequences of these in human behavior. For such a study of diverse social orders primitive peoples fortunately provide a laboratory not yet entirely vitiated by the spread of a standardized world-wide civilization. Dyaks and Hopis, Fijians and Yakuts are significant for psychological and sociological study because only among these simpler peoples has there been sufficient isolation to give opportunity for the development of localized social forms. In the higher cultures the standardization of custom and belief over a couple of continents has given a false sense of the inevitability of the particular forms that have gained currency, and we need to turn to a wider survey in order to check the conclusions we hastily base upon this near-universality of familiar customs. Most of the simpler cultures did not gain the wide currency of the one which, out of our experience, we identify with human nature, but this was for various historical reasons, and certainly not for any that gives us as its carriers a monopoly of social good or of social sanity. Modern civilization, from this point of view, becomes not a necessary pinnacle of human achievement but one entry in a long series of possible adjustments.

These adjustments, whether they are in mannerisms like the ways of showing anger, or joy, or grief in any society, or in major human drives like those of sex, prove to be far more variable than experience in any one culture would suggest. In certain fields, such as that of religion or of formal marriage arrangements, these wide limits of variability are well known and can be fairly described. In others it is not yet possible to give a generalized account, but that does not absolve us of the task of indicating the significance of the work that has been done and of the problems that have arisen.

One of these problems relates to the customary modern normal-abnormal categories and our conclusions regarding them. In how far are such categories culturally determined, or in how far can we with assurance regard them as absolute? In how far can we regard inability to function socially as diagnostic of abnormality, or in how far is it necessary to regard this as a function of the culture?

As a matter of fact, one of the most striking facts that emerge from a study of widely varying cultures is the ease with which our abnormals function in other cultures. It does not matter what kind of "abnormality" we choose for illustration, those which indicate extreme instability, or those which are more in the nature of character traits like sadism or delusions of grandeur or of persecution, there are well-described cultures in which these abnormals function at ease and with honor, and apparently without danger or difficulty to the society.

The most notorious of these is trance and catalepsy. Even a very mild mystic is aberrant in our culture. But most peoples have regarded even extreme psychic manifestations not only as normal and desirable, but even as characteristic of highly valued and gifted individuals. This was true even in our own cultural background in that period when Catholicism made the ecstatic experience the mark of sainthood. It is hard for us, born and brought up in a culture that makes no use of the experience, to realize how important a rôle it may play and how many individuals are capable of it, once it has been given an honorable place in any society.

Some of the Indian tribes of California accorded prestige principally to those who passed through certain trance experiences. Not all of these tribes believed that it was exclusively women who were so blessed, but among the Shasta (10) this was the convention. Their shamans were women, and they were accorded the greatest prestige in the community. They were chosen because of their constitutional liability to trance and allied manifestations. One day the woman who was so destined, while she was about her usual work, would fall suddenly to the ground. She had heard a voice speaking to her in tones of the greatest intensity. Turning, she had seen a man with drawn bow and arrow. He commanded her to sing on pain of being shot through the heart by his arrow, but under the stress of the experience she fell senseless. Her family gathered. She was lying rigid, hardly breathing. They knew that for some time she had had dreams of a special character which indicated a shamanistic calling, dreams of escaping grizzly bears, falling off cliffs or trees, or of being surrounded by swarms of yellow jackets. The community knew therefore what to expect. After a few hours the woman began to moan gently and to roll about upon the ground, trembling violently. She was supposed to be repeating the song which she had been told to sing and which during the trance had been taught her by the spirit. As she revived her moaning became more and more clearly the spirit's song until at last she called out the name of the spirit itself, and immediately blood oozed from her mouth.

When the woman had come to herself after the first encounter with her spirit she danced that night her first initiatory shamanistic dance, holding herself by a rope that was swung from the ceiling. For three nights she danced, and on the third night she had to receive in her body her power from her spirit. She was dancing, and as she felt the approach of the moment she called out, "He will shoot me, he will shoot me." Her friends stood close, for when she reeled in a kind of cataleptic seizure, they had to seize her before she fell or she would die. From this time on she had in her body a visible materialization of her spirit's power, an icicle-like object which in her dances thereafter she would exhibit, producing it from one part of her body and returning it to another part. From this time on she continued to validate her supernatural power by further cataleptic demonstrations, and she was called upon in great emergencies of life and death, for curing and for divination and for counsel. She became in other words by this procedure a woman of great power and importance.[1]

It is clear that, so far from regarding cataleptic seizures as blots upon the family escutcheon and as evidences of dreaded disease, cultural approval had seized upon them and made of them the pathway to authority over one's fellows. They were the outstanding characteristic of the most respected social type, the type which functioned with most honor and reward in the community. It was precisely the cataleptic individuals who in this culture were singled out for authority and leadership.

The availability of "abnormal" types in the social structure, provided they are types that are culturally selected by that group, is illustrated from every part of the world. The shamans of Siberia dominate their communities. According to the ideas of these peoples, they are individuals who by submission to the will of the spirits have been cured of a grievous illness—the onset of the seizures—and have acquired by this means great supernatural power and incomparable vigor and health. Some, during the period of the call, are violently insane for several years, others irresponsible to the point where they have to be watched constantly lest they wander off in the snow and freeze to death, others ill and emaciated to the point of death, sometimes with bloody sweat. It is the shamanistic practice which constitutes their cure, and the extreme physical exertion of a Siberian seance leaves them, they claim, rested and able to enter immediately upon a similar performance. Cataleptic seizures are regarded as an essential part of any shamanistic performance (8).

A good description of the neurotic condition of the shaman and the attention given him by his society is an old one by Canon Callaway (6, pp. 259 ff.) recorded in the words of an old Zulu of South Africa:

The condition of a man who is about to become a diviner is this; at first he is apparently robust, but in the process of time he begins to be delicate, not having any real disease, but being delicate. He habitually avoids certain kinds of food, choosing what he likes, and

he does not eat much of that; he is continually complaining of pains
in different parts of his body. And he tells them that he has dreamt
that he was carried away by a river. He dreams of many things, and
his body is muddied (as a river) and he becomes a house of dreams.
He dreams constantly of many things, and on awaking tells his
friends, 'My body is muddied today; I dreamt many men were killing me, and I escaped I know not how. On waking one part of my
body felt different from other parts; it was no longer alike all over.'
At last that man is very ill, and they go to the diviners to enquire.

The diviners do not at once see that he is about to have a soft head
(that is, the sensitivity associated with shamanism). It is difficult
for them to see the truth; they continually talk nonsense and make
false statements, until all the man's cattle are devoured at their command, they saying that the spirit of his people demands cattle, that
it may eat food. At length all the man's property is expended, he
still being ill; and they no longer know what to do, for he has no
more cattle, and his friends help him in such things as he needs.

At length a diviner comes and says that all the others are wrong.
He says, "He is possessed by the spirits. There is nothing else. They
move in him, being divided into two parties; some say, 'No, we do
not wish our child injured. We do not wish it.' It is for that reason
he does not get well. If you bar the way against the spirits, you will
be killing him. For he will not be a diviner; neither will he ever be a
man again."

So the man may be ill two years without getting better; perhaps
even longer than that. He is confined to his house. This continues till
his hair falls off. And his body is dry and scurfy; he does not like to
anoint himself. He shows that he is about to be a diviner by yawning
again and again, and by sneezing continually. It is apparent also
from his being very fond of snuff; not allowing any long time to pass
without taking some. And people begin to see that he has had what
is good given to him.

After that he is ill; he has convulsions, and when water has been
poured on him they then cease for a time. He habitually sheds tears,
at first slight, then at last he weeps aloud and when the people are
asleep he is heard making a noise and wakes the people by his singing; he has composed a song, and the men and women awake and go
to sing in concert with him. All the people of the village are troubled
by want of sleep; for a man who is becoming a diviner causes great
trouble, for he does not sleep, but works constantly with his brain;
his sleep is merely by snatches, and he wakes up singing many songs;
and people who are near quit their villages by night when they
hear him singing aloud and go to sing in concert. Perhaps he sings
till morning, no one having slept. And then he leaps about the house
like a frog; and the house becomes too small for him, and he goes
out leaping and singing, and shaking like a reed in the water, and
dripping with perspiration.

In this state of things they daily expect his death; he is now but
skin and bones, and they think that tomorrow's sun will not leave

him alive. At this time many cattle are eaten, for the people encourage his becoming a diviner. At length (in a dream) an ancient ancestral spirit is pointed out to him. This spirit says to him, "Go to So-and-so and he will churn for you an emetic (the medicine the drinking of which is a part of shamanistic initiation) that you may be a diviner altogether." Then he is quiet a few days, having gone to the diviner to have the medicine churned for him; and he comes back quite another man, being now cleansed and a diviner indeed.

Thereafter for life when he achieves possession, he foretells events, and finds lost articles.

It is clear that culture may value and make socially available even highly unstable human types. If it chooses to treat their peculiarities as the most valued variants of human behavior, the individuals in question will rise to the occasion and perform their social rôles without reference to our usual ideas of the types who can make social adjustments and those who cannot.

Cataleptic and trance phenomena are, of course, only one illustration of the fact that those whom we regard as abnormals may function adequately in other cultures. Many of our culturally discarded traits are selected for elaboration in different societies. Homosexuality is an excellent example, for in this case our attention is not constantly diverted, as in the consideration of trance, to the interruption of routine activity which it implies. Homosexuality poses the problem very simply. A tendency toward this trait in our culture exposes an individual to all the conflicts to which all aberrants are always exposed, and we tend to identify the consequences of this conflict with homosexuality. But these consequences are obviously local and cultural. Homosexuals in many societies are not incompetent, but they may be such if the culture asks adjustments of them that would strain any man's vitality. Wherever homosexuality has been given an honorable place in any society, those to whom it is congenial have filled adequately the honorable rôles society assigns to them. Plato's *Republic* is, of course, the most convincing statement of such a reading of homosexuality. It is presented as one of the major means to the good life, and it was generally so regarded in Greece at that time.

The cultural attitude toward homosexuals has not always been on such a high ethical plane, but it has been very varied. Among many American Indian tribes there exists the institution of the berdache (12, 15), as the French called them. These men-women were men who at puberty or thereafter took the dress and the occupations of women. Sometimes they married other men and lived with them. Sometimes they were men with no inversion, persons of weak sexual endowment who chose this rôle to avoid the jeers of the women. The berdaches were never regarded as of first-rate supernatural power, as similar

men-women were in Siberia, but rather as leaders in women's occupations, good healers in certain diseases, or, among certain tribes, as the
genial organizers of social affairs. In any case, they were socially placed.
They were not left exposed to the conflicts that visit the deviant who
is excluded from participation in the recognized patterns of his society.

The most spectacular illustrations of the extent to which normality
may be culturally defined are those cultures where an abnormality of
our culture is the cornerstone of their social structure. It is not possible
to do justice to these possibilities in a short discussion. A recent study
of an island of northwest Melanesia by Fortune (11) describes a society
built upon traits which we regard as beyond the border of paranoia.
In this tribe the exogamic groups look upon each other as prime manip-
ulators of black magic, so that one marries always into an enemy
group which remains for life one's deadly and unappeasable foes. They
look upon a good garden crop as a confession of theft, for everyone
is engaged in making magic to induce into his garden the productive-
ness of his neighbors'; therefore no secrecy in the island is so rigidly
insisted upon as the secrecy of a man's harvesting of his yams. Their
polite phrase at the acceptance of a gift is, "And if you now poison me,
how shall I repay you this present?" Their preoccupation with poison-
ing is constant; no woman ever leaves her cooking pot for a moment
untended. Even the great affinal economic exchanges that are characteristic of this Melanesian culture area are quite altered in Dobu since
they are incompatible with this fear and distrust that pervades the culture. They go farther and people the whole world outside their own
quarters with such malignant spirits that all-night feasts and ceremonials
simply do not occur here. They have even rigorous religiously enforced
customs that forbid the sharing of seed even in one family group. Anyone else's food is deadly poison to you, so that communality of stores
is out of the question. For some months before harvest the whole
society is on the verge of starvation, but if one falls to the temptation
and eats up one's seed yams, one is an outcast and a beachcomber for
life. There is no coming back. It involves, as a matter of course, divorce and the breaking of all social ties.

Now in this society where no one may work with another and no
one may share with another, Fortune describes the individual who
was regarded by all his fellows as crazy. He was not one of those who
periodically ran amok and, beside himself and frothing at the mouth,
fell with a knife upon anyone he could reach. Such behavior they did
not regard as putting anyone outside the pale. They did not even put
the individuals who were known to be liable to these attacks under any
kind of control. They merely fled when they saw the attack coming
on and kept out of the way. "He would be all right tomorrow." But
there was one man of sunny, kindly disposition who liked work and

liked to be helpful. The compulsion was too strong for him to repress it in favor of the opposite tendencies of his culture. Men and women never spoke of him without laughing; he was silly and simple and definitely crazy. Nevertheless, to the ethnologist used to a culture that has, in Christianity, made his type the model of all virtue, he seemed a pleasant fellow.

An even more extreme example, because it is of a culture that has built itself upon a more complex abnormality, is that of the North Pacific Coast of North America. The civilization of the Kwakiutl (1-5), at the time when it was first recorded in the last decades of the nineteenth century, was one of the most vigorous in North America. It was built up on an ample economic supply of goods, the fish which furnished their food staple being practically inexhaustible and obtainable with comparatively small labor, and the wood which furnished the material for their houses, their furnishings, and their arts being, with however much labor, always procurable. They lived in coastal villages that compared favorably in size with those of any other American Indians and they kept up constant communication by means of sea-going dug-out canoes.

It was one of the most vigorous and zestful of the aboriginal cultures of North America, with complex crafts and ceremonials, and elaborate and striking arts. It certainly had none of the earmarks of a sick civilization. The tribes of the Northwest Coast had wealth, and exactly in our terms. That is, they had not only a surplus of economic goods, but they made a game of the manipulation of wealth. It was by no means a mere direct transcription of economic needs and the filling of those needs. It involved the idea of capital, of interest, and of conspicuous waste. It was a game with all the binding rules of a game, and a person entered it as a child. His father distributed wealth for him, according to his ability, at a small feast or potlatch, and each gift the receiver was obliged to accept and to return after a short interval with interest that ran to about 100 per cent a year. By the time the child was grown, therefore, he was well launched, a larger potlatch had been given for him on various occasions of exploit or initiation, and he had wealth either out at usury or in his own possession. Nothing in the civilization could be enjoyed without validating it by the distribution of this wealth. Everything that was valued, names and songs as well as material objects, were passed down in family lines, but they were always publicly assumed with accompanying sufficient distributions of property. It was the game of validating and exercising all the privileges one could accumulate from one's various forebears, or by gift, or by marriage, that made the chief interest of the culture. Everyone in his degree took part in it, but many, of course, mainly as spectators. In its highest form it was played out between rival chiefs representing not only themselves and their family lines but their communities, and the object of the contest was to glorify oneself and to humiliate one's opponent. On this level of greatness the property involved was no longer represented by blankets, so many thousand of them to a potlatch, but by higher units of value. These higher units were like our bank notes. They were incised copper tablets, each of them named, and having a value that depended upon their illustrious history. This was as high as ten thousand blankets, and to possess one of them, still more to enhance its value at a great potlatch, was one of the greatest glories within the compass of the chiefs of the Northwest Coast.

The details of this manipulation of wealth are in many ways a parody on our own economic arrangements, but it is with the motivations that were recognized in this contest that we are concerned in this discussion. The drives were those which in our own culture we should call megalomaniac. There was an uncensored self-glorification and ridicule

Kwakiutl ritual mask. *Photo courtesy of American Museum of Natural History.*

of the opponent that it is hard to equal in other cultures outside of the monologues of the abnormal. Any of the songs and speeches of their chiefs at a potlatch illustrate the usual tenor:

. . . .

Wa, out of the way. Wa, out of the way. Turn your faces that I may give way to my anger by striking my fellow chiefs.

Wa, great potlatch, greatest potlatch.[2] The little ones[3] only pretend, the little stubborn ones, they only sell one copper again and again and give it away to the little chiefs of the tribe.
Ah, do not ask in vain for mercy. Ah, do not ask in vain for mercy and raise your hands, you with lolling tongues! I shall break,[4] I shall let disappear the great copper that has the name Kentsegum, the property of the great foolish one, the great extravagant one, the great surpassing one, the one farthest ahead, the great Cannibal dancer among the chiefs.[5]

I am the great chief who makes people ashamed.
I am the great chief who makes people ashamed.
Our chief brings shame to the faces.
Our chief brings jealousy to the faces.
Our chief makes people cover their faces by what he is continually doing in this world, from the beginning to the end of the year,
Giving again and again oil feasts to the tribes.

I am the great chief who vanquishes.
I am the great chief who vanquishes.
Only at those who continue running round and round in this world, working hard, losing their tails,[6] I sneer, at the chiefs below the true chief.[7]
Have mercy on them![8] Put oil on their dry heads with brittle hair, those who do not comb their hair!
I sneer at the chiefs below the true, real chief. I am the great chief who makes people ashamed.

. . . .

I am the only great tree, I the chief.
I am the only great tree, I the chief.
You are my subordinates, tribes.
You sit in the middle of the rear of the house, tribes.
Bring me your counter of property, tribes, that he may in vain try to count what is going to be given away by the great copper-maker, the chief.
Oh, I laugh at them, I sneer at them who empty boxes[9] in their houses, their potlatch houses, their inviting houses that are full only of hunger. They follow along after me like young sawbill ducks.
I am the only great tree, I the chief.

I have quoted a number of these hymns of self-glorification because by an association which psychiatrists will recognize as fundamental these delusions of grandeur were essential in the paranoid view of life which was so strikingly developed in this culture. All of existence was seen in terms of insult.[10] Not only derogatory acts performed by a neighbor or an enemy, but all untoward events, like a cut when one's axe slipped, or a ducking when one's canoe overturned, were insults. All alike threatened first and foremost one's ego security, and the first thought one was allowed was how to get even, how to wipe out the insult. Grief was little institutionalized, but sulking took its place. Until he had resolved upon a course of action by which to save his face after any misfortune, whether it was the slipping of a wedge in felling a tree, or the death of a favorite child, an Indian of the Northwest Coast retired to his pallet with his face to the wall and neither ate nor spoke. He rose from it to follow out some course which according to the traditional rules should reinstate him in his own eyes and those of the community: to distribute property enough to wipe out the stain, or to go head-hunting in order that somebody else should be made to mourn. His activities in neither case were specific responses to the bereavement he had just passed through, but were elaborately directed toward getting even. If he had not the money to distribute and did not succeed in killing someone to humiliate another, he might take his own life. He had staked everything, in his view of life, upon a certain picture of the self, and, when the bubble of his self-esteem was pricked, he had no interest, no occupation to fall back on, and the collapse of his inflated ego left him prostrate.

Every contingency of life was dealt with in these two traditional ways. To them the two were equivalent. Whether one fought with weapons or "fought with property," as they say, the same idea was at the bottom of both. In the olden times, they say, they fought with spears, but now they fight with property. One overcomes one's opponents in equivalent fashion in both, matching forces and seeing that one comes out ahead, and one can thumb one's nose at the vanquished rather more satisfactorily at a potlatch than on a battle field. Every occasion in life was noticed, not in its own terms, as a stage in the sex life of the individual or as a climax of joy or of grief, but as furthering this drama of consolidating one's own prestige and bringing shame to one's guests. Whether it was the occasion of the birth of a child, or a daughter's adolescence, or of the marriage of one's son, they were all equivalent raw material for the culture to use for this one traditionally selected end. They were all to raise one's personal status and to entrench oneself by the humiliation of one's fellows. A girl's adolescence among the Nootka (16) was an event for which her father gathered property from the time she was first able to run about. When she was adolescent he would demonstrate his greatness by an unheard of distribution of these goods, and put down all his rivals. It was not as a fact of the girl's sex life that it figured in their culture, but as the occasion for a major move in the great game of vindicating one's own greatness and humiliating one's associates.

In their behavior at great bereavements this set of the culture comes out most strongly. Among the Kwakiutl it did not matter whether a relative had died in bed of disease, or by the hand of an enemy, in either case death was an affront to be wiped out by the death of another person. The fact that one had been caused to mourn was proof that one had been put upon. A chief's sister and her daughter had gone up to Victoria, and either because they drank bad whiskey or because their boat capsized they never came back. The chief called together his warriors. "Now I ask you, tribes, who shall wail? Shall I do it or shall another?" The spokesman answered, of course, "Not you, Chief. Let some other of the tribes." Immediately they set up the war pole to announce their intention of wiping out the injury, and gathered a war party. They set out, and found seven men and two children asleep and killed them. "Then they felt good when they arrived at Sebaa in the evening."

The point which is of interest to us is that in our society those who on that occasion would feel good when they arrived at Sebaa that evening would be the definitely abnormal. There would be some, even in our society, but it is not a recognized and approved mood under the circumstances. On the Northwest Coast those are favored and fortunate to whom that mood under those circumstances is congenial, and those to whom it is repugnant are unlucky. This latter minority can register in their own culture only by doing violence to their congenial responses and acquiring others that are difficult for them. The person, for instance, who, like a Plains Indian whose wife has been taken from him, is too proud to fight, can deal with the Northwest Coast civilization only by ignoring its strongest bents. If he cannot achieve it, he is the deviant in that culture, their instance of abnormality.

This head-hunting that takes place on the Northwest Coast after a death is no matter of blood revenge or of organized vengeance. There is no effort to tie up the subsequent killing with any responsibility on the part of the victim for the death of the person who is being mourned. A chief whose son has died goes visiting wherever his fancy dictates, and he says to his host, "My prince has died today, and you go with him." Then he kills him. In this, according to their interpretation, he acts nobly because he has not been downed. He has thrust back in return. The whole procedure is meaningless without the fundamental paranoid reading of bereavement. Death, like all the other untoward accidents of existence, confounds man's pride and can only be handled in the category of insults.

Behavior honored upon the Northwest Coast is one which is recognized as abnormal in our civilization, and yet it is sufficiently close to the attitudes of our own culture to be intelligible to us and to have a definite vocabulary with which we may discuss it. The megalomaniac paranoid trend is a definite danger in our society. It is encouraged by some of our major preoccupations, and it confronts us with a choice of two possible attitudes. One is to brand it as abnormal and reprehensible, and is the attitude we have chosen in our civilization. The other is to make it an essential attribute of ideal man, and this is the solution in the culture of the Northwest Coast.

These illustrations, which it has been possible to indicate only in the briefest manner, force upon us the fact that normality is culturally defined. An adult shaped to the drives and standards of either of these cultures, if he were transported into our civilization, would fall into our categories of abnormality. He would be faced with the psychic dilemmas of the socially unavailable. In his own culture, however, he is the pillar of society, the end result of socially inculcated mores, and the problem of personal instability in his case simply does not arise.

No one civilization can possibly utilize in its mores the whole potential range of human behavior. Just as there are great numbers of possible phonetic articulations, and the possibility of language depends on a selection and standardization of a few of these in order that speech communication may be possible at all, so the possibility of organized behavior of every sort, from the fashions of local dress and houses to the dicta of a people's ethics and religion, depends upon a similar selection among the possible behavior traits. In the field of recognized economic obligations or sex tabus this selection is as nonrational and subconscious a process as it is in the field of phonetics. It is a process which goes on in the group for long periods of time and is historically conditioned by innumerable accidents of isolation or of contact of peoples. In any comprehensive study of psychology, the selection that different cultures have made in the course of history within the great circumference of potential behavior is of great significance.

Every society,[11] beginning with some slight inclination in one direction or another, carries its preference farther and farther, integrating itself more and more completely upon its chosen basis, and discarding those types of behavior that are uncongenial. Most of those organizations of personality that seem to us most incontrovertibly abnormal have been used by different civilizations in the very foundations of their institutional life. Conversely the most valued traits of our normal individuals have been looked on in differently organized cultures as aberrant. Normality, in short, within a very wide range, is culturally defined. It is primarily a term for the socially elaborated segment of human behavior in any culture; and abnormality, a term for the segment that that particular civilization does not use. The very eyes with which we see the problem are conditioned by the long traditional habits of our own society.

It is a point that has been made more often in relation to ethics than in relation to psychiatry. We do not any longer make the mistake of deriving the morality of our own locality and decade directly from the inevitable constitution of human nature. We do not elevate it to the dignity of a first principle. We recognize that morality differs in every society, and is a convenient term for socially approved habits. Mankind has always preferred to say, "It is a morally good," rather than "It is habitual," and the fact of this preference is matter enough for a critical science of ethics. But historically the two phrases are synonymous.

The concept of the normal is properly a variant of the concept of the good. It is that which society has approved. A normal action is one which falls well within the limits of expected behavior for a particular society. Its variability among different peoples is essentially a function of the variability of the behavior patterns that different societies have created for themselves, and can never be wholly divorced from a consideration of culturally institutionalized types of behavior.

Each culture is a more or less elaborate working-out of the potentialities of the segment it has chosen. In so far as a civilization is well integrated and consistent within itself, it will tend to carry farther and farther, according to its nature, its initial impulse toward a particular type of action, and from the point of view of any other culture those elaborations will include more and more extreme and aberrant traits.

Each of these traits, in proportion as it reinforces the chosen behavior patterns of that culture, is for that culture normal. Those individuals to whom it is congenial either congenitally, or as the result of childhood sets, are accorded prestige in that culture, and are not visited with the social contempt or disapproval which their traits would call down upon them in a society that was differently organized. On the other hand, those individuals whose characteristics are not congenial to the selected type of human behavior in that community are the deviants, no matter how valued their personality traits may be in a contrasted civilization.

The Dobuan who is not easily susceptible to fear of treachery, who enjoys work and likes to be helpful, is their neurotic and regarded as silly. On the Northwest Coast the person who finds it difficult to read life in terms of an insult contest will be the person upon whom fall all the difficulties of the culturally unprovided for. The person who does not find it easy to humiliate a neighbor, nor to see humiliation in his own experience, who is genial and loving, may, of course, find some unstandardized way of achieving satisfactions in his society, but not in the major patterned responses that his culture requires of him. If he is born to play an important rôle in a family with many hereditary privileges, he can succeed only by doing violence to his whole personality. If he does not succeed, he has betrayed his culture; that is, he is abnormal.

I have spoken of individuals as having sets toward certain types of behavior, and of these sets as running sometimes counter to the types of behavior which are institutionalized in the culture to which they belong. From all that we know of contrasting cultures it seems clear that differences of temperament occur in every society. The matter has never been made the subject of investigation, but from the available material it would appear that these temperament types are very likely of universal recurrence. That is, there is an ascertainable range of human behavior that is found wherever a sufficiently large series of individuals is observed. But the proportion in which behavior types stand to one another in different societies is not universal. The vast majority of the individuals in any group are shaped to the fashion of that culture. In other words, most individuals are plastic to the moulding force of the society into which they are born. In a society that values trance, as in India, they will have supernormal experience. In a society that institutionalizes homosexuality, they will be homosexual. In a society that sets the gathering of possessions as the chief human objective, they will amass property. The deviants, whatever the type of behavior the culture has institutionalized, will remain few in number, and there seems no more difficulty in moulding the vast malleable majority to the "normality" of what we consider an aberrant trait, such as delusions of reference, than to the normality of such accepted behavior patterns as acquisitiveness. The small proportion of the number of the deviants in any culture is not a function of the sure instinct with which that society has built itself upon the fundamental sanities, but of the universal fact that, happily, the majority of mankind quite readily take any shape that is presented to them.

The relativity of normality is not an academic issue. In the first place, it suggests that the apparent weakness of the aberrant is most often and in great measure illusory. It springs not from the fact that he is lacking in necessary vigor, but that he is an individual upon whom that culture has put more than the usual strain. His inability to adapt himself to society is a reflection of the fact that that adaptation involves a conflict in him that it does not in the so-called normal.

Therapeutically, it suggests that the inculcation of tolerance and appreciation in any society toward its less usual types is fundamentally important in successful mental hygiene. The complement of this tolerance, on the patients' side, is an education in self-reliance and honesty with himself. If he can be brought to realize that what has thrust him into his misery is despair at his lack of social backing he may be able to achieve a more independent and less tortured attitude and lay the foundation for an adequately functioning mode of existence.

There is a further corollary. From the point of view of absolute categories of abnormal psychology, we must expect in any culture to find a large proportion of the most extreme abnormal types among those who from the local point of view are farthest from belonging to this category. The culture, according to its major preoccupations, will increase and intensify hysterical, epileptic, or paranoid symptoms, at the same time relying socially in a greater and greater degree upon these very individuals. Western civilization allows and culturally honors gratifications of the ego which according to any absolute category would be regarded as abnormal. The portrayal of unbridled and arrogant egoists as family men, as officers of the law, and in business has been a favorite topic of novelists, and they are familiar in every community. Such individuals are probably mentally warped to a greater degree than many inmates of our institutions who are nevertheless socially unavailable. They are extreme types of those personality configurations which our civilization fosters.

This consideration throws into great prominence the confusion that follows, on the one hand, the use of social inadequacy as a criterion of abnormality and, on the other, of definite fixed symptoms. The confusion is present in practically all discussions of abnormal psychology, and it can be clarified chiefly by adequate consideration of the character of the culture, not of the constitution of the abnormal individual. Nevertheless, the bearing of social security upon the total situation of the abnormal cannot be exaggerated, and the study of comparative psychiatry will be fundamentally concerned with this aspect of the matter.

It is clear that statistical methods of defining normality, so long as they are based on studies in a selected civilization, only involve us, unless they are checked against the cultural configuration, in deeper and deeper provincialism. The recent tendency in abnormal psychology to take the laboratory mode as normal and to define abnormalities as they depart from this average has value in so far as it indicates that the aberrants in any culture are those individuals who are liable to serious disturbances because their habits are culturally unsupported. On the other hand, it overlooks the fact that every culture besides its abnormals of conflict has presumably its abnormals of extreme fulfillment of the cultural type. From the point of view of a universally valid abnormal psychology the extreme types of abnormality would probably be found in this very group—a group which in every study based upon one culture goes undescribed except in its end institutionalized forms.

The relativity of normality is important in what may some day come to be a true social engineering. Our picture of our own civilization is no longer in this generation in terms of a changeless and divinely derived set of categorical imperatives. We must face the problems our changed perspective has put upon us. In this matter of mental ailments, we must face the fact that even our normality is man-made, and is of our own seeking. Just as we have been handicapped in dealing with ethical problems so long as we held to an absolute definition of morality, so too in dealing with the problems of abnormality we are handicapped so long as we identify our local normalities with the universal sanities. I have taken illustrations from different cultures, because the conclusions are most inescapable from the contrasts as they are presented in unlike social groups. But the major problem is not a consequence of the variability of the normal from culture to culture, but its variability from era to era. This variability in time we cannot escape if we would, and it is not beyond the bounds of possibility that we may be able to face this inevitable change with full understanding and deal with it rationally (9). No society has yet achieved self-concious and critical analysis of its own normalities and attempted rationally to deal with its own social process of creating new normalities within its next generation. But the fact that it is unachieved is not therefore proof of its impossibility. It is a faint indication of how momentous it could be in human society.

There is another major factor in the cultural conditioning of abnormality. From the material that is available at the present time it seems a lesser factor than the one we have discussed. Nevertheless, disregard of its importance has led to many misconceptions. The particular forms of behavior to which unstable individuals of any group are liable are many of them matters of cultural patterning like any other behavior. It is for this obvious reason that the epidemic disorders of one continent or era are often rare or unreported from other parts of the world or other periods of history.

The baldest evidence of cultural patterning in the behavior of unstable individuals is in trance phenomena. The use to which such proclivities are put, the form their manifestations take, the things that are seen and felt in trance, are all culturally controlled. The tranced individual may come back with communications from the dead describing the minutiae of life in the hereafter, or he may visit the world of the unborn, or get information about lost objects in the camp, or experience cosmic unity, or acquire a life-long guardian spirit, or get information about coming events. Even in trance the individual holds strictly to the rules and expectations of his culture, and his experience is as locally patterned as a marriage rite or an economic exchange.

The conformity of trance experience to the expectations of waking life is well recognized. Now that we are no longer confused by the attempt to ascribe supernormal validity to the one or the other, and realize how trance experience bodies forth the preoccupations of the experiencing individual, the cultural patterning in ecstasy has become an accepted tenet.

But the matter does not end here. It is not only what is seen in trance experience that has clear-cut geographical and temporal distribution. It is equally true of forms of behavior which are affected by certain unstable individuals in any group. It is one of the prime difficulties in the use of such unprecise and casual information as we possess about the behavior of the unstable in different cultures, that the material does not correspond to data from our own society. It has even been thought that such definite types of instability as Arctic hysteria (14) and the Malay running-amok were racial diseases. But we know at least, in spite of the lack of good psychiatric accounts, that these phenomena do not coincide with racial distributions. Moreover, the same problem is quite as striking in cases where there is no possibility of a racial correlation. Running amok has been described as alike in symptoms and alike in the treatment accorded it by the rest of the group from such different parts of the world as Melanesia (11, pp. 54-55) and Tierra del Fuego (7).

The racial explanation is also ruled out of court in those instances of epidemic mania which are characteristic of our own cultural background. The dancing mania (13) that filled the streets of Europe with compulsively dancing men, women, and children in mediaeval times is recognized as an extreme instance of suggestibility in our own racial group.

These behaviors are capable of controlled elaboration that is often carried to great lengths. Unstable individuals in one culture achieve characteristic forms that may be excessively rare or absent in another, and this is very marked where social value has been attached to one form or another. Thus when some form of borderline behavior has been associated in any society with the shaman and he is a person of authority and influence, it is this particular indicated seizure to which he will be liable at every demonstration. Among the Shasta of California, as we have seen, and among many other tribes in various parts of the world, some form of cataleptic seizure is the passport to shamanism and must constantly accompany its practice. In other regions it is automatic vision or audition. In other societies behavior is perhaps closest to what we cover by the term hystero-epilepsy. In Siberia all the familiar characteristics of our spiritualistic seances are required for every performance of the shaman. In all these cases the particular experience that is thus socially chosen receives considerable elaboration and is usually patterned in detail according to local standards. That is, each culture, though it chooses quite narrowly in the great field of borderline experiences, without difficulty imposes its selected type upon certain of its individuals. The particular behavior of an unstable individual in these instances is not the single and inevitable mode in which his abnormality could express itself. He has taken up a traditionally conditioned pattern of behavior in this as in any other field. Conversely, in every society, our own included, there are forms of instability that are out of fashion. They are not at the present time at least being presented for imitation to the enormously suggestible individuals who constitute in any society a considerable group of the abnormals. It seems clear that this is no matter of the nature of sanity, or even of a biological, inherited tendency in a local group, but quite simply an affair of social patterning.

The problem of understanding abnormal human behavior in any absolute sense independent of cultural factors is still far in the future. The categories of borderline behavior which we derive from the study of the neuroses and psychoses of our civilization are categories of prevailing local types of instability. They give much information about the stresses and strains of Western civilization, but no final picture of inevitable human behavior. Any conclusions about such behavior must await the collection by trained observers of psychiatric data from other cultures. Since no adequate work of the kind has been done at the present time, it is impossible to say what core of definition of abnormality may be found valid from the comparative material. It is as it is in ethics: all our local conventions of moral behavior and of immoral are without absolute validity, and yet it is quite possible that a modicum of what is considered right and what wrong could be disentangled that is shared by the whole human race. When data are available in psychiatry, this minimum definition of abnormal human tendencies will be probably quite unlike our culturally conditioned, highly elaborated psychoses such as those that are described, for instance, under the terms of schizophrenia and manic-depressive.

NOTES

1. In all cultures behavior which is socially rewarded attracts persons who are attracted by the possibility of leadership, and such individuals may simulate the required behavior. This is as true when society rewards prodigality as when it rewards catalepsy. For the present argument the amount of shamming is not considered though it is of obvious importance. It is a matter which cultures standardize quite as much as they standardize the type of rewarded behavior.

2. The feast he is now engaged in giving.

3. His opponents.

4. To break a copper, showing in this way how far one rose above even the most superlatively valuable things, was the final mark of greatness.

5. Himself.

6. As salmon do.

7. Himself.

8. Irony, of course.

9. Of treasure.

10. Insult is used here in reference to the intense susceptibility to shame that is conspicuous in this culture. All possible contingencies were interpreted as rivalry situations, and the gamut of emotions swung between triumph and shame.

11. This phrasing of the process is deliberately animistic. It is used with no reference to a group mind or a superorganic, but in the same sense in which it is customary to say, "Every art has its own canons."

REFERENCES

1. BOAS, 1897
2. BOAS, 1921
3. BOAS, 1925
4. BOAS, 1930-b
5. BOAS and HUNT, 1905
6. CALLAWAY, 1868-70
7. CORIAT, n.d.
8. CZAPLICKA, 1914
9. DEWEY, 1922
10. DIXON, 1907
11. FORTUNE, 1932
12. GRINNELL, 1923
13. HECKER, J. F. C., 1885
14. NOVAKOVSKY, 1924
15. PARSONS, E. C., 1916
16. SAPIR, 1913

JOHN W. BENNETT

1946. "The Interpretation of Pueblo Culture: A Question of Values," *South-western Journal of Anthropology*, 2: 361-374. Reprinted by courtesy of the author and of the Editor of *Southwestern Journal of Anthropology*.

Before reading this essay, one should read two other papers included in the present book: one by Esther Goldfrank, the other by Laura Thompson. Perhaps *Patterns of Culture* by Ruth Benedict should be digested before reading any of these three. Dr. Bennett's analysis speaks for itself, and the student will have to make up his own mind—or seek further factual data. The issues involved, however, are broader than any local question of Pueblo culture.

THE INTERPRETATION OF PUEBLO CULTURE:
A QUESTION OF VALUES

John W. Bennett

It can be taken as a general rule that intensive research upon the same preliterate people by a variety of ethnologists gives rise to considerable controversy and disagreement over the nature of fundamental institutions and cultural expressions. Things which are accepted verbatim about groups reported on by single field workers are subjected to considerable scrutiny and argument when the area is opened up to additional members of the profession.

Studies of Pueblo Indians—especially the Hopi and Zuñi—are instances of the operation of this rule. Controversies of long standing over the relative definitions and composition of lineages, clans, and phratries are common; certain types of marriage, particularly cross-cousin marriage, have been equally debated; the kinship system has furnished considerable fuel for the argument over the relationship of terminology and social features. On the whole, such disputes are highly technical and concern only the inner circle of specialists. In most cases they have no great significance for wider philosophical and theoretical issues in social science.

A controversy over somewhat different issues and having a more direct importance for broader problems will be discussed in this paper. In a series of publications appearing during the past few years[1] two principal interpretations of the basic dynamics of Pueblo[2] society and culture have gradually emerged. These two interpretations have appeared not entirely as explicit, formal, theoretical positions, but more as implicit viewpoints within the matrix of methodological and empirical research on Pueblo communities.

As in the case of most other controversies, the respective adherents tend to imply, if not claim directly, that their respective interpretations are more "correct," "fundamental," and the like; there is no argument over or challenging of fact. In most cases the contrasting parties work with the same raw data. Hence the disagreement is purely one of manipulation of facts rather than of contradictory sets of facts.

The two perspectives are not to be viewed as polarites in diametric opposition. There is considerable cooperation in research and interchange of concepts and conclusions,[3] and in many cases the difference in viewpoint is not clear-cut. Yet the difference is there, and none of the ethnologists concerned have yet answered these questions: Can the two interpretations be held simultaneously, or are they contradictory; and, Are the differences a result of choice of problem, choice of fact, or of differing values held by the respective workers?

In the background of the controversy lie the criticisms of Benedict's and others' interpretation of Pueblo culture as "Apollonian," which often were not explicit denials of the truth of her characterization, but rather pointed out that there was another side to the story and that her method contained unexpressed value-orientations.[4] In a sense this older phase of the difference in perspective goes to the heart of the problem; namely, if interpretations of the same fact differ, must this not in part be a consequence of differing values?

I wish now to describe, by paraphrasing, the two viewpoints:

1. Pueblo culture and society are integrated to an unusual degree, all sectors being bound together by a consistent, harmonious set of values, which pervade and homogenize the categories of world view, ritual, art, social organization, economic activity, and social control.[5] Man is believed to have the ability to act freely and voluntarily in ordering his own affairs and fitting them into an harmonious universe. The outcome tends to be virtually a fulfillment of the ideal-typical folk-preliterate homogeneous, "sacred" society and culture. Associated with this integrated configuration is an ideal personality type which features the virtues of gentleness, nonaggression, cooperation, modesty, tranquillity, and so on.

In some analyses, this generalized ideal pattern is presented as the "real," that is, it is presented as lived up to more often than it is not.[6] In other writings the correct estimation of the ideal patterning is acknowledged, but qualifying materials from "real" patterns are added.[7] In still others, the ideal pattern is described as an ideal without *explicit* information as to its "real" manifestations or its consequences in other contexts of the society and culture.[8]

2. Pueblo society and culture are marked by considerable *covert* tension, suspicion, anxiety, hostility, fear, and ambition.[9] Children, despite a relatively permissive, gentle, and frictionless early training, are later coerced subtly and (from our viewpoint) brutally into behaving according to Pueblo norms. The ideals of free democratic election and expression are conspicuously lacking in Pueblo society, with authority in the hands of the group and chiefs, the latter formerly holding the power of life and death over his "subjects." The individual is suppressed and repressed. Witchcraft is covert, but highly developed.[10]

Like the first, this view is qualified in analysis in many ways, and as I have noted, is not necessarily in conflict at all points with the first.[11]

What is apparent, however, is a tendency among the workers on one side to avoid the conclusions and implications of the other, to "grind their own axes," so to speak. I believe, therefore, that the differences in interpretation, plus the relative avoidance by each of the views of the other, are evidence of a genuine difference in outlook and are not simply the result of conscious, objective choice of problem. I mean here that the social scientific research may have been directed and influenced in part by personal-cultural differences between the respective workers, and not merely by the division of scientific labor.

In order to suggest some possible approaches to the problem, I want to take up first the question of values or preferences represented in the two interpretations. I acknowledge the uncertainty and inconclusiveness of the imputations I may make, but I also believe that an inquiry of this sort—however preliminary—will have its value in stimulating further self-inquiry into the meaning of our cultural analyses in the wider culture of which they are a part.

The first view may be seen in a context of theory basic to much of anthropology, and which lays stress upon the organic wholeness of preliterate life in contrast to the heterogeneity and diffusiveness of modern civilization. One may trace this emphasis from the earliest American ethnological writings to the various manifestations of the configurational approach, and to Redfield's formal theory of the "folk society." This general viewpoint is in part an expectable outgrowth of the anthropological preoccupation with preliterate communities, in part traceable to certain perspectives in the culture of American social science.

In the latter case I refer to a general *critical* attitude of the social scientist toward the heterogeneity of modern life, and a fairly clear attitude toward the organic character of preliterate life as preferable.[12] Some direct statements of this value position can be found;[13] in other cases, one must perceive it more by the frequency of the choice of and emphasis on problems which deal with it.[14] In this paper, I wish to make the imputation by studying the general linguistic atmosphere. For example:

> Thus the Hopi have extended their harmonious, organic view of the universe logically and aesthetically through the world of nature and also through the world of man at both the personal and the social levels. Combining acute observation and induction with deduction and intuition, they have worked the flux of experience with its multitudinous, apparently unrelated details into a world view which is a notable achievement not only in pragmatic utility, but also in logic and aesthetics. . . . Under relentless environmental pressures, the Hopi has become a specialist in the arts of logical thinking, logical living, and logical character building . . . he even grows corn with the consummate skill of the artist. . . .[15]

The choice of such words and phrases as "harmonious," "acute," "notable achievement," "logical," and "consummate skill" in this passage, is, I think, fairly good evidence of the possibility that the author approves of the Hopi configuration. There is nothing to be condemned in such approval—one only asks perhaps for a more conscious recognition on her part of the value orientation, plus some thought as to its probable influences on the analysis of her data.

As to what such influences *might* be, we can consider the following passage:

> Actually the Hopi Way . . . sets up ideal conditions (in terms of external and internal pressures toward a single goal) for the development of an integrated system of social control, which functions effectively with a minimum of physical coercion, by fastening its internalization within the individual in the form of a super-ego or conscience consistent with the social goal.[16]

There are two things of importance here: (1) the statement that the Hopi configuration is imposed "with a minimum of physical coercion"; and (2) a generalized swallowing-down and obfuscation of the imposition of group will and authority upon the individual—"external and internal pressures," "fostering its internalization," "conscience consistent with the social goal," and so on. These can be viewed as circumlocutions of what the other approach calls "authority" and "totalitarianism."

Now my preliminary conclusion is as follows: In this first, or "organic" theory of Pueblo culture, there is an implicit value orientation toward solidified, homogeneous group life. At least in the case of the writer used as an example, it appears possible that this preference-position is inarticulate and may influence her conclusions in such a way as to render certain features of the Hopi social system and culture less clear to the reader.

The second, or "repression" theory of Pueblo culture stresses the very features which the "organic" viewpoint elides or ignores. In regard to "physical coercion," Goldfrank emphasizes the severe physical and mental tortures of Hopi child initiation and socialization,[17] including long descriptions of the horror and rigor of these rites. To these are added a multitude of subtle techniques for coercing the child into the norms. Whereas Thompson views Hopi participation in work as an example of "harmonious" and spontaneous cooperative attitudes toward fulfillment of the universal plan of Nature,[18] Goldfrank states,

> Large-scale cooperation deriving primarily from the needs of irrigation is therefore vitally important to the life and well-being of the Pueblo community. It is no spontaneous expression of good-will or sociability. What may seem "voluntary" to some is the end of a long process of conditioning, often persuasive, but frequently harsh, that commences in infancy and continues throughout adulthood.[19]

The point is that these views are not necessarily contradictory, but emphasize different aspects of Pueblo culture. The situation is made more complex by the fact that not only is there a difference in emphasis and choice of data, but that certain value orientations have intruded which influence the respective arguments in different ways.

While the "organic" approach tends to show a preference for homogeneous preliterate culture, the "repressed" theory has a fairly clear bias in the direction of egalitarian democracy and non-neurotic, "free" behavior. There tends to be a rejection of the hyper-personalized, inverted, "thick" atmosphere of the small, homogeneous society, in favor of the greater individuation and accessibility of urban life. The preference is not nearly as evident as the other orientation—at least it is not so in the published literature. But observe this conclusion from Goldfrank's paper:[20]

> It is, then, the "deeply disciplined" man, both at Hopi and at Zuñi, who is so desired and so necessary to the proper functioning of the community. Emotional restraint, reserve, avoidance, or the need to reject is the price he pays for achieving his society's social ideal.

Note the phrase, "the price he pays"—in other words, to become an ideal Hopi a man must repress his spontaneity, originality, enthusiasm, out-goingness, individualism, and so on, and become neurotic.[21] Clearly this is not a desirable situation in the eyes of the libertarian American anthropologist, who may have had his or her experiences with our own forms of coercion and who may be in process of rebellion against them.

I think something of this sort lay beneath Li An-che's observation of Bunzel's remark to the effect that Zuñi prayer is "not a spontaneous outpouring of the heart. It is rather the repetition of a fixed formula."[22] Li comments, "why . . . should 'spontaneous outpouring' . . . be . . . antithetical . . . to 'repetition'?" In Bunzel's case I think there may have been a tendency to follow a typical American value pattern which approves spontaneity, sincerity, originality and condemns rote repetitions as insincere, shallow, etc. But as Li points out, from a scientific standpoint it was not a question of the *form of prayer*, but rather the kind of cultural framework within which "feelings" take place. Bunzel unconsciously, and in a typically American-Western way identified "feeling" with "form."

Differences between the two points of view are also evident in the question of "environmental pressures." Both sides recognize the tremendous environmental difficulties faced by the Hopi, and the "successful" adjustment made to them. Thompson emphasizes man's "positive measure of control over the universe . . . the external world of nature";[23] "nature-man balance";[24] and the fact that "under relentless environmental pressure" the Hopi have become "specialists in logic," "artists," "experts,"[25] and so on.

Whether Goldfrank, Eggan, and others would grant all this I do not know, but what is apparent from their writings is an entirely different emphasis on the environmental question. Dorothy Eggan described the forbidding environment as productive of an attitude which I believe can be called "defeatist" (in Western culture); namely,

> Of course these sedentary people . . . worked out a religion designed to control the unappeasable elements.[26] But even this prop became a boomerang since their beliefs held no promise of virtue through suffering; rather *all* distress was equated with human failure, the consequence of "bad hearts."[27]

Goldfrank goes even farther, interpreting the religious pattern as a special response to agricultural needs; but even more significantly, the drastic Pueblo techniques for molding personality into "yielding" forms are seen as a result of the necessity to "achieve the coöperation necessary for a functioning irrigated agriculture."[28]

From Thompson and others we get a picture of Pueblo environmental adjustment as a kind of glorious fulfillment of a unique world view, a master plan. From Goldfrank and others, the adjustment is seen as a difficult, harsh experience, determinative of those phases of Pueblo culture and society which seem repressive and authoritarian.

By way of final illustration:

The Hopi Way may be used as illustration of what can be interpreted either as an ambivalence on the whole question or as merely a less definite specimen of the organic viewpoint. On the matter of tribal initiation, Thompson-Josephs cite the whipping and its severity as a flat statement of fact; then explain,

> This ceremony, in which the Mother Katchina may be interpreted from one point of view as symbolizing the mother . . . illustrates dramatically the complementary functions of the maternal and paternal kin in steering the child along the road of life. . . . And finally, through the discipliners' castigating of one another, it shows that the adult pattern of social control is not one in which one group, namely the children, terminate it, but one in which each adult individual is expected to exercise a certain amount of control over the others.[29]

In other words, the whipping is seen here as an incidental means to an end. There is nothing about the coercive severity of the means, yet the means are taken account of.

In a chapter on "Hopi Hostility" written by Alice Josephs, we find an account of certain hostile behavior patterns; but consider the following:

> To put it briefly, among the Hopi, not only work and spiritual activities, but even the emotional attachment to the various members of the group, father and mother included, seem to be consciously and practically under the direct, regulating influence of the society.[30]

This seems a curious method of avoiding a direct statement of coercion. What, one might ask, is "society" other than the collection of individuals who insist on obedience and order. The author seems to be saying, "Yes, there is hostility, but look how well it is controlled by society." Hostility becomes a kind of regrettable psychological artifact.

The feeling of ambivalence is strengthened by the passage which follows the above:

> The child who does not submit and tries to form deeper attachments of his own choice will most likely run the risk of finding himself without response from the object of his unruly affection. Repeated disappointments of this sort will usually lead to abandonment first of the open manifestation of such emotions, then of further attempts to establish new attachments.[31]

This flat statement of a pattern which we might well call "cruel frustration" contrasts oddly with the almost laudatory description of "the well-balanced and resilient character of the social structure . . . well integrated control system."[32]

In short one can find elements of both points of view scattered throughout The Hopi Way, and this reader must confess that he had difficulty seeing how the two really fit together. Stated flatly as they are, the two simply do not mix.

I believe it fairly clear, therefore, that over and above the objective choice of problem and method, there is some evidence of attitudes of approach ("organic" theory) and avoidance ("repressed" theory)[33] toward Pueblo culture. In cases of mixture or ambivalence, separate components of the two viewpoints stand out in a confused and unassimilated mixture, or the necessary facts of the whole case are not sufficiently interpreted.

Now, precisely what are the issues at stake in regard to the interpretation of Pueblo culture?

Lacking any close familiarity with Pueblo research, it is very difficult for me to assess the various specimens from the standpoint of excellence of field work and general scientific operations. As far I as know, the workers on both sides of the question are careful students of culture; they hold respectable jobs, have had considerable field experience, and are accepted within the academic fraternity as active professional anthropologists.

Their work on Pueblo culture, we have every reason to believe, has been done with due respect for basic rules of scientific method for the collection of data, and it is also highly probable that the actual field data collected by all would represent a highly homogeneous mass. This homogeneity would also hold true for the broadest generalizations and interpretations—in re social organization, technology, ritual forms, ideologies, and so on.

In other words, it is difficult to explain the difference in viewpoint from the standpoint of "good" and "bad" ethnology.

If, however, we attempt to appraise not the data and collection of data, but rather the suggestions as to conceptual tools for manipulation of the data, a somewhat different picture appears.

The "organic" approach can be charged with the following:

(a) The sin of omission of certain important sets of data; namely, those having to do with the severity and authoritarianism of Pueblo socialization processes. The "organic" point of view tends to avoid the apparent fact that the unique Pueblo homogeneity arises in a severe conflict process which is drastically suppressed, and from this standpoint I think we must award a laurel to the "repressed" school for facing the reality of the situation and seeing the process as well as the end product.

(b) A tendency to distort or misrepresent some facets of the Pueblo configuration. As Titiev notes:[34]

> Dr. Thompson, for instance, exhibits an unfortunate tendency to distort various items taken from the literature. A girlish pursuit game, somewhat comparable to following-the-leader, is magnified (p. 58) into a faithful portrayal of "the guidance role of the mother and the difficult and centripetal life course of the Hopi girl . . ." Moreover, in an effort to stress the cohesiveness of Hopi society, Dr. Thompson omits all but a casual reference to the split of 1906 that tore Oraibi to bits . . . etc.

(c) A tendency to make the interpretation in the long run an entirely personal, subjective affair. The *extreme* configurationist approach, which the "organic" approach represents, tends to assume the validity and demonstrability of its concepts and then use them on specific sets of data in an effort to reveal the "inner meaning" of these data. Thompson does not tell us what "logico-aesthetic integration" *is,* or where it fits into a general corpus of culture theory, or why she chose it as a major conceptual tool. Lacking the sound documentation of a *Balinese Character,* or the careful conceptual manipulation of a *Navaho Witchcraft,* a configurationist approach must inevitably slip into personalized impression.

What I am saying here is that all things considered, one is more likely to have scientific faith in the viewpoint which tries to see the whole picture and evaluate its various parts. But this is by no means the whole story. For beyond the issue of scientific completeness and validity lies a further question.

Let us assume that some of the difference in viewpoint stems from the fact that the respective authors have not published all their data or analyses of it, and that therefore if the "organic" group were to let us in on all their materials, their interpretation would not differ significantly from the other approach. Even if this were so—and I doubt it—it would be equally evident that the respective authors *choose* certain aspects of their data and conclusions for immediate publication. And further, the general controversy—if it can be called such—has been in progress for some years. Surely in this time the various differences would have been resolved if it were merely a matter of unequal publication.

The differences in viewpoint, therefore, cannot be explained entirely either on the basis of scientific goodness or badness, nor on the basis of publication differentials. Underneath both of these factors lies what I have already suggested may be a genuine difference in value orientation and outlook in the feeling about, the reaction toward, Pueblo society and culture in the light of the values in American culture brought to the scientific situation by the anthropologist.

For even if the methodological defects in the current "organic" approach were corrected, this group would still lay most of its emphasis upon the organic, horizontal, pervading world view. There is nothing "wrong" about this—I am convinced that this world view actually exists—just as I am also convinced that Pueblo society achieves homogeneity by repressive measures.

It is not so much a question of poor versus good anthropology, but rather a matter of the particular stress laid upon certain sets of facts—which facts could be identical for both sides—and the emphasis placed upon certain theoretical views of the materials. These, in turn, are bound up with the value question already discussed. This is really a very complex affair and the moral, if any, is that in cultural studies we can all be equally objective in the collection and ordering and interpretation of facts, but since social science is a part of our culture, research gets tangled in our attitudes toward the material. Why should Benedict, Thompson, *et al.*, choose the organic emphasis, and why should Goldfrank, Eggan, *et al.*, choose the repressive emphasis? This question quite transcends the fact that both groups of anthropologists may be equally reliable field workers and capable culture analysts.[35]

Inspecting the value question more closely, I think the issue can be resolved into one of means and ends. To Thompson's way of looking at things, the end is the most important and significant factor; the "end" in this case being the unique and rather remarkable Pueblo world view. To her this phenomenon has rare beauty and aesthetic appeal, and one receives the impression that the means of achieving this ideal really do not matter—at least she does not appear to be particularly concerned with them.

But to Goldfrank it is precisely the means that count—and that is *her* bias. She probably grants the organic, homogeneous, logico-aesthetic world view, and concerns herself almost entirely with the means for achieving this. These, to her, are the important factors; these are what the social scientist should study objectively. One suspects a kind of critical realism here, which contrasts sharply with the impressionistic, evocative approach of the extreme configurationist school.

Thompson and Goldfrank, then, clearly disagree over the respective values of means and ends,[36] and this question goes beyond any issue of scientific methodology, referring ultimately to current overt and covert value conflicts in our culture at large. Scientific anthropology is thus implicated in an on-going process in our own culture, and from this level of observation, it is "non-objective" and "culturally determined."

I do not believe, therefore, that we can definitely answer the questions: Who is right? Which emphasis is preferable? Who will decide? A decision on the grounds of scientific method alone does not provide an answer as to the "why" of choice of the different value positions, and this is the more fundamental and far-reaching question. Neither is it possible to say that one side or the other is less-influenced by values. Obviously Thompson is more subjective and possibly less aware of the influences upon her work, but at the same time we can show that the value orientation is just as marked in Goldfrank's work, only it is a different sort of value and one which happens to appeal strongly to the more literal-minded social scientist. It is possible that a "repressed" approach could conceal and distort to the same degree as do some specimens of the current "organic" approach.

The answers to these various questions can only be given in tentative form. First, the *fact* of influence upon anthropological research by values and personal preferences should be recognized and extraverted. At the present time we do not do so in sufficient degree. Secondly, as individual anthropologists we should be both more modest and more willing to think into and publish the implications and biases in our own analyses. I do not suggest an Olympian objectivity—only a serious concern with the problem. Third, we must be willing to turn to logical analysis to help decide the merits of such a case as the one reviewed in this paper.

What I mean in the last sentence is simply this: I do not believe that it is possible to decide, upon scientific grounds alone—that is, by repeated visits to Pueblo communities—whether it is more correct to emphasize organic wholeness or repression. The interpretation of Pueblo culture in these terms is a reflection of preference and value and I do not see how this can be eradicated or corrected by collecting more facts and making more interpretations. Therefore it becomes a problem for the sociologist of knowledge to deal with. He can, with greater detachment, make a reflexive analysis of the meaning of the respective interpretations in the culture of which they are a part; he can seek out biases and stresses obviously not completely apparent to the researchers. There is no reason why they should be. If we were completely objective about our own writings we would never be able to write anything because we would be in a state of constant self-disagreement.

It is my opinion that this case has a strict parallel in another major area of controversy in contemporary sociology and social anthropology: the question of "caste" as applied to American Negro society. Here, as in the Pueblo case, we can observe two conflicting viewpoints: The Negro is a caste and he is not. Both sides can present abundant documentation and "proof"; both sides betray conscious and unconscious value orientations. The matter cannot be decided entirely on the basis of whose facts are the better—for the simple reason that the controversy's major dimension is not scientific method but values.[37]

What is perhaps most interesting—and not a little amusing—is that these controversies, so plainly a matter of value and preference, endure as long as they do without some objective attempt to sit down and realistically arbitrate the matter. The Puebloists have been firing their respective interpretations back and forth for a decade, yet none have seen fit to dig into the real issues—at least in print. It is not, perhaps, an easy thing to do, since it requires a good deal of self-objectivity and humility. I do not pretend to be much more willing to go through that than the next fellow.

NOTES

1. See references throughout the footnotes of this article for the most important papers. In addition a partial bibliography of equally relevant articles may be cited here:

R. Bunzel, *Introduction to Zuñi Ceremonialism* (Forty-seventh Annual Report, Bureau of American Ethnology, pp. 467-544, 1932).

W. Dennis, *The Hopi Child* (New York, 1940).

A. E. Kennard, *Hopi Reactions to Death* (American Anthropologist, vol. 39, pp. 491-496, 1937).

K. A. Wittfogel and E. S. Goldfrank, *Some Aspects of Pueblo Mythology and Society* (Journal of American Folklore, vol. 56, pp. 17-30, 1943).

2. The literature actually covers only Hopi and Zuñi, but there are certain indications that the problem includes the Eastern Pueblos also. I will not attempt to discriminate carefully between Hopi and Zuñi, since the similarities are sufficient to permit generalization at the level of this paper. I wish to disavow any implication that I am setting myself up as a Pueblo expert, since I am merely examining published materials from the standpoint of logical analysis. My actual acquaintance with the Pueblo Indians consists of three Sun Dances at Hopi villages and two hours in Zuñi.

3. E. g., the Goldfrank-Josephs collaboration (E. S. Goldfrank, *Socialization, Personality, and the Structure of Pueblo Society*, American Anthropologist, vol. 47, pp. 516-539, 1945).

4. E. g., Li An-che, *Zuñi: Some Observations and Queries* (American Anthropologist, vol. 39, pp. 62-76, 1937), pp. 68-69; specifically in his criticisms of Benedict's analysis of Pueblo leadership. Li also criticises Kroeber's analysis of the men's attitude toward houses in the same vein.

5. See L. Thompson, *Logico-Aesthetic Integration in Hopi Culture* (American Anthropologist, vol. 47, pp. 540-553, 1945) for the most recent expression of this perspective. Her paper will be used as the conceptual model in most of the discussion.

6. E. g., R. Benedict, *Patterns of Culture* (New York, 1934; reprinted 1945). She would now recognize other possibilities, of course.

7. E. g., Li An-che, *Zuñi*, and D. Eggan, *The General Problem of Hopi Adjustment* (American Anthropologist, vol. 45, pp. 357-373, 1943).

8. E. g., Thompson, *Logico-Aesthetic Integration*.

9. See Goldfrank, *Socialization, Personality, and the Structure of Pueblo Society* for the most recent exposition.

10. Titiev has shown that witchcraft lies at the bottom of much of what appears to be Apollonian among the Hopi. Hopi men do not like to assume chieftainship for a particular ceremony which has been dropped from the calender because "the Hopi believe that a forward or aggressive person is a witch" (M. Titiev, *Old Oraibi: a Study of the Hopi Indians of Third Mesa*, Papers, Peabody Museum of American Archaeology and Ethnology, Harvard University, vol. 22, no. 1, 1944, p. 106). See also M. Titiev, *Notes on Hopi Witchcraft* (Papers, Michigan Academy of Science, Arts, and Letters, vol. 28, pt. 4, 1942).

11. E. g., L. Thompson and A. Joseph, *The Hopi Way* (Chicago, 1944), where elements of both views are represented, though not clearly analyzed in relation to each other.

12. The emphasis also appears strongly in the field of sociology, where a great many concepts like "social disorganization," "community," "social control," and so on have a basis in quasi-idealizations of rural society and culture.

13. E. g., E. Sapir's paper, *Culture; Genuine and Spurious* (American Journal of Sociology, vol. 29, pp. 401-429, 1924). See M. Tumin, *Culture, Genuine and Spurious: a Re-evaluation* (American Sociological Review, vol. 10, pp. 200-207, 1945) for an analysis of the value-orientation in Sapir's paper and the general problem it presents for cultural analysis. In a more general way, there is a large hint of the idea in the current stereotype of preliterate cultures as "simpler" than modern civilizations and therefore so much easier to study and learn from. In the case of Southwestern ethnology, these tendencies may often assume a special form conditioned by the pervading sense of mystery and glamour of the country itself. A good deal of ethnology and archaeology in the Southwest has been done with a kind of eager reverence for turquoise, concho belts, Snake Dances, and distant desert vistas, and while this need not materially distort the scientific conclusions, it provides the worker with a *favorable attitude* toward whatever he may work with. This attitude is, I think, particularly noticeable in the Thompson paper cited frequently in this essay.

14. E. g., Frank Speck's *Naskapi: The Savage Hunters of the Labrador Peninsula* (Norman, Oklahoma, 1935).

15. Thompson, *Logico-Aesthetic Integration*, p. 552. See also Benedict, *Patterns of Culture* (1945 edition), pp. 116-119 and others.

16. Thompson, op. cit., p. 546.

17. Goldfrank, *Socialization*, pp. 525-532. See also Eggan, *General Problem*, pp. 360, 369-370; Li An-che, *Zuñi*, pp. 69-72.

18. Thompson, *Logico-Aesthetic Integration*, pp. 541, 546.

19. Goldfrank, *Socialization*, p. 519. See also Li An-che, *Zuñi*, p. 66.

20. Goldfrank, *op. cit.*, p. 535.

21. A parallel view is expressed by John Collier in his foreword to the Thompson-Josephs volume (*The Hopi Way*): "The Hopi, thus making inner form and inner power of the limitations of their nature world, similarly have internalized their social limitations. The limitations are extremely severe. The Hopi have

achieved peace, and not through policing but through the disciplines and the affirmations planted within each of their several souls. The achievement has been maintained across millenia and is maintained now. And the Hopi pay for their peace, severe payments" (p. 9). This statement illustrates in some respects the ambivalent point of view of the whole Thompson-Josephs volume—the goal, "peace," is exalted along with the world view, but the price of this achievement is hinted at as being a high one.

22. Quoted in Li An-che, *Zuñi*, p. 64.

23. Thompson, *Logico-Aesthetic Integration*, p. 541.

24. Idem, p. 548.

25. Idem, p. 552.

26. To Thompson, this is a feature of not very great importance in Pueblo religion. The fact that ritual "reaffirms symbolically the Hopi world view" (p. 549), she appears to feel is of greater significance.

27. Eggan, *General Problem*, p. 359.

28. Goldfrank, *Socialization*, p. 527.

29. Thompson and Joseph, *The Hopi Way*, p. 56.

30. Idem, p. 122.

31. Ibid.

32. Idem, p. 128.

33. I am not so sure of this. It is quite possible that the adherents of the "repressed" approach are rejecting those features of Pueblo culture they emphasize simply because they like the rest of the culture so well that they wish to be "frank" and "objective" about the whole. To decide such questions one would need to interview the various anthropologists on both sides.

34. M. Titiev, *Review of "The Hopi Way"* (American Anthropologist, vol. 48, pp. 430-432, 1946), p. 431. The failure to tell the whole story, and to avoid or distort certain features of it, is best represented in the initiation situation. A study of any of the various accounts of Hopi initiation ceremonies leaves no doubt of the traumatic effect they must have upon the child. These ceremonies last for nine days, during which time the boys are under the domination and "rigid discipline" (Titiev, *Old Oraibi*, p. 139) of elders, supernatural beings, and ghosts, who subject them to bewildering and terrifying experiences. On the night of the Kwan ceremony the entire village is shut off from the outer world, and the spirits of the dead, along with bands of Kwan and Horn men, race through the streets with horrifying noises. The effect of this "night of mystery and terror" (*idem*, p. 135) on the boys can be imagined—the point is that because of them everyone in the village becomes involved in this incredible and dangerous business. All of what happens in the kivas is not yet known but Titiev's remarks clearly indicate the strenuous psychological shock involved, with or without physical injury: "What befalls the initiates in the presence of this weird assembly of living Hopi, visibly 'dead,' and unseen spirits, no white man can tell with assurance; but from the general context I think we may reasonably conjecture that in some manner the novices are ceremonially 'killed' . . ." (idem, p. 136).

35. In a sense, this problem is part of the wider problem of "objective" as *versus* "cultural" approach in social scientific studies (cf. K. H. Wolff, *A Methodological Note on the Empirical Establishment of Cultural Patterns*, American Sociological Review, vol. 10, pp. 176-184, 1945, pp. 177-179). The chief characteristics of the latter as contrasted to the former are: an attempt at explicit, conscious recognition of the fact that all cultural studies proceed *through* rather than *around* the biases, values, and choices of subject of the researcher; and that scientific method is not a goal in itself but rather a technical problem. The problem of choice which is outlined above is thus seen by the "cultural" worker as one of the important determinants and conditioning agents in social scientific work, not as something to be ignored or somehow conquered. The merits of the respec-

tive approaches are by no means easy to decide upon as a final judgment about the nature of social scientific research; however, at the moment I do feel that the "cultural" approach, being more willing to recognize the social matrix of scientific investigation, is thus more liable, other things being equal, to have somewhat more insight into these questions of value. The "other things being equal" is important, however—the adoption of the "cultural" approach does not justify, as in the Thompson case, the ignoring of important methodological procedures and rigor.

36. The further question—why do these two individuals possess these particular values—cannot be answered in this paper or any other logical analysis of the problem. To find out something of this sort one would have to interview the persons in question. Some interesting research might result from an inquiry into the possible correlations of wholeness—configurationist thinking and critical realism with contrasting personality types. The problem is by no means one of simple determinism, of course.

37. I am indebted to Kurt H. Wolff for suggesting the case of "caste."

GEORGE DEVEREUX

1953. "Cultural Factors in Psychoanalytic Therapy," *Journal of the American Psychoanalytic Association*, vol. *1*: 629-655. Reprinted by courtesy of the author and of the Editor of the *Journal of the American Psychoanalytic Association*.

Dr. Devereux's brilliant and varied contributions to the integrated study of cultural and social-psychological phenomena cannot be represented adequately by a single paper. (cf. Bibliography in this volume.)

For an appraisal of his earlier work, see the relevant paragraphs in Kluckhohn's paper, "The Influence of Psychiatry on Anthropology in America during the last 100 Years," reprinted in this book.

The reader should have some background in psychoanalytic theory and research findings in order to appreciate the discussion that follows. Nevertheless, many of the implications of Devereux's thinking will be clear to the thoughtful reader.

(Note: A few slight changes of wording in the present version of this paper were made with the approval of Dr. Devereux.—Ed.)

CULTURAL FACTORS IN PSYCHOANALYTIC THERAPY[1]

GEORGE DEVEREUX[2]

A technical discussion of the influence of cultural factors upon the course and technique of psychoanalytic therapy must begin with a preliminary analysis of the nature of culture, and of its fate in mental health, psychological illness, and psychoanalytic therapy. Since some of this material has already been touched upon in another study (11), it will be presented here only in a more or less axiomatic form.

I. Culture as a Characteristic Human Trait

Definition of Terms: In the following discussion we differentiate between *homo sapiens* or *genus homo* as a biological organism and *man* as a human being.

1. *Homo sapiens* is the current end product of an evolutionary process toward a high degree of differentiation and individualization. The principal and uniquely characteristic trait of *homo sapiens*—the "constant of human nature"—is the extreme plasticity and variability of his behavior.

2. The aforementioned four characteristics of *genus homo*—differentiation, individualization, plasticity, and variability of behavior—represent a unitary biological potentiality which is actualized in the acquisition of a distinctively human psyche and of culture.

3. The possession of a human psyche and the possession of culture are uniquely characteristic of man and further stimulate and expand *homo sapiens'* biologically determined tendency toward differentiation, individualization, plasticity, and variability of behavior.

4. Although the human psyche and culture are the resultants of a biological potentiality, whose actualization they represent, neither the human psyche nor culture may be thought of as *biological* characteristics of *genus homo*. They must be thought of as distinctively *human* characteristics of *man*.

5. Methodologically and functionally, the human psyche and culture are inseparable concepts.

6. Since culture represents an actualization of a basic biological potentiality of *genus homo*, whenever man functions as a "creator, creature, manipulator, and carrier" (21) of culture he satisfies one of

219

his most fundamental needs, which cannot be frustrated without dire consequences for the human psyche and for man's status as a human being. This is cogently demonstrated by Davis' study of a girl deprived more or less completely of cultural experiences (2).[3]

7. The "culturalization" of man is contingent upon, and is a resultant of, the replacing of the direct and massive *manifestation* of biological impulses—and especially of aggressive rather than of erotic impulses—by plastic, economical, and accurately context- and goal-adapted behavior. Such behavior has a high survival value and is in conformity with *homo sapiens'* biological potentialities for differentiation and individualization. In other words, in actualizing and in implementing his biological potentialities for differentiated, individualized, plastic, and variable behavior, *homo sapiens* acquires the status of man and functions as a human being.

8. It is an illusion that culture *constricts* behavior. If culture constricted behavior, then culture would not actualize but destroy *homo sapiens'* biological potentialities for differentiation, individualization, plasticity, and variability of behavior, so that the human being possessed of culture would be more *homo sapiens* than *man*, which is obviously a fallacy. In reality culture expands the scope, range, variability, efficiency, and appropriateness of behavior by substituting for massive and impulse-determined motility and affect discharge a partial, specific and goal- and context-determined motility and affect discharge. Several misconceptions are responsible for the illusion that culture constricts behavior. The first of these is the inappropriate use of a far too narrow biological frame of reference, which fits *genus homo* but not mankind and which ignores the biologically determined trend toward differentiation and individualization in the evolution of *homo sapiens*. The second misconception is derived from the observation of the effects of "sick" cultures upon human beings, whom such cultures force into patterns of passive and nonspontaneous adaptation. The source of the third misconception is clinical experience with analytic patients, who are in analysis precisely because they themselves constrict and distort, rather than sublimate, individualize, and adapt, their aggressive impulses.

9. A healthy society encourages, for its own sake, the fullest actualization of *homo sapiens'* potentialities for individualization and differentiation. As MacIver (17) pointed out long ago, maximum individualization and maximum socialization go hand in hand, since man cannot unfold all of his potentialities without the help of society, and society cannot derive the utmost benefit from any of its members unless each of these members is permitted and helped to unfold all of his potentialities to the fullest possible extent. A healthy society will therefore encourage individualized sublimations rather than dedifferentiating sup-

pressions and repressions. A successful sublimation disguises and distorts the underlying antisocial impulse to a far lesser extent than does a suppression or a repression. For example, if the underlying impulse happens to be a body-destruction fantasy, this impulse is more productively, more creatively, and more individualistically sublimated by the surgeon than by the butcher or by the antivivisectionist.

10. By contrast, a "sick society" cannot tolerate individualization and individualized sublimations and, therefore, favors dedifferentiation, loss of individuality, suppression, repression, reaction formation, etc.

11. The illusion that culture is constrictive and anti-instinctual is contradicted by the clinical fact that the analysis of the infantile and unconscious sources of a sublimation not only fails to destroy the sublimation in question but, on the contrary, actually strengthens it. This point was made with exceptional clarity by Jokl (15).

12. The cultural frame of reference enables the observer to "structure"—i.e., to understand, control, and predict—the behavior of normal persons. The psychoanalytic frame of reference enables the observer to "structure"—in the above sense—the behavior of abnormal persons.[4]

13. Personality disorders of various kinds—including those which arise in the course of the transference neuroses—represent a partial dedifferentiation and deindividualization, or, in other words, a partial regression of *man* to *homo sapiens*. For this reason children and abnormal persons belonging to our society resemble their counterparts in other cultures far more than the normal members of our society resemble the normal members of other ethnic groups, since normals are more highly differentiated and more fully individualized than are children and abnormal persons. These observed differences are best understandable in terms of the concept *man*, while the observed similarities are best understandable in terms of the concept *homo sapiens*.

14. The above considerations explain why the behavior of abnormal persons seems incomprehensible when we insist upon analyzing it in exclusively sociocultural terms. If, however, we view it also in biological terms, i.e., partly in terms of the concept *homo sapiens*, the behavior of such persons becomes understandable, predictable, and controllable—more understandable, predictable and controllable, in fact, than the far more complex, overdetermined, differentiated, and individualized behavior of normal man (10).

15. The preceding paragraphs explain why the manner in which abnormal persons manipulate and experience cultural material has a great diagnostic value. They also suggest that in really deep psychoanalytic therapy the analyst has to know the patient's specific cultural background *less* fully ahead of time than in more superficial forms of psychotherapy (11). This point will be elaborated more in detail below.

16. The psychoanalyst must, however, possess a very sound under-

standing of the nature and function of "culture per se"—as distinct from familiarity with any particular culture—because culture is a universal phenomenon and a trait uniquely characteristic of man, and because the broad categories of culture—as distinct from their concrete content in any particular culture—are also universal phenomena.[5] This statement is so complex that a simple illustrative example may help to clarify it. The writer once sought to diagnose an Indian of whose culture he knew next to nothing. This Indian reported that he had left his mother at the foot of the hill, ridden to the top of the hill, and met there his father and his mother. Although this sounded like a clearcut delusion or hallucination, the writer's knowledge of the *existence* of the cultural category "classificatory kinship systems" caused him to inquire whether the mother the patient had left at the bottom of the hill was the same mother he met on top of the hill. The patient immediately explained that the "mother" he met on top of the hill was actually his mother's sister, whom, in accordance with the kinship system of his tribe, he also called "mother." In brief, in this particular instance it was not the writer's nonexistent familiarity with the patient's tribal culture which enabled him to differentiate between a cultural practice and a delusion. What enabled him to do so was his familiarity with the categories of culture per se—of culture as a universal human phenomenon.

17. Whenever the psychotherapist utilizes his concrete familiarity with the patient's culture, he engages in the practice of *cross-cultural psychotherapy*. Whenever he utilizes his knowledge of the nature of culture per se and of universal cultural categories, he engages in the practice of *transcultural psychotherapy* (11).

II. The Relationship Between Psychoanalysis and Anthropology

Both psychoanalysis and anthropology study that which is distinctively human in mankind, i.e., that which differentiates man seen as a person-in-culture from *homo sapiens* seen in a biological frame of reference. Psychoanalysis is more particularly concerned with that which is distinctively human in the human psyche, while anthropology is primarily interested in that which is uniquely and characteristically human in culture and in society. In this sense both psychoanalysis and anthropology are branches of "Anthropology" as defined by Kant, i.e., of the science of that which is distinctively human in man. However, as pointed out elsewhere (6), psychoanalysis and anthropology do not yield additive, but complementary, insights. Indeed, the more fully we understand the deeper psychological factors which impelled John Doe to give his wife a pair of earrings on their first wedding anniversary, the less fully we understand this act in social and cultural terms, i.e., in terms of the customs, mores, and folkways regulating the relationship between spouses, the celebration of anniversaries, the choice of appropriate gifts, etc., in our own society. We may even assume that there exists a Heisenberg type of indeterminacy relationship between the psychoanalytic and the anthropological *understanding* of human behavior. We suggested elsewhere (6) that convenience and economy of effort alone determine at what point in one's investigation of a given action it is desirable and efficient to discontinue further inquiry in, e.g., psychoanalytic terms, and to start analyzing the phenomenon under consideration in social and cultural terms—and vice versa, of course. This is admittedly a purely heuristic solution of the problem, but one which is sufficiently accurate for our present purposes.

What we seek to stress in this context is that both psychoanalysis and anthropology study that which is distinctively and uniquely human and that both are sciences concerned with individuality and differentiation.

This does not mean that psychoanalysis and anthropology are not concerned also with similarities and uniformities. However, when psychoanalysts and anthropologists formulate general laws about the human psyche and about culture and cultural behavior, these laws usually pertain to various *processes* of differentiation and individualization rather than to the *end products* of these processes, which are extremely diversified. They are, in fact, so diversified that an attempt to strip them of their quality of variability frequently also deprives them of their very essence and reality. In brief, psychoanalytic and anthropological laws pertain to processes of differentiation and individualization, but leave relatively unexplained the phenomenological diversity of the end products of these processes. This is not a defect of psychoanalytic and anthropological theorizing. On the contrary, it is the natural consequence of a theoretical approach which is eminently suited to the nature of the phenomena which these sciences study.

III. The Vicissitudes of Culture in "Normality" and "Abnormality"

We are now prepared to examine in detail the transformations and vicissitudes to which cultural material is subjected in the total behavior of "normals" and "abnormals," especially in the course of psychoanalytic therapy.

It cannot be our purpose to summarize here the many insights into the differential significance of various concrete cultures for the etiology, symptomatology, and therapy of the neuroses and psychoses, which have accumulated in the last decades. Nor is it necessary to do so, since this matter has already been dealt with more or less adequately in another context (7). Rather do we propose to discuss the vicissitudes of culture per se—as distinct from American or Trobriand culture—in the experience and behavior of various types of psychiatric patients. It is our hope that a tentative formulation of these vicissitudes may eventually serve as a point of departure for the development of a genuine transcultural psychotherapy, based upon a real understanding of the generalized nature and function of culture per se, as it is experienced by normals and by various types of psychiatric patients. It seems probable that the practice of transcultural psychotherapy will require from the analyst a cultural neutrality similar to the emotional neutrality which he is expected to show in the analytic situation in regard to his own residual infantile and neurotic needs and attitudes (11).

The human being—be he a psychiatric patient or an unusually "normal" analytic candidate—experiences and manipulates cultural material in five characteristic ways:

1. *The present-synchronic and reality-adjusted use and experience of cultural material* is characteristic of mental health. Culture is experienced and recognized as an originally extrapsychic internalized "reality." The statement that culture is fundamentally an external reality is not intended to give support to the conception that culture is independent of, and wholly external to, Man. We refer simply to the empirical fact that every individual is "enculturated" by other individuals, who make him conform to existing cultural standards. The normal individual's awareness of the fact that culture is something first learned and then internalized is shown by the clinical observation that, after a successful analysis, the patient is aware of the extrapsychic origins of his superego. Another characteristic of the normal individual is his understanding and experiencing of culture as a system which "structures" man's life space, by defining "appropriate" ways of perceiving, evaluating, and experiencing, both natural (4) and social realities (5). It should be specified that culture not only ascribes meanings and values to the component parts of the life space, but also determines the manner in which these component parts must be patterned into a meaningful whole. In brief, the normal individual adjusts to, manipulates, and experiences cultural items in terms of meanings and values compatible both with the real contemporary social scene and with his true status and chronological age.

2. *Anachronistic adjustment to culture* is characteristic of socially and personally immature or regressed individuals, who need not *necessarily* exhibit also other types of neuroticisms. Such persons recognize and experience culture as culture, i.e., as something external which has been internalized, but they experience and manipulate cultural items in two anachronistic ways:

a. *In social anachronism* the cultural items are assigned meanings which they no longer possess in terms of contemporary realities. The socially anachronistic individual's cultural behavior is characterized by "cultural lag": he believes in the divine right of kings; he yearns for, and romanticizes, the good old days, etc. A depth-psychological investigation usually reveals that social anachronism is rooted in personal immaturity or in regression.

b. *In personal anachronism* cultural items are assigned meanings which are inappropriate in terms of, and incompatible with, the subject's true age and status. Such subjects cannot "really" believe that they are adults, married, and the parents of children, nor that their real social roles and tasks are more than make-believe play behavior. They view their employers as father figures, are convinced that all other adults are truly grown up, while they themselves are still children and react with surprise and relief-to the discovery that all other adults also have areas of infantilism, and occasionally doubt their own maturity.

Both types rapidly develop parent transferences, which sometimes manifest themselves first in the guise of "sexual" interests, whose spuriousness is revealed by their infantile, polymorphous-perverse, ambivalent, and unrealistic nature. When this "sexual" transference—which is actually a resistance, whose purpose is to destroy and degrade the analysis by turning it into immature sex play—is interpreted, it is rapidly replaced by pregenital types of demands. In fact, this shift may occur even if the analyst remains silent and offers no interpretation whatsoever.

3. *Culture in neurosis* continues to be recognized as culture—i.e., as something originally external which has been internalized. However, after it is internalized, the cultural material is reinterpreted in a manner which gratifies the neurotic's distorted needs. The new meaning assigned to a cultural trait is derived neither from some obsolete social meaning of that trait, nor from the meaning which that cultural trait has for children whose development was a fairly normal one.[6] For example, the neurotic may assign an oral significance to some practice whose accepted cultural meaning is primarily a phallic or genital one. One example of precisely this kind of neurotic distortion of the meaning of a rite will be cited in the next section of this study. The transference reactions of such patients are not only anachronistic and infantile, but they are also characterized by *systematic* distortions in the perception of the analyst's behavior. The pattern according to which the perception of the analyst's behavior is distorted is determined by the patient's neurotic needs. Thus, a "sexual"—or rather pseudosexual—interest in the analyst may perhaps be complicated from the start by the intrusion of paranoid elements, expressed perhaps in the form of accusations of seductiveness, in the feeling of being "tested," and the like.[7] The transference is usually not only based on severe distortions of perception, but is often also highly inconsistent, partly because of the presence of massive ambivalences, but partly also because of the intru-

sion of mutually inconsistent transference elements belonging to various stages of psychosexual development, which co-occur in every transference reaction, as, for example, in "sexual" interests complicated from the start by accusations of seductiveness.

4. *Culture in psychosis*—at least when the psychosis has more or less engulfed the patient's pre-psychotic personality—ceases to exist *as culture*. Culture traits continue to be utilized, but only in a subjective manner and almost without reference to their normal social context. They are, in Merton's sense (19), empty rituals, which have lost their intimate connection with the culture's means-end schemata and value systems. On an even deeper level of regression culture traits cease altogether to be treated as cultural materials which automatically imply a sense of common or shared experience. They are degraded and deculturalized, and become mere means or channels for the expression of psychotic needs. Thus, the manner in which a severely regressed schizophrenic utilizes "language" has been described elsewhere as follows:

> . . . the speech of the schizophrenic—the word salad—merely seems variable and complex, but is actually not. It has ceased to be speech in the strict sense, in that it is not intended as an interpersonal communication, but merely as a means of "self" expression. Furthermore, what the schizophrenic seeks to "express" most of the time is not what can actually be verbalized. In brief, words are being used as emotional vocalizations, i.e., as means of expressing subverbal instinctual urges.[8] "Reasoning" is used to express the irrational demands of the superego. In brief, cultural material continues to be utilized, but *for noncultural ends*. It suffers a loss of function and a degradation, as when a scalpel is used for murder [10].

In such cases a true transference usually cannot be established by the patient's own unaided efforts. The keystone of the entire psychotic edifice is its *private* character, which is an extreme manifestation of what we have previously denoted by the term "social negativism" (5, 9). In the early stages of analysis the therapist must therefore seek to deprive these structures of their private character (12, 16), by intruding into, finding a place within, and participating in the creation of, the psychotic edifice. Figuratively speaking, the patient must first learn to experience his psychosis as a kind of *folie à deux* before the psychotic edifice can be partly neutralized, by depriving it surreptitiously of its wholly "private" character. This is difficult, because the psychotic is not a proselytiser, but it is possible to achieve this aim nonetheless. Only after this partial neutralization of the psychotic system, now no longer completely "private" ("socially negativistic"), has been accomplished, can the psychoanalytic therapist once more resume his distance and "externality" and, instead of *sharing* the patient's psychosis in an artificial *folie à deux*, become the *object* thereof—"become the patient's psychosis," we might almost say—by the establishment of a transference relationship based upon, and rooted in, a constant reality testing, which gradually leads to a re-enculturation of the patient. The axiom that the psychosis cannot be abolished before its private character is destroyed, simply means that the re-establishment of some kind of object relationship—however minimal and distorted it may be—must always precede the cure. The patient must be partially *resocialized* before he can be *re-enculturated*. This view is fully compatible with what we know of the child's need for a relationship with the parent, before the parent can be accepted by, and can function with regard to, the child as a "mediator of culture." (3).

5. *Psychopathy* is characterized by a very special and complex vicissitude of culture. First of all, whereas the psychotic's social negativism leads him to repudiate culture per se, the psychopath is, in a sense, actually waging a systematic and provocative war against culture (5). However, we feel that, contrary to accepted views, the psychopath does not fight culture by giving free rein to his instincts, but by means of reaction formations both against his instincts and against sublimations suggested by culture. We have, therefore, proposed the term "defense-ridden psychopath" as a substitute for the term "instinct-ridden psychopath" (9). We also suggested that, unlike the immature person and the regressed schizophrenic, the psychopath does not behave in a truly infantile manner and does not seek to fight his way back to the instinctual "Garden of Eden" (20) of early childhood. We indicated that the psychopath seeks to "act out" the child's conception of adult behavior instead of conforming to a realistic definition of mature conduct. We hinted in particular that the psychopath patterns his conduct upon the conception of adult behavior which is held by frustrated children who, as a result of the traumata of weaning and of toilet training, delegate their own omnipotence to the frustrating adults. At that stage of development in the sense of reality, the child thinks of adulthood as a new avatar of the infantile instinctual paradise and defines adults as impulsive, autistic, unpredictable, and instinct-ridden autocrats, whom it can only hope to conciliate and to manipulate to its own advantage. It is this childish conception of adult behavior which the psychopath seeks to "act out" in his own conduct (13). The psychopath is fully aware of the external origin and reality of culture, but fails to internalize it to any appreciable extent. He understands intellectually the values and meanings wherewith cultural items are endowed, but fails to respond emotionally to these culturally determined values and meanings. In fact, the psychopath often specializes in exploiting the loyalty of other persons to cultural values. His predatory skill often consists simply in a callously and cold-bloodedly manipulative approach

to that which other persons most cherish. The true psychopath does not simply seduce lonely women "for the fun of it," nor does he burgle their homes at night. Instead, he exploits their yearning for matrimony —which is a cultural value—in order to swindle them out of their money. The psychopath is a plausible and successful confidence man precisely because he appeals to the basic cultural loyalties of his victims. An imaginary example may help us clarify this point. A feeble-minded thief may steal a woman's wedding band and be quite unaware of the fact that this woman values her ring far more highly than its monetary value warrants. He may therefore melt it down and sell it as bullion. The psychopath, on the other hand, is fully aware of the high "excess value" or "sentimental value," which this object has for his victim. Hence, instead of melting it down and turning it into bullion, he may try to induce the woman to ransom her ring, the amount of the ransom he demands being computed partly on the basis of the cash value of the gold and partly on the basis of the sentimental value which this ring has for the "sucker." In other words, the psychopath thinks of himself as a "realist" in a world of "suckers." It is in this sense only that we may define psychopathy as "semantic insanity" (1). The psychopath's "semantic insanity" is often simply an emotional scotoma. He is unable to internalize certain cultural meanings and values which he "knows" as well as the next person, and therefore cannot truly empathize with the cultural loyalties of normal persons. On the other hand, he is fully capable of taking a predatory advantage of other persons' allegiances to cultural values. The above considerations clearly indicate why—except under quite unusual circumstances—the psychopath is incapable of developing a genuine transference. With the utmost tentativeness it may be suggested that in the opening phases of therapy one might attempt to outdo the psychopath at his own game, thus forcing him to cease "acting out" the frustrated child's conception of the omnipotent and ruthless adult, and to accept instead the complementary role of the frustrated child, who is at the mercy of the "psychopathic" therapist. Since the writer has had no occasion to try out this technique, he mentions it only as a theoretical possibility, which in practice may fail as completely as many other theoretically plausible technical suggestions for the treatment of psychopaths have failed.

It is hardly necessary to add that the above remarks have definite diagnostic implications. The manner in which the patient manipulates cultural material indicates whether he is immature, neurotic, psychotic, or psychopathic. This finding, in turn, affects both the prognosis and the therapeutic policy to be adopted. In addition, it is to be remembered that we have described above only the *initial* state of the transference and the patient's *initial pattern* of manipulating cultural material. This does not mean, however, that the same diagnostic criteria cannot be used also at other stages of the psychoanalytic therapy. Precisely because, in the course of analytic therapy, the patient alternates between improvement and relapse, a continuous reappraisal of the patient's current diagnostic status, by means of an analysis of the manner in which he currently handles and experiences cultural material, is especially desirable.

It is implicit in the views presented in Part I of this paper that statements about "health," "maturity," "illness," or "immaturity," are *in terms of our present frame of reference* merely indirect ways of referring to degrees of differentiation and individualization—i.e., of sublimation. The "sicker" or "the more regressed" the patient is—be it all the time, or only at a given stage of the analysis—the smaller will be the role which *cultural items* play in his behavior, and the more frequently will he deculturalize such cultural items.

These considerations now enable us to examine in detail certain aspects of the role of cultural factors in psychoanalytic treatment.

IV. Cultural Factors in Psychoanalytic Therapy

The following remarks are based upon the research psychoanalyses of a Plains Indian woman and of some culturally marginal white patients, and upon psychoanalytically oriented diagnostic and psychotherapeutic research work with several American Indians.[9]

The most important of the influences exerted by cultural factors upon psychoanalytic therapy is, in a sense, the analyst's own interest in cultural factors. This interest represents a special aspect of the problem of countertransference as a whole and is closely related to the special countertransference problems which are bound to arise in any psychotherapeutic research situation. The analytic patient is usually quite sensitive to the analyst's cultural interests and, depending on the course of the analysis, will either gratify these interests by means of long discussions about the practices of his tribe—which is an indirect resistance—or else will use his analyst's cultural interests as means for manifesting more overt kinds of resistance.

In fact, the patient sometimes even manages to turn the tables on the analyst and, as a resistance, develops an interest in his analyst's native culture or degree of Americanization. Two of the writer's native-born, but culturally marginal, white American analytic patients were rather curious about his cultural background, and—since both of them were rather proud of their verbal skill—both confessed that they used stilted modes of expression in order to "teach" him new English words and better English.[10] They also speculated on whether he truly understood the *American* cultural meaning of some of their actions, and sometimes resisted certain ego-dystonic but correct interpretations of their inhibitions by making disparaging remarks about the manners and morals of foreigners.

It is probable that the writer, who happens to be an anthropologist, occasionally allowed his interest to be monopolized by his patient's description of some hitherto unrecorded custom, instead of focusing his attention primarily on the unconscious and characterological material revealed by such productions. Nonetheless, it is occasionally legitimate to stimulate deliberately the production of cultural material. This technique was used in the case of a highly acculturated (Americanized) Indian patient, in order to encourage a temporary regression, for the purpose of facilitating the recall of infantile experiences which took place in an aboriginal cultural setting. This technique occasionally works fairly well, though sometimes it leads only to dry, factual recitations, which have to be viewed as resistances.

It must also be admitted that on certain—happily very rare—occasions the writer's attempts to view a given event in the patient's life from the native point of view were ingenious rather than cogent. This happened primarily when the writer was "taken in" by a special kind of resistance representing the patient's negative response to his analyst's cultural interests. Indeed, the native patient soon becomes aware of the analyst's cultural interests, and evolves an "overcompliant resistance," which consists in the production of quantities of analytically more or less irrelevant cultural material. Such data play the role of a "red herring" (12) which, because it happens to interest the analyst, diverts him from his analytic duties. It might be added that spectacular "acting out," "telepathic" feats and other unusual performances in the course of the analysis also seek to divert the analyst's attention from the latent to the manifest content of the patient's productions (12).

One distinctive type of resistance evolved in response to the analyst's extra-analytic cultural interests is the patient's occasionally legitimate resentment over what he construes to be interest in him as an *Indian informant*, rather than as a *patient* and as a *person*. A querulous Indian patient mentioned with great anger that during her military service an illustrated magazine wanted to publish her photograph in order to show that not only Indian men, but also Indian women served in our Armed Forces. She emphasized very vigorously that she wanted neither favorable nor unfavorable notice as an *Indian*, but only as a *person*. This demand, which obviously had some bearing upon the transference relationship, was not altogether unreasonable, though it was primarily motivated by her tremendous need to deny her Indian origins, her femininity, and her sexuality as well. Another Indian patient, who was in research psychotherapy, had a dream in which he greatly resented the fact that some persons, whom he had just met, asked him whether he was an Indian before they even bothered to ask him his name (7). Such remarks are clear enough a warning to the analyst not to give too free a rein to his cultural interests in the analytic hour.

Yet, until a truly satisfactory technique of transcultural psychotherapy is evolved, the psychotherapist as well as the analyst must be genuinely interested in the cultural background of the patient, and must seek to understand the patient's productions in terms of the patient's own culture (7). In psychoanalysis, as distinct from psychotherapy, the analyst can sometimes obtain the necessary cultural perspective simply by remaining silent long enough to learn something about the patient's culture through the patient's own, spontaneous and naive, productions. This procedure is, however, far from ideal, not only because it is wasteful of the patient's time and money, but also because it is not in keeping with the principles governing the proper timing of confrontations and interpretations (8).

For the time being, the only way out of this difficulty is for the analyst to learn about the patient's culture beforehand, through reading and study. Then, when the patient mentions a custom with which the analyst is already familiar, the raw data provided by the patient will seem less fascinating to him, and will therefore fail to divert him from his strictly analytic tasks. This explains why the writer always prepares himself rather carefully for psychotherapeutic or psychoanalytic research work with patients belonging to cultures with which he is not thoroughly familiar. Unfortunately, there is probably no culture which has been fully described in the literature. Hence, even though the writer prepared himself for the analysis of his Plains Indian woman patient by reading all published data about her tribe, on one occasion this patient mentioned a hitherto unrecorded and extremely striking tribal custom. This information was so startling, that for a few minutes the writer was more interested in a further exploration of this cultural material than in asking himself what unconscious impulses motivated, and lay concealed behind, this narrative.

We have shown that the analyst's own culturally oriented interests sometimes play into the hands of the patient—a fact which the patient promptly exploits to the limit. The remedy for this state of affairs is an adequate preparation for the analysis of persons belonging to alien cultures, and, above all, a constant awareness of one's own true task, which is the analysis of the patient, rather than the collecting of anthropological data. Needless to say, this type of temptation is not restricted in the analysis of persons belonging to other cultures. The analyst who is an apprentice stamp collector and happens to analyze an expert stamp dealer, may likewise allow himself to be "seduced" and may listen entranced to the stamp dealer's lecture on "Antigua penny puce"—without ever asking himself what this monologue seeks to accomplish, or what it conceals. After the above lines were written, the writer was told by several well-informed colleagues that Freud himself is supposed to have transferred to another analyst a patient who happened to be an

Egyptologist, because Freud's own interest in Egyptology interfered with the analysis.

Traditional practices and attitudes can also be used as resistances. An Indian analysand often chose to play the role of the stolid Indian, when she did not wish to face some ego-dystonic insight. When confronted with the spuriousness of her stolidity, she laughingly admitted that she had deliberately used this typically Indian defense—the "ugh" resistance, as we came to call it—against "the meddling paleface." The same patient also exploited to the limit her very genuine grievance over the fact that she had been discriminated against because of her race. Since she knew that both reality and the analyst's sympathies were on her side in this connection, she blamed everything on discrimination. It finally became necessary to dispose of this resistance by showing her a cartoon clipped from *Time* magazine, in which an analyst tells his Indian patient: "I think we are getting somewhere, Mr. Great Cloud Shadow. Your neurosis apparently stems from a submerged resentment against your ancestors for disposing of Manhattan Island for only twenty-four dollars." This "interpretation" proved so effective that ever after even the most cursory reference to "Mr. Great Cloud Shadow" or to "Manhattan Island" sufficed to stop her previously interminable "Lo, the poor Indian" monologues. In fact, whenever the patient subsequently spoke of being discriminated against, this simply indicated that she was resorting to a last-ditch defense, by means of an already interpreted and notoriously ineffective resistance, before giving in and accepting some new and ego-dystonic insight.

The next point we wish to take up concerns the latent meaning of the patient's manifest behavior and productions. An Indian analysand just had her fourth psychotic episode—her first since the analysis began. Passive and mute, she stubbornly hid under her blanket, although her general attitude was obviously friendly and even seductive. Time-tested analytic interpretation: "You are playing dead—you have something to hide—you are playing the baby," etc., were tried with no effect. Finally the writer remembered that he was not only a research analyst, but also an anthropologist, and said: "You are playing the role of the Indian maiden, who silently hides under her buffalo robe, while her suitor is courting her." The next instant the patient literally popped out from under her blanket and behaved in an almost completely normal and rational manner for several days in a row. This incident stands in need of a detailed analysis.

The "culturalist" will perhaps exclaim: "This is an almost perfect instance of the culture-bound nature of symptoms and symbols! Had this patient belonged to our own society, her behavior would have meant that she was playing dead, or that she was playing the baby, etc., but in terms of her own culture it meant that she was the courted maiden."

Unfortunately, this interpretation of the facts is so excessively right in one sense, that it is absolutely wrong in another sense. Actually, the situation is far more complex.

It is quite correct to say that the patient did not *react* to the remark: "You are playing dead," but did *react* to the interpretation: "You are playing the bride." This simply meant that the writer had made a technical mistake. He had ignored the rule that one should interpret whatever fits the patient's current preoccupations, i.e., that which is uppermost in the patient's mind, and just on the threshold of the conscious. The interpretation: "You are playing dead" was ineffective, because it was an *untimely interpretation.* The remark: "You are playing the bride" was effective, because it was a *timely confrontation.*[11] and close enough to the conscious to be accepted.

Indeed, the patient had her fourth psychotic break precisely because she was unable to manage her incestuous positive transference, and was thrown into a panic by an envious fellow patient's accusation that her analyst saw her daily only because she let him cohabit with her. When the writer failed to act like a proper *Indian* suitor, and *interpreted* her behavior, instead of *courting* her, the patient openly asked the analyst to court her in the *European* manner, i.e., by kissing her hand. When this request too was interpreted, instead of being complied with, the patient repeated the "bride motif" in a third way—this time in terms of *American* culture. One day this patient, who had a slight, organically determined motor disability, stumbled so often while walking down the hospital corridor shod in clumsy hospital slippers ("scuffies"), that she "had" to lean on the arm of the analyst. After supporting her for a few steps, the writer noticed that the patient walked with half-closed eyes and that her face bore a conventional expression of bridal rapture. When the writer quietly remarked: "All we need now is Mendelssohn!" the patient immediately let go of his arm, and without a trace of resentment, began to march down the corridor with the step of a Grenadier Guard.

The above data indicate that the remark: "You are playing the role of a courted girl" was effective because it was timely, and pertained to the positive transference, which was at that time so close to the threshold of the patient's conscious that a very simple confrontation, couched in cultural terms, sufficed to make it understandable to her.

Our next task is to show that the "deep" interpretations: "You are playing dead," "You are playing the role of a baby," "You are hiding," etc., were not erroneous, but simply poorly timed. Everything we know of the formalized and traditional passivity of Plains Indian women in sex and courtship, of their striking masochistic and infantile approach to genital behavior, and of their attempts to pretend that they are chaste even when they are not, gives a clinical analytic *meaning* to

their culturally determined *practice* of passively submitting to courtship while hiding under a buffalo robe (7). Lack of space prevents us
from documenting here in detail this view of Plains Indian feminine
sexuality, which is supported by copious anthopological data (7).

The above characterization of the Plains Indian woman's attitude
toward sexuality is fully applicable to the patient in question. She in-
sistently assured the analyst that she had been a virginal bride, and even
told a long and entirely untrue story about the details of her deflora-
tion on her wedding night. She falsely alleged that she had been a
faithful wife. She had so often exposed herself to rape that it is hard to
understand how she had escaped unscathed. She placed all responsibility for her sexual acts upon the men who had allegedly "seduced"
her. She connected sexuality with castration and fantasied that prostitutes were oversexed women, whose internal genital organs had been
excised. She stated that, as a child, she had injured her vulva when,
while raiding the cookie jar, she slipped and fell astride on the open
door of the lower kitchen cabinet. In adult life she hemorrhaged for
months at a time and in her fantasies connected the idea of death with
sexual activity.

This being the case, it seems legitimate to suggest that the confrontation: "You are playing the role of the bride," was simply the more
timely formulation of such deeper, but untimely, interpretations as:
"You are playing dead," etc. The latter interpretations were also true—
"truer" perhaps than the confrontation which had proved effective—
but they were *premature*. This woman's unconscious did not differ
from that of other people, and her fantasies had nothing unique about
them. Like any other patient, she used symbols and symbolic acts to
express her conflicts and wishes, and the symbols she used were of the
type which a similarly motivated patient belonging to our own culture
would have used. The only distinctive thing about her symbolic acts
was the culturally determined *manner* in which she played the role of
the passive and symbolically dead bride. She hid under a blanket, where
a white American woman patient might perhaps have played the role
of a young bride in her coffin. The analyst was therefore confronted
with the necessity of understanding also the supplementary cultural
meaning of her symbolic acts. Such supplementary cultural meanings
are, needless to say, also implicit in the symbolic actions of members
of our own society, but we are so familiar with them that we sometimes tend to overlook them and to behave as though these supplementary cultural meanings did not exist or were parts of the basic
symbol. As regards analytic technique, the point to be stressed here is
that these supplementary cultural meanings lend themselves better to
confrontations than to interpretations, and that it is generally desirable
to make these confrontations before one proceeds to interpret the un-

derlying unconscious fantasy material which these symbols seek to express.

Another difficulty in the analysis of culturally alien patients is caused by the neurotic's tendency to distort the underlying, culturally and psychologically standardized meaning of his cultural experiences. An example will illustrate this point. One night in July the above-mentioned Indian woman dreamed that she sat on her bed, noticed that it was snowing outside, and felt surprised that it should snow in summer. Her associations referred to a variety of oral topics, including milk, breasts, the fact that she was given coffee as early as the sixth month of her life, her dislike of milk and her liking for a certain blood-red soft beverage, whose "bland taste" she praised extravagantly. The unconscious content of these associations was her resentment over the fact that, by the standards of her tribe, she had been weaned rather early, and had therefore developed a spiteful and almost conscious compensatory need to reject milk and to deny her obvious dependency cravings. She then proceeded to describe the principal rite of her tribe, in the course of which the *bare-breasted* wife of the ritual leader had to cohabit with a number of men. Since the analyst knew that the patient was—verbally at least—quite prudish, he expected her to denounce the sexual immorality of this rite. He was therefore greatly surprised to learn that what the patient actually objected to in this rite was the fact that the ritual leader's wife wore the aboriginal costume, *which left her breasts bare.* Although the patient's account of this previously not recorded detail of the rite fascinated the analyst a great deal, and tempted him to explore the matter further from the anthropological point of view, the startling nature of this theoretically prudish patient's objections to the rite served to remind him in time of his analytic obligations. The nature of the patient's diatribe revealed that she had assigned an oral meaning to a ritual whose true cultural meaning was a phallic and genital one. In other words, whereas the real focus of the aboriginal ceremony was a series of ritual sexual acts, to this neurotic and orally demanding patient the focus of the rite was the fact that the ritual leader's wife was bare-breasted. What she begrudged these men was not sexual pleasure, but the fact that, being men, they could, under the guise of sexual activity, gain access to a woman's breasts, which she, being a woman, could not do. This material, together with insights derived from the rest of her copious associations, only some of which could be mentioned in this context, enabled the analyst to understand this dream as an expression of the patient's desire to obtain (seminal?) milk from the analyst, while denying him oral access to her own breasts, which she carefully and even aggressively kept covered, in order to underscore her superiority over "wild Injuns," as she called them.

Occasionally special difficulties arise in connection with the proper interpretation of material produced by more or less fully acculturated (Americanized) patients. These difficulties are sometimes so considerable, that they are likely to enmesh the excessively "culturalistic" analyst in a logically fallacious and therapeutically deleterious network of "culturalistic" pseudoinsights into the patient's behavior. Thus, when a well-acculturated patient reports that, in a certain situation of stress, he behaved in the "aboriginal" manner, this may cause the extreme "culturalist" to become so preoccupied with problems of cultural duality, culture conflict, etc., that he may fail to give due consideration also to the regressive implications of that action. For example, when an Indian analysand, who had a college major in biology, contracted a minor chronic ailment which American physicians seemed unable to cure, she finally went to a native "therapeutic" peyote meeting, in the hope that this would cure her. From the analytic and therapeutic point of view her behavior has to be interpreted as a primarily regressive act, rather than simply as a bit of cultural traditionalism. In other words, this action of a highly acculturated Indian biology major has to be interpreted exactly as one would interpret the behavior of an American physician born of immigrant parents who, deeply disturbed by the discovery that he had a probably inoperable cancer, suddenly decided to consult the village witch, or her urban equivalent. Indeed, under normal circumstances this Indian patient sneered at those of her people who were naive enough to seek peyote cures. Hence, what is *analytically* relevant in this incident is not the fact that the patient has been raised by parents who believed in peyote cures—which makes her behavior only culturally, but not psychoanalytically, understandable[12]— but the fact that she had regressed sufficiently to resort to a subjectively anachronistic anxiety-allaying device, which she ordinarily ridiculed as a "wild Injun superstition."

It should be emphasized that nothing said in the preceding paragraph constitutes a denial of the empirically tested and theoretically defensible thesis that basic cultural attitudes and the tribal ethos continue to play a major role in the acculturated Indian's personality make-up long after he has forgotten the traditions and practices of his tribe (7). Every human being has many, partly repressed and partly sublimated, magical attitudes, and we cannot expect the acculturated Indian to be an exception to this rule. What was regressive in the behavior of this Indian patient was not the fact that she had certain unconscious magical attitudes, but the fact that there was a sudden return of these repressed attitudes, which were then *acted out* in the patient's attempt to seek a peyote cure.

The last technical problem we propose to discuss is, superficially at least, a fairly complex one, though in practice it can be handled strictly in accordance with the classical rule that one should interpret whatever is nearest to the threshold of the conscious. If, in the analysis of culturally alien patients, one seeks to adhere to this rule as strictly as one should, one is sometimes faced with the necessity of interpreting at a fairly early stage of the analysis certain matters which are usually not interpreted until after several months of analysis. When such situations arise, one is sometimes tempted to deviate from the classical rule, and to justify this deviation by assuming that the early production of seemingly very "deep" and "traumatic" material may possibly be indicative of a latent psychosis. While such a possibility should never be ruled out *a priori*, one must bear in mind that a given wish or conflict, which has to be very deeply repressed in one culture, may only be minimally repressed in another culture. For example, a tendency to indulge in magical thinking, or in fantasies of primary or delegated omnipotence, may be interpreted fairly early to an Indian, whose culture does not cathect cold rationality and objectivity to the same extent as ours is supposed to do. On the other hand, a Plains Indian male's cowardice, homosexual dependency cravings, and the like should be interpreted to him fairly cautiously, and, whenever possible, only after a fairly stable transference has been established. In a similar sense, castration anxiety may be interpreted fairly early to an Indian cowboy accustomed to castrating livestock, while his incestuous impulses will have to be handled rather carefully, since in many primitive tribes the incest taboo is very severe and applies not only to one's biological family, but also to most members of one's extended kin (7). An especially important corollary of the above considerations is the fact that, contrary to traditional rule-of-the-thumb practice, dreams may be interpreted even in the first analytic hour to a patient in whose culture dreaming—and especially stylized dreaming—plays an important role. One reason why it is fairly safe to do so is that, at least in the beginning, most dreams reported to the analyst are likely to be stylized dreams, whose actually dreamed manifest content will have been more or less consciously "corrected" or elaborated, in order to make these dreams conform to tribal ideas of what important dreams should be like.

CONCLUSION

Psychoanalysis and anthropology are the sciences most fundamentally concerned with man's *distinctively and uniquely human characteristics*. Though the human psyche and culture are functionally inseparable, the insights provided by psychoanalysis and those provided by anthropology are not additive but complementary. It is shown that culture is experienced in different ways by normals and by various types of psychiatric patients, and the characteristic transformations and vicissitudes of cultural material in normals, immature persons, neurotics, psychotics, and psychopaths are described in some detail.

On the basis of these findings certain technical rules for the analysis of culturally alien patients are outlined. The problems arising in the course of such analyses are illustrated by means of clinical examples.

NOTES

1. Read before the panel on "Cultural Factors in Psychoanalytic Therapy" at the Annual Meeting of the American Psychoanalytic Association, Cincinnati, Ohio, May 5, 1951.

2. Director of Research, The Devereux Foundation.

3. In so far as any reliance may be placed upon reports of so-called "wolf-children" in India (14, 18, 22) these data also support the views just expressed.

4. This formulation is in accordance with Mach's cautious dictum that there are no laws in nature, apart from those which we *put into*, or *ascribe to*, nature, in the course of our attempts to generalize from our observations of discrete phenomena.

5. This is implicit in Durkheim's conception of *les catégories de l'ésprit humain*. Indeed, every culture "has" a kinship system, an economic system, a system of laws, of knowledge, of religion, etc., though the actual kinship system, etc., may differ from tribe to tribe. In the present context—i.e., as regards the *use* one makes of these categories in scientific discourse—it is totally irrelevant whether these "structuring" categories *exist in* culture, or are *put into*, or *ascribed to*, culture by the observer, who may even be himself a member of the culture under consideration (6).

6. The term "normal development" is used here to denote a process in the course of which only the usual "developmental neuroses" (i.e., the so-called "infantile neuroses") occur. These developmental neuroses are uniquely characterized by the fact that they can be "outgrown" without psychiatric help, i.e., solely by means of the impetus inherent in psychosexual development and maturation. In addition, unlike true neuroses in children, such developmental neuroses cause no residual pathological distortions of the personality.

7. Nonpathological feelings of being "tested" may sometimes be culturally determined, as was shown by the psychotherapy of a Plains Indian, in whose culture the "test theme" played an important role (7).

8. The reverse of this procedure might be an attempt to translate Freud's *Three Contributions to the Theory of Sex* into the babbling of a baby.

9. The psychoanalyses were control analyses, and the research psychotherapies were conducted under the authority of a qualified psychiatrist, in a clinical setting.

10. The desire of these patients to "teach" their analyst English may have been partly motivated by the fact that, in his analytic work, the writer always uses the simplest and most homely modes of expression at his disposal. In addition, he usually avoids all abstractions, and uses instead figurative expressions consisting, whenever possible, of visual types of imagery, because his anthropological field experience has led him to believe that visual figures of speech are especially easily understood, and may even be particularly suitable for communication with at least the upper layers of the unconscious.

11. The distinction between confrontations and interpretations, especially as regards timing, was discussed elsewhere (8).

12. This incident is a good illustration of the complementarity relation between the cultural and the psychoanalytic understanding of human behavior.

BIBLIOGRAPHY

1. CLECKLEY, 1950
2. DAVIS, K., 1940
3. DEVEREUX, 1939-c
4. DEVEREUX, 1939-d
5. DEVEREUX, 1940-a
6. DEVEREUX, 1945
7. DEVEREUX, 1951-a
8. DEVEREUX, 1951-c
9. DEVEREUX, 1951-d
10. DEVEREUX, 1951-e
11. DEVEREUX, 1952
12. DEVEREUX, 1953, "The technique of analyzing 'telepathic' occurrences during analysis."
13. DEVEREUX, 1955
14. GESELL, 1940
15. JOKL, 1950
16. KUBIE, 1952
17. MACIVER, 1929
18. MANDELBAUM, 1943
19. MERTON, 1949, Chap. IV
20. RÓHEIM, 1940
21. SIMMONS, ed., 1942
22. SINGH & ZINGG, 1942

CORA DU BOIS

1941. "Attitudes toward Food and Hunger in Alor," from *Language, Culture, and Personality, Essays in Memory of Edward Sapir,* edited by Leslie Spier, A. Irving Hallowell, and Stanley S. Newman. Menasha, Wis. Pp. 272-281. Reprinted by courtesy of the author and of the Editors of *Language, Culture, and Personality.*

Dr. DuBois' field research in Alor, an Indonesian island about 600 miles east of Java and 700 miles west of northern New Guinea, is reported in full in her book, *The People of Alor.* A critical analysis of her data appears in *The Psychological Frontiers of Society* by Abram Kardiner. The essay in the following pages indicates the value of a careful reading of these two books.

ATTITUDES TOWARD FOOD AND HUNGER IN ALOR

Cora Du Bois

Dr. Sapir's great respect for the subtlety and complexity of human beings acted as a sobering influence on the growing interest of anthropologists in psychology and upon the contributions they made to social psychology. As an anthropologist he minimized in no way the tremendous power of society in shaping people but he never permitted his interests as a social scientist to blind him to the infinite variety of individuals within a culture. He went even farther and in conversation, at least, would support the probability of innate personality types. This sound caution against the environmentalists' inclination to overvalue conditioning was a great advantage to his students. At the same time he laid full stress on studying the socialization of the child.

It seems possible to combine these two principles in a preliminary and tentative fashion by making certain assumptions, following certain methods of reasoning and thereby arriving at certain generalizations about people within a given cultural framework, without at any time denying that the processes and symbols are going to have tremendously different values in the total economy of the individuals involved. It is with this in mind that I should like to discuss attitudes developed toward food and hunger in a particular culture.

It can be reasonably assumed that all human beings have certain physiologically determined tensions. One of the most obvious of these is hunger. But nowhere do human beings discharge this or any other basic tension directly. All societies have devices whereby such tensions are delayed, redirected, and often elaborated. To acquire these devices children everywhere must be subject to disciplines. Such disciplines may be of various types and undoubtedly the question deserves close comparative study. For our purposes it will suffice to point out that they may be permissive, restrictive, or absorptive. By permissive disciplines are meant those by which children are encouraged to acquire certain behaviors through a variety of immediate or delayed rewards. By restrictive disciplines are meant those which definitely deny the child certain types of activity by punishments ranging from physical violence to withdrawal of approval. The absorptive disciplines are those not consciously imparted, as are the permissive and restrictive, but rather those behavior patterns so consistently observed in other members of the group that the child acquires them by a kind of psychic osmosis.

It is important to stress that a single discipline of childhood or a single traumatic experience is rarely sufficient in itself to set cultural personality types. Repeated experiences in different behavioral, value, and institutional contexts alone will create personality constellations of such force and consistency that they may become apparent to ethnologists who, with the best will in the world, can never have more than a superficial insight into peoples of an alien culture.[1]

Lastly, there is so far no very definite knowledge of what ego mechanisms will be employed by the individual in reacting to frustrations associated with different kinds of disciplines and discipliners. However, from the psychoanalysts and the psychiatrists there is a growing insight into personality processes like projection, introjection, sublimation, and so on. I assume these processes to be universal to mankind, although I should expect variations in weighting from culture to culture.[2]

The procedure, therefore, is to consider a basic physiological tension, see how it is acted upon by disciplines of childhood, what repetitions it finds in a variety of contexts and how it is crystallized by (or into) institutional behavior through those personality mechanisms I have assumed to be universal to mankind.

Hunger, as one of the basic and obvious tensions of human beings, everywhere subject to delayed, redirected, and elaborated gratifications, suggests itself as a point of departure for testing the procedure outlined above. The people used for this purpose are the Atimelangers, who belong to a cluster of five mountain villages on the island of Alor in the Netherlands East Indies.[3]

The experiences of the Atimelang child with hunger and food are to be considered first. Immediately after birth the mother takes the child in her arms and offers it the breast to suckle at will. From four to six days after birth the mother remains in the house with the infant rather constantly in her arms. When the umbilical cord has dried and dropped off, the mother and child leave the house for the first time and from then onward the child is offered in addition to its mother's milk many different kinds of premasticated foods and vegetable gruels. Any refusal of the child to nurse freely and frequently when opportunity offers during this first period of life is considered a serious symptom of ill health and gives rise to considerable concern in parents. After the first week the child is given adult diet as fast as it will take it, and a child of about eighteen months can often be seen at a feast alternately nursing and sucking a cube of boiled pork fat.

Since, however, women are primarily responsible for garden work and the subsistence economy of the Atimelangers, they return to regular field work often ten days to two weeks after the birth of a child. It is not customary for the mother to work with the child on her back or even near her, as it is in some societies, so the infant is left at home in the care of some kin, usually the father or older sibling. There is great variation in solicitude and effectiveness of feeding care received by infants from these substitute mothers. Also some women have greater responsibilities than others in the number they must provide for and are therefore more pressed by field work. On the other hand some women may have given birth during the middle of the dry season when labor in the fields is slack. Still others may be lazy about gardening. As a result some infants receive more care and food during the first months of life. If an infant is left in the hands of a father or sibling, it is going to be fairly hungry part of that time. The person caring for the child may give it gruel or premasticated food more or less conscientiously, but to judge from the frequency with which infants spew out such nourishment, one may suggest that such feeding is not very effective or satisfactory. One repeatedly sees infants trying to nurse at the breast of a father or immature sibling only to be pushed away with an attitude of mild embarrassment.

Rilpada told an anecdote of his childhood which reveals both the frustration infants may suffer from this type of feeding as well as the older sibling's frequent resentment of the role of nurse maid.

> Once mother and I were living in a field house near our gardens. She told me to carry Senmani [younger brother] while she worked. At noon he was hungry and wanted to nurse. I gave him food but he only vomited it. He cried and cried and wouldn't stop. I cried too. Finally I went and told mother to come and nurse him but she wouldn't. So I took Senmani, laid him down on a mat in the house and ran off to Folafeng. There from the ridge I shouted, "Mother, your child lies in the house. If you want to care for it, good. If you don't want to, that is also good. I am going to Atimelang to play."

The point to be made is that even during infancy, when children are quite generally delighted-in, and when they are rarely out of someone's arms, or at least someone's carrying shawl, gratification of hunger is frequently a disappointing experience. Feeding is irregular; intervals between nursing are so long that acute hunger may arise with either no means of gratifying it or gratification is offered in foods obviously less satisfactory than that which the mother offers. When the mother is home and not too busy, she will offer the child the breast whenever it is restless. However, I never heard any woman speak of the pleasure of nursing, which probably means no more than that the culture has not maximized this particular physical pleasure. Women, when asked, did generally say that they preferred child bearing to intercourse but almost invariably added, "Because children will give my funeral feasts." There were several women who said that they did not wish any more children because feeding them meant so much work. Economic organization, therefore, acts directly upon attitudes toward children and conditions the child's earliest experiences in respect to food in this society.

In Atimelang, therefore, the hunger tension of infants is not maximally met as in some societies where children are constantly in contact with their mothers and where the pattern of nursing is a consciously fostered gratification of both mother and child.

A still more serious feeding problem may arise when the child begins to walk, approximately between the thirteenth and eighteenth months. By the time it can manage to get about alone, it is left to play near the house or on the dance place in the center of the village. An older sibling, real or classificatory, or an old woman may be near and will care for a whole group of children in a desultory fashion but no one is responsible for feeding the child and no one is greatly incommoded by his crying. When the mother goes off to work, the child is left from about eight in the morning until five in the afternoon without regular provision of food. This does not mean that he is left entirely without food, but that all he gets during that time may be odd bits an older child cedes more or less willingly and generously to him when he begs for it. Again, of course, there is marked variation in children's experiences during this period. They may have a solicitous older sister who can be spared from field work and who will provide relatively good care. There may be a grandmother who works less hard and frequently in the gardens. But, in any case, after the child learns to walk, his frustrations with respect to hunger are increased, and simultaneously he loses the constant handling and support he had during the first stage of life in the carrying shawl. That the acquisition of his first skill in the independent mastery of the outer world, i.e., walking, should be associated with two severe deprivations may well have larger personality repercussions in the realm of ego development than there is space to consider in this paper.

To add to the strain of this period and to reinforce it further, the weaning of the child may be hastened at this time because another sibling is expected. Rarely does one see a child of three or four still nursing. Although weaning is done simply by pushing the child away gently or placing the breast beyond its reach, there is no doubt that difficulties accumulate at this stage of development. Anal training, walking, and talking have not yet been deliberately instituted. They are allowed to take their own course. In other words, the child has acquired few skills during the first two or three years of life. Those which he has acquired have been by means of restrictive or absorptive disciplines. It is not surprising that this is the time par excellence of temper tantrums. These continue, as might be expected, with marked individual variation up to the ages of five to eight. Adult reactions to childrens' tantrums are characterized by great inconsistency. One day a mother will ignore the child; the next she may be irritated and strike it; on still another occasion she may deceive it into thinking she is not deserting it, only to slip away when the child has been diverted; or on still other occasions, especially at night, the child may be threatened with the local bogy-man who, incidentally, is not a very fearsome figure. In addition then to their inconsistency, all active disciplines are of the restrictive type. I have never seen a mother promise a child a reward for being good and then keep her promise.

A clear example of the needs of early childhood and the uncertainties of the persons on whom the child depends for its gratifications is found in a series of statements contained in Tilapada's autobiography. She tells of caring for a younger sister called Maliemai.

> On the way [to the fields] Maliemai cried a lot, so I put her down and slapped her. Then I talked nicely to her and we went on when she was quiet. . . . When Maliemai was a little older, she would cry to go to the fields with me. If I were not angry with her, I would take her along with me to dig sweet potatoes. I would give her the big ones and keep the small ones. She was always crying. She cried to be fed; she cried to go places. I hit her on the head with my knuckles and then I would feed her. She cried because she was hungry.

The inconsistent and restrictive quality of discipline which pervades the child's life might well be expected to breed in it a sense of insecurity and suspicious distrust. It has at its disposal only one weapon with which to meet frustration and that is rage. The alternative idea of being good in order to gain one's ends is not presented to the child. But that rage is an ineffectual weapon is learned at very latest during the first decade of life.

While the child is discovering the futility of protest, he is also discovering his own resources. He may expect his mother to prepare a morning meal at about seven o'clock and another at about the same time in the evening. During the intervening twelve hours he learns to forage for himself. He learns this from five or six onward in the fluid play groups of free roving children. Remnants may be scraped from the cooking pot. A variety of insects usually spurned by adults can be found. In the fields near the village are mangoes, bananas, sweet potatoes, young corn, and squash. They can be eaten raw or easily cooked. As a rule adults do not object to the minor depredations of their own children or their playmates, but if the raiding is too constant or if the crop is scarce, children may be scolded for it. Such objections are most apt to be voiced when children are reaching the age at which their labor might be expected and is not forthcoming. There are several anecdotes of reproaches on this score, and in one instance a mother and half-grown son came to blows over the matter. But an additional factor in adult objections to children using garden crops too freely is that it may actually disrupt friendships between age-mates. Mangma, in his autobiography, gives several such anecdotes, one of which is quoted below.

> Manimale said, "Let us go to the fields to dig sweet potatoes." My mother and father were away and I was hungry. For a month we played together going every day to dig sweet potatoes. But his mother was angry because we went to her garden to dig them. So after that first day we always went to my garden to dig them. Then my potatoes were finished. I was angry because we always went to my garden. I said to him, "You have lots of potatoes but we only went once to your garden and your mother was angry. Now you have many and you can't come to dig mine any more." I splashed water on him. Manimale said we would not play together any more.

Parental objections also pave the way for the thieving in which play groups of boys frequently indulge. The whole system of feeding reinforces one of the marked intracultural tensions centering on theft and fear of theft.

During this preadolescent play period boys may get occasional meals as guests. When an adult man visits a house in which a woman is at home, it is customary to set a calabash of food before him and any little boys who are about are invited to join him. Little boys very soon learn to attach themselves to any man who seems to be setting out on a "business" trip and in this way undoubtedly learn a great deal of the role expected of them as adults. Hunger is a motivation which leads to the acquisition of adult male skills. Little girls are not fed on these occasions, except rarely when they pick up a bit of food on the side while it is being prepared. There are still other sources of food available to small boys. During feasts those who help with the butchering are given the entrails or other less desirable bits of the pig to roast on the spot. Rat hunting, in which several boys assist a grown man or two, is another source of food. The rats are often roasted on the spot, and the children are given the bellies, entrails, and other less choice portions of the kill. In any event the day's food is as precariously and inconsistently procured as discipline is administered. Further, the food secured is the less choice kind which may, in conjunction with many other attitudes help to produce in the child the feeling of being undervalued.

As compared with this free play group period for boys, there is a slightly different adjustment for girls. Their play period is neither as long nor as free. They are more closely attached to their mothers, have more rigorous training in their adult role as providers for the family. They go out to work in the fields with their mothers and have therefore more regular access to food. I know of no cases in which little girls have been accused of pilfering from gardens, whereas such charges give rise to frequent if minor frictions with boys. On the other hand a girl does not have the guest privilege of the small boy. She gets no tidbits during butchering unless an unusually indulgent and thoughtful male kin happens to notice her on the edge of the group and gives her a bit of meat. Similarly, the meat at feasts is always distributed to the women but only in terms of the males in their household. That is, women get meat for their husbands and sons, but not for themselves or their daughters. Since food is taken home and eaten there, the women naturally get a share, but only as dependents of men. Also, since meat is eaten only in connection with a feast and is definitely a "treat," it becomes set in the children's minds as a symbol of masculine prestige. This coincides with theories of property which grant men the ownership of all flesh food as opposed to women who own the vegetable foods. The system of meat distribution at feasts helps to reinforce early in life and on a very basic level the role of masculine prestige in the culture. It is not that men are the providers; in fact they are quite the contrary. They are the ones provided for; yet they are the purveyors of a delicacy.

The girl, then is set during the preadolescent years in the essential and intimate relationship to the food cycle which she will follow all her life. Further, she has more systematic and deliberate training than boys in the role of adult existence. There is no sharp break in her life except the change of residence at marriage. It is significant that only after marriage is she allowed to make, independently of her mother, a food contribution to a feast. Public food contributions are the symbol of female adulthood.

Boys find themselves undervalued in comparison to men. Girls are valued in much the same terms as the adult women. Their role will always be somewhat underprivileged, but at least they do not experience the same marked discrepancy between childhood and the adult role expected of them as the boys do. The adolescent boy has a sudden adjustment to make and there are no crisis rites, no initiation ceremonies to help him. His change is not institutionalized or dramatized, and certainly he gets no direct education in it. At about fifteen he begins to ponder the purchase of a wife and that means entering upon the whole complex financial game which is the man's chief labor and honorific occupation. In the course of a few months he drifts away from the play groups, becomes a much more solitary figure, and interestingly enough often insists at this time on a midday meal, even if he must cook for himself. Three meals a day is the symbol of adulthood.

It is significant that food as a status symbol should be used at the time that adult sex drives and financial responsibilities first become pressing.

This situation at the end of a long series of childhood experiences probably helps to set the wife as a mother figure. The wife, like the mother, is the responsible provider of food. A high degree of identification between the parent-child and husband-wife relation is actually conscious and valued in the culture. When older men lecture a young couple who have quarrelled, they invariably tell the young woman that she should be a mother to her husband and tell the young man that he should be a father to his wife. One of the strongest expressions of this sentiment was given by a young informant who may have made the identification a little more strongly than was customary.

> Wives are like our mothers. When we were small our mothers fed us. When we are grown our wives cook for us. If there is something good, they keep it in the pot until we come home. When we were small we slept with our mothers; when we are grown we sleep with our wives. Sometimes when we are grown we wake in the night and call our wives "mother."

The mother is definitely the provider but, as we have seen, she is an uncertain one in many cases. It is not surprising therefore to find the relationship between spouses a precarious and mistrustful one. Even though the whole weight of the masculine financial system acts to stabilize marriages, Atimelangers average approximately 1.9 divorces apiece. This seems a high average when one considers the elaborate and cumbersome monetary negotiations involved in divorce.

So far I have been concerned with sketching briefly some of the hunger experience of childhood, the associated restrictive disciplines of adults, and the devices through which the culture somewhat negatively permits children to satisfy this basic need. There has been some indication how all of these affect human relationships. I should like to turn now to a series of institutionalized food attitudes and behavior.

The first and most striking is sacrifice, which is a matter of almost daily experience, representing practically all relationships to the supernatural. The word for sacrifice means literally "to feed," and every supernatural object is so placated. Individual and village tutelary spirits, the graves of the dead, the spirits of ancestors who have cultivated a field, wealth-bringing supernaturals, are all given their share of chicken blood, rice, and pig meat. Realistically enough, the offering is small and purely symbolic. The bulk of the sacrificial food is consumed by the people. In myths the sky heroes are always fed rice, millet, and eggs. Their revivification is achieved by pouring a pot of millet over their heads. The building of lineage houses must be accompanied by feasts at every stage of construction, and its importance is proportional to the number of pigs slaughtered in the course of building it.

Newly purchased gongs or *mokos*[4] must be fed. It is, in fact, difficult to find any aspect of religious and social ceremonial which does not involve "feeding." In this connection it is not without significance that throughout Indonesia is the concept of man's creation from molded clay. In Atimelang this widespread motif is altered so that man is created from molded rice and corn meal; that is, man is made from food.

Also food, rather than native currencies, is generally considered adequate pay for labor. The guest-workers who help cultivate a large rice field, who assist in erecting a lineage house who attend memorial funeral ceremonies, or who participate in similar ceremonial activities are all fed in return for their participation. When cooperative groups are formed for work in fields, the host of the day must furnish the midday meal.

There are other attitudes toward food which are perhaps less dramatic and institutionalized, but just as telling. If women are pounding rice or corn, any kernel which falls from the mortar is carefully picked up. Children of five or six have already absorbed this attitude and are as meticulous as the adults of both sexes. A single bean left in a pod during shelling will be retrieved by children as well as adults. In clearing ground even isolated food plants will be carefully preserved. The meticulous fashion in which all food articles are saved and used does not coincide with any actual scarcity.

The natives also refer frequently to the annual "hungry period." This is the end of the dry season when there is no actual want but only less of the preferred foods. For a month or two natives depend more on cassava and sweet potatoes than on corn. Yet the culture phrases this as a period of food stress. In addition there were references to periods of famine as though they were an ever present threat. Careful inquiry revealed only two periods of shortage within the memories of people between forty and fifty. Both of these were due to factors which had disorganized the community so that for one season the fields had not been as extensively planted and as carefully weeded as is customary. There is no doubt that food, especially of the preferred sort, was scarce on these two occasions, but it was procurable by purchase in nearby communities and there is no evidence that anyone died of hunger. There is, in fact, no indication that hunger is ever necessary if a proper amount of foresight and industry has been exercised. Perhaps one of the best indications that the concern over food scarcity is of psychological origin and not realistic is that there is no land hunger. No one ever expresses poverty or wealth in terms of land, although there is actually great variation between consumption units in the number and fertility of fields owned. This is so despite a strong preoccupation with wealth as status in the culture. Data on the yield of the fields indicate that crops are good and on the whole adequate not only to feed the consumption units but also to provide surpluses for contributions to feasts.

In addition there is a singular agricultural fiction in Alor. This concerns the so-called "good years" and "rat years" which come in alternate seasons. Theory has it that there is no use planting rice fields or any outlying plots during "rat years" because rodents will eat up the crop before it can be harvested. In the "good years" there are supposed to be fewer rats and there is a chance to lay in surpluses for large feasts. The theory of alternating years of rat plagues has no basis in reality. Essentially the idea is a fiction that every other year you are the helpless victim of depredations on your food supply. As one might expect, there are a few people who ignore the theory and plant extra corn fields or even occasional rice fields during "rat years." Yet the social fiction seems almost a rationalization of basic food attitudes in the individual. It appears to be almost an expression of infantile deprivation and helplessness. However, it is only with the utmost caution that I would suggest in any particular case that individual psychology is the direct source of an institutionalized form.

Theft and fear of theft are ramified phenomena whose implications extend beyond their application to food, but the most common type of theft is from gardens. This may be explained on two bases: one is the early theft habits of foraging play groups of boys; the other is that food is one of the few types of property which cannot be absolutely identified and which can be used without much fear of detection. For these reasons, perhaps, one sees the use of curses against theft erected most frequently in fields. These curses, made by specialists, are bamboo poles into whose cleft top are inserted the necessary combinations of magical objects. They are erected in fields where theft has occurred or where the owner fears such an occurrence. Once there, they are supposed to work automatically. A thief would develop leprosy or some other fatal or debilitating illness, and even the owner should call the specialist to remove the curse before harvesting the field. Although these curses are widely used, they seem actually to engender very little fear among most people. Certainly they in no way effectively stop pilfering. Many people are more realistic in the face of depredations and keep armed guard on their fields. A thief caught in the act runs the risk not only of having to pay a fine but also of being shot.

Another important food attitude is shown by the limited range of generosity in distributing it. An occasional guest is fed, but soon enough anyone who is obviously sponging is no longer asked to eat. In case a family runs short of corn or rice it has to buy or borrow from those who may have a surplus. But if food is borrowed, it is at

Alor: A little girl learns her adult task as water carrier.

Alor: Contributions from the wife's family in a dowry feast.
Photos courtesy of Cora Du Bois.

rates of interest running as high as one hundred percent. This holds even between brothers. Thus Fanseni wanted a hundred-ear corn bundle. He got it from his brother but had to repay it at harvest time with two corn bundles of the same size. Even feasts, which at first blush appear to be generous food distributions, are far from lavish in actuality. Each female guest brings to the feast a contribution of food. Everything brought by guests is pooled with the hosts' contributions and then redistributed so that women may carry back home but little more than they brought in the first place. Of course they do receive meat in addition, but most often the meat consists of only three or four cubes of boiled pork about two inches square. However, the quantities displayed are considerable and the hosts derive satisfaction therefrom.

I have been concerned with describing a series of childhood experiences and a series of institutionalized adult food attitudes. The experiences of individual children with respect to hunger gratifications and disciplines vary greatly; it is to be expected, therefore, that in adults these cultural attitudes toward food will vary in "the depth or shallowness of meaning in the individual's total economy." Mangma began his autobiography with early memories of a period of hunger, whereas Tilapada, who was the same age and of the same village, began the story of her childhood with quarrels between herself and other children. One man is conscientious and regular in making food sacrifices to his familiar spirits; another neglects them until illness indicates that he has angered his tutelaries. I have been concerned not with an attempt to uniformize personality among Atimelangers but with an attempt to show how individual childhood experiences with respect to hunger find constant outlets in institutionalized fields which reinforce early socialization and which persons may then invest with greater or lesser emotional energy.

Also, one must be careful not to use such nexi as exclusive causal sequences. I do not believe that the childhood food experiences of the Atimelangers have given rise to the system of sacrifice. They have merely reinforced and made significant to many individuals that widespread Indonesian custom. I would suggest, however, that it would be very difficult to eradicate sacrifice in Alor as long as its individual symbolic value can be so high. For example, a child who has learned that the gratification of hunger is a precarious and uncertain thing may well become an adult who shows obsessional attitudes toward the waste of food, especially if he sees adults who already reveal these attitudes. He has learned as a child that food is hard to get, that it can be stolen, and he has had no positive training in being generous with it. In fact, the whole pattern of discipline has been weighted on the restrictive rather than permissive side. All these individual experiences are reinforced by being reflected in adult behaviors (absorptive disciplines) and thereby become stable complexes that may have little relation to the reality of subsistence economy.

To avoid the possibility of simplistic interpretations, it must be stressed again that no single tension like hunger and the habits associated with its gratification will explain either the totality of the culture or the dominant and stressed personality traits of its bearers. It will be only by examining the whole variety of such individual life experiences and searching for the formalized and unformalized cultural correlates that any progress will be made, not only in defining more sharply the interaction of personality and culture, but also in elucidating the stability of attitudes and value systems. Institutions which may be invested with high emotional value because of patterns in child training are not the ones which can be lightly legislated out of existence. To eliminate such institutions without altering standardized methods of education, may well produce serious social and personal dislocations. The implications of these statements, if true, cannot be ignored by colonial administrators and legislators. It is possible that when we understand better our own culture we shall have learned that basic social changes of a non-disruptive nature must be anticipated in the early and intimate conditioning of children.

NOTES

1. I am indebted to Dr. A. Kardiner and some of his colleagues for their insistence on the need of repetition in many contexts to set certain personality trends.

2. For a discussion of these mechanisms see Anna Freud, *The Ego and the Mechanisms of Defence* (London, 1937).

3. The material used in this article was collected by the writer during eighteen months of residence on the island of Alor, extending from January 1938 through June 1939. Acknowledgments are gratefully made to the Social Science Research Council of Columbia University and to Dr. A. Kardiner who made this work possible.

4. Metal kettle drums used as currency.

ERIK HOMBURGER ERIKSON

1945. "Childhood and Tradition in Two American Indian Tribes," reprinted from *The Psychoanalytic Study of the Child*, vol. *1*: 319-350. (International Universities Press. 227 West 13th St., New York 11, N. Y.) By courtesy of the author and of the publisher.

Dr. Erikson is one of the few psychoanalysts who have studied non-Euro-American native peoples in the field by anthropological techniques. The paper reprinted here presents results of his studies. Subsequently this material was fitted into a larger perspective in his distinguished book, *Childhood and Society* (New York, 1950).

Two other important essays by Dr. Erikson would have been included here had space permitted: "Hitler's Imagery and German Youth," *Psychiatry 5*: 475-493; and "Ego Development and Historical Change," in *The Psychoanalytic Study of the Child. 2*: 359-396. Erikson's summary presentation of his ideas ("Growth and Crises of the 'Healthy Personality'," Supplement II, *Transactions of the Fourth Conference on Infancy and Childhood*, ed. by M. J. E. Senn, 1950) is accessible also in *Personality in Nature, Society, and Culture*, by Kluckhohn, Murray, and Schneider.

The field reports that underlie the paper quoted below are cited in the Bibliography of this book. Students may enjoy following up other writings of Dr. Erikson.

CHILDHOOD AND TRADITION IN TWO AMERICAN INDIAN TRIBES

Erik Homburger Erikson

I

Some years ago the writer, a psychoanalyst then studying infantile neuroses, had the double good fortune of accompanying the anthropologist H. Scudder Mekeel to a Sioux reservation on the Plains, and of visiting with A. L. Kroeber some Yurok Indians on the Pacific coast.

The original conditions and cultural systems of these two tribes differed strikingly. The Sioux were belligerent nomads, roaming the North Central plains in loosely organized groups, pursuing "dark masses of buffalo." Their economic life was dominated by the conviction that "you can't take it with you"—either here or there. Their possessions were few and changed hands readily. Generosity and fortitude were their cardinal virtues. The Yurok, on the other hand, lived in a narrow, densely wooded river valley which steeply descends into the Pacific. They were peaceful and sedentary, gathering acorns, fishing, and preparing themselves spiritually for the annual miracle of the salmon run, when an abundance of fish enters and ascends their river, coming like a gift from nowhere beyond the ocean. They owned real estate along the river, considered that to be virtuous which led to the storage of wealth, and gave monetary value to every named item in their small world.

A. L. Kroeber has written of the anthropology of the Yurok, H. S. Mekeel and others, that of the Sioux. It was the purpose of the writer's trips to collect additional data concerning the rapidly disintegrating systems of child training in both tribes; and this, in order to throw further light on present-day difficulties of reeducation among the Sioux, and for the Yurok, to interpret some of the compulsive weirdness of their ancient tradition. This he did in two impressionistic and speculative papers[1] a comparative abstract of which follows.

II

Today Indian tribes are American minorities. Remnants of their old concepts of childhood are compromised by attempts at acculturation, whether successful or not. But these remnants, whether still practised or hardly remembered, are all that will ever be known. For in the past child-training was an anthropological no-man's land. Even discerning white observers preferred to assume—with contempt or with elation—that Indian children were untrained "little animals." The Indians in the meantime have silently clung to items of child training which, as questioning quickly discloses, are of great emotional importance to them. In discussing "mental hygiene" problems in Indian re-education, white educators, too, reveal unofficial observations and private prejudices of great potency. In order to understand the cultural equation in his data the author found it necessary to review some of the successive images of themselves and of one another which the two groups had developed since they had first met.

The original image of the Sioux is that of the warrior and the hunter, endowed with manliness and mobility, cunning and cruelty. The very image of the Plains Indian with feather trophies in his bonnet now adorns the American "nickel" (as trophy or as ideal?). But since the olden days the Sioux has been beset by an apocalyptic sequence of catastrophes, as if nature and history had united to declare total war on their all-too-manly offspring. Only a few centuries before the whites settled among them, the Sioux had left their original home territory further East and had adjusted their lives to one creature: the buffalo.

> It is said that when the buffalo died, the Sioux died, ethnically and spiritually. The buffalo's body had provided not only food and material for clothing, covering and shelter, but such utilities as bags and boats, strings for bows and for sewing, cups and spoons. Medicine and ornaments were made of buffalo parts; his droppings, sun-dried, served as fuel in winter. Societies and seasons, ceremonies and dances, mythology and children's play extolled his name and image. (S. p. 106.)

The whites, eager for trade routes and territory, upset the hunting grounds and slaughtered buffalo by the hundred thousands. Eager for gold, they stampeded into the Black Hills, the Sioux' holy mountains, game reservoir, and winter refuge. The Sioux tried to deal with the U. S. generals, warrior to warrior, but found that the frontier knew neither federal nor Indian law. Forced to become cowboys, the Sioux soon found their grasslands destroyed by erosion, their herds decimated by selling booms and depressions. Finally there was nothing left but abhorred homesteading within the confines of reservations—on some of the poorest land in all the states. No wonder, then, that some missionaries convinced the older Sioux that they were the lost tribe of Israel.

During this historical period the Sioux encountered successive waves of white men who typified the restless search for space, power and new ethnic identity. The roaming trappers and fur traders seemed acceptable enough to the nomadic Sioux; certain American generals were almost deified for the very reason that they had fought them well; the Negro cavalry, because of its impressive charges, was given the precious name "Black Buffaloes." The consecrated belief in man demonstrated by the Quakers and missionaries did not fail to impress the dignified and religious leaders of the Sioux. But as they looked for fitting images to connect the past with the future, the Sioux found least acceptable the class of white man who was destined to teach them the blessing of civilization, namely, the government employee.

The young American democracy lost a battle with the Indian when it could not decide whether it was conquering, colonizing, converting, or liberating, and sent successive representatives who had one or another of these objectives in mind—a historical doubt which the Indians interpreted as insecurity, much as children do when faced with their parents' vacillations. The discrepancy between democratic ideology and practice, furthermore, is especially pronounced in the hierarchy of a centralized bureaucracy, for which fact the older Indian, who had been reared in the spirit of a hunter democracy leveling every potential dictator and every potential capitalist, had a good, if not malicious eye. (S. p. 123-124).

The destitute, malnourished, disease-ridden Indian of today has little similarity to his original image. Life on the reservation seems depressively arrested, like a slow-motion picture. While conversations with older individuals restore the impression of ancient decency and dignity, the tribe as a whole behaves in a fashion analogous to an oral-dependent compensation neurotic: the victim of a one-time catastrophe has adjusted to "government rations" and refuses to feed himself.

It seems only yesterday, especially for the older Indians, that the three inseparable horsemen of their history's apocalypse appeared on their horizon; the migration of foreign people, the death of the buffalo, and soil erosion. Somehow they still seem to expect that tomorrow the bad dream will be over . . . They have asked the United States Supreme Court to give back the Black Hills, the buffaloes, the gold—or to pay for them. Some day, they expect, there will be a notice on the bulletin board at the agency announcing that the court has heard them and has made them rich. In the meantime, why learn to farm? (S. p. 103-104.)

Thus the Indians' detailed problems of today are seen against a historical background:

Time for the older Indian, one gathers in talking with him, is empty waiting except for those vivid bits of the present in which he can be his old self, exchanging memories, gossiping, joking, or dancing, and in which he again feels connected with the boundless past wherein there was no one but himself, the game, and the enemy (the not-himself who could be fought). The space where he can feel at home is still without borders, allows for voluntary gatherings, and at the same time for sudden expansion and dispersion. He was glad to accept centrifugal items of white culture such as the horse and the gun . . . But so far he has shown little eagerness for the centers of centripetal existence and accumulation: the fireplace, the home-stead, the bank account. For these the educator encourages him to strive; they represent what the educator wants most for himself in life—although preferably far away from Pine Ridge. (S. p. 104).

As for the younger Sioux of today:

In their *early childhood* they were educated by members of the two older groups for whom the future is empty except for dreams of *restoration*. In their *later childhood* they were set an example of *reform* by the white man's educational system which was increasing in vitality and in perfection of organization. But the promise of vocational perfection, since it had a place neither in the individual's early impressions and childhood play nor among the virtues extolled in tales, cannot easily become generally meaningful. (S. p. 115-116.)

Therefore: Our curiosity in regard to the educational difficulties in the Indian Service was focused first on those psychological reali-ties in both groups in the light of which they characterize persons of the same or the other groups as difficult, disturbed, or abnormal. (S. p. 116.)

The Sioux lack any sense of property, whites say: and indeed, to the original Sioux, a "hoarder" was the poorest kind of a man because, apparently, irrational anxiety caused him to mistrust the abundance of the game and the generosity of his fellow men. The remnants of the old virtues of generosity, however, obviously represent not only a hindrance to federal indoctrination but also most practically interfere with attempts to help the Indian by special rations and subsidies. Re-cipients of relief are often beset by neighbors and relatives who good-naturedly and with the best of cultural conscience, demand that he provide for them as long as the supplies last. The Sioux are unclean, others complain: hygiene on the prairie was based on the principle that sand, wind and sun take care of the contaminating waste products of the body. Child-birth took place on a sand pile, excrements were deposited in the sunny outdoors, and corpses were left on scaffolds for the sun to dry. Mekeel knew of old Indians who when sick insisted on living in "draughty" tepees behind their new "hygienic" frame houses. The little Indian girl, however, who on entering a white school, is made to feel that she is dirty, and who learned to start the day with a shower, on returning home during late adolescence, is found to be "dirty" by her elders because she has not learned to ob-serve certain avoidances during menstruation. One of the outstanding complaints brought against Indian children is that they withdraw into themselves or become truant: in the nomadic days, families not only moved from place to place but children also moved from family to family, calling all their aunts "Mother" and all their uncles "Father," thus having at their disposal the welcome of a wide and generous family system. The tendency to pack up and leave when things get tense seems so "natural" to Indian parents that the truant officer finds them utterly indifferent to his complaints.

Every expressed white complaint has a silent counterpart in what the Indians consider the white man's immoral, lazy and dirty nature. The Indian feels that the white man is tense and thus a bad advertisement for his principles of conduct. Above all he beats his own children and is rude to them: an obvious sign of utter lack of "civilization." The Sioux used never to threaten their children with corporal punishment or abandonment. They told them that somebody was going to "come and get them," maybe the owl—and maybe "the white man." This judgment has its counterpart in the opinion of an experienced white educator who claimed that Indian parents "love their children less than animals do." He based his opinion on the fact that the notoriously shy and reticent Sioux parents, after not having seen their children for years, neither kiss them nor cry when they come to get them.

The more confidential a conversation with white or Indian, the more irrational became the accusations concerning the harm which each group assumed the other was deliberately planning to do to children on both sides. Representative is the Indian opinion that white people *teach* their newborn babies to cry, because they do not want them to enjoy life; and the opinion voiced by several whites, that Indians *teach* their children to masturbate, because they do not want them to crave higher things.

Thus, in trying to understand the grievances of both races, the author encountered "resistances" which, he believes, are not based on malice nor entirely on ignorance, but rather, on anachronistic *fears of extinction*, and *fear of loss of group identity;* for the Indian is unwilling to part with the past that provided him with the last cultural synthesis he was able to achieve.

But necessities change more suddenly than true virtues; and it is one of the most paradoxical problems of human evolution that virtues which originally were designed to safeguard an individual's or a group's self-preservation become rigid under pressure of anachronistic fears of extinction and thus can render a people unable to adapt to changed necessities. (S. p. 117-118.)

Most whites, on the other hand, find it difficult to face a minority problem that endangers what synthesis their hardly-won status seems to promise.

Every group, of whatever nature, demands sacrifices of its members which they can bear only in the firm belief that they are based on unquestionable absolutes of conduct. Thus the training of an effective and dependable government employee naturally tends to exclude automatically the ability to tolerate certain classes of people, their standards and habits. (S. p. 119.)

Such resistances—as the Office of Indian Affairs well knows—can not be overcome by administrative and moral coercion but only by gradual enlightenment and by planned historical change. Otherwise,

Plains tribes (not privileged as are the Pueblos to seclude themselves on self-sustained islands of archaic culture) will probably at best join the racial minorities in the poorer American population. Unavoidably, the psychological effects of unemployment and neurosis will be added to tuberculosis, syphilis, and alcoholism which the Indians have acquired so readily. In the long run, therefore, only a design which humanizes modern existence in general can deal adequately with the problems of Indian education. (S. p. 152.)

As for the "mental hygiene" problems encountered, the author suggests

. . . that it is necessary to confront a possible list of problems as the educator sees them with two other lists, namely those vices which can be traced to old virtues, and new virtues which, if adopted by Indian children, become behavior problems in the eyes of their elders. (S. p. 118.)

This, it seems, is the most astonishing single fact to be investigated: Indian children can live for years, without open rebellion or any signs of inner conflict, between two standards which are incomparably further apart than are those of any two generations or two classes in our culture.

We have been led to consider such discrepancies to be among the strongest factors in individual maladjustment. However, as far as the latent psychological prerequisites are concerned, it seems that at the moment there is more inclination towards delinquency, both in the narrower sense of actual juvenile delinquency and in the form of a general and intangible passive resistance against any further and more final impact of the white standards on the Indian conscience than toward neurotic tension, such as self-blame in the service of the white standards. In any event the Indian child of today does not seem to find himself confronted with a "bad conscience" when, in passive defiance of the white teacher, he retreats into himself; nor is he met by unsympathetic relatives when he chooses to run home. (S. p. 124.)

III

In introducing the data on Sioux childhood, the author points to the various resistances which stand in the way of conceptualizing a child as a gradually conditioned rather than a ready made member of his tribe, race, or nation. Pre-scientific narcissism caused man to project himself—in the form of Adam—into the beginning of the world; and made him assume the fetus in its beginning to be a tiny, but complete man: these images have given way to the insight into evolution, and into epigenetic development. We now want to learn how a child *develops* into a white or an Indian, a member of a clan or of a class.

In a recent article I found it helpful to base what we have learned from Freud about the critical periods in early childhood on an analogy between the effects of environmental interference with the first extrauterine impulse manifestations and those of experimental or accidental interference with fetal development. In both, modification or damage affected in the (epigenetically created) organization depends on the developmental time of interference. Any accidental or experimental interference in a given period of growth will change the rate of growth of the system "just budding up," and in doing so will rob this system of its potential supremacy over "its" period, thus endangering the whole hierarchy of developing systems. Furthermore, the whole organism as well as any of its systems is most deeply affected by interference so timed as to hit its first unfolding; at a later stage it might be restricted in its expression, but could not be destroyed as a potentiality (C. R. Stockard).

Educational environment, by choosing a focus for its interference with the unfolding set of given human elements, by timing this interference, and by regulating its intensity, accelerates and inhibits the child's impulse systems in such a way that the final outcome represents what is felt to be—and often is temporarily—the optimum configuration of given human impulses under certain natural and historic conditions. In thus creating "anthropological" variations of man, instinctive education apparently uses, systematically although unconsciously, the same possibilities for modification which become more spectacularly obvious in the abnormal deviations brought about by deficiency or accident. (S. p. 132-133.)

In making this statement, however, the author, to say the least, falls prey to semantic inertia. For environment cannot be said to "interfere with unfolding human elements." There is no social vacuum in which human elements could for a little while develop all by themselves, in order then—as similar phrases go—to be molded or "channelized" by society.

The libido-theory delineates the quality, the range of potentialities and the limitations of the psychological energy available at a given state of development. To be transformed into expressive and adaptive behavior, however, this energy needs a cultural medium; to develop human elements, i.e. to survive, a baby needs the seductive qualities of human organization. The same acts which help the baby to survive, help the culture to survive in him; and as he lives to grow, his first bodily sensations are also his first social experiences.

The initial "vocabulary" of social experience, in turn, is dictated by epigenetic facts: the successive erogeneity of orifices and peripheral systems, and the step for step expansion of mastery over space. The ready receptivity of mouth and senses (including the skin) establishes the organ-mode of incorporation. The muscle system (including the sphincters) expresses the discrimination between retention and elimination. The locomotor system and the genital organs serve the establishment of intrusion and (in girls) inception.[2]

Incorporation and assimilation, retention and elimination, intrusion and inception, are some of the basic problems of organismic existence. Emotional and intellectual, as well as physical, self-preservation demand that one accept, keep, digest, and eliminate; give and receive; take and be taken in *fair ratio*. This ratio is the firm foundation for the later development of the infinite variability and specialization of human existence.

IV

Before the Sioux child was born his mother's relatives and friends for many months gathered the best berries and herbs the prairie produced and prepared a juice in a buffalo bladder which served as the baby's first nursing bottle. A carefully selected woman stimulated his mouth with her finger and fed him the juice while two other selected women sucked the mother's breast till it was ready to give the real stuff of life in generous quantities. Thus the baby was saved the exertion of stimulating his mother's breasts and of digesting the colostrum which precedes the generous flow of milk. Once the baby had begun to enjoy the mother's breast, he was nursed whenever he whimpered and was permitted to play freely with the breast. The Sioux Indians did not believe that helpless crying would make a baby strong, although, as we shall see, they considered temper tantrums in the older child beneficial. Boys in particular, and especially the first boy, were breast-fed generously for a period of from three to five years, during which time the father was supposed not to interfere by making sexual advances to the mother; intercourse was said to spoil the milk. The author points out that the "length" of the breast-feeding period is a questionable concept if applied to a people like the Sioux, where the advent of a new baby often only temporarily interfered with the first child's breast-feeding. Even where a child had already learned to depend upon other food, he still was permitted to draw an occasional sip from his mother's or (for that matter) any other woman's breasts.

However, this paradise of a long and generous feeding history con-tained a forbidden fruit. Sioux grandmothers recount what trouble they had with these indulged babies when they began to bite with habitual abandon; how they would "thump" the baby's head and how he, in turn, would fly into infantile rage. The mother's apparent amuse-ment with these tantrums was justified by the explanation that rage makes a child strong. They apparently fostered it. The author makes two observations in this connection. He wonders how well the Sioux in-fant was able to abreact rage in muscular movement while still strapped in the traditional cradle board. While it is undoubtedly true that this tight container permitted the newborn to find a comfortable approxi-mation of the fetal state, the author considers the possibility that in-hibited expressions of provoked rage established a lasting reservoir of biting and muscular aggression which may well have contributed to the much described "trait" of anger and cruelty in Sioux character. The frustration of the biting period was also reflected in the most common nervous habit, the existence of which was admitted by the older Indians and was still observable in the younger ones:

> At any time, anywhere, one sees children (and adults, usually women) playing with their teeth, clicking or hitting something against them, snapping chewing gum or indulging in some play which involves teeth and finger nails on one or both hands. This seems rarely combined with thumb-sucking; the lips, even if both hands are as far inside the mouth as is at all possible, do not partici-pate in this Sioux habit par excellence." (S. p. 139.)

The author sees in the history of the Sioux child's pre-verbal condition-ing an ingenious arrangement which would secure in the Sioux per-sonality that combination of undiminished self-confidence, trust in the availability of food supply, and ready anger in the face of interference, the co-existence of which was necessary for the functioning of a hunter democracy. We shall come back to this point in connection with the conditioning of the Yurok child, the child of "capitalist" fish-ermen. As will be seen then, in both tribes, the first trauma in rela-tionship to the mother is dramatized in the rituals considered to be of highest spiritual meaning.

It seems to me that it is this unchannelized energy of frustrated impulses to bite and kick which is the contribution of the Sioux's child training to his cultural personality; it contributes to the urge for communal temper outbursts such as endless centrifugal "parties" setting out to hunt, kill, steal, and rape; to the Sioux Indian's pro-verbial cruelty both against enemies and against himself; and it finds its most exalted expression in the scene during the Sun dance when "little sticks driven through the breasts of the dancers and connected by strings to the Sun Pole, were pulled free so that the flesh was ripped open": a sacred turning against himself of suppressed—and long forgotten—wishes. (Y. p. 291.)[3]

The generosity manifested in the mother's initial handling of the child was continued in the family's respect for his property and the renunciation of adult claims wherever a conflict arose.

While a Sioux could not refuse a request for a gift, he could refuse to give away his child's possessions; the emphasis, however, was on the honor that would come to the child when he, of his own accord, would relinquish his property. The child was not taught that property was "bad," but given an example of extreme generosity by the parents, who even today, to the traders' horror, are willing to let the child waste money that should buy needed supplies.

> The first strict *taboos* expressed verbally and made inescapable by a tight net of ridiculing gossip did not concern the body and physical habits, but were of a social nature and first applied to the relationship of brother and sister: When a certain age after the sixth year was reached, brother and sister were not to speak with one another any more, and parents as well as the older siblings would urge the girl to confine herself to female play and to stay near the mother and tepee while the boy was encouraged to join the older boys in cowboy and hunter games. (S. p. 142.)

From then on, the daily patterns for boys and for girls differed radically. The boy was to become restless, brave and reckless; the girl, reticent, industrious and chaste. Boys used miniature bows and arrows and later ropes for an initial imitation and, as soon as possible, the real activation of a hunter's or cowboy's existence. Of interest are the "bone horses," small bones of phallic shape taken from killed animals and called "horses," "buffaloes," "cows," "bulls," etc. The author believes that the constant fingering of these dolls by small boys tended to connect the masturbatory tendencies of the phallic-locomotor stage with fantasies of becoming great hunters or cowboys. While thus sadistic, intrusive tendencies are cultivated in the boy, in the girl, corresponding inhibitions are used to teach her "an extreme state of passivity and fearfulness." Girls were taught to sit modestly, to walk in small, measured steps, later to sleep with their thighs tied together, and not to go beyond a certain radius around the tepee or the camp. It was understood by both sexes that any girls who habitually overstepped such restrictions could be raped by boys without their incurring punishment. The girl, however, who learned to conform could connect fantasies of the brother's greatness as a hunter with the skills she learned. She knew that the brother, as an adult, would be obliged to bring to her the best of what he could rob or hunt; she would butcher the buffalo and, on occasion, the enemy killed by him; her skill in embroidery would come to full display when she would be called upon to ornament the cradles and layettes of his wife's children. Moreover, at certain ceremonies, she would sing of his bravery, and in the Sun Dance she would assist him during his tortures. This is an example of the way in which homogeneous cultures pay in the currency of prestige for whatever restrictions they feel they have to impose. The girl was taught to serve hunters, to be on guard against them, but also to become a mother who would be willing and able to instil into her boys the fundamental traits of the plains hunter. The first basic avoidance between brother and sister thus used the energies of the phallic-loco-motor stage and of potential incestuous tendencies to establish a model of mutual respect and generosity among all the "brothers and sisters" of the extended kinship.

The author notes that such relationships were established without that estrangement between body and self which is effected by the idea of sin, and without that estrangement between parents and children which is caused where parents are the sole arbiters of seemingly arbitrary rules. Instead, older children would with ridiculing comment, enforce rules basic to the whole pattern of Sioux existence.

V

The psychopathologist will be especially interested in the way individuals were treated who for one reason or another were unable to conform to these clear-cut differentiations between masculinity or femininity. It seems that conformance, wherever humanly possible, was urged by ridicule. However, for the sincere nonconformer there was a ritual way out—right through the ridicule. The disturbed boy would seek a vision quest in lonesomeness and self-torture. The inventory of such visions were standardized and yet his vision had to be personally ·convincing to secure the deviant public recognition. One such role was the "Heyoka." A boy would dream that he had seen the Thunderbird, whereupon his father would tell him that he "must go through with it" or be struck by lightning. He was then obliged to behave as absurdly and clownishly as possible until his elders felt that he had cured himself of the curse. Descriptions of such activities make it plain that they are analogous to the involuntary self-debasing exhibitionism in neurotic men in our society. However, in further analogy to the more or less voluntary and conscious role played by great comedians in our culture, a Heyoka, in spite of the contempt freely bestowed upon him, could prove himself so victoriously funny that he would end up a leader among his people. Correspondingly a girl might dream that she must choose between certain objects that are typical for men's and women's activities. After that, it would be recognized that she must be "Witko," which means "crazy." She then would throw to the winds all feminine restraint and probably become a prostitute, sometimes a famous one. A boy may dream that the moon has two hands and tries to make him choose between certain objects, but that suddenly the hands cross and try to force the burden strap of a woman upon him (T. S. Lincoln). If the dreamer fails in his resistance, he is doomed to be like a woman. Such a man is called a "berdache"; he dresses like a woman and does woman's work. He is not necessarily a homosexual (although warriors before going on the war path are said to have visited such men in order to increase their own ferocity). Sometimes, because of his position between the sexes, a berdache could excel in the arts of companionship, cooking and embroidery.

Thus the dreamer's deepest urges present themselves to him as a prophecy and as a command from a spiritual source. The abnormal was not permitted to escape the elastic net of cultural meaning.

VI

The author's first anthropological impressions thus seemed to confirm Roheim's classical thesis that there is a "correlation between the habitual infancy situation" and . . . "the dominant ideas of a group." However, he cannot conceive of the second as being "derived" from the first nor of primitive societies as being solutions of specific infantile conflicts. Such quasi-causal formulations lead, it is true, to the hen-or-egg question,—what came first, the culture or the individual, specific infancy situation or dominant ideas. History, however, has beginnings only in myths; in reality it fuses into prehistory. And whatever the pre-human may have looked like, human beings always have attempted to derive a condensed design of group living that guarded against the *combined* dangers of physical harm (hunger, pain), group disintegration (panic), and individual anxiety; and had as their further goal: survival, accomplishment, self-expression. The treatment of children and other manifestations of a primitive culture evolve from an increasing synthetic tendency in the group-ego, situated as it is in its constituent individual egos. This tendency can be demonstrated somewhat more clearly in primitive societies because they represent condensed and homogeneous ways of dealing directly with one segment of nature. As we shall see later, the synthetic cultural tendency becomes less transparent where (1) tradition, i.e., previous syntheses, become a complicated "environment" that resists resynthesis; (2) the means of production as a whole lose their concreteness to the individual, and only segments of the economic system are immediate enough to permit practical and magic adaptation; (3) where consequently antagonistic social entities are created within the total group—with some entities in their particular segment bent on making other entities subservient to their syntheses.

For a member of such a complicated society it is, therefore, instructive to see how a homogeneous group like the American Indian tribes dealt with human existence. Let us compare the Sioux concepts of childhood with those among the Yurok. These two tribes stand in opposition in almost all the basic configurations of existence. The Sioux roamed the plains and cultivated spatial concepts of centrifugal mobility, the horizons of their existence coinciding with the limits of the buffalo's roaming and the beginnings of enemy hunting grounds. The Yurok not only lived largely in or at the mouth of a narrow, mountainous, densely-forested valley, but, in addition limited themselves within arbitrary borders. They considered a disc of about 150 miles in diameter, cut in half by the course of the Klamath river, to include all there was to this world. They ignored the rest and ostracized as "of ignoble birth" anyone who showed a marked tendency to venture into territories beyond. Instead they cried and prayed to their horizons which they thought contained the supernatural "homes" from which generous spirits sent the stuff of life to them: above all, salmon. The limitation of this world was manifested in its cardinal directions: there was an "upstream" and a "downstream," a "towards the river," and an "away from the river," and then, at the end of the world, an elliptic "in back and around."

Within this restricted radius of existence, extreme localization took place. Old Yuroks proudly point to hardly noticeable pits in the ground as their ancestors' home. Such pits retain the family name. The whole environment exists only in as far as human history has named certain locations. Their myths do not mention the gigantic redwoods which impress white travelers so much; yet the Yurok will point to certain insignificant looking rocks and trees as being the "origin" of the most far-reaching events. This localization finds its economic counterpart in a monetarization of values. Every person, relationship or act can be exactly valued and becomes the object of pride or ceaseless bickering. The acquisition and retention of possessions is and was what the Yurok thinks about, talks about and prays for.

This little well-defined world had, in the author's words, its "mouth open" towards the ocean and lived both in its practical and its magical pursuits for the yearly, mysterious appearance of tremendous numbers of salmon which came out of the ocean, climbed up the river, and usually having left an abundance of food supply in the Yurok's nets, disappeared up the river. The author debates the question as to whether the Yurok knew the complicated life history of the salmon, which, on reaching the spawning territory up river, procreates and dies; while some months later its diminutive progeny descends the river, disappears out in the ocean and two years later, as mature salmon, driven by a "homing instinct," returns to its very birthplace to fulfill its life cycle. The salmon, before entering the river, stops eating and therefore when caught has an empty stomach. As he ascends the river, his sexual organs develop and his fat content diminishes; at the optimum of his physical prowess and nutritional value, then, the salmon has ceased eating and has not commenced procreating. When the Yurok goes to catch him, he purifies himself, as we shall see, from contact with procreation and abstains from food.

It is the author's thesis that the Yurok show one extreme type of conceptual integration:

> Our preconception is this: Yurok thinking, so far as it is magic, tends to assimilate concepts derived from (1) observations of the geographic and biological environment, that is, (a) the lower part of a river valley with a mysterious periodical supply of fish, (b) a prey (salmon), with a particularly dramatic biology; and (2) experiences of the human body as a slowly maturing organism with periodical needs. In the non-magical sphere, of course, the Yurok reaches a certain degree of logic and technique, as do all human beings; but wherever magic behavior seems indicated—that is, wherever mysterious food sources beyond the Yurok's territory, technology, and causal comprehension need to be influenced, or whenever vague human impulses and fears need to be alleviated—the Yurok tries to understand nature around and within him by blending bodily and geographic configurations, both of which become parts of one geographic-anatomical environment. In this environment the periodical affluence of the waterway has a functional interrelation with the periodicity of vital juices in the body's nutritional, circulatory, and procreative systems. Therefore, the Yurok's main magic concern is that vital channels be kept open and that antagonistic fluids be kept apart from one another. (Y. p. 259.)

> . . . Every item of Yurok ethnology on which our demonstration can be based is shared by the Yurok's ethnic neighbors where it may have the same, a similar, a transformed, or a different meaning. Here, too, our attitude is clinical: we would expect an individual ego to synthesize individually experience typical for many; similarly, we assume that a group ego (or whatever we choose to name the organized and organizing core of a culture situated as it is in its constituent individual egos) tends to take stock of and to synthesize what has been selected, accepted, and preserved. It is this *synthetic tendency* which in the following pages is to be demonstrated *within one culture.* (Y. p. 259.)

One example of such primitive synthesis is the pervading importance of the "tube" configuration in Yurok thinking. According to Yurok mythology, the Klamath in prehistoric times flowed up on one side and down on the other. Now, it flows only in the downward direction and salmon ascend upward. To be sure that the river is open on both sides and thus an inviting waterway for the energetic salmon, the Yurok, magically concerned, attempts to keep all tubelike things within and around him unobstructed and all fluid-ways uncontaminated. He abhors the double-vector, i.e., a sac-like configuration which is entered and left through the same opening. Points in question are Yurok architecture and the Yurok concept of the human body.

The Yurok have two kinds of houses, the living house and the sweat house. Both are subterranean with a roof a few feet above the ground. The "doors" consist of oval openings just above the ground which admit one creeping human being at a time. The living house, however, has only one such opening (sac) while the sweat house has two (tube). The living house is a very crowded affair:

> Underneath the roof is a huge criss-cross of poles on which salmon is hanging in all possible states of age and eatenness, while a shelf bench between the dugout and the side walls is loaded with enormous baskets full of acorns and utensils in various states of use. The total impression is that of darkness, crowdedness, and endless accumulation. This is where women and children live; the man who comes to visit his home is careful not to sit on the floor, but on a block or stool of the form of a cylinder or mushroom. Otherwise, his place is in the sweat house, where he takes the older boys; there is one sweat house to six or seven living houses. . . .

> These two house forms not only serve woman and man, respectively, but also symbolize what the man's and woman's insides mean in Yurok culture: the family house, dark, unclean, full of food and utensils, and crowded with babies, the place from which a man emerges contaminated: the sweat house, lighter, cleaner, more orderly, with selectivity over who and what may enter, a place from which one emerges purified. (Y. p. 268.)

Living house and female anatomy are associated. After contact with either, the man has to pass the "test" of the sweat house. This he enters through the normal-sized door. However, he can leave it only through a very small opening which will permit only a man moderate in his eating habits and supple with the perspiration caused by the sacred fire to slip through. He is required to conclude the purification by swimming in the river. The conscientious fisherman passes this test every morning thus denying his contact with women and as it were, giving daily rebirth to himself through a tube-like womb.

What the Yurok calls "clean" living is an attempt to keep vectors clear, channels unobstructed, and to avoid the wombs of multiplication: woman; the lake upriver from which he thinks the waters of the Klamath flow; the place across the ocean where salmon originate; the origin of his shell money up the coast. The author describes an old Indian woman's melancholic apprehension when she saw a whale enter, play around in, and leave the mouth of the Klamath; the river should serve only one vector; that of ascending salmon. For that which flows in one channel of life, is said to be most eager not to come in contaminating contact with the objects of other channels or with "sac-like" configurations. Salmon and the river dislike it if food is eaten on a boat. Deer will stay away from the snare if deer meat has been brought in contact with water—even posthumously by washing the eating bowls. Salmon demands that women on their trip up or down river, at specified places, leave the boat and walk around a rock. Salmon also dislikes the man who is full of food, or, as we saw, has been in contact with the "woman's inside," and money will leave the house if intercourse took place while it was there. (Shell money is strung on thongs and carried in oblong tube-like purses.)

Only once a year, after the salmon run, these avoidances are set aside. At that time, following complicated ceremonies, a strong dam is built which obstructs the ascent of the salmon and permits the Yurok to catch a rich winter supply. The dam building is "the largest mechanical enterprise undertaken by the Yurok or, for that matter, by any California Indians, and the most communal attempt." After ten days of collective fishing, orgies of ridicule and of sexual freedom take place alongside the river, reminiscent of the ancient Satires of European spring ceremonials.

The author finds indications that these ceremonials dramatize the return, the ridicule, and the re-banishment of a "primal father" figure. For the Yurok's centripetal world was created by a most centrifugal and irresponsible father: The old man Wohpekumeu (the "widower from across the ocean") stood in the middle of the river which went up on one side and down on the other, and cried and claimed that he was lonely. Land appeared on both sides of him. He cried more. A water spout was rising in front of him, slowly coming up to the height of his breast. He cried again. The water came up to his brow. Upon further crying, the spout slowly developed into a woman, first her upper half and then, upon his further tearful insistence ("I want a whole woman") the lower part as well. After having created the rest of the world, the widower gave this woman to his son together with plenty of food, under the condition (which seems habitual with creators) that he must work. Later, however, he seduced his daughter-in-law and became so girl-crazy that he had to be banished. His sons decided that they would also overcome all centrifugal tendencies among themselves, henceforth love clean in their restricted, compulsive and phobic world.

This hysterical God, nostalgic but sly, powerful but inhibited, God-like but unreliable, is the originator across the ocean of the yearly salmon supply. In contrast to him, there is a more compulsive character, a "clean" God, who smoked but never ate, who never desired a woman, and accomplished the great historical deed of banning women from the sweat house. He represents all that the Yurok call "clean." And yet they know that they need a continuous, cautious, well-ritualized contact with the widower who provides food. The author interprets the rejuvenation ceremonial connected with the annual fish dam as dramatizing an early return of the primal father, who, having brought all the salmon (on a deeper level he is the salmon) is ceremoniously defeated by the dam chief, and after much ridicule, banned again. Whereupon the world for a short while is free of phobic restriction, sexual and otherwise. But then the Yurok again begins the "clean" life which helps him to be a conscientious warden of his segment of nature.

This interesting version of the primal father myth suggests some speculation concerning historical elements in its variations.

Let us assume that the Yurok came from somewhere else; with no chance or wish to turn back, they found their way blocked by the Pacific. They settled along the river, and, noticing the periodical salmon run, became fishermen—in technique and in magic.

The human mind is likely to feel guilty and, if necessary, to construct a guilt when it finds itself faced with sudden environmental limitation; adapting, it learns to see a virtue in the necessity imposed by the limitation; but it continues to look into the future for potential recurrences or intensifications of the trauma of limitation, anticipating punishment for not being virtuous enough. In this sense to the restricted Yurok, centrifugality may have become a vice in the past, centripetality a virtue; and the ocean's disfavor, anticipated punishment for centrifugal "mental sins" which Yurok ethics tries to avoid. (Y. p. 276.)

Thus an ontogenetic trauma (the banishment from the mother's body and house) and a historical task would appear synthesized, analagous to the spatial synthesis of geography and anatomy.

VII

In his attempts to gather information on the Yurok's ancient child training system, the author, in some areas, found himself among hostile, contemptuous and resistive people who apparently suspected him of trying to get information on their property rights. He thus not only met some of the old money-mindedness and suspicion; he also was quite aware that the inner distance between Yurok and whites is not so great as that between whites and Sioux. For there was much in the A. B. C. of Yurok life that did not have to be relearned when the whites came. The Yurok lived in frame houses and in fact now lives in superterranean structures next to pits in the ground which once contained his ancestors' subterranean dwellings. Unlike the Sioux, who, in the buffalo, lost overnight the focus of his economic and spiritual life, the Yurok still sees, catches, talks and eats salmon. When the Yurok man today steers a raft of logs, or the Yurok woman grows vegetables, their occupations are not too far removed from the original manufacture of dugouts, the gathering of acorns and the planting of tobacco. Above all, the Yurok concerned his life with property. "He schemed constantly to lodge a claim or to evade an obligation." According to the author, the Yurok need not forget this "primitive" tendency in the white world, and therefore his grievances with the United States find other than the inarticulate, smoldering expression of the prairie man's passive resistance. In fact, upriver, only twenty miles from a major U. S. highway, the author found himself treated (and saw visiting white officials treated) as definitely unwelcome white minority.

VIII

From a few wise old informants, however, the author gathered this information: The birth of a baby is surrounded with oral prohibitions. Father and mother eat neither deer meat nor salmon until the child's navel heals. Disregard of this taboo causes convulsions in the child. (The more "genital" Sioux thinks that a child's convulsions are caused by the parents' intercourse during pregnancy). During the birth, the mother must shut her mouth. The newborn is not breast-fed for ten days, but given a nut soup from a tiny shell. The breast-feeding begins with Indian generosity. However, there is a definite weaning time around the sixth month, that is, around the teething period. Yurok breast-feeding thus is maintained for a minimum period among American Indians. Weaning is called "forgetting the mother" and is enforced, if necessary, by the mother's going away for a few days. This relative acceleration of weaning seems to be part of a general tendency to encourage the baby to leave the mother and her support as soon as this is possible and bearable—and not to return. From his twentieth day on, the baby's legs, which are left uncovered in the Yurok version of the cradle board, are massaged by the grandmother. Early creeping is encouraged. The first postnatal crisis for the Yurok child, therefore, occurs much earlier than that of the Sioux, and consists of a relationship in time of enforced weaning, teething, and encouraged creeping. The shorter nursing period, of course, accelerates the advent of a second crisis, namely, the mother's next pregnancy.

We have referred to the contribution made by the Sioux baby's oral training to Sioux character structure. The Yurok child, as we saw, is weaned early and abruptly, before the full development of the biting stage, and after having been discouraged from feeling too comfortable with his mother. The author suggests that this expulsion—in its relation to other items—contributes to the Yurok character, a residue of potential nostalgia which consequently find its institutionalized form in the Yurok's ability to cry while he prays in order to gain influence over the food-sending powers behind the visible world. There is something of an early oral "hallucinatory wish fulfillment" implied in the adult Yurok's conviction that tearful words, such as "I see a salmon" will cause a salmon to come. It is as if he had to pretend that he had no teeth so that his food supply would not be cut off. In the meantime, however, he does not forget to build nets.

This concentration on the sources of food is not accomplished without a second oral training at the "sense" stage, i.e., when the child can repeat what he has been told. He is admonished to eat slowly, not to grab food, never to take it without asking for it, never to eat between meals and never to ask for a second helping—an oral puritanism hardly equaled among other primitives. During meals, a strict order of placement is maintained and the children are taught to eat in prescribed ways; for example, to put only a little food on the spoons, to take the spoons up to their mouths slowly, to put the spoon down while chewing the food—and above all, to think of becoming rich during the whole process. Nobody speaks during meals so that everybody can keep his own thoughts on money and salmon. Thus a maximum of preverbal avarice and need for intake, which may have been evoked by the combination of early weaning, not only from the breast but also from contact with the mother and from babyish ways in general is "tamed" and used for the development of those attitudes, which to the Yurok mind, will in the end assure the salmon's favor. The Yurok makes himself see money hanging from trees and salmon swimming in the river during off season. He learns to subordinate genital drives to the pursuit of money. In the sweat house the boy will learn the strange feat of thinking of money and at the same time *not* thinking of women.

These fables told to children in an interesting way underline the ugliness of lack of restraint. They isolate one outstanding item in the physiognomy of animals and use it as an argument for "clean behavior." The buzzard's baldness is the result of his having put his whole head into a dish of hot soup. The eel gambled his bones away. The hood of the angry bluejay is her clitoris which she tore off in "masculine protest." One fable which concerns itself with feces also emphasizes the need for cautious intake and incidentally illustrates the tube concept.

The bear was always hungry. He was married to the blue jay. One day they made a fire and the bear sent the blue jay to get some food. She brought back only one acorn. "Is that all?" the bear said. The blue jay got angry and threw the acorn in the fire. It popped all over the place and there was acorn all over the ground. The bear swallowed it all down and got awfully sick. Some birds tried to sing for him but it did not help. Nothing helped. Finally the hummingbird said, "Lie down and open your mouth," and then the hummingbird zipped right through him. That's why the bear has such a big anus and can't hold his feces. (Y. p. 286.)

Second in emphasis to cautious intake is the prohibition of swearing, that is, verbal offense committed especially by reference to death and dead people; i.e., verbal elimination.

In accordance with the Yurok's tendency to rush their children along on the path of maturation, they have an interesting concept of regression. It is bad for the child, they say, to sleep in the afternoon, for there is an affinity between dusk and death. In its time the fetus was kept awake in the afternoon by the mother's rubbing of her abdomen. At dusk, children are hurriedly called into the house, because then they may see some "wise" people, i.e., members of the race that inhabited the earth before the Yurok took possession of it. The description of these "wise" people seems to mark them as a materialization of pregenitality, their attraction as a regressive tendency. They are adult at six months of age. They procreate orally and have no genitals. They do not know what it means to be "clean" and they never die. The child who sees a member of this race develops symptoms such as lack of appetite, nightmares, disobedience. He may waste away if he is not given treatment.

There are various forms of treatment. The parents themselves should stay out of it; maybe the grandmother next door will sing the proper songs. In severe cases, however, a psychotherapist is consulted. The author was able to interview the last of these women shamans. Her techniques embrace the psychosomatic, the bisexual and the ambivalent nature of neurosis. The shaman sucks two "pains" out of the child's body—one residing always above the child's navel (where it obstructs the nutritional tube) and its "mate" from wherever the child feels pain. Then follows the interpretation and the group therapy. The child is laid on the floor and his parents and relatives gather around in a circle. After elaborate rituals, the shaman has a vision and describes it. She will see, for example, a man who had made a vow of abstinence, nevertheless have intercourse with a woman. Or she will see an old woman sitting in the hills trying to "sorcerize" somebody. Whatever it is, one or the other of the child's relatives will get up and confess that he has committed that crime. The fact that this procedure is said to result in cures can be attributed to the shaman's intuitive skill in making the child's relatives confess to whatever secret guilt caused ambivalent tension in the home and anxiety in the child, both of which are thus ameliorated.

The very healing power of the shaman is derived from a potentially pathogenic set of events.

Long before F., the daughter and granddaughter of shamans, reached puberty, people had predicted that she probably would turn into a shaman too because "she slept so much," that is, had a neurotic inclination to regress. During her premenarche, her grandmother tested her by taking a "pain" out of her own mouth and trying to make F. swallow it. F. ran away from home. The following night, however, she had an anxiety dream in which an old woman threw a basket over her mouth in such a way that she swallowed its "yellow, black bloody, nasty" content. She woke up in extreme anxiety but kept this dream to herself because she realized that people would force her to become a shaman if they knew that her grandmother's suggestion had invaded her dream life. At breakfast, however, she gave herself away by vomiting, whereupon the community made her confess and in great excitement prepared her novitiate. She now had to learn to transform this involuntary vomiting of stomach content into the ability to swallow and to throw up "pains" without throwing up food with it—a mastery over the oral-nutritional tube which gives F. the power to cure people. Here the abhorred double-vector becomes beneficial.

Unlike F., the ordinary Yurok girl when menstruating the first time, is forced to "close up" all around. Silently sitting in the corner of her home with her back turned to the fire, she moves as little as possible. On leaving the house once a day, she does not look about. For four days or longer, she abstains from food. Then she takes her food to a spot where she can not hear any sound except the noise of the river. To the girl who has thus learned to guard her receptivity, her mother demonstrates the purpose of her inceptive organization by putting in front of her twenty sticks, calling ten of them sons, and ten, daughters.

F., however, acquired all the prerogatives forbidden to other women. She could sleep in the sweat house, pray for money, and smoke a pipe. She became as rich as any man and stronger in magic power. From F.'s and other shaman's dreams, the author concludes that F. was destined to become her mother's successor because she, alone among her sisters, early showed hysterical traits of "masculine protest" which are promoted to a plane of magic usefulness by the community. The author secured fragments of the case history of another woman who had fled her home just as F. had, when the career of a shaman was suggested to her. However, no inner pressure made her produce ("against her will") either a dream or the symptom of vomiting, the two involuntary affirmations of shamanism that alone convince the people of a shaman's calling. This woman had lifelong chronic indigestion and compulsively spoke of her interrupted novitiate until her death.

IX

The author discusses the relationship of such institutionalized infantile behavior as the Yurok's crying and bickering to the problem of tribal character and to neurosis. The Yurok is, of course, helpless only in his magic protestations, not in his activities. He builds snares and nets and accomplishes the technical feat of the fish dam. The author believes that the closing of the two gigantic jaws of the dam is analogous to the Sioux Sun Dance in two respects: it is the event of highest collective significance in the tribe's life; and it dramatizes the oral (biting) taboo. The Yurok finds it necessary afterwards to assure his trapped prey that no malice was intended. In fact he claims that he really cannot harm his prey. "I will," says the salmon— according to Yurok Platonism—"leave my scales on nets and they will turn into salmon, but I, myself, will go by and not be killed." It is as if this combination of crying, snaring and protesting innocence, represented a collective play with the greatest dangers of both ontogeny and phylogeny: the loss of the mother at the biting stage; the mythical banishment of the creator from the women of this world; and historically: the loss of salmon supply during bad years. There are further indications that the salmon (the food which refuses to enter the mouth of the world if you desire it too voraciously) is associated with nipple and penis, the too highly cathexed life-giving organs.

Toward his fellow men, however, the Yurok's receptivity loses all its helplessness. He claims, demands, whines, fusses, bickers, and alibis— as the author puts it, "like a jealous child who, now so touchingly helpless in the presence of the mother, uses an instant of her absence to turn on his sibling and to protest that this or that object— anything will do—is his." As for the ontogenetic basis of this behavior, we mentioned that a child who is weaned early will find himself in the company of a younger rival.

It obviously would take detailed studies to establish the Yurok's collective character, including the way in which a Yurok manages to be an individual. For it is only within the official character of a given people that a personological inquiry can begin. Each system, whether it emphasizes generosity or avarice, admits of additions and exemptions of individual avarice and generosity. To know a people's character one has to know their laws of conduct and the way they circumvent them.

The author believes that neurosis and culture, although using the same inventory of human potentialities, are systematically different phenomena. Sioux "sadism" does, of course, not keep a Sioux man from being a devoted lover and husband. As for the Yurok's "helplessness":

Does it mean that the Yurok anywhere within his technology is more helpless, more paralyzed by sadness, than are members of a tribe which does not develop these "traits"? Certainly not; his institutionalized helplessness *eo ipso* is neither a trait nor a neurotic symptom. It is an infantile attitude which the culture chose to preserve and to put at the disposal of the individual, to be used by him and his fellow men in a limited area of existence. Such an institutionalized attitude neither spreads beyond its defined area nor makes impossible the development to full potency of its opposite: it is probable that the really successful Yurok was the one who could cry most heart-breakingly or bicker most convincingly in some situations and be full of fortitude in others, that is, the Yurok whose ego was strong enough to *synthesize orality and "sense."* In comparison, the oral types whom we may be able to discern today in our culture and to whom we would be inclined to liken what we have said about the Yurok, are bewildered people who find themselves victims of an overgrown and insatiable potentiality without the corresponding homogeneous cultural reality. (Y. p. 295-296.)

In contrast, an oral neurosis is non-adjustive and tends to be all inclusive. Most important, it interferes with the development of genital primacy in the individual.

Among our neurotics this retentiveness is common enough: it interferes with psychosexual development and genital potency. But here again the comparison between the cultural and the neurotic character ends; for, on this level too, the strong Yurok is he who never risks, over sexual matters, his property or his luck in hunting or fishing, but who would still be man enough to use with unimpaired sexual potency opportunities without danger of commitment. The understanding between the sexes in these matters goes so far (or can go so far) that one informant defined a "nice girl" as one who always tells the boy beforehand when she is menstruating, thus saving him ritual trouble and subsequent loss of working time. (Y. p. 298.)

Wherever the emphasis of the ontogenetic trauma lies, every culture must insure that the majority of its members will reach a certain amount of genitality—enough to support a strong personal ego and to secure a group-ego; but not more than is compatible with group living.

This applies to other pregenital factors as well. The collective or official character structure of the Yurok shows all the traits which Freud and Abraham found to be of typical significance in patients with "anal fixations," namely compulsiveness, suspiciousness, retentiveness, etc. The author, however was unable to find in Yurok childhood an emphasis on feces or on the anal zone that would fulfill the criteria of a collective "anal fixation." He feels that Yurok attitude toward property is alimentary in its incorporative aspects, and in its eliminative ones, rather concerns the total inside of the body with its mixture of excreta. This may be true for most primitives.

Anal character in our culture often appears to be a result of the impact on a retentive child of a certain type of maternal behavior in Western civilization, namely, a narcissistic and phobic over-concern with matters of elimination. This attitude helps to over-develop retentive and eliminative potentialities and to fixate them in the anal zone; it creates the strongest social ambivalence in the child, and it remains an isolating factor in his social and sexual development. Forms of "individualism" in Western culture which represent a mere insistence on the privilege to sit in isolation on possessions can be suspected of representing just such an inroad of anality into cultural and political life. Otherwise it seems that homogeneous cultural life and anality contradict one another. (Y. p. 297.)

The ground work for the Yurok's genital attitudes is laid in the child's earlier conditioning which teaches him to subordinate drive to economic considerations. Within such basic limits sex is viewed with leniency and humor. The fact that sex contact necessitates purification seems to be considered a duty or a nuisance, but does not reflect on sex as such or on individual women. There is no shame concerning the surface of the human body: it is its "inside" which, by implication, is covered when the young girl between menarche and marriage avoids bathing with others. Otherwise, everybody is free to bathe in the nude. But the girl knows that virtue, or shall we say an unblemished name, will gain her a husband who can pay well and that her status and that of her children and her children's children will depend on the amount her husband will offer to her father when asking for her. The boy, on the other hand, wishes to accumulate enough wealth to buy a worthwhile wife. If he were to make an unworthy girl pregnant, he would have to marry her. Above all, habitual deviant behavior is usually explained as a result of the delinquent's mother or grandmother not having been "paid for in full." This, it seems, means that the man in question was so eager to marry that he borrowed his wife on a down payment without being able to pay the installments; he thus proved that his ego was too weak to integrate sexual needs and economic virtues.

Exactly how genital the average genitality of any group can be said to be is debatable. The Sioux has an elaborate courtship during which, by restraint and the use of the love flute, he demonstrates to his girl that he has more than rape in mind. She, to be sure, brings a small knife along. Beyond this, intercourse in both tribes is mentioned by the men (of today!) as a primitive act of copulation without any aspiration to artfulness nor with any consciousness of a female orgasm. "After all," one Yurok said, "our women were bought." Since highly male societies restrict the verbal consciousness of women it probably would have been difficult under ancient circumstances to elicit data on female sex attitudes; at and during the time of the author's short trips, it was impossible.

As we saw, Sioux and Yurok children learned to associate both locomotor and genital modes with those of hunting and fishing. The Sioux, in his official sexuality, was more phallic-sadistic in that he pursued whatever roamed: game, enemy, woman. (Just as he could "count coup," i.e., gain prestige points by merely touching an enemy, a Sioux man could claim to have taken a girl's virtue by touching her vulva.) The Yurok was more phobic-compulsive in that, in his sexuality, he identified with his prey. He avoided being "snared" by the wrong woman or at the wrong time or place—*wrong* meaning any circumstances that would compromise his assets as an economic being. To this end he is said to have had intercourse in the open, outside the configuration of the living house, ostensibly in order to avoid offending the money in the house. The Yurok woman, in turn, took care not to be bought too cheaply. The snaring configuration occurs in one final item of the primal father story: having promised to be a good god, but venturing down the coast, he found the skate woman lying on the beach, invitingly spreading her legs.[4] ("The skatefish looks like a woman's inside.") He could not resist her. But as soon as he had inserted his penis, she held on to him with vagina and legs and abducted him. On the basis of an analogous equation (fish that looks like woman's inside = female genitals = woman) the author has tentatively assumed that the oblong salmon sent by the gods also represents the god's phallus and the god. In the fishdam ceremonials, then, all three are snared—without being harmed. Thus the symbolic meaning of catching the unwilling penis is added to that of holding on to the elusive nipple. This seems to enhance the enjoyment of the rejuvenation orgies for both sexes; for it gives reassurance that the incestuous and sadistic fantasies emphasized in the Yurok version of childhood dependence have not only not offended either the ontogenetic or the phylogenetic providers, but have been successfully applied to the common good for one more year. This permits the Yurok to accomplish a most precarious feat, namely, to eat their salmon and have it next year, too.

As these excerpts show, the author's data are largely data of verbal tradition, not of observation. They reflect what women remembered doing or saying to their children. There is no reason to doubt, however, that this selection, as far as it goes, is representative. To be sure, there is a great emphasis on feeding procedures; yet it may well be that in human groups who concentrate as homogeneous entities on a direct hand-to-mouth contact with one segment of nature, there is a communal and magic emphasis on first ontogenetic feeding problems.

In the primitive child's later childhood, as it fuses into community life, there probably is a diffusion of those pathogenic tensions that are typical for our each-family-for-itself training. It is in experiences connected with food that the primitive child is closest to his family, and especially to his mother, on whom falls the task in feeding him of laying the basis for his attitude toward the world as a whole. Some consciousness of this mission which gives female functions and modes equality in cultural importance with those of men, may prevent the vast majority of primitive women from resenting their restricted participation in the more spectacular activities of men.

X

The instinctive mental hygiene measures of homogeneous cultures are impressive: parent-fixations are diffused in extended families; children are largely educated by other children, are kept in check by fear of ridicule rather than by the bite of guilt feelings, and are encouraged to be virtuous by the promise of tangible and universal prestige points. On the plains at least, no threat of violence or abandonment estranges parent and child, no talk of sinfulness, body and self. As we consider our means of child rearing in a planned democracy, it may pay to ponder over the polarity of child training:

The Sioux baby is permitted to remain an individualist (for example, in the way he weans himself from his mother) while he builds an unequivocal trust in himself and in his surroundings. Then when strong in body and confident in himself, he is asked to bow to a tradition of unrelenting public opinion which focuses on his social behavior rather than on his bodily functions and their psychological concomitants. He is forced into a stern tradition which satisfies his social needs and conspires with him in projecting any possible source of sin and guilt into the supernatural. As long as he is able to conform, he can feel free. (S. p. 152-153).

In comparison,

the dominating classes in the Anglo-Saxon world tend more and more to regulate early functions and impulses in childhood. They implant the never silent metronome into the impressionable baby to regulate his first experiences with his body and with the immediate physical surroundings. After the establishment of these safety devices, he is encouraged to become an individualist. He pursues masculine strivings but often compulsively remains within standardized careers which tend to substitute themselves for communal conscience.

However, as just demonstrated, child training is not an isolated field governed or governable by attitudes of malice or love of children, insight or ignorance; it is a part of the totality of a culture's economic and ideational striving. The systematic difference between "primitive" and "civilized" cultures almost forbids comparison of details. What follows are reflections with some bearing on the study of childhood by clinical psychoanalytic means.

As we have seen, primitive cultures are exclusive. Their image of man coincides with their consciousness of being a strong or "clean" Yurok or Sioux. We do not know how and how long they would have succeeded in remaining homogeneous if left alone. In civilization the image of man is expanding and is ever more inclusive. New syntheses of economic and emotional safety are sought in inclusive formations of new entities and new identities: regions, nations, classes, races, ideologies. These new entities, however, overlap, and anachronistic fears of extinction cause some areas to seek archaic safety in spasms of reactionary exclusion. The viciousness of the battlefields is matched in that of the wars of standards (including those of child training) and in the conflicts which individuals wage with themselves.

Primitive tribes have a direct relation to the sources and means of production. Their techniques are extensions of the human body, their magic is a projection of body concepts. Children in these groups participate in technical and in magic pursuits; body and environment, childhood and culture may be full of dangers, but they are all one world. The expansiveness of civilization, its stratification and specialization make it impossible for children to include in their ego synthesis more than a section or sections of their society. Machines, far from remaining an extension of the body, destine whole classes to be extensions of machinery; magic becomes secondary, serving intermediate links only; and childhood, in some classes, becomes a separate segment of life with its own folklore. Neuroses, we find, are unconscious attempts to adjust to the heterogeneous present with the magic means of a homogeneous past. But individual neuroses are only parts of collective ones. It may well be, for example, that such mechanical child training as western civilization has developed during the last few decades, harbors an unconscious magic attempt to master machines by becoming more like them, comparable to the Sioux' identification with the buffalo, the Yurok's with the river and the salmon.

XI

According to the author, clinical description, i.e. the description of one or several successive segments of a historical process defines every item of human behavior according to at least three kinds of organization:

(1) The biological one, which reflects the nature of the human organism as a space-time organization of mammalian organ-systems (evolution, epigenesis, pregenitality),

(2) The social one, which reflects the fact that human organisms are organized into geographic-historical units,

(3) The ego-principle, reflecting the synthesis of experience and the resulting defensive and creative mastery (ego development).

None of these principles can "cause" a human event; but no human event is explained except by an investigation that pursues the Gestalten evoked by each principle in constant relativity to the two others.

In the psychoanalysis of the individual Freud has introduced this threefold investigation in the dynamic concepts of an id, a superego, and an ego.

What psychoanalysis has contributed to the knowledge of childhood, step by step, depended on the shifting foci of its theoretical attention. The id and its few basic drives were studied first. The initial focus of a science, however, threatens to impose its form on all further findings. Thus the next focus of study, namely the superego, which represents the first conceptualization of the influence of society on the individual, was primarily conceived of as an anti-id; it was said to be observable only when the id forced it to act. At best it behaved like the Victorian mother (quoted by Anna Freud) who sits in the parlor and periodically sends the nurse upstairs to tell the children not to do whatever it is they are doing. This mother never goes upstairs herself to tell the children what they *may* do—or even to do it with them. But this is what cultures, parents, neighborhoods do—and at least some of the ego's guiding ideals result from it. The ego, in turn, was at first conceived of as an ego both against the id and against the culture "with much emphasis on the poor little fellow's painful adjustment to the big bad environment" and with little emphasis on the fact that only a supporting society and a loving mother can make a functioning ego.

In his last writings Freud formulated the id and the superego in historical terms:

> During the whole of a man's life . . . the superego . . . represents the influence of his childhood, of the care and education given to him by his parents, of his dependence on them—of the childhood which is so greatly prolonged in human beings by a common family life. And in all this what is operating is not only the personal qualities of these parents but also everything that produced a determining effect upon themselves, the tastes and standards of the social class in which they live and the characteristics and traditions of the race from which they spring. Those who have a liking for generalizations and sharp distinctions may say that the external world, in which the individual finds himself exposed after being detached from his parents, represents the power of the present; that his id, with its inherited trends, represents the organic past; and that the superego, which later joins them, represents more than anything the cultural

past, of which the child has to pass through, as it were, an after-experience during the few years of his early childhood. ("An Outline of Psycho-Analysis," *International Journal of Psycho-Analysis,* XXI, p. 82.)

We are now studying the relationship of the ego to the "power of the present," that is the experience of perpetual change from the immediate past to the anticipated future.

In her book *The Ego and the Mechanisms of Defense,* Anna Freud asks whether or not the ego invents its defenses all by itself. She comes to the conclusion that the form of defense depends on the id content to be warded off, but does not discuss the relationship of ego mechanisms to the historical present.[5]

Anna Freud reports a case of altruism by identification and projection. A patient seems to have renounced all earthly pleasure. But far from being a Puritan, she does not insist that everybody else renounce these pleasures too. On the contrary, wherever possible she helps other people, even rivals, to enjoy what she herself seems neither to demand nor to need. This is called a defense mechanism, although at times it must have approached a symptom, and around it a personality must have been built. Beyond asking what infantile drives made such a mechanism necessary, and indeed pleasurable, we could inquire: Why, and at what stage of the patient's life did this mechanism develop and who was its model? Was it the parent of the same or of the other sex? Was it an ancestor, a priest, a teacher, a neighbor? Within what kind of a communal environment was this mechanism developed and within what kind of culture change: In what sections of her environment and at what period of her life did this kind of altruism secure to the patient glory and a halo, or shame and defamation, or indifference?

The need for clinical reconstructions that include the correlation of critical psychosexual phases with contemporaneous social changes becomes especially apparent—but it is by no means restricted to—American patients of psychoanalysis. This, I assume, is one major reason for the fact that the discussion of "social factors" that were energetically sought by some European workers in the field, has become more systematic and decisive in this country. This change of focus—like preceding ones—is accompanied by apologies and apostasies, and this for reasons intrinsic in the psychoanalytic movement, but not to be discussed here.

This dynamic country, by its very nature, subjects its inhabitants to more extreme contrasts and abrupt changes during a lifetime or a generation than is normally the case with other great nations. The national character is formed by what we hope will ultimately prove to be fruitful polarities: open roads of immigration and closed areas of settlement; free influences of immigration and jealous islands of tradition; outgoing internationalism and defiant isolationism; boisterous competition and self-effacing cooperation; and many others. Which of the resulting contradictory slogans has the greatest influence on the development of an individual ego, probably depends on the relationship of critical growth periods to the rate of change in the family history.

It was customary in some psychiatric circles in Europe to discuss what appeared to be a relative "ego weakness" in American patients. There are indications that in the depths of their hearts American neurotics, beyond seeking relief for guilt and inferiority feelings, desire to be cured of a basic vagueness and confusion in their identifications. Often they turn to psychoanalysis as a savior from the discrepancies of American life; abroad, they were willing to dissimulate their American identity for the sake of what promised to be a more comfortable one, made in "the old country."

The less neurotic American,[6] however, as long as he does not feel endangered by some too unexpected turn of events, paradoxically enough receives his very ego strength from a kind of proud refusal to settle on any form of group-ego too early, and too definitely. To be sure, he acknowledges some fundamental decencies and some—incredibly fleeting—common experiences on crossroads. Otherwise premature harmony disconcerts him; he is rather prepared for and willing to tackle discontinuities. In the meantime he lives by slogans which are, as it were, experimental crystallizations—a mode of life that can, of course, turn into perverse shiftiness.[7]

Such slogans as "let's get the hell out of here," or "let's stay no matter what happens"—to mention only two of the most sweeping ones—are in the sphere of ethos what rationalizations are in that of the intellect. Often outmoded, and without any pretense of logic, they are convincing enough to those involved to justify action whether within or just outside of the law insofar as it happens to be enforced. Slogans contain time and space perspectives as definite as those elaborated in the Sioux or Yurok systems—a collective ego time-space to which individual ego defenses are coordinated. But they change.

A cartoon in the *New Yorker* not long ago pictured an old lady who sat in her little garden before a little colonial house, knitting furiously but otherwise ignoring enormous bulldozers excavating the ground a hundred feet deep around her small property, to make space for the foundations of skyscrapers. Many a patient from Eastern mansions, finds himself regressing to such an *ego-space*, with all the defense mechanisms of exclusiveness, whenever he is frightened by competition outside, or by unbridled impulses from within.

Or take a patient whose grandparents came West "where never is heard a discouraging word." The grandfather, a powerful and powerfully driven man seeks ever new and challenging engineering tasks in widely separated regions. When the initial challenge is met, he hands the task over to others, and moves on. His wife sees him only for an occasional impregnation. According to a typical family pattern, his sons cannot keep pace with him and are left as respectable settlers by the wayside; only his daughter is and looks like him. Her very masculine identification, however, does not permit her to take a husband equal to her strong father. She marries a weak man and settles down. She brings her boy up to be God-fearing and industrious. He becomes reckless and shifting at times, depressed at others: somewhat of a juvenile delinquent now, later, maybe, a more enjoyable Westerner, with alcoholic moods.

What his worried mother does not know is that she herself all through his childhood has belittled the sedentary father; has decried the lack of mobility, geographic and social, of her marital existence; has idealized the grandfather's exploits; but has also reacted with panicky punitiveness to any display of friskiness in the boy, which was apt to disturb the now well-defined neighborhood.

In the course of a psychoanalysis patients repeat in transferences and regressions not only infantile instinctual tensions and ego defenses, but also their abortive (and often unconscious) infantile ego-ideals. These are often based on conditions and slogans which prevailed at the period of the family's greatest ascendancy. Specific conflicts and resistances result: the patient, on the one hand, is afraid that the brittleness of his ideal identity will be uncovered; on the other, he wishes the psychoanalyst, no matter with what means or terminologies, to free him from the ambiguity of his background and to provide him with the deceptive continuity of a magic psychoanalytic world.

This, however, is not the social function of psychoanalysis.

The individual is not merely the sum-total of his childhood identifications. Children—perhaps more pronouncedly in a highly mobile society—are early aware of their parents' position in the community; of their reactions to friends, servants, superiors; of their behavior in pleasant, pious, angry or alcoholized company; of Saturday nights in town and of mild enthusiasms and panics pervading neighborhoods, not to speak of lynchings and wars. If not impoverished too early by indifferent communities and selfish mothers, children early develop a nucleus of separate identity. Anxiety may cause them to sacrifice this individual awareness to blind identifications with parental persons. In the psychoanalytic treatment of adults this nucleus should be recovered. The patient, instead of blaming his parents (i.e. turning his positive over-identifications into negative ones), should learn to understand the social forces responsible for the deficiences of his childhood.

In our clinical attempts to reconstruct the childhood of adult patients we have studied "id resistances" as derivatives of the infantile fear of being deprived of urgent satisfactions; we have studied "super-ego resistances" as representatives of the infantile fear of being over-powered by such needs. The change in ego-potential or both these fears during maturational and psychological crises is well known to us. We perceive of the ego as a central regulator which, closest to the history of the day, guards a measure of safety, satisfaction and identity. As we add to our knowledge and technique the understanding of re-sistances that originate in contemporary conflicts of ego-ideals, we cannot fail to make new and, in a sense, perpetual contributions to the study of childhood in a world characterized by expanding identifica-tions and by great fears of losing hard-won identities.

NOTES

1. "Observations on Sioux Education," *Journal of Psychology*, 1939, 7, 101-156; and "Observations on the Yurok: Childhood and World Image," *University of California Press*, Berkeley and Los Angeles, 1943.

In the following, S, after a quotation refers to the first paper, Y, to the second.

2. For a diagrammatic representation of the interrelation of zones and modes see the author's contribution to Margaret Mead's chapter in the forthcoming edition of the *Handbook of Child Psychology*.

3. The author also considers the possibility that the remnants of such con-ditioning and its reflection in historical traits may contribute to the oral-depres-sive way in which the Sioux accept their—admittedly almost hopeless—lot.

4. This may indicate that the Yurok position in intercourse was the same as the most usual one among Indians and whites today.

5. See however, A. Freud and D. T. Burlingham, *Infants Without Families*. New York, 1944.

6. His elusive nature is only now being defined by anthropologists. See Mar-garet Mead, *And Keep Your Powder Dry*, 1942, for an attempt at such definition and for a relevant bibliography.

7. What is popularly called an "ego" in this country, seems to be the defiant expression of the owner's conviction that he is somebody without being identified with anybody in particular.

ALICE C. FLETCHER AND FRANCIS LA FLESCHE

1911. "Rites Pertaining to the Individual: Introduction of the Omaha Child to the Cosmos," from *The Omaha Tribe, Twenty-Seventh Annual Report of the Bureau of American Ethnology, 1905-06*. Washington, D. C., Government Printing Office. Pp. 115-133, *passim*.

It is easy to assume that the newest research must be the best; at least improvements in research technique make possible increasing accuracy, and developments in other sciences—as in psychiatry—induce ethnographers to observe aspects of native life that may have been neglected in the past. Nevertheless, some of the most precious documents of ethnography are old books and records made by persons innocent of special training in anthropology. One value of the older works inheres in their very age, for they record customs and conditions that have disappeared since they were written. Again, many older works will never go out of date, because their authors combined keen observation with decades of residence among the people whom they described. No matter how incisive and unique a new technique of field research may be, there can be no substitute for protracted intimate living among a people.

Alice Fletcher lived among the Omaha Indians for twenty-nine years before she wrote the book from which the following excerpt is reprinted. She did not rely exclusively on her own observations, for Francis La Flesche, son of the principal chief of the Omaha tribe, had dedicated himself to learning English and recording the lore of his people in that language. For twenty-five years he and Miss Fletcher worked together to produce a reliable picture of Omaha life.

The excerpt reprinted here presents only a part of the material on child-training from *The Omaha Tribe*. The section on "Care and Training of Children" (pp. 327 ff) is well worth study, against the background of the book as a whole.

THE OMAHA TRIBE:
INTRODUCTION OF THE CHILD
TO THE WORLD

Alice C. Fletcher and Francis LaFlesche

Introduction of the Omaha Child to the Cosmos

When a child was born it was not regarded as a member of its gens or of the tribe but simply as a living being coming forth into the universe, whose advent must be ceremonially announced in order to assure it an accepted place among the already existing forms. This ceremonial announcement took the form of an expression of the Omaha belief in the oneness of the universe through the bond of a common life-power that pervaded all things in nature animate and inanimate.

Although in the Teçin'de and Inshta' çunda gentes the custom survived of placing on the child, the fourth day after birth, certain symbols pertaining to the peculiar rites of those gentes, these acts did not serve the purpose of introducing the child into the teeming life of the universe. This ceremony of introduction took place on the eighth day after birth. Unfortunately the full details of the ceremony have been lost through the death of the priests who had charge of it. The hereditary right to perform the ceremony belonged in the Washe'ton subgens of the Inshta'çunda gens.

On the appointed day the priest was sent for. When he arrived he took his place at the door of the tent in which the child lay and raising his right hand to the sky, palm outward, he intoned the following in a loud voice:

Ho! Ye Sun, Moon, Stars, all ye that move in the heavens,
   I bid you hear me!
Into your midst has come a new life.
   Consent ye, I implore!
Make its path smooth, that it may reach the brow of the first hill!

Ho! Ye Winds, Clouds, Rain, Mist, all ye that move in the air.
   I bid you hear me!
Into your midst has come a new life.
   Consent ye, I implore!
Make its path smooth, that it may reach the brow of the second hill!

Ho! Ye Hills, Valleys, Rivers, Lakes, Trees, Grasses, all ye of the
   earth,
   I bid you hear me!
Into your midst has come a new life.
   Consent ye, I implore!
Make its path smooth, that it may reach the brow of the third hill!
Ho! Ye Birds, great and small, that fly in the air,
Ho! Ye Animals, great and small, that dwell in the forest,
Ho! Ye Insects that creep among the grasses and burrow in the
   ground—
   I bid you hear me!
Into your midst has come a new life.
   Consent ye, I implore!
Make its path smooth, that it may reach the brow of the fourth hill!
Ho! All ye of the heavens, all ye of the air, all ye of the earth:
   I bid you all to hear me!
Into your midst has come a new life.
   Consent ye, consent ye all, I implore!
Make its path smooth—then shall it travel beyond the four hills!

This ritual was a supplication to the powers of the heavens, the air,
and the earth for the safety of the child from birth to old age. In it the
life of the infant is pictured as about to travel a rugged road stretching
over four hills, marking the stages of infancy, youth, manhood, and
old age.

The ceremony which finds oral expression in this ritual voices in no
uncertain manner the Omaha belief in man's relation to the visible
powers of the heavens and in the interdependence of all forms of life.
The appeal bears evidence of its antiquity, breathing of a time ante-
dating established rites and ceremonies. It expresses the emotions of the
human soul, touched with the love of offspring, alone with the might
of nature, and companioned only by the living creatures whose friendliness must be sought if life is to be secure on its journey. . . .

INTRODUCTION OF THE CHILD INTO THE TRIBE
CEREMONY OF TURNING THE CHILD

The name of this ceremony was Thiku'wiⁿxe (thi, a prefix indicating action by the hand; ku'wiⁿxe, "to turn"). Although the child is not
mentioned, it is understood as being referred to. The translation of the
term, therefore, would be "turning the child."

All children, both boys and girls, passed through this ceremony,
which is a survival of that class of ceremonies belonging to the lowest
or oldest, stratum of tribal rites; it is directly related to the cosmic
forces—the wind, the earth, and the fire. Through this ceremony all the
children who had reached the period when they could move about
unaided, could direct their own steps, were symbolically "sent into the

midst of the winds"—that element essential to life and health; their feet were set upon the stone—emblem of long life upon the earth and of the wisdom derived from age; while the "flames," typical of the life-giving power, were invoked to give their aid toward insuring the capacity for a long, fruitful, and successful life within the tribe. Through this ceremony the child passed out of that stage in its life wherein it was hardly distinguished from all other living forms into its place as distinctively a human being, a member of its birth gens, and through this to a recognized place in the tribe. As it went forth its baby name was thrown away, its feet were clad in new moccasins made after the manner of the tribe, and its *ni'kie* name was proclaimed to all nature and to the assembled people.

The significance of the new moccasins put on the child will appear more clearly by the light of the following custom, still observed in families in which all the old traditions of the tribe are conserved: When moccasins are made for a little baby, a small hole is cut in the sole of one. This is done in order that "if a messenger from the spirit world should come and say to the child, 'I have come for you,' the child could answer, 'I can not go on a journey—my moccasins are worn out!' " A similar custom obtains in the Oto tribe. A little hole is cut in the first pair of moccasins made for a child. When the relatives come to see the little one they examine the moccasins, and, seeing the hole, they say: "Why, he (or she) has worn out his moccasins; he has traveled over the earth!" This is an indirect prayer that the child may live long. The new (whole) moccasins put on the child at the close of the ceremony of introducing it into the tribe constitute an assurance that it is prepared for the journey of life and that the journey will be a long one.

The ceremony of Turning the Child took place in the springtime, after the first thunders had been heard. When the grass was well up and the birds were singing, "particularly the meadow lark," the tribal herald proclaimed that the time for these ceremonies had come. A tent was set up for the purpose, made *xube*, or sacred, and the keeper of these rites, who belonged to the Washe'ton subgens of the Inshta'çunda gens, made himself ready and entered the tent. Meanwhile the parents whose children had arrived at the proper age, that is, could walk steadily unassisted, took their little ones and proceeded to the Sacred Tent. The only requisite for the child was a pair of new moccasins, but large fees were given to the priest for his services. . . .

The tent was always a large one, set facing the east, and open at the entrance, so that the bystanders, who kept at a respectful distance, could see something of what was going on within. As the ceremony was one of tribal interest, many flocked to the Sacred Tent to watch the proceedings. In the center was a fire. On the east of the fire was placed a stone. There was also a ball of grass, placed at the west of the fireplace near its edge. It was the mother who led the child to the tent. At the door she paused, and addressed the priest within, saying: "Venerable man! I desire my child to wear moccasins." Then she dropped the hand of the child, and the little one, carrying his new moccasins, entered the tent alone. He was met by the priest, who advanced to the door to receive the gifts brought by the mother as fees. Here she again addressed him, saying: "I desire my child to walk long upon the earth; I desire him to be content with the light of many days. We seek your protection; we hold to you for strength." The priest replied, addressing the child: " You shall reach the fourth hill sighing; you shall be bowed over; you shall have wrinkles; your staff shall bend under your weight. I speak to you that you may be strong." Laying his hand on the shoulder of the child, he added: "What you have brought me shall not be lost to you; you shall live long and enjoy many possessions; your eyes shall be satisfied with many good things." Then, moving with the child toward the fireplace in the center of the lodge, and speaking in the capacity of the Thunder, whose priest he was, he uttered these words: "I am a powerful being; I breathe from my lips over you." Then he began to sing the Invocation addressed to the Winds: . . .

Free translation

Ye four,* come hither and stand, near shall ye stand
In four groups shall ye stand
Here shall ye stand, in this place stand
(The Thunder Rolls)

The music of this invocation is in the five-toned scale. The voice dwells on the words *ti*, "come" and *she*, "near in this place." The roll of the Thunder is given in the relative minor.

At the close of this ritual song the priest faces the child to the east, lifting it by the shoulders; its feet are allowed to rest upon the stone. He then turns the child completely around, from left to right. If by any chance the child should struggle or move so as to turn from right to left the onlookers set up a cry of alarm. It was considered very disastrous to turn ever so little in the wrong way, so the priest was most careful to prevent any accident. When the child had been turned, its feet rested on the stone as it faced the south. The priest then lifted it by the arms, turned it, and set its feet on the stone as it faced the west; then he again lifted the child, turned it, and set its feet on the stone as it faced the north. Lastly the child was lifted to its feet and placed on the stone as it again faced the east. During this action the following ritual song was sung: . . .

---

*The four winds.

Free translation

Turned by the winds goes the one I send yonder;
Yonder he goes who is whirled by the winds;
Goes, where the four hills of life and the four winds are standing;
There, in the midst of the winds do I send him,
Into the midst of the winds, standing there.

(The Thunder Rolls)

The winds invoked by the priest stand in four groups, and receive the child, which is whirled by them, and by them enabled "to face in every direction." This action symbolizes that the winds will come and strengthen him as hereafter he shall traverse the earth and meet the vicissitudes he must encounter as he passes over the four hills and completes the circuit of a long life. It was believed that this ceremony exercised a marked influence on the child, and enabled it to grow in strength and in the ability to practise self-control.

The priest now put the new moccasins on the feet of the child, as the following ritual song was sung. Toward its close the child was lifted, set on its feet, and made to take four steps typical of its entrance into a long life. . . .

Free translation

Here unto you has been spoken the truth;
Because of this truth you shall stand.
Here, declared is the truth.
Here in this place has been shown you the truth.
Therefore, arise! go forth in its strength!

(The Thunder Rolls)

The *ni'kie* name of the child was now announced, after which the priest cried aloud: "Ye hills, ye grass, ye trees, ye creeping things both great and small, I bid you hear! This child has thrown away its baby name. Ho!" (a call to take notice).

The priest next instructed the child as to the tabu it must observe, and what would be the penalty for disobedience. If the child was a girl, she now passed out of the tent and rejoined her mother.

Up to this point the ceremony of introducing the child into the tribe was the same for male and female; but in the case of boys there was a supplemental rite which pertained to them as future warriors.

CONSECRATION OF THE BOY TO THUNDER

This ceremony was called We'bashna, meaning "to cut the hair." According to traditions, this specialized ceremony belonged to the period in the growth of the political development of the tribe when efforts were being made to hold the tribe more firmly together by checking the independence of the warriors and placing them under control—efforts that finally resulted in the placing of the rites of war in charge of the We'zhi^{n}shte gens.

In the ceremony of cutting the hair the priest in charge gathered a tuft from the crown of the boy's head, tied it, then cut it off and laid it away in a parfleche case, which was kept as a sacred repository, singing as he cut the lock a ritual song explanatory of the action. The severing of the lock was an act that implied the consecration of the life of the boy to Thunder, the symbol of the power that controlled the life and death of the warrior—for every man had to be a warrior in order to defend the home and the tribe. The ritual song which followed the cutting of the lock indicated the acceptance of the offering made; that is, the life of the warrior henceforth was under the control of the Thunder to prolong or to cut short at will.

The Washe'to^n subgens, which had charge of this rite of the consecration of the boy to the Thunder as the god of war, camped at the end of the I^{n}shta'çu^{n}da division, and formed the northern side of the entrance into the *hu'thuga** when the opening faced the east, while the We'zhi^{n}shte gens, which had charge of the rites pertaining to war, including the bestowal of honors, formed the southern side of the entrance. Thus the "door," through which all must pass who would enter the *hu'thuga,* was guarded on each side by gentes having charge of rites pertaining to Thunder, as the god of war, the power that could not only hold in check enemies from without, but which met each man child at his entrance into the tribe and controlled him even to the hour of his death.

In a community beginning to crystallize into organized social relations the sphere of the warrior would naturally rise above that of the mere fighter; and when the belief of the people concerning nature is taken into consideration it is not surprising that the movement toward social organization should tend to place the warriors—the men of power—in close relation to those natural manifestations of power seen in the fury of the storm and heard in the rolling of the thunder. Moreover, in the efforts toward political unification such rites as those which were connected with the Thunder would conduce to the welding of the people by the inculcation of a common dependence upon a powerful god and the sign of consecration to him would be put upon the head of every male member of the tribe.

The priest took the boy to the space west of the fire; there, facing the east, he cut a lock of hair from the crown of the boy's head, as he sang the following ritual song: . . .

**Húthuga:* the formal pattern of arrangement of the dwellings of members of the several gentes of the tribe.—Ed.

Free translation

Grandfather! far above on high,
The hair like a shadow passes before you.
Grandfather! far above on high,
Dark like a shadow the hair sweeps before you into the midst of
    your realm.
Grandfather! there above, on high,
Dark like a shadow the hair passes before you.
Grandfather! dwelling afar on high,
Like a dark shadow the hair sweeps before you into the midst of
    your realm.
Grandfather! far above on high,
The hair like a shadow passes before you.

From this ritual song we learn that the lock laid away in the sacred case in care of the Thunder priest symbolically was sent to the Thunder god dwelling "far above on high," who was ceremonially addressed as "Grandfather"—the term of highest respect in the language. The hair of a person was popularly believed to have a vital connection with the life of the body, so that anyone becoming possessed of a lock of hair might work his will on the individual from whom it came. In ceremonial expressions of grief the throwing of locks of hair upon the dead was indicative of the vital loss sustained. In the light of customs that obtained among the people the hair, under certain conditions, might be said to typify life. Because of the belief in the continuity of life a part could stand for the whole, so in this rite by the cutting off of a lock of the boy's hair and giving it to the Thunder the life of the child was given into the keeping of the god. It is to be noted that later, when the hair was suffered to grow on the boy's head, a lock on the crown of the head was parted in a circle from the rest of the hair and kept constantly distinct and neatly braided. Upon this lock the war honors of the warrior were worn, and it was this lock that was cut from the head of a slain enemy and formed the central object in the triumph ceremonies, for the reason that it preeminently represented the life of the man who had been slain in battle.

In the next ritual song the Thunder god speaks and proclaims his acceptance of the consecration of the life through the lock of hair and also declares his control over the life of the warrior. . . .

Free translation

What time I will, then only then,
A man lies dead, a gruesome thing.
What time I will, then suddenly
A man lies dead, a gruesome thing.
What time I will, then, only then,

Like a shadow dark, the man shall lie.
What time I will, then suddenly
A man lies dead, a gruesome thing.
What time I will, then, only then,
Reddened and stark a man lies dead.
What time I will, then suddenly
A man lies dead, a gruesome thing.

The word *shabe*, dark like a shadow, is used in the preceding song to describe the lock of hair that was cut from the child's head as a symbol that his life was offered to the god; in this song the same word, *shabe*, is applied to the man who, "like a shadow dark," "shall lie" when his life has been taken by the god. The use of this word bears out the meaning of the rite that accompanied the preceding song, that by the giving of the lock of hair the life of the person was given to the god. This song shows that the god intends to do as he wills with that life. There are other songs used in the tribe which iterate this belief that a man dies only when the gods decree.

The music is in the five-tone scale, and the phrase which carries the assertion of the god rises and dwells on the tonic, a movement rare in Omaha songs, the general trend being from higher to lower tones.

The imperfect account of this ritual makes it impossible to state whether or not the six songs here given were all that belonged to this ceremony. It is also uncertain whether or not the invocation to the winds was sung before the turning of every child; it may have been sung only once, at the opening of the general ceremony, there being indications that such was the case. It is probable that the song given below was also sung but once, at the close of the general ceremony, but it has been impossible to obtain accurate information on this point. Only one point is certain—that the following was the final song of the ceremony: . . .

Free translation

Come hither, haste to help me,
Ye flames, ye flames, O come!
O red-hot fire, hasten!
O haste, ye flames, to come.
Come speedily to help me,
Ye flames, ye flames, O come!
O red-hot fire, hasten!
O haste, ye flames, to come!
Come hither, haste, to help me!

As this song was sung the ball of grass to which reference has already been made was held aloft and then hurled to the ground, where it mysteriously burst into flames, which were regarded as symbolizing the lightning.

In this closing song there is a return to the cosmic forces which were appealed to and represented in the ceremony of Turning the Child. In early times before this ceremony had been arranged so as to include the rite of consecrating the boy to the Thunder god, the song which appears on the preceding page was sung probably soon after, if not immediately at the conclusion of, the third song given in this account.

At the conclusion of this tribal ceremony, when the child reached its home the father cut the hair of his son after the symbolic manner of his gens;[1] the hair was thus worn until the second dentition. Then the hair was allowed to grow, and the scalp lock, the sign of the warrior to which reference has already been made was parted off and kept carefully braided, no matter how frowzy and tangled the rest of the hair might be.

CEREMONIAL INTRODUCTION TO INDIVIDUAL LIFE AND TO THE SUPERNATURAL

The next stage in the life of the Omaha youth was marked by the rite known by the name of $No^{n'}zhi^{n}zho^{n}$. The literal meaning of the word is "to stand sleeping"; it here implies that during the rite the person stands as if oblivious of the outward world and conscious only of what transpires within himself, his own mind. This rite took place at puberty, when the mind of the child had "become white." This characterization was drawn from the passing of night into day. It should be remembered that in native symbolism night is the mother of day; so the mind of the new-born child is dark, like the night of its birth; gradually it begins to discern and remember things as objects seen in the early dawn; finally it is able to remember and observe discriminatingly; then its mind is said to be "white," as with the clear light of day. At the period when the youth is at the verge of his conscious individual life, is "old enough to know sorrow," it was considered time that through the rite $No^{n'}zhi^{n}zho^{n}$ he should enter into personal relations with the mysterious power that permeates and controls all nature as well as his own existence.

In the Sacred Legend, which recounts briefly the history of the people and from which quotations have been made, the origin of this rite is thus given:

The people felt themselves weak and poor. Then the old men gathered together and said: "Let us make our children cry to Wakon'da that he may give us strength." So all the parents took their children who were old enough to pray in earnest, put soft clay on their faces, and sent them forth to lonely places. The old men said to the youths: "You shall go forth to cry to Wakon'da. When on the hills you shall not ask for any particular thing. The answer may not come to you as you expect; whatever is good, that may Wakon'da give." Four days upon the hills shall the youths pray, crying. When they stop, they shall wipe their tears with the palms of their hands and lift their wet hands to the sky, then lay them to the earth. This was the people's first appeal to Wakon'da.

The closing statement as to "the first appeal" should not be taken literally, for the rite thus said to have been introduced is too complex, and embodies beliefs that must have required a long time for formulation into the dramatic forms observed in this rite.

The old men, when explaining the rite, said "It must be observed by all youths. After the first time, the youth could repeat the rite until he was old enough to marry and had children; by that time his life was fixed, and he prayed no more unless he was a priest, then he would continue to fast and pray." "In the Non'zhinzhon," it was further explained, "the appeal was to Wakon'da, the great power. There were other powers—the sun, the stars, the moon, the earth—but these were lesser; the prayer was not to them." The old men added: "The appeal was for help throughout life. As the youth goes forth to fast he thinks of a happy life, good health, success in hunting; in war he desires to secure spoils and escape the enemy; if he should be attacked that the weapons of his adversaries might fail to injure him. Such were the thoughts and hopes of the youth when he entered upon this fast, although he was forbidden to ask for any special favor." The rite Non'-zhinzhon was observed in the spring; never in the summer or winter. The meaning of putting clay on the head has been explained in different ways. Some have said it symbolized humility; others that it referred to the soft clay or mud brought up by the diving animals, out of which the earth was created. In the opinion of the writers the latter seems the more probable explanation.

In preparation the youth was taught the following prayer, which was to be sung during the ordeal of the fast. It was known to every youth in the tribe, no matter what his gens.[2] This prayer must be accepted, therefore, as voicing a fundamental belief of the entire Omaha tribe. The music is in keeping with the words, being unmistakably an earnest invocation. . . .

Literal translation: *Wakoᵃ'da*, the permeating life of nature and of man; the great mysterious power; *thethu*, here; *wahpathin*, poor, needy; *atonhe*, he stands, and I am he—a form of expression used to indicate humility. *Wakon'da!* here, needy, he stands, and I am he.

This prayer was called *Wakon'da gikon* (*gigikon*, "to weep from loss," as that of kindred, the prefix *gi* indicating possession; *gikon*, therefore, is to weep from the want of something not possessed, from conscious insufficiency and the desire for something that could bring happiness or prosperity). This prayer and the aspect of the suppliant, standing alone in the solitary place, with clay on his head, tears falling from his

eyes, and his hands lifted in supplication, were based on anthropomorphic ideas concerning Wako$^{n\prime}$da. The Omaha conceived that the
appeal from one so young and untried, who showed poverty and the
need of help, could not fail to move the power thus appealed to, even
as a man so importuned would render the aid that was asked. The words
of the prayer set forth the belief that Wako$^{n\prime}$da was able to understand
and to respond to the one who thus voiced his consciousness of dependence and his craving for help from a power higher than himself.

Four days and nights the youth was to fast and pray provided he
was physically able to bear so long a strain. No matter how hungry
he became, he was forbidden to use the bow and arrows put into his
hands by his father when he left his home for this solitary test of endurance. When he fell into a sleep or a trance, if he saw or heard anything, that thing was to become a special medium through which the
youth could receive supernatural aid. Generally with the sight of the
thing came an accompanying cadence. This cadence was the song or
call by which the man might summon aid in his time of need. The form,
animate or inanimate, which appeared to the man was drawn toward
him, it was believed, by the feeling of pity. The term used to express
this impelling of the form to the man was *i'thaethe*, meaning "to have
compassion on." If the youth at this time saw a buffalo, it would be
said: *Te i'thaethe*, "the buffalo had compassion on him"; if he heard
the thunder: *I^{n}gthu$^{n\prime}$ ithaethe*, "the thunder had compassion." The vision with its sacred call or song, was the one thing that the Omaha held
as his own, incapable of loss so long as life and memory lasted. It was
his personal connection with the vast universe, by which he could
strengthen his spirit and his physical powers. He never gave the details
of his vision to anyone, nor was it even casually spoken of; it was too
sacred for ordinary speech.

When going forth to fast, the youth went silently and unobserved.
No one accosted him or gave him counsel or direction. He passed
through his experience alone, and alone he returned to his father's
lodge. No one asked him of his absence, or even mentioned the fact that
he had been away. For four days he must rest, eat little, and speak
little. After that period he might go to an old and worthy man who
was known to have had a similar vision. After eating and smoking
with the old man, when they were quite alone it was permitted the
youth to mention that he had had a vision like that of his host, of
beast, or bird, or whatever it might have been. Should he speak of
his vision before the expiration of the four days, it would be the same
as lost to him. After the youth had spoken to the old man it became
his duty to travel until he should meet the animal or bird seen in his
vision, when he had to slay it, and preserve either the whole or a part
of its body. This trophy became the visible sign of his vision and the

most sacred of his possessions. He might wear it on his scalp lock or elsewhere on his person during sacred festivals, when going to war, or on some other important occasions. This article has been spoken of by some writers as the man's "personal totem." When the vision came in the form of a cloud or the sound of the thunder, these were symbolized by certain objects or were typified in designs painted on the man or on his belongings.

Some visions were regarded as "lucky," as giving special and helpful advantages to the man. Hawks were "lucky"—they helped to success and prowess in war. Bears, being slow and clumsy, were "not so good," although possessing great recuperative power. The elk was fleet. Snakes were "not good," etc. To dream of the moon might bring a great calamity. It is said that the moon would appear to a man having in one hand a burden strap, in the other a bow and arrows, and the man would be bidden to make a choice. When he reached for the bow, the moon would cross its hands and try to force the strap on the man. If he awaked before he took the strap, or if he succeeded in capturing the bow, he escaped the penalty of the dream. If, on the other hand, he failed and the strap came into his hand, he was doomed to forfeit his manhood and become like a woman. He must speak as a woman, pursue her avocations, adopt her dress, and sometimes become subject to gross actions. It is said that there have been those who, having dreamed of the moon and having had the burden strap forced on them, have tried to conceal their ill luck for a time, but that few have succeeded. Instances are known in which the unfortunate dreamer, even with the help of his parents, could not ward off the evil influence of the dream, and resorted to suicide as the only means of escape. . . .

Among the Omaha, as well as their cognates, there were societies whose membership was made up of men who had had visions of the same object. It has already been mentioned that the object seen in the vision was said to have had compassion on the man when it appeared to him. It was also thought that because the same form could come to certain men and be seen by them there was something in common in the nature of these men—that a sort of brotherhood existed among them. Out of this belief societies grew up based on the members having had similar visions, and the ceremonies of these societies, quasi religious in character, dealt with the special gifts vouchsafed by Wako$^{n\prime}$da through the particular form or the animal. The article which was the symbol of a man's dream, as a feather from a bird, a tuft of hair from an animal, or a black stone or translucent pebble representing the thunder or the water, was never an object of worship. It was a memento of the vision, a sort of credential that served to connect its possessor with the potentiality of the species or class represented by the form seen in the vision, through which the man's strength or faculties could be re-enforced by virtue of the continuity of life throughout the universe because of the ever-present power of Wako^n'da.

In the sequence of rites just detailed, which began at birth with the announcement to all created things that a new life had come into their midst, and later, when the child had acquired ability to move about of its own volition, its feet were set in the path of life, and it entered into membership in the tribe, are represented progressive steps in the life of the individual from a mere living form to a being with a recognized place. The entrance into manhood required a voluntary effort by which, through the rite of fasting and prayer, the man came into direct and personal relations with the supernatural and realized within himself the forceful power of the union of the seen with the unseen.

NOTES

1. The various styles of cutting the child's hair to symbolize the tabu of his gens are shown with the account given of the gentes. (Pp. 144-188 of *The Omaha Tribe.*)

2. Every male was obliged to pass through the rite of No^n'zhi^{n}zho^n when he reached the proper age; whether he should continue to practise the rite was left to his personal choice. The No^n'zhi^{n}zho^n was not obligatory on girls or women but they sometimes went through the fast, for the rite was open to them.

ESTHER GOLDFRANK

1945. "Socialization, Personality, and the Structure of Pueblo Society (With Particular Reference to Hopi and Zuni)," *American Anthropologist* vol. 47: 516-539. Reprinted by courtesy of the author and of the Editor of the *American Anthropologist*.

Numerous anthropologists and psychologists have studied Pueblo Indian tribes repeatedly and over many years. It is suggested that students begin with Ruth Benedict's *Patterns of Culture*, then read this article by Dr. Goldfrank and the one by Laura Thompson; after doing so, continue with John Bennett's article, also in this book.

The following essay by Dr. Goldfrank includes stimulating suggestions for guidance of students of personality among any people. In addition, she provides an excellent bibliography for further study of Pueblo tribes. Additional works on the Pueblos are cited in the Bibliography of this volume; such include Benedict, 1928, 1932; Bunzel, 1929; Dennis, 1941; Dennis and Dennis, 1940; Eggan, 1950; E. C. Parsons, 1916, 1929; Thompson, 1950-c; Titiev, 1942.

It is worthy of note that the Pueblo tribes and the Navaho occupy the same geographic region. The works of Kluckhohn and of Reichard, to name but two lifelong students of the Navaho, provide basis for comparing the two cultural types. The presence of two differing cultural patterns in the same geographic area indicates that man's use of nature, rather than nature as a mystical force, determines what kind of society will develop in any part of the world.

SOCIALIZATION, PERSONALITY, AND THE STRUCTURE OF PUEBLO SOCIETY
(With Particular Reference to Hopi and Zuni)

Esther Goldfrank

I

Anthropologists interested in personality and culture owe a considerable debt to the concepts of psychoanalysis for insights into problems of maturation. These concepts, developed by Freud and his followers on the basis of their experience with neurotics, are continually being tested in more normal situations in our society, and increasingly in primitive groups whose background differs widely from our own.[1]

Some years ago Malinowski, who worked extensively with the Trobriand Islanders, questioned the validity of the oedipus complex for societies where the mother's brother was recognized as the primary authority over his sister's son.[2] More recently, Dorothy Eggan has pointed out that, despite optimal conditioning in infancy, the Hopi Indians of Arizona exhibit an extreme degree of anxiety in adult life.[3] The present inquiry has much in common with both of these investigations. While not directly concerned with the problem of anxiety or with the oedipus complex as such, I should like to examine further into the relation between permissiveness in infancy and adult personality structure in a society where the weight of discipline *after* the first years of life rests, not with a parent or other near relative, but with the supernaturals, their temporary impersonators, or their more permanent surrogates, the priesthood.

Considerable attention has been paid in anthropological and psychological literature to birth, puberty, marriage and death—all crisis points in the life cycle of the individual which in many societies are marked by special rites and ceremonies. In the present investigation, however, the line is drawn between the years of infancy and those that follow, because, more and more, despite a lack of ceremonial recognition, extraordinary importance has been attached to the first years of training by analysts, educators, and pediatricians. A member of the last group, Dr. C. Anderson Aldrich, writing in a current issue of the Journal of the American Association of University Women, deplores the "aftermath" of exacting training schedules on mothers and children, and recommends that early habit-training be given at appropriate stages of growth in order to allay confusion, resistance and emotional storms. Instead of making children "eat from a spoon before their tongue and lip muscles have developed properly" or submit to "premature attempts to train bowel and bladder control," he advises "closer contact with their mothers during the first few weeks of life than they are usually allowed; a more self-reliant program, and to be fed, for instance, by their own feeding schedule. . . ."[4] Others may build their argument differently (at times the dichotomy between family and society is exaggerated); but in general the orientation is the same: emphasis on the importance of conditioning in the first years of life to the adult personality structure.

For the purposes of this paper, the period of infancy will comprise approximately the first two years; for, whatever the individual variations may be, in most societies at the end of this time, nursing is completed, the children walk (whether they have enjoyed freedom of movement from birth or been strapped to a cradle board[5]), and in varying degree they are able to make their wants felt through the use of language.

The "later" years are those between infancy and that time when an individual may be said to assume his role as an adult in community affairs. In some societies this moment remains uncertain; in many it is marked by serious and strenuous "rites de passage."

With these distinctions in mind, four categories of society may be postulated:

1) Societies where infant and later disciplines are weak.
2) Societies where infant and later disciplines are severe.
3) Societies where infant disciplines are severe and later disciplines are weak.
4) Societies where infant disciplines are weak and later disciplines are severe.

From the standpoint of logic, these categories pose no problem. However, difficulties may arise when an attempt is made to assign specific societies to any one of them, for permissiveness and pressure are present at all stages of development. Pressures of some sort are exerted during infancy even in those societies which exhibit the greatest leniency in nursing or toilet training, and some degree of permissiveness is present even when infant disciplines are manifestly severe. But despite this mixed situation, classification in many instances is comparatively simple. In others, it may appear highly subjective and debatable. It is, therefore, imperative when examining societies of this latter type to indicate the complexities clearly and to give the facts without prejudice.

Societies which reveal a marked discontinuity in disciplinary policy (see above, categories 3 and 4) offer the most fertile soil for investigating the relative significance of infant conditioning to adult personality structure. The present inquiry is concerned only with category 4 (societies where infant disciplines are weak and later disciplines are severe). More particularly, it is concerned with Pueblo society in New Mexico and Arizona.

Many who are familiar with certain recent anthropological and analytical discussions on Pueblo society may question this classification, but the reasons for it will, I trust, become increasingly clear as the descriptive material is presented.

II

Almost as soon as the Bureau of American Ethnology was established some sixty-six years ago, anthropologists were sent to the Southwest, several of them remaining in the region for extended periods. This early interest has been maintained. In the intervening years, an impressive number of archaeologists, ethnologists, and linguists have continued to study the area, and within the last decade, psychologists and psychoanalysts. The advantage to research is obvious. Unlike the all-too-frequent necessity of relying on the report of a single observer,[6] the student of the Southwest is fortunate in having at his disposal a wealth of data collected over almost three-quarters of a century by many trained social scientists. The bulk of the published literature deals with Hopi and Zûni, villages which were comparatively free from white contact and at the same time comparatively responsive to white inquiry. The present investigation, because of the fuller documentary evidence, is also concentrated on Hopi and Zuni, although there is every indication from the material at hand that the other pueblos, basically similar in structure despite certain divergencies, have utilized similar devices for fitting their young to their society.[7]

Today, there are twenty-five Indian pueblos in New Mexico and Arizona, small, settled, self-contained communities in what many would consider an arid waste-land. Yet the people are primarily farmers, and the staple food is maize. In regions of this kind, where the annual average rainfall is frequently less than ten inches, and where, in addition, this limited quantity may not fall at the most advantageous times, or may fall in such torrents that tender growths are uprooted and destroyed—in regions of this kind, irrigation of some sort is necessary to insure the successful maturing of a crop.[8] The Pueblos along the Rio Grande tap the river for their water; others, like Hopi and Zuni, depend more directly on rainfall for flood-irrigation, or on springs. But whatever the source of their water-supply, the tasks of clearing, terracing, braking, damming, and ditching, though variously combined and differing in intensity from locality to locality, are more than an individual or even a small family can accomplish working alone. At Isleta, the entire man-power of the village (some five hundred adult males) is called out at the annual overhauling of the ditches.[9] At Hopi, the larger family or clan seems to be the basic cooperative unit[10]—but when certain springs are to be cleaned *everyone* participates.[11]

Large-scale cooperation deriving primarily from the needs of irrigation[12] is therefore vitally important to the life and well-being of the Pueblo community. It is no spontaneous expression of good-will or sociability. What may seem "voluntary" to some[13] is the end of a long process of conditioning, often persuasive, but frequently harsh, that commences in infancy and continues through adulthood.

III

On one aspect of Pueblo behavior there is unanimity among observers: the permissiveness of parents to offspring during the first years of life. Dorothy Eggan, reporting on Hopi, writes: " . . . few societies have provided a more uninhibited infancy,"[14] and her subsequent discussion documents her statement fully. Mischa Titiev, who made four different visits to the pueblo, observes that "Hopi mothers are notoriously over-indulgent towards their children . . . . Mothers often scold and threaten punishment, but only rarely do they make good their threats."[15] Rarely also "does a father exercise his right of punishing."[16] Wayne Dennis, a psychologist, reports:

> . . . the Hopi infant is invariably breast fed, is seldom weaned under one year of age and frequently is not weaned before two years . . . . The Hopi infant . . . is nursed as soon as he cries, and consequently nurses frequently and cries very little. The breast is used as a pacifier even though the cause of crying is pain or fright and not hunger. Among the Hopi there is no feeling that crying is something to be expected from the infant; because of this there are few frustrations during infancy and but little adherence to predetermined routines.[17]

Regarding the establishment of toilet habits, he notes:

> No training in this respect is imposed upon the Hopi child until he can walk and can understand simple commands, when he is told to go outside the door. . . . Nor is he exhorted to keep himself clean.[18]

Sun Chief, a native of the Hopi village of Oraibi, while frankly admitting his inability to remember his own baby experiences, nevertheless writes in his autobiography, apparently from hearsay and observation of others:

> I had many kinds of soft food stuck into my mouth and I could get the breast almost any time I cried. . . . Of course the people talked baby talk to me, passed me from lap to lap on the cradle,

rocked or shook me to sleep on their knees, and often sang to me. I am sure my father and grandfather sang many songs with me on their laps at the close of the day, and before I could remember anything.[19]

And he continues:

By early fall I was permitted off the cradle during the day and crawled naked over the earthen floor or rolled about in the sunshine on the roof of our winter house. I urinated any time and at any place, but whenever I started to defecate, someone picked me up and held me just outside the door. Dogs, cats, and my brother were my constant companions. My sister became my nurse and often carried me wrapped in a blanket on her back. On other occasions my mother ground corn with me fastened to her back, or took me with her to the spring or rock cisterns for water. She often left me to play on the ground under the watchful eye of her crippled brother, Naquima, who lived with us. I had now learned to suck my thumb, my 'whole fist' reports my father. I had probably discovered pleasure in my penis too, for every male child was tickled in his private parts by adults who wished to win smiles and sometimes to stop crying. No doubt other children, including my brother and sister, played with me in the same way. . . . Before the snows came, we moved down the ladder to our winter house, where I could play on the floor all day and stay up by the fire at night until I wished to sleep. I still slept on my cradle after I had begun to walk and talk at about two. It seemed that I was restless without it. My mother has told me how I would drag it to her crying, 'Ache,' which means sleep. But several people have agreed that I was never a cry baby. I was healthy, grew rapidly, and surpassed other babies in size. I was still nursing when my mother gave birth to another child. This baby died, so I kept on getting the breast.[20]

The testimony for Zuni is similar.[21] One statement will suffice. Cushing writes of a Zuni infant:

She was the small "head of the household." All matters, however important, had to be calculated with reference to her. If she slept, the household duties had to be performed on tiptoe, or suspended. If she woke and howled, the mother or aunt would have to hold her, while "Old Ten" procured something bright-colored and waved it frantically before her. If she spoke, the whole family must be silent as a tomb, or else fear the indignation of three women and one man.[22]

While this treatment may have been somewhat excessive because the baby was a girl, there can be little doubt, if the whole literature on the subject is considered, that in the Pueblos infancy is characterized by great indulgence—indulgence of a kind that, according to Dr. Aldrich, would prevent individuals from becoming "confused, resistant and subject to emotional storms."[23] Yet while resistance and emotional storms find expression in the Pueblos only on the rarest occasions, the indulgence of infants does not seem to have resulted in secure, unconfused adults. Dorothy Eggan has pointed this out clearly. She writes: "In any prolonged contact with the Hopi Indians, an investigator who is interested in psychic as well as in the more tangible phenomena of culture is struck with the mass maladjustment of these people. . . ."[24] And Dr. Parsons observes: "Apprehensiveness is a noticeable Pueblo trait."[25] It must then be asked whether the docile behavior so often noted in the Pueblos results from favorable infant training at the hands of parents and near relatives, or from severe pressures consciously and consistently applied during the "later" years by responsible agents outside the family circle.

The answer must wait until all the evidence is in, but even during the obviously indulgent infancy period, a number of training devices give some hint of later developments. Cushing reports that as soon as an infant

> can creep about and begin to babble, the mother takes it in her arms and carries it with her when mealtimes come, and each time she takes a little pinch of each kind of food, and breathing upon it and presenting it to the lips of the little one also, whispers into its ear . . . a prayer to the beloved Gods and souls of the ancestors: "'Take, oh, ye ancients, this offering what though poor it be, and of it eat; and of all your abundant good fortune, difficult for us to have in life, unto us grant of it as ye will, and light of your favor withal."[26]

In other words, before there can be understanding, a child finds that something that is seemingly his is suddenly and frequently withdrawn. In view of the indulgent feeding habits, this may be only minimally frustrating, if it is frustrating at all. But at the first moment of comprehension, a child must realize that he can expect "abundant good fortune" from the gods *only* when he gives something up. In this society, the pattern for reward in return for ritualistic conformance and sacrifice is set at a very early age.

Another feature of infant training should also be mentioned. "The first time a member of the household puts the baby on her back to carry him the baby is whipped . . . four times, whipped on his buttocks with a bit of yucca,"[27] writes Elsie Clews Parsons. And she adds: "This measure will keep the baby from crying thereafter on being carried."[28] Again, neither fear nor frustration will result from such an act, whether the infant is crying or not, for in all probability the whipping is lightly done and done only once. But the explanation given reveals clearly that whipping, even if infrequent, is considered an effective means of preventing unsocial behavior.

The influence of the cradleboard on a child's physical and psychological development has long been a subject of discussion,[29] and there is no need to go into the general argument here. Nevertheless, it is relevant to record the Zunis' own reason for continuing, in a sedentary environment, a practice that, in a nomadic life, was obviously convenient and perhaps even necessary. Cushing, who considers this reason "very quaint but definite," reports that they place the infant on the board

> in order that it may learn to lie straight, yea, and to walk straight in the pathway of life, in order that it may learn the hardest lesson one has ever to learn in this life—namely, that it cannot have its own way, cannot have things as *it* would have them, but must e'en be content to take them as they come or are vouchsafed.[30]

Whatever the implications of such an attitude may be for the psychologist or analyst, particularly when it is associated with otherwise "kind and tender" treatment,[31] is not for me to say. But for the student of the structure of Pueblo society, the statement is instructive. Certainly, the Zunis, whose very existence depends upon large-scale cooperation, start early to inculcate "a yielding disposition,"[32] to train consciously for "sobriety and inoffensiveness"—those virtues which, according to Benedict, are valued above all others.[33] Certainly, also, the statement calls for a re-examination of the thesis that the Zuni child "is not broken or forcibly coerced into this pattern but is gradually fitted to it under the most subtle stress of social sanction."[34]

One more point must be made before leaving this indulgent period of infancy, a point on which all observers again agree—the omnipresence of ideas of witchcraft.[35] A baby runs a great risk if left alone in a room; and an ear of corn or ash smudge is employed to keep off the evil spirits. In the early months of life, such expressions of anxiety can have no meaning for him, but surely before the child is two years of age they, as well as spoken warnings, cannot fail to arouse feelings of uneasiness. As he grows older he learns that even those nearest him, even his parents, may be witches, and that he himself may be possessed without becoming aware of it. He learns that, once possessed, he cannot lay the evil power aside, nor can he expect effective help from relatives or friends. Only the medicine-men may be able to exorcise the "bad spirit." At times—and most frequently these times of drought or disaster—not even they would come to his aid. The accused was then tried and tortured before a body of his peers and his priests and, in most cases, executed by the War Chief and his assistants, since the need for trial was practically cause for conviction.[36]

"White law" has discouraged such legal practices. Now, the suspect merely disappears—a not uncommon procedure in certain totalitarian states today. But while the specific situation may be resolved thus, witchcraft remains the chief focus of anxiety in the Pueblos. Even the infant, indulged though he is, cannot long be unaware of his ever-threatening environment.

IV

The facts presented have been taken from many reports which, though made at different periods of time, are in substantial agreement. However, certain attitudes which in infancy may play only a small role have been discussed in considerable detail, since, in the "later" years, they assume increasing importance in the socialization process.

Education in the Pueblos, like education in every other society, depends largely on example and imitation. Writes F. C. Spencer, after "a somewhat extended personal contact" with these Indians:

> The Indian boy is provided with a bow and arrows and becomes a hunter, a battle axe and becomes a warrior, or he is given a plot of ground where he constructs miniature acequias and tills the soil or herds his flocks. With a few stones and some adobe he constructs miniature imitations of those buildings which have been the wonder of the ethnologist, or he may become a weaver, an arrow-maker or a skin-dresser. . . . Likewise, the little girl imitates in her plays those occupations which fall to the woman's lot among the Pueblos. . . .[37]

But Spencer also notes that spontaneous activity in the Pueblos is definitely limited. Imitation, far from being free, is "except in the earlier years of the child . . . brought about by external constraint."[38]

Parental exhortation, its least severe manifestation, becomes increasingly frequent after infancy—not, however, in regard to such matters as personal cleanliness or sexual behavior so important to us, but in regard to habits of eating and need for industry. Faced as the Pueblos frequently are with flood or drought and their dire consequence, famine, a grandfather may say: "Little man—when you ate this morning you did not lay your left hand across your stomach to keep the food from coming too high";[39] or knowing that laziness cannot be borne in a society where everyone must cooperate, he may say: "Whoever is caught napping when the [louse stars—stars of the milky way] pass will be spilled upon, and be a lousy good-for-nothing-lout";[40] or a mother bent on inculcating habits of neatness may say to her tiny girl who has left her painted doll lying on the floor instead of wrapping it up and tying it to a cradleboard: "My poor little mother of a girl, how she will cry when she loses the babies she has let to go as they will!"[41]

But besides admonitions of this kind, stories play a significant part in the early training process. Many merely suggest desirable behavior; others implement suggestion with threat. The tale that arouses the greatest fear in the mind of the little child is undoubtedly the one often recorded,[42] that tells of the ways of the Giant kachina gods.[43] In one Hopi version,[44] these monstrous creatures—one male, one female—are summoned by the kiva leader[45] who says: "Well, we've got a lot of children here . . . and they are getting out of control. We would like to get rid of some of them, so we want you to snatch and eat them for your food." The illuminating tale then goes on to relate how the male *So'yoko*, armed with a carrying basket, "would approach Oraibi mesa until he came upon some children, whereupon he would snatch up two of them, put them in his basket, and return home." The unfortunate captives were then handed over to his wife who might steam and bake them "to a turn."

The story ends on a happy note: the War Twins, the culture heroes, after a series of hair-raising adventures, decapitate the male Giant and throw his mate over the precipice to her death on the rocks below. However, it is more than doubtful whether even the happiest ending can completely reassure the child who is told by his mother when he is naughty and unruly: "I am going to send *Su'ukyi* to eat you up."[46] In addition, he knows that in former times when a victim was to be sacrificed to the gods, "the worst child in the place was selected."[47]

Many societies resort to bogey tales to scare children into being good; but for the Pueblos, this is not enough. They bring their bogeys to life. Once a year, these Giant kachinas and certain of their assistants (the number varies) visit the villages for what Cushing has characterized as a "dance expressly to frighten the children and keep them in good behavior the rest of the year."[48] At Hopi, writes Titiev, the group consists of "So'yoko male and female, each with a large carrying basket on the back; a We'e'e Katcina in a blue mask and carrying a long black and white ringed pole without snare; two Natackas with fierce, bulging eyes and huge black bills fashioned from large gourds, each with a bow in the left hand and a saw or a large knife in the right hand; two Masau Katcinas in regulation attire . . . and eight or ten Koyemsi, two of whom are equipped with lariats."[49] They brandish their weapons threateningly when they arrive at the houses of children whose parents have previously told the impersonators "all the naughty deeds, saucy words, or stubborn actions for which they want their offspring reprimanded."[50] The support of parents during the visitations can do but little to reduce the fright of the child whose small offerings of rats or birds or cornmeal are thrice rejected before they are accepted by the performers who play menacingly with their weapons and, at times, force the naked, frightened child "to run a mock race with one of the Katcinas, the little fellow dashing madly to win in the hope that it will help save his life."[51]

Matilda C. Stevenson, who made a number of visits to Zuni beginning in 1879 reports:

> Late in the afternoon the A'toshle and Ko'yemshi together visit a number of houses to learn if the inmates properly perform their duties. . . . The two gods lecture a boy of 4 years, while two

younger children of the family are held close in the arms of their parents, who cover the little ones' eyes with their hands. The boy receiving the lecture clings to his mother, and his knees shake as he replies to the questions of the gods. The fear of the child is great as the gods wave their stone knives above him and declare that if he is naughty they will cut off his head.[52]

In a paper cryptically entitled "Zuni A'doshlĕ and Suukĕ," Parsons tells of a visitation to the house in which she was staying:

> Owing to the special circumstances of the case . . . the a'Doshle was unaccompanied by his "old woman" or by the ko'yemshi. He ran up against the door twice only, striking it with his knife. In the house were three children, a baby asleep, a boy of three, a girl of four, and six adults. All but the infant and one man who was probably a visitor took part in the performance. The a'Doshle proceeded to harangue the little boy, punctuating his sentences with thrusts at the child with his knife. The boy stood at the woman's side, but although he showed great fear in his eyes and in his tense little body he did not flinch as he answered ae, "yes," to each injunction. . . . Meanwhile the girl covered her eyes with her hands and hid her head in the lap of the woman to whom she clung. When the a'Doshle approached her, the old woman made her look at him and answer despite her whimpering.[53]

Cushing, reporting on Zuni, writes: "They are never punished by whipping or other hurt, these little children. Their longing to be 'like big people' is constantly appealed to."[54] But he adds: "If they are bad they are shown how 'men and women do not behave like that.' And if still incorrigible, the masked demons they have heard of in stories with staring eyes, are summoned, and their resistance is at an end."[55]

Given such methods of socialization, whipping by parents or near relatives seems quite unnecessary. Writes Parsons: "Of that docility of the Pueblo child, so striking even to the least observant, the discipline of fear, I had often surmised, was an important factor, fear not so much of the elder *per se*—the Pueblo elder punishes very infrequently—as fear of the unknown or the supernatural inspired by their elders."[56] So great indeed is a child's fear of the supernatural at Zuni that even when the gods distribute presents, as they do at certain dances, the children "are stoical and will not cry, though they are sorely frightened by the singular beings. . . ."[57] Only after considerable "coaxing and talking and by explanations" are the small beneficiaries of godly largess "induced" to accept the proferred gifts.

At Hopi, children are equally ambivalent. Writes Dennis: "The general attitude of the child towards the kachinas is a favorable and expectant one, although the child may be afraid of the gods because of their strange appearance."[58] There is, however, every reason to believe that children beyond the period of infancy fear not only the gods' strange appearance but their punishing actions as well. Along with a dread of death, thirst, and famine, the childish image of *So'yoko* continues "to haunt Hopi dreams and the dark, to the day of their death."[59]

V

Because of their limited economic potential, the Pueblo peoples must live by their own efforts, with the exception of the Village Chief and, in former times, possibly a few others.[60] Primarily, these farmers are concerned with matters of subsistence. Given their difficult natural environment, it is not surprising that they appeal frequently to the gods for aid—mostly, however, under the directing leadership of their priests. But the religious sanctions required before action can be taken by no means indicate a lack of interest in economic affairs; rather they serve to underline the special needs of the agricultural situation.[61]

To achieve the cooperation necessary for a functioning irrigated agriculture, the Zunis and the Hopis strive from infancy for " a yielding disposition." From early childhood, quarrelling, even in play, is discouraged;[62] and the scare kachinas are summoned when parental admonition or story-telling fails to make the little ones industrious or to bring the desired conformity. To the unsophisticated outsider, resistance after such preliminary training may well have seemed at an end. To the Pueblo priesthoods, the mentors of social behavior, the children are still "unfinished."[63] Formal, painful, and terrifying ceremonies of initiation must be undergone before an individual can participate successfully in his society. It is perhaps no accident that the first of these ceremonies occurs when a boy begins to help his father or his mother's brother in the fields,[64] the second when it is felt that he can do a man's work, sacred and secular.

The first initiation at Zuni occurs when a child is between the ages of five and nine; at Hopi, between six and ten, but in former times it was more often the latter than the former.[65] However, at both Hopi and Zuni, this first initiation, which is held every fourth year, is an integral part of the ceremony that ushers in the new agricultural cycle, the ceremony at which the corn and beans that have been secretly grown by the authorized priests are distributed among the participating members of the various kivas to be used by them for seed corn and for luck.[66] Of the ear presented to the newly initiated boy at Zuni, Stevenson writes: "He plants the corn the coming year in his fields."[67]

At Hopi, both girls and boys are initiated, but the treatment accorded the girls is comparatively mild; at Zuni, except on rare occasions, only the boys are inducted. At Hopi, some choice is permitted, not however to the novice, but to his parents, for it is they who decide whether to place him in the Powamu Society where the children are given the necessary learning but are not flogged or in the Kachina Society where whipping is the distinctive feature. The more recalcitrant children are, not surprisingly, offered to the latter, the least conforming among them receiving the severest blows. At Zuni, there is only one society, the Kachina or Ko'tikili as it is locally called.[68]

Few outsiders have witnessed the first initiation at either pueblo; none has seen the more esoteric portions of the second. Certain divergencies between Hopi and Zuni practice are revealed in the different if fragmentary accounts. Some are significant; others are not. But, despite these divergencies, the general pattern in both places is strikingly similar, the conception and intent the same.

At Hopi, only Voth seems to have witnessed all parts of the first initiation. He writes of the final phase:

> The dreaded moment which the candidates have so often been told about and of which they stand in such great fear has arrived. They are about to go through the ordeal of being flogged. Presently a loud grunting noise, a rattling of turtle shell rattles and a jingling of bells is heard outside. The two Ho Katcinas and the Hahai-i have arrived at the kiva. . . . They first run around the kiva four times at a rapid rate, then dance on each side of the kiva a little while, beat the roof of the kiva with whips, jump on it, constantly howling the word *u'huhuhu* and finally enter the kiva. The two Ho Katcinas take a position on the east and west side of the large sand mosaic, the Hahai-i at its southeast corner, the latter holding a supply of whips. The children tremble and some begin to cry and to scream. The Ho Katcinas keep up their grunting, howling, rattling, trampling and brandishing of their yucca whips. All at once someone places a candidate on the sand mosaic, holds his (or her) hands upward and one of the Ho Katcinas whips the little victim quite severely. . . . It is said that four strokes are supposed to be applied, but the Katcinas do not always strictly adhere to this rule. The girls have their usual dress on, but the boys are entirely nude. The persons holding them are also nude except for a scant loin cloth, and they wear their hair loose, as is customary in all Hopi sacred ceremonies. When one child has been flogged another one is at once brought forward and beaten and then another and so on until all have gone through the ordeal. One is flogged by one Katcina, the next one by the other, the two Katcinas constantly changing about. When a whip is worn out it is handed to the Hahai-i Katcina who exchanges it for a fresh one. Some of the children go through the process with set teeth and without flinching, others squirm, try to jump away and scream. Occasionally a "sponsor," pitying his little ward, presents his own hip, snatching the child away, and receives a part of the flogging in the child's stead, in which case, however, the flogging is usually very severe.[69]

Voth continues:

> With the crying and screaming of the candidates men and women mingle their voices, some encouraging them, others accusing the Katcinas of partiality, claiming that they whip some harder than others; in short, pandemonium reigns in the kiva during this exciting half hour. But the scene has not only its exciting, but also its disgusting features. As the whips are quite long they frequently extend around the leg or hip of the little nude boys in such a manner that the points strike the pudibilia, and the author noticed on several occasions that the boys, when being placed on the sand mosaic, were warned to protect those parts, which they tried to do by either quickly freeing one hand and pushing the pudenda between the legs or by partly crossing the legs. It was also noticed on several occasions that some of the boys, probably as a result of fear and pain, involuntarily micturated and in one or two cases even defecated.[70]

Sun Chief, who at the age of nine was a "little victim" of these proceedings, substantiates Voth's account almost to the last detail.[71]

Zuni adults claim that "whipping is 'to take off the bad happenings',"[72] or that "boys are whipped . . . 'to save their lives'."[73] Such statements are understandable, for it is by no means unusual for those who impose hardship through violence to point out its benefits to the sufferer. Parsons, however, recognizing the dual function of the rite, notes that "whipping by the Blue Horns or by the disciplinary or bogey kachina of Zuni, of Cochiti, or of Tewa may take on a punitive character."[74] At Hopi, the matter is made most explicit by the Hopis themselves.

Steward, reporting the conversation between the whipping kachinas and the Kachina Chief, the head priest of the Kachina Society, at the commencement of the initiation ceremony, writes:

> Kachina chief asks them [the whippers] why they have come. Dü'mas kachina motions toward the children and says, "They do not obey their mothers and fathers. We are going to help you old people so that they will mind you." Kachina chief replies, "Of course they do not mind us. But I would rather be on my own children's side than on your side. They do not mind us, but I will take care of my children." Dü'mas kachina insists, however, that the children must be made to obey and the Kachina chief yields. But he asks them not to use the willows to whip the children. The kachinas consent to this and yucca blades, which have already been brought to the kiva for the purpose, are substituted. Kachina chief then says, "They do not mind us, so we will let you try to make them obey. We will let you force them to keep these things a secret."[75]

At the close of the ceremony, the Kachina Chief takes the whip from the punishing gods and says: "This is the way we initiate to the kachinas. You children must not tell how this thing is done to other children who have not been initiated. If you do tell, these kachinas will come around to you and whip you until they cut your flesh."[76]

The children then go home to be consoled by their mothers. For four days they perform certain propitiatory rites. On the night of the fourth day, they learn through a maskless dance that the gods they have come to know, those who have brought them presents and pain, are in reality merely impersonations—impersonations by their fathers, older brothers, uncles, and neighbors. According to Dorothy Eggan, all informants questioned by her (unfortunately she notes neither their sex nor their age) were emphatic in stressing their "intense disappointment in and resentment toward their elders which survived in consciousness for a long time."[77] She gives a direct quotation from one informant "which differs from the others only in its better English phrasing":

> I cried and cried into my sheepskin that night, feeling I had been made a fool of. How could I ever watch the Kachinas dance again; I hated my parents and thought I could never believe the old folks again, wondering if Gods had ever danced for the Hopi as they said and if people really lived after death. I hated to see the other children fooled and felt mad when they said I was a big girl now and should act like one. But I was afraid to tell the others the truth for they might whip me to death. I know now it was best and the only way to teach the children, but it took me a long time to know that. I hope my children won't feel like that.[78]

The second initiation takes place several years later, at adolescence. After numerous and exhausting tests of strength, the male candidates are again whipped severely, but—symbol of their newly acquired status—they emerge as victors over their ceremonial fathers after a mock battle. The Hopi boy is now "finished"; he is now a man,[79] and may impersonate the kachina gods.[80] How successful the Hopi socialization process is in creating the personality type that fits Hopi needs— the conforming and cooperating man—can be judged from the statement of the once mischievous and enterprising Sun Chief. After being inducted into the Wowochim, he writes:

> I had learned a great lesson and now knew that the ceremonies handed down by our fathers mean life and security, both now and hereafter. I regretted that I had ever joined the Y.M.C.A. and decided to set myself against Christianity once and for all. I could see that the old people were right when they insisted that Jesus Christ might do for modern Whites in a good climate, but that the Hopi gods had brought success to us in the desert ever since the world began.[81]

At Zuni, after a preliminary and seemingly mild whipping by some eleven gods at the commencement of the first initiation,

> one little boy kneels down in front of his father, with two women, one on each side, holding his blankets. The Sayalia stand in pairs facing each other, with the boy in the center. They are very terrible looking and jump around all the time shaking their rattles, and the little boys are terribly frightened . . . After each whipping the katcina chief and the katcina pekwin remove one blanket. If the father tries to shield the little boy by putting his own leg over the child's back, they will surely kill the father. The Koyemci stand beside them and count the strokes. The little boys cry terribly.[82]

Like their Hopi cousins, they are given the protection of their ceremonial fathers, who are also beaten by the Kachinas; they are also given a feather to tie in their hair and an ear of corn to take home, but—and this is most crucial—*they are not told the identity of the gods at this time.* Only at the close of the second initiation, another strenuous and painful procedure that occurs several years later when the boys are twelve or thirteen years of age, do the Zuni gods remove their masks.[83] These sacred objects are then placed on the heads of the boys who strike each god in turn. When this short but significant demonstration of power is over, the masks are returned to the impersonators. As at Hopi, the children are warned. But at Zuni, Kachina Chief threatens that if the novices "divulge the initiatory secrets, especially those associated with the masks, their heads will be cut off."[84]

Recently, projective tests have been given to the children of Hopi and Zuni. An illuminating analysis of the Hopi results is included in "The Hopi Way." Work on the Zuni material is still incomplete, but preliminary examination indicates much greater "constriction" among the children of this village, and a personality organization that differs markedly from the Hopis'.[85] In how far the configurations revealed by these tests are valid for adults is still an open question. Hallowell, who has collected Rorschachs from both children and adult Saulteaux, finds that trends seen in the older children's records appear in the adults'.[86]

But whatever the final decision on this point may be, variations in the personality organization of the children of Hopi and Zuni are quite compatible with the fact that the basic structure of Hopi and Zuni society is similar.[87] Geographic differences or specific historical experiences will—one might almost say will always—result in institutional modifications of some kind. Differences in natural resources, in the amount and reliability of the water-supply, in the technical means of production, in the vulnerability to attack from the outside, will lead to diverse developments. Among other things, the Hopis and Zunis reveal certain important differences in water-supply, for the Zunis have recourse to the flow from permanent and sizable springs as well as to the unpredictable rainfall for irrigation purposes.[88] Their more elaborate system of irrigation, which was commented on by the Spanish conquistadores,[89] demands a better organization of personnel and a tighter control over the group. Both the Hopi and Zuni governments are theocratic,[90] but the Zuni government seems infinitely less decentralized. One indication of the greater power vested in the Zuni authorities may be seen in the role of the War Chief. At Hopi, this important functionary, who was "given the duty of maintaining discipline," seems, at least as far as one can judge from the material, to have only "had the right of scolding miscreants, of boxing their ears, and, perhaps of thrashing them."[91] At Zuni, he could bring the suspected witch to trial and, on conviction, execute him for the evil he had brought upon the community.[92] In view of this and other disciplinary divergencies, the different personality organizations reported for Hopi and Zuni should cause little surprise.

But besides indicating significant differences between the pueblos, the Hopi tests reveal a variability within the pattern of personality organization not only as between boys and girls, but also in relation to different age levels.[93] Similar differences have been exposed by Rorschach tests in our society, but most frequently these have been correlated with stages in physical growth. The modifications in Hopi no doubt also reflect this aspect of maturation, but at one point at least it seems reasonable to assume that they result directly from a particular condition imposed by the socialization process. Dr. Alice Joseph writes:

> It is at about the age of eight to ten years that the average Hopi boy and girl seem to show the most natural and the happiest poise of the different forces of their personalities . . . they also seem to move in a world of greater reality, a world which is less bewildering and less frightening.[94]

And Dr. Joseph continues:

> At this age level the kind of work which the Hopi children have to do (i.e., for them, meaningful and comprehensible work that incorporates them closely into the household group) is in its regulating and assuring effect usually an excellent antidote against the vague anxieties of childhood.[95]

But much more important than his greater integration in the family group through work is the fact that it is just at this time that the Hopi child learns the identity of the gods who have given him presents but who have also severely disciplined him. At Zuni, where the child is also given more meaningful work at this age, but where he must wait until after his *second* initiation to learn the great secret, no such favorable adjustment seems to occur at the 8-10 year level.[96] Indeed, one might expect all the early tensions of childhood to be heightened after the first terrifying initiation, and to be further intensified by anticipation of the second. But such conjectures must wait for verification until the analysis of the Zuni material is completed.

At many other points the Hopi tests confirm ethnological observation, but only a few can be noted here.[97] In the emotional response test on FEAR, only 1.0% of the fears of midwestern, white children were attributable to the *supernatural*, but this category accounted for 25.4% of the Hopi children's fears. In the emotional response test on SADNESS, 2.6% of the sadness of white children was due to *discipline*, while 11.2% of the Hopi children's sorrow derived from this cause. In the emotional response test on the WORST THING, the white children's records gave *discipline* a 2.5% rating; the Hopi children's answers gave it a 17.8% rating. Such data reveal not only the role of coercion in Hopi socialization; they clearly indicate that, despite joint application, punishment is a painful and resented experience, whatever the final adjustment of the child to his social system may be.

That Hopi and Zuni society offer considerable compensations in adulthood for sufferings imposed in the earlier years is undeniable. In ancient Aztec Mexico and among the Inca of Peru (societies depending on large-scale water-control) social strata were very marked. No doubt, some degree of mobility was possible in these autocratic states, but essentially it was the sons of nobles who achieved the leading positions in military and priestly affairs.[98] The commoners cultivated their fields in the growing season, and, in the dormant months of the year, were liable to be called up for military or labor service.

Pueblo society is culturally peripheral to these great "oriental" complexes,[99] and, like them, it depends for survival upon water-control. Like them, also, it is theocratic. The early efforts of the Spaniards to weaken the power of the native hierarchy shortened in some instances the length of office tenure, but free elections are entirely foreign to Pueblo thought and action. Nominations are made by the priests and, almost invariably, they are unanimously accepted by the group. Now, as formerly, political power rests with the Village Chief and with the War Chief.[100]

But the low economic potential of Hopi and Zuni has made it possible for these pueblos to maintain a more equalitarian (sometimes called "democratic") social organization. Except for the Village Chief, every adult male is expected to cooperate with his fellows in the fields, in constructing and repairing irrigation works, in building houses and, in former times, in defending the village. Immediately after his second initiation—and this is most significant—every adult male may take an active part in the ceremonial life. In addition, eligibility for high office is subject to few restrictions.

For the women, the compensations are of a different order. As mothers and heads of households, as owners of houses and fields, they receive great respect, and in their homes they exercise (with other females) considerable authority. But they are excluded, even at Hopi, from high office and from dancing kachina. The satisfactions accruing to the male in his role of disciplining impersonator or priest are denied them. Until late adolescence the girls seem to harbor deeper resentments, particularly toward their mothers,[101] perhaps because of ceremonial and political deprivation, perhaps because they are so closely bound to the mother's household from the cradle to the grave. The males, on the other hand, despite their political and ceremonial dominance and the good maternal care given them in infancy, never seem to achieve sexual security, either in their mother's house in childhood, or in their wife's after marriage.[102]

But while satisfactions and resentments may be different in kind and in degree, both boys and girls, in the end, "appear deeply disciplined, to an extent which is truly astonishing."[103] Dr. Joseph continues:

> We do not find very often an average Hopi child who reveals inclinations towards emotional outbreaks and uncontrolled impulsiveness in his personality structure. On the contrary, from a relatively early age the Hopi children's attitude toward their own emotions and the open expression of them appears predominantly to be one of careful selection, cautious reserve and restraint, which in certain age groups tends even toward their complete avoidance and rejection.[104]

Without benefit of testing, Bunzel reports of Zuni:

> In all social relations, whether within the family group or outside, the most honored personality traits are a pleasing address, a yielding disposition, and a generous heart. All the sterner virtues—initiative, ambition, an uncompromising sense of honor and justice, intense personal loyalties—not only are not admired but are heartily deplored. The woman who cleaves to her husband through misfortune and family quarrels, the man who speaks his mind where flattery would be much more comfortable, the man, above all, who thirsts for power or knowledge, who wishes to be, as they scornfully phrase it, "a leader of his people," receives nothing but censure and will very likely be persecuted for sorcery.[105]

It is, then, the "deeply disciplined" man, both at Hopi and at Zuni, who is so desired and so necessary to the proper functioning of the community. Emotional restraint, reserve, avoidance, or the need to reject is the price he pays for achieving his society's social ideal.

VI

From the material presented, there can be little doubt, first, that the Pueblos belong among those societies where infant disciplines are weak and later disciplines are severe (category 4), and second, that adult personality in both Hopi and Zuni is moulded not so much by parental permissiveness during infancy as by the severe disciplines imposed after the period of infancy by external agents—by impersonators of the supernaturals and by the priesthoods. While the "normal" members of different societies may well "owe their varying personality configurations much less to their genes than to their nurseries,"[106] it seems equally obvious that, in some societies—and the Pueblos are one—the nurseries also play a secondary role in the socialization process. Not that good maternal care or easy habit formation does not significantly influence a child's development, even in societies which exhibit striking discontinuities in training. It is quite reasonable to assume that the good relation established between the Pueblo child and those nearest him in the first months of life make it possible for him to believe in the benevolence of his parents' gods—gods who bring the needed rain and many other benefits—and to believe in them even after they have painfully disciplined him. But his security in later life depends, not, as might be expected from his early experience, on the achievement of an independent spirit, but on his ability to fit into a carefully defined and strictly limited frame of adult activity.

That it is possible to bridge the gap between early training and adult performance without a complete disintegration of the personality is due to a number of cultural factors, primarily the form of the family and the way in which (and by whom) punishment and significant rewards are meted out.

The Pueblo family is, at least at Hopi and Zuni, a composite group comprising a mother, her unmarried offspring, her married daughters, their children, and the husbands of the adult females. In such a milieu,

Hopi Snake Dance Diorama. *Photo courtesy American Museum of Natural History.*

affection is diffused and loyalties do not reach the intensity usual in our society. A Pueblo child, upon discovering his parents' duplicity at initiations, feels considerable resentment towards them to be sure, but this resentment is inevitably watered down because his early affections were so broadly spread. In addition, he knows that it is the supernaturals and the priests who exercise the final authority, and that his parents, despite their intrigues against him, must also defer to them. The effect of the child's disillusionment, however, should not be underestimated. It may well be that it accounts in no small measure for the readiness of the Pueblo adult to accuse those nearest and dearest to him (and his priests and gods as well[107]) of the greatest crime against person and society—namely, witchcraft.

It should also be noted that while the child is little prepared by familial treatment in infancy for the harsh disciplines imposed in the "later" years by external agents, it is these external agents who are also the chief dispensers of rewards. The Pueblo parent who rarely disciplines is equally frugal with his praise. The tangible manifestations of his fatherly love and solicitude (the miniature bows and arrows, cradleboards and dolls which he has painstakingly constructed) are presented to his children at the public dances by the kachina impersonators. Even if the child accepts them "stoically," he comes to expect his benefits, not from his family, but from those who bring him the greatest pain. Most significantly, it is the kachinas (and the priests) who, after the severe rites of initiation, recognize the child's readiness to participate in the larger society and reward him accordingly.[108]

Much more could be said regarding the respective roles of the Pueblo family and the priesthoods in the socialization process, in adult performance, and in the organization of adult personality.[109] But it is eminently clear that a study of the period of infancy alone would give few clues to the personality structure exhibited by the Pueblo adult. It is possible that in some societies where infant disciplines are severe and later disciplines are weak (and ours may be one of them), the parent-child relationship during the first years of life has a more determining influence. But in the Pueblos where both severe disciplines and substantial rewards derive from external agents who function most importantly in the "later" years, a study of the society as a whole and over time is absolutely necessary for any satisfactory understanding of the building of adult personality.

NOTES

(See bibliography at end of article.)

1. See Kluckhohn, 1944.
2. Malinowski, 1927.
3. Eggan, 1943, pp. 357-374.

4. Aldrich, 1945, p. 74.

5. Dennis, 1940, pp. 95-98.

6. Bernard, 1945, pp. 284-291; see also Linton, 1945, p. 127.

7. In this connection, see Leslie A. White for Acoma, San Felipe, Santo Domingo and Santa Ana; Elsie Clews Parsons for Laguna, Isleta, Tewa, Taos; Father Noel Dumarest and Esther S. Goldfrank for Cochiti; William Whitman for San Ildefonso. Full titles can be found in the *Ethnographic Bibliography of North America*, Yale Anthropological Studies, Vol. 1, 1941, compiled by George Peter Murdock.

8. Irrigation for the Pueblos along the Rio Grande is well established, and most anthropologists have noted its long and continued use in Zuni as a primary agricultural technique. (For a short summary of the history of Zuni irrigation, see Wittfogel and Goldfrank, 1943, pp. 19-23.) But despite the clear statements of geologists and geographers (Gregory, 1916, p. 104; Bryan, 1929, pp. 444 ff; Hack, 1942, pp. XIX, 10 ff), and soil conservationists (particularly, Stewart, 1940, pp. 329 ff) that flood-water farming, the chief method of Hopi cultivation, is actually a type of irrigation, some ethnologists have failed to comprehend this fact. Parsons (1939, p. 111) has written, "The Hopi do not irrigate," and Thompson (1944, p. 127) in commenting on the Hopis' mastery of their physical environment refers to their perfected "methods of dry farming." Where such different statements are made, it seems advisable to accept the opinion of the soil and climate experts.

9. Lummis, 1897, p. 111.

10. Beaglehole, 1937, pp. 27 ff; Stewart, 1940, pp. 331 ff; Forde, 1931, p. 373.

11. Beaglehole, 1937, p. 30; Parsons, 1939, p. 111; Titiev, 1944, p. 187.

12. Parsons (1939, p. 110) speaking of the Pueblos in general, has written: "Of all the communal undertakings, work on the irrigation ditches is the most important." Without doubt, in a former time, the problems of defense reënforced the need for cooperative effort in the Pueblos; but this must be considered a secondary rather than a primary determinant; since the cessation of warfare in this area has had little if any effect on the character of the cooperation. To be sure, cooperation at some level is present in all societies, called forth under certain circumstances by the exigencies of such different activities as hunting, fishing, pastoralism, trading, defense, etc., as well as by agriculture. But while this fundamental fact must not be overlooked, it is equally necessary to be aware of the significant differences in the form and intensity of the various patterns of cooperation and discipline that result. (For a discussion of these points, see Wittfogel, *Oriental Society in Asia and Ancient America*, now in preparation.)

13. Aitken, 1930, p. 385.

14. Eggan, 1943, p. 361.

15. Titiev, 1944, p. 19.

16. *Ibid.*, p. 18.

17. Dennis, 1940, p. 99.

18. *Ibid.*, pp. 99 ff; cf. also, Beaglehole, 1935, pp. 38 ff. Somewhat more pressure after 15 months is indicated by the authors of *The Hopi Way*, p. 52.

19. *Sun Chief*, 1942, p. 33.

20. *Ibid.*, p. 34.

21. See Benedict, 1934, p. 101; Bunzel, 1932a, p. 477; Goldman, 1937, p. 339; Parsons, 1939, pp. 47 ff.; Spencer, 1899, p. 76; Stevenson, 1904, p. 293.

22. Cushing, 1882-1883a, p. 202.

23. Aldrich, 1945, p. 74.

24. Eggan, 1943, p. 357. Dr. Joseph (*The Hopi Way*, p. 109) writes of the Hopi children: "They do not tend to become confused but are rather determined in the acceptance or refusal of what is offered them . . . they seem to pursue what

once has been accepted with a tenacity that not rarely takes on features similar to an obsession. . . ." Such a constriction in personality development may well be the Hopi way of reacting to what we call "confusion." For a discussion of infantile indulgence, post-infancy traumas of socialization, and insecure adult personality, see Kluckhohn and Mowrer, 1944a, p. 96.

25. Parsons, 1939, p. 67.

26. Cushing, 1897, p. 35 ff.

27. Parsons, 1919, p. 173.

28. *Ibid.* As far as I know this practice is not reported for other pueblos. However, this does not necessarily imply its absence.

29. For influence on physical development, see Dennis, 1940, pp. 95-98, 101; on psychological development, see Kardiner, 1939, p. 468.

30. Cushing, 1897, p. 34. The italics are Cushing's. Dr. Joseph tells me she has never heard a similar verbalization at Hopi. It is possible that neither now nor formerly did the Hopi think in these terms. It is also possible that the Zuni, more sensitive to present white opinion, might refrain from making such a statement today.

31. Kardiner, 1939, p. 468.

32. Bunzel, 1932a, p. 480.

33. Benedict, 1934, p. 59.

34. Goldman, 1937, pp. 338 ff; see also Mead, 1937, p. 473, and Benedict, 1934, pp. 98-103 and 122.

35. For discussion of witchcraft see among others on Hopi, Beaglehole, 1935, pp. 5-10; Titiev, 1944, *passim; idem,* 1943, *passim; Sun Chief, passim;* Eggan, 1943, p. 357. For Zuni, Benedict, 1934, pp. 121 ff and 127; Bunzel, 1932a, p. 479; Cushing, 1882-83b, pp. 42 ff; Parsons, 1939, pp. 62-68; Stevenson, 1904, pp. 230, 393-406; Spencer, 1899, p. 66.

36. Recourse to trial is not reported for Hopi though it is known for the Rio Grande Pueblos.

37. Spencer, 1899, pp. 77 ff.

38. *Ibid.,* p. 76.

39. Cushing, 1897, p. 37.

40. *Ibid.*

41. *Ibid.*

42. For Hopi, see Titiev, 1944, pp. 216 ff; Stephen, 1936, p. 183; Voth, 1905, pp. 86 ff; Eggan, 1943, p. 366. For Zuni, Benedict, 1935, p. xxii; Cushing, 1901 ("The Coyote who killed the Demon Siuiuki and Atahsaia, the Cannibal Demon"); Parsons, 1916, p. 344; Bunzel, 1933, pp. 282 ff.

43. Bunzel (1932b, p. 844) writes: "The first katcinas were the children of humans lost through contact with contamination, unwilling sacrifices to atone for sin. By origin and later association they are identified with the dead . . . the katcinas are also especially associated with clouds and rain."

44. Titiev, 1944, pp. 216 ff.

45. Leader in the ceremonial chamber.

46. Parsons, 1939, p. 50.

47. Baxter, 1882, p. 90, based on interviews with Cushing at Zuni. For child sacrifice, see Parsons, 1939, p. 220, note, and 1017; also Bunzel, 1932b, pp. 846 ff.

48. Baxter, 1882, p. 90; For Zuni, see also Parsons, 1939, pp. 51 ff.; *idem,* 1916, *passim;* Stevenson, 1904, p. 229; Li An-che, 1937, pp. 71 ff; Bunzel, 1932b, p. 846; *idem,* 1933, pp. 84 ff. For Hopi, see Titiev, 1944, pp. 218-221; Voth, 1901, p. 118; Eggan, 1943, p. 370; Kennard, 1938, p. 26; Stephen, 1936, p. 183; Dennis, 1940, p. 44; Steward, 1931, pp. 68 ff.

49. Titiev, 1944, p. 220. For pictures of these kachinas see Kennard, 1938, Plates VII-XI drawn by Edwin Earle.

50. Titiev, 1944, p. 218.

51. *Ibid.*, p. 220.

52. Stevenson, 1904, p. 229; also p. 104. For other ways in which the threat of beheading can be made equally real, see description of dramatic "play" of kachinas at Hopi (Stephen, 1936, pp. 243, 254).

53. Parsons, 1916, pp. 345 ff.

54. Cushing, 1897, p. 37. At Hopi, punishment by near relatives seems to be more frequent (see Titiev, 1944, pp. 18, 25, 26; Eggan, 1943, p. 366, note; *Sun Chief*, pp. 56, 61, 70 ff; Dennis, 1940, pp. 45 ff), but even here it appears contrary to the social ideal.

55. Cushing, 1897, p. 37.

56. Parsons, 1916, p. 338.

57. Cushing, 1897, p. 37.

58. Dennis, 1940, p. 70; also pp. 162, 165.

59. Eggan, 1943, p. 370.

60. Recently at Zuni, I understand that the people have ceased to cultivate the Pekwin's fields. However, Bunzel (1932b, p. 846) points out that the impersonators of the great gods who are designated at the opening of the Zuni *ca'lako* ceremony to act the following year "do no work of their own" during the interval between appointment and performance. For Hopi, see Forde, 1931, p. 376.

61. For the same point, see Li An-che, 1937, p. 66; also Parsons, 1939, p. 111.

62. Spencer, 1899, p. 79.

63. *Ibid.*, p. 87.

64. Dennis, 1940, p. 40; Goldman, 1937, p. 340.

65. For Zuni, see Stevenson, 1904, p. 89; Benedict, 1934, p. 69. For Hopi, see Titiev, 1944, p. 109; Thompson and Joseph, 1944, pp. 55, 139.

66. Steward, 1931, p. 79.

67. Stevenson, 1904, p. 102.

68. For Zuni, see among others Stevenson, 1904, pp. 89, 99-102; Benedict, 1934, pp. 69 ff; Parsons, 1939, pp. 467 ff; Bunzel, 1932b, pp. 975-980. For Hopi, see Voth, 1901, particularly pp. 84-105; Stephen, 1936, pp. 200 ff; Steward, 1931, *passim;* Titiev, 1944, pp. 109-120; Thompson and Joseph, 1944, pp. 55 ff.

69. Voth, 1901, pp. 103 ff.

70. *Ibid.*, p. 104.

71. *Sun Chief*, pp. 79-87.

72. Benedict, 1934, p. 91.

73. Bunzel, 1932b, p. 975.

74. Parsons, 1939, p. 474.

75. Steward, 1931, pp. 64 ff.

76. *Ibid.*, p. 65. That they might indeed cut the flesh is evident from Sun Chief's experience (p. 83).

77. Eggan, 1943, p. 372.

78. *Ibid.*, note 34. For Zuni, as far as I know, no such explicit statement is available. However, the popularity of the tale about the abandoned children (see Benedict, 1935, pp. xvii ff) becomes comprehensible, not only as a psychological parallel to "the familiar daydreams of children in our civilization," but more particularly as an expression of the Zuni child's extreme disillusionment and resentment upon discovering at initiation his parents' duplicity. One woman in recounting the tale, said "with heat" "He [the child] made her cry all right" and, "Oh, she (the mother) was *ashamed*." Benedict continues: "The plots are all concerned with the supernatural assistance and human success of the poor child, and often the whole plot is directed toward the triumph of the abandoned

child over the mother or the parents. . . . The daydream, from the point of view of the child, is completed by the final largess of the children and their appointment to priestly rank."

79. *Sun Chief*, pp. 157-178; Titiev, 1944, pp. 130-141.

80. See editor's note in Stephen's *Journal*, p. 208. Girls, even at Hopi, despite participating in the initiation, never dance kachina.

81. *Sun Chief*, p. 178.

82. Bunzel, 1932b, pp. 979-980; see also Stevenson, 1904, pp. 99-102.

83. Stevenson, 1904, pp. 102 ff; also Bunzel, 1932b, pp. 998-1002. Stevenson refers to this second initiation as "voluntary" (1904, p. 102). Bunzel (1932b, p. 976, note 61) remarks: "The writer, however, fails to find any validity in Mrs. Stevenson's distinction between 'involuntary' and 'voluntary' initiations. The second initiation is no more voluntary than the first. The Zunis certainly do not use any such terms, nor have they any such feeling concerning them."

84. Stevenson, 1904, p. 104.

85. Dorothea Leighton, M.D., personal communication. Dr. Leighton also pointed out the relativeness of these tests and the possible differences of interpretation.

86. Hallowell, 1942, p. 47.

87. Compare pre-war France, England, and Germany, all modern industrialized states, whose nationals exhibited noticeable temperamental and behavioral differences.

88. Cushing, 1920, pp. 363-366.

89. Wittfogel and Goldfrank, 1943, pp. 21-23.

90. For Zuni, see among others, Benedict, 1934, p. 67; Cushing, 1882, pp. 186 ff; Parsons, 1939, *passim*; Bunzel, 1932a, p. 478. For Hopi, see Thompson and Joseph, 1944, p. 44. Titiev (1944, p. 59) raises certain objections to this conception of Hopi government. His reservations, however, are merely those of degree, not of kind.

91. Titiev, 1944, pp. 65 ff.

92. Stevenson, 1904, pp. 398 ff; Cushing, 1882-83b, p. 43; Parsons, 1939, pp. 65 ff; Bunzel, 1932a, p. 479; Benedict, 1934, pp. 99 and 100.

93. Linton (1945, pp. 129 ff) aptly refers to these as "status personalities."

94. Thompson and Joseph, 1944, p. 115.

95. *Ibid.*

96. Dr. Alice Joseph who made this statement most informally to the writer would be the first to point out its tentative character, for the analysis of the Zuni tests is still uncompleted.

97. Thompson and Joseph, 1944, pp. 145-146.

98. Vaillant, 1941, pp. 116-119; Means, 1925, pp. 440 ff, 448, 467 ff.

99. The meaning of the term "oriental" in this context, and the place of the Pueblos within the general complex is fully discussed by K. A. Wittfogel in his forthcoming publication, *Oriental Society in Asia and Ancient America*.

100. For Hopi, see Titiev, 1944, p. 64; for Zuni, see Bunzel, 1932a, p. 478.

101. Thompson and Joseph, 1944, Table XIV, p. 146. It would be particularly helpful if this figure could be broken down according to age and if tests from adult women were added so that the intensity of resentment over time could be ascertained.

102. The picture is somewhat different in the Rio Grande Pueblos where the matrilineal clans are weaker or non-existent (see Wittfogel and Goldfrank, 1943, pp. 26 ff).

103. Thompson and Joseph, 1944, p. 109.

104. *Ibid.*

105. Bunzel, 1932a, p. 480; cf. also Parsons, 1939, p. 76.

106. Linton, 1945, p. 143; see also Kardiner, 1939, pp. 20 ff.

107. Titiev, 1944, pp. 74, 251 and 252 text and note; *idem,* 1943, pp. 549, 553; Parsons, 1939, pp. 63 and 64.

108. Such a system of punishment and reward, however much it may lessen the tensions between parent and child, may give rise to other severe problems in personality organization. For comments on this point, see Kluckhohn and Mowrer, 1944a, p. 106 text and note.

109. No space has been given to the effects of acculturation on Pueblo personality, not because such effects are completely absent but because they have modified the socialization process to no significant degree (see Thompson and Joseph, 1944, pp. 123 ff).

BIBLIOGRAPHY (see General Bibliography)

AITKEN, 1930
ALDRICH, 1945
BAXTER, 1882
BEAGLEHOLE, 1937-a
BEAGLEHOLE, E. & P., 1935
BENEDICT, R., 1934-b, 1935
BERNARD, 1945
BRYAN, K., 1929
BUNZEL, 1932-a, 1932-b, 1933
CUSHING, 1882, 1882-3 (3 articles; *a* refers to I, *b* to III), 1897, 1901, 1920.
DENNIS, W., 1940-a
EGGAN, D., 1943
FORDE, 1931
GOLDMAN, I., 1937
GREGORY, 1916
HACK, 1942
HALLOWELL, 1942-d
KARDINER, 1939
KENNARD, 1938
KLUCKHOHN, 1944
KLUCKHOHN & MOWRER, 1944-b
LI, 1937
LINTON, 1945-a
LUMMIS, 1897
MALINOWSKI, 1927-b
MEAD, 1937-a, Interpretive statement
MEANS, 1925
PARSONS, E. C., 1916-a, 1919, 1939
SPENCER, F. C., 1899
STEPHEN, A. M., 1936
STEVENSON, M. C., 1904
STEWARD, 1931
STEWART, G., 1940
SUN CHIEF, 1942
THOMPSON & JOSEPH, 1944
TITIEV, 1943, 1944
VAILLANT, 1941
VOTH, 1901, 1905
WITTFOGEL & GOLDFRANK, 1943
WITTFOGEL, Ms. in preparation

GEOFFREY GORER

1955. "Modification of National Character: The Role of the Police in England," *The Journal of Social Issues*, vol. *11* #2: 24-32. Reprinted by courtesy of the author and of the Editor of *The Journal of Social Issues*. This article, slightly abridged, appears as Appendix One of Dr. Gorer's book, *Exploring English Character* (Criterion Books, Inc., New York, 1955); it is reprinted here in the original form by courtesy of Criterion Books, Inc., owners of the copyright.

Dr. Gorer's wide-ranging mind has produced reports of researches in Africa, the Himalayan foothills, the United States, and England, together with provocative analyses of "national character" of the Japanese and of the Russians (cf. General Bibliography). Former editions of this book included his study of the Japanese—an essay that evoked much discussion. Like Benedict's *The Chrysanthemum and the Sword*, that study was conducted during World War II when field research in Japan was impossible. Newer data from Japan and changing conditions in that nation suggest that Dr. Gorer might write somewhat differently about Japan were he to do so today. A glimpse of Gorer's recent work is afforded by the discussion of British character that follows, which is a fragment of the extensive research in Britain embodied in his *Exploring English Character*. In that work Gorer has applied ethnological techniques to study of his own country; his procedures and results invite careful study.

Gorer's approach to study of a non-literate people is embodied in *Himalayan Village* (1938)—a study of a Lepcha community. See also his contributions in *The Study of Culture at a Distance*, edited by Margaret Mead and Rhoda Métraux (Chicago, 1953).

MODIFICATION OF NATIONAL CHARACTER:
THE ROLE OF THE POLICE IN ENGLAND

Geoffrey Gorer

To my understanding, the concept of national character is essentially an aspect of social anthropology, and only becomes meaningful within the context of the social structure and component institutions which compose the culture of the society under investigation. The techniques of observation and interviewing that are habitual in all aspects of social anthropology are the necessary techniques for studying national character also. All anthropological statements tend to be generalizations or normative statements abstracted from a series of observed or recounted acts or expressions of opinion or belief. The study of national character describes the observed or deduced motives and values dominant within a given society at a given time in a way little different from that in which a study of primitive law describes the legal norms and sanctions operative in a given society at a given time. Studies of primitive law will often deduce generalizations that would probably not have occurred to any member of the society being studied, and will employ (often with a redefinition for the special circumstances) terms derived from the specialized study of jurisprudence as developed in the anthropologist's own society.

In quite an analogous way,[1] studies of national character have deduced unconscious motives as explanations for a variety of observed or recounted acts that would probably not have occurred to any member of the society being studied. But the observations or recorded information are primary; the deduced unconscious motives, like the deduced legal generalizations, have the status of *hypotheses* which are offered as being the principles underlying the disparate statements or behavior recorded. The usefulness of such hypotheses depends on their being applicable to a further series of observations within the same society; in other words the hypotheses concerning national character, like any other scientific hypotheses, are tested by the predictions that can be made when they are employed consistently.

Just as most generalizations about primitive law are phrased in terms drawn from contemporary jurisprudence, so are most generalizations about national character phrased in terms drawn from contemporary psychology and perhaps especially psychoanalysis. This has probably been a source of confusion; for though, to a certain extent, psycho-analysts and social anthropologists studying national character are deal-ing with the same endopsychic events, their observational viewpoints are different.

As an example of these different observational viewpoints, let us consider the attitudes towards authority. Both psychoanalysts and an-thropologists have noted that in many instances there is similarity or congruity in the attitudes felt or expressed towards the representatives of authority in varied institutions—parent, king or president, officer, priest, teacher, representative of the law, and so on. The psychoanalyst, engaged with the historical development of a single individual, knows or infers that the individual being studied had relations with his parents prior to relations with any other holder of authority, and therefore, *for that individual,* his attitude to kings, priests or teachers, and the like will tend to generalize from his attitude to his parents; and, within this individual context, it is legitimate to speak of kings, priests, and so on, as "father-surrogates."

The social anthropologist, on the other hand, takes as his basic obser-vation the fact that infants are born into a society in which the patterns of authority, of subordination and deference, are already established, and that these patterns include proper and expected, or improper and censured, behavior and attitudes for parents of young children. Despite the variations of personality and temperament, the parents' roles are to a very considerable extent determined before a child is born by the existing patterns of authority within the culture, so that, from an an-thropological point of view, a father can be considered a "king-surro-gate" or "policeman-surrogate," and so on.

In psychoanalytic theory, and within the aims of individual psycho-therapy, the parents' behavior is "given" or arbitrary, and the patient's adaptation to, or interpretation of, this parental behavior is the object of investigation. In the study of national character, the ideal and actual roles of parents are important objects of investigation; but they are considered to be no more "given" or arbitrary than any other aspect of the society under investigation. From this observational viewpoint, a change in the authority structure within a society can theoretically modify the expected role of the parent within the family and so, in course of time, the national character of the members of a given society.

In this paper, I wish to explore the hypothesis that the national char-acter of a society may be modified or transformed over a given period through the selection of the personnel for institutions that are in con-stant contact with the mass of the population and in a somewhat super-ordinate position, in a position of some authority. If the personnel of the institution are selected chiefly for their approximation to a certain type of character, rather than for specific intellectual or physical skills; if persons of this type of character have not hitherto been consistently given positions of authority; and if the authority of the institution is generally felt to be benevolent, protective, or succoring: then the character exemplified by the personnel of this institution will to a certain degree become part of the ego ideal of the mass of the population. The mass of the population will then tend to mold their own behavior in conformity with this ideal, and will reward and punish their children in conformity to this adopted pattern. As generations pass, the attempt to approximate this ideal will become less and less conscious, and increasingly part of the unconscious mechanisms that determine the content of the superego; with the ultimate consequence that a type of character that may have been relatively very uncommon when the institution was first manned will subsequently become relatively common, even perhaps typical of the society as a whole, or of those portions of it with which the members of the institution are in most continuous contact.

The English police forces are the institution that I propose to examine in detail; but the evidence that is available to me suggests that strictly analogous functions were performed by the public school teachers in the United States (3, 8), particularly during the period of the great ‘immigrations of the half century ending in 1914, when masses of immigrants' children were transformed into "hundred per cent Americans" and given new models of the parental roles. It also appears that a similar attempt is being made in the U.S.S.R. (1, 9) (and presumably in China), where the members of the Communist Party are consciously presented as models for the mass of the population.

The modern English police force had its inception in the Metropolitan Police Act of Sir Robert Peel in 1829; it was a generation before police forces became mandatory all over the country, through the County and Borough Police Act of 1856 (5). In one important respect the Metropolitan police is anomalous; it is directly responsible to the Home Secretary, to the centralized government; all the other police forces in the country are controlled by local authorities. In the counties the chief officer of the police has the legal power to promote and recruit other members of the force; in the borough forces of England and Wales the power of appointment lies (at least legally; in practice it is usually the chief constable who exercises the authority) in the hands of the watch committee (10). In its relationship to the community it serves and protects, the Metropolitan police is on a different footing from the numerous other forces in Britain (in 1857 there were 239 separate forces, a number gradually reduced by amalgamation to 129 in 1949); but its practices and standards have always served as a model to the other forces.

The chief novelties in Peel's conception of the police appear to be: (a) the institution of a force for the prevention of crimes and the maintenance of public order, rather than for the apprehension of criminals after the crime has been committed; (b) the high visibility of the police in a distinctive uniform, what Inspector J. L. Thomas has called the "scarecrow function" of the police (11); (c) the fact that the police were on continuous duty during the whole 24 hours (their immediate predecessors, the Bow Street runners, were not in uniform and only patrolled during the evenings, invariably finishing duty by midnight) (11); (d) the fact that the police were unarmed, except for the truncheon, which was no more formidable than the "life-preserver" which many gentlemen of the early nineteenth century carried on their walks abroad; (e) the fact that every complaint against the conduct of the police was publicly investigated, with considerable publicity in the earlier years (6); (f) the fact that the police were never segregated in barracks nor treated as a paramilitary formation, as occurred in a number of European countries; and (g) the fact that, apart from certain qualifications of height and age, the police were recruited entirely on the basis of their character, and not on their previous employment, or through patronage, or for the possession of any special skills beyond an unfixed minimum of education. Neither examinations nor tests (other than medical) have ever preceded recruitment into the English police force, though new entrants are naturally given training after they have been accepted.

The great bulk of the English police has almost continuously been drawn from the ranks of skilled and semiskilled labor, from the working, upper working, and lower middle classes. In 1832, three years after its inception, Peel's Metropolitan force was composed of former members of the following callings: 135 butchers, 109 bakers, 198 shoemakers, 51 tailors, 402 soldiers, 1,151 laborers, 205 servants, 141 carpenters, 75 bricklayers, 20 turners, 55 blacksmiths, 151 clerks, 141 shopkeepers, 141 "superior mechanics," 46 plumbers and painters, 101 sailors, 51 weavers and 8 stonemasons (12). The heterogeneity of this list is probably typical of the composition of most of the English police forces over the last 120 years, with two exceptions; the proportion of former military and naval personnel is rather high, except for recruitment in the years immediately following a major war (12); and in this first metropolitan force there is no special mention of the agricultural laborers (unless the "laborers" without specification were country workers) who for a great part of the nineteenth century made up a very high proportion of the police recruits (12). Agricultural laborers were considered to excel in physique and stamina; and in the words of a former Commissioner of the Metropolitan Police to the American writer, R. B. Fosdick: "They are slow but steady; you can mold them to any shape you please" (2). With the increasing industrialization and urbanization of England, the proportion of agricultural laborers has steadily dropped; and today most police recruits were formerly industrial workers, office workers, commercial travellers or shop assistants (12). It also seems probable that the type of character sought for in a police recruit was formerly much more common in the rural population than in the violent and lawless urban mobs; but with the modification of character that has been hypothesized in the mass of the English population, people of suitable character can be found in all strata of the English population, except possibly in the lower working class.

The following are the only conditions laid down by the Home Secretary for the selection of police recruits. He, or she, must be (a) within certain age limits; (b) not less than a stated height; (c) of a good character and with a satisfactory record in past employments; (d) physically and mentally fitted to perform the duties of a constable; and (d) sufficiently well educated(5). Apart from the criteria of age and height, this means in fact that the selection of recruits depends almost entirely on the result of interviews with the Chief Constable of the force concerned; his experience and skill in assessing character by unformalized techniques of observation and interrogation replace the selection boards, psychological tests, and other techniques of examination that are used for screening the entrants to most life-time careers of responsibility and authority.

In connection with the character of the members of the police force, the criterion of height may merit a little consideration. The minimum fixed by the Home Secretary is 5 feet, 8 inches for men, which already excludes more than half the male population, since the average height of the British male is 5 feet, 7½ inches (7). In point of fact, only three of the country's police forces, though of these two are the largest (Metropolitan, Birmingham and Buckinghamshire) in 1949 were content with the Home Secretary's permitted minimum; about 30 forces will take men of 5 feet, 9 inches, and another 20 of 5 feet, 9½ inches; the remainder—somewhat more than 70 forces—insist on a minimum of 5 feet, 10 inches (10). This means that most of the police recruits come from a small and (statistically speaking) physically unrepresentative section of the population, perhaps some 10 per cent of the whole; and, although the connection between physique and character is still comparatively undetermined,[2] the folk observation that big men are likely to be easy-going, even-tempered, just, and slow to anger may well have some foundation in fact. Although the minimum height was probably imposed with the intention of securing physically strong and impressive men, it may well have had the secondary effect of securing that recruits were selected from people of constitutionally equable temperament.

From its foundation, the emphasis of the British police force has been on the preservation of peace, on the prevention of crime and violence, rather than on the apprehension of criminals and rioters. The swearing-in oath, taken by each constable on entering the force, reads:

> I, A.B., do swear that I will well and truly serve our Sovereign Lady the Queen in the office of Constable ... without Favour or Affection, Malice or Ill-will; and that I will to the best of my Power cause the Peace to be kept and preserved, and prevent all offenses against the Persons and Properties of Her Majesty's Subjects; and that while I continue to hold the said Office I will to the best of my skill and knowledge discharge all the Duties thereof faithfully according to Law (5).

Similarly, the regulations drawn up in 1832 by Mr. Mayne, one of the first two Commissioners of the Metropolitan police, emphasize:

> The absence of crime will be considered the best proof of the complete efficiency of the police ... In divisions where this security and good order have been effected, the officers and men belonging to it may feel assured that such good conduct will be noticed by rewards and promotions ...

> The Constable must remember that there is no qualification more indispensable to a police officer than a perfect command of temper, never suffering himself to be moved in the slightest degree by any language or threats that may be used; if he do his duty in a quiet and determined manner, such conduct will probably induce well-disposed bystanders to assist him should he require it (6).

This emphasis on the prevention of aggression, on the preserving of the peace by a uniformed group of powerful men demonstrating self-restraint, would appear to have been a real novelty in English public life; it was not originally accepted without a great deal of opposition and abuse both from the press and from many representatives of the governing classes (6). Before the establishment of the Metropolitan police, wearers of uniform tended to be either symbolically or potentially oppressors and exploiters rather than protectors of the mass of the population: members of the armed forces, proverbially licentious and lawless, or the liveried servants of the rich and mighty. The policeman in uniform was still a member of his class in the hours off duty, had social as well as official contacts with his neighbors, and very much the same standard of living as most of the working class.

I have been able to find very little discussion of the motives that impel a young man or woman of "superior physique and character" to take up a profession or occupation that even today is not particularly rewarding financially. I do not think any systematic research has been done on the subject, but Inspector (now Chief Inspector) J. L. Thomas of the City of Bradford Police has some illuminating observations to make (12). He writes:

In other callings with a high age of entry such as the Church and the teaching profession, the tyro must previously devote a number of years to studying and training for his future work, and the Police Service is probably unique in taking on men aged twenty years and upwards, who have no preliminary training whatsoever for the work they are to perform. It follows therefore that it has to attract men already engaged in an occupation, and the question which presents itself is: What were the motives that induced young men to quit a diversity of jobs to become policemen?

Among the answers he suggests are: pay steady and not subject to the caprice of trade or industry, though not high; a reasonable pension at a comparatively early age; unemployment following a "dead end" job; lack of specialized training after a period in the armed forces; and similar circumstances. He continues:

> Minor causes, such as the power a policeman is supposed to wield may have influenced some men. . . . While it is acknowledged that some men now serving did cherish over a long period an ardent desire to become policemen, it is suggested that they are in the minority, and that most policemen more or less drifted into their present job, through force of circumstances, such as those already described, rather than having been impelled by a strong sense of vocation. . . . "How then," it may be asked, "has the English police service succeeded in gaining such a large measure of public approbation?" This can only be attributed to the rigid observance of a number of fundamental rules. . . . the principal ones are: selecting the best men available; preserving the civilian character of the Force by recruiting from the population at large and from a wide diversity of occupations; maintaining a high standard of discipline, integrity and *esprit de corps;* and observing the principle of promotion by merit. Consequently, the nature of the occupation previously followed by a policeman has little direct bearing on his new career. . . . The motive which prompted a man to enlist is not such a vital factor as may have been thought at first. As a matter of fact, it is often the men with the strongest inclination to become policemen who are the most unsuitable for the position.

These perspicacious remarks omit, I think, consideration of one motive which, though it may not play a large role in the decision to enlist, may quite probably be influential in keeping the new recruits in the calling they have chosen; that is the respect with which the members of the police force are regarded by their fellow-citizens. The evidence for the attitudes of the English towards their police in the nineteenth and early twentieth century is only anecdotal and inferential; music-hall songs, jokes, descriptions of members of the police in novels by Charles Dickens or Wilkie Collins and the like.[3] But today this affectionate respect is extremely widespread. In January, 1951, a scattered sample of 11,000 English men and women filled in for me a long and

Police constable, Metropolitan Police Force.
Photo supplied by British Information Services.

detailed questionnaire. One of the questions was: "What do you think of the police?" No answers were indicated, and four lines were left for volunteered comments.[4]

This large sample were overwhelmingly appreciative of the police, to the extent of 73 per cent; a mere 5 per cent were really hostile, though 13 per cent had some criticisms to make. The answers were categorized in a considerable number of ways; for this question the most significant is by social class, self-ascribed.

TABLE I

ENGLISH ATTITUDES TOWARD THE POLICE, BY SOCIAL CLASS

Question: *What do you think of the police?*

Social Class	Per cent Favorable	Per cent Neutral	Per cent Critical	Per cent Hostile	Per cent No answer or irrelevant
Upper middle	79	0	13	2	6
Middle	74	2	13	5	6
Lower middle	74	1	17	3	5
Upper working	72	1	17	3	3
Working	74	1	21	3	3
Lower working	65	2	12	7	14
Total Sample	73	2	13	5	7

Although, as could have been foreseen, appreciation of the police diminishes as one descends the social scale, it is only in the lower working class that appreciation falls below two-thirds of the total.

I should like to suggest that, increasingly during the past century, the English policeman has been for his fellow-citizens not only an object of respect but also a model of the ideal male character, self-controlled, possessing more strength than he has ever to call into use except in the gravest emergency, fair and impartial, serving the abstractions of Peace and Justice rather than any personal allegiance or sectional advantage. This model, distributed throughout the population (in 1949 there were 59,000 police officers, averaging one police officer for every 720 inhabitants (5)) has, I suggest, had an appreciable influence on the character of most of the population during recent decades, so that the bulk of the population has, so to speak, incorporated the police man or woman as an ideal and become progressively more "self-policing"; and with this incorporation there has been an increasing amount of identification, so that today, in the words of one typical respondent:

> I believe the police stand for all we English are, maybe at first appearances slow perhaps, but reliable stout and kindly. I have the greatest admiration for our police force and I am proud they are renowned abroad.

If this hypothesis be correct, then what started as an expedient to control the very great criminality and violence of large sections of the English urban population (6, 11) has resulted in a profound modification of the character of this urban population. In a somewhat similar fashion, the need to provide a common language and literacy for the children of immigrants to the United States placed the American public school teacher in a position of prestige that was not shared by her colleagues in any European society and turned her into a model of ideal American conduct. If the metaphor be allowed, the American has an incorporated schoolteacher as part of his or her superego, the English man or woman an incorporated policeman.

There is not yet sufficient evidence to show whether the Communist Party member in the U.S.S.R. is producing analogous results in the mass of the Soviet population. The Communist Party is a much more recent institution than the two others hitherto discussed, but its personnel are distributed throughout the population in much the same proportions and similar relationship as the policeman or the schoolteacher. The major contrasts are that the policy is quite self-conscious on the part of the regime, and that Communist Party members are publicly connected with the whole apparatus of state power, in a way that neither the police nor the teachers, both under the control of local authorities, are. This public connection with state power may interfere with the processes of identification by the powerless; and, it would seem, it is by means of the more-or-less complete and more-or-less conscious identification with the members of an admired and succoring institution that the characters of the mass of a population and the ways in which they interpret their roles as parents are gradually modified or transformed.

NOTES

1. It should perhaps be emphasized that the analogical elements lie in the deductions the anthropologist makes from his observations and interviews, rather than in any very close parallel between legal principles and unconscious motives. That there is a connection, however, is demonstrated in my forthcoming study of English character (4), where it is shown that unsophisticated English parents are likely to judge their children's conduct on the same basis as that which underlies the McNaghten rules for crimes committed by the legally insane.

2. Attempts to correlate physique and character or temperament have been made by a number of researchers, notably Kretschmer: *Physique and character* (English translation 1925) and W. H. Sheldon: *The Varieties of human physique* (1940), *The Varieties of temperament* (1942), and *Varieties of delinquent youth* (1949); but to date there has not been either general acceptance of their hypotheses, nor convincing application of them by other researchers.

3. E.g. Inspector Bucket in Charles Dickens' *Bleak house*, or Sergeant Cuff in Wilkie Collins' *The moonstone*.

4. For full details of the sample from which the following figures are drawn, see my forthcoming study (4). It was a mail survey, and had the very high return of 75 per cent of filled-out questionnaires. This study also gives the justification of the summary description of the ideal male character for the English outlined in the subsequent paragraphs.

REFERENCES

1. BAUER, R. A., 1952
2. FOSDICK, 1915
3. GORER, 1948
4. GORER, 1955-b
5. HART, J., 1951
6. LEE, W. L. M., 1901
7. MARTIN, J., 1949
8. MEAD, 1942-d
9. MEAD, 1951-b
10. *Oaksey Report*, 1949
11. THOMAS, J. L., 1945
12. THOMAS, J. L., 1946

A. IRVING HALLOWELL

1937. "Psychological Leads for Ethnological Field Workers." Prepared under the auspices of the Committee on Personality in Relation to Culture, Edward Sapir, Chairman, Division of Anthropology and Psychology, National Research Council, Washington, D. C. Mimeographed under the title, *"Introduction: Handbook of Psychological Leads for Ethnological Field Workers."* Published by courtesy of Dr. Hallowell.

1941. "The Social Function of Anxiety in a Primitive Society," *American Sociological Review* vol. 6: 869-881. Reprinted by courtesy of the author and of the Editor of the *American Sociological Review.*

Dr. Hallowell generously made his 1937 article available for the first edition of the present book, where it first appeared in print. It would be difficult to find a more satisfactory general introduction to the ethnographic study of patterns of personality. Unfortunately space does not permit inclusion of Hallowell's fruitful contributions to the use of Rorschach techniques in ethnography (see General Bibliography).

In *Anthropology Today: An Encyclopedic Inventory* (ed. by A. L. Kroeber, Chicago, 1953) appears another important discussion by Professor Hallowell: "Culture, Personality, and Society." The majority of Hallowell's contributions are scattered through professional journals; happily, most of them have been reproduced in his recent book, *Culture and Experience* (Philadelphia, 1955), to which students are referred. His paper, "Aggression in Saulteaux Society" is accessible in *Personality in Nature, Society, and Culture* by Kluckhohn, Murray and Schneider (N. Y., 1953). See also his articles, 1937-b, 1939-b, 1942-a, and 1950.

PSYCHOLOGICAL LEADS FOR ETHNOLOGICAL FIELD WORKERS

A. Irving Hallowell

Direct observation of human behavior cannot fail to impress one with two outstanding facts. On the one hand, certain behavior patterns of any particular individual are never entirely unique. The individual is only one of a series of persons exhibiting similar habits of speech, dress, economic activities, religious attitudes, etc. But the series of individuals characterized by these gross behavior traits is always limited. The persons involved may be those of a class, a community, a tribe, a nation or geographical area. And, if we had all the relevant historical data at our command, such behavior patterns would be found to have temporal limits as well.

On the other hand, it is also a matter of observation that these collectively shared patterns of behavior never obscure the uniqueness of the individual person. Nor is this individuality altogether a matter of distinctive physical traits or physiognomy, age or sex. No two individuals impress us as being precisely identical personalities, so that May has emphasized social stimulus value, the way an individual impresses others, as the differential of personality.

> It includes his physique, his dress, his manners, his voice and the way he handles it, his choice of language, his habitual modes of response, his general and special abilities. . . . All of these combine to make up his total social stimulus value.[1]

Depending upon the background of our interests, and our aims, if we are pursuing particular problems, attention may focus upon either the common behavior patterns shared by a series of individuals or upon the variations in the distinctive personality traits of individuals.

These two variables, of course, are by no means exclusively human. Students of animal life recognize parallel phenomena. Certain common as well as differential behavior traits are manifested by series of animal species. Indians have told me that they can distinguish the individual members of a beaver colony with which they are familiar; and marked variation in the personality traits of the higher primates is a matter of frequent comment by all experimenters with these animals.

Yet while this parallel in human and sub-human behavior is observed, a fundamental distinction must be drawn. No matter how individuals may differ, the supra-individual behavior patterns which characterize a series of animals tend to correspond fairly closely with the limits of the species, whereas in the case of man, supra-individual patterns of behavior of many different kinds are intra-specific.

In fact, specific identity in any series of living organisms ordinarily implies not only common anatomical and physiological characteristics, but common behavior traits as well. Thus, whatever the degree of differential behavior in beavers (*castor canadensis*) may be, throughout the range of their habitat they display the same predilection for certain types of food, are monogamous in their mating habits, and construct a typical form of dwelling. The organic form of the species and the reactive patterns of its individual members to the physical environment, as well as to other animals of their kind, appear to be not only closely correlated but stable from generation to generation. For some species of living creatures this correlation between organic form and behavior is assumed to be so close that Wheeler has not hesitated to infer, from the morphological features of ants preserved in Baltic amber recovered from Oligocene formations, that they had practically the same social habits as closely related contemporary species.[2]

When we turn to man, however, despite a common phylogeny and the specific identity of contemporary races (for taxonomically their differences are relatively insignificant), a contrasting picture presents itself. When viewed in the widest spatial and temporal perspectives, human behavior patterns of intra-specific incidence exhibit an enormous range of variability. The unity of our species offers no basis whatsoever for the inference of specific food preferences, mating habits, types of dwellings, or patterns of interpersonal relations. Consequently, the anthropologist cannot follow the procedure of Wheeler and infer the type of social organization characteristic of *Sinanthropus* or even *Neanderthal* man from the material evidence at his disposal in respect to the bodily form of these races. Faced with the known range of behavior patterns of *Homo sapiens*, there is no reason to suppose that the paleoanthropic members of our zoological family were necessarily confined to narrower behavior limits.

These facts of observation immediately suggest that the categories of explanation to which the biologist resorts most frequently in dealing with the determining factors in animal behavior—heredity, structure, physiology, the physical environment—are not altogether sufficient to explain all the multiform details of human behavior. The psychological equipment of man, as contrasted with even the most closely related species of primates, exhibits a capacity for plasticity in responses—learned, acquired reactions—that set *Homo sapiens* off from all other species of animals. The neurological basis of this differential in human behavior is rooted in the expansion of the cortical associational tissue which is so enormously increased as we pass from the higher apes to man, that the weight of the brain is practically doubled. As Herrick puts it:

> A neurological survey of the vertebrates reveals two patterns of behavior and of adjusting mechanism which may be characterized as (relatively) rigid and labile, innate and acquired, conservative and progressive. Between these tendencies there is, by the nature of things, more or less rivalry, competition, or conflict. In the lower vertebrates and in early embryonic stages of all vertebrates the stable patterns predominate; in the higher types, and especially in adult man, the labile, acquired or learned patterns predominate. This evolutionary sequence can be read in terms of both behavior and the structural organization of the brain.
>
> In the course of this evolution we can follow the transition from the simplest sort of mass-reaction to very complex reflex and instinctive patterns and from the latter to control behavior by individually learned and cortically directed analysis of experience which culminates in the fabrication of conscious symbols and rational control. On the structural side we see a gradual transfer of the center of physiological dominance and integration from the mid-brain to the strio-thalamic complex and, in the third stage, to the cerebral cortex parallel with the shift from physiological conditioning to intelligently directed motivation.[3]

Among infra-human organisms, of course, there is plenty of evidence that learned behavior is of adaptive importance to the animal.[4] There is no categorical distinction, then, between behavior of this type among the lower animals and man. There is no real break in continuity when viewed in broad evolutionary terms. But this mode of adjustment is of minor importance in infra-human organisms as compared with that of the functioning of innately determined behavior patterns. It is far from being characteristic, and it is not socially transmitted. On the other hand, the significant thing about human beings is the fact that their behavior *is* characterized by the quantitative dominance of socially acquired and transmitted idea-and-action patterns. "Much, perhaps nine-tenths of what commonly passes as distinctly human nature," says Thorndike,[5] "is . . . not in man originally but is put there by institutions, or grows there by the interaction of the world of natural forces and the capacity to learn."

In seeking to understand the determining factors in the behavior of human individuals, therefore, the role of acquired patterns assumes first rank. Until these are thoroughly understood an evaluation of innate factors must remain incomplete. Thus a category of explanation of relatively incidental importance in general biology assumes first importance in all the human sciences that do not confine their interests to the purely innate mechanisms involved in human behavior.

But the fact must not be overlooked that while human behavior in its gross observable aspects may be characterized in terms of the acquired patterns which distinguish it from the behavior of organisms on an infra-human level, the significance of its organically rooted dynamic energies must by no means be minimized. The chief point to be borne in mind is that the inherent impulses and strivings of human beings, as compared with other animals, are more constantly deflected and canalized or masked through the operation of acquired habit systems. These impose limits upon instinctual demands; condition the mode of expression tolerated, and act selectively with respect to the objects of possible gratification. This indirection in securing satisfaction suggests a qualitative difference of generic importance between human and animal psychology, particularly since man's phylogeny necessitates the assumption of certain consonant factors in the strivings of men and infra-human species. Since the acquired behavior patterns of man everywhere involve temporary or permanent inhibitions of one kind or another that delay or forbid the direct satisfaction of native impulses, inner psychic conflict would seem to be of the very essence of human existence. This fact, in turn, suggests complicated affective involvements that must be presumed to color human experience and provide important cues to the mechanisms of individual behavior.

These implications have been systematically developed in psychoanalytic psychology. It views the human psyche[6] "as the mediator between the individual's needs and the possibilities of their gratification in the external world." Psychic activity is assumed to be "inspired and sustained by instinctual drives and as directed either to securing the gratification of instinctual aims or to the resolution of the tension associated with instinctual frustration, that is, in the most modern terminology, to the mastery of anxiety." Since human life everywhere, whatever its dominant patterns of acquired behavior may be, precludes the direct satisfaction of native impulses, and since, as Freud has pointed out, these organically based inner stimuli, particularly sexual cravings, not only are constant but cannot be mastered by flight, human individuals are faced with the problem of maintaining a psychic equilibrium between instinctual drives, on the one hand, and the habitual patterns they have acquired, on the other. The psychoanalysts further emphasize that the control of a portion, at least, of the instinctual impulses is not consciously or volitionally centered. As a result of parental influences during the earliest phases of maturation, there is built up within the ego a "criticising faculty"—the super-ego—the nucleus of the moral conscience. It is not under the volitional control of the ego, and it tends to act as an unconscious restraining force upon native impulses, which often conflict with it. A portion of man's psychic energy is thus directed to the checking, deflecting and control of instinctual impulses at the unconscious as well as at the conscious level of behavior.

In dealing with the total range of human behavior, then, we are bound to consider: (1) The varieties of intra-specific patterns of acquired behavior shared by groups of human individuals and the psychological implications of these. (2) The processes by which these patterns become part of the integral responses of the individual and the moulding effect of these acquired patterns of thought and action upon the impulses, urges, and desires which arise from organic sources. (3) The differential behavior of the individual as compared with the responses shared with a series of other individuals.

Quite obviously, human behavior presents much more intricately woven chains of interdependent relations than that of any other animal. Again and again, however, over-simplification of the problems involved has resulted from attempts to cut the Gordian knot and to offer totalitarian explanations of human behavior by a direct appeal to single categories of factors such as heredity, bio-chemistry, racial type, constitutional type, a panel of instincts, climate, topography, etc. While all of these factors play some role in human behavior, a delicate weighing of each with due regard for the operation of other factors, rather than an insistence upon simple unitary explanations, is what is demanded.

II

To point out that in human life acquired behavior patterns dominate unlearned forms of thought and activity may seem obvious enough, yet the recognition of this fact and the systematic exploration of its implications have far-reaching consequences for all the human sciences. It leads directly to the observation that acquired modes of behavior are functions of inter-personal relations, and that the sources of these behavior patterns in the individual are to be sought in the behavior of other human individuals. Human societies, that is to say, function through systems of relations which bind the human beings who compose them to each other and to the physical environment in which they live; the specific patterning of these relations through acquired behavior responses constitutes the fundamental mode of human social integration. But it must not be concluded from this statement that acquired activity patterns are likewise the *sine qua non* of social life among all living organisms. On the contrary, part of the significance of acquired behavior patterns in human life lies in the fact that social integration is characteristically developed on *this* particular level.

In that other great phylum of organic life, the Arthropoda, e.g., the highly integrated social life of insect communities is maintained through the morphological differentiation of individuals and physiological processes of social significance like trophallaxis.[7] Acquired patterns of behavior are of no crucial importance in maintaining the general functioning of social relations, whether viewed from the standpoint of the individual insect or of the social group.

Among the vertebrates, wherever social life has developed, physiological mechanisms rather than acquired behavior appear to be the fundamental means of social integration. Zuckerman,[8] e.g., has stressed the direct correlation between reproductive physiology and social behavior among the mammals:

> The California sea-lion (*Eumetopias Stelleri*) has a breeding season that extends from June 15th to July 15th, and a gestation period of about eleven months. During the latter part of May, the cows band together, sometimes in the company of unmated bulls, in the neighborhood of the rookery where they will later meet the adult males. These arrive in early June, either singly or in groups of as many as six. By the middle of the month breeding activities are in full swing, and within a week or so of giving birth, the cows come into heat and seek the bull. Bull sea-lions do not form harems in the same way as the fur seal, although some take up positions in the rookery which they endeavor to keep by fighting. As soon as every female has been served, the animals take to the sea and the sexes separate.

> The pattern of social behavior exhibited by this species is clearly determined by its reproductive physiology. The sexes meet and engage in mating activity in only a small part of the year, because that is the only time when their reproductive organs are physiologically in a condition for mating. The fighting of the rutting males follows from the possession of physiologically active testes. The particular time that the females come into heat and seek the bull is determined by the fact that ovulation follows soon after parturition. The separation of the two sexes at the end of the season is due to the transition of the reproductive organs of the male from a functional to an inactive or *anoestrous* state, and to the fact that the physiological condition of mating or *oestrus* in the female is replaced by that of pregnancy.

> This example of the sea-lion illustrates how the framework of mammalian society is determined by physiological mechanisms. Reproductive physiology is the fundamental mechanism of society.

Even when we ascend still higher on the mammalian scale and reach the primates, where social life is characteristic of the order as a whole, it cannot be asserted that acquired behavior is the dominant integrative factor in the social relations of any of these species, although it is relatively more important than in the behavior of the sea-lions or the insects.

There is a deep-rooted qualitative difference, therefore, between the social life of man, chiefly integrated on the level of acquired behavior responses, and the social life of other animals where social integration is bound up so closely with, and limited by, physiological mechanisms and morphological adaptations. Since from a phylogenetic point of view man stems from a primate stock that is gregarious, no social contract ever was needed to induce human beings to adopt a social manner of life. Although the roots of man's social life undoubtedly lie below the predominant means of social integration now ubiquitously developed in our species, "nothing is known of intermediate social levels that may have existed between that of the subhuman primate and that of the most primitive food gatherers ever described."[9] But through the psychobiological changes that, among other things, gave the *Hominidae* their distinct zoological status, the potentialities for learned behavior came to be exploited to such a degree that a new level of social integration came into existence. Human social life has consequently been intensified, elaborated and diversified in terms of man's unique potentialities. Concomitantly, through the development of symbolic means of oral communication, a unique instrument arose which not only facilitated the transmission of acquired experience, but promoted the development of conceptual thought and functioned vitally in all aspects of social interaction. For, as de Laguna says:[10]

> Speech is the great medium through which human cooperation is brought about. It is the means by which the diverse activities of men are coordinated and correlated with each other for the attainment of common and reciprocal ends. Men do not speak simply to relieve their feelings or to air their views, but to awaken a response in their fellows and to influence their attitudes and acts. It is further the means by which men are brought into a new and momentous relationship with the external world, the very relationship which makes the world for them an objective order.
>
> Human speech has become the most complex and highly specialized of all vital functions; but the clue to the labyrinth of its complex forms lies in the fundamental function of social coordination it continues to perform. That it has itself become one of the chief human activities which it serves to correlate and coordinate, does not affect its fundamental nature, although it vastly complicates it. It is indeed the outstanding peculiarity of the function of speech that it is capable of this quasi-independence and self-determination. It marks in the evolution of life and mind a development as critical as the appearance of the distance receptors.[10]

Furthermore, the fact that acquired rather than innately determined behavior patterns became the outstanding differential of human behavior, together with the fact that these patterns were socially transmitted, ultimately led to the great diversity of idea and action patterns that characterizes our species today, and in the discernible past. Innate human needs were met in a host of ways, in a wide range of environments, and new needs were stimulated through the development of different acquired habit systems. Thus, aside from questions concerning the historic origins or determinants of this or that group pattern of acquired behavior, the typical patterns of living that characterize different human populations at any time can be distinguished from each other and discussed as individual units. It is also true, of course, that any particular mode of life has a temporal continuity of varying duration, the relative stability of which is explicable in terms of the degree to which the behavior patterns of one generation of individuals become the modal behavior of succeeding generations of their descendants.

In the social sciences the term culture has been increasingly employed to designate categorically and abstractly the traditional patterns of inter-personal and ecological relations which characterize populations. The particular patterns which exist must be defined in each case by investigation. But the concept of culture and its usefulness as a descriptive term is in itself symbolic of the central position which the category of acquired behavior patterns must occupy in all the human sciences.

To observe that man is a social animal is trite. Too often superficial analogies have been drawn between the social life of man and that of the lower animals, especially the insects. But a complete understanding of the nature and characteristic forms of human social integration, and particularly the psychological implications involved, awaits more complete and systematic investigation. Culture, therefore, sets man off from other animals, even from those whose social life is highly developed. It is not synonymous with the generic conception of the social. It implies, rather, the integration of social behavior on a unique and distinctive level. But this does not mean that culture is super-organic in the sense that a break is implied with infra-human species. The appearance of such a break is created only because of the profound degree to which our behavior has become dominated by learned responses of so many kinds.

Verbal communication is everywhere patterned by traditional linguistic forms. Interpersonal and ecological relations are guided by the conventional dictates of the social and economic order and the traditional technology. Conventional beliefs impose characteristic ideologies upon the minds of human beings, typical attitudes toward natural phenomena and spiritual beings are assumed, and so on. Such group patterns of thought and behavior are readily observable and innumerable accounts are available which describe how human populations in different parts of the world and at various historic periods differ in their cultural aspects. But there are more subtle implications which follow from the dominance of traditional behavior patterns in human life. Mental imagery, even perception itself, is not free from their influence; nor are motor habits, gestures, the expressions of the emotions and the motivations of the individual.

In perception, for instance, it seems that there is nothing final nor absolute about the color pyramid in use by psychologists of western civilization. Different cultural norms would dictate somewhat different pyramids, if these were developed out of the conventional color scales differentiated among peoples with other cultural backgrounds. Manus children, according to Mead,[11] "saw yellow, olive-green, blue-green, gray and lavender as variants of one color"; and while the Ashanti have distinct names for black, red and white, black is applied to any dark color—brown, blue, purple, etc.—while red includes what we differentiate as pink, orange and yellow.[12] As Professor Boas pointed out many years ago,[13] "the importance of the fact that in thought and speech these color-names convey the impression of quite different groups of sensations can hardly be over-rated."

In quite another field of perception, resemblances between relatives, Malinowski has indicated how the Trobriand culture patterns impose the recognition of similarity between certain classes of kin, and function to controvert the recognition of similarities between other relatives, which are obvious to the outsider. Among these people resemblance to the father is considered "natural, right and proper . . . and such similarity is always assumed and affirmed to exist," despite the theory of procreation which denies to him any physiological role. On the other hand, the dogma exists that children do not resemble their mothers or maternal kin. Even to hint that such is the case is an offense. "It is a phrase of serious bad language to say, 'thy face is thy sister's' which is the worst combination of kinship similarity." In still greater contrast to the "freedom" of perceptual impressions of this class permitted among other peoples, the Trobriands' dogma holds that while brothers resemble their father, they do not resemble each other. When Malinowski once drew attention to the striking likeness between two brothers, there came "a hush over all the assembly, while the brother present withdrew abruptly and the company was half-embarrassed, half offended at this breach of custom." In another instance in which five sons were said to be exactly like the father, when Malinowski "pointed out that this similarity to the father implied similarity among each other, such heresy was indignantly repudiated."[14]

The strength of conventional modes of perception among ourselves was once strikingly brought to my own attention in this way: I had been talking to a small group of students about this very point, and had been using the constellation Ursa Major as an example. I had reviewed the different names—bear, otter, plough, dipper, etc.—given to this group of stars, and discussed some of the associated folklore material. Just as I finished speaking, one of the students spoke up and said, "But it *does* look like a dipper."

Sherif,[15] who has reviewed the problem of social factors in perception, points out that, so far as primitive peoples are concerned, the variations observable are by no means made intelligible by some hypothesis of a "primitive" or "pre-logical" mind, but are reducible to the fundamental notion that "the nucleus of all perceiving and thinking lies in established norms or reference points." The core of the problem, then, is the relativity of these norms assimilated by the individual from the culture of his group and utilized as his standard reference points, or the scale, level or frame of reference the individual develops for himself in the context of a particular situation.

In a series of laboratory experiments designed to test this latter proposition, as well as to test the influence of controlled group factors, Sherif was able to demonstrate that, if subjects face a stimulus situation in individual sessions, the median values which they establish differ considerably; then in successive sessions, when they work together, their medians tend to converge. But when subjects start in group situations there is a convergence at once which is maintained in successive sessions, including the last individual session. There may even be a rise and fall of the median, but it is a rise and fall *as a group*. In the course of these experiments it was also found that suggestion was effective in giving definite direction to perception in an unstable stimulus situation. The subject continued to experience the patterning of perception originally initiated by suggestions.

The cultural patterning of perception, then, is one of the most fundamental aspects of the relation between culture and the individual, since through this process frames of reference are established basic to his relations to other persons and to the objects of the outer world.

Gait, the handling of tools and other motor habits also bear the stamp of cultural patterning and cannot be understood as purely individual modes of behavior. Nor, for that matter, can such commonplace organic functions as breathing. As Sapir[16] points out:

> . . . the regularized breathing of the Hindu Yogi, the subdued breathing of those who are in the presence of a recently deceased companion laid away in a coffin and surrounded by all the ritual of funeral observances, the style of breathing which one learns from an operatic singer who gives lessons on the proper control of the voice, are, each and every one of them, capable of isolation as socialized modes of conduct that have a definite place in the history of human culture, though they are obviously not a whit less facts of individual behavior than the most casual and normal style of breathing, such as one rarely imagines to have other than purely individual implica-

tions. Strange as it may seem at first blush, there is no hard and fast line of division as to class of behavior between a given style of breathing, *provided that it be socially interpreted,* and a religious doctrine or a form of political organization . . . such differences of analysis are merely imposed by the nature of the interest of the observer, and are not inherent in the phenomena themselves.

Gestures, too, are subtly patterned forms of bodily movement, as Sapir goes on to say, and hard to classify. It is also difficult

to make a conscious separation between that in gesture which is of merely individual origin and that which is referable to the habits of the group as a whole. In spite of these difficulties of conscious analysis, we respond to gestures with extreme alertness and, one might almost say, in accordance with an elaborate and secret code that is written nowhere, known by none, and understood by all. But this code is by no means referable to simple organic responses. On the contrary, it is as finely certain and artificial, as definitely a creation of social tradition, as language or religion or industrial technology. . . . A Jewish or Italian shrug of the shoulders is no more the same pattern of behavior as the shrug of a typical American than the forms and significant evocations of the Yiddish or Italian sentence are identical with those of any thinkable English sentence.

While emotion is often referred to as a "natural response," with the implication that it is one little varied by experience, this is a very inexact concept. "Emotional life," says Landis,[17] "is modified more rigorously in the growth and education of an individual than perhaps any other variety of human experience." And despite the immense amount of research that has already been devoted by physiologists and psychologists to the biochemistry and mechanisms of the emotions, Landis indicates that "the most important line of future research is that of the nature of the relation existing between emotion and learning in the broadest sense of each term."

In recent years child psychologists[18] and psychiatrists have been devoting more and more attention to the situational factors in emotional behavior from the genetic and psychopathological viewpoints respectively. But even more thorough-going investigations along these lines will leave a broader field of inquiry untouched. Once the social factors in emotional conditioning are recognized, it is obvious that these must vary in different societies in accordance with the culture patterns which characterize different groups. How wide this variation is may be judged from the fact that culture determines (1) the situations that will arouse certain emotional responses and not others; (2) the degree to which the response is supported by custom or inhibitions demanded; (3) the particular forms which the expression takes.[19] It is also probable that, as Klineberg[20] points out, the very emotions felt by one people may not occur in that same form elsewhere. When a Kwakiutl child dies, the father's emotional experience is a peculiar combination of grief and shame—grief at the loss of his child, and shame because he has been "insulted" by the universe, and because his prestige and security have been threatened. It may be that the Kwakiutl father never feels grief without its accompaniment or overtone of shame, and that as a consequence his felt emotion really differs markedly from what ours would be under similar circumstances.

Among the Kaingang Indians of Brazil, Henry[21] has called attention to another distinctive emotional pattern, "fear-anger, one emotion with two facets." A certain linguistic element when used with a postposition indicating "direction towards" functions as a verb and means angry. When used alone it means dangerous. Thus the former conveys something of the notion of directed danger and the latter of undirected anger. Consequently,

> if you say to A "I am angry with you," his reaction is not contrition nor repentance, or any kind of "negative self-feeling" but rage. This happens because even though he may know you do not intend bodily harm, there is an aura of danger about anger, and danger creates fear, which in turn begets anger.

That the typical motivations of individuals in different societies vary with relation to their traditional culture patterns, is demonstrable from many different angles of approach. Klineberg, for example, points out the indifference of Indian children to speed in the performance of psychological tests as contrasted with American children who respond so readily to this idea. Another psychologist, Porteus, noticed the same negative response among the Australians. Klineberg interprets this indifference to speed as due to cultural rather than innate factors, since he finds no physiological basis for the latter. Moreover, he found that Indian children "who have lived a long time among whites, or who attend a busy and progressive school, show a definite tendency to approximate white behavior in this respect. . . ."[22] Speed is at a premium in our culture, and children will even work quickly without special instruction. In other societies more cautious, deliberate behavior may be cultivated or even be necessary in particular economic pursuits. In hunting the Wallaby, or small kangaroo, in Australia, for instance, the natives need "sustained muscular control, an undivided attention, an extreme sensory wariness, inexhaustible patience and concentration of purpose."[23]

The values stressed by the economic institutions of a people considered as a whole also furnish significant clues to important differences in economic motivations. ". . . the acquirement of wealth is not to be lightly taken for granted as one of the basic drives of human beings. One accumulates property, one defers the immediate enjoyment of wealth only in so far as society sets the pace for these activities and inhibitions. . . ." Sapir[24] goes on to contrast the Indians of the West Coast of British Columbia with ourselves in this regard. The former

have often been quoted as a primitive society that has developed a philosophy of wealth which is somewhat comparable to our own, with its emphasis on "conspicuous waste" and on the sacrosanct character of property. The comparison is not essentially sound. The West Coast Indian does not handle wealth in a manner which we recognize as our own. We can find plenty of analogies, to be sure, but they are more likely to be misleading than helpful. No West Coast Indian, as far as we know, ever amassed wealth as an individual pure and simple, with the expectation of disposing of it in the fullness of time at his own sweet will. This is a dream of the modern European and American individualist, and it is a dream which not only brings no thrill to the heart of the West Coast Indian but is probably almost meaningless to him. The concepts of wealth and the display of honorific privileges, such as crests and dances and songs and names, which have been inherited from legendary ancestors, are inseparable among these Indians. One cannot publicly exhibit such a privilege without expending wealth in connection with it. Nor is there much object in accumulating wealth except to reaffirm privileges already possessed, or, in the spirit of a parvenu, to imply the possession of privileges none too clearly recognized as legitimate by one's fellow tribesmen. In other words, wealth, beyond a certain point, is with these people much more a token of status than it is a tool for the fulfilment of personal desires. We may go so far as to say that among the West Coast Indians it is not the individual at all who possesses wealth. It is primarily the ceremonial patrimony of which he is the temporary custodian that demands the symbolism of wealth. Arrived at a certain age, the West Coast Indian turns his privileges over to those who are by kin or marriage connection entitled to manipulate them. Henceforth he may be as poor as a church mouse, without loss of prestige. I should not like to go so far as to say that the concepts of wealth among ourselves and among the West Coast Indians are utterly different things. Obviously they are nothing of the kind, but they are measurably distinct and the nature of the difference must be sought in the total patterning of life in the two communities from which the particular pattern of wealth and its acquirement has been extracted. It should be fairly clear that where the patterns of manipulation of wealth are as different as they are in these two cases, it would be a mere exercise of the academic imagination to interpret the economic activities of one society in terms of the general economy which has been abstracted from the mode of life of the other.

These implications of culture for psychology are frequently lost sight of, especially in the course of inquiries dealing primarily with the behavior of individuals in western civilization where the cultural factor, common to both subject and investigator, has not been conceptualized by the latter as a human variable that must be properly controlled. Consequently, instead of taking familiar or widespread behavior patterns as constants which only define the limits of a group of individuals who have been subject to similar patterns of acquired behavior, they have been taken as common human constants. They have even been placed in the category of the "natural," "native" or "innate" responses, so that certain aspects of the behavior of man in western civilization have been considered as generically human.

The assumption once held that the syndrome of adolescence, as observed in western civilization, was a derivative of almost purely maturational processes is an outstanding example of this. Professor G. Murphy writes:[25]

> A generation ago, as a result of Stanley Hall's interest in and study of adolescence, this period was supposed to have special and peculiar characteristics dramatically developing at the moment of puberty. Subsequent investigations have tended to show that this clear-cut division of adolescence from the earlier and later periods is probably not justified; in fact, that for many young people, the changes which are involved in adolescence are no more startling and no more sudden (in our culture) in their development than the changes which come during, let us say, the period from 2 to 4 or 8 to 10 years. Some special studies of religion, e.g., and negativism, have shown that even such clear-cut characteristics of adolescence as we can now admit to exist are not completely dependent by any means on the mere effect of maturation. On the contrary, environmental differences of the sort which result from gross occupational or social differences, relations with one's immediate family, as well as the wider culture patterns of the group, are extremely important in determining not only the extent but the actual existence of the *Sturm und Drang* once considered an inevitable part of growing into manhood or womanhood. Indeed, it seems likely, as Mead[26] suggests, that even the emotional instabilities and tensions involved in the new sex adjustments of this period are in large part tied up with, if not the result of, the particular emotional and thought patterns which our civilization imposes upon our young.

The universality of masturbation in the maturational history of all human beings has also been inferred from the data obtained from relatively small samples of our own population,[27] and from clinical experience.[28] While it may be very well that the generalization is correct in respect to western society, it is not impossible that its prevalence in various classes of our population may even differ. One would also expect its incidence to vary with differences in the sex mores and the traditional attitudes toward early heterosexual experiences which exist in other societies.

At any rate, accurate generalizations in regard to generically human behavior responses must await the accumulation of much more detailed observations upon the lives of individuals subjected to diverse cultural patterns. Once this wider range of factual data is brought to bear upon problems of behavior, the importance of the cultural factor in human thought and action will be disclosed with more precision and clarity.

For the present, therefore, it is not only the recognition of objective differences in the culture patterns of the world's peoples and the delineation of them that is of importance; it is the significance of this fact in respect to the general psychological orientation and behavior of individuals.

III

It has not always been emphasized sufficiently that the very existence of varying culture patterns carries with it the psychological implication that the individuals of these societies actually live in different orders of reality. For the term reality can scarcely be regarded as having any absolute meaning content, unless it be used in a metaphysical sense to connote the ultimate nature of the phenomenal universe. But the physical sciences which, in western civilization, have aimed at a more definite interpretation of the phenomenal world than has ever been attempted before in human history, are less concerned with essences than with relations. Moreover, science itself looks with equanimity upon a changing interpretation of "reality." It is authoritative without being finalistic. Hypotheses are tested and retested and new interpretations emerge. Furthermore, denuded of the familiar sensory qualities that we ordinarily associate with physical objects, concepts of reality as defined by contemporary physicists have meaning chiefly within the context of the physical sciences themselves, and very little significance as such for the common man. But even within their own frame of scientific reference, one may now and again discern the reflection of western culture patterns. For surely the idea of a mathematically gifted creator of a mathematically patterned universe, as Jeans would have it, could only have been conceived in a society in which mathematics enjoyed special prestige.

Whatever the concept of reality arrived at through the procedures of the physical sciences may be, there remains a pragmatic usage of the term which is relevant to the comprehension of the determinants of human behavior and human psychology. Reality in this sense of the term does not primarily refer to discrete objects or persons as existents. The core of its connotations is functional. It defines the relations of human beings to the objects of their physical environment and other men in terms of the meanings and practical significance which these have had for them. These environmental and social relations of course involve psychological imponderables determined by the dynamic nature of the human organism on the one hand, and the content of the specific cultural heritage of human population on the other.

Human beings, that is to say, never live in a world of bare physical objects and events. They live in a meaningful universe. And the traditional culture patterns to which they become habituated define the specific meanings of that universe. Man's psychological responses to the physical objects of his external environment and to other human beings can only be understood, therefore, in terms of the traditional meanings which these latter have for him. He never views the outer world freshly or responds to his fellows entirely free from the influence which these meanings exert upon his thought and conduct. Celestial and meteorological phenomena, for example, or the plants and animals of man's habitat, even its inanimate forms, never are separated as such from the concepts of their essential nature and the beliefs about them that appear in the ideological tradition of a particular cultural heritage. Man's attitude toward them is a function of their reality as culturally defined, not in terms of their mere physical existence. Thus, to treat the physical environment in which a people lives, independently of the meaning that its multiform objects have for that people, involves a fundamental psychological distortion if we aim to comprehend the universe which is actually theirs. While useful in certain kinds of analysis, even the assertion that two peoples occupy the same natural environment because the regions inhabited by them exhibit the same climatic type, the same topography and biota can only have significance in the grossest physical sense. It is tantamount to ignoring the very data which have the most important psychological significance, namely the differences in meaning which similar objects of the phenomenal world have for peoples of different cultural traditions. Consequently, the objects of the external world *as meaningfully defined* in a traditional ideology constitute the reality to which the individuals habituated to a particular system of beliefs actually respond. As applied to the sphere of ecological relations, for example, an inventory of all the natural objects of a specific human habitat does not necessarily correspond to the "natural resources" of that habitat. The physical objects of the environment only enter the reality-order of the human population as a function of specific culture patterns. It is the knowledge and technological level of the culture of a people that determines their natural resources, not the mere presence of physical objects. To people without a tradition of pottery-making the presence of clay in their habitat is no more a natural resource than was the presence of coal and iron in the habitat of the pre-Columbian Indians of eastern North America. The economic geographer tacitly ignores this pragmatic fact when he lists the economic resources of the various regions of the world. They are only such from the standpoint of the culture to which he happens to belong.

Different concepts of time and space likewise create varying frameworks of reality as we pass from one cultural tradition to another. The non-quantitative concepts of most aboriginal peoples, for instance, tend to create such an enormous gap between this aspect of their thinking and the quantitative orientation of western thought that it is sometimes difficult or impossible to bridge. Among the Saulteaux, e.g., I found that it was extremely difficult for individuals concretely to grasp distances of a magnitude beyond their experience. Unable to employ any quantitative measure of distance that was intelligible to them, I do not believe that I ever succeeded in conveying any precise notion of the distance I had travelled to reach their country. Matters were further complicated by the fact that the *rate* of travel possible in different kinds of conveyances was not the sort of knowledge that could be taken for granted. Consequently, my attempt to convert distance into simple temporal units intelligible to them—nights on the "road," that is to say—made my home only twice the distance the mouth of the river lay from Lake Pekangikum, because I spent approximately the same number of nights on the boat and train between Philadelphia and the mouth of the river as I did in ascending the river to Lake Pekangikum. The differential factor, of course, was the speed of the train. This mode of conveyance not only was unknown to them except by hearsay, but there was no mode of travel in their experience that could, by analogy, convey in realistic fashion the speed of a train.

In western civilization temporal, like spatial concepts, have been elaborated and quantified to such a high degree that few activities of individuals escape their patterning. There are set hours for rising, eating, sleeping, working and so on. Trains leave at certain sub-divisions of the hour, and the feature picture at the movies or the speaker on the radio is scheduled to begin at a certain minute. Certain regular events take place weekly, monthly or yearly, which must be kept track of by means of a calendar or by memory, to say nothing of events at irregular intervals which may be scheduled by year, month, week, hour or minute.

This particular temporal emphasis in western culture, dependent as it is upon the invention of mechanical time-measuring and recording devices, is strikingly different from anything of the kind in earlier historic civilizations or in the cultures of non-literate peoples. Yet it is one of the basic realities to which individuals in our society must more or less successfully adapt themselves. Temporal orientation, moreover, is universally accepted as such a fundamental aspect of the individual's psychological adaptation in our society that disorientation in this regard alone is usually indicative of abnormality. A clinic patient so disoriented as to be unable to give the year, month or day of the week is almost sure to be suffering from amentia, senility or some psychic disorder. But a similar criterion would be entirely inapplicable in so far as year and day of the week are concerned, in some other culture in which the years are not even named, to say nothing of being numbered, and where the week as a unit of time-measurement does not exist. The absence of quantitative units of temporal measurement that can be applied to events in a past beyond the memory of living individuals, or their immediate forebears, likewise tends to induce a temporal order of reality among most primitive peoples that differentiates them from ourselves. Events of the distant past for them inevitably become entangled with mythological occurrences, thus creating an "historical" reality for them which is entirely divorced from any quantified scale of reference.

Beings of a purely conceptual nature also must be admitted to the culturally determined order of reality in which human beings live. Prayer, sacrifice, and worship are familiar activities that offer tangible evidence of the attitudes of man toward such beings. Sacred narratives in which they figure as protagonists also testify to the belief in their existence as do the more empirical tokens offered by the appearance of such beings in dreams or in other circumstances defined by cultural patterns. The malevolent force of witchcraft and demoniacal possession likewise must be reckoned among the pragmatic realities with which the patterns of human culture present us. Once indoctrinated with such concepts, human individuals tend to interpret particular events and experiences in a manner which offers empirical support to the traditional dogmas.

To dismiss all such beliefs as imaginary deflects attention from the determining role which they play in human behavior. Speaking in somewhat stricter psychological terms, conceptualization involves imaginative processes, but imagined objects may or may not be reified. Thus to point out that all conceptualized beings are imaginary objects is not equivalent to the assertion that such beliefs embody both imaginary *and* reified objects. Nor is it legitimate to equate the spiritual beings of primitive peoples with the imaginary playmates of children or other creations of the childish imagination. The imaginary playmates of children are temporary fantasies, however highly they may be reified in particular cases.[29] They are not the stabilized and culturally supported reifications of a traditional belief system. If a child maintained its belief in an imaginary playmate throughout life, it would obviously be no less than a psychotic symptom. On the other hand, the traditionally sanctioned concepts which are reified become real to the extent that they make demands upon human individuals in the same manner that physical objects and persons make demands. Spiritual beings no more can be ignored than can one's associates.

Thus, while belief systems that embody reified spiritual or supernatural beings may be compared to the delusional systems of individuals in the sense that they both belong to a category of false beliefs (as measured by objective evidence), their psychological importance is not at all diminished because of this fact. As an integral part of the traditional ideology of human populations, they are basic factors in determining the order of reality to which men adapt their behavior. Conduct is observed to be in accord with such beliefs. Human behavior, in fact, becomes unintelligible under certain circumstances unless it can be related to specific beliefs as a fundamental frame of reference.

But "delusional systems" whose matrix lies in traditional ideologies must be sharply distinguished from the private fantasies of individuals suffering from some type of mental disorder. So far as particular individuals are concerned, the etiological factors involved are quite distinct. To share the "delusional" beliefs traditional in one's own society is a normal phenomenon. To develop a private delusional system is abnormal, if not actually pathological. As a means of distinguishing between the etiology of such belief systems, however, the cultural background of the individual must be comprehended as well as his personal experiences.

Some years ago a negro committed to a mental hospital and thought to be suffering from private delusions was discovered by a psychiatrist to belong to a local religious cult of which his ideology was characteristic. In another case,

> an elderly Neapolitan cobbler comes to a hospital clinic with a rambling story told in broken English. His account wanders from headaches and listlessness to an old woman who has made him sick. He is referred to the neuro-psychiatric department with the comment: "Question of psychosis." Examination brings out little more than irrelevant detail about the enemy and how long she has wished him ill, and why, and how she makes his head hurt. There is all the first indication of a persecutory delusion. The man is told to come back with an interpreter. He returns with a fluent Italian-American who explains apologetically that the old man is illiterate and believes the woman is a witch and has cast the evil eye on him. The apparent delusion dissolves into a bit of superstition typical generally of the

lower orders of Neapolitan society. What is a normal belief there is a psychotic symptom in one of our hospitals. If the writer or reader of these lines were to harbor the same conviction as this Neapolitan, it would be *prima facie* evidence of mental derangement. The norm of one culture is a sign of nervous pathology in the other.[30]

Hence the necessity of taking the immediate cultural background of the individual into account as a primary frame of reference.

Cases of *folie a deux* indicate how occasionally delusional systems originally confined to one individual may be acquired by other persons through mechanisms of identification.[31] When the content of such ideologies is religious, a cult or sect may spring up as a whole series of persons becomes involved. The history of religions is replete with such instances.

In the sphere of interpersonal relations, the canalizing of social intercourse by different cultural patterns offers another level of reality to which the individual must adjust himself. One generic difference between all human societies, on the one hand, and infra-human primates, on the other, is the presence of incest restrictions in the former and the complete absence of them in the latter. This observational fact in itself implies a fundamental psychological difference in the reality orders of man as compared with the lower primates, so far as interpersonal relations are concerned. Again, human societies differ markedly among themselves in respect to the extension of incest tabus beyond the primary blood relatives—parents and children, and brother and sister—as well as in traditionally determined emotional attitudes toward the infringement of such restrictions. While we know a great deal about avoidances of the incest class from a formal point of view, we know very little about cases of deviation and their psychological involvements. In view of the emphasis laid by psychoanalysts upon the Oedipus complex and the determining influence of it in the subsequent life history of the individual, purely formal statements in regard to incest are of little psychological value. The concept "incest taboo" needs breaking down into the specific avoidances included; how they are built up in the individual; the responses of individuals to these inhibitions in terms of dreams, neurotic symptoms, or overt deviational behavior, as well as information on the punishment or rationalization of these latter responses when they occur. The significant psychological differences in the social realities imposed by different cultures, in terms of actual demands made upon the individual by the canalization of native impulses, may then emerge with greater clarity.

The culture patterns of human societies do more than determine the general framework of a reality-order to which all the individuals of a particular society are compelled more or less successfully to adjust themselves. The typical and even the specific situations with which individuals are faced during the course of their lives are derivations of different orders of the cosmic, ecological and social reality defined by different culture patterns. Situations arise in one society that might never occur in another; and what appears to be the same situation objectively is actually different because its cultural context is different.

In the economic sphere, for instance, the inability of millions of people to secure work during the depression, and the necessity for them to accept public or private relief while at the same time a surplus of certain commodities was available and the machinery of production unimpaired, is a situation which is inconceivable, perhaps, except within the context of western civilization. While game or crops may fail in societies with simpler economic patterns, and starvation may ensue, neither the unemployment nor relief situation would arise. Moreover, in societies which do not depend upon a market as the major distributive institution, goods on the one hand and human needs on the other are more closely integrated. That unique paradox—scarcity in the midst of plenty—could not arise.

On the other hand, illness is a universal situation to which all human beings are subject whatever their cultural heritage. But a belief that illness may be due to witchcraft, when typical of a culture, precipitates anxieties and fears if an individual falls sick that would not have to be faced by most persons in western civilization. Consequently, the necessity that a human individual face the fact of his illness is not the sole "reality" involved. Illness as such cannot be dissociated from theories of disease causation entertained. These are intrinsically bound up with the culture patterns of particular societies. In any disease situation the reality-order of one culture may induce psychological involvements which are entirely absent in a parallel situation in another.

The so-called "escape from reality" which the mental symptoms of deranged individuals are so often said to provide must be understood as a flight from some particular order of reality or some specific situation which the individual has difficulty in facing in terms of the conventional adjustments demanded by the culture patterns of that society.[32] It is never a flight from reality in an absolute sense. One might infer, however, from the comparisons which have often been drawn between the belief systems and mythologies of the so-called primitive peoples, the day dreams of children and the fantasies of psychotic individuals in western civilization, that all these types of thought were flights from "reality," and actually belonged in the same category. But if we accept this parallel at its face value, what status have the fantasies of children reared in societies whose culturally patterned beliefs are themselves a "flight from reality"? What of the dreams of adults? And what of the fantasies of deranged individuals of these societies? It is all very confusing unless we admit the relative connotation of reality and, taking different reality-orders at their face values, use them as the primary standards of reference with respect to the conformity or non-conformity of the ideology of individuals to them.

It would be unnecessary to stress this point were it not for the fact that the beliefs of primitive peoples have so frequently been taken indiscriminately to represent an earlier stage of mental evolution than that which has been achieved by the populations of western civilization.

Since, on this hypothesis of a biogenetic law, ontogeny recapitulates phylogeny, the mentality of children reared in western civilization is presumed to be comparable to that of primitives; and psychotics, at least in part, are assumed to have regressed to a more primitive level of mentality. Even if this hypothesis were true, however, there is a further difficulty. It involves the assumption of a racial mind or racial conscious to make it entirely plausible. Else the actual comparability of the *group* beliefs of primitive peoples of diverse historical origins with the day dreams or fantasies of individuals in western civilization remains in question, except as pure analogy. For no historic continuity can be demonstrated between these primitive cultures and that of western civilization. Moreover, by assuming the undifferentiated psychic life of individuals, genuine problems are ignored. How do individuals in these societies adjust to *their* worlds? What are the psychic strains and stresses of *their* social, economic and religious orders? Are their inner conflicts due to etiological factors similar to, or identical with, those which occur in western civilization? What are the characteristics of the fantasy levels to which *they* regress when psychoses occur? What are the terms of rationalization, compensation and sublimation which the culture patterns of their society provide? And so forth.

Inquiries along these lines assume nothing except comparable relations between individuals with similar native impulses and psychic mechanisms, and culturally defined reality orders which demand adaptation of varying kinds. The processes by which the individuals of a single organic species conform to, or the degree to which they depart from, the culture patterns of different societies, offer genuine control data for comparison with the observations already made in western civilization.

Thus the framework of the reality-order to which individuals of different human societies adjust as well as the situations encountered must be understood in their psychological aspects as functions of traditional culture patterns. Consequently it is not only vague but unintelligible to speak of human beings adjusting themselves to reality without a specific understanding of what is actually implied by this term. Adjustment is never to physical objects or persons as discrete entities, as we have attempted to show, nor to sickness as an event. The relations of man to physical objects and persons are everywhere defined traditionally, and these relations themselves are crucial to an understanding of the reality-order in which men live. And illness is psychologically unintelligible without an understanding of the cultural context of disease causation of which it is a specific manifestation, in the mind of the sufferer.

From a psychological point of view, therefore, human beings adjust to specific reality-orders, rather than to reality in an absolute or abstract sense. Life itself only has meaning and significance in terms of the traditionally determined universe with which men are familiar. So long as human beings act *as if* their beliefs were true, an understanding of their behavior must proceed from the premises implicit or explicit in their versions of reality. Whether their particular beliefs are true or false in any absolute sense is irrelevant for this type of inquiry.

Since the locus of different orders of reality lies in the traditional culture patterns of different societies, the reality-order in which these human beings live becomes the psychological counterpart of these patterns. They must be our primary frame of reference for an understanding of the behavior of the individual.

IV

Whether a community be viewed as a series of persons whose acquired idea and action patterns integrate their lives in characteristic fashion, or whether we describe the modal forms of behavior in any community in terms of culture patterns, it is obvious that new individuals constantly appear in the group through birth, and others withdraw by death. Such changes in the actual personnel of human communities are not observed to be concomitant with essential changes in the group's pattern of living; hence some writers have emphasized the supra-individual character of culture. Culture patterns thus are treated as something *sui generis*, independent of the individuals from whose thought and overt behavior such patterns have been generalized. The implicit assumption seems to be that cultural continuity is maintained by the continual birth of new individuals who will manifest the same behavior patterns as those who have died. It is quite true that the continuity of culture patterns over a series of generations is an observed fact, and also that gross cultural changes have received constant attention. A deeper understanding, however, of the very nature and functioning of culture—to say nothing of the forces effective in cultural change—requires a more detailed knowledge of what actually happens to the neonata who are precipitated into the midst of a group of human beings whose behavior conforms to established patterns, and who vary in degree of physical maturation.

We know, of course, that the human individual comes into the world provided at birth with a psychobiological equipment that permits the acquisition of a wide range of adaptive behavior patterns. But he is likewise equipped with instinctual urges that demand gratification. The cultural patterns of different societies, while tending to canalize his responses in different ways, inevitably permit some means, however restricted, of gratifying hunger, sex and ego assertion. In its ontological development, therefore, the human organism is faced with the problem of adapting itself on the one hand to the restrictions imposed by the particular cultural forms and on the other to achieving satisfaction for its instinctual impulses. Broadly speaking, the individual is primarily a resultant of these two sets of forces. The maturational process, according to Gesell,[33] exerts a regulatory function on the course of their interaction. The native endowment is

> built up through the selective stresses of growth, and is a product of growth as well as of inheritance. Not all potentialities are realized, but only those which pass the mesh of already attained organization. . . . The environment furnishes the foil and the milieu for the manifestations of development, but these manifestations come from inner compulsion and are primarily organized by inherent mechanisms and by an intrinsic physiology of development. The very plasticity of growth requires that there be limiting and regulatory mechanisms.
>
> Growth is a process so intricate and so sensitive that there must be powerful stabilizing factors, intrinsic rather than extrinsic, which preserve the balance of the total pattern and the direction of the growth trend. Maturation is, in a sense, a name for this regulatory mechanism. Just because we do not grant complete dichotomy of internal and external factors, it is necessary to explain what keeps the almost infinite fortuities of physical and social environment from dominating the organism of the developing individual. The organismal concept requires that the individual shall maintain an optimum or normal integrity. The phenomena of maturation suggest the stabilizing and inexpugnable factors which safeguard the basic patterns of growth. Just as the respiration of the organism depends upon the maintenance of constant hydrogen-ion concentration, so, probably on a vastly more intricate scale, the life-career of the individual is maintained by the physiological process of growth in which the maturational mechanisms play an important role. The role is not conspicuous in infancy, but it persists throughout the life-cycle until the growth potential completely subsides.[33]

Speaking in general terms we also know that the development of "mind" is a function of an adaptive process to the different reality-orders of particular human societies, rather than an unfolding of some entity within the confines of the organism itself,[34] independent of the individual's responses to persons and things. Many years ago Dewey pointed out[35] that one of Gabriel Tarde's most fruitful psychological conceptions, far ahead of his time, passed almost unnoticed. This was the idea that "all psychological phenomena can be divided into the physiological and the social, and that when we have relegated elementary sensation and appetite to the former head, all that is left of our mental life, our beliefs, ideas and desires falls within the scope of social psychology." More recent developments, writes Dewey, have provided "an unexpected confirmation of the insight of Tarde that what we call 'mind' means essentially the working of certain beliefs and desires, and that these in the concrete—in the only sense in which mind may be said to exist—are functions of associated behavior, varying with the structure and operation of social groups." Thus instead of being viewed as "an antecedent and ready-made thing," mind

> represents a reorganization of original activities through their operation in a given environment. It is a formation, not a datum, a product and a cause only after it has been produced. Now theoretically it is possible that the reorganization of native activities which constitute mind may occur, through their exercise within a purely physical medium. Empirically, however, this is highly improbable. A consideration of the dependence in infancy of the organization of the native activities into intelligence upon the presence of others, upon sharing in joint activities and upon language, makes it obvious that the sort of mind capable of development through the operation of native endowment in a non-social environment is of the moron order, and is practically if not theoretically negligible.

A limited amount of observational data, moreover, seems to support this view. Individuals cut off from interpersonal relations with their fellow human beings, whether through social isolation or sensory defects, appear to suffer from such marked mental retardation, even though natively equipped—as was Helen Keller—with potentially normal capacities, that they can at times scarcely be admitted to the human category except in a purely zoological sense.[36]

Thus, while full and complete mental maturation is as inseparable from social processes as bodily maturation is from physiological processes, and while the mechanisms involved in learning have commanded no less attention than the organic aspects of the human life cycle, the processes by which the varying culture patterns of different human societies become determining components in the behavior of individuals have been neglected almost completely.

These processes must be considered from a genetic point of view. To begin with, the individual is never exposed to the total cultural patterns of a society as such. In infancy only a single facet of them enters the world of the child—the aspect which pertains to the care of infants. As maturation proceeds, exposure to still other aspects occurs, and so on. Consequently, the world of the child is substantially a sub-cultural reality order. It is never precisely identical with that of parents or elders and the realities of adulthood.[37] This difference is partly due to maturational limitations—the development of childish versions of experiences and customs not yet fully understood in the same terms as adults understand them—and partly to specifically cultural factors. In western civilization, for example, fairy tales are considered to be the "natural" literary diet for the earlier years of childhood while in many aboriginal societies children and adults both listen to the same body of narratives. Thus the analogy, sometimes based upon this fact, between the mental level of primitives and children is scarcely to the point since the fairy tale diet of our children is culturally conditioned and not a natural demand. Besides, the function of mythology among pre-literate peoples—insofar as their oral narratives are sacred tales which support a religious ideology—is quite different from the function of fairy tales for children in our society. The real analogy in our society to the mythology of primitive peoples is much of the Old Testament literature.

Likewise, the concealment of sexual facts from children in western civilization is a specific cultural pattern, the argument sometimes advanced that the "child mind" is not prepared for such revelations being a patent rationalization of our practices. In other societies no such restrictions in knowledge may be found, and even a limited observation of the sexual life of adults is possible.

Furthermore, contrary to the tendency toward "spontaneous" animistic thinking on the part of the children of western civilization which has now and again been emphasized by students of child psychology, Mead's investigation of Manus children[38] revealed "a negativism towards explanations couched in animistic rather than actual cause and effect terms." She even found the Manus child to be less "spontaneously animistic and less traditionally animistic than is the Manus adult." The explanation lay in culturally determined conditions: (1) a language unenriched by metaphor, sex gender or developed imagery, (2) emphasis upon matter-of-fact adjustments to the physical conditions of the environment with no tendency upon the part of adults to suggest or encourage fanciful explanations like the English mother who told her child that "had already spent hours examining the internal structure of a piano that the sounds were made by little fairies who stood on the wires and sang,"[39] and (3) the practical exclusion of the child from religious ideology and mythical narratives which "are for men and women, not for children."[38]

Hence, cultural factors as well as physical and mental immaturity must be considered as determinants in the differentiation of the child's world from that of adults in different societies.

It must also be recognized that the specific acquisition of behavior

patterns by the individual must be conceived as a function of his relations to particular persons, things and situations. It is through processes of interaction that idea and action patterns are mediated to the
growing individual, and it is in terms of these patterns that subsequent
adult behavior must be understood.

Of primary importance in the initial stages of this process are the
relations of parents and children. Parents groom the child for its role
in the social, economic and religious structure of a given society. As
a part of this process also the acquisition of speech bit by bit must
not be overlooked. Speech is not only of importance in communication; from the start it is a fundamental mechanism for the control
of one's relations with other persons, whether from the standpoint
of the parent or that of the child, and, in a wider sense, for social
control. The differentiation of kin in all human societies is not only
a classificatory device, nor terms of relationship only a mode of address; the psychological attitudes toward different kin and conventional behavior toward them are inseparable from the terms themselves.
Without speech it is inconceivable how incest tabus could have developed or operated successfully.

The conditioning of the child to culturally approved modes of
behavior is not exclusively a conscious one,[40] or one involving intellectual processes alone. On the contrary, the affective aspects of the
process are of primary importance, however difficult they may be to
thoroughly unravel. Psychoanalytic hypotheses are the most important contributions to be considered in this connection, particularly
the emphasis laid upon infant sexuality.[41] From the very beginning
psychoanalysis laid stress upon inter-personal relations and in particular upon the unconscious affective involvements of the child in relation to its parents. The particular configuration of these affects which
run their course in the first five years of life is assumed to be crucial
for the inner organization of the instinctual impulses for the remainder
of the individual's life history. It is through the psychological process
of identification with parents and the introjection of their prescrip-
tive commands that a super-ego is built up which functions as an
inner source of control for the instinctual impulses.

The parents, then, are the first surrogates of the cultural patterns
of a particular society to which the individual is ordinarily exposed.
The physical dependency of the child upon them—the so-called pro-
longation of infancy—not only makes the latter the first objects of
vital affective interest, but in turn makes the affective bond a dynamic
fulcrum for the inculcation of the habits deemed conventional for
the child in the earliest years of its development when the organism
is the most plastic. The child does not acquire the culture patterns
of its group through the simple process of imitating the behavior of

parents, except to some degree in the field of speech. Even in the latter case the imitation of the speech sounds of parents is not accompanied by the meaning content which words have for adults. The use of language depends upon common experiences and the definition of the meaning of experiences. Its acquisition is not merely the process of acquiring a repertoire of sounds. What the child is encouraged to acquire are the patterns of child behavior typical of a particular society. A further problem, however, is involved here. Just as patterns of child behavior differ from culture to culture, so do the means by which parents and elders exercise their authority over the child. It is extremely important to know, then, the precise means employed to induce the child to conform to the behavior patterns considered appropriate for his age and sex, and particularly to what extent such behavior is motivated by the arousal of shame, fear, disgust, etc., and the emotional expression of approval and disapproval on the part of the parents.

If as in Samoa, writes Mead, the standard adult picture is of a grave and graceful personality, one which measures all things carefully and expends little emotion on any one of them, one which is concerned with the ordering of social life and profoundly uninterested in any form of individual experience, one which discredits haste or undue precocity, then we must know by what means the society moulds each generation into such a pattern, what types of individuals it finds most intractable, what devices it employs to discourage the precocious and mute the energy and enterprise of the over-aggressive. In the course of investigations such as this, which are essential to a final understanding of the adult culture, we can also test out the various theories of childhood experience as definitive in the formation of personality. The restless aggressive urge of a Manus man to get ahead, to attain economic security, to throw off his obligation of cooperating with an older relative, can only be understood thoroughly if we know of the uncontrolled social life which Manus children lead, the free rein which is given to their aggressiveness, the amount of security and self-confidence which they are permitted to develop, only to have it all suddenly taken away from them at marriage. Only by a record of the whole life span of the individual, and especially of the methods of education, formal and informal, can the adult personality be understood.[42]

V

The very fact that different human populations are characterized by distinguishable and persistent culture patterns indicates that the behavior of individuals added to these groups by birth tends to be moulded to the pre-existent culture. The processes of assimilation already referred to obviously function to this end, although our knowledge of them in detail is meager. That the processes of cultural acquisition by the individual are likewise among the primary forces involved in the formation of personality must also be recognized. For no matter what weight is given to innate factors, to unique experiences or early responses of particular children, the personality of individuals cannot escape the influences derived from the cultural configurations of some specific human society. It is to be expected, therefore, that individuals who have been exposed to the influences of a common cultural heritage will exhibit some personality traits and tendencies in common. This fact is popularly recognized in the distinguishable characteristics of individuals of different European national groups, although commonly attributed to innate "racial" factors. Actually, all that it is necessary to assume is some correlation between the cultural heritage of a population (in the case of Europe, sub-cultural areas of western civilization considered as a unit) and the specific integration in the individuals of that population of characteristic personality traits bound up with established culture patterns. This does not mean, of course, that individuals do not differ in specific personality traits or in the organization of them, nor that any one individual necessarily represents in microcosm a cultural configuration as a whole. But it does mean that common traits and personality trends are discernible in a series of individuals who have been subjected to the same culture patterns and that the former cannot be thoroughly understood without reference to the latter.

From this point of view, what have often been regarded as character and personality traits of racial derivation are seen to be individual responses commonly derived from the values intrinsic to the culture patterns of particular human societies. The stoical, imperturbable Red Man is one such personality stereotype. The suppression of emotional expression, however, which is really the nub of this characterization, is by no means biologically intrinsic to the Indian. It is connected demonstrably with different culture patterns. "Not all American Indians react in the same way. There is no stoical tradition, for example, among the Pueblos of the Southwest, or among many of the Mexican tribes; the Huichol in Mexico are lively and vociferous, differing greatly from the usual American Indian stereotype,"[43] Klineberg[44] describes them as "a gay and sociable group, emotional, laughing easily and often, quickly aroused to anger and as quickly appeased." Even among groups like the Plains Indians, where a stoical tradition actually exists, emotional expression under certain conditions, such as the death of a relative, is encouraged to an extreme degree. Moreover, the Assiniboine were actually known to early explorers as "The Weepers" because of their characteristic custom of profuse weeping upon meeting relatives after a considerable absence, or even when greeting strangers.

Thus, neither the inhibition nor the expression of emotion can be regarded as being a racial manifestation on the one hand, or a peculiarly intimate and individual response of the human personality on the other. The occasions when emotions are expressed or suppressed, the particular form of expression encouraged, as well as the degree considered desirable, can only be understood thoroughly in relation to the moulding forces of culture upon the individual.

Bravery has likewise been stressed as an essential character trait of many American Indian tribes, as if it were something peculiarly intrinsic to the individual. But little, if any, analysis has been made of the psychological and cultural factors that may be involved. In this connection Mr. David Rodnick tells me that no Assiniboine ever joined a war party or exposed himself to danger without a personal dream or vision in which he received assurance that he would remain unscathed. This supernatural support was essential to the enterprise, and obviously points to a psychological context, inseparable from a particular culture pattern and essential for an understanding of the bravery exhibited by these individuals.

A parallel ideology in the case of an individual came to my attention among the northern Saulteaux where there is no war tradition. At the time of the (first) World War a man had a dream which was interpreted to mean that he was invulnerable. He never enlisted but he assured me that if he had he would have come back safe and sound. In other cultures, of course, bravery of individuals would have a different psychological context.

Bravery in the abstract, then, has little meaning as a character trait. It is a mode of response that functions in a specific cultural context. Its psychological significance must be interpreted with reference to the cultural background of the individual, the supporting motivations which this supplies, as well as the situations which call forth its manifestation. Consequently, it may be assumed that bravery as a typical personality trait of individuals in particular societies is indissolubly linked with relevant culture patterns.[45]

Since the personality traits engendered by the culture patterns of one society may differ radically from those emphasized by another, it may happen that where individuals of these different cultural backgrounds come into contact the characteristic behavior of one group may fall into a category of conduct despised by the other. This seems to have occurred when the Ojibwa-speaking peoples moved westward in the late 18th century and later came into intimate contact with the white traders and settlers in Manitoba. One of the names by which they became known here was Bungi. This term seems to have been derived from a native word meaning "a little of something." The Indians were always asking the whites for a little of this and a little of that. From the white man's point of view they were persistent beggars. The name they received symbolized their outstanding character trait—begging, a habit for which they are reviled to this day. But this trait is simply the obverse of the emphasis laid in their native culture upon giving. Food, articles of clothing, even pipes and other items circulate freely among those who need them. If children are given food or candy, for instance, they will share it at once with their playmates. Among adults, those who have anything always share what they have with the "have-nots." It is not surprising that the Indians should have carried over these culturally determined habits in their social intercourse with traders, missionaries and settlers. How could they have done otherwise, particularly in view of the fact that they found themselves in the have-not class with respect to so many novelties that the whites possessed? So, to the white man with radically different institutionalized patterns of distributing commodities, and a different evaluation of the personality trait exhibited by the Saulteaux, they became Bungi-beggars.

But the common personality trends which receive the full stamp of approval by one society may, from the standpoint of the personality values familiar to another, involve departures much more radical than the habits of the Saulteaux. The personality characteristics engendered may actually be analogous to, although not identical in etiology with, the pathological traits of individuals in another society. An outstanding example of this is the paranoid traits of the Indians of the Northwest coast when considered from the standpoint of the clinical data on paranoia known to western civilization.

"All existence," writes Benedict of these Indians, "was seen in terms of insult." There was an amazing megalomania expressed, and self-glorification, on the one hand, combined with a withering ridicule of opponents, on the other. Correspondingly, the typical polarity of emotions swung between a sense of triumph over rivals and intensely experienced shame.

> Not only derogatory acts performed by a neighbor or an enemy, but all untoward events, like a cut when one's axe slipped, or a ducking when one's canoe overturned, were insults. All alike threatened first and foremost one's ego security, and the first thought one was allowed was how to get even, how to wipe out the insult. Grief was little institutionalized, but sulking took its place. Until he had resolved upon a course of action by which to save his face after any misfortune, whether it was the slipping of a wedge in felling a tree, or the death of a favorite child, an Indian of the Northwest Coast retired to his pallet with his face to the wall and neither ate nor spoke. He rose from it to follow some course which, according to the traditional rules, should reinstate him in

his own eyes and those of the community; to distribute property enough to wipe out the stain, or to go head-hunting in order that somebody else should be made to mourn. His activities in either case were specific responses to the bereavement he had just passed through, but were elaborately directed toward getting even. If he had not the money to distribute and did not succeed in killing someone to humiliate another, he might take his own life. He staked everything, in his view of life, upon a certain picture of the self, and, when the bubble of his self-esteem was pricked, he had no interest, no occupation to fall back on, and the collapse of his inflated ego left him prostrate.[46]

The psychoanalytic theories of character formation[47] were developed without taking into account the possible moulding influences which different cultural forms may exert upon personality structure. It seems likely, however, that the personality traits of adults which are assumed to be the result of a certain amount of libido fixation at the oral, anal and genital levels, may be influenced by different patterns of child care and thus vary in their incidence from culture to culture, as well as among the individuals of the same society. It is obviously more difficult to establish the general occurrence of the character types distinguished by the psychoanalysts than it is to differentiate these as a result of the personal analysis of individuals. The problem, nevertheless, is an interesting and important one. As a result of his observations among the Australians and other aboriginal peoples Róheim[48] has stressed the "oral optimist" and "oral sadist" strands in the character of the central Australians and has attempted to account for the prevalence of such character traits among them in terms of specific patterns in the parent and child relationships. He believes that it is possible to discover a formula for the collective or group character of a people in the typical traumata to which children habitually are subjected.[49]

The important difference between the Central Australian native and our individual neurotic is that in the former the libidinal shock or infantile trauma is conditioned by custom. It is an habitual trauma, a common experience, and will also be abreacted or dealt with collectively. . . . What I believe is that there is such a thing as a group character and that it is based on the collective sublimation of customary traumata, although, of course, not without individual deviations from the standard type. A primitive society might be defined as a society in which these deviations are small, i.e., in which the behavior of the parents is more uniform than in an advanced society. When we shall have more workers in the field trained in the use of analytic technique we shall probably find that the leading symptoms or characteristic features of primitive tribes can be explained as being derived from the infantile traumata which habitually occur in these societies. This is what I mean by an *onto-genetic theory of culture.* . . . This view of culture means an approach to theories put forward by the modern anthropological school (Malinowski, Mrs. Seligman) who, like myself, believe that the specific determining factors for the development of each type of civilization, and also for the character development of the individual, can be found in the family situation.[50]

A deeper and more thoroughly detailed elucidation of the relation between the culture patterns of different societies and associated personality traits should not blind us, however, to another problem of equal importance.

While it has been assumed from time to time that little, if any, variability in individual behavior was characteristic of the so-called primitive peoples, closer observation inevitably has disclosed the fact that even in these relatively homogeneous cultures variability in personality traits, as well as in talent, thought and behavior occurs.[51] Individuals are not completely moulded to a common pattern despite the forces at work which tend to produce this result. Perhaps a state of thorough-going regimentation of thought and action is impossible. It may conceivably be approached but never completely realized. Gross similarities must not be allowed to obscure the minutiae of genuine differences in thought and conduct. A great deal depends upon how our observations are scaled. The handwriting expert will detect individual peculiarities that escape the untrained eye, while the casual observer may be content to note generic similarities in styles of handwriting.

Indeed, the very nature of culture allows for such variations. It is not a die which stamps out succeeding generations of individuals indistinguishable in all their habits and beliefs. It defines ends for which individuals strive and at the same time provides correlative means for accomplishing them, for gratifying human desires within traditional limits. Even speech with all its established formalisms permits a certain amount of variability, provided that its functions of communication and social control can be served, within the context in which it is operative. As Allport[52] has shown, even the highly ritualized and repetitive act of crossing one's self with holy water, performed by Roman Catholics upon entering a church, varies widely among individuals. The significant thing here, as in many other aspects of culture, is the *purpose* of the act. Its form is subordinate to the end which it serves. Indeed, culture patterns as they actually function must be considered with reference to ends as well as means. For the individual to whom these ends are of primary importance, considerable latitude in ways of accomplishing them is often possible, unless the culture itself strongly emphasizes the formal aspects of act and thought. This is often the case in magic and ritual, and our own conscious emphasis upon grammatical speech is a further example. Emphasis upon strict tenets of established religious belief, as, e.g., the Trinity, is another instance, but on the other hand in many religious systems such precise formulations are unemphasized so that more variability in the conceptualization of deity may be expected, yet culturally determined notions of a characteristic form will no less prevail. Considered from the standpoint of the individual believer, the ends which religious behavior serves are important no matter what aspects of ritual or belief are traditionally emphasized. The same is true in the technological sphere, in economic life and in social life.

But since the attention of ethnologists has been principally centered upon the typical (or modal) aspects of group life and thought, as abstracted in terms of culture patterns, the problems connected with variability in individual behavior, the role of the individual as such in different societies and the extent to which its institutions serve his personal needs have been indifferently treated, if at all. No wonder, then, that investigators in other fields who dipped into older ethnological literature in order to discover something about the psychology of primitive man discovered a "group mind," a "pre-logical mentality," or came to the conclusion that myths could be equated with dreams, and neurotic compulsions and avoidances with primitive rites and taboos.[53] There was scarcely anything about the behavior of flesh and blood individuals and the degree to which their behavior conformed to, or departed from, the abstract culture patterns of the group. Individual and culture were practically identical. There were no dreams of individuals to be found, or, if so, they conformed to conveniently determined dream patterns. Hence, myths, having so many characteristics of the dreams of individuals in western civilization, became the dreams of a "group mind" or primitive mentality. Incest taboos likewise became exaggerated in their prohibitory incidence, since successful infractions were not ordinarily recorded and the severe penalties characteristic of some peoples were generalized into a generic horror of incest typical everywhere of primitive man. Consequently, the operation of exogamy was likewise overstressed since deviations were not systematically investigated. In the collection of myths Professor Boas was probably the first to insist that series of variants from the same people be collected rather than what was assumed to be a typical version by the investigator.

Nevertheless, the characteristic emphasis upon the typical behavior of different human groups among ethnologists led to the recognition of how profoundly different the cultural configurations of different human populations actually were, and to the exposure of specious generalizations about primitive man, primitive mind and primitive culture as unitary entities. Indeed, the task of accurately recording the culture patterns of innumerable human communities, to say nothing of determining the chronology of culture changes and the inter-relation between peoples with different culture patterns, has been an enormously difficult one. For the purposes of inter-group comparisons and gross chronological relations, generalizations in respect to typical modes of life, technologies, beliefs, etc., were sufficient. In this frame of reference the individual as such could be conveniently ignored, as could also variations in the significance of beliefs for different individuals, the infraction of custom by deviant individuals, to say nothing of variations in personality traits, dreams or psychic strains and stresses related to particular culture patterns or connected with specific situations arising under purely native conditions or as a result of acculturation processes and cultural change.

It is interesting to note that during the period when ethnologists were building up more and more detailed and comprehensive descriptions of the typical behavior patterns of human communities and paying little attention to the differential behavior of individuals, there arose in psychology, with Galton, a profound interest in individual differences themselves, which led to systematic inquiries that have grown to such marked proportions in recent decades of psychological investigation.

Due to the fact that such investigations at first gave almost exclusive emphasis to physiological and psychological variables,[54] dissociated for the most part from their social significance even in western civilization, no link seemed discernible between such inquiries and the culturally oriented studies that were being undertaken.

Contemporaneously, however, in one field of anthropological investigation, data on individual differences were accumulating. These were observations on the variations in bodily traits which had racial significance. But such anthropometric observations were inevitably undertaken to provide the basis for making *group* comparisons. Whether intra-community or tribal variations in the physical or physiological characteristics of individuals had any psychological, sociological or economic significance in terms of the culture patterns of the people, was a question not considered. Today it still remains a problem open for investigation. Yet in western civilization physique is a recognized qualification for certain occupations (policemen, soldiers), and perhaps an unformalized qualification for others.[55] Herskovits' study of the role of skin color differences in negro mating,[56] that is the tendency for dark men to marry light women, is an example of the social significance that individual variability within a racial type may possess.

Group differences in specific psychological capacities or general level of intelligence have likewise been the focus of attention in many investigations rather than inquiries into the possible functional significance of these differences in terms of the life histories, occupations and social adjustments of individuals in societies with different culture patterns.

Do measurable differences in general—musical ability, for example—act selectively in the emergence of prominent singers and drummers in primitive societies? Or is a good memory (the capacity to remember a large repertoire of songs) or some other quality more important? Is a high level of general intelligence actually a *sine qua non* for leadership in certain enterprises, for chieftainship, ceremonial leadership, etc.? Is there any correlation between sensory acuity or special abilities and success in any particular occupation or craft?

The investigation of such problems would require an adaptation of techniques and methodologies not yet even fully perfected for use in western civilization. But a specialized field for investigation lies open here which might be more fruitful than the gross comparison of group differences, as well as providing another angle of attack upon the functioning of the human individual in relation to the varying culture patterns of different societies.

While individual variations in discernible anatomical and physiological traits and in abilities of various kinds may have positive, negative or indifferent significance in relation to the culture patterns of different societies, a factor which M. A. May[57] has called an "integral variable," is perhaps of even greater importance. Individuals differ (a) in the degree and manner in which their respective organic traits, native capacities and acquired behavior patterns are organized, and (b) in the way they function as personalities in relation to the other members of the society in which they live. The former aspect of integral variability is one which only exceedingly intimate, detailed and prolonged studies of individuals can elucidate. The latter is open to more general observation.

It has already been pointed out that the culture patterns of a given society tend to engender certain personality traits which are favored to the exclusion of others. But it must be likewise recognized that the modes of personal integration stressed in different societies and the type of behavior demanded are by no means equally congenial to all individuals. Deviational behavior must consequently be taken into account to round out realistically the total picture of human behavior in a society. Data on deviational behavior also help to throw the typical behavior patterns of the society into stronger relief, and help to expose the functioning of social institutions. The relation of individual deviants to cultural change is a further problem.

The data on deviational behavior range all the way from idiosyncrasies in speech, dress, personal mannerisms, foibles, etc., through cases of immorality, crime, and religious heresy to pathological behavior.

But the frame of reference to be kept in mind is always the culturally defined series of norms of a particular society, not those derived from the scale of values of some other society (that of the observer in particular) or some ideal norm.

Homosexual behavior, for example, cannot be considered as morally or pathologically deviant in societies where the cultural patterns provide an established place for it.[58] Nor can homicide be considered in the category of crime where it occurs under culturally sanctioned conditions (e.g., war, human sacrifice, infanticide, blood feud, cases where aged persons or potential cannibals (windigos) are killed). Similarly, where dissociative phenomena[59] and catalepsy[60] are institutionalized, they do not fall within the category of morbidity or disease as defined by that society, although other pathological manifestations may. Even in western society the sharp distinction between the normal and the pathological that once prevailed is rapidly breaking down.

It is impossible to overemphasize the fact that there is no definite dividing line between the normal, the psychoneurotic and the psychotic reactions. The normal reactions shade imperceptibly into the neurotic and the neurotic into the psychotic. There will obviously, therefore, be many reactions which will be difficult to assign to any particular group. The greatest difficulty here is the deplorable lack of knowledge of what is normal. Despite the fact that we use the term 'normal' quite glibly, there has as yet been no extensive and satisfactory study of what is normal. The ignorance regarding the social history of the average individual is astounding. We know practically nothing about the average family; the questions of petty thievery and sex play among children. These occurrences and many others are thought to be of grave importance in maladjusted individuals, but the foundations for such beliefs are totally unknown.

It is entirely conceivable, therefore, that what is thought to be abnormal by one investigator may be considered quite within the range of normal by another. There is, however, considerable difference between the well-developed psychoneurosis and the normal, and between full-fledged psychoses and the neuroses.[61]

The terms "normal" and "abnormal," therefore, can be most satisfactorily employed in a statistical sense, normal corresponding to culturally sanctioned or prevailing modes of behavior, and abnormal designating departures from a central tendency or norm. From this point of view the term normal is completely divorced from the ideal or perfectionist overtones sometimes associated with it, and abnormal is dissociated from identification with the pathological or morbid, the latter being a variety of the abnormal.[62] There is also an obvious advantage to be gained in inter-societal comparisons, since the particular values of one civilization "cannot be naively employed as the standard measure for judging the behavior of individuals in another." We are

forced to consider as the immediate frame of reference the culture patterns and values of the particular society under observation,

> for if we define the "normal" as that particular behavior exhibited
> by the majority of the population in question, it becomes very neces-
> sary to have an intimate knowledge concerning the behavior of that
> population, the inculcation of such behavior in the individual mem-
> ber, and the relation of such behavior to that of similar and contrast-
> ing groups. It is this very community of behavior which serves as
> the distinguishing criterion of a psychological group, and any in-
> dividuals failing to develop such an institutionalized reaction equip-
> ment are considered aberrant to that culture. Thus correlated with
> the difference in mores from group to group may be found various
> "types" of abnormality; so classified because each shows a deviation
> from the norm or central tendency of the particular group in ques-
> tion; and the entire social structure of the group is devoted towards
> the further inculcation and development of behavior patterns which
> are "normal" to that specific group.[63]

Benedict, moreover, has called attention to the significant observation that—

> one of the most striking facts that emerge from a study of widely
> varying cultures is the ease with which our abnormals function in
> other cultures. It does not matter what kind of abnormality we
> choose for illustration, those which indicate extreme instability, or
> those which are more in the nature of character traits like sadism
> or delusions of grandeur or of persecution, there are well-described
> cultures in which these abnormals function at ease and with honor,
> and apparently without danger or difficulty to the society.[64]

In inter-social comparisons, as Foley points out, the individuals who
are closest to the central tendency of one culture will be the most
widely deviant from the individuals of a second or third culture who
occupy an analogous position. But deviant individuals from the standpoint of the modal behavior of one society may approach, or even fall
within, the central tendency of another.

It is on this account that, from a psychological point of view, the
most rigid and uncompromising conformity on the part of certain
individuals to the culturally approved manners and customs and ideals
of the society is as important an item of observation and analysis as
the deviant individual.[65] The "super-normal" behavior patterns of such
persons probably involve some mechanism of over-determination or
compensation for a repressed revolt against the very behavior which
they manifest. Their behavior represents the extreme of positive acceptance of the mores the negative reaction to which is typified by
the deviant. In western society adherence to the letter of the law,
the unrelenting pursuit of pecuniary values, the compulsion to be al-

ways properly attired, religious and moral fanaticism, undoubtedly have their analogies in the behavior of individuals in other societies who likewise feel compelled to give super-allegiance to their culture patterns.

The importance of comparative cultural data for abnormal psychology is thus apparent.

It enables the investigator to make intercomparisons between similar as well as dissimilar individuals reared in vastly different cultural milieux, and to isolate the fundamental stimulational factors making for certain types of behavior. Whether such behavior is abnormal to one or another culture makes but little difference so long as the basic mechanisms are understood.[66]

It is with reference to this last point that there are implications for psychiatry. The psychic strains and stresses to which human individuals are subject bear a direct relation to the traditional culture patterns of the society in which they live. Instinctual impulses are guided into approved channels of conventional release, and the occasions when fear, anger, shame, etc., are precipitated or inhibited are likewise linked with beliefs and customary activities. The precipitation, as well as the possibilities for the resolution, of psychic stresses are patterned differently, therefore, in different societies. The belief in sorcery as a source of illness is one such pattern and in communities where it exists there are always institutionalized means for combating its influence as well. The evangelical emphasis upon a sense of sin in Christian tradition is another instance which is associated with appropriate means for its resolution.

As I have pointed out elsewhere[67] supernatural sanctions have not only functioned in human history as a means whereby established institutions are supported; they have often afforded a court of appeal by means of which individuals have been enabled to resolve their personal conflicts. Dreams and visions, for example, as culturally interpreted, have often functioned in this way. A Saulteaux Indian was able to marry his own blood sister by invoking a supernaturally interpreted sanction of this sort.

F. L. Wells distinguishes three phases of what he calls "adaptive regression"—genetic, dynamic and social-ethical—as a correlate of sublimation. And he points out how regressive phenomena may have institutionalized cultural, as well as individual, aspects.[68]

So far as certain classes of mental disorder are concerned, it seems that the typical psychic strains and stresses engendered by the culture patterns of different societies, or the same society at different periods, must be taken into account. Psychogenic determinants connected with culture must be evaluated together with situational and organic factors. "The neurosis, for example," as Dollard has pointed out,[69] is an event which gets meaning only in a cultural frame of reference, and is an example of the malfunctioning of the culture. The prohibitory and frustrating aspects of the culture scheme have been more than the neurotic can bear. He has recourse, therefore, to a private solution of his instinctual problems. The essential notion is either that the culture itself is unendurably strict, from the standpoint of what the organism can tolerate in the way of frustration, or that a viciously frustrating substratum of the otherwise tolerable culture has been brought in contact with the neurotic individual. Those persons are normal who find the presented culture an endurable manner of expressing their affects. This manner of viewing the problem has some advantages over that of viewing the neurosis as a private matter of the individual's contact with other private persons. It brings the neurosis into its proper frame of reference as a deviation from a culturally established norm, on the one hand, and it points emphatically at the efficient source of the mischief, namely the culture itself.[70]

Among the psychoanalysts Fenichel[71] has likewise recognized the importance of cultural factors with reference to the form and etiology of the neuroses. He refers to

the demands of present day civilization with its contemporary manifestations which we find in the neurotic patients of today who come to seek treatment. So far as we know, other civilizations had produced neuroses, but these differed from the neuroses of today, because these civilizations demanded different instinctual privations. The taboo which we now designate "compulsion neurosis" is normal in civilizations other than ours; a "devil neurosis of the 17th century," once studied by Freud could not be fitted into our present diagnostic scheme. Indeed we are able to observe how the clinical pictures presented by the neuroses of today are changing, obviously parallel with changes in society and morality. It is the morality which prevails at the time which is directed against instinct in individuals, and morality is a relative power the nature of which depends on the structure of society. It is at this point that the psychologist must admit his inadequacy and agree that the problem of the etiology of neuroses is not a purely individual medical problem and that it needs supplementary sociological considerations.

It is also likely that acculturation processes, especially when they are rapid and lead to drastic changes in native life, particularly in religious beliefs, may engender, or be related to, manifestations of psychic disorder. Seligman[72] observed in British New Guinea that the population living in their undisturbed native villages did not suffer from discernible mental disorders, although both impulsive and ceremonial suicide were frequent, and there were occasional outbursts of maniacal excitement. But he cites several cases of insanity "in which the immediate cause (as evidenced by the history and delusions) was financial responsibility in connection with Europeans."

In other instances the difficulty was involved with mission contacts. In the new religious cults which arose among the natives in 1917, characterized by hysterical dissociation and mass contagion, conflict between new and old religions played an important part in all save one.[73]

Róheim, as a result of his field work among certain native peoples of Australia, New Guinea, Africa and America, is convinced that from the point of view of libido development the "savage is nearer the ideal genital stage than his cultured brother, and more free from disturbances of potency." "Among the savage and half savage peoples whom I know," he says, "masculine psycho-sexual impotence does not occur, female frigidity and perversions are relatively rare, and sadomasochistic perversions . . . are unknown except for a few doubtful symptoms."[74] These, of course, are all maladies of common occurrence in western civilization. To psycho-sexual impotence Freud once devoted a special essay.[75] He and other psychoanalysts[76] account for its etiology in terms of a disharmony between the tender and sensual currents of erotic feeling arising from the effects of strong incestuous fixations in the early infantile phases of sexual development. To achieve a full "normal" erotic life these two currents should be united. Freud then goes on to consider a still commoner phenomenon, psycho-sexual anesthesia, which he believes to be characteristic of "the erotic life of civilized peoples," and he finds the same etiological factors involved here as in psychical impotence in the narrower sense.

Despite the fact that Freud does not consider the possible relevance of western culture patterns as such to the dichotomy between tender and sensual feelings, he is obviously dealing with phenomena typical of our own culture rather than with humanity as a whole. And the question naturally arises whether in societies with different sexual attitudes psycho-sexual anesthesia would have such a high incidence. There are overtones throughout Freud's essay which suggest that he is aware of the possible significance of a cultural variable, particularly in his repeated reference to civilized man, education, up-bringing, etc. It is in view of these facts that Róheim's observations are of particular interest. Education, in short, as traditionally patterned in various societies, may facilitate or hinder the unification of tender and sensual feelings towards members of the opposite sex in addition to infantile fixations. This hypothesis would account for the relatively high incidence of psycho-sexual anesthesia in western civilization since our traditional attitude encourages such a dichotomy. It would also explain inter-societal variations, while at the same time recognizing the cogency of the Freudian etiology, particularly in cases of actual psychic impotence.

Although the clinically recognized disorders known in western society may be present or absent and may vary in their incidence among peoples with other cultural backgrounds, sometimes being recognized as abnormal by the latter or sometimes not, the problem is complicated by another factor. The *form* which the psychic disorders of individuals may take is patterned culturally.[77] From the point of view of western psychiatry this fact may mask the syndromes familiar in our culture and obscure the etiological factors as well unless detailed examination of individual cases is possible. One has only to consider the history of psychiatry itself in Western Europe in order to see the cogency of such factors in other cultures. In the early Renaissance, for instance, the prevalence of the belief in witchcraft, demoniacal possession and lycanthropy patterned the manifestation of psychic disorders to such a degree that individuals who now are recognized as being the victims of mental disorder, fell entirely within the jurisdiction of the Church, and were not considered to be medical problems at all. It was, in fact, even considered heretical to consider such cases from the latter point of view.[78]

In other cultures the phenomena of running-amok,[79] latah[79] and a cannibalistic (windigo) psychosis[80] represent culturally patterned abnormalities, the etiological factors involved in which and their possible relations to disorders familiar to western civilization have not yet been fully explored.

Psychic disorders of an epidemic variety, such as the dancing mania of the Middle Ages[81] and the Vailala madness of New Guinea, are likewise so deeply involved with their cultural backgrounds that any analyses of the etiological factors at work are inextricable from it.

The evaluation of cultural factors in the etiology, symptomatology and typology of psychic stress and mental disorders among some of the aboriginal peoples whose cultures are relatively homogeneous should provide data relevant to analogous, but more complex problems in western society. Here certain etiological aspects of mental disorder are apt to remain obscure owing to the difficulty of gaining the objective perspective upon our own culture patterns which is necessary to evaluate their psychogenic influences. Comparative data from other societies which we can view with relatively more complete objectivity are therefore highly desirable. It is not impossible that the tendency observable in psychoanalytic theory to trace more and more etiological factors of the neuroses and psychoses to the events of the first few years of life, and even beyond that to phylogenetic origins, is due to an under-evaluation of cultural factors as such. If these were given more weight, especially after more data are forthcoming upon the relation of such influences in societies other than our own, it might be found that culturally generic factors, rather than phylogenetic, might throw new light on certain problems. At any rate, Róheim, who, in his earlier writings was inclined to seek for the phylogenetic roots of some classes of mental disorder,[82] has receded somewhat from the general position which gave rise to these former speculations. He now believes it possible to assume that the primal horde really existed "without at the same time making it responsible for the human psyche in general. The oedipus complex is not a 'survival' of the primal horde but, on the contrary, the primal horde itself is to be regarded as an early form of social organization arising from the eternally human oedipus complex."[83]   Consequently,

> While the greater part of psychoanalytical anthropology, Freud's own work, as well as that of his followers, including my own, was concerned with prehistoric speculations (primal horde), my field work has demonstrated for me the predominant importance of ontogenesis, to such an extent that I now hold that practically all the actually functioning forms of social organization, belief or custom have their root in the infantile situation and ought to be first considered in connection with the personal experiences, desires and anxieties of the people who conform to them, believe in them, or practice them.[84]

While ultimately it may be possible to make some limited generalizations in regard to the incidence of different classes of mental disorder in societies with varying culture patterns, such comparisons can have little value unless a classification of mental disorders on a more strictly etiological basis is first evolved.   Otherwise the comparison is actually one of symptoms, the variability of which and the obscurity of the etiological factors involved has made the problem of classification a thorny one even when restricted to western society.   Consequently, inter-societal comparisons undertaken before the problem of culture-patterned symptoms and typology is cleared up have little meaning. For the present any such sweeping generalization as that the incidence of mental disorder increases with the advance of industrial civilization must remain undemonstrable.[85]

The variability in the culture patterns of mankind—the outcome of man's innate potentialities for acquiring and transmitting traditional modes of behavior—is thus as central to an understanding of varieties of abnormal behavior, whether pathological in a medical sense or not, as to a comprehension of the determinants of the typical behavior of human population groups.   Both differential behavior and community of behavior involve correlative problems which demand a uniform mode of attack.   In solving these problems the variability in human culture patterns and the influence exerted by them cannot be minimized.

REFERENCES

Author acknowledges permission to quote from all books listed in these References.

1. M. A. May, "The Adult in the Community," in *The Foundations of Experimental Psychology*, C. Murchison, ed., Worcester, Mass.: Clark University Press, 1929, p. 766.

2. J. M. Wheeler, *The Social Insects, Their Origin and Evolution*, International Library of Psych., Philos. and Scien. Method, London: K. Paul, Trench, Trubner and Co., 1928.

3. C. J. Herrick, "Factors of Neural Integration and Neural Disorder," in *The Problem of Mental Disorder*, Madison Bentley, ed., New York: McGraw-Hill Book Co., 1934, p. 213.

4. But the learning capacity of animals may not be fully called forth by their type of life; and learned behavior is usually confined to individuals and not transmitted.

5. E. L. Thorndike, *Educational Psychology*, Vol. I ("The Original Nature of Man"), New York: Bureau of Publications, Teachers College, Columbia University, 1913-14, p. 199.

6. M. Brierley, "Present Tendencies in Psychoanalysis," *Brit. J. Med. Psy.*, V. 14, 1934, 212.

7. I.e., food exchange, not only in the sense of equal quantities "as mere nutriment, but an exchange necessarily and immediately reciprocal," J. M. Wheeler, *op. cit.* (In this connection, see A. E. Emerson, "Why Termites?" *Scientific Monthly* 64: 337-345 (1947), especially discussion of exohormones on p. 340. Differentiated behavior within the swarm or hive stems from morphological differentiation apparently dependent upon exohormones. The analogue of these insect "societies" is the chemical controls within an organism, not the psychological-cultural differentiation within a human society—D. G. H.)

8. S. Zuckerman, *The Social Life of Monkeys and Apes*, London: Kegan Paul, Trench, Trubner and Co., 1932. pp. 29-30.

9. Zuckerman, *op. cit.*, p. 315.

10. Grace A. DeLaguna, *Speech: Its Functions and Development*, New Haven: Yale University Press, 1927, p. 19.

11. M. Mead, "The Primitive Child," in *Handbook of Child Psychology*, C. Murchison, ed., Worcester, Mass.: Clark University Press, .2nd ed. rev., 1933, p. 921.

12. R. S. Rattray, *Ashanti*, Oxford: Clarendon Press, 1923.

13. F. Boas, *The Mind of Primitive Man*, New York: The Macmillian Co., 1911, p. 128.

14. B. Malinowski, *The Father in Primitive Psychology*, New York: W. W. Norton & Co., 1927, pp. 87-92.

15. M. Sherif, "A Study of Some Social Factors in Perception," *Archives of Psychology*, No. 29, 1935.

16. E. Sapir, "The Unconscious Patterning of Behavior in Society," in *The Unconscious, A Symposium*, Chicago, University of Chicago Press, 1928.

17. C. Landis, "The Expression of Emotion," in *The Handbook of General Experimental Psychology*, 1934.

18. Mary C. Jones, "Emotional Development," in *The Handbook of Child Psychology*, 1935.

19. See O. Klineberg, *Race Differences*, Chap. XV, "Emotional Expression," (bibliography), New York: Harper and Brothers, 1935.

20. *Op. cit.*, p. 288.

21. J. Henry, "The Linguistic Expression of Emotion," *Am. Anthro.*, vol. 38, 1936.

22. Klineberg, *op. cit.*, pp. 159-160; and "An Experimental Study of Speed and Other Factors in 'Racial' Differences," *Arch. Psych.* No. 93, 1928.

23. S. D. Porteus, *The Psychology of a Primitive People; A Study of the Australian Aborigine*, 1931, p. 64, quoted by Klineberg, in *Race Differences.*

24. Sapir, *op. cit.*, pp. 139-41.

.25. G. Murphy, *Experimental Social Psychology*, New York: Harper and Brothers, 1931, p. 426.

26. M. Mead, *Coming of Age in Samoa*, New York: William Morrow and Co. 1928.

27. E.g. J. E. Nicole, *Psychopathology*, Baltimore: William Wood and Co. 2nd ed., 1934, p. 111. (For a study based on a more adequate sample, see A. C. Kinsey, W. B. Pomeroy, and C. E. Martin, *Sexual Behavior in the Human Male*, Philadelphia, 1948. This research amply documents Dr. Hallowell's suggestion, in the above paragraph, that social classes differ in their customs in this regard. At the same time, the study here cited might have been entitled more appropriately, "Sexual Behavior in the Human Male in the United States in the 1940 Decade,"– D. G. H.)

28. E.g., K. B. Davis, *Sex Factors in the Lives of Twenty-Two Hundred Women*, New York: Harper and Brothers, 1929; and G. V. Hamilton, *Research in Marriage*, New York: Boni and Liveright, 1928.

29. They are not hallucinations, See N. A. Harvey, *Imaginary Playmates and other Mental Phenomena of Children*, Ypsilanti, 1918.

30. A. L. Kroeber, "Cultural Anthropology," in *The Problems of Mental Disorder*, Madison Bentley, ed., New York: McGraw-Hill Book Co., 1934.

31. C. P. Oberndorf, "Folie a Deux," *Int. J. of Psychoanalysis*, vol. 15, 1934.

32. Cf. F. L. Wells, "Social Maladjustments: Adaptive Regression," in *Handbook of Social Psychology*, C. Murchison, Ed., Worcester, Mass., Clark University Press, 1935, p. 859: "It is clearer still that regression, like maladjustment, generally depends for its meaning on the cultural values involved, and the same kinds of overt reaction will vary in meaning accordingly."

33. A. Gesell, "Maturation and the Patterning of Behavior," *A Handbook of Child Psychology*, 2nd ed. rev. 1933, pp. 232-3.

34. R. B. Perry termed this concept of mind "subcutaneous."

35. "The Need for a Social Psychology," *Psych. Rev.*, No. 24, 1917.

36. R. Briffault, *The Mothers*, New York: The Macmillan Co., 3 Vols., 1927, vol. I, pp. 23-40.

37. In contrast with this human situation it is worth noting that Zuckerman (*op. cit.*, p. 268) states that "the young ape or monkey reproduces all the activities of its elders, and, so far as is physically possible, every sexual response of the sub-human primate is exhibited before puberty."

38. Margaret Mead, "An Investigation of the Thought of Primitive Children with Special Reference to Animism," *J. Royal Anthro. Inst.*, LXII, 1932, pp. 173-190.

39. Quoted by M. Mead from Susan Isaacs.

40. E. Sapir, *op. cit.*

41. S. Freud, *Three Contributions to the Theory of Sex*. A. A. Brill, ed. and trans., New York: Nervous and Mental Disease Publishing Co., 4th 'ed., 1930. Hug-Helmuth, *The Sexual Life of the Child*, 1919.

42. Margaret Mead, "The Use of Primitive Material in the Study of Personality," in *Character and Personality*, vol. III, Sept. 1934, no. 1, p. 14. See also Mead's *Growing up in New Guinea*, New York; William Morrow and Co., 1930.

43. O. Klineberg, *Race Differences*, p. 280.

44. O. Klineberg, "Notes on the Huichol," *Am. Anth.*, vol. 36, 1934.

45. The principles of analysis and interpretation involved are fundamentally the same as those employed by H. Hartshorne and M. A. May (*Studies in Deceit*, 1928). They found that honesty, e.g., was not a character trait which could be considered as innate or constant in the individual, but that it varied in relation to the specific situations to which the individual was exposed. In short, they insist upon "specificity of conduct" as the basic fact, and shift the emphasis from honest and dishonest persons to honest and dishonest acts. Similarly, the incidence of bravery in different human societies is a function of different cultural traditions and the situations which they engender.

46. R. Benedict, "Anthropology and the Abnormal," *J. of General Psychology*, vol. 10, 1934, p. 69, et seq.

47. S. Lorand, "Character Formation and Psychoanalysis," in *Psychoanalysis Today*, New York: Covici Friede and Co., 1933. (Complete bibliography.)

48. G. Róheim, "Psychoanalysis of Primitive Cultural Types," *Int. J. Psychoan.*, 13, 1932, pp. 77-78. A third variant of the oral character, the pessimistic type, does not occur, nor does the "anal character" (p. 85).

49. G. Róheim, "The Study of Character Development and the Ontogenetic Theory of Culture," in *Essays Presented to C. G. Seligman*, E. E. Evans-Pritchard and others, ed., London: K. Paul, Trench, Trubner & Co., 1934. Pp. 289-291.

50. Róheim recognizes a fundamental difficulty in his theory, p. 292: "It explains the adult in terms of his own infancy, and especially insofar as that infancy was conditioned by behavior of the previous generations of adults. Then that behavior again remains to be explained, and here we may be compelled to call for the aid of other facts, either psychological or constitutional." For further discussion, see his *The Riddle of the Sphinx*, 1934.

51. E. Sapir, "The Emergence of the Concept of Personality in a Study of Cultures," *J. of Social Psych.*, vol. 5, 1934, R. H. Lowie, "Individual Differences and Primitive Culture," *Schmidt Festschrift*, 1928; W. Koppers, "Individual forschung unter den Primitiven in besonderen unter den Yamina auf Feuerland," *ibid.*; C. G. Seligman, "Temperament, Conflict and Psychosis in a Stone-Age Population," *Brit. J. Med. Psych.*, vol. 9, 1929, pp. 189-190; the discussion and bibliography in G. Van Bulck, *Beitrage Zur Methodik Der Volkerkunde*, 1931, pp. 122-131; and J. H. Barnett, "Personality in Primitive Society," in *Character and Personality*, vol. 2, 1933.

52. F. Allport, "The J-curve Hypothesis of Conforming Behavior," *J. Soc. Psych.*, vol. 5, 1934, p. 141-183.

53. Róheim records the following impressions in his latest book, *The Riddle of the Sphinx*, London: Hogarth Press and the Institute of Psychoanalysis, 1934, p. 238, *after* having come in personal contact with primitives: "My first impression during my field work was that savages are not nearly so savage as the anthropologists; or, in other words, that they are not nearly as mysterious as one would think from reading Tylor, Frazer, Levy-Bruhl and Róheim. Because we read so much about animism and magic, totemism and demons, we come to identify primitive people with these things unintentionally and to imagine them as always plagued by demons, or running into taboos, and passing their lives in a chronic state of terror. Similarly, if we only knew Europe from the Catechism, the Talmud, and the books of Folklore, we might easily imagine that the main occupations of the inhabitants of this continent were confessing, fasting and telling fairy tales and legends. No savage occcupies himself as much with primitive religion as the anthropologist."

54. E.g., sensory activities, motor responses, difference in the so-called higher mental processes such as imagery, association, etc., and general capacities such as intelligence, musical and mechanical abilities.

55. Cf. May's (*op. cit.*) reference to Gowin's study of the height and weight of senators, governors, bishops, etc. The average height of the 1,037 eminent

men studied was nearly 3 inches greater than that of life insurance applicants, and the average weight 16 lbs. greater than the latter class.

56. M. J. Herskovits, *The American Negro*, New York, A. A. Knopf, 1928. pp. 62-66.

57. May, *op. cit.*, p. 750.

58. R. Benedict, *Patterns of Culture*, Boston: Houghton Mifflin Co., 1934, pp. 262-265.

59. See B. Z. Seligman, "The Part of the Unconscious in Social Heritage," in *Essays Presented to C. G. Seligman*, 1934; T. K. Oesterreich, *Possession, Demoniacal and Other*, 1930.

60. F. Alexander, "Buddhistic Training as an Artificial Catatonia." *Psychoanalytic Rev.*, vol. 18, 1931. Cf. Klineberg, *op. cit.*, "Fashions" in Abnormality, pp. 296-300.

61. R. M. Dorcus and G. W. Shaffer, *Textbook of Abnormal Psychology*, Baltimore: The Williams and Wilkens Co., 1st. ed. 1934, p. 265.

62. See J. P. Foley, Jr., "The Criterion of Abnormality," *J. Ab. and Soc. Psych.*, vol. 30, 1935 (bibliography); Aubrey Lewis, "The Psychopathology of Insight," *Brit. J. Med. Psych.*, vol. 14, 1934; Edward Glover, "Medico-Psychological Aspects of Normality," *ibid*, vol. 23, 1932; Ernest Jones, "The Concept of a Normal Mind," in *Our Neurotic Age*, ed. S. C. Schmallhausen; A. A. Roback, "What is Sanity?"

63. Foley, *op. cit.*, p. 283; Cf. Sapir, "Cultural Anthropology and Psychiatry," *J. Ab. and Social Psy.*, vol. 27, 1932.

64. R. Benedict, "Anthropology and the Abnormal," p. 60.

65. Cf. Benedict, "Anthropology and the Abnormal," pp. 77-78 and *Patterns of Culture*, pp. 275-277.

66. Foley, *ibid*. p. 290.

67. Cf. Hallowell, "Culture and Mental Disorder," *J. Ab. and Soc. Psych.* Vol. 29, 1934.

68. Wells, op. cit., p. 857 et seq.: "Intercultural comparisons: Escapes from 'Reality'." Attitudes towards death and the function of intoxicants are discussed, especially with reference to oriental and western cultures: "The characteristic intoxicant in Euro-American culture is alcohol, serving stimulating and narcotizing functions in not unequal proportions. Among Easterns as well as primitive cultures, intoxicants are apparently more valued for narcotizing effects; opium and hashish are the most important examples, coca rather an important exception. The narcotic function here is to accomplish a regression from secular reality, reinforced by stimulation of fantasy life. This accords well with larger cultural distinctions. To the westerner the mind is an instrument for molding a reality which is external. He thus seeks through intoxicants at least the sense of increased secular power ('Dutch courage'), in some cases a real access. To the Oriental the basic reality is the mental process itself; his favored intoxicants are such as play on activity as such, irrespective of relation to the external world." The author also examines the military, political, religious and anti-social aspects of western culture for regressive features, p. 861 seq.

69. J. Dollard, *Criteria for the Life History*, New Haven: Yale University Press, 1935, p 279. Cf. the same writer, "The Psychotic Person Seen Culturally," *Am. J. Soc.*; vol. 39, 1934.

70. Cf. Freud, *Civilization and its Discontents*, 1929, p. 45.

71. O. Fenichel, *Outline of Clinical Psychoanalysis*, New York: by permission of W. W. Norton & Co., Copyright 1934, by The Psychoanalytic Quarterly Press, pp. 3-4.

72. C. G. Seligman, "Temperament, Conflict and Psychosis in a Stone Age Population," *Brit. J. Psych.*, vol. 9, 1929.

73. For data on these see in addition: E. W. P. Chinnery and A. C. Haddon, "Five New Religious Cults in British New Guinea," *Hibbert Journal*, 15: 448-463, April 1917; F. E. Williams, "The Vailala Madness and the Destruction of Native Ceremonies in the Gulf Division, Territory of Papua," *Rept. No. 4*, 1932; and the last mentioned author's "The Vailala Madness in Retrospect," in *Essays Presented to C. G. Seligman*, 1934, pp. 369-379.

74. G. Róheim, *The Riddle of the Sphinx*, 1934, p. 237.

75. S. Freud, "The Most Prevalent Form of Degradations in Erotic Life," *Collected Papers*, vol. IV.

76. Cf. E. Jones, "Psychosexual Impotence and Anaesthesia," Chap. XXXI, *Papers on Psychoanalysis*, New York: William Wood and Co., 3rd ed. 1923.

77. Cf. Benedict, "Anthropology and the Abnormal," pp. 77-78.

78. See G. Zilboorg, *The Medical Man and the Witch in the Renaissance*, Baltimore: Johns Hopkins Press, 1935.

79. See J. M. Cooper, "Mental Disease Situations in Certain Cultures," *J. of Abn. and Soc. Psych.*, vol. 29, 1934, p. 13, no. 6, for specific references in the literature. Add also (80).

80. See J. M. Cooper, *op. cit.*, and "The Cree Witiko Psychosis," *Primitive Man*, vol. 6, 1933; and A. I. Hallowell, "Culture and Mental Disorder," *J. Abn. and Soc. Psych.*, vol. 29, 1934, pp. 1-9.

81. J. F. C. Hecker, *The Black Death and the Dancing Mania*, 1885.

82. Particularly as evidenced in his "Nach dem Tode des Urvaters," *Imago IX*, which, as Money-Kyrle has pointed out, required the assumption of some type of Lamarckian theory of transmission (*Brit. J. of Med. Psych.*, 1929, p. 274).

83. Róheim, "Primitive High Gods," *Psychoanal. Quart.*, vol. 3, 1934, p. 121.

84. Róheim, *op. cit.*, p. 62.

85. White queried it a number of years ago in his *Outlines of Psychiatry*, 10th ed., 1924, pp. 45-46; and on the basis of Mead's observations on functional disorders in Samoa it has more recently been challenged by Ella Winston, "The Alleged Lack of Mental Disease Among Primitive Groups," *Am. Anth.*, vol. 36, 1934.

THE SOCIAL FUNCTION OF ANXIETY IN
A PRIMITIVE SOCIETY

A. Irving Hallowell

In his discussion of anxiety, Freud emphasizes the fact that it is essentially an affective reaction to danger.[1] The relationship of anxiety to danger is anticipatory, the affect is a signal: "one feels anxiety *lest* something occur."[2] Anxiety is not confined to the human species. Freud states that it "is a reaction characteristic of probably all organisms, certainly of all of the higher ones."[3] He further suggests that since it has an indispensable biological function, anxiety may have developed differently in different organisms.[4] Freud does not elaborate the point, but I think it follows from the biological role he assigns to anxiety that it must be conceived as a function of the particular danger situations that the organism faces. These vary from species to species. What is dangerous for one species of animal would not necessarily be equivalent for another species, and danger situations in the human species may differ again from those faced by infrahuman animals. For the human species itself, Freud stresses another variable. Danger situations vary ontogenetically[5] and the birth process is the "prototype of anxiety in man."[6]

What Freud does not explicitly recognize is that the occurrence of anxiety in the human species is further complicated by another variable that I shall call "cultural." However, his assumption that anxiety reactions in man are based on experience and are in that sense learned,[7] leaves the door open for an evaluation of such variables within the framework of psychoanalytic principles. These cultural variables operate through the socialization process that all human beings undergo and result in the definition of situations as dangerous in one society which, in another, may be viewed as less dangerous or not dangerous at all. This means that individuals may manifest anxiety reactions that are appropriate in a particular culture but not in another.

Such cultural variables are of importance with respect to two problems: first, the basic question in which Freud himself was particularly interested, viz., the relation between anxiety and neurosis; secondly, the *positive* role of anxiety. This social function of anxiety is definitely linked, in principle, with the biological role which Freud stresses as a generic function of anxiety. I mean that an affective reaction to danger situations, as culturally defined, may motivate behavior on the part of individuals which is as significant in terms of societal values as comparable reactions are valuable in terms of biological utility. Anxiety-preparedness in the face of any danger is a very adaptive reaction.[8]

Before discussing this second problem, however, I wish to return to the first one, the relation between anxiety and neurosis. In this connection, Freud asks, "why it is that not all anxiety reactions are neurotic, why we recognize so many of them as normal," and he emphasizes the need for distinguishing between true anxiety (*Realangst*) and neurotic anxiety.[9] The conclusion to which he comes is this:

> A *real* danger is a danger which we know, a true anxiety the anxiety in regard to such a known danger. Neurotic anxiety is anxiety in regard to a danger which we do not know. The neurotic danger must first be sought, therefore: Analysis has taught us that it is an instinctual danger.[10] [That is, fear of the intensity of one's own impulses.]

This differentiation led to the terminological distinction often made between fear, *i.e.*, real or objective anxiety, and neurotic anxiety. I shall continue to use anxiety in its widest connotation, qualifying it with the adjectives "neurotic" or "objective" according to the meaning intended. In fact, I think there is a considerable conceptual advantage in considering fear-anxiety reactions as a broad affective continuum and not attempting to make categorical distinctions except in terms of known etiological factors, since what may seem to be instances of "pure" objective anxiety actually may have neurotic involvements when all the facts are known. On the other hand, as will appear later, there may be analogies to neurotic involvements in anxiety-laden situations which, in a particular culture, may present real objective dangers to the individual concerned.

Let us turn now to the second problem, the positive role of anxiety. I wish to show how anxiety is instigated and reduced in an American Indian society through the operation of cultural factors (beliefs and institutionalized procedures) which define certain situations as dangerous, how the motivations of individuals are affected, and how the resulting behavior is related to the maintenance of the approved social code.

The Indians to whose social system I have reference live in the bush country to the east of Lake Winnipeg (Manitoba, Canada).[11] Locally, they are known as Saulteaux and linguistically and culturally they are a branch of the Ojibwa. There are few white people in this area and the Indian population is sparse. The natives make their living principally by hunting, trapping, and fishing. Although the operation of acculturation processes makes it impossible to characterize their culture as "purely" aboriginal, not all of these Indians are Christians and in many other respects their manner of life approximates aboriginal conditions. The beliefs relevant to our discussion still flourish today and the more recent changes in their social system have not essentially affected the functioning of these beliefs.

One of the striking features of Saulteaux society is the anxiety with which certain disease situations are invested.[12] In order to understand *why* such situations are the focus of so much affect, we have to know something about native theories of disease. These theories reflect traditional notions. They represent an ideology which is culturally derived and they involve fundamental assumptions about the nature of the universe. From the standpoint of the Saulteaux themselves, such assumptions are taken a priori and are unchallengeable. They not only represent beliefs but are also a basis for action. The affect which arises in certain disease situations is a product of reflection upon the symptoms observed in the patient and the cause of the illness interpreted in terms of the native notions of disease causation. Thus, the anxiety aroused is intimately connected with a cultural variable.

There is a correlative fact, however, which gives *social* significance to the affect generated. Disease situations of any seriousness carry the implication that something wrong has been done. Illness is the penalty. Consequently, it is easy to see why illness tends to precipitate an affective reaction to a culturally defined danger situation. Furthermore, a closer examination of the dynamics of Saulteaux society reveals the fact that fear of disease is the major social sanction operative among these Indians. In this society, certain classes of sexual behavior[13] (incest, the so-called perversions in heterosexual intercourse, homosexuality, autoerotism, bestiality), various kinds of aggressive behavior (cruelty to animals, homicide, cruelty toward human beings, the use of bad medicine to cause suffering, rough or inconsiderate treatment of the dead, theft and a number of ego injuries like insult and ridicule, failure to share freely, etc.), behavior prescribed by guardian spirits, the acquisition of power to render specialized services to others (i.e., curing or clairvoyance), all fall under a disease sanction.

This leads us directly to the heart of one of the basic problems in the social sciences, viz., the determination of the specific conditions under which social codes are maintained and the means by which they operate under different cultural frames of reference. For despite the widest cultural variability in *homo sapiens*, we observe that all human societies are characterized by norms of conduct which, in MacIver's words, "assure some regularity, uniformity and predictability of behavior on the part of the members of a community."[14] Sheer anarchy, or literal rampant individualism, is unknown.

But this problem is not wholly a sociological one. It has important and far-reaching psychological implications, particularly in view of the fact that in many nonliterate societies, the institutions we associate with the maintenance of "law and order" are unelaborated or even absent. In the case of the Saulteaux, e. g., there were no chiefs nor any kind of political organization in aboriginal days. Nor were there any institutionalized juridical procedures or jails.

The psychological aspects of social control become evident when we examine the relation between the social sanctions operative in a given society and the motivations of individuals instigated by the prevailing sanctions. As Radcliffe-Brown has pointed out[15] "the sanctions existing in a community constitute motives in the individual for the regulation of his conduct in conformity with usage." Hence, there is an integral, inextricable relationship between sociological and psychological factors.

In Saulteaux society, it is not fear of the Gods or fear of punishment by the state that is the major sanction: it is the fear of disease.[16] Or, putting it in the terminology already employed, the motivating factor is the affect connected with certain disease situations. Individuals in Saulteaux society are highly sensitized to anxiety as an emotional reaction to a danger signal, the precipitating cause being illness interpreted as punishment. The manifest danger to which the anxiety is directed is the direct threat to someone's well-being or even life. But there is also a menace to the social code which is implied because some dissocial act has been committed. Insofar as individuals are motivated to avoid such acts through fear of disease, anxiety performs a distinct social function.

With this thesis in mind I should now like to analyze in more detail how disease operates as a social sanction in Saulteaux society in connection with anxiety-laden situations.

In the first place, health and a long life are very positive values to the Saulteaux. *Pīmädazīwin*, life in the fullest sense, is stressed again and again in their ceremonies. The supernaturals are asked for it. It is a prime value. In psychological terms, it is a major goal response. Disease interferes with achieving this goal. Ordinary cases of illness, however, colds, headaches, etc., do not arouse anxiety among the Saulteaux any more than they do among ourselves. They are not danger situations. But the nature of disease is such that it may become a threat to life itself, may be a real danger to the human organism. Real or "normal" anxiety is appropriate in such circumstances.[17]

A comparable affect under equivalent circumstances is found among the Saulteaux and ourselves. In both cases, the danger threatened is met with what are thought to be appropriate measures. Most disease situations among the Saulteaux, however, do not conform to this type. They correspond either to the nondangerous variety or they rapidly pass from this type into situations where the anxiety level is not only high, but where the *quality* of the affect suggests neurotic anxiety without its actually being so.   What are the conditions that bring this about? It is here that native beliefs about disease causation enter the picture.

In Saulteaux belief, one of the major causes of illness arises from what they term "bad conduct" (*madjīijīwé bazīwin*). "Because a person does bad things, that is where sickness (*ákwazīwin*) starts," is the way one informant phrased it.   In other words, a person may fall ill because of some transgression he has committed in the past. It is also possible that an individual may be suffering because of the bad conduct of his parents.   "When a man is young he may do something to cause his children trouble. They will suffer for this." Illness derived from this source is designated by a special native term *odjīneaúwaso*). Consequently, if a child falls seriously ill, it is often attributed to the transgression of a parent. It is easy to see the anxiety provoking possibilities in this theory of disease causation. In addition to the normal anxiety that the objective factors of the disease situation may stimulate, a sense of guilt may be aroused in one or both parents.   They are bound to reflect upon what they may have done to cause their child's suffering, or even death.   Their own acts are entangled with the disease situation.

Another cause of illness is witchcraft, the hostile action of some other human being. The significant fact to be observed in cases of this class is that the sick person almost always believes that his sickness is due to revenge. Some previous act of *his* has provoked retaliation in this form. Here the patient's own impulses, previously expressed in some form of dissocial behavior, are projected into the situation just as they are in those instances where disease is thought to have resulted from "bad conduct."   In cases of witchcraft, the penalty that threatens has acted in a mediate fashion instead of automatically as in the instances where "bad conduct" is thought to be the source.

An illuminating clue to the psychological significance of disease situations interpreted as a result of the causes just cited is obtained if we follow Freud's differentiation of what he terms a *traumatic* situation from a simple *danger* situation. He introduces this distinction by asking what the kernel of the danger situation is.[18] He finds that it revolves about the estimation of our strength in relation to the danger. If we feel a sense of helplessness in the face of it, an inability to cope with it, then he calls the situation *traumatic*. This is precisely the differentiation that applies to those disease situations among the Saulteaux where the cause of the illness is uncertain and obscure. In these situations, the quality of the anxiety aroused is different from that where illness is faced in the same way any danger situation is faced. It is disease situations of this *traumatic* type that operate as a social sanction.

The qualitative aspects of the anxiety aroused emerge from the combination of two determinants. The first is purely objective: ordinary medical treatment of the sick person has failed to produce improvement. The symptoms persist or the person gets worse. It is at this point that the situation becomes serious. Prior to this, the illness may not even have been considered dangerous, but when the medicine does not work, the situation rapidly becomes traumatic. This is because the suspicion is aroused in the patient or his associates that the cause of the illness is hidden. It may be a penalty for something done in the past. It may be due to "bad conduct" or witchcraft. But who knows? Yet if this is so, his very life is in jeopardy. Consequently, a feeling of helplessness arises which can only be alleviated if the precise cause of the sickness is discovered. Otherwise, appropriate measures cannot be undertaken. Meanwhile, the source of the danger remains uncertain and obscure; further suffering, even death, menace the patient.

Thus, while from an objective point of view we often may have displayed what seems to be a "disproportionality of affect" in disease situations, at the same time the definition of such situations in terms of Saulteaux beliefs presents dangers that are not comparable to those we would recognize in similar situations. This is an important qualitative difference. The affective reactions of the Saulteaux are a function of this difference.[19]

It would also appear that there are some analogies, although by no means an identity, between the anxiety created in some of these traumatic disease situations among the Saulteaux and neurotic anxiety. This is true, at least, in the cases where the danger that threatens is believed to have arisen out of the patient's own acts, so there is the closest integral relation between inner and outer danger as in neurotic anxiety, but there are no substitute formations in the individual which project the danger outwardly, as in animal phobias, while the real source of danger remains unknown. Nevertheless, it is true that the impulses of the individual become the *sine qua non* of the external danger, just as in neurotic anxiety. Consequently, these impulses are the ultimate source of the danger itself. The disease is not considered to be impersonal and objective in origin and for this reason it cannot be faced in the same terms as other kinds of illness or other objective hazards of life. The real source of danger is from within and, like neurotic anxiety, it is connected with forbidden acts.

Take the case of an Indian who believes himself bewitched, for example. At the first appearance of his illness, he may not have been worried because he may have thought that there was some other cause of his trouble, but as soon as he believes he is the victim of a hostile attack, he gets anxious. Why? Because he believes his illness is in retaliation for some previous act of aggression he has perpetrated. The assertion of these aggressive impulses on his part has led to a feeling of guilt and the illness from which he is suffering has aroused anxiety because he senses danger. His very life may be threatened. What this man fears is that he had endangered his life by acting as he did. He is afraid of the consequences of his own impulses. The source of the outwardly sensed danger lies in his own hostile impulses.

So far I have tried to explain how anxiety is integrated in disease situations among the Saulteaux and why it is that the emotion generated has qualitative features which suggest neurotic anxiety. I hope that I have made it clear, however, that these features are only analogies deduced from the manner in which the belief system of the Saulteaux compels the individual to interpret the objective aspects of disease situations under certain conditions. What we actually appear to have exhibited in these cases is an affective reaction on a fear-anxiety continuum that lies somewhere between true objective anxiety and real neurotic anxiety.[20] That this is indeed the case is supported by the fact that, on the one hand, we can point to occurrences of real anxiety in danger situations among the Saulteaux and, on the other, to cases of neurotic anxiety. An instance of the latter is the behavior of a man I have described at some length in another publication.[21] Among other things he had severe phobic symptoms, a kind of agoraphobia and fear of the dark. "Ask J. D. to go and fetch a kettle of water for you some night," one of the Indians said to me, "you'll find that he will refuse even if you offer to pay him well for it." Eye witnesses also told me the following episode. Once when J. D. was travelling in winter with some other Indians, the party was attempting to reach their camp late at night because they had no blankets with them. Before darkness fell, J. D. insisted that they help him collect birch bark so that torches could be made to carry with them during the rest of the journey. The bark was collected and the torches made but every now and then the wind would blow them out. When this happened and they were plunged into darkness, J. D. would fall to the ground and writhe and scream "like a crazy man."

The point I wish to emphasize particularly is that at both extremes of the fear-anxiety continuum the main function of the affect has reference to the individual alone. This is true whether he runs away from some objective danger or develops phobias which are reaction formations in self-defense against some instinctual danger. The anxiety associated with disease situations among the Saulteaux, on the other hand, has a social function insofar as it motivates individuals to avoid the danger (disease) by conforming to the dictates of the social code. This is accomplished by forcing the individual to reflect upon disapproved acts under the stress of the anxiety aroused by a disease situation or to anticipate possible discomfort through a knowledge of the experience of others. In either case, the disease sanction encourages the individual to be responsible for his own conduct.

The full implications of the social function of anxiety in Saulteaux society can best be exposed, however, if we return to the traumatic disease situation and inquire what steps are taken to reduce anxiety in the individual. I have already pointed out that, in such situations, the cause of the disease is at first problematical although the suspicion is aroused that the patient himself or some other person is responsible for the illness. This means that the true cause of the trouble must be sought before the disease can be alleviated. Once the cause of the illness is discovered, the disease situation loses some of its traumatic quality because the danger can be squarely faced like any other danger and some action taken to meet it. The therapeutic measures employed can be looked upon as anxiety-reducing devices.

Now one of the distinctive features of the Saulteaux belief system is this: if one who is ill because of "bad conduct" *confesses* his transgression, the medicine will then do its work and the patient will recover. This notion is the most typical feature of the operation of the disease sanction in cases where the penalty threatened is automatically induced. In fact, it adds considerable force to the sanction so far as the individual is concerned. It means that deviant conduct may not only lead to subsequent illness but that in order to get well one has to suffer the shame of self-exposure involved in confession. This is part of the punishment.   Since it is also believed that the medicine man's guardian spirits (*pawáganak*) will inform him of the cause of the trouble, there is no use withholding anything.[22] At the same time, confession provides the means of alleviating the guilt and anxiety of the individual, because, if a feeling of helplessness or being "trapped" is an intrinsic factor in these traumatic situations (or in any severe anxiety situation), confession provides a method of escape according to both Saulteaux belief and sound psychological principle.

From the standpoint of Saulteaux society as a whole, confession is also a means by which knowledge of confessed transgressions is put into social circulation. Confession among the Saulteaux is not equivalent to confession to a priest, a friend, or a psychoanalyst in western culture. In our society, it is assumed that what is exposed will be held in absolute confidence,[23] but among these Indians the notion is held that the very secrecy of the transgressions is one of the things that makes them particularly bad. This explains why it is that when one person confesses a sexual transgression in which he or she has participated with a second person, the latter will not become ill subsequently or have to confess. Once the transgression has been publicized, it is washed away or, as the Saulteaux phrase it, "bad conduct will not follow you any more."

Perhaps this attitude towards what is secret is connected with the lack of privacy that is intrinsic to the manner in which these people live. Anything that smacks of secrecy is always suspect. There is even an aura of potential menace about such things, fortified no doubt by the covert practice of magic and sorcery. Consequently, in disease situations where any hidden transgression is thought to be the cause of the trouble what is in effect a public exposure is a necessary step to regaining health.

In actual practice, this works out in a very simple way. When anyone is sick, there is no isolation of the patient; on the contrary, the wigwam is always full of people. Any statement on the part of the patient, although it may be made to the doctor, is not only public but also very quickly may become a matter of common gossip. Where conjuring is resorted to in cases where all other efforts have failed to reveal the hidden cause of the malady,[24] almost the whole community may be present en masse. Under these conditions, to confess a transgression is to reveal publicly a secret "sin." Consequently, the resistance to self-exposure is very great and the shame experienced by the individual extremely poignant. In terms of our own society it is as if the transgressions committed were exposed in open court or published in the newspapers so that everyone knew that Jerry had slept with his sister or that Kate had murdered her child. Among the Saulteaux, however, it is only after such a confession is made that the usual medicine can do its work and the patient can recover. In one case, three children of a married couple were all suffering from a discharge of mucous through the nose and mouth. They had been treated by a native doctor who was also a conjurer but his medicine had done no good. Finally, a conjuring performance was held. Despite the fact that the woman's husband, who was present, had threatened her with death if she ever told, she broke down in a flood of tears and confessed to everyone that he had forced fellatio upon her.

This public aspect of confession is one of the channels through which individuals growing up in Saulteaux society and overhearing the gossip of their elders *sense*, even though they may fail to understand fully, the general typology of disapproved patterns of behavior. Children do not have to be taught a concrete panel of transgressions in Saulteaux society any more than in our own. Nor does it have to be assumed that they have been present on numerous occasions when transgressions have been confessed. Even if they are present, they may not always understand what is meant. Yet some feeling is gained of the *kind* of conduct that is disapproved. The informant who told me about the case of the fellatio was present at the conjuring performance when this was confessed. She was about ten years old at the time and did not understand what was meant until later when her stepmother enlightened her.

In actual operation, the disease sanction among the Saulteaux does not completely deter individuals from committing socially disapproved acts but it functions as a brake by arousing anxiety at the very thought of such conduct. Functionally viewed, a society can well tolerate a few breaches of the rules if, through some means such as confession, a knowledge of dissocial conduct is publicized with the result that a large majority of individuals follow the approved types of behavior.

These deductions are by no means theoretical. That individuals in Saulteaux society actually are deterred from acting in forbidden ways by the disease sanction is illustrated by the following story.[25] In this case, illness did not follow incestuous intercourse. Perhaps this was because it occurred only once. In fact, this may be the moral of the story from the point of view of the Saulteaux themselves. At any rate, it gives a very clear picture of the conscious conflict between the impulses of the individual and socially sanctioned modes of conduct.

An unmarried woman had "adopted" her brother's son, a boy who was already a fairly good hunter.[26] They were camping by themselves alone in the bush. The boy had shot some meat and they were drying it. One night after they both lay down to sleep, he began to think about his *kisαgwas*.[27] After awhile he spoke to her. "How's chances?" he said.[28] "Are you crazy," she replied, "to talk like that? You are my brother's son." "Nothing will happen to us," the boy said. "Yes, there will," said his aunt, "we might suffer." "No we won't. Nothing will happen," her nephew replied.

Then he got up, went over to where she was lying and managed to get what he wanted. After he had finished, he went back to his own place and lay down again. He could not go to sleep. He began to worry about what he had done to his father's sister.

In the morning he said to her, "I'm going now." "Where?" she asked. "I'm going to live somewhere else, I'm ashamed of what I did. I'm going away. If I starve to death, all right." "No! No! Don't go," said his aunt, "If you leave who is going to make a living for me? I'll starve to death. It's not the first time people did what we did. It has happened elsewhere."

But the young man was much worried and determined to go. "No, you can't leave me," said his aunt. "I've brought you up and you must stay here." "I'll go for awhile, anyway," the boy said. "All right," said his aunt, "Just for a short time. No one knows and I'll never tell anyone. There might come a time to say it, but not now."

So the young fellow went off. He came to a high rock and sat down there. He thought over what he had done. He was sorry that he did it. He pulled out his penis and looked at it. He found a hair. He said to himself, "This is *nisαgwas*, her hair." He threw it away.

That night he camped by himself, half thinking all the time that he would go back to his aunt. In the morning, he did go back to where they had their camp. He arrived at sundown.

All during the night he was away his aunt had been crying. She was so very glad to see him now. He said to her, "I wonder if it would be all right if we lived together, just as if we were man and wife." "I don't think so," the woman said. "It would not look right if we did that. If you want a woman you better get one for yourself and if I want a man I better get one."

The trouble was this young man had tasted something new and he wanted more of it. He found a girl and got married in the spring. He and his wife lived with his aunt. Later his aunt got married, too.

The narrator commented that the boy's aunt was a sensible woman. They just made one slip and then stopped. This may explain why nothing happened to them, i.e., neither one got sick and had to confess.

Among the Saulteaux, then, desire for *pimädazīwin* can be assumed to be a major goal response. Everyone wants to be healthy, to live long and to enjoy life as much as possible. In order to achieve this aim, certain kinds of conduct should be avoided, not only for one's own sake, but for the sake of one's children. If one does commit transgressions and then falls ill, or if one's children become ill, it is better to suffer shame than more suffering or even death. This is the setting of confession and its individual motivation.[29] Confession, in turn, by making public the transgression committed permits the individual to recover. This is its ostensible purpose. But confession has a wider social function. It makes others aware of disapproved types of conduct which act as a warning to them. At the same time, since patients who confess usually recover, the publicity given to such cases supports both the native theory of disease causation on which the sanction rests, and the efficacy of confession itself. So while most individuals are motivated to avoid the risk of illness, there is consolation in the fact that even if one's sins find one out, there still is a means of regaining health.

In some traumatic disease situations where witchcraft is thought to be the cause of the illness, the anxiety of the patient and his associates is relieved by the removal of a material object from the patient's body by the doctor. This type of therapy is based upon the belief that it is possible to project material objects into the body of a person that will cause illness. Once the object is removed the patient is reputed to recover. The socio-psychological reverberations of cases diagnosed as due to witchcraft are much the same, however, as those in which confession has occurred. This follows because the same factors are involved: (a) a disease situation that requires explanation in terms of some previous behavior on the part of the patient; (b) the selection, perhaps with the help of the doctor, of some offensive act that is brought forward because the patient feels guilty about it; (c) the dissemination of the cause of the illness through gossip about the case;

(d) the resulting publicity given to socially disapproved types of conduct that act as a warning to others.

We can see, then, how the therapeutic measures utilized by these Indians in traumatic disease situations have the social function of anxiety-reduction, although this is not their ostensible purpose from the standpoint of the Saulteaux themselves. We can likewise understand how it is that in a society where so much anxiety is associated with disease that the persons who specialize in curative methods are individuals who enjoy the highest prestige. In psychological terms, this prestige accrues to those who are instrumental in reducing anxiety.

It is impossible to discuss here all the further ramifications of the functional aspects of anxiety, but we may point out that the whole magico-religious apparatus of the Saulteaux is a complex anxiety-reducing device.[30]

In summary, the thesis of this paper is that, by its very nature, disease may arouse "normal" or objective anxiety, but among the Saulteaux, native theories of disease causation invest certain disease situations with a traumatic quality which is a function of the beliefs held rather than of the actual danger threatened by the illness itself. The quality of the anxiety precipitated in the individuals affected by such situations suggests neurotic rather than objective anxiety because the ultimate cause of the disease is attributed to the expression of dissocial impulses. The illness is viewed as a punishment for such acts and the anxiety is a danger signal that heralds the imminence of this penalty. Insofar as individuals are motivated to avoid dissocial acts because of the penalty anticipated, the pseudoneurotic anxiety aroused in disease situations has a positive social function. It is a psychic mechanism that acts as a reinforcing agent in upholding the social code. Thus, in a society with such a relatively simple culture and one in which formalized institutions and devices for penalizing the individual for dissocial conduct are absent, the utilization of anxiety in connection with disease is an extremely effective means for supporting the patterns of interpersonal behavior that make Saulteaux society a going concern.

Finally, I should like to point out that this role of anxiety in Saulteaux society is consonant with the results that are emerging from certain researches in contemporary experimental psychology.[31] It has been found possible in Mowrer's view to recast the Freudian theory of anxiety in stimulus-response terms and to set up hypotheses which can be tested. In this paper, I have attempted to show how such a hypothesis is useful in interpreting observations made in a primitive society.

NOTES

1. S. Freud, *The Problem of Anxiety*, 94, 121 tr. H. A. Bunker, New York, 1936.

2. *Op. cit.*, 147.

3. *Op. cit.*, 93.

4. *Op. cit.*, 94.

5. *Op. cit.*, 116. Cf. page 108, "Psychic helplessness is the danger which is consonant with the period of immaturity of the ego, as object loss is the danger appertaining to the state of dependence of early childhood, the danger of castration to the phallic phase, and dread of the superego to the latency period. And yet all these danger situations and anxiety determinants may persist alongside one another and cause the ego to react with anxiety at a later period also than the appropriate one; or several of them may become operative simultaneously."

6. *Op. cit.*, 94. But Freud rejects O. Rank's theory "that those persons become neurotic who on account of the severity of the birth trauma have never succeeded in abreacting it completely" (page 123).

7. Cf. O. H. Mowrer, "A Stimulus-Response Analysis of Anxiety and Its Role as a Reinforcing Agent," *Psychol. Rev.*, 1939, 46: 554, note.

8. Cf. Mowrer, *op. cit.*, 563. "Anxiety is thus basically anticipatory in nature and has great biological utility in that it adaptively motivates living organisms to deal with (prepare for or flee from) traumatic events in advance of their actual occurrence, thereby diminishing their harmful effects." According to Mowrer, anxiety may be viewed as "the conditioned form of the pain reaction" (page 555).

9. Freud, *op. cit.*, 147.

10. Freud *op. cit.*, 147. In this paper, reference is made throughout to Freud's revised theory of anxiety. A discussion of the difference between his first and second theories will be found in chap. 4, *New Introductory Lectures on Psycho-Analysis*, New York, 1933.

11. The group that I have investigated personally lives on the Berens River.

12. In a previous paper, "Fear and Anxiety as Cultural and Individual Variables in a Primitive Society," *J. Social Psychol.*, 1938, 9: 25-47, I called attention to this affective differential as an explicit example of how cultural variables not only define situations for the individual but structuralize them emotionally.

13. Cf. A. I. Hallowell, "Sin, Sex and Sickness in Saulteaux Belief," *Brit. J. Med. Psychol.*, 18: 191-199, 1939.

14. R. M. MacIver, *Society, its Structure and Changes*, 248, New York, 1931.

15. A. R. Radcliffe-Brown, "Sanctions" in *Ency. of Soc. Sci.*: "What is called conscience is thus in the widest sense the reflex in the individual of the sanctions of the society."

16. In Radcliffe-Brown's terminology, disease is an example of a diffuse, negative sanction. Curiously enough, he does not mention disease at all in his article, despite the fact that it operates to some degree in many societies. Systematic attention has not been given to it as a sanction.

On the basis of the sketch of the Ojibwa given by Ruth Landes in *Cooperation and Competition among Primitive Peoples* (1937), Margaret Mead concludes (page 468) that "Although they know of and sometimes act in reference to concepts of social behavior characteristic of adjacent societies with higher integrations, they [the Ojibwa] lack effective sanctions to enforce any rule, either in mourning obligations or against incest or murder." Although Landes described Ojibwa in a different locale, the belief system and institutional set-up is equivalent to that of the Saulteaux. Mead's statement is, to my mind, completely misleading. A closer analysis would show, I think, that the disease sanction is both important and effective among all Ojibwa peoples.

17. Cf. Joseph C. Yaskin, "The Psychobiology of Anxiety," *Psychoanalytic Rev.,* 1937, vol. 24, Supplement page 53.

18. Freud, *op. cit.,* 149.

19. Cf. Mowrer, *op. cit.,* pages 563-564 who points out that ". . . experienced anxiety does not always vary in direct proportion to the objective danger in a given situation, with the result that living organisms, and human beings in particular, show tendencies to behave 'irrationally,' *i.e.,* to have anxiety in situations that are not dangerous or to have no anxiety in situations that are dangerous. Such a 'disproportionality of affect' may come about for a variety of reasons, and the analyses of these reasons throw light upon such diverse phenomena as magic, superstition, social exploitation, and the psychoneuroses."

20. While not offered in direct support of our contention, the following remarks of Freud (*op. cit.,* 148) seem worth citing: "There are cases in which the attributes of true and of neurotic anxiety are intermingled. The danger is known and of the real type, but the anxiety in regard to it is disproportionately great, greater than in our judgment it ought to be. It is by this excess that the neurotic element stands revealed. But these cases contribute nothing which is new in principle. Analysis shows that involved with the known reality danger is an unrecognized instinctual danger."

21. Hallowell, "Fear and Anxiety," etc., *op. cit.* 41-45.

22. There seems no doubt that this belief also opens the door wide to the use of suggestion on the part of the native doctor.

23. R. Pettazzoni, reviewing the ethnography of confession (*La Confession des Péchés,* Paris, 1931), makes the point that "la confession des primitifs en général n'est pas secrète," 128 ff.

24. Conjuring involves appeal to supernatural entities. The "bad conduct" of a parent may be discovered by this means and sometimes the spirits of the dead may be invoked for consultation if this seems relevant. Cf. A. I. Hallowell, "The Role of Conjuring in Saulteaux Society" (1942) and "The Spirits of the Dead in Saulteaux Life and Thought," *Royal Anthropol. Inst. of Great Britain and Ireland* (In press). [Both have been published. See general Bibliography.—Ed.]

25. Cf. Mowrer, the *op. cit.,* 558. "This capacity to be made uncomfortable by the mere prospect of traumatic experiences, in advance of their actual occurrence (or recurrence), and to be motivated thereby to take realistic precautions against them, is unquestionably a tremendously important and useful psychological mechanism, and the fact that the forward-looking, anxiety-arousing propensity of the human mind is more highly developed than it is in lower animals probably accounts for many of man's unique accomplishments. But it also accounts for some of his most conspicuous failures."

26. Probably 17 or 18 years of age. His aunt was not an "old" woman, I was told.

27. The term for father's sister and also for mother-in-law. Because of mother-in-law avoidance there was a double barrier to any erotic behavior.

28. The local English vernacular.

29. Among the Saulteaux there is absolutely no connection between confession and the Supreme Being, so that the disease sanction is not in any sense religious. Attention is drawn to this fact because of P. W. Schmidt's categorical interpretation of certain religious aspects of the *Urkulturen* to which, in his opinion, the Northern Algonkian peoples belong. Cf. Pettazzoni, *op. cit.,* 151-152, who discusses this problem. He stresses the dissociation of confession and supreme deities or supernaturals of lesser rank except in a few cases. After referring to these, he goes on to say that, "dans le reste des cas dont nous avons connaissance— c'est-à-dire le plus souvent—la confession a lieu en dehors de toute intervention directe ou indirecte d'êtres divins."

30. Cf. R. R. Willoughby, "Magic and Cognate Phenomena: an Hypothesis," in *A Handbook of Social Psychology*, Carl Murchison, ed. Worcester 1935.

31. Cf. O. H. Mowrer, *op. cit.*, 564, and his "Preparatory Set (Expectancy): Some Methods of Measurement," *Psychol. Monographs*, 52: 1-2, 39, number 2, 1940 and "Preparatory Set (Expectancy): A Determinant in Motivation and Learning," *Psychol. Rev.*, 1938, 45: 62-91.

DOUGLAS G. HARING

1943. Comment on Japanese Personal Character, from *Blood on the Rising Sun*, Philadelphia, Macrae Smith Co., pp. 22-25, 68-75, 125-126. Copyright by the author.

1946. "Aspects of Personal Character in Japan," *Far Eastern Quarterly*, vol. 6: 12-22. Reprinted by courtesy of the Editor of the *Far Eastern Quarterly*.

1953. "Japanese National Character: Cultural Anthropology, Psychoanalysis, and History," *The Yale Review*, vol. 42: 373-392. Reprinted by courtesy of the Editor of *The Yale Review*.

If the present book contains somewhat more material on the Japanese than on other peoples, that is partly due to the emphasis upon study of Japanese "national character" during and after World War II, and due also to the fact that the compiler is an anthropologist who has specialised in study of Japan. Background materials descriptive of Japanese culture are abundant; those who wish to survey this background are referred to Embree, 1939; Haring, 1946-a, 1949-a, 1955-a; Hulse, 1946; Lamott, 1944; Norbeck, 1954; Reischauer, 1950; and Sugimoto's novels. G. B. Sansom's *Japan, A Short Cultural History* (N. Y., 1931, 1943) is one of the best cultural histories of any nation.

The wartime studies of Japanese personality include Benedict's *The Chrysanthemum and the Sword*, which has been translated into Japanese. The *Japanese Journal of Ethnology* devoted an entire issue to discussion of her book (*Minzokugaku Kenkyū, 14 #4,* 1949; cf. Bennett & Nagai, 1953) and Japanese ethnologists and psychologists have turned to studies of national character. Other wartime studies are Gorer, 1943; LaBarre, 1945; Sikkema, 1947; and Spitzer, 1947. Relevant works, both prewar and postwar, include Anesaki, 1916; Bickerton, 1932; Buchanan, 1954; Caudill, 1952; W. Dening; Embree, 1950; Glacken, 1955; Hsiao, 1929; Kubo, 1938; Lyman, 1885; Matsumoto, 1946; Moloney, 1954 (cf. Haring, 1955-b); Seligman, 1931; and Stoetzel, 1955. Included in the present volume are new papers by Miss Lanham and by the Norbecks that indicate the emergence of more accurate information as a consequence of postwar field research.

Comparison of Haring's 1946 and 1953 papers suggests that the end of the war with its relaxation of police controls brought to the surface aspects of Japanese personality that had not been evident under militaristic controls. Probably "national character" is subject to modifications with changes in social and political organization. For example, between 1935 and 1950, economic conditions practically eliminated the hiring of nursemaids to care for babies, except in very well-to-do families and in backward, poverty-stricken rural areas. Take the nursemaid out of the picture given in Haring's 1946 article, and estimate the change in experience of infants.

COMMENT ON JAPANESE PERSONAL
CHARACTER: PRE-WAR

Douglas G. Haring

Every Japanese must attend primary school for six years. It is claimed that 98% of the people can read and write—a higher percentage of literacy than in the United States.* Large numbers of children whose births are unregistered, however, are not admitted to the schools. Apparently these illiterates are ignored in the statistics. Even allowing for this statistical trick, the proportion of literate persons still is high in Japan.

The aims of all education culminate in a single theme: the sanctity of the Emperor. Not for a moment in his school career may a Japanese forget that the purpose of life is to serve the Emperor. His history books—and above all, his "morality" courses—insure that every Japanese thinks of himself as a loyal subject. Whatever his social class, he is a subject, never a citizen. He learns to venerate the glorious warriors of Old Japan. Their bravery, their self-effacement for the sake of an overlord, their skill in strategy and deception, call for his emulation.

Shintō doctrines are impressed upon the young in their textbooks, by participation in rituals at the school, and by group worship at Government Shintō shrines. These cult activities are compulsory. Teachers lead their classes regularly to the shrines to worship the Imperial Ancestors, and nearly all pupils go with their schoolmates on pilgrimage to Tokyo at least once during their schooldays. There they humbly bow in worship before the Emperor's palace.

The official requirements for reading of the Imperial Rescript on Education illustrate the methods of impressing the doctrines upon the young. On national holidays all pupils must assemble at the schools, and this solemn document is intoned by each school principal while the pupils worship the Emperor—The Name That Cannot Be Uttered.

The principal must perform the ritual with meticulous attention to detail. Should he handle the sacred paper with gloves that have been worn previously, or should he stumble over a word, custom decrees suicide. For even a trivial error he will be demoted to an obscure country school.

In every school there is a sacred shrine, a holy place. There are en-

---

*Shortly before the cessation of hostilities in 1945, the Japanese Government admitted that 98% was too high, and suggested 80-90% as a reasonable estimate.

shrined the sacred portraits of the Emperor and the Empress (Those Who Are Too Awesome to Mention), together with other mystic objects such as the Imperial Rescript.

In case of fire or flood—and in Japan all wooden school buildings burn sooner or later—these treasures must be rescued at any cost. The principal is responsible for their safety. Many a pedagog has lost his life in an effort to save the Portraits. Small children have died in attempting to rescue the sacred objects, and those who succeed in salvaging them are honored. Thus every Japanese learns early that life is but a small sacrifice to offer the Manifest Deity Who reigns over the Land of the Gods.

The middle schools, junior colleges, and universities conform to similar standards. There is no relaxation of the duties of Emperor-worship in the higher institutions. The privileged few who receive higher education know that only the gracious beneficence of the Emperor allows them this privilege.

The educational system has achieved two major ends. First, all Japanese except the lowest peasants and coolies have learned to read. By the nature of the language and the system of writing with Chinese ideographs, the masses of the people cannot hope to acquire foreign ideas except as the officials permit their publication in Japanese. Isolation of the common people from foreign culture is maintained easily. Even the Chinese ideographs are used in such a way that Japanese primary school graduates cannot read Chinese.

Second, the relatively small numbers of persons who achieve higher education are rendered irrevocably Japanese in the formative years of childhood. By the time they encounter foreign ideas in the colleges, they have formed emotional habits which guarantee immunity against beliefs that might threaten their patriotic devotion. . . .

Shintō, schoolbooks, and synthetic *Bushidō* would be powerless to evoke the kind of mentality that militarists desire unless the Japanese were prepared to accept such propaganda. Shintō mythology is childish and irrational. So is much of the content of the schoolbooks. In comparison with Occidental ethical ideals, *Bushidō* is a ridiculous anachronism.

The ghost of feudalism, however, still stalks Japan. One asks constantly whether it be a ghost at all. Perhaps feudalism never really died.

Contemporary Japanese do not remember feudal days. Even persons who heard from grandparents the stirring tales of those times are not numerous. The departed grandparents, now worshipped as family ancestors, were nurtured in feudal discipline. That part of their heritage still endures. They viewed the world through eyes that could perceive nothing apart from a feudal context. Many of those grandparents hoped to rear their children for a different kind of world—the world from which Japan was receiving locomotives and bicycles and Hegelian philosophy. They could no more rear those children to be Occidentals than a mother in Omaha or Memphis could bring up her son to be a Hindu mystic. The babies of the eighteen-eighties often wore European clothing, but they drank in feudal habits of living and feeling with their mothers' milk.

Those babies grew up to fight Russia and to build the modernized façade of Japan. Their world was tense with conflict between old and new. Capitalism, Marxism, automobiles, heavy industry, beer, and Christianity—all were new, designated by the inclusive term *modan* (modern). All stood in contrast to the world of their infancy and challenged the inner emotions that are the essence of human personality. Unconsciously these men and women adapted and oriented the new ideas to the supposedly eternal values imparted by their parents.

Feudal mentality afforded a refuge against the psychological bombardment from the Occident—a refuge, however, which no one fully trusted. Shintō and *Bushidō* constituted a whistling in the graveyard, a bold front to cover an uneasy doubt. Perhaps after all *Yamato Damashii*—the Spirit of Japan—might go the way of brocaded kimonos and leather armor before the hot sun of Euro-American civilization. When in their turn this generation of the early nineteen-hundreds reared their children, they could impart no inner feeling patterns other than those which they themselves had learned in infancy. Filled with doubts, they concealed misgivings by aggressive emphasis upon the very things they doubted. Shintō and *Bushidō* symbolized the feudal orientation and received emphasis in proportion as the dream-world of Old Japan seemed to be threatened.

In its turn the modern generation cherishes the same inner dreams. The factory employee inhabits a private universe of fantasy. He is not merely a machine tender. He is a *samurai* in armor, brandishing his two swords in the face of Japan's enemies. In the movies, he relives the days when knighthood was in flower and his fantasies come alive. No longer is he bewildered by new ideas from abroad. Unlike his parents, he is certain of mastery of the foreign innovations. He may not think of them as foreign. The contemporary generation has been reared under electric lights and has eaten its vitamins from babyhood. The mechanical gadgets are not strange and awesome, they are objects of everyday use.

At the same time the modern Japanese is surer of his feudal heritage of intangibles. Like the *modan* contrivances, the feudal outlook has been his from the beginning. He perceives no incongruity—he simply accepts his world. He did not learn his feudal habits against a genuine feudal background; he learned them in modern Japan and they seem completely in harmony with his environment. This is a far cry from the insecure days when Japanese leaders strove to achieve national unity and turned inward upon Shintō for security in the midst of bewilderment. To the grandfathers' generation Shintō doctrine was a device manufactured to meet a need. To the contemporary generation it is *Kōdō*, the Imperial Way vouchsafed by the Sun Goddess and fixed in the eternal verities.

If a modern Japanese receives higher education and encounters Marx or Tolstoi, he takes them also in his stride, confident that the Occident offers nothing that Japanese cannot excel. If he should never advance beyond primary school, he accepts the ready-made world bequeathed by the Ancestors; his duties to superiors are clear and the mission of the Nation is beyond doubt. If conflicts arise in his inner world, the "pure impulses of the divine Japanese soul" ultimately dominate and resolve his dilemmas.

Feudal morality is unquestioning obedience, loyalty to one's superior, and frugality. Generations of proud feudal lords demanded these qualities in their subordinates on pain of death, and waxed fat on the yield of their estates. When feudal rights and titles were abolished, the Emperor replaced the overlord as the ultimate object of all obedience, loyalty, and self denial. The generations that achieved the transition, with their doubts and misgivings, have passed from the center of the stage. In this second quarter of the twentieth century the dominant generation is unaware of the doubts and misgivings. Feudal morality and modern technology have been reconciled by rationalizations which Japanese rarely question.

Thus it happens in the nineteen-twenties or thirties that a young engineer holds a responsible post in a Government utility. In the United States such a post would yield a salary of twenty-five thousand dollars. In Tokyo the engineer receives twenty-five hundred. The Dutch Government offers him a similar position in Java at twenty-five thousand. He talks about it with an American friend, who advises him to accept. Uncertain, he thinks it over. Two weeks later he meets his foreign friend, who asks, "When do you start for Java?"

Serenely the Japanese replies, "I'm not going. You Americans think in terms of money. You cannot understand the Japanese spirit. If I resign my government post, my wife and I lose court standing. It is better to keep our social position than to have the money."

Thus it happens also that a University student calls himself a radical and reads Karl Marx in secret. An American friend seeks his aid in rectifying an error of a few yen in a postal savings account. Boldly he answers, "Those stupid officials! They hide behind the Imperial Crest and cheat the people. Of course I'll go with you. I'll tell them off in style!"

He goes with the American. But when he enters the tiny postoffice he sees the Imperial Crest and bows from lifelong habit. He bows again to the old crone who serves as postmistress—is she not the representative of the Emperor's mails? Bravado gone, he mumbles timidly, "This foreigner says there must be a mistake in his account. Please deign to consider the matter!"

The old lady barks, "Mistake? The postoffice makes no mistakes. Probably the foreigner cannot add. All foreigners are ignorant of the abacus. His account is correct." The bold radical, thoroughly subdued, turns to the foreigner: "I am very sorry for you. There cannot be a mistake. We may not trouble the postoffice." There the matter ends. Intellectually he plays with Occidental dynamite; emotionally the core of him is feudal.

The streetcar conductor also knows his place. He carries a book of rules. Therein are printed all possible questions that passengers might ask, together with correct replies. His speech is confined to these prescribed sentences, and "whatsoever is more than these cometh of evil." Now and then the Electric Bureau holds a contest for the best sentence for conductors to use when asked thus-and-so. The winning sentence is added to the rule books and the conductor's repertory is enlarged. But originality transcends the conductor's imagination.

Perhaps the venturesome foreigner desires land on which to erect a summer cottage. He approaches the peasant who owns the site. After many cups of tea and much formality the peasant agrees that his land could be sold and names a reasonable price. The foreigner brings a lawyer and expects to carry away a deed to the land. The reasonable price is quoted again, but there is no sale. The buyer raises the ante. Still no sale. In desperation he seeks advice from a foreigner born in Japan who knows the ways of peasants. The old timer goes with him, but not to the peasant's cottage. He inquires, locates the local *tono sama*, descendant of the former feudal lord. The *tono sama* is devoid of authority and legal standing. He is sympathetic and reasonable though he makes no promises.

Next day the peasant seeks out the foreigner. Eagerly he sells his land at the original price. There is no mention of the higher price the foreigner had offered. The baffled Occidental gets his summer cottage, and writes a book about the mysterious Orient. Feudal habits and ideas are beyond his ken.

Or perhaps the foreigner lives in a port city among other foreigners. Unlike his neighbors he insures his house with a Japanese company. An earthquake destroys the city. No insurance company pays its losses. Earthquakes are Acts of God, and insurance companies are pious. His neighbors receive nothing from the foreign companies. He also receives nothing from the Japanese company. But after some months the mail brings a cheque for ten percent of his insurance. The company explains that while they do not recognize such losses, the divine Emperor in His infinite benevolence cannot bear the suffering of His people. So the Emperor has provided funds to enable Japanese insurance companies to mitigate suffering by token payments.

Japan remains feudal at heart. Vassals know their places, and overlords accept responsibilities. The Emperor is father to His people and divinity meets feudal obligations.

* * * *

Every Japanese has four souls.

First is his *nigi-mitama* or gentle spirit; second, the *ara-mitama* or rough, violent spirit; the other two are the *saki-mitama* or luck spirit, and the *kushi-mitama* or wonder spirit.

One's disposition and actions supposedly depend upon the balance between these souls. When the gentle spirit is ascendant, one is polite, kind, and friendly; when, as happens to everyone at times, the rough spirit is aroused, one gives way to temper and ungoverned fury. And one's fondest hopes come true of themselves when the luck spirit gains the upper hand.

Some people are so constituted that the gentle spirit is the strongest of the four. Others, like the Storm God, brother of the Sun Goddess, are dominated perpetually by their rough spirit. Evidence of unusual spiritual power in an individual calls forth the veneration of his fellow-Japanese, be he living or dead.

Thus a poet, scholar, or a saint manifests supernatural potency of the gentle spirit or the wonder spirit. An intractable rebel or a successful traitor is deemed to possess a rough spirit of more than natural violence. Such persons, after their death, are worshipped at Shintō shrines —the gentle spirits receive supplications from persons in distress, and rough spirits are propitiated and placated lest they work harm to the nation.

Quite in harmony with Japanese ways of thinking is the metaphor of Japan as a person with these four spirits. Many Japanese speak as if the nation were a living organism, and individuals are thought of as cells in the national body. In the mood of this symbol, one might interpret the liberal decade as a period when Japan's gentle spirit was partly ascendant. The succeeding decade, from 1929 to 1939, certainly could be viewed in terms of the resurgence and final dominance of the rough spirit.

Grandmother makes loops of straw rope for farm use. Japanese often work with their feet. *Photo by D. G. Haring.*

ASPECTS OF PERSONAL CHARACTER IN JAPAN*

Douglas G. Haring

Psychological characteristics of enemy peoples were studied almost frantically during the recent war with a view to more effective psychological warfare. Answers were sought to questions like the following: How does the average enemy individual think and feel? Can his mental-emotional constitution be exploited to disrupt his will to fight? And how did he get that way?

Prior to 1941 almost no one investigated the phenomena of personality development in Japanese society. Even the Germans were subjected to very little systematic study. After the bombs began to fall, when collection of essential data had become impossible, both governmental and private initiative backed research into "character structure" among enemy peoples.

Cessation of hostilities opened the way for this kind of research in both Germany and Japan. Simultaneously the official support of such studies collapsed. Yet with respect to both nations—Japan in particular—the practical need is even more pressing. Without foresight and almost unwittingly the people of the United States have become the ultimate rulers of seventy-five million Japanese for an undetermined period. No people can be ruled wisely unless the rulers know the mentality and emotional habits of their wards. Re-education of the Japanese poses a problem in American policy that carries profound implications for an orderly world. Such re-education cannot afford to proceed on assumptions current in education in the United States. Goals and methods must be adapted to Japanese psychology and to the traditional though changing Japanese cultural milieu. One may question the competence of American educators (with a capital E!) to determine policy for a people among whom they have not lived, whose language they do not speak, and whose cultural background is alien to their insight.

Critical examination of available resources for insight into the "Japanese mind" directs attention to certain recent studies of alleged

---

*The author is indebted deeply to Dr. George B. Wilbur for stimulating comment, criticism, and suggestions. Dr. Wilbur, however, has not seen the present paper and is innocent of responsibility for its contents.

typical features of Japanese personality. The background of these studies includes numerous investigations of personal character among peripheral peoples. During the past quarter-century some anthropologists have focussed attention upon the socially-conditioned aspects of individual development; in collaboration with psychoanalysts and sociologists research techniques have been tested and adapted, and results have been subjected to critical analysis.

Basic problems of such investigation were brought before a wider public by Ruth Benedict and Margaret Mead;[1] competent field studies of various peoples bear such names as Bateson, Beaglehole, DuBois, Erikson, Linton, Mead, Thompson, Whiting, Kluckhohn and Leighton.[2] Stimulating analyses have emerged through the collaboration of the psychoanalyst Kardiner with Linton and with DuBois.[3] Other similar studies have appeared in print and more are on the way. Appraisal of these investigations lies beyond the scope of the present paper, which is confined to studies of Japanese personal character.

The war emergency found this group of workers experienced in the use of fairly well-developed techniques. Their skill and knowledge were mobilized in connection with divers problems in many parts of the world. Often they were asked to make the most of inadequate data in default of opportunity for first-hand investigation; such was the case in the scramble for understanding of the motivations of the Japanese. Nevertheless, students of Eastern Asia cannot afford to neglect the implications of some of their hypotheses.

Superficial appraisals dismiss the study of "character structure" as a passing anthropological fad. Perhaps the term "character structure" and the allied jargon may go the way of fads to merited oblivion. But meticulous observation and analysis of the development of patterns of individual character in conformance with local cultural norms offers more than an academic amusement. Such investigation hews close to scientific explanation of the durable problem of *ethos*—"the soul of a people," "racial genius," or "national character." Ever since a remote forebear of *Gigantopithecus* first heaved a rock at a stranger, these catchwords have inspired blind ethnocentrism, tribal egotism, and national snobbery with malice toward all and charity for none. "National character" has provided a happy hunting ground for sentimentalists, demagogues, and collectors of curiosa. Scientific investigation is overdue.

An underlying hypothesis of the recent anthropological-psychoanalytic studies, *sans* technical jargon, may be summarized briefly. With due allowance for physical and regional limitations and for cultural history, the unique aspects of any society are determined and maintained by emotional habits learned in infancy by a majority of the participating individuals. Much of this learning occurs before the infant learns to talk. Consequently a variety of socially-important emotional habits continues vague and indefinite, even unconscious, throughout every individual's lifetime. One knows only that certain types of social situations are congenial and he feels at home in them, while in other situations he is ill at ease, even violently disturbed. The experiences of early infancy, reinforced by subsequent events, have developed in him unconscious criteria of social and cultural choice. Such preferences one takes for granted; despite fluent rationalizations, the ultimate criteria of his personal and social preferences lie beyond his ability to perceive objectively and to describe verbally.

Experience in infancy is by no means the sole determinant of an individual's social goals and preferences. He goes on learning and acquiring new tastes. But his pre-linguistic habits maintain a subtle primacy because they are buried beyond the reach of self-conscious analysis. The ways in which infants acquire feeling-habits with respect to personal relations invite further investigation. Apparently the baby learns habits of reciprocal behavior *vis à vis* each person in his small world—mother, father, nurse, siblings. Simultaneously he responds emotionally to their behavior toward each other. Thus he acquires the "feel of" the usual routines of interstimulation toward others, of others toward himself, and of others apart from himself. These feelings about human relations become deeply organic, a part of oneself too fundamental to analyze objectively in subsequent years. In such emotional habits arise the norms of conduct implicit in adult behavior.

These deep feelings of rightness or wickedness in conduct and in personal relationships gain force from the circumstance that they were learned at an age of maximum organic vigor and security. As an adult one strives unconsciously to recapture the perfection of a dimly sensed past in which warmth, sustenance, and the attention of others were provided without effort or uncertainty. Whatever persists in organic habit from that optimum epoch acquires symbolic values—values often dramatized in folklore and mythology. Hence Freud's definition of instinct: ". . . a tendency innate in living organic matter, impelling it toward the reinstatement of an earlier condition."[4] One's ideal constellation of persons and conduct is no intellectual scheme; it is a complex of emotional compulsions that impels him to seek a social milieu whose feeling-tone approximates the world of his infancy. Even when observers characterize an individual's infancy as "unhappy," the individual himself at least acts in terms of the emotional coloring of that half-forgotten but organically vital experience.

Thus one whose parents characteristically acted as equals motivated by affection and mutual respect subsequently may seek situations in which his associates hold each other in considerate, helpful regard. If, however, his father dominated the household, showed contempt for the mother, and dramatized the brutal aspects of living, the infant may grow up to create a household or to work for a political order that he can dominate in the mood of his father. Failing to achieve supreme command, he nevertheless feels at home under an authoritative ruler who enforces obedience. He tends to repress tender feelings associated with weakness and symbolized by the mother. The foregoing are by no means the only patterns that stem from the situations postulated. Given large numbers of similar households, however, the majority of their children in any generation develop along the lines indicated.

Each individual seeks to attain or to inhabit a social order in which personal relations are congruent with the feeling-patterns established in his infancy. To resort to a statistical analogy, the modal type of home determines the preferences of the modal type of person reared in any society. Autocratic regimes rest upon the habituation of infants to the folkways of autocracy. Democratic societies are composed of persons who in childhood learned to feel that each individual merits respect and consideration.

Democracy, therefore, cannot be created by fiat among a people whose deepest feelings run counter to democratic traditions. Only by changing the patterns of social experience in infancy can a society undergo permanent reform, either toward democracy or toward autocracy.[5] Nazism and Nipponism are possible in the long run only in populations where a majority of homes are patriarchal microcosms.

Wartime attempts to analyze Japanese personal character from this point of view produced hypotheses respecting various aspects of the development of Japanese individuals. Almost without exception, the principal contributors were handicapped by lack of first-hand experience in Japan. Their data came from books about Japan, biographies of Japanese, from Japanese cinema films, from *issei* and *nisei* in the United States, from experience in internment centers, from Japanese literature and schoolbooks. A sketchy outline of "typical" Japanese character emerged, and this outline contains features that probably will stand up in the face of new facts. Material thus far published includes papers by Geoffrey Gorer, Arnold Meadow, Ruth Benedict, Talcott Parsons, and Weston LaBarre.[6] Undoubtedly more will be printed. The present paper attempts to summarize synthetically some of the major contributions and to integrate them with residual impressions from personal residence in Japan between the years 1917 and 1926. Detailed critical analysis of the literature at present would be premature; further studies in the field by trained personnel are a *sine qua non* of any such evaluation.

In Japan infancy is a period of indulgence, especially for boys. Babies are fed to excess, fondled, and rarely restrained or punished.

Even excretion receives public attention; some writers have attempted to explain the less pleasant behavior of Japanese adults as a consequence of psychological injury through imposition of rigid toilet training before the infant has matured neurologically and physiologically to the point of effective control. Facetiously dubbed the scatological interpretation of personality, this hypothesis is amenable to verification by observation in Japan. Until such studies are made, it is pointless to argue the topic.*

One outstanding fact not stressed in the literature but amply verified involves the almost uninterrupted bodily contact of Japanese infants with mother or nursemaid. Practically never is a baby left to lie alone quietly. Always he rides on someone's back or sleeps close to someone. When he is restless his bearer sways or jiggles from one foot to the other. Some writers deem this jiggling a fearsome experience for the infant; whether this be so is another detail for field verification. My own unsystematic observations indicate that most Japanese think it soothes the child. At any rate the infant almost constantly feels the reassuring touch of human skin. When he cries he is given the breast, and in lower-class families his sexual organs are manipulated until he falls asleep. Many better-educated Japanese repudiate the latter practice, but they employ nursemaids versed in the folkways rather than in the niceties of genteel refinement.

In due season—perhaps at the birth of a sibling—the Japanese infant abruptly loses his warm, secure world of bodily contact with the mother. Although complete weaning may be deferred for several years, he no longer holds first claim on the breast. As he begins to walk he is "put on his own" quite drastically. He must conform to the implicit taboo on touching other people that still survives in Japan. Although relaxed in recent decades, the effects of this taboo still evoke from foreigners the verdict that Japanese society is cold and formal. Other taboos also restrict his behavior. He must learn never to reveal the inside of his mouth; the traditional frugality also is enforced and effects a sharp cessation of the practice of stuffing the infant with food. Simultaneously he is denied the pleasures of genital manipulation by mother or nursemaid, although children's play frequently includes such activities. He must learn his decorous way about the house and garden. Some writers have overemphasized the strictness of training with respect to the house; they allege that Japanese houses are so frail that even a baby's misstep can throw the building out of alignment. (My none-too-dainty feet have trod every part of many a Japanese house with no ill effects on the structure.) The baby, however, must learn to avoid the place of honor in the guest room and he must

---

*See Miss Lanham's preliminary report elsewhere in this book.—Ed.

learn to keep his fingers out of the firebox in wintertime. He must observe a rather neurotic taboo against stepping on the dividing lines between the straw floor-mats or on the threshold. He must learn not to injure or disturb the formal garden in the tiny yard—a fact that imposes considerable restriction upon his freedom of movement in play. His toys are few and he learns to make the most of a limited range of play activities.

The strict requirements of Japanese etiquette are with him from the time of his first step. Very early he learns to bow. He must approach his parents formally. When he leaves or enters the dwelling he approaches first his father, then his mother, bows, and recites the set formulas of departure and return (*Itte mairimasu; Tadaima kaerimashita*). The parents return the bow and utter the conventional responses (*Itte irasshai; Okaerinasai*). He does not rush home from play or school to the warm security of his mother's arms, nor do his childish woes find solace there. Some psychologists appraise this abrupt break in the sequence of habit formation as a psychological trauma fraught with consequences disruptive of later adult emotional life.

In any event the sudden break in the infant's habitual basic dependence on contact with other persons involves frustration. A normal response to frustration is a temper tantrum. In the case of a boy the mother resigns herself to the tantrum and accepts verbal and physical abuse from her son. The father, however, may suppress the outbreak. A girl encounters prompt suppression. The consequent vengeful desire to hurt someone finds no adequate outlet in the rigidly defined situations of Japanese life except perhaps through alcoholic intoxication. In girls the aggressive impulses apparently are repressed. In boys they may be indulged toward animals or women but not toward the father or elder brothers. Long postponed revenge for childhood frustration—a motivation of which the individual is unconscious—may be accomplished either in suicide or in the sadistic outbursts of war and torture of the helpless. In males these latter outlets receive social approval. Females apparently live with their repressions, unless the common neurotic malady called *hisuteri* (derived from the English hysteria —usually nymphomania) may be regarded as a consequence.

Another aspect of infantile frustration appears in the feelings of adolescent or adult males toward their own bodies. All those visceral functions that in infancy elicited lavish attention from others come to symbolize frustration. Even though they provide occasion for boasting, sexual functions may be repudiated in disgust. The unconscious conflict within the growing boy finds in sex a symbol of frustrated aggression and longing for dominance. Behavior related to sex is tinged with sadistic violence; the fierce obscenity of Japanese schoolboys, homosexuality, contempt for wives, and sexual mutilation of helpless enemies all stem perhaps from these unresolved conflicts. Throughout the history of Japanese fine arts the human body has been repudiated as a source of aesthetic pleasure—unless the pornographic *ukiyoye* can be called aesthetic. Perhaps this negative tradition in art and the self-deprecation inherent in Japanese etiquette found in similar repressions.

The family system places the child in a position of increasingly tense insecurity. Stress upon etiquette and fear of losing face are expressed in the training formulas: "Don't do that! People will laugh at our family!" and "When you grow up you must bring glory to the family." An individual's shortcomings expose an entire family to ridicule; hence children learn to fear outsiders and to cringe at the merest hint of ridicule. In time the child discovers that open affection and mutual confidence may not be forthcoming within the family. The unavoidable interdependence of kinsmen does not preclude bitter rivalries and hatreds behind the front of family face—all of which must be concealed beneath the polite rubrics of Confucian filial piety. Thus one is responsible to and absolutely dependent upon a group in which he feels no adequate psychological security.

Obligations to the family nevertheless color every contact with the outside world. For example, in Japanese primary schools every child in a class is promoted and every child receives some sort of prize lest a pupil lose face for his family and commit suicide. This utter domination of the individual by the family, coupled with the lack of psychological security within the family, have emerged dramatically in the writer's experience via the intimate confidences and correspondence of scores of Japanese friends. Youths feel alone and sorely beset—a condition in no way mitigated by rigid separation of the sexes. Only an occasional female cousin provides a confidante; what is said to her remains within the family even though she is not of the immediate household. Japanese conduct which Occidentals regard as erratic and inscrutable often stems from family situations; an individual cannot make a decision till the family council acts, and should it act counter to the individual's desires, he is forced to repudiate half-made commitments.

The growing boy learns to conform to stereotyped masculine roles explicitly set forth in precept and in story as part of Japanese cultural tradition. He is indoctrinated with Confucian loyalty and respect to elders, and with Japanese martial ideals. His mother and sisters minister to him, indulge him, and obey him; by masculine example and teaching he learns that no real man acknowledges tender feelings toward women. His affection for his mother—which may be very real—is repressed from the time that he discovers that it is his prerogative to lord it over any female.

Family experience, therefore, has provided him with emotionally based principles of conduct: he must be loyal to his family against a hostile, treacherous world; should his acts occasion loss of face for his family the offense is beyond forgiveness; tenderness and affection are unworthy of his status as male; the proper order of society is a hierarchy typified by his father, elder brothers, younger brothers, and women. Small wonder that he accepts the myths of Imperial divinity and of the hostility of all foreign nations toward poor little hemmed-in have-not Japan. He identifies himself with his nation, for the pattern of his inner emotional cosmos, learned before he could talk, is rationalized and projected in the dogmas of *Kōdō* nationalism while it remains inarticulate for him as an individual.

Neither space nor the writer's competence justifies detailed psychoanalytic interpretations. Those who offer such interpretations provide illuminating insights. For example, the approved pattern of masculine personality in Japan seems to be narcissistic and auto-erotic. Mutuality in love is excluded by the dogma of female inferiority—save for those hopeless extra-conventional passions that usually end in double suicide because they challenge the family system. The institutionalized prostitute caters to male narcissism and auto-eroticism; the wife is but a mechanism for perpetuating the family, so the prostitute offers a sanctioned escape from family controls. Such psychological phenomena underlie the loudly proclaimed Japanese devaluation of the individual. Life is worthless and may be discarded, other persons are of no value, love is obscene and may be thrown away. Such attitudes symbolize the repudiation of sex and consequently of the value of the human body. The male ego is inflated to a degree that demands revenge or suicide at the slightest hint of insult.

The average Japanese is faced with the reality of his own inferior social status. To compensate, he exalts the Emperor as ego-surrogate. By identification with the Emperor and death in battle one achieves that status as *kami* (deity) to which in his narcissistic feelings every Japanese male knows himself to be entitled. Foreigners, like women, are dirt and pollution, especially in view of their denial of the world of make-believe which the Japanese insist on maintaining through polite fictions. Observers comment that Japanese never feel sin or guilt, only shame at loss of face. This aspect of narcissistic, auto-erotic personalities is familar in clinical records everywhere.

Further details significant in analysis of Japanese personal character include compulsive preoccupation with small objects and the manual skills involved in their creation and manipulation. Perhaps this compulsion symbolizes the lost pleasures of infancy that centered in the manipulation of a highly interesting "little thing" by mother or nursemaid. The compulsive etiquette that treats eating as shameful is another detail significant to a psychoanalyst. Similarly meaningful practices include: the exclusion of children from adult concerns despite imposition of responsibility for family face; the near-pathological persistence and conscientiousness of most Japanese; the self-righteous fanaticism and arrogance typical of narcissistic persons; the orientation of Shintō rites to formal purification; the effects of the taboo against touching other persons on Japanese preferences for games and sports; and the unconscious criteria of selection in adoption of some foreign customs and the repudiation of others.[7]

The wartime studies of Japanese personality indicate that large numbers of Japanese behave in ways regarded by Euro-Americans as neurotic. Anthropologists tend to infer that such resemblances may be superficial, that tradition imposes upon individuals habits resembling those of Occidental neurotics without development of the inner conflicts in which true neuroses arise. Accessible evidence, however, favors the conclusion that genuine neurosis with its full weight of inner misery and social maladjustment occurs far more frequently in Japanese society than in many other societies. Japanese "culture"—of which militarism is both effect and cause—apparently places grievous burdens upon its carriers.

Further research, urgently needed, can determine the validity of these tentative hypotheses and can deal with important questions thus far unanswered. Are the patterns of personal development here suggested universal? Such universality is highly questionable. Perhaps the

Mealtime in the home of a rural Japanese mayor.
Formal meal in the guest room.

picture summarized here is more characteristic of urban Japanese and of those educated individuals who wrestle with the conflict of ideas engendered by cultural diffusion from the Occident. Is the cheerful, patient peasant developed in another sort of background, or perhaps in differing local backgrounds? What other patterns of personal character appear, and what is their statistical frequency of occurrence? Do the hypotheses thus far advanced account for Japanese women? Are all general formulations indefensible? In view of the insistence of psychoanalysts that a long and meticulous analysis must precede any diagnosis of individual psychological disturbances, what is the justification for vague interpretations of the behavior of large numbers of people in psychoanalytic terms?

In other words, present knowledge is inadequate, spotty, unverified, and non-specific. Probably also, it suffers from wartime bias. The issues can be clarified only by research in Japan by qualified specialists. Despite misgivings of personal bias, the caution is offered that those who do such research should spend years, not months, in Japan. The writer "learned all the answers" in his first year in Japan. The next six years taught him that practically all of those answers were misleading or false. Perhaps another seven years would have indicated the wisdom of saying nothing at all, and the motley throng who rush in where angels fear to tread would have numbered one less. The anthropologist who stays among a people for a mere six months or a year should avoid Japan or change his tactics and settle down. Assuming that a peripheral

Informal supper in the room next to the kitchen.
Photos by D. G. Haring.

people might be studied adequately in less than a year, the Japanese are not primitives, but a civilized society with a history and numbering over seventy millions. If protracted residence proves fatal to some brilliant deductions, the objective is not raw facts, but facts plus insight.

Consequently, research into Japanese mentality should be cooperative and organized on some such plan as the Field Laboratory conducted among the Pomo Indians at Ukiah, California, for over a decade by Drs. Bernard and Ethel Aginsky and their associates.[8] Such laboratories, operating in rural and urban centers in Japan over a period of years, could contribute mightily to practical policy as well as to the advancement of knowledge. If funds were forthcoming from private sources the advantages of non-governmental administration would be considerable. Personnel should be selected from anthropologists familiar with Japan and her history, psychologists and psychoanalysts, and sociologists. Caucasian personnel might well be minimized, with *nisei* and qualified native Japanese predominating; this policy would facilitate rapport with the subjects of investigation.

Meanwhile those who work with historical documents are invited to seek out and translate autobiographies, descriptions of child training and infantile experience, and of family situations. Such data may indicate the recency of alleged Japanese character traits, or may push their origin back to the horizons of history. Similar inquiries are in order with respect to other Oriental peoples, for coming decades will witness much study of contemporary psychological phenomena.

In any case attempts to apply American educational and political philosophy and the accompanying techniques in Japan are blind and foolish. Re-education of the Japanese demands fresh research, a pertinent philosophy, and a degree of insight and adaptability that victors in war rarely exhibit toward the vanquished. Persons who at heart are carpet-baggers cannot do the task; the Occupation Command will be justified in ruthless elimination of such individuals from its personnel. The immediate need is for research and for a flexible program that profits by the results of research as they emerge in verifiable form.

NOTES

1. See Ruth F. Benedict's "The concept of the guardian spirit in North America," *Memoir no. 29, American anthropological association* (1923) and *Patterns of culture* (Boston & New York, 1934); also Margaret Mead's *Coming of age in Samoa* (New York, 1928), *Growing up in New Guinea* (New York, 1930) and *Sex and temperament in three primitive societies* (New York, 1935). Edward Sapir's pioneer contributions, less directly pertinent here, are cited in detail in the paper by Kluckhohn (note 2, below).

2. Gregory Bateson, *Naven* (Cambridge, Eng., 1936) and Gregory Bateson and Margaret Mead, *Balinese character, a photographic analysis* (New York academy of sciences, 1942); Ernest Beaglehole "Character structure, its role in the analysis of interpersonal relations," *Psychiatry: journal of the biology and pathology of interpersonal relations*, 7 (May 1944), no. 2; Cora DuBois, *The people of Alor, a social psychological study of an East Indian island, with analyses by Abram Kardiner and Emil Oberholzer* (Minneapolis, 1944); Erik Homburger Erikson, "Hitler's imagery and German youth," *Psychiatry*, 5 (Nov. 1942), no. 4 and *Observations on the Yurok: childhood and world image*, University of California publications in American archaeology and ethnology, vol. 35, no. 10 (Berkeley, 1943); Ralph Linton, *The cultural background of personality* (New York, 1945); Margaret Mead, "Character formation in two South Sea societies," *American neurological association, transactions 66th annual meeting* (1940); Laura Thompson and Alice Joseph, *The Hopi way* (U.S. Indian Service, 1944); John W. M. Whiting, *Becoming a Kwoma: teaching and learning in a New Guinea tribe* (New Haven, 1941); Dorothea C. Leighton and Clyde Kluckhohn, *Children of the people: the Navaho individual and his development* (Cambridge, 1946). For a historical summary of the influence of psychiatry on anthropology, see Clyde Kluckhohn, "The influence of psychiatry on anthropology in America during the past one hundred years," *One hundred years of American psychiatry*, edited by J. K. Hall, G. Zilboorg, and H. A. Bunker (New York, 1944).

3. See DuBois (note 2, above) and the three works of Abram Kardiner, *The individual and his society, with a foreword and two ethnological reports by Ralph Linton* (New York, 1939), "The concept of basic personality structure as an operational tool in the social sciences," in *The science of man in the world crisis*, ed. by Ralph Linton (New York, 1945) and Kardiner with the collaboration of Ralph Linton, Cora DuBois, and James West, *The psychological frontiers of society* (New York, 1945).

4. Quoted without page citation by Fritz Wittels, *Freud and his time* (New York, 1931), p. 171.

5. Beaglehole, *op. cit.*, p. 155.

6. Studies frankly confined to Japanese internees in the United States are omitted from the scope of this paper. By the time this is in print, Ruth Benedict's forthcoming book on the Japanese probably will be available; it should be included among the papers listed below. Geoffrey Gorer, "Themes in Japanese culture," *Transactions New York academy of sciences*, ser. II, 5 (March 1943), 106-24; Arnold Meadow, *An analysis of Japanese character structure* (New York: distributed privately by The Institute for Intercultural Studies, 1944); Ruth F. Benedict, *Japanese behavior patterns*. Office of War Information, Area III, Overseas Branch, Foreign Morale Analysis Division, Report #25 (Washington, 1945); Talcott Parsons, "Population and social structure," chapter 4 in *Japan's prospect*, ed. by D. G. Haring (Cambridge, 1946). See also chapter 1 in the same book, *passim;* Weston LaBarre, "Some observations on character structure in the Orient: the Japanese," *Psychiatry*, 8 (August 1945), no. 3, an excellent summary; Herman M. Spitzer (in consultation with Dr. Ruth Fulton Benedict), *Bibliography of articles and books relating to Japanese psychology,* Office of War Information, Area III, Overseas Branch, Foreign Morale Analysis Division, Report #24 (Washington, 1945).

7. Unconscious criteria of selection on the part of the Japanese in the process of cultural diffusion are discussed in preliminary fashion by the present writer in chapter 7 of *Japan's prospect* (see Parsons entry, note 6, above).

8. William Henderson and B. W. Aginsky, "A social science field laboratory," *American sociological review*, 6 (February 1941), no. 1.

(Comment: The University of Michigan has maintained just such a field laboratory at Okayama, Japan, for a number of years, after the foregoing article was published.—Ed.)

JAPANESE NATIONAL CHARACTER: CULTURAL ANTHROPOLOGY, PSYCHOANALYSIS, AND HISTORY

Douglas G. Haring

National character, however conceived, perennially fascinates both scholar and layman. Psychoanalysts describe it in terms of the typical past experiences of individuals. Historians describe it in terms of those past events that circumscribe the future even as they open new doors to a people. Cultural anthropologists strive to attain Olympian detachment by combining history and psychology with field observation.

Some recent efforts of cultural anthropologists to organize our knowledge of national character betray greater reliance upon psychological techniques than upon history. Partly because psychoanalysis is fashionable, but more certainly because anthropologists usually observe nonliterate peoples who are unencumbered with recorded history, anthropological studies of literate peoples tend to stress field observation of present behavior without thorough study of the relevant history. The tie between psychology and cultural anthropology often is more conspicuous than the time-honored dependence of anthropology upon history.

Should cultural anthropologists therefore be censured for neglect of history? Some of them, brilliantly, have never weakened in their exploration of history; others are vulnerable to the charge of neglect. Sound investigations of national character recognize that the cultural heritage of a people furnishes the raw materials of personality and sets the limits of probability in the patterning of individual development. Every human being starts life as an unconditioned organism, who eventually makes himself into a person as he learns the customs and ways of thought of his local cultural milieu. By whatever name it may be called, cultural heritage is a historical phenomenon.

The past decade has witnessed attempts by numerous distinguished anthropologists to describe the national character of the Japanese. The verifiability of the resulting hypotheses holds absorbing interest for me because of a lifelong preoccupation with things Japanese. Unexpected circumstances recently placed me in a situation conducive to fresh perspective: I studied at first hand a Japanese community that had escaped the major influences that for four centuries have fashioned the rest of Japan. I emerged with new respect for Franz Boas' classic statement that "the material of anthropology is such that it needs must be a historical science."

The war demanded that Americans understand the Japanese in order to conduct hostilities and to effect a just peace. Agencies of the United States Government assembled anthropologists and psychologists, asked them to sift the evidence critically and to describe Japanese "national character." These scientists faced the problem of studying a people *in absentia;* direct observation was not possible. They rounded up hundreds of Japanese: immigrants, prisoners of war, and Nisei who had attended school in Japan. These individuals were interviewed, tested by psychologists, persuaded to write autobiographies, and studied in many other ways. Americans who had lived in Japan were questioned. Japanese motion pictures were analyzed to discover the sort of personality to which they appealed. Other investigators read books about Japan and translations of Japanese literature, history, popular magazines, political pamphlets, and schoolbooks.

The findings were used effectively in preparing broadcasts and printed matter for Japanese consumption, in training our Army and Navy officers for Military Government in Japan, in defining Occupation policy, and in working out the treaty of peace. Papers in scientific journals set forth the main conclusions of the investigation. Dr. Ruth Benedict, leader in the research and inspiration of the staff, assembled the outstanding findings in a remarkable book, "The Chrysanthemum and the Sword." An eagerly-read translation of this book has won the respect though not the unqualified agreement of Japanese scholars and critics.

Thus far, however, no one has commanded the funds and personnel necessary to verify these wartime studies on the spot in Japan, and indeed it no longer is possible to do so. The Japanese mode of living has changed too profoundly. The present situation could be studied; it would be feasible to discover much about prewar Japan while correcting our knowledge of contemporary Japanese character. Ruth Benedict's hopes of research in Japan were ended by her untimely death, though her book stands as a worthy monument to her insight. It states systematically the norms of conduct that nearly all prewar Japanese acknowledged. From this source and from other psychoanthropological studies of the war period, outstanding aspects of Japanese conduct and personal character may be inferred:

(1) Psychologically and culturally the Japanese people are unusually homogeneous. They act and think more alike than do Occidental peoples. The avowed aim of Japan's prewar Ministry of Education was to produce subjects of the Emperor so much alike as to be interchangeable for national purposes. Such homogeneity does not preclude differ-

ing norms for the sexes; the ideal man of Japanese tradition naturally differs from the ideal woman. American wartime studies concentrated upon norms for males and neglected the women as less pertinent to the immediate necessity of winning the war.

(2) The Japanese conform almost eagerly to numberless exact rules of conduct and exhibit bewilderment when required to act alone or in situations not anticipated in the codes. In the words of Frederick Hulse: "The most outstanding trait in Japanese behavior . . . is its thoroughly planned quality; . . . spontaneous action is uncalled for. . . . A stable individual is assumed to anticipate all emergencies and be ready to meet them calmly. . . . The display of emotion is dangerous."

(3) The major sanctions of conformity to Japanese codes of conduct are ridicule and shame. Early in life every child learns that the slightest breach of proper conduct may expose his family to ridicule, and that a lapse from propriety may leave him unsupported in the face of the ridicule of the world and the wrath of his own family. Hence individuals never face unflinchingly the adverse opinion of society and avoid assuming responsibility alone. Should a lone individual accept responsibility for something that has gone amiss, he commits suicide; ceremonial suicide is the sole recourse of one who "loses face" for his group. When loyalties conflict with codes of conduct, suicide again affords an honorable solution of the dilemma; thereby one demonstrates the purity of his motives as well as his respect for rules that circumstances have forced him to violate.

The complaint of Christian missionaries, that "the Japanese have no sense of sin," is understandable. For the Japanese exemplify the anthropological concept of a "shame culture"; the driving motive of individuals is fear of shame rather than sense of guilt. Societies like our own, in which guilt is an approved motive for good conduct, attach slight importance to shame, and are called "guilt cultures."

(4) The Japanese are extremely polite. Politeness is conceived of as adherence to a code that prescribes correct treatment of others in order to maintain one's own "face" and self-esteem. The test of Japanese politeness is ego-centered: "Have I acted correctly?" This contrasts with the concept of courtesy, as conduct motivated by consideration of the goals and welfare of the other person; the test of courtesy is alter-centered, i.e., "Is the other person better off because of what has occurred?" Thus defined, courtesy is alien to traditional Japanese codes. Weston La Barre observes pointedly, "The basic function of Japanese politeness is to use the conventional to mask the real, in emotional matters."

(5) Because Japanese families and Japanese society are rigid hierarchies, individuals must ascertain their precise status in every social

situation. Otherwise one may blunder and treat a superior as an inferior or vice versa. Any misgivings as to the exact status of someone else in a situation, as higher or lower than oneself, render a Japanese acutely uncomfortable—hence the need for vigilance concerning everyone's "proper place." This attitude transfers to international relations; American blindness to this motive helped to precipitate the war. Japanese diplomatic notes stressed the necessity of "enabling each nation to find its proper place"—clarification of the hierarchical ranking of nations was a compulsive necessity for the Japanese, even at the cost of war. Insight into this motive facilitates understanding of the postwar coöperativeness and relative lack of bitterness of the Japanese.

(6) Veneration of family ancestors and of the Emperor as surrogate of the national ancestors means that every individual has been reared to constant awareness of infinite blessings received from these sources. No effort of his, even death in battle, can repay one ten-thousandth part of the obligation to the Emperor and to his forebears. In addition, he has been impressed with his inflexible duties to the world (i.e., to family, to feudal lord, to benefactors) and equally stern duties to his own name (i.e., to avenge insults, admit no failure, to fulfil proprieties including vendetta). These latter duties, unlike the obligation of gratitude to ancestors and Emperor, are deemed onerous and burdensome.

(7) Pleasures of the flesh are regarded as in no way sinful or evil. They are subordinate, however, to the major goals of life. Ruth Benedict wrote: "The Japanese make life hard for themselves by cultivating physical pleasures and then setting up a code in which these pleasures are the very things which must not be indulged as a serious way of life. They cultivate the pleasures of the flesh like fine arts, and then, when they are fully savored, they sacrifice them to duty. . . . The strong, according to Japanese verdict, are those who disregard personal happiness and fulfil their obligations. Strength of character, they think, is shown in conforming, not in rebelling."

(8) The word *makoto*, mistranslated in dictionaries as "sincerity," is charged with emotional significance in Japan. Mrs. Benedict explains *makoto* as "zeal to follow the 'road' mapped out by the Japanese code and the Japanese Spirit." *Makoto* is not equivalent to sincerity; a *makoto* person uses every means, including deception and violence, to carry out his duty. The dictionary translation, "sincere," has occasioned endless misunderstanding between Japanese and Americans when both parties profess "sincerity" but attach quite different meanings to the word. In Japanese eyes *makoto*, utter devotion to codes of conduct, is one of the highest virtues.

This inadequate summary of Japanese characteristics cited in the wartime studies does not differ very greatly from what the Japanese say of themselves. Japanese analyses of their own character are highly stereotyped. From kindergarten through junior college, all of them were subjected—up to 1945—to the same standardized "ethics" courses. All Japanese learned by heart the official picture of a "splendid Japanese" drafted by a paternalistic Ministry of Education. Inquiries concerning Japanese personality evoke that standardized response. In emphasis and vocabulary it differs from the list just presented, but it tends to embody many of the same themes. Its central emphasis is upon the duty of every Japanese to be a loyal subject of the divine Emperor.

Granting that this pattern of personal character was indoctrinated by the government, how is such a set of norms to be explained? Most of the wartime studies rely heavily upon psychoanalysis; most of them go beyond Ruth Benedict in accepting that approach. The concept of a "compulsive personality" is invoked frequently. In the words of Weston La Barre: "The traits of the compulsive personality . . . are: secretiveness, hiding of emotions and attitudes; perseveration and persistency; conscientiousness; self-righteousness; a tendency to project attitudes; fanaticism; arrogance; 'touchiness,' precision and perfectionism; neatness and ritualistic cleanliness; ceremoniousness; conformity to rule; sadomasochistic behavior; hypochondriasis; suspiciousness; jealousy and enviousness; pedantry; sentimentality; love of scatological obscenity and anal sexuality. . . . This list of characteristics . . . occurs with great consistency in typical Japanese character structure," Geoffrey Gorer has pointed out that descriptions of compulsive behavior usually also include miserliness and parsimony, but that no one has accused the Japanese of being stingy.

Like many other writers, both Gorer and La Barre insist that Japanese compulsiveness derives from too early and too severe toilet training of infants. Granted that in American neurotics compulsive traits often are related to overstrict infant toilet training, I do not rest content with this explanation, though I agree that prewar Japanese behavior characteristically resembled that of "compulsive personalities." During eight years' residence in Japan I did not observe early or severe toilet training, although observation is facilitated by the custom of holding babies over the gutter in front of the house. I admit, however, that I am not trained to observe infant behavior and that toilet training is not one of my major interests.

Does history offer a surer guide? Ever since their adoption of Chinese writing in the eighth century A.D., the Japanese have produced historical chronicles, novels, poetry, religious treatises, and discourses that range in content from painting to economics. Prior to the seventeenth century, this rich literature fails to disclose some of the traits of Japanese character cited in the wartime studies—save perhaps in rudimentary form. No reader of the "Manyoshu"—an eighth-century anthology of poetry—or of the eleventh-century novel, "Tale of Genji," would apply the formula "compulsive personality" to the Japanese of those far-off centuries. They loved and brawled with abandon, bore obligations lightly, were not overawed by ancestors or Emperor, and manifested no taut preoccupation with ceremonial suicide. Court nobles and their ladies dallied preciously in Chinese aesthetics with never a glance at·Confucian moral codes; Buddhist theology was attenuated till it became a fashionable, genteel stimulus to refined melancholy while its asceticism and philosophical pessimism were ignored blandly. Edwin Reischauer comments:

The Japanese . . seem to have been an openly emotional and unrepressed people during much of their history, perhaps until as late as the sixteenth or seventeenth century. The unending quest for love and beauty . . . typified the courtier of ancient times. Murder and treachery, uprisings and feuding, passionate outbursts and equally passionate devotion characterized the feudal age. The Confucian insistence on decorum and the "doctrine of the mean" . . . made relatively little impression on the ancient Japanese. There was nothing moderate about them. The Portuguese and Spaniards in the sixteenth century did not find them unduly repressed emotionally or more prone to conformity than the Europeans themselves.

How did it happen that the Japanese changed so radically between, say, 1600 and 1900 A.D.? History offers a dramatic answer. The Japanese of modern times are products of a dictatorship that foreshadowed the totalitarian police states of the twentieth century. Prewar militaristic Japan emerged naturally and without break from this background of three centuries' preparation.

The great Japanese dictators were preceded by prolonged civil war and cumulative governmental impotence, beginning roughly with the thirteenth century. Late in the sixteenth century three outstanding dictators followed in close succession, unified the nation, and laid the basis of three centuries of peace. First arose Oda Nobunaga, a rough soldier who met force with greater force and coerced the local lords into submission; then came Japan's foremost military genius, Toyotomi Hideyoshi, who rose from stable boy to general and consolidated the feudal duchies by force and clever manipulation; and finally, Tokugawa Iyeyasu, supreme genius of dictatorial organization. Iyeyasu aimed to establish his rule so firmly that the House of Tokugawa would dominate Japan indefinitely, no matter how stupid his individual descendants might be. This goal was realized for two and a half centuries—the centuries that shaped the Japanese character as it continued up to the Second World War.

The Tokugawa technique of holding the nation in subjection was based on strict division of the people into social classes. Houses, dress, food, and etiquette were prescribed for each class by incredibly detailed sumptuary laws. The highest class, the *daimyo*, were compelled to reside at the capital in alternate years lest they foment rebellion at their local fiefs; when they returned home their families remained as hostages at the capital. Loyalty to overlord was enforced as the supreme virtue. This ideal was inculcated so deeply that retainers gladly sacrificed wife, children, friends, possessions, and life itself for their lords. Omniscient espionage kept everyone suspicious of his own household. Enforcement of the codes devolved upon the two-sworded samurai, professional warriors who were authorized to decapitate on the spot anyone of lesser status whose conduct was "other than expected." The price of survival was constant vigilance, meticulous conformity to the numerous codes, and cultivation of a smiling face—or at least a "deadpan"—regardless of real emotions. The survivors were those who learned in early childhood to keep their own counsel, trust no one, and conform fanatically to whatever might be ordered. With prolonged peace the despised merchant class waxed rich despite capital levies and confiscations; they were abetted by the plight of samurai who fell into debt and hesitated to use their privilege of cutting off heads. Unlike the knights of feudal Europe, samurai rarely held land and were totally dependent upon grants of rice from their lords; loyalty and conformity were the price of life.

Lafcadio Hearn was among the first foreign observers correctly to estimate the effect of three centuries of dictatorship upon the Japanese character. His writings are marred by blind adulation of everything Japanese, to the amusement of the Japanese themselves. They sincerely adore his memory, however, because he viewed so much of their culture with appreciative, accurate insight. Hearn's account of the dictatorship merits quotation:

Every detail of the farmer's existence was prescribed for by law,—from the size, form, and cost of his dwelling, down even to such trifling matters as the number and quality of the dishes to be served to him at meal-times. A farmer with an income of 100 *koku* of rice . . . might build a house 60 feet long, but no longer: he was forbidden to construct it with a room containing an alcove. . . . None of his family were permitted to wear silk; and in case of the marriage of his daughter to a person legally entitled to wear silk, the bridegroom was to be requested not to wear silk at the wedding. Three kinds of viands only were to be served at the wedding of such a farmer's daughter or son; and the quality as well as the quantity of the soup, fish, or sweetmeats offered to the wedding-guests, were legally fixed. So likewise the number of the wedding-gifts: even the cost of the presents of rice-wine and dried fish was prescribed, and the quality of the single fan which it was permissible to offer the bride. . . .

A farmer whose property was assessed at 50 *koku* was forbidden to build a house more than 45 feet long. At the wedding of his daughter the gift-girdle was not to exceed 50 *sen* in value; and it was forbidden to serve more than one kind of soup at the wedding-feast. . . . A farmer with a property assessed at 20 *koku* was not allowed to build a house more than 36 feet long, or to use . . . superior qualities of wood. . . . The roof of his house was to be made of bamboo-thatch or straw; and he was strictly forbidden the comfort of floor mats.

The regulations specified the kind of combs, if any, the hair ornaments, and even the thongs of sandals worn by women of each class; the dolls permitted to the children were listed in detail, by classes, to say nothing of kinds of food and even the forms of speech. The latter prescription accounts for the elaborate "courtesy language" that has made it difficult for a foreigner to learn to speak Japanese well; there are different vocabularies adapted to every difference in status between the speaker and the person addressed.

Although Hearn gives no hint that the sumptuary regulation was distasteful to the people, Japanese writers have portrayed the oppression that accompanied it. In a book published about 1700, Kumazawa Banzan wrote:

The peasant toils all year long and everything he produces is taken by the annual tax. Moreover, if he does not produce enough and falls behind in his payment, pressure is applied and he is obliged to sell wife and children, even fields, forests, and domestic animals. This breaks up his home and he is cast adrift. Those with no place to go become beggars. Even if he remains in his own village he cannot avoid starvation in famine years; in desperation he may lose his mind. He is tortured by the water cure, by the bamboo blinds, or on the wooden horse. Thus he may fall ill or else grow so weak that he cannot work. No matter how shocking the situation, there is no avenue of appeal or redress.

During the Tokugawa era there occurred some twelve hundred peasant rebellions. Invariably the leaders were executed, even though the feudal lord against whom they had rebelled might be punished for having permitted the rebellion.

In "modern Japan"—at least that phase of it which extended from 1868 to 1945—the ancient discipline was modified and redirected in the interests of imperialistic militarism. Samurai no longer strutted with their two swords, proud of their right to decapitate lesser folk. In their stead an efficient centralized police combined the experience of two centuries of control with the police lore of European monarchies. More potent than the ubiquitous police was the state cult of Shintō, fashioned deliberately from elements of local folk-religion to unify the people and give backbone to national morale. Originally, Shintō ideology exalting the divine Emperor inspired the overthrow of the Tokugawas and the restoration of the Emperor to the visible headship of the state. Subsequently the astute makers of modern Japan took cues from Bismarck and Herbert Spencer and remolded Shintō into a cult of fanatic loyalty to the Emperor and supreme devotion to His state. Always the police stood in the background, ready to deal with those whose patriotic zeal became suspect.

The police aspect of authoritarian societies is outstanding because ordinary folk know little and care less about high policy. Especially in the Orient, the common man is convinced that such affairs are none of his business. The police, however, he knows at first hand. Japan's police were both paternalistic and censoring; in their way they cared for the people and the people expected it. They also supervised popular thinking, watched the acts of every individual, and reminded him of any unfulfilled duty.

In 1925 I became a confidant of a high police officer in Tokyo. On one occasion he demonstrated the efficiency of the system by telling me of the mass of information recorded about myself: every trip, every friend, every letter sent or received, every telephone call—and to cap the climax, a detailed account of my activities while in the United States from 1922 to 1924. Not that I was particularly suspect; all foreigners were subject to minute scrutiny, and Japanese subjects were watched almost as closely. Under such a regime one learns to trust no one, to keep his own counsel, and to conceal his emotions. Japanese personality was compelled, not compulsive.

All the features of the alleged "compulsive personality" of the Japanese are logical fruits of the police state. An explanation centered in diapers is suspect if it neglects three centuries of fear-inspired discipline. To say this does not refute psychoanalytic interpretations, for relentless police supervision modifies the human psyche profoundly. Psychological explanations, however, should be oriented to the facts of inescapable absolutism and sumptuary control of individuals. The psychological tensions habitual in parents outweigh details of specific practices such as toilet training. Police controls impose strains on individuals—strains that multiply and become more rigorous as adulthood is reached. Whatever psychological concepts be invoked to characterize the Japanese, there is agreement that in prewar days strain and tension were outstanding aspects of Japanese personalities.

Granted that thorough, extensive researches into Japanese character have not yet been conducted in Japan, is it still possible to discover general checks upon the adequacy of this hypothesis that a long-continued police state is the major influence in Japanese national character?

Two possibilities of verification suggest themselves. If the police state were relaxed and the perpetual espionage lifted, would the character of the people change accordingly? Again, are there places not reached by Tokugawa discipline, where pre-Tokugawa customs survive and, if so, what light do they shed upon Japanese character?

To both of these possibilities positive answers are available.

The police state has vanished, temporarily at least. I spent nearly four months of 1952 in Japan, both in cities and as a guest in a farm household. Such brief observation falls short of scientific adequacy, but Japanese behavior had changed profoundly during the twenty-six years that I had been absent from Japan. People now go where they wish, choose friends and write letters as they please, speak their minds with apparent freedom. The complex language of social status is falling into disuse. The drab colors of daily clothing—and of houses, formerly unpainted—have given way to gay brilliance. Occidental music has been assimilated and "everyone" sings and dances. Men and women associate freely. The number of persons who speak from the shoulder in straightforward fashion has increased. In short, the people have responded ebulliently to wider freedom. Modern Japan indeed faces grave problems, perhaps in the shadow of reviving tyranny; meanwhile, however, the people ardently sample the joys of freedom. Contemporary Japan is a land of swift change in mentality and character, no matter how unfortunate some of the changes may seem. Stalwart defenders of the old order deplore the trend in national character; their very protests, however, lend color to the hypothesis that the police state created the typical features of Japanese character. The spokesman for a group of farmers said to me spontaneously, "When you return home, thank the Americans for taking the police off our necks. It is such a relief to be free from prying supervision, to go and come as we please, to read what we wish, and to say what we think!"

No nation changes over night. Older people in particular are not silkworms that can metamorphose into moths. Many young people, however, know little of some aspects of the older Japan; thanks to the movies they are more familiar with America, Hollywood version. Even among scholars the younger men recall the past so vaguely that they resent descriptions of Japan in terms of customs that were universal thirty-five years ago. It is too early to estimate the durability of these changes. Should totalitarianism—Communist or fascist—revive in Japan, its appeal may reside in provision of authoritative norms of conduct for many who find freedom a burden, who are ill at ease when faced with independent decisions. There is a fair chance, however, that the Japanese will rally to defend their new freedoms against the Asiatic tide of Communism, and will vindicate the soundness of their new ways of feeling and living.

What of the second possible check upon the hypothesis that Tokugawa sumptuary legislation molded traditional Japanese character? Can there exist in this day and age any Japanese whose forebears escaped Tokugawa domination and whose customs still preserve traces of pre-Tokugawa Japan?

It would be pleasant to report that my scientific acumen had envisioned the possibility that pre-Tokugawa institutions might survive on some remote Japanese islet; that in pursuit of this triumph of scientific insight I had searched diligently, found just the right island, studied it on the spot, and returned home waving the banner of discovery. The facts are less romantic. Never had I dreamed of the existence of a community overlooked by Tokugawa meticulosity. I never had heard of Amami Ōshima, situated between Kyushu and Okinawa. When the Pacific Science Board unexpectedly asked me to conduct an anthropological survey of Amami Ōshima for the United States Army, I looked at a map and said yes. In the field, it was months before I realized that when Amami customs differed from those of Japan Proper, all the differences occurred in matters stressed by Tokugawa restrictive legislation. Thereafter I gradually dug out an answer from history.

Amami Ōshima is the scene of a fascinating history recorded with fair accuracy from the twelfth century of the Christian era. The earlier centuries, important to both anthropologists and historians, must be omitted in the present context. The last three or four centuries call for scrutiny. Unlike Okinawa and the southern Ryukyus, Amami Ōshima and the adjoining islands have been thoroughly Japanese throughout their history. For some time prior to 1600 A.D., Amami Ōshima was incorporated in the ancient Liu Ch'iu kingdom on Okinawa; this interlude is remembered happily because the Liu Ch'iu kings waxed rich by smuggling and levied no taxes. About 1611 the ambitious Japanese duchy of Satsuma on Southern Kyushu expanded southward and

Amami Ōshima woodcutter's wife and children. *Photo by D. G. Haring.*

subjugated Amami Ōshima. Chronologically this expansion coincided with the establishment of Tokugawa power over Japan's main islands. Satsuma's expansion was possible because the Tokugawa rulers never gained absolute control over the great southwestern feudatories of Satsuma and Chōshū. At the battle of Sekigahara (1600) these duchies submitted outwardly to Tokugawa Iyeyasu; thenceforth they were held in check by Tokugawa vassals placed strategically to check their ambitions within Japan Proper. Expansion of Satsuma to the southern islands, however, was not blocked because the Tokugawas had no navy. Satsuma and Chōshū were reckoned among the *Tozama* ("outer lords") whose fiefs were remote from the capital at Yedo and whose submission to the Tokugawa power continued suspect.

Satsuma soon found that Amami Ōshima could yield substantial revenues. Amami produced, and still produces, sugar cane, from which the peasants make "black sugar" that became the favorite candy of Japanese peasants. To monopolize this product, the lords of Satsuma reduced Amamians to serfdom, treated them as beasts of burden, and jealously excluded Tokugawa interest or control from the island. From 1615 till 1870, Satsuma managed to keep Amami Ōshima out of Tokugawa hands, held its people in virtual slavery, and resisted introduction of external influences and new ideas to this profitable island. Partly from this source, Satsuma accumulated the wealth through which, in combination with Chōshū, Tosa, and Hizen, they overthrew the Tokugawa dictators in 1868 and instituted the modern government of Japan. The new Tokyo government accepted European political patterns; among other reforms, they freed all serfs including the Amamians. Since the 1870's, Amami people have shared in the modern development of Japan, and because to them the Emperor's rule symbolizes liberation, they continue unusually loyal to Tokyo.

In Amami Ōshima, therefore, the culture of contemporary Japan is superimposed upon an archaic "cultural base" that preserves some ideas and beliefs long extinct in Japan Proper, but recorded in ancient Japanese documents. Their dialects, close to archaic Japanese, are unintelligible to people from Japan Proper. Some of their genealogies go back to court nobles of the twelfth-century capital at Kyōto. Despite the influence of modern Japanese schools and textbooks, their conduct and patterns of personality exhibit few of the features distinctive of prewar Japanese national character and are reminiscent of the singing, dancing, carefree peoples of the Philippines and southern Pacific islands. The marks of grinding poverty and protracted slavery under Satsuma are readily apparent; nevertheless, the folkways of an earlier era survive. Again and again the Amanians remind one of the recorded pictures of life in Japan Proper from the tenth century up to the Tokugawa era. The people are cheerful, affectionate, frank, hospitable; their emotions are open and unrepressed. Reischauer's description of the pre-Tokugawa Japanese fits them nicely: "The unending quest for love and beauty . . . murder and treachery . . . passionate outbursts and equally passionate devotion."

Amamians meet friendly advances more than halfway. American G.I.'s stationed there soon became attached to them. To stress these aspects of Amamian character detracts nothing from the hospitality and friendliness, usually unfeigned, of the people of Japan Proper. In Japan Proper, however, frankness and friendliness without suspicion are new, cultivated with a bit of effort; the Tokugawa mask is not quickly discarded. In Amami there never was any Tokugawa mask. As far as the "planned quality" of Japanese behavior goes, Amamian behavior is less cast in the rigid mold of codes of conduct, more spontaneous and fun-loving. Their rich and durable sense of humor withstands the disasters of storm and famine that sweep their island; they "kid" each other with the same abandon that American young people manifest; they even poke fun at Japanese ceremonial suicide, saying, "Why commit suicide? Living is too much fun!" True, they retain the habit of watchful attention to the whims of authority; two hundred and fifty years of slavery taught them to anticipate the wishes of rulers and avoid torture. But their folk songs run the gamut of human emotions, their folk dancing is superb, and the carefree abandon of the southern islanders has not been destroyed by prolonged serfdom.

Ridicule and shame carry weight in Amami but do not pass endurance. The child who blunders in public still is loved and cherished by his family. Never have I seen families whose members openly, unselfconsciously love each other more devotedly. The reverse of this affection appears in sudden rages that may end in murder if a mate is unfaithful or love is rejected. There is none of the impassivity so characteristic of the prewar Japanese. As for politeness, Tokugawa etiquette reached only the small ruling class on Amami. Spontaneous hospitality, consideration of others, and kindness outweigh the equally open tokens of hostility under frustration; genuine emotions are not camouflaged by poker faces. As one Amami gentleman said to me at a party when a geisha danced: "That's a Japanese dance. She looks like a funeral: deadpan. Now wait for an Amami dance; the girls will smile and laugh, and everyone will be happy." So indeed it happened.

Perhaps because Amamians were serfs together under Satsuma oppression, class differences are not keenly felt. Formal Japanese "courtesy language" is heard only from those who have been educated in Japan Proper. Ancestors are venerated mildly and without intensity of devotion. Save for a minority of Buddhists, Roman Catholics, adherents of modern Japanese cults, and remnants of an ancient folk cult of female deities called *noro*, most of the people claim to follow no religion. Women are freer, more assured, and participate more readily in social and political life than the women of prewar Japan. The picture of the neurotic "compulsive personality" does not fit Amami Ōshima. Local physicians deny the occurrence of neuroses; I saw a few apparently neurotic individuals, all of whom had been educated in Japan or in the United States. The taut repressions of the prewar Japanese do not appear in Amamians; they are not secretive, do not conceal emotions, are not unduly persistent, are free from self-righteousness and exaggerated conscientiousness, are neither fanatical nor arrogant, lack ceremoniousness, and, to put it mildly, hold their passion for ritual cleanliness within bounds. They do exhibit a full measure of sentimentality; it is reminiscent of the sentimentality of tenth-century Japanese poetry, echoes of which survive in Amami Ōshima.

If this sketch justifies any conclusion, it is that, in the formation of national character, police coercion shapes and outweighs infant training. Police tyranny is a fearful thing; it eliminates everyone who fails to adopt habits of conformity, suspicion, and tense watchfulness. Such habits doubtless begin with rigorous training of infants by parents ever vigilant under strain, and the orientation of that training is fixed by the police state. In the long run, however, human daring can curb tyranny. Diapers go on forever and need not bar a free people from the pursuit of happiness.

SOURCES OF QUOTATIONS IN THE FOREGOING

P. 426: Hulse, F., 1946, pp. 219-223, *passim.*
        LaBarre, W., 1945, p. 327.
P. 427: Benedict, R. F., 1946-b, pp. 178, 207.
P. 428: LaBarre, *op. cit.*, pp. 326-327.
P. 429: Reischauer, E. O., 1950, p. 134.
Pp. 430-431: Hearn, Lafcadio, *Japan, an Interpretation* (N. Y., 1904), pp. 182-184, *passim.*
P. 431. Kumazawa Banzan, quoted by M. Takikawa, *Nihon Shakaishi* (Tokyo, 1929), p. 296. From unpublished translation by W. Tsuneishi and D. G. Haring.

JOHN J. HONIGMANN

1953. "Toward a distinction between Psychiatric and Social Abnormality," *Social Forces* vol. *31*: 274-277. Reprinted by courtesy of the author and of the Editor of *Social Forces*.

Dr. Honigmann's recent book, *Culture and Personality* (New York, 1954) is one of the few specialized textbooks devoted to problems of culturally fostered patterns of personal character.

The article that follows deals with issues discussed in other essays in the present volume, notably in "Anthropology and the Abnormal" by Ruth Benedict, and in "Cultural Factors in Psychoanalytic Therapy" by George Devereux.

Honigmann's field researches among the Kaska Indians of northwestern Canada are reported in his *Culture and Ethos of Kaska Society* (Yale Univ. Publ. in Anthrop., #40. 1949), and *The Kaska Indians; An Ethnographic Reconstruction* (Yale Univ. Publ. in Anthrop., #51. 1954). The former presents an enlightening discussion of the concepts, "culture" and "ethos," together with a careful statement of research procedures. A glimpse of Kaska child-training appears in the present volume in the paper by Mrs. Honigmann and Frances Underwood.

TOWARD A DISTINCTION BETWEEN PSYCHIATRIC AND SOCIAL ABNORMALITY*

JOHN J. HONIGMANN

We are probably all familiar with the knowledge that certain behavior which one community regards as psychopathological would be "perfectly normal" in some other society. It has even been said that where nearly everybody has tuberculosis or syphilis—and such communities are not unknown—those diseases would be normal. A popular anthropology textbook contains the sentence: "The very definition of what is normal or abnormal is relative to the cultural frame of reference." A text in social disorganization begins discussion of mental abnormality with these words: "There can, then, be no universal and objective definition of insanity. It must be defined in relation to the cultural context."

One of the principal aims of this paper is to demonstrate that statements affirming the cultural basis of abnormality apply better to what is commonly meant by "deviance" rather than to what the psychiatrist designates by the term "abnormal."[1]

I

Social scientists will generally agree that cross-cultural research would benefit from an objective, universal definition of personality dysfunction, one opening the way to measurement and facilitating comparative studies. Further, we may expect that carefully undertaken comparative studies will fruitfully illuminate the social and cultural determinants of mental illness. While the construction of even a provisional and relatively culture-free definition of psychopathology scarcely comes within the competence of the sociologist or anthropologist, we have available for a start those signs of personality dysfunction that constitute the diagnostic tools of Western psychiatry. There can be no serious objection to employing such indicators, provided that we use them objectively. After all, what difference is there between employing the psychiatric definition of psychopathology in cross-cultural research and using the anthropological definition of clan

*Read before the fifteenth annual meeting of the Southern Sociological Society, Atlanta, Georgia, March 28, 1952.

or religion for research in other societies? In each case, a conceptual frame of reference, constructed within the framework of Western culture, provides an instrument with which to understand facts in an exotic social setting.

In order to follow the argument which follows, we must avoid attaching insidious or extraneous connotations to terms like "psycho-pathological" or "psychiatrically abnormal." As William James pointed out, to classify behavior with mental derangement decides nothing about the social value of the behavior in question. Similarly, because of the intense anxiety conditioned to psychopathology in our society, the term "normal" when used in its psychiatric meaning connotes desirable security. This connotation remains unimportant for present purposes.

For materials, then, with which to construct a relatively culture-free definition of psychopathology, we turn to psychiatry. Despite the diversity of that field, most clinicians would readily agree upon some half dozen indicators of abnormality. Such signs, which we adapt from Jules Massermann's book, *Principles of Dynamic Psychiatry*, afford a useful point of departure for an initial, relatively culture-free defi-nition.[2]

Anxiety with its several manifestations can well stand as the initial indicator of psychopathology. Manifestations of anxiety include the racing, pounding heart; rapid, shallow or difficult breathing; trembling; a sweaty, flushed, or pale skin; incontinence, and a feeling of impending catastrophe and panic that has been labeled "fear of catastrophic breakdown."[3] That everybody at some time or other experiences anxiety in one or another of these forms, is, of course, no serious ar-gument against the utility of the definition as far as its intended purpose is concerned. Episodes of anxiety, whether transitory or persistent, may be regarded as evidence of psychiatric abnormality, if we remem-ber that no clear line separates the psychiatrically normal from the abnormal. For the purpose of this paper, we have no need for a practical distinction, such as makes the difference between mental health and ill health a matter of degree and not of kind.

Individuals learn in one way or another to guard against the full impact of anxiety. Pervasive defenses like phobias, obsessions, and compulsions, furnish additional criteria by which to recognize psy-chiatric abnormality. Incidentally, such defenses often prove to be as incapacitating and unadaptive as chronic anxiety itself although they may be more economical and bearable. Handwashing exemplifies a familiar compulsion and one which we observed dominating a Cree Indian youth living in far northern Ontario. Apparently he spontan-eously hit upon the compulsion to relieve feelings of tension whose source remained hidden to the anthropologist.

Often anxiety comes to be experienced in sensory or motor dysfunctions, as, for example, in the familiar instance of hysterical blindness. The whole organism may show an unwillingness to respond to a wide range of stimuli, as in combat fatigue. The notion of psychosomatic illness is to be included in the term "sensory and motor dysfunctions." Accident proneness must also be included. To digress for an instant, there is evidence suggesting that accident proneness may appear in a community as an alternative culture pattern which people—especially men—may select in order to meet some unremitting and intense stress.[4]

Disorders of affect ranging from mild to serious depression, and including emotional blunting, or disproportionate (i.e., manic) excitement are other signs on the basis of which psychiatrists identify both neurotic and psychotic tendencies, the diagnosis depending on the degree to which the behavior departs from customary patterns. The criterion of affective disorder involves us more than we would prefer in cultural relativity. Undoubtedly we have to know something about the way of life before we can establish lack of correspondence between idea and affect. Armed with this criterion, the researcher looks for individuals who depart from the affective norms prescribed for particular situations.

Coming next to reality distortion as a sign of psychopathology, we encounter another mark by which neurosis may be distinguished from psychosis—although such distinctions are not pertinent for present purposes. With reality distortion we have an indicator again involving cultural relativity. Loss of contact with or marked distortions of reality can be useful criteria of psychopathology only when we first ascertain the social definition of the reality situation. Obviously it does not constitute a hallucination for a shaman to see his familiars under conditions where the community expects that he may see them. It is not a delusion for an Athapaskan Indian to believe that dangerous emanations come from a corpse because in this belief the community fully concurs. Some day, however, as schooling and other influences of Euro-American culture increase in Athapaskan culture the community may gradually cease defining reality to include ghosts. Ghost beliefs will then become delusional. While short term distortions of reality may deliberately be induced by the ingestion of drugs or alcohol, the spontaneous and recurrent episodes are often regarded gravely in whatever community they occur.

With regression considered as a sign of psychopathology we once more stand on relatively culture-free territory. The term regression includes behavior analogous to the responses of the unsocialized child, including extreme passivity, profound withdrawal from social relations, extreme aggressiveness and open masturbation or soiling. Regression may represent a frank disinclination—for whatever reason—to try any longer to cope with social demands. Extreme passive behavior has sometimes been revealed by entire communities refusing to till fields or tend cattle because they expect that the ancestors are on the verge of returning with abundant gifts.[5] The so-called Vailala Madness in New Guinea in 1919 constitutes such a pattern, which has also been manifested elsewhere.

Without quite showing the quality of regression, personality may evidence a degree of disintegration in which hostile, erotic, and other impulses are severed from control. Alcohol promotes such severance in many people.[6] The phenomenon also indicates psychopathology.

We may complete our provisional definition of psychopathology by adding as another sign any acute or chronic inability to perceive, interpret, or manipulate reality. Here is a pattern of dissociation familiar in drunkenness, trance, and senility. Illustration is hardly necessary, but, on the other hand, a quotation from an interview with a Balinese trance principal is highly illuminating. The subject told the anthropologist, "When I go in trance . . . my body suddenly gets hot, and gradually I lose consciousness. The hotness comes from below, rising. When I go in trance in the temple, suddenly my thoughts are different . . ."[7] The hypothesis has been offered that the frequency of trance in a community is a function of stress experienced by the members of that group.[8]

II

Having defined psychiatric abnormality in these terms, it remains to point out that social abnormality or deviance is usually—and usefully—recognized by different marks. The deviant does not stand out because of his high level of anxiety, sensori-motor dysfunctions, or reality distortion. He is conspicuous through the fact that he underplays or overplays socially standardized behavior or innovates behavior. The policeman who becomes an authoritarian colossus overplays his role; the Crow Indian who holds back from battle because of the fear that he may be killed underplays a role. The purveyor of a new religion represents an innovator. All are deviants, but we cannot without further information classify them as also psychopathic. To classify the policeman, warrior, and prophet as psychiatrically abnormal, each must be judged by the criteria which we adopted from psychiatry—anxiety, regression and the others.

Deviance, by definition, is relative only to a particular community. A deviant becomes apparent by conspicuously departing from the norms of his group. The deviant theoretically has a greater chance of finding his behavior becoming normal by shifting his group than the psychopath does.

We therefore distinguish deviance from psychopathology by defining the deviant with reference to the values and standards of his group while identifying the psychopath through the use of universal indicators borrowed from psychiatry. We suggest that the deviant, more often than the psychopath, can find adjustment by shifting to a group where his behavior is accepted. Now it must be apparent that an individual may simultaneously be both deviant and psychopathological. For example, the compulsive tendency to step on every, or no, crack in the sidewalk if it is rooted in anxiety, also makes a man deviant in every American city.

Most social scientists would agree that deviance may occur in approved as well as disapproved directions. The saint wins approval in a Christian community but he will probably be deviant from customary norms of behavior. The thief earns disapproval in the same community and is also a deviant. In one of the so-called criminal tribes of India, the burglar merits neither disapproval nor can he properly be considered deviant.[9] The psychopath is similar to the deviant in this respect. Like the latter, the behavior of the psychiatrically abnormal individual may be honored or rejected in his group. In a number of communities known to anthropologists, the person prone to trance wins regular rewards for experiencing dissociation. On the other hand, the individual whose hostile impulses flee beyond his control will nearly always find his behavior meeting with punishment rather than approval.

III

Perhaps our definition of psychopathology provides a new perspective from which to understand the relationship of group membership to psychiatric abnormality.[10] For example, crudely speaking, it is much more likely that we would find ourselves saddled with an obsessive fear of cannibalism had we been bred as members of a Cree Indian band in northern Canada rather than as members of rural or urban American communities.[11] Not likely will any one of us become sick or die of magical fright provoked by the report that an enemy has sent his sorcery against us. Yet had we been reared in parts of Africa or Australia, the chances would be much greater of thanatomania striking. Such extreme anxiety about death, Cannon points out, can depress the bodily functions to the point of death itself.[12] Continuing with these examples, had we been bred in Bali, our capacities for trance would be stimulated far more than is the case. In Bali we would probably experience such dissociation periodically.[13] As it is, as members of a professional group, we have an ascertainable and probably high chance of achieving mild dissociation through convivial intoxication— a form of psychopathology unknown in other parts of the world. Were we in highland South America, however, our binges on occasions of fiestas would be more frequent and prolonged.[14] Were we Indians living in Oklahoma, peyote rather than alcohol would provide the toxic lift and we would know the experience of multi-hued visions and a feeling of living as if in a picture.[15]

Whether the total incidence of psychopathology—especially psychiatric abnormality of the involuntary kind—varies between societies is something about which we are highly uncertain. An African mental hospital differs from an American institution of the same scope by housing few cases of obsessional neurosis but relatively many cases of acute mania.[16] In India schizophrenia is two or three times less common than in America.[17] We know that the incidence of certain types of mental illness may vary between groups but this tells us nothing about total incidence.

Questions concerning the comparative incidence of psychopathology and the socio-cultural factors which contribute to mental abnormality represent some of the foremost problems in psychiatry. These problems also provide a meeting ground between the social and medical sciences. It would seem to be worthwhile for us as social scientists to continue cooperating with psychiatry to refine further a universal conception of abnormality. Then, with a clear idea of what we want to find out and using some universal definition of psychopathology, we can undertake cross-cultural research into the incidence and etiology of psychopathology. Extensive comparative study appears indispensable if we want to control abnormal phenomena in our society.

NOTES

1. Cf., John Gillin, *The Ways of Men* (1948), p. 589.

2. Jules Massermann, *Principles of Dynamic Psychiatry* (1946). See terms like "neurosis," "psychosis," and "anxiety syndrome" in the glossary of this book.

3. The term is used by A. H. Maslow and Bela Mittelmann, *Principles of Abnormal Psychology* (1941), pp. 56-60, 106, 174.

4. John J. Honigmann, Foodways of a Muskeg Community (1948). Manuscript report.

5. The writer is indebted to Mr. Nathan Altshuler for this interpretation of certain forms of nativism.

6. John J. Honigmann, *Culture and Ethos of Kaska Society* (1949), p. 238.

7. Jane Belo, *Bali: Rangda and Barong* (1949), p. 56.

8. *Ibid.*, p. 12; Erwin H. Ackerknecht, "Psychopathology, Primitive Medicine and Primitive Culture," *Bulletin of the History of Medicine*, 14 (1943), pp. 30-67, esp. pp. 63-64.

9. D. N. Majumdar, *The Fortunes of Primitive Tribes* (1944), p. 185.

10. John J. Honigmann, "Culture Patterns and Human Stress," *Psychiatry*, 13 (1950), pp. 25-34.

11. John Cooper, "The Cree Witiko Psychosis," *Primitive Man*, 6 (1933), pp. 20-24.

12. W. B. Cannon, "Voodoo Death," *American Anthropologist,* 44 (1942), pp. 169-180.

13. Jane Belo, *op. cit.*

14. Elsie Clews Parsons, *Peguche* (1945), pp. 122-123.

15. Charles Brant, "Peyotism among the Kiowa-Apache and Neighboring Tribes," *Southwestern Journal of Anthropology,* 6 (1950), pp. 212-222.

16. J. E. Carothers, "A Study of Mental Derangement in Africans, and an Attempt to Explain Its Peculiarities, More Especially in Relation to the African Attitude to Life," *Psychiatry,* 11 (1948), pp. 47-86; Geoffrey Tooth, *Studies in Mental Illness in the Gold Coast,* Colonial Research Publication No. 6 (1950), p. 38.

17. J. E. Dhunjibhoy, "A Brief *Resumé* of the Types of Insanity Commonly Met With in India," *Journal of Mental Science,* 76 (1930), pp. 254-264.

HU HSIEN-CHIN

1944. "The Chinese Concepts of 'Face'," *American Anthropologist*, vol. 46: 45-64. Reprinted by courtesy of the author and of the Editor of the *American Anthropologist*.
(The surname of this author is Hu; Chinese names are written correctly with the surname first.)

If this paper appears to be concerned only indirectly with problems of "culture and personality" such a view is superficial. For every people cherish ideals of personal character that are inculcated in the young in many ways. Clear statement of such ideals is prerequisite to understanding by the student of the process by which children are led in developing the kind of personality that their society approves. Here is a clear picture of vital aspects of Chinese cultural behavior that often baffle foreign observers. Present conditions make it difficult—perhaps impossible—to determine the extent to which the ideas of "face" have been modified by Communist indoctrination.

Miss Hu is also the author of a clarifying monograph, *The Common Descent Group in China and its Functions* (Viking Fund Publications in Anthropology, #10. New York, 1948).

The General Bibliography at the end of the present volume cites a number of studies pertinent to Chinese personality: Hsiao, 1929; Hsu, 1948, 1949-b; LaBarre, 1946-b; Lang, 1946; Liu, tr. by Shyrock, 1937; Pruitt, 1945; Tao, 1934; Tretiakov, 1934; Waley, 1938.

Since Chinese culture has influenced Japan much as European culture influences the United States, effort may be directed to discovering the extent to which Chinese ideas of "face" survive in modern Japan.

THE CHINESE CONCEPTS OF FACE

Hu Hsien-Chin

Investigations by anthropologists and psychologists have shown that while the desire for prestige exists in every human society, the value placed upon it and the means for attaining it vary considerably. In the analysis of a culture different in emphasis and basic attitudes from our own it is important to keep in mind that that society may have formed different conceptions of even the most universal aspects of human life. Very often this difference in conception is reflected in the vocabulary, but a careful investigation of the situations in which such concepts figure is required to interpret their full meaning for the bearers of the culture. The study of the concepts of "face" in China is particularly interesting because it reveals two sets of criteria by which prestige is gained and status secured or improved, and also how different attitudes can be reconciled within the framework of the same culture.

Verbally the two sets of criteria are distinguished by two words which on the physical level both mean "face." One of these *mien-tzŭ*, stands for the kind of prestige that is emphasized in this country: a reputation achieved through getting on in life, through success and ostentation. This is prestige that is accumulated by means of personal effort or clever maneuvering. For this kind of recognition ego is dependent at all times on his external environment. The other kind of "face," *lien*, is also known to Americans without being accorded formal recognition. It is the respect of the group for a man with a good moral reputation: the man who will fulfill his obligations regardless of the hardships involved, who under all circumstances shows himself a decent human being. It represents the confidence of society in the integrity of ego's moral character,[1] the loss of which makes it impossible for him to function properly within the community. *Lien* is both a social sanction for enforcing moral standards and an internalized sanction.

As no observer has so far noticed the difference between these two sets of criteria for prestige, a detailed analysis has been made of the two concepts and their application in social situations.[2]

Of the two words for "face": *lien* and *mien*,[3] the latter is by far the older, being found in ancient literature. *Mien* had acquired a figurative meaning referring to the relation between ego and society as early as the fourth century B.C. *Lien* is a more modern term, the earliest reference cited in the K'ang-hsi Dictionary dating from the Yuan Dynasty (1277-1367). This word seems to have originated somewhere in North China and gradually to have supplanted *mien* in the physical sense, and also to have acquired some of its figurative meaning. Meanwhile, *mien*, with the meaningless syllable *-tzŭ* attached, had developed different connotations. Both words are now current in North and Central China,[4] though in Central China, that is the Yangtze provinces, *lien* is not used to the extent it is in the north. However, here the difference in the referents for *lien* and *mien* is understood, though it is not always consciously realized.[5]

LIEN

1. *Tiu-lien*—"to lose *lien*" is a condemnation by the group for immoral or socially disagreeable behavior. A serious infraction of the moral code of society, once come to the notice of the public, is a blemish on the character of the individual and excites a great deal of comment. A fraud detected, a crime exposed, meanness, poor judgment, lies told for one's own profit, unfaithfulness while in office, a broken promise, the cheating of a customer, a married man making love to a young girl, these are just some of the acts that incur the criticism of society, and are rated as "losing *lien*" for ego.

A simple case of *lien*-losing is afforded by the experience of an American traveller in the interior of China. In a little village she had made a deal with a peasant to use his donkey for transportation. On the day agreed upon the owner appeared only to declare that his donkey was not available, the lady would have to wait for one day. Yet he would not allow her to hire another animal, because she had consented to use his ass. They argued back and forth first in the inn, then in the courtyard; a crowd gathered around them, as each stated his point of view over and over again. No comment was made, but some of the older people shook their heads and muttered something, the peasant getting more and more excited all the time trying to prove his right. Finally he turned and left the place without any more arguments, and the American was free to hire another beast. The man had felt the disapproval of the group. The condemnation of his community of his attempt to take advantage of the plight of the traveller made him feel he had "lost *lien*."

A criminal case that occurred in Peiping in 1935 is a good example of the seriousness of "losing *lien*." A college student had come to be on very intimate terms with a girl-student. He had promised to marry her, but when she found herself pregnant, he denied his promise in a letter. Thereupon she went to see him in his dormitory. Not finding him in, she hanged herself then and there. The student was arrested at once and given a sentence of ten years. The feeling of the public against the irresponsibility of the young man which drove the young girl to despair ran high indeed. The suicide was the most severe accusation and caused many discussions of his bad character, making him "lose *lien*" completely. However, the judgment of the public does not always follow the grooves of the law. When a person commits a crime which is regarded as justified, though he be subject to punishment by justice, society will not think of him as one who flaunts moral standards for his own profit; he does not "lose *lien*."

In the above case the victim exposed the character of the culprit by her suicide. This may be effected by less serious means. A mistreated servant may turn on his master in exasperation and denounce him for his inhuman behavior. A student may show up his teacher for making a mistake. A customer who finds a business-man trying to get the better in a bargain can expose him by attracting a crowd and telling them what sort of a man the merchant is. As business-men are very careful of their reputation, they will often give in to a particularly quarrelsome customer, so as to avoid arousing unwelcome attention. The servant, the student and the customer maintain their rights by making the other party "lose *lien*."

Although righteous indignation is a legitimate weapon in the hand of an inferior, or of a victim of fraud or injustice, a person of high status, such as a member of the gentry in a village, or the professional or scholar in the city has to be more circumspect in dealing with people of lower status. Such a person would be entitled to the respect of the younger and inferior, but this respect would be impaired if ego lost dignity by behavior very contrary to the expectation of society. Except in extreme cases, the higher the social standing of a person the more dignity he has to maintain, and the more vulnerable this *lien* becomes. While a poor man is justified in husbanding his resources, the wealthy man who shows himself stingy offends the code of decency and incurs public censure. For a person of education to be drawn into a violent argument with a rough country-fellow is much beneath his dignity. Education is regarded as training of character as much as the accumulation of knowledge, so "those who have drunk ink" should achieve greater self-control in social behavior than people who never had such a chance. Therefore an open quarrel with an illiterate person greatly damages the dignity of ego and causes him to "lose *lien*."

Status is graded within the family too. The father of the family occupies a higher standing and commands more respect than a younger brother attached to the household. A *faux pas* on his part in dealing with people of lesser status would cause much more comment and "loss of *lien*." Again, of two boys of the same age living in the same extended family, one may have achieved higher status through marriage. This confers the position of a responsible adult on him and he will have to refrain from childish behavior such as enjoying candy and firecrackers, which would be all right for his unmarried cousin.

It once happened to me to slap the face of a boy-servant for dishonesty. It is bad manners to hit anyone; for a young lady to administer physical punishment to a male servant is altogether beneath her dignity. For a long time I had to endure the reproaches of my family and in the eyes of the servants I had definitely "lost *lien*." No one had sympathy for me, but the boy went unreprimanded by the others.

To choose an example from international politics: The appeasement policy of Chamberlain up to the outbreak of the European War, in the face of Britain's treaty obligations to smaller nations, was felt as extremely "*lien*-losing" in China. To be unwilling to keep promises to weaker nations because of its own interests was neither compatible with its claim to status as the most powerful empire of the world, nor with the desire of the leaders of the nation to be termed gentlemen.

Thus, the "loss of *lien*" varies in intensity with the status of ego. Condoning factors in the life of the poor and downtrodden are taken into account when the public voices its opinion, while the misbehavior of the well-to-do is contrasted with their social eminence. A position of economic advantage has to be exploited without offending moral standards. Persons in subordinate positions can use the fact that their superiors must maintain their *lien* at a high level. Students at certain universities used to subject every new instructor to an intense questioning during his first lectures. Should he prove unable to answer, his incapability would be proven and his *lien* lost. The creditor, too, in a business transaction who cannot collect from a powerful debtor may press his debtor knowing that the latter will lose *lien* if he is called irresponsible and dishonest in public. The debtor for this reason often hides himself from his creditor, and by this act is regarded as having acknowledged his incapacity. The creditor is satisfied that the other is anxious to maintain his *lien* and will eventually pay his debt. He feels he has gained a moral advantage.

The consciousness that an amorphous public is so-to-say supervising the conduct of ego, relentlessly condemning every breach of morals and punishing with ridicule, has bred extreme sensitivity in some people. This is particularly obvious where the taking of the initiative may incur failure. The wooing situation provides a good example: Modern China does not believe in marriages arranged by parents. Yet a boy, though he knows a girl quite well, will often hesitate a long time before making up his mind to ask the decisive question, because he dreads a refusal and the consequent ridicule of his fellows. Similarly, boys are shy in approaching girls, fearing to make a clumsy impression and thus "losing *lien*." So they will ask friends to introduce them to the girl of their choice. A young person who fails to pass an examination will sometimes feel the shame so keenly as to commit suicide. To understand this aspect of *lien* we have to investigate a little further its relation to personality as conceived in this culture.

Western observers have often remarked that Chinese are excessively modest about their attainments and status; they sometimes go as far as accusing them of hypocrisy. The exaggerated modesty is not a sign of lack of self-confidence, as it appears to the objective observer at the first glance. The over-estimation of one's ability, the exaggeration of one's capacity, designed to elevate one above one's fellows, is frowned upon by society. As physical violence is discountenanced, so is every action that might call forth unpleasant feelings, such as envy and dislike, in other people. A person given to boasting will not have the sympathy of his group when he fails; rather will he incur ridicule. A person with such poor judgment of his powers is termed "light and floating" (*ch'ing-fou*) in character; a person serious in his endeavors but careful in reckoning his abilities and circumspect in his dealing with others is called "sinking and steady" (*ch'ên-chuo*) or "reliably heavy" (*wên-chung*). The former type of personality cannot be trusted, but the latter is a good citizen and trustworthy friend. Now it is not easy to gauge one's capacity at every point nor is it possible to foresee the outcome of every venture, so it is wise to underestimate one's value. In this way one will always have the satisfaction of hearing friends deny this inferiority and thus gain greater conviction of the possibility of success. The fear of being considered "light and floating" is similar to that of being blamed for immoral behavior. So ego will depreciate his intelligence and capacity on every occasion, always confident that people will have an all the higher opinion of him.

This emphasis on modesty seems to be linked to the importance attributed to "self-training" (*hsiu-yang*). Since Confucius described the sequence of training through which ego has to pass to prepare for leadership in the state, scholars have often stressed the responsibility of the individual for the formation of his character. A person "without self-training" is one who shows no consideration for others or is given to boasting. Thus the failure of ego's venture demonstrates his immaturity and uncertainty, and so impairs the confidence of the community in his performance within his status.

This attitude also explains why a person's *lien* is lost if, after criticizing somebody, ego commits the same mistake. We have here identical behavior in A and B. On the part of B it may be unwitting or unintentional, or its import may not have been realized. By his reproof of B, A has shown himself superior in knowledge; at least, he has shown that he understands how unwise such conduct is. By committing the same mistake, he demonstrates either a weak will or an untrained character. The conception of human nature as inherently evil is absent in China;[6] the training of the personality should accompany the growing understanding of the mind. To be insincere in one's efforts to achieve a better character and at the same time to call attention to another's faults is like throwing stones when one lives in a glass house. The contempt of society is expressed in terms of "loss of *lien*."

We have seen that all infringements of the moral code, all acts contrary to behavior of a person of ego's status cause a depreciation of character. The loss of esteem is felt acutely and is symbolically expressed as "loss of *lien*." The fear of "losing *lien*" keeps up the consciousness of moral boundaries, maintains moral values, and expresses the force of social sanctions. Behavior that is usually not classed as immoral: the self-confidence of the opportunist, the criticism of another in the absence of control of one's own conduct, the failure of an undertaking through lack of judgment, also are punished by "loss of *lien*." "Loss of *lien*" is felt acutely, for it entails not only the condemnation of society, but the loss of its confidence in the integrity of ego's character. Much of the activity of Chinese life is operated on the basis of trust. As the confidence of society is essential to the functioning of the ego, the "loss of *lien*" has come to constitute a real dread affecting the nervous system of ego more strongly than physical fear.

Another expression for "losing *lien*" is *tiu-jên*—"to lose man." *Jên*, "man," here probably stands for *jên-kê*—"character." It is possible that *tiu-jên* is a newer expression that will eventually come to displace *tiu-lien*.

In the following pages other uses of *lien* are given, none of them as important as "to lose *lien*."

2. *Kei mou-mou-jên tiu-lien*—"to lose *lien* for so-and-so." Ego almost always belongs to a closely integrated group on which is reflected some of his glory or shame. His family, the wider community of friends, and his superiors, all have an interest in his advancement or set-backs. So a person does not simply "lose his own face." Public disgrace or ridicule of a serious nature is bound to have an effect on the reputation of the family. A boy or girl involved in a scandal will be severely reprimanded by his or her relatives for "losing their *lien*." In the case of the broken promise of marriage cited above, the family of the girl felt the disgrace very strongly and insisted on the maximum penalty for the culprit. They lost *lien* because her careless behavior was proclaimed by her suicide. Students who call forth through their behavior the ridicule of society "lose *lien* for their college." Many Chinese feel particularly embarrassed when meeting Americans in this country: they fear that by unwittingly breaking conventions they may "lose the face of their country."

The expression is often used by elders to stimulate the young to greater effort and correct behavior. "Don't lose *lien* for us!" not only implants in the mind of the young person the concept of *lien*, but gives him or her the consciousness of the collective responsibility which his family bears in regard to his behavior. He will be impressed by the fact that his character should befit the standing of his family. Occasionally the phrase is used jocularly. Thus a boy about eleven years old tried to add a few inches to his ego-stature by saying to his niece who was three years his senior: "You are always displaying yourself with these eccentric dresses. You are really losing *lien* for me." Over-dressing so as to attract attention is as bad as boasting and therefore frowned upon by decent society.

Outside the family the teacher bears some responsibility for the success of his pupil. By teacher is meant the person who trains ego for his work, be he a university professor, a master craftsman or any other person selected to guide the young individual. Only a teacher with whom the pupil has entered into close personal relations will feel concern for the welfare and achievements of the latter. Ego will feel the disgrace doubly because he "lost the *lien* for his teacher," that is, proved his teacher incapable.

Serious infringements of the social code on the part of ego will cast a shadow not only on his own character and the reputation of his family, but will raise doubts as to the judgment and integrity of all those who educated and promoted him in life. To be sure, the "loss of *lien*" entailed differs quantitatively for those in closer or less close association with ego, as it differs with the seriousness of the offense or failure.

3. *Pu-yao lien*—"not to want *lien*," is a serious accusation meaning that ego does not care what society thinks of his character, that he is ready to obtain benefits for himself in defiance of moral standards. On such a person social sanctions lose their effect, as he does not recognize the rules of the game. Moreover, should he be in the habit of "not wanting *lien*" his fellows would find it impossible to predict his behavior. Such an individual few people will care to deal with unless under the force of circumstances.

It should be understood that this expression applies mainly to taking advantage of others for one's own ends; a disregard for conventions is considered eccentricity, but does not cause "loss of *lien*." A businessman who is known to sell mediocre wares for first-rate goods, or one who frequently resorts to methods of high-pressure salesmanship; a person who lies for his own profit; a politician who grants favors for pecuniary benefits; a young girl who exploits her boyfriends, or worse, sells her favors; all these are declared as not "wanting *lien*" or, sometimes, as "not having *lien*."

Very often the conduct of these people cannot be punished by law, and public censure may not be open, but should a time come when they find themselves in a disadvantageous position, society will withdraw its moral and material support. They can no longer count on the network of social relationships to help them out, for they have isolated themselves by flaunting moral standards. Indeed society will point to their failure or misfortune as deserved punishment for defying its injunctions.

"Not to want *lien*" is a reproach which is very commonly heard during a quarrel: "Don't you want any *lien*, to make allegations which you know to be false?" "It's you, who denies these charges, who does not want *lien!*" In this way the accusations fly back and forth. It is most serious when used by a person of inferior status to one of superior standing. The habit of students to grill new instructors with questions was mentioned before. On one occasion the lecturer had failed to satisfy his students; when he did not take the hint that they were through with him, he was told squarely that "he did not want *lien*," before the class filed out. This is an extreme case, however. Where the accusation is made with good reason, the victim will not be able to show himself again. The students successfully prevented the instructor from continuing his course at this university.

There are times when *pu-yao lien* is used with a touch of humor. During old age the conventions and moral restrictions which encompass the life of younger people are relaxed. Where excess in food and enjoyment is condemned in a young person, it is condoned in an old fellow. Society knows him as a good citizen and forgives small weaknesses. So when he takes liberties he will excuse himself with a "I am old enough not to want *lien*." Though this has been reported only from one community in Shantung it is quite typical of the greater freedom from conventions enjoyed by old people. This does not mean, that *lien* is no longer a sanction for old age. It means that the confidence of society in the integrity of ego cannot be shaken by disregard for its conventions.

At the other end of the age-ladder, children are not held down strictly to regard for the sanction of *lien*. A child behaving like one of a lower age-group, for example, a boy of eight or nine who still fights for the largest piece of cake, will be ridiculed with this expression "you don't want *lien*, to do so-and-so." However, it is not taken seriously. Adolescents are quite conscious of *lien*, and in a quarrel will accuse each other of "not wanting *lien*," but the feeling of intense humiliation is not developed to the extent it is in adults.

4. *Mei-yu lien*— "to have no *lien*" is today used almost interchangeably with *pu-yao lien*. This is about the most severe condemnation that can be made of a person. For example, people who turned traitors against their country in its hour of greatest need are said to "have no

lien" at all, meaning that they have laid aside all pretensions of being decent human beings. In a similar way, individuals who accept a religion[7] as a step for material advantage and social advancement "have no *lien*" in the eyes of the public.

The last two expressions analyzed, "not to want *lien*" and "not to have *lien*" are at times stronger than to "lose *lien*." One may "lose *lien*" through behavior due to ignorance or inexperience; the use of this expression serves to call to consciousness the error of the individual. "Not to want *lien*" emphasizes the will of the individual: he intends to leave *lien* out of consideration. "Not to have *lien*" is the strongest of all perhaps: ego has lost the feeling for *lien*, he has no conscience about flaunting moral standards.

There are no records to show how early the expression "to lose *lien*" was used. But we do know that "not to have *lien*" has been in use at least since the fourth century B.C. The word *lien* had not been coined at the time, the old word for "face," *mien*, was employed instead. Two examples may be cited from history.

During the period of the later Chou Dynasty all feudal states were striving for supremacy. Duke Huan of Ch'i succeeded in making himself the dominant power among the feudal lords, thanks to the ability of his prime minister Kuan Chung. The latter, on his death-bed, enjoined his master to dismiss certain persons from court. The Duke promised to do so, but subsequently found these people indispensable. Once back in power they schemed successfully to bring about the downfall of their master. Finally the troops of the insurgents occupied the palace. Forsaken by all, the Duke found himself reduced to starvation. Recalling the advice of his former prime minister which he had ignored, he said to himself: "If the dead have no consciousness, it will be all right. But if they should have consciousness, what *mien-mu* would I have to see Chung-fu under the ground."[8]

During the struggles for the throne following the downfall of the Ch'in Dynasty in 207 B.C. the two main contestants were Hsiang Yü and Liu Pang. The former lost out in the end. When, after several defeats, his forces were finally surrounded by the enemy, Hsiang Yü knew that his fight had been in vain. Fleeing with a few cavalry men and hotly pursued by the army of his rival, he arrived at the crossing of a river, where he was welcomed by the head of the borough, who advised him to take this road to safety. Once in his home in Chiang-tung[9] he might yet be able to maintain himself. He answered him: "I came with eight thousand of the youths of Chiang-tung. If I return defeated and alone, though the elders of Chiang-tung should pity me and make me their king, what *mien-mu* would I have to see them?"[10] *Mien-mu* in these two cases mean "face" and "eyes," and is still much used in Central China, whereas in Northern Chinese *lien* has taken its place. When starting out on his campaign, Hsiang Yü had spoken with confidence of winning the throne. He was not only disappointing those who had believed in his ability, but had involved in his defeat all the young people for whom he had assumed responsibility as a leader.

The expression "I have no *lien* to see so-and-so" is often used when ego feels he has disappointed somebody through his own fault. A son who has dissipated the hard-earned money of his father, an official who has squandered public funds or otherwise betrayed the trust of the ruler or the nation, the subordinate who has failed to carry out successfully the orders of his boss, the officer who loses a battle through carelessness, the leader who involves others in his defeat, these are the persons who feel that "they have no *lien*" to see their elders or superiors. There is no necessity for ego to confront public opinion; even though there be only one person present, or none at all, the consciousness of trust betrayed will be in his mind.

This demonstrates the complete internalization of a social sanction. Very often ego will carry out what he thinks should be the verdict of society in order to retrieve his *lien*.

5. *Lien-p'i hou* or *po*—"the skin on the *lien* is thick" or "thin." A "thick skin on the *lien*" is similar in meaning to *pu-yao lien*, but it is milder. Figuratively speaking the skin is still in place, only it is hard to penetrate it with social disapproval. It means defiance of public censure or disregard for the injunctions of elders trying to impress on the young the moral standards of society. It is very often applied when friends have hinted to ego that his conduct is offensive and those hints have gone unheeded. A very mild case: a guest had overstayed her time, although the hostess had tried hard to make her understand that she wanted her to leave. After the lady had finally left, the hostess told me: "What a thick skin that woman has on her *lien!*" Chinese place high value on hospitality; they avoid making visitors feel that they are not wanted. Therefore it is up to the visitor to sense how far friendship can be stretched.

A person with a thin skin on his *lien* is highly sensitive to public opinion, and will go to a great deal of trouble to retain his good name. But there are cases when an individual has "too thin a skin on his *lien*," so that he is offended at the least criticism offered by his friends. A friend speaking of a political career told me that a person needs a "thick skin on his *lien*" in order to carry out many acts against his conscience. Many a scholar called upon to perform administrative duties finds himself unable to sustain his position. He will then acknowledge that " the skin on his *lien* is too thin" for public life.

Yet on the whole, society favors the person with a thin skin, for he conforms more readily to social standards.

From the above it can be seen that the preoccupation with *lien* is a real concern. "Loss of *lien*" entails an intense humiliation for the ego. As a person who does not care for *lien* is unamenable to social sanctions, so society exerts the greatest possible pressure to implant in him the consciousness of *lien*.

The main criterion for *lien* consists of the virtues of a decent man. A single lapse is punished by ridicule and comments on "loss of *lien*"; repeated offenses arouse strong disapproval and cause the withdrawal, psychologically speaking, of the community from ego. The consciousness that "loss of *lien*" means that the confidence of society in his character is impaired, and places him in danger of being despised and isolated, usually acts as a strong deterrent on the individual.

MIEN-TZU

While *lien* is a word with one concrete and one figurative meaning, the word *mien* has developed a variety of meanings, both concrete and figurative.

1. *Mien* originally signified "face" in the physiological sense. It is still occasionally so used in the combinations *mien-mao* and *mien-mu*. *Mao* also means "face," though rarely used so except with *mien*, meaning the same as the English noun "looks." *Mien* is used also in the oft-quoted phrases "girl's face and peach flower";[11] and "white-faced student," that is, a scholar whose sole occupation is his books.

2. *Mien* may mean the surface of an object, as in *piao-mien* "outer appearance," *chuo-mien* "surface of the table," *ti-mien* "surface of the earth."

3. It may mean direction, as in *tung-mien* "east" or *hsi-mien* "west."

4. It may refer to aspect, as in *chêng-mien* "front view," *tuei-mien* "opposite."

In these combinations *mien* stands for a concrete concept. The figurative meanings it has acquired are:

1. "Side" in the social sense, as in *pa-mien ling-lung* "smooth in dealing with different people under all circumstances."

2. It may refer to occasions when people face each other, as in *huei-mien* "meet face to face," or in *tang-mien shang-liang* "talk over face to face."

3. In *t'i-mien*, "good looking," the concept of beauty is associated with that of social approval. A person good to look at is said to be *t'i-mien*, but he may also "act *t'i-mien*" by showing himself generous.

4. It has been mentioned already that in some parts of China *mien* is still used where other regions use *lien*. Thus in the Yangtze Valley it is common to say *mien-p'i hou* instead of *lien-p'i hou*.

5. *Ku mien-tzŭ*—"to consider *mien-tzŭ*." Ego has had to consider his *mien-tzŭ* in order to advance his prestige. Thus the head of a gentry family will give a big feast for his birthday, arranging theatricals to last

for several days for all the members of the community. The favorable comment of society will increase his *mien tzŭ*.

Or, ego may have consideration for another's *mien-tzŭ*. For example, he will avoid any depreciation of his neighbors that might excite the least unfavorable comment. Particularly teachers often will exercise such tact in regard to poor work done by students. A clerk may be doing very mediocre work, but out of consideration for the *mien-tzŭ* of his family the boss will keep him on the job and give him an opportunity to improve.

There are times when consideration for someone's *mien-tzŭ* is in opposition to the best advantage of society or of the individual concerned. It is evident that too considerate a teacher will not be able to correct his students; too considerate an administrator or family head will find himself devoid of authority. This is why throughout Chinese literature we find many an individual extolled for not considering anyone's *mien-tzŭ* when it interfered with the carrying out of duty.

6. *Mien-tzŭ shang pu hoa-k'an*—"(something) does not look good on someone's *mien-tzŭ*" describes the feelings of a person when confronted with the disapproval of society. This is related to the conception of *lien*. Indeed, *lien* is often used in the same way. But the feeling of shame in this case is much milder than in the case of "losing *lien*." Whereas the latter refers most often to the contravention of moral standards, "bad looks on one's *mien-tzŭ*" are due to some *faux pas* or neglect of a social convention that is not bound up with the integrity of the character. Ego will feel his prestige impaired to some extent, but the feeling of intense humiliation and social isolation is absent.

8. *Tsêng-chia mien-tzŭ*—"to add to one's *mien-tzŭ*." This is achieved by endowing an institution of public welfare, by aiding people with little direct claim on ego to get on in life, by attaching one's name to important documents or petitions, by founding a school, an orphanage, etc. These are actions that bring an individual into the public limelight, and they are bound to meet with favorable comment. Such expression of public approval adds to one's *mien-tzŭ*.

9. *Chêng mien-tzŭ*—"to struggle for *mien-tzŭ*." Two individuals struggle for *mien-tzŭ* by endeavoring to outdo one another by entertainments, by wealth display, in all ways of attracting favorable attention from the public. The college ball team struggles to add to the *mien-tzŭ* of the alma mater.

10. *Kei mien-tzŭ*—"to give *mien-tzŭ*," is the action of A to increase B's prestige in front of other people. There are many ways of doing so: To praise B in public, to stress B's title or ability, to show deference for his advice (even though A may not think much of it), all these are means to increase someone's *mien-tzŭ* or, in other words, "to make it look good on B's *mien-tzŭ*."

"*Mien-tzŭ* is given" very often to people who are not well known in society. It acts as an important stimulation to greater effort. The approbation of a leading scientist for the research of a student, for example, will encourage the latter to work all the harder.

The slighting of a person is often felt as "not giving *mien-tzŭ.*" When a person of some social standing refuses to see an individual of little account or to grant his request, he fails "to give him *mien-tzŭ,*" causing him to feel small and insignificant. While there are some people who indulge in this form of self-aggrandizement, the really cultured person who is valued by society will take care not to slight people.

"To give *mien-tzŭ*" is not always approved of by society. Sometimes an individual is elected or appointed to an honorary position without being properly qualified. Some person may criticize such an action, but his friends, wise in the affairs of the world, will tell him: "He is an eminent scholar (etc.), so they decided to give him *mien-tzŭ.*" It may be used in quite a derogatory sense: "Everybody knows that X is incapable of holding that job. But of course, he and so-and-so were school-mates, so so-and-so wanted to give him some *mien-tzŭ.*" Or, "that fellow X is a most obnoxious fellow. Let's give him some *mien-tzŭ* to keep him quiet."

11. *Liu mien-tzŭ*—"to leave *mien-tzŭ*" for someone. To expose a person's mistake, or even to allude to the disapproved action on his part and thus provoke public comment, will make a person feel that "it does not look good on his *mien-tzŭ,*" if it does not constitute down-right "loss of *lien.*" In this case the individual who so tactlessly cast a doubt on ego's character "does not leave him any *mien-tzŭ.*" But any decent individual will avoid mention of the affair and allow ego to retain his self-respect. The absence of comment will make the latter feel that his offense will be overlooked, and his prestige remains unimpaired.

Officials of high standing when accused of a crime used to be subjected to trial and examination in secret. The public did not learn about the proceedings, so public comment was avoided, and the official was "left some *mien-tzŭ.*"

It is regarded as essential not to touch the prestige of a person, not to ruin his reputation, for though the punishment be justified, the sudden loss of prestige built up through years of effort might be too much of a shock for the personality. A culprit should be left some *mien-tzŭ,* if we expect him to change his behavior; that is, we must "give him a chance for self-renewal." For example, an individual who has become impossible on the political stage, cannot be put aside without ado. He is sent out of the country on an official mission of little importance, or is offered a post with a good-sounding title, but little authority.

These examples chosen from the political sphere show that as the person becomes more exposed to the public eye, susceptibility tends to be greater. But even in ordinary life it is not good to accuse a person in public. Experience has shown that the publicity given to crimes ruining the reputation of the culprit often has caused tragedies.

From the above discussion it is clear that the motive is to avoid any action or words that might make the other fellow feel insignificant; rather it is believed that by elevating his self-esteem his good performance will be assured. This parallels a principle often applied in home education: a young child is encouraged to develop the desired qualities by treating him as an adult, or by giving him tasks beyond his age.

Individuals of good standing in society, whose words carry weight with their fellows, are particularly expected to "leave other people some *mien-tzŭ*," an attitude also described as "great in capacity," as opposed to narrowness in dealing with others.

12. *Yao mien-tzŭ*—"to want *mien-tzŭ*" is to attempt to acquire reputation by ostentation or subterfuge. A person "who wants *mien-tzŭ*" strives to show himself better situated, more capable, possessing better social connections or a better character than actually is the case. It is the closest Chinese approximation for the English "to save face."

Custom demands that a man provide his daughter with a dowry befitting his own station in life. But a wedding being a ceremony of the utmost importance a person who "wants *mien-tzŭ*" will give as rich a dowry as he possibly can, even to the point of incurring debts that will take years to pay off. For in this way *mien-tzŭ* is increased.

The following story illustrates well this expression: As a consequence of the Revolution (1911) the Manchus had lost their privileged position. Incapable of working for a living in spite of their education, many were reduced to utmost poverty. But they had the pride of aristocrats. One day a Manchu visited a tea-house. He was hungry, but had only just enough money to buy one small piece of pastry covered with sesame-seeds. As his grumbling stomach could not be pacified by such a small piece, he looked longingly at the seeds dropped on the table. He desired very much to pick them up, but feared to lose prestige in front of all the people. A bright idea hit him: using his finger as a brush and saliva as ink he wrote on the table, thus picking up the seeds and conveying them to his mouth. Some seeds had fallen into a crack and he had to use ingenuity to get at those. So he pretended to become angry and banged his fist on the table, jerking the seeds out of the crack. Then he started writing again and picked up the seeds. This story is told to ridicule the exaggerated desire for *mien-tzŭ* among Manchus, a weakness they share with poor aristocrats in many parts of the world.

The tendency of human beings lacking in education or talent to insist all the more on social recognition, once they have achieved a certain social position, is well known. A man of humble birth had risen to the post of police chief in some city. He was most anxious to demonstrate his connections with officials of high standing. So he bought a calligraphic scroll written by General Tsêng Kuo-fan, the best known military man in China during the latter part of the last century. The name of the original recipient of the scroll was erased and that of the police chief placed there instead, so that people might think him a friend of the general. Little did he realize that General Tsêng died well before his time.

Here is an example of this expression as applied to international politics. Some time ago a New York newspaper reported Hitler as accusing the Russians of using only antiquated equipment in the Finnish war, reserving their best arms for the fight against Germany. He very obviously was trying to explain his reverses and thus maintain his *mien-tzŭ*. Unfortunately this allegation annoyed the Finns, who would in this way be proved poor fighters. Feeling their *mien-tzŭ* depreciated, they repudiated Hitler's assertion. Hitler "wanted *mien-tzŭ*" very much in front of his own people, but did not care to "leave *mien-tzŭ*" to his allies.

13. *Fu-yen mien-tzŭ*—"padding (someone's) *mien-tzŭ*." A may not have much regard for B; but in order to obtain his goodwill, A will show him some deference, just enough to avoid making him feel uncomfortable. An example from international politics: A Chinese student remarked one day that all through the Sino-Japanese war the British had been *fu-yenning* China's *mien-tzŭ*, encouraging her to fight on, and making promises when necessary, but sending only a minimum of effective aid. This expressed clearly that this student had no confidence in Britain's sincerity. In order to retain the goodwill of the other fellow, ego will often hide his true judgment, even when he is held responsible for his opinion. Thus a critic reviewing a book may find it very poor but either because the author is a well-known personality or because he is a personal friend, he will express his criticism very mildly. Close friends of the critic will know his motives for padding the author's *mien-tzŭ* even though they may not approve of it.

Needless to say, this expression denotes an expedient adopted against the feeling of the person acting. An administrator coming into a new locality may heartily despise the people who regard themselves as the peaks of local society, but for reasons of prudence he will pad their *mien-tzŭ*.

14. *Chiang-chiu mien-tzŭ*—"to be particular about *mien-tzŭ*" is very similar to "to consider *mien-tzŭ*."

15. *Mei-yu mien-tzŭ*—"to have no *mien-tzŭ*" means that ego does not command enough prestige to attain a certain objective. He may want

to speak to a prominent person for some particular reason, but, not being well-known in that circle, he will ask a friend who is in a better position to undertake the task.

16. *Wo-men yu mien-tzŭ*—"we have *mien-tzŭ*" or *ta-chia yu mien-tzŭ*—"we all have *mien-tzŭ*." In the first form the "we" is inclusive of the person spoken to. Here *mien-tzŭ* stands for the friendship bond on which one can count. Thus, if A has *mien-tzŭ* with B, he can be certain that B will render him friendship services on occasion, and also that B will increase A's *mien-tzŭ* in front of other people in every possible way. This bond ensures reciprocity, so that the greater the circle of those with whom "one has *mien-tzŭ*," the better one can encounter adversity.

17. *Ho wo yu mien-tzŭ*—"to have *mien-tzŭ* with me" is similar to the above. For example, someone needs a person to intercede for him with his superior. I happen to know the superior quite well. "Having *mien-tzŭ* with me" he would not refuse me a favor. So his subordinate will try to ask me to speak to his boss. To ignore the obligation symbolized by this expression is a bad breach of etiquette. Actually a person is rarely reminded of the bond openly. Sometimes the phrase is used to exert pressure on an individual, as when inviting someone to dinner who tries to refuse, ego may say "Don't I have this little *mien-tzŭ* with you?" Although meant as a joke, it is not easy to overlook such a plea.

18. *K'an wo-ti mien-tzŭ*—"look at my *mien-tzŭ*," or better, "have regard for my *mien-tzŭ*." This expression is used when a person attempts to separate two individuals who are fighting or quarrelling. The idea of a "fair fight" does not exist in China: to resort to brute force is the acknowledgment that reason cannot work any longer; the result depends on the muscle of the disputants but can never show who is right and who wrong. So, as soon as two people lose control of themselves in a quarrel, a mediator, usually an older person, will appear at once, separate the two and argue with them till they stop. To give his words effect he asks each person to stop "out of regards for my *mien-tzŭ*." Such an appeal by an individual of some standing, made for ego's own good, must not be disregarded.

19. *Chieh mo-mo-jên-ti mien-tzŭ* "to borrow someone's *mien-tzŭ*" is used when somebody takes advantage of his acquaintance with some person of prestige in the community. Ego when applying for a job will give so-and-so as a reference though he may be a bare acquaintance, but this being a prominent person his chances of being accepted are better. On the other hand, most individuals are proud of being given as reference, as it constitutes a good gauge of their own prestige. Though knowing ego only slightly, the prominent person will gladly give the requested recommendation for ego's character. A concrete example: A well-known industrialist found a distant cousin

of his claiming to be his son in order to get on in life. When his own son objected, he reprimanded him. If his cousin claimed relationship with him, it was because of his standing in society. As no one was the loser, why call the young man a liar.

20. *T'uo mo-mo-jên-ti mien-tzŭ*—"to ask that so-and-so's *mien-tzŭ* be exerted in one's behalf" is similar to the above. But where *chieh mien-tzŭ* makes use of the name of a person of good standing, this expression refers to a request by ego that this person do something for ego, for example, write a letter of recommendation or make some inquiries.

21. *Mien-tzŭ shih-ch'ing*—"it is a matter of *mien-tzŭ*," is the explanation given for an action undertaken purely for the reason of maintaining one's own *mien-tzŭ*, or to give someone else *mien-tzŭ*. A rather objectionable young man is included in the list of guests for a party, because his father is a high official and the host has to keep on good terms with the latter. This is "just a matter of *mien-tzŭ*." Or, on New Year's Day ego feels it necessary to pay his respects to his superior, because this is "a matter of *mien-tzŭ*."

"A matter of *mien-tzŭ*" is often an action not quite welcome to the sentiments of ego, but to maintain his prestige and extend the net of social relationships a man has to undertake it. On the other hand, a close friend may make demands on ego involving considerable discomfort and sacrifice. They will be fulfilled without objection, as a matter of sentiment, not of *mien-tzŭ*.

CONCLUSION

The examples given have demonstrated the importance of the concepts *lien* and *mien-tzŭ* in the relations of ego to his environment. Both symbolize the regard of the group for ego, but they are based on different criteria.

Lien refers to the confidence of society in the moral character of ego. The concept of sin does not figure to any great extent in Chinese culture although it is not unknown. But the assumption of human nature as inherently good places on the individual the responsibility of training his character according to his own light and the demands of his status. A disregard for the standards of behavior causes the group to doubt the moral character of the individual and to question his ability to perform his roles. This "loss of *lien*" puts ego outside the society of decent human beings and threatens him with isolation and insecurity. *Lien* is not only an external sanction for behavior that violates moral standards, but constitutes an internal sanction as well. It will have been noticed that *lien* is conceived of as being maintained or lost as a whole; it forms an indivisible entity as experienced by ego, though its loss may be felt more or less strongly. In extreme cases the realization that one's conduct has been damned by group standards drives an individual to suicide.

Mien-tzŭ differs greatly from *lien* in that it can be borrowed, struggled for, added to, padded,—all terms indicating a gradual increase in volume. It is built up through initial high position, wealth, power, ability, through cleverly established social ties to a number of prominent people, as well as through avoidance of acts that would cause unfavorable comment. The value that society attaches to *mientzŭ* is ambivalent. On the one hand, it refers to well-earned popularity which is called *ming-yü*—"reputation" in its best sense; on the other, it implies a desire for self-aggrandizement. While moral criteria are basic in evaluating a person's worth to his group, self-maximation is allowed as a motive for greater exertion.

That *lien* and *mien-tzŭ* constitute separate concepts is well shown in the difference of reaction to the expressions "to have no *lien*" and "to have no *mien-tzŭ*." The former is the worst insult, casting doubt on the integrity of ego's moral character; the latter signifies merely the failure of ego to achieve a reputation through success in life. Again "to want *mien-tzŭ*" is by no means the opposite of "not to want *lien*." As explained before, the latter means that society considers ego's action a deliberate flaunting of moral standards in order to obtain practical advantages. "To want *mien-tzŭ*" is to increase or maintain prestige beyond one's station in life. As soon as the motive behind ego's actions becomes apparent in this case, he is shamed by loss of *lien*. Ego's lack of ability to influence his fellow-men or to convince them that he is a valuable asset to the community may be regrettable from his point of view, but it does not provide a shock to his self-respect that the loss of the confidence of society in his character does.

As the basic prerequisite for the personality, *lien* is included among the conditions determining the amount of ego's *mien-tzŭ*. Once *lien* is lost, *mien-tzŭ* will be hard to maintain. Because of this interrelationship the concept of *lien* is bound to overlap with that of *mien-tzŭ*. Deliberately to make a person "lose *lien*" is termed non-consideration for so-and-so's *mien-tzŭ*. Very frequently what a sensitive person feels as "loss of *lien*" may be regarded as no more than "looking bad on his or her *mien-tzŭ*" by an outsider. Besides, the mores differing to some extent in different parts of the country, the line differentiating behavior leading to "loss of *lien*" or to a depreciation of *mien-tzŭ* varies considerably. Thus *lien* and *mien-tzŭ* are not two entirely independent concepts. Nevertheless, their referents clearly belong to two distinct sets of criteria for judging conduct.

The importance of *lien* and *mien-tzŭ* varies with the social circumstances of ego. All persons growing up in any community have the same claim to *lien*, an honest, decent "face"; but their *mien-tzŭ* will differ with the status of the family, personal ties, ego's ability to impress people, etc. In a tightly-knit community the minimum requirements for the status of each person are well recognized. Anyone who does not fulfill the responsibilities associated with his roles will throw out of gear some part of the mechanism of well-ordered social life. For example, the head of a family who neglects his duties will place the burden for his dependents on the shoulders of his relatives or the village. Such irresponsible behavior in ego will arouse doubts as to his competence in maintaining his status. So society decrees that the "light-and-floating" character cannot be trusted, for such a person does not take his duties and obligations seriously; he does not have enough concern for *lien*. At the same time, the small farmer, the storekeeper, the laborer, etc. know that the "heavy-steady" type can be trusted, for he prizes his *lien* above the riches of the world; they know that they themselves can always rely on the help of friends as long as they maintain their *lien* intact.

Thus *lien* operates within the community as a means for insuring the social-economic security of ego and for maintaining his self-respect. In order that the community may form an opinion of his moral character an individual necessarily has to live continually in the same locality. A change of residence will put him in a new environment, out of reach of the constant reminder of "loss of *lien*" when this has occurred. So the city with its many opportunities for work is the welcome refuge for many an individual who has lost the respect of his group through lack of virtue. But even in the city the criteria for *lien* operate when one seeks steady employment. A craftsman taking an apprentice will want to know more about his character and the character of his family; a firm hiring an accountant will demand that the good conduct of the candidate be endorsed by respectable people. Thus the custom has arisen that anyone who seeks employment, anyone who intends to conclude a deal with someone in a locality far from home brings a written guarantee from a shop with a good reputation in his own neighborhood. These people would know how much concern ego has shown for his *lien* when staying with his family.

To be able to count on the confidence of his fellowmen even the poorest peasant or laborer will be anxious to preserve his *lien*. He cannot achieve *mien-tzŭ*, the reward for success in life, but he can conduct his life so that no blemish can be cast on his character. This will assure him work when he is in need of it, sympathy in adversity, moral support in disputes, and recommendations to employers in other parts when it becomes necessary to leave home.

In the middle classes the individual has a good start in life and has many opportunities for rising higher, but he must also be on guard not to slip down the social scale. Here *lien* is still very important.

However, *mien-tzŭ* has become a serious concern for ego, for he knows that by the manipulation of all possibilities to increase his prestige he is certain of social advancement. To make use of the opportunities offered by society he has to exert his efforts to demonstrate his ability, enlarge his friendship circle and follow in detail the conventions regulating social intercourse. The higher he ascends the social ladder, the wider the circle of eyes fastened upon his career, the more he must try to impress people. "Loss of *lien*" must be avoided, of course; a question regarding the integrity of his moral character would cause him to sink low in the esteem of his group. But no politician, no lawyer, no doctor, no scholar will expect to rise in social standing without building up his *mien-tzŭ*.

Lien also figures in the business world, although *mien-tzŭ* is a prime consideration. Once the community has acknowledged that a person is honest in his dealings and lives up to his obligations, he has credit far beyond his perhaps very modest possessions. For his creditors know that concern for keeping the respect of the community will force him to the utmost effort in satisfying their claims. This is the reason that up to recent times Chinese business men, though among the most prudent in the world, very often concluded deals without written contract. A person with a feeling for *lien* can be trusted implicitly, for *lien* is worth more than a fortune to those who value it. However, some merchants are unscrupulous. The fluidity of the city population has made it possible for these people to make profits in flagrant violation of the moral code. Much of the dislike for business men as a class is due to this emphasis on the profit motive. The feeling is that a person acting on such incentives cannot care for his moral character. Business thrives best where the mechanism of supply-and-demand is trusted to keep all parties satisfied. In Chinese society it had to accommodate itself to the insistence on *lien* as part of one's reputation; in those instances, for example, when business deals were at the expense of the seller or borrower, the businessman was assailed by all classes.

Lien is prized even by people living outside the pale of organized society. Banditry is often the result of famines and depressions. Even though defying the law, some outlaws do not lose their sense of decency, and will confine themselves to looting those who have too much, while on occasion helping the poor. In recent years before the war a thief in Peiping had achieved a good deal of popularity by stealing from the rich and handing a good deal of his wealth to the indigent. Such individuals naturally have not the slightest *mien-tzŭ*, but their actions show a respect for virtue which indicates that they were compelled by circumstances to become outlaws. They are not people who "do not want *lien*."

We have seen how important the idea of *lien* is for judging the personality; how *mien-tzŭ* confers on a person social standing far above one's fellows; how the middle classes have to struggle to maintain *lien* and increase their prestige. As the upper class is recruited largely from a middle class base, the highest executives in the government have always striven for both. Many a minister has ended his life by his own hands because he felt that on account of his inefficiency he had "no *lien* to see his emperor." Yet among the people who rise on top, particularly in times of stress and strain, there are those who care for *mien-tzŭ* far more than for *lien*. Opportunists often build up their reputation by all possible means, avoiding social censure for a time. Then, once wealth is acquired, power attained and position consolidated, they trust their *mien-tzŭ* to be strong enough to hush talk about their moral character. The warlords during the early part of the Republic are a good example. Each of them maintained his power by military force, perpetrating many crimes for the sake of money, but not allowing these to become public, meanwhile attracting to them politicians to help them devise taxing systems. They found the troubled conditions an easy opportunity to achieve success and sought to do so without regard to the moral standards of society, so that their liquidation was treated with rejoicing by all classes. They believed that they could maintain their position and prestige by means of money and military force, but their disregard for *lien* earned for them the contempt of their nation.

NOTES

1. Throughout this paper the word "character" has been used in its colloquial sense. It does not refer to character structure, but to the opinion that society forms of ego.

2. The writer is indebted to Dr. Meng-hsiu Chang for discussing with her the difference in the two concepts, clarifying some points and confirming others.

3. In rendering Chinese words into English the Giles system has been used throughout the paper.

4. The writer is not conversant enough with the southern Chinese dialects to know how far *lien* has penetrated. It seems that Kwangtung at least has not been reached.

5. In the lower Yangtze Valley the word *mien-k'ung* is used for *lien*.

6. We are speaking here of the society as a whole. Individual thinkers have discussed the probability of man's nature being inherently evil and needing training to fit it for a well-ordered social life. Foremost among these was Hsün-tzu, a disciple of Confucius. But in the long run, his philosophy could not prevail against that of Mencius, also a disciple of Confucius, who maintained the inborn tendency to goodness in man. Through the centuries Mencius has been read by every schoolboy, Hsün-tzu only by a few philosophers.

7. In particular some Chinese Christians in the early part of this century.

8. *Kuan-tzu* (Shanghai edition, 1934), pp. 40-41. Chung-fu was the name which the Duke used for Kuan Chung.

9. Chiang-tung was the southern part of the present province of Kiangsu, where Hsiang Yü started his campaign.

10. Shih-chi, chapt. 7: *The Annals of Hsiang Yü*.

11. An abbreviation of the verse "girl's face and peach flower reflect each other," meaning "youth and spring."

ABRAM KARDINER

1945. "The Concept of Basic Personality Structure as an Operational Tool in the Social Sciences," from *The Science of Man in the World Crisis,* ed. by Ralph Linton. New York. Reprinted by courtesy of Columbia University Press, the Editor, and the author.

Together with Ralph Linton, the psychoanalyst Abram Kardiner has presented the underlying ideas of the "culture and personality" school of research to wide audiences of scholars and laymen. Dr. Kardiner is known for two epoch-making books in the field: *The Individual and His Society, The Psychodynamics of Primitive Social Organization* (with a foreword and two ethnological reports by Ralph Linton), New York, 1939; and *The Psychological Frontiers of Society,* with the collaboration of Ralph Linton, Cora DuBois, and James West, New York, 1945.

The brief article that follows will take on added meaning to anyone who goes on to read the above-cited works. Students should master Kardiner's approach to the point where they can show clearly the resemblances and differences between Kardiner and other writers such as Benedict, Hallowell, and Mead—to name but three.

THE CONCEPT OF BASIC PERSONALITY STRUCTURE AS AN OPERATIONAL TOOL IN THE SOCIAL SCIENCES

ABRAM KARDINER

The processes of adaptation in man have been treated in various ways. The biologist limits the meaning of the term to those autoplastic changes in bodily structure which take place presumably to accommodate the organism to its physical environment. On this basis he can describe certain long-term phases of human adjustment, but he has to treat his subject with bold strokes and in relation to long periods of time. Morphological criteria cannot be used to describe the adaptive maneuvers of man covering short periods of time. Morphological adaptation in our species seems to have become almost stabilized, in spite of a long series of minor variations which now form the basis for the concept of race. Moreover, such adaptations record only the response of man to his external physical environment. What has become more important in the thinking of the past century is the adaptation of man to his human environment, the behavioral adjustments which he has had to make to the conditions imposed by social living.

While the morphological adjustments of our species could be studied and described in the familiar terms of biology, new techniques had to be devised for the description of behavioral and psychological adjustments. The concept which showed the greatest usefulness and viability in this connection was that of culture. The concept was purely descriptive, but it furnished a definite way of identifying at least the end products of the processes of adaptation and hence laid a basis for the comparison of various types of adaptive maneuvers.

The culture concept was first used with relation to the culture trait, an item of behavior common to the members of a particular society. Such a culture trait was presumably isolated and idiosyncratic. Later, the sociologists developed the concept of institutions—configurations of functionally interrelated culture traits, which are the dynamic units within culture. Although comparative studies of the forms of the institutions within various cultures could now be made, no significant conclusions concerning the relations of institutions within the same culture were possible without the aid of new techniques. Up to now only one technique has been able to yield decisive results in the interpretation of the variations in institutional combinations—and this technique is a psychological one. This psychological technique has shown itself capable of investigating the minutiae of those adaptive processes which cover short spans of time and represent reactions to both the natural and the human environment.

Preliminary attempts to establish relationships between institutions within the same culture had to draw heavily upon our knowledge of psychopathology. From this contact there emerged the concept of the psychological culture pattern.[1] However, early attempts based on too close analogies between society and the individual did not furnish a basis for a dynamic concept of society. The culture pattern merely gave recognition to the fact that personality and institutions were always to be found in some persistent relationship. It remained a difficult technical problem to demonstrate this relationship in an empirically verifiable manner without merely referring in a descriptive way to certain pathological configurations of frequent occurrence in individuals.

The study of "primitive" societies offered the best opportunity for the working out of such a technique. It could be legitimately anticipated that "primitive" societies would prove simpler in structure than our own and that the psychological constellations there found would be more consistent and more naïve in character. By far the most difficult problem was that of selecting a psychological technique suited to this particular assignment. Neither the classical psychologies, behaviorism, nor Gestalt psychology had made more than sporadic attempts to apply themselves to this problem. Psychoanalysis seemed the technique best suited to the task; yet Freud himself, in spite of his application of psychoanalysis to sociology, did not develop an empirically verifiable technique. On the whole, his efforts were dedicated to the verification in primitive society of those constellations found in modern man. This endeavor was consistent with the evolutionary hypothesis regarding the development of society and culture which was in vogue at the end of the nineteenth century. Among the most valuable suggestions made by Freud was that of an analogy between the practices of primitive people and neurotic symptoms. Some rather unproductive hypotheses resulted from the pursuit of this analogy to too great lengths; nevertheless, the study of the origin of neurotic symptoms in the individual laid a basis for the understanding of the minimal adaptive tools of man. Thus, even though the neurotic symptom is a special case, the principles upon which symptom formations are based cannot be very different from those involved in the development of any of the habitual modes of behavior which we identify in the character of the individual.

The integration of the two techniques, anthropological and psychological, was later facilitated by the abandonment of the evolutionary hypothesis exploited by the early anthropologists. For this was substituted the concept of cultures as functional wholes and the study of primitive societies as entities, a point of view of which Malinowski was the earliest exponent. All that was gained by the application of the concept of psychological culture pattern to primitive societies was the impression that institutions within a society were in large measure consistent with each other and that this consistency could be described in terms of analogies with entities found in psychopathology. This was a definite gain, but it was not a technique.

The most obvious approach to the problem of devising a definite technique was to utilize the known facts that cultures are transmitted within a society from generation to generation. It was natural, therefore, to attempt to develop such a technique with the aid of learning-theory formulations. However, what we know about acculturation and diffusion indicates that there is a limit to the sort of culture content which can be transmitted by direct learning processes. Though no one can deny the role of direct learning in culture transmission, qualified of course by the age of the individual who is exposed to culture change, there seems to be a high degree of selection in the acceptance of elements from any culture by individuals reared in another. Moreover, if learning process alone could account for the transmission of culture, it is difficult to see how culture change without borrowing from other cultures could ever take place. The point is that learning processes do not account for the integrative character of the human mind in so far as the emotional relationships of the individual to his environment are concerned. There is another factor at work, a factor upon which psychoanalytic technique can throw much light. In addition to direct learning processes, the individual builds up a highly complicated series of integrative systems which are not a result of direct learning. The concept of basic personality structure was established on the basis of a recognition of these factors.

The purely descriptive use of very similar concepts is an exceedingly old one. One can easily find it, by implication, in the writings of Herodotus and Caesar. Both of these authors recognize that the various peoples they described not only had unique customs and practices but were also unique in temperament, disposition, and character. Caesar took this factor into account and used it to the advantage of Rome in his dealings with the various barbarian tribes. However, the recognition that there are different basic personality structures for different societies really takes us no farther than did the concept of psychological culture pattern. It can acquire an operational significance only when the formation of this basic personality structure can be tracked down to identifiable causes and if significant generalizations can be made concerning the relation between the formation of basic personality structure and the individual's specific potentialities for adaptation.

The realization that the concept of basic personality structure was a dynamic instrument of sociological research was not an a priori judgment. It was a conclusion reached after two cultures described by Linton—the Tanala and the Marquesan—had been analyzed with the objective of correlating personality with institutions. In the analysis of these two cultures the potentialities of psychoanalytic principles were first shown. The analyses began with the study of the integrational systems formed in the child by the direct experiences during the process of growth. In other words, the approach was a genetic one. It followed two standards: (1) that integrative processes were at work, and (2) that the end results of these integrative processes could be identified. A technique which follows this line is, however, bound to have limitations. The first limitation is that, if the investigator is a citizen of Western society, and if he is moreover a psychopathologist, he will usually be able to identify only those end products which have significance in the neurotic and psychotic disturbances in his own society. But it must be recognized that, simultaneously, other end products were formed which we in our society could not possibly identify. Notwithstanding these limitations, some significant results were obtained in the first few attempts. The first correlation to be observed was that, in any given culture, religious systems were replicas of the experiences of the child with parental disciplines. It was noted that the concept of deity was universal, but that the technique for soliciting divine aid varied according to the specific experiences of the child and the particular life goals defined by the society. In one culture this technique for solicitation was merely to demonstrate endurance; in another it was to punish oneself in order to be reinstated in the good graces of the deity, a position that had been lost by some transgression clearly defined in the actual life practices sanctioned by the community. These variations in the technique of soliciting divine aid pointed, therefore, to different influences which shaped the personality in each specific culture.

From this first correlation several important conclusions could be drawn. The first of these was that certain culturally established techniques of child treatment had the effect of shaping basic attitudes toward parents and that these attitudes enjoyed a permanent existence in the mental equipment of the individual. The institutions from which the growing child received the experience responsible for the production of these basic constellations were, therefore, called primary institutions. The religious ideologies and methods of solicitation were, for the most part, consistent with these basic constellations and had presumably been derived from them by a process known as projection. In other words, primary institutions laid the basis for the projective system which was subsequently reflected in the development of other institutions. Institutions developed as a result of the projective systems were, therefore, called secondary institutions. If this correlation proved to be correct, it followed that between the primary experiences and the end results, identifiable through their projective manifestations, there stood this entity which could now be called the basic personality structure. Primary institutions were responsible for the basic personality structure which, in turn, was responsible for the secondary institutions. It must be emphasized that the important feature of this concept is not its name—although a good many investigators have since attempted variations in the name without any effort to modify or criticize the technique by which it was derived. This name stands for a special technique. Its importance depends upon the fact that it is possible to demonstrate that certain practices are significant for the individual during his period of growth and that the constellations thus formed remain as a continuity in the personality. This technique is an achievement of psychodynamics.

Although the development of these correlations began with a demonstration of the relation of religion to childhood experiences, as time went on, the technique was extended to include more and more factors. When all the institutions of a culture had been described, it became possible to classify them and to point out many which were instrumental in the creation of specific disposition, temperament, and values. Furthermore, many of the institutions proved to be oriented toward specific conditions in the life of a particular society as, for example, food supply. It was shown conclusively that in the Marquesas Islands anxiety about food created within the individual a specific series of integrative systems from which were derived special value systems, as well as certain religious practices.

Because of its many strange contrasts with the conditions of life and the value systems of our society, the Marquesans[2] furnished the first opportunity to establish the influence of early constellations. In this culture the ratio of men to women was 2½ to 1. It was a society much occupied with the threat of periodic starvation. Accordingly, its folktales showed that the relationship of men to women was strikingly different from that in our society. The initiative seemed to be decidedly in the hands of the women, and in many of the tales the young boy occupied precisely the same position that the innocent girl in our culture occupies in relation to the sex-hungry, brutal male. It was the woman who appeared in the place of the bad man of our society. The boy was subject to the sexual wishes of the woman. It was clear to see from these folktales that certain processes not present in our society were at work. It was the woman who was desired and hated, yet there was little overt hostility of the men toward each other in their competition for women. In other words, here was another evidence of areas of repression that differ from those in our culture.

In Tanala, as described by Linton,[3] another important aspect of basic personality structure was uncovered. There the important lesson was the demonstration of the confusion created by social changes when the basic personality remained intact. The old Tanala society had as its economic basis the cultivation of dry rice. This technique permitted a certain type of social organization, based on communal ownership of land, in which produce was divided under the extremely authoritarian rule of the father. The basic needs of the individual (that is, particularly of the younger sons upon whose labor the economy chiefly depended) were completely satisfied, notwithstanding what we should call in our society submission to despotic rule. Passive adaptation to a father was perfectly satisfactory as long as the basic needs of the individual were met. When the wet method of rice cultivation was introduced, communal ownership of land had to be abandoned. The individual suddenly became important, and his rights were threatened by the competitive needs of other individuals for the same means of subsistence. In other words, private property was introduced. The mad scramble for the favored valleys led to the disruption of the whole family organization. This resulted in a great increase in crime, homosexuality, magic, and hysterical illnesses. These social phenomena indicated quite clearly that when the personality, as shaped by the customs suited to the old method of economy, encountered, in the new economy, psychological tasks it was in no way prepared to meet, the result was an enormous outbreak of anxiety with various manifestations. Defensive measures had to be introduced by both the "haves" and the "have-nots."

Still another facet of basic personality structure was clearly demonstrated in Linton's description of the Comanche. These were a predatory people. Enterprise, courage, and initiative were the attributes needed in the individual to perpetuate the society. It was a society in which the young and able-bodied male bore all the burdens. Moreover it was a society which demanded a high degree of coöperation between the young males. It is clearly predictable from these demands that the greatest anxiety for the individual would come at that period in life when his powers, endurance, and courage were on the wane. Since there were no vested interests in this society, the individual could not accumulate any emblems of social value to perpetuate a status once achieved. Perforce, the society was a democracy in which status must be constantly validated. The discipline to which the individual must conform in childhood could not therefore be of a kind that would impede development and growth, especially along those lines most valuable to the society. Accordingly we find that no impediments were placed in the path of development; the self-esteem, courage and enterprise of the individual were fostered by every possible device, and the qualifications he had to meet in later life were consistent with the constellations created in childhood. It is therefore not surprising to find that the projective systems in Comanche were extremely uncomplicated. In their religion there was no concept of sin and no complicated ritual for reinstatement in the good graces of the deity. A Comanche who wanted "power" simply asked for it, or demonstrated his fortitude. In other words, the practical religion was merely a replica of those conventions which guaranteed the fullest coöperation between the males for their common enterprise.

Up to this point we have been using source material of a limited kind. We have used only the institutional set-up of a given society and have established a relationship between the various institutions by demonstrating their consistency with the basic experiences of the individual during the process of growth. Even if our conclusions are valid, no more can be said for the result obtained than that it is a good guess. But thus far we have no way of checking the validity of our conclusions. New data are imperative. If there is such a thing as a basic personality, we should be able to identify it in the individuals composing a particular society. However, we are obliged to reckon with the fact that all individuals are different, that is, each has a different character. Therefore, how is it possible to reconcile the idea of basic personality with the known fact that each individual in a given culture has his own individual character?

This question is readily answered when we examine the structure of the personalities of one hundred individuals in our own society. Each of them will have a specific character-structure shaped partly by potentialities at birth and by innate predispositions, but also by those specific influences encountered during the process of growth. Were it not for the fact that there is a basic personality among these one hundred people, we could never identify such specific constellations as Oedipus complex, castration complex, and so on, which were made so noteworthy by Freud. Freud, however, did not know that these constellations, which were so universal in the people in our society, were specific to our culture. He believed that they were universal to all mankind, and therefore that many of them were of phylogenetic origin. One can define such a thing as a basic personality among these one hundred individuals in our society by the fact that they all have been shaped by situations which have their origin in institutional practices. Each individual handles the specific influences in a characteristic way, but this notwithstanding, the character-structure is formed within an ambit of a certain range of potentialities, and within this latter the basic personality is to be found.

A study of biographies therefore became imperative for the further development of our work. It was important also that there should be a series of biographies for each society—in fact, the more the better. But the study of a dozen biographies including both sexes and representing variations in status and age could give us not only those features which all had in common but could also indicate for us those places at which the variations occurred. It might be mentioned parenthetically that the technique of taking such a biography is not an easy task, because when individuals are invited to recount the story of their lives they take for granted all the background of value systems and socially approved objectives and therefore all one gets is a *curriculum vitae*. Such a record is of no value. What is needed is a cross-section of the individual which embraces the influences of his childhood, the history of his entire development, and a cross-section of his adaptation at the time the history is taken.

The opportunity for such an experiment presented itself in the description of Alorese culture by Dr. Cora DuBois. She brought back from this culture not only a description of the institutional set-up, but a series of eight biographies together with Porteus intelligence tests, children's drawings, and a series of thirty-seven Rorschach tests. The study of this culture revealed the following: The conclusions already reached in the study of Marquesans, Tanala, and Comanche were corroborated. From the institutional description of Alor it was not difficult to reconstruct the basic personality. The influences to which the child was subjected in this society were of a unique character. Owing to the peculiar division of function between the males and the females, the woman bore the brunt of the vegetable food economy. She worked in the fields all day and could take care of her children only before she went out to the fields and after she returned. Maternal neglect was therefore the rule, and by that is meant that the supportive influences of the mother in establishing the structure of the ego were in default. Tensions from hunger, the need for support, for emotional response, were therefore greatly neglected, and the child was left in the care of older siblings, relatives, or other persons. The consistency of the disciplines was therefore destroyed; the image of the parent as a persistent and solicitous helper in case of need was not built up. The ego was feeble in development and filled with anxiety. The patterns of aggression remained amorphous. Accordingly, although we find in the projective systems the concept of a deity, there is no effort at idealization of the divine image and the Alorese perform their religious rituals only under the pressure of urgent circumstances, and then in a reluctant manner. The interpersonal tensions within the society run high, distrust is universal, and the emotional development retarded and filled with anxiety.

We then turned our attention to the study of the individual biographies. Fortunately they were documented in such a way that the basic requirements for our specific needs were fully met, notwithstanding the fact that many of them were faulty from the point of view of a fully documented life history. Many things concerning the character structure of the individuals were picked up by observing these subjects in the actual process of living from day to day, and moreover by observing their reactions to the ethnographer and by studying their dream life. In connection with the studies of these individuals certain new features concerning basic personality were unraveled. It was an extraordinary fact to find in half a dozen of these biographies that, whenever the subject of hunger was touched upon, the associations led to some form of natural catastrophe, such as earthquake or flood. This was quite in accordance with what we would expect and what we predicted from the study of the basic personality structure. Each of these eight people had an individual character, but nevertheless all had certain features in common, not because they followed certain conventions in common but because the deeper fabric of their personalities was molded on similar lines. Furthermore, the points at which the individuals differed in character structure could be clearly tracked down to variations in the influences at work during the period of growth. Where the parental care was good, specific variations in character appeared. For example, one of the men proved to have a conscience molded upon lines similar to those found in our society. He had moreover a patent Oedipus complex. But all these factors were clearly traceable to the influence of a powerful father who had more than the usual amount of solicitude for his son. Conscience was a rare phenomenon among the Alorese, and the relation of conscience to the absence of good parental care was therefore· clearly demonstrated. Moreover all the individuals showed similar sequences in aggression patterns and in the absence of specific constellations that are found in our society.

But we still had, in addition to these biographical studies, a new series of data which could be used to corroborate, amplify, or refute the findings up to this point. These were the conclusions of the Rorschach tests, which were made by Dr. Emil Oberholzer "blind," that is, without knowledge either of the personalities or of the specific features of the culture. Dr. Oberholzer's report concerning these Rorschach findings was to me the most astonishing confirmation of the validity of the concept of basic personality. First of all, he identified certain features which all Alorese had in common. Secondly, the specific individuals all showed individual variations from this basic pattern. But to me these findings were less important than another order of data revealed by the Rorschach tests. As previously stated, the psychologist who operates only within the knowledge of the psychopathological entities found in our society has an insuperable handicap —he is capable of identifying only those entities found in our society. It is at this point that the Rorschach test adds a new series of data. Whereas the Rorschach test can give no information concerning the genesis of distinctive traits in the individual or in the group, the test nevertheless demonstrates emotional combinations which are not identifiable in the psychopathological entities common in our society. With the aid of those features, revealed by the Rorschach but which do not appear either in the basic personality or in the study of biographies, it is now possible to rework the original genetic picture so as to describe how the new entities came into existence. The Rorschach test therefore is an instrument not only for checking conclusions already reached but for discovering new entities inaccessible to the other techniques. It may be objected that, after all, the Rorschach is a projective test and therefore its utility may be limited by the fact that its norm has been based upon the study of our society, or, to be more specific, upon the citizens of Switzerland. In actual operation this limitation proves to be unimportant.

In studies undertaken after the Alorese only three yielded significant results: a description by Mr. James West of a community in the United States called Plainville; a study of Sikh culture, described by Dr. Marian W. Smith; and a study of the Ojibwa, described by Miss Ernestine Friedl.

The first study showed that Plainville, a small, rural community in the Middle West, had distinctive features which deviated in a considerable number of respects from urban communities. Furthermore, it precipitated the entire question of whether one can study such large groups as nations with the aid of the concept of basic personality. The answer seems to be in the affirmative, since the Plainville variations from the norm established in urban centers are not very wide. The study of Plainville also precipitated the issue of whether or not the concept of basic personality may be profitably applied to the history of Western society. This is a problem yet to be resolved.

In the study of Sikh we again found some unique features. Here we worked largely with a description of the institutions and with Rorschach tests. The consistency of the two kinds of data was again quite remarkable. The same was true of Ojibwa. It was clearly demonstrated that the Rorschach was indispensable in checking up essential features of basic personality which could not be identified from the genetic picture alone. For example, it was noted in Ojibwa that the disciplines of childhood and the folktales concerning Wenebojo (the

Ojibwa culture hero) all pointed to the fact that the claims the child made upon the parent were definitely limited. He was discouraged from believing that the parent had magical powers which could be used for the benefit of the child. The tenor of the early disciplines was all in the direction of informing the child that he could make but limited claims upon the parent, all this notwithstanding the fact that the child was given excellent care. We had here, therefore, a combination not to be found in our society: the personality was given a good foundation, but emotional development was limited in a manner very different from anything we find in our society. This limitation could not be completely identified from the genetic picture of the development of the child. It required the Rorschach test to demonstrate quite conclusively the peculiar limitations of the Ojibwa in his emotional contact with others. A second feature of Ojibwa was that it afforded an excellent opportunity for the study of the acculturation processes and the specific manner in which acculturation took place. It was very clear from the Rorschach picture that these processes introduced factors into the emotional life of the individual which were common in our society but unknown to Ojibwa, who had not been exposed to the ways of white men or to Catholicism.

The technique of deriving the basic personality as it has been described up to this point is open to some serious objections. One may say that people are what they are because they grow up under certain conditions; we have known that for some thousands of years. Quite true. But the technique as described furnishes a specific bill of particulars as to what conditions give rise to precisely what results in the personality; moreover, because of the integrational processes at work and the unforeseen combinations, it is able to derive some indirect results. But so far the technique is open to a still more serious objection: It gives no answer to the question of why one people finds it necessary to institute certain disciplines, impulse controls, and so on, while others do not. This objection finally reduces the technique to a refinement of the old saw that some people do one thing and some do another, a position not far removed from that furnished by the use of the culture pattern.

The crucial question then becomes: What determines the parental attitude toward children and hence the specific influences to which the child is subject? In general, one can say that these parental attitudes are determined by the social organization and the subsistence techniques. Whereas this statement is, strictly speaking, true, we are likely to get many surprises unless we qualify it with several conditions. And these conditions are of the highest importance in relation to cultural change.

If we attempt to define those conditions which qualify the socio-economic determinants of parental attitudes, apparently we immediately run into the problem of social origins. This is a hopeless task, and theories at this point are no substitute for demonstrable evidence. An excellent case in point is Comanche culture. As we compare the institutions of the old Plateau culture from which the Comanche derived, we notice that some institutions are the same in both, some are modified, and some disappear in the new conditions. Hunting medicine, though common in the old culture, disappears in the new. The reason is obvious. In the new environment game was plentiful, which meant no anxiety and no need for supernatural aid, skill being the only requirement. The raising of the young, especially the young male, was not the same in the new culture as in the old. But there was an *Anlage* in the old culture for the new development; and the new economy could not be aided in any way by impulse control over the young. On the contrary, everything was to be gained from an unobstructed development of the young male.

In old Tanala the parental attitudes were likewise consistent with the economy of communal ownership of land; but when private property was introduced, chaos resulted because the disciplines in the old culture qualified the individual for a very passive adaptation to an economy devoid of opportunities for competition. The new economy demanded strong competitive attitudes; the result was only an increase in anxiety, symptomatic of the absence of executive capacities to deal with the situation.

One would be inclined to generalize from the illustration of Comanche and to conclude that, of course, when economic and social conditions change, attitudes to children and hence the conditions for growth change. This might be true if the parental attitude were determined by factors which were perfectly well known to the parents. They are not. And hence one cannot generalize from Comanche, which is the exception and not the rule. We have long since heard of the "cultural lag," which some attempt to account for on the basis of an inertia principle. Such philosophical formulae, even if true, do not explain the facts.

The case of Alor is one in which the rearing of the child and the influences to which it is exposed are in keeping with the socioeconomic conditions. But we do not know the origins of the particular type of economy, nor does it appear to make any sense to us. In Alor the division of labor is such that the female carries the entire burden—with sporadic help—of the main diet of vegetable food. She is thus taken away from the children all day, caring for them before she leaves for the fields and after she returns. The fields are not contiguous and are sometimes quite far from the village. The effects of the absent mother we have already described, but we cannot answer the question of why labor is so unevenly and capriciously divided. The remote effect of this single institution on the culture as a whole is surely not known to the Alorese. If we say that this institution is not rationally determined, or that it is an illustration of cultural lag, we are not saying much. This cultural lag is no abstract principle of inertia; it is caused by the accumulation of vested emotional interests, which in this instance accrue on the side of the males. To discontinue these interests would cause enormous resistance and discomfort, even if the women had imagination enough to demand that some of the burden of the food economy be lifted from their shoulders. This is an illustration of how "rights" of a certain group in a society (in this instance the males) are established and maintained. To alter the economy would be to alter the entire psychological adaptation of both males and females. This is precisely the point at which anxiety and defensive maneuvers became necessary to retain a system of adaptation and to resist change.

We must pause to make a parenthetical observation on the relative usefulness of a descriptive versus an operational concept. To call the phenomena described in the preceding paragraph a principle of inertia is not incorrect—even though it calls to mind the physical phenomena on which the principle of inertia was based and is hence a false analogy. The real objection to it is that the concept does not reach the facts. Moreover, to a law of inertia one can only bow with humility. But if we point out that this inertia is localized in specific emotional factors, we can mobilize some specific antidotes at these points.

What we have been saying is that the operational value of the concept of basic personality is not only to diagnose the factors which mold the personality but also to furnish some clues about why these influences are what they are. The concept therefore implies a technique which will explore with some degree of accuracy the widest ramifications between culture and personality.

It remains a question whether this technique can be used to describe the dynamics of Western society and to attempt an analysis of the dynamics of culture change over long spans of time. Such an attempt would really be the proof of the technique. But this problem is not as simple as the one in "primitive society." "Western" society is not a single culture but a conglomeration of cultures in which the socio-economic order has gone through a host of vicissitudes. The number of factors which must be brought into correlation is much greater than any we have encountered in primitive society. Whether the attempt at such correlation can succeed remains to be seen; meanwhile there have been enough efforts to solve the problem by other techniques to show us what to avoid. We cannot work on the basis of physiological analogies as did Spengler. One can tell a good story by comparing the rise and fall of civilizations with the physiological life cycle of individuals, but societies are organisms of a quite different order. Following the fate of elites, as does Pareto, leaves many questions unanswered. We can get no real guidance from Toynbee, who tries to follow the process of adaptation of large groups according to various ideas—successful or unsuccessful struggle with the external environment, and so on—without benefit of a psychology to track down the minutiae of adaptation. Least of all can we extract much benefit from a long series of correlations such as Mumford[4] marshals and then proceeds to evaluate on the basis of a highly personal system of value judgments. Endeavors like these give no empirical basis for action based on rational principles. They must degenerate into doctrines which one may endorse or reject according to personal predilection or in defense of interests, whether conscious or unconscious.

The outline for a plan of research derived from our present knowledge of basic personality type is given elsewhere.[5] Here we can only make a few suggestions about technique. One can determine the basic personality for a few communities, both urban and rural. There are appreciable differences between the two. One can then see where the points of difference lie and try to ascertain their causes. The same procedure can be used for communities in other countries as, for example, England and France. Once a dozen such studies have been made, accompanied by biographies, Rorschachs and other projective tests, we can tell what clues to follow in our historical researches. We have already done enough of this to know that there are three systems whose vicissitudes we must follow historically: (1) the projective systems, (2) the empirically derived rational systems, such as technologies, and (3) the endless labyrinths or rationalizations whereby actions are justified but the sources of which lie in projective systems of which man is not aware. One cannot follow the reactions of man to his physical and human environment without the aid of these psychological guides.

The promise which this new technique offers lies in a direction quite different from the current condition of decisions by force or the defense of personal or class interests. It offers a greater insight into personal and social motivations and points the way toward the introduction of controls over the anxieties of men and the defenses mobilized by these anxieties. Any plan for social action based on these principles must, however, compete with powerful forces lined up on the side of simpler principles, such as race theories of superiority, of eugenic selection of elites, of the "rights" of certain classes, and so on, which derive from the projective systems of contemporary man. These forces are all polarized toward the dominance-submission principle. The triumph of empirically derived directives for social action can only follow in the wake of a triumph for greater democracy and of an increased desire to gain insight into the psychological fabric of the forces that can either hold society together or tear it apart and destroy it.

NOTES

1. Ruth Benedict, *Patterns of Culture* (New York, 1934).
2. See A. Kardiner, *The Individual and His Society* (New York, 1939).
3. *Ibid.*
4. Lewis Mumford, *The Condition of Man* (New York, 1944).
5. A. Kardiner, *The Psychological Frontiers of Society* (New York, 1945).

CLYDE KLUCKHOHN

1944. "The Influence of Psychiatry on Anthropology in America during the last 100 years," from *One Hundred Years of American Psychiatry*, edited by J. K. Hall, G. Zilboorg, and H. A. Bunker. Columbia University Press, New York. Reprinted by permission of the author and of Columbia University Press. The compiler acknowledges permission of the owners of copyrights covering the quoted excerpts in this article; sources are given in detail in the footnotes.

1945. "A Navaho Personal Document with a brief Paretian analysis," *Southwestern Journal of Anthropology*, vol. 1: 260-283. Reprinted by courtesy of the author and of the Editor of the *Southwestern Journal of Anthropology*.

Perhaps the outstanding publication in the field of "culture and personality" is the textbook by Kluckhohn, Murray, and Schneider: *Personality in Nature, Society, and Culture* (New York, A. A. Knopf; rev. ed., 1953). Students are urged to familiarize themselves with *Personality in Nature, Society, and Culture*, for many important articles omitted from the present book are reprinted there. Neither book, unfortunately, contains some of Dr. Kluckhohn's important research reports (see Bibliography: Kluckhohn, 1943, 1946, 1947, 1954—to name but a few).

The story of the relations of psychiatry and anthropology, as told in the following pages, affords scholarly perspective on the whole development of research and thinking denoted by the phrase, "culturally fostered patterns of personal character." The second paper, an analysis of a Navaho autobiography, is pertinent for its narrative content; the merits of Pareto's sociology are not an issue in the present context. It is possible here only to suggest the wealth of material accumulated on the Navaho Indians and the important role of Kluckhohn in collecting much of it.

THE INFLUENCE OF PSYCHIATRY ON ANTHROPOLOGY IN AMERICA DURING THE PAST ONE HUNDRED YEARS

Clyde Kluckhohn

A presentation of this subject matter will be simplified if it is pointed out at the outset that American anthropologists have been influenced almost exclusively by psychoanalytic psychiatry. It may be argued whether this circumstance has resulted, as Allport[1] has suggested, because psychoanalysis "is the most effortless type of psychology to lean upon," or because of genuine convergence upon a series of fundamental assumptions,[2] or because of an intricate network of historical accidents. But the fact is beyond dispute. A few anthropologists, of course, have had intellectual contacts with nonanalytic psychiatrists; but the name of Dr. Adolf Meyer is the only one which recurs frequently enough in informal conversations within the profession to indicate any influence transcending the purely casual or that which a chance personal relationship happened to bring to an individual anthropologist. Even in the case of Dr. Meyer, one may suspect that most anthropologists of psychiatric orientation have at most a hazy conception of his point of view.

Certainly from the study of anthropological literature one gets an overwhelming impression that it is only psychoanalytic writers who are extensively read by anthropologists in this country. One would be hard pressed to discover five citations to nonanalytic psychiatrists, with the exception of Rorschach.

This generalization as to the predominance of psychoanalysis in anthropological thought may be both widened and narrowed. It may be widened by calling attention to the fact that anthropologists have obtained much more than psychiatric notions, in any limited sense, from the psychoanalytic movement. Although a few American anthropologists have shown some interest in the problems of perception and of intelligence tests, academic psychology has had a surprising minimum of influence upon anthropology. Almost the only concept of any wide currency which has been taken over from academic psychology is that of the sentiment (which came mainly via Radcliffe-Brown and other British anthropologists). The influence of Gestalt psychology upon Benedict and others may also be noted. With these qualifications, it

485

must be said that American anthropology, for good or for ill, has seemed to find only in psychoanalysis the bases for a workable social psychology.

The generalization may be narrowed by noting that we need say little of the older psychiatries which originated in, but diverged from, Freudian psychoanalysis. Jung is talked about by anthropologists fairly occasionally, and one sees references to his work, especially to the personality types, now and then.[3] Radin[4] discussed the implications of Jung's theories for ethnology and predicted that Jung would have a greater influence than any of the scientific group. This prediction has thus far notably failed of justification. Jung's systematic influence in this country in contrast to Great Britain seems to have been restricted to one psychiatrist who used ethnological data and published in anthropological media.[5] Of Rank there is barely casual mention,[6] and in the professional literature I have discovered but three incidental references to Adler.[7] The so-called "Neo-Freudians" (Horney, Kardiner, Fromm, and others) have, as is well known, been highly influential in anthropological circles during the past few years.

The dominant currents in American anthropology prior to, roughly, 1920 were descriptive and historical. Anthropologists were, understandably, obsessed with the necessity of making adequate records of nonliterate societies before these had disappeared or been altered beyond recognition by contact with European cultures. To this day, anthropologists as a group are relatively unsophisticated in broad intellectual matters. In large part, this tendency may be traced to a major condition of their intellectual lives: The time which other social scientists may give to work in the library the anthropologist must give to field work, to preparation for field trips, to the study of difficult non-Indo-European tongues. Such attention as the earlier American anthropologists gave to strictly theoretical questions was almost entirely confined to diffusion versus independent invention and various other "historical" issues.

These statements are as true as any assertions of comparable breadth can be. Naturally, some writers treated problems in which a psychiatrist would be interested. Thus Brinton has a chapter on "Pathological Variation in the Ethnic Mind," in which he repeats that fallacious and persistent dogma of the folklore of science: "Diseases of nervous and mental exhaustion belong exclusively among nations of advanced culture."[8] Writers of monographs often, but not always, devoted a page or two to a description of "mental abnormalities" found within the tribe.[9] But of awareness of psychiatry—in other than the most diffuse sense that there was such a thing as "mental disease"—there is almost no evidence. Indeed, most anthropologists of the period before 1920 seem almost apologetic when they incidentally allude to individual variations. Anthropology was focused upon the standard, the average, the abstracted culture patterns. It is hardly too much to say that the prevalent trend of American anthropology was "anti-psychological."

Gradually there developed a realization that, after all, even culture was manifested in the concrete only by individuals, and that hence it was valuable to obtain personal documents. This method of attack seems to have been stimulated by Professor Boas. In 1906 Kroeber published three brief personal narratives of war experience as told by Gros Ventre Indians. In 1913 Radin provided a short Winnebago autobiography, and in 1920 a considerably more substantial one. In 1922 a group of American anthropologists, under the editorship of E. C. Parsons, produced a volume of personal sketches, short autobiographies, and other personalized material. A little later Michelson published the autobiography of a Fox woman.

The importance of such endeavors as a preliminary to an interest in strictly psychiatric questions must not be underestimated. Once the individual is admitted as a legitimate object of anthropological study, the way is opened for collaboration with psychiatrists. On the other hand, it must be stressed that these early life histories from nonliterate societies were viewed by anthropologists as strictly ethnological documents. They were regarded as useful leads on hitherto undiscovered cultural items and as source material on the legitimate problem of cultural variation. In no one of them is there a reference to a psychiatric source, nor is there any attempt to interpret or illumine them with psychiatric concepts.

Psychiatrists were much quicker to appreciate the value of anthropological materials than were anthropologists to seize upon psychiatric knowledge. I have heard a distinguished American historian of psychiatry remark that even during the middle portion of the last century psychiatrists were searching for a usable anthropology. In any case, before 1920 European psychiatrists had made considerable use of material from "primitives." Kraepelin[10] and others had begun to construct a comparative psychiatry. Freud, Reik, Rank, and other European psychoanalysts had ransacked the older ethnological literature. In this country at least three psychiatrists had published upon nonliterate groups: Brill on the Eskimo;[11] Coriat on the Yaghan Indians of South America;[12] Brown on various groups.[13]

Publications of English anthropologists show that they were seriously affected by psychoanalysis about ten years before their American colleagues. In the published record in this country prior to 1920, I have been able to find only three small evidences of contact. One American ethnologist, Parsons, published a brief note in a psychoanalytical periodical.[14] She indicated some familiarity with psychoanalytic theory but carefully eschewed all interpretation. A casual footnote in another paper first published in 1918 evidences that another American anthropologist, Goldenweiser, had become aware of Freud.[15] In the same year Kroeber published in the *American Anthropologist* a brief review of two books by Jung.[16]

In 1920 came the first proof that some of the leaders in American anthropological thought were giving serious consideration to psychoanalysis. Lowie devoted several pages of his *Primitive Society* to a "refutation" of the Freudian explanation of the mother-in-law taboo.[17] Professor Boas had repeatedly insisted upon the importance to anthropology of studies of the individual—even though most of the empirical work done by Boas in cultural anthropology had, like that of his pupils, been preoccupied with descriptive and historical matters. Now, in a general discussion of "The Methods of Ethnology," he stated explicitly his belief that "some of the ideas underlying Freud's psychoanalytic studies may be fruitfully applied to ethnological problems." However, he ended his article with some cautious remarks which are representative of the difficulties felt by even the more sympathetic anthropologists from that day to this:

> The theologians who interpreted the Bible on the basis of religious symbolism were no less certain of the correctness of their views, than the psychoanalysts are of their interpretations of thought and conduct based on sexual symbolism. The results of a symbolic interpretation depend primarily upon the subjective attitude of the investigator who arranges phenomena according to his leading concept. In order to prove the applicability of the symbolism of psychoanalysis, it would be necessary to show that a symbolic interpretation from other entirely different points of view would not be equally plausible, and that explanations that leave out symbolic significance or reduce it to a minimum would not be adequate.
>
> While, therefore, we may welcome the application of every advance in the method of psychological investigation, we cannot accept as an advance in ethnological method the crude transfer of a novel, one-sided method of psychological investigation of individual to social phenomena the origin of which can be shown to be historically determined and to be subject to influences that are not at all comparable to those that control the psychology of the individual.[18]

In this same year (1920) there appeared the first article in an American anthropological publication to be devoted entirely to psychiatric questions.[19] In this consideration of *Totem and Taboo* Professor Kroeber rejected Freud's conclusions but praised many of his concepts and insights: "But, with all the essential failure of its finally avowed purpose, the book is an important and valuable contribution" (p. 63); "the book . . . thus is one that no ethnologist can afford to neglect" (p. 55). Herein Kroeber appeared much wiser than many American anthropologists, down to the present. The fact that Freud, in this and other works, relied mainly upon anthropologists of "the English evolutionary school" was a major stumbling block to professional acceptance in America. Here it was felt that these data (themselves dubious because culled without too much discrimination from the accounts of travelers and missionaries) had been processed into spurious generalizations by invalid methods. The conventional American anthropologist dismissed Freud's anthropology as bad and his conclusions as worthless. With regrettable but familiar illogic, psychoanalytic method and theory were therewith rejected.

To some ·degree, this may be merely the rationalization covering a deeper psychological factor. Perhaps the tendency to ignore or to be resistive to psychiatry springs from a temperamental selectivity of the anthropological profession. Anthropology as it was conceived (and still is, by many) in this country was a refuge for those who were impelled by inner, largely unconscious, needs to escape from the personal or "to crawl back into the womb of the cultural past." Sapir was keenly aware of the temperamental antithesis:

> What is the genesis of our duality of interest in the facts of behavior? Why is it necessary to discover the contrast, real or fictitious, between culture and personality, or, to speak more accurately, between a segment of behavior seen as cultural pattern and a segment of behavior interpreted as having a person-defining value? Why cannot our interest in behavior maintain the undifferentiated character which it possessed in early childhood? The answer, presumably, is that each type of interest is necessary for the psychic preservation of the individual in an environment which experience makes increasingly complex and unassimilable on its own simple terms. The interests denoted by the terms culture and personality are necessary for intelligent and helpful growth because each is based on a distinctive kind of imaginative participation by the observer in the life around him. The observer may dramatize such behavior as he takes note of in terms of values, a conscience which is beyond self and to which he must conform, actually or imaginatively, if he is to preserve his place in the world of authority or impersonal social necessity. Or, on the other hand, he may feel the behavior as self-expressive, as defining the reality of individual consciousness against the mass of environing determinants. Observations coming within the framework of the former of these two kinds of participation constitute our knowledge of culture. Those which come within the framework of the latter constitute our knowledge of personality. One is as subjective or objective as the other, for both are essentially modes of projection of personal experience into the analysis of social phenomena. Culture may be psychoanalytically reinterpreted as the supposedly impersonal aspect of those values and definitions which come to the child with the irresistible authority of

the father, mother, or other individuals of their class. The child does not feel itself to be contributing to culture through his personal interaction but is the passive recipient of values which lie completely beyond his control and which have a necessity and excellence that he dare not question. We may therefore venture to surmise that one's earliest configurations of experience have more of the character of what is later to be rationalized as culture than of what the psychologist is likely to abstract as personality. We have all had the disillusioning experience of revising our father and mother images down from the institutional plane to the purely personal one. The discovery of the world of personality is apparently dependent upon the ability of the individual to become aware of and to attach value to his resistance to authority. It could probably be shown that naturally conservative people find it difficult to take personality valuations seriously, while temperamental radicals tend to be impatient with purely cultural analysis of human behavior.[20]

It is an induction from my own observation that a majority of American anthropologists, at least of those of the older generation, seem to be made uncomfortable by discussion of topics which relate to persons or individuals rather than to cultural forms. This discomfort is manifested by nuances of behavior as well as by a hasty displacement of responsibility ("Yes, I suppose I have to admit that those questions are important but they are none of our business as anthropologists. Let the psychiatrists and psychologists worry about them."), or by an impatient deathblow with threadbare professional clichés ("You know perfectly well that Kroeber and Opler showed that Freud was absurd and that Malinowski proved there was no such thing as the oedipus complex in the Trobriand Islands.").

This interpretation may be questioned, but there can be no doubt that until roughly fifteen years ago one could gorge oneself upon anthropological literature without ever coming face to face with the type of problem which is all important in psychiatric thinking. There were, to be sure, temporary and occasional exceptions, but they deviated from the main currents. For example, Goldenweiser in his *Early Civilization*[21] referred to Freud many times and gave a number of pages to a systematic exposition of psychoanalytic theory. But much more representative of the general trend is the astonishing fact that in 1924 Lowie published a general treatise on primitive religion in which he did not so much as mention Freud, psychoanalysis, or psychiatry.

Of the acknowledged leaders of the profession only Boas and Kroeber uncompromisingly recognized the significance of psychological issues in anthropological research. Boas was constantly stressing "man's mental life," "psychic attitudes," and "subjective worlds"[22] in his publications and seems consistently to have adhered to this point of view in his teaching. We find Kroeber making this critical stricture upon Lowie's *Primitive Society*: "There is scarcely even anything that psychology, which underlies anthropology, can take hold of and utilize."[23] Kroeber made other similar comments from time to time, yet neither Kroeber nor Boas ever followed psychological lines in his own researches. Boas did stimulate some of his students to do such research—Benedict, Mead, and others; presumably he also influenced Sapir somewhat in this direction. Kroeber's case is curious. He reviewed Jung's *Analytical Psychology*[24] and has published (besides the two discussions of *Totem and Taboo* in 1920 and 1939) two incidental papers dealing with the contribution of anthropology to psychiatry.[25] Although I am told that he has recently engaged in collaborative research with E. Homburger Erikson, one may search in vain throughout the enormous bulk of his published ethnographic contributions for any application of psychiatric concepts. Of all his many and distinguished students, only Du Bois, Devereux, and Loeb have shown any psychiatric interests, and in each of these cases there is reason to believe that other influences were operative, and that those anthropologists moved toward psychiatry in spite of Kroeber rather than because of him. The question can fairly be put: Was Kroeber's relentless pursuit of "objective" and "historical" enquiries and his avoidance of research into the genesis and functioning of personalities (to which he would unquestionably have brought tremendous and unusual talents) based upon deep-seated, unconscious factors,[26] or was it primarily the submission to an occupational psychosis of his profession?

In the period between 1928 and 1939 the growing rapprochement between anthropology and psychiatry is reflected in the greatly increased number of personal documents and other materials on personality which anthropologists published.[27] This trend is paralleled by more frequent, though often grudging, allusions in theoretical statements. The papers by Lowie[28] and Wissler[29] in which the whole subject of anthropology's relation to psychology was treated without a single allusion to psychoanalysis could hardly have appeared after 1928. A more general awareness of psychoanalysis on the part of anthropologists in this country must be connected with the publications in England by Rivers and Malinowski of extended applications of psychoanalytic concepts to ethnological data.

The new directions seem to have been instigated (and later intensified through teaching and publication) primarily by three persons: Ruth Benedict, Margaret Mead, and Edward Sapir. Although these three tended always to rephrase psychiatric insights in cultural terms, and although others (such as Hallowell and the Oplers) have made more sustained and more direct applications of psychiatric concepts to their own empirical data, still the fundamental theoretical groundwork must be credited to Benedict, Mead and Sapir.

In 1928 Ruth Benedict, pupil and colleague of Boas, published "Psychological Types in the Cultures of the Southwest."[30] This was followed in 1932 by her "Configurations of Culture in North America."[31] In neither of these papers is there explicit reference to psychiatric sources. The stated acknowledgments are to the Gestalt psychologists and to philosophers of history, notably Dilthey. But every page is colored by an attitude which can only be described as "psychiatric," and which must be traced eventually from the influence of psychiatry. Mead has cogently summarized their essence: "In these first papers Dr. Benedict advanced the hypotheses that cultures and the use which they make of the traditional matter which was the stock of a widespread area could be interpreted as we interpret the choices of an individual personality.[32] In a later paper of Benedict's there is manifest attention to psychiatry, but mainly from the angle of anthropology's contribution to it[33] rather than the reverse. The following lines give perhaps the conceptual nucleus of this paper:

> The categories of borderline behavior which we derive from the study of the neuroses and psychoses of our civilization are categories of prevailing local types of instability. They give much information about the stresses and strains of Western civilization, but no final picture of inevitable human behavior. . . . When data are available in psychiatry, this minimum will be probably quite unlike our culturally conditioned, highly elaborated psychoses such as those that are described, for instance, under the terms of schizophrenia and manic-depressive.[34]

In Benedict's *Patterns of Culture*,[35] the approach is primarily cultural: a restatement and a testing, on the materials from three tribes, of her basic analogy "between the variations in human personality and the variations between cultures." There is, however, systematic treatment of the problems of the individual deviant. She again shows how the idiosyncratic component[36] of some personalities can find cultural expectations so ineluctably incongenial as to prevent these individuals from fitting acceptably into the patterns, and even drive them to mental illness. A later article[37] develops another variation upon this same theme of the connection between cultural patterns and individual personality development. It is argued that discontinuities in cultural conditioning, rather than "physiological necessity," are often responsible for maladjustments and personality upheavals. Once again, even though implicitly pointing the way to new types of anthropological research, Benedict is mainly concerned with indicating the relevance of anthropological materials to the psychiatrist:

> The anthropologist's role is not to question the facts of nature, but to insist upon the interposition of a middle term between "nature" and "human behavior"; his role is to analyze that term, to document

man-made doctorings of nature and to insist that these doctorings should not be read off in any one culture as nature itself. Although it is a fact of nature that the child becomes a man, the way in which this transition is effected varies from one society to another, and no one of these particular bridges should be regarded as the "natural path to maturity.[38]

The conceptions set forth in the lines just quoted from Benedict constitute a clear statement of the central thread which runs through at least the earlier writings of Margaret Mead. Mead was a pupil of Benedict (and of Boas). Her *Coming of Age in Samoa*[39] is a report on the first major piece of empirical research by an American anthropologist to be organized along psychiatric lines. Although she was avowedly testing the hypotheses on adolescence set forth by the psychologist G. Stanley Hall, still much of her approach is patently influenced by psychoanalysis. Boas refers to psychoanalysis in his introduction to the book, and Mead's own interest and knowledge are reflected in a paper published two years later.[40] Her subsequent researches, best known through the popular publications *Growing Up in New Guinea*[41] and *Sex and Temperament in Three Primitive Societies*,[42] similarly had orientations which converged with the psychiatric. During her first three field expeditions Mead's method was that of the crucial experiment. She focused her efforts upon obtaining evidence which might confirm or disprove some very general hypothesis. She has herself[43] indicated this succession of focal questions very clearly:

1925: How flexible is human nature? How much can we learn about its limits and its potentialities from studies of societies so very different from, so conveniently simpler than, our own?

1930: Is human nature elastic as well as flexible? Will it tend to return to the form that was impressed upon it in earliest years?

1935: In judging human nature may human societies make assumptions which their educational systems are unable to carry out?

The asking of these questions is patently contingent upon some cross-fertilization between anthropology and psychiatry. Not only was Mead's material organized in a fashion which appealed to psychiatrists, but she wrote in an idiom which they found intelligible. Besides the books which have been cited and a number of monographs addressed primarily to an anthropological audience, her work is embodied in an extensive series of papers—many of them on subjects of great psychiatric interest.[44] It is hardly surprising that Mead is possibly the best-known anthropologist in psychiatric circles. For many years her work has been discussed in the journals of the psychiatric profession, and these discussions have resulted in secondary stimulations to anthropology.[45]

In one of her more recent papers[46] Mead acknowledges more explicitly than she was earlier wont to do the psychiatric sources which had
influenced her. We learn that the work of Abraham, Spitz and Róheim
on "oral" and "anal" characters proved suggestive to her for her field
work and for theoretical analysis. Homburger Erikson's system of
dealing with zones in relation to character formation is likewise mentioned.[47] The concept of plot in culture, which seems to have formed
the focal point of Mead's most recent field work in Bali, is attributed to
Róheim.[48] The extent to which Mead's point of view remains incompatible with presuppositions which would doubtless be shared by most
psychiatrists is indicated by a recent controversy with Dr. Alexander.[49]

If Boas is always somehow in the background of the influence of
psychiatry upon anthropology, the third of the three persons most
influential in laying a fundamental theoretical groundwork for a rapprochement between the two sciences—Sapir—is forever in the foreground. Psychiatry, for Benedict, is merely ancillary to a number of
other extra-anthropological approaches; but psychiatry is central in Sapir's theoretical contribution. Mead is probably better known to psychiatrists because she has published more and provided a greater abundance of field data which appealed to them. Yet it was Sapir who made
possible some real fusion between the two disciplines. Benedict and
Mead were importantly influenced by psychiatry as to the topics they
chose to study, and they were able to show the utility to psychiatry
of the raw materials provided by anthropological field work. Only
Sapir, however, supplied the necessary corrections to anthropological
theory which were demanded by psychiatric knowledge. To him,
more than to any other single person, must be traced the growth of
psychiatric thinking in anthropology. His conceptual refinements made
possible something more than an interchange of facts and ideas. He
perceived a certain flatness, a certain unrealism, in the current conceptual scheme of American anthropology, when he checked this
scheme against what psychiatry had learned. The tough insights which
Sapir drew from psychiatry not only forced a basic reconstruction of
anthropological postulates but lead to new types of specifically pointed
field work. The subtle, tantalizing leads he threw out shaped the basic
conceptualizations not only of his immediate pupils and associates
(such as Opler, Mekeel, and Dollard) but of many other workers who
had no formal relationship to him (Linton, Hallowell, and many
others).[50] Sapir had no formal psychiatric training, so far as I am aware,
and was not himself analyzed. But he had intimate personal relationships with a number of psychiatrists, notably Dr. Harry Stack Sullivan.
Sapir's psychiatric outlook was discriminating, eclectic, generalized.
While deeply swayed by psychoanalysis, he was highly critical of psychoanalytic theory in many respects.[51] Himself exquisitely sensitive to

the nuances of personal behavior and a consummate master of the English language, he was able to translate psychiatric conceptions into terms which struck home to even the least imaginative ethnologists.

The preliminary formulation of the fusion which Sapir was able to make is best seen in his brilliant and much neglected "The Unconscious Patterning of Behavior in Society,"[52] although this essay contains no citations to psychiatric literature and indeed no overt references to psychiatry. The essentials of Sapir's contribution and the primary sources of that portion of his influence which did not spring from direct personal contact are to be found in two brief papers.[53] It is doubtful that so small a number of pages has ever had such momentous consequences for anthropology.

What, precisely, are the critical issues which anthropological theory had ignored or evaded and which Sapir compelled anthropologists to face? Digests or paraphrases of Sapir are always notably unsatisfactory. Perhaps a series of quotations, even though the intervening passages are not given, will be most nearly adequate:

> But all these [anthropological] approaches agree in thinking of the individual as a more or less passive carrier of tradition or, to speak more dynamically, as the infinitely variable actualizer of ideas and modes of behavior which are implicit in the structure and traditions of a given society. It is what all the individuals of a society have in common which is supposed to constitute the true subject matter of cultural anthropology and sociology. If the testimony of an individual is set down as such, as often happens in our anthropological monographs, it is not because of an interest in the individual himself as a matured and single organization of ideas but in his assumed typicality for the community as a whole. . . . He [the anthropologist] always hopes that the individual informant is near enough to the understandings and intentions of his society to report them duly, thereby implicitly eliminating himself as a factor in the method of research. . . . Our ethnological monographs present a kaleidoscopic picture of varying degrees of generality, often within the covers of a single volume.[54]

There is reason, then, to think that while cultural anthropology and psychiatry have distinct problems to begin with, they must, at some point, join hands in a highly significant way. That culture is a superorganic, impersonal whole is a useful enough methodological principle to begin with but becomes a serious deterrent in the long run to the more dynamic study of the genesis and development of cultural patterns because these cannot be realistically disconnected from those organizations of ideas and feelings which constitute the individual. . . . We are not, therefore, to begin with a simple contrast between social patterns and individual behavior, whether normal or abnormal, but we are, rather, to ask what is the meaning of culture in terms of individual behavior and whether the individual can, in a sense, be looked upon as the effective carrier of the culture of his group. As we follow tangible problems of behavior rather than the selected problems set by recognized disciplines, we discover the field of social psychology, which is not a whit more social than it is individual and which is, or should be, the mother science from which stem both the abstracted impersonal problems as phrased by the cultural anthropologist and the almost impertinently realistic explorations into behavior which are the province of the psychiatrist.[55]

The so-called culture of a group of human beings, as it is ordinarily treated by the cultural anthropologist, is essentially a systematic list of all the socially inherited patterns of behavior which may be illustrated in the actual behavior of all or most of the individuals of the group. The true locus, however, of these processes which, when abstracted into a totality, constitute culture is not in a theoretical community of human beings known as society, for the term "society" is itself a cultural construct which is employed by individuals who stand in significant relations to each other in order to help them in the interpretation of certain aspects of their behavior. The true locus of culture is in the interactions of specific individuals and, on the subjective side, in the world of meanings which each one of these individuals may unconsciously abstract for himself from his participation in these interactions. . . . Such differences of culture never seem as significant as they really are; partly because in the workaday world of experience they are not often given the opportunity to emerge into sharp consciousness, partly because the economy of interpersonal relations and the friendly ambiguities of language conspire to reinterpret for each individual all behavior which he has under observation in terms of those meanings which are relevant to his own life. The concept of culture, as it is handled by the cultural anthropologist, is necessarily something of a statistical fiction and it is easy to see that the social psychologist and the psychiatrist must eventually induce him to reconsider his terms.[56]

Culture, as it is ordinarily constructed by the anthropologist, is a more or less mechanical sum of the more striking or picturesque generalized patterns of behavior which he has either abstracted for himself out of the sum total of his observations or has had abstracted for him by his informants in verbal communication. Such a "culture," because generally constructed of unfamiliar terms, has an almost unavoidable picturesqueness about it, which suggests a vitality which it does not, as a matter of scrupulous psychological fact, embody. The cultures so carefully described in our ethnological and sociological monographs are not, and cannot be, the truly objective entities they claim to be. No matter how accurate their individual itemization, their integrations into suggested structures are uniformly fallacious and unreal. This cannot be helped so long as we confine ourselves to the procedures recognized as sound by orthodox ethnology. If we make the test of imputing the contents of an ethnological monograph to a known individual in the community which it describes we would inevitably be led to discover that, while every single statement in it may, in the favorable case, be recognized as holding true in some sense, the complex of patterns as described cannot, without considerable absurdity, be interpreted as a significant configuration of experience, both actual and potential, in the life of the person appealed to. Cultures, as ordinarily dealt with, are merely abstracted configurations of idea and action patterns, which have endlessly different meanings for the various individuals in the group, and which, if they are to build up into any kind of significant psychic structure, whether for the individual or the small group or the larger group, must be set in relation to each other in a complex configuration of evaluations, inclusive and exclusive implications, priorities, and potentialities of realization which cannot be discovered from an enquiry into the described patterns.[57]

... the tight, "objectified" culture loosens up at once and is eventually seen to be a convenient fiction of thought . . . Many problems which are now in the forefront of investigation sink into a secondary position and patterns of behavior which seem so obvious or universal as not to be worthy of the distinctive attention of the ethnologist leap into a new and unexpected importance. The ethnologist may some day have to face the uncomfortable predicament of inquiring into such humble facts as whether the father is in the habit of acting as indulgent guide or as disciplinarian to his son and regarding the problem of the child's membership inside or outside of his father's clan as a relatively subsidiary question. In short, the application of the personality point of view tends to minimize the bizarre or exotic in alien cultures and to reveal to us more and more clearly the broad human base on which all culture has developed. The profound commonplace that all culture starts from the needs of a common humanity is believed by all anthropologists, but it is not demonstrated by their writings.[58]

Two of Sapir's later papers[59] add little that is new conceptually and are remarkable chiefly for some unforgettably felicitous phrases, such as:

... the pages of Freud, with their haunting imagery of society as censor and of culture as a beautiful extortion from the sinister depths of desire. . . .[60]

In an atmosphere of mollified contrasts one may hope to escape the policemen of rival conceptual headquarters.[61]

One of these papers also contains a warning (presumably addressed to anthropologists tending to move in the Benedict-Mead direction):

It is these actual relationships that matter, not society. This simple and intuitively necessary viewpoint of the psychiatrist is shared, of course, by the man in the street. He cannot be dislodged from it by any amount of social scientific sophistication. It is to be hoped that no psychiatrist will ever surrender this naive and powerful view of the reality of personality to a system of secondary concepts about people and their relations to each other which flow from an analysis of social forms. . . . Certain recent attempts, in part brilliant and stimulating, to impose upon the actual psychologies of actual people, in continuous and tangible relations to each other, a generalized psychology based on the real or supposed psychological implications of cultural forms, show clearly what confusions in our thinking are likely to result when social science turns psychiatric without, in the process, allowing its own historically determined concepts to dissolve in those larger ones which have meaning for psychology and psychiatry.[62]

Another important figure, Géza Róheim, was trained as a psychoanalyst, but he has done anthropological field work of no little interest and importance and must be regarded as also, in some sense, an anthropologist. He has been a worker of prodigious industry and has published prolifically upon anthropological subjects. Róheim's position is a curious one. To many, perhaps to most, American anthropologists his writings are both violently irritating and simply opaque. A passage like the following, for example, is enough to make the hair of even mildly conservative anthropologists stand on end.

This is the origin of the world beyond the grave. The soul enters heaven as the sperm enters the ovum, and for the same reason. The idea of the loss of the semen or of death would not be bearable without this consolation. There are certain individuals in savage society in whom this castration complex is particularly strong and who manage to get rid of it by castrating others instead of being castrated themselves. These are the wizards, the ancestors of savage medicine-men. It is because coitus is a sort of self-castration that the savage needs a castrator, and projects the image of the castrator into space. The black magician is the man who consents to play the part.[63]

Discourse of this sort is both cryptic and repugnant to the modal anthropological reader. Nevertheless there is evidence that those few anthropologists who have closely studied Róheim, and especially his more recent writings, have gained a great deal. One passage in Mead's review of The Riddle of the Sphinx may stand out as a representative reaction of those anthropologists who really know Róheim:

Dr. Róheim presents an argument bewildering in its tangle of unresolved complexities, elisions, and condensations. After a short introduction posing the problem of the origin of culture, he presents a long description of Australian aboriginal ceremonialism which is practically unintelligible in the terms in which he describes it here. If his previous publications on Australia have been read with great care, and if the reader possesses a good working knowledge of

Freudian theory, and a detailed knowledge of the ethnology of Central Australian tribes drawn from other more formal sources, this section becomes relatively intelligible and also very stimulating.[64]

In the period between 1928 and 1939 the published record indicates that the work of at least seven other American anthropologists had received major influences from psychiatry: Ernest and Pearl Beaglehole,[65] Cora Du Bois, John Dollard, A. I. Hallowell, Scudder Mekeel, and M. E. Opler. Four of these can be dealt with very briefly. The papers of the Beagleholes of special interest to us which have thus far appeared are relatively slight but, like the contributions of Hallowell and Opler, they have the great merit of being direct applications to personally gathered empirical data.[66] Whether Dollard is an "anthropologist" or a "sociologist" is an academic question; certainly his influence on anthropologists has been very considerable. Mekeel's publications thus far[67] have been of an exclusively programmatic order.

Du Bois worked with psychiatrists at the Harvard Psychological Clinic. She published what anthropologists regard as an eminently sound critique of the use of ethnological data by psychoanalysts[68] and a most helpful digest of some of the aids which psychiatry (and psychology) can offer to the techniques of field work.[69] "Some Anthropological Perspectives on Psychoanalysis" is something more than a sane synthesis of the criticisms which anthropologists had made of the use of their data by psychoanalysts; it is equally a theoretical essay of unusual insight, posing new problems for anthropological research and rephrasing more sharply some which had been previously presented. For instance:

> Are we to assume that the psychological change preceded and induced the cultural change? Or is it necessary to assume the priority of one or the other? If we assume the priority of cultural change, then psychological interpretations of culture are purely descriptive and not explanatory. If we assume the priority of psychological changes, we are faced with the problem of accounting for their origin.[70]
>
> Are psychoses merely culturally defined and simply cultural judgments? In other words, how far are psychoses problems in psychic or social pathology? Or are psychoses everywhere constant but are certain types of psychotics culturally protected? For example, does Buddhism in prizing and rewarding the schizoid personality actually protect and conceal the real schizophrenic who unconsciously denies reality because his culture permits its conscious denial in ascetic practices?[71]
>
> Roheim has suggested that ritual is a group catharsis for traumata produced by the socialization of the child. For instance, does a heavily ritualized life, whether that of the Pueblo Indian, the Roman Catholic or the orthodox Jew, drain off anxieties by a multiplicity

of cultural behavior comparable to that devised in compulsion neuroses and thereby produce a sense of safety and security? ... How does ritual not only enact but also discharge social tensions, if at all? What light will demographic studies of populations crumbling under the impact of European colonization throw on such trends?[72]

At least in the period prior to 1939, M. E. Opler seems to me to have produced the most impressive empirical testing of psychiatric concepts on materials from nonliterate societies. He did not stop (as have too many anthropologists!) with a general discussion of the psychoanalytic treatment of culture;[73] he went on[74] to compare the Apache shamans' therapy of functional disorders with that of modern psychiatrists. His scrutiny of Freudian theories of ambivalence in terms of his Apache data[75] has convincing workmanship of detail and received at least partial validation from field materials obtained later.[76] However, for complete acceptance of his valuable thesis it would be necessary to show that those persons whose life experience and situation necessitated a maximal repression of aggressive reactions then feared the dead more than those whose need for repression was minimal. A methodological contribution[77] demonstrates the extent to which Opler has thought through the more general implications of psychiatry for anthropology.

In a massive sequence of papers that have appeared largely since 1938, A. I. Hallowell has tenaciously applied psychiatric knowledge to his own field materials.[78] His achievement is remarkable for its sanity and for the uncommonly high order of workmanship at both psychiatric and ethnological levels.

In addition to these anthropologists for whom psychiatry has supplied a major directive of research, there are a number of others whom psychiatry has touched at least casually. On the one hand, there are those who have been stimulated to write systematic descriptions of mental disorders among "primitive" peoples;[79] on the other, there are those who show psychiatric influence in at least a single publication.[80]

There has been a greatly intensified collaboration of anthropology and psychiatry during the last five years. In great part this heightened psychiatric influence is indicated by enlargement of the trends which have already been delineated. A much greater number of more substantial life-history documents have been produced. Names of psychiatrists and psychiatric terms appear much more frequently in the pages of anthropological periodicals. In theory, there is increased focusing upon the role of culture in the formation of personality.[81] Anthropological field work is more commonly directed to problems of psychiatric interest; the research of various anthropologists widens and deepens in psychiatric directions,[82] and new names appear in the list.[83]

Quantitatively, the publications of George Devereux[84] bulk larger than those of any other of the newcomers. The papers of Devereux are marked by great breadth of knowledge and by fertility of ideas; their effect in some cases is marred by apparent haste and carelessness of workmanship. In certain respects, however, Devereux is representative of developments which tend to demarcate the last five years from the earlier period under discussion. He did not learn his psychiatry merely by reading books and listening to lectures. He spent a year on the staff of the Worcester State Hospital.

An appreciable number of anthropologists have now emerged from the category of complete laymen in the field of psychiatry. They can speak with firsthand familiarity of, and to a degree use, psychiatric techniques; they are no longer restricted to "learning from" psychiatry and making crude analogical applications. Before 1939 there was, I believe, only one psychoanalyzed professional anthropologist in the United States. Today there are about a dozen. Some anthropologists have also learned to administer, and even to interpret, the Rorschach Tests.[85]

The point to be understood is that the influence of psychiatry has proceeded beyond the stage of general talk. A period of calling attention to the relevance of psychiatric knowledge was inevitable, a period of fumbling translations between the two idioms was necessary. But this preliminary groundwork seems to have been covered to a first approximation. Active collaboration is now supplanting polite gestures. There is coöperation in research—Aginsky and Wilbur, Chapple and Lindemann[86]—and particularly in field work—Erikson with Mekeel;[87] Levy with the Henrys, with Mirsky, and with Bunzel;[88] Kardiner with DuBois; Fries with Kluckhohn;[89] Alexander and Dorothea Leighton with Kluckhohn.[90] There are coöperative seminars in universities—Kardiner with Linton at Columbia, Murray with Kluckhohn at Harvard.[91]

The product of the Kardiner-Linton seminar is perhaps the most substantial evidence (in the generalized, theoretical field) of the fruitfulness of such coöperation.[92] It is important to notice that, even at the written level, this was not merely a matter of an anthropologist providing raw materials for a psychiatrist to analyze. In Kardiner's book Linton wrote a theoretical introduction as well as the two ethnographic chapters. Three other publications[93] attest to the extent of psychiatric influence upon Linton's thinking. The Kardiner-Linton volume is undoubtedly the outstanding integration of anthropology and psychiatry to date, but since it is a case of true synthesis rather than of "the influence of anthropology upon psychiatry," it will not be discussed at length here.[94]

The position of anthropology and psychiatry today, then, is roughly this: A conceptual *modus vivendi* has been established; data to test and refine this conceptual scheme are being gathered in a number of specific studies; the work of many anthropologists for whom the psychiatric type of interest is not at all central shows, nevertheless, an appreciable amount of psychiatric influence. It would be a great mistake, however, to conclude that psychiatric orientations are universally accepted at least to some degree. Lowie's *History of Ethnological Theory* (1937) gives exceedingly brief shrift to all psychiatrists; indeed a few paragraphs discussing the work of Rivers and Malinowski constitute the only systematic attention to this subject. Chapple and Coon[95] have published a general text in anthropology which does devote a number of pages to psychoses and to psychotics in society, but contains not a single mention of psychoanalysis nor of any one psychoanalyst.

The persistent resistance of anthropology is forcefully documented by two more general facts. First, by far the greater number of articles which reflect the psychiatric interests of anthropologists have been published in *non*-anthropological journals. Only within the last two or three years have there been any appreciable number of papers in the *American Anthropologist*, for example, which directly show psychiatric influence. Second, the reviews in the leading journal of a profession may be presumed to mirror major bents. The record in the *American Anthropologist* is astonishing. There are the two reviews by Kroeber which have been mentioned.[96] A psychiatrist reviewed one of Róheim's works and, as we have noted, Mekeel reviewed Kardiner.[97] That is all! The other contributions of Freud and Róheim, the books of Abraham, Reik, Rank, and many others which treat anthropological subjects unequivocally have never been noticed in the standard American journal of the anthropological profession. And, unfortunately, the conventions of field work still leave much to be desired. So far as many ethnologists are concerned, the observations of Devereux are still all too apropos:

> Linton's Tanala chapter invites, however, melancholy reflections on anthropological waste. It contains all the human material which Linton could not include in his great Tanala monograph. One wonders how much material of this type, invaluable to social psychologists, is at present floating around in the discarded notes and in the heads of other anthropologists, who never thought these data worthy of publication. It is hoped that Kardiner's book will help to rearrange the peculiar scale of values pervading anthropology, which induces anthropologists to devote ten pages to the making of pots, and ten lines to infancy.[98]

Finally, a word must be said about a propensity which has been frequently noticeable in the last few years. Sometimes the enthusiasm for psychological explanations is not associated with a firm grasp of the essentials of psychiatric methods. Fragmentary cultural data are linked without the requisite support in case materials.[99] Anthropologists, as well as psychiatrists, are tending to indulge in highly disjunctive arguments. The starting point for psychological interpretations must surely always rest in studies of specific individuals.

There is one question which requires further exploration: Why has the development between anthropology and psychiatry been so slow, why is the permeation of psychiatric ideas so incomplete even today? I have already suggested that there might be a basic factor of temperamental selection for the two professions. In addition, there is the discomfort which laymen from whatever group frequently feel about association with psychiatrists. The fact that the psychiatrists who have dealt with anthropological matters have mostly been psychoanalysts has tended to mobilize another host of resistances which are essentially irrational in their bases and manifestations, whatever degree of rationality may be mustered for each specific criticism. In many American universities there is a pronounced *nolite me tangere* attitude with regard to psychoanalysis. Psychoanalysts are too often felt to be intrinsically rather nasty people who wallow in sex and brood over the morbidities of human life. With some greater show of rationality, psychoanalysis is denied a place in the intellectual community because of its own excessive cultism. There are other familiar objections, but the simple fact is that some of the more timorous anthropological brethren have been deterred from collaboration because of their conviction that psychoanalysis wasn't really quite respectable and that they would be damaged as to professional advancement if they sullied themselves by contact with it.

Over and above such irrational resistances, however, there are certain respects in which psychiatrists themselves have needlessly diminished the scope of their influence. Granted that it is always unjustifiable to reject a method in its entirety (without further examination) because certain aspects of it can be shown to be incompatible with other technical evidence, or because the conclusions reached by it can be refuted on other grounds, still we must face the fact that this is a very general tendency in science. In the past, almost all psychiatrists forfeited the potential attention of a larger anthropological audience because they so flagrantly violated various canons of anthropological theory and method which were regarded by anthropologists as definitive. To greater or lesser degree, this remains true of a sizeable proportion of psychiatrists who utilize anthropologic data. For a variety of reasons, psychoanalysts as a group have tended to be most familiar with the works of the classical British evolutionary anthropologists, in particular with the great compendia of Frazer. These still serve too much as inexhaustible storehouses from which psychoanalysts pilfer illustrative ornaments for this or that theory. While a gratifying number of psychiatrists have made "culture" a solid part of their conceptual repertory, many have failed to make this notion part of their habitual thinking. Although

Freud himself was abundantly aware of the social dimensions of human living (the family situation and the like), it may be doubted whether he ever grasped the full import of "social heredity."

Although many good critiques have been published,[100] it may be useful to summarize the points on which all anthropological critics agree in substance. If psychiatrists would bear this simple list (as a minimum) in mind, they could avoid unnecessary shock to anthropological sensibilities and thus maximize the weight which psychiatrists have in anthropological quarters.

1. "Primitive" societies must not be lumped together. All anthropologists would deny such equivalence, except to the limited extent that these societies may share features in common as a result of their tendency to small size and relative simplicity in many (but not necessarily all) aspects of their cultural inventory, and as a consequence of their all being outside a written language tradition.[101]

2. Psychiatrists must cease to equate "primitive" with "childlike" or "archaic" or, in any unqualified sense, with "simple" (as opposed to "complex").[102]

3. The anecdotal approach is worthless. Ethnological data must be used with a fair regard for their context, both historical[103] and situational.

4. Cultures must be regarded as wholes, having organization as well as content. Data must not be too cavalierly torn from their configurational context (any more than from their historical or situational contexts).

5. The premises of theoretical arguments must be congruent with anthropological theorems (or cause must be shown for rejecting or disregarding the latter). That is, psychiatrists must not tacitly or uncritically accept a conceptual scheme (for example, that of "evolutionary" anthropology) which professional opinion unanimously regards as unacceptable (in the traditional sense, at least). This means further that for psychiatrists to use such hypotheses as that of the "racial unconscious," for which, anthropologists would argue, there never was evidence admissible in the court of science, is inevitably to wave a red flag at the anthropological bull.

6. At least before indulging in far-flung theories, psychiatrists must acquire a fuller control of the relevant anthropological literature than they have commonly shown in the past. There must be less uncritical use of data, as well as less snatching of data out of context.

If psychiatrists will respect these six points and their implications, anthropologists will reciprocate with an enthusiasm for psychiatry less sharply restricted to a small though growing intellectual clique within the anthropological profession.

Let us now, in conclusion, summarize the gains which this clique may claim to have attained from their study of psychiatry.

1. In the techniques of field research, a completely new conception of the number and character of informants needed has come as much from psychiatry (especially through Sapir)[104] as from sampling theory in statistics. Many anthropologists now feel an obligation to provide their readers with much more information and controls on this subject.[105]

The need for more systematic attention to interpersonal relations between ethnographer, informants, and interpreters has gained some recognition.[106] While anthropologists are still notably inarticulate (at least in print) about their interview methods and their relationships with the "natives" generally, still evidence is not lacking that the more sophisticated have at any rate begun seriously to consider such matters—which were formerly handled by very crude rules of thumb. Anthropologists have learned much from psychiatry about the technique of the interview, including how to get anxiety-protected material. Although the precise parallels to the transference situation have yet to receive an extended published discussion, there are hints that thought is proceeding along these lines.[107]

Under the impact of psychiatry, anthropology has come to recognize the incompleteness of the question and answer method. The need for passive interviews, for controlled observations, even for simple experiments, for personal documents, dreams, phantasies of individuals, and other informal materials is now seen by a large number of field workers.

The content of field research—that is, the topics upon which the investigator must report if he is to be considered professionally respectable—has been much enlarged and sharply revised.[108] Though there is still great room for improvement in this direction, even those changes which are generally accepted are considerable.

In general, greater attention should be paid to intensive as opposed to extensive procedures.[109]

2. In theoretical anthropology new topics have been added. Psychiatry is primarily responsible for the granting of full recognition to interpretative studies of such subjects as the following: "the individual in culture"; "culture and personality"; child socialization; transmission of culture through child-training; the "abnormal" or "deviant" person; life histories; culture and motivation; the origin of culture (in a new sense); a new attack on configurational analysis ("To what degree can we understand the plot or theme of a culture by reference to the recurrent traumatic situations to which the child is subjected in the family situations?");[110] a different approach to "the instinct problem";[111] psychosomatic problems: the relationship of disease pictures to culturally determined forms of character structure.[112]

And there are new conceptual tools. There is wide variation in the extent to which even psychiatrically oriented anthropologists accept and utilize psychiatric concepts. But it may be said that, save among the die-hard conservatives, such notions as "ambivalence," "identification," and "latent content" are now part of the standard conceptual currency.

Concepts derived from psychiatry have proved of peculiar value in the theoretical interpretations which anthropologists must make of such phenomena as family behavior,[113] religion,[114] clowns and formalized joking,[115] suicide,[116] narcotics and alcoholism.[117]

In conclusion, it may be noted that anthropologists have altered many of their postulates. The whole thinking about the individual informant as a cultural specimen has been sharply refashioned.[118] The false antimony of "the individual vs. society" is gradually being abandoned. Assumptions as to the relative proportions of irrational, nonrational, and rational elements in human behavior have been revised; although this last trend was independently forced upon anthropology by its own materials, the trend was given increased momentum by pressure from psychiatry.

NOTES

1. Gordon W. Allport, *The Use of Personal Documents in Psychological Science* (Social Science Research Council, Bull. 49, New York, 1942), p. 47.

2. O. H. Mowrer and C. Kluckhohn, "Dynamic Theory of Personality," in *Personality and the Behavior Disorders* (ed. J. Hunt, New York, The Ronald Press, 1944), pp. 69-75.

3. Margaret Mead, "The Use of Primitive Material in the Study of Personality," *Character and Personality*, III (1934), 11.

4. Paul Radin, "History of Ethnological Theories," *Am. Anthropol.*, XXXI (1929), 26-30.

5. William Morgan: "Navajo Diagnosticians," *Am. Anthropol.* XXXIII (1931), 390-402; "Navajo Dreams," *ibid.*, XXXIV (1932), 390-405; *Human-wolves among the Navaho* (Yale Univ. Publications in Anthropology, No. 11, 1936), pp. 3-43.

6. Cf. J. S. Lincoln, *The Dream in Primitive Cultures* (London, The Cresset Press, 1935), p. 12; Alexander Goldenweiser, "Some Contributions of Psychoanalysis to the Interpretation of Social Facts," in *Contemporary Social Theory* (ed. H. Barnes and F. B. Becker, New York, D. Appleton Century, 1940), p. 402.

7. Radin, *op. cit.*, p. 26; Edward Sapir, "Personality," in *Encyclopedia of the Social Sciences*, XII (1934), 86; Goldenweiser, *op. cit.*, pp. 401-402.

8. Daniel G. Brinton, *The Basis of Social Relations* (New York and London, G. P. Putnam's Sons, 1902), p. 118.

9. For example, A. L. Kroeber, "The Arapaho," *Bull. Am. Mus. Nat. Hist.*, VIII (1902), p. 20.

10. E. Kraepelin, "Vergleichende Psychiatrie," *Centralblatt für Nervenheilkunde und Psychiatrie*, XXVII (1904), 433-438.

11. "Publokto or Hysteria among Peary's Eskimos," *J. Mental and Nerv. Dis.*, XL (1913), 514-526.

12. "Psychoneurosis among Primitive Tribes," *J. Abnormal Psychol.*, X (1915-16), 201-208.

13. Sanger Brown, "The Sex Worship and Symbolism of Primitive Races," *J. Abnormal Psychol.*, X (1915-16), 297-314, 418-432.

14. E. C. Parsons, "Ceremonial Consummation," *Psychoanalytic Rev.*, II (1915), 358-359.

15. Goldenweiser, *History, Psychology, and Culture* (New York, Knopf, 1933), p. 67.

16. Review of Jung's *Collected Papers in Analytical Psychology* and *The Psychology of the Unconscious*, in *Am. Anthropol.*, XX (1918), 323-324.

17. New York, Boni & Liveright, 1920, pp. 91-94.

18. *Am. Anthropol.*, XXII (1920), 321.

19. A. L. Kroeber, "*Totem and Taboo:* an Ethnologic Psychoanalysis," *Am. Anthropol.*, XXII (1920), 48-55.

20. Edward Sapir, "The Emergence of the Concept of Personality in a Study of Cultures," *J. Soc. Psychol.*, V (1934), 408-415.

21. New York, Knopf, 1922.

22. Cf. Ruth F. Benedict, "Franz Boas as an Ethnologist," *Franz Boas, 1858-1942* (Memoir 61 of the Am. Anthropol. Assn., 1943), pp. 27-38.

23. *Am. Anthropol.*, XXII (1920), 380.

24. *Am. Anthropol.*, XX (1918), 323-324.

25. "Cultural Anthropology," Chap. XIX in *The Problem of Mental Disorder* (ed. Bentley, New York, McGraw Hill, 1934); "Psychosis or Social Sanction," *Character and Personality*, VIII (1940), 204-215.

26. Cf. Goldenweiser, "Recent Trends in American Anthropology," *Am. Anthropol.*, XLIII (1941), 151-163.

27. For a fairly complete bibliography see John Gillin, "Personality in Preliterate Societies," *Am. Soc. Rev.*, V (1940), 371-380.

28. "Psychology and Sociology," *Am. J. Soc.*, XXI (1915), 217-230.

29. "Opportunities for Coordination in Anthropological and Psychological Research," *Am. Anthropol.*, XXII (1920), 1-12.

30. Intnl. Congress of Americanists, *Proceedings*, XXIII (1928), 572-581.

31. *Am. Anthropol.*, XXXIV (1932), 1-27.

32. Mead, *op. cit.*, *Character and Personality*, III (1934), 9.

33. For a psychiatric reply, see H. J. Wegrocki, *J. Abnormal and Soc. Psychol.*, XXXIV (1939), 166-178, and for a further development, see Schilder, *J. Soc. Psychol.*, XV (1942), 3-21.

34. Benedict, "Anthropology and the Abnormal," *J. Gen. Psychol.*, X (1934), 79.

35. Boston and New York, Houghton Mifflin, 1934.

36. C. Kluckhohn and O. H. Mowrer, "Culture and Personality," *Am. Anthropol.*, XLVI (Jan., 1944).

37. "Continuities and Discontinuities in Cultural Conditioning," *Psychiatry*, I (1938), 161-167.

38. *Ibid.*, p. 161.

39. New York, William Morrow, 1928.

40. "An Ethnologist's Footnote to 'Totem and Taboo,'" *Psychoanalytic Rev.*, XVII (1930), 297-304.

41. New York, William Morrow, 1930.

42. New York, William Morrow, 1935.

43. *From the South Seas* (New York, William Morrow, 1939), pp. ix-xxxi.

44. For a list of her earlier papers which are psychiatrically oriented, see Mead, *op. cit.*, *Character and Personality*, III (1934), 10, note 11; for more recent ones, see the Mead bibliography in Bateson and Mead, *Balinese Character* (New York Academy of Sciences, Special Publications Vol. II, 1942).

45. See, for example, R. A. Spitz, "Frühkindliches Erleben und Erwachsenen Kultur bei den Primitiven," *Imago*, XXI (1935), 367-387.

46. "The Mountain Arapesh. II. Supernaturalism," *Anthrop. Papers of the Am. Mus. Nat. Hist.*, XXXVII (1940), 330-331.

47. Cf. also Mead, "Educative Effects of Social Environment as Disclosed by Studies of Primitive Societies," *Environment and Education*, Supplementary Monographs, No. 54 (Chicago, Univ. of Chicago Press, 1942).

48. Mead, "Researches in Bali," N. Y. Acad. Sci., *Transactions*, Ser. 2, II, 1-8.

49. Mead, "Educative Effects of Social Environment as Disclosed by Studies of Primitive Societies," *Environment and Education*, pp. 48-61; Franz Alexander, "Educative Influence of Personality Factors in the Environment," *ibid.*, pp. 29-47.

50. How much of the parallelism in the writings of Benedict, Mead, and Sapir is pure convergence and how much represents the influence of Sapir upon Benedict and Mead is a difficult question. I agree with Goldenweiser ("Leading Contributions of Anthropology to Social Theory," in *Contemporary Social Theory*, p. 489) that a careful reading of *Patterns of Culture* "can leave no doubt that on several occasions Benedict found inspiration in the writings of the late Edward Sapir."

51. "Cultural Anthropology and Psychiatry," *J. Abnormal and Soc. Psychol.*, XXVII (1932), 234-235.

52. In *The Unconscious: a Symposium* (New York, Knopf, 1929), pp. 114-142. A still earlier paper, "Culture, Genuine and Spurious," *Am. J. Soc.*, XXIX (1924), 401-430, should probably also be cited in this connection.

53. "Cultural Anthropology and Psychiatry," and "The Emergence of the Concept of Personality in a Study of Cultures," *J. Soc. Psychol.*, V (1934), 408-415.

54. "Cultural Anthropology and Psychiatry," pp. 229-230.

55. *Ibid.*, p. 233.

56. *Ibid.*, pp. 235-237.

57. "The Emergence of the Concept of Personality in a Study of Cultures," *J. Soc. Psychol.*, XXIX (1934), 408-415.

58. *Ibid.*, p. 413.

59. "The Contribution of Psychiatry to an Understanding of Behavior in Society," *Am. J. Soc.*, XXIX (1937), 862-871; "Anthropology and the Psychiatrist," *Psychiatry*, I (1938), 7-13.

60. "The Contribution of Psychiatry to an Understanding of Behavior in Society," pp. 862-863.

61. *Ibid.*, p. 863.

62. *Ibid.*, p. 867.

63. *Animism, Magic, and the Divine King* (London, Kegan Paul, Trench, Trubner & Co., 1930), p. 381.
A very partial list of Róheim's anthropological writings includes: "Ethnology and Folk-Psychology," *Int. J. Psycho-analysis*, III (1922), 189-222; *Australian Totemism* (London, Allen and Unwin, 1925); "Psychoanalysis of Primitive Cultural Types," *Int. J. Psycho-analysis*, XIII (1932), 6-22; "Women and Their Life in Central America," *J. Royal Anthropol. Inst.*, LXIII (1933), 207-265; *The Riddle of the Sphinx* (London, Hogarth, 1934); "The Study of Character Development and the Ontogenetic Theory of Culture," in *Essays Presented to C. G. Seligman* (ed. Evans-Pritchard *et al.*, London, Kegan Paul, 1934); "The Nescience of the Aranda," *Brit. J. Med. Psychology*, VII (1938), 343-360; "Racial Differences in the Neurosis and Psychosis," *Psychiatry*, II (1939), 375-390; "Dreams of a Somali Prostitute," *J. Criminal Psychopathol.*, II (1940), 162-170; "Society and the Individual," *Psychoanalytic Q.*, IX (1940), 526-545; "Myth and Folk-Tale," *Am. Imago*, II (1941), 266-279; "Play Analysis with Normanby Island Children," *Am. J. Orthopsychiatry*, XI (1941), 524-529; "The Psycho-analytic Interpretation of

Culture," *Int. J. Psycho-analysis*, XXII (1941), 1-23; "The Origin and Function of Culture," *Psychoanalytic Rev.*, XXIX (1942), 131-164.

64. *Character and Personality*, IV (1935), 85.

65. In this and other cases I have interpreted "American anthropologist" rather liberally. This is a typical example. The Beagleholes are not American by nationality, but they studied in this country, published in American media, and were in sustained face-to-face contact with large numbers of American anthropologists.

66. See Ernest and Pearl Beaglehole, "Personality Development in Pukapukan Children," in *Language, Culture and Personality* (ed. Spier, Hallowell, and Newman, Menasha, Wis., Sapir Memorial Publication Fund, 1941); Ernest Beaglehole, "Emotional Release in a Polynesian Community," *J. Abnormal and Soc. Psychol.*, XXXII (1937), 319-328; Ernest Beaglehole, "A Note on Cultural Compensation," *J. Abnormal and Soc. Psychol.*, XXXIII (1938), 121-123.

67. H. Scudder Mekeel, "Clinic and Culture," *J. Abnormal and Soc. Psychol.*, XXX (1935), 292-300; "A Psychoanalytic Approach to Culture," *J. Soc. Philos.*, II (1937), 232-236; Review of Kardiner, *The Individual and His Society*, in *Am. Anthropol.*, XLII (1940), 526-530; "Education, Child-training, and Culture," *Am. J. Soc.*, XLVIII (1943), 676-681.

68. "Some Anthropological Perspectives on Psychoanalysis," *Psychoanalytic Rev.*, XXIV (1937), 246-263.

69. "Some Psychological Objectives and Techniques in Ethnography," *J. Soc. Psychol.*, VIII (1937), 285-301.

70. *Op. cit.*, p. 250.

71. *Ibid.*, p. 261.

72. *Ibid.*, pp. 261-262.

73. "The Psychoanalytic Treatment of Culture," *Psychoanalytic Rev.*, XXII (1935), 138-157.

74. "Some Points of Comparison and Contrast between the Treatment of Functional Disorders by Apache Shamans and Modern Psychiatric Practice," *Am. J. Psychiatry*, XCII (1936), 1371-1387.

75. "An Interpretation of Ambivalence of Two American Indian Tribes," *J. Soc. Psychol.*, VII (1936), 82-116.

76. "Further Comparative Anthropological Data Bearing on the Solution of a Psychological Problem," *J. Soc. Psychol.*, IX (1938), 477-483.

77. "Personality and Culture," *Psychiatry*, I (1938), 217-220.

78. "Culture and Mental Disorder," *J. Abnormal and Soc. Psychol.*, XXIX (1934), 1-9; "Psychic Stresses and Cultural Patterns," *Am. J. Psychiatry*, XCIII (1936), 1291-1310; "Fear and Anxiety as Cultural and Individual Variables in a Primitive Society," *J. Abnormal and Soc. Psychol.*, XXXIII (1938), 25-47; "Shabwan," *Am. J. Orthopsychiatry*, VIII (1938), 329-340; "Sin, Sex and Sickness in Saulteaux Belief," *Brit. J. Med. Psychol.*, VIII (1939), 191-197; "Aggression in Saulteaux Society," *Psychiatry*, III (1940), 395-407; "The Rorschach Method as an Aid in the Study of Personalities in Primitive Societies," *Character and Personality*, IX (1941), 235-245.

79. J. E. Saindon, "Mental Disorders among the James Bay Cree," *Primitive Man*, VI (1933), 1-12; D. Jenness, " An Indian Method of Teaching Hysteria," *ibid.*, pp. 13-20; J. M. Cooper, "The Cree Witiko Psychosis," *ibid.*, pp. 20-24, and "Mental Disease Situation in Certain Cultures," *J. Abnormal and Soc. Psychol.*, XXIX (1934), 10-17; N. S. Demerath, "Schizophrenia among Primitives," *Am. J. Psychiatry*, XCVIII (1942), 703-708.

80. J. H. Barnett, "Personality in Primitive Society," *Character and Personality*, II (1933), 152-167; Jules Henry, "The Personality of the Kaingang Indians," *ibid.*, V (1936), 113-123; M. J. Herskovits, "Freudian Mechanisms in Primitive Negro Psychology," in *Essays Presented to C. G. Seligman* (London, Kegan Paul, 1934),

pp. 75-84; R. Landis, "The Personality of the Ojibwa," *Character and Personality*, VI (1937), 51-60, and "The Abnormal among the Ojibwa," *J. Abnormal and Soc. Psychol.*, XXXIII (1938), 14-33; Gertrude Toffelmier and Katherine Luomala, "Dreams and Dream Interpretation of the Diegueño Indians of Southern California," *Psychoanalytic Q.*, V (1936), 195-225; W. L. Warner, "The Society, the Individual, and His Mental Disorders," *Am. J. Psychiatry*, XCIV (1937), 275-284.

81. Ralph Linton, "Psychology and Anthropology," *J. Soc. Philos.*, V (1940), 115-127; C. Kluckhohn and O. H. Mowrer, "Culture and Personality," *Am. Anthropol.*, XLVI (Jan., 1944).

82. Jules and Zunia Henry, "Speech Disturbances in Pilaga Indian Children," *Am. J. Orthopsychiatry*, X (1940), 362-369; Jules Henry, "Some Cultural Determinants of Hostility in Pilaga Indian Children," *ibid.*, 111-119.

83. M. F. Ashley-Montagu, "Nescience, Science, and Psycho-analysis," *Psychiatry*, IV (1941), 45-60; Ann Barnard, "Patterns of Masculine Protest among the Buka," *Character and Personality*, XI (1943), 152-167; Gregory Bateson, "Some Systematic Approaches to the Study of Culture and Personality," *Character and Personality*, XI (1942), 76-82, and "Cultural Determinants of Personality," *Personality and the Behavior Disorders* (ed. J. Hunt, New York, Ronald Press, 1944), 714-736; Dorothy Eggan, "The General Problem of Hopi Adjustment," *Am. Anthropol.*, XLV (1943), 357-373; John Gillin, "Personality in Preliterate Societies," *Am. Soc. Rev.*, IV (1939), 681-702; Gillin and Victor Raimy, "Acculturation and Personality," *ibid.*, V (1940), 371-380; E. S. Goldfrank, "Historic Change and Social Character," *Am. Anthropol.*, XLV (1943), 67-83; C. Kluckhohn, "Theoretical Bases for an Empirical Method of Studying the Acquisition of Culture by Individuals," *Man*, XXXIX (1939), 98-103, "Myths and Rituals: a General Theory," *Harvard Theological Rev.*, XXXV (1942), 45-79, and "Navaho Witchcraft," *Papers of the Peabody Mus. of Am. Archaeol. and Ethnol.*, Vol. XXII, No. 3 (1943); Weston LaBarre, "A Cultist Drug-addiction in an Indian Alcoholic," *Menninger Clinic Bull.*, V (1941), 40-46; E. M. Loeb and G. Toffelmier, "Kin Marriage and Exogamy," *J. Gen. Psychol.*, XX (1939), 181-223; D. McAllester, "Water as a Disciplinary Agent among the Crow and Blackfoot," *Am. Anthropol.* n.s. XLIII (1941), No. 4, Pt. 1, 593-604; M. K. Opler, "Psychoanalytic Techniques in Social Analysis," *J. Soc. Psychol.*, XV (1942), 91-127; J. W. M. Whiting, *Becoming a Kwoma* (New Haven, Yale Univ. Press, 1941).

84. "Maladjustment and Social Neurosis," *Am. Soc. Rev.*, IV (1939), 844-851; "Mohave Culture and Personality," *Character and Personality*, VIII (1939), 91-109; "The Social and Cultural Implications of Incest among the Mohave Indians," *Psychoanalytic Q.*, VIII (1939), 510-533; "A Sociological Theory of Schizophrenia," *Psychoanalytic Rev.*, XXVI (1939), 315-342; "A Conceptual Scheme of Society," *Am. J. Soc.*, XLV (1940), 687-706; Review of *The Individual and His Society* (Kardiner), *Character and Personality*, VIII (1940), 253-256; "Social Negativism and Criminal Psychopathology," *J. Criminal Psychopathol.*, I (1940), 323-338; "The Mental Hygiene of the American Indian," *Mental Hygiene*, XXVI (1942), 71-84; "Motivation and Control of Crime," *J. Criminal Psychopathol.*, III (1942), 553-584; "Primitive Psychiatry, II: Funeral Suicide and the Mohave Social Structure," *Bulletin of the Hist. of Med.*, XI (1942), 522-542; "Social Structure and Economy of Affective Bonds," *Psychoanalytic Rev.*, XXIX (1942), 303-314. Devereux, and E. M. Loeb, "Antagonistic Acculturation," *Am. Soc. Rev.*, VIII (1943), 133-147; "Some Notes on Apache Criminality." *J. Criminal Psychopathol.*, IV (1943), 424-430; see also, Karl Menninger, "An Anthropological Note on the Theory of Pre-natal Instinctual Conflict," *Inter. J. Psycho-analysis*, XX (1939).

85. Hallowell, "The Rorschach Method as an Aid in the Study of Personalities in Primitive Societies," *Character and Personality*, IX (1941), 235-245; Hallowell, "Acculturation Processes and Personality Changes as Indicated by the Rorschach Technique," *Rorschach Research Exchange*, VI (1942), 42-50; Henry, "Rorschach Technique in Primitive Cultures," *Am. J. Orthopsychiatry*, XI (1941), 230-234;

A. H. Schachtel and Jules and Zunia Henry, "Rorschach Analysis of Pilaga Indian Children," *ibid.*, XII (1942), 679-712.

86. B. W. Aginsky, "The Socio-psychological Significance of Death among the Pomo Indians," *Am. Imago*, I (1940), 1-11, and G. B. Wilbur, Comments (on the foregoing), *ibid.*, 12-18; E. D. Chapple and E. Lindemann, "Clinical Implications of Measurements of Interaction Rates in Psychiatric Interviews," *Applied Anthropol.*, I (1942), 1-10.

87. E. H. Erikson, "Some Observations on Sioux Education," *J. Psychol.*, VII (1937), 101-156.

88. David M. Levy, "Sibling Rivalry Studies in Children of Primitive Groups," *Am. J. Orthopsychiatry*, IX (1939), 205-215.

89. Margaret E. Fries, "National and International Difficulties," *ibid.*, XI (1941), 562-573.

90. (It is worth pointing out that the Drs. Leighton are not psychoanalysts.) A. and D. Leighton, "Elements of Psychotherapy in Navaho Religion," *Psychiatry*, IV (1941), 515-523, and "Some Types of Uneasiness and Fear in a Navaho Indian Community," *Am. Anthropol.*, XLIV (1942), 194-209.

91. The Sapir-Dollard seminar on the Impact of Culture on Personality (held at Yale University, 1932-33) was at least a partial precursor.

92. Kardiner, *The Individual and His Society* (New York, Columbia Univ. Press, 1939).

93. Linton, "Culture, Society, and the Individual," *J. Abnormal and Soc. Psychol.*, XXXIII (1938), 425-436; "The Effects of Culture on Mental and Emotional Processes," Assn. for Research in Nerv. and Mental Dis., *Research Publications*, XIX (1939), 293-304; "Psychology and Anthropology," *J. Soc. Philos.*, V (1940), 115-127.

94. For sympathetic but discriminating reviews of this work by anthropologists, see Devereux, *Character and Personality*, VIII (1940), 253-256, and Mekeel, *Am. Anthropol.*, XLII (1940), 526-530.

95. *Principles of Anthropology* (New York, Henry Holt, 1942).

96. See notes 23 and 24.

97. William Morgan, Review of Róheim's *Psychoanalysis of Primitive Cultural Types*, in *Am. Anthropol.*, XXXIV (1932), pp. 705-710; for Mekeel's review, see note 94.

98. *Character and Personality*, VIII (1940), 254.

99. Jane Richardson and L. M. Hanks, Jr., "Water Discipline and Water Imagery among the Blackfoot," *Am. Anthropol.*, XLIV (1942), 331-333.

100. Du Bois, *Psychoanalytic Rev.*, XXIV (1937), 246-263; Hallowell, "The Child, the Savage, and Human Experience" (in "Progress of Scientific Research in the Field of the Exceptional Child") *Proceedings* of the Sixth Institute on the Exceptional Child, of the Child Research Clinic of the Woods School, 1939, pp. 8-34; Kroeber, Reviews of *Totem and Taboo*, *Am. Anthropol.*, XXII (1920), 48-55, and *Am. J. Soc.*, XLV (1939), 446-451; Mead, *Character and Personality*, III (1934), 3-16; Opler, "The Psychoanalytic Treatment of Culture," *Psychoanalytic Rev.*, XXII (1935), 138-157.

101. Cf. Mead, *op. cit.*: "The significance of primitive societies for the study of personality lies not in the similarities between them but in their differences."

102. There might be a gain to clarity in communication, if the multivalued word "primitive" were at least temporarily stricken from our professional vocabularies. "Nonliterate" is unequivocal and objective. "Preliterate" must be strictly avoided as question-begging, specifically as implying acceptance of the evolutionary schema.

103. Cf. Mead, *op. cit.*, p. 13: "Each culture must be studied against the back-

ground of the general area to which it belongs"; that is, diffusion must not be ignored.

104. See notes 52-59.

105. Kluckhohn, "Theoretical Bases for an Empirical Method of Studying the Acquisition of Culture by Individuals," *Man* XXXIX (1939), 98-103.

106. Du Bois, "Some Psychological Objectives and Techniques in Ethnography," *J. Soc. Psychol.*, VIII (1937), 246-263.

107. An obvious limitation upon the full use of psychiatric techniques in interviews is the lamentable fact that only a trifling number of anthropological field workers have an adequate command of the native idiom.

108. Mead, "More Comprehensive Field Methods," *Am. Anthropol.*, XXXV (1933), 1-15.

109. H. D. Lasswell, *World Politics and Personal Insecurity* (New York, McGraw Hill, 1935), pp. 210-211.

110. Mead, "Review of 'The Riddle of the Sphinx' by G. Róheim," *Character and Personality*, IV (1935), 86.

111. Mead, "Anthropological Data on the Problem of Instinct," *Psychosomatic Med.*, IV (1942), 396, 397.

112. Mead, "Character Formation in Two South Seas Societies," Am. Neurol. Assn. *Transactions*, 66th Annual Meeting, June, 1940, pp. 99-103. Gregory Bateson and Margaret Mead, *Balinese Character*.

113. Kardiner, *op. cit.*

114. Kluckhohn, "Myths and Rituals," *Harvard Theol. Rev.*, XXXV (1942), 45-79.

115. J. J. Honigman, "An Interpretation of the Social-psychological Functions of the Ritual Clown," *Character and Personality*, X, (1942), 220-226.

116. B. W. Aginsky, "The Socio-psychological Significance of Death among the Pomo Indians," *Am. Imago*, I (1940), 1-11.

117. Kluckhohn, *Navaho Witchcraft*.

118. Sapir, "Cultural Anthropology and Psychiatry," *J. Abnormal and Soc. Psychol.*, XXVII (1932), 229-242; "The Emergence of the Concept of Personality in a Study of Cultures," *J. Soc. Psychol.*, V (1934), 408-415; "Personality," in *Encyclopaedia of the Social Sciences*, XII, 85-87.

A NAVAHO PERSONAL DOCUMENT WITH A BRIEF PARETIAN ANALYSIS

CLYDE KLUCKHOHN

One of the accusations most frequently leveled at anthropological investigations and reports by others working in the field of general sociology is that statements made are too seldom reducible to their specific behavioral references.[1] In particular, anthropologists have often seemed to work and talk as if there were no such thing as the concrete individual. They have tended to hypostatize an interesting and important but abstract "culture."

For example, it has been said that the anthropologists who have described the Hopi Indian Snake Dance gave the reader the right to assume (if the problem occurs to them at all) that all of the Indians participating in this ritual share essentially identical emotions. Or, in our terminology here, they make the tacit assumption that the derivations which would be made by various Hopis about the ceremony would not show differences of any interest or importance. Although, as a matter of fact, it is a crude induction from my experience with the Hopi that the uniformities of the derivations[2] would actually be more striking than the individual variations, it is equally true that anyone who has had any first-hand experience with the Hopi could predict with full confidence that the derivations observed would show some interesting differences. In short, anthropologists have tended to neglect certain aspects of the problem of the heterogeneity of persons in the social system. In many monographs in the past statements were couched almost entirely in the general mode—"the Navaho do so and so" rather than "I saw Navaho A, Navaho B, Navaho C, etc., do so and so" or "Navahos X, Y, Z independently told me that they had seen Navaho A do so and so" or even "I have spent eight months among the Navaho of such and such a region and under circumstances f, g, h I have never failed to see a Navaho behave as follows." The reader of ethnological monographs has too often had to guess whether a given statement was based on six months or six years of observation, on observation of one incident or a hundred, on the say-so of two informants or twenty.

Similarly, except in the most platitudinous and general way we know almost nothing about how particular culture elements are transmitted from individual to individual within a given society or how they spread from one society to another. In our conceptual scheme here: precisely how are characteristic residues and derivations passed on in a given society? This is another set of problems from the ones which are the center of our interest here, but parenthetically I should like to suggest that if we are to "ask the right questions" about residues and derivations as such it would be helpful to have more precise knowledge of the mechanisms of their social heredity. When it comes down to cases and to details, our ignorance as to how social and cultural conditioning is carried on is abysmal. "Diffusion" is one of the bywords of cultural anthropologists and a great many more or less plausible theories as to the mechanisms of the process have been formulated. But they have been documented, in the main, only by the striking example or, at best, by the method of highly imperfect induction. In short, anthropologists have seldom given us descriptions of any features of behavior (including what people say) except those which they have recognized as pretty well formalized.

The case which I am going to present is that of the life story of an old Navaho Indian precisely as I got it in 1936 from the interpreter who was translating his words. It is not an ambitious and extended "life history" in the technical sense.[3] But my seeking this kind of material arose, so far as I am conscious of my motivations, out of considerations of the kind I have just presented to you. I believe that the document does give certain valuable hints as to the way in which social conditioning is carried on among the Navaho and at the same time provides some nice data on the values institutionalized and approved in this society. These, I think, are important problems. I have no thought of making this case the basis for pretentious and sweeping conclusions—even for this one society it is most clearly inadequate. It is, however, an authentic sample of concrete material bearing on such issues. It may also have some claim on your attention as coming out of a cultural setting which is not a part of the Western European tradition.

Indeed one of the central problems of general sociology could perhaps be posed as follows: which uniformities in the interactions between persons are essentially universal (even though their specific forms may be culturally patterned) and which tend to appear only in certain cultures or types of cultures? Some uniformities do appear to present themselves wherever human beings interact and most of the residues and derivations which Pareto has classified seem indeed to fall into this class, though, as he and others have pointed out, the relative prominence of different residues and derivations varies from society to society—which is one of the merits of the Paretian scheme. It is a fact of experience that the individuals in different social systems often react to the same stimulus in characteristically different ways. But perhaps if this case has no other interest it will at least provide one bit of evidence that residues and derivations are not phenomena manifested solely by speakers of Indo-European languages.

Before turning directly to the story, you will also want to know the sociological context in which this material was gathered. The interactions of three persons: the narrator, the interpreter, and myself are involved, and so there must be a few words about each and their relations.

The narrator we shall call Mr. Moustache (7),[4] the literal translation of the name by which the Navaho in this region most often call him. The following facts about him seem particularly worth enumerating before presenting the document itself. (It does not seem worth while here to go into detail as to how all of these facts were established. I shall simply make the general statement that I have what seems to me good reason to believe that these *are* facts.)

He was about sixty-eight years old at the time of giving me this story of his life, for he was born the year after the Navaho were released from Fort Sumner, New Mexico (1868). His father and mother were the first Navaho to settle permanently in this region a few years after the Fort Sumner captivity. A large proportion of the other early settlers were related to his father and mother. Indeed there is a recognized blood relationship between Mr. Moustache and fully sixty percent of the living members of this society. His clan is the largest in this community, that of his wife being second. The father of Mr. Moustache was for many years the headman or "chief" of this community. When he felt too feeble with age to continue, Mr. Moustache succeeded him and was "chief" for thirty years. Some five years before the narration Mr. Moustache in his turn relinquished the "chieftainship" to a younger and more active man (13), the husband of his younger half-sister. (But Mr. Moustache is in no sense senile, either from the Navaho point of view or from ours.) The two "deputy chiefs" are respectively sororal nephew and younger half-brother of Mr. Moustache. The father of Moustache had two wives, his second wife being the sororal niece of the first. A number of informants independently volunteered the information that the father and his wives never quarreled nor did the wives quarrel with each other.

Mr. Moustache has had three wives and has twelve living children. From the economic point of view he and his immediate family fall into that quarter of the group which is least well off, although previous to a heavy snowstorm which occurred five years earlier and resulted in the death of much livestock, my data indicate that his consumption unit would have fallen into the third rather than the bottom quarter. He is a curer, carrying out the Blessing Way ceremonial. (I might mention, in passing, that becoming a singer or curer is perhaps the principal mechanism for the "circulation of the elite" in Navaho society as a whole.[5])

My first acquaintance with this old man went back fourteen years. When I was a freshman at college I visited on a ranch with whose owner the old man was friendly. He used to come to visit the ranch occasionally and he took some interest in me, largely, I believe, because I was trying to learn to speak Navaho. He invited me to visit him at his house and I went out there two or three times for short periods. Likewise I continued to see him at the ranch and at the trading store from time to time and we would exchange such jokes and small talk as my knowledge of Navaho and his equally meager knowledge of Spanish permitted. At four subsequent summer visits to this ranch this contact was renewed on a basis which was friendly but casual. These visits were interspaced over a number of years but all preceded my formal training in anthropology. The point of importance here is that this was the first occasion on which I had interviewed him in the role of an ethnologist. Some three years previous to this another ethnologist (W. W. Hill), interested primarily in the agricultural and hunting methods of the Navaho, had spent most of a day questioning the old man on these subjects. He had never had any direct contact with a missionary or anyone else who would have had a trained or specially pointed interest in culture. My approach to him with the request that he tell me about his life was not only the first time that I had talked to him as an ethnologist but also on the first day I ever did formal ethnological work among the Navaho. I therefore feel justified in assuming that the data he gave were not selected to accord with any views he might have had as to what I, as an ethnologist, wanted. I took the trouble to write down at the time the words which I asked the interpreter to translate to Mr. Moustache and the replies he made before beginning on the actual story of his life. They are, I think, to the point:

"You are the first Navaho I ever knew. Lots of what I have learned about the Navaho has come from you. We have been friends a long time. Now I am a teacher. My job is to tell the people way off in the East about the Indians out here in New Mexico and Arizona, especially the Navahos. I want to tell them true things, not lies. I want you to help me. What I want to tell them about is how the Navaho live. You have had a long life; you have seen and done many things. You were chief here many years and I know that these Navaho here believe that what you say is right. So I wish you would tell me about your life, right from the beginning. I want to hear everything that you remember just as it comes into your head. I know this will be hard work for you and that you have other things to do. So every day that you work, telling me about your life, I will pay you two dollars. Will you do this for me?"

"What you said is right. We have been friends since you were just a young boy. You have always been good to Navahos and done what was right. I want to help you. But I've got to be sure that it would be all right for the people for me to talk to you like this. Lately since we've got this new Indian commissioner the government has sent some white people out here to ask us questions. Then they started to take our sheep and goats away. The people don't like that. Are you going to tell Washington everything I tell you?"

I assured him that I had no connection whatsoever with "Washington." Then he continued:

"I don't see just exactly why you want to know these things. Some things are for Indians and some things are for white people."

"In the schools we've built for your children we try to teach them what we've found out about how to get along. Some of us think that maybe you Indians have learned things too that would help us. That's why I've come to you."

"All right. What do you want me to tell you first?"

"The first things you remember in your life. I want you to start right there and go on right until now. I don't want to ask you any more questions after you get started. I want you to go on by yourself just as things come into your mind."

But before giving you the actual narrative which he began at this point, something must be said about Frank Pino (31), the interpreter. He was about forty years old and a sororal nephew of Mr. Moustache. He had gone through the eighth grade in the Indian School in Albuquerque and was one of three Indians in this particular community who had sufficient knowledge of English to be able to act as interpreter. Although he had worked for a number of years in the local trading store, his ability as a translator had sharp limitations. Eight times he interrupted his rendering to say "That old man, he uses hard words, and I'm kinda stuck." He would then discuss the Navaho and ask Mr. Moustache to repeat his statement in another way. Frank would also sometimes fail to translate certain Navaho words or phrases of a more or less technical nature with which he knew I was familiar. Apart from these qualifications I give you the old man's life story in precisely the words in which I got it from Frank Pino. I have not tampered with it editorially to rearrange the order, to eliminate repetitions, nor in any manner whatsoever. I should like to emphasize the circumstance that this is "passive interview" material. I asked no questions after he started to talk, and the only interruptions were those incidental to the interpreting and a few queries on the part of members of his family as to his wishes with regard to various work activities and meals. (The interview took place in his own house and members of his extended family group came and went, often stopping for periods of an hour or more to hear the old man's tale). There were pauses, some of them of several minutes, on the part of Mr. Moustache while he "thought things over." These interruptions and pauses account in some part for the relative shortness of the document, considering that the narration required a whole day. The principal explanation, however, rests in the fact that the translation required a considerable amount of time, and after Frank Pino had "figured it out" he had to give it to me slowly enough so that I could write each word exactly as it came.

"I never went any place as a kid. My folks wouldn't let me go to sings. They made me work, getting wood and things like that. I always stayed at home. Now children want to go around as they please. These young Navahos around here—they don't know anything. I'm about the only old Navaho left around here. Soon I'll be dead.

"In the old days we didn't have much food. We were often hungry. We didn't have any clothes—just rags around our bodies. We didn't have any sheep. We hunted deer and other animals. We dug up wild potatoes. The women used to dig these up all day. Then they'd boil them. Sometimes we used to eat dirt even. We used to eat weeds in the summer time. We'd go out and gather Indian millet and pile it up as high as our house. Then we'd thrash it and the women would grind it and make bread. We gathered piñon nuts then just like we do now. We used to gather cactus fruit too. We'd tell each other when we saw it. We had very few horses. We'd walk mostly.

"After a while we heard that Washington would give us groceries at Fort Defiance. Every once in a while they had a meeting there too. I went twice and I remember it. They put us in big corrals twice as high as this house. They gave us iron. The Navaho chief talked to us. They gave us iron—hoe, pick, axe, shovel, and other things and white thick cloth too. The chief said the tools were to work with—build the fields. They didn't use to farm around here. They only started about the time I was able to work in the fields. We had hoes but no plough. The first seed corn was brought from near Lukachukai, the second from near Tohaci.

"We got goats from the Mexicans and Pueblo Indians. Traded for them. We used goat milk—boiled it, stuck a stick in it and sucked it. Then the government bought Mexican sheep and gave them to us at Fort Defiance, one sheep for each person, and we brought them back here. We put the goats and sheep together and started a herd. The Mexicans around here had cheap sheep and the women sold blankets and bought sheep and horses from the Mexicans and from the Apaches and Americans. That's how we got started again after we lost everything in that big war with the white people.

"My father and mother told me 'Take care of these sheep.' My father spanked me and scared me so that I took good care of the sheep. We got sheep the third trip we made to Fort Defiance. Then they stopped giving sheep. The women got sheep last. They went over this third time alone. They got wool carders and dyes this time too.

"There weren't any stores around here at all then. Later the closest was over at Fort Wingate. Bob Masters built the first store near here about twenty-five years ago. When I heard the chief at Fort Defiance say that after a while we were going to get other tools—plough, harness, and wagons, I didn't know what he meant. I had never seen those things.

"After that we raised lots of sheep and horses. Then something happened. There was much less grass than there had been. Big snows came in winter and no rain in summer. They do bad things now. The reason there is no rain on the reservation these days is because they start dancing those dances with masks too early. I can see it now around here like that.

"The first sing I saw was Night Way when I was about five or six years old. That was over by Fort Wingate. I didn't see the masks taken off then. You mustn't see that the first time or you'll go blind. Then I saw a Mountain Top Way a year or so later and that same year a Corral Way. Then about two years after that I saw another Night Way and that time I saw the masks.

"I was the first child in our family. Before I could talk this man's [the interpreter's] mother was born when we were living not far from Tohaci. I was glad. I like all my brothers and sisters and we have always got on well.

"When I was a little boy I thought I was going to live a long time. I thought I was going to live to get old. Now I think I am going to die tomorrow or the next day. I don't know anything about that night. When I was a young man I was always well. Sometimes I was a little sick. My head ached and things like that. But I never laid down during the day when I was young like I have to now.

"My father was a smart man. He told me lots of stories about way back. I don't remember all of it. My father told me how to get along. I have tried to live like my father told me. I don't want to do bad things. They had some kind of story of very old times. My father told me just part—just little things.

"My father said not to sleep too long. Get up early and run a race.[6] That way be stronger. If you sleep until sun-up, you'll never get anything good—sheep or horses. Be poor all the time. I had to work all the time. My father made me. He didn't want to let me fool around. That way I'd never get lazy.

"My father told me about Zuñis, Mexicans, Lagunas, and some white men. Navahos are scared of Mexicans, whites and some Navahos. That's why they have to get up early in the morning. Roll in the snow and get your body hard and strong. Roll in water. If you do that way, never get scared of anyone. That's why they have to practise. If you don't do that, somebody is going to beat you up right now. You can't beat him. That's what my father always told me.

"These people [Mexicans and other Indians] had guns and knives. So they kill you. You can't beat him, but you have to fight a little. Might kill him some way. My father said: 'Better get good guns and powder in a sack. Then enemies be afraid. If sometimes at midnight when you're asleep a bunch of people come and are going to get you. If you've got good guns, you can jump out of bed and try to fight them and if you've worked hard, then you can scare them. If you are a good man, you needn't be afraid of them. If you think you are strong.' That's what my father said and that's why he said I had to be stronger. If I had some children I'd have to chase away these people trying to get my family; that's what he said. I'd have to chase them back away.

"When the snow was a foot deep, sometimes I was scared of rolling in the snow—just like water with ice in it. It's the same thing as being scared of a snake or bear. That's why you have to be strong. Get up early in the morning. That's why you don't scare. If you don't get in water and snow somebody sure to get you right now. You be weak and faint. Get killed right here. People get your family.

"Things were that way a long time ago. When we came here from Tohaci, my father told me not to fight any more. He told me I didn't need to run a race any more or get in snow or water. He thinks everything is all right now. People can sleep all they want to.

"My father said: 'Get in sweat-house: sweat-house good for Navaho. When you get in, put all kinds of weeds and brush in water and boil it. After boiling it, cool it a little, drink every bit of it. Then go into sweat-house. Then vomit when you come out. Must do this because when you were a baby maybe you swallowed some of your mother's blood. If you get in the sweat-house and do these things, you'll be strong and not lazy. You'll be a runner. You'll never get hungry either—just a little.'

"Then he'd tell me: 'Run a race about a mile in the morning, when you're fast like horses, when the snow comes about six feet deep.' I could run like a jack rabbit. I could catch them. Two or three of us used to run a deer down at sun-down. The Navahos used to run all the way from Canyon de Chelly to Laguna and steal some sheep from the Lagunas.

"My father used to say: 'Try to make a farm. Plant some corn.' He was thinking that I might be thinking about getting married. He thought that when I got my wife, pretty soon I'd have some children. Then I'd need some corn or something; then my family'd never starve. If I didn't try to farm or plant, how would we get along then? If a man is a worker, he sure gets along all right. Some men think they'll go to another place where they got something to eat. But that doesn't do any good. That's not right. You got to think things over in your own mind. That's the only way to do.

"When a boy gets married, he has to build up his house and stay there and try to make his field bigger—five or six acres—ten or fifteen. Try to plant all what he wants—pumpkins, beans, wheat. Then make some place to put it up for winter. That way never get hungry. If you do that people would say 'Good man, good worker, not lazy man.'[7]

"You have to think about things for home—dishes and so on. Try to get all kinds of dishes so they can eat with them. Then other people think: 'Good man. He is getting along all right. Just as well as anyone else.' If you do that, they call you a good man.

"When a couple is going to get married, the boy's mother or father comes across and asks the girl's mother or father. The girl takes part of the mother's dishes for a few months or nearly a year. After a while get some themselves. Boy works. Builds a house near the girl's mother's place. The boy takes care of things. After they get started well, the boy brings his sheep and puts with the girl's.

"My father told me not to forget what he said. He said if I did I'd never get broke or poor. I've obeyed my father. That's why I've gotten on so well. If I hadn't minded my father and mother, I'd be without anything. I'd go broke all the time—no shoes, no blankets, sheep, horses. I've told my sons the same thing. I've made them roll in the snow too. My mother told me some things too and her brother. But my father told me most.

"My father said if I knew lots of stories in my head, that way some-one (like you) might come and ask me to tell story. I might tell lots of things all right. If I didn't get what my father told me right, I couldn't talk. If a good man comes to my place, I tell him to camp for the night; I ask story and news. In the morning I feed him again. Then the visitor goes home feeling better. My father told me to do this to be a good man.

"I think I am about like what my father wanted me to be. The people from up there around Fort Defiance and Tohaci, they think I know lots of old stories. I don't know. My father knew almost every-thing. I used to have lots of horses. People came from the reservation and asked for a horse. I gave them one. I think I am a good man with a good head. That's why all my children still have some sheep and horses yet. I think what my father told me.

"What I tell is true. My father always told me to tell the truth. It's

all wrong to lie. My father said not to lie or steal. Don't touch anybody else's rope or anything. Try not to think about stealing. Behave.
Don't try to catch girls. I never did. Don't gamble or you'll forget
other things. Don't drink, my father said, or you'll spend all your
money. Even if I had lots of sheep, it wouldn't last long if I drank.
My father said: 'Take care of yourself. Have good horses, bridle,
saddle blankets so I could go anywhere to a sing without being
ashamed!'[8] Without good clothes you couldn't go anywhere there
were lots of people. Might get ashamed where they had good times.

"I minded my father and mother. I believed what they said was true.
And so I got along all right. I never got poor. I could go any place.
Well, that was right. That is why I don't try to touch bad things. I
never think about bad business. I don't like it. I know now my father
was right. Sometimes people go wrong. My father told me to plant
corn. That is the main thing. Fire also counts. Also sheep and horses.
Attend to these four things, my father said. When you sell or trade,
you can get anything else you want. Don't lose sheep.

"If I use my head all the time, my boys and girls would be just like
me. I knew that. Live a long time that way. Living like this was told
to people a long time ago when they made the world. People were told
to teach each other. Fathers and mothers ought to teach their children.
Some people didn't have sheep. They had little to eat. Better to have
a little bunch of sheep. Sheep are very, very good, I think. Even the
white traders like to buy wool, pelts, lambs, and build up their store.
Sheep are better than cattle. You make blankets from wool. The
government has been making many mistakes. Shouldn't cut the sheep
down. Many fewer sheep around here now. Shouldn't make them sell.
Had to reduce here unequal to the reservation.

"That's about all, I think. I've been talking since early this morning
and I'm tired. You must be tired writing. Young men around here
never wanted to know these things I remember, like you. My own
sons never asked me for my songs and my medicine. If they asked me,
I would tell them. I never tried to learn all my father's medicine. I
don't know why. Maybe I didn't understand. I learned just part of
Blessing Way. My father knew it all. I learned the songs you sing before you plant corn and other good luck songs; before eating you pray
for rain, for food and piñons. Only the people who know the meaning
of Blessing Way can have those. Well, that's the end of the story."

To relate this document adequately to any specific series of events
would require more extended descriptions and more exhaustive
analysis than are possible here. I shall limit myself to drawing
attention to some considerations relevant to generalized classes of
behavior in this social system.

The first thing we notice, I think, in this story is that it is hardly

even a meager autobiography in our sense. He mentions very few
particular events and no persons except his father enter more than
casually into his story. What he says constitutes much more a kind
of philosophic homily than a proper life history. In part, this is to
be understood in the context that the man had been a chief for many
years and was accustomed to have people come to him for advice of a
general nature.[9] It may be also that to another person or under other
circumstances he might have given a more chronologically ordered
account of particular happenings in his life. All of my experience,
however, gives me grounds to doubt this. In any case the fact remains
that this was his response to my request that he start at the beginning
and tell me about all the things he had seen and done in his own life.
Had I questioned him, I feel sure that I could have got a chronological framework to the story, but I repeat that the significance of the
material rests in considerable degree precisely in the circumstance
that I did not in any way attempt to direct or control the content.
He said what he felt as most significant. And so Navaho cultural patterns and not our own stand out. For instance, Navahos, like Pueblo
Indians, have little historical sense. In their myths, legends, and folktales distant past and immediate present are telescoped. In this respect
they contrast, as Professor Leslie Spier has pointed out, with other
Southwestern Indians such as the Maricopa where the sense for the
historical sequence of events is strongly developed. A non-psychotic
person in our culture, asked to tell the story of his life and not
interrupted during the process, would undoubtedly digress a great
deal, but at the same time would, with little doubt, be at some pains
to give some sort of backbone of events and sequences of events to
his story. Likewise, it is my observation that Navahos, with few exceptions, seldom talk spontaneously about their relations with other
persons out of the context of an immediate social situation.

The exceptions mainly come out of the class of relationships which
the Navaho individuals feel as of peculiar significance. Such a case is
clearly that of Mr. Moustache's relationship to his father, perhaps an
example of Pareto's. class 2b "persistence of relations between the
living and the dead." This is surely one of the most striking features
of the story as a human document. It seems perfectly evident that the
interactions of Mr. Moustache with his father have great influence in
determining the former's speech reactions and other behavior. The
father seems definitely to have been the principal agency in conditioning the child to the behavior and attitudes socially approved by
Navaho culture. The emotional tone of this conditioning is patent.

The syndrome of sentiments and behavior stands out unmistakably throughout. At the same time the preoccupation with economic
interests must not be overlooked even though clearly set in a matrix

of the sentiments. He begins and he ends with the struggle for making a living, and one continually gets the feeling of a human being whose thoughts never escape very long from a realization of uneasy dependence upon the natural environment for very existence. The early part of the narrative deals mainly with the reestablishment of the equilibrium of the society *vis à vis* nature which had been disturbed by the war with the whites—almost constantly from 1848 until 1864 there were raids and large or small punitive expeditions—and the captivity at Fort Sumner (1864-1868). Considering the time and attention given to ceremonial interests in this society (my rather full figures indicate that the men in this Navaho community give one productive day out of four to ceremonial activity[10]), it is a little surprising that this topic bulks so small. It is conceivable that this is due in part to the reticences observed with outsiders on esoteric matters, but my notes on casual conversations carried on without reference to my presence on hundreds of occasions during my field work among this group afford basis for this sort of rough induction: economic subjects (corn, sheep, horses, weather, etc.) recur more frequently than do subjects relating to the supernatural and the ceremonial. The point perhaps is that the ceremonials themselves exist, in Navaho theory, mainly to maintain the society's equilibrium *vis à vis* nature, by controlling the supernatural. Nevertheless, from the standpoint of behavioral events and from the standpoint indeed of how economic resources are utilized, the central focus of behavior in this society appears to consist in ritual activities. Here we have a nice case of interdependence of the sentiments. Take almost any set of events or sayings and it is easy to detect in them manifestations of different sets of organized sentiments in a complicated and somewhat fluid state of mutual interdependence.

Analysis of casual conversations gives a decided impression that the fundamental manifest motivations are basically economic in character. This impression is reinforced by such statements as we get in the life story about being ashamed to go to "sings" unless nice clothes could be bought and by certain of the statements wherein members of the community express their opinions of their fellows. In enumerating the qualities desirable in a prospective son-in-law every informant without exception gave first place to industry and general ability to make a living. For example, Dick Pino (1), a younger brother of Mr. Moustache, a leading singer, and one of the most respected men in the community, said in referring to Jolio (universally characterized as the lowest of the low)— and as a kind of final devastation— "Why, he hasn't even got a dog." In short, by selecting evidence, the view that economic prosperity is the principal criterion of success in life could be documented. But this view cannot be sustained without serious qualification in the face of all the pertinent evidence. The present chief and Mr. Moustache, the former chief, both fall into the lowest economic quarter. And both word and deed make it absolutely certain that their prestige is of the very highest. Of the three singers two fall into the lowest economic quarter, one into the quarter next to the bottom. Singers receive fees which in terms of the culture's standards are excellent. But the cultural ideology also demands that they make many gifts and be unusually liberal in their hospitality. A singer of more than mean prosperity is *ipso facto* suspect of witchcraft. So, as a matter of fact, is Jolio. In other words, in this culture to have either too much or too little gives grounds for suspicion on the part of your neighbors. At odd times I have collected independently from more than fifty men and women of varying ages their list of the five or six individuals whom they regarded as most nearly embodying the ideal of the "good man." The lists show remarkable uniformities. For example, Mr. Moustache appeared in every list save his own. The five or six persons in this group who are really very well off (even by our standards) appeared in few lists—two of them did not appear in any—nor did any of the individuals who are essentially destitute. It seems likely that anyone who is really very poor is thought of as not only lacking in industry and other qualities of character but also as (probably) violating "religious" tabus and hence not enjoying the favor of supernatural forces.

At any rate, the two types of activity—"ceremonial" and "economic" —are highly dependent at every point. It takes economic resources to have ceremonials. This is therefore one conscious motivation for working: laying a surplus by. Otherwise the family could not procure a good singer when someone was ill. "Sickness," as a matter of fact, is defined somewhat liberally by this culture, and ceremonials are held when the family has "bad luck," especially economic bad luck— for instance if some of the sheep die. On the other side, the ceremonials act as economic levellers. They tend to prevent excessive accumulations, for unusually wealthy families feel social pressure to give long and expensive ceremonials to which the people can come. As the activities are so intertwined so also are the sentiment systems bearing on the two types.

To return to the preoccupations of casual conversation,[11] sex is an easy third, and here I must postulate a factor of individual variation influencing the content of Mr. Moustache's narrative. I know from experience that most of the other men of his age group in this community would not have talked all day (unless the conversation were rigidly controlled by my questions) without giving far more abundant expression to the sexual residue than did Mr. Moustache. He talks about marriage in the abstract, and it is a fair guess that when he gives the generalized account of Navaho marriage that he is thinking of his own marriage. But he never once refers explicitly to any one of his own three marriages. Perhaps this must be partly understood in terms of an attitude that this would have been improper or indelicate in talking with a comparative stranger. I know from other sources that one of his wives left him about thirty years ago for one of his younger brothers. This was almost certainly an event of some emotional significance at the time at least, and it may well be a fair inference that he is consciously reticent on such topics. Nevertheless I suspect that his silence on these matters is much more related to the Navaho tendency to take marriage and divorce (though not sex) for granted. There is no (or almost no) romantic love among the Navaho. Men and women marry just as in the normal course of things they eat every day. There is nothing in marriage as such that seems to require mention or comment. It is only non-marriage which requires comment by them. One wife is about like another—unless she brought an exceptionally large dowry, or was a particularly famous rug-weaver, or was a singer, or was exceptionally "mean." At least this seems the determinant view when a Navaho is not speaking of an immediate situation but is looking back over his whole life and singling out the really noteworthy for comment. In the other "life histories" which I collected from the Navaho of this group there are a fair number of sexual anecdotes, but again marriages as events are not mentioned, though the deaths of wives and husbands are.

Interests bulk large in his discourse, and there is more than one logico-experimental statement such as "If I drink all the time, I would spend all my money." But interests and logico-experimental statements are most obviously imbedded in a context of strong sentiments. He links his statement about drink with the insistence that this was one of the things his father had urged upon him. The material simply reeks with residues and derivations. Let us single some of these out and try to see how they exist in a state of complex mutual interdependence with the interests and logico-experimental statements.

Early in the document we meet a straightforward example of a residue of class 1b: "You mustn't see the masks the first time or you'll go blind." This clearly combines a rare event (initiation), somewhat terrifying, with a terrible eventuality. Residues of this sub-class are very commonly manifested by the Navaho, as by almost all non-literate peoples. A similar example is the argument which may be paraphrased as follows: "If you make yourself tough by rolling in the snow, you will be able to stand up under other situations that call for toughness, such as fights, meeting snakes and bears, etc." Incidentally, this citation of snakes and bears must not be regarded as logico-experimental for it includes harmless bull snakes as well as actually noxious rattlers. It is the manifestation of another residue characteristic of this culture: Pareto's sub-class 1c, "mysterious powers ascribed to certain things and certain acts." Another example of this sub-class is afforded in Mr. Moustache's mentioning *four* things that are important to the Navaho: corn, fire, sheep, and horses. Everything is done in Navaho culture by fours. Knowledge of this fact is experimentally useful to the ethnologist, for if he is having difficulty in getting a particular bit of information, if he will repeat the question four times in rapid succession the unacculturated Navaho finds it difficult not to answer.

The story gives us an interesting example of combinations solidified into persistent aggregates. You may have noticed that at one point in the recital Mr. Moustache states that his father said that since conditions were now peaceful the combination "roll in the snow—attain hardihood against all dangers" could be dissolved. But presently Mr. Moustache is saying that he taught his own children (who grew up under quite stable conditions) to roll in the snow and the like. The injunctions to roll in the snow, to run races, to rise early, and in general to develop physical hardiness and industry, all have in them a logico-experimental element related to the interests, but nothing could be more patent than that the appeal to carry them out is not put solely, or even mainly, on such bases.

The residue 4b3, "neophobia," is manifested in more than one place. The discourse opens indeed with a manifestation of this residue linked with residues of the fifth class, "integrity of the individual," and especially 5a, "sentiments opposing alteration in the social equilibrium": "I never went any place as a kid. My folks wouldn't let me go to sings. They made me work, getting wood and things like that. I always stayed at home. Now children want to go around as they please. These young Navahos around here—they don't know anything." What an inescapably familiar ring all this has! Residues of the fourth class, "residues of sociability," are likewise recurrently manifested. Particularly frequent of appearance are those of sub-class 4e3, "need of social approval." He points out that people think he "knows a lot"; that people from way off on the Navaho Reservation came to see him and admired his stories. Some remarks of his on another occasion, when I asked him how it was that he had not cut his long hair (as have all of the other male Navaho in the region with five other exceptions), manifest this and other characteristic residues of Mr. Moustache:

"A Navaho man ought to leave his hair long. That is the Navaho way. When Navahos cut their hair, they get mixed up with whites and Mexicans. They forget the prayers for rain. If you leave your hair long, you keep strong. That's why I have always gotten on all right. That's why all the people around here come to me to settle their fights."

Just as one can dip into the document essentially at random and find examples of diverse residues, with equal or greater ease one can pick out examples of various derivations. There are simple affirmations, such as "It's all wrong to lie," which appears to be specifically a case of sub-class 1c, "mixture of facts and sentiments." Derivations of class 2, "authority," are as numerous as we might expect from the representative of a relatively homogeneous, relatively conservative, non-literate culture. Sub-class 2a, "of one or many men," recurs constantly with reference to the father. Class 2b, "of traditions and customs," appears more than once: "Living like this was told to people a long time ago when they made the world." There are plenty of examples of class 3b, "individual interest": "If you sleep until sun-up you'll never get anything good—horses or sheep." Of course, there is a logico-experimental element in this, but the tone and form are clearly that of a derivation. There are cases of 4b, "terms exciting accessory sentiments": "I minded my mother and father . . . I never got poor." Remember that "poor" is a term with a strong pejorative connotation to the Navaho.

Obviously I have not catalogued anything like completely the manifestations of residues and derivations which may be observed in Mr. Moustache's story of his life. It seems sufficient here simply to point the finger at some of those that happened to strike me first and thus to show the applicability of the conceptual scheme. It seems clear to me that data of this type do gain new meanings if considered in terms of Paretian concepts. It is true, of course, that these are the residues and derivations of a single individual. But data which I have not time to present here show that most of these are shared—with varying emphasis—by most other members of this society. Just as one sample I shall give you a brief excerpt from the life story of Dick Pino, the younger brother of Mr. Moustache whom I have already mentioned. This material was gathered quite independently a few days later at Dick Pino's home thirty miles from that of Mr. Moustache.

"My father taught me most. My father taught me almost everything —just like when you sweep up clean. My father didn't need a pencil like you do. He just remembered things. My mother also used to talk to me about some things. Told me not to steal. Be honest. I try to be like my father. That's why I don't like to do what is bad."

Both content and emphasis differ somewhat in similar documents which I have from other individuals in this group and the differences bear importantly on the heterogeneity of persons in this society and its consequences for the general workings of the society. I should like to underline the fact that if I had made up a composite "cultural personality" from bits of acts and theory observed in different individuals my reconstruction would have been misleading. Now it is possible to speak meaningfully of, for example, "cultural values" in a statistical sense. That is, data of the sort I have presented in this case indicate that if an observer were to go into this society and pick out an adult male at random the betting odds are about eight out of ten that he, for example, will have been made to roll in the snow as a boy and about six out of ten that he will be making his children do so. At the same time this material brings out very clearly the hazards of supposing that (in other than a statistical sense) one can drop a kind of perpendicular from "culture" to the behavior of any given culture carrier. From reading certain general accounts of the Navaho one could well be confident that the person who would figure most strongly in the derivations in this document would be the mother's brother, not the father. This prediction is false, of course,[12] and this brings out the necessity for stating not only the statistical mean or mode (which the pattern putatively represents) but also the range and intensity of variation. Note, with reference to this particular point, that while it is of interest and of importance in some contexts that very often in Navaho culture it is the mother's brother rather than the father who instructs and disciplines, this circumstance appears to be of considerably less significance than the almost universal uniformity (residue) in human societies that there is some person from the older generation who is in a position of authority with reference to every maturing organism.

In any event, for our purposes here, one circumstance of importance to notice is that these are the residues and derivations of an individual whom his group consider as a "good man." Pareto in his discussion of "utility and equilibrium" has shown the significance of conceptions of "good men" and of ideals generally in any society. The values that are set high are important even though they are seldom or never fully actualized in the behavior of particular individuals. They exist at least as a series of goals to shoot at and there seems reason to believe that as such they have some influence upon the character of the actual behavior. My fellow anthropologists have tended to neglect this question.

Finally, I should like to take up very briefly and schematically a kind of sub-case which arises out of the case I have presented. You will remember that before undertaking to tell his life story and again at the conclusion of that story Mr. Moustache referred with some acrimony to the recent policy of the United States Indian Service in reducing the number of sheep and goats owned by the Navaho. The facts of this matter afford another neat illustration of the difficulties which arise when, in situations involving the interaction of persons, the attempt is made to alter fundamental economic conditions much more rapidly than the relevant residues and the underlying sentiments can be expected to change.

There can be no reasonable doubt that range conditions in the Navaho country are very much worse than they were two generations or even a single generation ago. Comparison of photographs of the same locality reveal that where it was possible around 1880 actually to cut hay, today there is either the most meager cover on the ground or the former meadow has been eaten away by arroyos. The inference that the change is due—at least in part—to over-grazing consequent upon great increases in Navaho population and in concomitant increases in the size of flocks and herds seems well established, as does the contention of the Indian Service that the standard of living of Navaho families would not be undermined by a certain reduction in the numbers of their livestock.

In brief, the policy of the Indian Service seems justified from a logico-experimental point of view and the officials of the Indian Service have been at great pains to explain to the Navaho at many meetings the details of the bases for their decision and how the policy would benefit the Navaho both in the immediate future and for future generations. But the Indian Service has had in the past few years more difficulties with the Navaho — and difficulties of the most varied sorts—than they have ever had since the Navaho were subjugated. And this is in spite of the fact that many things for which the Navaho have been crying for many years have only been granted during the same past few years. Under the present Indian commissioner far more deep wells have been dug than ever before, fine new hospitals have been built, excellent breeding rams have been given the Navaho, etc., etc. But the great majority of the Navaho tend to react to all of these things in terms of the stock-reduction program, in terms of the logic of the sentiments. Almost never do you hear a Navaho say anything of this sort: "Well, I don't like the stock-reduction program. But the present commissioner has done so many other things for us that I am not going to protest too much about that one thing." Rather, the views which are expressed constantly and on every hand afford magnificent examples of the determination of the premises of arguments by the conclusions which have already been arrived at. Mr. Moustache's statement is typical enough. It may be paraphrased as follows: "Stock are the basis of Navaho well-being. My father said so. Now the government is taking horses, sheep, and goats away. I don't like it." I need not point out to you the residues and derivations manifested in these words. The sentiments which essentially every Navaho centers on the range animals were revealed by more than one statement in Mr. Moustache's story.[13]

The government's logico-experimental program for stock-reduction as a means to erosion control and the restoring of the range has disturbed those sentiments and, so to speak, nothing else matters. The disturbance of these sentiments has activated other latent accessory sentiments against the whites. When the anti-white Ghost Dance religion of the last century was presented to the Navaho, they simply were not interested. Today in more than one quarter of the Navaho country violently anti-white revivalistic cults have attained wide popularity. Demonstrations which show great intensity of feeling have occurred. The present administrative officers of the Indian Service were, for the most part, realistic enough and well enough informed to anticipate resistance to the stock-reduction program itself. But it is my impression that many of them have been amazed because their troubles with the Navaho became so hydra-headed. Opposition to interference with the flocks (the sheep, especially) and herds has been, to be sure, the core of the anti-Indian Service feeling, but resentment has flared in many other, not obviously related, sectors as well.

It seems clearly one more instance of an attempt to improve conditions in a society by certain "rational" means which to the surprise of many actually makes things worse all along the line (even though the particular condition against which the measures were directed may itself be ameliorated) because a nicely adjusted equilibrium has been disturbed too suddenly and too violently. Perhaps those in authority might have proceeded more skillfully had they been familiar with Pareto's concept of social equilibrium.

NOTES

1. Between 1935 and 1941 the distinguished physiologist, L. J. Henderson, conducted a course at Harvard University which was known as "Concrete Sociology." Physicians, lawyers, business executives, governmental administrators, and representatives of the various social sciences presented and discussed a "case" with which they were personally familiar. The conceptual scheme in terms of which all the concrete materials were considered was that of Pareto.

The present paper represents the substance of the case presented by the writer in 1938. Background materials on the Navaho have been deleted, as being generally known to an anthropological audience. Those who wish to consult a general work on the Navaho (with data on the specific Navaho group from which the subject of this personal document came) are referred to Dorothea Leighton and Clyde Kluckhohn, The People and their Children (Chicago, 1945).

The writer does not consider the analysis at all complete from the anthropological point of view. But war duties prevent a more detailed treatment at present, and it is felt that the document itself ought to be spread on the record without further delay since a number of other Navaho personal documents have now appeared and invite comparison (cf. Clyde Kluckhohn, The Personal Document in Anthropological Science [in The Use of Personal Documents in History, Anthropology, and Sociology, Bulletin, Social Science Research Council, no. 53, pp. 79-173, 1945], pp. 100-101).

2. The principal technical concepts used by Pareto are those of "derivation," "residue," and "equilibrium." The first two refer to isolable elements in a body of verbal subject matter. In simple language, the "derivations" are the variable elements, the "residues," the constants. Or, one might say that the "residues" are the actual though implicit premises of the discourse, whereas the "derivations" are the explicit justifications for a given line of reasoning. More technically, the "residues" are those relatively simple uniformities that are observed in a large number of phenomena and that may be interpreted as manifestations of perduring sentiments. A "derivation" is a rationalization or a non-logical (which does *not* mean necessarily irrational or *il*logical) argument, explanation, assertion, appeal to authority, or association of ideas in words. In any given society the residues change slowly, the derivations more rapidly. Pareto defines "equilibrium" as "a state such that if a small modification different from that which will otherwise occur is impressed upon a system, a reaction will at once appear tending toward the conditions that would have existed if the modification had not been impressed." See W. Pareto, *The Mind and Society* (New York, 1935); cf. also G. Homans and C. Curtis, *An Introduction to Pareto* (New York, 1934); L. J. Henderson, *Pareto's General Sociology* (Cambridge, 1935).

3. More correctly it may be described as what an old Navaho Indian told me when I asked him to tell me the story of his life. True autobiographies have been published by Walter Dyk (*Son of Old Man Hat*, New York, 1938) and by A. H. and D. C. Leighton (*The Navaho Door*, Cambridge, 1944.) For a comprehensive report upon American Indian personal documents see Kluckhohn, *The Use of Personal Documents in Anthropological Science.*

4. In the various publications dealing with the Navaho of Ramah, New Mexico, a standard set of numbers has been used to refer to the individuals of the group. For the benefit of any who may ever wish to collate, these numbers are here introduced (in parenthesis) immediately following the first mention of the person.

5. See Clyde Kluckhohn, *Some Personal and Social Aspects of Navaho Ceremonial Practice* (Harvard Theological Review, vol. 32, pp. 57-82, 1939), esp. pp. 80-81.

6. Cf. Dyk, *Son of Old Man Hat*, pp. 8, 70 ff., 172. The collations of Dyk's material given in this paper are merely suggestive of the many which exist—by no means exhaustive.

7. Cf. Dyk, *op. cit.*, pp. 71, 246.

8. Cf. Dyk, *op. cit.*, p. 322.

9. The fact that he had been so long a chief likewise throws light upon a certain stylistic distinction which not even translation could destroy. The Navaho prize oratory highly, and any chief is expected to have some rhetorical proficiency and to observe, more or less, certain recognized canons.

10. See Clyde Kluckhohn, *Participation in Ceremonials in a Navaho Community* (American Anthropologist, vol. 40, pp. 359-369, 1938).

11. It is recognized, of course, that each culture has its characteristic repressions and that sometimes the best index of interest is that of the subjects most strenuously avoided in conversation. There are, however, grounds for thinking that here the topics of manifest interest are significant.

12. That it would have been false also for Dick Pino is indicated not merely by the brief quotations given but also by abundant material (in varying contexts) in my later field notes. For example, I once complimented Dick on the excellence of his memory. He replied immediately, "I remember because my father told me." This influence of the father upon Mr. Moustache and Dick might be usefully commented upon from a number of points of view, including the psychoanalytic, but—for our purposes here—it is probably sufficient to say that the testimony of the members of the community is unanimous in ascribing to him what would, in our idiom, be called "an unusually strong personality." For other instances

of father or *father's* brother (rather than mother's brother) playing a dominant role, cf. Dyk, *Son of Old Man Hat,* pp. 226, 230, 236-237, 251, 297, 371.

13. Cf. also Dyk, *op. cit.,* pp. 103 ("Everything comes from the sheep"), 8f., 65f., 70f., 103, 136f., 172f., 240, 253f. These pages also afford additional evidence for the supposition that the Navaho child's "super-ego" is formed mainly by the father.

WESTON LABARRE

1946. "Social Cynosure and Social Structure," *Journal of Personality*, vol. *14*: 169-183. Reprinted by courtesy of the author and of the Editor of the *Journal of Personality*.

1947. "The Cultural Basis of Emotions and Gestures," *Journal of Personality*, vol. *16*: 49-68. Reprinted by courtesy of the author and of the Editor of the *Journal of Personality*. (Duke University Press).

These two articles by the distinguished author of *The Human Animal* (Chicago, 1954) should be read almost at the beginning of any study of personality differences in various societies. For here are basic facts of ethnology—commonplaces in the thinking of anthropologists, yet stated by Dr. LaBarre with fresh and sensitive insight.

Dr. LaBarre was among the first to attempt systematic analysis of character patterns in Asiatic countries (LaBarre, 1954, 1946-b). He has studied the peyote cult among American Indians (LaBarre, 1938) and his report of field research among the Aymara of South America (LaBarre, 1948) is an excellent example of ethnographic description.

SOCIAL CYNOSURE AND SOCIAL STRUCTURE

Weston LaBarre

Advertisements, movies, popular fiction, and other vehicles of publicity, amusement, and fantasy unite in demonstrating to us that in our society it is the nubile young female who achieves the most attention, who is the cynosure of all eyes. Indeed, this is so true that the statement itself appears a naïve laboring of the obvious. But although this situation may seem to us inevitable, and indeed quasi-biological, a closer study reveals that it is a culturally arbitrary and historically conditioned phenomenon.[1]

The status of women in American society is derived partly from the prior culture of the west-European settlers in our country, and partly from later historical accidents. Under the conditions of frontier society, woman achieved high status through an economically useful contribution that was enhanced by her scarcity value.

This achieved status has never been abdicated in later American culture-history, though it has been greatly modified. Most of the economic functions of woman, in the manufacture and preparation of food and clothing and the like, have been removed from the home, to be performed by specialized extra-familial commercial institutions. With woman no longer valuable in terms of her sex-patterned economic activity, and no longer valuable as a statistical rarity, she seeks to retain her status through an artificial scarcity, a competitive, cultivated invidiousness of sexual appeal.

This is so evident that prestige now accrues to woman as *consumer*, rather than as producer: it is as a suitable vehicle for the display of male buying power that a woman is now valued. Her socially useful contributions as a producer or worker carry no prestige at all, save in competitive-masculine terms. It is woman as a cosmetic creation, as clothes-horse, and as conspicuous consumer who is valued.

In this competition for overt sexual desirability, youth on the part of the woman is the greatest ally. Thus it is that our advertisements are, with heavy preponderance, concerned with pictures of young women.

A striking exception to this occurs in wartime; and was as true of the advertisements of the first World War as of the second. With the same unanimity, advertisements become preoccupied with the young male

535

as soldier. Usually he is nude and bathing in groups overseas, or alone at home in a bathtub; or he is presented as sleeping, eating, and drinking, or in other appealing circumstances. The sentimentality (overly patterned affects) toward the soldier is as stereotyped in wartime as the corresponding attitudes toward the nubile female are in peacetime.

But the social usefulness of the male appears nowhere so clearly and so poignantly as in his potential sacrifice in the ultimate defense of the society. His temporary position as cynosure is regarded by most people as earned, together with the increase in narcissism signalized by the uniform, etc. (we feel that there is distinctly nothing unvirile in a paratrooper's insignia, corps identification, or in the bright colors of ribbons won for courage and unselfish valor).

The most excruciating of advertisements are those which attempt in wartime to indicate that face-powder and lipstick are somehow subtly more important than gunpowder and airplanes. The picture of leisure-class women at home gallantly buying the right perfume in order magically to succor their men in the raddled agony of battle and death is extravagantly absurd. Yet even here, such a woman is by implication a mere appanage of the male, and hardly a person in her own right.

That clothes-narcissism *is* permitted women in our contemporary society and is regarded as appropriate to their role, while it is *not* permitted or appropriate to the male in peacetime, is indicated, I believe, by the rather usual adult male attitude toward the pastel sweaters, the green pork-pie hats, the ravishing ties, and the fancy shoes of the fashion plates in certain self-announced "magazines for men." Here the appeal is to the collegiate adolescent, the tout, and the sharpy; the bachelor man-about-town over-protesting his virility; and to other persons unsure of or dubious in their masculinity and maturity.

Most adult men find such advertisements obscurely effeminate. The socially approved male exhibitionism in our society is largely the symbolic one of competitive accomplishment in athletics, business, or science, rather than the direct exhibition of the person. This is so much the case that, however undeserved, there clings about the radio crooner, the male actor, dancer, and movie star (and even the professional strong man with his spectacularly masculine body) a distinct aura of the effeminate or the sexually inappropriate act. Even the politician dare not be too unusually handsome lest, like several British and Americans who could be named, his real abilities be overshadowed and obscured. And, however indulgent and approving we may feel toward the public nudity of the female in contexts of entertainment, by contrast the ultimate horror and crime is the exhibition of male genitals.

Thus it is, as I have stated, that the great majority of our advertisements are centered around pictures of young women. These pictures are doubly significant: they constitute reader appeal for both sexes (evidencing that the young woman *is* the cynosure of our society), and they further make appeal to the woman as consumer (in their concern for the correct bodily shape, texture, cleanliness, scent, haberdashery, sartorial *brouhaha*, and general impedimenta of the female).

The unhappiness of modern woman is traceable in part to her recognition that her status is somehow factitious in its grounds. As clothes-horse her status is dependent upon the logically prior activity of the male, and woman is the mere vehicle of the masculine prestige gained· through competitive achievement of buying power. Her value is her sexual marketability, not her value as a human being or as a person. Her real social value as mother and wife is by no means as conspicuously attended to and rewarded; still less her value in the economic production of goods and services. She may well feel that this is a most unfair evaluation of the relative worth of womanly roles.

But in movies and popular fiction, the focus of attention is upon the competitive nubility of the young woman. The type fantasy is the Cinderella saga, of irresistible feminine beauty winning the bearer of masculine status and wealth. She need not know how to cook, she need not be able to read a newspaper intelligently, she need not even belong to the right book club: cutaneous texture and subcutaneous contour are all she needs to bring buying power ravening at her feet. The appalling emptiness of values in this transaction is highlighted by the fact that the male, too, is depersonalized. It is true that he is required to have cosmetic charm, though of a recognizably lower candle power than the female's, but he need possess none of the variety of signs of masculine worth, provided he embodies buying power.

The startling fact is that the movie ends in the "final clinch," after the cut-and-dried vicissitudes of the boy meeting, losing, and refinding the girl. For all that the bulk of movie fare gives witness, life ends at this point. The excitements, the problems, and the rewards of maturity are, comparatively speaking, little noticed in this art. Popular music is even more exclusively obsessed with the anxieties of mate-finding and mate-losing, so drearily and so masochistically so that one is moved, with profane exasperation, to wish for, at least once, a forthright cock-crow of possession and triumph.

But the status of glamour girl can be lost through the years, or indeed, in a season. So compelling is the pattern, however, that even when it is no longer useful or appropriate to the legal spouse and matron, the woman still endlessly strives toward it. Thus our society is witness to the obscenity of grandmothers still archly affecting the bobby socks, the jumpers, and the youthfully styled haircuts of their remoter descendants, still smearing onto their sagging jowls the greases and the colored dirts of synthetic youth. The fripperies of dress and the general hallucinations of attitude continue with a sad shamelessness, all the more tragic in that the patterned imprisonment in immaturity disenfranchises the woman of the far richer experiences open to her as a functioning adult.

Thus, the status of cynosure is by no means a blessing to its bearer. And when thus realistically dissected, the arbitrariness and extravagance of popular myth and behavior make it clear that the status of cynosure is a cultural construct, and the contingent product of social, economic, and historical forces.

* * *

Success in our society is invidious. And yet, in its essence, it need not necessarily be so, nor it is the case in a number of societies which we could cite. The fundamental problem of the stability and even of the viability of a given culture may be involved with the question of the extent to which individual members of the society may really achieve "success," in the terms with which the society defines success. *By definition* success in our capitalistic society means the obtaining of what others may not have; it is the exclusiveness of achieving the statistically rare. Yet, strangely, perhaps a majority of humble supporters of this dispensation empathize the figure on the dizzy pinnacle, ignore their own statistical chances of this invidious success, and delude themselves with the fantasy that it could be they. The "hard-headed" small businessman planning his empire is as equally capable of this empathy and this cavalier and irresponsible attitude toward the cold statistics of the matter as the shopgirl dreaming of the movie queen. Were this not true, the society would not enjoy such stability as it does. But with this definition of success, the majority of people are permanently infantilized as mere spectators of the feast of life. However, it is an open question whether mass satisfactions need be real or merely empathized, and the anthropologist is by no means prepared to insist that stability requires genuine rather than fantasied satisfactions, when he observes our own society in the thirteenth century.

We may now summarize two points: (a) The cynosure of a society may be an individual, an age and/or sex group, a class-, caste-, or occupational-group, such that some individuals, and not others, receive the bulk of attention, gratification of narcissism, and public prestige. One may be born to the status of cynosure, one may achieve it, and one may in some cases lose it. (b) Not all individuals in a given society are permitted to achieve success, within the culture's definition of success; therefore some individuals must be emotionally disenfranchised for the benefit of those others. Although success is not necessarily invidious in all societies, the percentage of those in a given society who achieve it may differ widely from the percentage of those who achieve success in the terms of another society.

The ideal society would possess a *variety* of cynosures such that every age, sex, occupational and other group could fit into a number of respectable alternatives, or at least such that the total list would exhaust the whole variety of conditions of man in that society. This is merely to say that such an ideal society would achieve a democratization of prestige and would abolish its single or exclusive cynosure status. Or, put in other words, a stable and satisfying society would embrace within its patterns of success the greatest possible number of individuals.

It is possible that we may find relationships between the conservatism and the tempo of social change, the percentality of success, and the nature of cynosures? The following information from a variety of cultures other than our own will illustrate, if it does not answer, some of these questions.

*   *   *

We have noted that the status of cynosure or focus of attention and prestige may be reached in a wide variety of ways. In one of the most stable, conservative, and perhaps individually most satisfying of all cultures, the Chinese, *any individual may achieve it in time if he is biologically normal.* For here parenthood is the criterion of cynosure-ship. While it may appear that age makes one the cynosure, this is not strictly the case; for without the creation of a family during the years one is attaining to that age, in the familial organization of Chinese society, one would be a cynosure without an audience, an absurdity. The aged eunuch and the celibate Buddhist monk lack this respect. And while it may appear that the father is the cynosure (for he can demand the obedience and respect of even a middle-aged married son), nevertheless, the mother too, for all the alleged superiority in status of the male to the female, may similarly enjoy the status. That the true criterion is parenthood, and not age or sex, is evidenced by the fact that the matriarch, too, shares in the ultimate prestige, and also perhaps by the fact that these same values are extrapolated further into the supernatural world, in ancestor worship. For all its faults (and it has them) Chinese culture does in time embrace within its forms of prestige and success the vast majority of the members of its society. The reverence and respect for the parent is also involved with the teacher and preceptor as cynosure, and it is certainly true that the scholar in China is similarly a social cynosure. But with intelligence and hard work any man can achieve the status whatever his social origins, and the system remains democratically open. By contrast the occupations traditionally admired in many other societies, those of warrior and merchant, in China are despised and held far below the occupation of husbandman, that other promoter of increase.

Or all individuals may achieve the status of cynosure *in time if of the requisite sex.* In the Central Australian gerontocracy, every male need only survive to old age to be its beneficiary. Here the exclusion of the women from ceremonial and other prestigeful areas of life is striking, so that half the society, unlike the Chinese, is disenfranchised by the accident of birth. It is important to note that the cynosure also has considerable significance in the economic and social functioning of Central Australian culture. It is no trick at all to manipulate food taboos in such a manner that the most desirable food is taboo to youngsters and to women, although as in the case of exploiters of most societies the process is hardly conscious. The tempo of change in a gerontocracy is also notable. By contrast with the breathless faddism and precipitate change in our own youth-oriented society, Central Australian native culture is among the most unchanging in the world, and the most conservative. It is not without significance, perhaps, that its mythology is oriented into the remote past, and the sanction for behavior is that it has always been done this way, not that this way is "new."

This suggests a dynamism perhaps significant in Western society. In America the authority figure has been dethroned by a successful revolution against a British tyrant, and in the resultant sibling society, youth and dizzy change reign. The symbolic Oedipal revolution is won. In British society, however, the king still reigns, though he does not rule. Undethroned, he is reduced to political impotence, but remains still the cynosure of an empire. Thus, English affects cluster around the familiar, the old and the loved, in a word, the traditional; and social change comes with some reluctance, lagging far behind the indubitably intelligent and realistic judgment of the electorate. Modern England has had economic and political revolution, but without a complete social and symbolic revolution. Modern America has had a political and symbolic revolution, but without a complete social and economic revolution. Modern Russia has presumably undergone a social and economic revolution, but in its retention of absolutism, it has completed neither the political nor the symbolic revolution. And, quite clearly, Catholic and dictatorial South American countries, for all their many spurious revolutions, have achieved neither political, social, economic, nor symbolic revolution, for although the personnel changes, the system and the practices remain.

An extreme of catholicity in cynosure selection is reached in parts of Indonesia. Here the status is achieved *automatically in time by every individual.* It is, however, a somewhat empty status from our own unbelieving point of view, since it is reached only in death. Not so to the Indonesians:

> Powerful though the beliefs in magic and spirits are, probably the most important cult in Indonesia has to do with the ghosts of the dead and the ancestors. In few other places in the world do funeral ceremonies involve so much time, energy, and sacrifice. In many tribes the dead receive not only one, but two and even three successive funerals, at each of which the bones of the deceased are exhumed or removed from their tombs for cleaning. The ways of dis-

posing of mortal remains are extremely varied. In the island of Sumatra alone, for instance, the different tribes bury, cremate, entomb, abandon, conceal in caves, and seal in trees the bodies of their dead. Even within the same tribe diverse methods of disposal may be employed, depending upon the age, rank, sex, and manner of death of the deceased.

This obsession with death and the dead reaches its culmination in the all-important ancestor cult. The ancestors have passed beyond, to the realm of the spirits, and, if kept satisfied, are in an excellent position to aid the living. Therefore they receive endless sacrifices, and the people dread offending them in any way. This, indeed, is a great reason for the conservativism of the Indonesians, as the ancestors are likely to be angered by any alteration in the ways they were used to on earth.[2]

Thus, whatever the frustrations and failures of this life, one could at least look forward to becoming dead in Indonesia, and to enjoying the lively revenge of an ancestral ghost. However, this raises the question (if it has not already been suggested by our own culture) of the social cost of the cynosure, and whether its support is ultimately worth while in terms of return to the society.

Alternatively, cynosure status can be closely exclusive, *achieved by birth by one individual in each generation, or by one family only.* Here should be mentioned the Emperor of Japan, in whom the cynosureship of his society was dazzlingly focused as the descendant of the Sun Goddess, Amaterasu ō Mikami. This is wholly consonant with the male orientation and the tightly feudal structure of prewar Japan. The Royal Family of England is an excellent example of the second. The breathless concern with Royal household trivia by the citizens of a far-flung Empire equals, indeed, the tireless voyeurism of the sexuality of the cinema great by the avid readers of movie magazines in America.

The individual may become a cynosure *by election* of one sort or another. The "divine kings" described in such detail by Sir James Frazer in *The Golden Bough* probably belong in this category. The divine king, somewhat in the manner of the President among us, is the scapegoat of the society, however, and is regarded as being magically responsible, both positively and negatively, for the success or failure of the crops, the well-being of the cattle, and the like. The position of cynosure here is subject to sudden vacation by death, if weakness and old age, or anything untoward like a drought or crop failure reveals the senescence of the cynosure. In Mexico, the Aztec youths chosen to impersonate the gods enjoyed all the available delights and prestige which the society could give them; but this was for a term only, and ended in the use of such individuals in human sacrifice. In the case of the divine king and the god impersonator, therefore, the status of cynosure, though elective, carried many prerogatives and great prestige, but it was paid for by the individual's death. The dynamics of hostile affect in the ruthless Aztec society and in absolutist societies with divine kings would be an interesting subject for study. The question of the price of being cynosure to the individual is also obvious.

Similarly punishing to the individual may be the cynosureship won *by either sex if the right activities are performed*, as in the case of ascetics in India. The enormous prestige which accrues to the "holy" person practicing austerities in India must be witnessed to be believed; even the Hindu gods can compel one another to their will, and at times the very structure of the universe has been threatened in Hindu myth by ascetic individuals piling up the capital of supernatural virtue in extraordinary amounts through their penances. The institutionalized masochism of these individuals is functionally of a piece with the fantastically sadomasochistic structure of Indian culture.

In some societies the individual may become the cynosure *by sex, age and activity*. The case of the soldier in Germany from the time at least of Frederick the Great is an illustration of this. The saber-scarred cheek of the duelist was the badge of this society, and the soldier was the darling of German society in the last war to the extent that economic, social, and sexual values were bent to his service. The extent to which military values and the philosophy of force have permeated German history is evident to any student of German history and German philosophy. The history of Hitler is the shrewd implementation of his magical political formulae with police and military power.[3]

The warrior as cynosure is not an uncommon phenomenon, as a matter of fact, among primitive societies; thus one may attain the status *by successful sex-patterned activity*. Possibly the culture of the Plains Indians carried this to the greatest logical extreme. The idea of *power*, a sort of male *mana*, underlies Plains culture. One may acquire supernatural power through the vision quest, or through purchase (as with the Blackfoot medicine bundles), but only two formal roles were open to men in the exploitation and display of this power. A man might become a warrior or a medicine man—and little else. Secular success in warfare probably carried greater prestige than magic success in doctoring, but between the two of them, these roles absorbed practically all the prestige of cynosureship available in the society. The fiercely competitive and individualistic struggle for success in war, through scalp-taking, horse-stealing, counting coup, and other quixotic displays of daring, has given to the typical Plains Indian the qualities of character, the aggressiveness and the extroversion, which we regard as fundamentally "masculine" since they conform to our own cultural male-ideal.

But the psychological pressures of the male pattern in Plains society— the systematic and repeated exposure of oneself to mutilation and death

—must have been enormous indeed; for success in its terms was commonly so threatening and impossible that a semiofficial status was set up for the frequent enough "failures" in this society. This was the famous institution of the *berdache*, the non-man who did not go to war like other males, signalized by the feminine dress and feminine activities (and sometimes quasi-female sexuality) of these individuals. The *berdache* is the product of the fierce exclusiveness of concentration upon the warrior as cynosure, and not all men in the gamut of individual temperament and character variation could take on the severely defined traits of the warrior's role. Our own concentration upon the acquisition of economic buying power as the prime and essential masculine value, and the central and only worth-while male activity, might well be examined in the light of the psychodynamics of Plains culture.

Successful sex-patterned activity finds a less traumatogenic expression elsewhere. In France, in my opinion, it is the mature and sexually functioning woman who is the cynosure of the society. Nowhere, certainly not in Europe, is there so well-developed an appreciation of woman as woman, as sexual object and mother alike. That there is the split-image of woman as official wife and as mistress in French society does not negate this fact; it is rather an evidence of the double role of woman as mother and as sexual object, which in no society may be the same individual. It is in France that femininity reaches its highest *chic*, and Paris is the true home of feminine *haute couture*, millinery, and perfume.[4] It is the France of that feminine Don Juan, George Sand, of the ageless Ninon de l'Enclos, the imperishable Sarah Bernhardt, the fabled Kiki, and the indestructible Mistinguette.

For the achievement of cynosure-status by successful sex-patterned activity is by no means undesirable in itself: it all depends upon what the sexually patterned activities and roles are, and what their social usefulness may be. In late medieval and early modern times, the condition and outward appearance of pregnancy and approaching motherhood brought such prestige and was considered aesthetically so satisfying that stomachers were introduced into fashionable dress to imitate the condition. Similarly, in the prolific Victorian period, fashion emphasized the elegance and importance of the female pelvis in the bustle. Inasmuch as maternity is a genuine social value, and since there is much to be gained for all individuals concerned through its satisfactions, the value of the mother as cynosure is easily recognized. Indeed, whatever of stability medieval Europe knew, after the disintegration of the classical cultures, centered around the forms and institutions of mariolatry and recrudescent Mediterranean mother-goddess religions. That this same culture can in other times produce institutionalized social, economic, and emotional infantilisms is another problem, and an instance of the dangers of overemphasizing any one human role.

On the other hand, since one male can produce many pregnancies and his own role in child-bearing is a relatively minor one, the appurtenances of individual virility are biologically and socially less valuable and indispensable. Thus, the similar expression of male exhibitionism in dress, in the late fifteenth and early sixteenth century codpiece, quickly reached competitive extremes which were ridiculously and patently spurious. The well-established psychiatric significance of suckling children at the breast, as an undeniable social value, gives, on the other hand, a dignity and a perennial satisfaction to the display in dress of the female bosom throughout the history of style. But these are *functional* values of woman as mother and as mate, and of incomparably greater worth than woman as conspicuous consumer in the competitive seeking to capture male buying power. It is surely at least arguable that a focused cultural appreciation of wise maternity and a connoisseurship of the finesses and intricacies of intelligent and well-considered motherhood constitute as worth while and as satisfying a social cynosure as the French connoisseurship of woman as sexual object. And certainly both are more real creatures than the cold, compulsive-masked, cosmetic beauty of the professional glamour girl and cinema queen, who is less the maturely functioning female than prenuptial mantrap.

Other cultures, too, have been aware of the charm of youth. Our somewhat antisexual and youth-oriented American society chooses to concentrate attention upon the young female before the time of sexual fulfillment. This is a cynosureship achieved *by the appropriate sex at a given age and subsequently lost.* Among the Greeks of the fifth century before Christ, the cynosure of society was just as distinctly the adolescent and maturing young male. There are rich philosophical, metaphysical, theological, psychiatric and didactic overtones to this fact, both in classic times and later, but these as much merit extended study elsewhere as does our own social cynosure.

The case of Bali, in which the very young, preadolescent girl is the social cynosure, is even more striking, but the choice of the breastless female child is quite probably another index of the pathology of this ignorantly admired and profoundly schizothymic culture. Her fate is to grow up and become the wicked witch of a mother, whose frustrations (subjective and objective, active and passive) regenerate the whole trauma and tragedy.

One final type of cynosureship comes to mind in this not necessarily exhaustive list. This is the case of the Northwest Coast Indians, in whose society the cynosure is the prestige-creating, property-destroying potlatching chief. In one sense he is the cynosure as recipient of prestige created by his ancestors, and in another sense he is the cynosure as creator of prestige for his descendants. However, a *nouveau riche* or *arriviste* potlatch-giver cannot gain prestige *for himself*, but only *for his descendants.* The cynosureship is here, more correctly, a *property-purchased prestige which is inherited.* Something of the sort is familiar to us in our own society, in which full gentility lags a generation, and in which the length of time the family has had money is significant.

Indeed, it is in terms of the social cynosure that we might most usefully view the Northwest Coast culture. Ruth Benedict's *Patterns of Culture* has had the well-deserved influence of a pioneering attempt to apply the insights of psychiatry to ethnology. And like all truly significant books, it instructs us even in its errors. Not the least of its values has been the teaching of caution about the extrapolation of clinical categories from the field of *psychiatric* description of *individuals* to the *ethnological* description of *cultures.* Sapir, like many another later investigator, has pointed out that if Northwest Coast culture is descriptively "megalomaniac," then the megalomaniac individual in it is in close, nonconflictful conformity with the culture. That is, the individual who (in our clinical sense) is megalomaniac there, is then *well adjusted* to his culture; while the nonmegalomaniac individual (the "sane" man in our judgment) is a bad misfit. It is clear that the dynamic situations of the descriptively megalomaniac individual in Northwest Coast culture on the one hand, and such an individual in our culture on the other hand, are not only different, but diametrically opposite.

The danger of this line of thought is evident when would-be scientific description and analysis degenerate into name-calling. Spengler labels cultures "carnivorous" and "herbivorous," and leaves us in no doubt as to which he regards as superior. But it is equally crude on our part to call Nazi culture "paranoid." Casting aside nationalistic emotion and ethnocentric value judgment, such description is to be criticized on the same grounds as the Northwest Coast instance. If we are satisfied with an impressionistic first approximation of *description,* well and good; Nazi culture *was* arrogantly "megalomaniac" in its racism, "persecutory" in its political ideology, "amoral" in its behavior, and pathological in its sexuality. Its leader, Hitler, *was* hypochondriac, and from abundant evidence very possibly a classical clinical case of paranoia. Descriptively there is much evidence of the paranoid here; but we must consider more deeply the problem of the *dynamics* of the "abnormal" milieu, in which the abnormal individual is at home.

The concept of cynosure may be a useful refinement of description in dealing with the Northwest Coast culture. Actually it is only the potlatching chief who is the functioning megalomaniac, in one sense. It is he who is the focus of his group's economic activity; it is he who recklessly and arrogantly destroys great amounts of property in the social manufacture of prestige. Of course the group empathizes its potlatch chief and of course its members share the cultural values of their chief, but it is the chief who is the cynosure. And although other individuals share the culture of the chief, to what extent are the commoner and the chief actually identical in their psychological functioning as individuals?

In so far as the Northwest Coast culture and our own are wry caricatures of each other, its study is illuminating in the critical examination of our capitalist culture. Has not Veblen already adequately demonstrated that property among us is utilized not so much for its sound biological contributions to our well-being as for its prestige value? Do we not "consume" (destroy, or withhold from the use of needful others), motivated by invidious conspicuousness, and are we not thus grossly wasteful of social effort? Does not the invidiousness of success as we define it exact a fearful emotional toll in the psychological disenfranchisement of the majority of men and women, and their systematic infantilization as voyeurs rather than partakers of success? And, since all our values must be cast in pecuniary terms, do we really have the best cynosures that money can buy?

NOTES

1. The illuminating studies by Dr. Helene Deutsch on the origins and development of feminine narcissism (in *The psychology of women,* 2 vols., New York, 1944 & 1945), impressive and convincing as they are, may need to be qualified as applying perhaps only to women *in our culture, now.*

2. Raymond Kennedy, *Islands and peoples of the Indies,* Smithsonian Institution, War Background Studies, No. 14, p. 48.

3. If the magic force of Hitler was in the political realm, the Marxist and Russian faith is in the magic of economics—but it nevertheless implements itself with a tight social, cultural, political, and military control of its communicants. The British-American faith is in law and orderly social process.

4. If, as it may indeed be contended, the English cynosure is the young statesman and public servant (the young Pitt, the Anthony Edens), then it is appropriate to find London the analogous center of male style.

THE CULTURAL BASIS OF EMOTIONS AND GESTURES

WESTON LABARRE

Psychologists have long concerned themselves with the physiological problems of emotion, as for example, whether the psychic state is prior to the physiological changes and causes them, or whether the conscious perception of the inner physiological changes in itself constitutes the "emotion." The physiologists also, notably Cannon, have described the various bodily concomitants of fear, pain, rage, and the like. Not much attention, however, has been directed toward another potential dimension of meaning in the field of emotions, that is to say the *cultural* dimension.

The anthropologist is wary of those who speak of an "instinctive" gesture on the part of a human being. One important reason is that a sensitivity to meanings which are culturally different from his own stereotypes may on occasion be crucial for the anthropologist's own physical survival among at least some groups he studies, and he must at the very least be a student of this area of symbolism if he would avoid embarrassment.[1] He cannot safely rely upon his own culturally subjective understandings of emotional expression in his relations with persons of another tribe. The advisability and the value of a correct reading of any cultural symbolism whatsoever have alerted him to the possibility of culturally arbitrary, quasilinguistic (that is, noninstinctual but learned and purely agreed-upon) meanings in the behavior he observes.

A rocking of the skull forward and backward upon its condyles, which rest on the atlas vertebra, as an indication of affirmation and the rotation upon the axis vertebra for negation have so far been accepted as "natural" and "instinctive" gestures that one psychologist at least[2] has sought an explanation of the supposedly universal phenomenon in ascribing the motions of "yes" to the infant's seeking of the mother's breast, and "no" to its avoidance and refusal of the breast. This is ingenious, but it is arguing without one's host, since the phenomenon to be explained is by no means as widespread ethnologically, even among humans, as is mammalian behavior biologically.

Indeed, the Orient alone is rich in alternatives. Among the Ainu of northern Japan, for example, our particular head noddings are unknown:

the right hand is usually used in negation, passing from right to left
and back in front of the chest; and both hands are gracefully brought
up to the chest and gracefully waved downwards—palms upwards—
in sign of affirmation.[3]

The Semang, pygmy Negroes of interior Malaya, thrust the head
sharply forward for "yes" and cast the eyes down for "no."[4]

The Abyssinians say "no" by jerking the head to the right shoulder, and "yes" by throwing the head back and raising the eyebrows.
The Dyaks of Borneo raise their eyebrows to mean "yes" and contract them slightly to mean "no." The Maori say "yes" by raising the
head and chin: the Sicilians say "no" in exactly the same manner.[5]

A Bengali servant in Calcutta rocks his head rapidly in an arc from
shoulder to shoulder, usually four times, in assent; in Delhi a Moslem boy throws his head diagonally backward with a slight turning
of the neck for the same purpose; and the Kandyan Singhalese bends
the head diagonally forward toward the right, with an indescribably
graceful turning in of the chin, often accompanying this with a
cross-legged curtsey, arms partly crossed, palms upward—the whole
performance extraordinarily beautiful and ingratiating. Indeed, did
my own cultural difference not tell me it already, I would know that
the Singhalese manner of receiving an object (with the right hand,
the left palm supporting the right elbow) is not instinctive, for I
have seen a Singhalese mother *teaching* her little boy to do this when
I gave him a chunk of palm-tree sugar. I only regretted, later, that my
own manners must have seemed boorish or subhuman, since I handed
it to him with my right hand, instead of with both, as would any
courteous Singhalese. Alas, if I handed it to a little Moslem beggar in
Sind or the Punjab with my *left* hand, he would probably have dashed
the gift to the ground, spat, and called me by the name of an animal
whose flesh he had been taught to dislike, but which I have not—for
such use of the left hand would be insulting, since it is supposed to
be confined to attending to personal functions, while the right hand
is the only proper one for food.

Those persons with a passion for easy dominance, the professional
dog-lovers, must often be exasperated at the stupidity of a dog which
does not respond to so obvious a command as the pointed forefinger.
The defense of man's best friend might be that this "instinctively"
human gesture does not correspond to the kinaesthesias of a nonhanded
animal. Nevertheless, even for an intelligent human baby, at the exact
period when he is busily using the forefinger in exploring the world,
"pointing" by an adult is an arbitrary, sublinguistic gesture which is
not automatically understood and which must be *taught*. I am the less
inclined to berate the obtuseness to the obvious of either dog or baby,

because of an early field experience of my own. One day I asked a favorite informant of mine among the Kiowa, old Mary Buffalo, where something was in the *ramada* or willow-branch "shade" where we were working. It was clear she had heard me, for her eighty-eight-year-old ears were by no means deaf; but she kept on busying both hands with her work. I wondered at her rudeness and repeated the request several times, until finally with a puzzled exasperation which matched my own, she dropped her work and fetched it for me from in plain sight: she had been repeatedly pointing with her lips in approved American Indian fashion, as any Caucasian numbskull should have been able to see.

Some time afterward I asked a somewhat naive question of a very great anthropologist, the late Edward Sapir: "Do other tribes cry and laugh as we do?" In appropriate response, Sapir himself laughed, but with an instant grasping of the point of the question: In which of these things are men alike everywhere, in which different? Where are the international boundaries between physiology and culture? What are the extremes of variability, and what are the scope and range of cultural differences in emotional and gestural expression? Probably one of the most learned linguists who have ever lived, Sapir was extremely sensitive to emotional and sublinguistic gesture—an area of deep illiteracy for most "Anglo-Saxon" Americans—and my present interest was founded on our conversation at that time.

Smiling, indeed, I have found may almost be mapped after the fashion of any other culture trait; and laughter is in some senses a geographic variable. On a map of the Southwest Pacific one could perhaps even draw lines between areas of "Papuan hilarity" and others where a Dobuan, Melanesian dourness reigned. In Africa, Gorer noted that

> laughter is used by the negro to express surprise, wonder, embarrassment and even discomfiture; it is not necessarily, or even often a sign of amusement; the significance given to "black laughter" is due to a mistake of supposing that similar symbols have identical meanings.[6]

Thus it is that even if the physiological behavior be present, its cultural and emotional functions may differ. Indeed, even within the same culture, the laughter of adolescent girls and the laughter of corporation presidents can be functionally different things; so too the laughter of an American Negro and that of the white he addresses.

The behaviorist Holt "physiologized" the smile as being ontogenetically the relaxation of the muscles of the face in a baby replete from nursing. Explanations of this order may well be the case, if the phenomenon of the smile is truly a physiological expression of generalized pleasure, which is caught up later in ever more complex conditioned reflexes. And yet, even in its basis here, I am not sure that this is the whole story: for the "smile" of a child in its sleep is certainly in at least some cases the grimace of *pain* from colic, rather than the relaxation of pleasure. Other explanations such as that the smile is *phylogenetically* a snarl suffer from much the same *ad hoc* quality.

Klineberg writes:

It is quite possible, however, that a smile or a laugh may have a different meaning for groups other than our own. Lafcadio Hearn has remarked that the Japanese smile is not necessarily a spontaneous expression of amusement, but a law of etiquette, elaborated and cultivated from early times. It is a silent language, often seemingly inexplicable to Europeans, and it may arouse violent anger in them as a consequence. The Japanese child is taught to smile as a social duty, just as he is taught to bow or prostrate himself; he must always show an appearance of happiness to avoid inflicting his sorrow upon his friends. The story is told of a woman servant who smilingly asked her mistress if she might go to her husband's funeral. Later she returned with his ashes in a vase and said, actually laughing, "Here is my husband." Her White mistress regarded her as a cynical creature; Hearn suggests that this may have been pure heroism.[7]

Many in fact of these motor habits in one culture are open to grave misunderstanding in another. The Copper Eskimo welcome strangers with a buffet on the head or shoulders with the fist, while the northwest Amazonians slap one another on the back in greeting. Polynesian men greet each other by embracing and rubbing each other's back; Spanish-American males greet one another by a stereotyped embrace, head over right shoulder of the partner, three pats on the back, head over reciprocal left shoulder, three more pats. In the Torres Straits islands "the old form of greeting was to bend slightly the fingers of the right hand, hook them with those of the person greeted, and then draw them away so as to scratch the palm of the hand; this is repeated several times."[8] The Ainu of Yezo have a peculiar greeting; on the occasion of a man meeting his sister, "The man held the woman's hands for a few seconds, then suddenly releasing his hold, grasped her by both ears and uttered the Aino cry. Then they stroked one another down the face and shoulders."[9] Kayan males in Borneo embrace or grasp each other by the forearm, while a host throws his arm over the shoulder of a guest and strokes him endearingly with the palm of his hand. When two Kurd males meet, "they grasp each other's right hand, which they simultaneously raise, and each kisses the hand of the other."[10] Among the Andaman Islanders of the Gulf of Bengal:

When two friends or relatives meet who have been separated from each other for a few weeks or longer, they greet each other by sitting down, one on the lap of the other, with their arms around each other's necks, and weeping or wailing for two or three minutes till they are tired. Two brothers greet each other in this way, and so do father and son, mother and daughter, and husband and wife. When husband and wife meet, it is the man who sits in the lap of the woman. When two friends part from one another, one of them lifts up the hand of the other towards his mouth and gently blows on it.[11]

Some of these expressions of "joy" seem more lugubrious than otherwise. One old voyager, John Turnbull, writes as follows:

The arrival of a ship brings them to the scene of action from far and near. Many of them meet at Matavai who have not seen each other for some length of time. The ceremony of these meetings is not without singularity; taking a shark's tooth, they strike it into their head and temples with great violence, so as to produce a copious bleeding; and this they will repeat, till they become clotted with blood and gore.

The honest mariner confesses to be nonplussed at this behavior.

I cannot explain the origin of this custom nor its analogy with what it is intended to express. It has no other meaning with them than to express the excess of their joy. By what construction it is considered symbolical of this emotion I do not understand.[12]

Quite possibly, then, the weeping of an American woman "because she is so happy" may merely indicate that the poverty of our gamut of physiological responses is such as to require using the same response for opposite meanings. Certainly weeping does not obey social stereotypes in other cultures. Consider old Mary Buffalo at her brother's funeral: she wept in a frenzy, tore her hair, scratched her cheeks, and even tried to jump into the grave (being conveniently restrained from this by remoter relatives). I happened to know that she had not seen her brother for some time, and there was no particular love lost between them: she was merely carrying on the way a decent woman should among the Kiowa. Away from the grave, she was immediately chatting vivaciously about some other topic. Weeping is *used* differently among the Kiowa. Any stereotypes I may have had about the strong and silent American Indian, whose speech is limited to an infrequent "ugh" and whose stoicism to pain is limitless, were once rudely shattered in a public religious meeting. A great burly Wichita Indian who had come with me to a peyote meeting, after a word with the leader which I did not understand (it was probably permission to take his turn in a prayer) suddenly burst out blubbering with an abandon which no Occidental male adult would permit himself in public. In time I learned that this was a stereotyped approach to the supernatural powers, enthusiastic weeping to indicate that he was powerless as a child, to invoke their pity, and to beseech their gift of medicine power. Everyone in the tipi understood this except me.

So much for the expression of emotion in one culture, which is open to serious misinterpretation in another: there is no "natural" language of emotional gesture. To return a moment to the earlier topic of emotional expression in greetings: West Africans in particular have developed highly the ritual gestures and language of greeting. What Gorer says of the Wolof would stand for many another tribe:

> The gestures and language of polite intercourse are stylized and graceful; a greeting is a formal litany of question and answer embracing everyone and everything connected with the two people meeting (the questions are merely formal and a dying person is stated to be in good health so as not to break the rhythm of the responses) and continuing for several minutes; women accompany it with a swaying movement of the body; with people to whom a special deference is due the formula is resumed several times during the conversation; saying goodbye is equally elaborate.[13]

But here the sublinguistic gesture language has clearly emerged into pure formalisms of language which are quite plainly cultural.

The allegedly "instinctive" nature of such motor habits in personal relationships is difficult to maintain in the face of the fact that in many cases the same gesture means exactly opposite, or incommensurable things, in different cultures. Hissing in Japan is a polite deference to social superiors; the Basuto applaud by hissing, but in England hissing is rude and public disapprobation of an actor or a speaker. Spitting in very many parts of the world is a sign of utmost contempt; and yet among the Masai of Africa it is a sign of affection and benediction, while the spitting of an American Indian medicine man upon a patient is one of the kindly offices of the curer. Urination upon another (as in a famous case at the Sands Point, Long Island, country club, involving a congressman since assassinated) is a grave insult among Occidentals, but it is part of the transfer of power from an African medicine man in initiations and curing rituals. As for other opposite meanings, Western man stands up in the presence of a superior; the Fijians and the Tongans sit down. In some contexts we put on more clothes as a sign of respect; the Friendly Islanders take them off. The Toda of South India raise the open right hand to the face, with the thumb on the bridge of the nose, to express respect; a gesture almost identical among Europeans is an obscene expression of extreme disrespect. Placing to the tip of the nose the projecting knuckle of the right forefinger bent at the second joint was among the Maori of New Zealand a sign of friendship and often of protection;[14] but in eighteenth-century England the placing of the same forefinger to the right side of the nose expressed dubiousness about the intelligence and sanity of a speaker—much as does the twentieth-century clockwise motion of the forefinger above the right hemisphere of the head. The sticking out of the tongue among Europeans (often at the same time "making a face") is an insulting, almost obscene act of provocative challenge and mocking contempt for the adversary, so undignified as to be used only by children; so long as Maya writing remains undeciphered we do not know the meaning of the exposure of the tongue in some religious sculptures of the gods, but we can be sure it scarcely has the same significance as with us. In Bengali statues of the dread black mother goddess Kali, the tongue is protruded to signify great raging anger and shock; but the Chinese of the Sung dynasty protruded the tongue playfully to pretend to mock terror, as if to "make fun of" the ridiculous and unfeared anger of another person.[15] Modern Chinese, in South China at least, protrude the tongue for a moment and then retract it, to express embarrassment at a *faux pas*.

Kissing, as is well known, is in the Orient an act of private loveplay and arouses only disgust when indulged in publicly: in Japan it is necessary to censor out the major portion of love scenes in American-made movies for this reason. Correspondingly, some of the old *kagura* dances of the Japanese strike Occidentals as revolting overt obscenities, yet it is doubtful if they arouse this response in Japanese onlookers. Manchu kissing is purely a private sexual act, and though husband and wife or lovers might kiss each other, they would do it stealthily since it is shameful to do in public; yet Manchu mothers have the pattern of putting the penis of the baby boy into their mouths, a practice which probably shocks Westerners even more than kissing in public shocks the Manchu.[16] Tapuya men in South America kiss as a sign of peace, but men do not kiss women because the latter wear labrets or lip plugs. Nose-rubbing is Eskimo and Polynesian, and the Djuka Negroes of Surinam[17] show pleasure at a particularly interesting or amusing dance step by embracing the dancer and touching cheek to cheek, now on one side, now on the other—which is the identical attenuation of the "social kiss" between American women who do not wish to spoil each other's makeup.

In the language of gesture all over the world there are varying mixtures of the physiologically conditioned response and the purely cultural one, and it is frequently difficult to analyze out and segregate the two. The Chukchee of Siberia, for example, have a phenomenal quickness to anger, which they express by showing the teeth and growling like an animal—yet man's snout has long ceased being functionally useful in offensive or defensive biting as it has phylogenetically and continuously retreated from effective prognathism. But this behavior reappears again and again: the Malayan pagans, for example, raise the lip over the canine tooth when sneering and jeering. Is this instinctual reflex or mere motor habit? The Tasmanians stamped rapidly on the ground to express surprise or pleasure; Occidentals beat the palms of their hands together for the same purpose ordinarily, but in some rowdier contexts this is accompanied by whistling and a similar stamping of the feet. Europeans "snort" with contempt; and the non-Mohammedan primitives of interior Malaya express disgust with a sudden expiration of the breath. In this particular instance, it is difficult to rid oneself of the notion that this is a consciously controlled act, to be sure, but nevertheless at least a "symbolic sneeze" based upon a purely physiological reflex which does rid the nostrils of irritating matter. The favorite gesture of contempt of the Menomini Indians of Wisconsin—raising the clenched fist palm down up to the level of the mouth, then bringing it swiftly downwards, throwing forth the thumb and first two fingers—would seem to be based on the same "instinctual" notion of rejection.

However, American Indian gestures soon pass over into the undisputedly linguistic area, as when two old men of different tribes who do not know a word of each other's spoken language, sit side by side and tell each other improper stories in the complex and highly articulate intertribal sign language of the Plains. These conventionalized gestures of the Plains sign language must of course be learned as a language is learned, for they are a kind of kinaesthetic ideograph, resembling written Chinese. The written Chinese may be "read" in the Japanese and the Korean and any number of mutually unintelligible spoken Chinese dialects; similarly, the sign language may be "read" in Comanche, in Cheyenne, or in Pawnee, all of which belong to different language families. The primitive Australian sign language was evidently of the conventionalized Plains type also, for it reproduced words, not mere letters (since of course they had no written language), but unfortunately little is known in detail of its mechanisms.

Like the writing of the Chinese, Occidental man has a number of ideographs, but they are sublinguistic and primarily *signs to action* or *expressions of action*. Thus, in the standard symbolism of cartoons, a "balloon" encircling print has signified *speaking* since at least the eighteenth century. Interestingly, in a Maya painting on a vase from Guatemala of pre-Columbian times, we have the same speech "balloons" enclosing ideographs representing what a chief and his vassal are saying, though what that is we do not know.[18] In Toltec frescoes speech is symbolized by foliated or noded crooks or scrolls, sometimes double, proceeding out of the mouths of human figures, although *what* is said is not indicated.[19] In the later Aztec codices written on wild fig-bark paper, speech is conventionalized by one or more little scrolls like miniature curled ostrich feathers coming out of the mouths of human beings, while motion or walking is indicated by footprints leading to where the person is now standing in the picture.[20] In American cartoons the same simple idea of footprints is also used. The ideograph of "sawing wood" indicates the action of *snoring* or *sleeping*. A light bulb with radial lines means that a "bright idea" has just occurred in the mind of the character above whose head it is written. While even children learn in time to understand these signs in context, no one would maintain that the electric-light "sign" could naturally be understood by an individual from another tribe than our own. Birds singing, a spiral, or a five-pointed star means unconsciousness or semi-consciousness through concussion. A dotted line, if curved, indicates the past trajectory of a moving object; if straight and from eye to object, the action of seeing. None of these visual aids to understanding is part of objective nature. Sweat drops symbolize surprise or dumfounding, although the physiology of this sign is thoroughly implausible. And]%!*/=‡?[& very often says the unspeakable, quite as ? signifies queries and ! surprise.

Many languages have *spoken* punctuation marks, which English grievously lacks. On the other hand, the speakers of English have a few *phonetic* "ideographs," at least two of which invite to action. An imitation of a kiss, loudly performed, summons a dog, if that dog understands this much of English. A bilateral clucking of the tongue adjures a horse to "giddyap," i.e., to commence moving or to move more smartly; and in some parts of the country at least, it has a secondary semantic employment in summoning barnyard fowl to their feeding. The dental-alveolar repeated clicking of the tongue, on the other hand, is not a symbolic ideophone to action, but a *moral comment* upon action, a strongly critical disapprobation largely confined in use to elderly females preoccupied with such moral commentary. These symbolic ideophones are used in no other way in our language; but in African Bushman and Hottentot languages, of course, these three sounds plus two others phonetically classified as "clicks" (as opposed to sonants like b, d, g, z and surds like p, t, k, s, etc.) are regularly employed in words like any other consonants. It is nonsense to suppose that dogs, horses, or chickens are equipped for "instinctive" understanding or response to these human-made sounds, as much as that speakers of English have an instinctive understanding of Hottentot and Bushman. Certainly the sounds used in the Lake Titicaca plateau to handle llamas are entirely different.[21]

Sublinguistic "language" can take a number of related forms. Among the Neolithic population of the Canary Islands there was a curious auxiliary "language" of conventionalized whistles, signals which could be understood at greater distances than mere spoken speech. On four bugle tones, differently configured, we can similarly order soldiers to such various actions as arising, assembling, eating, lowering a flag, and burying the dead. The drum language of West Africa, however, is more strictly linguistic than bugle calls. Many West African languages are tonemic, that is, they have pitch-accent somewhat like Chinese or Navaho. Drum language, therefore, by reproducing not only the rhythm, but also the tonal configurations of familiar phrases and sentences, is able to send messages of high semantic sophistication and complexity, as easily recognizable as our "Star-Spangled Banner" sung with rhythm and melody, but without words. The Kru send battle signals on multiple-pitched horns, but these are not conventional tunes like our bugle calls, but fully articulated sentences and phrases whose tonemic patterns they reproduce on an instrument other than the human vocal cords. The Morse and International telegraph codes and Boy Scout and Navy flag communication (either with hand semaphores or with strings of variously shaped and colored flags) are of course mere auditory or visual alphabets, tied down except for very minor conventionalized abbreviations to the *spelling* of a given language. (The advantages of a phonetic script, however, are very evident when it comes to sending messages via a Morselike code for Chinese, which is written in ideographs which have different phonetic pronunciations in different dialects; Japanese has some advantage in this situation over Chinese in that its ideographs are already cumbrously paralleled in *katakana* and *hiragana* writing, which is quasi-phonetic.) Deaf-and-dumb language, if it is the mere spelling of words, is similarly bound to an alphabet; but as it becomes highly conventionalized it approaches the international supralinguistic nature of the Plains Indian sign language. Of this order are the symbols of mathematics, the conventionalizations on maps for topography, the symbol language for expressing meteorological happenings on weather maps, and international flag signals for weather. Modern musical notation is similarly international: a supralinguistic system which orders in great detail what to do, and with what intensity, rhythm, tempo, timbre, and manner. Possibly the international nature of musical notation was influenced by the fact that medieval neume notation arose at a time when Latin was an international lingua franca, and also by the international nature of late feudal culture, rather than being an internationally-agreed-upon consensus of scientific symbolism. Based on the principles of musical notation, there have been several experimental attempts to construct an international system of dance notation, with signs to designate the position and motions of all parts of the body, with diacritical modifications to indicate tempo and the like. But while the motions of the classical ballet are highly stereotyped, they are semantically meaningless (unlike *natya* dancing in India and Ceylon, and Chinese and other Asiatic theatrics), so that this dance notation is mere *orders to action* like musical notation, with no other semantic content. Western dancing as an art form must appear insipid in its semantic emptiness to an Oriental who is used to articulate literary *meaning* in his dance forms. This is not to deny, however, that Occidental kinaesthetic language *may* be heavily imbued with great subtleties of meaning: the pantomime of the early Charlie Chaplin achieved at least a pan-European understanding and appreciation, while the implicit conventionalizations and stereotypes of Mickey Mouse (a psychiatrically most interesting figure!) are achieving currently an intercontinental recognition and enjoyment.

If all these various ways of *talking* be generously conceded to be purely cultural behavior, surely *walking*—although learned—is a purely physiological phenomenon since it is undeniably a panhuman trait which has brought about far-reaching functional and morphological changes in man as an animal. Perhaps it is, basically. And yet, there would seem to be clear evidence of cultural conditioning here. There is a distinct contrast in the gait of the Shans of Burma versus that of the hill people: the Kachins and the Palaungs keep time to each step by swinging the arms from side to side in front of the body in semicircular movements, but the Shans swing their arms in a straight line and do not bring the arms in front of the body. Experts among the American missionaries can detect the Shan from the Palaung and the Kachin, even though they are dressed in the same kinds of garment, purely from observing their respective gaits, and as surely as the character in a Mark Twain story detected a boy in girl's clothes by throwing a rat-chunker in his lap (the boy closed his legs, whereas a girl would spread her skirt). If an American Indian and an adult American male stride with discernible mechanical differences which may be imputed to the kinds of shoes worn and the varying hardness of the ground in woods or city, the argument will not convince those who know—but would find it hard to describe—that the Singhalese and the Chinese simply and unquestionably just do walk differently, even when both are barefooted. Amazonian tribes show marked sexual contrasts in their styles of walking; men place one foot directly in front of the other, toes straight forward, while women walk in a rather stilted, pigeon-toed fashion, the toes turned inward at an angle of some thirty degrees; it is regarded as a sign of power if the muscles of the thighs are made to come in contact with each other in walking. To pick a more familiar example, it is probable that a great many persons would agree with Sapir's contention that there does exist a peculiarly East European Jewish gait—a kind of kyphotic Ashkenazim shuffle or trudge—which is lost by the very first generation brought up in this country, and which, moreover, may not be observed in the Sephardic Jews of the Iberian Peninsula. Similar evidence comes from a recent news article: "Vienna boasts that it has civilized the Russians ... has taught them how to walk like Europeans (some Russians from the steppes had a curious gait, left arm and left foot swinging forward at the same time)."[22] The last parenthesis plays havoc with behavioristic notions concerning allegedly quadrupedal engrams behind our "normal" way of walking!

It is very clear that the would-be "natural" and "instinctive" gestures of actors change both culturally and historically. The back-of-the-hand-to-the-forehead and sideways-stagger of the early silent films to express intense emotion is expressed nowadays, for example, by making the already expressionless compulsive sullen mask of the actress one shade still more flat: the former technique of exaggerated panto-mime is no doubt related to the limitations of the silent film, the latter to the fact that even a raised eyebrow may travel six feet in the modern close-up. The "deathless acting" of the immortal Bernhardt, witnessed now in ancient movies, is scarcely more dated than the middle-Garbo style, and hardly more artificially stylized than Hepburn's or Crawford's. Indeed, for whatever reason, Bernhardt herself is reported to have fainted upon viewing her own acting in an early movie of *Camille*.[23] There are undoubtedly both fashions and individual styles in acting, just as there are in painting and in music composition and performance, and all are surely far removed from the instinctual gesture. The fact that each contemporary audience can receive the communication of the actor's gestures is a false argument concerning the "naturalness" of that gesture: behavior of the order of the "linguistic" (communication in terms of culturally agreed-upon arbitrary symbols) goes far beyond the purely verbal and the spoken.

That this is true can be decisively proved by a glance at Oriental theatrics. Chinese acting is full of stylized gestures which "mean" to the audience that the actor is stepping over the threshold into a house, mounting a horse, or the like; and these conventionalizations are just as stereotyped as the colors of the acting masks which indicate the formalized personalities of the stock characters, villains or heroes or supernaturals. In Tamil movies made in South India, the audience is quickly informed as to who is the villain and who the hero by the fact that the former wears Europeanized clothing, whereas the latter wears the native *dhoti*. But this is elementary: for the intricate *natya* dancing of India, the postural dance dramas of Bali, and the sacred *hula* of Polynesia are all telling articulated stories in detailed gestural language. That one is himself illiterate in this language, while even the child or the ignorant countryman sitting beside one on the ground has an avid and understanding enjoyment of the tableau, leaves no doubt in the mind that this *is* a gestural language and that there *are* sublinguistic kinaesthetic symbolisms of an arbitrary but learnable kind.

Hindu movies are extraordinarily difficult for the Occidental man to follow and to comprehend, not only because he must be fortified with much reading and knowledge to recognize mythological themes and such stereotypes as the *deus-ex-machina* appearance of Hanuman the monkey-god, but also because Americans are characteristically illiterate in the area of gesture language. The kinaesthetic "business" of even accomplished and imaginative stage actors like Sir Laurence Olivier and Ethel Barrymore is limited by the rudimentary comprehension of their audiences. Americans watch enthusiastically the muscular skills of an athlete in *doing* something, but they display a proud muckerism toward the dance as an art form which attempts to *mean* something. There are exceptions to this illiteracy, of course, notably among some psychiatrists and some ethnologists. Dr. H. S. Sullivan, for example, is known to many for his acute understanding of the postural tonuses of his patients. Another psychiatrist, Dr. E. J. Kempf, evidences in the copious illustrations of his "Psychopathology" a highly cultivated sense of the kinaesthetic language of tonuses in painting and sculpture, and can undoubtedly discover a great deal about a patient merely by glancing at him. The linguist, Dr. Stanley Newman, has a preternatural skill in recognizing psychiatric syndromes through the individual styles of tempo, stress, and intonation.[24] The gifted cartoonist, Mr. William Steig, has produced in *The Lonely Ones*, highly sophisticated and authentic drawings of the postures and tonuses of schizophrenia, depression, mania, paranoia, hysteria, and in fact the whole gamut of psychiatric syndromes. Among anthropologists, Dr. W. H. Sheldon is peculiarly sensitive and alert to the emotional and temperamental significance of constitutional tonuses.[25] I believe that it is by no means entirely an illusion that an experienced teacher can come into a classroom of new students and predict with some accuracy the probable quality of individual scholastic accomplishment—even as judged by other professors—by distinguishing the unreachable, unteachable *Apperceptions masse*-less sprawl of one student, from the edge-of-the-seat starved avidity and intentness of another. Likewise, an experienced lecturer can become acutely aware of the body language of his listeners and respond to it appropriately until the room fairly dances with communication and counter-communication, head-noddings, and the tenseness of listeners soon to be prodded into public speech.

The "body language" of speakers in face-to-face conversation may often be seen to subserve the purposes of outright linguistic communication. The peoples of Mediterranean origin have developed this to a high degree. In Argentina,[26] for example, the gesture language of the hands is called "ademanes" or "with the hands." Often the signs are in no need of language accompaniment: "What a crowd!" is stated by forming the fingers into a tight cluster and shaking them before you at eye level; "Do you take me for a sucker?" is asked by touching just beneath the eye with a finger, accompanying this with appropriate facial expressions of jeering or reproach as the case might be; and "I haven't the faintest idea" is indicated by stroking beneath the chin with the back of the palm. One Argentine gentleman, reflecting the common notion that *ademanes* have the same vulgarity and undignified nature as slang—appropriate only for youngsters or lower-class folk—nevertheless within five minutes of this statement, had himself twirled an imaginary moustache ("How swell!") and stroked one hand over the other, nodding his head wisely ("Ah ha! there's hanky-panky going on there somewhere!"). Argentine gesture-language is nearly as automatic and unconscious as spoken language itself, for when one attempts to collect a "vocabulary" of *ademanes*, the Argentine has to stop and think of situations first which recall the *ademanes* that "naturally" follow. The naturalness of at least one of these might be disputed by Americans, for the American hand-gesture meaning "go away" (palm out and vertical), elbow somewhat bent, arm extended vigorously as the palm is bent to a face-downward horizontal position, somewhat as a baseball is thrown and in a manner which could be rationalized as a threatened or symbolic blow or projectile-hurling) is the same which in Buenos Aires would serve to summon half the waiters in a restaurant, since it means exactly the opposite, "Come here!" When the Argentines use the word "mañana" in the familiar sense of the distant and improbable future, they accompany the word by moving the hand forward, palm down, and extending the fingers lackadaisically—a motion which is kinaesthetically and semantically related perhaps to the Argentine "come here!" since this symbolically *brings*, while "mañana" *pushes off*. Kissing the bunched fingertips, raising them from the mouth and turning the head with rolled or closed eyes, means "Wonderful! Magnificent!," basically perhaps as a comment or allusion to a lady, but in many remotely derived senses as well. "Wonderful!" may also be expressed by shaking one of the hands smartly so that the fingers make an audible clacking sound, similar to the snapping of the fingers, but much louder. But this gesture may signify pain as well as enjoyment, for if one steps on an Argentine's toes, he may shake his fingers as well as saying "Ai yai!" for "ouch!" The same gesture, furthermore, can be one of impatience, "Get a move on!" Were one to define this gesture semantically, then, in a lexicon of *ademanes*, it would have to be classified as a nondescript intensificative adverb whose predication is indicated by the context. In fast repartee an Argentine, even though he may not be able to get a word in edgewise, can make caustic and devastating critiques of the speaker and his opinions, solely through the subtle, timed use of *ademanes*.

A study of conventional gesture language (including even those obscene ones of the *mano cornuta*, the thumbed nose, the *mano fica*, the thumbnail snapped out from the point of the canine tooth, and so forth,[27] as well as those more articulated ones of the Oriental dance dramas), a study of the body language of constitutional types (the uncorticated, spinal-reflex spontaneity and *legato* feline quality of the musclebound athletosome, his body knit into rubbery bouncing tonuses even in repose; the collapsed colloid quality of the epicurean viscerotonic whose tensest tonus is at best no more than that of the chorion holding the yolk advantageously centered in the albumen of an egg, or the muscle habituated into a tendon supporting a flitch of bacon; and the multiple-vectored, tangled-stringiness of the complex "highstrung" cerebrotonic, whose conceptual alternatives and nuances of control are so intricately involved in his cortex as to inhibit action), and the study of psychiatric types (the Egyptian-statue grandeur and hauteur of the paranoiac's pose; the catatonic who offers his motor control to the outsider because he has withdrawn his own executive ego into an inner, autistic cerebral world and has left no one at the switchboard; the impermanent, varying, puppet-on-a-string, spastic tonuses of the compulsive neurotic which picture myotonically his ambivalence, his rigidities, and his perfectionism; the broken-lute despair of the depressive; and the distractable, *staccato*, canine, benzedrine-muscledness of the maniac)—all might offer us new insights into psychology, psychiatry, ethnology and linguistics alike.

NOTES

1. The notorious Massey murder in Hawaii arose from the fact that a native beach boy perhaps understandably mistook the Occidental "flirting" of a white woman for a *bona fide* sexual invitation. On the other hand, there are known cases which have ended in the death of American ethnographers who misread the cultural signs while in the field.

2. E. B. Holt, *Animal drive and the learning process* (New York, 1931), p. 111, and personal conversations.

The idea is originally Darwin's, I believe (Charles Darwin, *The expression of the emotions in man and animals*, New York, 1873), but he himself pointed out that the lateral shake of the head is by no means universally the sign of negation. Holt has further noted the interesting point that in a surprising number of languages, quite unrelated to each other, the word for "mother" is a variant of the sound "ma." One can collect dozens of such instances, representing all the continents, which would seem to confirm his conjecture: the genuinely universal "sucking reflex" which brings the lips into approximation (m), plus the simplest of the simple open vowel sounds (a), are "recognized" by the mother as referring to her when the baby first pronounces them; hence they become the lexical designation of the maternal parent. Although this phenomenon becomes a linguistic one, it is only on some such physiological basis that one can explain the recurrence of the identical sound combinations in wholly unrelated languages referring to the same person, the mother. But there is no absolute semantic association involved: one baby boy I have observed used "mama" both to connote and to denote older persons of either sex.

3. A. H. Landor, *Alone with the Hairy Ainu* (London, 1893), pp. 6, 233-234.

4. W. W. Skeat and C. O. Blagden, *Pagan races of the Malay Peninsula* (London, 1906; 2 vols).

5. Otto Klineberg, *Race differences* (New York, 1935), p. 282.

6. Geoffrey Gorer, *Africa dances* (New York, 1935), p. 10.

7. Lafcadio Hearn, The Japanese smile, in *Glimpses of unfamiliar Japan* (New York, 1894; 2 vols.), quoted in Klineberg, *op. cit.*

8. *Report on the Cambridge expedition to the Torres Straits*, ed. A. C. Haddon (Cambridge, 1904; 5 vols.), IV, p. 306; Thomas Whiffen, *The North West Amazons* (London, 1905), p. 259.

9. R. Hitchcock, The Ainos of Yezo, in *Papers on Japan*, pp. 464-465. See also Landor, *op. cit.*, pp. 6, 233-234.

10. J. Perkins, Journal of a tour from Oroomish to Mosul, through the Koordish Mountains, and a visit to the ruins of Nineveh, *Journal of the American Oriental Society*, 1851, *2*, 101; Charles Hose & William MacDougall, *The pagan tribes of Borneo* (London, 1912; 2 vols.), *1*, 124-125.

11. A. R. Radcliffe-Brown, *The Andaman Islanders* (Cambridge, 1922), p. 117 and p. 74 n. 1.

12. John Turnbull, *A voyage round the world* (London, 1813), pp. 301-302.

13. Gorer, *op. cit.*, p. 38. Cf. Hollis, *The Masai, their language and folklore* (Oxford, 1905), pp. 284-287; E. Torday & T. A. Joyce, *Notes ethnographiques sur les peuples communément appelés Bakuba, ainsi que sur les peuplades apparentées, les Bushonga* (Brussels, 1910), pp. 233-234, 284, *et passim*. West Africans have developed the etiquette and protocol of greeting to a high degree, adjusting it to sex, age, relative rank, relationship degrees, and the like. Probably there is more than a trace of this ceremoniousness surviving in American Negro greetings in the South.

14. Klineberg, *op. cit.*, pp. 286-287, citing J. Lubbock, *Prehistoric times* (New York, 1872); E. Best, *The Maori* (Wellington [N. Z.], 1924, 2 vols.); R. H. Lowie, *Are we civilized?* (New York, 1929); and A. C. Hollis, *The Masai, their language and folklore* (Oxford, 1905), p. 315.

15. *Chin P'ing Mei* (Shanghai, n. d.), Introduction by Arthur Waley. The sixteenth-century Chinese also had the expressions to act "with seven hands and eight feet" for awkwardness, and "to sweat two handfuls of anxiety."

16. S. M. Shirokogoroff, *Social organization of the Manchus* (Extra Vol. III, North China Branch, Royal Asiatic Society, Shanghai, 1924), pp. 122-123.

17. M. C. Kahn, Notes on the Saramaccaner Bush Negroes of Dutch Guiana, *Amer. Anthrop.*, 1929, *31*, 473.

18. George C. Vaillant, *The Aztecs of Mexico* (Garden City, N. Y., 1941), plate 7, top.

19. *Ibid.*, plate 24.

20. *Ibid.*, plates 42, 57, 61.

21. Weston La Barre, *The Aymara Indians of the Lake Titicaca Plateau*, Memoir 68, Amer. Anthrop. Assn. (Menasha, Wisconsin, 1947). All the tribes of the Provincia Oriental of Ecuador had the "cluck of satisfaction" (Alfred Simpson, *Travels in the wilds of Ecuador and exploration of the Putumayo River*, 1886, p. 94), which among the tribes of the Issa-Japura rivers is a "sign of assent and pleasure" (Whiffen, *op. cit.*, p. 249).

22. Paula Hoffman, Twilight in the Heldenplatz, *Time*, June 9, 1947, *49*:23, 31. A related kind of motor habit—which is of course conscious—was that of the Plains Indian men who wore the buffalo robe "gathered . . . about the person in a way that emphasized their action or the expression of emotion" (*Handbook of American Indians north of Mexico*, Bulletin 30, Bureau Amer. Ethnol., Washington, D. C., 1907-1910; 2 vols.). For the Amazonians, see Whiffen, *op. cit.*, p. 271.

23. Maurice Bardèche and Robert Brasillach, *The history of motion pictures* (New York, 1938), p. 130.

24. Stanley S. Newman, Personal symbolism in language patterns, *Psychiatry*, 1939, *2*, 177-184; Cultural and psychological features in English intonation, *Trans. N. Y. Acad. Sci.*, 1944, ser. II, *7*, 45-54; (with Vera G. Mather), Analysis of spoken language of patients with affective disorders, *Amer. J. Psychiat.*, 1938, *94*, 913-942; Further experiments in phonetic symbolism, *Amer. J. Psychol.*, 1933, *45*, 53-57; Behavior patterns in linguistic structure, a case history, in *Language, culture and personality, Essays in honor of Edward Sapir* (Menasha, Wis., 1931), pp. 94-106. The Witoto and Bororo have a curious motor habit: "When an Indian talks he sits down—no conversation is ever carried on when the speakers are standing unless it is a serious difference of opinion under discussion; nor, when he speaks, does the Indian look at the person addressed, any more than the latter watches the speaker. Both look at some outside objects. This is the attitude also of the Indian when addressing more than one listener, so that he appears to be talking to some one not visibly present." A story-teller turns his back on the listener and talks to the wall of the hut (Whiffen, *op. cit.*, p. 254).

25. W. H. Sheldon, *The varieties of temperament* (New York & London, 1942). The argument of one variety of athletosome or somatotonic scientist that Sheldon is unable or unconcerned to muscle his findings into manageable, manipulable statistical forms wherewith to bludgeon and compel the belief of the unperceiving, is of course peculiarly irrelevant. The psychiatrist soaked in clinical experience is similarly helpless in his didactic relations with a public which either has not, or cannot, or will not see what he has repeatedly observed clinically.

26. Arthur Daniels, Hand-made repartee, New York *Times*, October 5, 1941.

27. The only place I have seen this discussed recently is in an article by Sandor Feldman, The blessing of the Kohenites, *American Imago*, 1941, *2*, 315-318. In the same periodical is an exquisitely sensitive interpretation of one person's interpretation of the signs of the zodiac in terms of positions and tonuses of the human body (Doris Webster, The origin of the signs of the zodiac, *ibid.*, 1940, *1*, 31-47). Other papers, of the few which could be cited with relevance to the present problem, would include: Macdonald Critchley, *The language of gesture* (New York, 1939); G. W. Allport and P. E. Vernon, *Studies in expressive movement* (New York, 1933); F. C. Hayes, Should we have a dictionary of gestures? *Southern Folk-Lore Quarterly*, 1940, *4*, 239-245; Felix Deutsch, Analysis of postural behavior, *Psychoanal. Quart.*, 1947, *16*, 195-213; Paul Schilder, *The image and appearance of the human body*, Psyche Monographs (London, 1935); Th. Pear, Suggested parallels between speaking and clothing, *Acta Psychol.*, Hague, 1935, *1*, 191-201; J. C. Flugel, On the mental attitude to present-day clothing, *Brit. J. med. Psychol.*, 1929, *9*: 97; La Meri, *Gesture language of the Hindu dance* (New York, c. 1940); Rudolf von Laban, *Laban's dance notations* (New York, c. 1928).

BETTY B. LANHAM

1956. Aspects of Child Care in Japan: Preliminary Report. Not published previously.

Discussions of Japanese "national character" sometimes have stressed the son's domination of his mother, even to maternal endurance of beating and abuse. It has been alleged that Japanese children never are punished, save for the severe social disapproval encountered after they have grown beyond the indulgent years of infancy. Again, it is alleged that Japanese babies undergo rigorous toilet training before physiological maturation has reached the point of voluntary control; from this supposed fact explanations are offered to account for the cruelty and reckless abandon in battle manifested by Japanese soldiers (cf. footnote 1 in the following article for sources).

Miss Lanham spent more than a year in Wakayama, Japan, investigating family behavior, especially among lacquer craftsmen, in a nearby city, and testing allegations that have appeared in print about Japanese character. The sifting of data and organization of her report are incomplete; nevertheless she generously provided summaries of part of her statistical data for inclusion here. Her findings may be compared with those of the Norbecks (elsewhere in this book), who observed a fishing village in another part of Japan, and with other discussions of Japanese personality. The data that follow are limited to one locality and to a single postwar year. No claim is made respecting other times and places. Obviously, Japanese habits of living are changing rapidly. Women's magazines have provided an entire generation with scientific and unscientific advice about the rearing of children, and "baby books" are found in every home. There is reason to bewail the lack of data on child-rearing of a generation ago.

ASPECTS OF CHILD CARE IN JAPAN: PRELIMINARY REPORT[1]

Betty B. Lanham

Voluminous data on child care in Japan were obtained from a questionnaire submitted to parents in the city of Kainan (pop. 35,000), located fifty miles south of Ōsaka. The present paper includes a brief resume of early tabulations and significant findings, together with detailed information concerning certain controversial issues. Japanese child-rearing practices have been discussed widely;[2] this paper is confined to statistical tabulations with interpretative comment.

The questionnaires, in Japanese, were distributed through public schools, in envelopes bearing the investigator's name and return address. Respondents were instructed not to sign the completed forms; individuals were not identifiable in the tabulation. To insure completeness of coverage, teachers checked each pupil's name when he returned the sealed envelope. The many families who answered the questionnaires cooperated generously despite the twenty-one pages of inquiry.

Each household was asked to complete three forms: one covering the children of the household, one covering the father's own childhood, and the other the mother's childhood. Of 500 questionnaires, 449 were returned. Of these, 441 gave information about children, 433 were filled out for the childhood of the adult female, and 414 were filled out for the childhood of the adult male. All respondents claimed Japanese nationality for themselves and for both parents. In only three families was the youngest child over nine years of age.

The accompanying tables present numbers of responses in the indicated categories. The term "respondents" refers to the number of forms on which an answer was entered, exclusive of questions left blank. Totals therefore do not reach the possible number of 449. Entries under the headings "Father" and "Mother" include nine male and nine female respondents who filled out forms in lieu of parents. Some tables are based on preliminary tabulations made by hand and do not include all of the returns.[3]

For any given aspect of child training, the range and distribution of variations are rather extraordinary (cf. Tables 1 and 2). Moreover, many contingencies and correlations that seemed probable logically, do not appear. For example: many children who are punished by use of moxa[4] are not those whose parents were punished in this way, broadly speaking; the number of children in a family is not appreciably contingent upon income or occupation of parents; and the low income group frequently is closer to the high income group than to the middle —in ways of toilet training, family member held in highest affection, and extent of promise fulfilment.

The data nevertheless manifest internal consistency. For example, returns from three different sections of Kainan City show closely similar answers. Again, fulfilment of promises made to children bears an inverse relation to extent of teasing. On the whole, punishment experienced by parents in their childhood (excepting incidence of moxa cautery) closely resembles that meted out to present-day children.

Most of the tables are based on families as units. Data were tabulated in terms of whole families, then in terms of the number of children involved; comparison of the distributions shows almost identical results (e.g., Table 2). Consequently the tables do not give the data in terms of the number of children affected, although the data can be organized to do so.

Ages of weaning appear in Table 1; the figures present family averages.[5] The earliest reports of the beginning of weaning fall between three months and eight months; the lowest age for completion

TABLE 1

REPORTS OF FAMILY PRACTICES WITH
RESPECT TO WEANING

Age class* yr.-mo.	Weaning Began no. of families†	Weaning Completed no. of families
0-3 to 0-8	17	—
0-9 to 1-2	76	27
1-3 to 1-8	108	90
1-9 to 2-2	70	87
2-3 to 2-8	36	49
2-9 to 3-2	23	34
3-3 to 3-8	10	8
3-9 to 4-2	8	9
4-3 to 4-8	4	6
4-9 to 5-2	—	2
5-3 to 5-8	2	1
5-9 to 6-2	—	—
6-3 to 6-8	1	1
TOTAL (respondents)	355	314

*Some persons may have used the older "Japanese" form of reckoning age in spite of instructions to the contrary.

†Differing ages for the various children within one family were averaged for tabulation purposes.

of weaning falls between nine months and one year and two months. For both initiation and completion of weaning, the highest ages cited are between six years three months and six years eight months. In both categories—initiation and completion—the modal age class is the same, viz., between one year three months and one year eight months. These figures do not reveal the precise duration of the weaning process, but they suggest that the interval between beginning and completion of weaning is less than six months.

Since a child who for all practical purposes has been weaned may return occasionally to the mother's breast, the interpretation of "completion" by respondents is open to question. Reasons of superstition and convenience—perhaps of affection and of good health practices—govern the beginning and completion of weaning. Some mothers say that continued nursing prevents another pregnancy. Age at weaning might be expected to differ from American practice: nursing a baby in public is inherent in the folkways, and a Japanese mother finds enjoyment and entertainment in her baby in lieu of activities outside the home. On the other hand, Japan's high birth rate may decrease the age at which weaning otherwise might occur.

Data on toilet training appear in Table 2, which gives the number of respondents by age intervals for the beginning of toilet training, the first punishment for mishaps, and the "age at which mishaps are not supposed to occur or at which they occur on rare occasions."[6] In all three categories the minimum age entry is between two and eight months. The latest entry under "Began" appears in the class whose midpoint is five years eleven months; "First punished," six years five months; "Completion," eight years five months. Each of the stages in toilet training shows considerable age variation.

With respect to toilet training it is especially difficult to ascertain the respondents' interpretations of ages at beginning, completion, and even of punishment. A mother may hold her baby over a toilet or gutter at regular intervals even though she is quite aware that the child is too young to control his physical functions or to inform her of need. The idea is to condition the child gradually to proper procedure and perhaps to save diaper washing. Punishment may be intended to indicate disapproval and not designed to hurt. Some children unavoidably wet the bed at night even though sphincter controls during the waking hours have long been established; mothers of these children may have overstated the age at which mishaps are not supposed to occur.

Methods of training children in toilet habits vary greatly. The words *shi, shikko, unn,* and *unko,* are often spoken during the act. In time the child comes to use these words to notify the mother of his needs. In other instances the child is not "trained" until able to go by himself. At this age the mother may remind him at frequent intervals. In Japan

TABLE 2

REPORTS OF FAMILY PRACTICES WITH RESPECT TO TOILET TRAINING

Toilet training: Age classes*	Began				Child 1st punished no. families	Age at which mishap is not expected no. families
	Families no.	%	Children no.	%		
yr.-mo.						
0-2	3	1%	8	1%	—	—
0-3 to 0-8	55	17	183	18	1	1
0-9 to 1-2	73	22	231	22	26	6
1-3 to 1-8	57	17	179	17	43	30
1-9 to 2-2	53	16	162	16	72	62
2-3 to 2-8	27	8	88	9	21	50
2-9 to 3-2	33	10	107	10	57	43
3-3 to 3-8	11	3	27	3	11	22
3-9 to 4-2	10	3	30	3	35	47
4-3 to 4-8	1	0	4	0	4	7
4-9 to 5-2	2	1	7	1	19	24
5-3 to 5-8	1	0	2	0	6	4
5-9 to 6-2	1	0	3	0	6	16
6-3 to 6-8	—	—	—	—	2	1
6-9 to 7-2	—	—	—	—	—	5
7-3 to 7-8	—	—	—	—	—	—
7-9 to 8-2	—	—	—	—	—	4
8-3 to 8-8	—	—	—	—	—	1
TOTAL (respondents)	324 (100%)		1031 (100%)		303	323

*Some persons may have used the older "Japanese" form of reckoning age in spite of instructions to the contrary.

the design of toilet facilities reduces the difficulty of the child's un-aided performance.

This is not to contend that punishment is never severe. On a sample of a hundred forms for children, two report moxa cautery; one of these began punishment at age one. Six, however, reply that no punishment was inflicted; nineteen say that they merely reprove the child. Five parents provide rewards for proper behavior. Twenty-seven report a slap on the buttocks, six pinching, and three spanking. Thirteen speci-fy threats of various sorts including illness or the use of terms of re-proof connoting uncleanliness. Where indicated the age range for each form of punishment is considerable—from one to five years in the case of slapping. Other methods are used but less frequently mentioned.

Respondents were asked to list the first things they taught their chil-dren to do and not to do. Space for six items was provided under each question. The answers on a sample of a hundred questionnaires follow on page 571.

Ten-months-old baby stays with mother as she works.

Japanese infancy and childhood. *Photos by Betty B. Lanham.*
See also "Child Training in a Japanese Fishing Community"
by Edward and Margaret Norbeck, page 651.

The baby bathes with adults.

Mother and month-old baby.   Father teaches daughter *O-Bon* dance.

Midwife bathing week-old baby.   Sister caresses ten-months-old brother.

LIST OF PARENTS' ANSWERS TO: "What are the first things you taught your child to do other than walk or talk? Examples: forms of etiquette, sitting position, etc."*

Manners and courtesies: (how to perform, as well as occasions on which to do so)

Properly to sit, stand, bow, and eat

Express gratitude for something the child is given

Traditional hand position when receiving anything

Greet a visitor

When to visit another's house

Bow before and after meals

Properly to give a good answer; how to answer "yes" and "no"

Speak quietly

Eat everything that is served

Appearance and cleanliness:

How to wash face and limbs

Wash hands before meals, face in the morning, and hands when he returns home

Keep one's limbs clean

Wipe feet when one returns home

Brush teeth

Blow his nose cleanly always

Comb his hair

Discipline and training:

Toilet habits

Parents' bidding

Go on errands

Help mother

Come home at mealtime

Study hard

Tell everything that happens in school each day

Return things to their places

Place things neatly

Treat various articles carefully

Arrange *zori* (sandals) in the doorway when returning home

Cautions in traffic

Go to sleep alone

Play alone with toys and picture books

Go to bed and rise early

Worship gods

Put one's hands together in worship

Skills

A-baba (patting on the mouth)

Choncho (clapping of hands)

---

*Based on a sample of a hundred questionnaires.

O-tsumu-tenten (patting of head with one's hands)

Kaiguri (Simple game: elbows flexed, hands in front of chest, turn them as if pulling in a rope)

Roll over on stomach

Crawl

Build blocks

Clap one's hands

Beckoning

Wave hand *Bai-Bai* (Japanese spelling and pronunciation for the English "bye-bye")

Names of things—flowers, foods, animals

Names and faces of family members

Words: (in Japanese)
   thank you; mother and father; please

Words to say:
   Preceding and following a meal
   When entering and leaving the house
   In greeting and bidding farewell to someone

The meaning of "come here" (in Japanese)

The words, *banzai* and *gutto-bai* ("good bye")

Distinguish trains, streetcars, automobiles and other vehicles

Distinguish colors

Distinguish sounds, one from another

Songs and music

Dance to music

Count

The child's own name and address

Picture books, Paper folding, Drawing, Reading, Writing

Simple characters and figures as the child asks

How to hold and use a pen, brush, spoon

How a bowl should be held in the hands

Wear *zori*

Independence—to stand when he falls, to arrange his toys neatly by himself

Behavior toward others:
   Friendliness
   Select good friends
   Offer toys and sweets to others
   Play harmoniously with others
   Distinguish another's property

LIST OF PARENTS' ANSWERS TO: "What are the things you taught your child *not* to do? Examples: wet his clothing, go barefooted outside the house, etc."*

Cautions: *Do not*
   Touch anything hot or dangerous

---

*Based on a sample of a hundred questionnaires.

Play in a dangerous place
Go far away alone
Go into the street
Go without a hat in the summer
Play with cutlery
Play with fire
Go out without giving notice

Cleanliness and health measures: *Do not*
Soil one's limbs
Enter the house with soiled feet
Let your nose run
Put your fingers in your mouth
Put a toy in the mouth
Sit down and play on the ground
Pick up soiled things in the street
Eat filth
Go into the rain without an umbrella
Drink water
Soil one's clothes when urinating
Wet the bed
Urinate at the gate

Relations to others: *Do not*
Quarrel
Envy (want anything a child has or is holding)
Make another child cry
Say spiteful things to another
Ill treat another child
Hit or beat anyone with hand or stick
Have a vicious thought
Trouble others
Trouble others when walking
Do mischief to a stranger
Take another's toy
Bring home another's property
Throw stones

Discipline and manners: *Do not*
Oppose the teachings of your parents
Answer or talk back
Touch books or anything that is set neatly one on top of another
Scribble on the walls
Break anything
Tear the paper on the *shoji* (sliding inner doors)
Throw or tear anything
Touch paints or india ink
Play in a disorderly manner
Get into mischief

Be naughty
Eat sweets without permission
Act peevish in front of a shop to get something
Tell a lie
Play without clothes
Suck your mother's breast
Waste money
Fail to study hard
Lie down after eating
Tumble down the veranda
Get your head off the pillow
Eat at another's house
Confuse the outside with the inside of the house

Mentioned most frequently on a sample of fifty forms were: (beginning with the first, given in order of frequency):

TO DO: Toilet habits, polite sitting position, eat properly, manners, wash hands before meals, use chopsticks, say *arigatō* ("thank you"), words to say preceding and following a meal, return things to their places.

NOT TO DO: Play outside without footgear, soil clothes with urine, quarrel, let food fall from the table, envy (want things others have), throw stones.

Following the question of what children are taught not to do, parents were asked the means of obtaining compliance. On a sampling of fifty forms there were 29 reports of explaining to the child the real reason why he should refrain. "Irrational" explanations consisted of twelve forms of threat, six of which were that sickness would ensue. Four words that convey a previously established derogatory meaning to the child, were used: bad child, unsightly, dirty, quarrel. Verbal reproval was mentioned five times, reward twice. Eight acted to prevent the desire to misbehave from arising; e.g. one mother provided sweets in the afternoon so that the child might not be tempted to buy unsanitary candies.

On other more direct questions respondents were to indicate with a mark the use or non-use of a given practice. These data appear in Tables 3 and 4. With respect to forms of punishment the number of questions left blank increases as the percent. of affirmative answers decreases. Perhaps respondents tended to ignore the question when a practice did not exist, as may have been the case with punishment by deprival, or they may have not wished to admit the existence of a practice, or both. The latter explanation seems more likely for punishment by embarrassing the child. As the figures were reported for children, threat and slapping are as high as 90%, deprival and shame a little over 40%, and embarrassment 12%. Fathers' reports of punishment administered to them range from 3 to 15% higher than for mothers: for children 1% to 16% higher than for fathers except for deprival. Under this category the figure for fathers is 9% higher than for children. Although parents' answers indicate some difference in the treatment of boys and girls, it is not necessary to compare data for the two sexes to show that children now receive more varieties of punishment than did their parents, or that more children are being punished, or both. Faulty reporting, of course, is possible. Respondents may have failed to recall certain forms of punishment administered to themselves.

TABLE 3

PERCENT AFFIRMING USE OF GENERAL TYPES OF PUNISHMENT IN THE PAST UPON THEMSELVES AND NOW UPON THEIR CHILDREN*

Form of punishment	% affirming practice		
	CHILD	MOTHER	FATHER
Threat	93%	84%	88%
Slap†	90%	62%	74%
Deprival	41%	35%	50%
Shame	45%	20%	31%
Embarrass	12%	8%	11%

*Data on this table were taken from a sample of 200 questionnaires rather than from 449. For each category under *Child, Mother & Father*, percent represents the number affirming use of the practice, of the total reporting—a possible 200. The actual number of respondents ranged from 117 to 186.
†Includes spanking.

Within categories under the main headings mentioned above (Table 4), the same general trend is evident: maximum punishment for the children, next that meted out to the father as a child, and thirdly the mother's childhood experience. This is true of use of a parent or religious deity as a threat, of slapping the buttocks or other part of the body,[7] and of ridiculing the child or making him feel he will bring shame upon himself or family. There are three exceptions: deprival by isolation is reported least frequently for children; deprival of pleasures is higher for children than mothers but less than for fathers; frightening by ghosts apparently is on the decrease with a younger generation.

Answers on a sample of a hundred questionnaires as to the kind of religious deity feared were Buddha, tutelary god, ancestors, sun god, Inari, Tenjin, Yama, and just the word "gods." The latter term as used by parents is rather indefinite and vague; no specific god is intended. The greater number of answers falls under this latter category. Some mothers told their children, the gods see and know everything and will punish you. The child is made to fear that divine judgment will

TABLE 4

PERCENT AFFIRMING USE OF SPECIFIED FORMS OF PUNISHMENT IN
THE PAST UPON THEMSELVES AND NOW UPON THEIR CHILDREN*

Form of punishment	CHILD	% affirming practice MOTHER	FATHER
Frightened by threat of:			
Religious deity	47%	40%	44%
Ghost	24%	27%	34%
Parents	90%	79%	81%
Physical punishment by slapping:			
Buttocks†	85%	55%	63%
Body‡	51%	39%	50%
Deprival:			
Of pleasures	28%	23%	35%
By isolation	23%	24%	31%
Shame will be brought on the			
Child	43%	18%§	27%§
Family	18%	13%	17%
Embarrass by:			
Ridicule	10%	6%	8%

*Data on this table were taken from a sample of 200 questionnaires rather than from 449. For each category under *Child, Mother,* and *Father,* percent represents the number affirming use of the practice, of the total reporting—a possible 200. The actual number of respondents ranged from 98 to 175.

†Includes spanking.

‡The probable interpretation of this category by respondents was slapping on a part of the body other than the buttocks.

§The explanation "(people will dislike you)" was added to this question as it appeared on the parents' forms but not on the children's form.

bring illness, injury, or stupidity. Other threats were of the Image of Buddha, and that the child would be put in inferno.

Cited as ghost figures were *yurei, obake,* fox, devil, thunder god, badger, cat, dog, wolf, long-nosed goblin, and the dead. According to Japanese legends ghosts of animals are thought upon occasion to assume human form, appeal to the weakness of an individual, and then at the propitious moment revert to their ghostly form leaving the victim contaminated by contact. One answer given by parents as to what they feared most as a child was a lonely or dark road. On such occasions these ghost forms are thought to appear. *Yurei* generally refers to a soul of the dead which could not enter nirvana and thus remains on earth. *Obake* covers both animal and human forms. The thunder god is said to be fond of stealing the human navel. To the child this is presented in the form of a threat. (An additional symbolism may be significant here since children are sometimes told that a baby is born by bursting forth from the mother's stomach or navel.) One parent's unsolicited response to the question on ghost-threats was, "I never let the children have fears of imaginary beings."

On a list of living persons used as a threat to the child (Table 5), the answer "parents" appears most frequently. It should be noted that in some families the mother, and not the father, is used as a threat although the latter is the more frequently mentioned. Often threat is contingent upon which parent is reproving the child. Each uses the absent spouse.

TABLE 5

INDIVIDUALS USED AS A THREAT TO THE CHILD: CHILDREN'S AND PARENTS' EXPERIENCE* (no. of citations)†

Threatened of	CHILD	MOTHER	FATHER
Mother	6	7	7
Father	38	24	18
Both parents	17	15	15
Other	33	22	32
TOTAL (citations)	94	68	72

*Data on this table were taken from a sample of 100 questionnaires rather than from 449. Figures have not been verified from the original questionnaire with as much care as in other tables.

†The first three categories—*Mother, Father, Both parents*—are mutually exclusive but a respondent who answered for one of these three might also have designated one or more persons under *Other*. All citations have been included.

Other individuals used in threats were grandmother, grandfather, older brother or sister, uncle, teacher, policeman, kidnapper, beggar, woodsman, lunatic, ragman, and neighbors. Aside from parents, the teacher was most frequently mentioned. Answers to a question on education reveal that the form of threat experienced by parents and by present day children is somewhat different. Previously the parent stood in awe and fear of this learned person who was both stern and severe in discipline. Today the child is respectful but not reverential. He admires and sometimes idolizes this symbol of new learning and freedom. Hardly would he wish to be belittled in the sight of such a person. A child in kindergarten may simply be told that his teacher will not like him if he does such a thing. Threats with respect to a beggar or lunatic generally refer to a specific person in the neighborhood by whom the child is told he will be taken away. A child may also be told that a policeman will take him away or that he will be punished by him.

Respondents listed the following pleasures of which they or their children were, or are deprived: candy, new clothes, eating between meals, a meal, reading books, magazines, having books bought for them, going out to play or playing with friends, seeing a moving picture, a promised reward, toys, being bought toys or a desired article, having a wish fulfilled, pocket money, attending a festival, sunbathing, playing house, and being taken on a trip, outing, or a visit.

Forms of isolation were given as being placed in a closet, a storehouse, a room—sometimes darkened—and a barn. Two mothers report having been shut out of the house, and one father the same treatment at night. Through interviews, not questionnaires, it was learned that the child is sometimes put in a *futon* box, the old style container of sleeping mats and quilts.

Although the percentage of children now being punished by slapping may not have been as high as the 90% indicated by respondents on Table 3, it is quite certain that well over half used this form of punishment—inferred from the fact that 323 of a possible 441 respondents report use of the hand in punishment. Two hundred forty-seven persons apply the hand to the buttocks.

The number of citations of instruments used on respondents' children and bodily regions to which applied appears on Table 6. In order of frequency, regions other than buttocks were back, head, legs, face, and hand. One each mentions use of a stick and flipping a finger on the child's forehead; four specify pinching.

Information on punishment administered in toilet training indicates that spanking is not too frequent as compared with a slap on the buttocks. The fact that translators mistakenly used the categories "slap on the buttocks" and "slap on the body" instead of the intended "slap" and "spank," also would suggest that the practice is not too common.

As judged from parents' reported experience, slapping is definitely on the increase, greater than that administered to either parent with a slight preference now being shown for the bodily region of the buttocks. Table 7 would seem to indicate that slapping the buttocks is being done increasingly by mothers instead of fathers.

Punishment of children is more often identical to that of mothers than fathers with respect to instrument used and bodily regions to which applied—46% as compared with 38%.

Tabulations from a sample of a hundred questionnaires show the range in age and frequency of slapping to be quite similar to what might be expected in the United States. Ages at which administered range from two to thirteen years, extended to older ages when applied to parts of the body other than buttocks. The frequency ranges from three times a day to once a year with modal points at once or twice a week, month, or year.

The use of moxa is not decreasing, perhaps increasing with the younger generation. Seventeen per cent of the parents report use of

TABLE 6

Instruments Used in Punishment of Respondents' Children and Bodily Regions to Which Applied

Where applied	No. of citations*	Instrument	No. of citations*
Buttocks	248	Hand	323
Head	26	Stick	1
Face	12	Forefinger‡	1
Back	56	Pinch	4
Legs	14	Other	—
Hand	11		
Forehead	2	TOTAL (citations)	329
Fingers	1		
Body†	12	TOTAL (respondents)	325
Other	12		
TOTAL (citations)	394		
TOTAL (respondents)	322		

*Where one respondent indicated more than one instrument or region to which applied, all cited are included.

†Includes both indefinite replies and answers specifying "anywhere on the body."

‡Snapped somewhere on the body.

TABLE 7

Reports on Individuals by Whom Punishment is Administered to Children and Was Administered to Parents* (no. of citations)†

Adminis-tered by	Slapped: CHILD	MO.	FA.	On other part of body CHILD	MO.	FA.
Mother	34	15	9	8	10	7
Father	13	11	13	9	6	15
Both parents	13	4	7	7	—	3
Other	2	3	5	1	3	3
TOTAL (citations)	62	33	34	25	19	28

*Data on this table were taken from a sample of 100 questionnaires rather than from 449. Figures have not been verified from the original questionnaires with the same care as on other tables.

†The first three categories—*Mother, Father, Both parents*—are mutually exclusive but a respondent who answered under one of these might also have designated one or more persons under *Other*. All citations have been included.

moxa upon their children, as compared with 14% for the mothers, and 15% for the fathers. About half the respondents who report that moxa was used upon themselves, report its use on their children; this is also true when it was used on both adult family members (Table 8).

Increased use on the children is accounted for by the number of parents on whom it was not used who now apply it to their children. It should be noted that use of moxa, to the parent and sometimes the child, is something more than a severe form of punishment; generally regarded as a medical treatment, there is the implication of a cure for ill behavior as well as for sickness.

TABLE 8

Use of Moxa on Children Compared With Parents'
Own Experience*

CHILD	MOTHER		FATHER		MO. & FA.	
	used	not used	used	not used	used	not used
Used	13	15	11	28	4	11
Not used	14	144	24	166	5	103
TOTAL (respondents)	27	159	35	194	9	114

*Of the 53 reporting past use of moxa on either the father or mother of a family, 38% report its use on the children.

On a sample of a hundred questionnaires there are relatively few answers to the questions of what the parent would say or do in case masturbation or sex play were discovered among his own children. Action taken with respect to girls did not differ substantially from that for boys. Where answers for the two sexes are combined, the results are: 19 threats of forthcoming sickness or disease; 14 other threats, scoldings, or warnings; 10 admonishments that the behavior was dirty or unclean; and others less frequently mentioned. To the question on sex play, answers were higher for threat, scold, or warn, than for a threatened illness; none mentioned that it was dirty. In some cases the warning was severe such as a threat of disowning the offspring. For small children, the answer was sometimes "do nothing," "not punish because he is too young to understand," but instead instruct him, or divert the child's attention.

Affirmative answers to respondents' stimulation of their baby's genitals appeared on seven of 441 forms. Purposes for the practice were given as quieting crying, inducing sleep, provoking laughter, and making him cease sucking the breast. All affirmative responses were from parents in the middle and upper income brackets. It is possible that some of lower income simply did not admit this form of behavior. It should be noted, however, that many responses were vehemently negative.

In summary, two assumed forms of child-rearing in Japan would stand contradicted by data that appear above. Some writers allege that

Japanese mothers acquiesce without retaliation to physical abuse by their young sons. Results on Tables 5 and 6 show that in a majority of families the mother as well as (or instead of) the father, is used as a threat to enforce proper behavior on the part of her young son. In slightly under half the families reporting, the mother punishes by slapping the boy.

The wide range and distribution of practices with respect to toilet training could hardly be interpreted as meaning that in Japan punishment or completion occur at an unduly early age. In a like manner, the forms of punishment administered are not indicative of severity.

In Japan forms of child training vary so greatly that any attempt to generalize about adult behavior on this basis is open to question. Probably such variability might normally be expected in a civilized nation, particularly among a literate people in contact with the outside world and as highly adaptive as the Japanese.

For data to be meaningful there must be a voluntary or unconscious comparison of practices in Japan with those that exist among another people. Comments that follow represent the writer's unsystematized observations of similarities and dissimilarities between forms of training in the United States and information about Japan appearing above. Of course, valid comparison would necessitate circulation of a comparable questionnaire in this country.

Toilet training may not be too different from what occurs in the United States. Weaning is much more protracted or deferred. As reported there is perhaps more similarity than dissimilarity with respect to punishment. American children are threatened by use of parents and ghosts, slapped, deprived of pleasures, placed in isolation and sometimes ridiculed. They are more frequently spanked. Moxa is not used. Punishment by God is not generally threatened but they are warned of his disapproval. The American child is less often shamed and practically never with respect to disgrace of his family.

Perhaps surprising to an American mother would be the early emphasis upon orderliness, cleanliness, manners, and neatness. The early establishment of proper behavior and attitudes in relation to other children with whom the child plays is interesting, particularly the frequent admonition to refrain from envy. Although the Ten Commandments forbid covetousness, mothers in the United States probably would not begin teaching this concept at so young an age, or emphasize it to any marked extent as the child grows older. Buddhist precepts may have something to do with this form of child training in Japan.

Non-valid threats of subsequent illness or stupidity[8] are not generally used in the United States. In Japan, the belief as a child that one of these conditions would be caused by the gods in return for misbehavior, might have a psychological implication.

Data yet to be tabulated suggest that unfulfilled promises are quite common, but that this practice and physical punishment (including the use of moxa), rarely occasion unhappiness beyond the momentary effect. On the other hand, reaction to quarreling seemingly is of a different nature. Respondents' reports indicate a strong emotional barrier developed in childhood, in addition to the severe social sanction against it.

Tabulated information appearing above would hardly account for any important personality differences in the behavior of Japanese and American children or adults unless certain minor differences in practice be assigned major influence in determining behavior of the child. Suggested are the limitations of statistical data derived from questionnaires. Even interviewing is not altogether successful; yet an anthropologist is all too aware that when he returns to the United States and hears a child say "no" to a parent, he is observing something that does not occur in Japan. Subtle differences are difficult to ascertain. A mother is generally unaware of the number of times she says "no" to a child when he misbehaves before she punishes or otherwise forces compliance. The parent's facial expressions are important and meaningful but how often used and exactly what they convey to the child are extremely difficult to ascertain. The nature and extent of positive instruction in establishing approved behavior, instead of verbal admonitions or punishment are likewise significant. Much additional work on child care and relevant adult behavior will have to be done before a clear picture emerges.

NOTES

1. Research partly financed by a pre-doctoral fellowship from the Wenner-Gren Foundation for Anthropological Research, Inc. The writer spent from Oct. 1951 to Nov. 1952 studying child training and family behavior in Kainan, Wakayama Prefecture, Japan, and served concurrently on the faculty of Wakayama University. The Wenner-Gren Foundation is in no way responsible for statements made here.

2. Benedict, R. F., 1946-b; Bennett & Nagai, 1953; Boutflower, 1939; Buchanan, D. C., 1954; Caudill, 1952; Dening, W., AsJ *19* pt. 1; Dillaway, 1947; Embree, J. F., 1950; Glacken, 1955; Gorer, 1943; Haring, 1946-b, 1953-a, 1955-b; Hasegawa, n.d.; Hsiao, 1929; Hulse, 1948; Kubo, 1938; LaBarre, 1945; Moloney, 1945, 1951, 1954; Norbeck, 1954 and article in this book; Reischauer, 1950; Seligman, 1931; Sikkema, 1947; Spitzer, 1947; Stoetzel, 1955; Warner, L., 1952, Chap. 2.

3. Tables 3 and 4 are based on a sample of 200 rather than 449 questionnaires. Unless otherwise specified, information on open-ended questions, necessarily hand tabulated, comes from only 100 of the questionnaires, and is presented as summary comment on the statistical data; figures given in the text refer to number of citations rather than to number of respondents. Tables 5 and 7 are based on 100 questionnaires.

4. Cauterization with moxa consists in burning a pinch of dried herbs on the skin. A permanent scar results.

5. Data were obtained separately for each child. Tabulations in terms of individual children will be published later.

6. Although the original question on completion was phrased in this manner, the word "completed" is used hereafter to denote this category. In Table 2, it is denoted by the phrase, "Age at which mishap is not expected."

7. Although the original questionnaire specified "buttocks" and "body," translation and results indicate the interpretation given by parents was "buttocks" and "other part of body." Material presented in this paper is based upon this assumption.

8. In Japan the threat of stupidity is real. One seldom recovers mentally from B-encephalitis.

MARGARET MEAD

1947. "On the Implications for Anthropology of the Gesell-Ilg Approach to Maturation," *American Anthropologist*, vol. *49*: 69-77. Reprinted by courtesy of the author and of the Editor of *American Anthropologist*.

1947. "The Concept of Culture and the Psychosomatic Approach," *Psychiatry: Journal of the Biology and the Pathology of Interpersonal Relations*, vol. *10*: 57-76. Reprinted by courtesy of the author and of the Editor of *Psychiatry*.

1947. "The Implications of Culture Change for Personality Development," *American Journal of Orthopsychiatry*, vol. *17*: 633-646. Reprinted by courtesy of the author and of the Editor of the *American Journal of Orthopsychiatry*.

1954. "Some Theoretical Considerations on the Problem of Mother-Child Separation," *American Journal of Orthopsychiatry*, vol. *24*: 471-483. Reprinted by courtesy of the author and of the Editor of the *American Journal of Orthopsychiatry*.

A glance at the selection from Margaret Mead's writings included in the General Bibliography indicates that four papers cannot represent the range and variety of her studies. A wide public reads *Coming of Age in Samoa, Growing up in New Guinea, Sex and Temperament in Three Primitive Societies,* and *Male and Female.* All of these books are important in understanding personality development in different cultural situations. No serious student of the subject can afford to neglect the impressive photographic studies: *Balinese Character, A Photographic Analysis,* by Gregory Bateson and Margaret Mead (1942); and *Growth and Culture: A Photographic Study of Balinese Childhood,* by Margaret Mead and Frances Cooke MacGregor (1951). Dr. Mead's article on "Some Uses of Photography in Culture and Personality Studies" in the present book sets the stage for appreciation of *Balinese Character* and *Growth and Culture.*

Anthropology suffers—perhaps more than any other science—from the expense of publishing complete data of field research. Mathematical statement and symbolic logic enable physicists and chemists to compress even years of research into brief compass. Thus far there is no way to present the complex life of an exotic people other than literary (and sometimes statistical) description. This requires many hundreds of pages to report even a short field expedition; witness the bulk of the present book, in which only brief snatches of researches can be set forth. These facts explain the impossibility of publishing all of the data of Dr. Mead's many field trips. It is noteworthy that of the tribes she has studied, the fullest publication of data occurs in her works on the Arapesh of New Guinea (1938, 1940-c, 1947-a, 1949-e). Thoughtful readers who wish fuller documentation of her conclusions are referred to *The Mountain Arapesh* as a sample of what every anthropologist would like to put on record.

In the case of one tribe—Manus—Dr. Mead has been able to revisit a people studied in 1928 and to report on conditions observed nearly a quarter-century later. Data of the second visit have been published in Mead, 1954-b and 1956.

ON THE IMPLICATIONS FOR ANTHROPOLOGY OF THE GESELL-ILG APPROACH TO MATURATION

Margaret Mead

One of the recurrent problems[1] which face the anthropologist is the selection from current researches in our own culture of concepts which have cross-cultural promise, which are capable of a sufficient degree of heightened abstraction, or of extrapolation, so as to be useful in increasing our interpretation of other cultures.[2] Each time that a field of research is developed, by a scientist in our own society, there is a chance that a new tool will be provided to the field anthropologist. In remaining alert to such possibilities there are two cautions which are worth making. The anthropologist who goes into the field, well equipped with the most rewarding conceptual frame which he has found in some current psychological research, may confine himself to illustration of that theme, paying so much attention to the relationship between his data and the hypothesis in which he is interested that he will have no time or energy to spare for a fresh responsive approach to the *new* relationships among his data. When this is done, the results will be less rich because while it may be useful to have some illustrations from primitive cultures of an hypothesis which was constructed to include, at least partially, the concept of culture, finding such illustrations is incomparably less important to the advance of science than is draining the last drop of new suggestive meaning from the culture being studied. If we arrange in a sequence work done among primitive peoples by individuals, either psychologists, psychiatrists, or anthropologists, with varying degrees of specificity in the hypotheses which they wished to test out, we find a correlated difference among their results in the richness and suggestiveness of the new hypotheses which are brought back.[3]

But while there is real danger that some of the rewards of months of painstaking field work, under difficult conditions, may be lost if the material is observed too rigorously from a predetermined point of view, there is also the danger that without theoretical tools, the field anthropologist may not see enough and may not sense the significance of what he does see.

In selecting the developmental point of view, especially some of the recent aspects of the Gesell-Ilg[4] approach to the study of maturation, for discussion in an anthropological context, I have done so because I believe that certain of the concepts emerging from this approach may be of the very greatest importance to the field worker, especially the field worker who is concerned with child development as a major approach to the study of culture, and also to the theoretical student who is looking for convenient terms for expressing differences in the culturally determined character structure of members of different cultures. But because I think it is so important, I am going to discuss initially in some detail ways in which it could be used which would lead not to greater insight but rather to the opposite. Gesell has delineated a sequence in maturation, and, allowing for individual differences—individual differences within which it may ultimately be possible to discriminate types of maturation—he has located nodal points in this sequence at definite chronological-age points, with a plus or minus two months, or six months or more, systematically implied if not always explicitly stated. This sequence has been determined by the detailed study of middle-class children in New Haven and its environs and is based on a very large number of exceedingly detailed records. If the field worker should take into the field the series of descriptive norms which Gesell has established and simply attempt to verify that the same norms did or did not obtain in a given primitive culture, this would be of relatively little final value for science. His conditions of observation would be infinitely inferior to some of the highly controlled situations in which Gesell has worked; he would not be able to extend his observations over anything like the number of years nor with the same large staff and battery of recording devices. The chance of his having enough cases to make his results in any way comparable would be minimal.

Nor approaching the matter from another angle is it possible to take the Gesell standards as a way of placing the age of infants whose age is not known. The field worker comes into the field to find some children whose age is already beyond the point at which accuracy of maternal reporting can be expected, although this point will vary from five or six days in some cultures to 210 days or larger calendrical units in others. It is then necessary to place the children which are being observed in some approximate age group, and the observer calls upon past clinical experience of infants, combined with such data as appearance of a first tooth, as a partial guide, supplemented whenever possible with other data, such as relative age of other children, puppies, ceremonial events with a known time-span or calendrical placing, etc.[5] But even though the Gesell descriptions of characteristic age behavior are so complete and contain statements of range, they would only provide an approximation, and because they are stated in relationship to a concrete American environment might easily be misleading.

However, there is another level at which the Gesell-Ilg findings can be of the very greatest significance if we recognize that their observations provide us with a model, a basic way of thinking about the maturation of the individual, in terms of which any given culture's expectations and demands can be calibrated. They themselves use their description of maturation rates and rhythms, differential capabilities, and individual differences in development as a set of criteria which culture, at least a democratic culture, should meet. However, for research purposes we can use these descriptions which, properly abstracted from the cultural matrix, give us a picture of the pattern of human growth, as a means of *studying* cultural developmental mechanisms without necessarily evaluating them. (Such study should lead in turn to further criteria for evaluation if we find, for instance, that the effect of asking a child to do a too difficult task, or keeping him at a too simple one, may contain sufficient rewards in general personality differentiation to justify it, in spite of its demonstrated discrepancy with an innate growth rhythm.)

Although the progressive application of this type of thinking will doubtless show a series of more complex problems, it will be sufficient here to point out a few major ways in which it can be used. Dr. Ilg uses the spiral as her mechanical model, which provides for the concept of continuous growth that nevertheless contains both upward and downward gradients, and allows for the systematic inclusion of repetitions of behavior characteristic of previous stages, as part of growth, rather than as regression. This is an exceedingly important distinction to bear in mind, because the quite different psychiatric concept of regression,[6] in which an individual fails to conquer his reality problems on one level of maturity and so regresses to an earlier technique of adjustment, is itself a useful concept and one with cross-cultural validity. (We may for instance study the extent to which different cultures institutionalize regression—lying in bed, being nursed and fed, etc., in the case of illness or in various life crises, and *rites de passage*. We may also with adequate psychiatric equipment study the types of regression which are characteristic of different cultural character structures.) But there is an important difference between temporary or permanent failure to adjust and consequent regression, and the discontinuities of normal growth, by which the growing child concentrates now upon one segment of behavior, now upon another, learns a new skill only temporarily to relinquish mastery in another. The intermediate periods, when some former interest or skill seems to have vanished, and when behavior characteristic of an earlier period of growth appears, are seen as the downsweep of the spiral, while the forerunners of a new period are seen as the upsweep.

In the maturation process, certain nodal points of consolidation may be recognized, stages in the sequence in which there are no extreme discontinuities apparent so that the child seems especially well balanced and able to confront life. Furthermore, this spiral model can be used to express another phenomenon which has been observed in the Yale clinic, the recurrence of certain types of adjusting, as to eating, or reading, etc., in definite sequences. So Dr. Ilg is able to place the periods at which a child's appetite is likely to alter, and say, "If it does not happen within the next two or three months, then it will not happen for another two years. At about age 'Y' you can expect another period of potential shift, etc." Or she can say: "If a child has not shown some interest in letters by Y age, it is probable that at the next period of paying attention he will not fully learn to read,— but that reading will not come until about such and such a time." As individual differences are discernible in the duration and intensity of different interrelated points on this growth spiral, it becomes possible to characterize different types of children as those who show different patterns of sequential repeat, stressing more the type of development which comes around 4, 6, and 8 years, for instance, or around 5, 7, and 9 years. (The exact and probably logarithmic relationships between these repetitive emphases in sequential development have yet to be determined.)

We can now take these three concepts, a rhythm of growth with a definite sequence which can be distorted or by-passed, but not hurried; a concept of growth as proceeding from periods of consolidation to periods of expansion to new consolidation, so that different points on the spiral will have a different quality (in ability to adjust, vulnerability to external pressures, accidents, etc.); and a concept of patterned individual differences expressed in differing emphases on different phases of the growth process. If we attempt to apply these concepts to studies of culture, we find that we may look at any culture as to whether the cultural expectations of growth anticipate, coincide with, lag behind or fail to recognize altogether, the innate growth pattern in the generalized form in which it may be attributed to all human infants. There are cultures like the Arapesh[7] in which crawling is discouraged before the appearance of teeth, or like the Balinese[8] in which a child cannot set foot on the ground—and therefore has little freedom off the carrier's hip—until it is six and one-half months old. Cultures which strap or bind their infants interfere with the child's capacity for certain types of motor activity. While it has been reported that students found that Balkan infants who had been swaddled, in a very few days attained to the level of movement which other infants would have arrived at through a series of stages, we do not yet have any way of measuring the change in quality which is introduced when an activity is engaged in later than was organically possible. There seems every possibility that the pattern will be altered and that, while children in all cultures learn to walk, the way in which they learn to walk and the time at which they learn to walk, in relation to their actual innate maturational capacity, may be very significant as a factor in personality formation. For instance, the Balinese child is encouraged to walk earlier, as creeping is culturally abhorred, and the child has frequent experiences of overextension and loss of balance; and loss of balance is a preoccupation of Balinese throughout their lives, playing a role in their rejection of alcohol, disorientation after traveling in motor cars, etc. At each stage the degree of discrepancy or exact correspondence will be registered at a deutero level,[9] and become a factor in later development. So throughout the maturation cycle, the cultural pattern is one factor in the development of the total personality. The innate rhythmic maturation potential is a second.

If one compares this hypothesis with the *tabula rasa* school of thought, it will be seen how much more complicated and how much more systematic it is. Each act of learning will have occurred in one of a series of definite relationships to the organism's degree of readiness for that act, and from these relationships deutero learnings will occur which may be finally stated in such terms as attitude towards effort, trust in physical environment or in own skill, etc. The differences among cultures in which readiness for a given piece of learning is looked for, and cultures in which the importance of a given item of learning is so emphasized that the child is prematurely hurried into it, and cultures in which it is felt that capacities for behavior are revealed at socially premature points and so need be retarded or interfered with are very striking. Once we seriously begin to explore cultures from this point of view, we may find, for instance, that the learnings which a culture most successfully transmits are those which are most closely attuned to the human growth rhythm, or we may find that hypertrophy of certain skills or arts may be due to such a coincidence of emphasis and timing. Throughout such inquiries it is necessary to recognize that such differences may be due for instance not to the age at which a child is taught to draw, but to the presence or absence of opportunities for certain sorts of free and certain sorts of precision movements, at a stage before the child would be capable of drawing. The Gesell-Ilg method makes it possible to follow through the development of special bodily emphases, or special emphases on segments of the body, as on arm movements, leg movements, or the importance of the head, as these reappear in different stages in the maturation sequence.

The most striking differences will be found between those cultures in which learning is regarded as an individual matter, where the appearance of walking, talking, heterosexual expression, etc., is waited for until the individual displays readiness, and those cultures in which by the use of a calendar, or through a ceremonial of initiating novices in groups, or because of the extreme fluctuations of seasonal life, a new step of development is enforced, either upon an individual or upon a group with very slight recognition of degree of readiness. Initiation ceremonies for adolescents which include the eight-year-old children of especially important men, and the twenty-year-old who went away to work before he was initiated, are examples of this order. So are such pediatric dicta in our society as that a "baby should feed itself at fifteen months," and that an infant which weighs seven pounds and over should be fed at four-hour intervals—from birth on, while an infant that weighs one ounce less should be fed at three-hour intervals. Although measurements enormously enhance this tendency to substitute man-made patterns for innate patterns by the use of calendar, clock, scales, calipers, etc., essential contrasts of this sort may be found in cultures in which there is nothing but the rhythm of the seasons and the sun to go on, or in which through ceremonial calendars there is artificial structuring of behavior. A striking instance of numerical imposition is the frequent relationship between the sacred number of a group and the day on which the umbilical cord "falls off": in Bali, where the mother is in a special state for the first three days after birth, the cord falls off in three days; in Iatmul,[10] where five is the magic number, it falls off in five. Such usages reinforce the imputation to the organism of the cultural pattern, an imputation which is justified in detail in the case of hunger at meal-times or sleepiness at bedtime, where innate rhythms have been altered to suit a cultural time-scale. However, the difference between the sleep of those who went to sleep when they were tired as children rather than by the clock, and those whose sleep has been patterned and decreed is probably something which will ulti-mately be measured and studied.

The second relevant concept is the concept of periods of varying degrees of consolidation and expansion, as the child learns, consolidates its learning, casts back towards older forms, and projects forward new forms. Some of these periods may be sufficiently well defined—for all children—so that it is possible to discuss the way in which some cultural demands coincide with periods of relative stability or vulnerability. According to Gesell and Ilg, our national custom of sending children to school for the first time at six is an example of such a significant lack of correspondence, five being a period when a higher state of con-solidation is to be expected. We do not of course yet have any way of knowing to what extent these periods are internally regulated and to what extent culture can alter them. The characteristic behavior of a six-year-old, especially in dependence upon parents, may be as related to an intensification in some earlier period of some items in our child pattern, as it is to the current state of the growing organism.

However, the systematic occurrence of such periods of varying consolidation presents a good case for the possibility of an innate pattern of growth which provides a ground plan. Adolescence is of course the most striking instance of this phenomenon. There are very few cultures in which the disruptive concomitants of adolescence are so successfully muted as in Samoa.[11] It is possible that one might use care of the sick as a model in thinking about this problem. An individual may have a disease which will run its course so that recovery will set in quickly under conditions of mild rest. In some cultures, however, under such circumstances, sweat baths, religious pilgrimages, blood-letting or other measures will be decreed which will aggravate the condition, while in other cultures—of which our own has been a sample, in the upper economic levels—a degree of total rest may be imposed which is also inappropriate and which will also aggravate the patient's state. The more intense and complex the state of the patient becomes, however, the more chance there is that the treatment may lack certain necessary elements. When we are dealing not with a temporary illness but with a state of temporary out-of-phaseness peculiar to a stage of growth, the situation becomes all the more complicated because many of the cultural conditions necessary for an easy adolescence may be enhanced by patterns laid down in early childhood, in methods of feeding, in relationships to parents and siblings, etc. For example, if a child makes a successful separation away from his mother *before* the next child is born, so that the separation is seen not as due to the entrance of a rival but as part of the child's own natural exploratory tendencies, the break with the parents which comes with leaving home, or marriage, may be of a very different character.

In spite of these necessary considerations, the extent to which in different cultures individuals are put under pressure at points of maximum or minimum ability to stand those pressures is exceedingly important. Where, for any reason, there is anxiety lest a child display behavior characteristic of an earlier age (as among some American Indians watching their male children for signs of manhood or in our cultural attitudes towards enuresis), or where there is anxiety about precocity, as in Samoa, in regard to the overt display of social initiative, and among us in regard to sex, either characteristic of the growth spiral, the downgrade with recurrence of earlier forms of behavior or the upgrade with its premonitory bits of future behavior may selectively come in for cultural disapproval. A mother may fly into a tantrum when her knee baby begins to crawl or seeks her breast at the funeral of its younger sibling. A flirtatious glance from a girl who has not passed through her puberty ceremony may arouse harsh measures.

So there are useful implications in this delineation of periods of differential degrees of consolidation, whether we consider the degree to which in a given culture a given period, like adolescence, is made difficult or easy, whether we consider the extent to which precocity or slow development is culturally disapproved, or whether we consider the extent to which cultural devices protect the individual during periods of vulnerability, such as "weaning," "acquiring a new skill like walking or talking," "birth of a sibling," puberty, first parenthood, climacteric, etc. (It will be noted that I am assuming that the Gesell-Ilg approach should apply to the whole life cycle and not only to the rising curve from conception to maturity.) Even such cultural attitudes as the Samoan acceptance of a "state of unwillingness or disgruntlement," or the English acceptance of "mood" in children may provide a sheltering state within which the individual can develop more easily.

The third facet of the Gesell-Ilg approach, the possibility of discerning a series of patterns or types among the individual differences, still awaits more work and need only be mentioned here. If it becomes possible to discriminate types of maturation and to place them schematically on different sides of the spiral-of-growth model, we will then have an instrument which will make it possible to deal systematically with the hypothesis that in different cultures different constitutional types have been institutionalized. It has seemed clear for a long time that the best approach to this problem would be through differentiating types of maturation as opposed to working with types of adult constitutional difference. But the material has never been available to do this. If it were found—from the examination of Gesell's data and other similar types of data—that types of innate maturation style could be distinguished, these differences could be counterpoised against detailed records of cultural expectations, and we would be able to study these cultures which had come to specialize in exactly hitting a natural rhythm, peculiar to one constitutional type, and also those cultures where child-rearing practices tend towards smoothing out the differences by superimposing patterns specifically congenial to no type, or intermediate patterns which blur the distinctions between types. It should also provide a device by which such problems as class and sex typing, and regional differences in larger cultures can be approached. Finally by giving us a conceptual tool with which to handle the question of deviance, it will provide a method for studying social change, which may be seen as becoming effective to the extent that the customary patterning of maturation is altered for part or all of the population, thus embodying in their character formation the character changes appropriate to the changed cultural state.

NOTES

1. This paper appeared on the program of the American Anthropological Association, December 1945, and was read at a Viking Fund dinner, in February, 1946.

2. For discussions of this problem of cross-disciplinary borrowing of abstractions see: Mead, M., 1930-d, 1932, 1942-a, 1942-b, 1944, 1946-b; Bateson, G., 1932, 1941.

3. Compare for instance the studies of S. F. Nadel on memory in different African cultures, 1937-b, 1937-c, or the study of Lepcha childhood by Geoffrey Gorer, 1938, with the work of W. Dennis, 1940-a, who used but was not primarily concerned with validating psychoanalytic hypotheses; or E. H. Erikson, 1943-a, with such studies as John Whiting, 1941, and C. Dubois, 1944.

4. Gesell, A., Ilg, F. L., and others, 1943, contains a bibliography of the earlier Gesell literature. This paper was delivered by Dr. Gesell at a meeting of the N. Y. Neurological Society, January 8, 1946. For earlier bibliography of this general field, see McGraw, Myrtle B., 1935.

5. In Bali, normally ages are not given accurately beyond the second *oton* (210 day unit), but because the date of the earthquake in 1918 was known, and because the Balinese had named children born during the earthquake, I Gedjer (I Earthquake) it was possible to identify 21-year olds in 1939.

6. Kris, Ernst, 1944.

7. Mead, M., 1935-a.

8. Bateson, G., and Mead, M., 1942.

9. Bateson, G., 1942-c.

10. Unpublished field work, New Guinea, 1939.

11. Mead, M., 1928-b.

BIBLIOGRAPHY

BATESON, G., 1932, 1941, 1942-c
BATESON & MEAD, 1942
DENNIS, 1940-a
DuBOIS, 1944
ERIKSON, 1943-a
GESELL, A., Paper delivered at a meeting of the N. Y. Neurological Soc., Jan. 8, 1946
GESELL, ILG, et al, 1943
GORER, 1938
KRIS, 1944
MEAD, M., 1928-b, 1930-d, 1932-b, 1935-a, 1939 (unpublished field work), 1942-a, 1942-b, 1944, 1946-b
NADEL, 1937-b, 1937-c
WHITING, 1941
Bibliographies: Gesell, Ilg et al, 1943; McGraw, 1935

THE CONCEPT OF CULTURE AND THE PSYCHOSOMATIC APPROACH †

MARGARET MEAD‡

The concept with which psychosomatic medicine operates at present is that a personality which develops according to definite laws of growth is limited and defined by constitutional type, is subject to the accidents of social development, and is acted upon by environmental pressures; these pressures vary as to whether they occur during the period of earlier development or after the personality organization has been defined. The personality may develop psychosomatic defects which are the result of the reactivation of earlier difficulties or the failure of the personality to adjust to contemporary pressures. These defects may be either reversible or irreversible.

This formulation leaves culture outside the individual, in fact does not consider culture at all, and merely considers the social environment which is conceived as external to the individual, as represented by one or more persons who, in addition to acting upon the individual, are also responding to the individual. There is the further assumption that

†*Editor's note:* This paper which was prepared first in 1940 and has been the basis for considerable critical collaboration is published as presented by the author without the editorial revisions which are customary in the Journal.

‡*Author's note:* This paper is the outcome of a piece of exploratory research undertaken with the help of a grant from the Josiah H. Macy Jr. Foundation during the summer of 1940. Publication was delayed because some of the criticisms which I received in reply to preliminary circulation of the draft of the paper were so contradictory and lacking in internal consistency that it was obvious that some unidentified factor was at work. I finally identified this in 1941 as a confusion between the argument which I was presenting and internal theoretical disagreements in contemporary psychoanalysis in which the word culture has been used with a rather different connotation. I also found, in these discussions through which I attempted to clarify the discrepancies in the criticisms which I received, that there was some well-justified fear that I was recommending a type of therapy which would substitute cultural categorization for the intensive study of individual cases, as for example encouraging a diagnosis which said the patient was "suffering from the Depression" or a "victim of culture contact" and took no account of the individual dynamics of the case. In regard to the first type of criticism, I can only label it. As to the second, I find on carefully rereading the paper that I have discussed cultural understanding as a desirable *component* of psychosomatic theory, as a *basis for planning* in preventive medicine, and only as a *background*—in most instances taken for granted by the practitioner—for individual therapy. I have endeavored to correct any phrasing which would suggest that knowledge of culture is in some way a primary therapeutic tool or that

there is a *normal* as represented by those individuals in our society who do not come actively to the attention of the various therapeutic agencies—medicine, the law, social work—and who manifest only that degree of mild breakdown which we have included within our definition of the term *normal*. Variations of this normal personality are to be referred to the interaction of the forces listed above, and this interaction may be handled as a contemporary unit, without invoking the past, in terms of the "personality organization" or the psychodynamic mechanisms of the individual. Regardless of the weight which may be given to one or another aspect of this picture—whether, for example, special emphasis is laid upon an asthenic habitus, or whooping cough at the age of three, or an over-protective mother who is compensating for hostility to the child, or an employer who is a father surrogate—the individual under discussion is seen in terms of deviation from the normal and the normal is identified as basic human functioning. Within this conception, two ideas of health obtain. We have the phrasing "normal healthy," which permits by implication the deviations from an ideal state of health which are statistically usual and do not result in any form of breakdown, and the ideal of perfect health or "textbook normal" which seldom if ever occurs.[1]

This conception of the individual who would pursue a normal course of development, in accordance with his constitutional type, subject only to such vulnerabilities as may be identified as existing or developing within his body in terms of its own internal organization,—if not interfered with by an environment expressing itself in such forms as infection, over-protection, trauma, and malnutrition—is only one degree less hampering than was the old approach in which single organs were considered without regard to their interrelationship with the rest of the body, and the body was conceived as a system of independent organs, one of which—through internal defect or external influences—became diseased, and ultimately, because diseased, affected the other organs and finally the whole body, or collection of organs.[2] However, now that the students of psychosomatic medicine have done such far-

---

the categorization of maladjustment in cultural terms is any less undesirable than any other system of categorizations which would neglect the individual in favor of systematic attempts to classify the disorders from which he suffers.

Final revision of the paper for publication was further delayed by the war. The literature quoted all falls within the pre-war years, but no material has been brought to my attention which would seem to invalidate the position taken here, although much distinguished new material has been published since that time, notably: Richardson, H. B., *Patients Have Families*, New York, Commonwealth Fund 1945; Mittlemann, Bela, Wolff, H. G. and Scharf, M. P., Emotions and Gastroduodenal Functions: Experimental Studies on Patients with Gastritis, Duodenitis and Peptic Ulcer, *Psychosomatic Med.* (1942) 4:5-61; and Booth, G. C. Variety in Personality and its Relation to Health, *The Review of Religion*, New York 1946.

reaching theoretical work[3] in bringing the organism as a whole into the focus of attention, so that it is no longer regarded as a mere collection of organs and faculties or as a dualism between mind and body, the widening of the psychosomatic approach to include the concept of culture should not be difficult, because such an inclusion is merely an extension of the same kind of thinking which has gone into building up the psychosomatic approach.

If we accept the full implications of the statement that man is not merely an "animal" but that "man is a culture-building animal," we may fairly take—as our working definition of a human being—an individual member of the species, *Homo sapiens*, who has been submitted throughout his entire individual existence to systematic cultural pressures. Although a newborn member of the species might conceivably be adopted by parents of some other species and survive, that individual would not be *human* in the sense in which I am using the term. It would be without language, without human tradition, dependent upon its immediate capacity to deal with the environment unassisted either by tools or the accumulated experience of the human race.[4] In a sufficiently benign environment, safe from attacks of enemy species, with foods available which required no implements or techniques to collect or catch or prepare, and in the absence of poisons, such individuals might survive, mate, reproduce, suckle, and rear their young, and die, in almost a state of nature, depending almost entirely upon the wisdom of the body. But, if we encountered them, we would not call them human beings. There is no guarantee that their descendants would ever become such human beings, nor any guarantee that the long historical sequence of improbable discovery and invention which is human culture would ever occur again.

The student of human disease who speaks of "normal" and thinks that he means by that term the form that human behavior would "naturally" take if it were not distorted by environmental pressures, who thinks in fact that he is speaking of a biological or basically human normal, is really always including in his definition that particular variant of human culture which his subjects use as their basic instrument of survival. In this sense it may be said that it is "normal" for human beings to learn to talk, since human beings are, by definition, born into cultures which include language, so that only those human beings who are constitutionally defective or subject to some accident fail to learn to talk. But while *learning to talk* is normal human behavior, there is no normal language. If we are to make any further generalization, we can only say: *it is normal for a child to learn to speak the language or languages spoken by the adults and older children with whom he comes in contact, if those persons expect him to learn.* There are cases on record in which children learn to understand languages which they never speak. We cannot say that it is normal to learn a single language or even one language better than another, nor can we say that it is normal to learn, as a young child, the form of the language which will be later spoken as an adult. There are communities on linguistic frontiers where everyone speaks two languages; there are cultures which have developed baby talk which is used to all children by adults and so becomes the child's first language; there are cultures in which men and women speak differentiated forms of the language, and the small boys learn first their mothers' speech and later their fathers'. In our society it is abnormal for children to make up a complete special language, and only special accidents in his life history will predispose a child to such behavior. But there are cultures in which it is normal for children to speak a secret language which they constantly alter, in which creative linguistic manipulation is expected behavior from children of certain ages. Our statement that children normally learn to talk between the first and second year simply means that in all known societies children will be exposed to language, some form of which they will be expected and, if necessary, forced to master, and that they should be able, in terms of their neurological development, to start to master it between the first and second year. Out of the random sounds that the child makes, older people will select, repeat, and reward certain sounds, until a certain set of sounds which are systematically related to one another become standardized,[5] and other sounds, some of which the infant once made systematically, become, first, less easy to make, and finally, for most adults impossible to make. We do not even know that the child who was not so taught would continue to babble its random series of sounds; it might become mute or almost mute except in cases of extreme emotion. All we can say is that the human infant living in a world in which people communicate with each other by sounds, systematically related to each other in patterns, will first babble, and later learn to imitate such sounds as the adults think it should learn. We do not know that all subspecies of *Homo sapiens* would be capable of learning to speak; we merely know that all the subspecies known to live on the earth now are capable of learning language. Furthermore, data from orphan asylums have demonstrated[6] that learning to talk may be postponed for a whole group of children by isolating them from any contact with individuals who might either talk to them or talk among themselves.

This discussion of learning to talk may seem unduly labored and a mere restatement of something with which every educated person is well acquainted. But current discussions in psychosomatic medicine have not yet incorporated the implications of this sort of knowledge. Followed through, these implications are that every human being has had some of his potentialities selected by culture for elaboration, other

potentialities ignored, and others suppressed, and that the fully socialized human being is *normal*, in the sense that he is *socialized*, but that
no single item in the socialization is a biologically given piece of behavior which has not been moulded, and systematically moulded, by
his culture. The nature of human maturation limits this moulding of
course. Infants of five days cannot be made to walk alone. Human
physiology provides clues which a cultural system may elaborate into
endless diversity, and the structure of the human body may to some
extent determine the pattern of the cultural symbolism. So we find that
a culture which relies extensively upon eating as a clue elaborates the
idea in many ways; such a culture (for example, that of the Arapesh
of New Guinea) may also stress a tie between the eater and what remains after he has eaten; and the relationships between parent and
child, between husband and wife, between elders and youth, are conceived of in terms of feeding; vomiting is exceedingly dreaded behavior, and defecation becomes the automatic reaction to extreme disgust. All of these attitudes and ceremonies reveal a pattern which can be
related to the structure of the body and the physiology of eating, but
no direct necessity compelled the culture to adopt this set of symbols.

Similarly an emphasis upon the perfection of the individual person
and upon the importance of an unimpaired body surface may express
itself in a tendency towards quick wound healing, in a social rule de-
barring an individual with an open sore from participation in religious
ceremonies, and in a series of mortuary rites which extend over many
years and involve repeated attempts to eliminate the corpse and surrogates of the corpse, balanced by a continuous creation of new surrogates.[7]

There are basic mammalian problems, such as feeding the young,
which every human society must meet, but whether these problems
will be met in part by stimulating the breasts of nonlactating women
so that they can suckle adopted children, by giving infants food as
well as mothers' milk from birth on, by wet nurses, or by cows' milk,
mares' milk, or goats' milk, will vary from culture to culture. Further,
the form of socialization in every culture is probably limited to some
extent not only by the rate of maturation but also by a systematic
interrelationship between the socialization process, the child's biological
makeup, and the whole cultural system. For example, parental preoccupation with the intake of food may result in the child's preoccupation with evacuation, which is a function of the child's response to
the combination of parental pressure and his own physiological functions. This derivative preoccupation of the child will in turn help to
shape the parental attitude towards the child's evacuation habits. The
form of the socialization process at any given time represents a historically developed working adjustment which reflects this interdepen-

dence between the organism and the cultural forms. The training given children in sphincter control will therefore depend on the previous training given them in regard to eating, on their response to that previous training, and on the parent's response to that response; but it will also depend upon behavior which is culturally standard for adults at a stage in life not yet reached even by the parent. In the parent's training of the child will be reflected, for instance, the cultural imperative that dying old men must still attempt to control their bodily functions and drag themselves to the edge of the village to defecate.

Any given moulding of the young organism is then limited by the nature of the young organism; it is a function of the entire cultural scheme, and in homogeneous and stable cultures is systematically related to every other bit of moulding. No culture is completely homogeneous, for this would require that every individual within it had been socialized with the same success; nor is it completely stable, because, even in the absence of external pressure, this very fact of differential socialization has within it potentialities for change. A culture may be said to be homogeneous to the extent that the processes of socialization and the forms of living available to adults have not lost their systematic relationship. (A Spanish community which contains a group of gypsies and is situated in a town which contains remnants of Moorish architecture does not necessarily have a heterogeneous culture, for if we know that a given individual is a gypsy or a Spaniard born in that town, we know at once most of the other important things about his upbringing, beliefs, and expected behavior: we know in fact what his character or basic personality structure is.[8] On the other hand, an individual may be said to belong to a heterogeneous culture, simply in terms of the fewness of the number of elements of his past experience and probable future behavior which we can derive from a mere statement of his general cultural position. If we are told that Mr. A is a third generation American, that still does not tell us whether he is white or Negro, what was the language spoken in his home as a child, what is the character of the food he eats—starch with very little meat, or a balanced collection of fats, proteins, and carbohydrates—whether his religion demands unflagging moral vigilance or permits periodic obliteration of past misbehavior, whether he is a banker or a thief, whether his wife will go to a hospital when she has a baby or call in a midwife, and whether he has lived all his life among scenes of drunkenness, brawling, and violence or never seen a blow given except on the screen or stage. In fact one of the most systematic things that we can say about a heterogeneous culture is that in many respects each individual's cultural experience[9] will be profoundly different from the experience of the other individuals with whom he associates. We can further find, in our culture, various standardized handlings of this cultural uniqueness: (1) *The alibi of the past.* In our society where it is evident to everyone that many things have happened to any one individual which have not happened, in the same combination, to any other individual, he is permitted to blame upon past events many present shortcomings or failures. Such statements form a great part of a social history.[10] "I never had a chance." "There were ten of us at home, and my mother sick, and father always drank up most of what he made, and that's the way it went." "I never had a chance to get an education." "We all went to work at twelve in the mills ten hours a day, and then often enough a beating at home."[11] (2) *The use of the past as a foil for any positive achievement in the present.* "I had to go to work when I was sixteen but I was determined to be somebody and I studied at night and finally I got a degree." "My parents were poor and ignorant and didn't want us to go to school but I went anyway." (3) *The protective coloration of highly similar manners and clothing which requires little more than money to enable an individual to blur the question of who his parents were and what his background is.* The attitudes described in Middletown,[12] of regarding clothes as sometimes the only available clue to another person's standing, reflect this position. In a society in which each man's origins may be not only different but shamefully different from those of his neighbor, and capable of being invoked to explain any depravity or failure, the protective cloak of facilely similar clothes and manners is spread far and thin. Deviation from the ordinary standards of American behavior—whether class-typed or not—is felt as dangerous and the pressure towards protective conformity is great.[13]

When we realize how important and widespread, in American urban culture, is this emphasis on the responsibility which may be placed on the events of the individual's past, we see another force acting upon the research worker who attempts to see the patient, not in isolation, but in terms of his social environment. The special circumstances of the patient's life—the various shocks, deprivations, and extraordinary experiences—stand out in relief, and the typical cultural picture, of which the patient is just one representative, is obscured. Each patient is seen, not as a slightly variant representative of a cultural type, moulded since birth, but as a special distortion of what would otherwise have been a "normal" personality. This word *"normal"* has two meanings: it may refer to the statistically usual in the culture—usually without any recognition that this is culturally relative—so that the statistically usual is identified with the basically human; or it may be used as a synonym for health or medically negative. If the conception of the norm has been built up on a group of human beings in which a given condition, such as tryptophane deficiency, is statistically unusual and identified as a dysgenic state, and if a group, like certain underprivileged white groups in the South, is subsequently discovered among whom such a deficiency is statistically usual, the state of these individuals in the South will not be identified as "normal" or "healthy" but will be contrasted with the "normal" or "healthy" state previously identified as statistically usual in the other group. Even without comparative data of this sort, somatic conditions which in one generation are so statistically usual as to be hardly worthy of note, such as summer complaint in infants, may, owing to some new discovery in bacterial control, suddenly be seen in a new light, as disorders associated with a certain way of life, not merely the inevitable fate of infants who are born at a time of year which will make their second summer difficult.

But each time that medical science has taken a step towards the removal of some formerly prevalent condition of malnutrition, for example dental caries, the new state of the population becomes identified with the basic human normal, from which rachitic children or young people with decayed teeth are regarded as pathological deviations. Mention should perhaps also be made of the tendency to attribute all such conditions as decay of teeth to some simple element in the civilized environment, and to conceive of a hypothetical primitive man whose teeth were strong and resistant to decay because he ate plenty of raw meat and no bonbons. But the more usual procedure is to ascribe disease conditions, about the etiology of which modern medicine has a working hypothesis, to ignorance of the natural laws which govern the human body, or to ignorance of specific treatments for constitutional defects under which heading the discovery of antigens for the treatment of allergies might be placed.

Thus any identifiable pathological condition could be pigeonholed, on the one hand, with conditions fostered by ignorance, dirt, bad ventilation, poor sewerage, etc., with faulty and defective cultural adjustments of one sort or another which had only to be overcome to obliterate the condition; or, on the other hand, it could be considered as attributable to constitution or accident, in which it is the progress of the science of therapy rather than the progress of the understanding of etiology which will enable the person who is constitutionally abnormal, or who has suffered some accident, to live longer or to live more comfortably. In either case, we are conceived as proceeding, with the help of medicine, towards a *normal* human functioning which would be medically negative in the particular respects.

Once a given symptom, or syndrome, has been identified as pathology, and objectively described as pathology, it is possible for the physician to collect data on a group in which the pathological condition is statistically usual, compare it with data on a group in which the pathological condition is unusual and perhaps isolate the special contributing conditions in the environment which foster the condition in one case and not in the other.[14] It has been fairly easy to recognize that Eskimos have good teeth or that native peoples who have never been exposed to tuberculosis infection have textbook normal chests. Such a recognition proceeds however against a background of already identified pathologies. The expectation that the functioning of every part of the human body is moulded by the culture within which the individual has been reared—not only in terms of diet, sunlight, exposure to contagious and infectious diseases, overstrain, occupational disease hazards, catastrophes and traumatic experiences, but also by the way that he, born into a society with a definite culture, has been fed and disciplined, fondled and put to sleep, punished and rewarded—had to wait for the psychosomatic approach. As soon as it was realized that the *character* of the individual—the psychodynamic mechanisms which enabled him to function in society and reproduce his kind—was integrally related to various somatic manifestations which brought him into the clinic, the necessary bridge was laid between medicine and the science of culture. For the last fifteen years, students of medicine have been making the investigations which show that cardiac conditions, fractures, asthma, essential hypertension, anorexemia nervosa, migraine, etc., cannot be explained merely by reference to some constitutional deficiency or accident in the life history of the individual patient, but must be seen as systematically related to the total mode of behavior of the patient, to his total personality. During the same period, students of culture were collecting material to show that not only could the contrasts in the behavior of individuals who were members of different cultures not be laid to racial differences, but that they must be laid to the systematically different ways in which historically developed cultural systems are embodied in the developing organism. The student of disease was saying that if we were to understand essential hypertension[15] we must look at the character of the patient, and expect to find significant relationships of the order of an interaction between his passivity cravings and the restrictions upon satisfying these cravings and his aggressive tendencies and the restrictions upon his expressing them, as well as to some possible constitutional defect in his circulatory system. At the same time, the student of culture was saying that if we want to understand the way in which a Zuni Indian lives peaceably in his crowded village with a minimum of formal government, we must not invoke his racial constitution nor even a physical type special in terms of a local area of characterization,[16] but we must invoke the pattern of psychodynamics within the Zuni individual which reflects the historical cultural forms which the Zuni Indians have built up through centuries of selection and invention. The student of psychosomatic medicine was saying that in order to understand the pattern of psychodynamics, we had to go to the life history of the individual patient, to the peculiar way in which events had impinged upon his development. The student of culture was saying we must go to the process of socialization of the child, peculiar to Zuni culture, if we are to understand the adult Zuni Indian as he differs from members of other societies. During this process of socialization a certain pattern of behavior is built into the growing organism and becomes a part of him, in the same sense that a certain pattern of capillary behavior is a part of a patient with Reynaud's disease. Culture is seen, not as a set of external impacts and catastrophes to which an organism, whose normal functioning is just like the functioning of a member of a different society, is subjected, but as a principal element in the development of the individual, which will result in his having a structure, a type of functioning and a pattern of irritability, different in kind from that of individuals who have been socialized within another culture. In this conception, immersion in a culture, through continuous intercourse with individuals all of whom have been similarly immersed, sets up in the developing organism a large number of tendencies which become steadily more irreversible, not so much in the sense that each tendency has a precise counterpart in the soma, as in Jelliffe's hypothesis concerning Dupuytren's Contracture[17] but in the sense that the total functioning of the individual is dependent upon the systematic interrelationships between a large number of tendencies.

To take a very simple example: the Samoan is habituated from birth to sitting upon the floor. He sits cross-legged for hours with perfect ease and without fatigue, but if he is compelled to sit upon a chair, even for a half hour, he experiences the most acute fatigue. This, however, is in no sense an inalterable state. Any Samoan can learn with practice to sit upon a chair so that he will no longer feel special fatigue when he does so. But at the same time that the Samoan child is learning to sit upon the floor, he is also learning a whole set of behavior items which are related to this sitting position: that it is rude to speak while standing; that before one decides to use the right or the left hand, or both hands in accepting a cup, attention must be given to the relative distances at which one's neighbors on the right and the left are seated; that one's back, which on formal occasions will rest against a post, is outside the formal circle (so that one can wipe one's hands on the back of one's head, or the back of the post); that the person who stands when another person is seated is the person of higher rank; that if one passes in front of a seated person of equal or higher rank, one should bend low, etc. In turn all of these motor adjustments are tied up with the whole complicated question of status and the fact that in Samoa among the same individuals, a man who takes first place in one setting may take the lowest place in a different setting. This appreciation of status, as a place in a *seating plan* which may be varied in many ways is maintained by an emotional organization which is habituated to respond only to defined situations, to feel anger only when a special set of circumstances calls for it—for example, being presented with a cocoanut into which an improperly bent twig has been inserted, or being offered a meal of roast chicken which has stones in its crop. Such a specialized and flexible emotional organization is related to an absence of strong attachments or strong antagonisms, early experience of a large number of parent surrogates, and freedom from any early or rigorously imposed frustrations. If now, we ask a Samoan to sit upon a chair, and from that position to act as an integrated human being within the occidental social setting, we are asking more of him than to stretch his legs in an unaccustomed way. In making the unaccustomed postural adjustment, he is also upsetting his whole orientation in personal relations; he is no longer an individual moving smoothly within known social grooves to which he is accustomed, but a disoriented person, and his disorientation will be of another order from that of a member of some other culture to whom sitting has a different symbolic significance.

So, though the adult Samoan may learn his way about in social relations with Europeans, he will not become a European, and if we record his behavior and compare it with the behavior of other Samoans who, as adults, have been brought into contact with Europeans, there will be found to be systematic similarities in their behavior, in their approach to speaking English, for instance. A Samoan who knows only one English sentence will attempt to make that sentence grammatically perfect, he will resist speaking a pidgin. An adult Samoan may learn to adapt to the new culture but he will not do so by unlearning all that he has learnt as a child, but by attacking the new problem in terms of his personality structure which has been built up from birth through contact with other Samoans, within whose habituated bodies the implications of Samoan culture are carried.

When a physician, writing a psychosomatic case history, writes down: "The patient is an unmarried woman of twenty-five and a devout Roman Catholic," he is making a cultural statement. Any physician who has had experience with Roman Catholics knows at once that the patient will have absorbed certain attitudes towards sex and towards authority, and that whether the patient comes for the treatment of migraine, asthma, or anorexia nervosa, the personality which will be revealed in the course of the anamnesis will contain the attitudes in which every Roman Catholic girl is trained. Yet the physician who writes down this statement has not completely placed his patient in a cultural frame of reference, because in recognizing the Roman Catholic variant of the personality types that come before him as contrasting with the personality types of Methodists or Quakers or those who have had no religious training, he still thinks of it as a variant on a universal human personality type. Such a young woman may be recognized as having strong sexual inhibitions and a dependence upon authority, and a strong sense of guilt; but sexual inhibitions, dependence and guilt—to some degree—are regarded as the normal fate of all human beings. In other words, in the present type of psychosomatic case history, each patient's history is treated as a deviation from the normal, and the deviation is classified as more or less systematic. If we say a patient is a Catholic, we already know a good deal about her; if we say she is a Protestant, we know less and it is necessary to qualify our description still further; while, if we say she has had no religious background, the details of her position will require still further definition. If we say, "'The patient is a clerk with a high school education," we let the matter rest there because it conforms to the expected. But the statement that "the patient who holds a Ph.D. degree is a silk-stocking salesman" would require further qualification, unless it was known that the patient was a recent refugee in which case we would feel that we could fall back again upon the normal and expected.

Every such case history is a combination of statements of greater and less specificity. The age and sex of the patient can be referred to our knowledge of the incidence within an age-sex range of the particular complaint for which the patient comes to be treated; the occupation and the address will give a clue to the degree of economic pressure under which the patient lives; statements about religion are taken as clues to ethical attitudes. Within this picture, in which each item about the patient stands in orderly relationship to the physician's knowledge of similar classifications of human beings, the physician then seeks for the exceptional circumstance—that element in the patient's life history which will differentiate him or her from other individuals.[18]

The great contribution of Freudian psychology as it has been applied in psychosomatic studies has been to make this search systematic, to teach the physician to expect similar predetermining conditions, or more sophisticatedly, similar responses to precipitating events in the outer world, in patients who show similar disorders. So students of hypertension working with Alexander's[19] phrasing will look for a frustrated dependency relationship as one component of the personality of the patient; students of asthma who follow Deutsch's[20] phrasing will look for an upper respiratory infection, particularly whooping cough, during the period when oral phantasies were still active, and for an over-response to the child's eating difficulties on the part of the parent or parent-surrogate. They will look always for an over- or an underemphasis, for a series of reinforcing traumatic circumstances, for an over-dominating mother or an over-rejecting mother, a too-early imposed responsibility, etc. Throughout the investigation one will find that if the physician does not rely supinely upon a constitutional predisposition, but attempts to see the disease picture in terms of the patient's total personality, he is continually invoking deviations from the expected, deviations from the course of development which he considers normal. This invocation carries with it the assumption that if no such deviations are found, then the disease picture has to be put down as due to constitutional predisposition or defect, with a verdict, *social history negative*, just as when the heart and lungs of an individual are found to conform to the statistical norm for the age, sex, weight, and occupation of the patient, the verdict is heart and lungs *negative*. The implication of this verdict is that the growing individual would develop spontaneously within his environment, subject only to constitutional limitations, if the environment did not interfere in some way with what would otherwise be *normal human* development.

Analogously, in examining individuals for dietary deficiencies there are two alternative points of view. Forty years ago a physician might have had a series of cases; individuals who, because of poverty, had never had enough meat, individuals with excessive food fads, an ascetic who regularly fasted for long intervals, a political prisoner on a hunger strike, a woman found dead in her bed from starvation, and a man who regularly ate well and heartily according to the conventions of the time, with chicken and corn on the cob and two kinds of pie for Sunday dinner. This last man would have been dismissed as *dietary history negative*, for the usual diet would have been regarded as the proper diet. With the development of dietetics, however, a second physician looking over those records of forty years ago, might find that the usual diet of those days was sadly lacking in certain vitamins and minerals, and so find no *dietary history negative* in the whole set. But among his own patients, if there were children whose diet he had succeeded in supervising from birth, he might, when considering one of them in terms of some illness, write down *dietary history negative*. Both of these responses, either condemning all dietary regimes of forty years ago, or regarding the history of a properly supervised child as *ipso facto* negative, assume that there are no relevant events except wrong events. The individual's dietary history is negative except when he eats the wrong food, or too much food, or too little food, or the wrong combination of foods. The man who eats poisoned crabs has a positive experience and the man who eats unpoisoned crabs has no medically relevant experience at all. If, however, it is found upon questioning him that he has eaten crabs every day, then there is the possibility that the crabs may again be given attention, on the assumption that he has eaten too many of them.

So the practicing physician works with his concept of the normal, interpreted either as the usual or the known-to-be-desirable, as his base line. At any given moment the proportions to which the usual and the ideal are represented in this picture of the normal at the back of his mind is a matter of the history of the culture in general and of the history of medicine in particular. Fifty years ago the item, "nursed until a year old" would have been classified as normal in a case history; today many physicians would classify "nursed until three months" as normal, and so *negative*, while certain physicians with special theories about the importance of the sucking reflex[21] would base their diagnoses on a nine-month nursing period as desirable (or negative), and any shorter period of nursing would be classified as positive in the sense that the child might be assumed to have suffered a deprivation. But whatever criteria the physician was using in evaluating this item in the life history, either his idea of what was statistically usual and therefore normal or his idea of what was desirable, the history would be counted as negative on the particular point if it conformed to the criteria he was using. When we consider then what would happen if a physician planning to use the psychosomatic approach took a life history in which every single item came out *negative*,[22] we come face to face with the need for a cultural frame of reference in the development of psychosomatic theory. In terms of present practice, the physician who had been prepared to see the case in a psychosomatic frame of reference alone would be logically forced to refer the disorder either to constitutional defect, or to some definite somatic pathology which would have to be given an etiology independent of the total personality organization of the patient. Furthermore, the problem arises as to what an individual whose entire history was negative would die of.[23]

The basis of this dilemma lies in the tendency to identify only the unusual and deviant events, the too much, too little, too early, too late, too frequent, too rare events in a life history as those which are given integrated expression in the organism, and to regard the organism which is not subjected to pressures and events of an extraordinary nature as outside the psychosomatic frame of reference because it is outside the therapeutic frame of reference.

Systematically the psychosomatic approach still bears the imprint of the conceptions of conversion hysteria, in which a given individual was said to express his psychic conflicts in somatic terms while another individual expressed his conflict in psychic terms. Cases of the sort that Jelliffe[24] cites in which "successful" psychotherapy has resulted in the appearance of organic disease, or "successful" removal of a somatic disturbance has resulted in the appearance of a psychosis, have tended to reinforce this all or nothing point of view in the interpretation of individual cases. Ripley, Rahman, and Richardson's[25] classification of cases of anorexia nervosa into severe cases, those in which the somatic symptoms of the patient have specific symbolic value, and lighter cases in which the patient's anxiety has expressed itself in a failure to eat but might presumably have expressed itself in some other way—in which in fact a different sort of nexus between psychic breakdown and physical breakdown is postulated—is another current study unintentionally reinforcing this point of view. So also is the McDermott and Cobb[26] classification of asthma cases into the neurotic and the nonneurotic, in which the difference in the life history materials and the responses of the patients to psychoneurotic inventories is regarded as crucial.

If the psychosomatic theory is to be developed to its fullest usefulness, the dramatic correspondence between psychic conflict and somatic symptom, as it appears for instance in anorexia nervosa[27] may most fruitfully be regarded as one end of a continuum, while the gradual wear and tear on the body due to general strain in the response of the whole personality to the demands of life, special to that social environment, may be regarded as the other. Any such continuum can be set against the background of the culture, against the whole complexity of learnings and experiences which occur in a social history which is *negative*, that is to say, uneventfully typical of every individual born into it. It is necessary to realize that every individual born into a society is from birth—and in all probability from before birth—subjected to a progressive moulding by the culture, mediated through all of those with whom he comes in contact, so that the cultural pattern is built into his whole personality in one process in which no dualism exists, so that the temper tantrum, the tautened muscles, the change in the manufacture of blood sugar, and the verbal insults hurled at an offending parent, all become patterned and integrated. Then we see that every individual, and not merely every patient, may be viewed from the psychosomatic point of view, within which individuals who show definite organ neuroses are merely extreme and special developments of one potentiality of the total personality. And we further see that there is no basic *human* personality, but that every individual must be seen against the cultural base line, that he is a special idiosyncratic variant of one of many culturally unique ways in which human personality is developed.

The sort of life history that is *negative* is then seen as a document of the successful moulding of the personality of the individual to the cultural norm, of the successful over- and under-emphases, development and disallowance of parts of the personality, and this successful moulding invokes as great or greater specialization of human nature as does the creation of the personality whose life history is *positive*, that is, filled with deviant events which have so moulded his personality that he cannot adjust to his culture without betraying certain symptoms. In this sense, every human being is paying many definite psychosomatic prices for his adjustment; when these prices are special

or extreme we see him as diseased, as potentially *dying;* when they are
similar to those paid by his neighbors, we set them down as normal
fatigue, normal aging, normal effects of urban living, or normal exposure to the elements, and we see the individual as *living*. But the
difference between the man who is sick and the man who is well is
only one of degree; both men are integrated and specialized compromises between psychosomatic functioning and cultural pressures.

We may, of course, if we wish, rank cultures in terms of what type
of moulding in any given respect is imposed upon the developing
human organism. Erikson[28] has pointed out that American Indian education relies on early indulgence of the young child, followed by
rather strict discipline at a later period when the child, who is secure
because it has not been heavily frustrated, can take the discipline. On
the other hand, other native peoples[29] and we ourselves rely upon a
very early imposition of special forms of behavior, coupled with strong
enough sanctions, parental disapproval, withdrawal of parental love,
and parental punishment to maintain these early-instilled disciplines.
Ratings of cultures as expressed in gross modifications of the human
life span can of course be made. We can arrange cultures in a series
as to the extent to which they include practices conducive to or
inimical to infant survival. So cultures which impose a taboo upon
sexual intercourse during the lactation period give infants not only a
better chance of survival but alter the age ranges of sibling rivalry so
that the operation of the lactation taboo may be seen not only in a
better nourished child but in a different conformation of the character. At one step more removed, the way in which the lactation taboo
is phrased—so as to combine with warm parental feelings, observed for
the child's sake, or so as to conflict with specific sexual motivations so
that it has to be maintained by fear of injury to the parent's health—
will affect the willingness of the mother to nurse the child, the health
of the child, and the spacing of children. A custom of carrying infants
may determine whether or not they get any sunlight under a year old,
and this in turn may be referred not only to the method of punting
canoes, which requires that the adult have both hands free so that the
baby must be able to hold on by itself, but to a system of cultural
values which emphasizes the importance of will power. So the Manus
do not take children out of doors until they are old enough to be
trusted to hold on, although their neighbors have net bags in which
they carry their babies, and in which the Manus could carry their
babies and still punt their canoes. But carrying the children relaxed in
net bags would not fit in with the Manus insistence that children become morally and physically responsible as early as possible. So the
babies are kept indoors and get no sunlight; the Manus infant death
rate is very high.

Alexander[30] and his associates have shown that certain psychodynamics may be summarized by the formula: "I do not need to take or receive, therefore I do not need to give" in which the refusal to give is expressed symbolically by constipation. But degree of constipation or looseness of the bowels is itself subject to cultural standardization. The Iatmul of New Guinea, who expend a great deal of energy teaching their children not to step in feces, human or animal, but are uninterested in points of extreme prudery or rigid routine, have loose and frequent stools. The Manus, living on approximately the same diet, of sago, yams, and fish, and in the same climate, as the Iatmul, have hard-formed stools and defecate only once a day, at a fixed time and place in the early morning. This behavior is consistent with their prudery, rigidity, with their general character structure. If it can be maintained, on the basis of intensive study of selected cases in which constipation has become a chronic means of symbolic expression, that a general somatic alteration which can become irreversible may thus be set up, then it may also be postulated that a lifetime of enjoined routines of defecation may also be expected to produce definite somatic changes. But as long as every member of a society is expressing a general character formula, such as, "I am a good person because I defecate every day and rigidly confine myself to one difficult and constipated stool so that there is no danger of my being caught unawares and out of control and so outraging the feelings of other people," one hard stool a day will be described as "normal," and a medical history which reported this would be *negative*.[31]

Abundant evidence is accumulating for the close relationship between the total personality and skin disorders such as eczema, etc.[32] Differences between the organization of the personality in different cultures may also be expressed through the skin. In New Guinea, when one is treating cuts and wounds, the problem is to make the wound close up, and it has become standard practice among medical assistants and dispensers to wash the wound with a disinfectant and seal it up with zinc adhesive plaster. In Bali where there is an extreme fear of any mutilation or injury to the perfection of the body, an attitude which contrasts strongly with the New Guinea natives' casualness towards wounds, this sealing up treatment cannot be used at all. It is necessary to keep even the smallest and most innocuous looking cut open for several days with continual wet dressings, to combat the tendency of a cut to heal too quickly and then fester. Undoubtedly psychoanalytic exploration of the personalities of individuals who show these contrasting healing tendencies would reveal the formula which summarized the specific attitudes which they express in these ways, but it is also possible for such tendencies to become the standard equipment of every well-adjusted individual who is fully representative of a particular culture.

If students of psychosomatic medicine included in the point of view from which they organize case histories the recognition that to the extent that the patient is "normal" and his life history "negative," to that extent he is a specimen of the special type of moulding peculiar to his culture, not only of the local cultural variation characteristic of his class and occupational group and geographical location, but also of that basic American culture which he shares in its major emphases with all other Americans—if they saw every individual as having been shaped in the functioning of the whole body into an expression of his culture—each special disease picture would assume a very different significance. The so-called healthy or normal individual would be seen as he who had made the same compromises with his body and the same somatic symbolizations as the majority of his fellows, and the student could then proceed to identify what these standard compromises were. Some of these compromises are partially identified: the relationship between bottle-feeding from birth and constipation; the emphasis upon a single daily bowel movement coupled with anxiety if this is not fulfilled and the concomitant use of cathartics and enemas; central heating, increase in children's colds and the consequences; arbitrary sleep periods for children and the accompanying disorders of sleeping later in life; inhibition of childhood sexuality and the inculcation of sexual taboos so stringent that full genital functioning is impaired, etc. It is only necessary to arrange these points and others like them in a systematic order to see the ordinary "healthy" adult American as a product of progressive and regular patterning in a given direction which will make him, other things being equal, specially subject to certain ways of dying, each a function of the fundamentally patterned way of living within which he has grown up.[33]

The effect of culture upon the total functioning of the human being may be viewed in different lights according to whether the primary emphasis is upon the single sick individual or upon the understanding of psychosomatic relationships in their most general and fundamental sense. If the emphasis is primarily upon the individual case the psychosomatic theorist will have made a considerable advance in the invocation of culture in his thinking, if he can think of two individuals from different cultural backgrounds, as he might think of the manifestations of Reynaud's disease under different temperature conditions, a lower temperature providing a more permissive and predisposing environmental setting for the specific pathological condition, than a higher temperature. In this way, American culture might be seen as more permissive to the development of angina pectoris than Chinese culture.[34] Such an understanding of the cultural positions, however, is only a first step although it serves to place the patient, who, through constitution-temperament and personal history, comes to reveal the presence of a disorder in greater or less degree, dependent upon the cultural pressures to which he has been subjected all of his life. The next step is taken when the cultural process is conceptualized, not in terms of a generalized raising or lowering of thresholds so that few or many individuals will succumb to a disease condition to which their specific idiosyncratic circumstances make them liable, but as the *pattern* of interaction between the psychosomatic functioning organism and the cultural system. This pattern will then be found to be as specific as the sort of pattern which is found in the study of the individual psychodynamics of particular pathological conditions.

We may take Graves' disease as an example. It is recognized that the incidence of Graves' disease is related to the amount of anxiety under which the individual lives.[35] This anxiety may then be considered as an idiosyncratic feature of the individual life history; or when we consider the increased incidence of Graves' disease among both military and civilian population in the first World War[36] and the fact that the incidence is again increasing,[37] the increase in anxiety may be seen as a function of the general social situation in which a large number of persons, individually vulnerable to Graves' disease, develop positive symptoms. If we now further postulate not a passing emergency like a depression or a threat of war, but a type of culture which systematically exerts upon the developing organism this sort of anxiety-producing pressure at critical stages in maturation, we might expect an alteration in thyroid metabolism which would become chronic and to which many other homeostatic systems would make a systematic adjustment. The average representative of such a culture would show a consistent variation in homeostatic pattern in the same direction as that in patients suffering from disturbances of thyroid metabolism. In the light of this approach, every socialized individual is seen as so profoundly moulded by his culture that the most fundamental life processes will have systematically different patterns even though these patterns may all lie within the margin of safety for human functioning.

We may now examine the significance for the individual organism of the degree of homogeneity of a culture and the possibility that there is a correlation between concentration of deviant attitudes in specific somatic symptoms and the lack of homogeneity of the culture. In the most homogeneous culture we may expect to find consistent slight pathologies, as well as consistent and systematic somatic modifications. Furthermore we may expect to find a certain amount of aggravation of the consistent pathology in individuals with greater constitutional vulnerability or among those who have been subjected to unusually severe pressures. But the extent to which we find an *exuberance* of somatic expressions of varieties of psychic conflict or persistent character strain may well be correlated with cultural heterogeneity. In a heterogeneous culture, individual life experiences differ so markedly from one another that almost every individual may find the existing cultural forms of expression inadequate to express his peculiar bent, and so be driven into more and more special forms of psychosomatic expression. It is well known that mass hysterias tend to occur among primitive peoples during periods of rapid cultural change when individuals are extremely disoriented. Movements like the Ghost Dance,[38] or the Vailala Madness,[39] simply sweep through a whole district. It is quite possible that the speed with which a disturbed population seizes upon one of these standard hysterias is a function of the extent to which large numbers of individuals have been using divergent idiosyncratic symptoms to express disorientation, all of which will be replaced by the new socially acceptable form of behavior. As periods of cultural change inevitably carry with them a greater degree of heterogeneity, in the history of any culture or sub-culture, periods will be found in which adequate social forms for the expression of points of strain and tension in the personality will be lacking, and the individual will be forced back upon his own body for symbolic expression. In attempting to find systematic relationships in the life histories of patients who suffer from certain psychosomatic disorders, it is important to consider how far the individual patient differs from other members of his class, age, sex, and occupational groups (all of which are indices of the cultural forms which he embodies) and the extent to which standard forms of symbolic expression are denied to him. For instance in the Bruch and Touraine[40] study, one of the most conspicuous common elements in the case histories presented is the isolation of the parents, particularly the mother, from community contacts. The authors comment upon this relationship in a paragraph: "The social contacts and cultural interests of the family generally did not reach beyond the narrowest family limits." They present evidence to show that the homes from which these obese children came were well kept, that the mothers, in fact, were using rubber plants and furniture to express their strivings for individual achievement, just as they were using the bodies of their children as a medium through which to make amends for their hostility to their children for standing in the way of their own achievement. Ordinary community outlets for striving feminine ambitions—comparison of their cooking with the cooking of others, comparison with other mothers of the standard of independence which their children had attained, office and activity in church clubs, etc.—all were absent from the home setting. These mothers who were revealed as specially ambitious and not specially gifted, were, because of their isolation in large urban communities, left with no external media in which to work out their individual conflicts except their homes and their children. They were completely removed from the check of public opinion on which we depend to regularize maternal behavior so that it does not become so idiosyncratic.

During periods of change, of emigration, or rapid movements of labor, of rapid growth of cities with populations of mixed origin, during war and revolution, more and more people get out of reach or out of touch with the social forms which through generations of slow adjustment have become the techniques for resolving the routine strains associated with membership in that culture. Under these circumstances two mutually reinforcing tendencies appear; the culturally disoriented person is subject to new strains of loneliness and isolation which exacerbate the tensions within the personality, and he is at the same time robbed of culturally usual means of reducing these tensions. The available materials on which to work out psychic conflict become one's own body and its immediate extensions in the environment, and one's own family, especially children. If the latter form of expression is chosen it may in turn add to psychosomatic expressions of conflict by affecting the child concerned during critical periods in its development. Similarly, a husband and wife, with a constitutional or developmental vulnerability to some disorder, may be pushed into expressing a psychosomatic illness by the spouse. A vicious circle is set up which has enormous possibilities for disastrous social repercussions, for the patient may also be in significant contact with other members of society, as a foreman, or a teacher, or an executive. The regularity with which psychosomatic disorders of the same type recur in the family history, as for example in the McDermott and Cobb[41] asthma life histories, demonstrates how the tendency to use the body symbolically may be perpetuated within the family, in which an accidental or constitutional weakness in each new member is seized upon for elaboration. Isolated from continual interchange with other persons, who, if not free from psychosomatic disorders, will at least have a different set of them, these family conditions flourish and effloresce and become steadily more expensive to society in terms of lowered efficiency, medical costs, and wrecked human lives.

The Balinese have a form of ordeal in which everyone who takes an oath of innocence of some offense invokes upon himself and his descendants a long list of horrible and incurable diseases. If one of those who has taken the oath subsequently is proved guilty, the community will pay the costs of having the oath ritually nullified, because, they argue, people might forget and someday one of his descendants might marry one of *our* descendants and upon *our* great-grandchildren the punishments would fall. Modern communities might take the same attitude towards permitting the isolation and deculturalization of individuals who thereby become much more likely to develop psychosomatic disorders which may become self-perpetuating.

At the present time, psychosomatic research has set itself the task of identifying the type of character, the order of psychodynamics, which is associated with definite disease pictures. Dunbar and Wolfe have described cardiac and accident fracture types;[42] Deutsch has described the asthmatic male and the asthmatic female;[43] H. G. Wolff has described the migraine character[44] which checks extremely closely with Jensen's description[45] which is based upon a quite different theoretical approach; Alexander[46] and his associates are seeking to identify the character structures of those who are suffering from gastro-intestinal disorders and hypertension. Whether the emphasis is placed upon the present psychodynamics, or upon the developmental background which establishes what Deutsch[47] has called a psychosomatic unit which becomes the inevitable locus of a conflict, the attempt is being made throughout to establish systematic relationships. Inclusion of the concept of culture would involve one more level of such systematic relationships. Running through the contrasting character structures shown by the asthmatic and the sufferer from migraine, the sufferer from essential hypertension and the victim of Graves' disease, there is a significant regularity which involves processes of the same order as those which have already been invoked to explain the separate syndromes. We cannot go directly from the details of the special character structure of the asthmatic to the basic human nature, assuming that the only middle term involved is the modification which has resulted in the asthma. Nor can we dismiss the problem with a vague reference to the pressures of civilization. For a complete and systematic psychosomatic approach it is necessary to identify that which is common to every individual who is reared in our society, and to see these special character types, which are found in association with special disease pictures, as variants of this basic cultural type. Although related mechanisms can undoubtedly be found in individuals from other societies, the special character types would have to be placed against a different base, because in another culture the human organism would have been moulded in a different way. If one wishes to study dietary deficiency, it is not enough to identify the apparent lack of some essential vitamin in the diet of one group of individuals, its apparent presence in another. It is necessary to study the whole diet of the group, if we are to understand the interaction of very different articles of diet, in nourishing human beings who are able to function in society and reproduce their kind. The absence of one ingredient may make the difference as to whether a given diet, that of mountain whites, or Eskimos, or Singhalese, results in a definite deficiency picture, but that one ingredient is only significant when seen in terms of the total diet, as well as in terms of the known facts about human nutrition.

The culture may be likened to the standard diet on which the individual members have subsisted since birth. In merely assaying the effects of various specific factors—extreme unsatisfied dependency cravings, or maternal over-emphasis upon eating when the child had whooping cough at two years old, or the fear of falling short of expectations and so losing love—the student of psychosomatic medicine is in the position of the specialist in diet who is assaying the effects of few green vegetables, or very little fat, without taking systematic account of the whole diet. It is necessary to consider explicitly the relationship of the specific factors to the whole socialization process. The specific factors must all be referred to general cultural conditions: the role played by extreme dependency cravings in a male is partly a function of our insistence upon a contrasting ethos between the sexes[48] so that dependency becomes identified with femininity and arouses homosexual fears; the maternal over-preoccupation with eating is tied up with our stereotyping of the maternal role as making children eat what is good for them (in some cultures the mother's care is directed towards keeping the children from eating too much), and the fear of falling short is a function of the way in which, in this culture, mother-love is made conditional upon the child's achievement. Just as the extreme expressions of these cultural emphases, when they are expressed in individuals with certain constitutional vulnerabilities and certain special life histories, are found in somatic processes which in time become irreversible, so the primary cultural emphases must be regarded as having also systematic somatic concomitants which also become differentially irreversible.

But if this is so, if an understanding of the culture is essential to the understanding of the individual psychosomatic picture, one may well ask why the psychosomatic approach has got as far as it has, when an essential factor was not included in the working hypotheses. No student of diet could get as far, if he studied only certain significant abnormalities and neglected to consider the whole diet. The answer is that because the physician is a member of the culture himself, he *has* taken the culture into account, only he has identified the particular type of cultural moulding which he sees in himself, his colleagues and his patients, as *human nature*. It is as if a special kind of delivery with high forceps, which resulted in a distinctive moulding of the neonate's head, had become a universal obstetrical pattern in our society and all infants were delivered in this manner. Every physician who examined the head of a two-day-old infant would take this moulding into account in making diagnoses and prognoses. It is only necessary to forget or not to know that infants were ever delivered without resulting head moulding, for head moulding to be regarded as the inevitable effect of human birth. For practical purposes the physician would make allowance for the head moulding, and it would not matter very much whether he regarded head moulding as the inseparable accompaniment of human birth, or as a mere item of cultural behavior, local in time and place. When, however, the physician, in addition to being a healer, is also a scientist interested in systematizing his knowledge of human heads and the significance of deviations in the shape of the head at two days old, then it would be absolutely essential that he should realize that this head moulding, which he always encountered, was something imposed upon the human organism by agents of the culture into which it was born and not the inevitable result of its humanity. So the psychiatrist, the psychoanalyst, and the wise physician have always operated with a working knowledge of our culturally standardized character structure and called it *"human nature."* But the physician, *qua* research worker, needs to include in his conceptual scheme a recognition that man's biological potentialities can only be inferred from a study of human beings who have been subjected to many kinds of cultural pressures, and that no human being's behavior can be referred directly to these potentialities.

Such a recognition has profound significance for preventive medicine. If the form of behavior which is manifested with more or less completeness by every representative of our culture were unchangeable, as the phrase *"human nature"* implies, then it would be the physician's task to alter the conditions within the individual, or at most, the conditions within the individual's immediate environment which contribute to his ill health. He could do no more. He would be as hampered as would the dietary expert who assumed that human beings necessarily live on corn meal and salt pork, so that his preventive work would consist of persuading people to eat niacin, or at the widest remove, persuading social agencies to provide niacin which the individual patient was too poor to buy. Assuming corn meal and salt pork to be the inevitable human diet, no purpose would be served by examining the effects of these particular foods upon the human organism. They could be taken for granted. Once, however, it is recognized that no basic diet, neither macaroni, nor rice, nor wheat bread, nor potatoes, nor yams, nor sago, nor seal and walrus meat, is an inevitable human diet, but that all are man-selected, then it becomes possible and necessary to assay the effects upon the human organism of the particular basic diet as well as of the crucial elements in the diet which result in the illness or health of specified individuals.

So the findings of psychosomatic medicine, when placed in a cultural frame, become relevant for education, become basic data for social planning. It will be possible to assemble evidence to show that certain types of psychosomatic modification, carrying within them definite possibilities of a pathology which becomes in time structural and irreversible, are associated with our whole way of life and so are circumstances with which we must reckon. This is so whether the reckoning takes the form of developing compensating cultural forms which will relieve the somatic strain, or dignifying, for example, hypertension as a way of dying, or altering some of our cultural emphases so that the individual organisms will not pay the particular prices which they now pay for being socialized. In planning for any of these forms of preventive medicine, "society is the patient"[49] and it is the research physician who is in a position to provide relevant data and make constructive plans for a health program so inclusive that it concerns itself with the way in which the new organism is socialized and the sort of world in which an individual, so socialized, can live with minimum strain and maximum good adjustment.[50]

NOTES

1. In 1925, I met in Samoa a tuberculosis specialist who had made the three weeks' trip to Samoa in order to hear a "textbook normal" chest, a chest without a single trace of past or present tubercular infection, because he claimed that he could not find such a chest in the United States.

2. For a discussion of the weakness of this approach see Dunbar, H. Flanders, *Emotions and Bodily Changes*, Columbia University Press, New York, 1938; Introduction to the Second Edition, xvii-xl.

3. See especially: Alexander, Franz, Psychological Aspects of Medicine, *Psychosomatic Med.* (1939) 1:7-18; Symposium on Hypertension: Psychoanalytic Study of a Case of Essential Hypertension, *Psychosomatic Med.* (1939) 1:139-152. Duetsch, Felix, The Choice of Organ in Organ Neuroses, *Internat. J. Psychoanal.* (1939) 20: nos. 3 and 4. Dunbar, reference footnote 2; also Character and Symptom Formation: Some Preliminary Notes with Special Reference to Patients with Hypertensive, Rheumatic and Coronary Disease, *Psychoanalytic Quart.* (1939) 8:18-47. Fremont-Smith, Frank, The Influence of Emotional Factors upon Physiological and Pathological Processes, *Bull. N. Y. Acad. Med.* (1939) 15:560-569. Jelliffe, Smith Ely, Sketches in Psychosomatic Medicine, *Nervous and Mental Disease Monographs*, No. 65, New York 1939.

For other approaches to the same problem see: Robinson, G. Canby, *The Patient as a Person*; Commonwealth Fund, New York 1939. Propst, Duane W., *The Patient is the Unit of Practice*; Charles C. Thomas, Springfield, Ill., 1939. Wolfe, Theodore P., Emotion and Organic Heart Disease, *Amer. J. Psychiatry* (1936) 93:681-691.

4. I am not raising the issue here as to whether animals, and particularly domestic animals, may not have some "culture," as it is sufficient for the terms of this discussion to confine ourselves to "human culture."

5. Sapir, Edward, Sound Patterns in Language, *Language* (1925) 1:37-51.

6. Personal Communication from Professor Franz Boas.

7. Based on field work in Bali, by Gregory Bateson and Margaret Mead, 1936-1939. *Balinese Character: A Photographic Analysis*; New York Academy of Sciences, 1942.

8. The terminology here is in such a confused state that it demands more than the fiat of a single individual to straighten it out. It is necessary to distinguish between: the constitution-temperament of the individual—determined by heredity; that part of the individual's functioning which is due to the interaction between him and his cultural forms, which I prefer to call character structure, and which

Abram Kardiner has recently called "basic personality structure" (*The Individual and His Society:* Columbia University Press, New York, 1939; p. 12); and the idiosyncratic aspects of the individual for which there is no satisfactory term in use. The term personality may be used to include all of these different aspects.

9. By the term cultural experience, I mean to indicate that I am dealing not with the vagaries of the individual life, such as the effect of a parent's death in a railway accident or of being locked into a closet by an unstable nurse, but with the sort of experience which in a homogeneous culture would be systematic and shared with a group of other individuals so that knowledge of one detail would permit us to fill in the others.

10. They are not, of course, taken at their face value by a sophisticated physician skilled in anamnesis.

11. This sort of general attribution of responsibility to the past is so familiar to us and so congruent with present theories of the interrelationship between the individual and his environment that it may seem strange to call it a cultural phenomenon. But the Balinese, commenting on a misfortune or failure—if he recognizes the present misfortune as congruent with his past experiences—will merely remark: "I am just not having any good luck this incarnation; well, turn and turn about," in which he conceives of his soul as taking turns with itself, as well as with other souls in succeeding reincarnations, in sampling the good and the bad of life. And where we tend to blame the whole unfortunate past for some single current misstep or failure, the Iatmul native of New Guinea will attribute a whole galaxy of misfortunes resulting in the illness, death, and bad luck of twenty or thirty people to some single event in the past which antagonized another group into invoking black magic.

It is worth remarking that one of the points at which it is most difficult to identify cultural influences is where the cultural phrasing agrees with the current scientific phrasing. I once included in a monograph a description of the Samoan beliefs about birth, which happened to agree in most respects with our own,—and the manuscript was returned to me with an editorial note: "Same all over the world." That editor meant that pregnancy, as far as *we* know, did take about nine months, and so the Samoan belief on the subject was not worth recording; whereas if I had been recording the Iatmul willingness to accept a three-month pregnancy—when a child which is born three months after its father's return from work is said to have "hurried up to see its father,"—I would have encountered no such opposition. Similarly there may be no difference between the content of scientific theory and the individual's belief in vitamins, but the latter may be based on very different psychological mechanics.

There is danger in failing to realize that congruence between cultural behavior and scientific theory may be of many different orders: the scientific theory may have been shaped by the folk belief; both folk belief and scientific theory may have come from observing the same set of data; folk belief may be the result of popularization and diffusion of the scientific theory; and the congruence may be a mere coincidence. Such a failure leads to statements like that made by Ross Stagner and M. H. Krout (A Correlational Study of Personality Development and Structure, *J. Abnormal and Social Psychol.* (1940) 35:339-355; p. 350): "Perhaps the most interesting phase of our data relates to the study of the way our subjects have associated childhood treatment with present reports of their attitudes. (Let us emphasize again that our subjects could not be reacting to conscious associations or suggested theories of these relationships.)"

12. Lynd, Robert S. and Helen M., *Middletown;* Harcourt, Brace and Company, New York, 1929.

13. This may be contrasted with the position of the aristocrat in a homogeneous culture who makes every effort to differentiate himself by idiosyncratic behavior.

14. It would also be interesting to speculate what would be the effect upon the theories of immunization to infantile paralysis as to whether the original experi-

ments were conducted in a population which showed thirty percent, a low immunity, or, as is credited to the Fijians, one hundred percent immunity.

15. See *Psychosomatic Med.* (1939) 1:93-179; Symposium on Hypertension.

16. Benedict, Ruth, *Race, Science and Politics;* Modern Age Books, New York, 1940.

17. Jelliffe, reference footnote 3; see chapter on Dupuytren's Contracture, pp. 36-51.

18. In most cases the physician thinks in terms of vulnerabilities. This patient manifests a disease from which most other individuals of her age and sex are free. What is there in her constitution, her history, and her present character structure which has given her this vulnerability? Usually only under research, as contrasted with therapeutic situations, is the question asked, not why is this individual vulnerable, but why is this individual immune, why does the disease picture which might be expected to appear not appear? Such questions are related to the problem raised by Dunbar of the way in which one type of pathology, e.g., a tendency to fractures, may to some extent, because of the incompatibility of underlying tendencies in the personality, exclude a tendency to some other pathology, e.g., cardiac disorders. Such a distinction may be seen expressed systematically in the difference between two cultures, one of which will encourage a type of behavior which forms the basis upon which a tendency to fractures can develop, while the other culture encourages a type of behavior more congenial to the cardiac symptoms. Immunity, either in individual or in cultural terms, may be expressed as a vulnerability to some other disorder, and the question can reasonably be expressed in either way. Every culture would then be seen as endowing individuals within it with a systematic set of immunities and vulnerabilities; whether a given individual succumbed to the pressures of life and developed a given pathology would then be due to his constitution and life history, and idiosyncratic phrasing of experience on this cultural base. The same individual, in a different culture, but with similar constitution and similar life history and idiosyncratic phrasing, might develop a very different pathology.

19. Alexander, reference footnote 3; Symposium on Hypertension; pp. 139-152 and 173-179.

20. Deutsch, reference footnote 3.

21. See particularly: Levy, David, Fingersucking and Accessory Movements in Early Infancy, *Amer. J. Psychiatry* (1928) 7:881-918.

22. This discussion is purely theoretical in that it assumes that the physician can get an accurate and complete history. In practice it has been found that patients systematically exhibit amnesia concerning just those very events in their lives which have the greatest relevance to their pathological condition. Fremont-Smith, reference footnote 3. Sargant, William, and Slater, Eliot, Acute War Neuroses, *The Lancet*, Vol. II, July 1940.

23. Cowdry, E. V. (ed.), *Problems of Aging;* Williams and Wilkins Co., Baltimore 1939.

24. Jelliffe, reference footnote 3; ch. I *passim.*

25. Rahman, Lincoln, Richardson, Henry B., and Ripley, Herbert S., Anorexia Nervosa with Psychiatric Observations, *Psychosomatic Med.* (1939) 1:335-365.

26. McDermott, Neil T., and Cobb, Stanley, A Psychiatric Survey of Bronchial Asthma. *Psychosomatic Med.* (1939) 1:203-244.

27. Waller, John V., Kaufman, Ralph M., and Deutsch, Felix, Anorexia Nervosa: A Psychosomatic Entity, *Psychosomatic Med.* (1940)) 2:3-16.

28. Erikson, Erik Homburger, Observations on Sioux Education, *J. of Psychol.* (1939) 7:101-156.

29. For example, the Manus of the Admiralty Islands. Mead, *Growing up in New Guinea;* W. Morrow and Co., New York 1930.

30. Summarized in Review in *Psychosomatic Med.* (1939) 1:429-430: Alexander, Franz, The Influence of Psychologic Factors upon Gastro-Intestinal Disturbances: A Symposium: A Report upon Research Carried on at the Chicago Institute for Psychoanalysis. I. General Principles, Objectives and Preliminary Results.

31. A further problem remains as to how much the strain incident to a disordered functioning in any given individual is increased or decreased in terms of the congruence between his symptoms and the standardized but less extreme manifestations of cultural moulding which are common to all members of his culture. In a given individual whose special personality configuration has expressed itself in constipation the degree of strain involved will be a function, not only of the alterations in the intestinal track, the pain, the "energy" diverted from other types of functioning, the secondary repercussions of his symptoms, the degree to which his digestive track has already been moulded in one direction or another by cultural pressure, etc., but also the standard of digestive functioning in his culture. Upon the congruençe between the individual symptom and the cultural emphasis will depend not only the extent to which his symptoms make him conspicuous and subject to immediate social pressures, but also the degree of strain resulting from a conflict between his idiosyncratic symbolism and the standard cultural symbolism. If, for instance, in the symbolic language of the culture, constipation=control=goodness, his problem will be quite different from what it will be if constipation=withholding=stinginess. The ramifications of this problem are too extensive to discuss in this introductory paper.

32. Stokes, John H., Beerman, Herman, and Ingraham, Norman R., The Psychoneurogenous Component of Cutaneous Reaction Mechanisms, *Amer. J. Med. Sciences* (1939) 198:577-588; and especially The Psychoneurogenous Component of Cutaneous Reaction Mechanisms (Part II), *Amer. J. Med. Sciences* (1940) 200:560-576.

33. In this discussion there is no moral valuation involved, nor is the assumption made that there is any dichotomy between a "natural" or "spontaneous" way of life as over against a culturally ordered way of life. In accepting cultural modification of the human organism, one assumes patterning in the sense that the interaction between the new organism and the social environment is continuous, systematic and inescapable.

34. Dunbar, reference footnote 2; especially p. 219.

35. Dunbar, reference footnote 2; especially pp. 151-163. Miller, Emanuel, and Crichton-Miller, H., *The Neuroses in War;* Macmillan, New York 1940.

36. Maranon, G., quoted by Dunbar, reference footnote 2; p. 152.

37. Shorr, Ephraim, Personal communication, December 3, 1940:
"Although I have not had an opportunity to assemble the actual figures as to the admissions of patients with Graves' disease to the New York Hospital during the past eight years, I think it can be safely said that the following fluctuations in their number occurred:
"A. From 1932 through 1935 the number of admissions was great.
"B. From 1935 through the fall of 1939 there was a distinct diminution in the number of patients seen which was particularly noticeable during the first eight months of 1939.
"C. The number of patients then began to increase slowly until early spring of 1940 when there was a very extraordinary rise in the number of patients.
"Psychiatric histories have been taken of a large number of these patients with a view to assembling this material at some time. My impression is that cases in the years 1932 through 1935 were related to the economic conditions at the time. The low incidence in the next three years may be related to the moderate amelioration of the economic distress. The sharp rise in the spring of 1940 represents cases which for the most part had been of many months' duration when they were seen. They did not seem to be related directly to the war situation but may very well have represented the influence of the increased tension in relation to the usual type of problem seen in patients with this disease."

38. Mooney, J., The Ghost-dance Religion and the Sioux Outbreak of 1890, Bureau of Amer. Ethnology, Fourteenth Annual Report, 1892-1893.

39. Williams, F. E., *The Vailala Madness in Retrospect:* In Essays Presented to C. G. Seligman; edited by E. E. Evans-Pritchard, *et al;* Kegan Paul, London, 1934; pp. 368-379.

40. Bruch, Hilde and Touraine, Grace, Obesity in Childhood: V. The Family Frame of Obese Children, *Psychosomatic Med.* (1940) 2:141-206.

41. Reference footnote 26.

42. Dunbar, H. F., Wolfe, Theodore P., and Rioch, J. McK., The Psychic Component of the Disease Process (including Convalescence) in Cardiac, Diabetic, and Fracture Patients, *Amer. J. Psychiatry* (1936) 93:649-679. Dunbar, H. F., Wolfe, Theodore P., Tauber, E. S., and Brush, A. L., with assistance of Rioch, J. McK. and Coffin, Marian, The Psychic Component of the Disease Process (including Convalescence) in Cardiac, Diabetic and Fracture Patients (Part II), *Amer. J. Psychiatry* (1939) 95:1319-1342.

43. Deutsch, Felix, Emotional Factors in Asthma, in forthcoming *Psychoanalytic Quart.*

44. Wolfe, H. G., Personality Features and Reactions of Subjects with Migraine, *Arch. Neurol. and Psychiat.* (1937) 37:895-921.

45. Jensen, M. B., Some Psychological Aspects of Migraine, *Psychol. Record* (1938) 2: December Issue.

46. Alexander, reference footnote 30.

47. Deutsch, reference footnote 3.

48. As more and more evidence accumulates on the importance of the bisexuality of human beings, the significance for psychosomatic theory of the cultural standardization of sexual roles is brought further into relief. All rigid cultural regimentation of individuals with varying degrees of masculinity and femininity are bound to have important psychosomatic manifestation. *Cf.,* the contrast in Deutsch's asthmatic male who shows "feminine" traits and the asthmatic female who shows "masculine" traits.

49. Frank, Lawrence K., Society as the Patient, *Amer. J. Sociology* (1936) 42: 335-344.

50. Dollard, John, Mental Hygiene and a Scientific Culture, *Internat. J. Ethics* (1935) 45:431-439.

THE IMPLICATIONS OF CULTURE CHANGE
FOR PERSONALITY DEVELOPMENT

Margaret Mead

In our current thinking about the development of human personality there is a tendency to discuss the effects of culture change—whether that change be between generations, or between the former and present environment, as though it were an interruption, however frequent, in normal development. Case histories note faithfully that one or other of the parents or spouses were immigrants, that the family has moved many times, or there was a shift from a rural environment to an urban. Allowances are made for these factors as one might make allowance for a physical handicap or the results of a railroad accident.

The assumption implicit in the case history is that the normal course of a human life would be cast under conditions where all the ancestors had lived for several generations in the same place, where social change as registered in the living habits of two successive generations was slow enough to be easily assimilable by adults, and where young people would in turn grow up to marry others of almost exactly the same background. This implicit model, derived as it is from the statistically more frequent types of family life in earlier centuries, has such important implications for education and therapy that it seems worthwhile to do two things: 1) to examine it in reality and not as a construct. That can only be done through field material on primitive or very isolated folk populations, so as to bring into relief the construct quality of the model with which we deal today. 2) To challenge the validity of the model for present-day thinking, and suggest an alternative formulation which seems closer to the observed facts of modern life.

When we examine personality development in a homogeneous, slowly changing culture we find certain outstanding characteristics. Every individual in the human environment will carry the same cultural assumption; both he who observes the social forms gladly, and he who flouts and ignores them; the man who is admitted to the ceremony, and the woman who is excluded; the chief who sets his foot on the slave's neck, and the slave who kneels to receive the stepping foot. If the child is influenced more by the phrasing of one parent than of the other, because of some temperamental identification or accident

623

of upbringing, he will still make a choice that is completely encompassed within his culture.

In a polygamous culture the wife who accepts her co-wife and the wife who rejects her co-wife, both act on a common premise that polygamy is a way in which marriage is normally organized. The gentleness of a grandmother may be contrasted with rough handling, or even cruel practical joking on the part of the grandfather, but the grandmother's gentleness allows for and in a sense contains the joking of the grandfather. She can be gentler because his harshness will prevent her grandson from being too softened by her behavior. He can be harsh because the solace of her gentleness can be relied upon.

The knee baby may be weaned with great suddenness and apparent lack of care because an earlier period has been, as it were, included in the weaning process. The child has learned that suddenness is not necessarily cruelty,[1] or that all periods of deprivation are followed by periods of indulgence, or that whenever he has been the victim, he has in turn been able to retaliate. The single act, or special treatment accorded the child at one period—at teething, weaning, or in learning sphincter control—does not stand alone to traumatize or provide some life-long obsessive pattern.

Adults and older children, within whose personality the culturally distinctive learning sequence has been integrated, are able to impart simultaneously the place of the present bit of learning in a longer sequence, that which the child has already experienced and the part which is to come. The trembling hand of old age, as it strokes a child's feverish skin, contains in it a promise not only of the bearableness of illness, but also of the bearableness of death itself, or of the unbearableness of both.

I do not mean to indicate that because a culture is homogeneous and very slowly changing, this means that growing up within it is necessarily a smooth, painless, or untraumatic process. However traumatic or frustrating the life experience is, it can nevertheless be presented to each growing individual as *viable*, and to that extent bearable. The demands made in traditional Japanese culture (2) on the child and on every individual in the society may seem on inspection to go beyond the limits of human tolerance. Yet Japanese culture has survived and provided philosophical and aesthetic statements of life which made life significant and meaningful, if not pleasant, to those who were born within it.

This *simultaneity of impact* is carried not only by the behavior of each individual with whom the child comes in contact, but is also mediated by ritual, drama, and the arts. The shape of a pot, the design on the temple door, the pattern of the courtyard, the form of the bed, the grave posts or the funeral urn, the dancer's headdress and the clown's mask, are again reinforcements and whole statements of the same pattern which the child himself is experiencing serially.

Significant contrasts can be drawn between the course of personality development in which children are majorly reared by grandparents who have almost completed the cycle of life,[2] by parents who stand at the maximum point of contrast with the child, or by older children, themselves but recently emerged from the state in which their younger charges now are. Even though differences in emphasis of this sort, or the comparable differences when the nurse is of a different class, or because of the intervention of the boarding school as determinative factors in the distinctive differences between cultures, it is seldom an all or none matter. Children are not reared entirely by children, entirely by parents, or entirely by nurses. Many different people of different ages and both sexes, different temperaments and contrasting kinship positions, play counterpuntal roles in the life of the growing child.

Two further characteristics of growing up in a homogeneous, slowly changing society may be described as the effective *prefiguring of future experience* and *reinforcement and consolidation of past experience*. As soon as the child is able to assimilate the behavior of those about him, he sees older children living out the next steps in his own emerging life pattern, sees the dying and the dead completing it. On the other hand he sees the child at the mother's breast suckled as he was suckled, soothed or scolded in the same words which were so recently used to him. His own infancy—with its uncontrolled outbursts of anger, unmanageable fears, unregulated excretion, and exorbitant hungers and thirsts—does not remain as the same kind of partly repressed, partly remembered record of ignominy and licentiousness with which clinical pictures in our type of society make us so familiar.

Again and again the individual memory, so treacherous, so subject to distortion, is corrected and quieted by the child's experiences as a spectator of many other similar situations, which other babies are living through just as he is emerging from that stage himself. As a five- to ten-year old he observes the differently loaded behavior of early childhood from a quite different set of preoccupations.

At adolescence, the reassurance provided by such repetition is available when the rapidity of physical changes within the body revives some of the early childhood patterns, or as the mother awaits the birth of her first baby, or the father anticipates parenthood. When extreme old age again brings early childhood experience dangerously or temptingly close to consciousness, infants are still present to scream and tauten their bodies like a bent bow, to defecate in anger, to pound the breast, or cling to it for comfort too long. Man lives through these events, which loom so conspicuously in his own overinflated memory, and comes out a quite usual person, neither a great criminal nor a great hero.

When an individual grows up in a homogeneous slowly changing culture, the older he grows, the surer he grows, and the better acquainted he becomes with the form which other peoples' behavior will take. Behavior can become automatic; for example, as those who drive motor cars in only one city can let more of their driving behavior sink below the level of consciousness. When to turn right and when to turn left, who should enter a door first and who second, who must be seated first, who will help themselves first from the common dish, when the ceremony will really begin, how much error to allow on any calculation, when people mean what they say and when their speech is only ceremonial self-deprecation or shrewd bargaining—all these the child learns as he grows.

As old age approaches and the immediate memory dims, the past is a reliable guide to the present, and the old grandfather threads his way with assurance through the most intricate social situation. Whether the culture is one in which consciousness is valued or deprecated, whether all of life flows smoothly or parts of it are designed to contrast sharply, there are nevertheless wide areas in which the freedom to act habitually lessens fatigue, makes motor behavior more economical, and provides a steady compensation for the decrease in spontaneity and zest which usually accompanies the aging process (13).

If we consider carefully these real characteristics of life in a homogeneous society, it becomes immediately apparent that these conditions are true for such a limited number of our population today that those few are placed in a position so deviant that it becomes a liability through its unusualness. The carefully fitted together internally coherent sequences of behavior and the implications for learning of their presence in the behavior of others, the prefiguration of the future and the consolidation of the past, or finally, the increase in automatic behavior and sureness with age—all these are missing. The rapidity of social change alone during the last few decades has, for most people, eliminated all of these features. Each person who approaches an infant is likely to approach it with behavior which embodies sequences to which the child will not otherwise be exposed. The behavior of the adults is discrepant and confused because of the breaks in continuity in their own upbringing.

The growing child sees old people sicken (although seldom allowed to see them die) and fail in a way congruent with *their* past. Children only a few years younger than himself are reared along entirely different lines—they are rocked where he was put firmly in his cradle; fed on self-demand where he was kept to schedule, given a pacifier where he was denied one, or the reverse. Instead of being able to develop more and more automatic behavior, he must learn to be increasingly on the alert for lights that turn off differently, lavatories with a different flushing system, games which have the same names but are played with different rules, etc. Far more important, on the social level, he meets ever-changing standards of manners and morals, shifting criteria of refusal and acceptance. There is no chance for relaxation, for, even as he becomes adept and in part accustomed to the ways of his adult contemporaries, his own children begin to display new forms of behavior to which he has no clues. By the time grandchildren arrive, the gap is so great that many grandparents are refusing even to try to bridge it.

Seen in this light, it will be recognized that the normal expectancy today is for a type of personality development with different characteristics, and that there is urgent need to define these characteristics and integrate them into our systematic expectations of human beings. Since our systematic knowledge of personality formation in homogeneous societies far outstrips our knowledge of the process or even of the effects of heterogeneity and social change, the next step must be to indicate some of the problems involved; that is, to alert the research worker and begin to clarify the task of the educator and therapist.

We may begin with the type of case in which an individual reared in *one homogeneous culture enters, as an adult, a quite different culture*.[3] By this I mean such contrasts as between an Italian village and the city of Detroit, or between a Puerto Rican village and an American factory, or correspondingly when a member of western Euro-American culture goes to live permanently in an isolated part of the Arctic, or in a Southeast Asian jungle. In this case the individual has already a coherent personality, nurtured under the conditions which we have already described. (The Italian villager or the Puerto Rican will have come from a more coherent background than the member of a modern urbanized culture, but it is still possible to find living individuals in England or Germany who grew up within a culture which was still relatively homogeneous and not yet completely disrupted by unassimilated change.) It will be useful to indicate here some of the types of adjustment which may occur.

The immigrant may keep intact his cultural picture of the world, his cultural ideas of hierarchy or order of the way in which events "naturally" occur, and merely accept from his environment concrete information and points of references. He will learn the address of a restaurant, how to read the menu, what a meal will cost and how much of a tip to give. The significance of the restaurant itself—as a place where men go to be away from their women folk, where one takes one's whole family on a holiday, as a place where one takes a mistress but never a wife, where one drinks alone in a curtained booth—will retain its original configurational meaning for him. When he goes there he will experience the sense of irresponsible masculinity, the pater familias role, the sense of pleasant sin, or rather repellent sin for which restaurant life stood in his original culture. He may learn the names of many restaurants, their street numbers and days of closing, but each item remains simply a concrete, more or less imperfect substitution of a foreign element in an unaltered scheme. He may marry a wife from the new culture, and only perceive her behavior at the points where it can be interpreted in terms of his own conception of the wife and mother role. If from her cultural background she expects him to carve the roast, while he comes from a culture in which one honors the man by never letting him serve a spoonful of peas or even ask for the salt, her behavior will symbolize lack of respect to him to the end of his days.

We see an interesting illustration of the relationship between the substitution of such concrete and historical bits of a preexisting pattern as contrasted with the substitution of new patterns in the phenomenon known as "tropical memory." After several years in a completely alien environment, where the physical environment, the food, the tempo, the very premises of life are different, the occidental often finds that he has forgotten most of the proper names which were completely available to him in his western life. Practically every item in his former life which would have been spelled in English with a capital letter disappears, while the life which they stood for is remembered perfectly clearly. Conversations on one's return to the old scene after several years' absence have an extraordinary quality. There is conversation of the respective merits of two actors whose names are forgotten, of a play, the name lost, at two theaters, once familiar and now designated as "that theater near the center of town with the very wide single balcony." As each of these fantastic conversations, studded with omitted proper names goes on, the names begin to come back and, after a few weeks in the home environment, again become parts of the ordinary memory store. It will take much research to describe this process which gives the impression of a different "setting" of the human organism on a concrete historical level on the one hand, and the cultural pattern level on the other.

A second type of conflict occurs when the immigrant or colonist attempts to establish a new pattern by trying to alter his expectations and standards to fit into the new society. Here a variety of effects may be seen. His previous cultural experience may become almost inaccessible, even to the point where a language spoken until adulthood appears to be forgotten, so intense is his acceptance of the new and the need for blocking out the "interference" of the old. If the individual later leaves the new culture and returns to the old, a similar type of apparent loss of memory may occur. In this type of "culture contact adjustment," the individual does not fit the two cultures together, but puts, as it were, the whole of his personality in a position to learn the new culture. What this means in terms of psychosomatic cost, we have as yet no method of assaying.

Even a relatively homogeneous culture may utilize such sharp contrasts in the course of the developmental sequence that a related type of forgetting may occur and some items be almost completely removed from memory availability. In tracing personality development under such circumstances, there is, I believe, adequate data to show that these intervals of extreme contrast in the life history, although sinking below the level of availability, are part of the personality structure of the individual. It is possible that some of these contrasts, whether in structure of situation within the life history in a homogeneous culture, or between two cultures, each learned at a different period of life, may be found to have a variety of systematic and identifiable effects. In some cases they may be part of a vertical structure, and an essential part of it; in others, mere horizontal supplements to the rest of life in which the "years I spent in Paris" are regarded essentially as duplications of years spent learning and enjoying another culture. They may also play into a more abstract definition of life in which the individual who has shared intensely in two contrasting cultures may include contrasts in culture in his widened gestalt. In the case of children, exposed serially to two cultures, some scattered evidence suggests that the premises of the earlier may persist as distortions of perception into later experience, so that years later errors in syntax or reasoning may be traced to the earlier and "forgotten" cultural experience.[4]

Another order of complication occurs when the split between the old and the new culture is made, not as a split between the conceptual and the concrete, or completely in time and attention, but instead as between different areas of life, such as home and work, family life and public life, etc. Materials on immigrant families provide abundant illustrations of these various splits, of groups who live in enclaves where the native language is still spoken and the whole pattern of living conforms to the original culture. Leaving it daily for the working world, they speak the language of that outside world, handle the currency, fill out the forms, and meet the work expectations of the new culture. Where such a split is made, the older conceptual framework in which home and work had their own significance is likely to survive to invest the culture of the "working world" with the glamor or drudgery assigned to work, versus home life, in the older culture. Where the living habits of the new culture are taken over for everyday life, but festival patterns of the old cultures are invoked for weddings, funerals, and all high holidays, the new culture becomes invested with the aura of the ordinary; the old keeps a nostalgia-invoking quality (6).

A still different type of split occurs with the need to adjust to the new culture through the person of a relative or spouse, as when an immigrant boy comes to live with a highly acculturated uncle, or a recently arrived immigrant marries a girl who is thoroughly representative of the new culture. Whatever patterned significance the particular relationship had, if a wife was seen as comfort or responsibility, a mentor and curber of errant impulses, or a partner in indulgence, becomes the conceptual form in which the new culture is perceived and assimilated.

Changes in status as an immigrant moves from one country to another may also deliver such a shock that the perception of the new culture contains a sharp gradient, or sharp discontinuities as a major element. The shock may be so great that no systematic perception of the new culture is ever achieved or a systematic distortion may result.

I have discussed first the type of change which occurs when an individual is reared in one culture, and migrates to the second culture in which he establishes a relationship of some duration. These are the dramatic situations, easy to delineate, extremely conspicuous and familiar in the American scene. Lesser types of migration, especially from rural to urban life, or from class to class, present the same features in less dramatic form.[5]

In generation change, we can find the analogue of the individual who keeps his original cultural orientation and merely adjusts superficially to the new culture. Those who live in the past, while transacting their everyday business on a contemporary level, are familiar figures in societies which combine rapid change with class mobility. An adjustment may be "frozen" at an earlier level by identification with parents whose way of life belonged to another generation, because the individual, now adult, cannot live at the same class level or in the same way they did. Without models for his new life, he may make only the most superficial adjustment, and his values and patterns of human relationships may be completely referred to the past. Conversely, we have the type of adjustment in which the individual "migrates" into the next generation, assumes the manners and attitudes of the child generation, often suppressing completely all the values of his own generation. The present trend in American life to keep the mother perennially young is tending to standardize this type of generation displacement. It is developing compensatory or defensive reactions on the part of the young as they attempt to distinguish themselves—the real inhabitants of adolescence in 1947—from the invading forty-year-olds.

Fragmented types of development may occur as the growing child patterns his conscience on some member of the older generation, and shapes his ideal of himself upon the expressed day dreams of some other member who belongs to a different generation or possibly to both a different generation and a different original culture. Serious distortions occur when the mechanisms of inter-generation behavior, whatever that may be, break down. This occurs when an epidemic selectively kills off the grandparent generation, which happened in many parts of the South Seas in World War I, or where a work or war pattern takes the young men during the years when they would have been models or disciplinarians of their younger brothers, or buffers between the younger and the older. Memory distortions as severe as those which cover a change from one culture to another may occur, as the elders retrospectively falsify their own past behavior either to make it conform to the demands which *their* parents implanted in them as children, or to the world of their children to which they do not belong. Both types of distortion create difficulties, as both violate the original consistencies of the real behavior and make it possible either to perpetuate an increasingly untenable behavioral ideal[6] of imputed past conservatism, or to obscure the possible difficulties and contradictions involved in some new experimental step being taken by the adolescent generation. Thus a parent insisting that his youth conformed to the highest standards, rather than admitting he often failed to conform and paid heavily in anxiety or guilt, will introduce a disorienting factor into the child's adjustment. Likewise, the over-complacent parent who takes advantage of loosening standards to live out vicariously some license which was not permitted in his own youth, may equally cast a shadow of sin over some adolescent practice which would otherwise have its own workable ethics.

There remain to consider those types of generation contrast which occur with cumulative, rapidly accelerating change such as the world has experienced in the last two or three hundred years.[7] A new set of contrasts become conspicuous. The previous generation seems surer because of having been reared under more homogeneous conditions which are gone, and the contemporary generation is both up to date and unsure (9).

Culture change aggravates the effects of oscillatory changes between the members of different generations within the same family, as when an indulgent mother spoils and over-protects a daughter, who then makes heavy demands on *her* daughter. She, in turn, schooled to self-denying service, becomes an indulgent mother. It is probable also that those trends within single family structure in which there is some deep instability (11), will have a greater tendency to become cumulative and result in disaster during a period of rapid accelerating change.

It should furthermore be recognized that the types of contrast due to contrast of culture and those due to contrast between generations are of course interwoven in every possible way, with the culture contrast being at least superficially easier to describe.

Both types of contrast—those introduced by migration of individuals between cultures, and those introduced by a rapidity of change which places the members of succeeding generations who do not migrate in very strongly contrasted position—may be described as primary effects of cultural change. The disorganizations they produce have a kind of clarity of outline which may be attributed to the existing degrees of homogeneity in the cultures or generation behavior patterns involved. We face in the present day world a form of personality which reflects these primary contrasts, at a second and third remove in the children and grandchildren of those whose personalities have been subjected to pressures and changes of the order which has been described. Where the first generation of sharp culture contact, between different cultures or between different periods of rapid cultural change, manifested the various types of amnesia, distortion, and confusion between different perceptions of cultural and historical reality, the second generation shows the effects of having been reared among individuals who were in various degrees representative of the first type.[8]

This second stage of manifestation of extremely rapid change combined with increasing mobility of peoples so that both temporal and local roots are gone, is becoming the expected personality type for the world. This is so provided the breakdown of European feudal institutions on the one hand and of Oriental agrarian societies on the other, proceed piecemeal under various unrelated auspices rather than under the auspices of any group powerful enough to handle their own orthodoxy as a homogeneity which must be accepted. Although data are lacking, it is probable that such a purposive westernization or modernization of a society, under the guidance of a self-consistent ideology, will produce merely another example of primary culture contact. In North and South America, in Western Europe, and in Britain the war has loosened the old locality ties which preserved some cultural and local orientation in the face of great technological change. We may therefore expect to find as the emerging type of personality the child who has been reared among persons who have themselves been subjected to profound cultural and historical disorientation. The same is true of all those parts of the orient where modernization and the importation of western ideas is unaccompanied by power sufficient to regularize and integrate the change. This power did exist in nineteenth century Japan, so that Japanese culture maintained its cultural integrity through industrial revolution, as Britain had done earlier.

In this group of partially disoriented and partially reoriented persons, certain characteristic forms of behavior may be examined systematically in the effect on the children who grow up under their influence. Among them may be found: 1) a nostalgia for a homogeneous and internally consistent view of life which becomes an available focus for various forms of religious and political propaganda offering a unitary solution of all problems; 2) a disturbance between memories of the past and expectations of the future; 3) internal discrepancies in habits of disciplining children, conducting domestic relations, and managing work contacts; 4) disturbed and inconsistent images of their children's future; 5) unevennesses in grasp of the contemporary culture in which they live, ranging from formal literacy without any real ability to handle reading as a tool, to isolated professional patterns of behavior thoroughly discrepant with the rest of their habits of living. It is necessary to add to this picture that in most instances no single pair of parents will show the same pattern. Teachers, friends, and relatives will show other variants, so that to the internal contradictions and inconsistencies existing in each rearing adult, must be added the whole set of intricate relationships among a group of such adults.

As it was possible to describe the characteristics of personality development within a homogeneous, slowly changing society, when members of such societies were subjected to sharp and prolonged exposures to other cultures or to very rapid technological change, so it should also be possible to begin to describe the characteristics of this group who show the secondary effects of the spatial and temporal disturbances of modern times. This secondary effect has been described by Charles Eastman (son of a Sioux Indian mother and a father who was part Sioux, part Caucasian) who lived as a boy the life of his grandparents, and as an adult, the life of an educated modern American.

As a child I understood how to give, I have forgotten this grace since I became civilized. I lived the natural life, whereas I now live the artificial. Any pretty pebble was valuable to me then; every growing tree an object of reverence. Now I worship with the white man before a painted landscape whose value is estimated in dollars! Thus the Indian is reconstructed, as the *natural rocks are ground to powder and made into artificial blocks* which may be built into the walls of modern society (1) (italics mine).

Here speaks the representative of the primary stage who already sees the young in the next stage where values are no longer multiple and incommensurate but estimated in dollars; that is, estimated *on a single scale*.[9]

The capacity to organize experience in terms of a cultural reality inherent in growing up in a homogeneous culture, is lost among the children of those who have themselves undergone the first impact of change. As a result perceived experience becomes *atomized* into units which have no structural relationship to a whole that can no longer be perceived. The shape of the blocks themselves is seen as arbitrary in contrast to the "natural rocks," those whose form was not imposed upon an aggregation of meaningless units.

Individuals reared in this secondary stage develop an approach to life which Erikson (7) has called "tentative" and I have described as "situational" (15). Erickson has pointed out that the modern American, who is perhaps the best studied example of this modern type of human being, must be able to be *sedentary* as well as *migratory*. His tentativeness must cover not only a range of situations but a range which actually involves polarization.

A fourth characteristic of this personality type may be described as a tendency to fragment, unsystematically, the counterpart within personality development of the tendency to perceive the world atomistically. This lack of coherence, this tendency toward fragmentation under strain provides an opening for propagandist movements offering a coherent view of life just as the nostalgia of the primary stage presents an opening to such movements.

Meanwhile modern American culture has developed a variety of therapeutic and educational measures designed to protect and strengthen the individuals who are exposed to this terrific cultural strain, especially during childhood. Conspicuous among these socially self-corrective devices are: 1) emphasis on a new type of child rearing which takes "self-demand" (the child's own individual physiological rhythm) as the framework for habit formation; 2) the progressive education movement with its philosophy of letting the child strike its own pace; 3) types of social case work and psychiatry which stress the need for helping the individual work out his own problems and achieve a new integration.[10] (5) These methods may be seen in historical perspective as the efforts of a disoriented society to develop human beings who will be strong enough to survive and participate constructively in creating new cultural forms which will again restore some order to human life.

Kepes (10) has described the modern artist as fasting from the indigestibility of the visual forms of this muddled modern world and turning entirely to inner experience as the only reliable contemporary guide. Movements which turn to "inner rhythms" may be expected to develop in almost every field of life during this period of unprecedented strain which now faces the human race. They need not be seen as a final rejection of cultural form or traditional, ethical, or aesthetic discipline, but rather as a blessed expedient, imaginatively devised, for the present human emergency.

NOTES

1. For a discussion of these deutero learning effects see (3).

2. Typical of many Plains Indian Tribes.

3. I am excluding, for lack of space, the situations in which an individual from one culture may live for most of his life in another culture, in which there is a traditional allowance for his presence which does not presume any change occurring in her personality. The Dutch or British colonial administrator, the gold miner in New Guinea, the Arab money lender, the foreign trader who lives in the country with which he trades—are all examples of individuals whose own cultural position may actually be intensified by their residence within a society with a different culture. In some cases this intensification will also be found in immigrant groups such as Irish-Americans in Boston whose original relationship to the United States was postulated upon a possible return to a liberated Ireland.

4. I have observed scattered instances of such behavior. One instance is the case of an American child who lived during the period when he was learning to talk in American Samoa; he learned to speak both languages. He returned to America, "forgot" his Samoan and, at the age of 7 and 8, greeted any attempt to speak Samoan to him as a sign that the speaker was discussing something pornographic. But as a high school student with a very high IQ he often had difficulties with the simplest syntax, which could be referred to the Samoan linguistic forms. A comparable case occurred with an American Indian girl who spoke idiomatic American, but in the seventh grade of an ordinary grade school wrote an English which was filled with errors characteristic of literal translations from her Indian language (16).

5. The type of contrast occurring between generations in a rapidly changing society is related to the type of contact with two distinct cultures, but is subtler and more difficult to delineate. We may again profitably distinguish different types and preserve, for the sake of ease, a parallel organization. It must be recognized that in culture change, the relationship of each generation's distinctive style of life to the common base is usually though not necessarily closer to the basic premises of the former generation. However, it is open to question whether an immigrant from England to Australia has to adjust within a less comparable conceptual frame than does a modernly educated Chinese youth who returns to his village in a far off Chinese province after having absorbed the premises of western education. A distinguishable difference in culture, as when a national boundary is crossed or a different language is spoken, serves as a sort of warning to the self and to others that a change has occurred and must be dealt with. Changes in the same culture between generations, or within the same society between classes or regions not identified as different because less labelled, may be dealt with differently by the adjusting personality and produce a more confused pattern lacking the systematic amnesias and distortions of the conspicuous culture contact situation.

6. See especially the role played by the Mundugumor who insisted on clinging to the ideal of a culture that functioned along lines which the actual present day society had abandoned, and so slowed down the much needed adjustments between ideal and reality (12). A further complication occurs when the ideal is conceived in a given generation and projected into the future, so that the whole question of ideological loyalty takes on a quality of extreme idealism, in turn breeding a compensatory cynicism or hedonism as a form of adjustment in the contemporary scene. This is characteristic of the American attitude toward ideals set forth in the Declaration of Independence and in the Constitution. This is a possible development in the Soviet Union where a single generation constructed the ideal for the future, defined as a break with the past. The British convention, under which the most radical departure is integrated with the past as a "step long overdue," simplifies the relationship of each generation to the past in Britain, but complicates relationships toward those next steps which those who initiate them insist on defining as *new as* well as overdue, as is the case with colonial possessions and dependencies.

7. Contrasts between generations of these sorts have of course occurred to some extent for many centuries and occur in many societies, even in primitive societies like Mundugumor where change is rapid enough to introduce conspicuous breaks in traditional behavior. Interestingly enough, styles of clothing, which change rapidly in New Guinea, had become fixed by generation. The old women wore, not a costume of the elderly nor the newest style of the day, but an outworn style of yesterday.

8. I make no attempt here to locate these various types firmly in time or in a generation sequence. With the differences in age of contact, in presence or absence of grandparents and other two-generation ascendant relatives, in residence inside or outside an enclave, in the rapidity of intermarriage with other immigrant or emigrant groups, or with the native group, to the extent in which change of national culture also represents a change from one technological level to another, or one class position to another, it is not possible to specify just which groups in the population of any country will consistently show the reflections of the first type, and which the second type. I limit myself here to describing types of personality which emerge when certain structural conditions of change obtain.

9. The limiting effects of estimating all the values of life in a single unit have often been described as inevitable in a money economy. Actually, money is simply a particularly convenient counter in periods when most of the members of a society are seeking to reduce life to a single, manageable scale. See (4) (7) (8), and my own discussion of the single scale point (14).

10. These movements have often been phrased as revolts against previous cultural forms, against puritanism or classicism, because in many cases they are initiated by percipient individuals who themselves represent a primary type of culture contact or generation change, but who sense acutely the greater need of those who represent the secondary type.

BIBLIOGRAPHY

1. ASTROV, 1946
2. BENEDICT, R., 1946-b
3. BATESON, 1942-c
4. BATESON, 1949-a
5. COBB, 1947
6. Comm. on Food Habits, 1942
7. ERIKSON, 1947
8. FRANK, 1940
9. HICKS, 1946
10. KEPES, 1947
11. LEHMANN, 1945
12. MEAD, 1935-a, Part II, pp. 167-233
13. BURGESS, E. W., 1942
14. MEAD, 1942-d, pp. 138-158
15. MEAD, 1946-c
16. SAER, 1923
17. VONNEUMANN & MORGENSTERN, 1943

SOME THEORETICAL CONSIDERATIONS ON THE PROBLEM OF MOTHER-CHILD SEPARATION

Margaret Mead

The publication by the World Health Organization of John Bowl-by's study of mother-child separation (5) has highlighted the extreme importance of this area of research. The International Seminar on Mental Health and Infant Development held at Chichester in the summer of 1952 (27) further emphasized the extent to which findings in the field of child care may now be rapidly generalized, affecting medical practice, hospital design, and public health practices all over the world. This new capacity for the rapid dissemination and translation into practice of research findings places an extra burden of responsibility for the very careful examination of the theoretical basis of research on those of us concerned in either the research itself or the experimental translation of the research into practice. In this paper I want to consider the present status of our knowledge about mother-child separation, attempt to define some of the most immediate questions for research, and suggest the lines along which this research may perhaps be pursued most profitably.

We may first consider the type of research on which the theory has been developed. Research in the field of cultural anthropology and research in fields basic to the exercise of therapeutic skills have in common a sense of urgency on the one hand and a subject matter of great complexity on the other. Field anthropologists have never been able to wait until newer and better methods of research were devised. If we waited, our material would disappear. We have always worked on the edge of possibility, in cultures which had already come into some contact with a higher culture and which were being subjected to more European contact with every day that passed. In comparable fashion, the therapist cannot wait, because the patient now in the consulting room must be dealt with *now*. It is perhaps this combination of urgency and complexity which gives anthropological and psychiatric research other common features—a refusal to oversimplify in order to appear scientific and a continued use of the highly trained human being as a diagnostic instrument. We have refused to give our material spurious quantification by translating subjective judgments or poor observations into numbers, as is done for instance when three judges are asked to rate poor material and the research worker then acts as if the addition of the three judges somehow alters the quality of the original observation (48). We have continued to rely on the speed of multiple observation of which human beings and human beings alone are capable, knowing that the clinical observation "the child is frightened" can be made, but that no observer or set of observers could record rapidly enough the multiple observations on which the clinician's statement is based when, using all his senses plus a stored memory of the child in previous states, allowing for respiration, pallor, tensity of muscles, direction of vision, etc., he makes the judgment on the child.

To make the statement "Charles showed more fright on his second visit," or to say "In the 'X' tribe babies make a passive adjustment to the bodies of their carriers" (28) requires thousands of such units, the utilization of an enormous number of stored memories, thousands of cross-correlations. Furthermore, all of these are made without tearing apart the texture of Charles's behavior as a whole reacting human being responding to a real situation, as is necessary if one attempts to substitute indicators of states (such as, for example, the psychogalvanic reflex) on the one hand, or to standardize stimuli, on the other, as is done in standard word-association tests. Similarly, the anthropologist must be able to observe many infants at many times in many situations—noting, remembering, recording mentally—in order finally to make the statement about "passive adjustment." Whether the observations of the clinician or the anthropologist stand up when subjected to interpretation within some wider theoretical framework which makes prediction possible—as prediction from one clinical hour to another, or from one body of observations on a culture to another body of observations on the same culture—is primarily a function of how good a clinician or how good an anthropologist the reporter is, "good" in the sense of having acquired trained and disciplined sensitivity to the particular type of phenomena being observed.

These statements may appear truistic to this audience, accustomed as clinicians to include the worker within the observation, again often unconsciously, as when a psychiatrist makes a different sort of rapid correction for a report coming from one social caseworker than he does for one coming from another, or from one psychologist rather than another. If the statement "Charles showed more fright on his second visit" comes from a worker he has found sensitive and trustworthy, it will be given immediately a weight different from that given the same statement from a less sensitive worker, while a statement from an unknown caseworker will be evaluated in terms of the psychiatrist's general judgment of the degree of precision that can be expected from caseworkers in general. Judgment on a mother's report on a child will include the psychiatrist's knowledge of the particular mother, his response to her at the moment she makes the report, and probably also something of his general theory about the accuracy of maternal reporting or the reporting of special types of mothers who have been classified as "overprotective," "compulsive," and so forth. In the same way, an anthropologist reading a field worker's statement includes the personality, training, and theoretical framework of the writer, the period of history, the size of population on which observations were made, the length of stay, etc., in evaluating his statements about such a matter as infant care.[1] An extreme example of failure to take such factors into account is given by Orlansky's statement.

When anthropologists work in groups, the same care which the clinician uses is exercised. Observations are analyzed in terms of what X's informant, Y, said to X; they are not merely taken at their face value.[2] Most of our information about the way in which methods of child rearing are expressed in character formation is of this order—careful reports by trained people, actually summaries of millions of unrecorded and unrecordable observations which have been coded and correlated by the particular human being who made them. These observations stand up well when submitted to theoretical analysis or appropriate internal cross-checking for congruence. The current efforts to handle "scientifically" the importance of early child training in shaping character have attempted either to use incomparable data (Whiting, 48), putting observations made by the trained and the untrained, the interested and the uninterested, side by side; to test correspondences between single factors, i.e., breast feeding and some index of adjustment (Peterson, 32); or to use retrospective accounts of exceedingly complex behavior (Sewell, 40; Dennis, 8 [on walking in Hopi][3]) in order to claim that differences in child-rearing practices have no effect. None of these attempts to test "scientifically" the hypothesis that child-rearing practices are represented in character formation has taken proper account either of the hypotheses or of the methods and theoretical structure of the anthropologists and psychiatrists who have been responsible for the research involved and its interpretation.[4] Stated broadly, the position for which I believe we have evidence we ourselves can trust is that the character formation of the child represents the child's total environmental situation (15) as it is responded to and introcepted by that child in terms of its constitution and individual life history. Neither anthropologists nor psychiatrists would expect (a) that a single activity like breast feeding would have consistent effects, (b) that the statement "the child was breast-fed" could be interpreted meaningfully unless a trained person had made a detailed study over time of the behavior of both mother and child during the breast feeding, or that (c) a mother's report several years later would indicate anything of what was actually done with enough precision to be valuable in a study of personality. Studies like those of Sewell (40) in which questionnaire results are correlated with test results need not concern us seriously to the point of arousing doubts in our own minds. They are, however, very serious in that they use inadmissible over-simplification to bring into disrepute findings on which recommendations for breast feeding, rooming-in, and self-demand feeding have been based. It is important that the unjustified claims of such research should not be permitted to becloud the climate of opinion.

The second set of researches, the experiments provided by the study of children who have been subjected to a variety of practices in institutions, have given us one valuable set of data (1, 5, 7, 36, 42, 43). It has been, I believe, effectively demonstrated that children do not thrive, in spite of good physical care, if kept as young infants in impersonal institutions, and that separation from the mother—especially at certain periods—has serious deleterious effects on the child. Retardation, failure to learn to talk, apathy, regression, and death all appear as accompaniments to institutionalization when no mother surrogate is provided.

But now let us examine where our recommendations in regard to mother-child relations have gone on the basis of these sets of materials. The institutional experiments suggest that some continuity of interpersonal contact is essential if the child is to thrive. The clinical and anthropological studies point to the great importance of the configuration of that care, both in terms of the total adults-child relationship and of the biologically given, constitutionally specified pattern of the child's development as it is involved in the different zones, modes, senses, etc. (11). Stated concretely, breast feeding provided by an angry mother or an anxious mother may differ more from that given by a relaxed happy mother than breast feeding will differ from bottle feeding given by any of these. To see the exact effects of breast feeding alone, one would need sets of identical twins in whose lives every factor except manner of feeding in infancy was held absolutely constant. The most we can do is to establish the existence of recognizable patterns, which themselves take their consistency and systematic character from the structure of *Homo sapiens* as expressed in culture, so that we can compare the general character formation of children of compulsive, overorderly, time-conscious mothers, or of children reared in societies where compulsive orderliness is manifested regularly by members of that culture as part of the formal child-rearing practices. Sensitive pediatricians are well aware that small changes in procedure will not alter to any appreciable degree the impact of the total situation on the child as long as the personality of mother or nurse is

actively involved in whatever procedure is followed. We are beginning to accumulate records (Jackson, 16) of what happens when modern women with different personality configurations insist on nursing
their babies or practicing natural childbirth. It is on the basis of a
large number of such patterned situations that most of the new procedures recommended for child care have been based, not on simple,
uncritical beliefs that breast feeding was *ipso facto* a single item
which could be relied upon to produce specific good results. To state
the case broadly, those who apply the current findings of psychiatry,
anthropology, and child development research insist that the closer,
warmer, and more frequent the mother's contact with the child, the
more the mother studies the child's own rhythm and the less she imposes an external rhythm, and the better adjusted to developmental
stages the child rearing is—food to chew on when there are teeth to
chew with, toilet training when the child can understand and talk, etc.
—the better the chance that the child will grow up in good communication with his own body and with other people. All the procedures
about feeding, weaning, sleeping, toilet training, etc., are simply prescriptions for implementing this more general attempt to establish new
kinds of child-rearing patterns. It is recognized also that something will
change in those who must administer the new cultural practices, and
that new methods of rearing children are actually a very important
way of making changes in adult attitudes.

This was where the matter stood five years ago (21), and we could
say, I think in all honesty, that we were making recommendations which
were congruent with our research findings, neither claiming too much
nor being unjustifiably cautious in putting what we believed to be true
into practice for the benefit of the contemporary generation.

But during the past few years a whole new set of factors has entered the picture. These may be briefly enumerated as: 1) Exaggerated
statements about the role of single procedures (30), which, although
usually made by critics (31, 39, 48) rather than advocates of the procedures, having affected the climate of opinion on such matters as
breast feeding. 2) Exaggerated and poorly supported claims of the
importance of the mother as a single figure in the infant's life (of
which Ribble's work [34] is an outstanding example; cf. Pinneau [33])
which have included drawing extreme conclusions from the type of
work summarized by Bowlby (5). 3) The use of still photographs,
moving pictures, and sound recordings in the study of interpersonal
relationships, so that we can now make precise recordings of events
which are so complex that we previously had to summarize verbally
what could not be recorded (2, 3, 4, 12, 13, 35, 36, 41, 46). 4) The
possibility of tackling from a new point of view—that of comparative
ethnology (Lorenz [18], Tinbergen [45])—the whole question of the

instinctual elements in parent-child relationships.

Taken together, they should make it possible for us to distinguish much better than we have in the past the biologically given elements in maternity and infancy and to measure the extent to which these are intractable or subject to modification. This means that it is necessary to distinguish between practices surrounding conception, pregnancy, gestation, delivery, and lactation, as far as the mother is concerned, and birth, sucking, and the subsequent set of experiences of the child in which the patterning is given during growth in the total interpersonal situation of the first two or three years of life. Put concretely, how much better and in what ways for mother and for infant are a "natural delivery," and putting the infant to the breast early and often, and how much better and in what ways is the mother's relation to the child established if she is conscious during delivery, has the child with her from birth, etc.? I have purposely phrased this as an applied problem rather than a pure research problem, because whatever research is done will immediately be subject to application. We need to know not only what part is played by consciousness or pain in establishing maternal feeling, but also what practices seem best suited to our stated child-rearing goals.

We need to know such detailed things as the effects of the infant's cry on the contraction of the uterus, whether there are definable stages during labor in which the mother shifts from positive to negative attitudes (which would have serious implications for the point at which an anesthetic is administered, etc.). We need to know whether there is something in the early days of sucking behavior which is precursor behavior for thumb-sucking, as is suggested by the specific absence of reported thumb-sucking among even very oral primitive people. We need to know whether specific accession to pregnancy cravings has any effect on maternal feelings. We need to define and specify situations like these and distinguish them sharply from the generalized needs of the child for interpersonal interaction with other human beings.

At present, the specific biological situation of the continuing relationship of the child to its biological mother and its need for care by human beings are being hopelessly confused in the growing insistence that child and biological mother, or mother surrogate, must never be separated, that all separation even for a few days is inevitably damaging, and that if long enough it does irreversible damage. This, as Hilde Bruch (6) has cogently pointed out, is a new and subtle form of anti-feminism in which men—under the guise of exalting the importance of maternity—are tying women more tightly to their children than has been thought necessary since the invention of bottle feeding and baby carriages. Actually, anthropological evidence gives no support at present to the value of such an accentuation of the tie between mother and child (20). On the contrary, cross-cultural studies suggest that adjustment is most facilitated if the child is cared for by many warm friendly people. Clinical studies and anthropological studies support the relationship between strong attachments to single individuals in childhood and capacity for a limited number of intense, exclusive relationships in adulthood. It may well be, of course, that limiting a child's contacts to its biological mother may be the most efficient way to produce a character suited to lifelong monogamous marriage, but if so then we should be clear that that is what we are doing, that the biological mother is necessary for a sort of "imprinting" strong enough for monogamy, and that that is the reason we insist that mothers alone care for their children without help from fathers, grandparents, servants, or siblings.

Present anthropological studies give us little help when we approach the questions of specificity in the mother-child tie. All peoples have introduced various types of artificiality into the birth process. They have patterned posture, decreed whether birth is to be viewed as painful or easy, set up some sort of rules about when and by whom the neonate is to be first suckled. It may well be that there are a large number of instinctual elements in this relationship, like those found in the behavior of birds, and that one item in the child's behavior is the cue for the next item in the mother's as the shadow of the parent bird makes the nestlings open their mouths which in turn cues the parent to push food into the nestlings' mouths. Spitz's work on the smile (41) and reported work on responses to snakes in Vienna by institutionalized children who had never seen snakes (44) suggest that there may well be in human beings hereditary structures for which there are specific releasing elements in the behavior of parent, child or mate. On the other hand, man is a domestic animal, and so is comparable not with wild birds but with domesticated animals, among whom these hereditary structured mechanisms are found in a much more irregular and less highly patterned form, any detail of which is likely to be present or absent in any given individual. Survival may have depended upon man's developing socially patterned behavior which lacked a precise fit to any given hereditary pattern, because such precisely fitted behavior might contain lethal elements. For example, if some mothers' expulsion of the afterbirth were triggered by the child's cry, and no other means of expulsion were provided for in a given culture for any mother, mothers who did not have this particular mechanism would suffer. Some infants may depend for the beginning of breathing on one type of situation, some on another. As far as nutritive behavior is concerned we know that, although human beings probably have a high capacity for correct nutritional choices, a balanced diet with suitable devices for teaching all children to eat it seems to allow a wider margin of safety than relying on idiosyncratic elements of choice (19).

But whichever turns out to be the case, whether there are certain elements of maternal and infant behavior which are human and include all individuals (and here Spitz's findings on the cues for a smile—an oval shape with two eyeholes, nodding—are very suggestive), or whether there are a large number of specific elements distributed in a variety of ways through the population, it is most essential that they be identified. Those which are common to all human beings could then be built into our cultural practices to give additional protection to mother and child. Consider, for example, three possibilities for infant feeding—cues given by the state of the mother's breasts (as among Russian peasants), cues given by the child's expressed hunger, or cues given by some impersonal standard such as a feeding schedule implemented by a clock. If it is demonstrated that building the *child's* cues into an individualized schedule results in a different order of adjustment between mother and child than either of the other two, then self-regulatory schedules ("self-demand") could be established as universal practice. (It is important to point out that self-regulatory scheduling is not a return to a primitive style of child feeding, but a method of conscious, disciplined, recorded adjustment of the feeding schedule for which a clock and pencil and paper—all absent at the primitive level—are essential; without them it is not possible to identify the personal schedule the infant gradually establishes.) Or, if it were found that the capacity for self-regulation is associated, for example, with some particular strength of the sucking reflex or with some identifiable peculiarity of that reflex, and that infants capable of establishing a viable demand schedule could be identified at birth, then this method of feeding could be institutionalized as *one* formal alternative in the culture. Similarly, sufficiently detailed research might indicate that there are identifying characteristics in women who lose their milk unless they give their infants a night feeding which are not present in other women. Some women might be found to establish a relationship to the child immediately if they see it within five minutes of its birth but to take days to establish the same relationship if the child is not seen for two hours after birth, and so forth.

From the research side, these new questions are made possible by the theoretical framework of ethology and also by our new techniques of recording. Specificity of instinctual manifestations was abandoned in our working theories of psychology, partly under the tremendous impetus given to understanding personality by Freud, modern anthropology, and learning theory, all of which stressed the importance of learning and experience, and partly because instinct theory was so gross and undifferentiated, and concepts like the sex instinct, the maternal instinct, the instinct of self-preservation were found to be unworkable. The concept of drives which succeeded it (cf. 10, for example) stressed the enormous capacity for modification of drives and the importance of learned cues, but it neglected the possibility of much finer, more precise mechanisms, such as "imprinting" and "internal releasing mechanisms." This neglect was probably due in part to our lack of tools for sufficiently precise recording, but that lack has now been overcome, and we can begin to work with moving pictures and sound recordings, preserving details which formerly had to be organized by single clinical observers. It is notable that it is the "impressionistic" and "intuitive" clinicians and anthropologists who have welcomed these finer tools which permit behavior to be analyzed without changing its internal organization by intervening operations (48).

Very possibly we may find that the kind of negative results which David Levy (17) got for most of the criteria which he used in his study of maternal feeling will be reduced to order when we look for patterned sets of constitutionally determined mechanisms which differ in pattern rather than along a continuum. Thus we may find that sets of internally consistent patterns would emerge, all of them differentially responsive to experience, if any one of Levy's factors (such as the size of the areola, baby carriage peeking, or the copiousness and duration of menstrual flow) is examined in the light of other factors—age at menarche, uterus size as determined by X ray rather than simply by pelvic measurements, shape of breasts, copiousness and type of lactation, etc. The circumstance that some cultures regard prepubertal, and others pubertal, girls as most subject to maternal impulses is suggestive.

The discovery of much more precise patterns of interrelationship might also throw light on the frequent baffling cases in which it is possible to predict backwards but not forward. We find, for instance, that a large number of children who have asthma had whooping cough at a time when they were having feeding conflicts with their mothers (23), but we also find that we have no criteria for explaining the children who have whooping cough and feeding problems at the same time but do not develop asthma. Here Arthur Mirsky's type of research, in which he attempts to make such predictions with the help of specific physiological measures, is relevant.[5]

Anthropologists have contributed to the tendency to emphasize the learned nature and flexibility of human responses and the importance of such learning, no doubt because they work specifically with those human inventions constructed so that they *can* be learned. A "natural language" is precisely a language every nondefective human child of whatever race or constitution can learn to speak and understand; an artificial language differs in that the economy produced by a reduction in redundancy lowers the margin of safety. All cultures that survive have to contain sufficient leeway for the gamut of human potentialities. The increases in crime, alcoholism, drug addiction, and mental disease which occur in periods of culture breakdown are negative illustrations of this aspect of culture. But it is exceedingly probable that when we have done enough detailed research we may find that no culture that has ever existed is as well adapted to the actual range of human needs as a culture could be, even when such an adaptation is culture-wide— i.e., fixed-time feeding schedules adjusted to weight and weight gain alone, with a fixed habitual pattern to which radio schedules, commuter trains, and Fuller Brush men can adapt. It may be possible to make a new cultural invention, on the other hand, to enable us to discriminate and cater to widely varying individual needs, which may themselves be systematic and recurrent from culture to culture and period to period or unsystematic and nonrecurrent.

I would like to indicate briefly two further problems which deserve consideration. The first is the question as to whether we may have to speak of paternal as well as maternal instinctual responses (21), at least insofar as they are elaborations of protectiveness toward the small and helpless, and whether it is not possible that with the invention of social organization, marriage, and division of labor, men relinquished an expression of paternal behavior for which, however, the needed mechanisms still exist. It is true that specific paternal behavior is extraordinarily undeveloped among primates and, in general is low among mammals, although primates do respond to the cry for help of very young animals. The degree to which the capacity to identify a mate or a child (men share with birds a dependence on vision for this identification) plays an important role in establishing specificity of paternal responses, as distinct from generalized male protective responses, needs investigation (18, 44).

The second problem is the question of hereditary fit between mother and child. The functioning of the RH-factor in blood demonstrates vividly that our tremendous range of fertility which permits any member of *Homo sapiens* to mate with any other (man's alternative to establishing small, mutually infertile races) can carry significant lethal elements (20). It may be that the cues for maternal feeling which result in increased capacity for maternal performance, in lactation, tenderness, patience, and playfulness, depend on the types of congruity between the parent's hereditary equipment and the child's. The birth cry of some children may not be the cry for which some mothers are constitutionally prepared, and the quality of the mother-child tie may be 'determined by interaction between mutually reinforcing and releasing mechanisms, on the one hand, or by mechanisms which negate, mute, extinguish each other, on the other. Spitz's findings (42) suggest that separation is more traumatic for the child who has had a good mother-child relationship than for the child who has not. It has been claimed that famine is harder on those who have been well nourished than upon those who have been subjected to an inadequate diet since birth, and lack of proper nourishment may, under certain conditions, have survival value. Arthur Mirsky[6] has pointed out that we must not only think of the rejecting mother, but also of the insatiable baby, whose hypersecretive stomach makes it impossible for even the best mother to satisfy it. It may be, unless we can discover discriminating indices for maternal and child reaction types, that cultural arrangements which minimize such lack of fit may be essential; certainly a "rejecting baby" is less trying if bottle-fed, when the pediatrician can be consulted for a change in formula and blamed if it doesn't work, than if it is breast-fed and the mother feels that it is she who is inadequate. The great decrease in infant mortality with the introduction of numerous artificial methods—anesthesia at childbirth, artificial feeding, cribs, baby carriages, etc.—may be due to the development of more emotionally neutral practices in which constitutional discrepancies between parent and child are less important. Even if this should prove to be so, it would of course be possible to claim that the price is too high, that an individual reared in closer human contact, while subject to all these discrepancies of rhythm and response, is still a more integrated human being than one reared with precautionary artificial devices. Perhaps it is better for a child to be breast-fed *and* have colic. But these are the things which we do not yet know.

Only by *using* each new theoretical and practical tool as it becomes available can we discharge our responsibility to substitute specific research for best guesses as rapidly as possible.

NOTES

1. For example, Orlansky (31) writes: "Mead's unqualified statement (*sic*) that 'no primitive child whom I have ever seen or heard of sucks its thumb or fingers,' which appears in an authoritative handbook of child psychology and which was repeated at the May 29th, 1948 meeting of the Society for Applied Anthropology in Philadelphia, can only be deplored as an inaccuracy. . . . Ward Goodenough informs me that cases of thumb sucking are to be observed among children on the island of Truk, despite unlimited breast feeding throughout the first year...." The points to be noted are: 1) I included in my statement the careful qualification, "whom I have ever seen or heard of." To this Orlansky should have added the date as of vital significance. This statement was written for the first edition of the *Handbook of Child Psychology* in 1931 (23). 2) The article revised and brought up to date for publication in the *Manual of Child Psychology* (24) does not contain this sentence, as I subsequently found primitive children (among the Arapesh) who sucked their fingers, and I had published an extensive account of their orality (*Sex and Temperament*, 1935). At the Society for Applied Anthropology meeting in 1949, I specifically said that so far thumb-sucking was unreported, even where fingers were sucked. But Orlansky, apparently in ignorance of any possible theoretical importance as to whether it was a thumb or a finger

that was sucked, mistakenly credited me with the old statement. 3) In a conversation with Ward Goodenough, I found that he was not prepared to say that he had seen children *suck* their thumbs—a very different matter from putting a thumb into the mouth for some immediate purpose like removing a bit of food from a tooth. Here the question at issue is whether very early, frequent, unscheduled access to the mother's breast prevents the subsequent resort to thumb-sucking, as this seems to be the only pertinent feature common to the primitive peoples on whom we have reports. (For purposes of this discussion, the Hopi with their long exposure to white contact who displayed an obsessive objection to thumb-sucking when observed by Wayne Dennis in 1937-38 [8] cannot be regarded as primitive.) The most striking material on this subject comes from people where there is a great deal of oral play, so that the nonoccurrence of thumb-sucking becomes the more remarkable. Dr. K. Wolf has recently suggested that the prone position commonly used for our infants may promote thumb-sucking (personal communication).

2. For a further discussion of this point, see Mead and Métraux (29).

3. Cf. also (25).

4. For general discussion of anthropological method and for bibliography, see Mead (22), Métraux (29), Gorer (14). For general discussion of interdisciplinary research on problems of infancy, see Senn (38, 39).

5. Ongoing research at the University of Pittsburgh, as described in a personal communication by Arthur Mirsky.

6. Personal communication.

REFERENCES

1. BAKWIN, 1944
2. BATESON & MEAD, 1942
3. BATESON, 1951-53
4. BATESON, RUESCH, & KEES, n.d.
5. BOWLBY, 1951
6. BRUCH, 1952
7. BURLINGHAM & FREUD, 1942
8. DENNIS, 1940-a
9. DEUTSCH, 1939
10. DOLLARD & MILLER, 1950
11. ERIKSON, 1950-a
12. ESCALONA & LEITCH, n.d.
13. FRIES & WOOLF, n.d.
14. GORER, 1950-b
15. HENRY, J., & BOGGS, 1952
16. JACKSON & KLATSKIN, 1950
17. LEVY, D., 1929
18. LORENZ, K., 1952
19. MEAD, 1950-a
20. MEAD, 1955-a
21. MEAD, 1949-b
22. MEAD, 1953-a
23. MEAD, 1931
24. MEAD, 1946-b
25. MEAD, 1941-b
26. MEAD, 1935-a
27. MEAD, 1952-b
28. MEAD & MACGREGOR, 1951
29. MEAD & METRAUX, 1953
30. MOLONEY, n.d.

31. ORLANSKY, 1949
32. PETERSON & SPANO, 1941
33. PINNEAU, 1950
34. RIBBLE, 1943
35. ROBERTSON, J., 1953
36. ROUDINESCO, 1952
37. ROUDINESCO, J. & APPELL, n.d.
38. SENN, M. J. E., ed., 1950
39. SENN, M. J. E., ed., 1947-1950
40. SEWELL, 1952
41. SPITZ, 1946
42. SPITZ, 1945
43. SPITZ & WOLF, 1946
44. TANNER, J., ed., (in preparation).
45. TINBERGEN, 1951
46. VASSAR COLL., Dept. Child Study, n.d.
47. WEAVER, 1948
48. WHITING & CHILD, 1953

EDWARD AND MARGARET NORBECK

1956. Child Training in a Japanese Fishing Community. Not published previously.

When World War II brought the United States into conflict with Japan, not many Americans knew Japan well. The only anthropological study of a Japanese community was John Embree's *Suye Mura, A Japanese Village* (1939), and no one could be certain whether *Suye Mura* should be accepted as typical. Of numerous postwar studies, Norbeck's *Takashima, a Japanese Fishing Community* (1954), is outstanding. Dr. and Mrs. Norbeck amplify the details of child-rearing in Takashima in the article that follows. Their field research was nearly synchronous with that of Miss Lanham (see her article in this book), and comparison of the findings of these investigations is invited.

Other postwar studies, weighted heavily toward rural villages, and not always easy of access, include: Bennett & Ishino, 1955; Cornell, 1953; Glacken, 1955; Grad, 1952, 1955; Ishino, 1953; Nishikiori, 1945; Odaka, 1950; Pelzel, 1949; Raper, 1950; and Titiev, 1953. None of these is oriented specifically to "national character" or to child-training. See "Community Studies in Japan and China, A Symposium," *Far Eastern Quarterly 14* (1954): 3-53. Studies in the Japanese language, however, are appearing frequently; some of these reveal important cultural differences in various parts of Japan. (E.g., Izumi and Gamō, *Regionalism in Japanese Society*, in *Nihon chiri shin taikei*, Tokyo, 1952; Ms. translation by H. Befu.)

CHILD TRAINING IN A JAPANESE FISHING COMMUNITY

Edward and Margaret Norbeck

The community of Takashima, a hamlet of Okayama Prefecture, Japan, is located on a small island bearing the same name in the Inland Sea approximately a quarter-mile off Kojima Peninsula. Its residents numbered 188 in 1951, and comprised 33 separate households. For a living they rely chiefly upon net fishing from small motor craft in neighboring waters. Cultivation of table crops in small unirrigated farm plots affords a subsidiary but economically vital source of livelihood. Generally, men fish and women farm. Despite its island location, Takashima is not isolated, but relies for many purposes upon daily contact with neighboring mainland communities.

Takashima residents are poor, although by local standards few are poverty-stricken. Their culture, like that of all Japan, is in a state of rapid change that began approximately a century ago and has been accelerated since 1945. In degree of change from the traditional, Takashima probably is slightly more "advanced" than the average rural community. As elsewhere in Japan, traditional and modern ways co-exist and sometimes vie with each other. The old in years cherish the old in custom and give way only slowly to the new. The young are part of modern Japan, literate and modestly acquainted through school with the broader world and with Western scientific thought. Much that is traditional remains, however, and in many matters youth defers to age. Many aspects of child training reflect the changing ways, but the changes do not greatly alter the traditional patterns of relationship between adults and children. Life in the community revolves about the family—the group of relatives living under one roof—who continue to regard and conduct themselves as a closely knit unit, although shrunken in size as compared with the past. One's social position is that of his family, and the affairs of any family member are the intimate concern of all other members.

The statements that follow are based upon eight months' joint field work of the authors during 1950-1951. Data were gathered by observation and by formal and informal interviews. Virtually all members of the community served as informants. At least one adult female of each household was interviewed in detail concerning the care and training of infants and small children.

* * * *

Conscious nurture of the child born in Takashima begins as soon as the mother knows she has conceived. Pre-natal conditions are thought to affect the future welfare of the child. The conduct of the mother and other relatives during the prenatal period relates to both the natural and the supernatural worlds.

When a married woman of child-bearing age ceases to menstruate, the cause is assumed to be pregnancy. Unless a household already has many children the birth is awaited eagerly. One male child to inherit the household property and continue the patrilineal family is considered a necessity, but female children are welcome and a balanced family of both sexes is considered most desirable. A woman who previously has borne no children ordinarily seeks the advice of a licensed midwife in a nearby community. Experienced women who already are mothers frequently do not engage a midwife; they rely upon their own experience and the aid of other females of the household. The average woman sees a midwife two or three times before parturition, but the midwife offers little or no advice unless it is solicited. Knowledge of proper and beneficial conduct during pregnancy is assumed to be the common property of all pregnant women.

The expectant mother performs her customary work and participates in most of her usual activities. Numerous dietary restrictions presumably conducive to the health and well-being of mother and child are traditional and known if not observed by all women. Some of these are regarded as tested common-sense measures; others relate to the supernatural. The pregnant woman should avoid foods considered difficult to digest, such as condiments and excessively oily foods. To insure the growth of a sturdy child she should eat seaweed and the bones of small fish. The exceptional young woman who has consulted a physician, or has read of the practice in women's magazines, may supplement her diet with calcium. Other diet restrictions rest on supernaturalistic beliefs sometimes laughed at but usually observed. To eat crab, squid, octopus, shrimp, or any misshapen vegetable or fruit will result in the birth of a malformed child or one boneless like an octopus or squid, hunchbacked like a shrimp, or otherwise grotesque. Numerous other beliefs and customs of this kind may be observed.

The pregnant mother's behavior is thought to influence the future personality of the child. Cravings for special foods are common, but if the mother indulges herself by resting and eating the foods she craves, her child will be selfish, indulgent, and lazy. She must not be angry or sad lest the child be quarrelsome or melancholy; she must "keep a quiet feeling." If during pregnancy her expression is gentle and calm (*yasashii*), her child will be a female; if her expression is stern and forceful (*kitsui*), she will bear a boy.

During the Day of the Dog in the fifth lunar month of pregnancy, a woman winds about her abdomen a narrow cloth sash about ten feet long, and continues to wear this abdominal support until the child is delivered. The sash usually is purchased at a temple with the blessings of Kannon, Goddess of Mercy, and presented to the pregnant woman by a relative—most frequently by her mother. Supernatural blessing also is sought in other ways. The pregnant woman is encouraged to visit Shintō shrines and Buddhist temples to make offerings to the deities. Her mother, mother-in-law, or other relatives also may make pilgrimages in her behalf. Most frequently, she herself or a close relative makes offerings to Kannon at a nearby temple, whence protective and magical objects are received: an inscribed paper talisman to be placed in the dwelling to protect the mother and child, and a second talisman consisting of a piece of bamboo in which is inserted a paper containing a blessing. The sex of the unborn child is divined from the number of nodes on the bamboo—one if a boy, two if a girl. A bottle of divine water is obtained from a well on the temple grounds for possible future use in eradicating birthmarks.

Until she feels the birth contractions, a woman continues her usual round of activities. Then she retires to the innermost room of the dwelling—a room that contains no shrines or religious objects. Sterile cloths and other equipment ordinarily have been prepared. If the services of a midwife have been engaged, someone hurriedly summons her. Otherwise older women of the household officiate. When contractions have become frequent and severe, the woman assumes a kneeling position on the floor on the padded cotton comforter that constitutes her bed. She holds or rests her arms on a pile of folded comforters or other high object. The waiting attendant receives the child from the rear. If a midwife attends, the woman is instructed to lie supine in Western fashion—a practice that Takashima women say renders delivery difficult. After parturition the mother lies down and is encouraged to bite the wooden handle of a dipper—a practice said to produce retching that expedites passage of the placenta.

The newborn child utters its first cries without the stimulus of slapping; such practice is unknown. The baby is cleaned with sterile cloths, and if a midwife is in attendance, the eyes are wiped with a solution of boric acid. A bath in a small wooden tub or other container follows. The infant is then liberally powdered with talc, applied with a puff, and dressed with an abdominal band, diapers, rubber-lined diaper cover, and, dependent upon the season, two or more loose-fitting cotton wrappers tied with strings. The garmented child is wrapped loosely in a blanket and held in someone's arms or placed on the usual bed—between padded comforters on the floor. In cold weather a container of hot water may be placed with the infant. Within a few days babies usually share their parents' bed.

The flowing of blood is a traditional source of pollution; hence the new mother is ceremonially unclean and is a source of pollution and danger to others until the thirty-third day after the birth. She is restricted from all contact with Shintō supernatural beings, and traditionally the period of pollution is also a time of rest. The seventh day, however, ends the period of strongest pollution; she may then assume a few of her normal duties, especially the washing of clothes for the infant and herself. Ordinarily she does little work until the fifteenth day after the birth. Pollution ends on the thirty-third day, when the mother purifies herself ritually and resumes domestic and farm work.

Beliefs about pollution include the child as well as the mother, although with respect to the child they are less clearly defined. Until the thirty-third day, the clothing of the mother and child may not be dried directly in the sun, but must be placed in the shadow of the eaves lest it offend the Sun Goddess. For the same reason the new mother and infant in traditionally-minded households may not step into the sunlight with uncovered heads during this period. The baby is bathed in a special tub rather than in the household bathtub for at least six days after birth, and the period may extend to a month. This practice is likely to be ascribed to practical convenience rather than to need for isolating a "polluted" infant.

Differentiation of male and female roles begins immediately after birth. If the neonate is female the placenta is buried just outside the principal entrance to the dwelling; if a male, in the earthen floor just inside the entrance. These customs, observed but only half-believed, insure that at maturity the girl will marry out of the household and that the male will remain in the household after marriage. Clothing of male and female infants is identical in shape but differs in color and decorative design. Clothing of the boy, especially the firstborn male, is likely to be of better quality.

The infant's first feeding, a few hours after birth, is a bitter or sour infusion of one, three, or five traditionally-used herbs, briefly steeped in warm water. Bog rhubarb is used most frequently as it grows on the island; the others must usually be purchased. A round, compressed wad of absorbent cotton or fabric is tied in a piece of silk to make a ball about the size of a marble. This is soaked in about an ounce of the infusion and placed in the child's mouth. If the child will accept the infusion, several feedings of this kind may be given in the first day. Most infants refuse more than a small amount. Until the mother is ready to nurse the child—usually on the second or third day—additional feedings consist of small amounts of sugar water given by means of the ball when the child cries. Tea with a little added sugar may be substituted.

Infants usually are suckled whenever they cry and will accept the breast. A few young mothers have learned from women's magazines to nurse their children according to a schedule. Exposure of the breasts to nurse a child in the home, garden, or even in public, occasions no embarrassment and arouses no curiosity in others. The young mother usually kneels to allow her child to suckle and cradles the infant in her arms. Some women, especially the middle-aged, fold a cushion to form a right angle, kneel, and place the improvised seat with the open angle toward them. The infant is placed on the cushion in a sitting position so that it faces the mother with its back against the upright portion of the cushion, which is supported by the mother's outstretched arms. Mothers hold children in this manner at other times; when agricultural or other duties are pressing and a very young child is fretful, the mother may "deceive" the child by placing it, half reclining, in its customary seat on the cushion, supported by folded comforters, the wall, or other objects. The mother then leaves quietly.

The occasional mother whose breast milk is scanty supplements nursing with bottle feeding of thin strained rice gruel or the white fluid remaining in the pot after cooking soy bean curd. The rare mother who has no breast milk purchases powdered cow's milk and prepares according to directions on the container a formula that is fed by bottle—a practice regarded by all as a poor substitute for nursing.

Only two events in the first six months of life of the average child are regarded by adults as special: the naming ceremony, and the introduction to the tutelary god of the community. A simple name-giving ceremony is held on the seventh day, counting the day of birth as the first day. Offerings to household gods are made at the small shrines within the dwelling but ordinarily no special prayers are said. The infant's head is shaved so that it will be acceptable to the gods and it is dressed in its best clothing—its finest bright red outer garment—and placed on a bed laid for the occasion in the best room of the dwelling. A tray of solid adult food of special quality is offered symbolically to the child by placing it on the floor near the baby's head. A rounded beach stone may be placed on a dish as "food" to impart to the child the qualities of firmness and strength. Subsequently the food on the tray is eaten by adults with additional food of the same kind. Close relatives and friends may be invited to participate, especially when the child is the firstborn. Guests bring small gifts of fruit or sweets for the mother and clothing for the child. Close relatives outside the household, especially the child's maternal grandmother, usually send gifts of clothing for the infant. In a poor household the naming ceremony may be omitted for children other than the firstborn, although a name usually is selected on the traditional day.

A child takes its father's surname, and the single given name is chosen variously. The parents—the father's wishes carry the greater weight—may select the name of a hero of the past, a name that the grandfather or some other knowledgeable person regards as felicitous, or a name fancied for no special reason. Boys' names commonly express approved virtues such as bravery or honesty or other lofty moral sentiments; the variety of names from which a choice is made is enormously greater for boys than for girls. Boys' names also may indicate, by incorporation of the ordinal numerals, primacy of birth among male offspring. Girls' names seldom reflect noble sentiments, and, since girls do not ordinarily inherit household property, primacy of their birth is of slight concern. Girls' names are usually those regarded as "pretty" or as connoting gentle feminine qualities.

The formal introduction to the tutelary god of the community occurs on the 110th day of a boy's life and the 120th of that of a girl. The mother or a close relative carries the child to the shrine of the tutelary god—a small wooden building amid the pines a few hundred yards from the dwellings. Some grains of rice and a little money are placed in the offertory and obeisance is made before the shrine. An unvoiced prayer may be offered for the child's welfare, and the ceremony is ended.

Most infants sleep in the same bed as their parents and close to the mother. A few have their own beds, like those of adults but smaller, and laid in the sleeping room of the parents. An infant usually is nursed when it appears to demand food by crying, and its diapers are changed when soiled or as the exigencies of the mother's work allow. A crying child is comforted by nursing; if it refuses to nurse it is held, patted, and spoken to soothingly. Patting, jostling, and pressing the child's abdomen to relieve pain due to gas are unknown practices. Throughout its infancy the child is ordinarily the center of household attention and receives solicitous care.

In its first months of life an infant is almost constantly in the mother's company. The household grandmother may assist with its care, and after a few months an older sibling may assume responsibility for its care for short periods. While in the dwelling an infant usually is in bed or in its mother's arms. Frequently the mother takes it with her when she must work in the garden plot, where she places it on the ground and arranges it comfortably with its face in the shade. When it cries the child may be nursed in the field.

About the home a child is carried in the arms. If the mother must travel outside the community or take the child away from the dwelling for more than a few minutes, it is transported on her back, secured by a square of cloth with tapes at the corners; two of these are passed under the bearer's arms and two are tied around her waist. The infant's legs are partially spread to embrace the bearer's back, and it faces in the same direction as its bearer. Freedom of movement is limited, and until the child is tall enough to look over the bearer's shoulders, its vision is restricted principally to narrow lateral views.

The first hot bath in the household tub may occur as early as the seventh day after birth. More frequently this experience comes when the baby is about a month old. Before entering the tub it is cleansed by soap and water in the same manner as are adults. The baby is then held in the arms of an adult who is immersed to the shoulders in the tub. Removed from the bath, its skin heavily flushed from the high temperature, the baby is powdered, dressed, and put to bed. Until a baby has become accustomed to the high temperature of the bath, special treatment is accorded it. The water in the cast iron tub may be cooled slightly, and after the infant is in the water the temperature is raised gradually by regulating the fire beneath the tub. After several weeks the child is said to be adjusted to the high bath temperature customary for adults and no regulation is necessary.

The Japanese bath is as much a bodily comfort as it is a hygienic or ritual measure. The standard procedure is to scrub and rinse the body thoroughly before entering the tub. Soaking in the very hot water is a pleasant, approved form of relaxation, particularly comforting on cold winter days. Children quickly learn to like hot baths and soon remain immersed as long as do the adults with whom they bathe. One tubful of water suffices for the entire family. The baby, male or female, usually is allowed the privilege of bathing first when the water is fresh. Thus its earliest adult bath-companion is usually the father, who takes precedence in order of bathing as in other matters.

Most households do not prepare a bath daily because of the labor required to haul water in buckets and the expense of firewood. Three or four baths during the week, taken in the evening after dinner, are customary, and one tub of water sometimes serves for two days' bathing. Children continue to bathe with adults, entering the tub at the same time, until they are too large comfortably to do so. For several years they continue to bathe in the presence of adults. After the first year of infancy, children may bathe with their mothers, especially if they are girls. When a new baby is born, the next older sibling may then bathe with an adult other than its mother—frequently an older sibling or the grandmother. Most bathhouses accommodate only one adult with any comfort. If the bath is large enough, mother, father and small children may bathe together.

Toilet training usually begins in the sixth month, but it may be postponed if the sixth month of life is reached during the winter. Several times daily the child is partially disrobed and held over the family toilet, over a special container placed on the porch, or, among less fastidious households, over a spot of ground in a corner of the yard. Other than disrobing and holding the child at a generally invariable place at times thought to be appropriate, no action is taken. The infant is not shaken, scolded or subjected to any other kind of harsh treatment as a signal or as a punishment when diapers are soiled. Months usually pass before the child learns what it is expected to do. After a child has begun to speak, verbal admonition to inform the mother before the event occurs is repeated every time the child soils itself. By two years of age most children are fairly well trained to report their needs during daylight hours, but retention at night is seldom learned until a child is three. Girls are said to be more quickly trained than boys. Most mothers arise once or twice during the night to awaken partially-trained children. The effort of arising is considered much the lesser unpleasantness. At or shortly before the age of three, children begin to awaken by themselves and inform their mothers, usually by crying. Because most people fear the dark, buckets are placed near the entrances of houses at night so that no one need expose himself to the fright of traveling the few steps to the detached latrine.

Foods other than milk are added to an infant's diet at about six months of age. The new foods are customarily small amounts of rice gruel from which most of the rice grains have been removed, clear soups, weak tea with sugar, small quantities of tangerine juice, and grated apple. As the infant matures, the rice gruel is gradually thickened, and whole pieces of tangerine from which the stringy membrane has been removed are substituted for its juice. Following an old custom, a mother does not ordinarily give her child fish until it has begun to talk. Other soft foods in small pieces are added after a few months of life, and by the time a child has passed its first year its diet includes foods in solid form. Sitting on its mother's lap, it may now join the family at meals, where the mother gives it bits of her food as she eats.

Training in table etiquette ordinarily begins after children have learned to understand speech and can themselves speak a few words. Most children begin to eat food with a spoon at or before eighteen months of age, and soon thereafter receive introduction to chopsticks. Months of practice are required before infant fingers can handle chopsticks effectively. At first the child grasps both chopsticks in the fist and uses them principally to push food into its mouth from a bowl held close to the face by the other hand. By the time a child is three it can usually manage chopsticks with little spilling of food, but most mothers are reluctant to encourage their consistent use until a child is well over two, because inexperienced hands allow much food to drop to the floor. Until the child is old enough to understand clearly words of instruction and reproof, a mother prefers for the sake of tidiness to feed it with her own implements, or, if she is a modern young wife, with chopsticks or a spoon used only for the child. Once the use of chopsticks is habitual, the mother repeatedly admonishes against dropping food, and her words may be seconded by any other member of the household. The tone of voice is soft but instruction is insistent and unfailing.

Instruction in proper postures for sitting and kneeling is given in the same persistent manner after a child is old enough to sit securely by itself. The mother places the arms and legs of the child in the traditional positions; patiently and repeatedly she corrects the positions as the child moves. Later, verbal instruction is added, and kneeling and bowing also are taught; the mother manipulates the child's head and body until the desired positions are attained. Takashima adults state that because they do not often have occasion to sit, kneel, and bow in approved formal fashion, they find the positions uncomfortable and therefore do not strongly emphasize these traditional customs in training their children. With considerable variation from household to household, however, the usual practice is to give boys a little training and girls considerable training in those polite conventions, shaping their bodies into the desired positions as if they were objects being molded.

Weaning is most frequently done at about two years of age or, if another child is expected, shortly before its birth. Otherwise, some mothers continue nursing until a child is about three. Mothers state that weaning is no problem. The standard practice is to rub the nipples with crushed pieces of fresh but mature chili pepper. One attempt to suckle from breasts treated with chili pepper is sufficient for many children. Weaning is said to be accompanied by no apparent disturbance of the child; his diet has long included a substantial amount of solid foods.

Until they have become fairly adept at walking, children wear loose, wrap-around clothing of traditional style, with some substitution of Western-derived pull-over and buttoned under-garments after the first year. When a child begins to walk, its coat-like kimono is folded under the sash so that the hem of the garment is raised about to the knees and does not impede movement. Once children have learned to walk, Western clothes are the rule for boys and the most common garments for girls.

Until the arrival of another baby, the youngest child is the center of attention and affection. Its wants and whims are indulged, and its welfare superintended with loving care. Relegated to a less-favored position by the birth of a new baby, a child is, nevertheless, seldom reported to be jealous of the new favorite. Deposed babies are said sometimes to be irritable and given to crying, and they often attempt to push the new baby off its mother's lap. These are regarded as normal ways for a child to behave under the circumstances and are not construed as jealousy. If the household includes a grandmother or an older female sibling, the older baby usually is turned over principally to her care for the first months of the new baby's life. The child then sleeps, bathes, and spends most of its waking hours with the grandmother or elder sister until it is old enough to associate with other children. Adjustment to the altered conditions is said to be accomplished by the child with little distress.

Until a child enters primary school at the age of six it is treated with great indulgence. Behavior is sanctioned by punishment and reward as soon as it has learned to comprehend words or actions; greater conformance to patterns considered proper is demanded of girls than of boys. Tolerance toward children of both sexes, however, is the rule. A small child "has no sense" and conformance to the standards imposed upon older children and adults cannot be expected. Temper tantrums during which a child may shriek repeatedly and strike its parents, especially the mother, are not uncommon among boys of age three or four though rare among girls. Such displays are embarrassing if they occur in public, but they are not considered serious offenses and are countered with mild measures. Attempts are made to soothe the child and to divert its attention, or it may be urged to desist.

Discipline for non-conformance is not solely the responsibility or prerogative of the parents; any member of the household may discipline the very young. Most frequently the mother is the disciplinarian because it is she with whom a child has the most frequent contact. The father is often away from the dwelling, and grandparents, who feel under less obligation to intrude into unpleasantness, tend to indulge or reward rather than to punish. The words and actions of the father carry more weight than those of others and, although he may seldom discipline children, fear of his disapproval becomes important. Unlike the words of the mother, those of the father must ordinarily be heeded.

Many forms of punishment are used. Physical punishment of the very young is common but mild in form, consisting most frequently of light blows, little more than pats of the hand or raps of the fingers. The hands of infants are often struck lightly when the undesirable behavior has involved use of the hands. Otherwise, avoiding the face, blows are directed at no particular area of the body but fall wherever the single casual stroke might land. Pinching parts of the body lightly, pricking the fingers with needles, and, occasionally, brief seclusion in another room or in a dark and windowless closet are sometimes also used as punishment. Most mothers over thirty subject their children to moxacautery. The use of moxa, a highly inflammable tinder made from the leaves of a variety of sage, is considered both a therapeutic measure and an effective punishment for unruly small children. Most mothers who subject their children to moxacautery view it principally as a cure for fretfulness rather than a punishment. Traditionally, the burning of moxa on the skin of a child improves its health. Few women doubt that once a child has experienced moxacautery the threat of its use serves effectively to control behavior. But most mothers dislike to subject their children to the painful burns, and a single application, almost always done by a specialist in a nearby community rather than by the mother herself, is the standard practice. A child should traditionally receive a series of treatments; the amount of moxa (i.e., the number of places to which it is applied at one time) varies with the age of the child. Tiny quantities of the powder, the size of a grain of rice, are placed by the specialist on the small of the back or near the spine just above the shoulders. Lighted with a match, the powdered leaf burns instantly, causing pain, evoking tears and cries, and leaving small scars. At the first treatment women usually purchase moxa to take home, but they seldom continue with the traditional series and only threaten to do so.

Despite its use in controlling behavior, physical punishment is in disfavor. Striking a child, the most common form, is not favored because "if the mother strikes her child, the child will strike other children." Young mothers think moxa valueless as a form of therapy and unnecessarily cruel as a disciplinary device, and its use is declining. Fathers rarely resort to physical punishment of any kind.

In the early years the most common sanction for behavior is persistent instruction and reproof. Common offenses of the very young are dropping and scattering food at the table, spreading ashes from the charcoal brazier over the floor, and poking holes in the paper-covered sliding partitions that separate rooms. For these acts they may receive both physical punishment—light slaps of the hands—and verbal reproof. The soiling of diapers is not ordinarily regarded as an offense of the same order and is not an occasion for physical punishment. Instead, repeated instruction and admonition are used to rectify errors after a child is old enough to understand. Among children past three or four years of age, disobedience and quarreling are the most common offenses. The most serious misbehavior of older children is quarreling with persons outside the family. Transgression against the property of other households, such as taking fruit or vegetables from garden plots, is an extremely serious though uncommon offense which, if known to the parents of the offending child, meets with quick action.

As a child matures, disciplinary measures tend increasingly away from physical punishment and stress censure designed to make the child feel ashamed. By the time a child is eight or nine, physical punishment has usually entirely stopped; he now responds quickly to censure and ridicule, which may be communicated by silence, by facial expression, or by speech.

Rewards constitute important techniques of child training. Material rewards, however, in the form of sweets, money or privileges, although sometimes given, are frowned upon as encouraging the child to look only for the reward and failing to teach that proper behavior is desirable for its own sake. The appropriate form of reward is praise for conformance and for deeds well accomplished. In addition to verbal praise, a small child may receive approving pats on the top of the head. Grandparents are particularly prone to sanction the behavior of toddlers with extravagant praise.

Quarrels among siblings of comparable ages are common and among the very young may include physical aggression. Dissension among small children most frequently arises over the use of toys or charges of usurped privileges. Each child customarily has a prescribed private place to store its small possessions, and these are often jealously guarded. Physical aggression, usually confined to small boys, consists of striking with the hand or with objects held in the hand, striking by throwing objects, and pushing. Biting and pulling hair are said never to be done. By the time a child has reached five or six years of age, quarrels involving blows are uncommon, although verbal quarrels may continue long past puberty. Quarrels among siblings of school age are limited principally to age-mates of the same sex. Causes of friction are numerous; they most commonly revolve about contentions of inequality in treatment by parents or charges of unfairness in sharing work or privileges. Those who sleep together complain that one or the other takes an unequal share of the bed or bed covers. Sisters jointly responsible for putting away the beds of the household may accuse each other of shirking. Sisters of about the same age quarrel most frequently over dresses, and dissension on this ground may arise up to the time of their marriage. Mothers are usually careful to avoid grounds for contention in this important sector of their daughters' lives, but real or fancied inequalities arise frequently. When quarrels occur among siblings, adults of the household—most frequently the mother—intervene to placate and admonish. Quarrels in the presence of the father are uncommon. Whoever the intervening person, the procedure follows a standard pattern of adjuring the very young not to quarrel. Older children are ordinarily admonished to conduct themselves more properly and their behavior is ridiculed as unbecoming for their age and sex. Although sides are seldom taken and both siblings are told that their behavior is improper, the almost invariable course is to instruct the elder to defer to the younger "because you are older." Quarrels among siblings, although deprecated, are not considered serious transgressions unless they recur frequently. Parents also sometimes quarrel, usually over domestic finance and matters of child rearing, and their children hear them.

Quarrels with children of other households are far more serious and elicit heavier censure. Small boys under six years of age may quarrel with and strike other children, but otherwise physical aggression is uncommon. Older boys and, much less frequently, girls, sometimes quarrel with their friends verbally, or they silently take offense and avoid each other. A few boys under ten bear the reputation of having bad dispositions and of quarreling frequently with other boys. Parents, informed of quarrels involving children outside the family, are usually non-partisan. A child is told that he also must have been at fault or the quarrel would never have arisen, that quarreling is improper behavior, and that he must not repeat the offense. A child may be consoled if it appears that he is the injured party, but consolation should not be emphasized lest it encourage the child to quarrel.

Quarrels among siblings or unrelated but very young children are usually quickly forgotten, but dissension among near-adults and adults with persons outside the family most frequently results in long-harbored feelings of resentment and future avoidance of contact. Aggressive behavior of any kind extended to persons who are not family members is considered reprehensible. A quick temper is a serious defect of character.

Life of the child until it reaches school age continues to be a period of amusement and indulgence, but certain precautionary rules are enforced. Small children are forbidden to go alone to dangerous places, the community pier, the shore, and the steep cliffs on the island. Children are warned against climbing trees on the ground that such action will damage the trees, and they rarely do so. No instance is known of the injury of a child in the community from climbing trees or in falls from the cliffs, and no child has ever drowned.

Amusements for children are numerous. They congregate to play games in an open area near the community hall. Simple games using cards decorated with pictures of traditional heroes, baseball players, and comic strip characters—some of them Western—are popular among children of both sexes of ages five to ten or twelve. Hopscotch-like games and hide-and-seek are played by both girls and boys. Girls bounce balls, play jacks, jump rope, draw pictures, and play house with dolls. Elaborate and delicately constructed traditional dolls, kept in glass cases, are owned by households which can afford them, but they are for the visual enjoyment of girls only upon special occasions and may not be handled. Most girls have one or more durable dolls designed for everyday use, and those who have none may fold cushions to represent dolls. Infant boys also have dolls of traditional style but show little or no interest in them once they have begun to talk and associate with other children.

Children of any age are seldom allowed to go swimming, but most children of nine or ten have mastered a clumsy dog-paddle adequate to keep them afloat. Older boys catch white-eyes, a species of small wild bird, and keep them in cages. Mothers and grandparents occasionally tell stories and teach songs, but this kind of entertainment is afforded principally by the school or by older siblings who have learned the tales and songs at school. Spinning tops and playing games with glass marbles are favorite occupations of small boys. Toys of various kinds, including noise-making and mobile animals pulled by strings, picture books, tricycles, and wagons, are owned by children of financially fortunate households. Most households buy as many toys as finances will allow. Play activities of children follow cycles; at one time tops and jacks are in fashion and at another time colored decalcomanias applied to the back of the hands, hopscotch, or other forms of diversion prevail.

The brightest spots in the life of the child as well as of its elders are afforded by the annual round of traditional ceremonial holidays, when outside relatives arrive as guests, special clothing is worn, and special food is eaten. New Year's, the Buddhist Bon summer festival in honor of the dead, and the community autumn festival are the greatest occasions. Several traditional festival days of lesser importance honor children, but they are not always observed by poor households. An infant's first birthday is honored by special food and gifts, although subsequent birthdays receive no attention. On March 3rd girls traditionally receive presents of good clothing and the elaborate dolls in glass cases, and special food is eaten. Boys are honored in similar but somewhat more elaborate fashion on May 5th, when inflated paper carp, symbolic of strength and endurance, are suspended from bamboo poles by the dwelling, special food is eaten, and presents of clothing are given to them. Children who have reached the age of three during the year are taken on November 15th to the shrine of the tutelary god, where an offering is made. On this date children traditionally receive their first clothes of adult pattern. Girls usually receive at least one fine kimono of Japanese style and boys receive new Western clothing.

Other traditional religious events, today observed principally by persons of the grandparental generation, may mean diversion and new experiences for the young child, who is sometimes allowed the privilege of accompanying the grandmother or, less frequently, the grandfather, on trips to shrines or temples in other communities. The annual family pilgrimage to the famous shrine of Kompira on the island of Shikoku, a trip made during the slack work months of winter and covering several days, is an eagerly-awaited period of treats, shopping, and other diversions.

Children ordinarily begin school at the age of six, travelling to and fro in a school-boat which transports them in a few minutes over the quarter-mile of sea to the school on the mainland. Public kindergarten is available for children of ages four and five, but it is not compulsory and Takashima parents usually do not enroll their children in school until they are six and enter primary school. The inconvenience of water transportation and of specially dressing children for only a few hours of school attendance outweighs in importance the benefits of this early school training.

Entering school marks a break in childhood training. Until this time little is expected of the child although he has been subjected to many social sanctions. The actions of the school child, who has become a representative of the household in contact with a world outside that of the home and immediate neighbors, now reflect upon the whole household. Social sanctions for the non-conformist tend increasingly to emphasize ridicule and the danger that improper behavior will disgrace not only the miscreant but also the whole family; these ideas are impressed upon the child at home and in school. A child has now begun to have sense, and it may be subjected to the patterns of social relations prevailing among adults. The attitudes and instructions of parents and teachers are reinforced by schoolfellows, and fear of censure or ridicule and consequent loss of prestige becomes a dominant motive to conform. A child of this age has become aware, too, of the great effect of censure and ridicule upon its elders and the importance they attach to conformance to avoid feelings of shame and loss of face.

Fights among boys from different communities in the lowest primary classes are almost daily events during recesses, but teachers are rarely obliged to intervene. Few blows are struck and quarrels are quickly ended. Older boys seldom fight, and girls quarrel only rarely, almost never coming to blows. Pupils respect their teachers, and strong disciplinary measures seldom are needed. Physical punishment is repugnant to teachers and is forbidden by law. Adherence to standards expected of pupils is achieved principally by drawing attention to conformance or its lack. Children who have done what is expected of them—completed home assignments, brushed their teeth, or cleaned their fingernails—are asked to put up their hands or are otherwise noted. The occasional noisy or troublesome boy is scolded and thus held up to ridicule, and he may be required to stand alone at the front or back of the room. Truancy, called "eating the roadside grass," is rare; although the school district has a truant officer, his services have never been requested. Certain boys assume positions as informal leaders in school work and in play; in the eyes of the teachers some of the leaders are "good," and others—those who bully or lead in mischief—are "bad." Leadership among girls is far less clearly marked.

The extra-curricular school education of Takashima children involves a gradual awareness of social distinctions. In addition to absorbing the formal instruction of the school curriculum, they learn that their social status as sons and daughters of fishermen is lower than that of most of their schoolmates, whose fathers are farmers or engage in other occupations. Takashima children are usually eager to don the black, Western-style uniforms mandatory for school children. For the first few years, their scholastic records are on a par with those of children of other communities which the school serves. Their interest in studies gradually wanes, however, and records of Takashima students in the advanced grades are below the average. Teachers attribute this poor scholarship to Takashima parents, who, as fishermen, do not value education as highly as do farmers or parents who follow a more respected calling. Certain Takashima adults say that they hold education in less esteem than do people in neighboring farm communities because the amount of formal education which they can afford to give their children (usually only the nine years of compulsory public education) gives no special advantage in their adult lives. Literacy, however, is considered an absolute necessity.

Competition in school is not stressed, although awards of pencils, notebooks, and citations are given for outstanding scholarship and are cherished by their recipients. Badges are sometimes awarded for the consistent use of very polite speech. Exams are given regularly "to test progress and teaching techniques," but they have virtually no bearing on promotion. All children are automatically passed to the next higher class unless they have been ill or absent for a substantial part of the school year. At the several annual school athletic meets each participant in competitive games and athletic contests receives some kind of present, although the winner receives acclaim and perhaps a prize of greater value.

Japanese boy receiving winner's certificate in school athletic meet.
Photo by D. G. Haring.

Instruction in reading, writing, arithmetic, drawing, vocal and instrumental music of both native and Western derivation, natural science, and "social studies," which includes history, geography, civic affairs, and ethics, forms the principal part of the curriculum. As in pre-war times, students stand to recite, but many other pre-war practices have been abandoned. Joint studying by reading aloud is done "in soft voices" during the first three years only. The practice of bowing before a picture of the emperor and the pre-war nationalistic subject called *shūshin*, "morality," which stressed devotion to parents, emperor and country, no longer form a part of school training. Ethics in less nationalistic form is taught under "social studies."

After the completion of primary school, the Takashima child must go to another community three miles away to attend the three-year middle school. Although middle school is free and attendance is required by law, Takashima children of poorer families do not always complete all three years. No punitive action is taken by school authorities. Parents advance as reasons for keeping their children out of school a lack of money to pay for clothing, school supplies, and school lunches (pupils may not bring their own), and the belief that a middle school education is of no economic value to them or their children. Formal education of the Takashima child ordinarily ends with completion or partial completion of middle school. Few parents can afford further education, and few regard the three years of high school as economically warranted for young people who will become fishermen or housewives.

Until boys and girls reach the end of their schooling, life is principally school and play. The activities and interests of children from six to about fifteen revolve principally about school. If studies are sometimes not relished, other school affairs such as athletic meets, plays, educational movies, and the music, singing, and games are important and interesting events. Annual class excursions under the supervision of teachers to famous historic or scenic places are particularly memorable events. The distances covered by school excursions increase with each grade so that students of the last years of middle school may visit points one hundred or more miles away, spending several days on the trips and lodging in inns which offer low rates for student excursionists. For many individuals these trips represent the most distant travel of the life-span.

Separation of the sexes begins without active intervention on the part of parents at the time children enter school. Boys and girls of pre-school age and, less frequently, children in the lowest primary classes, play together at home. After reaching five or six years of age, they associate increasingly with members of their own sex. Voluntary play groups at school are ordinarily composed of only one sex. By the time children are nine or ten, except for one's family and in school classes and events, association is almost wholly with one's own sex, a state of affairs wholly approved by adults.

Small duties and responsibilities are regularly assigned to school children by their parents. Boys are ordinarily asked to do less than girls. Girls are taught early to fold and put away their beds in the morning and to help their mothers with domestic duties—boiling water for tea, watching the cookstove, digging clams at the beach, preparing food, and, most frequently, the care of younger siblings. Transporting small brothers and sisters on their backs, ten- and twelve-year-old girls indulge in customary play while the heads of the sleeping infants wobble about perilously as the girls run, bounce balls, and play hopscotch. Boys of twelve or less sometimes also aid with the care of younger brothers and sisters and, like their fathers, they help the women with agricultural tasks during the rush seasons of planting and harvesting. Older boys help their fathers with the repair and treatment of fishing nets, as do some girls, and sturdy boys may go out in the fishing boats as helpers.

Regular work as economically contributing members of the household does not begin until schooling has ended, although by this time most boys and girls have had some introduction to their future tasks. From the age of fifteen to twenty-one or twenty-two, when a girl marries, she ordinarily learns and participates actively in women's work, helping with tasks in the dwelling and also with farm duties. If the family lacks enough males to operate the household fishing boat, she may serve as a crew member, helping with the laying and drawing in of nets, and their manufacture, maintenance and repair. Some girls take employment before marriage as clerks or employees in small clothing factories in larger communities nearby; they may commute to work daily or reside in company dormitories.

The conduct of girls is more strictly supervised than that of young men. They receive frequent instruction directly and indirectly in the proper attributes of their roles as females—obedience to elders and deference to males, gentleness, self-effacement, politeness, and a cheerful, quiet manner. But the life of the unmarried girl who has finished school is not limited to drudgery and subservience to household males. A girl's position is honored and secure and she is allowed many privileges and avenues of pleasure. The extreme subordination of females to males traditional in Japan is less strongly marked among the fishing households of Takashima where women, as operators of the vital farm plots, are economically important, and where wives and mothers, although generally submissive to their husbands, sometimes express their own views and interests forcefully.

Pretty clothing, spending money on festival days, and considerable free time for amusement are regarded as the normal and just privileges of any girl. It is considered permissible, if something of an unwelcome break with tradition, for girls to take a keen and active interest in clothing and beauty of face and figure. Girls spend much time sewing and knitting in the company of friends, chatting meanwhile about clothes and other interests. Lessons in machine and hand sewing of both native and Western style clothing are a post-war innovation for most girls of late teen age. Movies, both Western and Japanese, attended in nearby towns in the company of other girls during festival periods afford glimpses of romantic ways of life that are admired and serve as subjects of discussion.

To achieve minimum standards of beauty a girl must have curly hair, and she receives her first permanent wave at about age sixteen. Girls admire Western ideas of dress and adornment and, in addition to per-

Japanese girl carrying her brother. *Photo courtesy of Edward Norbeck.* (See also illustrations on pages 569 and 570.)

manent waves and Western clothing of many kinds, they possess a few cosmetics—powder, rouge, lipstick, and, more rarely, perfume—which are treasured and displayed only among intimate friends. If used at all, only traces of these cosmetics may be applied by anyone except a bride on her wedding day. A girl with an obviously made-up face is a target for ridicule; the habitual use of cosmetics of this kind is regarded as the trade-mark of professionally loose women—waitresses, geishas and prostitutes.

Many girls like to read magazines and novels, and, although they can usually buy only a small number, those purchased are exchanged among friends. Western and native popular music played on the phonograph or radio are popular and most girls have some knowledge of the foxtrot and other Western styles of social dancing. Girls who have taken employment in larger communities learn the dances from more sophisticated dormitory mates, and transmit these glamorous and daring accomplishments to sisters and friends on Takashima. Most girls secretly—at least outside the range of vision of elders—practice Western dancing in the home, but none would dare to attend a public dance or to dance with males.

Unmarried girls usually appear more contented than their male age-mates. Their status as females entails strictly bounded roles, but they may look forward with security and assurance to the only course open to them: a future as wives and mothers. Generally shy, docile and extremely sensitive to ridicule or criticism, they are also good-natured and happy; viewing the future with equanimity, they enjoy their girl-hood.

When an eldest son finishes middle school he usually begins work as a full-time fisherman under the direction of his father. Several years of experience are necessary before he has mastered all the skills and knowledge of a seasoned fisherman. Younger sons more frequently seek employment outside the community; following traditional custom, they cannot expect to succeed their fathers as household heads and heirs to the household property. Although primogeniture was abolished officially by post-war legislation, family property is seldom great enough to bear division among two or more persons and the eldest son continues as the heir.

Boys who take outside employment—most frequently as deck hands on small cargo ships in the Inland Sea—are usually lost to the community and settle down elsewhere. For young men who stay in the community, life from sixteen to about twenty-five, when they marry, is generally a period of unrest, discontent, and extreme susceptibility to fear of criticism or ridicule. Few want to be fishermen; still less do they want to be farmers. Untrained for any occupation of higher prestige and income than fishing, they are nevertheless aware from schooling and contacts with the world of the possibilities open to others. At home and on the fishing boats, the father is indisputably in command, and the growth of initiative or the assumption of responsibility for decisions finds little encouragement. The proceeds of a young man's productive labor are a part of common household earnings, and funds at the control of the young man are ordinarily limited to spending money given to him during festival seasons.

Young men who have finished school have ample leisure but fewer sources of satisfactory amusement and entertainment than girls of the same age. They continue to attend plays and track meets at the elementary school, as do their sisters and parents, and they sometimes play baseball on the school grounds when school is not in session. Hobbies such as collecting postage stamps are known but uncommon, as most hobbies require more money than a young man has at his disposal. Japanese chess and Western games of cards are sometimes played. Card games must usually be played in secrecy for fear of the censure of elders because they are viewed as gambling and in fact usually are so. Gambling, sometimes financially disastrous and feared and hated by women, is an addiction of many adult males and household heads, who nevertheless reprove their sons for the same behavior. Many boys read such popular magazines and books as come to their hands, but they are less interested in reading than are young women. During festival seasons, when the building is left open for this purpose, they sometimes play ping-pong in the community hall.

The happiest occasions in a young man's life are the festivals, when he is given spending money—more than is allowed to sisters of equivalent age—and may visit other and larger communities. In the company of other young men he attends movies, sees the sights, and occasionally drinks a little rice wine. The consumption of liquor by young men in anything but small amounts on special occasions is strongly disapproved, but all unmarried young men may once annually, at the autumn festival, drink to the point of intoxication without parental censure. A young man participates in this ancient ceremonial—formerly religious but today supernaturalistic only in form—for the first time at sixteen or when he has finished middle school. Each household contributes funds for food and liquor, which are consumed jointly by the young men in the mid-afternoon. Most youths, in expected fashion, drink to the point of drunkenness. After the feasting and drinking have ended they may wander in groups of two and three about the community in a sodden state with arms about their friends—behavior which is avoided at all other times—until sleep overcomes them. Traditionally all enmities incurred among the young men during the year are settled by this ceremonial and are henceforth forgotten.

Joint activities of unmarried young men and women are rare. Occasionally a few girls join the men in games of ping-pong in the community hall on festival days, the only instance when the mingling of sexes on an individual basis among the unmarried is approved. Dancing during the Bon festival, one of the rare traditional occasions when young people of both sexes mingled, is seldom performed today, and on the increasingly rare occasions when the community does perform the dances only the middle-aged and aged participate. Young people are bashful and they regard Bon dancing as very old-fashioned. Until marriage, both men and women belong to the Takashima sections of the Young People's Association, whose stated purpose is to promote community welfare. Young men's units and young women's units form complementary parts, and, although the infrequent meetings of the several local subsections often include both male and female units, attendance and seating are in the company of others of one's own sex. Young men and young women are usually extremely ill at ease in the presence of unrelated young people of opposite sex and avoid them.

Education in sexual matters comes chiefly from friends of one's own sex. In recent years knowledge of human reproduction has been gained from middle school classes in physiology and from magazine articles. Most young men and women of marriageable age acquire more scientifically sound information on matters of sex than did their parents. Except among old men, who may with impunity indulge jokingly in much behavior prohibited to others, reference to sex is an occasion for embarrassment or secrecy. Some mothers give their daughters instruction in procedures to follow during menses, but ordinarily only if the daughters inform them at the first occurrence and have not by this time acquired instruction from other sources. Mothers and fathers give their children no instruction regarding sexual relations. Instead, boys and girls "hear things" from other boys and girls, who in turn hear them from other boys and girls or from sources no one knows or remembers. The cohabitation of spouses is hurried and secret, but walls are thin and houses are small so that chance observation may sometimes be instructive.

Although parents seldom or never include direct reference to sexual relations in instruction regarding the proper deportment of girls, by the time a girl has reached puberty she has learned thoroughly that pre-marital sex experience is not only prohibited but also that it may be disastrous. To make a desirable marriage a girl must be a virginal bride, a condition which is demanded by the family of the prospective groom. Adolescent girls and young women are allowed to visit outside communities in the company of other girls, but their whereabouts are always known and few opportunities for any kind of misstep are afforded. No girl would ordinarily ever want to go anywhere alone. Within the closely juxtaposed community of Takashima all acts performed

outside the walls of the dwelling and many of the activities that trans-
pire within are common knowledge—a condition which serves to inhibit socially unapproved behavior of any kind. Takashima brides are
almost invariably virginal, a state which they regard as both appropriate and desirable.

Young men are allowed greater latitude, and it is expected that they
will have some sexual experience by the time they marry. Such experience begins for most young men at eighteen or nineteen and consists
of a few visits during festival seasons, when they have money in their
pockets, to houses of prostitution in nearby towns. A young man seldom visits prostitutes alone but instead goes encouraged and supported
by the company of one or more age-mates intent upon the same errand,
all of the party frequently emboldened by liquor. A few experiences
of this kind are expected and tacitly approved, although a young man
who habitually visits prostitutes is looked upon with strong disapproval. No girl expects a virginal groom, and all parties concerned with a
marriage consider it appropriate that a bride's instruction in sexual relations be provided by the experienced groom.

As young men and young women approach marriageable age, parents ordinarily have little reason to fear that their behavior will not
meet the approved standard. For most young adults the socially approved patterns have become ends in themselves. The young adult is
no longer simply an individual whose wants are to be indulged; he
has long been an integral part of a larger aggregation, the family, whose
united welfare is of greater importance than that of any single member. Each of the individual's acts reflects upon others of the family, an
idea which has been impressed both consciously and unconsciously from
earliest childhood. The sanctions imposed have changed from the mild
physical punishment and repeated instruction of the indulgent period
of early childhood to increasing emphasis and finally total reliance
upon acts which shame—censure or ridicule, either verbal or implied
by facial expression and ostracism through silence or physical avoidance. The dread of humiliation and loss of prestige that non-conformance brings extends even to the fear of inadvertent missteps; the
young adult is diffident about any kind of public performance unless
he is exceptionally skilled. The number of persons who exert control
over the behavior of the individual also has increased as he has matured.
His range of social relationships has grown; at first it includes only the
close relatives of his household, then increases to embrace his peers and
teachers in the school and members of his community, and finally, includes the whole world. Self-respect and family-respect, now viewed
as vital necessities, are practical necessities if one is to make a desirable
marriage. The family, the community, and the whole world watch to
see that standards are met, and few individuals fail to conform.

RONALD L. OLSON

1956. Channelling of Character in Tlingit Society. Not published previously.

An anthropologist whose special interest focuses on the Indians of the Pacific coast of North America, Dr. Olson offers a picture of the inevitable adjustment of the Tlingit Indian youth to the clan or sib organization of his society. Ever since Freud demonstrated the priority of infant experiences in determining certain main lines of personality, increasing numbers of anthropologists have labored to fill gaps in ethnographic data by studying the care of infants in various societies. Few if any would question the importance of observing the childhood and adolescent situations in which adult personality is achieved; at the moment, however, post-infancy experiences have received somewhat less than their due. Dr. Olson, in this paper, shifts the emphasis from infancy to childhood and youth without denying the basic experiences of infancy.

Other relevant papers by the same author are cited in the General Bibliography. See also Goldenweiser, 1922; Krause, 1956; Swanton, 1908.

CHANNELING OF CHARACTER IN TLINGIT SOCIETY

Ronald L. Olson

The Tlingit language was spoken by about a dozen tribes that occupied some five hundred miles of the coastal zone of southeast Alaska from the Canadian boundary to Yakutat Bay. Usually they have been referred to as if they were a single tribe. With their southern neighbors, the Tsimshian and Haida, they represented the highest development of "Northwest Coast Culture."[1]

The climate is relatively mild despite the far northern location between 44° and 60° North latitude. Temperatures at sea level seldom fall below 0°F.; on the open coast the tempering effect of the warm Japan Current is pronounced. The rugged, broken coast is fringed with innumerable islands and nearly everywhere mountains rise sharply from the water's edge. A maze of sheltered waterways—deep narrow channels and fjords—reflects the landscape sculpturing of heavy glaciation in the last ice age. Precipitation is heavy in winter, with rain in the warmer sections and snow at altitudes above 1000 feet and along the margin of the Cascade range. At Ketchikan and Sitka the annual rainfall often exceeds 100 inches; rain or snow falls on more than half of the days of the year.

Heavy forests of hemlock, cedar, and spruce, with undergrowth of brush and bushes, cover most of the land below 3000 feet. The dense rain forest and rugged terrain make land travel almost impossible, although the waterways provide easy communication. The sea and rivers were the chief source of food; the Tlingit had no agriculture and no domestic animals other than the dog. The abundant game—chiefly bear, deer, and mountain goat—were of minor economic importance, for the sea insured a boundless supply of food. Shellfish and crustaceans, seals, sea lions, and other sea mammals are plentiful, and the ocean teems with codfish, herring, and halibut, to name but a few species of fish. During the summer, salmon ascend the streams in numbers almost beyond belief; properly smoke-dried, these formed the major food staple. The struggle for existence was never severe and the Tlingit exploited but a fraction of the food supply. This abundance enabled the people to secure food for the entire year in a few months, and allowed them to spend the winter in large permanent villages; at this season they made dugout canoes, built houses, and manufactured household and hunting gear. This was the time for visiting, and above all for the famed ceremonial festivals called "potlatches." Concentration of population, plus a season of respite from food-getting, perhaps contributed to the high development of art and ceremonial activities.

The highly distinctive art style of this area was executed mainly in wood carving and painting. While the most spectacular item was totem-pole art, house posts, boxes, dishes, canoes, and other objects were embellished. Nearly all of this art was totemic; that is, it reflected the legends, crests, and other symbols of clans and various kin groups.

While Tlingit culture exhibits a decided masculine bias, the social structure is wholly matrilineal. Men are far more important than women in food-getting and manufacturing; they own the houses, canoes, and hunting and fishing grounds, and residence is patrilocal. These facts might well have led to patrilineal rather than matrilineal descent and inheritance. The reasons for this anomaly probably lie far back in history.

The Tlingit had little sense of national, tribal, or village solidarity. The basic features of their organization were the moieties (or super-clans) and the clans. The moieties were named Raven and Wolf (in some tribes, Raven and Eagle). Each moiety was divided into several clans that bore animal names—often derived from legendary places of origin. By birth, every Tlingit belonged to the clan of his mother and derivatively to her moiety. Loyalty to the clan was paramount, and clan affiliation determined nearly every aspect of social life. Clanship dictated choice of mates, social behavior toward clansmen and non-clansmen, and a thousand other things.

The clans "owned" houses, salmon streams, hunting and berrying grounds, overland trade routes to the interior, etc. More important than these was clan ownership of a multitude of intangibles: these included rights to crests, sets of personal names, house names, canoe names, even names of famous dishes and baskets. Clans also owned legends, songs, dances, ceremonial titles, and even such things as the right to build an especially big fire at a potlatch. All these were of the greatest value in the Tlingit mind.[2] The result was that clan loyalty far outweighed family, village, or tribal loyalty. Feuds, wars, and potlatch rivalry occurred between clan and clan, not between village and village or tribe and tribe.

The enormous emphasis on clanship acted disruptively in Tlingit society. The father of a family belonged to one clan, his wife and children to another. Always in the multiple-family household, two and usually more clans were represented. Males above the age of ten years or so belonged to one clan, the women and children to another. In every village the houses of the respective clans were grouped together.

Tlingit Indians, Yakutat Bay, Alaska. Sketched by the Malaspina Expedition in 1792. *From the Archives of the Museo Naval, Madrid.*

Consequently there were no tribal or village chiefs as such, but only house chiefs. One of these, because of his higher social rank, was regarded as clan chief.

So fierce was clan loyalty that in the event of an inter-clan, intra-village blood feud the women and children of each household fled to houses of their own clans. It was feared that to even the score a wife might kill her husband or vice versa. So rarely was a man "untrue to his clan" that an instance of it is cited in the semi-historical legend of a war. Clan membership is the one aspect of Tlingit society that has largely withstood the destructive influence of the white man. Thus, in an Indian Claims case decided in 1954, the original claim was made by a clan, not by a village group or tribe.

The emphasis on clan rather than on family resulted in some curious usages. Thus, women going on a berrying trip always were of a single clan, lest in case of accident the clan that had lost a member, or had lost more than another clan had lost, might bring a claim for compensation. A few years ago, D. C. took his son to the salmon trolling grounds and the son was lost. The wife's clan held a meeting to decide whether to press a claim against the father's clan. They decided not to do so, because the father had lost a valuable boat and had offered a large reward for the finding of the boy's body. In earlier times nephews rather than sons would accompany the elders.

The dilemma of conflict between a father's affection for his children and the necessity of educating the young in "clanship" was solved in part by having boys leave their homes for the house of the maternal uncle at the age of eight or ten. Who else could train them and teach the many things necessary to becoming a true and full clan member? The education of girls could be accomplished by the mother, but a boy's learning could not be imparted by the father, who automatically was a member of another clan.

However, since one half of a person's ancestry came through the father and it was desirable that a boy should know something of this part of his family history, a father usually gave some instruction to his sons during their early years. One of my informants described how his father had done this:

"As soon as I was old enough, 'when I came to myself,' my father began by telling me about the clans. He told me how it was that a child belonged to the clan of the mother. It has always been that way. Then he explained that the father and mother were always of different clans, for persons of the same clan (and generation) were brothers and sisters. Next he explained that each of the clans belonged either to the Wolf (Eagle) or Raven 'side' (moiety), and that within the 'side,' in the same way as within the clan, persons are brothers and sisters.

"He told me how important it was that every person should know about his ancestry. It is a disgrace if they do not know. Each child must be told what kind or class of people his ancestors were.[3] If there is a case of slavery, or other blot on the family escutcheon, the child must be told of it.

"My father told me, 'Son, I am going to die, but you will become a man. It is important that you know that on my side there is a disgrace. My grandfather was captured in war and became a slave until he was ransomed. (But on your mother's side everything is clean.) So be careful of your words. When people speak 'hard words' to you, you must hold your tongue or they will throw this disgrace in your face. But if you keep silent, people will say, 'His father has told him things and he has listened.'[4]

"Persons who are not careful of their words, who care for nothing or for no one, who speak their minds brazenly, show that they have had no training. Such persons are nitchkayadki."[5]

Although there was little formal education or child training, definite attempts were made to mold character according to the ideal pattern and there was a considerable amount of indoctrination in the chief virtues of bravery, fortitude, industry, thrift, and pride in family and clan. Training included long homilies, ritualistic corporal punishment for boys, and tales of the behavior of idealized ancestors. Both practical and magical methods were used.

Education was considered as beginning at birth. A newborn boy was held and his umbilical cord rubbed with an adze so that he would become a skilled workman. He was moved about as if "fighting" with the implement. This also made him quick-tempered and strong. A quick temper in our sense was not a desired quality, but he should be quick to resent slurs and insults. He was cradled with the skin of a bear or wolf for the same effect. Later, boys were taught the use of tools and weapons.

As soon as a child began to crawl the mother or maternal grandmother made as if spitting in each ear and said, "Be smart! Be smart!" If the baby cried too much or otherwise misbehaved, the mother said, "Slave's child you are."

When a child began to understand things, he was told how to behave and how not to behave: he must not be extravagant; he should spend money for food rather than foolish things; he should always keep some money hidden away. The mother did most of this sort of training. At the age of about eight years, however, boys were turned over to their maternal uncles. Girls remained with the parents. The boy's uncle continued the early training, stressing the virtues of industriousness and efficiency. This was so that the boy would not become a beggar. The uncle would tell him always to save, to have wealth put away, to aspire to owning slaves, to try to become greater than the uncle himself.

The father had now (after the boy left home) nothing whatever to do with training his son. A girl was often given masculine advice by her mother's brother. A boy's uncle made him work hard. He must build the fires, keep them going, get wood and water, and help keep the house clean.

Punishment of children for misbehavior was done chiefly by the mother until they reached the age of seven or eight. Before this age they were considered as "not knowing their own minds." Whipping for misbehavior was employed but rarely. More usual were scolding or keeping indoors. Long "lectures" on proper behavior were frequent. This discipline was to "make them smart," to teach them that they must work, save, get wealth and goods. It is said that girls were punished more frequently than boys. In a sense this was because the perpetuation of the family line within the clan depended on them. Girls were told, "You may come to be the only woman of the family. It is important that you grow up to bear children. You alone can give them the names of the noted people of our line."

For boys, more emphasis was placed on a long life and success so that they "would not have to go from place to place," or "fall down" (die) by middle age, or be considered of little account by everyone. Boys were expected to become brave and industrious. Pride in one's clan was a part of this indoctrination, especially within those clans ranked as "high" or noble. Since there were marked differences in the status of households and lineages within the clan, there were corresponding differences in training. Children and youths were taught to live up to a certain station in life. But for all except those classed as "noble" there was also the obligation not to aspire to or attempt things beyond one's status in society.[6]

The uncle became the "social father." He taught the virtues and warned against the vices. In some aspects of this training severe discipline was involved. In former times the uncle would pull off the boy's blankets at daybreak and order him to the river or beach. There the lad waded into the water up to his neck and remained for a time. In winter this might involve breaking the ice. Reluctance was met with a forcible ducking. When the lad emerged the uncle whipped him with birch boughs.

The nephew was sent for wood, wearing only trousers and moccasins. He carried birch switches with him and on his return was met by his uncle or another clansman who made liberal use of the boughs in a ceremonial lashing. All this was supposed to make the nephew strong, tough, and full of courage. It insured that "the house of the mother's father's father would not die out" or be "lost." J. B. stated that her family had failed in this in recent generations. Hence two clan houses at Klukwan (Raven House and Whale House) stand empty.

In former times a chief or chiefs would call the people of the clan together for a night meeting. There the smartest old man would talk to them, directing his remarks especially to the young. The "sermon" emphasized that children should listen to the advice of their parents; that lying, gossiping, and failure to pay debts were bad. An especially promising lad might be told to stand up and the speaker would extol his virtues. "Here is a young fellow who can be trusted, one to whom it will be safe to leave property," and so on.

The old people would say of a wayward or disobedient child, "He will not live long. He doesn't mind his father, his mother, his uncle, or even his grandparents."

Even to the present time parents employ various methods of insuring exemplary conduct. When the infant is but a few months old the mother talks to him, tells him moral tales, "trains" him. Each morning the infant's lips are rubbed with a good luck charm of jade or serpentine, often carved in the form of one of the clan crests. This is done until the child is grown, to insure that the child will be peaceable and quiet, one who would "hold his hand over his mouth." Even adults apply these amulets to themselves.

Grandfathers were expected to sermonize to their grandsons, grandmothers to their granddaughters. Boys were told, "Don't get angry at anyone, don't bother people or make trouble."

Children guilty of misbehavior, especially theft, formerly were punished as follows: two or three times a year a chief called the people of the clan together in a large house. Here a fire was built and huge boxes placed on either side. Wayward children were put in the boxes, as many as six in a box. The boxes were covered and the fire built up. Soon the heat inside the boxes became almost unbearable. The fire side of the box was like hot iron. Those inside began to despair for their lives. Some would cry but others out of pride would not even whimper. The elders would weep for the children. Perhaps when the fire had eaten through the side of the box the children were let out.

D. C. and another lad once played at "keeping house" with some little girls. Each had two "wives." The play included childish sex activity. D. C.'s father found them and gave the boys a severe lecture. Some months later the two boys were tied together at the wrists and put through the hot box ordeal.

G. M.'s uncle used to rouse him at daybreak and tell him to build up the fire. Each morning the uncle would admonish him, tell him that he didn't wish him ever to be dependent on other houses for food, that he must learn to do for himself, that he must rise early and be about the business of earning his living.

When G. M. was a lad his aged uncle Shaklen used to call all his nephews together and tell them the tribal and clan history. He would repeat each legend, each account of events, several times until the lads knew them well.

Each morning Shaklen also took his nephews to the water to bathe. When they emerged he whipped each with a bundle of red huckleberry brush until their chests bled. He used eight bundles every morning. As he whipped them he would say, "This is so you will not be like Dikgeh."

Dikgeh, according to the legend, was a Ganaxadi lad of very high birth, in fact too high for his own good. His uncle's slaves did everything for him. He learned nothing about how to do anything practical. When he was to board a canoe the slaves placed a painted gangplank for him and stood alongside to hand him into the canoe. In the middle of the canoe he was placed in an arrangement of painted planks, almost like a little room, to screen him from wind and spray. There he sat, instead of with the others. But finally all his kin and the slaves died. He became poor because he could do nothing. He could not even fix the cracks in his canoe because his hands were so tender they blistered when he tried to use the drill. He then foolishly tried to patch the cracks with pitch and feathers.

In the training of a girl, she was put into one of the bedrooms at the rear ("head") of the house (or behind a screen or curtain) at her first menses. Her mother slept at her side. For eight days the girl must not eat or drink. Each morning her mother wiped her mouth with a pad of shredded bark, so that when she grew up she would be careful in her speech and not be gossipy or quarrelsome. After the eight-day fast this bark was driven into a crevice in a rock with a wedge and maul. The girl was kept in the room one or two months and then was allowed to come out. But she still slept beside her mother and when she went to the beach on errands of nature her mother went with her. Food was brought to her in bed, and she drank through a bone tube. She wore a hat with a fringe around the brim and a stone "bustle" under her robe. She was treated much like a widow.

After some months (or even a year) there was a ceremonial removal of her hat. Her father invited all those of his own moiety to the house. Several women of his clan led the girl out (from behind the screen) and removed her hat and wiped her face. A feast followed, the girl joining the others in eating. Her father piled the blankets and other goods to be given to the guests and these were distributed. It was as if the girl's clan were giving the feast. The largest gifts were to the women who led her out and removed her hat. The girl was now free, a woman, and waited for someone to come and take her as wife.

If during the eight-day fast she should take a drink, she would, after the menopause, have a compulsion to steal. If she should take food, she would become a glutton. If she were of good birth and faithfully carried out the rituals, she would come to be called anTlingi'ddi ("High caste woman"), a title reserved only for women of high birth who possessed the womanly virtues.

Should her puberty observances be violated, she was sure to be a loose woman, quick to look for a man other than her husband if she had the chance. Of a loose woman, it is said, "Yetlte't katye'h wutsgi't" ("She did it on purpose"), meaning she had violated the puberty taboos.

High caste girls in particular were kept chaste. At the first menses the girl was shut up in one of the alcoves or "bedrooms" of the house. Here was a box which served as toilet. Ideally, she never left this room for a year, but it might be necessary for the family to move to a camp for the summer's hunting or fishing and she would go along. This period of seclusion is called wuwedi'h (lit., "menstruating time"). Her mother and other adult female kin kept a close watch over her. The prolonged seclusion resulted in some lightening or bleaching of the skin and this was considered desirable. It was hoped that during or shortly after the seclusion some worthy lad's parents would come with a proposal of marriage. In practice marriage arrangements were often made years earlier.

In case an unmarried girl became pregnant, every attempt was made to keep it secret. When the child was born it often was killed and disposed of secretly. If the father was of low caste while the girl was high caste, the child, if allowed to live, would be adopted by the girl's close kin. If the girl and her lover were of equal rank, marriage was forced on them. If both were of the same moiety or clan the child was invariably killed, for this was incest. A chief reason is that such a child was almost without clan ties. No one would give the child a name. The mother's clan refused absolutely to recognize it and the father's side scarcely took note of it. Since names must come from the mother's clan, such a child would grow up nameless and altogether outside the pale.

As might be expected, there were (and are) children born out of wedlock. No stigma attached to them, but there would be some gossip about the parents. In recent times a number of Tlingit women have borne children by white fathers. These belong to the clan of the mother and take their place in Tlingit society readily enough, though the lack of rank from the father's side is a handicap. The natives say of such cases, "The world is turning over. Every day new things come."

Girls were given special training in regard to gossiping and quarreling, for according to tradition and current attitude most intra-group social difficulties arose through the failure of women to hold their tongues, or through their infidelities. Therefore, each morning from infancy on, the good Tlingit mother whispered in her daughter's ear, "We are women and always the cause of trouble." She then went on to admonish her to be careful with her tongue, to mind her virtue, and so on.

The Tlingit put great emphasis on integrity, honor, bravery, and "face" in social and personal relations. No insult, wrong, indignity, or injury could pass unnoticed or unresolved. The passage of time healed no breaches. The injured person or group never forgot and the story of the grounds for enmity was passed from generation to generation. Wrongs were regarded as acts not so much against individuals as against the clan. The individual in such cases merely represented the group. From a casual slur to murder, every wrong called for settlement. There was no mechanism for punishment of acts, even murder, within the clan.

The reputation and honor of the clan rather than the individual were at stake. Thus in blood feuds (always inter-clan) Tlingit law did not call for punishment of the killer but for payment of a blood price dependent on the social rank of the slain man. If the injured clan decided to demand a life for a life, the clan met and chose a victim whose social rank was equal to that of the slain man. If the murderer was a commoner and the victim a high class person, the killing of the murderer would not even the score. The injured clan named the man chosen as stand-in for the murderer and the man so chosen must come out of his house at a designated time, and be shot down "against" the murdered man. There was no escape, for the honor of the clan was at stake. There is a legend of one man whose bravery was not up to making this sacrifice. During the night he ran away. His clan then offered his nephew, a mere lad, in his stead. Since the boy was the heir of the chosen man and therefore equal in rank, he was acceptable and at the appointed time came out and was killed. The uncle's behavior is cited as an example of cowardice, dishonor, and shame.

Boys were given a thorough indoctrination in the code of bravery in feuds and wars. The code demanded complete disregard for one's own life. The enemy must be met with a cry of defiance. Even a wounded man or one faced with imminent and inevitable death must make no plea for mercy but die with a challenge on his lips. I was told of one instance in which a man was badly wounded and left lying until his enemy could return to finish him off. The wounded man appealed to a neutral clan member for help and later begged his enemy for mercy, only to be killed in scorn. Later, his mother learned of his cowardice and, in utter shame at the disgrace to the clan and family line, committed suicide.

Deep insults between men called for revenge but did not usually involve the clans. Calling a man a descendant of a slave or reference to an ancestor as "bought back" (ransomed from war captivity) could not be overlooked.[7] In such cases the insulted man went to his clansmen and stated, "I have been insulted by so-and-so. I am going to die." From that time on he went armed. The other man likewise went about armed. When they met, one or the other would be killed. Killing from ambush was unknown, the code dictating that there must be a face-to-face meeting. Since the insult was a matter of public knowledge (insults were always passed publicly) the killing seldom gave rise to a feud and no payment of blood price was necessary. Minor insults could be forgiven and forgotten, though it was customary for the households or clans involved to "wash away" the matter by giving minor reciprocal feasts. But serious or not, insults were remembered and the families and clans in question often remained bad friends for several generations.

Women were regarded as much more inclined to bicker and quarrel than were men. But their insults were taken less seriously than those between men and never called for feuds. Settlements were achieved by each side giving a minor feast with the other party as guests. The commonest insults were usually public references to slavery or witchcraft in the family, or to clan ancestry. Such an insult usually could be countered by saying, "I wonder if they never told her about herself," i.e., if she knew her own ancestry she would not imply that her family tree was without blemish. Some women would hurl public insults at a man. It was considered beneath a man's dignity to answer; it was enough merely to walk away. Children were admonished repeatedly never to repeat gossip which they might hear, lest they initiate trouble.

Although much has been made of the arrogance of high caste persons in Northwest Coast society[8] such behavior was regarded by the Tlingit as uncalled for and unnecessary. On ceremonial occasions a man might relate the great deeds of his ancestors but not his own. Each individual had a personal name which was a measure of his social rank and there was no need to boast of rank. Only persons of no account would be ignorant of the social position of the high born.

No person of high birth would demean himself by unworthy behavior or words. The concept of *noblesse oblige* was clear. A man who spoke foolishly or boastfully marked himself as common. Only in the heat of battle would a man hurl insults at an enemy. However, even a high caste person who had spoken or acted on the fringe of impropriety might be put in his place by innuendo or sly indirection or implication.

The ramification of clanship was the outstanding feature of Tlingit society. Family, household, tribe, social class, and personal achievement were of far less importance. Even in the most important ceremonials, the great potlatches, the "host" or giver was merely the representative of the clan. The affair was one which enhanced the reputation of the entire clan and every member was a participant in the collection of food and wealth distributed. Clanship represented Durkheim's "collectivism" almost ideally. The individual felt himself a part of the clan almost in an organic sense. So far as I could learn there was no feeling of resentment or frustration on the part of those in the middle and lower ranks of society. Every person could feel pride in his clan and in his kinship, however distant, with the great ones of the present and past. The social scheme and the social life were not things to be fought against, they just *were*.

In the social world of the Tlingit there was little of neurosis, psychosis, or personality conflicts resulting from experiences of infancy or childhood. Character was channeled to harmonize with the most important social group, the clan, and for most individuals the participation which they experienced was rewarding and satisfying. To an unusual degree Tlingit personality was channeled by the social environment imposed by clan membership and social rank. In the give-and-take of social life the individual was conditioned to keep his clan and its history and reputation constantly in mind. The major part of the whole system of values was clan-oriented. It is said that the high born, upon waking in the morning, would lie in bed for a time, thinking of the great names and deeds of their respective clans and of their own roles in a social world dominated by clanship.

NOTES

1. Tlingit culture has all but disappeared, save for matrilineal clans, the rule of exogamy, and some related features. Accordingly I describe it in the past tense. The rush to Alaska on discovery of gold in the Klondike accelerated Tlingit cultural disintegration.

2. Although some of these things are referred to as "owned" by individuals, such persons in reality were only trustees. They could not sell or otherwise dispose of such things, but must pass them on within the clan, usually to a sister's son.

3. Northwest Coast society was far from democratic. There were marked class distinctions, from low class commoners to high class "nobles." Social rank depended largely on birth and wealth. Rank could be changed somewhat by striving, especially in giving potlatches. But the right to give these was a prerogative of the well-born. Slaves, chiefly war captives and their descendants, were outside the pale.

4. The Tlingit were very warlike and the strong clans often raided for slaves both on other Tlingit tribes and farther afield. Women and children were often taken captive and held as slaves if not ransomed. Even if ransomed the captivity was a disgrace. For a man it was far more honorable to die fighting than to be taken captive.

5. Literally "children of Nitchkakau." Once upon a time a group of Tlingit met a young man who was a stranger. In order to learn how to behave toward him they asked his name, to learn his clan. But he answered that his name was "Nitchkakau," a name which belonged to no family, no clan. The term nitchkayadki is a "hard word," far worse than our "bastard."

6. The members of the Kagwantan clan had certain special prides. By repute they had high foreheads and accentuated this by plucking some of the hair at the margin of the scalp. They practiced wearing a scowl (yĕssiga'ni, "angry face") to bear out their reputation of being quick-tempered and proud. This is reflected in certain features of joking relationships when joking kin say to a Kagwantan, "Kagwantan duwa'h" ("Kagwantan face") in feigned ridicule. This always pleased the Kagwantan or "child" of Kagwantan so addressed.

7. Persons low in the social scale would take such insults less seriously and often pretend not to hear.

8. See, e.g., Benedict's *Patterns of Culture.*

BENJAMIN D. PAUL

1953. "Mental Disorder and Self-Regulating Processes in Culture: A Guatemalan Illustration." In *Interrelations between the Social Environment and Psychiatric Disorders,* Milbank Memorial Fund, New York. Reprinted by courtesy of the author and of the Milbank Memorial Fund.

Careless reasoning that brands as fraud the activities of shamans and other healers, charismatics, and agents of the supernatural in peripheral and ancient societies has led some writers to minimize the role of these activities. If science requires that all relevant facts be taken into account, such pre-medical (or, rather pre-scientific) rituals and techniques require understanding. Dr. Paul, in the pages that follow, places a pre-scientific treatment of psychotic behavior in its social and cultural context. No one need be surprised that the treatment "worked." Psychiatrists constantly reiterate the importance of the relations of the patient to his companions, and some of them view all emotional illness in terms of strain in social relations. Scientifically-trained medical men often fail to cure illness that yields readily to native methods of treatment; the native "healer" is at home in the culture of his patient, accepts whatever beliefs in witches or evil magic the patient accepts, and consequently deals with the cultural basis of the illness. The "modern" physician may be handicapped seriously if he cannot enter into the thoughts and fears of his patient. People act in terms of what they believe, not in terms of what someone else can "prove false." The student of cultural behavior must take into account the beliefs of his subjects, together with what they do *not* know that otherwise he might take for granted.

MENTAL DISORDER AND SELF-REGULATING PROCESSES IN CULTURE: A GUATEMALAN ILLUSTRATION

BENJAMIN D. PAUL

The concept of culture, like the proverbial elephant, has been seen from many sides. To some, culture appears primarily as a pattern. To others, it is a process, a frame of perception, a precipitate of history, a mechanism for survival. These are all mutually reconcilable. The particular view depends on one's line of vision and on one's immediate purposes. From where I stand, and for purposes of this meeting, culture can be viewed as a type of "self-correcting" mechanism.

Culture, if it is in working order, lends purpose and direction to the lives of those it serves. All forms of organization, however, are achieved at some price. The costs may be widely distributed throughout the society in the form of strains built into the "typical" personality, or they can be borne disproportionately by a minority of individuals, those typed as "deviants" by their fellows.

My concern here is with the deviant person, and more especially with a process in group behavior which first works in the direction of pushing the individual deeper into deviancy and then, in response to a behavioral signal from the deviant, reverses its direction to bring the disturbed individual back into a better state of balance with society. It is this reversible process which suggests comparison with self-regulating mechanisms, such as the thermostat on the governor of a steam engine.

Abstractly and generally considered, the conception is both simple and familiar. But its applicability to the socio-cultural sphere remains to be clarified. It is my hope that presentation of a detailed and concrete case will help to communicate the conception of self-regulating forces within culture and possibly stimulate productive comparisons. The case that follows will also raise other problems such as the relation of social role structure to individual deviance in simple societies, and the nature of the interchange between cultural and personality dynamics.

When my wife and I settled down as anthropologists in an Indian village on Lake Atitlán in Guatemala, we made the mistake of hiring the wrong girl as household helper. She soon proved inadequate in many respects, but it was no easy matter to discharge her in view of the fact that her father was an important person whose good will we were eager to preserve. We did manage to dismiss her on some face-saving pretext, proceeding with caution before hiring another girl. After a careful inspection of the field of choice, we selected Maria, the central figure in this case, a person who eventually deserted our household, abandoned her own baby and suffered a psychotic episode.

These unexpected events occurred after Maria had been working with us daily for ten weeks. During this time she had proved herself a good helper in the house, a lively and engaging companion, and a good source of information, if not always a source of good information. We came to know her as well as we knew anyone in the village, recording observations on what turned out to be a pre-morbid period in her life.

Who was Maria? She was a very attractive girl of eighteen, commanding attention even in a village renowned for its beautiful women. She was separated from her husband—her second—at the time she came to work for us and had a nine-month old baby girl. She was the daughter of a man named Manuel, who was, in some ways, an "operator." Manuel and a brother were early orphaned and raised by a kinsman who was a strict disciplinarian and taskmaster. Manuel's brother turned out to be a ne'er-do-well who was living with his seventh wife, and barely eking out a living at the time we arrived. Manuel had enjoyed better fortune. He had married strategically, thereby acquiring a house and land, and had managed to become a shaman, one of about six in the village. Shamanism can be a road to power, and though there was some question as to the legitimacy of his credentials (supernatural signs), he exerted a fair amount of influence in community councils. He was also regarded by some as a man who was lazy, and who sought to escape honest effort in a culture which extols the virtue of diligent labor in the fields. His wife's original inheritance had dwindled somewhat under his mediocre management.

Maria's mother came from one of the wealthy families with a considerable admixture of *ladino* (non-Indian) blood. She was a handsome woman of lighter-than-average complexion, a conscientious housekeeper, and a dutiful wife. But her life was punctuated by violent arguments with her husband, typically touched off by Manuel's habit of coming home drunk from a *fiesta*, and by her complaints that he was dissolving her inheritance in drinking debts. Manuel finally gave up drinking and took to smoking a pipe.

Maria was the oldest of six surviving children. Three children had died in infancy before Maria was born. According to relatives and neighbors, Maria had received much attention and affection as a baby. She was a sickly child, requiring more than ordinary care. When she was old enough to travel, her father took her on trips and to the fields as his traveling companion, a privilege commonly reserved for sons rather than daughters. But later on her father's indulgent attitude changed to one of criticism and punishment. He scolded and beat her for carrying tales ("She was always a great liar and troublemaker"), for her laziness around the house, and for getting into fights with her younger siblings.

Another girl, Juana, was born when Maria was fifteen months old. When Maria came to work for us, Juana was sixteen or seventeen years old. She was married, lived with her husband in her parents' home, and was pregnant with her first child. There was no love lost between Maria and Juana. They had a history of frequent quarrels and had even been rivals for the same beau. While Maria had more attractive features, Juana's lighter skin color carried more prestige. In marked contrast to Maria, Juana was a "good daughter," conforming to cultural expectations which distinguished sharply between the behavior prescribed for men and the behavior prescribed for women. Juana was obedient and respectful toward her parents, worked hard about the house, seldom sought to leave the house for idle purposes, and remained properly reticent in the presence of outsiders.

Some of Maria's traits suggested psychological affinity with masculine rather than with feminine standards. In a community where Maya is the native language, most of the women quickly forget what Spanish they learn as girls in grade school and feel ashamed to use the little they can remember. Men, in contrast, find Spanish useful in their commerce with the outside world. Maria not only had a fair command of Spanish but seemed to take pride in using it. She used her charm to attract men, but her attitude toward them was essentially competitive and hostile. By local standards, she was immodest and aggressive. She was disobedient and resisted authority; at home she was quarrelsome, dominating her younger siblings and engaging in arguments with her father.

Her first marriage lasted only a few months; her husband had accused her of carrying on flirtations with other men. Her second marriage, which had dissolved before we arrived, had been to a culturally marginal man of unstable character. The son of a wealthy family, he had been educated in the capital of Guatemala and had become a schoolteacher, but later lost his job because of excessive drinking. Maria quarreled with her husband and her mother-in-law, the marriage broke up, and she returned with a baby to live with her parents, having no other place to go.

Maria "happened" to be around when we needed a helper. Men and children visited our house freely from the beginning, but women and girls, deterred by fear of public disapproval, tended to keep a polite distance. Maria was one of our first female visitors. She volunteered her assistance about the house and kitchen and immediately began to help us with our Spanish. We thought the decision to hire her was ours, but in retrospect, it seems that Maria in fact selected us.

She was vivacious, gossipy, and an avid informant, but she embroidered nimbly. She was witty and a very clever mimic, but would occasionally lapse into morose silences. She seldom assumed a submissive attitude. When she was corrected in her household duties, she would respond by correcting our Spanish or by withdrawing into dignified silence.

Maria had a flair for the gruesome and the destructive. Once she helped a young man remove a chigger-like insect from his toe. This is done with a needle. She laughed and joked about sticking the needle into his eyes and all over his body. Another time she gave us an account of a celebrated murder that had occurred when she was only a few years old. With the aid of an accomplice, one man had killed another, over a woman. The culprits were apprehended and sent to the penitentiary, where the accomplice eventually died. These were the facts, and Maria presented them, but she allowed her imagination to embellish the story with a wealth of colorful and improbable details. According to her vivid version, the assassin hacked up the body, split the head open, extracted the brain and put it in his pocket. The victim was also shot but wasn't killed until he received the fifth bullet. The accomplice did not merely die during his imprisonment, according to Maria; he was hacked to death, just as the original victim had been.

Maria worked for us part-time, and we paid her weekly. Sometimes she brought along her daughter and let her crawl about our floor. Most of the time the baby was left in the care of her mother or younger siblings. Their house was only a short distance from ours, and Maria could go home to breast-feed the baby. She seemed, in general, to be quite unconcerned about her child.

In our house, where she could escape the protective vigilance of her kinsmen, she had the rare opportunity of meeting the men who came to visit us. This enabled her to carry on conversations and surreptitiously arrange to run away and marry José, one of our informants. Like her previous husband, José was culturally marginal and was hoping to leave his native village when he could find employment in the capital. To disguise their plans, both Maria and José assured us that they wouldn't think of marrying since they were cousins and that their sustained conversations had to do with intrigues involving third parties. One evening when we left Maria alone for a moment, washing the supper dishes, she disappeared, eloping with José to his house. In Maria's village, at the present time, eloping with the boy and leaving the unsuspecting parents is the dominant form of marriage. In this case, Maria found it more convenient to use our house rather than her own as a staging area for the elopement.

Inevitably, Maria's parents learned the facts of the case by the following morning. Manuel, her father, came to our house and asked when we could give him the money he assumed we owed his daughter for the ten weeks of her employment. She apparently had told him that we had not yet begun to pay her. She had told us that her father kept her salary and that she had nothing left to buy essential clothes. In sympathy for her plight, we had presented her a blouse and other items for the Easter holidays.

Following local practices in connection with the elopement pattern, Manuel went to the village court house the day after Maria's disappearance to bring suit against her and José. He wanted to see her punished severely for having caused him anger and humiliation and especially for having abandoned her baby. This was a heartless thing to do to the baby, he contended, and it placed a heavy responsibility on his family, especially since the child was still nursing. The court imposed a fine on the couple, which José's father paid, terminating the court case but not the marriage. Maria returned to live with José and his parents. Her baby was awarded by the court to relatives of the child's real father. They claimed the baby on grounds that they had materially contributed to its support, and they claimed to be able to provide a wet-nurse, a paternal aunt who was then nursing a baby of her own.

People in the village spoke ill of Maria, not so much for eloping from her parents as for deserting her baby. There is no bottle feeding in the village, wet-nursing is regarded as a temporary expedient at best, and it is generally assumed that a baby under one year of age has a poor chance to survive if separated from its mother. Apparently feeling that the baby would be an obstacle in her new marriage, Maria made no effort to keep or regain her. Manuel remained bitter; relationships between Maria and her own family were completely ruptured.

Having alienated nearly everybody else, Maria could still count on José and his parents—but not for long. She promptly antagonized her new mother-in-law, whose named happened to be Juana, the same as the name of Maria's next younger sister. Her mother-in-law charged Maria with indolence and insubordination, and with giving orders to children of the household over whom Maria had no authority.

About a month after their marriage, Maria had a violent argument with José. He accused her of flirting with another man, and she accused him of making overtures to another girl. She reviled José and his parents. He responded by beating her. She in turn suffered a violent attack of *cólera* (rage), a culturally patterned syndrome consisting, according to local conceptions, of a swelling of the heart due to an excess of "bad blood," and consequent symptoms of gasping and suffocation. An attack of *cólera* is nearly always the product of an acrimonious quarrel. It gives the appearance of being a kind of adult temper-tantrum with screaming generally suppressed, and some of the anger directed at the self. The local culture frowns on the expression of overt hostility but nevertheless heated arguments sometimes occur, engendering secondary anxiety which can lead to *cólera*.

Later that night, after the quarrel and the attack of *cólera*, Maria lapsed into a state of unconsciousness which turned out to be the onset of a dissociated episode. Her husband tried to rouse her but could not. He summoned his father, Francisco, but he too was unsuccessful in trying to wake her. In their own words, they found her "cold and stiff as though dead for good." The Maya word *kamik* refers both to death and to unconsciousness, hence the phrase "dead for good" is a Spanish rendering to distinguish death from other losses of consciousness.

José and Francisco were frightened. Francisco shook his son and demanded, "What have you done to her?" He supposed that José might have beaten his wife to death. Francisco then called in a *ladina* (non-Indian) school mistress temporarily residing in the village. The schoolteacher tried some remedies, but without effect. Francisco next summoned one of the village shamans (native medico-magical specialists). The shaman came but was reluctant to try one of his medicines because, as he remarked, "She already looks so serious." He feared she would die, and he did not want to assume any responsibility. He remained in the house, however, and in about two hours Maria showed signs of life. She began to wail that spirits of the dead were surrounding her and were trying to take her to the realm of the dead. This heightened the fears of those present. The shaman left abruptly, saying that this was not a case for him. Ghosts are not taken lightly by people of this village; their arrival suggests that death is imminent.

Maria was in a state of fugue; she did not respond to overtures and did not recognize what was happening about her. She walked about the house talking and arguing, but only with the spirits. She told the spirits that she did not want to go along.

Realizing that she was *loca* (crazy), Francisco sent for the appropriate shaman. Of the six or seven shamans in the village, only one was qualified by his calling and by experience to deal with insanity. That person, it so happened, was Manuel, Maria's father.

Until this moment, Francisco and Manuel had not been on speaking terms owing to the elopement and the subsequent court case. But that night the breach was speedily remedied. Now in the role of a critical specialist and not in the role of an injured father, Manuel swung into action. He advised that Maria be taken immediately to the neighboring town of Atitlán, regarded as the seat of sorcery, to see a still more powerful shaman, a person who had once cured Manuel of a stubborn illness and had thus become Manuel's mentor in the shamanistic arts.

At two o'clock at night the party set out by canoe—Maria, her father, José, and José's parents. Maria resisted, but she was forcibly taken by the arm. Just before dawn they arrived in Atitlán. Manuel called on the other shaman, and they all paid a visit to the abode of the powerful and dreaded *Maximon*, the master of insanity and black magic. Candles were burned, incense was offered, and the two shamans held conversations with the mystic power, unseen in the darkness of the night.

The seance ended with the diagnosis that Maria had fallen victim to the power of malignant supernatural forces. The cause lay in a history of sinful behavior on the part of any or all of the following: Maria, her father and mother; her husband José, his father and mother. Hence, the first step in the course of treatment was to be a ritual whipping administered to all six by a senior relative. This could be done only by the aged mother of Francisco, the only living grandparent of the couple. The party returned to the village and asked the grandmother to carry out the whipping. This was to be done as a gesture and as a symbol, and not as an act of corporal punishment. Even though it involved more exorcism than exercise, the old lady refused to cooperate. Like the first shaman who had run out on the case, she feared that someone would die, and did not want to incur any blame. But many other steps were taken. Considerable time, money, and effort were expended by both sets of parents in an effort to placate the threatening spirits. Resort was made to additional shamans and new remedies. The details of the course of cure are not relevant here. The significant thing is that the onset of Maria's illness created a marked change in the pattern of interpersonal activity within her kinship circle and that Maria was aware that not she alone but a group of people were locked in battle with the threatening forces.

Within about a week, Maria had a remission. For awhile she was not as gay as she had been, but she resumed her normal round of activities and no longer suffered from hallucinations. During the six or seven additional months we continued to reside in the village, Maria lived a normal life.

What was Maria's own version of events at the time of her seizure? Several days after the onset of her symptoms, my wife interviewed Maria, visiting her in the home of her own parents. After the night she first experienced hallucinations, she was afraid to remain in the household of Francisco, her father-in-law, for fear of ghosts. "I am afraid to go out of the house," Maria told my wife. "When I go out I feel as though someone were following me. I feel that the spirits are around me." Then virtually without questioning, she gave the following account.

"Saturday night at 11:00 o'clock, I felt that I had left the house of Francisco, that I was walking around strange streets and places, accompanied by spirits of dead women who had come for me. It is absolutely true that I was dead [unconscious] for two or three hours. I didn't feel a thing. My body was completely cold, but my spirit was walking around with the dead.

"They took me to a place where a man brought out a very big book. He looked in it and asked, 'Are you Juana?' and I told him, 'No.' He asked my mother's name and my father's name and other things about me, and then he said, 'No, you are not Juana. Your name is not here, but her name is. You must return. We don't want you here yet.' It wasn't me they wanted but my mother-in-law."

It should be recalled that Maria's sister and her mother-in-law are both called Juana. It is possible that the two persons were merged in Maria's imagery; she had reportedly told another informant that the Juana in her hallucinations was her own sister rather than her husband's mother.

"It was Rosario, the dead sister of my mother-in-law, who took me there, and she was the one who was with me all the time. When I got there, I saw all the dead people whom I had known. They were all there. But the Lord told me to return, that my name was not recorded. Rosario was angry. She had wanted her sister, Juana, called in to confront her dead parents and answer to the charge of stealing all the inheritance which the parents had left. Rosario argued that I should remain, saying 'This one is at least her daughter-in-law. Let her stay.' She was angry.

"Then some of the others [here she names a number of actual women who had recently died in childbirth] wouldn't let me leave. Whenever I tried to pass by in the road, they blocked my path. They said to me, 'You must stay here and help us give milk to the babies.' There were babies all over the ground, without any clothes on, rolling around and playing on the ground. One of the dead women said she was very tired from having nursed the babies and wanted me to stay and help them because there were so many [dead] babies there, but I don't have any milk now." This last statement of Maria's was contrary to fact. According to her own mother, Maria did have milk.

"Finally I didn't want to leave; I wanted to remain there with them, but the father of Juana [José's grandfather] came along the road and beat me with a whip and threw me on the ground and told me to leave." She then recounted how she journeyed home and how her spirit traveled through distant lands for a period of four days under the guidance of Rosario's spirit.

Though she spoke of her spirit as having wandered for four days, Maria actually went to stay in her father's house after the first night of her seizure. This was the first time she had appeared in her parents' home since the evening she had eloped from our house.

But shifting residence had no immediate effect on Maria's condition. According to information that we received from José's sister, for three days "Maria talked out loud, constantly addressing the spirits, protesting that she had no milk, exclaiming that they were trying to take her. When her husband tried to calm her, she would shake off his hand or hit him." According to Maria's mother, Maria was unable to sleep but walked up and down talking to the spirits and intermittently singing and dancing.

The songs she sang were snatches of esoteric, shamanistic incantations she had overheard her father chanting at times when he had come home drunk. Shamans are not supposed to sing their songs or to recite their verses in the presence of children. The words and the tunes are powerful, and capable of bringing disaster to those who sing them without warrant. When Maria's father heard her burst into these songs during the period of her breakdown, he scolded her severely, and ordered her to desist immediately. "This is why you have gone crazy," he told her, "from singing sacred songs that you have no business with."

By the end of a week, Maria was well enough to go out for a walk with her husband. Instead of returning to her father's home, the couple again went to live with José's parents. Maria greeted her father-in-law: "How would you like two laborers who are seeking work and lodging?" To this Francisco replied, "Where are the laborers?" "Why, José and I," said Maria, "I no longer wish to stay in my own father's house." She then offered Francisco a cup of soft drink as a gesture of amity. Francisco hesitated, pointing out that Maria's father might become vexed over the couple's unannounced departure from Manuel's household, especially "since I asked him to do us the favor of curing your illness." Francisco finally consented and accepted the drink after Maria protested that there was nothing wrong with her, that if she were ill she would be in bed. At eight or nine o'clock they all went to sleep.

That same night at one o'clock Maria rose from her bed in a rage and began beating José furiously. His cries aroused his sister's husband who rushed in to investigate, but Maria knocked him to the floor and reached for an axe handle. By this time Francisco appeared in the room. As Francisco reported it, he found Maria climbing over the prostrate brother-in-law and lunging for the latter's testicles. With the aid of his son and son-in-law, Francisco managed to seize Maria and tie her with ropes.

She pleaded for mercy. "I don't want you to kill my son [or son-in-law]," Francisco replied, "So I am going to have you sent away to prison." But her pleas prevailed. She promised never again to misbehave. Thereafter indeed her disturbing symptoms lifted and she resumed her normal activities, continuing to live with José. Of course, "normal" does not preclude occasional quarrels.

How did people in the community explain Maria's strange behavior? Some said the basic fault resided with Manuel, her father—that he had performed unethical acts in the past, and that he was now being punished through his daughter. Others said the fault was Maria's directly. Still others blamed José; others said the sickness was brought on by misdeeds on the part of José's parents. Others thought it to be a combination.

What are the general implications of this case? Let me first raise, in order to dispose of them, two issues which this case does little to resolve. The first issue is this: Do the dynamics of mental disorder remain constant from culture to culture, or do they vary? An easy but equivocal answer is that the psychodynamic *process* is essentially the same, but the *content* (the specific symptoms and manifestations) differs with the cultural milieu. This partly begs the question as to what is content and what is process. In this particular case I should suppose that content refers to the nature of Maria's visual and auditory hallucinations. Perhaps the processes revealed in her behavior fall into place as those characteristic of a "castrating female." Maria was both seductive and hostile towards men; she had met with failure in her effort to escape her culturally-prescribed feminine role, and had finally resorted to a temporary retreat from reality.

The second issue I want to dispose of briefly is this: Do the roots of psychopathology lie tangled in the skein of interpersonal relations, that is, in the social process; or do they reach deeper, originating in hereditary predispositions? Again, the case is necessarily ambiguous in this regard. The data can be so interpreted as to support either view. Maria's social history is certainly an etiological factor, but whether her life experience is the ultimate cause or only the proximate cause must remain an open question. It takes a carefully devised experimental design and not just a case to probe a problem of this kind effectively.

I come now to three general implications that are somewhat more positive. The first of these has to do with the range of role-choice available in a given society. Some authorities say that middle-class women in the United States are torn between competing roles, those of mother, glamor girl, careerist, and the like. There is the wear of indecision arising from excessive latitude of choice, leading to emotional conflict and in some cases to psychopathology. This viewpoint implies that a more unitary, more well defined, feminine role would provoke less anxiety. The case of Maria makes one wonder. The society in which she lived, with its clear definition of the female role, stands as a reminder that the pinch may only be shifted to another foot. There is essentially but one allowed feminine role, the wife-mother-housekeeper role, one that is socially subordinate to the male role. The system works reasonably well for most women in the society. There is no indication that women as a group are more unhappy than men in this Guatemalan village. But in the case of a person like Maria, who was unconventional for reasons of predisposition or socialization or both, the culture provided no role alternatives, no legitimate means of escape into non-domestic activity. Maria tried desperately to evade the demands of her milieu by marrying a succession of culturally marginal men who might have had the means and the motivation to leave the village to live in a less constricting urban environment. In the United States she might have become absorbed in a professional career. In her village she could only rebel, and eventually break with reality when the battle became unbearable. As a matter of fact, Maria did eventually escape from the village. Five years later when we revisited Guatemala, we learned that she and José had moved to Guatemala City and were raising a family.

The second of my concluding points relates to the question of secondary guilt in mental patients. If emotional illness connotes personal inadequacy in the judgment of society and hence also in the self-estimation of the patient, this should arouse secondary guilt, or blaming one's self for being emotionally disturbed. This in turn might aggravate the illness in spiral fashion. If secondary guilt can be a handicap to recovery, then the culture of the Guatemalan village tends to mitigate this particular handicap and thus encourage remission or recovery. Two cultural features permit escape from a sense of secondary guilt. One is the fact that hallucinations are not culturally defined as products of fantasy. Sights and sounds of ghosts are regarded by most normal people in Maria's village not as fears and fancies but as real occurrences. It was never doubted by others that dead women actually surrounded Maria during her illness. Maria thought so at the time, and she continued to think so after recovery. In Maria's village people do not share our quip: "I'm hallucinating again."

The difference between Maria and her kinsmen was that she could see and hear the spirits that were present, while they could not see or hear them. Spirits are believed capable of making themselves selectively visible and invisible. Maria was sick in the eyes of her neighbors not because she imagined visitations, but because she was host to visitations, just as we might consider a person sick because he is host to microbes we cannot see but know to be present on the basis of our cultural information.

The other cultural circumstance that minimizes secondary guilt is the merciful ambiguity of the blameful agent in bringing on Maria's sickness. Spirits are sent for a cause (bad behavior) but who committed the transgression? Was Manuel really the intended target? Some thought he was. If so, was it because he himself had done evil things or was it because of hidden enemies who wished him ill? Both these thoughts were expressed. Was it Francisco? Was it José? Was it Maria herself? Some certainly thought so. Was the malefactor Maria's mother-in-law, Juana? Maria certainly thought so, and some agreed with her. Each judge could cast blame where he would and find cultural justification for his judgment. It is locally believed that supernatural retribution is sometimes ineffective against people with "strong" characters, and that in such cases the punishment is deflected onto more suscepti-ble kinsmen, usually offspring. It is likely that in her own mind, Maria was only an innocent bystander who fell victim to ghostly vengeance directed at someone else in the household. Our culture, having dis-credited these non-rational escapes, makes it more difficult for the men-tal patient to avoid a sense of secondary guilt or conscious self-blame.

The last of my three general points reverts to the concept of self-regulation in the socio-cultural process. When a ribbon in a typewriter moves far enough in one direction it trips a hammer and the move-ment is reversed. A like process appears to have occurred in Maria's human environment. The more she tried to evade the feminine role, the more she was renounced by society. Progressively alienating her parents, her parents-in-law, and finally her husband—her last social prop—she and her society had reached a state of complete mutual re-jection. At this point, quantitative saturation brought a qualitative change; unable to proceed further in the same direction, Maria sudden-ly and dramatically altered her mode of behavior from argument and rebellion to psychological withdrawal. This culturally available act redefined the social situation. She was no longer an active threat to society and its norms; she was now regarded by those about her as the passive target of a more sinister threat, the forces of literal death. Any kinsman might be struck when ghosts are around. Any relative might in fact be to blame. To save themselves, for purely personal reasons if for no others, her relatives had to work for Maria and with Maria to repel the invading spirits. The process of social alienation was now reversed; the ribbon was winding the other way. Community of con-cern and anxiety is an important form of social solidarity. Groups of relatives who had been at odds with each other—her husband's family and her own family—now came together in common action. From an attitude of scorn and avoidance, her own father switched to one of sympathy and assistance. Once shunned by society, Maria was now the center of attention. She became the center of attention in a very literal sense. It is believed that the soul of anyone who is gravely sick, whether the disease is emotional or organic, is in peril of being seized by were-animals who wait for the weakened patient to be left unguarded. It is therefore necessary for relatives and neighbors to be in constant protec-tive attendance. Maria was under day-and-night vigilance during most of the time that she (and her kinsmen) were in deepest danger.

Maria recovered. I should like to think that the process of redefinition and reversal just described was instrumental in the remission of her symptoms. What differs in Maria's society from our own is not so much the actual process of mental disorder as the *cultural definition* of this process—belief in an external threat and in joint jeopardy. By an abrupt switch in her mode of deviance, Maria was able to trip the cultural lever that set restitutive processes in motion. Having no hospitals to hide her in, the community provided Maria with a key to reenter their own society.

This baby was learning to walk "because it was getting too heavy to carry."

Family group.

Guatemala Indians. *Photos by Richard Hirshberg.*

Boy playmates. Note shoes, rarely worn.

Terrain near Lake Atitlán.

O. F. RAUM

1938. "Some Aspects of Indigenous Education among the Chaga," *Journal of the Royal Anthropological Institute of Great Britain and Ireland*, vol. *68:* 209-221. Reprinted by courtesy of the author and of the Editor of the *Journal of the Royal Anthropological Institute*.

A keen observer and long-time student of native tradition, Professor Raum of University College, Fort Hare, in South Africa has spent most of a lifetime among the Chaga of Tanganyika Territory. A detailed account of the development of the Chaga individual and of the cultural ideals of the Chaga is available in Raum's notable book, *Chaga Childhood; a description of indigenous education in an East African Tribe,* published in 1940 by Oxford University Press, for the International Institute of African Languages and Cultures.

For descriptions of educational procedures among some other African tribes, see Stayt, 1931; Fortes, 1949; H. Thurnwald, 1935; Childs, 1949; M. M. Edel in Mead, 1937-a; and I. Goldman in Mead, 1937-a.

SOME ASPECTS OF INDIGENOUS EDUCATION AMONG THE CHAGA[1]

O. F. RAUM

PRELIMINARY METHODOLOGICAL REMARKS

Of all the sociological sciences, Education is the least advanced. The reasons for this are partly to be found in the past connexions of Education with Philosophy and partly in the educational situation itself. It is obviously difficult for an outsider to *observe* the educational process in a family fairly. This difficulty is increased among native peoples, as parental sensitiveness and the shyness of children are often fixed by tradition at a much higher pitch than in our society. It may, for instance, be assumed that the scarcity of observed cases of corporal punishment is partly due to this modifying factor.

Reliance on informants clearly suffers from the presence of many sources of error, such as the suggestibility of children, intentional bias in statements made by parents, and the unconscious colouring of reminiscences by natives who are neither parents nor children. Statistical methods, so useful in other sociological sciences, could therefore only be applied with great caution, and are in fact seldom or never used.

It is clear that the fundamental difficulty is the definition and classification of educational phenomena. From the educational point of view it is necessary to find an answer to the question of how a given people, such as the Chaga,[2] deal with a certain educational situation, e.g., how they treat a disobedient child. We would falsify our observations if we did not consider under the heading of disobedience the type of behaviour to which the Chaga themselves apply that word, but used European standards. Viewing it from this angle, the field-worker, by a careful combination of methods and by avoiding generalisations at an early stage of his study, will be able to collect adequate material on indigenous education.

Sociologically education can be defined as the relation between consecutive generations. This relationship, like all other social relations, possesses the characteristics of mutuality and reciprocity. It is usually assumed that in the educational process the child is subjected to a multiplicity of formative forces, e.g., family, play group and tribal organisation. If one tries to visualise the situation, one is easily led to imagine the child crushed by the action of many social forces. There are, however, three factors which restore the balance.

First, the sociological significance of the child is extraordinarily great and contrasts strongly with its biological dependence. The possession of a child raises the status of the parents among the Chaga. A young woman, who is called *mbora* from the time of her circumcision, receives the status of a *malyi* after the birth of her first child and that of *nka* after the arrival of her second. The status of her husband, too, is raised. His father gives a heifer to the young couple when the first child is born. On the other hand, barrenness in woman or man is considered a fault in character and leads to divorce. The death of a child is put down to the agency of sterile women or co-wives resorting to sorcery out of envy. Sociologically the Chaga child is therefore the founder of a stable marriage, just as marriage procures for the child the status of legitimacy.

Secondly, the psychological significance of the child for the parents must not be forgotten. Its trustfulness, simplicity, light-heartedness and fancifulness produce pleasurable emotional responses. Even the polygynous Chaga father cannot escape these influences. He fondles his baby, tickles it and addresses it respectfully by his father's name. The mother's lullabies have not only the purpose of quieting the child, but are an expression of her own experiences in adult society, as an examination of the texts reveals. Very significant in this respect are the names given to children. In many cases they embody a story, or hint at an event which is of importance to the parents.

Thirdly, the child is not a passive object of education. He is a very active agent in it. There is an irrepressible tendency in the child to become an adult, to rise to the status of being allowed to enjoy the privileges of a grown-up Chaga. The child attempts to force the pace of his "social promotion." Thus, at five or six years of age, a little boy will surprise his mother one day by telling her that he wants to be circumcised. The mother will hear nothing of it and threatens to beat him if he repeats the request. But the demand will be made with increasing insistence as the child grows up. In former times it was the clamour and restiveness of the adolescents which decided the older section of Chaga society to start the formal education of the initiation camp.

THE CHILD'S SOCIAL ENVIRONMENT

The child's position in the Chaga family is determined by the fact that Chaga marriage is as a rule patrilocal, and not infrequently polygynous. Since the households of the wives do not form a kraal but are scattered over the district, this means that the father is only an occasional visitor to the child's home. The early intimacies between father and child are superseded by a period when the father is held up as a bugbear to the toddler by the mother. Later he comes to be feared for his disciplinary interventions. The mother's mediation prevents this fear from becoming a permanent mental state. But when the father departs from the compound the children cannot but make merry, and the mother joins in laughingly, saying: "When the bull is gone, the lizards slip out to sun themselves!"

The child's attitude towards the mother is determined by the closeness and continuity of the contact. She knows the worries and troubles of her little flock. The sharing of trivial experiences in field and hut and her partial exclusion from affairs of court and community make a woman a member of the children's group. She stands out in it because of her wider knowledge, but the confidential relationship which she maintains with her children often makes it difficult for her to enforce discipline. She allies herself, therefore, to the father's authority and reports to him when the children have broken rules of conduct. As her mediation may, however, be favourable to a particular child the children are ready to do their mother a good turn; e.g., the boys, by taking a piece of roasted meat from the slaughtering place, circumvent for their mothers the taboo which prohibits them from cooking meat before the husband's return from the butchering party.

The Chaga family can thus be looked upon as having three layers of disciplinary authority. The bottom layer is formed by the children, for even among them the boys and the older girls rule the others. The top layer is represented by the father and the central one by the mother. She holds a crucial position, much more so than she can possibly do in a monogamous marriage, where the attempt is usually made for the parents to take up an identical attitude. The three layers find their expression in the rules of etiquette observed.

These rules can be sub-divided into terms of address and polite manners. Within the first two or three years a child learns all the names, proper, descriptive, and classificatory, of the members of the family group. The parents, notably the father, occasionally test the knowledge of the child as regards these names. The parents are differentiated from the children's group by the descriptive terms *awu* and *mai*, or the classificatory terms *baba* and *mama*, respectively. The latter terms are used by smaller children, who also, when they want to confide something to one parent, use the proper name of the other parent.

The teaching of polite manners starts later than that of terms of address, as I was able to establish in my observation of Chaga family life during a number of years. It takes place between three and six years of age. The formalised kinds of behaviour comprise such acts as handing over things to older people with two hands and getting up from seats on the arrival of important persons. Polite manners to some extent imply the employment of a new and elaborate set of terms of address, involving the use of the clan name and other ceremonial phrases. Confusion with the ordinary set is unavoidable and is looked upon as normal. The method of training used is not one of attempting to ensure that "right for the first time is right for all time," but rather of gradually restricting the originally vague boundaries of application to the appropriate persons.

Etiquette undoubtedly enhances the authority of the parents. Yet it is not a mere bolstering up of prestige, but a necessary factor in all family life, as it helps to create "social distance" under the levelling conditions of close contact. That this is so is shown by the fact that parents observe some sort of etiquette towards the children, as they do, in turn, among themselves. The parents are particularly polite to the eldest son, and there is a formalised way of dealing with the youngest child. Again, the children, besides taking up a "parental" attitude towards their younger brothers and sisters, address the eldest brother as *wawa* and habitually submit to his authority and give him precedence. This is not only of educational significance, but is an important element in the social organisation of the Chaga. The classificatory application of the term *wawa* to eldest sibling, father, and paternal uncles implies potential identity of sociological function: if the father dies, the paternal uncle or the eldest brother assumes his position as regards ritual leadership and control of hereditaments.

The terms of address and manners which the child should adopt in its relations with grandparents, paternal and maternal uncles and aunts are first taught so early that the child cannot have the slightest idea of what it is all about. When the infant is a little more advanced, it is the members of the child's narrower family circle who comment on or check any misbehaviour in the presence of these relatives. The male members of the parental generation are all addressed as *baba*, the female ones as *mama*.

The attitude of the children towards the kindred has three components. First, according to native theory, the behaviour of the children towards their parents is also extended to uncles and aunts, since they, on their part, exercise disciplinary authority like that of the parents over the children. To this corresponds the system of vocative terminology. Secondly, the general attitude towards the parental generation is modified in practice by the behaviour of the parents towards the individual members of the kindred group. The greater deference shown by the parents towards the senior mother's brother and father's brother, as well as the more confidential relationship between a man and his eldest sister, are reflected in the children's attitude and symbolised by indices of individuation, e.g., the father's brother is called *awu o kawi*, "second father." Thirdly, special attitudes are ingrained towards those persons who are of ritual or social importance to the child, e.g., the mother's brother who carries out the ear-piercing ceremony. Behaviour towards these relatives is less static than that examined so far. It looms large when the control of a relative becomes decisive to the child, e.g., at the state of initiation or marriage, and may weaken when the ties are not reinforced by social intercourse, e.g., if spatial separation makes such intercourse difficult.

The relations of the children with their grandparents, especially the paternal ones, are very close. Frequent visits are paid to them. In fact, the parents' possessive rights in their children are restricted in favour of the grandparents. The first child is claimed by the paternal grandfather. The claim rests on the assistance which he rendered the young couple in setting up a household. The second child is claimed by the maternal grandfather. However, he must compensate its parents by the payment of a goat. If the first child is a girl and the second one a boy, the father usually insists on having his heir left with him. But the mother's people's claim is only postponed, not cancelled thereby. It appears from this and other factors that the system of child transference to kindred is different from what has been called fosterage, where children are sent to friends of their father's for their education. In fosterage a definite educational purpose is present, while in the Chaga system, as in the similar one reported of the Baganda, the emphasis lies on fulfilling a kinship obligation. Accordingly the claim of the maternal grandfather is inherited by the maternal uncle.

Children are generally sent to their paternal grandparents at the time of weaning. The grandmother attempts to console the child for the separation by cooking food which it likes, and care is taken not to beat it lest it be reminded of home. This laxity in grandparental education is said to result in rudeness of manners and stupidity. However, the statement may very well be only an expression of jealousy, as the boy who grows up with grandparents may inherit from them.

The relationship of cross- and parallel-cousins among the Chaga is not based on common play, but on more or less ceremonial meetings. Thus when an animal has been butchered, the mother allows the children to invite their half-siblings and the children of the father's brothers to eat with them those parts of the animal which are reserved for children. The children of the other kindred are only invited if they happen to be neighbours. Similar children's parties take place at harvest time, and when a cow is newly in milk, for the beestings are consumed by children only. In adolescence the motive for meeting shifts gradually from the ceremonial to the utilitarian. It is especially paternal parallel-cousins who are bound together by the reciprocity of co-operation.

Within the cousin-group marriage is prohibited, with the exception that in certain circumstances marriage with the daughter of a mother's brother is allowed, but this is not a preferential marriage. It is only allowed after Ego's mother is dead. Cousin relationship, however, does not involve avoidance in play groups. Erotic elements enter very early into play imitative of married life. It sometimes happens that boys play such games with their sisters or cousins. When this is discovered the children are not scolded. They are asked in a sarcastic tone, "Who would ever marry his sister?" As this happens at a time when the erotic impulse is vague, the boys' choice of playmates for wives becomes by degrees canalised, i.e., limited to girls that stand outside the cousin relationship. Boys who ask their parents why one does not marry one's cousin are simply told, "It is bad!"

In the foregoing sketch two types of relationship can be distinguished. First, the relationship to a definite individual, such as a mother or a father's father. This is the only type experienced by the smaller child. The primary relationships to members of the family are gradually extended to members of the kindred, and form a set of derived individual relationships. Secondly, there is the relationship of the child to a social unit as such. The older the child grows the more intimately his interests are interwoven with the welfare of the family. Through evasions of kinship obligations, through the fear experienced by the family as a whole regarding neighbours suspected of practising witchcraft, through petty quarrels between the different households of a polygynous family, loyalties are formed which have unique emotional value. By analogous processes the child finds its place in the play group, the clan and later the tribe.

THE PARENTAL MEANS OF EDUCATION

The Chaga parent is fully aware of the process of education. There exists a great number of proverbs and tales concerning the effects of negligence, bias, harshness and other educational factors.

One of the most important means employed by parents is supervision of the smaller child. Infants are hidden in the "sleeping corner" of the hut when anybody suspected of possessing the evil eye comes to call on the parents. This area is separated from the central passage by a beam which serves both as seat for the mother when cooking and as boundary for the infant in the crawling stage. The storage place for food and milk is forbidden territory to children of both sexes. For boys, in addition, it is considered a disgrace to touch a calabash. The Chaga child is prevented from handling the many implements which might injure it; they are tucked away out of reach in the thatch of the hut. A small child is also watched lest it come too near the open fire on the hearth.

However, the essential problem of education is how direct means of behaviour control, such as supervision, punishment and reward, which have only a temporary effect, can be superseded by an indirect mechanism which will determine the actions of the child in the absence of the parents and for a longer period than an ordinary command. This can only be done by the creation of a set of inhibitive factors in the mental make-up of the child itself. Accordingly, the older children are warned by terrifying, but quite probable, stories concerning the fate of disobedient children who kindled a fire or stole honey from the storage place.

In this indirect control of the child's behaviour magic plays an important role. If the mother wants the child to stop crying she calls the *irumbu*-spectre. If the baby does not drink its soup, a brother is sent behind the Dracaena hedge to produce the growl of this ghost. A loitering child is warned that the low-sailing clouds will carry it off. The speedy return of a child messenger is secured by spitting on the palm of his hand saying, "If you are not back before the spittle is dried up, you will vanish like it!"

Taboos can be classed with this kind of magical behaviour control. The effect of these rules is to place the children into definite behaviour groups as they grow up, since the taboos differ according to age and sex. It is unnecessary to describe them in detail. It is of educational importance, however, to examine the way in which they are supposed to act. In general, the transgression is said either to have a detrimental effect on some person to whom the child is attached, usually the mother, or to react on the child itself by handicapping its future assumption of full adult status. Many food taboos are sanctioned by the threat that the mother will die, or that the transgressor will behave in a cowardly way during circumcision. Appeal is therefore made to the two most powerful sentiments, those centring round one's mother and one's own social aspirations. The educative function of these taboos consists thus in ensuring that the prescribed behaviour should appear to serve the interests of the children themselves.

A special class of sanctions, best called religious, threatens the child with death if it breaks certain rules. The mother tells the child in angry tones, "If you won't obey, I shall call the spirits to kill you!" When the excitement has subsided, the parents usually repudiate the curse in a solemn manner. Of special efficacy are grandparental curses. Hence children who live with their grandparents are warned not to enrage them. Their nearness to death magnifies, in the eyes of the Chaga, their potentiality for interference.

Among the Chaga several kinds of punishment can be distinguished according to their nature, such as deprival of food, incarceration, disgrace, corporal punishment, and torture. But it is also possible to define them with reference to the situation from which the conflict ending in punishment arises. There is first the class of punishments which is inhibitive, conditioning or habituating. They occur mainly during the first half of childhood and can be easily observed. The kind of punishment most suitable for this purpose is a quick unexpected slap, and the Chaga mother makes frequent use of it, e.g., when the child comes too near the fire, eats earth or dung, or refuses food when it is being weaned. When punishing, mothers act under an affective strain. Then the physiological exhaustion of the emotion of anger being complete, the opposite reaction is released. The mother who slapped her baby a minute ago proceeds to fondle and even lick it.

The other type of punishment is much more difficult to observe. It arises out of a conflict between the paternal and filial generations, and increases in frequency the older the boys grow. During the first six years there is little disciplinary differentiation between sons and daughters. Between eight and ten the girls enter into effective co-operation with their mother and gradually come to share all her burdens and rights, except marital ones. The occasions on which mother and daughters may fall out with each other are therefore limited to cases where the degree of diligence or thoroughness considered necessary for a particular job is in dispute. When the boys start looking after the cattle, however, the growing cleavage between mother and sons shows its effect in an increased disciplinary tension. It is at this time that boys become attached to a play group, and its influence makes the separation irrevocable. Moreover, the father deems it fit to inculcate in his sons a feeling of contempt for all womenfolk. But boys do not quarrel only with their mothers. Soon they will be passing out of their father's tutelage also, and at puberty a struggle ensues as to the time at which full adult status is to be granted to the striplings.

In this struggle deprival of liberty is a recognised form of punishment. Disobedient children may be shut up in an empty hut and left there without food for some time. Loiterers may be tied to the middle post of the hut and sometimes have to spend the whole night in this uncomfortable position. Deprival of food is common, probably because it lends itself to being administered in varying degrees. A lazy child does not get its share when an animal is slaughtered. The nurse who eats the baby's food may not get anything to eat for one or two days.

Degradation, the public deprival of one's honour, is not unknown as an educational method. A negligent herd-boy gets the excrements of a slaughtered animal smeared on his face in the presence of all the male members of the kinship group, who forgather on such an occasion. A persistent loiterer is given a goat's horn to drink out of during a carousal, a sign of utter disgrace. Quite distinct from degradation is humiliation, which is employed when the child has not given cause for complaint. For instance, a child that is being brought up in the home of his grandparents is made to remove their faeces from inside the hut without showing any signs of disgust. It is in this way that one earns the grandparents' blessing. Again when an elderly person emits wind, it is the child who is blamed for it. Children must not deny any such charge, because they are told that by their acquiescence they prevent the disgrace of their fathers.

Corporal punishment is also used as a means for settling disputes between father and son. A boy who loses a cow on the pasture gets fifteen strokes with a stick, this being the traditional measure. In the exercise of their disciplinary rights, parents are subject to the control of the community in which they live. Cruelty is condemned and indulgence ridiculed. Individual cases are dealt with on their own merits. In spite of this check, the existence of stories of torture and the use made of them for intimidating a child into obedience suggest that they might in certain circumstances serve as justification for the summary punishment of young offenders.

When an interval is placed between the punishable act and the corrective reaction, opportunity is given for the elaboration of the punitive process. The necessity is felt, especially with adolescent children, for a confession to justify the punishment. When the child is young the reconciliation ritual may be a quite informal act, such as seizing the father's beard. But if the boy already possesses a semi-independent household of his own, the procedure is quite formal and takes place in the presence of the kindred, some of whom may act as mediators. Usually the ceremony consists in expressions of repentance, the handing over of a fine by the son to his father, and a symbolisation of restored confidence on the father's part. It is important to notice that both the affective reconciliation noted above, and the ceremonial one, are initiated by the parent concerned. The explanation of this is the fact that not only the punishable act but also the punishment itself violates the principle of mutual assistance upon which family life is based. It is restored only if the parents resume the relations of affectionate attachment which amplify the biological bond existing between parents and children. These attempts at reconciliation clearly distinguish educational from legal punishment.

Rewards are, of course, extensively used by parents in their attempt to make the children conform to their standards. The technique of rewards implies the lavish use of promises, controlling child behaviour by anticipation. Thus when the mother goes to market, the children are promised a small present, such as a locust, a banana or a few beads, if they do not cry. The father who interests himself in his sons at a later stage deviates sometimes from the customary law of inheritance by assigning special gifts to a son who is obedient and exhibits good manners, thrift and diligence, and he ensures the carrying out of his will by a curse on anyone who should deprive his favourite of his claims.

A most important educational factor is training in work. It is impossible to distinguish play and work genetically. A great amount of childish energy is directed to the acquisition of techniques, and this is done spontaneously and in a style which differs little, if at all, from play activities. A condition of this state of affairs is the simplicity of the tools employed and the scarcity of toys. It is sometimes difficult to decide whether at a particular moment a child is using an implement as a tool or as a toy.

Actual training in work takes place at a much later date and consists chiefly in an impressive lesson in the necessity of diligence and thoroughness in work. From the above generalisation professional training in one of the non-hereditary crafts must be excluded. This takes place after initiation and is surrounded by elaborate ceremonies to ensure the secrecy of the methods taught and to protect the teacher from future competition by the pupil.

As regards the content of training in work, the education of the girls is concluded much earlier than that of the boys. Both sexes learn first together all the domestic tasks of a Chaga household. At about eight years of age the division of labour is gradually imposed on this common base. For the girl this means continuation lessons in domestic tasks, with greater refinement and independence. For the boy this is the opening of a new chapter in life. As an informal process of social education he is taken to public meetings, where he gleans information about the political authorities, the distribution of wealth and influence, and legal procedure. He is also introduced to tasks reserved for men only, such as hunting and forest work.

We must next consider some of the methods employed in training for work. Extensive use is made of models. Oral explanation is rarely given, except to a very inquisitive child. The degree of skill attained in the basic tasks is ascertained, and proficiency made a pre-condition of advance in status. The training terminates in the handing over of some of the parental stock and land to the care and for the use of the adolescent child. The first-fruits of his labours are expected to be given to the parents, and later on annual gifts are the rule. Thus the adolescents grow into the adult system of kinship obligations.

Ceremonies hold a special position in the educational process. The Chaga *rites de passage* divide childhood into different stages. The infant has to undergo the rite of the "First Tooth" and of receiving a name. From the time of the latter rite to the appearance of the second set of teeth the child is called a *mwana*, but thenceforward a *ndentewura*. About three years later the ear-piercing ceremony takes place and simultaneously the two lower incisors are knocked out, the child acquiring the status of a *ndaka*. At adolescence the boys form groups that loiter about and make a nuisance of themselves. In some districts a special *kisusa* rite is held to discipline the most forward of these stripling individuals. If the *"kisusa* spirit," as the rebelliousness of youth is called, cannot be curbed, the demand for tribal initiation and the formation of a new age-class is raised before the chief.

The educational function of these rites has often been described. The special diet, the quaintness of the ceremonies and the tiring repetition of the ethical teaching all help to make the impression indelible. Yet if one has seen native children during the longer rites, haggard, drowsy, often insensible to what is going on around them, one doubts whether the educational importance of ritual lies entirely in its immediate effects. Much more important are, indeed, two other factors neglected hitherto. First, the anticipation of the rite influences childish behaviour long beforehand. Negatively this means that the parents make admission to the rite conditional on conformity to their demands, and positively that the child definitely strives to make himself worthy of acceptance. Secondly, the rites introduce the child into wider social circles. This rise in status, implying ever-increasing responsibilities, is the topic most discussed among the children. Their wish for social advancement is so strong that the children of third-generation Christian families are some-times "infected" by it and run away from their parents to take part in the rites, showing how effectively social pressure is still diffused in the society of the children.

THE SELF-EDUCATION OF THE CHILDREN

It is important that we should try to discover in what manner the society of the children reacts to the educational efforts of the parents. To some of them it makes a positive adjustment, others it dislikes be-cause of the discrimination in status which they imply. It makes, in fact, an attempt to create in its play activities its own social life, with its own laws and cultural features.

It is possible to classify Chaga play activities into three groups. First, there is the playful exercise of the sensory and motor apparatus, re-sulting in the physical adaptation of the individual organism. Secondly, there is imitative play, consisting in an adaptation of adult life to the social needs and understanding of the children. Thirdly, there are com-petitive games, which test not only physical fitness but also intellectual and social qualities. These three groups follow one another in a rough time sequence, the first corresponding to infancy, the second to child-hood, and the third to adolescence. Corresponding with this develop-ment there proceeds an increasing socialisation of the children's group, and its gradual separation from adult society.

While the play of physical adaptation is performed by infants in iso-lation, the mimicry type of play draws the child into a community of players who enact the daily round, the activities of the annual cycle, and scenes from individual life-histories and the different social classes. In calling these play activities imitative, we must be careful to describe what we mean by this term. Imitation among people having the same status in society must clearly be distinguished from imitation which cuts across boundaries of status, such as is seen in the native's craze for European clothes and the child's copying of the adult. In the latter case the mental outlook of the imitator differs from that of the imitated, and the copy performs a different function from that of the original. For instance, in considering the mimicry of married life the fact must not be forgotten that most children know of the marriage ceremony only by hearsay, as they are forbidden to attend weddings. Much of the subject-matter of imitation is in fact relayed through the medium of speech only. This kind of imitation may therefore be described as "blind," i.e., the children's performance is a free reconstruction of more or less imagined happenings.

It must also be noted that such imitative play is not a complete taking over of the example, but selective. Certain traits important or striking to the child are chosen from the adult pattern. This becomes apparent in the "imitation" of so-called "bride-lifting." This practice has long fallen into desuetude. The reasons which caused this exceptional custom to be resorted to were in most cases economic. With children out on the pasture the economic justification for "marriage by capture" obviously does not weigh. But it would also be an insufficient explanation to call their imitation of this custom a survival, a mere form without meaning. As a matter of fact, the "lifting" is to them a vital part of all play weddings, a symbol of marriage as they understand and practice it.

Having guarded against certain ambiguities arising from the use of the term "imitation," it must be admitted that the accuracy of the copying process increases as the child grows up and approaches adult status. Younger children insist on the meticulous repetition of isolated bits of behaviour, which are taken as representative of the corresponding adult activities. But this insistence becomes less and less pronounced with increasing conceptual specialisation in the minds of the children, which goes hand in hand with greater variation and realism in mimicry. This is the result of a mutually corrective process in which that child is accorded the approval of his associates who, by the standards of the play group, deviates least from the adult pattern.

The imitative play activities which copy family and tribal life also afford an opportunity for the exchange of experience regarding persons and institutions with which some children have little chance to become directly acquainted. The framework of social organisation in its practical working is learned through the boys' participation in organising the play group. This educates them to accept voluntarily a social system into which they would otherwise have to be forced when entering adult society. Besides, the element of secrecy which attaches to the copying of the more intimate scenes from the life of the parents and of the political authorities draws the boys into a close social unit with a sense of common interests and needs.

The play group on the pasture must be distinguished on the one hand from the very much smaller group of infants who meet in the yards and groves near the huts, and on the other hand from the age-class, an institution with a ritual and a significance which go beyond childish interests. The boys' group is altogether independent; it is not established by a ceremony controlled by adults, but is a spontaneous growth. While in the family and the tribal age-class a strict authoritarian order prevails, the boys' group is an entirely democratic affair. Every boy enters it with equal chances of rising to a leading position. The qualities which decide his promotion are not the rank and wealth of his parents, but intelligence, physical prowess, and social adaptability. It is true that the chief's son is supposed to be treated with deference, and he has strict injunctions to be affable to his playmates; but his privileges count for little if he is a stupid or socially disagreeable fellow.

The methods by which the selection of the leaders in the boys' group is carried out begin with practical jokes and tests of endurance for the younger members. The tests later assume the form of competitive games, such as wrestling, fist-fights, bird-shooting and battles with a hard green fruit the size of an orange, exercises which resemble those which were part of the former military training of the Chaga. Besides competitive games, the distribution of food (originally supplied by the mother) is a means of obtaining at least temporary allegiance from others. Finally, the leadership in certain games, etc., is decided by mere chance, e.g., by drawing straws or lots.

The Chief of the Pasture, if he has risen to his post through pluck and perseverance, often holds it for a considerable time. He appoints his henchmen and orders the other boys about on serious business. For instance, when during a heavy shower the boys have retired to the hut which they have built for themselves, he may command a boy to go out and look for the cattle, which often bolt into the bush on such an occasion. He also has a decisive voice in the choice and arrangement of the games and play activities. However, it is inherent in the democratic nature of the group that he may be superseded. His ascendancy may be resented by a number of boys whom he has defeated, and jealousy may develop into open conflict, serious fights, and his final deposition.

In assessing the position and function of the boys' group within the general scheme of Chaga society, we realised that the traditional system of play activities offers the children opportunities for obtaining more or less correct notions about married life and the social organisation of the tribe. With the development of their own capabilities, this process assumes a more positive aspect and may well be described as an attempt by the children to create a society for themselves, keeping closely to the original from which they are still excluded. In a sense it is true to say that the children's society has its own culture, which on the one hand can be described as a system of instruments with which the children satisfy their needs, and on the other hand consists in the re-creation of the values possessed by the paternal generation. But the expressions "re-creation of values" and "children's society" must not mislead us. In its fundamental nature the society of the children has not developed far from its adult prototype. The reasons for this are obvious. The time and capacities at the children's disposal in their striving towards independence are too limited to allow of the creation of something absolutely original, if such a thing were possible. And yet, within the cultural tradition, the function of play as an autonomous means of self-education seems to be fairly well established, for the children's society achieves a set of distinctive cultural features which are absent in adult culture.

With regard to language it is a well-known fact that children have what has been called "age-dialects." But over and above these natural developmental stages, the children evolve special secret languages, which resemble our "Double Dutch," by transposing syllables, inserting infixes and saying words backwards.

In the economic substratum of culture, the boys' group attempts to be independent by stealing food either at home or from strangers, and by bird-shooting and buck-hunting expeditions. Moreover, as they approach adolescence, boys and girls are given their own gardens and a few chickens and goats as a reward for having helped their parents. As regards material objects, the boys use bows and arrows, which are not employed by the Chaga warriors, and the children's tops, small toboggans used on grassy slopes, and other toys have no equivalents in the adult culture.

Concerning magic, taboos which are binding on grown-up men are not observed by the boys on the pasture. Chaga men are not allowed to eat fowls, but the boys relish them. Again the strong, unchecked desires of play-life lead the children to invent their own magic. Girls use wish-magic to make their breasts grow, and I know of a boy who, to ensure the capture of his hiding playfellows, cut himself in the finger. Also with regard to law and order the children's society has its own distinctive features, handed down by tradition in the play groups. Thus girls have an ordeal for detecting nurses who eat the food of their charges, while boys more frequently use more forceful methods, such as bombardment with missiles, to discipline a social misfit.

From the educational point of view it is very important to realize that the fundamental sentiments of loyalty to social groups and the authorities, upon which life in all its various kinds of organisation depends, are not necessarily formed by teaching and the giving of instructions. They emerge naturally from the sentiments attaching to the "imitative" institutions of childhood which are created through play activities.

NOTES

1. The author wishes to express his indebtedness to Professor Malinowski, in whose seminar this paper was discussed.

2. The Chaga live on the slopes of Mt. Kilimanjaro, in northern Tanganyika; aspects of their culture have been described by B. Gutmann in *Das Recht der Dschagga* (München, C. H. Beck'sche Verl., 1926) and *Die Stammeslehren der Dschagga* (München, C. H. Beck, 1932-5), and by C. Dundas in *Kilimanjaro and its People* (London, 1924).

EDWARD SAPIR

1938. "Why Cultural Anthropology Needs the Psychiatrist," *Psychiatry: Journal of the Biology and Pathology of Interpersonal Relations*, vol. *1*: 7-12. Reprinted by courtesy of Philip Sapir and by special permission of the William Alanson White Psychiatric Foundation, Inc., and Patrick Mullahy from *A Study of Interpersonal Relations*, edited by Patrick Mullahy and published by Thomas Nelson and Sons, New York. Copyright, 1949, by Hermitage Press. Originally published in *Psychiatry*, 1938, *1*:7-12.

Comment on the influence of Edward Sapir in bringing together psychiatrists and anthropologists is superfluous; the student is referred to Kluckhohn's article, "The Influence of Psychiatry on Anthropology in America during the last 100 Years."

Most of Sapir's published work has been assembled in one volume by David Mandelbaum (*Selected Writings of Edward Sapir*. Berkeley, 1949) and many of his essays are basic in the present field of interest. To compile a source book on the cultural aspects of individual character, however, without including any of Sapir's work would be inexcusable. The paper that follows pointed the way that many anthropologists have since attempted to follow, but its thesis still is pertinent.

WHY CULTURAL ANTHROPOLOGY NEEDS THE PSYCHIATRIST

Edward Sapir

Until not so many years ago cultural anthropology and psychiatry seemed miles apart. Cultural anthropology was conceived of as a social science which concerned itself little, if at all, with the individual. Its province was rather to emphasize those aspects of behavior which belonged to society as such, more particularly societies of the dim past or exotic societies whose way of life seemed so different from that of our own people that one could hope to construct a generalized picture of the life of society at large, particularly in its more archaic stages of development. There was little need in the anthropology of a Tylor or Frazer to ask questions which demanded a more intimate knowledge of the individual than could be assumed on the basis of common experience. The important distinctions were felt to be distinctions of race, of geographical setting, of chronology, of cultural province. The whole temper of cultural anthropology was impersonal to a degree. In this earlier period of the development of the science it seemed almost indelicate, not to say indecent, to obtrude observations that smacked of the personal or anecdotal. The assumption was that in some way not in the least clearly defined as to observational method it was possible for the anthropologist to arrive at conclusive statements which would hold for a given society as such. One was rarely in a position to say whether such an inclusive statement was a tacit quotation from a primitive "John Doe" or a carefully tested generalization abstracted from hundreds of personal observations or hundreds of statements excerpted from conversations with many John Does.

Perhaps it is just as well that no strict methodology of field inquiry was perfected and that embarrassing questions as to the factual nature of the evidence which led to anthropological generalizations were courteously withheld by a sort of gentlemen's agreement. I remember being rather shocked than pleased when in my student days I came across such statements in J. O. Dorsey's "Omaha Sociology" as "Two Crows denies this." This looked a little as though the writer had not squarely met the challenge of assaying his source material and giving us the kind of data that we, as respectable anthropologists, could live on. It was as though he "passed the buck" to the reader, expecting him by some miracle of cultural insight to segregate truth from error. We see now that Dorsey was ahead of his age. Living as he did in close touch with the Omaha Indians, he knew that he was dealing, not with a society nor with a specimen of primitive man nor with a cross-section of the history of primitive culture, but with a finite, though indefinite number of human beings, who gave themselves the privilege of differing from each other not only in matters generally considered as "one's own business" but even on questions which clearly transcended the private individual's concern and were, by the anthropologist's definition, implied in the conception of a definitely delimited society with a definitely discoverable culture. Apparently Two Crows, a perfectly good and authoritative Indian, could presume to rule out of court the very existence of a custom or attitude or belief vouched for by some other Indian, equally good and authoritative. Unless one wishes to dismiss the implicit problem raised by contradictory statements by assuming that Dorsey, the anthropologist, misunderstood one, or both, of his informants, one would have to pause for a while and ponder the meaning of the statement that "Two Crows denies this."

This is not the place to introduce anything like a complete analysis of the meaning of such contradictory statements, real or supposed. The only thing that we need to be clear about is whether a completely impersonal anthropological description and analysis of custom in terms which tacitly assume the unimportance of individual needs and preferences is, in the long run, truly possible for a social discipline. There has been so much talk of ideal objectivity in social science and such eager willingness to take the ideals of physical and chemical workmanship as translatable into the procedures of social research that we really ought not to blink this problem. Suppose we take a test case. John Doe and an Indian named Two Feathers agree that two and two make four. Someone reports that "Two Crows denies this." Inasmuch as we know that the testimony of the first two informants is the testimony of all human beings who are normally considered as entitled to a hearing, we do not attach much importance to Two Crows' denial. We do not even say that he is mistaken. We suspect that he is crazy. In the case of more abstruse problems in the world of natural science, we narrow the field of authority to those individuals who are known, or believed, to be in full command of techniques that enable them to interpret the impersonal testimony of the physical universe. Everyone knows that the history of science is full of corrective statements on errors of judgment but no value is attached to such errors beyond the necessity of ruling them out of the record. Though the mistaken scientist's hurt feelings may be of great interest to a psychologist or psychiatrist, they are nothing for the votaries of pure science to worry about.

Are correspondingly ruthless judgments possible in the field of social science? Hardly. Let us take a desperately extreme case. All the members of a given community agree in arranging the letters of the alphabet in a certain historically determined order, an order so fixed and so thoroughly ingrained in the minds of all normal children who go to school that the attempt to tamper with this order has, to the man in the street, the same ridiculous, one might almost say unholy, impossibility as an attempt to have the sun rise half an hour earlier or later than celestial mechanics decree to be proper. There is one member of this hypothetical society who takes the liberty of interchanging A and Z. If he keeps his strange departure from custom to himself, no one need ever know how queer he really is. If he contradicts his children's teacher and tries to tell them that they should put Z first and A last, he is almost certain to run foul of his fellow beings. His own children may desert him in spite of their natural tendency to recognize parental authority. Certainly we should agree that this very peculiar kind of a Two Crows is crazy, and we may even agree as psychiatrists that so far as an understanding of his aberrant phantasies and behavior is concerned, it really makes little difference whether what he is impelled to deny is that two and two are four or the order of the letters of the alphabet as a conventionally, or naturally, fixed order.

At this point we have misgivings. Is the parallel as accurate as it seems to be? There is an important difference, which we have perhaps overlooked in our joint condemnation. This difference may be expressed in terms of possibility. No matter how many Two Crows deny that two and two make four, the actual history of mathematics, however retarded by such perversity, cannot be seriously modified by it. But if we get enough Two Crows to agree on the interchange of A and Z, we have what we call a new tradition, or a new dogma, or a new theory, or a new procedure, in the handling of that particular pattern of culture which is known as the alphabet. What starts as a thoroughly irresponsible and perhaps psychotic aberration seems to have the power, by some kind of "social infection," to lose its purely personal quality and to take on something of that very impersonality of custom which, in the first instance, it seemed to contradict so flatly. The reason for this is very simple. Whatever the majority of the members of a given society may say, there is no inherent human impossibility in an alphabet which starts with a symbol for the sound or sounds represented by the letter Z and ends up with a symbol for the vocalic sound or sounds represented by the letter A. The consensus of history, anthropology, and common sense leads us to maintain that the actually accepted order of letters is "necessary" only in a very conditional sense and that this necessity can, under appropriate conditions of human interrelationship, yield to a conflict of possibilities, which may ultimately iron out into an entirely different "necessity."

The truth of the matter is that if we think long enough about Two Crows and his persistent denials, we shall have to admit that in some sense Two Crows is never wrong. It may not be a very useful sense for social science but in a strict methodology of science in general it dare not be completely ignored. The fact that this rebel, Two Crows, can in turn bend others to his own view of fact or theory or to his own preference in action shows that his divergence from custom had, from the very beginning, the essential possibility of culturalized behavior. It seems, therefore, that we must regretfully admit that the rebel who tampers with the truths of mathematics or physics or chemistry is not really the same kind of rebel as the one who plays nine-pins with custom, whether in theory or practice. The latter is likely to make more of a nuisance of himself than the former. No doubt he runs the risk of being condemned with far greater heat by his fellow men but he just cannot be proved to contradict some mysterious essence of things. He can only be said, at best, to disagree completely with everybody else in a matter in which opinion or preference, in however humble and useless a degree, is after all possible.

We have said nothing so far that is not utterly commonplace. What is strange is that the ultimate importance of these commonplaces seems not to be thoroughly grasped by social scientists at the present time. If the ultimate criterion of value interpretation, and even "existence," in the world of socialized behavior is nothing more than consensus of opinion, it is difficult to see how cultural anthropology can escape the ultimate necessity of testing out its analysis of patterns called "social" or "cultural" in terms of individual realities. If people tend to become illiterate, owing to a troubled political atmosphere, the "reality" of the alphabet weakens. It may still be true that the order of the letters is, in the minds of those relatively few people who know anything about the alphabet, precisely what it always was, but in a cultural atmosphere of unrest and growing illiteracy a Two Crows who interchanges A and Z is certainly not as crazy as he would have been at a more fortunate time in the past. We are quick to see the importance of the individual in those more flexible fields of cultural patterning that are referred to as ideals or tastes or personal preferences. A truly rigorous analysis of any arbitrarily selected phase of individualized "social behavior" or "culture" would show two things: First, that no matter how flexible, how individually variable, it may in the first instance be thought to be, it is as a matter of fact the complex resultant of an incredibly elaborate cultural history, in which many diverse strands intercross at that point in place and time at which the individual judgment of preference is expressed [this terminology is *cultural*]; second, that, conversely, no matter how rigorously necessary in practice the analyzed pattern may seem to be, it is always possible in principle, if not in experiential fact, for the lone individual to effect a transformation of form or meaning which is capable of communication to other individuals [this terminology is *psychiatric* or *personalistic*]. What this means is that problems of social science differ from problems of individual behavior in degree of specificity, not in kind. Every statement about behavior which throws the emphasis, explicitly or implicitly, on the actual, integral, experiences of defined personalities or types of personalities is a datum of psychology or psychiatry rather than of social science. Every statement about behavior which aims, not to be accurate about the behavior of an actual individual or individuals or about the expected behavior of a physically and psychologically defined type of individuals, but which abstracts from such behavior in order to bring out in clear relief certain expectancies with regard to those aspects of individual behavior which various people share, as an interpersonal or "social" pattern, is a datum, however crudely expressed, of social science.

If Dorsey tells us that "Two Crows denies this," surely there is a reason for his statement. We need not say that Two Crows is badly informed or that he is fooling the anthropologist. Is it not more reasonable to say that the totality of socialized habits, in short the "culture," that he was familiar with was not in all respects the same entity as the corresponding totality presented to the observation or introspection of some other Indian, or perhaps of all other Indians? If the question asked by the anthropologist involved a mere question of personal affirmation, we need have no difficulty in understanding his denial. But even if it involved the question of "objective fact," we need not be too greatly shocked by the denial. Let us suppose that the anthropologist asked the simple question, "Are there seven clans or eight clans in moiety A of your tribe?", or words to that effect. All other Indians that he has asked about this sheer question of "fact" have said eight, we will assume. Two Crows claims there are only seven. How can this be? If we look more closely to the facts, we should undoubtedly find that the contradiction is not as puzzling as it seems. It may turn out that one of the clans had been extinct for a long time, most of the informants, however, remembering some old man, now deceased, who had been said to be the last survivor of it. They might feel that while the clan no longer exists in a practical sense, it has a theoretical place in the ordered description of the tribe's social organization. Perhaps there is some ceremonial function or placement, properly belonging to the extinct clan, which is remembered as such and which makes it a little difficult to completely overlook its claims to "existence." Various things, on the other hand, may be true of Two Crows. He may have belonged to a clan which had good reason to detest the extinct clan, perhaps because it had humiliated a relative of his in the dim past. It is certainly conceivable that the factual nonexistence of the clan coupled with his personal reason for thinking as little about it as possible might give him the perfectly honest conviction that one need speak of only seven clans in the tribe. There is no reason why the normal anthropological investigator should, in an inquiry of this kind, look much beneath the surface of a simple answer to a simple question. It almost looks as though either seven clans or eight clans might be the "correct" answer to an apparently unambiguous question. The problem is very simple here. By thinking a little about Two Crows himself, we are enabled to show that he was not wrong, though he seemed to disagree with all his fellow Indians. He had a special kind of rightness, which was partly factual, partly personal.

Have we not the right to go on from simple instances of this sort and advance to the position that any statement, no matter how general, which can be made about culture needs the supporting testimony of a tangible person or persons, to whom such a statement is of real value in his system of interrelationships with other human beings? If this is so, we shall, at last analysis, have to admit that any individual of a group has cultural definitions which do not apply to all the members of his group, which even, in specific instances, apply to him alone. Instead, therefore, of arguing from a supposed objectivity of culture to the problem of individual variation, we shall, for certain kinds of analysis, have to proceed in the opposite direction. We shall have to operate as though we knew nothing about culture but were interested in analyzing as well as we could what a given number of human beings accustomed to live with each other actually think and do in their day to day relationships. We shall then find that we are driven, willy-nilly, to the recognition of certain permanencies, in a relative sense, in these interrelationships, permanencies which can reasonably be counted on to perdure but which must also be recognized to be eternally subject to serious modification of form and meaning with the lapse of time and with those changes of personnel which are unavoidable in the history of any group of human beings.

This mode of thinking is, of course, essentially psychiatric. Psychiatrists may, or may not, believe in cultural patterns, in group minds, in historic tendencies, or even missions; they cannot avoid believing in particular people. Personalities may be dubbed fictions by sociologists, anthropologists, and even by certain psychologists, but they must be accepted as bread and butter realities by the psychiatrist. Nothing, in short, can be more real to a psychiatrist than a personality organization, its modification from infancy to death, its essential persistence in terms of consciousness and ego reference. From this point of view culture cannot be accepted as anything more than a convenient assemblage, or at best total theory, of real or possible modes of behavior

abstracted from the experienced realities of communication, whether
in the form of overt behavior or in the form of fantasy. Even the alphabet from this standpoint becomes a datum of personality research!
As a matter of fact, the alphabet does mean different things to different people. It is loved by some, hated by others, an object of indifference to most. It is a purely instrumental thing to a few; it has varying
kinds of overtones of meaning for most, ranging all the way from the
weakly sentimental to the passionately poetic. No one in his senses
would wish the alphabet studied from this highly personalistic point
of view. In plain English, it would not be worth the trouble. The total
meaning of the alphabet for X is so very nearly the same as that for
any other individual, Y, that one does much better to analyze it and
explain its relation to other cultural patterns in terms of an impersonal,
or cultural, or anthropological, mode of description. The fact, however,
that X has had more difficulty in learning the alphabet than Y, or that
in old age X may forget the alphabet or some part of it more readily
than Y, shows clearly enough that there is a psychiatric side to even
the coldest and most indifferent of cultural patterns. Even such cold
and indifferent cultural patterns have locked in them psychiatric meanings which are ordinarily of no moment to the student of society but
which may under peculiar circumstances come to the foreground of
attention. When this happens, anthropological data need to be translated into psychiatric terms.

What we have tried to advance is little more than a plea for the assistance of the psychiatrist in the study of certain problems which
come up in an analysis of socialized behavior. In spite of all that has
been claimed to the contrary, we cannot thoroughly understand the
dynamics of culture, of society, of history, without sooner or later
taking account of the actual interrelationships of human beings. We
can postpone this psychiatric analysis indefinitely but we cannot theoretically eliminate it. With the modern growth of interest in the study
of personality and with the growing conviction of the enormous flexibility of personality adjustment to one's fellow men, it is difficult to
see how one's intellectual curiosity about the problems of human
intercourse can be forever satisfied by schematic statements about society and its stock of cultural patterns. The very variations and uncertainties which the earlier anthropologists ignored seem to be the
very aspects of human behavior that future students of society will
have to look to with a special concern, for it is only through an analysis
of variation that the reality and meaning of a norm can be established
at all, and it is only through a minute and sympathetic study of individual behavior in the state in which normal human beings find themselves, namely in a state of society, that it will ultimately be possible
to say things about society itself and culture that are more than fairly

convenient abstractions. Surely, if the social scientist is interested in effective consistencies, in tendencies, and in values, he must not dodge the task of studying the effects produced by individuals of varying temperaments and backgrounds on each other. Anthropology, sociology, indeed social science in general, is notoriously weak in the discovery of effective consistencies. This weakness, it seems, is not unrelated to a fatal fallacy with regard to the objective reality of social and cultural patterns defined impersonally.

Causation implies continuity, as does personality itself. The social scientist's world of reality is generally expressed in discontinuous terms. An effective philosophy of causation in the realm of social phenomena seems impossible so long as these phenomena are judged to have a valid existence and sequence in their own right. It is only when they are translated into the underlying facts of behavior from which they have never been divorced in reality that one can hope to advance to an understanding of causes. The test can be made easily enough. We have no difficulty in understanding how a given human being's experiences tend to produce certain results in the further conduct of his life. Our knowledge is far too fragmentary to allow us to understand fully, but there is never a serious difficulty in principle in imputing to the stream of his experiences that causative quality which we take for granted in the physical universe. To the extent that we can similarly speak of causative sequences in social phenomena, what we are really doing is to pyramid, as skilfully and as rapidly as possible, the sorts of cause and effect relations that we are familiar with in individual experience, imputing these to a social reality which has been constructed out of our need for a maximally economical expression of typically human events. It will be the future task of the psychiatrist to read cause and effect in human history. He cannot do it now because his theory of personality is too weak and because he tends to accept with too little criticism the impersonal mode of social and cultural analysis which anthropology has made fashionable. If, therefore, we answer our initial question, "Why cultural anthropology needs the psychiatrist," in a sense entirely favorable to the psychiatrist, that is, to the systematic student of human personality, we do not for a moment mean to assert that any psychiatry that has as yet been evolved is in a position to do much more than to ask intelligent questions.

LAURA THOMPSON

1945. "Logico-Aesthetic Integration in Hopi Culture," *American Anthropologist*, vol. 47:540-553. Reprinted by courtesy of the author and of the Editor of *American Anthropologist*.

As suggested elsewhere, this paper should be read along with Benedict's *Patterns of Culture* and the essay on socialization and personality in Pueblo society by Esther Goldfrank. When these discussions have been digested, the student should read John W. Bennett's article, "The Interpretation of Pueblo Culture."

Attention is directed to the more comprehensive reports of Dr. Thompson's field research: *The Hopi Way*, by Laura Thompson and Alice Joseph; and *Culture in Crisis, a Study of the Hopi Indians* by Miss Thompson. Another investigation by the same author, oriented to patterns of personality, is the third revised edition of *Guam and its People* (Princeton, 1947).

LOGICO-AESTHETIC INTEGRATION
IN HOPI CULTURE

Laura Thompson

The Hopi, a tribe of less than four thousand Indians living in the heart of the northern Arizona desert, have developed one of the most integrated cultures known to man.[1] For some fifteen centuries this small group, without the use of metal tools, succeeded in mastering almost overwhelming environmental odds and, with group survival at stake, built up a truly functional way of life. Arts and artifacts, institutions and customs, myth and ritual have been integrated into a complex and unified whole, every essential part of which contributes to, and is conditioned by, the over-all structural totality. Indeed, as standard tests have indicated, even the personalities of the individual members of the group have been sharpened and molded toward a particular pattern of mentality.[2]

The Hopi psycho-socio-cultural totality manifests a high degree of the functional dependency type of integration; that is, the type of interdependency of the parts and the whole which results when a change in one part tends in the course of time to be reflected in a change in all the other parts and in the whole.[3] The functional dependency type of integration is sometimes called organic, since it is the type that characterizes organic structures. I have discussed this point elsewhere.[4] Here I wish to point out that a close study of the covert aspects of the Hopi culture reveals that it is characterized by a high degree of still another, more subtle and distinctively human type of integration, namely, an abstract, logical unity which reinforces its organic wholeness at both the conceptual and the aesthetic levels. The purpose of this paper is to describe this *logico-aesthetic integration*[5] as it is manifest especially in the key unverbalized premises and the explicit concepts which form the covert core of Hopi traditional culture.[5a]

THE NATURE-MAN COOPERATIVE

The Hopi conceive the cosmos as a complex, ordered structure regulated by an inherent, logical Principle. According to Hopi ideology, all phenomena relevant to Hopi life—including man, the animals and plants, the earth, sun, moon, and clouds, the ancestors and the spirits—are interdependent through an innate, dynamic Law. According to this Law, the various orders and sub-orders of the over-all universal scheme work together for the common weal by exchanging values or services, which are essentially equivalent but not identical. Man, the elements, the animals, plants, and the super-natural powers interact in an orderly fashion, by means of a complex set of correlative interrelationships, for the good of all. Thus the Hopi cosmos is inherently harmonious and cooperative.[6]

The Hopi classify all phenomena relevant to their life way according to principles which are similar to, but not so refined as, those upon which Western science is based—that is, they recognize various classes or species of animals, plants, men, etc. But they also have a system of cross-classification, not recognized by Western science, which cuts across the empirically established, mutually exclusive orders, and close-ly relates phenomena from the different classes or species into higher orders, which function as interdependent wholes in the cosmic scheme. Such a higher order, for example, may include a group of men related by kinship (namely, a clan) a species of animals, of birds, of plants, or supernatural beings, of elements, etc. It also may have other attributes, such as direction, color, sex, etc. These century-long established, cross-classified higher orders may be thought of as forming a sort of super-society which functions as a universal nature-man cooperative. They form the backbone of the system of interdependent relationships which gives basic structure to the universe.

In this system each individual—human and non-human—has its proper place in relation to all the other phenomena and each has a definite role in the cosmic order. The scheme does not operate mechanically, however, on account of the special role played by man. Whereas, according to Hopi theory, the non-human universe is controlled automatically by the reciprocity Principle, man is a responsible agent who may or may not completely fulfill his function in it. While the world of nature is compelled to respond in certain fixed ways to certain stimuli, man has a margin of choice and also man has the power to elicit response. Thus, in contrast to the non-human world, man can exercise a certain limited but positive measure of control over the universe. Indeed the Hopi believe not only that man can positively affect the functioning of the external world of nature to a limited extent, but that in the measure that he fails to do so, the harmonious functioning of the universe will be impaired. To the Hopi the move-ments of the sun, the coming of rain, the growth of crops, the reproduction of animals and of human beings depend (to a certain extent at least) on man's correct, complete, and active participation in the fulfillment of the cosmic Law.

Moreover, the Law requires that, to be effective, man must participate in the universal scheme not only at the overt behavioral level—that is, by performing certain rites at prescribed intervals in certain ways—but he must participate also at the emotional and ideational levels—that is, by a concentration of his psychical energy on praying or willing. In the Hopi language the word for "to pray" also means "to will."[7] And an appreciation of the Hopi "pray-will" formulation, which has no equivalent in English, is crucial in understanding the Hopi culture and character. The individual's success in life, the welfare of the tribe, and to a certain extent the smooth functioning of the whole cosmic order, depend on man's carrying out the rules, in cooperation with his non-human partners, wholeheartedly and with an effort of the will.

Hopi traditional philosophy, therefore, ascribes to man a purposive, creative role in the universe, a role which is dependent on the development of his volition. The universe is not conceived as a sort of machine at the mercy of mechanical law and blind chance. Nor is it viewed as a system of hostile, competitive forces struggling for existence. It is a harmonious, integrated system operating on the principle of immanent justice, and in it the key role is played by man's will.

COSMIC FULFILLMENT

To the Hopi, time is not cut up into segments which can be measured, like an hour, a day, or a year, but it is rather conceived as a duration, in which the Law is being fulfilled.[8] Time is a becoming-later-and-later in which the existing phenomena develop or change from one phase to another, each according to its own intrinsic dynamic pattern. In the nature of each phenomenon which manifests as a whole entity is the power or energy of its own mode of fulfillment. Some phenomena, according to Hopi theory, have a growth cycle like plants, others change by means of a repetitive or vibratory movement pattern, others take form, diffuse and vanish, still others, like the earth, develop by a series of metamorphoses.[9] Thus there is a great diversity in the modes of duration and fulfillment of various phenomena within the unity of the great cosmic Law. And the present manifestation of each phenomenon is one phase of its development, which has been prepared by earlier phases and will be succeeded by later ones now in process of preparation, according to its own inherent dynamics.

Against this ever-becoming-later background of the cosmos, the Hopi conception of history becomes that of the unfolding of Hopi destiny according to the Law. This unfolding takes place in a sequence of phases. These phases are marked by legendary events, important to the tribe, such as the emergence of mankind from the Underworld, and the series of settlements along the clan migration routes from the Place of Emergence to the present site of the tribe.

THE IDEAL SOCIETY

Within this over-all cosmic scheme the Hopi conceive the ideal society as a theocratic pueblo state which reflects, at the social level, the structure and Law of the universe. That is, the ideal society is also a unified, dynamic whole composed of various parts and sub-parts, interrelated by a network of correlative obligations and responsibilities on the fulfillment of which depends the mutual welfare of all. And each part and sub-part of the social system consists not only of human orders and sub-orders, but also of other categories of phenomena such as classes of animals, plants, natural elements, and supernatural beings, which may be thought of as intimately associated with, or partners to, the human orders, and which together with them form the nature-man super-society.[10]

Moreover, social groups based on kinship—namely, clans—are closely interrelated with social groups based on ritual ties—namely, secret societies—through the equipoise of the female-centered clan system versus the male-centered ceremonial system. The chief priests of the major secret societies, who are also members of certain leading clans, form a "Chief's Talk" or council. This group is headed by the chief priest of the ranking society who, by virtue of his ceremonial position, is the pueblo chief responsible for the welfare of the group. His main duty is to concentrate on and "pray-will" for the common weal, in accordance with the Law, and he is protected from secular matters and revered as the leader or "Father" of the pueblo.

Under this system the religious, judicial, political, social, and economic functions of the pueblo are merged into a single unit, in which every part is interrelated and given significance in respect to the whole. Kinship and ceremonial groups are subtly equilibrated through mutual correlativity in a highly integrated and cohesive pueblo theocracy, which reflects the dynamic structure of the cosmos.

Reproduction of this organically conceived society is ideally by means of budding. As the Hopi matrilineal clan grows by adding daughter households to the mother unit, so the pueblo expands by the budding[11] of daughter colonies from the original nucleus. Thus ideally the society is able to segment and completely reconstitute itself.[12]

THE IDEAL MAN

As has been noted, to fulfill his key role in the universal scheme of things, man must actively participate in the Law. This means full assumption of personal responsibility by the whole man—including mind, emotions, and body. To the Hopi, as to modern psychiatry, man is a complex psycho-physiological whole. Moreover, the Hopi believe that each individual is a responsible agent through the creative development of his will, and Hopi interest in the whole man centers in the psycho-physiological development of the will. Man is a sculptor who can mold himself from within. This assumption is the basic adjustive and generative postulate of their cosmogony.

To the Hopi the traditional ideal of man or woman is the individual of maximum psycho-physiological effectiveness in the fulfillment of the Law. This means that he or she operates at high intensity in his or her own particular place and role in the cosmic scheme. But since every Hopi's place and role are defined in terms of his obligations and responsibilities as a part of the social whole, the ideal man is envisaged not only within the framework of the cosmos, but also and always very specifically within the setting of the pueblo state.

The Hopi's ideal is to live, to the utmost of his powers, for society as envisaged in Hopi terms—i.e., the pueblo unit composed of groups of human beings in association with their non-human partners, interacting correlatively in fulfillment of the Law. And hence the one who approaches most nearly the ideal would be the individual who is most completely socialized (in Hopi terms).

The Hopi have set up a definite standard for the individual and this standard is expressed by the term _hòpi_.[13] Whereas much of Hopi ideology is expressed only by implication in the culture, Hopi tradition is explicit and detailed on this point. The word _hopi_ is usually translated as "peaceful, good, happy." But as far as can be determined, it also includes all those attributes which to the Hopi make up the balanced, Law-fulfilling, psycho-physiological whole which is man as he should be—that is, it connotes the ideal, dynamic totality at the level of the individual (hence, of society). Thus the _hopi_ individual is: (1) strong (in the Hopi sense, i.e., he is psychically strong—self-controlled, intelligent, and wise—and he is physically strong); (2) poised (in the Hopi sense, i.e., he is balanced, free of anxiety, tranquil, "quiet of heart" and concentrated on "good" thoughts); (3) law-abiding (i.e., responsible, actively cooperative, kind and unselfish); (4) peaceful (i.e., non-aggressive, non-quarrelsome, modest); (5) protective (i.e., fertility-promoting and life-preserving, rather than injurious or destructive to life in any of its manifestations, including human beings, animals, and plants); and (6) free of illness. These are the main positive qualities which make up the subtly balanced, integrated (in Hopi terms, "one-hearted") personality which fulfills the Law and hence is good, happy, and healthy (from the Hopi point of view). The Hopi ideal is highlighted in the personality of the village chief. As the human embodiment of the ideal, he is the most revered person in the pueblo. And his word, as the certification and interpretation of the Law, is honored and obeyed.

The ideal or _hopi_ personality is better understood by contrast to its antithesis, namely, that which is *kahopi*. Whereas the idea-complex signified by the term *hopi* represents one pole in the personality potential, that of *kahopi* represents the other. The term *kahopi* includes all those qualities which, to the Hopi, are anti-social in terms of the pueblo state; for example, lack of integrity, quarrelsomeness, jealousy, envy, boastfulness, self-assertion, irresponsibility, non-cooperativeness and sickness. And the personality type which represents the *kahopi* pole, the antithesis of the ideal, is sharply drawn in the Hopi concept of the witch.[14] The witch is "two-hearted" and personifies all that to the Hopi is anti-social, unlawful, illness-bringing, death-dealing; in a word, all that is "bad."

THE HOPI WAY

Whereas the non-human orders fulfill their obligations more or less automatically under the Law, man has definite responsibilities which have to be carried out according to a rather complicated set of rules. These rules embody the immanent, cosmic Law reduced to the level of human thought, feeling and behavior, and they form an unwritten ethical canon known as the Hopi Way.

The Hopi Way is a unified code of practical rules covering every role which a Hopi person, male or female, is expected to assume during his journey through life from birth to death. It sets up a standard not only for his overt behavior but for his thoughts and emotions as well. And the individual's success in life, as well as the welfare of the group, depends on active cultivation of the Hopi Way.

The training of the child is directed toward progressively learning and practising the basic precepts of this code. Each individual, however, is expected to master only those over-all principles and detailed rules which apply to his particular sex, age-grade, status, and ceremonial responsibilities, the learning process being adjusted to the maturation curve. Those selected for high ceremonial offices are required, during their period of training and apprenticeship, also to become adept in the more esoteric aspects of the code, the village chief's successor being initiated gradually into the most intricate forms and meanings of the whole system as it is related to the over-all Law.

The Hopi Way, besides being an ethical code for the individual, thus functions as an unwritten constitution for the pueblo state. It embodies the traditional pueblo legal system—guarded, certified, and interpreted by the Village Chief. And this functionary, besides his other offices, is the chief judiciary officer of the pueblo.

Hence Hopi traditional ethics form a simple, integrated canon which serves as the ideal standard for the individual and, at the same time, for the group. And since the rules for individual conduct and the laws for the government of the state are part and parcel of the innate, logical Principle of the universe, both are sacred and absolute.

Actually the Hopi Way, by equating the personal and the social ideal within a cosmic frame of reference, and by placing full and specific moral responsibility for fulfillment of the Law on each and every individual in the group, as indispensable parts of the whole, sets up ideal conditions (in terms of external and internal pressures toward a single goal) for the development of an integrated system of social control, which functions effectively with a minimum of physical coercion, by fostering its internalization within the individual in the form of a super-ego or conscience consistent with the social goal. Traditional sanctions—whether for the group or the individual, whether external or internal—are thus unified by, and directed toward, a single ideal.

THE ROLE OF RITE

Complete participation in the Law, according to Hopi ideology, means not only that the business of every-day living must be regulated by the Code, but that man must also discharge his full responsibilities in regard to the cosmos. This is done mainly by the rhythmic, psycho-physiological performance of a cycle of ceremonies which constitute the main machinery of the pueblo theocracy.[15]

Hopi ritual is a complex, but logical and ordered, system which represents symbolically the Hopi conception of the universe, the Law and the life process. It consists mainly of an annual series of interrelated episodes, the rendition of which, through the media of art and concentrated "will-prayer," is believed to facilitate the harmonious functioning of the universe. The ceremonial is thus an indispensable part of man's fulfillment of the Law.

The ritual serves mainly as a mechanism symbolically to forecast and prepare for, and hence (according to the Hopi view) to participate in, and facilitate the fulfillment of, phases of the multidimensional cosmic Process according to the ordered sequence in which they are expected to occur and at various levels relevant to the whole of life as the Hopi envisage it. Thus, the ritual is a logical outgrowth of the unverbalized premises regarding the nature of the universe and the concept of time which underlie the Hopi life way.

To consider the Hopi ceremonial as an instrumentality designed solely to enable the crops to grow by bringing moisture to the fields is to throw out of focus the whole picture of Hopi religion, and indeed to misunderstand the basic orientation of their culture and character. Each main ceremony, it is true, includes within its rite complex instrumentalities believed to facilitate the coming of rain and the germination, growth, and maturation of the crops. For example, the Powamu or so-called "Bean Dance" in February involves the forced growth of beans and corn in the *kivas* and the arrival of large numbers of *kachinas* (ancestral deities associated with rain clouds and other life-promoting phenomena) and it opens the season for racing which is believed to speed growth. All these ritual practices obviously are intended to promote the germination and aid the growth of food plants.[16] But this is only one aspect of their over-all significance. The so-called "whipping rite" or first initiation of children is included quadrennially in the Powamu complex, and at this time the four phases of the journey through life are graphically portrayed,[17] and the discipline pattern of the Hopi as it changes from childhood to adulthood is dramatized. Thus, it is clear that the early growth and psycho-physiological development of human beings is also associated with this rite complex. Moreover, the "road of life," as depicted through sand paintings and other media, symbolizes not only the human life cycle, but also the migration of the tribe from the Place of Emergence. Viewed at a higher level of abstraction, the "road of life" motif expresses, with a nice simplicity and mastery of the relevant, the Hopi pre-supposition regarding the unfolding of the Law by intrinsic, multiordinal, episodic process. Thus it may be inferred through internal evidence that the Powamu ceremonies have multidimensional implications from the Hopi point of view, consistent with the basic dynamic structure of Hopi cosmogony.

This extensive character of the Hopi ceremonial is clearly evident in the pivotal Winter Solstice ceremony which inaugurates the annual cycle in December. Although dramatic rites are performed to turn the Sun back northward from his winter "house," giving the complex a cosmic focus, as a part of these rites prayer-sticks are made for practically every order important to Hopi life—for individual human beings and the ancestors, for non-human clan partners, for useful animals and plants, for dwelling houses, fields, shrines, growing crops and even for points along the traditional migration routes. Thus while the ceremony emphasizes the yearly cycle of the Sun and its significance in the universal scheme, it also expresses the entire Hopi cosmogony with its stress on correlative interdependence, the emergence of the tribe from the Underworld and the migration to its present site, as well as the cosmic life process. Hence, it is clear that the Winter Solstice rites are also multidimensional in their underlying significance.

The Hopi emphasis on ritual mechanisms directed toward the active promotion of the life process in all its manifestations which they consider important to their life needs has just been noted. This emphasis is clearly reflected in their formulation of the ideal personality. Also of fundamental importance to the problem under consideration is their stress on the active conservation of life. Stress on the promotion of life on the one hand, and on its protection on the other, should be recognized as logical complements in a single, purposive idea-complex.

Interest in the conservation and protection of life is well illustrated in the Hopi hunting rites. The ancient rites involve the propitiation of the particular kind of game animal being hunted, with prayer-sticks and an entreaty to the "animal people" not to become angry when killed but to forgive the Hopi who take their lives only because of great need.[18] A Hopi should never kill more than he needs and must use every part of the animal, even the bones, hoofs, horns and skull.

A similar protective and conciliatory attitude is manifest toward the plant world, and Hopi children are taught never to destroy or pick anything they do not need to use, not even a weed, and to use everything they pick.

These life-promoting and live-conserving attitudes and values reiterate the fundamental Hopi precept that human beings are actively responsible for maintaining the harmonious nature-man balance which is indispensable for the welfare of all. Moreover, they are apparently closely related to the Hopi view of premature death. Death from old age is regarded as the natural and proper transition from the last phase of the life cycle to rebirth in the Underworld. Premature death, however, seems to indicate to the Hopi some interference with the harmonious unfolding of the life process—some disturbance of the subtly balanced and intricately interdependent life web. There seems to be a definite feeling that the individual himself can develop the psycho-physiological power to keep his own life properly balanced so as to avoid such affliction, and that in failing to do so he has displayed a lack of concern for others in the group.

This ideology also plays a part in the Hopi attitude toward sickness. Thus the psycho-physiological condition of imbalance in the individual, eventuating from a failure to fulfill the Law, may be punished by means of a disease or "whip" inflicted through the agency of a secret society or a witch.[19] The sickness may be eliminated by the restoration of the proper balance through various mechanisms.[20]

RITUAL AS ART

The implicit concept of ceremonial, which has just been discussed very briefly, is inextricably bound up with the Hopi concept of art. From the aesthetic point of view the ceremonial cycle, as a whole, is a multimediary, polyphonic work of art, and only by viewing it from this angle may its full significance and power be appreciated.

The ceremonial cycle may be thought of as super-drama which requires a period of one year for its complete rendition. This super-drama is composed of a series of dramas or mystery plays, each complete in itself but an integral part of the whole, and each extending from nine to seventeen days and nights.

Each ceremonial or drama in the Hopi over-all ritual whole is in itself a subtly orchestrated unit, combining, in a highly stylized manner, many creative media—chiefly rhythmic movement, singing, drumming, impersonation, and painting—to express one ever-recurring master theme.[21] Thus the Hopi cycle forms an exceedingly complex, serialized, fugue-like structure which each year expresses and reaffirms symbolically the Hopi world view, as a whole and in its intricately interwoven details.

The ceremonial cycle, therefore, is an aesthetic formulation of the Hopi creed. It is a representation of a configuration of abstract principles. As a whole and throughout the various media used, it always seeks to portray not an event or an object which may be perceived through the senses, but a conventionalized concept of such an event or object, whether it be a cosmic event like a solstice, an elementary force like the sun, a plant like corn, or a creature like the butterfly. Always Hopi art seeks to portray the Hopi idea or ideal of the event, of the force, of the plant, or of the creature, rather than the particularized occasion or object itself. Thus it should be differentiated from the realistic type of art and also from the type of conventionalized art (like that of the Eskimo or the Northwest coast Indians) which seeks stylistically to portray an experience itself rather than an idea or an ideal of an experience. Hopi aesthetic representations are highly abstract and should be classified as that type of conventionalized art which is primarily abstract.[22]

In this respect it is important to bear in mind that in each single Hopi creation (such as a sand painting or a pottery design) as well as in each creation-complex (such as the Winter Solstice or the Powamu ritual) there is a reflection of the Hopi world view as a whole. And this holistic quality of each particular design unit will be recognized as an indispensable attribute of highly abstract art throughout history.

It should also be noted that Hopi works of art, in whatever medium or combination of media, are characterized by a particular type of balance. This balance is not based on the principle of symmetry. It is a subtle type of balance between different artistic factors which have no common denominator and therefore cannot be numerically measured. For example, line is balanced against shade, surface quality against color. It is as if, instead of balancing one black square against another, we counterpose a red circle with a black square. This is the organic or asymmetrical sort of balance found in nature. To achieve it the artist must see the problem and at the same time see its solution.

Another outstanding quality of Hopi art is its characteristic rhythm. Hopi designs move both around in a circle and toward the center. That is, the movement is circular and centripetal. For example, take the design on the concave surface of a Hopi bowl. The border design moves around the inside of the rim, while the main central section moves inward toward the center of the bowl. Similarly, the ceremonial cycle moves in a circular or spiral annual orbit, while at the same time it moves inward through various levels of abstraction toward a central creed or core. Viewed within the Hopi concept of time, the main ceremonials would be episodes or occasions in an annual cycle which describes a spiral movement.

Hopi art is therefore a symbolic, formalized expression of an idea or an ideal rendered in fulfillment of the Law. Each creation is an organic unit in which every detail has meaning in relation to the whole, and the whole implies an over-all canon or principle. Hopi art, viewed in its totality, gives a complete representation of the Hopi creed and also an insight into Hopi mentality. From this point of view it is a rich, unexplored field which may be expected, upon analysis, to yield objective, internal evidence of those covert aspects of Hopi culture which are unverbalized and often unconscious.

EDUCATION TOWARD THE IDEAL

Dr. Joseph and the writer have described the Hopi educative process in detail elsewhere and analyzed its effects on the individual by age grades from birth to adulthood.[23] Here I wish merely to point out that the Hopi utilize the creative potentialities of the educative process to an extraordinary high degree. The Hopi conceive of the human life process as a gradual unfolding of the whole human being through four phases of the journey through life: childhood, youth, adulthood, and old age. Education commences at birth and consists of a life-long process of molding the individual toward the ideal through actual experience which, while effectively meeting the problems of the present life phase, is also preparatory to the life phases that are to come. Through the centuries a uniquely Hopi educational system has developed which actually does orient the individual toward the social ideal with remarkable effectiveness. It gradually molds the whole individual (emotions, mind and body) for greatest social usefulness in the fulfillment of the Law. The process is directed toward an explicit standard or ideal, namely that which is *hopi* in contrast to that which is *kahopi*, and it involves the mastering of a code, the Hopi Way. And the ideal is most assiduously pursued in regard to those destined for the highest ceremonial positions.

FREEDOM AND CONTROL

We have also discussed at length elsewhere the remarkable Hopi control-system as expressed in the society-personality integrate.[24] Here the writer wishes merely to note some of the implications of the Hopi control-system regarding the problem of individual freedom. To the Hopi, freedom is not phrased negatively as it often is in modern

Western civilization (e. g., freedom from want, freedom from fear.) Freedom is a positive formulation.

Freedom to the Hopi means peace, prosperity and happiness. It may be compared to the Greek concept of *eudaemonia*, raised to the group level. It is man's richest harvest for harmonious living, his precious reward for fulfillment of the Law. Thus freedom is an inherent, positive attribute of the Law. Nothing in the universe can ever be free from the Law. But every being can be free through the Law. Inexorable cosmic process is inherent in the nature of things. It behooves man to study it, to understand it, and to bring his life-way into harmony with it. Only thus may he be free.

AN ORGANIC WORLD VIEW

This brief survey of the major premises and values of Hopi culture reveals first that the Hopi tend to think and formulate in terms of complex, abstract, structural wholes, not in the static sense but in terms of structural wholes as inherently dynamic. Structure is conceived by the Hopi in terms of subtly balanced, changing relationships. These relationships are between the orders, sub-orders, sub-sub-orders, etc., which comprise the whole entities, viewed at various levels of abstraction, and they change according to definite rhythms or periodicities, which vary according to the innate nature of each entity which manifests itself as a structural whole. There is a sense of the unfolding of these diverse, changing structures in fulfillment of the immanent Law. And the unfolding of each structural whole is interdependently related to that of every other in the over-all multiordinal totality.

These findings show, secondly, that the Hopi tend to think of cosmic fulfillment as multimodal, in time viewed as a duration. The evolution of each structural whole, mentioned above, is characterized by phases which are marked by events, and these events, viewed as wholes, are epochs in the over-all duration which is time. Time itself is a gradually-becoming-later-and-later which is logically divisible only through the epochal character of events. Thus the cosmic Process unfolds through rhythmic, epochal types of evolutionary movement in the duration of time.

And finally, by his insight into this multidimensional cosmic Process, man can foresee and prepare for its harmonious realization. Through concentration on the "good," through rite, art, and "will-prayer," he can, with the aid of his non-human partners, facilitate its fulfillment.

To this end the Hopi has organized his world into what might be called a super-society, which cuts across what to Western science are empirically established classes or species, and closely relates both human and non-human phenomena into higher orders which function ceremonially as interdependent wholes in the cosmic scheme. It is mainly through these cross-classified higher orders that man is able to exercise his key role in the cosmos.

Here is recognized an organic view of the universe. The cosmos is formulated as a living whole in which the subtly balanced relationships of the various parts to one another and to the multidimensional totality are similar to those which characterize living organisms. The parts and the whole operate together for the good of all, according to a single, harmonious, immanent Law. Man is a psycho-physiological whole, differentiated from the rest of nature by his power of volition, which is an integral part of the scheme, to be used for the common weal. He cooperates with other men and with his non-human partners in fulfilling the Law, through kinship and ceremonial groups. And the main mechanisms through which he expresses symbolically the cosmic Process are ritual and art, reinforced by concentrated "will-prayer." Human life is a developmental cycle which is but one of the many diverse, evolutionary modes of Law-fulfillment existent in the universe, each with its own intrinsic dynamic pattern, in the ever-becoming-later duration of time.

Thus the Hopi have extended their harmonious, organic view of the universe logically and aesthetically through the world of nature and also through the world of man at both the personal and the social levels. Combining acute observation and induction with deduction and intuition, they have worked the flux of experience with its multitudinous, apparently unrelated details into a world view which is a notable achievement not only in pragmatic utility, but also in logic and aesthetics.

Hopi philosophy is not something apart from life; most of it is not even explicitly stated. It is implicity woven into the very fabric of Hopi life—into institutions, child-training patterns, customs, arts, values and cosmogony—even into Hopi character and mentality. Under relentless environmental pressures, the Hopi has become a specialist in the arts of logical thinking, logical living, and logical character building. Indeed he has become an artist of great versatility. He dances, sings, drums, paints; he weaves, makes pottery, and plaits; he even grows corn with the consummate skill of an artist. But although he has raised his achievements in these varous media to the creative level of the expert, his focus of attention is not solely on any one of them or in a combination of them, but in the mastery of the supreme art of Law-fulfillment, in which all lesser arts play a role.

By relentless concentration on the whole life process as an art, the Hopi has given his culture a high degree of logico-aesthetic integration which is revealed in that crowning attribute of specialism, namely "configuration" or style. Whitehead's apt remark that style is the particular contribution of specialism to culture[25] here is demonstrated on a multidimensional scale. Through systematic specialization the Hopi have developed a unique style which not only characterizes their arts but permeates their culture and even is expressed in their personality structure. And the Hopi "configuration" or style is the overt expression of logico-aesthetic integration in the Hopi psycho-socio-cultural totality.

NOTES

1. This study is based on an analysis of the Hopi psycho-socio-cultural totality presented in "The Hopi Way," by Laura Thompson and Alice Joseph, University of Chicago Press, 1944. See also the writer's forthcoming monograph, *Implicit Configuration in Hopi Symbolism*, for further systematic, detailed documentation of this study. (See bibliography at end of article.)

2. Thompson and Joseph, 1944, pp. 129 *et seq.*

3. For an analysis of the functional dependency type of integration, see Chapple and Coon, 1942, p. 4 *et seq.*

4. Thompson and Joseph, 1944, pp. 127-133.

5. This type of integration is similar to what Sorokin describes as "logico-meaningful." See Sorokin, Vol. I, 1937, p. 18 *et seq.*

5a. The Hopi tradition is still functioning at high intensity in eleven out of the thirteen Hopi villages.

6. Thompson and Joseph, 1944, p. 36 *et seq.*

7. *Ibid.,* p. 41.

8. *Ibid.,* p. 39 *et seq.*

9. Whorf, 1941, p. 84.

10. Thompson and Joseph, 1944, p. 33 *et seq.,* 44 *et seq.*

11. See Parsons, 1939, Vol. I, p. 6.

12. It should be noted that the Hopi conceive the ideal society in terms of the autonomous pueblo unit, not the tribal unit. The Hopi tribe is not traditionally a formal political unit. It is merely an aggregation of historically autonomous pueblo states of common breed, language and culture, united by kinship, ritual, economic and geographic bonds and by a millennia-long tradition of common and similar experiences. Hopi social thought is centered not on the tribe but on the pueblo unit of mother and daughter groups.

13. The full connotation of the word *hopi* and its significance in Hopi life seem to be difficult, if not impossible, for anyone who is not a Hopi himself to appreciate. Some of its implications may be grasped if it is realized that this word, which represents the ideal standard for the individual, is used also as a generic term for the whole tribe and thus expresses dramatically the concept of the complete identification of the individual and of the group with the ideal.

14. Thompson and Joseph, 1944, p. 41.

15. *Ibid.,* p. 42 *et seq.*

16. *Ibid.,* pp. 42-43.

17. *Ibid.,* pp. 50, 65.

18. *Ibid.,* p. 24; Whiting, 1939, pp. 6-7.

19. Thompson and Joseph, 1944, p. 46.

20. These include rites conducted by the society owning the "whip" or by a medicine man. They also include the concentration on "good" thoughts and the driving away of "bad" thoughts by the sick person himself for the purpose of self-cure.

21. Thompson and Joseph, 1944, p. 42 *et seq.*

22. I am indebted to Rene d'Harnoncourt for clarification of the type of abstraction and the balance pattern expressed in Hopi graphic art.

23. Thompson and Joseph, 1944.

24. *Ibid.*

25. Whitehead, 1929, p. 20.

BIBLIOGRAPHY

CHAPPLE & COON, 1942
PARSONS, E. C., 1939
SOROKIN, P. A., 1937
THOMPSON & JOSEPH, 1944
WHITEHEAD, 1929
WHITING, A. F., 1939
WHORF, 1941

FRANCES W. UNDERWOOD AND IRMA HONIGMANN

1947. "A Comparison of Socialization and Personality in Two Simple Societies," *American Anthropologist*, vol. *49*: 557-577. Reprinted by courtesy of the authors and of the Editor of the *American Anthropologist*.

This report of direct observations in the field among two quite different peoples may be supplemented by reading of John Honigmann's reports on the Kaska (cf. General Bibliography and citations on face sheet of article by John Honigmann).

On Haitian societies, two important ethnographic reports are Herskovits, 1937; and Leyburn, 1941.

A COMPARISON OF SOCIALIZATION AND PERSONALITY IN TWO SIMPLE SOCIETIES

FRANCES W. UNDERWOOD AND IRMA HONIGMANN

INTRODUCTION

This paper presents infancy and childhood data from two societies. Those aspects of childhood are stressed which seem to be important in the formation of the more readily apparent personality qualities of the people studied. The conclusions, based upon a comparison of the materials, represent generalizations directed toward problems currently facing the field of personality development.

It is coincidental that the societies discussed offer direct contrasts in two significant aspects of personality development—discipline and the induction of emotionality. In the fall of 1944 a group of students, recently returned from the field, met at a discussion meeting of the Yale Anthropology Club to compare their notes on child development. The members of this group, with varying interests, had each gone to a different society. Nevertheless, the data brought back covered comparable categories of infancy and socialization. The diverse childhood pictures described for each society provoked inquiry into consequences for the adult personalities. This paper was written to show the relationship between patterns of child development and the adult personality. It is unfortunate that not all the groups originally discussed could be represented here.

Although extended knowledge of infancy and childhood is vital in understanding the adult personality in any society, the insight gained from such data alone is very partial indeed. A richer, more complete understanding of personality would depend upon a comprehensive knowledge of the total culture. Kardiner has made this point. He denies that personality formation can be predicted from life-cycle data alone. Rather "the indicators of what are the permanent effects of traumatic experiences in childhood are found in religion, folklore, and a host of other facts gathered from the description of the institutional set-up."[1]

It is with this limitation in mind that the studies below are offered. Comprehensive ethnographies are being prepared for both the Haitians of Beaumont Plateau[2] and the Kaska.[3]

SOME ASPECTS OF PERSONALITY
PATTERNING IN KASKA INDIAN CHILDREN

The Kaska Indians today inhabit the northern area of British Columbia and southern Yukon Territory from the Continental Divide on the west to the Rocky Mountains on the east. Climatically this area is in the polar continental zone of extremely cold winters and warm, even hot, summer days. Biotically it is in the forest belt of spruce, jack-pine and poplar, a region hospitable to moose, bear, caribou and a number of smaller, fur-bearing animals.

Lower Post, the trading post for this region, is located at the confluence of the Dease and Liard Rivers, about 150 miles below the headwaters of the Liard. The settlement extends from the Liard River to the Alaska Highway, a distance of about a quarter of a mile, and is about a mile long. Three trading stores are the nucleus of the town, the merchant personnel, the policeman and the game warden constituting the permanent residents of the community. During the summer months, when the Indian families and white trappers return from the bush, the population swells to about 200 persons. Most of the Indians are Kaska. From about May to September the Indians remain in Lower Post. They trade their furs and then relax after the strain of the rigorous winter life. Before they leave they also stock up for the new trapping season, which begins in November after the first heavy snowfalls.

The data presented below were collected during a three months' stay in Lower Post, from June to September, 1944, and a six months' stay in 1945. June to August was spent in Lower Post, September to December at a winter settlement of Kaska Indians on the Upper Liard River. Rapport was such that at the trading post I exchanged visits with eight Indian women who had children, and in addition could observe the activities of other children and parents as they loitered around the trading stores. The presence of my own two children undoubtedly aided in establishing rapport. In the bush we were completely accepted as participant members of the small community and were fitted into the matrilocal set-up by being assigned appropriate native kinship terms. In spite of these advantages, however, it was not easy to obtain specific information by verbal communication. For one thing most of the culture patterns are highly unformalized, so that a mother could not say what general procedures people followed with relation to children. Also, although most of the Indians speak a simple English, they are extremely introverted and taciturn so that spontaneous discussions were limited. The most frequent Indian contribution to a conversation was "Yes" or "No." Most of my information, therefore, was gained through participant observation.

The hunting-trapping-trading economy of the Kaska Indians necessitates a long winter stay in the bush. Late in July families begin to pull out of Lower Post for their trapping areas. By the middle of September the last stragglers have rolled up their tents and are busy transporting their winter outfit to their trap lines. Trap lines are owned by individuals, usually the men, but occasionally by an unattached woman. Until spring a single family or a matrilocal group of three or four families lives in isolation in its winter cabins with only a rare visitor. Winters are long, dark and intensely cold. By October the rivers begin to freeze, not to run again until March. Winter temperatures average about 35 degrees below zero, Fahrenheit, occasionally dropping to 60 and 70 below. Daylight is at a premium during winter; in December there are days of almost 20 hours of darkness. This is balanced in June and early July when it is light almost 24 hours a day. On the trap line a woman may frequently remain home alone for days with her young children and daughters while her husband, sons and sons-in-law are visiting and setting traps. All Indian women interviewed said they liked the winter life with its work and isolation. The cabin in the bush is referred to as "home." But by winter's end the people are again eagerly looking forward to their summer's visit to the post, with its opportunities for sociability.

The atomistic nature of the Indian community in Lower Post is quickly perceived. No attempt is made to set up a planned community. Each family pitches its tent where it pleases, usually at a spot near the river bank having sufficient trees and brush around to insure privacy from other dwellings. Occasionally, related families will set up adjacent tents.

Sociability takes the form of groups of men, women and children loitering in front of trading stores, exchanging visits, drinking and dancing together, participating in gambling games. Dances, gambling and drinking parties are eagerly anticipated and almost every night during midsummer one or another of these activities will take place. Nevertheless, unless stimulated by alcohol, social interaction is rarely intense. At a dance it may take an hour or even two before the ten or fifteen participants are sufficiently at ease with one another to venture onto the dance floor. There is somewhat more spontaneous interaction between adolescents, particularly of the same sex. Intra-sexual chasing, tickling, hugging, wrestling are readily provoked and greatly enjoyed. Similar inter-sexual "horsing around" is more inhibited and usually initiated after dark, or after the ice between the sexes has already been broken by a dance or a few drinks.

The individualistic manner in which the Kaska participate in group activities can be illustrated in the following situations: Arrangements for a dance are made without prior planning and in a completely informal manner. On the spur of the moment someone will say, "Ask

Pete to play fiddle tonight?" Word will get around that Pete is being asked "to make dance." At about midnight folks begin to drift toward an empty cabin usually used for dancing. Should Pete not feel like playing that night, the group disperses. Pete is under no compulsion to cooperate, although he usually does. In the same way anyone may leave the dance on impulse without any apparent thought as to how his absence will affect the party. Alcoholic beverages are prepared by individuals, on rare occasions by two individuals, who then invite a few friends to share them. This is in sharp contrast to the practice of the whites at Lower Post who cooperate in making brews, five or six individuals contributing supplies, money and services toward making liquor which may later be shared among ten persons.

Sanctions in this loosely knit Indian community are rarely severe. Although there is a nominal chief appointed by the Canadian government he exercises no authority whatsoever. Criticism is the strongest sanction. No matter how much a man's behavior may be disapproved of, barring actual endangering of the life of others, he will be accepted, respected and supported by his kin and friends, although they may tell him he is doing a bad thing, scold him and urge him to mend his ways in the case of severe misconduct, or simply gossip about his faults. This was graphically illustrated with relation to sexual misbehavior. Promiscuity of the girls with visiting soldiers was severely disapproved of by the older people. Nevertheless the girls were not ostracized nor were they disrespected as individuals. They were lectured by one of the old men, criticized and gossiped about, but no one denied them friendship or hospitality. In general people prefer to avoid the resentment of others by minding their own business.

Rorschach tests interpreted for 28 Indians confirm the picture of introversion and emotional aloofness observable in much of Kaska behavior.[4]

THE DEVELOPING PERSONALITY

Children are wanted and welcomed by their parents. The actual birth is dealt with casually, no ceremonies marking the occasion. Some mothers are up and active in a week, some take it easy for about a month. The baby is wrapped in a velvet, embroidered "moss bag," now frequently modernized with the substitution of flannel for moss. The infant's legs are firmly bound, but its hands are usually free. I observed no restriction on thumb sucking. The baby is comforted whenever it cries, fed whenever it appears hungry. Babies are breast fed although some take a supplementary bottle. (It is not at all unusual to see a discarded whiskey bottle or cologne bottle used for this purpose.) The mother takes the baby with her wherever she goes, packing it in its moss bag. Around the camp the child is held in arms; on the trail it is packed on its mother's back, its face toward the mother. A baby rests contentedly on its mother's back and can sleep comfortably with its head nestled on her neck. An older baby has its legs free, but continues to be packed around by its mother or father until it can walk. It appears that the child's initial experiences in life are such as to foster a sense of security. Since the people are undemonstrative and emotionally aloof, however, there is not much open demonstration of affection.

Weaning usually occurs between one and three years of age and is a gradual process. The child is urged to stop suckling by being talked to and scolded. A persistent child, however, will be allowed to the breast till he stops the habit of his own accord. An older child goes to his mother's breast, undoes her dress and helps himself whenever he wants to.

Training for elimination control occurs at about two years and is not severe. The mother takes the child with her into the bush to indicate to him the expected behavior. Conformity is expected to come from the child. As one mother put it, "I never say nothing. He learn himself." Young boys from about a year and a half to about two years have a large hole slit in their pants for ease in self-training. Others wear no pants at all during this period. By three years most children go alone into the bush around the camp to eliminate in privacy. A child who persistently soils beyond this age is criticized and scolded.

A more severe attitude is taken with regard to masturbation. Such activity is discouraged with threats of insanity. It is important to note, however, that parents sincerely believe insanity to be a possible consequence of masturbation.

A child walks and talks when he is developmentally motivated to do so. He receives no pressure from others. The taciturnity of the parents offers little stimulation for a child to express himself verbally. My own young son was always a source of amusement to the little Indian children because of his constant stream of chatter.

When a child can walk he is left more and more to himself; a process of emotional weaning taking place. He fulfills his activities with little parental supervision. If he hurts himself he must go to his mother or father for comfort. Only in situations of immediate danger—if a child walks too close to the cutbank above the river, or approaches too near the fire—will a parent interrupt the child's activity. The laissez faire attitude of parents in many cases is not an active rejection of the child; "passive acceptance" would probably better describe the relationship. This is particularly so for the child living with both his true parents. The child living with but one true parent and a step-parent is more isolated emotionally since a step-parent usually considers his spouse's child by a former marriage to be out of his jurisdiction. One seven-year-old orphaned child presented a picture of very severe isolation. The boy exhibited attachment to no one, not even to his grandfather with whom he lived. He roamed around alone, usually failed to respond to his grandfather's requests, and frequently prepared his own meals from cans. When his grandfather nagged him to go to the summer missionary school he simply "disappeared," sleeping on a white trapper's porch and eating whatever left-over food he could find at our camp. Food was one of the few things this boy responded to with enthusiasm. About 10 per cent of the children live with at least one step-parent. Often a two-year-old can be seen walking alone, playing or crying out of sight and hearing of his parents. For example, I twice had to remove two-year-olds from the road to permit trucks to pass, the parents of the children being nowhere in sight. One two-year-old was sitting in the road howling while his parents were shopping in the trading store. Finally someone picked him up and brought him to his mother who then held him and patted him while she continued making her purchases. It is generally the case that if the crying child is brought to his mother, or if he goes to her, he will be picked up and quieted. A petulant child, hanging around his mother's skirts, is absently indulged so long as he hangs around.

Rather than directly refuse a child anything, the parent will use sly tricks to distract a child from an object. For example, a two-year-old wanted some of his mother's chewing gum. In her pocket the mother slipped the gum out of its wrapper and showed the child the empty wrapper, saying she had no gum left. Later when she wanted the gum for herself she pointed out an airplane to the boy and, as he looked up, popped the gum into her mouth. Being caught in a lie by the child did not appear to disturb this parent. Such experiences reinforced the child's loss of faith in his parents.

The only temper tantrums that were observed occurred in children eighteen to twenty-four months of age. The child was either ignored or picked up and removed from the frustrating situation. That these temper tantrums may be an expression of resentment against the early emotional weaning is suggested by the fact that the ages of the two phenomena coincide.

It seems likely that being thrown on his own at so early an age involves a serious threat to the child's sense of security. Psychologists have pointed out for children in our society that a very frequent reaction to lack and loss of love is a withdrawal from affectional relationships.[5] The early emotional weaning experienced by the Kaska child may well be an etiological factor in the emotional isolation and introversion exhibited by these Indians. The childhood situation appears to offer some compensations to the child. Warm sibling ties develop; for sisters particularly, this warm tie is retained all through life. The child is also given ample opportunity to develop self-sufficiency and to acquire a sense of independence. These are qualities which permit at least conscious adjustment to a sense of aloneness.[6]

A low energy level prevails among children, manifested in little gross motor activity. This is undoubtedly related to poor nutrition. A good deal of the time young children sit quietly close to their parents, who discourage too great boisterousness. Children who run about constantly, shout and are more aggressive toward their playmates are thought of as too wild.

Play groups are small, consisting of close-aged siblings or relatives. The structure of these groups is atomistic. There is little cooperative play and even this is at a low level of organization. For example, a child may throw a toy boat to which a rope is attached into the river and another child will pull it in, entirely spontaneously and with no pre-discussion of roles. When the second boy tires of pulling it in, the first does his own pulling without comment. Cooperation is accepted but not expected. There is no formalized or organized group play. Predominantly there is parallel play. As an example take two or three boys, each sailing his own boat in the river with little reference to each other, outside of occasional comments or exclamations. A new child joining the group adds his presence and activity but leaves the structure of the group undisturbed. A child motivated to leave simply walks off without disturbing the activities of the others. Nevertheless children usually play in groups of twos and threes, apparently finding gratification and stimulation in the mere presence and exclamations of fellow mates.

From the foregoing it can be seen that the qualities of emotional aloofness and individualism also manifest themselves in the play relationships among children. Group interaction in play is weak and the child maintains his identity in group activity.

Sibling relationships are good. As stated above, close-aged siblings invariably play together. Indeed, being isolated in the bush for nine long winter months they are likely to see few children other than siblings and maternal parallel cousins until they return to the post. Physical aggression among children is infrequent. Cultural values are strongly oriented against aggression. An older child being beaten by his younger sibling smiles as he disengages himself from the onslaught. Should he fight back his parent will scold, "That's your brother. Don't hit your brother." Children may tease one another, for example, by taking away another's pet toy.

Without strong positive pressure from adults and without formal education the young child readily learns cultural activities. A little two-year-old can occasionally be seen fetching water from the river in a small pot. The child's voluntary contributions to camp chores are accepted. Children are permitted to use sharp knives, scissors and axes as soon as their activities demand the need of these tools. A five-year-old was seen making a rolling toy for himself. He nailed the round top of a coffee tin to a thin pole, using the flat side of a sharp ax to pound the nail through. This same boy was playing with a fly hook at the river front. No one paid any attention to him till the hook got caught in my daughter's overalls. Then the boy was scolded for his carelessness.

Older children are expected to help around the camp. A girl of six or seven is asked to pack small wood into the house and attend to other routines commensurate with her abilities. A ten- or eleven-year-old girl is assisting in the bulk of the housework. In addition she sets and visits rabbit snares, assists in sawing and splitting wood. In winter she may set a few traps, the fur from which will become her own to sell. A boy's education for his economic role in the family begins at about ten years of age when he starts to accompany his father or brothers fishing, hunting and trapping, and watches them prepare the various manufactures needed by the family. He is also expected to haul, saw and split wood. Educational methods are extremely flexible and indirect. A child learns primarily by observing how a thing is done. So long as he can fairly well approximate the finished product, the steps whereby he managed to achieve it are not rigorously prescribed. For example a six-year-old child was asked to build a fire in the stove. No further instruction was offered. The child put the kindling on top of the heavy wood and consequently the fire failed to catch. Her guardian said nothing but rebuilt and set the fire herself.

No one in this society is bogged down with work. A girl contributing heavily to household chores still has a great deal of free time. During her leisure she is her own boss, although she is expected to return quickly to camp whenever her assistance is needed. A boy enjoys even more free time.

It appears to be not so much the pressure of other people that brings about socialization but more importantly the values inherent in the cultural patterns as answers to the problems that the individual will face growing up in his milieu. For example, a boy eagerly accompanies his father on the trap line. To subsist in the adult culture the boy needs trapping experience and knowledge. A good hunter and trapper is respected, has a definite prestige with girls and can reassure himself as to his self-sufficiency. Therefore, although trapping is an extremely rigorous business, the task has a strong enough positive valence to make the boy eager to begin it. On the other hand the boy who fails to become a good trapper and who, upon marriage, cannot support his wife and family does not face severe deprivation, for he will be assisted in supporting his family by his wife's family.

From the above it can be seen that socialization for the Kaska is a consistent process which steadily re-enforces the personality qualities which were initiated at the break between infancy and childhood.

SUMMARY AND CONCLUSIONS

Two cultural trends appear to influence Kaska personality development. The first trend makes its appearance with the early emotional weaning of the child. The parents, particularly the mother, withdraw themselves from any intensive emotional interaction with the two- and three-year-old. Their attitudes may be described as being compounded of passive affection and emotional indifference. The result in the child appears to be an emotional aloofness which later manifests itself in the withdrawn, taciturn adult personality which we have described as introverted. The impetus to strong social interaction having been removed from the developing individual, the child is thrown upon his own resources.

The second cultural trend influential in Kaska personality formation stems from the opportunities for independent development afforded by the atomistic social structure of the community and society. Discipline is lax, frustrations are minimal, and social sanctions, such as aggression, scarcely elaborated. The individual developing in this milieu is stimulated along strongly individualistic lines, a development that is highly compatible with his emotionally aloof personality. Only the expectation of rewards like social approval, sexual opportunities, and economic independence instigate definite behavioral trends. Negative sanctions are far less effective as motives of behavior, since the atomistic structure of the society makes such sanctions of minor importance to the strongly individualistic personality of the Kaska Indian.

IRMA HONIGMANN

PEASANT CHILD REARING IN RURAL SOUTHWESTERN HAITI

The observations recorded below were made during the summer of 1944 in rural villages scattered over the Beaumont Plateau[7] which lies approximately in the center (both north-south and east-west) of the mountainous southern peninsula of Haiti.[8] They are not as complete as the author could wish, since rapport with peasant women was difficult, but it is hoped that such information as it is possible to give may help fill out gaps in our knowledge of this phase of life in simple societies.

The term "child" (êfê)[9] has two cultural meanings: (1) all sub-adults, and (2) individuals of age six months to five or six years. The first is a generalized meaning; the second's practicality in cultural terms is demonstrated by the acquisition of pants for boys and knee-length dresses for girls at the latter age, and by the economic fact that children of five or six are put to work in towns as domestics.

Within childhood, then, two categories are defined and recognized: infants (*ti êfê,* or *bébé*), comprising babies from the day of birth to approximately six months, and children, or individuals from six months to approximately six years.

A word about the organization of this section is in order here. Young humans must make two types of adjustment to life, and society must solve two sets of problems in regard to new individuals. One is the result of the physiological weaknesses of the baby; the second is the result of societal living. These two aspects have, therefore, been set off as categories, and pertinent information subsumed under them. At the end a summary will be attempted.

CHILD CARE

Feeding. Babies are breast fed, the hours seeming to depend on the child's needs and desires in the matter. During the nursing period some other forms of nourishment are given to babies. These are of the gruel type and made of cornmeal, wheat flour, or manioc boiled in water.

Weaning. This takes place at fifteen to seventeen months, according to my informant, and children of two years or more were never seen breast feeding but were given solid foods, such as fruit or cassava cakes, when they asked for a bite. Presumably their regular meals correspond with the adult diet.

Teething. The baby's gums are massaged by the mother to soothe them, and she may let him chew on a lime or piece of orange to aid the dental eruption.

Cleanliness. New babies wear a diaper arrangement to facilitate cleaning, but later (about four months) have one piece of clothing only—a little dress for a girl, a shirt for a boy—or nothing at all, a costume most practical and functional. From birth through the crawling stage few restrictions seem to be placed on the children, as they were observed urinating and defecating in the houses and on the porches with no one taking any notice except to clean the spot if it interfered with adult activities. Since the floors are of earth and lime, liquid is easily absorbed; every family owns a chamber pot which no doubt is utilized if the child is caught in time. In some cases, it was noticed that the baby was cleaned. Although no information was secured on the techniques of toilet training, with the exception of mild intrasibling ridicule among some upper class boys, the fact that after five years children are fully clothed in most instances would indicate that they are expected to have learned control by that time.

Frequency of bathing was not observed, but each peasant washes his face and mouth the first thing in the morning, using either fingers or a wooden stick to clean the teeth. Presumably these practices extend to the children.

Sleeping. Babies sleep with the mother at night. They nap during midday and during the first few months sleep much of the twenty-four hours. If the mother must be away during the day, the grandmother or other elder female relative will rest or sleep with the baby. An instance of this was observed in Cassonette one morning about eleven. The baby was lying on some rags within the curve of the old woman's arm. Both were peacefully asleep in the cookhouse near the banked fire.

Health. Attention to this varies with the individual family. For example, two cases of hernia in young boys were seen. One family is literate and expects to see that the child gets an operation; the other is of average peasant level and the child will probably go without help. Another factor enters here. The peasant does not like to spend money on children—it is with the greatest reluctance that he will buy clothes for them, hence the preponderance of nudity in young children. Most of the minor ailments, however, have folk remedies which are applied when needed.

Clothing. Only for infants is clothing a protection. The climate is so mild and salubrious that clothing after infancy serves the functions of adornment and modesty. A new baby is clothed in a diaper, sometimes an undershirt, cap, and little dress, then wrapped in a cloth or blanket. The six-week-old girl I met my first day in the area was wrapped in a dirty, ragged cloth, with equally soiled cap and dress the only other items of clothing seen. Booties are optional. After three or four months, as mentioned before, this is changed to the single garment. From birth to death the average peasant is barefooted.

Crying. Children are not encouraged to cry; if they do so except when they have been punished, the nearest adult will attempt to soothe them; if they are in the hands of an older sibling, the latter will usually pick up the child and try to quiet it by cuddling or directing its attention elsewhere. The children observed seem to have a rather low frustration threshold. Even older children will cry if teased, and young ones will howl if someone accidentally pushes them or will not pick them up when they want it, or does not allow them whatever they wish at the moment. They always cry when disciplined, but in such case they get no attention—or if any, it is a sharp word to keep quiet.

Walking. No pressure to walk was observed; babies are put on the floor after a few months and allowed to crawl as much as they like. Presumably children imitate siblings or other youngsters who care for them. By two years of age they are walking.

Play. Babies' play is about half and half baby-adult and baby-child in composition. They enjoy peek-a-boo, patting or grasping at objects held for them, being jiggled, trying to participate in the activities of the older youngsters.

After the toddling stage, play is in sex-differentiated gangs. Frequently, however, a girl was seen attempting to join the boys. Most play after toddling is done on the way to or from an errand, or when the family has not assigned a task.

Favorite forms noticed include: tag, chasing each other in an apparently aimless fashion (this is confined to young children), teasing (verbal and otherwise), pretending activities of their elders, and practical joking. These are all child-and-child games. Verbal teasing is mainly confined to older children and was not so easily observed as the more active type. Every time a group of youngsters gathered at a water supply spot there was much splashing, screaming, and laughing, evidencing dousing. One youngster was observed teasing a playmate by practically wiping him with a kitten. Only one case of practical joking was observed. A group of her contemporaries set a puppy at the heels of the girl dwarf of Lachicotte Valley as she was on her way home with a water-filled bamboo stalk balanced on her head. Pretending ranges all the way from imitating the characteristics of relatives, strangers, and others to riding sticks with fiber tassels as horses.

Play with animals is fairly frequently to be seen, smaller children confining themselves to dogs and cats, while older ones love to ride every chance they get. The boys prefer horses for the speed.

Sex play. Masturbation is a prohibited form of behavior and my informant (R. Hs. Etienne) insisted he knew of no incidence of it or of a child trying it. My own observations agree with his, but the suspicion is that the children do attempt it, only to come up against one of the strongest cultural taboos. The way they are dressed (or undressed) would enable elders to inhibit its occurrence easily. The efficacy of training here is indicated by the fact that not once was a native boy seen with an erect penis.

About the age of puberty (fifteen) great interest in sex relations is manifest, and my informant is sure that there is considerable experimentation. Sex relations are not considered obscene or wicked, but fun; there are no taboos on speaking of the sex organs; work songs mention them, and sexual jokes are frequent. Also houses are small (mainly one or two rooms only) and members of the family have a minimum of privacy so that children must learn much of the sex act early.

Responsibility for care. The mother is primarily responsible in caring for the children. No one replaces her for feeding, but a relative (either sex and any age from two on) will watch a baby or child for her. These surrogates are permitted discipline privileges, but tend to be less severe than the parents.

Amount of care. Supervision and attention are continuous for children until the walking age. After that they are not under direct supervision, but parents can ask any villager going by the door and usually get an answer as to where the children are. Total impressions are that the culture follows physiological lines closely here as care is continuous until the child is talking and walking. Then, casualness replaces the previous pattern.

TRAINING FOR SOCIAL LIVING

Talking. Since only upper-class Haitians were observed trying to encourage speaking in children, it is assumed that little pressure in this direction is exerted among the peasants who do, however, teach the talking baby mannerly address in short order. In addition another factor comes into play. Society is organized either in terms of a village which is relatively heterogeneous as regards lineages, or of a village composed of several lines within the same family tree. These units are high in daily interaction levels, so that a growing child would move in a very verbal world and probably be rewarded by forms of adult activity for intelligible speech.

Diet. Information on this point is negligible. Two meals a day are eaten by the peasants with snacks in between. Children of two were seen nibbling on cassava cakes between meals, and older ones eating bread or fruits, such as oranges or mangoes. Children attending the market ate rice and beans together with their mothers, so that the diet tends to approximate that of adults soon after weaning.

Clothing. Reference has been made previously to infants' and young children's apparel. After five or six, children always wear clothes: shirt and short trousers for boys until puberty; slip and dress for girls. After changing voice and other secondary sexual characteristics appear in a boy, he dons long pants, although two boys of seventeen were observed still wearing short ones. Generally two sets of clothing are maintained for each individual, the old ones being used for work or sleeping garments and being replaced when necessary. No shoes are worn, though sandals are now being used to a slight degree.

Work. At an early age children are given the responsibility of certain tasks. Girls and boys of two or more watch their younger siblings, and take care of them in the sense of providing companionship and entertainment as well as supervising how far they toddle, crawl, or otherwise motivate themselves. A boy of four was noticed walking with a younger brother and holding him by the hand to aid if he stumbled over a stone or depression in the ground; two girls of four and five were seen playing hide-and-seek, cuddling, and rolling about with three younger siblings. A little fellow of about three was frequently observed picking up his year-and-a-half old sister whenever she cried or strayed. Other examples are found above under *Crying*.

The children are the water-getters; they are sent for it the first thing in the morning and the last thing at night, and as often in between as necessity and distance demand. They are also the family messengers. A little girl of about four carried a communication to me from her father, the total distance going and returning being about a mile.

After six or seven, children become economic cogs in the family wheel. At that age a child may be sent into town to work as a domestic, or, if he stays at home, he takes an active part in daily activities. Two young girls were encountered one day on their way from home in Cassonette village to Andre village where they were going to market the produce carried on their heads. A girl of eight was observed helping her mother with the exacting task of fixing manioc for cassava cakes. Boys will help the father cultivate, make saddles, run long errands, and so on. A six-year-old boy was seen one morning with a small mâchete on his head, on his way to join his father at cutting branches for the production of charcoal. Both sexes learn to ride early, but boys were more often seen playing at riding and more often in the saddle than the girls, even though the latter will grow up to ride donkeys to market.

Especially at a communal work project, like building a house or preparing coffee for market or doing a major farm task such as working the ground for cultivation, the children are pressed into service in many ways. At the gathering of a sosiété datribusiô to help a Centre d'Avezac man get his stored coffee ready to sell, young boys were playing the musical instruments to which the men sang and worked; young girls were carrying water and assisting in the cooking. In the same village, neighbors of another man were helping him build his new house. The little fellows carried stones to the site in company with adult males; little girls carried baskets of lime from the kiln and, together with the women, brought in water.

Sex differentiation. Distinction between male and female runs through every aspect of peasant culture and children are early made aware of it. Differentiation starts before birth, for boys are much more desired than girls since they are the ones who will bear the family name and be responsible for their elders in old age. This continues throughout life in the relationship between parents and children. Ambitions are had and planned for the son—more money will be spent on him; if any education is to be had, the son is given it.

Clothing, ornamentation, and hair style are differentiated after three months. In church, baby girls were seen with caps or hats and earrings. The heads of boys are shaved; the hair of the girls is parted in squares over the head and the hair in each square braided. Frequently bright ribbons or string are tied to the braids.

Distinction in tasks performed was not noticeable until five or six, when the dress of the children shows that they are now in a semi-adult category. Then girls are set to helping the mother to cook, bearing responsibility for youngsters in the family, and marketing goods. The boys at this age begin to operate within the adult male circle of activities—farming, musicianship, cock fighting, housebuilding, charcoal making.

In sleeping arrangements boys and girls are separated after they leave the mother's side (about six months?), so that siblings of the same sex sleep together. This division seems to have more than an incest-prevention function since it is carried so far back into childhood. Still wider chasms separate the home environments of boy and girl at puberty, because the peasant family in the majority of cases keeps the girls home at night as a check on their sexual life, while the boys are out late courting or trying to. Thus the ideal is for the girl to be virginal, but cultural allowance is made for experimentation by the boy in maturing.

Control measures. Treatment of infants and children up to two years is indulgent. By that age they are walking and saying some words, and real discipline begins here. The father is the primary disciplinarian because of his position as head of the family, and much of the discipline is directed toward teaching children the father's role and that they must always obey him. A mother may have to go and get a child after she has called it, but he will always appear when the father calls, though he may move slowly enough to show he resents being disturbed.

One could say that almost any adult may discipline a child, although there is a definite ranking in terms of authority. The godfather (*paren*) is obeyed and respected almost on a par with the natural father. The same is true of the grandfather.

The measures used for discipline which were observed are: (1) scolding; (2) sharp tone of voice; (3) withholding of affectionate behavior; (4) force, in the sense of picking a child up, dragging it, and so on; (5) force, in the sense of the use of pain, such as switching. Only one case of the latter was seen. Back of the market place one Tuesday (market day) a boy of about five was noticed crying; a few seconds later his mother appeared with a switch she had pulled from a nearby tree. She grabbed the boy roughly and switched his bare legs and back about a half dozen times, scolding during and after the performance. An instance of spanking was heard one evening before dusk. A little four-year-old boy had been shooed from our premises by my cook and a few minutes later was given two spanks on his buttocks by one of the farm workers. The child ran home screaming and crying. A father was seen to go across the street one morning in Beaumont, pull his crying daughter of four or five away from her playmates and back to her home, set her in a chair, go into the house, and come out with a horsewhip which he handed her with a lecture. During the whole time his voice was raised, loud, and angry.

As indicated above, the use of stern measures seems confined to immediate parents; surrogates will slap, speak sharply, or just take the child away from the spot of misbehavior, or, if possible, remove the cause. Naturally, individual parents vary in the application of discipline. One mother asked her young son to let his younger brother have a ride on the horse which the elder was galloping up and down the path. As an answer, the rider whipped the horse off down the lane. The mother just shrugged her shoulders and went her way, leaving the younger boy to get his ride as best he could.

Rewards for good performance by a child were observed as follows: (1) tokens of affection, such as caressing head, face, arms, shoulders, back, or legs by rubbing and stroking; hugging; kissing; cuddling or cradling in lap or arms or both;[10] (2) verbal praise; (3) verbal thanks; (4) food, such as a sweet, a fruit, cassava cake, and so on.

The learning situation. There are several interesting points to be considered in the learning situation of the peasant child on the Beaumont plateau.

One which contrasts strongly with our own is the lack of painful pressure surrounding the toilet and sex areas of the training process. Due to the "realistic" handling of these two problems, the potential psychological stresses involved are almost eliminated as factors. This is interpreted as contributing to the friendliness and openness noticeable in the personality of the people studied, since the child does not develop aggression toward his social environment at this time but receives cooperation and understanding.

On the surface it might seem that feeding could be added to the above list, but although mothers tend to feed children when they desire it, there is not much quantity of food so that a large proportion of the youngsters are undernourished. It is suspected that nursing children fare a little better in this respect than their older brothers and sisters. This, plus the sudden change from indulgence to stern discipline at the walking stage, may be the important factors in the production of the low frustration threshold which characterizes these people. None of the indications of oral fixation was noted, with the exception of grass chewing by all ages and both sexes.

A more important aspect of conditioning is the radical variation in the social environment after a youngster has become intelligibly verbal and physically coordinated. The previous pattern, as outlined, was highly protective (stemming from the high infant mortality rate and the cultural pressure for large families), attentive, and coddling. The new one, on the other hand, is restrictive of the child's whims and desires, casual in attentive reaction, and rather oppressive where elders are involved. For it is at this time that the training for adult roles takes place and, presumably due to reasons of economics (both lack of adult time and a constant need for added labor) and of status (respect and obedience must be accorded all elders), this educational process is hurried along through the mechanism of strong discipline. Enforcement, moreover, is in the hands of volatile individuals. This means that the psychological atmosphere in which the child must learn is productive of insecurity and ambivalence in emotion.

Lastly, there is the structural aspect of the social environment of the child. Figures available on peasant families (Lachicotte Valley) show that they average five children per family, the range being from one (newly married couple) to thirteen. In addition, at least a third of the families are polygamous. Further, three of the six villages visited are what is known as *aglomerasiô de famiye* (Aux Pommes—part of Beaumont, Digotrie, and Guinée). This is the result of the sharing of the same area of land by several branches of the same family or several related families. In such communities one is struck by the African compound-like aspect they exhibit, the houses clustering around a central clearing. Still further, a set of godparents, with concomitant co-siblings, is added to the child's list of blood and affinal relatives. With all these facts in mind one can vision the continuity and density of social interaction affecting growing youngsters.

SUMMARY

It is assumed by workers in the field of culture and personality that child-training patterns correlate directly with the adult personality configuration and the institutional emphases of a given culture.[11] Therefore, in summary, we will briefly examine the validity of this assumption for Beaumont plateau.

Adult character structure in this culture has, as components, (1) extroversion (indicated by easy friendliness, openness, curiosity toward the novel, social initiative), (2) volatility, (3) relative aggressiveness, (4) relative individualism, and (5) relative insecurity. The possible role of non-painful toilet and sex training in contributing to elements of extroversion has been mentioned already. Other factors include the structure of the physical and social environments. In the case of the former, there are few dangers for the growing child. For example, houses are usually small, one-storied, with a minimum of furniture. An eating table, several rush-seated chairs of the straight-backed variety, water jug, a cabinet for the necessary eating equipment, and beds or mats comprise the average household articles. Lamps are hung or put out of reach of a child; mats and baskets are fairly easily replaced, so that a youngster moves in relative freedom about his or another home.

His social environment is extended, rewarding (in terms of food, affection, and novelty[12]), and consistently group-oriented in every phase of life. Agricultural activity is carried on mainly by groups; relaxation is gained in group dances, sings, and pageants (such as the Kombit revus and Easter Rara festival); marketing is communal; death involves kinship and local-group participation; even laundry is frequently done in a group. Security is so strongly a function of group activity that only a few instances of solitary activity were noted during the six weeks. One was by a man who had been drinking; another was the singing, as he worked alone, by a man who had been a laborer in Cuba for several years. He was not an average member of the community.

Individualism is noticeable, however, in the personality of the plateau peasant. It is especially so in two spheres—political and emotional. By political is not meant reference to the Haitian government, but a say in the affairs of the community. One evening, while passing the house of the local policeman of Beaumont, a group of persons was seen gathered around him in what seemed to be a heated debate. It was discovered that a man had been accused of killing four goats which had wandered onto his property. It is perfectly permissible to kill one or two which have done damage, but to kill four was to be wantonly destructive of the meat resources of the village. Some of the individuals gathered to participate in the "trial" were owners of the animals killed; others were just interested members of the town. Anyone going by could have stopped and added his opinion and argument to the informal proceedings. Several had. Such an occurrence has analogies in many areas of village life.

Emotionally, the individual is allowed considerable freedom of expression, which not only adds to his individuality but is basic to the norm of volatility or excitability. Perhaps a convenient generalization would be that these people are emotional. They laugh easily, cry easily (at least as children), are angered easily and so on. This seems to be related to the sharp change in the character of child care from indulgence to strict discipline, the latter administered by adults whose self-control is weak.

This same constellation is responsible for an amount of insecurity noted among the inhabitants of Beaumont plateau and gives rise to aggressiveness. The latter can be dissipated culturally through gossip, teasing and joking, black magic (via the bokor or vodù priest), cock fighting and verbosity. Mistreatment of wives and children is common, as might be expected.

From the foregoing, there is seen to be a direct relationship between the patterns of child training in this section of Haiti and the adult character structure which supports and is implemented by the institutional life of the communities mentioned. Children become adults who find congeniality in the group activity which makes possible a better economic existence. The same groupings provide the necessary entertainment and relaxation to offset hard work and in-group tensions growing out of individual aggressiveness and excitability. Babies are well enough treated to support the cultural pressure for many of them; older youngsters, under the impact of relatively harsh discipline and loss of permitted willfulness, develop the temperamentality and aggressiveness which are characteristic of adult personality.

From the facts of child training presented in this paper, there is a temptation to predict great sibling rivalry and the presence of the Oedipus complex. Unfortunately insufficient data were gathered to support such predictions. More information would probably yield clues, at least, to their existence.

FRANCES W. UNDERWOOD

CONCLUSIONS

The existence of a causal relationship between the child-training process of a society and the adult character structure exhibited by its members is an accepted axiom in the social sciences. Data from simple human aggregates, however, have frequently been declared to offer an especially fertile field for insight into the various operative factors involved, and it is with the hope of thus adding further information on these forces that the present authors have undertaken to conclude with a qualitative and comparative analysis of the material presented in the foregoing sections.

Psychoanalysis has placed particular emphasis on the role of infant years of experience in the production of the mature personality on the thesis that initial handling of basic drives forms the ultimate source for the direction of adult character. It is interesting, then, that the Kaska personality norm is introvert and the Haitian extrovert, although in both societies babies are fed when they so desire, receive no pressure to control elimination, are comforted and handled when irritable or playful, and suffer no discipline for emotional willfulness. The indication is that other criteria than those associated with physiological urges are important in personality structuring, and moreover, that these may lie in the childhood rather than infant experiences, at least for the two societies under discussion.

Goldfrank, in an important recent article,[13] has pointed out that the period beyond infancy may be the critical stage for molding adult character in some cases. On the basis of disciplinary policy, she sets up four categories: (1) societies where discipline is weak throughout infancy and childhood; (2) societies where it is severe throughout; (3) societies where it is severe in infancy and weak later; and (4) societies where infant discipline is weak and that of childhood is severe. Following her outline, the Indian group is seen to fall into class one, as lax discipline is continued into later years and the culture itself exhibits atomistic features of organization plus mild sanctions for non-normal behavior. The Negro communities of the Haitian plateau, on the other hand, fit into category four, since, after two years of permissive and indulgent treatment from its elders, a child is subject to increasingly stern and widespread discipline from these same persons. In other words, Kaska society offers continuity in this sphere, and Haitian peasant groups are characterized by discontinuity as between babyhood and childhood. It should be pointed out, however, that despite the fact that Kaska conditioning shows continuity in regard to the single feature of discipline, after infancy there is a demonstrable withdrawal of maternal warmth and affection which seems to have a qualitative effect upon the growing organism. Both societies, at the transition period between the helpless, unsocial, verbally uncommunicative baby and the coordinated, relatively socialized, talking child show a discontinuity in the affective relationship between the youngster and its parents plus/or surrogates, whether it be gradual withdrawal of overt emotionality or the imposition of rather harsh discipline. In either case, there appears to be a traumatic effect on the personality produced by the change itself (shown by temper tantrums among the Kaska and sullen malingering in Haiti). In addition, the new configuration is measured against an initial secure, pleasurable pattern of infancy, thus furthering its impact. We conclude, therefore, that a positive correlation exists here between the affective environment of an individual's formative years and his personality structure.

Within the total discipline picture, the mechanisms of reward and punishment may also offer further clues to character formation. Consistency in the agencies by which and the areas in which specific rewards and punishments are administered is thought to have quite different implications in personality development than lack of it. The Haitian peasant child entering the stage of sub-adult, but non-infant, is punished or rewarded according to the whims of the volatile elders of his family and community. He may be brutally spanked today when bawling because his mother had just quarreled with his father, or the same misdemeanor may be ignored tomorrow if his mother had made some extra money at the market. But the Kaska child can depend upon a minimum of discipline and a passively permissive parent. Thus, in Haitian plateau society, added to the discontinuity of discipline as a whole, inconsistency in dispensing punishments and rewards by adults with weak self-control is characteristic, while continuity of discipline policy and relative consistency in its mechanisms is an attribute of the Indian group.

Cultural bases for these opposite traits are readily observable. The Haitian pattern contributes to an ambivalence of feelings toward elders, which is exploited culturally to hurry the sub-adult into the period of maturity; the Kaska constellation permits the development of a self-reliant, independent individual who will maintain the atomistic social organization. This interaction may also be seen in the fact that the severe discipline of peasant society operates greatly as external pressure to take on cultural skills. At the same time the child loses the right of emotional spontaneity within the family, so that he is provided with an external drive to regain a volatile state (adulthood) where these crafts will be utilized. Conversely, among the Kaska, there is a low degree of outside compulsion to acquire customary aptitudes, while the child's independence is supported by emotional withdrawal on the part of his parents. Thus, he receives progressive impetus toward self-reliance over the years, and due to the lack of attention and direction by senior members in regard to traditional techniques, his learning is by a gradual process of imitation.

In summary, the data from Kaska and Beaumont plateau point up several possible elements in personality formation. Firstly, the total socialization process must be examined in attempting to understand the production of character type in any group. Secondly, we agree with Goldfrank and Benedict[14] that where this continuum shows discontinuity over its course or inconsistency in its application, these in themselves can be important factors in personality development. Further, the imposition of a changed affective pattern may have a traumatic effect upon the organism. As a corollary of this latter fact, it is felt that additional support is given the thesis of a human need for affection.[15] Still another inference to be drawn is that where a secondary period of disciplinary policy can be distinguished, its impact upon the personality of the individual is a function of the initial experiences of that individual.

Lastly, our examination of socialization in two simple societies shows that in addition to the handling of hunger, weaning, elimination, and sexuality, other diagnostics are to be looked for in explaining personality structuring. Those reaffirmed by analysis of Kaska and Haitian material are (1) affectional relationship, and (2) the nature of discipline and its administration.

NOTES

1. Kardiner, 1945, p. 102.
2. Underwood, Mss.
3. Honigmann, Mss.
4. Honigmann, Mss.
5. Levy, 1937, pp. 643-652.

6. Horney finds for the detached personality type "a need for *self-sufficiency*. Its most positive expression is resourcefulness. . . . It is the only way he can compensate for his isolation." Horney, 1945, p. 75.

7. The following villages were visited in the six-week's stay: Beaumont, Cassonette, Centre d'Avezac, Digotrie, Guinée, and Lachicotte Valley.

8. Funds for anthropological research in Haiti were supplied through a grant to the Department of Anthropology at Yale University from the Viking Fund, Inc.

9. Spelling of Créole words follows the official phonetic script adopted by the Haitian government.^ indicates nasalization of the vowel. All vowels and consonants indicated are pronounced, and with the usual French qualities.

10. Public display of affection is reserved for children only.

11. This correlation has been explored most thoroughly recently by Cora Du Bois, 1944.

12. This term subsumes play, attentive interaction of other individuals in the group with the child, and the varied experiences offered a youngster in a community. The word is used in recognition of a social need (possibly with a physiological basis) which has been well outlined by Linton, 1944, pp. 9-10.

13. Goldfrank, 1945.

14. Benedict, 1938.

15. Ribble, 1943, p. 4.

BIBLIOGRAPHY

Benedict, R., 1938
DuBois, 1944
Goldfrank, 1945-b.
Henry, J., 1940
Honigmann, J., 1949-a
Horney, 1945
Kardiner, 1945-a
Levy, D. M., 1936
Linton, 1945-a
Ribble, 1943
Underwood, F. W., Ms., *The Ethnography of Beaumont Plateau, Haiti.*

GENERAL BIBLIOGRAPHY

In an overcrowded university the library constitutes a major bottle-neck. When books are hard to come by, an ample list of references increases the chances that a student will find useful readings.

This is a Bibliography of cultural aspects of personality, plus a near-random selection of ethnographic field reports (usually indicated by an asterisk if general in character) from which the reader can glean something of the cultural patterns within which individuals adjust in various societies. Any anthropologist can add important titles. A generalized field report not directly oriented to the study of personal character still may enable one to visualize the conditions under which individuals face life in the society described.

Works on psychology, psychiatry, and psychoanalysis are omitted except for a baker's dozen of outstanding titles. The present interest is anthropological; specialists in the psychological sciences can recommend ample bibliographies in their own fields. Omission of an important title from this Bibliography carries no invidious implications. Some items that have been left out because of their advanced character will be discovered by any student who builds himself a sound foundation of reading. Those who do not intend to go deeply into the field will not miss the omitted items. A re-reading of the page at the beginning of Part II, headed "The Use of Ethnographic Reports on Cultural Behavior in Different Societies," is suggested.

Since this entire compilation is directed to the problem of readings for students handicapped by overtaxed libraries, reference generally is made to the inclusion of important papers in books of readings or symposia that might be accessible when an original journal could not be obtained.

The bibliographies originally appearing at the end of articles reprinted in this book have been incorporated in the following list, and in the text are replaced by abbreviated citations of author and date. The items herewith incorporated from such sources, however, have not been verified, and are printed as cited by the authors who originally referred to them.

GENERAL BIBLIOGRAPHY

Revised June, 1956

Journals and Serial Publications
With Abbreviations

Note: The following arrangement of abbreviations and titles does not conform strictly to alphabetical principles. For example: Journals whose title begins with the world *American* appear before entries such as *Africa* in order to use the letter *A* as an efficient abbreviation. Similarly, items whose abbreviation contains a lower case letter usually appear after the items denoted by the same capital letter, e.g.:

JPY	*The Journal of Psychology*	precedes
JPol	*Journal of the Polynesian Society*	

In some cases, to avoid clumsy abbreviations, a *Journal* is entered under the name of the organization publishing it, thus:

RAI *Royal Anthropological Institute, Journal*

It is hoped that this compromise with strict alphabetical principles may be efficient in practice. Dates indicate first appearance of a series.

A *Anthropos.* Vienna. 1906—

AA *American Anthropologist.* American Anthropological Association. Menasha, Wis. 1888—

AAAS Amer. Assn. for Advancement of Science.

AAM Amer. Anthropological Assn., *Memoirs.*

AAN *American Antiquity.* Menasha, Wis. 1935—

AASPS *Annals,* American Academy of Social & Political Science. Phila. 1890—

AEM American Ethnological Society, N. Y., *Monographs.* 1940—

AEP ———*Publications,* 1907—

AFLM American Folklore Society, *Memoirs.* Phila., 1894— Cf., also JAF.

AGO American Geographical Society, New York. *Oriental Explorations and Studies, 1-6.* 1926-28.

AGSp ———*Special Publications.* 1915—

AI *American Imago.* South Dennis, Mass. 1939—

AIn *America Indigena.* Mexico, D. F. 1941—

AJO *American Journal of Orthopsychiatry.* American Orthopsychiatric Association. New York. 1930—

AJP *American Journal of Psychiatry.* American Psychiatric Association, N. Y. 1844—

AJPA *American Journal of Physical Anthropology.* American Assn. of Physical Anthropologists. Philadelphia. 1918—

AJPy   *American Journal of Psychology*. Ithaca, N. Y. 1887–

AJS   *American Journal of Sociology*. Chicago. 1894–

American Museum of Natural History, New York:

AMA   ———*Anthropological Papers*.

AMB   ———*Bulletin*.

AMH   ———*Handbook Series*.

AMJ   ———*Publications*. Jesup North Pacific Expedition (Leiden).

AMM   ———*Memoirs*.

ANP   American Neurological Association. *Proceedings*. New York.

AOR   American Orthopsychiatric Association. *Research Monographs*. New York.

American Philosophical Society. Philadelphia:

APSM   ———*Memoirs*. 1935–

APSP   ———*Proceedings*. 1838–. n. s. from 1939–

APST   ———*Transactions*. 1769-1801. n.s. from 1818–

APSR   *American Political Science Review*. Washington. 1906–

AS   *The American Scholar*. New York. 1932–

ASC   *American Scientist*. Society of the Sigma Xi. New Haven. 1913–

ASL   *American Slavic and East European Review*. Cambridge, Mass. 1941–

American Sociological Society: (see also So)

ASP   ———*Publications*. Chicago.

ASR   ———*American Sociological Review*. Menasha. 1936–

AcA   *Acta Americana*. Inter-American Society of Anthropology and Geography, Los Angeles. 1943–

Af   *Africa*. London. 1928–

AnPC   *Anthropological Papers, University of Calcutta*. Calcutta. 1920-21; n.s., 1927–

An Q   *Anthropological Quarterly* (formerly *Primitive Man*). Catholic University of America Press. Washington. 1927–

AnR   *Anthropological Records*. Univ. of Calif. Press, Berkeley. 1937–

Applied Anthropology: see *Human Organization*.

ArA   *Archiv für Anthropologie*. Braunschweig. 1866–

ArB   *The Art Bulletin*. College Art Assn. of America, New York. 1913–

As   *Asia*, later called *Asia and the Americas*. New York. 1898–1946.

AsJ   *Asiatic Society of Japan: Transactions*. Tokyo.
      O. S.: 1872-1922, vols. 1-50
      2nd ser.: 1924-1940, vols. 1-19.
      3rd ser.: 1949– vol. 1–

AsR   *Association for Research in Nervous and Mental Disease, Research Publications*. New York. 1920–

BMB   Bernice P. Bishop Museum, *Bulletins*. Honolulu. 1922–

BMM   ———*Memoirs*, 1899–

BMS   ———Special *Publications*. 1903–

BMP   *British Journal of Medical Psychology*. Cambridge, Eng. 1921–

BRJP   *British Journal of Psychology*. London. 1904–

BRJS   *British Journal of Sociology*. London. 1950–

BlHM   *Bulletin of the History of Medicine*. Baltimore. 1933–

Bureau of American Ethnology, Smithsonian Institution. Washington, D. C.:

BuER   ———*Annual Reports*. 1879-80 (Publ. 1881)–.

BuEB   ———*Bulletins*. 1887–

CA   *Carnegie Institution, Publications*. Washington. 1902–

Catholic University of America:

CAC   *Catholic Anthropological Congress, Publications.* Washington. 1929–

CAS   *Anthropological Series.* Washington, D. C. 1930–

Chicago: *Natural History Museum,* see under FM:*Fieldiana.*

CP   *Character and Personality.* Title changed to *Journal of Personality.*

CUCA   *Columbia University Contributions to Anthropology.* New York. 1910–

CoPM   *Comparative Psychology Monographs* (supersedes *Behavior Monographs*). Baltimore. 1922–

CoSPR   *Symposia, Conference on Science, Philosophy, and Religion in Their Relation to the Democratic Way of Life.* Garden City, N. Y. 1940–

ConNAE *Contributions to North American Ethnology.* U. S. Geographical and Geological Survey of the Rocky Mt. Region. Washington. 1877-1893.

DM   *Dominion Museum: Monographs.* Wellington, N. Z. 1922-1924.

DMB   *––––Bulletin.* Wellington, N. Z. 1905-1929.

DMR   *––––Records in Ethnology.* do. 1946–

E   *Ethnos.* Stockholm. 1936–

EA   *Eastern Anthropologist.* Ethnographic & Folk Culture Society. Lucknow Univ. 1947–

ESS   *Encyclopedia of the Social Sciences.* N. Y. 1930-1935.

ETC   *ETC.,* a Review of General Semantics. N. Y. 1954–

ETH   *Ethics: An International Journal of Social, Political, and Legal Philosophy.* Chicago. 1890–

EX   *Explorations.* University of Toronto.

FEQ   *Far Eastern Quarterly.* Far Eastern Association. Ann Arbor. 1941–

FES   *Far Eastern Survey.* Fortnightly. Amer. Institute of Pacific Relations. N. Y. 1932–

FM   *Fieldiana: Anthropology* (formerly *Anthropological Series, Field Museum of Natural History*), Chicago Natural History Museum. 1895–

FO   *Folklore.* London. 1878–

FoA   *Foreign Affairs.* N. Y. 1922–

GA   *General Series in Anthropology.* Menasha, Wis. 1935–

GPM   *Genetic Psychology Monographs.* Provincetown, Mass. 1926–

GR   *Geographical Review.* American Geographical Society, New York. 1916–

HAA   *Harvard African Studies.* Cambridge, Mass. 1917–

HAE   *Harvard Educational Review.* Cambridge, Mass. 1931–

HAT   *Harvard Theological Review.* Cambridge, Mass. 1908–

HB   *Human Biology.* Baltimore. 1929–

HO   *Human Organization* (formerly *Applied Anthropology*). Society for Applied Anthropology. New York. 1941–

HR   *Human Relations.* London. 1947–

I   *Imago.* Leipzig; Vienna. 1912-1937.

ICA   International Congress of Americanists. *Proceedings.* (Biennially, or less frequently.) 1875–

IJAL   *International Journal of American Linguistics.* New York. 1917–

IJOAR   *International Journal of Opinion and Attitude Research.* Mexico. 1947-1951.

IJP   *International Journal of Psycho-Analysis.* London. 1920–

IPR   Institute of Pacific Relations, N. Y. *Publications.*

JASL   *Japan Society of London, Proceedings.* London. 1892–

JAF   *Journal of American Folklore.* American Folklore Society. Menasha, Wis. 1888–

JASP   *Journal of Abnormal and Social Psychology.* Washington, D. C. 1906–

JAmDA *Journal of the American Dietetic Association.* Chicago. 1935–

JAmO   *Journal of the American Oriental Society.* New Haven. 1843–

JAmP   *Journal of the American Psychoanalytic Association,* N. Y. Jan. 1953–

JAp   *Journal of Applied Psychology.* American Psychological Assn. Washington, D. C. 1917–

JCE   *Journal of Clinical Endocrinology.* London. 1939–

JCP   *Journal of Clinical Psychopathology.* (Since 1950, called *Journal of Clinical and Experimental Psychopathology.*) N. Y. 1939–

JCoP   *Journal of Comparative Psychology.* (Since 1946, entitled *Journal of Comparative and Physiological Psychology.*) Washington. 1921–

JES   *Journal of Educational Sociology.* New York. 1927–

JEZ   *Journal of Experimental Zoology.* Baltimore. 1904–

JGE   *The Journal of General Education.* Chicago. 1946–

JGP   *Journal of General Psychology.* Worcester & Provincetown, Mass. 1927–

JGeP   *Journal of Genetic Psychology* (formerly *Pedagogical Seminary and Journal of Genetic Psychology*). Worcester, Mass. 1891–

JMS   *Journal of Mental Science.* London. 1855–

JNMD   *Journal of Nervous and Mental Disease.* Chicago. 1874–

JP   *Journal of Personality* (formerly *Character and Personality*). Durham, N. C. 1932–

JPD   *Journal of Pediatrics.* St. Louis. 1932–

JPH   *Journal of Philosophy* (formerly *Journal of Philosophy, Psychology, and Scientific Method*), New York. 1904–

JPPSM *Journal of Philosophy, Psychology, and Scientific Method.* (Title changed in 1920 to *Journal of Philosophy.*) New York. 1904-1920.

JPS   *Journal of Politics.* Gainesville, Fla. 1939–

JPT   *Journal of Projective Techniques* (formerly *Rorschach Research Exchange,* etc. Cf. under R). New York. 1936–

JPY   *The Journal of Psychology.* Provincetown, Mass. 1936–

JPol   *Journal of the Polynesian Society* (c/o Alexander Turnbull Library, Wellington C-1, N. Z.). Wellington, N. Z. 1892–

JSI   *Journal of Social Issues.* New York. 1945–

JSP   *Journal of Social Psychology,* Provincetown, Mass. 1929–

JSPh   *Journal of Social Philosophy and Jurisprudence.* New York. 1935-1941–

JSpP   *Journal of Speculative Philosophy.* St. Louis, Mo. 1867-1893.

L   *Language, Journal of the Linguistic Society of America.* Baltimore. 1924–

M   *Man.* Royal Anthropological Institute. London. 1901–

MA   *Mankind.* Anthropological Society of New South Wales. Sidney. 1931–

MFL   *Marriage and Family Living.* Chicago. 1939–

MH   *Mental Hygiene.* National Committee for Mental Hygiene. New York. 1917–

MI   *Man in India.* Quarterly. Ranchi. 1921–

MIA   *Michigan Academy of Science, Arts, and Letters: Papers.* New York. 1921–

MPol   *Memoirs, The Polynesian Society.* Wellington, N. Z. 1910-1934. (Continued as signatures in JPol.)

N   *Nature*. London. 1869–

NAS   National Academy of Science: *Proceedings*. Washington. 1915–

NC   *The Nervous Child*. Baltimore. 1941–

NMDM   *Nervous and Mental Disease Monograph Series*. New York. 1908–

NUS   *Northwestern University, Studies in the Social Sciences*. Evanston, Ill. 1936–

New York Academy of Sciences, New York:

NYA   –––*Annals*. 1877–

NYT   –––*Transactions*. 1881–

NYM   New York State Museum. *Bulletin*. Albany. 1887–

Australian National Research Council. Melbourne:

O   –––*Oceania*. 1930–

OM   –––*Oceania Monographs*. Melbourne & London. 1931–

PA   *Pacific Affairs*. International Institute of Pacific Relations, Quarterly. New York. 1926–

PACS   *Proceedings, Pacific Science Congress*. (Formerly Pan-Pacific Science Congress.) Various places and dates.

PHS   *Philosophy of Science*. Philosophy of Science Assn. Baltimore. 1934–

PHa   *Papers of the Peabody Museum of American Archaeology and Ethnology, Harvard University*. Cambridge, Mass. 1888–

PLA   *Polynesian Anthropological Studies*. Wellington, N. Z.

PM   *Primitive Man*. Catholic Anthropological Conference. (Changed to *Anthropological Quarterly*. 1954. AnQ.) Washington, D. C. 1928–

POLQ   *Political Science Quarterly*. Boston & N. Y. 1886–

PS   *Psychiatry: Journal for the Study of Interpersonal Relations*. Washington, D. C. (Sub-title has varied.) 1938–

PSQ   *Psychiatric .Quarterly*. Utica, N. Y. 1927–

PSS   *Psychoanalysis and the Social Sciences*. Annual. New York. 1947–

PSY   *Psyche: Eine Zeitschrift für Tiefenpsychologie u. Menschenkunde in Forschung u. Praxis*. Stuttgart. 1948–

PYQ   *Psychoanalytic Quarterly*. Albany, N. Y. 1932–

PYR   *Psychoanalytic Review*. New York. 1913–

PaC   *The Psychoanalytic Study of the Child*. Annual. New York. 1945–

PsB   *Psychological Bulletin*. American Psychological Association. Evanston, Ill. 1904–

PsM   *Psychological Monographs*. American Psychological Association. Evanston, Ill. 1895–

PsR   *Psychological Review*. American Psychological Association. Washington, D. C. 1894–

PsRe   *Psychological Record*. Bloomington, Ind. 1937–

Psm   *Psychosomatic Medicine*. American Society for Research in Psychosomatic Problems. New York. 1939–

PuQ   *Public Opinion Quarterly*. Princeton. 1927–

QJS   *Quarterly Journal of Speech*. Speech Assn. of America. Columbia, Missouri. 1914–

QJSA   *Quarterly Journal of Studies on Alcohol*. New Haven. 1940–

R   *Rorschach Research Exchange and Journal of Projective Techniques*. New York. 1936–
         (Prior to 1947, title was *Rorschach Research Exchange;* since 1949, title is *Journal of Projective Techniques*.)

RAI   *Royal Anthropological Institute of Great Britain and Ireland: Journal.* London. 1875–

RAIO   *——Occasional Papers.*

RS   *Rural Sociology.* Lexington, Ky. 1936–

S   *Science.* American Assn. for Advancement of Science. Washington, D. C. 1883–

SCAm   *The Scientific American.* New form with vol. 178 (1948). New York. 1845–

SCM   *Scientific Monthly.* Lancaster, Pa. American Assn. for Adv. of Science, Washington, D. C. 1915–

Smithsonian Institution, Washington, D. C.:

SIAR   *——Annual Report of the Board of Regents.*

SIO   *——Occasional Papers.*

SIC   *——Contributions to Knowledge.*

SIM   *——Miscellaneous Collection.*

SIP   *——Publications. Institute of Social Anthropology.*

SIWB   *——War Background Series.*

SLF   *Social Forces.* Baltimore. 1922–

Social Science Research Council. New York:

SRCB   *——Bulletins.* 1930–

SRCP   *——Pamphlets.*

SRCD   *Society for Research in Child Development: Monographs.* Washington, D. C. 1935–

SSR   *Sociology and Social Research.* Los Angeles. 1916–

Sl   *Sociologus,* n.s. Berlin. 1951–

So   *Sociometry.* Amer. Sociological Soc., New York. 1937–

SwA   *Southwestern Journal of Anthropology.* Albuquerque. 1945–

UC   *Understanding the Child: A Magazine for Teachers.* New York. 1931–

USNM   United States National Museum. *Reports.* Washington.

USNMP   *——Proceedings.*

UnCa   *University of California Publications in American Archaeology and Ethnology.* Berkeley. 1903–

UnCaCS *University of California Publications in Culture and Society.* Berkeley & Los Angeles. 1945–

University of Chicago. Chicago.

UnCh   *——Publications in Anthropology, Ethnological Series.*

UnCh   *——Publications in Social Anthropology.*

UnChE   *——Supplementary Educational Monographs.* Chicago.

UnM   *University of Minnesota Studies in the Social Sciences.* Minneapolis. 1913-1929.

UnMi   Univ. of Michigan Center for Japanese Studies. *Occasional Papers.* 1951–

UnNM   University of New Mexico. *Bulletin, Anthropological Series.* Albuquerque. 1930–

UnW   *University of Washington Publications in Anthropology.* Seattle. 1920–

V   *Viking Fund Publications in Anthropology.* New York. 1943–

WASJ   *Washington Academy of Science, Journal.* Washington, D. C. 1911–

WHO   *World Health Organization,* Monographs and other publications. Geneva.

WP   *World Politics.* New Haven. 1948–

WS   *Woods Schools, Child Research Clinic and Conferences: Proceedings,* etc. Langhorne, Pa. 1934–

YAS   *Yale Anthropological Studies*. New Haven. v.d.

YPA   Yale University. *Publications in Anthropology*. New Haven. 1936–

YR   *The Yale Review*. New Haven. 1892–

YbA   *Yearbook of Anthropology*. Wenner-Gren Foundation for Anthropological Research, Inc. New York. 1955–

YbP   *Yearbook of Psychoanalysis*. Ed. by Sandor Lorand. New York. 1945–

Articles, Books and Monographs

Abegg, Lily
1952. *The Mind of East Asia.* London.

Abel, Theodora M.
1948. The Rorschach Test in the Study of Culture, R *12* #2:79-93.

Abel, Theodora M., and F. L. K. Hsu
1949. Some Aspects of Personality of Chinese as Revealed by the Rorschach Test, R *13*:285-301.

Aberle, David Friend
1951. Psychosocial analysis of a Hopi life history, CoPM *21*:1-133.
1952. "Arctic Hysteria" and Latah in Mongolia. NYT *14:* 291-297.

Aberle, David F., A. Cohen, A. Davis, M. Levy, and F. Sutton
1950. The Functional Prerequisites of a Society, ETH *60*:100-111.

Abt, Lawrence E., and Leopold Bellak
1950. *Projective Psychology.* New York.

Ackerknecht, Erwin H.
1943. Psychopathology, Primitive Medicine and Primitive Culture. BlHM *14:* 30-67.
1945. On the Collection of Data Concerning Primitive Medicine, AA *47*:427-432.

Adams, Inez
1949. An Asiatic Subsistence Pattern. EA *2*:182-185.

Adorno, T. W., E. Frenkel-Brunswik, D. J. Levinson, and R. N. Sanford
1950. *The Authoritarian Personality.* New York.

Aginsky, Burt W.
1939. Psychopathic Trends in Culture, CP *7:*331-343.
1940-a. The Socio-psychological Significance of Death Among the Pomo Indians, AI *1*:1-11. (Cf. also G. B. Wilbur, 1940.)
1940-b. An Indian's Soliloquy, AJS *46* #1.

Aginsky, Burt W., and Ethel G. Aginsky
1947. A Resultant of Intercultural Relations, SLF *26*:84-87.

Aginsky, Burt W., and Peter H. Buck
1940. Interacting Forces in the Maori Family, AA *42*:195-210.

Aitken, Barbara
1930. Temperament in Native American Religion, RAI *60*:363-387.

Akhilananda, Swami
1946. *Hindu Psychology: Its Meaning for the West.* New York.

Aldrich, C. Anderson
1945. Applying What We Know, *Jnl. Amer. Assn. Univ. Women, 38* #2.

Alexander, Franz
1931. Buddhistic Training as an Artificial Catatonia, PYR *18*:129-145.
1937. Psychoanalysis and Social Disorganization, AJS *42*:781-813.
1942-a. Educative Influence of Personality Factors in the Environment, UnChE *54*:29-47. (Reprinted in Kluckhohn, Murray, and Schneider, 1953.)
1942-b. *Our Age of Unreason.* Philadelphia.
1950. *Psychosomatic Medicine: Its Principles and Applications.* New York.

*The asterisk identifies well-known ethnographic reports.

ALEXANDER, H. G.
  1936. Linguistic Morphology in Relation to Thinking. JPPSM *33*:261-269.
ALLPORT, FLOYD H.
  1934. The J-Curve Hypothesis of Conforming Behavior, JSP *5*:141-183. (Reprinted in Newcomb, Hartley et al, *Readings in Social Psychology:* 55-67.)
  1939. Rule and Custom as Individual Variations of Behavior Distributed upon a Continuum of Conformity, AJS *44*:897-921.
  1955. *Theories of Perception and the Concept of Structure.* New York.
ALLPORT, GORDON W.
  1937. *Personality.* New York.
  n.d. *The ABC's of Scapegoating.* Pamphlet. Central Y. M. C. A. College, Chicago.
ALLPORT, GORDON W., J. S. BRUNER, AND E. M. JANDORF
  1941. Personality under Social Catastrophe: Ninety Life-Histories of the Nazi Revolution, CP *10*:1-22. (Reprinted in Kluckhohn, Murray & Schneider, 1953.)
ANESAKI MASAHARU
  1916. *Nichiren, the Buddhist Prophet.* Cambridge, Mass.
Applied Anthropology
  1955. Unsigned editorial, HO *14:* #2:2-3.
ARENSBERG, CONRAD M.
  1937. **The Irish Countryman.* New York.
ARENSBERG, C. M. et al
  1953. *Techniques and Cultures.* For. Service Inst., Dept. of State. Washington.
ARENSBERG, C. M., AND S. T. KIMBALL
  1940. **Family and Community in Ireland.* Cambridge, Mass.
AREY, LESLIE BRAINERD
  1940. *Developmental Anatomy, a Textbook and Laboratory Manual of Embryology.* 4th ed., rev. Philadelphia.
ARIETI, SILVANO
  1956. Some Basic Problems Common to Anthropology and Modern Psychiatry. AA *58*:26-39.
ARIGA KIZAEMON
  1954. The Family in Japan, MFL *16*:362-368.
ARSENIAN, JOHN, AND JEAN M. ARSENIAN
  1948. Tough and Easy Cultures, PS *11*:377-385.
ASTROV, MARGOT
  1946. *The Winged Serpent.* New York.
  1950. The Concept of Motion as the Psychological Leitmotif of Navaho Life and Literature, JAF *63*:45-56.
BABCOCK, CHARLOTTE G.
  1947. Psychologically Significant Factors in the Nutrition Interview, JAmDA *23*:8-12.
  1948. Food and its Emotional Significance, JAmDA *24*:390-393.
BAILEY, FLORA L.
  1942. Navaho Motor Habits, AA *44*:210-234.
BAKWIN, H.
  1944. Psychogenic Fever in Infants, *Am. J. Dis. Child,* 67:176-181.
BALES, ROBERT F.
  1946. Cultural differences in rates of alcoholism, QJSA *6*:480-493.
BARBER, B.
  1941. Acculturation and Messianic Movements, ASR *6*:663-669.
BARNARD, ANN
  1943. Patterns of Masculine Protest among the Buka. CP *11*:302-311.

BARNETT, H. G.
  1941. Personal Conflicts and Cultural Change, SLF *20*:171.
BARNETT, J. H.
  1933. Personality in Primitive Society, CP *2*:152-167.
BARNOUW, VICTOR
  1949. The Phantasy World of a Chippewa Woman, PS *12*:67-76.
  1950. *Acculturation and Personality among the Wisconsin Chippewa.* AAM *72.*
  1955. A Psychological Interpretation of a Chippewa Origin Legend, JAF *68*:73-85; 211-223; 341-355.
BARTLETT, F. C.
  1923. *Psychology and Primitive Culture.* Cambridge.
  1932. *Remembering.* Cambridge.
    (Excerpt reprinted in Newcomb, Hartley et al, *Readings in Social Psychology:* 69-76.)
  1937. Psychological Methods and Anthropological Problems, Af *10*:401-419.
BARTLETT, H. H.
  1928. Color Nomenclature in Batak and Malay. MIA *10:* 1-52.
BARTON, ROY F.
  1919. *Ifugao Law. UnCa *15.*
  1938. *Philippine Pagans, the Autobiographies of Three Ifugaos.* London.
  1947. **The Religion of the Ifugaos.* AAM *65.*
  1949. **The Kalingas.* UnCh.
BASCOM, WILLIAM R.
  1953. Folklore and Anthropology, JAF *66*:283-290.
  1954. Four Functions of Folklore, JAF *67*:333-349.
BASTIDE, R.
  1952. Field Methods and Problems of the Basic Personality School, BRJS *3*:1-13.
BATESON, GREGORY
  1932. The Social Structure of the Iatmul People, OM *IV.*
  1935. Culture Contact and Schismogenesis, M *35* #199:178-183.
  1936. **Naven: A Survey of the Problems Suggested by a Composite Picture of the Culture of a New Guinea Tribe Drawn from Three Points of View,* Cambridge, Eng. (See also Wolff, K. H.)
  1941. The Frustration-Aggression Hypothesis and Culture, PsR *48*:350-355. (Reprinted in Newcomb, Hartley et al, *Readings in Social Psychology,* 267-268.)
  1942-a. Morale and National Character, *In Civilian Morale,* Goodwin Watson, ed.:74-89. Boston. 2nd Yearbook, Soc. for the Psych'l Study of Soc. Issues.
  1942-b. Some Systematic Approaches to the Study of Culture and Personality, CP *11*:76-84. (Reproduced herewith.)
  1942-c. Social Planning and the Concept of "Deutero-Learning," CoSPR *2*:81-97. (Reprinted in Newcomb, Hartley et al, *Readings in Social Psychology:* 121-128.)
  1943. Cultural and Thematic Analysis of Fictional Films, NYT *ll-5*:72-78. (Reproduced herewith.)
  1944. Cultural Determinants of Personality, In J. M. Hunt, ed., *Personality and the Behavior Disorders, ll*:714-735. New York.
  1946-a. Physical Thinking and Social Problems, S *103*:717-718.
  1946-b. The Pattern of an Armaments Race, *Bulletin of the Atomic Scientists 2*:1-11, 26-28.
  1947. Sex and Culture, NYA *47,* Art. 5:647-660. (Reproduced herewith.)
  1949-a. Bali: the Value System of a Steady State, In M. Fortes, ed., *Studies in Social Structure . . .* London.
  1949-b. See under Ruesch, J.; also Ruesch & Bateson, 1951.
  1951-53. *Character Formation in Different Cultures.* Six films. N. Y. Univ. Film Library, N. Y.

1953. The Position of Humor in Human Communication. In *Cybernetics*. . . . (Trans. 9th Conf.) Macy Foundation, N. Y. Pp. 1-47.

BATESON, GREGORY, AND MARGARET MEAD
1942. *Balinese Character: A Photographic Analysis*. New York.

BATESON, GREGORY, J. RUESCH, AND W. KEES
n.d. *Communication and Interaction in Three Families*. Kinesis Films, San Francisco.

BAUER, RAYMOND A.
1952. *The New Man in Soviet Psychology*. Cambridge, Mass.
1954. The Psycho-cultural Approach to Soviet Studies, WP 7:118-132. (Review of Mead, 1951-b and Tomasic, 1953.)

BAUR, JULIUS
1945. *Constitution and Disease: Applied Constitutional Pathology*, 2nd ed. New York.

BAXTER, SYLVESTER
1882. The Fathers of the Pueblos, *Harpers 65*.

BEADLE, GEORGE M.
1948. Genes and Biological Enigmas, ASC *36*:69-74.

BEAGLEHOLE, ERNEST
1937-a. *Notes on Hopi Economic Life*. YPA *15*.
1937-b. Emotional Release in a Polynesian Community, JASP *32*:319-328.
1939-a. Culture and Psychosis in Hawaii. *Some Modern Hawaiians*, Univ. of Hawaii Research Publ. #*19*:156-171.
1939-b. Culture and Psychosis in New Zealand, JPol *48*:144-155.
1939-c. Psychic Stress in a Tongan Village. PACS *VI* vol. 4:43-52.
1940. Cultural Complexity and Psychological Problems, PS *3*:329-339.
1944-a. Character Structure, its Role in the Analysis of Interpersonal Relations, PS 7:145-162.
1944-b. **Islands of Danger*. Wellington, N. Z.

BEAGLEHOLE, ERNEST AND PEARL BEAGLEHOLE
1935. *Hopi of the Second Mesa*. AAM *44*.
1938. **Ethnology of Pukapuka*. BMB *150*.
1941. Personality Development in Pukapukan Children, *In Language, Culture and Personality, Essays in Memory of Edward Sapir*, ed. by Leslie Spier et. al. Pp. 282-298. Menasha.
1946. *Some Modern Maoris*. Wellington, N. Z.

BEALS, RALPH L.
1946. **Cherán: A Sierra Tarascan Village*. SIP *2*.

BECK, SAMUEL J.
1944. *Rorschach's Test: I. Basic Processes*. New York.
1945. *Rorschach's Test: II. A Variety of Personality Pictures*. New York.

BELO, JANE
1935. The Balinese Temper, CP *4*:120-146. (Reproduced herewith.)
1936. A Study of a Balinese Family, AA *38*:12-31.
1949. *Bali: Rangda and Barong*. AEM *16*.
1953. *Bali: Temple Festival*. AEM *22*.

BENEDICT, PAUL K., AND IRVING JACKS
1954. Mental Illness in Primitive Societies. PS *17*:377-390.

BENEDICT, RUTH FULTON
1922. The Vision in Plains Culture, AA *24*:1-23.
1923. *The Concept of the Guardian Spirit in North America*. AAM *29*.
1928. Psychological Types in the Cultures of the Southwest, ICA *23*:572-581. (Reprinted in Newcomb, Hartley, et al, *Readings in Social Psychology*: 14-23.)
1932. Configurations of Culture in North America, AA *34*:1-27.

1934-a. Anthropology and the Abnormal, JGP *10:59-80*. (Reprinted herewith.)

1934-b. *Patterns of Culture*. Boston. (Penguin Books, 1946.)

1935. *Zuni Mythology*. 2 vol. CUCA *21*.

1938. Continuities and Discontinuities in Cultural Conditioning, PS *1:161-167*. (Reprinted, Kluckhohn, Murray & Schneider, 1953.)

1939. A Reply to Dr. Aginsky, CP 7:344-345.

1940. Discussion of J. Henry, Some Cultural Determinants of Hostility in Pilagá Indian Children, AJO *10:*120-122.

1946-a. The Study of Cultural Patterns in European Nations, NYT II, *8 #8:* 274-279.

1946-b. *The Chrysanthemum and the Sword*. Boston.

1949. Child-rearing in certain European Countries, AJO *19:342-350*. (Cf. obituary by M. Mead, AA *51:457-468*.)

BENET, SULA

1951. *Song, Dance and Customs of Peasant Poland*. N. Y.

BENNETT, JOHN W.

1946. The Interpretation of Pueblo Culture: A Question of Values, SwA *2:361-* 374. (Reprinted herewith.)

1948. The Study of Cultures: A Survey of Techniques and Methodology in Field Work. ASR *13:672-687*.

BENNETT, JOHN W., AND IWAO ISHINO

1955. Futomi: A Case Study of the Socio-Economic Adjustments of a Marginal Community in Japan, RS *20:41-50*.

BENNETT, JOHN W. AND MICHIO NAGAI

1953. The Japanese Critique of the Methodology of Benedict's *Chrysanthemum and the Sword*. AA *55:404-410*.

BENNETT, WENDELL C., AND R. M. ZINGG

1935. *The Tarahumara*. Chicago.

BERGER, MORROE

1951. Understanding "National Character"—and War. *Commentary 11 #4:375-* 386.

BERGLER, EDMUND

1948. *The Battle of the Conscience*. Washington, D. C.

BERNARD, JESSIE

1945. Observation and Generalization in Cultural Anthropology, AJS *50 #4*.

BERNDT, RONALD M.

1953. A Day in the Life of a Dieri Man before Alien Contact, A *48:171-201*.

BERNDT, RONALD M. AND CATHERINE H. BERNDT

1951-a. *Sexual Behavior in Western Arnhem Land*. V *16*.

1951-b. The Concept of Abnormality in an Australian Aboriginal Society, In Wilbur & Muensterberger, 1951.

BEST, ELSDON

1923. The Maori School of Learning, Its Objects, Methods and Ceremonial, DM *6:3-29*.

1924. *The Maori*. 2 vols. Wellington, N. Z.

BETTELHEIM, BRUNO

1954. *Symbolic Wounds: Puberty Rites and the Envious Male*. Glencoe, Ill.

BETTELHEIM, BRUNO, AND EMMY SYLVESTER

1950. Notes on the impact of parental occupations: some cultural determinants of symptom choice in emotionally disturbed children, AJO *20:785-795*.

BICKERTON, MAX

1932. Issa's Life and Poetry, AsJ 2nd. ser., *9:111-154*.

BIDNEY, DAVID

1944. On the Concept of Culture and Some Cultural Fallacies, AA *46:30-44*.

1947-a. Human Nature and the Cultural Process, AA *49:375-399*.

1947-b. Human Nature and Culture, CoSPR 7:179-196.
1953. *Theoretical Anthropology*. New York.

BIENENSTOCK, THEODORE
1950. Social Life and Authority in the Eastern European *Shtetl* Community, SwA 6:238-254.
1951. Antiauthoritarian Attitudes in the Eastern European.*Shtetl* Community, AJS 57:150-158.

BILLIG, OTTO, JOHN GILLIN, & WM. DAVIDSON
1947-1948. Aspects of Personality and Culture in a Guatemalan Community: Ethnological and Rorschach Approaches. JP 16:153-187; 326-368.

BIRDWHISTELL, RAY L.
1952. Body Motion Research and Interviewing. HO 11 #1:37-38.
1954. Kinesics and Communication. EX No. 3:31-41.
(In Press) *An Introduction to Kinesics*. Louisville.

BLACKWOOD, BEATRICE
1935. *Both Sides of Buka Passage*. Oxford.

BLUEMEL, C. S.
1950. *War, Politics, and Insanity*. Denver. Rev. ed.

BOAS, FRANZ
1884-5. *The Central Eskimo*. BuER 6.
1897. *Social Organization and Secret Societies of the Kwakiutl Indians, USNM 1895:311-738.
1910. Psychological Problems in Anthropology, AJPy 21:371-384.
1911. *The Mind of Primitive Man*. New York.
1921. *Ethnology of the Kwakiutl*. BuER 35. 2 vols.
1925. *Contributions to the Ethnology of the Kwakiutl*. CUCA 3.
1927. *Primitive Art*. Oslo.
1930-a. Anthropology, ESS 2:73-110.
1930-b. *Religion of the Kwakiutl*. 2 vol. CUCA 10.
1932-a. *Anthropology and Modern Life*. Rev. ed., New York.
1932-b. The Aims of Anthropological Research, S 76:605-613.
1938. *The Mind of Primitive Man*. Rev. ed. New York.
1940. *Race, Language, and Culture*. New York. (Collected essays.)
For complete bibliography, cf. AAM 61:67-109 (1943).
For summary of Boas' work, cf. Spier, L., 1943.

BOAS, FRANZ AND G. HUNT
1905. *Kwakiutl Texts*. AMJ 3.

BODDE, DERK
1939. Types of Chinese Categorical Thinking, JAmO 59:200-219.

BOGGS, STEPHEN T.
1956. An Interactional Study of Ojibwa Socialization. ASR 21:191-198.

BOGORAS, WALDEMAR
1904-1909. *The Chukchee*. 3 vols. AMJ-AMM 11.

BOHANNON, LAURA
1952. A genealogical charter, Af 22:301-315.

BOHANNON, PAUL
1953. Concepts of Time among the Tiv of Nigeria. SwA 9:251-262.

BOULDING, KENNETH
1955. Notes on the Information Concept, EX # 5:103-112.

BOUTFLOWER, CECIL H.
1939. The Individual versus Society in Japan. JASL 36:1-18.

BOWERS, ALFRED W.
1950. *Mandan Social and Ceremonial Organization*. UnCh.

BOWLBY, J.
1951. Maternal Care and Mental Health, WHO *Monogr. 2*. Geneva.

BOYD, WILLIAM C.
1950. *Genetics and the Races of Man: An Introduction to Modern Physical Anthropology.* Boston.

BRAND, HOWARD, comp.
1955. *The Study of Personality, A Book of Readings.* New York.

BRANDT, RICHARD E.
1954. *Hopi Ethics.* Chicago.

BRANT, CHARLES
1950. Peyotism among the Kiowa-Apache and Neighboring Tribes. SwA *6*:212-222.

BRAY, D.
1913. *The Life History of a Brannul.* London.

BRICKNER, R.
1942. The German Cultural Paranoid Trend, AJO *12*:611-632.
1943. *Is Germany Incurable?* Philadelphia.

BRILL, A. A.
1913. Piblokto or Hysteria among Peary's Eskimos. JNMD *40*:514-520.

BRONFENBRENNER, URIE
1951. Toward an Integrated Theory of Personality. In Robt. R. Blake and G. W. Ramsey, eds., *Perception: An Approach to Personality.* New York.

BROWN, A. R. RADCLIFFE-
1931. *The Social Organization of Australian Tribes.* OM *1*.
1933. **The Andaman Islanders.* London.
See also M. Fortes, ed., 1949.

BROWN, G. GORDON
1951. Culture, Society and Personality: A Restatement, AJP *108*:173-175.

BROWN, STEPHEN J.
1927. *The World of Imagery.* London.

BRUCH, H.
1952. *Don't be Afraid of Your Child.* New York.

BRUNER, EDWARD M., AND J. B. ROTTER
1953. A Level-of-Aspiration Study among the Ramah Navaho. JP *21*:375-385.

BRUNER, J. S. AND R. TAGIURI
1954. The Perception of the People, In *Handbook of Social Psychology,* ed. by G. Lindzey, vol. II, chap. 17. Cambridge, Mass.

BRUNSWIK, ELSE FRENKEL
See Frenkel-Brunswik, Else.

BRUNSWIK, ELSE F. AND R. N. SANFORD
1947. The Anti-Semitic Personality, A Research Report, YbP *3*.

BRYAN, KIRK
1929. Flood Water Farming, GR *19* #3.

BRYK, F.
1939. *Dark Rapture.* New York.

BRYSON, LYMAN
1952. *The Next America.* New York.
1954. *The Drive Toward Reason.* New York.

BUCHANAN, DANIEL CRUMP
1954. Japanese Character and Personality as Revealed in their Culture, In *Understanding Other Cultures,* ed. by Wm. A. Parker; Amer. Council of Learned Societies, Washington, D. C.

BUHLER, CHARLOTTE
1952. National Differences in "World Test" Projective Patterns, JPT *16*:42-55.

BULLEN, ADELAIDE K.
1945. A Cross-cultural Approach to the Problem of Stuttering. *Child Development*, *16*:1-88.

BUNZEL, RUTH L.
1929. *The Pueblo Potter*. New York (Section on dreams).
1932-a. *Introduction to Zuni Ceremonialism*. BuER *47*.
1932-b. *Zuni Katcinas*. BuER *47*.
1933. *Zuni Texts*. AEP *15*.
1940. The Role of Alcoholism in Two Central American Cultures, PS *3*:361-387.
1953. *Chichicastenango: A Guatemalan Village*. AEP *22*.

BURGESS, ERNEST W.
1930. The Cultural Approach to the Study of Personality, MH *14*:307-325.
1942. Educative Effects of Social Environment as Disclosed by Studies of Primitive Societies, In *Environment and Education*, Human Development Series, *1*:54:48-61.

BURLINGHAM, D. T. AND A. FREUD
1942. *Young Children in Wartime: A Year's Work in a War Nursery*. London.

BURROWS, EDWIN G.
1952. From Value to Ethos on Ifaluk Atoll. SwA *8*:13-35.

BURROWS, EDWIN G., & M. SPIRO
1953. *An Atoll Culture: Ethnography of Ifaluk*. Human Relations Area Files, New Haven.

CADY, EDWIN HARRISON
1949. *The Gentleman in America*. Syracuse, N. Y.

CALLAWAY, REV. HENRY
1868-1870. *The Religious System of the Amazulu*. Natal and London. Republished 1884.

CAMPBELL, A. A.
1943. St. Thomas Negroes, a Study in Personality and Culture, PsM *55* #5 (Whole #253).

CAMPBELL, J. G. D.
1902. *Siam in the Twentieth Century*. New York.

CANNON, WALTER B.
1932. *The Wisdom of the Body*. New York.

CANTRIL, HADLEY
1950. *The "Why" of Man's Experience*. New York.

CANTRIL, HADLEY, ed., et al
1950. *Tensions that Cause Wars*. Urbana, Ill.

CAPLAN, GERALD, ed.,
1955. *Emotional Problems of Early Childhood*. New York.

CARMICHAEL, LEONARD, ed.
1946, 1953. *Manual of Child Psychology*. N. Y.

CAROTHERS, J. C.
1948. A Study of Mental Derangement in Africans . . . PS *11*:47-86.
1953. The African Mind in Health and Disease: Ethnopsychiatry, WHO.

CARTWRIGHT, DORWIN, AND JOHN R. P. FRENCH, JR.
1939. The Reliability of Life-History Studies. CP *8*:110-119.

CARPENTER, CLARENCE R.
1940. Field Study in Siam of the Behavior and Social Relations of the Gibbon. CoPM *16* #5. (Reprinted in Coon, 1948.)

CASSIRER, ERNST
1944. *An Essay on Man*. New Haven.

CATTELL, RAYMOND B.
1950. The Principal Culture Patterns Discoverable in the Syntal Dimensions of Existing Nations, JSP *32*:215-253.

CAUDILL, WILLIAM
1949. Psychological Characteristics of Acculturated Wisconsin Ojibwa Children, AA *51*:409-427.
1952. *Japanese-American Personality and Acculturation.* GPM *45*:3-102.
1953. Cultural Perspectives on Stress. In *Symposium on Stress.* Army Med. Srvc. Grad. School. Washington.
1955. Comments (on J. Henry, Projective Testing . . .), AA *57*:250-253.

CAVAN, RUTH SHONLE, ERNEST W. BURGESS, ROBERT J. HAVIGHURST, AND HERBERT GOLDHAMER
1949. *Personal Adjustment in Old Age.* Chicago.

CHANG TUNG-SUN.
1939. A Chinese Philosopher's Theory of Knowledge. *Yenching Jnl. Soc. Studies.* Reprinted in *ETC.*, 1952: *9*:203-226.

CHAO, B. Y.
1947. *Autobiography of a Chinese Woman.* New York.

CHAPPLE, ELIOT D.
1940. *Measuring Human Relations; An Introduction to the Study of the Interaction of Individuals.* GPM *22*.
1949. The Interaction Chronograph: Its Evaluation and Present Application, *Personnel* *25*:295-307.

CHAPPLE, ELIOT D., MARTHA F. CHAPPLE, AND J. A. REPP
1955. Behavioral Definitions of Personality and Temperament Characteristics, HO *13* #*4*:34-39.

CHAPPLE, ELIOT D., AND CARLETON S. COON
1942. *Principles of Anthropology.* New York.

CHASE, STUART
1948. *The Proper Study of Mankind, an Inquiry into the Science of Human Relations.* New York. Rev. ed. 1955.

CHILDS, GLADWYN MURRAY
1949. *Umbundu Kinship and Character.* London.

CHIN AI-LI S.
1948. Some Problems of Chinese Youth in Transition, AJS *54*:1-9.

CHINNERY, E. W. P. AND A. C. HADDON
1917. Five New Religious Cults in British New Guinea, *Hibbert Journal, 15*: 448-463

CHRISTENSEN, JAMES BOYD
1954. **Double Descent Among the Fanti.* New Haven.

CLECKLEY, H. M.
1950. *The Mask of Sanity.* 2nd ed., St. Louis.

COBB, EDITH
1947. *The Therapeutic Function of the Creative Phantasy in Childhood During Latency Period.* Social Survey Work, New York.

CODERE, HELEN
1956. The Amiable Side of Kwakiutl Life: The Potlatch and the Play Potlatch, AA *58*:334-351.

CODRINGTON, R. H.
1891. **The Melanesians.* Oxford.

COHEN, ALBERT K.
1948. On the Place of "Themes" and Kindred Concepts in Social Theory, AA *50*:436-443.

COHEN, YEHUDI A.
1955. Character Formation and Social Structure in a Jamaican Community, PS *18*:275-296.

COLLINS, J. M.
1949. John Fornsby: The Personal Document of a Coast Salish Indian. CUCA *36*:287-342. (Smith, Marian W., 1949.)

COMMITTEE ON FOOD HABITS
  1942. *The Relationship Between Food Habits and Problems of Wartime Emergency Feeding.* National Research Council.
COOK, P. H.
  1942. Mental Structure and the Psychological Field: Some Samoan Observations. CP *10*:296-308.
COON, CARLETON S.
  1931. **Tribes of the Rif.* HAA *9*.
  1942. See under Chapple, E. D.
  1948. Ed., *A Reader in General Anthropology.* New York.
  1954. Climate and Race. SIAR, *1953*:277-298.
  1954-b. *The Story of Man.* New York.
COON, CARLETON S., S. M. GARN, AND J. B. BIRDSELL
  1950. *Races: A Study of the Problems of Race Formation in Man.* Springfield, Ill.
COOPER, JOHN M.
  1928. Child Training Among Primitive Peoples, PM *1*:10-16.
  1933. The Cree Witiko Psychosis. PM *6*:20-24.
  1946. The Culture of the Northeastern Hunters: A Reconstructive Interpretation. In F. Johnson, ed., *Man in Northeastern North America.* (Papers, R. S. Peabody Foundation for Archaeology, #3.)
CORIAT, I. H.
  n.d. Psychoneuroses among Primitive Tribes, In *Studies in Abnormal Psychology,* Ser. 6, Boston.
CORNELL, JOHN B.
  1953. *Matsunagi: The Life and Social Organization of a Japanese Mountain Community.* UnMi *5*.
COTTRELL, LEONARD S., JR.
  1942. The Adjustment of the Individual to his Age and Sex Roles, ASR *7*:617-620.
COUNT, EARL W., ed.
  1950. *This is Race: An Anthology Selected from the International Literature on the Races of Man.* New York.
  1955. *Dynamic Anthropometry* (papers from a Conference on Dynamic Anthropometry, Section on Biology, New York Acad. Sci.) NYA *63*, Art. 4: 433-636.
COVARRUBIAS, MIGUEL
  1937. *Island of Bali.* N. Y.
CRAWLEY, ERNEST
  1927. *The Mystic Rose.* (rev. ed.) New York (orig. 1902).
CRILE, GEORGE, JR.
  1955. *Cancer and Common Sense.* New York.
CUSHING, FRANK H.
  1882. The Zuni Social, Mythic and Religious Systems, *Popular Sci. Monthly 21.*
  1882-1883. My Adventures in Zuni, *Century Magazine,* n.s., nos. 3-4.
  1897. Primitive Motherhood. *Proc. Nat. Congress of Mothers.* Washington, D. C.
  1901. *Zuni Folk Tales.* New York.
  1920. *Zuni Breadstuff.* Indian Notes & Monographs, *8.* Heye Foundation, N. Y.
CZAPLICKA, M. A.
  1914. **Aboriginal Siberia.* Oxford.
DAI, BINGHAM
  1945. Some Problems of Personality Development among Negro Children, WS *12*:67-100. (Reprinted in Kluckhohn, Murray & Schneider, 1953.)
  1952. A Socio-Psychiatric Approach to Personality Organization, ASR *17*:44-49.
DARWIN, CHARLES
  1872, 1955. *Expression of Emotion in Men and Animals.* London. New York.

DAVIS, ALLISON
1941. American Status Systems and the Socialization of the Child, ASR *6*:345-354. (Reprinted, Kluckhohn, Murray & Schneider, 1953.)
1948. *Social Class Influences on Learning*. Cambridge, Mass.

DAVIS, ALLISON AND JOHN DOLLARD
1940. *Children of Bondage*. Washington, D. C.

DAVIS, ALLISON AND R. J. HAVIGHURST
1946. Social Class and Color Differences in Child-Rearing, ASR *11*:698-710. (Reprinted in Kluckhohn, Murray, & Schneider, 1953.)
1947. *Father of the Man*. Boston.

DAVIS, K.
1940. Extreme Social Isolation of a Child, AJS *45*:554-565.

DEANE, W.
1921. *Fijian Society, or the Sociology and Psychology of the Fijians*. London.

DEGRAZIA, S.
1948. *Political Community, A Study of Anomie*. Chicago.

DE LAGUNA, FREDERICA
1954. Tlingit Ideas about the Individual. SwA *10*:172-191.

DE LAGUNA, GRACE A.
1949. Culture and Rationality. AA *51*:379-391.

DENING, WALTER
1891. Mental Characteristics of the Japanese People. AsJ *19* pt. 1:17-36.

DENNIS, WAYNE
1940-a. *The Hopi Child*. New York. (Rev. by M. Mead, AA *43*:95-97.)
1940-b. Does Culture Appreciably Affect Patterns of Infant Behavior? JSP *12*: 305-317 (Reprinted in Newcomb, Hartley, et al, *Readings in Social Psych.*)
1941. Socialization of the Hopi Child, in *Language, Culture, and Personality*, ed. by Spier et al. Menasha. Wis. Pp. 259-271.
1942. The performance of Hopi children on the Goodenough "Draw a Man" test, JCoP *34*:341-348.
1943. *Re* animism in Hopi children, JASP *38*:21-36.

DENNIS, WAYNE AND MARSENA G. DENNIS
1940. Cradles and Cradling Practices of the Pueblo Indians, AA *42*:107-115.

DEUTSCH, F.
1939. The Choice of Organ in Organ Neurosis. IJP *20* # 3 & 4.

DEUTSCH, KARL W.
1953. The Growth of Nations: Some Recurrent Patterns of Political and Social Integration. WP *6*:168-195.

DEVEREUX, GEORGE
1937-a. Institutionalized Homosexuality of the Mohave Indians, HB *9*:498-527.
1937-b. Mohave Soul Concepts, AA *39*:417-422.
1939-a. Mohave Culture and Personality, CP *8*:91-109.
1939-b. The Social and Cultural Implications of Incest Among the Mohave Indians, PYQ *8*:510-533.
1939-c. A Sociological Theory of Schizophrenia, PYR *26*:315-342.
1939-d. Maladjustment and Social Neurosis, ASR *4*:844-51.
1940-a. Social Negativism and Criminal Psychopathology, *Jnl. Crim. Pyscho-pathology* *1*:325-338.
1940-b. Primitive Psychiatry, Pt. I. BlHM *8*:1194-1213.
1941. Mohave Beliefs Concerning Twins, AA *43*:573-592.
1942. The Mental Hygiene of the American Indian, MH *26*:71-84.
1945. The Logical Foundations of Culture and Personality Studies, NYT *II*-7 #*5*:110-130.
1947. Mohave Orality: Analysis of Nursing and Weaning Customs, PYQ *16*: 519-546.

1948-a. The Mohave Neonate and its Cradle. PM *21*:1-18.
1948-b. Mohave Etiquette. *Southwest Museum Leaflet 22.*
1948-c. Mohave Indian Obstetrics. AI *5*:95-139.
1948-d. The Function of Alcohol in Mohave Society. QJSA *9*:207-251.
1948-e. The Mohave Indian Kamalo:y, JCP *9*:433-457.
1950-a. Heterosexual Behavior of the Mohave Indians, PSS *2*:85-128.
1950-b. Education and Discipline in Mohave Society. PM *23*:85-102.
1950-c. Amusements and Sports of Mohave Children. *The Masterkey 24*:143-152.
1950-d. Status, Socialization, and Interpersonal Relations of Mohave Children, PS *13*:489-502.
1951-a. *Reality and Dream: The Psychotherapy of a Plains Indian.* New York.
1951-b. Mohave Indian Verbal and Motor Profanity, PSS *3*:99-127.
1951-c. Some Criteria for the Timing of Confrontations and Interpretations, IJP *32*:19-24.
1951-d. Neurotic Crime vs. Criminal Behavior, PSQ *25*:73ff.
1951-e. Logical Status and Methodological Problems of Research in Clinical Psychiatry, PS *14*:327-330.
1951-f. The Primal Scene and Juvenile Heterosexuality in Mohave Society, In Wilbur & Muensterberger, 1951.
1952. Psychiatry and Anthropology: Some Research Objectives, *Bull. Menninger Clinic* 16:167-177.
1953-a. ed. & contrib., *Psychoanalysis and the Occult.* New York.
1953-b. Cultural Factors in Psychoanalytic Therapy, JAmP *1*:629-655. (Reprinted herewith.)
1955-a. Charismatic Leadership and Crisis, In PSS *4.*
1955-b. *A Study of Abortion in Primitive Societies.* New York.

DEWEY, JOHN
1922. *Human Nature and Conduct: An Introduction to Social Psychology.* New York.

DHUNJIBHOY, J. E.
1930. A Brief Resume of the Types of Insanity Commonly Met with in India. JMS 76:254-264.

DICKS, HENRY V.
1950. Personality Traits and National Socialist Ideology, HR *3*:111-154.
1952. Observations on Contemporary Russian Behavior, HR *5*:111-175.

DILLAWAY, NEWTON
1947. *The Lesson of Okinawa.* Wakefield, Mass.

DIXON, ROLAND B.
1905. *The Northern Maidu.* AMB *17*:119-346.
1907. *The Shasta.* AMB *17*:381-498.
1928. *The Building of Cultures.* New York.

DJAMOUR, JUDITH
1952. Adoption of Children among Singapore Malaysians, RAI *82*:159-168.

DOBRIZHOFER, M.
1822. *An Account of the Abipones.* London.

DODDS, E. R.
1951. *The Greeks and the Irrational.* Berkeley & Los Angeles.

DOI, L. TAKEO
1955. Some Aspects of Japanese Psychiatry. AJP *111*:691-695.

DOLLARD, JOHN
1935. *Criteria for the Life History.* New Haven.
1938. The Life History in Community Studies, ASR *3*:724-737. (Reprinted, Kluckhohn et al, 1953.)
1939. Culture, Society, Impulse, and Socialization, AJS *45*:50-63.

DOLLARD, JOHN AND NEAL E. MILLER
1950. *Personality and Psychotherapy.* New York.

DOLLARD, JOHN, N. E. MILLER, L. W. DOOB, O. H. MOWRER, AND R. R. SEARS
1939. *Frustration and Aggression.* New Haven.

DONNER, KAI (tr. by R. Kyler)
1954. **Among the Samoyed in Siberia.* New Haven.

DOOB, LEONARD W.
1952. *Social Psychology.* New York.

DOOLEY, C. T.
1934-1936. Child Training among the Wanguru, PM 7:22-31; 8:73-80; 9:1-12.

DRUCKER, PHILIP
1951. **The Northern and Central Nootkan Tribes.* BuEB *144.*

DUBE, LEELA
1949. Pregnancy and Childbirth among the Amat Gonds. EA *2:153-159.*

DUBOIS, CORA
1937-a. Some Anthropological Perspectives on Psychoanalysis, PYR *24:246-263.*
1937-b. Some Psychological Objectives and Techniques in Ethnography, JSP *8:285-300.*
1941. Attitudes toward Food and Hunger in Alor, In *Language, Culture, and Personality,* ed. by L. Spier et al, Menasha. Pp. 272-281. (Reprinted herewith.)
1944. *The People of Alor.* Minneapolis. (Cf. A. Kardiner, *The Psychological Frontiers of Society,* for discussion.)

DUBOIS, J. A. AND H. K. BEAUCHAMP
1928. **Hindu Manners, Customs, and Ceremonies.* Rev. ed., Oxford. (Early 19th century observations.)

DUNN, L. C. AND TH. DOBZHANSKY
1946. *Heredity, Race and Society.* Pelican Books.

DYK, WALTER
1938. *Son of Old Man Hat: A Navaho Autobiography.* New York.
1947. *A Navaho Autobiography.* V *8.*
1951. Notes and Illustrations of Navaho Sex Behavior, In Wilbur and Muensterberger, 1951.

EASTMAN, CHARLES
1915. *Indian Boyhood.* New York.

EATON, JOSEPH W. AND ROBERT J. WEIL
1955. *Culture and Mental Disorders: A Comparative Study of the Hutterites and Other Populations.* Glencoe, Ill.

EBERHARD, WOLFRAM
1937. *Chinese Fairy Tales and Folk Tales.* London.

EFRON, DAVID
1941. *Gesture and Environment.* New York.

EGGAN, DOROTHY
1943. The General Problem of Hopi Adjustment, AA *45:357-373.* (Reprinted in Kluckhohn, Murray, & Schneider, 1953.)
1949. The Significance of Dreams for Anthropological Research, AA *51:177-198.*
1952. The Manifest Content of Dreams: A Challenge to Social Science. AA *54:469-485.*
1955. The Personal Use of Myth in Dreams, JAF *68:445-453.*

EGGAN, FRED
1950. **Social Organization of the Western Pueblos.* Chicago.

EGGAN, FRED, ed.
1937. **Social Anthropology of North American Tribes.* Chicago.

EISSLER, K. R.
1944. Balinese Character, PS 7:139-144.

ELKIN, A. P.
1932. The Secret Life of the Australian Aborigines. O *3*:119-138.
1953. *Social Anthropology in Melanesia.* Oxford. (Excellent guide to literature.)

ELKIN, H.
1940. The Northern Arapaho of Wyoming, In R. Linton, ed. *Acculturation in Seven American Indian Tribes.* New York.

ELLIS, W. G.
1893. The *amok* of the Malays. JMS *39*:325-328.
1895-7. Latah. JMS *41*:527-538; *42*:209-212; *43*:32-40.

ELWIN, VERRIER
1937. A Note on the Theory and Symbolism of Dreams among the Baiga, BMP *16*:237-259.
1943. *Muria Murder and Suicide.* Oxford.
1947. **The Muria and Their Ghotul.* Bombay.

EMBREE, JOHN F.
1939. **Suye Mura, A Japanese Village.* Chicago.
1950. Standardized Error and Japanese Character: A Note on Political Interpretation, WP *2*:439-443.

EMERSON, ALFRED E.
1947. Why Termites? SCM *64*:337-345.

ENDLEMAN, ROBERT
1949. The New Anthropology and Its Ambitions, The Science of Man in Messianic Dress. *Commentary* (September): 284-291.

ENGLISH, O. S., & G. H. J. PEARSON
1945. *Emotional Problems of Living: Avoiding the Neurotic Pattern.* New York.

ERIKSON, ERIK HOMBURGER
1939. Observations on Sioux Education, JPY *7*:101-156.
1942. Hitler's Imagery and German Youth, PS *5*:475-493. (Revised version in Kluckhohn & Murray, 1948, pp. 485-510.)
1943-a. *Observations on the Yurok: Childhood and World Image.* UnCa *35* No. 10.
1943-b. Problems of Infancy & Early Childhood, In *Cyclopedia of Medicine, Surgery & Specialties.* 2nd ed. Philadelphia.
1945. Childhood and Tradition in Two American Indian Tribes, PaC *1*:319-350. (Reproduced herewith.)
1947. Ego Development and Historical Change, PaC *2*:359-396.
1950-a. *Childhood and Society.* New York.
1950-b. Growth and Crises of the "Healthy Personality," In *Symposium on the Healthy Personality,* ed. by M. Senn. N. Y. (reprinted, Kluckhohn et al, 1953).
1951. Sex Differences in the Play Configurations of Preadolescents, AJO *21*:667-692.

ESCALONA, S., AND M. LEITCH
n.d. *Eight Infants: Tension Manifestations in Response to Perceptual Stimuli.* N. Y. Univ. Film Library, N. Y. (Film.)

ESCALONA, S. K., R. R. SEARS, G. W. WISE, AND J. P. BENJAMIN
1950. Approaches to a Dynamic Theory of Development. Round Table. AJO *20*:123-160.

EVANS-PRITCHARD, E. E.
1934. Editor, *Essays Presented to C. G. Seligman.* London.
1937. *Witchcraft, Oracles, and Magic Among the Azande.* Oxford.
1940. **The Nuer.* Oxford.
1951-a. *Kinship and Marriage Among the Nuer.* Oxford.
1951-b. *Social Anthropology.* London.
1953. The Sacrificial Role of Cattle Among the Nuer, Af *23*:181-198.
1954. The Meaning of Sacrifice Among the Nuer, RAI *81*:21-33.

FARBER, MAURICE L.
1950. The Problem of National Character: a Methodological Analysis, JPY *30*:307-316.
1955. The Study of National Character. JSI *11* #2:52-56.

FARIS, ELLSWORTH
1934. Culture and Personality among the Forest Bantu, ASP *28*:3ff.

FARIS, ROBERT E. L.
1934-a. Some Observations on the Incidence of Schizophrenia in Primitive Society, JASP *29*:30-31.
1934-b. Cultural Isolation and the Schizophrenic Personality, AJS *40*:155-164.

FEJOS, PAUL
1943. *Ethnography of the Yagua*. V *1*.

FENICHEL, OTTO
1934. *Outline of Clinical Psychoanalysis*. New York.
1954. *The Psychoanalytic Theory of Neurosis*. N. Y.

FENTON, WILLIAM N.
1941. Iroquois Suicide: A Study in the Stability of a Culture Pattern, BuEB *128*:80-137.
1948. The Present Status of Anthropology in Northeastern North America: A Review Article. AA *50*:494-515.
1951. Ed., *Symposium on Local Diversity in Iroquois Culture*. BuEB *149*.

FIRTH, RAYMOND W.
1934. The Meaning of Dreams in Tikopia, *Essays Presented to C. G. Seligman*, ed. by E. E. Evans-Pritchard. London. Pp. 63-74.
1936. *We the Tikopia*. New York.
1940. *The Work of the Gods in Tikopia*. London.
1948. Religious Belief and Personal Adjustment. RAI *78*:25-43.
1951. *Elements of Social Organization*. New York.

FISCHER, J. L.
1956. The Position of Men and Women in Truk and Ponape: A Comparative Analysis of Kinship Terminology and Folktales. JAF *69*:55-62.

FISHER, SEYMOUR AND DAVID MENDELL
1956. The Communication of Neurotic Patterns over Two and Three Generations. PS *19*:41-46.

FISKE, DONALD W.
1955. Comments. (On J. Henry, Projective Testing . . .) AA *57*:258-259.

FLANNERY, REGINA
1937. Child Behavior from the Point of View of the Cultural Anthropologists. JES *10*:470-478.

FLETCHER, ALICE, AND FRANCIS LaFLESCHE
1911. *The Omaha Tribe*. BuER 27. Esp. pp. 327-337. (Excerpt reprinted herewith.)

FLETCHER, W.
1938. Latah and Amok. *British Encyclop. Medical Pract.* 641-650.

FLÜGEL, J. C.
1931. *The Psychoanalytic Study of the Family*. London.

FORD, CLELLAN S.
1939. Society, Culture, and the Human Organism, JGP *20*:135-179.
1941. *Smoke from Their Fires*. (Kwakiutl.) New Haven.
1943. Culture and Human Behavior, SCM *55*:546-557.
1945. *A Comparative Study of Human Reproduction*. YPA *32*.

FORD, CLELLAN S., AND FRANK A. BEACH
1951. *Patterns of Sexual Behavior*. New York.

FORDE, C. DARYLL
1931. Hopi Agriculture and Land Ownership, RAI *61*.

FORTES, MEYER
  1936. Ritual Festivals and Social Cohesion in the Hinterland of the Gold Coast,
    AA *38*:590-604.
  1945. *The Dynamics of Clanship Among the Tallensi.* Oxford.
  1949. *The Web of Kinship Among the Tallensi.* London.

FORTES, MEYER, ed.
  1949. *Social Structure, Studies Presented to A. R. Radcliffe-Brown.* Oxford.

FORTES, MEYER, AND E. E. EVANS-PRITCHARD, eds.
  1940. *African Political Systems.* London & New York.

FORTUNE, REO F.
  1931. Manus Religion. O *2*:74-108.
  1932-a. *Sorcerers of Dobu.* London & N. Y.
  1932-b. *Omaha Secret Societies.* CUCA *14.*
  1935. *Manus Religion.* APSP. Philadelphia.
  1940. Arapesh Warfare, AA *41*:22-41.
  1943. Arapesh Maternity, N *152*:164.

FOSDICK, RAYMOND B.
  1915. *European Police Systems.* New York.

FOSTER, GEORGE M., assisted by G. OSPINA
  1948. *Empire's Children: The People of Tzintzuntzan.* SIP *6.*

FRANK, LAWRENCE K.
  1938. Cultural Control and Physiological Autonomy, AJO *8*:622-626. (Reprinted,
    Kluckhohn et al, 1953.)
  1939. Projective Methods for the Study of Personality, JPY *8*:389-413.
  1940-a. The Cost of Competition. *Plan Age 6*:9 & 10.
  1940-b. Freedom for the Personality, PS *3*:341-350.
  1949. *Society as the Patient, Essays on Culture and Personality.* New Brunswick,
    N. J.
  1951. *Nature and Human Nature.* New Brunswick, N. J.
  1952. Psycho-Cultural Approaches to Medical Care, JSI *8* #4:45-54.
  1953. Education for World Community through Cultural Dynamics, *The Aryan
    Path* (July), Indian Inst. of Culture.

FRANKFORT, HENRI
  1948. *Kingship and the Gods.* Chicago.

FRANKFORT, HENRIETTE A.
  1951. *Arrest and Movement: Space and Time in the Near East.* Chicago.

FREEDMAN, LAWRENCE A. AND VERA M. FERGUSON
  1950. The Question of "Painless Childbirth" in Primitive Cultures. AJO
    20:363-372.

FRENCH, DAVID H.
  1948. *Factionalism in Isleta Pueblo.* AEM *14.*

FRENKEL-BRUNSWIK, ELSE
  1948. A Study of Prejudice in Children. HR *1*:295-306.
  1954. Meaning of Psychoanalytic Concepts and Confirmation of Psychoanalytic
    Theories, SCM *79*:293-299.
  (See also Brunswik.)

FREUD, ANNA
  1937. *The Ego and the Mechanisms of Defense.* London.

FREUD, SIGMUND
  1918. *Totem and Taboo.* New York.
  1930. *Three Contributions to the Theory of Sex.* 4th ed. New York.
  1933. *New Introductory Lectures on Psychoanalysis.* N. Y.
  1938. *The Basic Writings of Sigmund Freud*, tr. and ed. by A. A. Brill. New
    York. (Contains 1918, 1930, above and other writings.)

FRICK, JOHANN
  1955. Mutter und Kind bei den Chinesen in Tsinghai. A *50*:337-374.

FRIED, JACOB
1953. The Relation of Ideal Norms to Actual Behavior in Tarahumara Society, SwA 9:286-295.

FRIEDGOOD, HARRY B.
1951. On the Psychological Aspects of Authoritarian and Democratic Political Systems, ASC 39:432-440, 451.

FRIES, M., AND P. J. WOOLF
n.d. Series of Studies on Integrated Environment: The Interaction Between Child and Environment. (5 films) N. Y. University Film Library. New York.

FROMM, ERICH
1931. Die Entwicklung des Christusdogmas. Vienna.
1941. Escape from Freedom. New York.
1944. Individual and Social Origins of Neurosis, ASR 9:380-384. (Reprinted in Kluckhohn, Murray, & Schneider, 1953.)
1948. Man for Himself. N. Y.
1949. Psychoanalytic Characterology and its Application to the Understanding of Culture. In S. S. Sargent & M. W. Smith, eds., Culture and Personality.
1955. The Sane Society. New York & Toronto.

FROMM-REICHMANN, FRIEDA
1950. Principles of Intensive Psychotherapy. Chicago.

FÜRER-HAIMENDORF, CHRISTOPH VON
1943. *The Chenchus, Jungle Folk of the Deccan. London.
1950. Youth Dormitories and Community Houses in India, A 45:119-144.

FYFE, HENRY HAMILTON
1940. The Illusion of National Character. London.

GARTH, THOMAS R., JR.
1945. Emphasis on Industriousness among the Atsuwegi, AA 47:554-566.

GATES, R. RUGGLES
1946. Human Genetics. 2 vols. New York.
1948. Human Ancestry from a Genetical Point of View. Cambridge, Mass.

GERTH, HANS AND C. WRIGHT MILLS
1953. Character and Social Structure. New York.

GESELL, ARNOLD
1928. Infancy and Human Growth. New York.
1940. Wolf Child and Human Child. New York.
1949. Human Infancy and the Ontogenesis of Behavior, ASC 37:529-553.
1950. Growth Potentials of the Human Infant, In Centennial, A.A.A.S., Washington.

GESELL, ARNOLD et al
1934. An Atlas of Infant Behavior. New Haven.

GESELL, ARNOLD, AND FRANCES L. ILG
1950. Child Development: An Introduction to the Study of Human Growth. New York.

GESELL, ARNOLD, FRANCES ILG, et al
1943. Infant and Child in the Culture of Today. New York.
1946. The Child from Five to Ten. N. Y.

GIDDINGS, FRANKLIN H.
1922. Studies in the Theory of Human Society. New York. (Especially chaps. I, IX, X, XII.)

GIFFORD, E. W.
1933. *The Cocopa. UnCa 31 #5.

GILLIN, JOHN PHILLIP
1936. *The Barama River Caribs of British Guiana. PHa 14 #2.
1939. Personality in Preliterate Societies, ASR 4:681-702.

1944-a. Custom and the Range of Human Response, CP *13*:101-134.

1944-b. Cultural Adjustment, AA *46*:429-447.

1945. Parallel Cultures and the Inhibitions to Acculturation in a Guatemalan Community, SLF, *24*:1-14.

1946. Personality Formation from the Comparative Cultural Point of View, WS: *Sociological Foundations of the Psychiatric Disorders of Childhood.*

1947. *Moche: A Peruvian Coastal Community. SIP 3.*

1948-a. *The Ways of Men: An Introduction to Anthropology.* New York.

1948-b. Magical Fright, PS *11*:387-400.

1951. *The Culture of Security in San Carlos.* New Orleans.

1952. Ethos and Cultural Aspects of Personality. In Sol Tax, ed., *Heritage of Conquest.* Glencoe, Ill.

1956. The Making of a Witch Doctor. PS *19*:131-136.

GILLIN, JOHN, O. BILLIG AND W. DAVIDSON

1947-1948. Aspects of Personality and Culture in a Guatemalan Community, JP *16*:153-187, 326-368.

GILLIN, JOHN, AND VICTOR RAIMY

1940. Acculturation and Personality, ASR *5*:371-380.

GLACKEN, CLARENCE J.

1955. *The Great Loochoo: A Study of Okinawan Village Life.* Berkeley. Esp. chapters 10, 11.

GLADWIN, THOMAS

1948. Comanche Kin Behavior. AA *50*:73-94.

GLADWIN, THOMAS AND SEYMOUR B. SARASON

1953. *Truk: Man in Paradise.* V *20*.

GLENN, EDMUND S.

1954. Semantic Difficulties in International Communication. *Etc.: A Review of General Semantics, 11*:163-180.

GLOVER, E.

1932. Common Problems in Psychoanalysis and Anthropology, BMP *12*:109-131.

GLOYNE, HOWARD F.

1950. Tarantism: Mass Hysterical Reaction to Spider Bite in the Middle Ages, AI *7*:29-41.

GODDARD, PLINY E.

1903. *Life and Culture of the Hupa.* UnCa *1* #1.

GOLDENWEISER, ALEXANDER A.

1922. *Early Civilization.* New York.

1933. *History, Psychology, and Culture.* New York.

1936. The Individual, Pattern, and Involution in Primitive Society, *Essays in Anthropology Presented to A. L. Kroeber*, Berkeley. Pp. 99-104.

1937. *Anthropology.* New York.

GOLDFRANK, ESTHER S.

1943. Historic Change and Social Character, AA *45*:67-83.

1945-a. *Changing Configurations in the Social Organization of a Blackfoot Tribe During the Reserve Period.* AEM *8*. New York.

1945-b. Socialization, Personality, and the Structure of Pueblo Society, AA *47*: 516-539. (Reproduced herewith.)

1948. The Impact of Socialization and Personality on four Hopi Emergence Myths. SwA *4*:241-262.

1951-a. Observations on Sexuality among the Blood Indians of Alberta, Canada, PSS *3*:71-98.

1951-b. "Old Man" and the Father Image in Blood (Blackfoot) Society, In Wilbur and Muensterberger, 1951.

GOLDHAMER, HERBERT

1948. Recent Developments in Personality Studies. ASR *13*:555-565.

GOLDMAN, IRVING
  1937. The Zuni Indians of New Mexico, in M. Mead, ed., *Cooperation & Competition Among Primitive Peoples*. N. Y.
  1950-a. Cultural Factors in Education, JGE *4*:234-240.
  1950-b. Psychiatric Interpretation of Russian History: a Reply to Geoffrey Gorer, ASL *9*:151-161.

GOLDMAN-EISLER, FRIEDA
  1948. Breast Feeding and Character Formation, JP *17*:83-103.
  1950. Breast Feeding and Character Formation, II, JP *19*:189-196.
  1951. The Problem of "Orality" and of its Origin in Early Childhood. JMS *97*: 765-782.
  1948, 1950, 1951. Breast Feeding and Character Formation, (Based on three other papers, dated as indicated). In Kluckhohn, Murray, & Schneider, 1953.

GOLDSCHMIDT, WALTER
  1951. Ethics and the Structure of Society: An Ethnological Contribution to the Sociology of Knowledge. AA *53*:506-524.

GOODE, WM. J., & PAUL K. HATT
  1952. *Methods in Social Research*. New York.

GOODENOUGH, FLORENCE L.
  1936. The Measurement of Mental Functions in Primitive Groups, AA *38*:1-11.

GOODENOUGH, FLORENCE L., AND JOHN E. ANDERSON
  1947. Psychology and Anthropology: Some Problems of Joint Import for the Two Fields, SwA *3*:5-14.

GOODENOUGH, WARD H.
  1949. Premarital Freedom on Truk: Theory and Practice. AA *51*:615-620.
  1951. *Property, Kin, and Community on Truk*, YPA *46*

GOODMAN, MARY ELLEN
  1952. *Race Awareness in Young Children*. Cambridge, Mass.

GORER, GEOFFREY
  1936. *Bali and Angkor or Looking at Life and Death*. London.
  1938. **Himalayan Village*. London.
  1943. Themes in Japanese Culture, NYT *2-5*:106-124.
  1945. *Burmese Personality*. Institute for Intercultural Studies. (mimeo.) New York.
  1948. *The American People*. London and New York.
  1949. Some Aspects of the Psychology of the People of Great Russia, ASL *8*: 155-166.
  1950-a. The Erotic Myth of America, *Partisan Rev.* *17*:589-594.
  1950-b. The Concept of National Character, *Science News* #18:105-122. Penguin Books, England. (Reprinted, Kluckhohn, Murray & Schneider, 1953.)
  1950-c. Some Notes on the British Character, *Horizon 20:* Nos. 120-121, 369-379.
  1951. Swaddling and the Russians, *New Leader*, May 21, pp. 19-20.
  1953. National Character: Theory and Practice. In Mead & Metraux, eds., *The Study of Culture at a Distance*. Chicago.
  1955-a. Modification of National Character: the Role of the Police in England. JSI *11* #2:24-32. (Reprinted herewith.)
  1955-b. *Exploring English Character*. New York.

GORER, GEOFFREY AND JOHN RICKMAN
  1950. *The People of Great Russia*. New York.

GOTTSCHALK, LOUIS, CLYDE KLUCKHOHN, AND ROBERT ANGELL
  1945. *The Use of Personal Documents in History, Anthropology, and Sociology*. SRCB *53*.

GRAD, ANDREW J.
  1952. *Land and Peasant in Japan*. (Mimeo.) New York, IPR.
  1955. *Fukaya, A Japanese Town*. New York, IPR.

GRANQVIST, HILMA
  1947. *Birth and Childhood Among the Arabs, Studies in a Muhammadan Village in Palestine.* Helsingfors.
  1950. *Child Problems Among the Arabs, Studies in a Muhammadan Village in Palestine.* Helsingfors.

GREEN, ARNOLD W.
  1946. Social Values and Psychotherapy. JP *14*:199-228.
  1948. Culture, Normality, and Personality Conflict. AA *50*:225-237.

GREENACRE, PHYLLIS
  1944. Infant Reactions to Restraint, AJO *14*:204-218. (Reprinted in Kluckhohn, Murray, & Schneider, 1953.)

GREENMAN, E. F.
  1948. The Extraorganic, AA *50*:181-199.

GREGORY, H. E.
  1916. The Navaho Country. Dept. of the Interior, U. S. Geolog. Survey, Water Supply Paper 380. Wash'n.

GRIMBLE, ARTHUR
  1921. From Birth to Death in the Gilbert Islands. RAI *51*:25-54.

GRINNELL, G. B.
  1923. *The Cheyenne Indians.* New Haven.

GRÜNBAUM, ADOLF
  1952. Causality and the Science of Human Behavior, ASC *40*:665-676.

GUILLAIN, ROBERT (tr. by J. C. Weightman)
  1954. *Japan.* In Werner Bischof, *Japan,* pp. 5-26. London.

GUNTHER, ERNA, TR.
  1956. *The Tlingit Indians,* by Aurel Krause. Seattle.

HACK, JOHN T.
  1942. *The Changing Physical Environment of the Hopi Indians of Arizona.* PHa *35* #1.

HADLEY, C. V. D.
  1949. Personality Patterns, Social Class, and Aggression in the British West Indies, HR *2*:349-362.

HAEBERLIN, HERMAN K.
  1916. The Idea of Fertilization in the Culture of the Pueblo Indians, AAM *3*: 1-55.

HAGER, DON J.
  1950. Some Observations on the Relationship Between Genetics and Social Science, PS *13*:371-379.

HALL, EDWARD T., JR.
  1955. The Anthropology of Manners. SCAm *192* #4:84-90.

HALL, J. K., G. ZILBOORG, & H. A. BUNKER, eds.
  1944. *One Hundred Years of American Psychiatry.* New York.

HALLOWELL, A. IRVING
  1934. Culture and Mental Disorder, JASP *29*:1-9.
  1936. Psychic Stresses and Cultural Patterns, AJP *92*:1291-1310.
  1937-a. *Introduction: Handbook of Psychological Leads for Ethnological Field Workers.* (Mimeo.) Nat. Research Council. (Reproduced herewith.)
  1937-b. Temporal Orientation in Western Civilization and in a Preliterate Society, AA *39*:647-670.
  1938-a. Fear and Anxiety as Cultural and Individual Variables in a Primitive Society, JSP *9*:25-47.
  1938-b. Shabwan: a Dissociated Indian Girl, AJO *8*:328-340.
  1939-a. Sin, Sex, and Sickness in Saulteaux Belief, BMP *8*:191-197.
  1939-b. The Child, the Savage, and Human Experience, WS *6*:8-34.

1940. Aggression in Saulteaux Society, PS *3*:395-407. (Reprinted, Kluckhohn et al, 1953.)

1941-a. The Rorschach Method as an Aid in the Study of Personalities in Primitive Societies, JP *9*:235-245.

1941-b. The Social Function of Anxiety in a Primitive Society, ASR *6*:869-881. (Reprinted herewith.)

1942-a. Some Psychological Aspects of Measurement among the Saulteaux, AA *44*:62-77.

1942-b. *The Role of Conjuring in Saulteaux Society*. Philadelphia.

1942-c. Psychology and Anthropology, *Proc. 8th Amer. Sci. Congress.*

1942-d. Acculturation Processes and Personality Changes as Indicated by the Rorschach Technique. R *6* #2.

1945-a. The Rorschach Technique in the Study of Personality and Culture, AA *47*:195-210.

1945-b. Sociopsychological Aspects of Acculturation, In R. Linton, ed., *The Science of Man in the World Crisis*, New York. Pp. 171-200.

1946. Some Psychological Characteristics of the Northeastern Indians, *In Man in Northeastern North America*, Papers, R. S. Peabody Foundation for Archaeology, *3*:195-225. Andover, Mass.

1947. Myth, Culture, and Personality, AA *49*:544-556.

1949. Psychosexual Adjustment, Personality, and the Good Life in a Non-Literate Culture, In *Psychosexual Adjustment in Health and Disease*, N. Y. Pp. 102-123.

1950-a. Personality Structure and the Evolution of Man, AA *52*:159-173.

1950-b. Values, Acculturation, and Mental Health, AJO *20*:732-743.

1951-a. Cultural Factors in the Structuralization of Perception. In J. Rohrer & M. Sherif, eds., *Social Psychology at the Crossroads*. New York.

1951-b. The Use of Projective Techniques in the Study of Sociopsychological Aspects of Acculturation, JPT *15*:26-44.

1952. Ojibwa Personality and Acculturation, In Sol Tax, ed. *Acculturation in the Americas*, vol. II of *Selected Papers of the XXIXth I. C. A.* Chicago, pp. 105-112.

1953. Culture, Personality, and Society, In A. L. Kroeber, ed., *Anthropology Today*. Chicago. Pp. 597-620.

1955-a. Comments. (On J. Henry, Projective Testing . . .) AA *57*:262-264.

1955-b. *Culture and Experience*. Philadelphia.

HAMBLY, W. D.
1937. *Source Book for African Anthropology*. FM *26*: Nos. 394, 396.

HANDY, EDWARD S. C.
1923. **The Native Culture in the Marquesas*. BMB *9*.

1927. **Polynesian Religion*. BMB *34*.

1936. Dreaming in Relation to Spirit Kindred and Sickness in Hawaii, In *Essays in Anthropology Presented to A. L. Kroeber*. Berkeley. Pp. 119-127.

1940. **The Hawaiian Planter*, vol. I. BMB *161*.

HANKS, L. M., JR.
1949-a. The Locus of Individual Differences in Certain Primitive Cultures. In Sargent, S. S. & M. W. Smith, eds., *Culture and Personality*. New York. Pp. 107-126.

1949-b. The Quest for Individual Autonomy in Burmese Personality, with particular Reference to the Arakan. PS *12*:285-300.

HANKS, L. M., JR., AND JANE RICHARDSON
1945. *Observations on Northern Blackfoot Kinship*. AEM *9*.

HARDIN, GARRETT
1956. Meaninglessness of the word Protoplasm, SCM *82*:112-120.

HARDING, CHARLES F., III
1953. A Plea for an Anthropological Approach to the Study of Personality, HO *12* #3:13-16.

HARING, DOUGLAS G.
   1929. *The Land of Gods and Earthquakes.* New York.
   1941. Social Behavior, Nine chapters in W. E. Mosher and associates, *Introduction to Responsible Citizenship.* New York.
   1943. *Blood on the Rising Sun.* Philadelphia. (Excerpt reprinted herewith.)
   1946-a. Ed. & Contrib., *Japan's Prospect.* Cambridge, Mass.
   1946-b. Aspects of Personal Character in Japan, FEQ *6*:12-22. (Reproduced herewith.)
   1947-a. *Racial Differences and Human Resemblances.* Rev. ed. Pamphlet. Syracuse.
   1947-b. Science and Social Phenomena, ASC *35*:351-363. (Reproduced herewith.)
   1949-a. Japan and the Japanese, In R. Linton, ed., *Most of the World.* New York. Pp. 814-875.
   1949-b. Is Culture Definable? ASR *14*:26-32.
   1950. The Social Sciences and Biology, In *Beiträge Zur Gesellungs- u. Völker-Wissenschaft: Prof. Dr. R. Thurnwald Zu Seinem Achtzigsten Geburtstag Gewidmet.* Berlin. Pp. 125-135.
   1951. Cultural Contexts of Thought and Communication, QJS *37*:161-172.
   1953-a. Japanese National Character: Cultural Anthropology, Psychoanalysis, and History, YR *42*:375-392. (Reprinted herewith.)
   1953-b. The Noro Cult of Amami Ōshima: Divine Priestesses of the Ryūkyū Islands, Sl *3*:108-121.
   1954. *Folk Music of the Amami Islands.* (Pamphlet and LP record, P448) Folkways Records, New York.
   1955-a. Japan: Changing Cultural Patterns, In article *Japan. Encyclopedia Americana,* 1955 ed.
   1955-b. Review of *Understanding the Japanese Mind* by James Clark Moloney. PA *28*:176-180.

HARING, DOUGLAS G. AND MARY E. JOHNSON
   1940. *Order and Possibility in Social Life.* New York.

HARRIS, Z. S.
   1951. *Methods in Structural Linguistics.* Chicago.

HARSH, C. M. AND H. G. SCHRICKEL
   1950. *Personality Development and Assessment.* New York.

HART, C. W. M.
   1954. Sons of Turimpi (sibling differentiation in Australia), AA *56*:242ff.

HART, J. M.
   1951. *The British Police.* London.

HARTMANN, H.
   1948. Relationship of Social Structure and Personality Types. *Bull. Amer. Psychoanalytic Assn.* 4:12.

HARTMANN, H., E. KRIS, AND R. M. LOEWENSTEIN
   1949. Notes on the Theory of Aggression, In PaC. III-IV. N. Y.
   1951. Some Psychoanalytic Comments on "Culture and Personality," In G. B. Wilbur & W. Muensterberger, eds., *Psychoanalysis and Culture.*

HASEGAWA NYOZEKAN
   n.d. *Japanese National Character.* Tokyo. (Japan Tourist Library, #40.)

HAVIGHURST, ROBERT J.
   1946. Environment and the Draw-a-man Test, the Performance of Indian Children, JASP *41*:50-63.

HAVIGHURST, ROBT. J. AND BERNICE L. NEUGARTEN
   1954. *American Indian and White Children: A Socio-Psychological Investigation.* Chicago.

HAVIGHURST, ROBERT J., AND HILDA TABA
   1949. *Adolescent Character and Personality.* New York.

HAWARD, L. R. C., AND W. A. ROLAND
  1954. Some Inter-cultural Differences on the Draw-a-man Test: Goodenough Scores, M *54*:86-88.

HAWLEY, FLORENCE AND DONOVAN SENTER
  1946. Group-designated Behavior Patterns in Two Acculturating Groups, SwA *2*:133-151.

HAWTHORN, HARRY B., ed.
  1955. *The Doukhobors of British Columbia.* Vancouver.

HAYES, CATHY
  1951. *The Ape in Our House.* New York.

HEBB, D. O.
  1949. *The Organization of Behavior.* N. Y.

HECKER, J. F. C., TR. BY B. G. BABBINGTON
  1885. *The Black Death and the Dancing Mania.* New York.

HEINICKE, CHRISTOPH, comp.
  1953. *Bibliography on Personality and Social Development of the Child.* (Bound with Beatrice B. Whiting, *Selected Ethnographic Sources on Child Training.*) SRCP #10. N. Y.

HELLERSBERG, ELIZABETH F.
  1947. Social and Cultural Aspects in Guidance Work and Psychotherapy. AJO, *17*:647-651.
  1950. *The Individual's Relation to Reality in our Culture.* Springfield, Ill.

HELSER, A. D.
  1934. *Education of Primitive People.* New York.

HENRY, JULES
  1936-37. The Personality of the Kaingang Indians, CP *5*:113-123.
  1940. Some Cultural Determinants of Hostility in Pilagá Indian Children, AJO *10*:111-120. (Cf. R. Benedict, 1940.)
  1941-a. *Jungle People.* New York. (Kaingang of Brazil.)
  1941-b. Rorschach Technique in Primitive Cultures, AJO *11*:230-234.
  1947. Environment and Symptom Formation, AJO *17*:628-632.
  1948-a. Cultural Discontinuity and the Shadow of the Past, SCM *66*:248-254.
  1948-b. Anthropology and Orthopsychiatry, In *Orthopsychiatry 1923-1948: Retrospect and Prospect.* New York.
  1949. The Social Function of Child Sexuality in Pilagá Indian Culture, In *Psychosexual Development in Health and Disease.* New York.
  1951-a. The Inner Experience of Culture, PS *14*:87-103.
  1951-b. Family Structure and Psychic Development, AJO *21*:59-73.
  1951-c. Family Structure and Transmission of Neurotic Behavior, AJO *21*:801-818.
  1955-a. Projective Testing in Ethnography. AA *57*:245-247. Rejoinder. ibid., 264-270.
  1955-b. Docility, or Giving Teacher What She Wants. JSI *11* #2:33-41.

HENRY, JULES, AND JOAN WHITEHORN BOGGS
  1952. Child Rearing, Culture, and the Natural World. PS *15*:261-272.

HENRY, JULES, AND ZUNIA HENRY
  1940. Speech disturbances in Pilagá Indian Children, AJO *10*:362-369.
  1944. *Doll Play of Pilagá Indian Children.* AOR *4*. (Reprinted, abridged, in Kluckhohn et al, 1953.)

HENRY, JULES, AND GEORGE WINOKUR
  1952. Some Aspects of the Relationship Between Psychoanalysis and Anthropology, AJO *22*:644-648.

HENRY, WILLIAM E.
  1947. *The Thematic Apperception Technique in the Study of Culture-Personality Relations.* GPM *35: #1*.

HERRICK, C. JUDSON
1931. *Introduction to Neurology.* 5th ed. Philadelphia.
1949-a. *George Ellett Coghill, Naturalist and Philosopher.* Chicago.
1949-b. A Biological Survey of Integrative Levels, In *Philosophy for the Future,* ed. by Roy Wood Sellars, V. J. McGill, and Marvin Farber. New York.

HERSKOVITS, MELVILLE J.
1934. Freudian Mechanisms in Primitive Negro Psychology, In *Essays Presented to C. G. Seligman,* ed. by E. E. Evans-Pritchard. Pp. 75-84. London.
1937. **Life in a Haitian Valley.* New York.
1938. **Dahomey.* 2 vols. New York.
1948. *Man and His Works, The Science of Cultural Anthropology.* New York. Chapter 4.
1951. On Cultural and Psychological Reality, in Rohrer & Sherif, 1951.
1952. Some Psychological Implications of Afroamerican Studies, In Sol Tax, ed., *Acculturation in the Americas,* vol. II of *Selected Papers of the XXIXth* I. C. A. Chicago. pp. 152-160.
1953. *Franz Boas: The Science of Man in the Making.* New York.

HERSKOVITS, MELVILLE J. AND FRANCES S.
1934. **Rebel Destiny.* New York. (Saramacca tribe, Dutch Guiana.)
1947. **Trinidad Village.* New York.

HEUSE, GEORGES A.
1953. *La Psychologie Ethnique.* Paris.

HEWES, GORDON W.
1955. World Distribution of Certain Postural Habits. AA 57:231-244.

HICKS, GRANVILLE
1946. *Small Town.* New York.

HIGHBAUGH, IRMA
1948. *Family Life in West China.* New York.

HILGARD, E. R. & D. G. MARQUIS
1940. *Conditioning and Learning.* New York.

HILGER, SISTER M. INEZ
1946. Notes on Cheyenne Child life, AA 48:60-69.
1951-a. Some Customs Related to Arikara Indian Child Life, PM 24:67-71.
1951-b. Chippewa Child Life in its Cultural Background, BuEB 146.
1952. Arapaho Child Life and its Cultural Background, BuEB 148.

HILL, W. W.
1935. The Status of the Hermaphrodite and Transvestite in Navaho Culture, AA 37:273-279.
1936. Navaho Rites for Dispelling Insanity and Delirium, *El Palacio* 41:71-74.
1938. Notes on the Pima Berdache. AA 40:338-340.
1943. *Navaho Humor.* GA 9.

HISS, PHILIP HANSON
1941. *Bali.* New York.

HOAGLAND, HUDSON
1949. Schizophrenia and Stress, SCAm 181:44 et seq.
1950. Rhythmic Behavior of the Nervous System, In *Centennial, A. A. A. S.* Washington.

HOCART, A. M.
1915. Ethnology and Psychology. FO 75:115-138.
1927. *Kingship.* Oxford.

HOEBEL, E. ADAMSON
1939. Comanche and Hekandika Shoshone Relationship Systems. AA 41:440-457.
1940. *The Political Organization and Law-Ways of the Comanche Indians.* AAM 54.
1941. The Comanche Sun Dance and Messianic Outbreak of 1873. AA 43:301-303.

1948. Joint ed. and tr., B. terHaar, *Adat Law in Indonesia*. New York.
1949. *Man in the Primitive World, an Introduction to Anthropology*. New York. Chapter 32.
1954. *The Law of Primitive Man: A Study in Comparative Legal Dynamics*, Cambridge, Mass.

HOEBEL, E. A., J. D. JENNINGS, & E. R. SMITH
1955. *Readings in Anthropology*. New York.

HOFSTRA, S.
1937. Personality and Differentiation in the Political Life of the Mendi, Af *10*:436-457.

HOGBIN, H. IAN
1931-a. The Social Organization of Ontong Java. O *1*:399-425.
1931-b. Education at Ontong Java. AA *33*:601-614.
1935. Native Culture of Wogeo. O *5*:308-337.
1939. Native Land Tenure in New Guinea. O *10*:113-165.
1943. A New Guinea Infancy: From Conception to Weaning in Wogeo. O *13*:285-309.
1945. Marriage in Wogeo, New Guinea. O *15*:324-352.
1946-a. Puberty to Marriage: a Study of the Sexual Life of the Natives of Wogeo, New Guinea. O *16*:185-209.
1946-b. A New Guinea Childhood: from Weaning till the Eighth Year in Wogeo. O *16*:275-296.
1947. Shame: a Study of Social Conformity in a New Guinea Village. O *17*:273-288.

HOIJER, HARRY
1951. Cultural Implications of Some Navaho Linguistic Categories, L *27*:111-120.

HOIJER, HARRY, ed.
1954. *Language in Culture: Proceedings of a Conference on the Interrelations of Language and Other Aspects of Culture*. AAM 79. Chicago.

HOLLIS, A. C.
1905. *The Masai*. Oxford.

HOLMBERG, ALLEN R.
1950. *Nomads of the Long Bow*. Publ. #10, SIP.

HOMANS, GEORGE C.
1941. Anxiety and Ritual: The Theories of Malinowski and Radcliffe-Brown, AA *43*:164ff.
1950. *The Human Group*. New York.

HONIGMANN, JOHN J.
1942. An Interpretation of the Social-Psychological Functions of the Ritual Clown. CP *10*:220-226.
1944. Morale in a Primitive Society, CP *12*:228-236
1947. Cultural Dynamics of Sex (Kaska Indians), PS *10*:37-47.
1949-a. *Culture & Ethos of Kaska Society*. YPA *40*.
1949-b. Incentives to Work in a Canadian Indian Society, HO *8* #4:23-28.
1950. Culture Patterns and Human Stress, PS *13*:25-34.
1952. Community Relations in Great Whale River, AA *54*:510-522.
1953-a. A Comparative Analysis of Divorce, MFL *15*:37-43.
1953-b. Toward a Distinction between Psychiatric and Social Abnormality, SLF *31*:274-277. (Reprinted herewith.)
1954. *Culture and Personality*. New York.
1955. Comments, (On J. Henry, "Projective Testing . . ." AA *57*:253-256.

HONIGMANN, JOHN J. AND IRMA
1945. Alcoholic Drinking in an Indian-White Community, QJSA *5*:575-619.
1953. Some Patterns of Child Rearing among the Great Whale River Eskimo, *Anthrop. Papers*, Univ. Alaska. *2*:31-51.

HOOTON, EARNEST A.
    1946. *Up from the Ape.* Rev. ed. New York.
HOPKINS, PRYNS
    1939. A Personality Study of an Avatar of Krishna. CP *8:*71-80.
HORNEY, KAREN
    1937. *The Neurotic Personality of our Time.* New York.
    1939. *New Ways in Psychoanalysis.* New York.
    1945. *Our Inner Conflicts.* New York.
    1950. *Neurosis and Human Growth.* New York.
HORTON, DONALD
    1943. The Functions of Alcohol in Primitive Societies: A Cross-Cultural Study,
        QJSA *4:*199-320. (Reprinted in Kluckhohn, Murray & Schneider, 1953.)
HOSKINS, R. G.
    1941. *Endocrinology.* New York.
    1946. *The Biology of Schizophrenia.* New York.
HOWITT, A. W.
    1904. **Native Tribes of Southeast Australia.* London.
HSIAO, H. H.
    1929. Mentality of the Chinese and Japanese, JAp *13:*9-31.
HSU, FRANCIS L. K.
    1942. The Differential Functions of Relationship Terms, AA *44:*248-256.
    1943. Incentives to Work in Primitive Communities, ASR *8:*638-642.
    1945. Observations on Cross-cousin Marriage in China, AA *47:*83-103.
    1948. *Under the Ancestors' Shadow, Chinese Culture and Personality.* New
        York.
    1949-a. Suppression versus Repression: A Limited Psychological Interpretation
        of Four Cultures, PS *12:*223-242.
    1949-b. China, In *Most of the World,* ed. by Ralph Linton. New York. Pp.
        731-813.
    1951. Sex Crime and Personality: a Study in Comparative Cultural Patterns, AS
        *20:*57-66.
    1952-a. *Religion, Science, and Human Crises: A Study of China in Transition*
        . . . London.
    1952-b. Anthropology or Psychiatry, SwA *8:*227-250.
    1953. *Americans and Chinese: Two Ways of Life.* New York.
    1954. Ed., *Aspects of Culture and Personality: A Symposium.* New York.
HU HSIEN-CHIN
    1944. The Chinese Concepts of "Face," AA *46:*45-64. (Reproduced herewith.)
    1947. *The Common Descent Group in China and Its Functions.* V *10.*
HUDSON, ALFRED E., AND ELIZABETH BACON
    1941. Social Control and the Individual in Eastern Hazara Culture, In L. Spier
        et al, ed., *Language, Culture, and Personality.* Menasha. Pp. 239-258.
HULSE, FREDERICK S.
    1946. A Sketch of Japanese Society, JAmO *66:*219-229.
    1947. Technological Development and Personal Incentive in Japan, SwA *3:*
        124-129.
    1948. Convention and Reality in Japanese Culture, SwA *4:*345-355.
HUNT, J. McV.
    1938. An Instance of the Social Origin of Conflict Resulting in Psychoses, AJO
        *8:*158-164. (Reprinted, Kluckhohn, Murray & Schneider, 1953.)
    1944. Ed., *Personality and the Behavior Disorders.* New York.
HUNTER, EDWARD
    1951. *Brain-Washing in Red China.* Toronto and Tokyo.
HUTTON, J. H.
    1951. **Caste in India.* Rev. ed. Oxford.

HUXLEY, JULIAN
1942. *Evolution, the Modern Synthesis.* New York.

HYMAN, HERBERT H. AND ASSOCIATES
1954. *Interviewing in Social Research.* Chicago.

ILG, FRANCES, AND LOUISE B. AMES
1955. *Child Behavior.* New York

INKELES, ALEX
1953. Some Sociological Observations on Culture and Personality Studies, In Kluckhohn, Murray, and Schneider, 1953: pp. 577-592.
1955. Social Change and Social Character: The Role of Parental Mediation. JSI *11* #2:12-23.

INKELES, ALEX AND DANIEL LEVINSON
1954. National Character: the Study of Modal Personality and Sociocultural Systems, in *Handbook of Social Psychology,* vol. II., ed. by ·Gardner Lindzey. Cambridge.

Interrelations Between the Social Environment and Psychiatric Disorders
1953. Milbank Memorial Fund, New York.

ISHINO IWAO
1953. The *Oyabun-kobun:* A Japanese Ritual Kinship Institution, AA *55:*695-707.

JACKSON, E., AND E. H. KLATSKIN
1950. Rooming-in research project: Development of Methodology of Parent-Child Relationship in a Clinical Setting, PaC *5:*236-274.

JAHODA, MARIE, AND RICHARD CHRISTIE, eds.
1954. *Studies in the Scope and Method of "The Authoritarian Personality."* Glencoe, Ill.

JAMES, BERNARD F.
1954. Some Critical Observations Concerning Analyses of Chippewa "Atomism" and Chippewa Personality, AA *56:*283-286.

JENNESS, DIAMOND
1933. An Indian Method of Treating Hysteria. PM *6:*13-20.

JENNINGS, HERBERT SPENCER
1906. The Method of Regulation in Behavior and Other Fields, JEZ *2:*473ff. (Reprinted in Haring & Johnson, *Order & Possibility in Social Life,* 1940.)
1942. The Transition from the Individual to the Social Level, In R. Redfield, ed., *Levels of Integration in Biological and Social Systems* (Biological Symposia *8*). Lancaster, Pa. pp. 105-119.

JENSEN, BARRY T.
1952. Reading Habits and left-right orientation in Profile Drawings by Japanese children. AJPy. *65:*306-307.

JEWELL, DONALD P.
1952. A Case of a "Psychotic" Navaho Indian Male, HO *11* #1:32-36.

JOHNSON, MARY E.
1929. Review of M. Mead, *Coming of Age in Samoa. Sat. Rev. of Lit.,* *5:*778. Cf. also Haring & Johnson, 1940.

JOKL, R. H.
1950. Psychic Determinism and Preservation of Sublimation in Classical Psychoanalytic Procedure, *Bull. Menninger Clin., 14:*207-219.

JONES, ERNEST
1924. Psycho-Analysis and Anthropology. RAI *54:*47-66.

JOSEPH, ALICE AND VERONICA F. MURRAY
1948. Chamorros and Carolinians of Saipan. Personality Studies of Saipanese Children and Adults, Including a Report on Psychopathology. *CIMA Report, Pacific Science Board, National Research Council.* Washington, D. C.
1951. *Chamorros and Carolinians of Saipan.* Cambridge, Mass.

JOSEPH, ALICE, ROSAMOND B. SPICER, AND JANE CHESKY
　1949. *The Desert People*. Chicago. (Papago.)

JOST, HUDSON, AND LESTER W. SONTAG
　1944. The Genetic Factor in Autonomic Nervous System Function, Psm *6*:308-
　　310. (Reproduced in Kluckhohn, Murray & Schneider, 1953.)

JUNG, CARL GUSTAV
　1916. *Psychology of the Unconscious*. New York.

JUNOD, H. A.
　1912, 1927. * *The Life of a South African Tribe*. 2 vols. Neuchatel & London.

KABAT, ELVIN A.
　1949. Allergic Mechanisms in Nervous Disease, SCAm *181*:16-19.

KANTOR, J. R.
　1942. Toward a Scientific Analysis of Motivation. PsRe *5*:225-275.

KAPLAN, BERT
　1954. *A Study of Rorschach Responses in Four Cultures*. Reports of the Ramah
　　Project, No. 6. PHa *42* #2.

KARDINER, ABRAM
　1939. *The Individual and His Society*. New York.
　1945-a. *The Psychological Frontiers of Society*. New York. With the collabora-
　　tion of Ralph Linton, Cora DuBois, and James West.
　1945-b. The Concept of Basic Personality Structure as an Operational Tool in
　　the Social Sciences, In *The Science of Man in the World Crisis*, ed. by
　　Ralph Linton. New York. (Reprinted herewith.)

KARDINER, ABRAM AND L. OVERSEY
　1951. *The Mark of Oppression: a Psychological Study of the American Negro*.
　　New York.

KEESING, FELIX M.
　1953. *Social Anthropology in Polynesia*. Oxford. (Excellent guide to literature.)

KELLOGG, W. N. & L. A.
　1933. *The Ape and the Child*. New York.

KELLY, GEORGE A.
　1955. *The Psychology of Personal Constructs*. 2 vol.. New York.

KENNARD, EDWARD
　1938. *Hopi Kachinas*. New York.

KENNEDY, RAYMOND
　1945. *Bibliography of Indonesian Peoples and Cultures*. YAS *4*.

KEPES, G.
　1947. *Art as Circumstantial Organization, Creative Discipline of the Visual En-
　　vironment*. Presented at 35th Ann. Meeting of College Art Association of
　　America, New York.

KERLINGER, FRED N.
　1953. Behavior and Personality in Japan: a Critique of three Studies of Japanese
　　Personality. SLF *31*:250-258.

KEUR, JOHN Y., AND DOROTHY L. KEUR
　1955. *The Deeply Rooted: A Study of a Drents Community in the Netherlands*.
　　AEM *25*.

KHAING, MI MI
　1946. *Burmese Family*. London

KIDD, DUDLEY
　1906. *Savage Childhood, A Study of Kafir Children*. London.

KING, ARDEN R.
　1943. The Dream Biography of a Mountain Maidü. CP *11*:227-234.

KING, L. M.
　1927. *China in Turmoil: Studies in Personality*. London.

KINSEY, ALFRED C., W. B. POMEROY, AND C. E. MARTIN
1948. *Sexual Behavior in the Human Male*. Philadelphia.

KINSEY, A. C., W. B. POMEROY, C. E. MARTIN, AND P. H. GEBHARD
1953. *Sexual Behavior in the Human Female*. Philadelphia.

KLATSKIN, E. H.
1952. Shifts in Child Care in Three Social Classes Under an Infant Care Program of Flexible Methodology. AJO *22*:52-61.

KLEIN, VIOLA
1946. *The Feminine Character, History of an Ideology*. New York.

KLER, JOSEPH
1938. Birth, Infancy, and Childhood among the Ordos Mongols, PM *11* #3, 4.

KLINE, NATHAN S., ED.
1956. *Approaches to the Study of Human Personality*. Amer. Psychiatric Assn., Psychiatric Research Reports, *2*, Washington.

KLINEBERG, OTTO
1934. Notes on the Huichol, AA *36*:446-460.
1935. *Race Differences*. New York.
1938. Emotional Expression in Chinese Literature. JASP *33*:517-520.
1944. A Science of National Character, JSP *19*:147-162.
1950. *Tensions Affecting International Understanding, A Survey of Research*. SRCB *62*.
1953. Cultural Factors in Personality Adjustment of Children, AJO *23*:465-471.

KLOPFER, BRUNO AND DOUGLAS McG. KELLEY
1942. *The Rorschach Technique*. Yonkers.

KLUCKHOHN, CLYDE
1938. Participation in Ceremonials in a Navaho Community, AA *40*:359-369. (Reproduced herewith.)
1939. Theoretical Bases for an Empirical Method of Studying the Acquisition of Culture by Individuals, M *39*:98-103.
1941. Patterning as Exemplified in Navaho Culture, In Spier, Hallowell & Newman, eds., 1941.
1942. Myths and Rituals: A General Theory, HAT *35*:45-79.
1943. *Navaho Witchcraft*. PHa *22* #3.
1944. The Influence of Psychiatry on Anthropology in America During the Last 100 Years, In *One Hundred Years of American Psychiatry*, ed. by J. K. Hall, G. Zilboorg, and H. A. Bunker. New York. (Reprinted herewith.)
1945-a. A Navaho Personal Document with a Brief Paretian Analysis. SwA *1*:260-283. (Reproduced herewith.)
1945-b. Group Tensions: Analysis of a Case History, *Fifth Symposium*, CoSPR: pp. 222-243.
1946. Personality Formation among the Navaho Indians, So *9*.
1947. Some Aspects of Navaho Infancy and Early Childhood, PSS *1*:37-86.
1948. As an Anthropologist Views it. In *Sex Habits of American Men*, ed. by A. Deutsch. New York. pp. 88-104.
1949-a. *Mirror for Man, The Relation of Anthropology to Modern Life*. New York.
1949-b. The Philosophy of the Navaho Indians, In *Ideological Differences and World Order*. New Haven.
1951. The Study of Culture, In D. Lerner, ed., *The Policy Sciences*. Pp. 86-101.
1953. Universal Categories of Culture. In *Anthropology Today*, ed. by A. L. Kroeber, New York.
1954. Southwestern Studies of Culture and Personality. AA *56*:685-696.

KLUCKHOHN, CLYDE AND FLORENCE KLUCKHOHN
1948. American Culture: Generalized Orientations and Class Patterns. In *Conflicts of Power in Modern Culture*, CoSPR 1947 Symposium.

KLUCKHOHN, CLYDE, AND DOROTHEA LEIGHTON
  1947. *The Navaho. Cambridge, Mass.
KLUCKHOHN, CLYDE AND WILLIAM MORGAN
  1951. Some Notes on Navaho Dreams, In Wilbur and Muensterberger, 1951.
KLUCKHOHN, CLYDE, AND O. H. MOWRER
  1944-a. "Culture and Personality"; A Conceptual Scheme, AA 46:1-29.
  1944-b. Dynamic Theory of Personality, in J. McV. Hunt, ed., Personality and
    the Behavior Disorders. New York.
KLUCKHOHN, CLYDE, AND HENRY A. MURRAY
  1948. Personality in Nature, Society, and Culture. New York.
KLUCKHOHN, CLYDE, HENRY A. MURRAY, AND D. M. SCHNEIDER
  1953. Personality in Nature, Society, and Culture. Revised Edition. New York.
KLUCKHOHN, CLYDE AND J. ROSENZWEIG.
  1949. Two Navaho Children over a Five-year Period. AJO 19: 266-278.
KLUCKHOHN, CLYDE, AND L. C. WYMAN
  1940. An Introduction to Navaho Chant Practice. AAM 53.
KLUCKHOHN, FLORENCE R.
  1940. The Participant-Observer Technique in Small Communities, AJS 46:331-
    342.
  1950. Dominant and Substitute Profiles of Cultural Orientations, SLF 28:376-
    393.
  1951. Dominant and Variant Cultural Value Orientations, Social Welfare Forum:
    97-113. (The 1950 and 1951 items are reprinted in revised form in Kluck-
    hohn, Murray, & Schneider, 1953.)
KRADER, LAWRENCE
  1956. A Nativistic Movement in Western Siberia, AA 58:282-292.
KRAMER, SAMUEL N.
  1949. Schooldays: A Sumerian Composition relating to the Education of a
    Scribe, JAmO 69:199-215.
KRAUSE, AUREL, TR. BY ERNA GUNTHER
  1956. *The Tlingit Indians: Results of a Trip to the Northwest Coast of Amer-
    ica and the Bering Straits. Seattle, 1956. (Original German edition, Jena,
    1885)
KRETSCHMER, E., (tr. by W. J. H. SPROTT)
  1925. Physique and Character. London.
KRIS, E.
  1944. Art and Regression. N. Y. Acad. Sciences, N. Y.
KROEBER, ALFRED L.
  1917. The Superorganic, AA 19:163-213.
  1918. The Possibility of a Social Psychology, AJS 23:635-650.
  1920. Totem and Taboo: An Ethnologic Psychoanalysis, AA 22:48-55.
  1925. *Handbook of the Indians of California. BuEB 78.
  1935-a. Ed. with associates, *Walapai Ethnography. AAM 42.
  1935-b. Review, R. Benedict, Patterns of Culture. AA 37:689-690.
  1939. Totem and Taboo in Retrospect, AJS 45:446-451.
  1940. Psychosis or Social Sanction, CP 8:204-215.
  1944. Configurations of Culture Growth. Berkeley.
  1945. The Use of Autobiographical Evidence, SwA 1:318-322. (Original title:
    A Yurok War Reminiscence.)
  1947. A Southwestern Personality Type, SwA 3:108-113.
  1948. Anthropology. Rev. ed. New York. Esp. Chap. 15.
  1953. Ed., Anthropology Today, an Encyclopedic Inventory. Chicago.
  1955-a. The Nature of Culture. Chicago. (Contains above items: 1917, 1918, 1920,
    1939, 1940, 1945, 1947.) See especially pp. 299-300.
  1955-b. History of Anthropological Thought, In YbA:293-311.

1956. The Place of Boas in Anthropology. AA *58*:151-159.
(Complete bibliography to 1936 in R. Lowie, ed., *Essays in Anthropology Presented to A. L. Kroeber*, Berkeley, 1936.)

KROEBER, A. L., AND CLYDE KLUCKHOHN
1952. *Culture: A Critical Review of Concepts and Definitions*. PHa *47*.

KUBIE, L. S.
1952. Problems and Techniques of Psychoanalytic Validation and Progress, In *Psychoanalysis as Science*, ed. by E. Pumpian-Mindlin. Stanford.

KUBO, Y.
1938. The Behavior Inventories and Examinations of Japanese Children, JGeP *53*:87-99.

LABARRE, WESTON
1938. *The Peyote Cult*. YPA *19*.
1942. Hitler's Imagery and German Youth, PS *5*:475-493.
1945. Some Observations on Character Structure in the Orient: The Japanese, PS *8* #3.
1946-a. Social Cynosure and Social Structure, JP *14*:169-183. (Reprinted herewith.)
1946-b. Some Observations on Character Structure in the Orient: The Chinese, PS *9* #3, 4.
1947-a. Primitive Psychotherapy in Native American Cultures: Peyotism and Confession, JASP *42*:294-309.
1947-b. The Cultural Basis of Emotions and Gestures, JP *16*:49-68. (Reproduced herewith.)
1948-a. *The Aymara Indians of the Lake Titicaca Plateau, Bolivia*. AAM *68*.
1948-b. Folklore and Psychology. JAF *61*:382-390.
1949-a. Wanted: A Pattern for Modern Man, MH *33*:209-221.
1949-b. Child Care and World Peace, *The Child*. Federal Security Agency.
1949-c. Rev., first ed., *Personal Character and Cultural Milieu*, AA *51*:626-628.
1950. Aymara Folktales. IJAL *16*:40-45.
1954-a. Bibliography, Culture and Personality. (Mimeo.) Durham, N. C.
1954-b. *The Human Animal*. Chicago.

LAMOTT, W. C.
1944. *Nippon, the Crime and Punishment of Japan*. New York.

LANDES, RUTH
1937. The Personality of the Ojibwa, CP *6*:51-60.
1938-a. *The Ojibwa Woman*. CUCA *31*.
1938-b.The Abnormal among the Ojibwa Indians, JASP *33*:14-33.
1940. A Cult Matriarchiate and Male Homosexuality, JASP *35*:386-397.

LANDES, RUTH AND MARK ZBOROWSKI
1950. Hypotheses Concerning the Eastern European Jewish Family, PS *13*: 447-464.

LANDMAN, RUTH H.
1952. Studies in Drinking in Jewish Culture: III. Drinking Patterns of Children and Adolescents Attending Religious Schools. QJSA *13*:89-94.

LANG, OLGA
1946. *Chinese Family and Society*. New Haven.

LANTIS, MARGARET
1947. *Alaskan Eskimo Ceremonialism*. AEM *11*.
1953. Nunivak Eskimo Personality as Revealed in the Mythology, *Anthrop. Papers, Univ. of Alaska*, 2:109-174.
1955. Ed., The USA as Anthropologists See It, AA 57 #6. (Special issue, fourteen collaborators.)

LASSWELL, HAROLD D.
1949-a. The Language of Power. In H. D. Lasswell and N. Leites, eds., *Language and Politics*. New York.

1949-b. Style and the Language of Politics. In Lasswell and Leites, eds., *Language and Politics*.
1950. Propaganda and Mass Insecurity, PS *13*:283-299.

LAUBSCHER, B. J. F.
1938. *Sex, Custom, and Psychopathology*. New York. (African data.)

LAWRENCE, W. E.
1937. Alternating Generations in Australia, In *Studies in the Science of Society Presented to A. G. Keller*, ed. by G. P. Murdock. New Haven.

LEE, DOROTHY D.
1938. Conceptual Implications of an Indian Language, PHS *5*:89-102.
1940. A Primitive System of Values, PHS 7:355-378.
1944-a. Categories of the Generic and the Particular in Wintu. AA *46*:362-369.
1944-b. Linguistic Reflection of the Wintu Thought. IJAL *10*:181-187.
1948. Are Basic Needs Ultimate? JASP *43*:391-395. (Reprinted in Kluckhohn, Murray & Schneider, 1953.)
1949. Being and Value in a Primitive Culture, JPH *46*:401-415.
1950. Lineal and Nonlineal Codifications of Reality, Psm *12*:89-97.

LEE, S. G.
1950. Some Zulu Concepts of Mental Disorder. *So. Afr. Jnl. Soc. Research 1*:9-19.

LEE, W. L. M.
1901. *A History of Police in England*. London.

LEHMANN, ROSAMOND
1945. *The Ballad and the Source*. New York.

LEIGHTON, ALEXANDER
1949. *Human Relations in a Changing World*. New York.
1955. Psychiatric Disorder and Social Environment, PS *18*:367-383.

LEIGHTON, ALEXANDER H., AND DOROTHEA C. LEIGHTON
1942. Some Types of Uneasiness and Fear in a Navaho Indian Community, AA *44*:194-209.
1944. *The Navaho Door, an Introduction to Navaho Life*. Cambridge.
1945. *The Governing of Men*. Princeton.
1949. *Gregorio, The Hand Trembler: A Psycho-Biological Personality Study of a Navaho Indian*. PHa *40* #1.

LEIGHTON, DOROTHEA, AND CLYDE KLUCKHOHN
1947. *Children of the People: The Navaho Individual and His Development*. Cambridge, Mass.

LEITES, NATHAN
1947. Trends in Affectlessness. AI *4* #2:89-112. (Reprinted in Kluckhohn, Murray & Schneider, 1953.)
1948. Psycho-Cultural Hypotheses about Political Acts, WP *1*:102-119.
1953. *A Study of Bolshevism*. Glencoe, Ill.

LEITES, NATHAN, AND ELSE BERNAUT
1954. *Ritual of Liquidation: Communists on Trial*. Glencoe, Ill.

LEITES, NATHAN, AND MARTHA WOLFENSTEIN
1947. An Analysis of Themes and Plots, AASPS *254*:41-48.

LESSA, WILLIAM A.
1956. Oedipus-type Tales in Oceania, JAF *69*:63-73.

LESSA, WM. A. AND MARVIN SPIEGELMAN
1954. Ulithian Personality as Seen through Ethnological Materials and Thematic Test Analysis. UnCaCS *2* #5:243-301.

LEVIN, A. J.
1948. Maine, McLennan, and Freud, PS *11*:177-191.

LEVI-STRAUSS, CLAUDE
1949. *Les Structures Élémentaires de la Parenté*. Paris.

1956. The Family. In *Man, Culture, and Society,* ed. by H. L. Shapiro. New York.

LEVY, DAVID M.
1929. A Method of Integrating Physical and Psychiatric Examination, AJP *9*:121-194.
1936. Primary Affect Hunger, AJP *94*:643-652.
1939. Sibling Rivalry Studies in Children of Primitive Groups, AJO *9*:205-215.
1942. Psychosomatic Studies of Some Aspects of Maternal Behavior, Psm *4*:223-227. (Reprinted in Kluckhohn, Murray & Schneider, 1953.)
1946. The German Anti-Nazi: A Case Study, AJO *16*:505-515.
1948. Anti-Nazis: Criteria of Differentiation, PS *11*:125-167.

LEVY, MARION J., JR.
1949. *The Family Revolution in Modern China.* Cambridge, Mass.

LEWIN, K.
1935. Some Social-Psychological Differences Between the United States and Germany, CP *4*:265-293.
1943. Forces behind Food Habits and Methods of Change, In *The Problem of Changing Food Habits,* National Research Council Bulletin *108.*
1948. *Resolving Social Conflicts: Selected Papers on Group Dynamics,* 1935-1946. Ed. by G. W. Lewin. New York.

LEWIS, HYLAN
1955. *Blackways of Kent.* Chapel Hill.

LEWIS, OSCAR
1941. Manly-Hearted Women among the North Piegan, AA *43*:173-187.
1951. *Life in a Mexican Village.* Chicago.
1953. Controls and Experiments in Field Work, In A. L. Kroeber, ed., *Anthropology Today.* Chicago.

LEYBURN, JAMES G.
1931. *Handbook of Ethnography.* New Haven. (Index of tribal names and locations.)
1941. *The Haitian People.* Oxford and New York.

LI AN-CHE
1937. Zuni: Some Observations and Queries. AA *39*:62-76.

LIFTON, ROBERT J.
1956. "Thought Reform" of Western Civilians in Chinese Communist Prisons. PS *19*:173-195

LIN TSUNG-YI
1953. A Study of the Incidence of Mental Disorder in Chinese and other Cultures, PS *16*:313-336.

LIN YUEH-HWA
1947. *The Golden Wing.* London, 2nd. ed. (Story of Chinese family.)

LINCOLN, J. S.
1936. *The Dream in Primitive Cultures.* Baltimore.

LINDESMITH, ALFRED R., AND ANSELM L. STRAUSS
1950. A Critique of Culture-Personality Writings, ASR *15*:587-600.

LINEBARGER, PAUL M. A.
1954. Asian Nationalism. PS *17*:261-266.

LINK, MARGARET S. AND J. L. HENDERSON
1956. *The Pollen Path.* Stanford. (Navaho)

LINTON, RALPH
1933. *The Tanala, a Hill Tribe of Madagascar.* FM *22* (Publ. #317).
1936. *The Study of Man.* New York.
1938. Culture, Society, and the Individual, JASP *33*:425-436.
1939. The Effects of Culture on Mental and Emotional Processes, AsR *19*:293-304.

1943. Nativistic Movements. AA *45*:230-240.

1945-a. *The Cultural Background of Personality.* New York.

1945-b. Ed., *The Science of Man in the World Crisis.* New York.

1949-a. Ed., *Most of the World: The Peoples of Africa, Latin America, and the East Today.* New York.

1949-b. The Personality of Peoples, SCAm *181*:11-15.

1955. *The Tree of Culture.* New York.

LIPMAN, MATTHEW AND SALVATORE PIZZURO
1956. Charismatic Participation as a Sociopathic Process. PS *19*:11-30.

LITTLE, K. L.
1950. Methodology in the Study of Adult Personality and "National Character," AA *52*:279-282.

LIU SHAO, *see under* J. K. SHRYOCK

LLEWELLYN, K., AND E. A. HOEBEL
1941. *The Cheyenne Way.* Norman, Okla.

LLOYD, WESLEY P.
1953. *Student Counseling in Japan.* Minneapolis.

LOEB, EDWIN M.
1929. Tribal Initiations and Secret Societies, UnCa *25*.

LOEB, EDWIN M. AND JAN O. M. BROEK
1947. Social Organization and the Long House in Southeast Asia, AA *49*:414-425.

LOEB, EDWIN M., AND R. HEINE-GELDERN
1935. **Sumatra.* Vienna.

LOEWENSTEIN, RUDOLPH M.
1947. The Historical and Cultural Roots of Anti-Semitism, PSS *1*:313-356.

1951. *Christians and Jews, a Psychoanalytic Study.* New York. (Tr. by V. Damman.)

LOLLI, G., ET AL
1952. The Use of Wine and other alcoholic Beverages by a Group of Italians and Americans of Italian Extraction. QJSA *13*:27-48.

LOMMEL, A.
1949. Notes on Sexual Behavior and Initiation, Wunambal tribe, northwestern Australia, O *20*:158-164.

LORENZ, K.
1952. *King Solomon's Ring.* London.

LOWENFELD, MARGARET
1954. *The Lowenfeld Mosaic Test.* London.

LOWREY, LAWSON G.
1946. *Psychiatry for Social Workers.* New York.

LOWERY, LAWSON G. AND VICTORIA SLOANE, Asst., Eds.
1948. *Orthopsychiatry, 1923-1948. Retrospect and Prospect. Twenty-Five Years of Orthopsychiatric Endeavor to Obtain Straightness of Mind and Spirit.* Amer. Orthopsychiatric Assn., N. Y.

LOWIE, ROBERT H.
1915. Ceremonialism in North America, In *Anthropology in North America.* New York. Pp. 229-258.

1917. Notes on the Social Organization and Customs of the Mandan, Hidatsa, and Crow Indians, AMA *21*:1-96.

1920. *Primitive Society.* New York.

1927. Prestige Among Indians, *Amer. Mercury 12*:446-448.

1935. **The Crow Indians.* New York.

1936. Ed. *Essays in Anthropology Presented to A. L. Kroeber.* Berkeley.

1945. *The German People, a Social Portrait to 1914.* New York.

1949. *Social Organization.* New York.

1950. Observations on the Literary Style of the Crow Indians. In *Beiträge zur Gesellungs-u. Völkerwissenschaft . . . Richard Thurnwald*, Berlin.

1954. *Toward Understanding Germany*. Chicago.

1956. Boas once more. AA *58*:159-164.

LUDWIG, ALFRED O.

1948. Some Psycho-social Factors in Cases of Severe Medical Disease, HO *7:* 1-5.

LUMMIS, CHARLES F.

1897. *The Land of Poco Tiempo*. New York.

LUOMALA, KATHERINE

1936. Dreams and Dream Interpretations of the Diegueño Indians of Southern California, PYQ 195-225.

LYMAN, BENJAMIN SMITH

1885. The Character of the Japanese, JSpP *19*:133-172.

MAAS, HENRY S., C. H. PRINCE, AND G. E. DAVIE

1953. Personal-Social Disequilibria in a Bureaucratic System. PS *16*:129-138.

MACGREGOR, FRANCES COOKE, T. M. ABEL, A. BRYT, E. LAUER, AND S. WEISSMANN

1956. *Facial Deformities and Plastic Surgery, a Psychosocial Study*. Springfield, Ill.

MACGREGOR, GORDON

1946. *Warriors without Weapons, A Study of the Society and Personality of the Pine Ridge Sioux*. Chicago.

MACIVER, R. M.

1929. *Community*. New York.

MAIR, L. P.

1951. Marriage and the Family in the Dedza district of Nyasaland, RAI *81*:103-119.

MAJUMDAR, D. N.

1944. *The Fortunes of Primitive Tribes*. Lucknow.

MALINOWSKI, BRONISLAW

1922. *Argonauts of the Western Pacific*. London.

1927-a. *The Father in Primitive Psychology*. New York.

1927-b. *Sex and Repression in Savage Society*. New York.

1929. *The Sexual Life of Savages*. New York.

1935. *Coral Gardens and Their Magic*. 2 vol. New York.

1939. The Group and the Individual in Functional Analysis, AJS *44*:938-964.

1948. *Magic, Science and Religion*. Glencoe, Ill. and Anchor Books.

MANDELBAUM, DAVID G.

1943. Wolf-Child Histories from India, JSP *17*:25-44.

1953-a. On the Study of National Character, AA *55*:174-187.

1953-b. Comments; see Index, In *An Appraisal of Anthropology Today*, ed. by Sol Tax et al. Chicago.

MANDELBAUM, DAVID, ed.

1949. *Selected Writings of Edward Sapir, In Language, Culture, and Personality*. Berkeley.

MARINER, WILLIAM

1827. *Account of the Natives of the Tonga Islands*. Edinburgh.

MARKS, ROSE W.

1951. The Effect of Probability, Desirability, and "Privilege" on the Stated Expectations of Children, JP *19*:332-351.

MARRIOTT, A.

1948. *Maria, The Potter of San Ildefonso*. Norman, Okla.

MARTIN, J.

1949. *The Physique of Young Adult Males*. Memor. Med. Res. Coun. *20*. London.

MARWICK, M. G.

1952. The Social Context of Cewa Witch Beliefs, Af *22*:120-135, 215-233.

Maslow, Abraham H.
  1942. The Dynamics of Psychological Security-Insecurity, JP *10*:331-344.
  1943-a. The Authoritarian Character Structure, JSP *18*:401-411.
  1943-b. Dynamics of Personality Organization, PsR *50*:514-539, 541-558.
  1943-c. Preface to Motivation Theory, Psm *5*:85-92.
  1951. Ed., American Culture and Personality Issue, JSI 7 #4.

Maslow, Abraham H., and Bela Mittelmann
  1941. *Principles of Abnormal Psychology*. New York.

Mathews, J. J.
  1932. *Wah' Kon-Tah, the Osage and the White Man's Road*. Norman, Okla.

Matsumoto Toru and Marion O. Lerrigo
  1946. *A Brother is a Stranger*. New York. (Japanese autobiography.)

May, L. Carlyle
  1954. The Dancing Religion: A Japanese Messianic Sect. SwA *10*:119-137.
  1956. A Survey of Glossolalia and Related Phenomena in Non-Christian Religions. AA *58*:75-96.

Mayer, Philip
  1953. Gusii Initiation Ceremonies, RAI *83*:9-36.

McAllester, D.
  1941. Water as a Disciplinary Agent among the Crow and Blackfoot, AA *43*: 593-604.

McArthur, Charles
  1956. Personalities of First and Second Children. PS *19*:47-54.

McGill, V. J.
  1954. *Emotions and Reason*. Springfield, Ill.

McGranahan, D. J.
  1936. The Psychology of Language, PsB *33*:178-216.

McGraw, Myrtle
  1935. *Growth*. New York.

McIlwraith, Thomas F.
  1949. *The Bella Coola Indians*. 2 vol. Toronto.

McPhee, Colin
  1940. *Balinese Ceremonial Music*. Schirmer, N. Y.
  1941. *Music in Bali*. Schirmer's Library of Recorded Music, Set No. 17. N. Y.
  1947. *A House in Bali*. N. Y.
  1948. Dance in Bali. *Dance Index* 7 Nos. 7, 8.

Mead, Margaret
  1928-a. The Role of the Individual in Samoan Culture, RAI *58*:481-495.
  1928-b. *Coming of Age in Samoa*, New York. (Cf. Johnson, M., 1929.)
  1930-a. *Social Organization of Manu'a*. BMB 76. (Samoa.)
  1930-b. Adolescence in Primitive and Modern Society, In V. Calverton & S. Schmalhausen, eds., *The New Generation*, N. Y. (Reprinted: Newcomb, Hartley et al, *Readings in Social Psychology*, pp. 6-13.)
  1930-c. *Growing up in New Guinea*. New York.
  1930-d. An ethnologist's footnote to "Totem and Taboo," PYR *17*:297-304.
  1931. The Primitive Child, In *Handbook of Child Psychology* ed. by C. Murchison. Worcester.
  1932-a. *The Changing Culture of an Indian Tribe*. New York.
  1932-b. An Investigation of the Thought of Primitive Children with Special Reference to Animism, RAI *42*:173ff.
  1934. The Use of Primitive Material in the Study of Personality, CP *3*:3-16.
  1935-a. *Sex and Temperament in Three Primitive Societies*. New York.
  1935-b. Review of G. Róheim, *The Riddle of the Sphinx*. CP *4*:85-90.
  1936. Culture and Personality, AJS *42*:84-87.
  1937-a. Ed. & contrib. *Cooperation and Competition among Primitive Peoples*. New York.

1937-b. Public Opinion Mechanisms among Primitive Peoples, PuQ *1* #6.

1938. *The Mountain Arapesh*, Part I. AMA *36* pt. 3. (Cf. also 1940, 1947, 1949.)

1939-a. *From the South Seas*. New York. (Contains 1928, 1930-c, and 1935-a.)

1939-b. The Concept of Plot in Culture, NYT *2-2*:24-31.

1940-a. Character Formation in Two South Sea Societies, ANP, 66th Ann. Meeting. Pp. 99-103.

1940-b. Social Change and Cultural Surrogates, JES *14*:92-100. (Reprinted, Kluckhohn et al, 1953.)

1940-c. *The Mountain Arapesh*, Part II. AMA *37* pt. 3.

1940-d. Conflict of Cultures in America, *Proceedings* 5th Ann'l Conv'n, Middle States Assn. Coll. & Secondary Schools.

1940-e. The Arts in Bali, YR *30*:335-347.

1941-a. Administrative Contributions to Democratic Character Formation at the Adolescent Level, *Jnl. Nat. Assn. Deans of Women* 4:51-57. (Reprinted in Kluckhohn, Murray, & Schneider, 1953.)

1941-b. Review of W. Dennis, *The Hopi Child*. AA *43*:95-97.

1941-c. Back of Adolescence Lies Early Childhood, *Childhood Education 18:* 58-61.

1942-a. Educative Effects of Social Environment as Disclosed by Studies of Primitive Societies, In E. W. Burgess et al, *Environment & Education*, UnChE *54*:48-61. (Reprinted in Newcomb, Hartley, et al, *Readings in Social Psychology*, pp. 151-158.)

1942-b. Anthropological Data on the Problem of Instinct. Psm *4*:396-397. (Reprinted, Kluckhohn et al, 1953.)

1942-c. The Comparative Study of Culture and the Purposive Cultivation of Democratic Values, CoSPR *2*:59-69. (Cf. also G. Bateson, 1942-c.)

1942-d. *And Keep Your Powder Dry*. New York.

1944. Cultural Approach to Personality, Anthropological Comment on . . Andreas Angyal, NYT, ser II, *6*, *3*:93-101.

1946-a. Fundamental Education and Cultural Values, In *Fundamental Education: Common Ground for all Peoples*, Report, Spec. Comm. to the Preparatory Comm'n of UNESCO. Paris. Pp. 132-135.

1946-b. Research on Primitive Children, in L. Carmichael, ed., *Manual of Child Psychology*, N. Y. Pp. 667ff.

1946-c. Trends in Personal Life, *New Republic 115* #12, pp. 346-348. (Complete bibliography to 1947 in PS *10*:117-120.)

1947-a. *The Mountain Arapesh*, Parts III, IV. AMA *40:* pt. 3.

1947-b. On the Implications for Anthropology of the Gesell-Ilg Approach to Maturation, AA *49*:69-77. (Reproduced herewith.)

1947-c. The Concept of Culture and the Psychosomatic Approach, PS *10*:57-76. (Reproduced herewith.)

1947-d. Age Patterning in Personality Development, AJO *17*:231-240.

1947-e. The Implications of Culture Change for Personality Development, AJO *17*:633-646. (Reproduced herewith.)

1948. The Contemporary American Family as an Anthropologist sees it, AJS *53*:453-459.

1949-a. Male and Female, *Ladies Home Journal 66* #9.

1949-b. *Male and Female*. New York.

1949-c. Character Formation and Diachronic Theory, In M. Fortes, ed., *Social Structure* . . . London.

1949-d. Psychologic Weaning: Childhood and Adolescence, In *Psychosexual Development in Health and Disease*. N. Y.

1949-e. *The Mountain Arapesh*, Part V. AMA *41* pt. 3.

1950-a. Cultural Contexts of Nutritional Patterns, In *Centennial*, A.A.A.S. Washington.

1950-b. Some Anthropological Considerations Concerning Guilt, In *Feelings and Emotions, the Mooseheart Symposium*, ed. by M. L. Reymert. N. Y.

1951-a. Anthropologist and Historian: Their Common Problems. *American Quarterly, 3* #1:3-13.

1951-b. *Soviet Attitudes Toward Authority.* N. Y.

1951-c. What Makes Soviet Character? *Natural History 60 #7*:296-303, 336.

1951-d. The Study of National Character In *The Policy Sciences,* ed. by D. Lerner & H. D. Lasswell. Stanford.

1952-a. Some relationships between Social Anthropology and Psychiatry, In *Dynamic Psychiatry,* ed. by F. Alexander and H. Ross. Chicago.

1952-b. Sharing Child Development Insights around the Globe, *Understanding the Child, 21*:98.

1953-a. National character, In *Anthropology Today,* ed. by A. L. Kroeber. Chicago.

1953-b. Ed., *Cultural Patterns & Technical Change.* UNESCO, Paris (Mentor Books, 1955.)

1954-a. The Swaddling Hypothesis: Its Reception, AA *56*:395-409.

1954-b. Manus restudied: an interim report, NYT *ll* vol. *16 # 8*:426-432.

1954-c. Some Theoretical Considerations on the Problem of Mother-child Separation, AJO *24*:471-483. (Reprinted herewith.)

1954-d. Cultural Discontinuities and Personality Transformation, JSI Supp. Ser. *#8.*

1955-a. Cultural Patterning of Sexual Behavior, In E. Dempsey, ed., *Sex and Internal Secretions.*

1955-b. Effects of Anthropological Field Work Models on Interdisciplinary Communication in the Study of National Character, JSI *11 #2*:3-11.

1955-c. Applied Anthropology, 1955, In *Some Uses of Anthropology,* ed. by J. Casagrande & T. Gladwin. Washington.

1956. *New Lives for Old: Cultural Transformation—Manus, 1928-1953.* New York.

MEAD, MARGARET AND FRANCES COOKE MACGREGOR

1951. *Growth and Culture: A Photographic Study of Balinese Childhood.* New York.

MEAD, MARGARET, AND MARTHA WOLFENSTEIN, eds.

1955. *Childhood in Contemporary Cultures.* Chicago.

MEAD, MARGARET, AND RHODA MÉTRAUX, eds.

1953. *The Study of Culture at a Distance.* Chicago.

MEANS, PHILIP AINSWORTH

1925. A Study of Ancient Andean Social Institutions, *Transactions,* Connecticut Acad. Arts & Sciences, *27.* New Haven.

MEERLOO, JOOST A. M.

1950. *Patterns of Panic.* New York.

MEGGERS, BETTY J.

1946. Recent Trends in American Ethnology, AA *48*:176-214.

MEKEEL, SCUDDER

1934. Education, Child-training, and Culture. AJS *47*:676ff.

1935. Clinic and Culture. JASP *30*:292-300.

1937. A Psychoanalytic Approach to Culture. JSPh *2*:232-236.

MENNINGER, KARL A.

1951. Totemic Aspects of Contemporary Attitudes toward Animals, In Wilbur and Muensterberger, 1951.

MENSH, IVAN M. AND JULES HENRY

1953. Direct Observation and Psychological Tests in Anthropological Field Work. AA *55*:461-480.

MERTON, ROBERT K.

1940. Bureaucratic Structure and Personality, SLF *18*:560-568. (Reprinted in Kluckhohn, Murray & Schneider, 1953.)

1949. *Social Theory and Social Structure.* Glencoe, Ill.

MÉTRAUX, ALFRED

1942. *The Native Tribes of Eastern Bolivia and Western Matto Grosso.* BuEB

MÉTRAUX, RHODA
1952. Some Aspects of Hierarchical Structure in Haiti, In Sol Tax, ed., *Acculturation in the Americas*, vol. II of *Selected Papers of the XXIXth* I. C. A. Chicago. pp. 185-194.

MICHELSON, TRUMAN
1926. The Autobiography of a Fox Indian Woman, BuER *40*:291-350.
1932. The Narrative of a Southern Cheyenne Woman, SIM *85* #5:1-13.

MEYERS, M., AND H. M. CUSHING
1936. Types and Incidence of Behavior Problems in Relation to Cultural Background, AJO *6*:110-117.

MICKEY, MARGARET PORTIA
1947. *The Cowrie Shell Miao of Kweichow*. PHa *32* #1.

MILLER, DANIEL K. AND M. L. HUTT
1949. Value Interiorization and Personality Development. JSI *5*:2-30.

MILLER, NATHAN
1928. *The Child in Primitive Society*. New York.

MILLER, N. E. AND J. DOLLARD
1941. *Social Learning and Imitation*. New Haven.

MILLS, CLARENCE A.
1942-a. Climatic Effects on Growth and Development, with particular Reference to the Effects of Tropical Residence, AA *44*:1-13.
1942-b. *Climate Makes the Man*. New York. (Cf. review by W. M. Krogman, AA *45*:290-291.)

MILNE, MRS. LESLIE
1924. *The Home of an Eastern Clan, a Study of the Palaungs of the Shan States*. Oxford.

MINAMI HIROSHI
1953. *Nihonjin No Shinri* (The Psychology of the Japanese.) Tōkyō. (Translation in process, A. Hōbō and D. Haring.)

MOFOLO, T.
1931. *Chaka*. London.

MOLINA, M. F.
1947. Study of a Psychopathic Personality in Guatemala. PS *10*:31-36.

MOLONEY, JAMES CLARK
n.d. *Child Rearing on Okinawa*, (a film). Birmingham, Mich.
1945. Psychiatric Observations on Okinawa Shima. PS *8*:391-399.
1946. On Oriental Stoicism, AJP *103*:60-64.
1949. *The Magic Cloak*. Wakefield, Mass.
1951. A Study in Neurotic Conformity: The Japanese. *Complex 5*:26-32.
1952. *The Battle for Mental Health*. New York.
1953. Understanding the Paradox of Japanese Psychoanalysis. IJP *34* Pt. IV.
1954. *Understanding the Japanese Mind*. New York.
1955-a. Psychic Self-Abandon and Extortion of Confessions. IJP *36* pt. I.
1955-b. Etiology of Mental Health, *Child-Family Digest*, *12* #5.

MONEY-KYRLE, ROGER
1939. *Superstition and Society*. London.
1951. Some Aspects of State and Character in Germany, In Wilbur, G. B. and W. Muensterberger, *Psychoanalysis and Culture*. N. Y.

MONTAGU, M. F. ASHLEY
1937. *Coming into Being Among the Australian Aborigines*. London.
1942. *Man's Most Dangerous Myth: the Fallacy of Race*. New York.
1945. *An Introduction to Physical Anthropology*. Springfield, Ill.
1946. *Adolescent Sterility*. Springfield, Ill.
1955. *The Direction of Human Development: Biological and Social Bases*. New York.

MOONEY, JAMES
　　1896. The Ghost-dance Religion and the Sioux Outbreak of 1890, BuER *14:*
　　　　641-1110.
　　1905-1907. *The Cheyenne Indians.* AAM *1,* pt. 6
MORGAN, THOMAS HUNT
　　1932. *The Scientific Basis of Evolution.* New York.
MORGAN, WILLIAM
　　1932-a. Navaho Dreams, AA *34:*390-405.
　　1932-b. Review of G. Róheim, *Psycho-Analysis of Primitive Cultural Types,*
　　　　AA *34:*705-710.
　　1936. *Human Wolves Among the Navaho.* YPA *11.*
MOSELY, PHILIP E.
　　1953. The Nineteenth Party Congress, FoA *31:*238-256.
MOUBRAY, G. A. DEC. DE
　　1931. *Matriarchy in the Malay Peninsula.* London.
MOWRER, O. H. AND CLYDE KLUCKHOHN
　　1944. Dynamic Theory of Personality, In *Personality and the Behavior Dis-*
　　　　orders, ed. by J. Hunt. Pp. 69-135. New York.
MUENSTERBERGER, WARNER
　　1950. Oral Trauma and Taboo, a Psychoanalytic Study of an Indonesian Tribe,
　　　　PSS *2:*129-172.
　　1951. Orality and Dependence, PSS *3:*37-69.
　　(See also under G. B. Wilbur.)
MUKERJI, DHAN GOPAL
　　1927. *Caste and Outcaste.* New York. (First published, 1923.) Autobiography.
MULLAHY, PATRICK
　　1948. *Oedipus: Myth and Complex, a Review of Psychoanalytic Theory.* New
　　　　York. (Includes text of the Oedipus trilogy.)
　　1949. Ed., *A Study of Interpersonal Relations: New Contributions to Psychiatry.*
　　　　(Articles from PS.) New York.
　　1950. A Philosophy of Personality, PS *13:*417-437.
MUNROE, RUTH L.
　　1955. *Schools of Psychoanalytic Thought.* New York.
MURDOCK, GEORGE PETER
　　1934. *Our Primitive Contemporaries.* New York.
　　1949-a. *Social Structure.* New York.
　　1949-b. The Science of Human Learning, Society, Culture, and Personality.
　　　　SCM *69:*377-381.
　　1953. *Ethnographic Bibliography of North America.* Rev. ed. New Haven.
MURDOCK, GEORGE P., C. S. FORD, A. E. HUDSON, RAYMOND KENNEDY, L. W.
　　SIMMONS, AND J. W. M. WHITING
　　1950. *Outline of Cultural Materials.* 3rd rev. ed. New Haven.
MURDOCK, GEORGE P. AND J. W. M. WHITING
　　1951. Cultural Determination of Parental Attitudes: The Relationship between
　　　　Social Structure, particularly Family Structure and Parental Behavior.
　　　　In *Problems of Infancy and Childhood: Transactions of the Fourth Con-*
　　　　ference, March 6-7, 1950. Macy Foundation, New York.
MURPHY, GARDNER
　　1947. *Personality.* New York.
MURRAY, HENRY A.
　　1943. *Thematic Apperception Test Manual.* Cambridge.
MURRAY, J. M.
　　1932. Anthropological Significance of the Oedipus Complex. PYR *19:*327-330.
MURRAY, VERONICA F., AND ALICE JOSEPH
　　1950. The Rorschach Test as a Tool in Action Research, JPT *14:*362-384.
　　　　(Chamorros in Saipan.)

Musil, Alois
  1928. *Manners and Customs of the Rwala Bedouins. AGO 6.
Nadel, Siegfried F.
  1937-a. The Typological Approach to Culture, CP 5:267-284.
  1937-b. Experiments in Cultural Psychology, Af 10:421-435.
  1937-c. A Field Experiment in Racial Psychology, BRJP 28:195-211.
  1942. *A Black Byzantium, the Kingdom of Nupe in Nigeria. London.
  1951. The Foundations of Social Anthropology. London and Glencoe.
  1955. Comments. (On J. Henry, Projective Testing . . .) AA 57:247-250.
Neumann, John von, and Oskar Morgenstern
  1947. Theory of Games and Economic Behavior, 2nd. ed. Princeton. (First edition, 1943.)
Newcomb, Theodore M.
  1950. Social Psychology. New York.
Newcomb, T. M., E. L. Hartley, et al,
  1947. Readings in Social Psychology. New York.
Newton, N. R.
  1951. The Relationship between Infant Feeding Experience and Later Behavior. JPD 38:28-40.
Nimuendaju, Curt (R. H. Lowie, tr.)
  1939. *The Apinaye. CAS 8.
  1942. *The Serente. Los Angeles.
  1946-a. *The Eastern Timbira. UnCa 41.
  1946-b. Social Organization and Beliefs of the Botocudo of Eastern Brazil, SwA 2:93-115.
  1952. *The Tukuna. UnCa 45.
Nishikiori Hideo, tr. by Sano Toshiō
  1945. Togo Mura, A Village in Northern Japan. (Mimeo) I. P. R., New York.
Norbeck, Edward
  1953. Age-grading in Japan. AA 55:373-384.
  1954. Takashima, a Japanese Fishing Community. Salt Lake City
Northrop, F. S. C.
  1946. The Meeting of East and West. New York.
  1949. Ideological Differences and World Order. New York.
Novakovsky, S.
  1924. Arctic or Siberian Hysteria as a Reflex of the Geographic Environment, Ecology 5:113-127.
Ntara, S. Y.
  1935. Man of Africa. London.
Nyabonga, A. K.
  1935. The Story of an African Chief. New York.
Oaksey Report on Police Conditions of Service.
  1949. Part II. London.
Oberg, Kalervo
  1953. *Indian Tribes of Northern Mato Grosso, Brazil. SIP 15.
Odaka Kunio
  1950. An Iron-workers' Community in Japan, ASR 15:186ff.
Oesterreich, T. K.
  1930. Possession: Primitive, Middle Ages, and Modern. New York.
Olbrechts, Frans M.
  1931. Cherokee Belief and Practice with Regard to Childbirth. A 26:17-33.
Oliver, Douglas L.
  1949. Human Relations and Language in a Papuan-Speaking Tribe of Southern Bougainville, Solomon Islands, PHa, 29: #2.

OLSON, RONALD L.

1927. Adze, Canoe, and House Types of the Northwest Coast, UnW 2 #1.

1930. Chumash Prehistory, UnCa 28 #1.

1933. Clan and Moiety in Native America, UnCa 33 #4.

1936-a. The Quinault Indians, UnW 6 #1.

1936-b. Some Trading Customs of the Chilkat Tlingit, In *Essays in Anthropology Presented to A. L. Kroeber*, ed. by R. H. Lowie. Berkeley.

1940. The Social Organization of the Haisla, AnR 2:169-200.

1954. Social Life of the Owikeno Kwakiutl, AnR 14 #3.

OPLER, MARVIN K.

1942. Psychoanalytic Techniques in Social Analysis, JSP 15:91-127.

1955-a. Cultural Perspectives in Mental Health Research, AJO 25:51-59.

1955-b. *Culture, Psychiatry and Human Values*. Springfield, Ill.

1956. Cultural Anthropology and Social Psychiatry. (In press.)

OPLER, MORRIS E.

1935-a. The Concept of Supernatural Power among the Chiricahua and Mescalero Apaches, AA 37:65-70.

1935-b. The Psychoanalytic Treatment of Culture, PYR 22:138-157.

1936-a. An Interpretation of Ambivalence of Two American Indian Tribes, JSP 7:82-116.

1936-b. Some Points of Comparison and Contrast Between the Treatment of Functional Disorders by Apache Shamans and Modern Psychiatric Practice, AJP 92:1371-1387.

1938-a. Personality and Culture: A Methodological Suggestion, PS 1:217-220.

1938-b. The Use of Peyote by the Carrizo and Lipan Apache Tribes, AA 40: 271ff.

1938-c. Further Comparative Anthropological Data Bearing on the Solution of a Psychological Problem, JSP 9:477ff.

1938-d. *Dirty Boy: A Jicarilla Tale of Raid and War*. AAM 52.

1941. *An Apache Life-Way: The Economic, Social and Religious Institutions of the Chiricahua Indians*. UnCh.

1942. *Myths and Tales of the Chiricahua Apache Indians*. AFLM 37.

1943. The Character and Derivation of the Jicarilla Holiness Rite. UnNM 4 #3.

1945. Themes as Dynamic Forces in Culture, AJS 51:198-206.

1946. Mountain Spirits of the Chiricahua Apache, *Masterkey* 20:121-131.

1947. Notes on Chiricahua Apache Culture: 1. Supernatural Power and the Shaman, PM 20:1-14.

1948. Some Implications of Culture Theory for Anthropology and Psychology, AJO 18:611-621.

ORLANSKY, HAROLD

1949. Infant Care and Personality, PsB 46:1-48.

OSGOOD, CORNELIUS V.

1937. *The Ethnography of the Tanaina*. YPA 16.

1951. *The Koreans and Their Culture*. New York. (Especially Chap. 17.)

OSTROW, MORTIMER

1955. Behavior Correlates of Neural Function. ASC 43:127-133.

PAGET, G. W.

1932. Some Drawings of Men and Women Made by Children of Certain Non-European Races, RAI 62:127-144.

PARK, W. Z.

1938. *Shamanism in Western North America*. NUS 2.

PARKER, A. C.

1913. *The Code of Handsome Lake*. NYM 163.

PARKER, WILLIAM A., ed., et al

1954. *Understanding Other Cultures*. Washington, D. C. American Council of Learned Societies.

PARSONS, ELSIE CLEWS
  1906. *The Family*. New York. (Esp. pp. 90-111.)
  1916-a. The Zuni A'doshlĕ and Suukĕ, AA *18*:338-347.
  1916-b. The Zuni La'mana, AA *18*:521-528.
  1919. Mothers and Children at Zuni, M *19*:168-173.
  1920. The Study of Variants, JAF *33*:87-90.
  1929. *The Social Organization of the Tewa of New Mexico*. AAM *36*.
  1939. *Pueblo Indian Religion*. 2 vol. Chicago.
  1945. *Peguche*. Chicago.

PARSONS, TALCOTT
  1942. Age and Sex in the Social Structure of the United States, ASR 7:604-616.
    (Reprinted, Kluckhohn, Murray, & Schneider, 1953.)
  1943. The Kinship System of the Contemporary United States, AA *45*:22-38.
  1946. Population and Social Structure (of Japan), In *Japan's Prospect*, ed. by D.
    Haring. Cambridge, Mass. Chapter IV.
  1947. Certain Primary Sources and Patterns of Aggression in the Social Struc-
    ture of the Western World, PS *10*:167-181.
  1949. *Essays in Sociological Theory, Pure and Applied*. Glencoe, Ill.
  1950. The Social Environment of the Educational Process, In *Centennial*, A. A.
    A. S., Washington.
  1951-a. *The Social System*. Glencoe, Ill.
  1951-b. Illness and the Role of the Physician: A Sociological Perspective, AJO
    21:452-460. (Reprinted, Kluckhohn, Murray & Schneider, 1953.)
  1952. The Superego and the Theory of Social Systems, PS *15*:15-26.

PARSONS, TALCOTT, AND R. F. BALES
  1955. *Family, Socialization and Interaction Process*. Glencoe, Ill.

PARSONS, TALCOTT, AND EWARD A. SHILS, eds.,
  1951. *Toward a General Theory of Action*. Cambridge, Mass.

PAUL, BENJAMIN D.
  1949. Review, first edition of *Personal Character and Cultural Milieu*, comp. by
    D. Haring. JASP *44*:132-135.
  1950. Symbolic Sibling Rivalry in a Guatemalan Indian Village, AA *52*:205-218.
    (Reprinted in Kluckhohn, Murray & Schneider, 1953.)
  1953-a. Mental Disorder and Self-Regulating Processes in Culture: A Guate-
    malan Illustration, In *Interrelations between the Social Environment and
    Psychiatric Disorders*, Milbank Memorial Fund, N. Y. Pp. 51-67. (Re-
    printed herewith.)
  1953-b. The Cultural Context of Health Education, *Symposium Proceedings
    1953*, School of Social Work, Univ. of Pittsburgh. Pp. 31-38.

PAUL, BENJAMIN D., ed.
  1955. *Health, Culture, and Community*. New York.

PELZEL, JOHN C.
  1949. *Social Stratification in Japanese Urban Economic Life*. Microfilm. Har-
    vard University.

PERHAM, M. F., ed.
  1936. *Ten Africans*. London.

PETER, PRINCE (HRH of Greece and Denmark)
  1955. The Todas: some additions and corrections to W. H. R. Rivers' book, as
    observed in the field, M *55*:89-93.

PETERSEN, WILLIAM F.
  1943. *Lincoln-Douglas, the Weather as Destiny*. Springfield, Ill.

PETERSON, C. H. AND F. L. SPANO
  1941. Breast Feeding, Maternal Rejection and Child Personality, CP *10*:62-66.

PETRULLO, VINCENZO
  1934. *The Diabolic Root, a Study of Peyotism, the New Indian Religion Among
    the Delawares*. Philadelphia.

PETTITT, GEORGE A.
  1946. *Primitive Education in North America.* UnCa *43 #1.*
PIAGET, JEAN
  1929. *The Moral Judgment of the Child.* New York.
  1952. *The Language and Thought of the Child.* New York.
PIDDINGTON, RALPH
  1932. *Karadjeri Initiation. O *3:46-87.*
PIERIS, RALPH
  1952. Character Formation in the Evolution of the Acquisitive Society, PS *15:*
    53-60.
PIERS, GERHART AND MILTON B. SINGER
  1954. *Shame and Guilt: a Psychoanalytic and a Cultural Study.* Springfield, Ill.
PIERSON, DONALD, et al
  1951. *Cruz das Almas: a Brazilian Village.* SIP *12.*
PINCUS, GREGORY, AND HUDSON HOAGLAND
  1950. Adrenal Cortical Responses to Stress in Normal Men and in those with
    Personality Disorders, AJP *106:641-659.*
PINCUS, GREGORY, HUDSON HOAGLAND, HARRY FREEMAN, FRED ELMADJIAN, AND
  LOUISE P. ROMANOFF
  1949. A Study of Pituitary-Adrenocortical Function in Normal and Psychotic
    Men, Psm *11:74* et seq.
PINNEAU, S. R.
  1950. A critique on the articles by Margaret Ribble, *Child Development 21:*
    203-228.
PITTS, F. R., W. P. LEBRA AND W. P. SUTTLES
  1955. *Postwar Okinawa.* S. I. R. I. Report #8, Pacific Science Board, National
    Research Council, (Mimeo). Washington.
PLANT, JAMES S.
  1937. *Personality and the Cultural Pattern.* New York.
  1950. *The Envelope, a Study of the Impact of the World Upon the Child.*
    New York.
PLOSS, HERMANN HEINRICH
  1911-12. *Das Kind.* 2 vol. 3rd Ed. Leipzig.
PORTEUS, STANLEY D.
  1931. *The Psychology of a Primitive People: a Study of the Australian Abor-
    igine.* New York.
POTTER, DAVID M.
  1954. *People of Plenty: Economic Abundance and the American Character.*
    Chicago.
POWDERMAKER, HORTENSE
  1933. *Life in Lesu.* New York.
  1950. *Hollywood: The Dream Factory.* Boston.
PRESSEY, S. L. AND L. C. PRESSEY
  1933. A Comparison of the Emotional Development of Indians Belonging to
    Different Tribes, JAp *17:535-541.*
PRUITT, IDA
  1945. *A Daughter of Han: The Autobiography of a Chinese Working Woman.*
    New Haven.
PUNER, HELEN
  1956. Gesell's Children Grow Up. *Harper's Magazine,* March: 37-43.
QUAIN, BUELL
  1937. The Iroquois, In M. Mead, ed., 1937-a.
  1948. *Fijian Village.* Chicago.
RADCLIFFE-BROWN, A. R.
    See Brown, A. R. Radcliffe—

RADIN, PAUL
1926. *Crashing Thunder, The Autobiography of an American Indian.* New York.
1927. *Primitive Man as Philosopher.* New York.
1936. Ojibwa and Ottawa Puberty Dreams, in R. Lowie, ed., *Essays in Anthropology Presented to A. L. Kroeber.* Berkeley. Pp. 233-264.

RADIN, PAUL, ed.
1946. Japanese Ceremonies and Festivals in California, SwA *2*:152-179.

RAPAPORT, DAVID
1942. Principles Underlying Projective Techniques. CP *10*:213-219.
1950. *Emotions and Memory.* New York.

RAPAPORT, DAVID, tr. & comment.
1951. *Organization and Pathology of Thought: Selected Sources.* New York.

RAPER, ARTHUR F., et al.
1950. *The Japanese Village in Transition.* GHQ, SCAP, Nat. Resources Section, Report #136. Tokyo.

RAPOPORT, ROBERT N.
1954. *Changing Navaho Religious Values: A Study of Christian Missions to the Rimrock Navahos.* PHa *41* #2.

RATTRAY, R. S.
1923. **Ashanti.* Oxford.
1929. **Ashanti Law and Constitution.* Oxford.
1932. **The Tribes of the Ashanti Hinterland.* 2 vol. London.

RAUM, O. F.
1938. Some Aspects of Indigenous Education Among the Chaga. RAI *68*:209-221. (Reprinted herewith.)
1940. *Chaga Childhood.* London.

RAY, VERNE F.
1956. Rejoinder (to Kroeber and Lowie on Boas). AA *58*:164-170.

READ, K. E.
1955. Morality and the Concept of the Person Among the Gahuku-Gama (New Guinea), O *25*:233-282.

REAY, MARIE
1949. Native Thought in Rural New South Wales. O *20*:89-118.

REDFIELD, ROBERT
1930. **Tepoztlan, A Mexican Village.* UnCh.
1941. **The Folk Culture of Yucatan.* UnCh.

REDFIELD, ROBERT, AND R. A. VILLA
1934. **Chan Kom, a Maya Village. CA #448.*

REICHARD, GLADYS A.
1928. **Social Life of the Navaho Indians.* CUCA 7.
1934. *Spider Woman.* New York.
1936. *Navajo Shepherd and Weaver.* New York.
1938. *Dezba, Woman of the Desert.* New York.
1944. *Prayer: The Compulsive Word.* AEM 7.
1950. *Navaho Religion, A Study of Symbolism.* 2 vol. New York. (Complete bibliography in obituary: AA *58*).

REIK, THEODOR
1936. (Margaret M. Green, tr.) *Surprise and the Psycho-Analyst.* London.
1951. Jessica, My Child! AI *8*:1-27.

REISCHAUER, EDWIN O.
1950. *The United States and Japan.* Cambridge, Mass. Part III: The Japanese Character, pp. 99-204.

REYHER, REBECCA H.
1948. *Zulu Woman.* New York.

RIBBLE, M. A.
　1943. *The Rights of Infants: Early Psychological Needs & Their Satisfaction.*
　　New York.

RICHARDS, A. I.
　1932. **Hunger and Work in a Savage Tribe.* London.
　1939. **Land, Labour and Diet in Northern Rhodesia.* London.

RICHARDSON, JANE AND L. M. HANKS, JR.
　1942. Water Discipline and Water Imagery Among the Blackfoot. AA *44*:331-
　　333.

RICHFIELD, JEROME
　1954. On the Scientific Status of Psychoanalysis, SCM *79*:306-308.

RIESMAN, DAVID
　1950. *The Lonely Crowd: A Study of the Changing American Character.* New
　　Haven.
　1952. *Faces in the Crowd.* New Haven.
　1953. Psychological Types and National Character. *Amer. Quar. 5*:325-343.
　1953. *Thorstein Veblen: A Critical Interpretation.* New York.

RIESMAN, DAVID AND N. GLAZER
　1948-9. Social Structure, Character Structure, and Opinion. IJOAR *2*:1-16.

RIVERS, G. H. PITT
　1927. *The Clash of Culture and Contact of Races.* London.

RIVERS, WM. H. R.
　1906. **The Todas.* London & New York.
　1922. *The Depopulation of Melanesia.* Cambridge, Eng.
　1926. *Psychology and Ethnology.* New York & London.

ROBERTS, JOHN M.
　1951. *Three Navaho Households: A Comparative Study of Small Group Cul-
　　ture.* PHa *40 #3.*

ROBERTS, R. G.
　1954. **Mind over Matter—Magical Performances in the Gilbert Islands. JPol
　　63*:17-25.

ROBERTSON, J.
　1953. *A Two-Year Old Goes to the Hospital.* (Film) World Federation for
　　Mental Health, London.

ROCKER, RUDOLPH
　1937. *Nationalism and Culture.* New York.

RODNICK, DAVID
　1948. *Postwar Germans: An Anthropologist's Account.* New Haven.

RÓHEIM, GÉZA
　1922. Ethnology and Folk-Psychology, IJP *3*:189-222.
　1925. *Australian Totemism.* London.
　1932. Psycho-analysis of Primitive Types: Doketa, IJP *13*:1-224. (Rev., W.
　　Morgan, AA *34*:705-710.)
　1933. Women and Their Life in Central Australia, RAI *63*:241-250.
　1934-a. *The Riddle of the Sphinx.* London.
　1934-b. The Study of Character Development and the Ontogenetic Theory of
　　Culture, In *Essays in Honor of C. G. Seligman,* ed. by E. Evans-Pritchard.
　　London. Pp. 281ff.
　1940. The Garden of Eden, PYR *27*:1-26, 177-199.
　1941. Play Analysis with Normanby Island Children, AJO *11*:524-530.
　1943-a. *The Origin and Function of Culture.* NMDM *63*.
　1943-b. Children's Games and Rhythms in Duau, AA *45*:99-119.
　1945. *The Eternal Ones of the Dream, A Psycho-Analytic Interpretation of
　　Australian Myth and Ritual.* New York.
　1947. Ed., *Psychoanalysis and the Social Sciences,* vol. I. New York. Contains
　　his "Psychoanalysis and Anthropology," and "Dream Analysis and Field
　　Work in Anthropology."

1948. Ed., *Psychoanalysis and the Social Sciences*, vol. II. New York. Contains his "The Oedipus Complex, Magic and Culture."
1950. *Psychoanalysis and Anthropology.* New York.
1951. Hungarian Shamanism, PSS *3*:131-169.
1952. The Anthropological Evidence and the Oedipus Complex, PYQ *21*:537-542.
(Complete bibliography in G. B. Wilbur & W. Muensterberger, eds., *Psychoanalysis and Culture*, N. Y. 1951, pp. 455-462.)

ROHRER, JOHN H., AND MUZAFER SHERIF, eds.
1951. *Social Psychology at the Crossroads.* New York.

RORSCHACH, HERMANN (tr. by P. Lemkau & B. Kronenberg)
1942. *Psychodiagnostics: A Diagnostic Test Based on Perception.* Berne

ROSCOE, JOHN
1911. *The Baganda.* London.
1923-a. *The Bakitara or Banyoro.* London.
1923-b. *The Banyankole.* London.

ROSE, ARNOLD, ed.
1955. *Mental Health and Mental Disease.* New York.

ROSS, GEORGE L., AND THELMA E. BROWN
1950. The Psychosomatic Concept in Working Clothes, AJP *106*:680-685.

ROTH, H. LING
1896. *The Natives of Sarawak and British North Borneo.* 2 vol. London.

ROUDINESCO, J.
1952. Severe Maternal Deprivation and Personality Development in Early Childhood, UC *21*:104-108.

ROUDINESCO, J. AND G. APPELL
n.d. *Maternal Deprivation in Young Children.* (Film) Association pour la Santé Mentale de l'Enfance. Paris.

ROUTLEDGE, W. S. AND K.
1910. *With a Prehistoric People, The Akikuyu of British East Africa.* London.

ROY (RAYA), SARAT-CHANDRA
1915. *The Oroans of Chota Nagpur.* Ranchi (India).
1935. *The Hill Bhuiyas of Orissa.* Ranchi.

ROYAL ANTHROPOLOGICAL INSTITUTE
1951. *Notes and Queries on Anthropology.* 6th ed., rev. and rewritten by a committee of the Royal Anthropological Institute of Great Britain and Ireland. London.

RUESCH, JURGEN
1953. Social Technique, Social Status, and Social Change in Illness, In Kluckhohn, Murray, and Schneider, 1953.

RUESCH, JURGEN, AND GREGORY BATESON
1949. Structure and Process in Social Relations, PS *12*:105-124.
1951. *Communication: The Social Matrix of Psychiatry.* New York.

RÜMKE, H. C.
1955. Solved and Unsolved Problems in Mental Health, MH *39*:178-195.

RYAN, BRYCE F.
1950. Socio-Cultural Regions of Ceylon. RS *15*:3-19.
1952. The Ceylonese Village and the New Value System. RS *18*:9-28.
1953. *Caste in Modern Ceylon: The Sinhalese System in Transition.* New Brunswick, N. J.

RYAN, BRYCE F., AND MURRAY A. STRAUS
1954. The Integration of Sinhalese Society. *Research Studies of the State College of Washington, 22* #4:179-227.

SACHS, HANNS
1941. Psychotherapy and the Pursuit of Happiness, AI *2*:356-364.

SACHS, WULF
   1947. *Black Hamlet.* London. (Psychoanalysis of an African native.)
SAER, D. J.
   1923. The Effect of Bilingualism on Intelligence, *British Jnl. Psychiatry, 14:*35.
SAINDON, J. ÉMILE
   1933. Mental Disorders Among the James Bay Cree, PM *6:*1-12.
SANDERS, IRWIN T., ed., et al
   1953. *Societies Around the World.* 2 vol. New York.
SANDS, SIDNEY L., AND ELIOT H. RODNICK
   1950. Concept and Experimental Design in the Study of Stress and Personality,
      AJP *106:*673-679.
SANFORD, R. NEVITT et al
   1943. *Physique, Personality, and Scholarship.* SRCD *8*, Ser. #34, No. 1. (Excerpt
      reprinted in Kluckhohn and Murray, 1948.)
SAPIR, EDWARD
   1913. A Girl's Puberty Ceremony Among the Nootka, *Transactions*, Royal
      Society of Canada, ser. 3, 7:67-80.
   1928. The Unconscious Patterning of Behavior in Society, In C. M. Child et al,
      eds., *The Unconscious, a Symposium.*
   1932. Cultural Anthropology and Psychiatry, JASP *27:*229-242.
   1934-a. Personality, ESS *12:*85-87.
   1934-b. The Emergence of the Concept of Personality in a Study of Cultures,
      JSP *5:*408-415.
   1937. The Contribution of Psychiatry to an Understanding of Behavior in So-
      ciety, AJS *42:*862-870.
   1938. Why Cultural Anthropology Needs the Psychiatrist, PS *1:*7-13. (Reprint-
      ed herewith.)
   1949. *Selected Writings of Edward Sapir in Language, Culture, and Personality,*
      ed. by D. G. Mandelbaum. Berkeley and Los Angeles.
   See also SPIER, L., A. HALLOWELL, & S. NEWMAN, 1941.
SARGENT, S. STANSFELD
   1950. *Social Psychology: An Integrative Discipline.* New York.
SARGENT, S. STANSFELD AND MARIAN W. SMITH, eds.
   1949. *Culture and Personality.* Proceedings of an Inter-Disciplinary Conference
      Under the Auspices of the Viking Fund, Nov. 1947. N. Y.
SARHAN, EL-DEMARDASH ABDEL MEGUID
   1950. *Interests and Culture.* New York.
SAUNDERS, LYLE
   1954. *Cultural Difference and Medical Care.* N. Y.
SAYRES, WILLIAM C.
   1955. *Sammy Louis: The Life History of a Young Micmac.* New Haven.
SCHACHTEL, ANNA H., J. HENRY, AND Z. HENRY
   1942. Rorschach Analysis of Pilagá Indian Children. AJO *12:*670-712.
SCHACHTEL, ERNEST G.
   1947. On Memory and Childhood Amnesia, PS *10:*1-26.
SCHAFFNER, BERTRAM
   1948. *Father Land, a Study of Authoritarianism in the German Family.* New
      York.
SCHAPERA, ISAAC
   1930, 1935. *The Khoisan Peoples of South Africa: Bushmen and Hottentots.*
      London.
   1941. *Married Life in an African Tribe.* New York.
SCHEIN, EDGAR H.
   1956. The Chinese Indoctrination Program for Prisoners of War: A Study of
      Attempted "Brainwashing." PS *19:*149-172.

SCHILDER, PAUL
  1935. *The Image and Appearance of the Human Body.* New York.
  1942. *Goals and Desires of Men.* New York.
SEEMAN, M.
  1946. An Evaluation of Current Approaches to Personality Differences in Folk and Urban Societies, SLF *25*:160-165.
SELIGMAN, BRENDA Z.
  1934. The Part of the Unconscious in Social Heritage, In *Essays in Honor of C. G. Seligman,* ed. by E. E. Evans-Pritchard. Pp. 307-317. London.
SELIGMAN, CHARLES G.
  1923. Anthropology and Psychology: a Study of Some Points of Contact, RAI *54*:13-46.
  1929. Temperament, Conflict, and Psychosis in a Stone-age Population, BMP *9*:189-190.
  1931. Japanese Temperament and Character, JASL *28*:123-125.
  1935. Anthropological Perspective and Psychological Theory, RAI *62*:193-228. (Cf. also E. E. Evans-Pritchard, ed., 1934.)
SELIGMAN, CHARLES G. AND BRENDA Z.
  1911. *The Veddas.* London. (Ceylon.)
  1918. *The Kababish, a Sudan Arab Tribe.* HAA *2.*
  1932. *Pagan Tribes of the Nilotic Sudan.* London.
SELTZER, CARL C.
  1945. The Relation Between the Masculine Component and Personality, AJPA *3*:33-47. (Reprinted in Kluckhohn & Murray, 1948.)
SELYE, HANS
  1946. The General Adaptation Syndrome, JCE *6*:117-230.
  1950-a. *The Physiology and Pathology of Exposure to Stress.* Montreal.
  1950-b. *Stress. Acta Endocrinologia.*
SELYE, HANS, AND CLAUDE FORTIER
  1950. Adaptive Reaction to Stress, Psm *12*:149-157.
SENN, M. J. E., ed.
  1947, 1948, 1949, 1950. *Transactions: Problems of Infancy and Childhood.* Macy Foundation, N. Y.
  1950. *Symposium on the Healthy Personality.* Macy Foundation, N. Y.
SENTER, DONOVAN
  1947. Witches and Psychiatrists, PS *10*:49-56.
SERENO, RENZO
  1948. Obeah: Magic and Social Structure in the Lesser Antilles. PS *11*:15-32.
  1949. Boricua: A Study of Language, Transculturation, and Politics, PS *12*:167-184. (Puerto Rico.)
SERVICE, ELMAN R. AND HELEN S.
  1954. *Tobati: Paraguayan Town.* Chicago.
SEWELL, W. H.
  1952. Infant Training and the Personality of the Child, AJS *58*:150-159.
SHAFER, BOYD C.
  1952. Men are More Alike. *American Historical Review,* *57*:593-612.
SHAPIRO, HARRY L.
  1939. *Migration and Environment.* Oxford.
  1956. Ed., *Man, Culture, and Soceity.* New York.
SHELDON, WILLIAM H.
  1944. Constitutional Factors in Personality, In *Personality and the Behavior Disorders,* ed. by J. McV. Hunt, vol. II:529-549, New York.
SHELDON, WILLIAM H., AND S. S. STEVENS
  1942. *The Varieties of Temperament.* New York.

SHELDON, W. H., S. S. STEVENS, AND W. B. TUCKER
  1940. *The Varieties of Human Physique.* New York.

SHERIF, MUZAFER
  1936. *The Psychology of Social Norms.* New York.
  1948. *An Outline of Social Psychology.* New York.

SHERRINGTON, SIR CHARLES S.
  1941. *Man on His Nature.* London and New York.
  1948. *The Integrative Action of the Nervous System.* 6th ed. New Haven.

SHIMKIN, DMITRI B.
  1947. Childhood and Development Among the Wind River Shoshone. AnR
    5 #5:289-325.

SHRYOCK, JOHN KNIGHT, tr. and ed.
  1937. *Jen Wu Chih,* by Liu Shao. (*The Study of Human Abilities* by Liu Shao).
    With Introduction, etc. New Haven. (On types of personality; 3rd cen-
    tury A. D.)

SIKKEMA, MILDRED
  1947. Observations on Japanese Early Training, PS *10:*423-432.

SIMMONS, LEO W.
  1945. *The Role of the Aged in Primitive Society.* New Haven.

SIMMONS, LEO, ed.
  1942. *Sun Chief, the Autobiography of a Hopi Indian.* New Haven.

SIMMONS, LEO W., AND H. G. WOLFF
  1954. *Social Science in Medicine.* New York.

SINGH, J. A. L., AND R. M. ZINGG
  1942. *Wolf Children and Feral Man.* New York.

SKEAT, W. W. AND C. O. BLAGDEN
  1906. **Pagan Races of the Malay Peninsula.* London.

SKINNER, A. B.
  1913. *Social Life and Ceremonial Bundles of the Menomini Indians, AMA *13.*
  1915. *Associations and Ceremonies of the Menomini Indians, AMA *13.*

SKINNER, B. F.
  1954. Critique of Psychoanalytic Concepts and Theories, SCM *79:*300-305.

SLOTKIN, J. S.
  1950. *Social Anthropology.* New York.
  1952. *Personality Development.* New York.
  1953. Social Psychiatry of a Menomini Community, JASP *48:*10-17.
  1955. Peyotism, 1521-1891. AA *57:*202-230.

SMITH, EDWIN W.
  1934. Indigenous Education in Africa, In E. E. Evans-Pritchard, ed., *Essays in
    Honor of C. G. Seligman,* pp. 319-334. London.

SMITH, M. BREWSTER, J. S. BRUNER, AND ROBERT W. WHITE
  1956. *Opinions and Personality.* New York & London.

SMITH, MARIAN W.
  1940. **The Puyallup-Nisqually.* New York.
  1946. Village Notes from Bengal, AA *48:*574-592.
  1948. Synthesis and Other Processes in Sikhism, AA *50:*457-462.
  1952. Different Cultural Concepts of Past, Present, and Future. PS *15:*395-400.

SMITH, MARIAN W., ed., et al
  1949. *Indians of the Urban Northwest.* New York. CUCA *36.*

SMITH, ROBERT J.
  1956. Kurusu: A Japanese Agricultural Community. UnMi *5.*

SMITH, RUSSELL GORDON
  1930. *Fugitive Papers.* New York.

SMITH, S. PERCY
1913. *The Lore of the Whare Wananga*, Pt. I. New Plymouth.
1913-1915. *The Lore of the Whare Wananga*, Pt. II. Serially in JPol *22, 23, 24.* (Maori training of boys.)
SMITH, WILLIAM A.
1955. *Ancient Education.* New York.
SMITH, WILLIAM CARLSON
1925. **The Ao Naga Tribe of Assam.* London.
1949. The Stepmother, SSR *33:*342-347.
SNYDER, LAURENCE H.
1950. The Genetic Approach to Human Individuality, In *Centennial*, A.A.A.S., Washington.
SOKOLOV, Y. M. (Catherine R. Smith, tr.)
1950. *Russian Folklore.* New York.
SONTAG, LESTER W.
1946. Some Psychosomatic Aspects of Childhood, NC *5:*296-304. (Reprinted in Kluckhohn, Murray & Schneider, 1953.)
1950. The Genetics of Differences in Psychosomatic Patterns in Childhood, AJO *20:*479-489.
SOROKIN, PITIRIM A.
1937. *Social and Cultural Dynamics.* New York.
SPECK, FRANK G.
1933. Ethical Attributes of the Labrador Indians, AA *35:*559-594.
1945. **The Iroquois, A Study in Cultural Evolution.* Bloomfield Hills, Mich.
SPENCER, BALDWIN, AND F. J. GILLIN
1904. **The Northern Tribes of Central Australia.* London.
1914. **Native Tribes of the Northern Territory of Australia.* London.
1927. **The Arunta.* 2 vols., London.
SPENCER, DOROTHY M.
1937. Fijian Dreams and Visions. In D. S. Davidson, ed., *25th Anniversary Studies, Publ. Phila. Anthropological Soc.*
1939. The Composition of the Family as a Factor in the Behavior of Children in Fijian Society, So *2* #1.
1941. *Disease, Religion and Society in the Fiji Islands.* AEM *2.*
SPENCER, FRANK C.
1899. *The Education of a Pueblo Child.* New York.
SPICER, E.
1940. *Pascua: A Yaqui Village in Arizona.* Chicago.
SPIER, LESLIE
1921. **The Sun Dance of the Plains Indians, AMA *14.*
1927. The Ghost Dance of 1870 among the Klamath of Oregon. UnW *2:*39-56.
1930. **Klamath Ethnography.* UnCa *30.*
1933. **Yuman Tribes of the Gila River.* UnCh.
1935. *The Prophet Dance of the Northwest and its Derivatives.* GA *1.*
1943. Franz Boas and Some of His Views, AcA *1:*108-127. (Despite printer's blunders, one of the best sources on Boas' work.)
1954. Some Aspects of the Nature of Culture, *New Mexico Quar., 24* #3.
SPIER, LESLIE, A. I. HALLOWELL AND S. S. NEWMAN, eds.
1941. *Language, Culture and Personality, Essays in Memory of Edward Sapir.* Menasha, Wis.
SPINDLER, GEORGE DEARBORN
1952. Personality and Peyotism in Menomini Indian Acculturation. PS *15:*151-160.
1955-a. *Sociocultural and Psychological Processes in Menomini Acculturation.* UnCaCS *5.*
1955-b. Comments (on J. Henry, Projective Testing . . .), AA *57:*259-262.

SPINDLER, G. D. AND WALTER GOLDSCHMIDT
1952. Experimental Design in the Study of Culture Change. SwA *8*:68-83.

SPIRO, MELFORD E.
1950. A Psychotic Personality in the South Seas, PS *13*:189-204.
1951. Culture and Personality: The Natural History of a False Dichotomy, PS *14*:19-46.
1952. Ghosts, Ifaluk, and Teleological Functionalism. AA *54*:497-503.
1954-a. Human Nature in Its Psychological Dimensions, AA *56*:19-30.
1954-b. Is the Family Universal? AA *56*:839-846. (Study of Israeli *kibbutz*.)
1955-a. Comments (on J. Henry, Projective Testing . . .) AA *57*:256-258.
1955-b. Education in a Communal Village in Israel, AJO *25*:283-292.

SPITZ, R. A.
1945. Hospitalism, PaC *1*:53-74.
1946. *The Smiling Response.* (Film.) N. Y. Univ. Film Library. (Article: GPM *34*:47-125.)

SPITZ, R. A. AND K. M. WOLF
1946. Anaclitic Depression, PaC *2*:313-342.

SPITZER, HERMAN M.
1945. *Bibliography of Articles and Books Relating to Japanese Psychology.* (Mimeo.) Office of War Information, Area III, Overseas Branch, Foreign Morale Analysis Division, Report #24.
1947. Psychoanalytic Approaches to the Japanese Character, PSS *1*:131-156.

SPRINGER, DORIS V.
1950. Awareness of Racial Differences by Pre-school children. GPM *41*:215-271.

STAGNER, ROSS
1948. *Psychology of Personality.* 2nd. ed., New York.

STANTON, ALFRED H., AND MORRIS S. SCHWARTZ
1954. *The Mental Hospital: A Study of Institutional Participation in Psychiatric Illness and Treatment.* New York.

STAYT, HUGH A.
1931. *The Bavenda.* London.

STEPHEN, A. M., ed. by E. C. PARSONS
1936. *Hopi Journal.* New York.

STEVENSON, MATILDA C.
1904. *The Zuni Indians.* BuER *23* (1901-1902).

STEVENSON, MRS. SINCLAIR
1920. *The Rites of the Twice-Born.* Oxford. (Hindu caste ceremonies.)

STEWARD, JULIAN H.
1931. Notes on Hopi Ceremonies in Their Initiatory Form in 1927-1928. AA *33*:56-79.
1934. Two Paiute Autobiographies. UnCa *33* #5.
1938. Panatübiji', An Owens Valley Paiute, BuEB *119*.
1946. et seq. Ed., *Handbook of South American Indians.* 7 vols. BuEB *143*.
1949. Cultural Causality and Law: A Trial Formulation of the Development of Early Civilizations, AA *51*:1-27.
1955. *Theory of Culture Change: the Methodology of Multilinear Evolution.* Urbana, Ill.

STEWART, GUY R.
1940. Conservation in Pueblo Agriculture, SCM *51*:201-220, 329-340.

STEWART, K.
1951. Dream Theory in Malaya. *Complex* 6:21-33.

STEWART, OMER C.
1944. Washo-Northern Paiute Peyotism, UnCa *40* #3.

STIRLING, MATTHEW W.
1933. Jivaro Shamanism. PYR *20*:412-420.

STOETZEL, JEAN
　1955. *Without the Chrysanthemum and the Sword: A Study of the Attitudes of Youth in Postwar Japan.* New York.

STOUFFER, SAMUEL A., AND JACKSON TOBY
　1951. Role Conflict and Personality, AJS *56*:395-406.

STOUT, DAVID B.
　1947. **San Blas Cuna Acculturation: An Introduction.* V *9*.

STRATTON, G. M. AND F. M. HENRY
　1943. Emotion in Chinese, Japanese, and Whites . . . AJPy *56*:161-180.

STRAUS, J. H., AND M. A.
　1953. Suicide, Homicide, and the Social Structure of Ceylon. AJS *59*:461-469.

STRAUS, MURRAY A.
　1954. Childhood Experience and Emotional Security in the Context of Sinhalese Social Organization. SLF *33*:153-160.

STRAUS, ROBERT AND SELDEN D. BACON
　1953. *Drinking in College.* New Haven.

STRODTBECK, F. L.
　1951. Husband-wife Interaction over Revealed Differences, ASR *16*:468-473. (Re: Navaho, Texan, Mormon couples.)

STUNKARD, ALBERT
　1951. Some Interpersonal Aspects of an Oriental Religion, PS *14*:419-431.

STURTEVANT, A. H.
　1948. The Evolution and Function of Genes, ASC *36*:225-236.

SUGIMOTO, MRS. ETSU I.
　1925. *A Daughter of the Samurai.* Garden City. (Japanese Autobiography.)
　1932. *A Daughter of the Narikin.* Garden City. (Novel; Japanese parvenu life.)
　1935. *A Daughter of the Nohfu.* Garden City. (Novel; Japanese peasant life.)

SULLIVAN, HARRY STACK
　1937. A Note on the Implications of Psychiatry, the Study of Interpersonal Relations, for Investigation in the Social Sciences, AJS *42*:848-861.
　1939. A Note on Formulating the Relationship of the Individual and the Group, AJS *44*:932-937.
　1940. The Human Organism and its Necessary Environment, PS *3*:14-27.
　1946. *Conceptions of Modern Psychiatry.* Washington.
　1947. The Study of Psychiatry: Three Orienting Lectures, PS *10*:355-371.
　1948. Towards a Psychiatry of Peoples, PS *11*:105-116.
　1950. Tensions Interpersonal and International: A Psychiatrist's View, In *Tensions that Cause Wars*, ed. by Hadley Cantril. Urbana, Ill.
　1953. *The Interpersonal Theory of Psychiatry.* N. Y.
　1954. *The Psychiatric Interview.* New York.

SUN CHIEF, ed. by LEO W. SIMMONS
　1942. *The Autobiography of a Hopi Indian.* New Haven.

SUN, JOE TOM
　1923. Symbolism in the Chinese Written Language, PYR *10*:183ff.

SWANTON, JOHN R.
　1905. **Contributions to the Ethnology of the Haida.* AMM *8*.
　1908. **Social Conditions, Beliefs, and Linguistic Relationships of the Tlingit Indians.* BuER *26*.
　1911. **Indian Tribes of the Lower Mississippi Valley.* BuEB *43*.

TALBOT, P. A.
　1926. **The Peoples of Southern Nigeria.* 3 vol. London.

TANNENBAUM, FRANK
　1945. On Certain Characteristics of American Democracy, POLQ *60*:343-350.
　1946. The Balance of Power in Society, POLQ *61*:481-504.
　1951. The American Tradition in Foreign Relations, FoA, *30*:31-50.

TANNER, J., ed.
Proceedings of the Study Group on the Psychobiological Development of the Child, 1952. WHO, Geneva (In preparation).

TAO, L. K.
1934. Some Chinese Characteristics in the Light of the Chinese Family, In E. E. Evans-Pritchard, ed., *Essays Presented to C. G. Seligman*, pp. 335-344. London.

TAX, SOL, L. C. EISELEY, I. ROUSE, AND C. VOEGELIN, eds.
1953. *An Appraisal of Anthropology Today*. Chicago. Esp. Ch. VIII.

TAYLOR, DOUGLAS MACRAE
1951. **The Black Carib of British Honduras*. V *17*.

TER HAAR, B. (tr. and ed. by E. A. Hoebel & A. A. Schiller)
1948. *Adat Law in Indonesia*. New York.

THOMAS, DOROTHY SWAINE and associates
1946. *The Spoilage*. Berkeley.

THOMAS, J. L.
1945. The Scarecrow Function of the Police, *Police Journal 18*. London.
1946. Recruits for the Police Service, *Police Journal 19*. London.

THOMAS, WM. I.
1909. *Source Book for Social Origins*. Boston.
1937. *Primitive Behavior*. New York. (Excellent bibliographies in both of the above.)

THOMPSON, CLARA (with Patrick Mullahy)
1950. *Psychoanalysis: Evolution and Development*. New York.

THOMPSON, LAURA
1940. *Fijian Frontier*. New York.
1945. Logico-Aesthetic Integration in Hopi Culture, AA *47*:540-553. (Reproduced herewith.)
1946. In Quest of an Heuristic Approach to the Study of Mankind, PHS *13*: 53-66.
1947. *Guam and its People*. Rev. 3rd ed. Princeton.
1948. Attitudes and Acculturation, AA *50*:200-215.
1950-a. Action Research Among American Indians, SCM *70*:34-40.
1950-b. Personality and Government, AIn *10*:7-43.
1950-c. *Culture in Crisis: A Study of the Hopi Indians*. New York.
1951-a. Perception Patterns in Three Indian Tribes. PS *14*:255-264.
1951-b. *Personality and Government*. Mexico, D. F.

THOMPSON, LAURA, AND ALICE JOSEPH
1944. **The Hopi Way*. Chicago.
1947. White Pressures on Indian Personality and Culture, AJS *53*:17-22.

THOMPSON, STITH
1953. Advances in Folklore Studies, in *Anthropology Today*, ed. A. L. Kroeber. New York. Pp. 587-596.

THORNER, ISIDORE
1953. Ascetic Protestantism and Alcoholism. PS *16*:167-176.

THURNWALD, HILDE
1935. **Die Schwarze Frau Im Wandel Africas*, Stuttgart. (English version is Chap. 4 in R. Thurnwald, *Black and White in East Africa*, London, 1935.)
1937. *Menschen Der Südsee: Charaktere Und Schicksale*. Stuttgart. (Deals with Buin, Bougainville.)
1938. Ehe und Mutterschaft in Buin, ArA *24*:214-246.

THURNWALD, RICHARD C.
1916. **Banaro Society*. AAM *3* #4.
1933. The Social Function of Personality, SSR *17*:203-218.
1934. Pigs and Currency in Buin, *Oceania*, *5*:119-141.
1931-1935. *Die Menschliche Gesellschaft*. Berlin & Leipzig. 5 vols.

1937. Cultural Rotation, Its Propulsion and Rhythm, ASR *2*:26-42.
1940. Der Kulturhintergrund des Primitiven Denkens, *Zeitschrift für Psychologie 147*:328-357.
1949. Probleme der Fremdheit, *Psychologische Forschung 23*:25-68.
1950-a. *Der Mensch Geringer Natur-Beherrschung: Sein Aufstieg Zwischen Vernunft und Wahn.* Berlin.
1950-b. (Anniversary Volume). *Beiträge zur Gesellungs- und Völkerwissenschaft: Professor Dr. Richard Thurnwald zu Seinem Achtzigsten Geburtstag Gewidmet.* Berlin. (Complete bibliography of R. Thurnwald, pp. 469-477.)

THURSTON, JOHN R. AND P. H. MOSSEN
1951. Infant Feeding Gratification and Adult Personality, JP *19*:449ff.

TILAK, LAKSHMIBAI (tr. by E. JOSEPHINE INKSTER)
1950. *I Follow After: An Autobiography.* Madras.

TINBERGEN, N.
1951. *The Study of Instinct.* Oxford & London.

TITIEV, MISCHA
1942. Notes on Hopi Witchcraft, MIA *28*:549-557.
1944. **Old Oraibi, A Study of the Hopi Indians of Third Mesa.* PHa *22* #1.
1953. Changing Patterns of *Kumiai* Structure in Rural Okayama, UnMi *4*:1-28.
1954. *The Science of Man.* New York.

TITIEV, MISCHA AND HSING-CHIH TIEN
1947. (Publ. 1949.) A Primer of Filial Piety, MIA *33*:259 et seq. (Chinese schoolbook.)

TODD, A. J.
1913. *The Primitive Family as an Educational Agency.* New York.

TOFFELMIER, G., AND KATHERINE LUOMALA
1936. Dreams and Dream Interpretation of the Diegueno Indians of Southern California, PYQ *2*:195-225.

TOMAŠIĆ, DINKO
1942. Personality Development in the Zadruga Society, PS *5*:229-261. (Croatia.)
1946. The Structure of Balkan Society, AJS *52*:132-140.
1948-a. Ideologies and the Structure of Eastern European Society, AJS *53*:367-375.
1948-b. *Personality and Culture in Eastern European Politics.* New York.
1953. *The Impact of Russian Culture on Soviet Communism.* Glencoe.

TOOTH, GEOFFREY
1950. *Studies in Mental Illness on the Gold Coast.* (H. M. Stationery Office, Colonial Research Publ. #6.) London.

TOZZER, ALFRED M.
1933. Biography and Biology, AA *35*:418-432. (Reprinted in part in Kluckhohn, Murray & Schneider, 1953.)

TRAGER, G. L., AND EDWARD T. HALL
1954. Culture and Communication. EX, No. *3*:137-149.

TRETIAKOV, S.
1934. *A Chinese Testament, the Autobiography of Tan Shih Hua.* New York.

TSCHOPIK, HARRY, JR.
1946. The Aymara, In *Handbook of South American Indians*, BuEB *143*, vol. II, pp. 501-573.
1951. The Aymara of Chucuito, Peru. I. Magic. AMA *44 pt. 2.*

TUMIN, MELVIN M.
1950-a. The Dynamics of Discontinuity in a Peasant Society. (Guatemala.) SLF *29*:135-141.
1950-b. The Hero and the Scapegoat in a Peasant Community. JP *19*:197-211.
1952. *Caste in a Peasant Society.* Princeton.
1953. Some Principles of Stratification: A Critical Analysis. ASR *18*:387-394.

TUMIN, MELVIN M., AND ARNOLD S. FELDMAN
1955. The Miracle at Sabana Grande. PuQ *19*:125-139.

TURNER, SIDNEY
1938. Infant Life in Yüanling, PM *11* #1, #2:1-25.

TURNEY-HIGH, HARRY HOLBERT
1949-a. *General Anthropology.* New York.
1949-b. *Primitive War, Its Practice and Concepts.* Columbia, S. C.

UNDERHILL, RUTH
1936. *The Autobiography of a Papago Woman.* AAM *46.*
1946. *Papago Indian Religion.* CUCA *33.*
1948. *Ceremonial Patterns in the Greater Southwest.* AEM *13.*
1953. **Red Man's America.* Chicago.

UNDERWOOD, FRANCES W., AND IRMA HONIGMANN
1947. A Comparison of Socialization and Personality in Two Simple Societies, AA *49*:557-577. (Reproduced herewith.)

UNWIN, J. D.
1935. *Sexual Regulations and Cultural Behavior.* London.

VAILLANT, GEORGE C.
1941. **Aztecs of Mexico.* Garden City.

VAN LOON, F. H. G.
1927. Amok and Latah, JASP *21*:434-444.

VANSINA, J.
1955. Initiation Rituals of the Bushong, Af *25*:138-153.

VASSAR COLLEGE, Dept. of Child Study
n.d. *Studies in Normal Personality Development.* (10 films; notes by L. J. Stone.) N. Y. University Film Library. New York.

VAUGHAN, ELIZABETH HEAD
1949. *Community Under Stress: An Internment Camp Culture.* Princeton.

VEBLEN, THORSTEIN
1899. *The Theory of the Leisure Class.* New York.
1914, 1918. *The Instinct of Workmanship and the State of the Industrial Arts.* New York.

VINACKE, W. E.
1949. The Judgment of Facial Expression by Three National Racial Groups in Hawaii, JP *17*:407-429.

VOGT, EVON Z.
1951. *Navaho Veterans: A Study of Changing Values.* PHa *41* #1.

VOGT, EVON Z. AND JOHN M. ROBERTS
1956. A Study of Values. SCAm *195* #1:25-31.

VOGT, EVON Z., AND T. F. O'DEA
1953. A Comparative Study of the Role of Values in Social Action in Two Southwestern Communities, ASR *18*:645-654.

VOLKART, EDMUND H.
1951. *Social Behavior and Personality: Contributions of W. I. Thomas to Theory and Social Research.* N. Y.

VOTH, H. R.
1901. The Oraibi Powamu Ceremony, FM *3*:67-158.
1905-a. Oraibi Natal Customs and Ceremonies, FM *6*:47-61.
1905-b. The Traditions of the Hopi, FM *8*:1-319.

VOWINCKEL-WEIGERT, EDITH
See Weigert, Edith Vowinckel-.

WAGLEY, CHARLES
1949. *Social and Religious Life of a Guatemalan Village.* AAM *71.*
1953. *Amazon Town: A Study of Man in the Tropics.* New York.

WAGLEY, CHARLES, AND EDUARDO GALVAO
  1949. *The Tenetehara Indians of Brazil, a Culture in Transition.* New York. CUCA #35.

WALES, H. G. Q.
  1933. Siamese Theory and Ritual Connected with Pregnancy, Birth, and Infancy, RAI 63:441-451.

WALEY, ARTHUR, tr. and commentator
  1938. *The Analects of Confucius.* New York & London. (Esp. Introduction.)
  1955. *The Nine Songs, A Study of Shamanism in Ancient China.* London.

WALLACE, ANTHONY F. C.
  1950. A Possible Technique for Recognizing Psychological Characteristics of the Ancient Maya from Their Art, AI 7:239-253.
  1951. Some Psychological Determinants of Culture Change in an Iroquoian Community, In Wm. N. Fenton, ed. *Symposium on Local Diversity in Iroquois Culture.* BuEB 149.
  1952-a. The Modal Personality Structure of the Tuscarora Indians, as Revealed by the Rorschach Test. BuEB 150.
  1952-b. Individual Differences and Cultural Uniformities, ASR 17:747-750.
  1956. Revitalization Movements, AA 58:264-281.

WALLACE, E. AND E. A. HOEBEL
  1952. *The Comanches: Lords of the South Plains.* Norman, Okla.

WALLACE, WM. J.
  1947-a. Personality Variation in a Primitive Society, JP 15:321-328.
  1947-b. The Dream in Mohave Life, JAF 60:252-258.
  1948. Infancy and Childhood Among the Mohave Indians, PM 21:19-38.

WALN, NORA
  1933. *The House of Exile.* (China) Boston.

WANG KUNG-HSING
  1946. *The Chinese Mind.* New York.

WARE, C. F., ed.
  1940. *The Cultural Approach to History.* New York.

WARNER, LANGDON
  1948. Shintō, Nurse of the Arts, ArB 30:279-281.
  1952. *The Enduring Art of Japan.* Cambridge, Mass. (His 1948 article appears as Chapter II.)

WARNER, W. LLOYD
  1931. *Murngin Warfare. O 1:417-494.
  1937-a. *A Black Civilization.* (Australia) New York.
  1937-b. The Society, the Individual, and His Mental Disorders. AJP 94:275-284.

WATERMAN, T. T.
  1918. The Yana Indians. UnCa 13.

WAX, MURRAY
  1956. The Limitations of Boas' Anthropology. AA 58:63-74.

WEAKLAND, JOHN HART
  1950. The Organization of Action in Chinese Culture. PS 13:361-370.
  1951. Method in Cultural Anthropology, PHS 18:55-69.
  1953. Chinese Family Images in International Affairs. In M. Mead & R. Metraux, *The Study of Culture at a Distance.*

WEAVER, WARREN
  1948. Science and Complexity, ASC 36:536-544.

WEDGWOOD, CAMILLA H.
  1938. The Life of Children in Manam, O 9:101-108. (New Guinea.)

WEGROCKI, HENRY J.
  1939. A Critique of Cultural and Statistical Concepts of Abnormality, JASP 34: 166-178. (Reprinted in Kluckhohn & Murray, 1948.)

WEIDENREICH, FRANZ
1948. The Human Brain in the Light of its Phylogenetic Development, SCM 67:103-109.

WEIGERT, EDITH VOWINCKEL-
1938. The Cult and Mythology of the Magna Mater from the Standpoint of Psychoanalysis. PS 1:347-378.

WEINBERG, S. KIRSON
1952. Society and Personality Disorders. New York.

WERNER, HEINZ
1948. The Comparative Psychology of Mental Development. Chicago.

WEST, JAMES (pseud.)
1945. Plainville, U. S. A. New York.

WEYER, EDWARD M.
1932. *The Eskimos. New Haven.

WHITE, LESLIE A.
1925. Personality and Culture. Open Court 39:145-149.
1947. Culturological vs. Psychological Interpretations of Human Behavior, ASR 12:686-698.
1949. The Science of Culture. New York.
1950. The Individual and the Culture Process, In Centennial, A. A. A. S. Washington.

WHITEHEAD, ALFRED NORTH
1929. The Aims of Education. New York.

WHITING, A. F.
1939. Ethnobotany of the Hopi. Bull. Museum N. Arizona, 15. Flagstaff.

WHITING, BEATRICE BLYTH
1950. Paiute Sorcery. V 15.
1953. Comp., Selected Ethnographic Sources on Child Training. Social Science Research Council Pamphlet 10. New York.

WHITING, JOHN W. M.
1941. Becoming a Kwoma: Teaching and Learning in a New Guinea Tribe. New Haven.
1944. The Frustration Complex in Kwoma Society. M 44:140-144. (Reprinted. Kluckhohn et al, 1953.)

WHITING, JOHN W. M., AND IRVIN L. CHILD
1953. Child Training and Personality: a Cross-Cultural Study. New Haven.

WHORF, BENJAMIN LEE
1941. The Relation of Habitual Thought and Behavior to Language, In Language, Culture, and Personality, ed. by L. Spier et al., pp. 75-94. Menasha.
1950. An American Indian Model of the Universe. IJAL 16:67-72.
1956. Language, Thought and Reality. Cambridge and New York.

WIELAWSKI, J., & W. WINIARZ
1936. Some Observations from Three Years of Study of Psychotherapy and Genetic Psychology in Asia, PYR 23:173-180.

WIENER, NORBERT
1948. Cybernetics, or Control and Communication in the Animal and the Machine. New York.
1954. The Human Use of Human Beings: Cybernetics and Society. Garden City.

WIESCHOFF, H. A.
1943. Concepts of Abnormality Among the Ibo of Nigeria. JAmO 63:262ff.

WILBUR, GEORGE B.
1940. Comments (On B. W. Aginsky, 1940) AI 1:12-18.
1946. The Reciprocal Relationship of Man and His Ideological Milieu, AI 3 #4:3-48.

WILBUR, GEORGE B., AND WARNER MUENSTERBERGER, eds.
1951. *Psychoanalysis and Culture: Essays in Honor of Géza Róheim.* New York.

WILE, IRA S., AND ROSE DAVIS
1941. The Relation of Birth to Behavior, AJO *11*:320-334. (Reprinted in Kluckhohn and Murray, 1948.)

WILLIAMS, A. N.
1950. A Psychological Study of Indian Soldiers in the Arakan. BMP *23*:130-181.

WILLIAMS, ELGIN
1947. Anthropology for the Common Man, AA *49*:84-90. (*Re* R. Benedict, *Patterns of Culture.*)

WILLIAMS, F. E.
1923. The Vailala Madness and the Destruction of Native Ceremonies in the Gulf Division, *Territory of Papua, Anthropological Report,* No. 4. Port Moresby, New Guinea.
1930. *Orokaiva Society.* London.
1934. The Vailala Madness in Retrospect, In *Essays Presented to C. G. Seligman,* ed. by E. E. Evans-Pritchard, London.
1936. *Papuans of the Trans-fly.* Oxford.

WILSON, ARTHUR JESS
1950. *The Emotional Life of the Ill and Injured.* New York.

WILSON, MONICA
1949. Nyakusa Age-Villages. RAI *79*:21-25.
1951. Witch Beliefs and Social Structure, AJS *56*:307-313.

WINOKUR, GEORGE
1955. "Brainwashing"—a Social Phenomenon of Our Time, HO 13 #4:16-18.

WINSTON, ELLA
1934. The Alleged Lack of Mental Diseases Among Primitive Groups, AA *36*:234-238.

WISER, WILLIAM H.
1936. *The Hindu Jajmani System.* Lucknow.

WISSLER, CLARK
1912. The Psychological Aspects of the Culture-Environment Relation, AA *14*:217-225.
1916. Psychological and Historical Interpretations for Culture, S *43*:193-201.

WITTELS, FRITZ
1931. *Freud and His Time.* New York.

WITTFOGEL, KARL A., AND E. S. GOLDFRANK
1943. Some Aspects of Pueblo Mythology and Society. JAF *56*:17-30.

WOLF, KATHLEEN L.
1952. Growing Up and Its Price in Three Puerto Rican Subcultures, PS *15*:401-434.

WOLF, STEWART
1948. Experimental Research into Psychosomatic Phenomena in Medicine, S *107*:637-639.

WOLFENSTEIN, MARTHA
1953. Trends in Infant Care, AJO *23*:120-130.
1954. *Children's Humor: A Psychological Analysis.* Glencoe, Ill.

WOLFENSTEIN, MARTHA, AND NATHAN LEITES
1950. *The Movies, A Psychological Study.* Glencoe, Ill.
1955. Trends in French Films. JSI *11* #2:42-51.

WOLFF, HAROLD G.
1954. *Stress and Disease.* Springfield, Ill.

WOLFF, KURT H.
1944. A Critique of Bateson's *Naven*. RAI 74:59-74.

WOODY, THOMAS
1949. *Life and Education in Early Societies*. New York.

WYMAN, LELAND C.
1936. Navaho Diagnosticians. AA *38*:236-246.

WYMAN, LELAND C. AND BETTY THORNE
1945. Notes on Navaho Suicide. AA *47*:278-287.

WYNDHAM, H. A.
1933. *Native Education*. London.

YEE CHING
1940. *A Chinese Childhood*. London.

YOGANANDA, PARAMHANSA
1947. *Autobiography of a Yogi*. New York.

ZBOROWSKI, MARK
1949. The Place of Book-Learning in Traditional Jewish Culture, HAE *19*:87-109.
1952. Cultural Components in Response to Pain, JSI *8* #4: 16-30.

ZBOROWSKI, MARK AND ELIZABETH HERZOG
1952. *Life Is With People: the Jewish Little-Town of Eastern Europe*. New York.

ZILBOORG, GREGORY
1938. Culture and Personality, AJO *8*:596-601.
1942. Psychology and Culture, PYQ *11*:1-16.
1944. Masculine and Feminine: Some Biological and Cultural Aspects. PS *7*:257-296.

ZINGG, ROBERT M.
1942. The Genuine and Spurious Values in Tarahumara Culture. AA *44*:78-92.

ZOETE, BERYL DE, AND W. SPIES
1939. *Dance and Drama in Bali*. N. Y. & London.

ZUCKERMAN, S.
1932. *The Social Life of Monkeys and Apes*. New York.